THE NEW

Milton Cross'

Complete Stories

OF THE

Great Operas

*REVISED AND
ENLARGED EDITION*

Edited by Karl Kohrs

DOUBLEDAY & COMPANY, INC.

Garden City, New York

Author's Note

This revision of COMPLETE STORIES OF THE GREAT OPERAS *has been dictated largely by a steadily expanding operatic repertoire. In the eight years since the original volume was published, this expansion has been reflected in a number of ways: Operas by Twentieth-Century composers have won new audiences. Some works have been frankly experimental—atonal in musical design and stylized in dramatic presentation. Other highly interesting works have been written to meet the specialized demands of television performance. In still another category are older classics that have enjoyed successful revivals, and contemporary works that blend classic forms with a modern approach. In the present volume, ten operas considered representative of current repertoire have been added to the original, so that the reader may keep pace with the progress of opera today.*

To

LILLIAN

and to the memory of
Our Little Daughter
LILLIAN GALE

ISBN: 0-385-0434-4
Library of Congress Catalog Card Number 55–10505

Foreword

THIS is a book of stories—the stories of the great and enduring operas. Most of them I have told on the air many times in the twenty-odd years that I've been privileged to work with opera broadcasts. Some of them have become so familiar that I return to them each year almost as one returns each season to the Christmas story.

To me the stories in this volume are never old, never timeworn. I've enjoyed retelling them here as I have on the air. Indeed, this book has in a sense grown out of the broadcasts, for through the years nothing has given me more pleasure, I think, than the letters from listeners, newcomers, and seasoned operagoers alike, telling me how important the stories had been in the appreciation and enjoyment of the music. A disturbing element, however, has been the number of people who told me that they wanted to know the stories in greater detail than we could tell them. I can't say how many thousands of times I have explained that the synopses preceding the broadcasts were brief only because of the limitation of time. I do know, though, with what pleasure I have tried to work into the stories in the book the color and flavor and detail that I have never had the opportunity to use on the air. I have retold them here as fully, as clearly, and as carefully as I could. Whatever faults there may be this time are mine alone.

This book then is an attempt to fill a need—to tell the stories of the best-known operas completely and accurately, with every bit of essential action described, with every important musical section indicated, with the relationship between action and music clearly defined. In later sections of the book the study of the libretti and the scores themselves is recommended. But I am fully aware, of course, that frequently the libretti and scores are not available and that, even when they are, many readers are not yet ready to study the operas in such detail. Then, too, even the most ardent opera enthusiast must admit that libretti in English translation are too often both inaccurate and dull. I hope that as the stories are retold here, with all of the distinctive passages—such as the opening lines of each aria—given in the language in which the opera is sung, they will provide all of the essential landmarks so necessary to a true understanding of the operas.

To preserve the utmost accuracy and to avoid the errors which have crept into many of the translations, the stories in this volume have been taken from the scores and the libretti in the original languages. There is, however, an element of risk even in complete accuracy, for many performances today abbreviate or deviate from the script. In many cases these deviations have become traditional, so that throughout this book it has been necessary to indicate the exact plot of the opera not only as it is written, but also as it is normally produced. This situation has been further complicated by the fact that the variations are not always uniform, and considerable effort has frequently been necessary to trace the pattern of the stories as they are actually produced in the important opera houses of the world.

Needless to say, there are many and varied opinions as to what constitutes "standard" or "favorite" repertoire. Some will consider many of the seventy-six operas in this volume too infrequently performed to be worthy of inclusion. Others will surely think the list too short and will point to one or several operas which they rate as worthy as others included here. It is worth stressing that the list has not been compiled on the basis of personal preference. It is based fundamentally on an analysis of actual frequency-of-performance statistics of leading opera houses for the last fifty years. Obviously such a method is, in itself, not completely satisfactory, and to prevent the list from becoming a mere mathematical computation, a group of people closely associated with the opera were queried and the benefits of their knowledge superimposed on the statistical results. I have tried—and, I hope, successfully—to keep my own personal preferences from interfering with a more desirable system.

The reasons for including in a book of opera stories sections on the history of the opera, on the ballet in opera, and on how to enjoy an opera must be obvious. In them are embodied answers to the questions most frequently asked by those anxious to create a richer background for the enjoyment of operatic music. Actually each section is intended to serve a dual purpose: to provide at least a minimum foundation for the more casual reader and to indicate the more important fields of study for those serious students who wish to go further.

The writing and compilation of this book represents the work of five years, and without the aid, advice, and encouragement of many persons, it would almost certainly never have been completed. Inadequate though my thanks may be, I want to express my gratitude to a few of those who have helped.

First, to Karl Kohrs, whose assistance has been invaluable. The burden of research was his, and his careful checking and rechecking of doubtful points insure the accuracy of this book. In addition, much of the credit for final rewriting goes to him, because his choice of word and phrase has frequently made possible the logical clarification of a scene which the librettist had left only half told, half implied.

To Ralph Beebe and Mel Evans, who believed in this book from the start. Their ideas and their encouragement gave the book its broad plan and purpose, and they guided it through difficult periods.

To Miss Gladys E. Chamberlain, librarian of the Music Branch, New York Public Library, and to her assistants Mary Lee Daniels, Elsa Hollister, Louise Howe, Eleanor Chasan, Lily Goldberg, and Hilda Stolov, for their co-operation in making available scores, libretti, books, and other research sources.

To Paul Weiss, of Boosey & Hawkes, Inc., and to Alfred Mapleson of the Mapleson Music Library, for their understanding kindness in allowing the use of materials otherwise difficult to obtain.

To Goddard Lieberson, of Columbia Recording Corporation, and to music critic Irving Kolodin, of the New York *Sun* and the *Saturday Review of Literature*, for their aid in selecting the operas to be included.

To Madame Zinaïda Lisichkina for her transliterations of arias from the Russian to the Latin alphabet.

To Nelson Lansdale, of Columbia Concerts, Inc., for his generous advice on opera décor.

To Richard Crooks, who made the initial contact between author and publisher that brought this book into being.

To Mark Woods, Charles Barry, Helen Guy, Harold Strickland, Ruth Crawford, Ruth Smith, and numerous other associates at American Broadcasting Company who have helped in many ways to ease the way for this book. Also to my many friends at the National Broadcasting Company, the Metropolitan Opera Association, and others associated with the opera broadcasts over the years, because the knowledge and the help I obtained in working with them have contributed both directly and indirectly to this book.

To Mr. Chandler Cowles and his staff for making available the original score of *The Saint of Bleecker Street*.

And finally to my wife. Her assistance was no passive encouragement from the side lines. Not only did she read and listen to the stories hour upon hour; she participated in the work directly, and many of the most felicitous words and phrases are hers. Her patience and competence have frequently rescued a scene or an act from my hands and given it new life.

M. J. C.

Contents

L'Africaine

by GIACOMO MEYERBEER

[1791–1864]

Libretto by
EUGÈNE SCRIBE

CHARACTERS

Inez, daughter of Don Diego............................*Soprano*
Anna, her maid....................................*Mezzo-soprano*
Don Diego, member of the Royal Council.......................*Bass*
Don Pedro, president of the Royal Council.......................*Bass*
Grand Inquisitor ....*Bass*
Don Alvar, member of the Royal Council.......................*Tenor*
Vasco da Gama, an officer in the Portuguese Navy................*Tenor*
Nelusko ⎱ slaves.......................................⎧ *Baritone*
Selika ⎰ ....⎩ *Soprano*
High Priest of Brahma..................................*Baritone*

Councilors, bishops, sailors, Hindus,
soldiers, Brahmans, dancers

Place: Lisbon and India
Time: Fifteenth century
First performance: Grand Opéra, Paris, April 28, 1865
Original language: French

GIACOMO MEYERBEER, born Jakob Liebmann Beer in Germany, studied in Italy and climaxed his career in Paris, where he became the virtual dictator of opera. He represents the point in operatic history where opera broke away from classic traditions and began to reflect the new romantic spirit of the nineteenth century. A master of musical expression in the heroic vein, Meyerbeer, being an experienced man of the theater as well as a composer, strove primarily for dramatic effect—sometimes at the expense of plot coherence. He was, however, one of the strongest influences on the development of opera before Wagner. *L'Africaine* was his last opera. Although written in French, it is usually sung in Italian.

There is a brief prelude which opens with a phrase of an aria sung by Inez in the first act. Around this dominating theme are woven fragments of other themes which will be heard in the climactic scenes of the opera.

ACT ONE

The Council Chamber in the palace of the King of Portugal. There are doors at the rear and at the sides. On one side is the chair of the president of the Council, flanked by seats of the councilors. Inez comes in followed by her maid, Anna, who tells her that she is to appear in the Council Chamber on her father's urgent orders. Inez wonders if there has been news of the fleet of Bartolomeu Diaz (the great Portuguese navigator who discovered the Cape of Good Hope), who had set out to find a route to the Indies. Inez's interest in the venture is solely concerned with Vasco da Gama, a young officer in the fleet, with whom she is in love. Anna asks if she still hopes to hear from him after a year of silence. Inez replies that she knows Vasco will return a conqueror, and then, in a beautiful aria, she recalls the parting song he sang beneath her balcony ("Del Tago sponde addio"— "Adieu mon doux rivage"). He sang farewell to the shores of the Tagus, his beloved homeland, and farewell to her whom he loved. Inez ends her song in a thrilling cadenza.

Don Diego enters. He informs Inez that the King has ordained that she is to marry Don Pedro, president of the Royal Council. Inez starts in dismay, for Don Pedro is notorious for his ruthlessness, cruelty, and lust for power. When she protests, her father sternly tells her that he approves the King's decision and advises her to forget her infatuation for a mere officer.

At that moment Don Pedro himself approaches. Don Diego asks him if there has been any news of Diaz's fleet. To the horror of Inez, Pedro answers that Diaz and his entire fleet have been reported lost in a storm. When Inez asks about Vasco da Gama, Pedro remarks that no one would waste a thought on the fate of an unknown officer. Scanning a list of officers and crew aboard the ill-fated ships, he announces that Vasco is among those reported dead. He hands the document to Inez, who glances at it and cries out in anguish.

Dismissing her maid, Inez goes to her father, who tries to comfort her. A trio follows ("O per dover"—"Ou par devoir") in which the three express their thoughts. Diego warns his daughter to hide her feelings lest they arouse Pedro's suspicions. Pedro himself sings that he will soon find out the reason for Inez's agitation over the news of Vasco's death. Lamenting that Vasco has sacrificed his life in the flower of his youth, Inez declares that her heart has died with his. After the trio she leaves. Pedro sharply asks Diego why Inez is so concerned over Vasco's fate. Diego hastily assures him that he has nothing to fear from a rival.

Heralded by a brief martial interlude, the Grand Inquisitor, a number of bishops, Don Alvar, and other members of the Council enter the chamber. The councilors acclaim the Inquisitor in a vigorous chorus ("Tu che la terra adora"—"Dieu, que le monde révère"), after which they take their places. Don Pedro rises to speak. Since Columbus discovered America, he begins, His Majesty has hoped that Portugal's navigators would add to the glory of their country by being the first to chart a new route to the Indies. The Inquisitor angrily murmurs that these efforts will bring not glory but ruin.

The great Diaz sought a passage through the Cape of Storms, Pedro goes on. Interrupting again, the Inquisitor says that it was a fool's errand which, as everyone now knows, ended in disaster. Now, Pedro continues, the King has asked the councilors to decide if another expedition is to be sent to ascertain Diaz's fate or—in the event that he and his men are still alive—bring them aid. The Council is divided into two factions on the issue—one, led by the Inquisitor, is against any further exploration, while the younger element, led by Don Alvar, favors continued efforts. After a brief prayer for divine guidance ("Colla tua santa face"—"Dieu, que ta sainte lumière"), the councilors settle down to discuss the situation.

When Don Alvar is asked his opinion, he astounds the Council with the information that one survivor of the Diaz expedition is waiting outside and asks the privilege of addressing the Council. The survivor, Alvar says, is Vasco da Gama. Pedro and Diego look at each other in dismay. Brought before the Council, Vasco bows and then, in a ringing aria, makes his petition ("Io vidi miei signori"—"J'ai vu, nobles seigneurs"). Often while battling the sea's fierce storms, he says, he has resolved to conquer them for the glory of Portugal. If the King will but grant him men and vessels he will dare the Cape of Storms once again, so that Portugal's ships may range the seas and enrich the country through foreign commerce. When the Grand Inquisitor asks what reward he expects, Vasco replies that he desires only the immortal fame that success will bring. He will die, if necessary, in this great attempt.

In a lively chorus ("Ah, se dovesi il sangue"—"Oui, fallut-il perdre la vie"), the two factions argue the matter—the conservatives scorning Vasco's foolhardiness and Alvar's adherents praising the officer's courage. Vasco asks one word more. To prove the worth of his quest, he says, he has brought back two slaves whom he bought in Africa. Their features and characteristics, he explains, indicate the existence of an unknown race in an undiscovered realm beyond the seas. Dramatically Vasco asks that they be brought in so that the councilors may judge for themselves.

As the councilors stare in astonishment, Selika, a dark-skinned woman of imperious mien, and Nelusko, her tall and dignified companion, are brought before the Grand Inquisitor. Although they were purchased as slaves, Selika is in reality a Hindu queen and Nelusko a member of her court. At first they both refuse to answer Don Pedro's questions about their country. Finally Selika relates how they were taken captive in the region of the Cape of Storms when their ship was blown far from the shores of their native land by tempests. She refuses, however, to answer any further questions until Vasco entreats her to speak. Gazing at him ardently, she murmurs that she cannot resist his voice. Noticing her look, Nelusko, in an aside, begs her, in the name of Brahma and her people, not to speak, even though she is at the mercy of tyrants.

Don Pedro commands her to answer, but both Selika and Nelusko steadfastly refuse—Selika quietly but firmly, Nelusko with an expression of intense rage. Vasco interrupts to say that further questioning is useless. It must suffice that the appearance and manner of these two slaves prove the existence of a land beyond Africa, which he, Vasco, promises to discover for the glory of Portugal if the King will give him men and ships.

As Pedro and the councilors are about to retire for their deliberations Alvar leaps to his feet and declares himself in favor of Vasco's plan ("Secondare si deve un tanto"—"Il faut avec ardeur"), which marks the beginning of an agitated chorus in which the two factions violently dispute the issue. The Inquisitor and the bishops finally halt the quarrel with a majestic prayer for divine guidance ("Dio cui la terra adora"—"Dieu, que le monde révère"), and the uproar momentarily subsides. During a brief orchestral interlude Pedro talks with the councilors and then turns to Vasco. His voice edged with contempt, he informs Vasco that the Council, acting in the name of the King, considers his plan fantastic and senseless and refuses his request. In a dramatic refrain ("Insensati voi dite"—"Insensés, dites-vous!"), Vasco reminds the councilors that the great Columbus also was considered a madman by those who deemed themselves wise.

Don Pedro angrily warns him to hold his tongue, while the Inquisitor and the bishops urge him to be calm. But Vasco furiously denounces them for their blindness and obstinacy, whereupon the councilors exclaim that he must be punished for his defiance. Don Alvar loyally tries to speak in Vasco's defense, but his voice is lost in the clamor. The dispute now breaks out more violently than before. It is expressed in the powerful chorus which concludes the act ("O giovin imprudente"—"Vasco, jeune imprudent"). The Inquisitor and his faction hurl their denunciations at Vasco for daring to question the authority of the Council. Alvar and his followers defiantly acclaim Vasco's courage and daring. In brief interludes both Vasco and Alvar warn the Council that history will judge their ignoble repudiation and will exact its vengeance. Suddenly the Grand Inquisitor rises and in stentorian tones proclaims that Vasco will be put under the papal ban as punishment for his rebellious remarks. As the councilors repeat the Inquisitor's words in a thunderous phrase, Vasco, Selika, and Nelusko are led away.

ACT TWO

A gloomy room in the prison of the Inquisition. At the rear, to one side, is a bench on which Vasco is lying asleep. In the center of the room is a huge pillar on which hangs a large map. Selika stands looking tenderly down at the sleeping officer. She muses that he sleeps restlessly, as though he dreamed of nothing but fame and immortality. He is suffering imprisonment for her sake, she murmurs, and yet he does not know how deep her love is for him. Vasco stirs in his sleep and softly calls Inez's name. Selika sighs that he loves someone else. But she will sing to him, she goes on, so that her song will bring him the rest and calm which she herself is denied.

Kneeling at his side, Selika sings a plaintive slumber song ("In grembo a me"—"Sur mes genous, fils du soleil"). It expresses her desire to cradle this child of the sun in her arms and bring him the profound peace of tropical nights she has known. The mood of her song changes as the torment of her love for him makes her cry out against her suffering. So much does she love him, she cries, that she scarcely regrets the throne she has lost or the gods she has forsaken. Her song ends in a passionate avowal of her love.

Just as she bends down to kiss his brow she sees Nelusko approaching.

Rising, she conceals herself behind the pillar. Slowly going toward Vasco, Nelusko murmurs that the honor of his queen and his burning hatred of this man drive him to kill. He draws his dagger. As he is about to plunge it into Vasco's breast Selika rushes from her hiding place and seizes his arm. A dramatic colloquy ensues as Selika implores Nelusko to remember that Vasco saved their lives by buying them in the slave market. She asks if he, proud warrior of a proud race, will stoop to stain his hands with the blood of a defenseless man. Nelusko replies in a long aria ("Figlia di re, a te l'omaggio"—"Fille des rois, à toi l'hommage"). His loyalty, he declares, belongs to Selika, daughter of kings, whose glory will not be tarnished by slavery or exile. He recalls that in her native land priest and warrior alike knelt before her in the dust. But even as hate drove him on in his attempt to kill this Christian, Nelusko cries, he knew that he was being impelled by an even stronger force—his jealous love for Selika. He says that he is haunted by a certain premonition (betraying his suspicion that Selika is in love with Vasco). But even if this foreboding proves baseless, he declares, he has sworn to kill Vasco. As he again raises his dagger Selika quickly steps to Vasco's side and rouses him.

Nelusko conceals his dagger. When Selika notices Vasco looking questioningly at Nelusko she hastily says that the slave has come to bring him food. Vasco curtly dismisses him. With a glance of fierce ardor at Selika, Nelusko slowly leaves. In a dramatic phrase he wonders if Brahma will tolerate the spectacle of his queen kneeling abjectly before a Christian ("O gran Brama"—"O Brahma, Dieu puissant").

Ignoring Selika, Vasco murmurs that he is resolved to escape from the prison and make his way to his beloved Inez. Watching him closely, Selika prays that he may not discern her anguish. Going over to the map, Vasco traces a route with his finger, musing that the passage to the unknown land must lie in that direction. Approaching quietly, Selika remarks that the correct passage lies to the right. As Vasco turns to her in eager surprise she tells him that beyond the passage is the land that is dear to Brahma—her native land. It was from there that her ship was driven into hostile waters.

Looking at the map, Vasco joyfully exclaims that this bears out his own calculations about the location of the passage. Impetuously clasping Selika in his arms, he fervently thanks her in a ringing refrain ("Ah! quanto m'è caro"—"Combien tu m'es chère"). Selika's voice blends with his as she expresses her mingled fear and ecstasy.

As they stand in an embrace Don Pedro enters with Inez, Alvar, and Anna. Pointing to Selika and Vasco, Pedro sardonically remarks that certain rumors about them are obviously true ("Avevan detto il ver"—"On nous l'avait bien dit!"). This marks the beginning of the magnificent septet which concludes the act. Looking at Inez, Selika murmurs enviously of her fair beauty. Vasco ecstatically greets Inez. Regarding him in cold anger, Inez hands him a document, saying that it is his pardon. And now, she adds, they must part forever.

Thinking that the reason for her anger is her jealousy of Selika, Vasco offers Selika to Inez as her slave. As Selika cries out in dismay Nelusko strides out of the shadows at the back of the room and asks what is to become of him. He may follow Selika, Vasco answers carelessly, and then turns to Inez and passionately avows his love. The seven voices blend in an ensemble interlude in which Inez laments that though she still loves Vasco fate has now sealed her lips. Selika gives way to her despair, while Anna comments on the conflicting emotions which are torturing Inez and Vasco. Alvar wishes that he could aid the unhappy lovers. Nelusko reiterates his determination to have revenge, while Pedro exults in his victory over his rival.

Pedro then tells Vasco that he will buy the slaves and take them with him on his voyage of exploration. As Vasco gasps in surprise Pedro triumphantly informs him that the King has commissioned him to make the voyage in search of the eastward passage. When Vasco, wild with anger, asks if he intends to use the secret charts that he himself so laboriously prepared, Pedro scornfully replies that those useless maps were burned. Turning away in dismay and wrath, Vasco protests that the right to the discovery is his alone. At that moment Nelusko, in an aside, tells Pedro that he will gladly serve him as pilot. Pedro coldly informs him that it was for that reason he was purchased.

As Vasco turns back to Pedro the latter tells him that the King already has appointed him governor of the lands he discovers. Saying that his fleet will sail this very day, Pedro takes Inez's hand and prepares to leave. Inez pauses, turns to Vasco, and tells him sadly that in order to win his freedom she consented to marry Pedro and accompany him on his voyage. At this point the ensemble is resumed. Inez bitterly grieves that her evil destiny forced her to betray the man she loves. Vasco curses her treachery and rages over Pedro's triumph. Anna comments that her mistress's marriage vows have condemned her to a life of sorrow and anguish. Selika declares that she is glad Vasco is now racked by the selfsame tortures of unrequited love that she has endured for him. Nelusko rejoices over Vasco's defeat and repeats his vows of vengeance, while Pedro gloats that Inez is his bride and that he can laugh at his hapless rival.

In a solo interlude Inez brokenheartedly bids Vasco farewell. She implores him not to pass her grave unheeding in years to come and assures him that they will be united in heaven. Selika cries out against the fate that separates her from Vasco, who declares that death itself would be more welcome than the torment of parting from Inez. The ensemble rises to a brilliant climax and then dies away to a dramatic, whispered phrase. Pedro escorts Inez from the chamber, while Vasco collapses on a bench. Selika rushes toward him, but Nelusko bars her way and forces her to follow Pedro and Inez. As Selika leaves she looks at Vasco in passionate despair. The curtain falls.

ACT THREE

The interior of Don Pedro's ship. It is shown in cross section, with the main deck above and passenger quarters below. The vessel is on the high seas, nearing the Cape of Storms on the voyage in search of the eastward passage. It is early morning. Sailors and officers are seen about. On the passenger deck Inez, attended by Selika and her serving-women, is lying on a couch. Don Pedro approaches and stands fondly watching her, while the maids sing a tuneful chorus ("Leggiero e rapido il naviglio"—"Le rapide et leger navire"), telling of the gentle winds that are driving the ship along over a calm sea. Don Pedro interrupts momentarily to remind them pompously that the ship is safe in his hands and that he fears neither wind nor wave.

At the conclusion of the chorus the sailors sing a lusty chanty ("Su, su, marinar"—"Debout! matelots"), in which they urge one another to be up and about their work. As a bell rings for morning prayer the sailors, joined later by Inez, Selika, and the other women, intone an impressive prayer to Saint Dominic, protector of the mariner ("O grande San Dominico"—"O grand Saint Dominique").

After the prayer Nelusko strides on deck, shouting that the wind has changed. He orders the ship to be brought about on a northerly course, warning that a typhoon is threatening. Repeating his warning to keep to the north, Nelusko comes down from the main deck. Passing Alvar and Pedro, he overhears Alvar remark that Nelusko is not to be trusted as a pilot. Turning quickly to Pedro, Nelusko, with pretended servility, asks why he should be suspected, when it was he who stole Vasco's maps and charts and delivered them into Pedro's hands.

When Pedro nods approvingly Alvar reminds him that two ships already have been lost. Nelusko interrupts, saying that they were doomed by Adamastor, the dreaded king of storms. He will destroy this ship, too, Nelusko goes on, if the course is not quickly changed to the north. Pedro thereupon orders him to change the course accordingly. Arrogantly taking his place at the helm, Nelusko begins singing to himself. When a sailor asks what he is singing about, he answers that his song is about the legend of Adamastor. Urged by the sailors, he relates the legend in a dramatic aria ("Adamastor, re dell'onde profonde"—"Adamastor, roi des vagues profondes").

He describes how the terrible monarch rides on the wings of the storm, ready to destroy any luckless ship in his path. With a maniacal laugh Nelusko orders the sailors to unfurl more sail so that the ship may escape the wrath of Adamastor. The sailors respond in a lusty chorus. A lookout suddenly calls that a vessel flying Portuguese colors is approaching—a boat has been launched and a man is rowing toward the ship. Nelusko, in alarm, wonders if someone is coming to warn Pedro of the danger ahead. Nelusko, of course, has been steering toward a dangerous reef, hoping to wreck the vessel and thus avenge himself on the Portuguese.

In the next moment Vasco da Gama climbs aboard. Pedro and Alvar greet him in astonishment. Rushing up to them, Vasco cries that they are heading full sail for the reef on which Diaz was lost with all his ships. They have more than the sea to fear, he cautions. Once the ship is helpless on the reef, hordes of savage warriors will swarm aboard for pillage and murder. A dramatic conversation follows as Pedro sarcastically remarks that Vasco undoubtedly had another reason for following his worst enemy and attempting to save him from destruction. Vasco answers that the sons of Portugal must forget their differences in time of danger. But finally, goaded by Pedro's sneering disbelief, he admits that his main thought was for Inez. He must rescue her, he cries, and his hated rival with her. When Vasco frantically tries to persuade Pedro to change the course Pedro warns him that he alone is master aboard the ship and that he will punish any interference with his authority by death. Vasco recoils at this insult from a man of his own rank and race. Their voices blend in a fiery refrain as Vasco dares Pedro to do his worst, while Pedro repeats his threat of dire punishment.

Suddenly Pedro orders the sailors to seize Vasco, bind him to the mainmast, and shoot him at once. Attracted by the scuffling, Inez, Selika, and the women crowd on deck. Inez and Selika cry out in surprise and dismay and then kneel before Pedro and beg him to spare Vasco's life. The voice of a sailor breaks through, warning that the storm is upon them. Before the infuriated Pedro can give the order to fire, the tempest engulfs the ship and drives it on the reef.[1]

An instant later a band of Indian warriors swarms aboard the ship. Nelusko's voice is heard above the tumult, urging them on. Selika remains at his side, while Inez and the women seek refuge below. As the warriors savagely strike down Don Pedro and his desperately resisting crew they sing an exultant chorus calling on Brahma to bring them victory ("Gran Brama! La forza, il coraggio"—"Brahma! force et courage!"). Gazing triumphantly down on the slain, the warriors bring the chorus to a thunderous climax.

ACT FOUR

An open space before a Hindu temple, which is seen at one side. Opposite is an oriental palace. The buildings are in a setting of tropical splendor. During the playing of an exotic intermezzo there is a ritual procession of Brahman priests and votaries, followed by a ballet. Selika appears, accompanied by Nelusko, the High Priest of Brahma, and other dignitaries. In a colorful ceremony Selika is welcomed back to her throne and is invested with the crown.

The High Priest then steps forward and intones the oath of allegiance to the Hindu gods—Brahma, Vishnu, and Siva. He is answered by priests and temple worshipers. Turning to Selika, he holds forth the sacred Golden Book. Placing her hand upon it, she promises to uphold the Brahman laws. In an aside she reveals her anxiety over the fate of Vasco da Gama. From the distance comes the throbbing of a drum followed by a scream, the grim reminder that one of the women brought ashore with Inez after the massacre aboard ship is being tortured. As Selika betrays her fear and terror the High Priest sternly exhorts her to complete the oath. She swears that she will allow no stranger to defile the sacred soil of Hindustan.

[1] At this point in some versions, Selika draws a dagger and tells Pedro that she will kill Inez unless he releases Vasco. Pedro orders the sailors to release him. Selika relinquishes her dagger. Thereupon Pedro orders Vasco to be seized again and put in irons, and then commands the sailors to bind Selika to the mast and flog her in the presence of the entire crew. While his orders are being executed the warriors rush on deck. As the fighting begins the women kneel and sing a prayer for the protection of the embattled crew. At the end of the chorus the curtain falls.

After she has taken the oath Nelusko approaches and informs her that Don Pedro and all his officers and men were slain. A priest steps up to Nelusko and whispers that one survivor was found chained in the wreckage. Angrily muttering that perhaps this survivor is Vasco, he orders the priest to see that the captive is dispatched at once. Selika enters the temple with the High Priest. From the distance come the cries and screams of the women, who have been condemned to inhale the poisonous perfume of the mancanilla tree. Ordering the soldiers to lead them into the sacred grove where they are to die, Nelusko goes into the temple.

Vasco is led in by soldiers. Looking around in wonder and awe, he voices his emotions in the magnificent aria, "O Paradiso in terra sceso"—"O Paradis sorti de l'onde," one of the most beautiful arias in operatic tenor repertoire. Oblivious to the fact that he is surrounded by his would-be executioners, Vasco sings fervently of this wonderful paradise on earth, with its lush verdure under azure skies. This land, so long his goal, he cries, will be a gift from him to his native country. He brings his aria to a thrilling climax as he claims this new and radiant world for his own.

The soldiers break in on his reflections, crowding around and threatening to put him to death. Vasco fiercely demands that he be released so that he may sail home at once to announce his discovery and claim the honor that is due him. But the soldiers shout that the stranger who has invaded their sacred land must die. Frantically Vasco entreats them to allow him at least to send a messenger back to his homeland. He will gladly die, he says, if he can but secure his fame by informing the world of his discovery. In answer, the soldiers raise their weapons. Vasco, now resigned to his fate, declares that he will die like a Christian and a hero and bids the soldiers proceed.

At that moment Selika appears, followed by Nelusko, the High Priest, and other Indians. Seeing her, Vasco cries out her name. The soldiers lower their weapons. Selika rushes to Vasco's side. When the High Priest and the others grimly demand death for the stranger she faces them and asserts that Vasco is not a stranger. Determined to save him, Selika tells her people that she married Vasco after he had bought her as a slave in a foreign land and set her free.

She calls on Nelusko to bear out her story, warning him softly not to contradict her, for if Vasco is condemned to death she will die with him. Gazing at Selika in despair, Nelusko murmurs that he is forced by fate to surrender to his rival the woman he loves ("Averla tanto amata"—"L'avoir tant adorée"). These words mark the beginning of the dramatic aria—sung over the accompaniment of the chorus—in which he voices his confusion and despair. As a priest brings forth the Golden Book on which Nelusko is to swear that Selika's story is true, Selika entreats him not to reveal her deception. Nelusko laments that he must sacrifice not only his honor but his dream of love, while the priests crowd around and urge him to take the oath for the sake of his queen.

With a supreme effort Nelusko steps forward, places his hand on the Golden Book, and swears that Selika loves Vasco and that he is her husband. As the priests offer thanks to the gods Nelusko gives way to his misery, calling down lightning from heaven on himself and the interloper who robbed him of Selika's love ("Al mio penar da fine"—"Ecrase moi tonnerre"). Shaken by grief and humiliation, he rushes away. The High Priest proclaims that the marriage of Selika and Vasco must be solemnized at the altar of the Hindu gods. After singing a great chorus of praise to the gods ("O Brama! O Vishnu! O Shiva!"—"Brahma! Vichnou! Siva!"), the priests march into the temple in solemn procession.

Alone with Vasco, Selika speaks to him of the disaster that overtook Don Pedro's ship and of the sentence of death that has been imposed on Inez and the other women. Lost in thought, Vasco scarcely listens to her. Selika sadly muses that the vows at the nuptial altar bind her alone. As her royal consort Vasco is free to do as he wishes. Tomorrow—perhaps even today—he can order a ship made ready and sail away from this land which he sought so long and hoped to conquer.

As though dreaming, Vasco suddenly exults over the strange happiness that is flooding his heart, sweeping away all recollection of the past and its suffering ("Dove son? O qual gioia"—"O transport, O douce exstase"). It is the opening phrase of the passionate love duet which is one of the finest numbers of the opera. Still pursuing her own thoughts, Selika asks Vasco if he will leave her now. Surprised at the question, Vasco declares that he will never leave her and wonders how he could have been so blind to her love. When she reminds him that he gave her to Inez, he kneels humbly at her feet and asks forgiveness. In momentary doubt Selika implores him not to torture her with protestations of love. Vasco declares that before her god and his own he asks her to be his wife. Selika replies that as his wife she will be jealous even of the memory of the woman he once loved. He swears that he will tear her memory from his heart. Their voices blend in ecstatic phrases as they sing of their bliss and pledge each other eternal fidelity. The duet ends in a phrase of passionate tenderness.

The High Priest reappears with his retinue and approaches Selika and Vasco. As they kneel before him he invokes the blessing of the gods on their union. Dancing girls surround Selika, crown her with flowers, and cover her with a veil. They sing a charming chorus about the happiness of the bridal pair ("Siepe leggeria"—"Remparts de gaze"). This builds into the ensemble which concludes the act. Blending with the chorus, the voices of Inez and the women are heard in the distance, singing a mournful farewell to the river Tagus of their homeland ("Addio, sponde del Tago"—"Adieu, mon beau rivage"). The melody is that of Inez's aria in the first act, when she sang of Vasco's farewell serenade.

Turning away from Selika, Vasco listens as though spellbound and then cries out that the spirit of Inez is bidding him a last farewell. He tries to rush away in the direction in which the voices are heard, but the dancers restrain him and push him toward Selika, who is walking slowly toward the palace. As they enter under an archway formed by the veils of the dancers the curtain falls.

ACT FIVE

[*Scene One*] The tropical garden of Selika's palace.[2] The entrance to the palace is at one side. Selika comes out of the palace, and a moment

[2] This scene is sometimes omitted.

later Inez, under guard, is brought before her. Selika has learned that Vasco found his way to Inez and she furiously upbraids her for abetting his faithlessness. Inez begs forgiveness, but Selika cuts her short, declaring that she is speaking not as the outraged wife but as a queen—and as a queen she will impose severe punishment. A long and tempestuous duet ensues ("In pria che mia vendetta"—"Avant que ma vengeance"). Selika demands to know what Vasco said. Inez answers that he told her he was bound to Selika in holy wedlock and henceforth belonged to her. Despite her anger, Selika muses that Vasco is still in love with Inez. Crying that all happiness has fled, Inez begs to be put to death. Gazing at her compassionately, Selika admits to herself that Inez is not to blame and that they both are torn by the same conflicting emotions of love and hate.

Again Inez implores for death—not only for herself but for Vasco. Selika recoils at the thought. She asks Inez if she would go to Vasco if she were free to do so. Inez replies that she would spurn him, for he is Selika's husband, and only death can break the ties of wedlock. Moved by Inez's sincerity, Selika confesses quietly that the fever of her hate is subsiding and that a mood of calm resignation is stealing over her heart. Gazing at her, Inez prays that she will be merciful. The duet ends in a ringing unison phrase.

Summoning Nelusko and the soldiers, Selika announces that Inez and Vasco are to be liberated and put aboard a ship bound for Portugal. As the soldiers lead Inez away, Selika turns to Nelusko. When he sees the sails of the departing ship in the distance, she tells him, he is to join her on the farthest tip of the promontory which rises above the sea. In terror Nelusko begs her not to go to that fatal spot, for there grows the dreaded mancanilla tree, with its fatal perfume. Selika quietly replies that she realizes the tree is there but adds that it is her wish to look out over the sea from that point. Nelusko hurries away, while Selika slowly enters the palace.

[*Scene Two*]　A promontory high above the sea, which can be seen in the background. At one side is the deadly mancanilla tree, casting an ominous shadow. To the somber music of a brief prelude Selika appears and walks slowly to the edge of the cliff. Addressing the sea, she murmurs that it is as boundless as her misery ("Di qui io vedo il mar"—"D'ici je vois la mer immense"). Then she turns to the tree and in the dramatic aria, "O tempio sontuoso"—"O temple magnifique," she sings that she has come to find the eternal peace which its fatal perfume can give. Gathering up several blossoms which have fallen from the tree, she inhales their fragrance.

In the delirium brought on by the initial effect of the deadly perfume Selika cries rapturously that she sees Brahma in all his celestial splendor and Vasco returning to her arms again. An unseen chorus hums a murmuring accompaniment. As the lethal effect of the perfume overcomes her Selika sinks slowly to the ground. The sails of Vasco's ship are seen on the horizon. Watching them for a moment, Selika closes her eyes in deathlike slumber.

Nelusko hurriedly appears, exclaiming in triumph that the foreigners have gone at last. Seeing that Selika is in the grip of the fatal sleep, he takes her in his arms and makes a desperate attempt to rouse her. When Selika slowly opens her eyes he realizes that she is beyond help. Crying that he will die with her, he snatches up a mancanilla blossom and deeply inhales its perfume. Suddenly he takes Selika's hand. It is icy cold, he gasps in horror; it is death. It is joy eternal, Selika whispers, and dies in his arms. As Nelusko sinks lifeless at her side an unseen chorus softly sings that in love's eternal kingdom all are equal ("Questo sol è il soggiorno"—"C'est ici le séjour").

Aïda

by GIUSEPPE VERDI

[1813–1901]

Libretto by
ANTONIO GHISLANZONI

Based on a sketch by Mariette Bey which was later used as a basis for a
prose drama written by Camille du Locle in collaboration with Verdi

CHARACTERS

The King of Egypt	*Bass*
Amneris, his daughter	*Mezzo-soprano*
Aïda, an Ethiopian girl and slave to Amneris	*Soprano*
Radames, an Egyptian captain of the guard	*Tenor*
Ramfis, a high priest of Isis	*Bass*
Amonasro, King of Ethiopia and father of Aïda	*Baritone*
Messenger	*Tenor*
Priestess	*Soprano*

Priests and priestesses, guards, slaves, dancers, soldiers,
Egyptians, prisoners

Place: Memphis and Thebes in ancient Egypt
Time: The dynasty of the Pharaohs
First performance: Cairo Opera House, Cairo, Egypt, December 24, 1871
Original language: Italian

VERDI was nearing sixty when he composed *Aïda* at the invitation of
the Khedive of Egypt, who had asked him to write an opera on an
Egyptian subject for the opening of the Italian Opera House in Cairo
in 1869 as part of the celebration in honor of the dedication of the Suez
Canal. The opera, however, was not completed in time for the festivities.

The composer had become interested in a scenario by the French Egyp-
tologist, Mariette Bey, who, it is said, based it on an incident in ancient
Egyptian history disclosed during his archaeological excavations at Memphis. Verdi and the dramatist, Du Locle, expanded the scenario into a prose
drama, and the composer also collaborated with Ghislanzoni in turning the
drama into a libretto.

The prelude begins with the violins softly stating the theme associated
with Aïda throughout the opera. This gives way to the somber motive of
the priests of Isis, foreshadowing the final doom pronounced by those
priests on Aïda and Radames. The Aïda theme then recurs briefly.

ACT ONE

[*Scene One*] A great hall in the palace of the Egyptian King at Memphis. Ramfis and Radames are seen in conversation. The High Priest reveals that the Ethiopians are again challenging Egypt's power in the Nile Valley and are threatening Thebes. He expects word from messengers shortly. Radames inquires if the goddess Isis has been consulted. Isis has named the man who is to lead the Egyptians, Ramfis replies, looking significantly at Radames. He then leaves to report the sacred decree to the King.

Radames exclaims that perhaps now he will realize his greatest ambition —to lead Egypt's army to victory. Then he will return in triumph to Memphis—and to his beloved Aïda. In the aria, "Celeste Aïda, forma divina," he reveals his secret love for the captive Ethiopian girl who is the slave of Amneris. He envisions her in the homeland she longs for, reigning as a beautiful queen on a throne near the sun. Radames concludes the aria on a high ringing note of exaltation.

At the conclusion of the number Amneris enters, and Radames tells her that today he has achieved his proudest desire. She asks pointedly if no other feeling touches his heart—thoughts of someone in Memphis, perhaps. As the theme of Amneris's jealousy stirs in the orchestra, Radames, in an aside, wonders if in his enthusiasm he has betrayed his love for Aïda. Amneris, also to herself, voices her haunting suspicion that Aïda is her rival.

Aïda appears as her characteristic theme is heard. Amneris asks her why she is sad ("Vieni, O diletta, appressati"), and these words introduce an impressive trio. The talk of war frightens her, Aïda replies, and she is distressed by the country's danger. By this subterfuge Aïda successfully conceals her grief for her own country. Her Egyptian captors do not suspect that she is the daughter of Amonasro, King of Ethiopia. Over the jealousy theme Amneris fumes in an aside that Aïda's efforts to deceive her are in vain. Aïda expresses her foreboding, while Radames frets over Amneris's malevolent look, fearing that her suspicions will ruin all his plans.

Suddenly there is a fanfare of trumpets. The King enters, preceded by his guards and followed by Ramfis, ministers, priests, and officers. A courier reports that the Ethiopians have invaded Egypt and are marching on Thebes. The enemy troops are under the command of Amonasro, their King. The throng shouts in anger, while Aïda cries out in fear and alarm as she hears her father's name. Turning to Radames, the King announces that Isis has decreed that he is to lead the attack, then bids him enter the Temple of Vulcan to be vested with the sacred armor. In a martial strain, "Su! del Nilo al sacro lido!" he calls on his people to fight. Singing a chorus of triumph, the throng leaves the great hall, acclaiming Radames with the shout, "Ritorna vincitor!" Aïda, left alone, repeats the phrase, "Ritorna vincitor!" which introduces the aria thus familiarly titled. Wondering how she can say, "Return victorious," she describes how she is torn between devotion to her father and love for Radames. Bitterly she reproaches herself for daring to utter the unholy words which mean the conquest of her own father. She visions the conqueror, stained with the blood of her brothers, riding trium-

phantly in his chariot—and behind his chariot her father in chains. In poignant phrases ("O Numi, sperdete") she implores the gods to give her father
the victory. Then, recalling her love for Radames, she wails that she can
pray neither for father nor lover without blaspheming one or the other.
Again her voice soars in an eloquent prayer ("Numi, pietà"). At the end of
the aria her voice dies away in a mournful sigh. The curtain falls.

[*Scene Two*] The Temple of Vulcan in Memphis. In the center of the
stage is an altar carved with sacred emblems. Clouds of incense rise from
the great golden tripods. Ramfis stands at the foot of the altar with priests
and priestesses around him. The priestesses chant an invocation to the god
Phtha ("Possente, Phtha!"), to which the priests respond. The ritual dance
of the priestesses then begins. Radames enters and proceeds to the altar. A
silver veil is draped over his head, and in his outstretched hands Ramfis
places the sacred sword. The High Priest invokes the aid of the gods in protecting Egypt ("Nume, custode e vindice"). Radames repeats the prayer.
The chorus breaks out into a tremendous cry to the great Phtha ("Immenso
Phtha!") as the curtain falls.

ACT TWO

[*Scene One*] An open court outside the palace apartments of Amneris.
Her serving-women are attiring her for the victory festival in honor of the
returning armies. Moorish slave boys dance for her, while slave girls sing of
the delights of love that await the victor ("Chi mai fra gli inni e i plausi").
The voice of Amneris rises above the chorus as she bids her hero hasten to
her arms ("Vieni, amor mio").
    Suddenly she sees Aïda approaching. She dismisses her slaves, resolving
to wring from Aïda the confession of her love for Radames. A powerfully
dramatic duet ensues ("Fu la sorte dell' armi"). Amneris first tells Aïda
that Radames has been slain. When Aïda's deep grief betrays her love,
Amneris says that she has trapped her with a lie—Radames is alive! Overcome with joy, Aïda thanks the gods. Amneris furiously commands her slave
to look upon the one whom she dares oppose in love—a daughter of the
Pharaohs. Aïda is about to disclose that she, too, is of royal blood, but she
checks herself. Falling to her knees, she pleads for mercy and confesses her
love. From outside comes a blare of trumpets, followed by the shouts of the
crowd hailing the conqueror. Amneris tells Aïda that in the victory festival
she shall play her true role—a slave groveling in the dust. She herself will be
seated on the throne in triumph at the King's side. Aïda implores once
again for mercy. The curtain falls.

[*Scene Two*] A great palm-bordered avenue at an entrance to the city
of Memphis. On one side is the Temple of Ammon, on the other a canopied
throne. At the rear is a triumphal arch. The scene is crowded with people.
The King enters with his vast retinue. Followed by Aïda and her other
slaves, Amneris appears and takes her place on the throne at the King's
side. A massive chorus ("Gloria all' Egitto") bursts forth, acclaiming the

glory of Egypt. Then the priests thunder a chorus of thanksgiving ("Della vittoria agli arbitri") for the deliverance of the nation.

Led by a phalanx of trumpeters playing the *Grand March*, the Egyptian troops enter in a glittering pageant of banners, arms, chariots, sacred vessels, and statues of the gods. The warriors arrange themselves on either side. Dancing girls, carrying the spoils of victory, perform a ballet symbolic of the Egyptian triumph. The chorus rises to a great crescendo as Radames rides up in his chariot.

As the theme of Amneris's infatuation for Radames vibrates in the orchestra, she bestows upon him the victor's crown. In response to his request the Ethiopian captives are led forth in chains, the last prisoner being Amonasro, dressed as an officer. Aïda gasps that he is her father. All exclaim in surprise. When she embraces him he warns her not to disclose his kingly identity. Amonasro tells the King that as an officer he fought for his sovereign, who was slain in battle. In a melody of noble dignity ("Ma tu, o Re, tu possente") he beseeches the King to be merciful to the defeated.

Amonasro is joined in his entreaty by Aïda, the other slaves, and the captives. In a great ensemble ("Struggi, o Re, queste ciurme feroci"), the priests grimly demand revenge, while the people urge the King to heed the pleas of the conquered. As Radames expresses his love for Aïda, Amneris, watching them both, cries out for revenge. The King mourns that he must bow to the will of the gods. This ensemble is interrupted when Radames requests the King to free the Ethiopian captives. Ramfis, however, objects, saying he will consent to their release only if Aïda's father is held as hostage. The King agrees. Turning to Radames, he declares that his reward for winning the victory will be the hand of Amneris. Another triumphal chorus concludes the act.

ACT THREE

The banks of the Nile. Granite rocks, partially hidden by palm trees, rise from its edge. Near the top of the ramparts is the Temple of Isis. From within come the voices of the priests chanting a hymn to Isis. Amneris and Ramfis, followed by a group of heavily veiled women, step from a boat which has glided to the shore. Ramfis invites Amneris to the temple, where she may invoke the blessing of the goddess on her wedding eve. All then enter the sanctuary.

With her face veiled, Aïda now appears and sings the famous aria which is familiarly known as "O patria mia." Beginning with the phrase, "O cieli azzuri," Aïda poignantly expresses her hopeless longing for her homeland. As she stands bowed in sorrow Amonasro suddenly enters. Sternly he says that he has learned that she is in love with Radames, the conqueror of her people. He angrily reminds her that the Egyptian hordes have devastated her homeland and commands her to forget her love in thoughts of revenge. The Ethiopians are now poised to strike back, Amonasro says, but they must first know the name of the pass through which the Egyptians will march. Aïda herself must betray Radames into revealing that secret, Amonasro declares. When her protests prove useless Aïda yields and promises to obey. Amonasro hides among the palms as Radames approaches.

Radames greets Aïda with an ecstatic cry. She responds coldly, reminding him that he is soon to wed Amneris. He swears that he loves Aïda alone and will never forsake her. Yielding at length to his fervent declarations, Aïda says that only one course remains—they must flee from this inhospitable country to her native land, where they can share the bliss of love ("Fuggiam gli ardori inospiti"). Radames at first hesitates but finally resolves to go with her ("Ah! no! fuggiamo!"). Together they sing of the joys that await them. Aïda then asks Radames what route they will take to avoid the opposing armies. Through the pass, he answers, where the Egyptians have planned to ambush the Ethiopians—it will be unguarded until morning. Deliberately Aïda asks him to name it. The pass of Napata, he replies.

Scarcely has he spoken when Amonasro springs from his hiding place, reveals himself as King of the Ethiopians, and exclaims that he will order his troops to the pass at once. Radames cries that for Aïda's sake he has unwittingly become a traitor ("Io son disonorato!"). Amonasro and Aïda try to calm him, saying that he is guiltless and that his actions were decreed by destiny. At that moment Amneris rushes from the temple, shouting "Traitor!" She is followed by Ramfis, the priests, and the temple guards. Amonasro, dagger in hand, lunges at Amneris but is restrained by Radames, who urges him to flee with Aïda. Ramfis orders his guards to follow the fleeing pair. With a cry of surrender ("Sacerdote, io resto a te") Radames hands his sword to the High Priest. The curtain falls.

ACT FOUR

[*Scene One*]   A hall in the palace of the Egyptian King. At right is the portal of the prison where Radames is waiting to hear the traitor's doom from the lips of the priests. At left is the entrance to the subterranean hall of judgment. Before it stands Amneris in an attitude of dejection. In recitative she expresses her conflicting emotions of jealousy and love. Resolving to make one final attempt to save Radames, she orders the soldiers to bring him before her.

An intensely dramatic duet follows ("Già i sacerdoti adunansi"). Amneris entreats him to confess his guilt, throw himself on the mercy of the priests, and clear his name. Radames scorns her pleas. She has robbed him of Aïda, he says—perhaps even caused her death—and now nothing is left him but infamy. Aïda lives, Amneris answers. She tells Radames that only Amonasro was killed, while Aïda escaped. Amneris offers to save him if he will promise to forget Aïda, but Radames calmly refuses to bargain, saying he is prepared to die.

Radames is returned to his cell by the guards as the grim theme of the priests sounds in the orchestra. Amneris sings that in her jealous fury she has condemned Radames to death and herself to unending woe ("Ohimè! morir mi sento"). She cowers in terror as the priests cross the stage to the entrance of the judgment hall. Below, in an unaccompanied chorus ("Spirto del Nume sovra noi discendi!"), they call upon the gods to witness the justice of their sentence.

Now Radames, between guards, crosses the stage and descends to the judgment hall. We hear the voice of Ramfis stating the charge of treason. The priests command him to defend himself ("Discolpati!"). There is no answer. Three times Ramfis calls, "Radames"; three times the priests exhort him to reply. He remains silent. During the pauses Amneris implores the gods for mercy.

Suddenly, in a powerful chorus, the sentence is pronounced: Radames is to be buried alive in a tomb under the altar of the god whose wrath he has provoked ("Radames, è deciso il tuo fato"). The priests emerge from the hall, chanting that justice has been done. Amneris rages that in their lust for revenge they have condemned an innocent man. In answer they intone that the traitor must die ("È traditor! morrà!"). As they slowly move off, Amneris screams a curse after them. The curtain falls.

[*Scene Two*]   This is the famous double scene. The upper part is the Temple of Vulcan, flooded with light. The lower portion is a tomb, deep in shadow. Radames is seated on the steps leading down from above. Two priests move a great stone slab into place over the tomb. Radames sings that the stone has now closed over him ("La fatal pietra") and laments that he will never see Aïda again. Suddenly a figure emerges from the shadows. Recognizing Aïda, he cries out in astonishment at seeing her in the tomb ("Tu—in questa tomba!"). Now begins the moving duet which dominates the opera's great closing scene. Aïda tells Radames that she stole unseen into the tomb to share death with him ("Presago il core della tua condanna"). Radames protests that she must not thus doom herself.

Meanwhile the ritual dance begins in the temple above and we hear the voices of the priests in the death chant. In a last frenzied effort Radames tries to move the stone. Then he clasps Aïda in his arms, and together they sing their farewell to earth ("O terra, addio"). Amneris appears above and flings herself on the stone of the vault, sobbing a prayer to Isis. Her voice and the chanting of the priests blend with the final phrases of the lovers' duet. Aïda dies in the arms of Radames. As the curtain slowly descends we hear the prayer of Amneris imploring peace ("Pace t'imploro") and the priests' final invocation to Phtha.

Amahl and the Night Visitors

by GIAN-CARLO MENOTTI

[1911–   ]

Libretto by the Composer

Inspired by the painting, *Adoration of the Magi,* by
Hieronymus van Aeken (Bosch), the sixteenth-century Dutch painter

CHARACTERS

Amahl, a crippled boy of about 12 . . . . *Boy soprano*
His Mother . . . . *Soprano*
The Page . . . . *Bass*
King Kaspar (somewhat deaf) . . . . *Tenor*
King Balthazar . . . . *Bass*
King Melchior . . . . *Baritone*
Shepherds and villagers

Place: Legendary
Time: Antiquity
First performance: World première, NBC Television Opera Theatre, New
York, Christmas Eve, 1951. First professional stage pre-
mière, New York City Opera Company, April 9, 1952.
Original language: English

A MAHL AND THE NIGHT VISITORS is the first opera expressly commissioned
for television, and as such it marks an important milestone in operatic
history. Given its première by the NBC Television Opera Theatre, the
55-minute work is a lyrical interpretation of the Christmas legend of the
Three Kings. The entire production was staged by the composer himself.
Since its première, *Amahl* has been televised regularly every Christmas Eve.
The opera is in one act.

The stage is divided into two sets. One is the poor hut where the
crippled shepherd boy Amahl and his mother live. The other is an exterior
representing the countryside, with hamlets visible in the distance. A road
that leads past the door of the hut winds back into the distance. The dividing element of the stage is the third wall of the hut, which has a door and a
window. Snow covers the ground. Above, the stars glitter; the brightest of
all is the Star of the East.

There is a soft, sustained orchestral introduction of a few brief measures.
The curtain rises to show the hut and the cold, clear winter sky. Near the
door, Amahl sits on a stone. Wrapped in a huge cloak, he is playing his
shepherd's pipe. His mother, busy with chores, can be seen inside the hut.

After a while she pauses to listen to the sweet, plaintive shepherd's tune, then calls to Amahl, telling him it is time to go to bed.

He answers, but then continues playing. When his mother calls again, this time more sharply, he pleads to be allowed to stay outside a little longer. His cloak is warm, he says, and the sky is light. There will be a weeping child, his mother answers, if he doesn't do as he is told. Sighing, Amahl picks up his crutch and hobbles into the hut.

His mother is kneeling in front of the fireplace, trying to coax up the flame with a handful of twigs. Amahl hangs up his cap and cloak, carefully puts away his shepherd's pipe, then hobbles back to the open door. A melodic dialogue ensues. Exclaiming in wonder over the beauty of the winter sky, the boy describes it to his mother. The clouds have swept it clean, he sings, as though in preparation for a royal ball. Lanterns are glittering like crystal. And over our roof, he goes on, there is a great star with a blazing tail, moving across the sky like a fiery chariot.

In a continuation of the melody, his mother speaks. She scolds him for mooning about in his dream world, while in the house there is nothing to eat, no wood for the fire, no oil for the lamp. And what is more, he is telling lies again—after he had promised not to. Amahl begs her to believe him this time. Tugging at her skirt, he asks her to come and see for herself. She impatiently pushes him away, saying she knows only too well what sort of things he makes up out of his childish fantasies—a leopard with a woman's head, a bleeding tree, a fish with horns and wings. Now he is talking about a star as big as a window, with its tail on fire.

But, Amahl insists, there *is* a star that big, right above the house. He indicates its size with his outstretched arms. When his mother looks at him sternly, he cuts down the indicated size by half. Overcome with tenderness and pity, the Mother goes over to the boy and takes him in her arms. Poor Amahl, she sings, hunger has made him lose his senses. Giving way to despair, she sinks down beside the cold and cheerless fireplace, sobbing that money and food are gone. Now they must beg or die.

Amahl tries to comfort her. If they must beg, he sings, he'll make the best of it and be a good beggar. He can sing tunes that will set people dancing. And so they will go from town to town—he as a clown, she as a gypsy. They will eat roast goose and almonds. The King, riding by, will hear their piping and singing and will throw them some gold to stop the noise. Despite herself, the Mother is charmed by the boy's fancies. Her voice blends with his in a brief but lyrical conclusion of the dialogue.

The two then bid each other good night. Amahl curls up beside the fireplace. The Mother fastens the door, covers Amahl with his cloak, snuffs out the lamp, and lies down on the bench near the fireplace. The orchestral accompaniment dies away into silence.

Then, as from far off, come the voices of the Three Kings, heard in trio form to the accompaniment of sonorous chords in the orchestra. Following the Biblical version of the Christmas story, they sing of following the great star while shepherds sleep on the hillsides. The night is bitter cold—even the incense freezes in their hands, and the gold they carry is heavy.

Awakened by their singing, Amahl sits up and listens intently. Then he gets up, takes his crutch and goes over to the window just as the Three

Kings appear at a bend in the road not far from the hut. First comes Melchior, carrying the coffer of gold; then Balthazar, with the urn of incense; and finally Kaspar, with the chalice of myrrh. Before them walks the Page, lighting the way with a lantern. He is bent under a great load of bundles, including an oriental rug, a caged parrot, and a jeweled casket.

The trio of the Kings continues. It comes to an end as they slowly approach the door of the hut and Melchior knocks. Without getting up, the Mother tells Amahl to see who is at the door. The boy opens it slightly and peers out. With a gasp of surprise, he slams it shut and runs back to his mother. An agitated figure in the orchestra reflects his excitement. A rather amusing dialogue follows. To the accompaniment of a rhythmic orchestral pattern, Amahl begs his mother to come and look, so he can be sure she sees what he sees. Sitting up, the Mother impatiently asks what all the fuss is about. When the boy replies hesitantly that a King is standing outside the door, she scolds him for lying and threatens to spank him. Just then there is another knock on the door.

Sinking back on the bed, the Mother orders Amahl to answer. He does as before, to a repetition of the orchestral pattern. Timidly Amahl tells his mother he really wasn't telling the truth before: there isn't one King, there are two. Exasperated, the Mother complains she doesn't know what to do with this boy . . . he will not stop lying. Again there is a knock. Find out who's there, the Mother tells Amahl, and try telling the truth for a change.

For the third time, Amahl looks, comes back and reports. It's true, he says solemnly, there aren't two Kings at all. There are three—and one of them is black. Still rather gentle with the boy, though completely out of patience, the Mother gets up wearily and starts toward the door. This time, she tells him grimly, there will be a reckoning. Amahl, clutching her skirt, follows. She opens the door. There stand the Three Kings and the Page. The Mother staggers back in amazement.

With regal dignity the Kings bid her good evening. Balthazar asks if they may warm themselves by the fire. Saying she is a poor widow, the Mother tells them they are welcome to all she has to offer—a cold fireplace and a pallet of straw. The deaf Kaspar,[1] straining to hear, asks the others what the Mother has said. They tell him, and then in chorus the Three Kings express their thanks.

To the accompaniment of a stately march, the visitors enter the hut, preceded by the Page. He places his lantern on a stool by the fire, then drops his bundles. Kaspar strides across the room to the bench, while the Page runs to hold his train. The King sits down. In the same dignified manner, Balthazar and Melchior, with the Page holding their trains in turn, go over and sit down on the bench with Kaspar. Amahl, meanwhile, watches the proceedings in open-mouthed wonder. The Page spreads out the oriental rug before them and places on it the gifts the Kings are bringing to the Child.

A brief recitative passage follows. Melchior says the place is "nice." The

---

[1] Menotti modeled Kaspar after one of the "Three Kings" who came to his childhood home in Italy at Christmas, bringing presents—the Italian version of the visit of Santa Claus. This real-life Kaspar was deaf.

Mother puts on her shawl and says she will go out and try to gather up some wood. Melchior tells her they cannot stay long because they must not lose sight of their Star. The Mother, warning Amahl not to make a nuisance of himself, goes out. The moment she leaves, of course, the boy begins asking questions. Confronting Balthazar, he asks him if he is a real king and if he has royal blood. Balthazar nods gravely. Could he see some, Amahl asks. With quiet amusement, the King says it is just like his own. When Balthazar, in turn, asks Amahl about himself, the boy answers in a touching, minor refrain. He is a shepherd, he sings, but his mother has sold all the sheep. He had a black goat that gave him sweet milk, but she died of old age. Now there is nothing left, and he and his mother will have to go begging.

Next, Amahl goes over to Kaspar, who is feeding the parrot. There is an amusing colloquy between the two, with Amahl shouting his questions into Kaspar's deaf ears. When he asks if the parrot bites, Kaspar ruefully holds up a bandaged finger. Then the boy wants to know what is in the jeweled casket. In a richly melodic passage, Kaspar enumerates its contents drawer by drawer. The first contains magic stones—carnelian, moonstone, coral, lapis lazuli, jasper, topaz, and ruby. The second contains glittering beads. The third, says Kaspar with deliberate emphasis, has licorice. He offers some to Amahl, who seizes a handful and hungrily wolfs it down.

As he does so his mother comes in carrying a few branches. In recitative, she scolds Amahl for annoying the visitors. The boy artfully explains that they kept asking *him* questions. In low tones, the Mother tells the boy to go to the other shepherds, tell them about the visitors, and ask them to bring whatever they have as presents. Here, she reminds him, there is nothing at all. Putting on his cloak and cap, Amahl hobbles out as fast as he can. When the Mother goes over to the fireplace to put down the wood she has gathered, she sees the array of wonderful gifts on the rug. She is overwhelmed by the sight.

Melchior explains that these are gifts for the Child. Greatly excited, the Mother asks who the Child is. That they do not know, Melchior replies, but the Star will lead the way to Him. What is He like? the Mother asks. To the accompaniment of descending triads, Melchior tries to describe Him—a child the color of dawn, with hands like a king. For Him, they bring gold, incense, and myrrh. In a similar refrain, the Mother sings—half to herself—that she knows just such a child. But no one will bring him gifts, even though he is sick and cold and hungry. That child, she goes on, is her own darling son.

A moving ensemble now ensues. It begins as Melchior and Balthazar, in duet form, ask if the Mother has really ever seen a child "the color of earth"—a child of the poor. The Mother takes up the theme, repeating that she knows this child—her own son. The Kings then go on to describe the Child they are seeking: He holds the seas and the winds in His hands . . . moon and stars are at His feet . . . He tames eagle and lion alike. . . .

The four voices then blend in a chorale-like conclusion. The Kings sing of a child over whom angels watch and whose mother is "both Virgin and Queen." The Mother sings of a child who holds her heart in his hands. His name is Amahl.

There is a moment of complete silence. Then from the outside comes the joyous call of the shepherds. The Mother, with a housewifely glance around the room, hurries to the door and flings it open. Then follows the Shepherd's Chorus, the opera's chief concerted number. Coming from all directions in small groups, they gather in a crowd and approach the hut. They are carrying baskets of fruits and vegetables. Leading them is Amahl, limping excitedly along on his crutch.

As they draw near, the shepherds sing an unaccompanied chorus, a sort of naïve doggerel made up of the names of children in the village. Though meaningless, it is very gay and charming. Crowding together at the open door of the hut, they suddenly catch sight of the Kings. They exclaim in wonder and awe, then stare open-mouthed. Meanwhile, Amahl makes his way to his mother's side.

When the Mother urges the shepherds to come inside and show the Kings what they have brought, they shrink back in embarrassment, each one trying to push his neighbor ahead of him. Finally they are all crowded in one corner of the room, each trying to egg the other on. One shepherd eventually plucks up enough courage to walk up and place his gifts before the Kings. He bows, then goes back to his place.

Then begins a melodious ensemble in a rhythmic 6/8 tempo. Still crowded in the corner, the shepherds shyly sing that they have nothing to offer but the products of their toil—fruits, vegetables, spices, nuts, and cheese. The Three Kings respond in a sort of antiphon. During the chorus, two more shepherds come forward with their offerings.

Then the Mother asks the shepherds to dance for the Kings. A young girl tries to break away from the crowd. There is much excitement as the young men try to pull her back. During this byplay, Amahl gets his shepherd's pipe, goes over to the fireplace, and sits down beside a shepherd who has his own pipe. He and Amahl begin to play. The shepherds listen for a moment, then start to dance.

Hesitantly at first, they swing into a kind of folk dance that is at the same time a ceremony of welcome. They are self-conscious in the presence of the Kings, but as they get into the mood of the dance they forget their shyness. When the music rises to an *allegro vivace*, they throw off all restraint and bring the dance to a joyous climax.

Balthazar thanks them for their dancing and their gifts, then bids them good night, saying he and his companions must rest for their long journey ahead. As the shepherds leave, bowing before the Kings, they say good night in a tuneful chorus, which fades out as the Mother closes the door.

While she is arranging a pile of sheepskins for her bed, Amahl steals over to Kaspar. In a whispered aside, he asks the King if he has a magic stone that could heal a crippled boy. But Kaspar cannot hear. Disappointed, Amahl turns away and lies down on his straw pallet. As a soft, sustained theme runs through the orchestra, silence settles over the hut. The Three Kings, still seated on the bench, go to sleep leaning against each other. The Page lies down at their feet, one arm curled around their gifts. His lantern sheds a dim light on the scene.

Suddenly the Mother sits bolt upright and stares at the royal treasures. She then begins a dramatic soliloquy which is the outstanding solo number in the opera. All that gold, she murmurs. Do rich people who have it know what could be done with their gold . . . do they know it could feed a child, buy logs to warm a house, buy corn to roast on the fire, or fill a courtyard with doves? If the rich only knew, the Mother goes on in tense, brooding tones, what she could do for her child if she had all that gold.

As though hypnotized by the sight of the treasure, the Mother drags herself over to it, whispering hoarsely, "For my child." She reaches out and clutches a handful of gold and jewels. Instantly the Page awakens and grabs her arm. The Mother struggles desperately to free herself. The Kings wake up and cry out in alarm. Over a stormy passage in the orchestra, the Page shouts that he caught the Mother stealing the treasure. The Kings cry "shame" and order her to give it back.

The uproar awakens Amahl. When he sees his mother struggling with the Page, he rushes over and begins pummeling him furiously. In an *agitato* refrain, he threatens to knock the Page's teeth out if he dares touch his mother. Desperately, he runs to Kaspar for help, then returns to the attack. As Amahl's frenzy rises, Kaspar gestures to the Page, who then releases the Mother. Kneeling, she turns to Amahl with open arms. He rushes to her, sobbing bitterly. The furor of the music gradually subsides, and then Melchior steps forward.

He speaks to the Mother in a refrain of great dignity. She may keep the gold, he tells her, because the Child the Kings seek does not need it. His kingdom is built on love alone—He is a king without sceptre or crown. He will come as suddenly as lightning and bring new life with Him. The keys to His kingdom belong to the poor. Concluding, Melchior looks down at the Mother for a moment in forgiveness and pity, then motions to the other Kings to leave with him.

Gently pushing Amahl to one side, the Mother kneels before the Kings. The treasure she has taken scatters on the rug. In recitative, she asks them to take it back. She has waited all her life for the King whom Melchior has described, she says, and now only wishes she could send Him a gift of her own.

Thereupon Amahl says he will send this Child his crutch—the one he made himself. Perhaps the Child might need it. Standing unaided, Amahl lifts the crutch. There is a long, tense silence. Then the boy takes one step toward the Kings. In an awed whisper he gasps that he can walk. Holding his crutch in his outstretched hands, Amahl walks step by step toward the Kings. They and the Mother murmur in wonder at this miracle. Then in a brief trio phrase, the Kings sing that this is a sign from God Himself.

Amahl hands the crutch to Kaspar. In boyish delight he begins to jump and dance about the room. The Mother and the Kings watch him breathlessly, ready to catch him if he falls. He does fall when he rashly tries to do a pirouette. The Mother catches him and anxiously warns him to be careful. Reassuring her, the Kings say the boy is truly loved by the Son of God.

One by one, the Kings lay their hands on Amahl's head, first asking his permission to touch him. They then gather up their gifts in readiness to leave. Finally the Page comes over and humbly asks if he, too, may touch Amahl. Hugely enjoying the situation, Amahl gives his permission with amusing condescension.

Joyously shouting that now he can fight and work and play, Amahl begs to be allowed to go with the Kings and take the crutch to the Child himself. The Kings urge the Mother to let him come along, promising to return him on the back of a camel. Leading Amahl to one side, the Mother kneels before him. A brief but touching duet follows. The Mother asks Amahl if he is sure he wants to go. Very sure, Amahl answers. Then, says the Mother, he should go and thank the Child himself for his good fortune. Amahl is beside himself with joy. As for his crutch, he tells her, it can be tied on his back. Then, like any mother, she gives him last-minute advice: He must remember to wear his hat—and he must not tell any lies. They both sing that they will miss each other very much.

Their farewells are interrupted by the voices of the shepherds offstage. As the chorus rises in beautiful, triumphant phrases, the Kings go out of the hut and begin their stately procession. The Page, carrying his huge bundle and his lantern, goes before them. Amahl hugs his mother once more, then runs to catch up with the Kings. Walking proudly in front of them he begins to play a merry tune on his shepherd's pipe.

From the door of the hut, the Mother fondly watches him. Amahl turns and waves. She waves back just as he disappears around the bend of the road. As the music softly dies away on a high clear chord in the strings, the curtain slowly falls.

L'Amore Dei Tre Re

(The Love of Three Kings)

by ITALO MONTEMEZZI

[1875–1952]

Libretto by
SEM BENELLI

Adapted from his own tragic poem of the same title

CHARACTERS

Archibaldo, King of Altura	*Bass*
Flaminio, a servant	*Tenor*
Avito, former Prince of Altura	*Tenor*
Fiora, Manfredo's wife	*Soprano*
Manfredo, Archibaldo's son	*Baritone*
A handmaiden	*Soprano*
A young girl	*Soprano*
A youth	*Tenor*
An old woman	*Mezzo-soprano*

People of Altura

Place: A remote castle in Italy
Time: In the Middle Ages, forty years after a barbarian invasion led by Archibaldo
First performance: La Scala, Milan, April 10, 1913
Original language: Italian

T HE LOVE OF THREE KINGS is the story of the love of Archibaldo, an ancient barbarian conqueror, for his son, Manfredo; of Manfredo's love for Fiora, princess of the conquered country, given to him in marriage; and of the love of Avito, prince of the conquered country, for Fiora, whom he was to have married.

The symbolism in Sem Benelli's great tragedy may be stated as follows: Fiora, representing Italy, despises and defies the conqueror. She rejects Manfredo, who portrays the conqueror's attempt to win over a subjugated people. Fiora sacrifices herself for Avito, who embodies loyalty and love of country.

ACT ONE

A spacious hall in the castle of Archibaldo. Through the curves of ornamented arches can be seen a terrace over which a lantern spreads a reddish glow. The sky shows the pale, dim light of early dawn above the hilly terrain.

There is a brief silence. Archibaldo enters from the left, guided by Flaminio, one of the castle guards. Archibaldo is old and blind. Pointing to a door at the right, he asks if it is shut. Flaminio answers that it is slightly open. Archibaldo tells him to close the door but suddenly changes his mind. "Who sleeps there?" he asks. "Fiora, your son's wife," answers Flaminio. "Then let her sleep," the King says. "But for me there is no sleep.

"Look out into the valley," the King orders Flaminio. "I feel that Manfredo will return." "Not if he still fights our men in the mountains," answers Flaminio. "Our men?" the King asks in surprise. Flaminio reminds the old King that he is one of the Alturans whom Archibaldo conquered many years ago and that Princess Fiora was given in marriage to Archibaldo's son, Manfredo, for the sake of peace; she was to have wed Avito, a young prince of the Alturans.

Again Archibaldo tells Flaminio to look across the valley for some sign of Manfredo's returning, but Flaminio tells him all is quiet. Archibaldo has been spending the weary, sleepless night thinking of the past. In a dramatic aria he proudly reminisces of his younger days as a conqueror ("Italia! Italia! e tutto il mio ricordo!"). He recalls how forty years earlier he led his band of picked warriors into this land and drove out its people. He has loved the beautiful countryside ever since his first sight of it. "But the country is our slave and not our mother," he finishes, "for if she were our mother, she would teach us to dominate the world."

It is almost dawn. Feeling that Manfredo will not come, the King has Flaminio extinguish the lantern. A rustic flute is heard in the distance. At the sound of it Flaminio uneasily hurries the King away. Avito comes stealthily out of Fiora's room, walks toward the terrace, then turns back. At that moment the beautiful Fiora, her hair in disorder, appears in the doorway. She is clad in an ivory-white gown. Avito voices his apprehension because it is still dark, which means that Geronte, the shepherd, has given the flute signal too soon—before the coming of dawn. Fiora asks him to return to her chamber, but Avito demurs, answering that now is the moment for farewell to their night of love. They cling to each other in ecstatic embrace. Nervously Avito points to the door leading to Archibaldo's room and asks if it is closed, but Fiora seeks to calm him, singing of the profound peace in her heart. Her lover replies that that very peace fills him with fear. Passionately Fiora asks Avito for a kiss, that he may share her serenity. Then follows a short duet in which the two sing rapturously of their love.

Avito now notices that the lantern has been extinguished and tears himself from Fiora's arms. Terror-stricken, he says someone has been on the terrace during the night. It was the wind, Fiora reassures him, but Avito reminds her that the night has been calm. Suddenly Fiora warns him to flee. He escapes while she runs toward her door.

At that moment Archibaldo enters, calling Fiora's name. She vainly tries to elude him, but he calls out that he knows she is near, that he can hear her breathing. He demands to know to whom she has been speaking. To herself, Fiora lies. Archibaldo comes slowly nearer, commanding her to remain where she is. Sensing her lie, he expresses his incredulity at her attempt to deceive him. His manner grows tender and fatherly as he again asks who was with her. Resolutely Fiora repeats her lie.

Touching her, the old man asks why she is trembling if she is telling the truth. Fiora craftily replies that he also trembles, even though he is not lying. Archibaldo retorts that he trembles only for her lie. Quickly Fiora says she came out on the terrace because her thoughts of someone had banished sleep. When Archibaldo angrily demands to know of whom she was thinking, Fiora calmly replies it was of her husband, Manfredo.

Archibaldo, in despair because he cannot see the deceit in her face, cries out against his blindness. Then, in bitter wrath, he dramatically denounces her duplicity and commands her to go lest he slay her.

Flaminio comes in to announce that the Baron Manfredo has returned home at the head of his troops. There is a fanfare of trumpets. Archibaldo excitedly orders Flaminio to go and welcome Manfredo. In grim anger he forbids Fiora to meet her husband and orders her to her room. Fiora slowly leaves, a triumphant smile on her face.

Manfredo enters. Archibaldo joyously embraces his son, saying he brings the light with him. Manfredo replies that he grew impatient with the siege and decided to return home for a few days. The war, he adds, will soon be over. When he asks for Fiora, Archibaldo tells him she is sleeping. In a brief but impassioned aria ("Oh, padre mio"), Manfredo sings that this return is dearer to him than any long-expected reward. Through war and victory he has kept his virtue stainless for the sake of Fiora's love, nurtured by his father. Archibaldo bids him enjoy his happiness to the utmost and tells him that Fiora is approaching.

Although her manner is cold, Fiora tries to mask it with an air of friendliness. She tells Manfredo that she came out on the battlements before dawn to look for him, then with deliberate cunning asks affirmation of Archibaldo. Off guard, the old King blurts out that he "caught" her, but quickly corrects himself and says he found her waiting.

Manfredo holds out his arms to Fiora and begins a tender, impassioned song of love and longing. He turns to his father, saying that, despite his blindness, he now must surely see his son's happiness because of the light that streams from his son's soul. Manfredo gently leads Fiora to her room. Left alone, Archibaldo bitterly implores God—who has taken away his eyes —to let him be truly blind.

ACT TWO

A circular terrace high on the castle walls, overlooking the valley. At the rear a stairway leads to the upper part of the battlement, and a stone bench curves around the lower part. As the curtain rises there is a brief, melodious introduction, followed by the sound of trumpets, coming as if from the valley below.

Manfredo enters with Fiora, his arms affectionately about her. He sings a profoundly moving aria expressive of his longing for Fiora's love and his sorrow at parting ("Dimmi, Fiora, perchè ti veggo ancora"). Anxiously he inquires why she is so restrained and aloof at this moment, while his own intense grief makes him feel as though he were leaving her forever. Fiora continues the majestic, sweeping melody as she responds that his untimely parting has robbed her of the joy she had in his arrival. His journeyings have kept them strangers, she adds wistfully, and when he returns it is only to tell her that he must soon leave again.

Deeply troubled, Manfredo protests that she speaks to him as would an enemy asking for peace. He implores her to speak frankly, but Fiora repeats that her mood is only the result of his parting. Dramatically Manfredo assures her that he will return, then quietly asks for a token of her love to take with him on his journey. Momentarily overcome by her secret sorrow, Fiora cries out that he is demanding her very life. Tenderly Manfredo replies that there is only one gift he would have. Within a few minutes he will be riding down the valley with his men. As the tower on which they now stand will be the last bit of home he will see, he entreats her to stay there and wave a white scarf, which he will send to her, until he has disappeared from view. This will seem, he tells her, as though she were drying the tears of his heart.

Fiora, sincerely touched by compassion, promises to grant his request. Almost overcome by his emotions, Manfredo tells her that her wave of farewell will almost make this parting a joy. He embraces her passionately; then, shaken and sobbing, rushes off.

A galloping rhythm in the orchestra vividly portrays Manfredo and his troops riding down the valley. With a gesture of distaste at the thought of Manfredo's embrace, Fiora ascends the stairs to the top of the battlement. A moment later Avito enters, disguised as a castle guard. Ecstatically he calls her name. At first Fiora does not recognize him, then expresses astonishment at his being there. He explains that, with Flaminio's connivance, he has been hiding in the castle and watching her.

Fiora now tells him that she must renounce his love. Stunned at her words, Avito refuses to believe her. She cries out that now her life is enshrouded in gloom, that she has been conquered by her husband's kindness and devotion. She entreats Avito to leave her. In helpless bewilderment he asks where he is to go—how he is to live without her. Suddenly Fiora warns Avito to hide, for someone is coming. Dazed, Avito leaves.

Fiora comes down from the battlement. A maid enters and hands her a casket, saying that it is an offering from Baron Manfredo. Slowly opening the casket, Fiora takes out a long white scarf. For several moments she stands motionless, holding the scarf, her arms listlessly hanging at her sides. The rhythm of the galloping horses, heard previously in the introduction to this act, echoes in the orchestra. Fiora again ascends to the battlement and, to the accompaniment of sweeping musical phrases, waves the scarf three times.

As the music grows quieter, Avito enters. Softly he sings farewell, telling her he shall never return. He asks only that, if she refuse him a kiss, she permit him to caress the scarf. She forbids him to touch it. Then her manner changes and she expresses alarm at his pallor. It is the poison of love, Avito replies. Marveling at how his love is overwhelming her, Fiora remorsefully says that the evil she has done is destroying her lover. Avito beseeches her to come down, but Fiora refuses. She turns and waves the scarf.

Avito starts for the staircase, but Fiora warns him away and again waves the scarf. Crushed, Avito says he will leave, although he is almost too weary to drag himself away. Relenting, Fiora calls him back and asks him to kiss the golden fringe which she had embroidered on her gown. Avito complies and in soaring phrases sings of his ecstasy. His kisses sting, he cries, as though she had left her needle in the embroidery. Rapturously he sings that he will no longer listen to Fiora's protests.

In vain Fiora cries that his pleading is like heavy lead that is dragging her down. Ardently Avito begs for her lips. At last, Fiora, helpless in her passion, yields to Avito, saying that she bows down to him as a tree bows over someone dying of thirst. Gasping, "Ho sete! Ho sete!" ("I thirst! I thirst!"), Avito draws her into his arms. Then, after a long kiss, the lovers seat themselves on the stone bench and begin a rhapsodic duet. It rises to an overpowering climax as Avito sings of a kiss which shall be the last of an infinity of kisses and the first of an eternity.

Suddenly Archibaldo's voice is heard, calling Fiora's name. The lovers, completely oblivious, remain in their embrace. An instant later Archibaldo strides out on the terrace, followed by Flaminio. Leaping to his feet, Avito rushes toward the old man with drawn dagger, but Flaminio stops him. Fiora answers Archibaldo while frantically signaling Avito to leave. Suspiciously Archibaldo asks Flaminio to tell him who else is present. As Avito escapes, Flaminio answers that no one is there. Again Archibaldo calls Fiora's name and again she answers.

The old man, having heard footsteps and knowing Flaminio has lied to him, angrily orders the servant to leave. Flaminio leaps to the battlement and announces that Manfredo is returning. Fiora exclaims in terror, while Archibaldo, surprised and confused, orders Flaminio to go and meet Manfredo.

Turning on Fiora, Archibaldo wrathfully denounces her treachery, then demands to know who has betrayed him. Fiora first denies everything, then defiantly proclaims that the one who fled was her lover. He orders her to speak her lover's name. She retorts that she will tell only Manfredo, because she can trust his kindness. Raging, Archibaldo strikes her down on the bench, crying out that Manfredo would only forgive her—because he himself taught his son forgiveness.

Then in terrible fury he seizes Fiora by the throat, again demanding her lover's name. Fiora answers that he is nameless. Archibaldo brands her a traitress, saying that the name he seeks is in her throat—the throat that is now in his hands. He warns her that, though Manfredo may pardon, he himself will not. Furiously he bids her speak. She quietly answers that her lover's name is Death. The old man tells her that even after she is dead he will hunt the betrayer down. In frantic despair Fiora begs to be allowed to live to defend her lover. With a fearful cry Archibaldo strangles her to death.

As a series of powerful chords sound in the orchestra, Archibaldo draws back horrified from Fiora's body. There is a long pause. Then Archibaldo sings of the utter silence and the deepening night about him. Only the tor-

rent of his anger can be heard. In sudden anguish and terror he remembers
that Manfredo is approaching to greet his wife. The old man places himself
before Fiora's body as if to conceal it, and thus awaits his son.

Manfredo's voice is heard, excitedly calling for Fiora. He rushes in, fear-
stricken, and asks his father if Fiora has fallen from the wall. As he watched
her waving her scarf, he continues, she suddenly disappeared. Archibaldo
despairingly asks Manfredo for his sword, so that he may perish with her
who is dead. Manfredo gasps. Brokenly the old man confesses that he killed
Fiora. When Manfredo cries out in agony, Archibaldo, shouting "Impura!"
declares that Fiora's impurity was as black as night. Dazed, Manfredo exclaims that this is madness.

Archibaldo tells Manfredo that he was betrayed in his own house, that
even while Fiora waved her scarf she was dragged from the battlement for
a tryst with her lover and thus he found her. In calm resignation Manfredo
muses that, though Fiora's heart was capable of such great love, that love
was not for him. Manfredo begs to be allowed to weep on his wife's body.
The old man asks how he can bear thus to join his lips with those of the betrayer. Manfredo asks his name. Bitterly Archibaldo replies that he could
not see him but that the fires of his revenge will light the shadows in which
he will hunt down the guilty lover for his son's sake.

Again Manfredo begs to look upon Fiora. Imperiously the old King refuses, telling his son that he would only see the marks of his father's fingers
around her throat. He commands Manfredo to lead him from the terrace,
showing the way by the sound of his footsteps. As he obeys, Archibaldo lifts
Fiora's lifeless body into his arms and slowly follows his son. The curtain
falls.

ACT THREE

The chapel crypt beneath the castle, with steps leading down from
above. On a catafalque in the center lies the body of Fiora, robed in white.
As the curtain rises, a group of mourners are seen kneeling near the body.
After several measures of introduction, voices of the choir within the chapel
begin a solemn requiem. They sing of the torpor of Death and the darkness
of Desire that will brood over the world until the day on which the Creator
will redeem mankind. Then love will triumph and man will at last be lifted
to the light.

A young girl sings, lamenting that she has returned weeping to this place
to see her princess and she has found the whole world in tears. In hushed
voices the chorus of mourners calls Fiora's name, beseeching her to answer.
A young man sings that Fiora seems alive, and yet so weary. The lamentation grows louder.

Suddenly an old woman cries out that on Fiora's face is written "Vengeance!" The other women look closely. Excitedly they chatter that her eyes
seem to accuse the old man. They angrily denounce the foul crime and cry
out that they will have revenge. Their outburst is interrupted by the chanting of the choir and the tolling of a bell. The women sink to their knees
again. The men tell them to be silent. The mourners now rise to go, bidding

Fiora a final farewell. Avito appears on the steps. The old woman says it is the Prince of Altura. The mourners murmur his name as they leave.

Standing motionless until all have left the crypt, Avito walks toward Fiora's bier. He sings a deeply moving aria voicing his bitter grief ("Fiora . . . È silenzio"). Calling her name, he entreats her to speak. Her hands will be cold, he sings, and cold, too, the lips he has so often kissed. No more can he hold what once he could claim his own. But one last breath must surely be within her yet, and that breath lingers on her mouth. In a frenzy of despair he kisses Fiora's lips.

The next instant Avito staggers back, crying, "Miracle!" He feels himself perishing with Fiora. He exults that his heart is being racked and marvels at the power of pain. Walking a few paces toward the steps, he reels as if struck. The chains that bind him to the "rock" of his life are strong, he muses. In sudden fear he hears someone approaching.

Then out of the shadow steps Manfredo. The betrayer is caught at last, he sings in grim satisfaction. He is dumfounded as he recognizes Avito, who gasps out that he is barely able to speak. Exultingly Manfredo tells him that he is doomed, that Fiora's lips have been smeared with a powerful poison to trap her guilty lover. Avito recoils in horror. He has desecrated her lips with his kiss, Manfredo goes on, and for that he shall die. In agony Avito asks Manfredo how he could thus defile Fiora's hallowed mouth. Then Manfredo reveals that it was Archibaldo who did this odious thing to snare Fiora's lover for his son's satisfaction.

Quietly Avito says that justice has been done and that Manfredo may exult in his death. In bitter anguish Manfredo asks Avito if Fiora really loved him. Far more than the life of which she has been robbed, Avito replies, then urges Manfredo to make haste if he wishes to exact revenge, because death is near.

Avito staggers forward and Manfredo eases him gently to the ground. From the chapel come the voices of the choir. In a paroxysm of despair Manfredo raises his arms and cries out to God that he cannot hate. Wildly he turns to Fiora's body and exclaims that she must not leave him in his utter desolation. He implores her to let him join her once again, and throwing himself on Fiora's lifeless form, he too kisses her lips. He lies there shuddering as the poison works its fatal power.

And now the old King Archibaldo gropes his way into the crypt. He hears a groan. In phrases partly sung and partly spoken, he declares triumphantly that he has caught the thief. He reaches out and touches Manfredo, saying that he wants to feel his victim's last heartbeats. The dying Manfredo gasps out that he is wrong. The terrible truth dawns on Archibaldo. In a stricken voice he sings that now Manfredo, too, is with him, past all redemption in the eternal shadows. The curtain falls.

Andrea Chénier

by UMBERTO GIORDANO

[1867–1948]

Libretto by
LUIGI ILLICA

CHARACTERS

Major-domo ....*Baritone*
Charles Gérard ....*Baritone*
Madeleine de Coigny......................................*Soprano*
Countess de Coigny, her mother.......................*Mezzo-soprano*
Bersi, Madeleine's maid..............................*Mezzo-soprano*
Fléville, a cavalier.....................................*Baritone*
The Abbé ....*Tenor*
Andrea Chénier, a poet....................................*Tenor*
Mathieu, a waiter..*Baritone*
Incredibile (the spy)......................................*Tenor*
Roucher, a friend of Chénier...............................*Bass*
Madelon (Vecchia—the old woman) ....*Mezzo-soprano*
Dumas, president of the revolutionary tribunal.................*Baritone*
Fouquier-Tinville, attorney general of the tribunal.............*Baritone*
Schmidt, jailer at St. Lazare prison.........................*Baritone*
Ladies and gentlemen of the court, citizens of Paris, soldiers, servants,
dancers, peasants, prisoners, members of the revolutionary tribunal

Place: Paris
Time: Before and during the French Revolution
First performance: Teatro La Scala, Milan, March 23, 1896
Original language: Italian

GIORDANO is identified with the modern Italian operatic composers of the *verismo,* or realistic, school, which includes such men as Puccini, Mascagni, Leoncavallo, and Montemezzi. His technique is a projection of the methods developed by Wagner and (in his later years) by Verdi to effect a merging of music and drama. There are no set arias in the fashion of earlier Italian opera.

The story of Andrea Chénier, though highly fictionized, is taken from history and is based on events in the life of André Marie de Chénier, a French poet of the eighteenth century. He supported the Revolution but later incurred the enmity of Robespierre by writing pamphlets protesting the lack of discipline and order in the movement. Chénier was proscribed and beheaded in the prison of St. Lazare.

ACT ONE

The ballroom in the château of the Countess de Coigny. The major-domo and other servants are decorating the room in preparation for a ball. Directed by Gérard, himself a servant and secretly a revolutionist, the servants bring in a large sofa. When they leave, Gérard dusts it off and straightens the cushions, meanwhile soliloquizing over the events it has witnessed ("Compiacente a'colloqui"). Many a cavalier, he muses, has sat here and whispered vapid nothings into the ear of a painted and bedizened lady of fashion. As Gérard addresses his thoughts to the sofa he mimics the simpering and posturing of a dandy.

He stops short when he sees his father, long a retainer in the household, enter the room carrying a flower stand. Trembling from his efforts, the old man is forced to sit down and rest for a moment. Gérard goes to his father, helps him to his feet, and then assists him from the room. Returning, he murmurs bitterly over the fact that for sixty years his father has given his strength in the service of his haughty and unappreciative masters. Now, added to the burden of his years, he must bear the shame of seeing his son as a slave in the same household.

Looking around the luxurious room, Gérard gives vent to his rage over the selfishness and arrogance of the aristocracy, the hateful breed that fattens on the misery of the oppressed and is heedless of everything except its own pleasures ("T'odio casa dorata"). Fiercely cursing them, he cries that he, a despised lackey, will yet pronounce their doom. Hearing voices outside, he controls his anger and assumes the impassive mien of a servant.

The Countess de Coigny and Madeleine appear, attended by Bersi, Madeleine's maid, and the major-domo. As the Countess pauses at the door to speak to the major-domo, Madeleine and Bersi enter the room. Madeleine murmurs poetically about the deepening twilight and the serenity of the evening hours. Gérard, secretly in love with her, looks passionately at her and remarks in an aside over her beauty. Bustling into the room, the Countess asks Gérard if the singers, musicians, and actors who are to provide the evening's entertainment have arrived. Gérard assures her that everything is in readiness. After a brief conversation with Madeleine regarding the guests, the Countess leaves, admonishing her daughter to make all haste in dressing for the party.

In a sprightly air ("Si, io penso all'tortura"), Madeleine complains to Bersi over the various forms of torture devised by the dictators of fashion in the name of feminine adornment. First of all, there is that worst of all nuisances, the corset, holding the waist in a viselike grip. Then comes the gown, fitted like a sheath and designed to make every movement as painful as possible. The crowning absurdity is the enormous hat, which succeeds in hiding the wearer's features. The general effect of all this frippery, Madeleine observes, is to change a beautiful woman into an apparition. When the Countess reappears to supervise last-minute preparations, Madeleine informs her that she has decided to wear a simple white gown and a rose in her hair. She leaves with Bersi to attend to her toilette.

Fluttering about, the Countess besieges Gérard and the other servants with useless questions concerning the pastoral which is to be the feature of the entertainment. She is repeatedly assured that the singers and musicians are ready and that the shepherds and shepherdesses are dressed in their costumes. The guests then begin to arrive and are greeted by the Countess with much excitement and chatter. There is a stir as the Chevalier Fléville and the Abbé are announced. As the ladies crowd around the Abbé, Fléville introduces to the Countess his two companions, Signor Fiorinelli, an Italian musician, and Andrea Chénier, whom Fléville describes as a rather gifted poet.

Attention centers for the moment on the Abbé, who, having lately come from Paris, is bombarded with questions about the latest political developments. The King, he informs his eager listeners, is being misled by his advisers, particularly by Necker, one of the craftiest of his ministers. The ladies and gentlemen beg him not to speak of this unpleasant individual. And what is worse, the Abbé goes on, the people have profaned the statue of Henry IV. There are polite exclamations of indignation over this dreadful news.

Mincing forward, Fléville observes that all these things really do not matter and urges the guests to give their attention to the pastoral, which is now to be performed. It is a typical eighteenth-century court playlet, mimed by a ballet to the accompaniment of a tuneful chorus sung by shepherds and shepherdesses ("O Pastorelli, addio! Ne andiamo verso"). The guests murmur their approval of the presentation and dutifully applaud the performers.

After the entertainment the Countess, moving about among her guests, approaches Chénier and asks him if he will favor the company with one of his poems. Chénier rather curtly declines. Madeleine, seated with her friends, takes note of his refusal and wagers that she can persuade the poet to speak of love. Going over to Chénier, she courteously asks him if he will oblige her by reading a poem—perhaps some amusing trifle about love. With a bow Chénier gallantly answers that though he considers her request a command the Muse is not readily invoked and is as elusive as love itself. Hearing him mention the word, Madeleine and her friends laugh mockingly over the fact that she has made good her wager.

Nettled by their disdainful laughter, Chénier tells Madeleine that he will comply with her request. He will read a poem which will reveal to her the profound truths that are hidden in the word "love." He discourses in a dramatic and moving refrain ("Un di all'azzuro spazio"). One day, he says, he looked at the glories of nature about him and his heart was filled with love for his beautiful country. Deeply moved, he went into a church to express his thoughts in prayer. But there, at the fountainhead of divine love and mercy, he saw a priest greedily collecting contributions, all the while spurning a wretched beggar who held out his hand for alms.

Ignoring the looks of surprise and displeasure from the guests, Chénier goes on with rising intensity. He tells how he visited the hovel of a workingman and heard him curse his rich employers, who denied him a living wage and forced him into a life of hopeless poverty. Chénier bitterly inveighs against the selfishness and greed of politicians and prelates. Looking at Madeleine, Chénier says that he seemed at first to see compassion and love for mankind shining in her eyes. But he has learned to his sorrow that there is nothing but mockery. In ringing phrases he cries out that she knows nothing of love—nothing of the divine emotion that embraces all mankind.

As the guests exclaim angrily over Chénier's audacious sentiments Madeleine quietly asks his pardon and turns away in embarrassment and confusion. Clapping her hands, the Countess orders the musicians to begin the gavotte and invites everyone to dance. Just as they take their places Gérard bursts into the salon, followed by a group of beggars who hold out their hands and intone a mournful plea for alms ("La notte e giorno"). Imitating the major-domo, Gérard strikes a pose and sardonically announces "His Lordship, Misery." Furiously the Countess demands to know who allowed these creatures in her home. He himself, Gérard replies. The Countess orders him to drive the beggars out at once and tells him to go with them.

Tearing off his livery, Gérard rages that he will rid himself once and for all of this detested badge of slavery ("Si, me ne vo, Contessa"). No more will he eat the food that chokes him when he thinks of the millions starving in the streets outside. When Gérard's father makes pathetic attempts to silence his son Gérard strips the old man of his lackey's coat. Hurling it to the floor, he cries that never again will he be forced to bow in servile respect before these people who have no pity in their hearts. There is a great uproar as footmen rush forward and push Gérard, his father, and the cringing beggars out of the room. Chénier quickly follows after them. In sorrow and dismay Madeleine watches him go.

The Countess sinks half fainting on the sofa, wailing that Gérard's rebellion has been brought on by his bad habit of reading. She does not deserve such ingratitude, she moans—she who gives to the poor every day and even gowns herself with appropriate simplicity when going among them to attend to their wants. Assured by the major-domo that the rabble is safely out of the house, the Countess instantly becomes herself again. As though nothing had happened, she invites the guests to continue dancing. They resume the gavotte as the curtain falls.

ACT TWO

The Café Hottot in Paris. At one side is an altarlike affair on which is a bust of Marat. A street and one of the bridges of the Seine are visible in the background. Mathieu and another waiter are busy wiping off tables. Mathieu pauses to dust off the bust of Marat. Bersi and Incredibile, the spy, are seated at a table. At another, Chénier is seated alone. Mathieu buys a paper from a newsboy, looks at it, and then growls that the brat has sold him a paper that is five months old. As the waiter goes on about his duties Bersi asks Incredibile if it is true that Robespierre is employing spies against the revolutionaries. Rather call them "observers of the people," Incredibile comments dryly. He casually asks Bersi if she has anything to fear.

In a spirited aria ("Temer? Perchè? Perchè temer dovrò?") Bersi replies that she is afraid of nothing, for she, like himself, is a true child of the Revolution. She revels in the excitement of being with the surging crowds, sharing their triumphs, drinking champagne while the blood of the aristocrats flows in the gutters. She enjoys walking among her friends in the market place, pausing occasionally to watch the tumbrels pass. At that moment a cart carrying doomed prisoners to the guillotine rattles by, followed by a howling throng.

As she watches, Incredibile, aside, reads aloud the notes he makes about Bersi in his spy's report. He is sure he saw her with a certain blond woman —very beautiful—obviously an aristocrat. Citizeness Bersi, he writes, is definitely under suspicion. She is to be watched closely, as is Chénier, who is undoubtedly waiting here to make contact with a counterrevolutionary. Saying good-by to Incredibile, Bersi leaves. The spy pockets his notebook and slowly follows her.

Roucher appears, looks carefully around, and hurries to Chénier's table. Handing Chénier a passport, Roucher warns him to leave at once, for his enemies are trailing him and every moment of delay is dangerous. Chénier scorns the thought of running away from his foes and in a dramatic refrain declares that he puts his faith in his destiny ("Credo a una possanza arcana"). Fate, he says, makes one man a poet, another a soldier. Perhaps fate has decreed that he, the poet Chénier, is to remain here. In passionate phrases Chénier goes on to say that, for him, love and destiny are one. He confesses that he is being inspired to this conclusion by certain wonderful letters from a mysterious woman. She is the creature of his dreams, he exclaims, surpassingly beautiful. He hears her voice in the night, singing that her love belongs only to him. Her very letters blaze with passion, Chénier says, adding, however, that he has had no success in his attempts to find her.

Confiding that he has hopes for a rendezvous with the unknown woman he adores, he shows Roucher one of the letters he has received. Examining it, Roucher remarks that it is obviously in a woman's hand and cynically implies that it is merely a communication from someone desiring an assignation. He advises Chénier to give his attention to his passport and to throw the letter away. His adored unknown, he says, is probably a painted courtesan who has been hired to spy on him.

Outraged at the thought, Chénier is about to rush away when Robespierre passes along the street, a clamoring mob at his heels. Hailing Robespierre, the people shout the names of the revolutionary heroes. Seeing Gérard, who is approaching the café, the crowd acclaims him as one of their newest favorites. As Gérard pauses in front of the café and looks around, Incredibile suddenly appears and walks up to him. In low tones he asks him to describe the lady whom he is seeking. Gérard launches into an extravagant description ("Azzuro occhio di cielo"), his refrain continuing as an obbligato to the choral phrases sung by the mob as they hail the revolutionaries. Gérard fervently tells the spy that if he can find this paragon of womanhood he can have anything he asks. Incredibile murmurs that Gérard will see her this very evening. Gérard goes on his way.

Approaching Roucher in the manner of a woman of the streets, Bersi leads him aside and in a hurried whisper tells him that he must detain Chénier, for someone wishes to see him. She warns that she is being watched. Seeing the spy walking toward her, Bersi turns, casually greets him, and accepts his invitation to go into the café for refreshments.

A crowd of people appears, singing a devil-may-care chorus about drinking and loving while there is time, for those who kiss today may die tomorrow ("Ah, riderem davver"). After they surge into the café, shouting for wine, Roucher and Chénier prepare to leave, Chénier lamenting that his dream of love has been shattered. Just at that moment Bersi hurries out of the café, calls to Chénier, and tells him that a lady is coming here in a few moments to ask for his help. Her name, Bersi says, is "Speranza." With that she goes back into the café. When Roucher warns Chénier of an ambush Chénier decides to get his sword. They both hurry away.

The scene grows darker. Mathieu emerges from the café and places a lighted lantern on Marat's altar. The spy now appears and conceals himself in the shadows. A woman, heavily veiled and enveloped in a long cloak, cautiously approaches the altar. The light from the lantern reveals her as Madeleine. Shortly afterward Chénier arrives, hurries over to her, and asks for whom she is seeking help. For herself, she answers. When he asks who she is, she repeats the words he spoke to her on the evening of the ball at the château—when he told her that she knew nothing of love. With that she lifts her veil. Chénier starts back in surprise when he recognizes her. At that moment the spy steps from his hiding place, softly exclaiming that she is the blond woman he has been seeking. Murmuring that he will inform Gérard, he glides away.

Noticing a figure disappearing into the shadows, Madeleine exclaims in terror. Chénier tries to calm her but expresses concern over the unknown dangers that surround them. It was Bersi who selected this spot, Madeleine says, adding that if anyone should challenge her she will pretend that she is a maid who is bringing a cloak for her mistress. Gazing tenderly at her, Chénier asks if she is the writer of the mysterious letters. Madeleine replies in a lovely, flowing melody ("Eravate possente"). When he was at the height of his power as a revolutionary, Madeleine says, she hoped that perhaps he would be able to save her from the fate of the other aristocrats. But then they were kept apart by unhappy circumstances. Now, through a caprice of fate, they meet—a woman who has espoused the revolutionary cause but is being hounded by spies, and a revolutionary who has been condemned by his own comrades.

She goes on to say that she never lost faith in the possibility of meeting him. For that reason, she says, she wrote the letters which she knew would move him to sympathy, even though she had once sneered at his ideals. When she learned that he had been denounced by the revolutionaries she decided to come to him, hoping that they—both outcasts—could share their fate. Poignantly she entreats him to aid her.

Chénier replies in an ecstatic refrain ("Ora soave, sublime ora d'amore"), crying that this is the moment of which he has been dreaming. Love has turned his sorrow into joy, and even death cannot frighten him now. Their voices blend in rapturous phrases as they pledge themselves to each other. They are about to rush away when Gérard suddenly appears in their path, crying Madeleine's name. Roucher dashes in, followed by the spy. Pushing Madeleine toward Roucher, Chénier shouts to his friend to take her to safety. The spy tries to bar Roucher's way, but the latter hurls him aside and escapes with Madeleine.

Gérard and Chénier draw their swords, neither recognizing the other in the darkness. Gérard lunges at Chénier, who feints, thrusts, and wounds him, taunting him for his poor swordmanship. As Chénier bends over him Gérard sees who he is, warns him that he is on the death list of Fouquier-Tinville of the tribunal, and urges him to flee for his life. Chénier rushes away.

The spy, who has meanwhile gone to summon gendarmes, now returns. As the men surround Gérard, he manages, by dint of frantic effort, to prevent the spy from speaking Chénier's name. Declaring that he did not recognize his assailant, Gérard faints. The crowd shouts for vengeance as the curtain falls.

ACT THREE

The revolutionary tribunal. On the president's dais at the rear, on which the judges are seated, stands a huge urn. As a succession of harsh, powerful chords sounds in the orchestra Mathieu rises and moves among the crowd gathered to witness the session of the tribunal. After inveighing against those who have turned traitor to the cause and declaring that all Europe has turned against the revolutionaries, he asks for contributions. The crowd hears him listlessly, and only a few people shuffle up to the urn and drop in coins. Looking at them in disgust, Mathieu sits down.

Gérard, still weak from his wounds, walks slowly into the room, bringing a shout of welcome from the crowd. Mathieu asks him to plead with the people, saying that he undoubtedly can speak the words which will drag the necessary funds out of the pockets of his listeners. Quietly, but with intense earnestness, Gérard makes his appeal ("Lacrime e sangue dà la Francia"). France, he says, is shedding tears of blood. Some of her provinces are in flames. Austria, Prussia, England, Europe—all have risen against those who fight for liberty. Gérard asks the women to contribute their jewelry and trinkets, and as he finishes they come forward and drop earrings, brooches, bracelets, and money into the urn.

Led by a boy of about fifteen, an old blind woman makes her way through the crowd and stands before the dais. Her name is Madelon, she says. Her son was slain in the storming of the Bastille and his eldest son perished for the cause. Now she offers the youngest and the last. He is a child, but he is strong and brave enough to die for France. Deeply moved, Gérard tells her that the boy will be accepted. In poignant phrases the old woman bids her grandson farewell and then is led away. As though at a signal, the people strike up the *Carmagnole*, one of the famous songs of the Revolution ("Amici, ancor cantiam, beviam"). In fiery unison phrases they sing that they will drink to Freedom and to the death of all tyrants. After the song they gradually disperse.

While the throng is milling about, the spy enters and approaches Gérard, telling him that Chénier has been traced and that the trap is closing on him. Gérard inquires about Madeleine. The spy remarks that once Chénier is in the net she will appear of her own accord. When Gérard expresses doubt, Incredibile bids him listen to the cry of a passing newsboy, who shouts the news of Andrea Chénier's arrest.

In a cynical, mocking refrain the spy describes how a lovelorn lady will go in search of the one she adores if he fails to come to her of his own volition ("Donnina innamorata che d'aspettar s'annoia"). She will watch and wait. Suddenly she learns that her lover is in danger. Inspired with magic courage by this stupid emotion called "love," she will risk all to fly to his aid. The spy assures Gérard that he will see the lady before nightfall.

Shocked by Incredibile's sneering contempt, Gérard cries that Madeleine will hate him and reject him utterly when she discovers that Chénier is at his mercy. Incredibile dismisses his misgivings with the coarse remark that a woman is made up of soul and body—and the latter is the more important consideration. He urges Gérard to write Chénier's indictment—the poet must be denounced before the tribunal.

Gérard, seating himself at a table, begins writing and then throws down his pen in disgust, saying he cannot do so vile a thing. The crowds are gathering outside, Incredibile murmurs over his shoulder. Gérard then gives expression to the struggle in his heart in one of the most magnificent numbers in the opera, the great aria, "Nemico della patria?" The accusation that a man is "an enemy of his country" always sways the mob, he reflects with a bitter laugh. He reads aloud as he begins writing Chénier's record: Born in Constantinople . . . student at St. Cyr . . . soldier . . . traitor . . . poet . . . a dangerous seditionist.

Laying down his pen, Gérard gives himself over to reflection about the past. Once he was a brave and honest man, he muses, a man who could not be swayed by ignoble impulses of revenge. Now he has merely changed masters—now he is a slave to passion and a cynical murderer in the name of Freedom—a son of the Revolution. A phrase of the *Marseillaise* flashes through the orchestra as he sings. He thinks of how he has repudiated the idealism of his early days, when in his revolutionary zeal he burned with the desire to make this earth a paradise where all men could live as brothers. Now he has crushed this idealism to make room for hate and lust in his heart. And it is love, he muses sardonically, that has brought about this change in him. Goaded by his desire for Madeleine, he cries that nothing exists—only passion is real. Shaken by his emotions, he hastily finishes writing the indictment and signs his name. Incredibile glides to his side, reads the indictment with a murmur of satisfaction, and shuffles away.

Madeleine is escorted in by Mathieu. Gérard tells her that it is through his own spies that she was brought here. To make sure that she would appear, he has arrested her lover. Madeleine quietly tells him to take his revenge. With passionate intensity Gérard declares that he has not brought her here because he desires revenge but because he loves her and fate has decreed that he shall have her ("Perchè ciò volle il mio voler possente").

He has longed for her since she was a child—since the days he first served as lackey in her château. Her beauty and allure are driving him mad. If only for one short hour, he must feast on her caresses. Gazing avidly at her, he asks who will now save her from his love. Crying that she will rush into the street and give herself up to the mob rather than submit to him,

Madeleine tries to escape, but Gérard bars her way. She screams in terror, then suddenly, with icy calm, tells him that she will surrender to him if he will save Chénier. Bowing his head, Gérard murmurs in wonder and despair over her great love for the poet.

Staring before her with unseeing eyes, Madeleine recalls, in a poignant and moving aria, the terrible night when her mother perished in the flames of her home ("La mamma morta"). She remembers how she fled with Bersi, who took her to a place of safety and cared for her when she was homeless and ill. And then, after many days of misery and loneliness, she heard the voice of love. In rapturous phrases she sings of the joy that love brought into her life—how its magic power transported her to paradise. Madeleine's voice dies away to a hopeless whisper as she turns to Gérard and tells him that he may have his way, for now her heart has died within her.

Moved by her tragic story, Gérard looks at her in sadness and pity. A courier enters and hands him a message. Reading it, Gérard groans that Chénier is lost. His enemies have hastened his case and he is being brought to the tribunal at this very moment. The clamor of the crowd is heard outside. In response to Madeleine's frantic plea Gérard promises to do what he can to save Chénier. As he writes a note to be presented to the president of the tribunal the mob storms into the room. Pandemonium reigns as the members of the tribunal file in and take their places. The people excitedly cry out the names of the men they recognize—Dumas, the president; Vilate, the painter; Fouquier-Tinville, the attorney general, and so on.

Then the prisoners are brought in, and Madeleine exclaims as she sees Chénier. Several of the accused are quickly disposed of, after which Dumas reads the name of Andrea Chénier. The crowd stirs expectantly. Fouquier begins reading the indictment, which charges that Chénier has written against the Revolution. Chénier shouts that it is a lie. Gérard remorsefully murmurs to Madeleine that it is he who has brought these accusations against Chénier. Dumas refuses Chénier permission to answer the indictment. Rising quickly, Gérard, backed by the crowd, demands that Chénier be allowed to answer. Yielding, Dumas gives his consent.

In a ringing refrain ("Si, fui soldato e floriosa affrontata") Chénier speaks in his own defense. He was once a soldier of the Revolution, he says, a soldier who faced an honorable death for his country—not the ignoble doom of a traitor which is being imposed on him here. As a writer he fought with his pen, striking out at hypocrisy and oppression wherever he found them. He compares his life then to a ship sailing proudly and freely on a sunlit sea. But now, he says, the ship has been driven on the shoals. Yet even if it is wrecked the banner of his faith will float from the mast, and on that banner is written "Patria." Looking up at Fouquier, Chénier defiantly tells him to take his life but to leave his honor unstained.

As Fouquier proclaims that witnesses will be called, Gérard electrifies the court by striding forward and declaring that the indictment is a lie. When Fouquier asks why he wrote it Gérard answers that it was done out of personal hatred and jealousy. As Dumas pounds for order the crowd howls that Gérard has no doubt been bribed.

Defying the crowd and the court, Gérard furiously denounces the proceedings of the tribunal as an orgy of hatred and revenge ("La patria? La giustizia osi tu dire?"). Rather than condemn Chénier, who has the interest of France at heart, he cries, they should hail him as a hero. Bidding them listen to the sounds of fighting outside, Gérard shouts that there the real France speaks—there, where her patriots are dying—not in this court, where her poets are being unjustly condemned to a traitor's death. Impetuously he rushes up to Chénier and embraces him.

As the jury retires he whispers to Chénier that Madeleine is in the courtroom. Looking ardently at her, Chénier murmurs that, having seen her once again, he will gladly die. The jury returns. Fouquier announces the verdict: Death. As Chénier is led away, Madeleine cries out his name in terror and despair. The curtain falls.

ACT FOUR

The courtyard of St. Lazare prison. Chénier is writing at a table. Roucher is seated beside him. It is midnight, only a few hours before Chénier is to go to the guillotine. Schmidt, the jailer, comes in to tell Roucher that he must leave. Roucher gives him some money and asks to be allowed to remain a few moments longer. As Schmidt leaves, Chénier lays down his pen, saying that he has finished. In a beautiful aria ("Come un bel di di maggio") he reads to Roucher the poem he has written. It is, in effect, the last will and testament of a poet. Chénier speaks of his life as a summer day that is drawing to a close. The bliss of living and loving are gone forever and there is only time for a last farewell to his Muse before the headsman summons him. Carried away by his emotions, Chénier sings a flaming invocation to Poetry, his goddess, and to her sublime inspiration, dedicating to her his last song. As he finishes, Roucher embraces him in farewell and leaves. Chénier is taken back to his cell.

A knock is heard at the prison gate. Schmidt, swinging his lantern and singing to himself, goes to the gate and opens it. He bows respectfully as he recognizes Gérard, who enters with Madeleine. She bribes the jailer to permit her to take the place of a certain Idia Legray, who is among the condemned. Schmidt then leaves to bring Chénier, reminding Madeleine to come forward when he calls the name of Legray.

As she says farewell to Gérard he cries that the nobility of her love puts even death to shame. He turns away, murmuring in an aside that he will make one last appeal to Robespierre. Schmidt returns with Chénier, who rushes into Madeleine's arms. In a profoundly moving duet ("Vicino a te s'aqueta") Madeleine and Chénier hail their love and exult that death will forever unite them. In the magnificent climax they sing that love and death are one. As they stand in a passionate embrace Schmidt enters with guardsmen and gendarmes. He calls out the names of Andrea Chénier and Idia Legray. With an exultant cry of "Viva la morte!" Madeleine and Chénier walk hand in hand to the guillotine. The curtain falls.

Arabella

by RICHARD STRAUSS

[1864–1949]

Libretto by
HUGO von HOFMANNSTHAL

Based on a novelized sketch, by him, entitled "Lucidor" (1917) and
designated as "Figures for an Unwritten Comedy"

CHARACTERS

A fortuneteller .... *Mezzo-soprano*
Adelaide, the Countess Waldner...................... *Mezzo-soprano*
Zdenka, her younger daughter.............................. *Soprano*
Matteo, a young officer...................................... *Tenor*
Arabella, elder daughter of Count and Countess Waldner.......... *Soprano*
Elemer ⎤   ⎧ *Baritone*
Dominik ⎬ Counts and suitors of Arabella................... ⎨ *Tenor*
Lamoral ⎦   ⎩ *Tenor*
Theodor Waldner, a retired captain......................... *Baritone*
Mandryka, a wealthy landowner of Slavonia..................... *Bass*
Fiakermilli, a music-hall singer............................... *Soprano*
Welko ⎤
Djura ⎬ hussars and Mandryka's servants.................. *Acting roles*
Jankel ⎦

A waiter, Arabella's woman companion, three gamblers, a physician, a
groom, coachmen, guests at the Coachmen's Ball, hotel residents, other
waiters

Place: Vienna
Time: 1860
First performance: Dresden Opera House, Dresden, Germany, July 1, 1933
Original language: German

RICHARD STRAUSS was in his sixties when he started writing the score of
Arabella in 1927. It represents the last collaboration with his famous
librettist, Hugo von Hofmannsthal. The composer completed the
score in 1933. The libretto is admittedly rather weak, while the score itself
is not considered one of Strauss's best. Although there are certain arid spots,
Arabella does contain some of Strauss's most skillful musical characterization, and, in general, the opera's faults are lost in the thrilling outpour-
ing of Straussian melody. As is usual with Strauss, the orchestra, in its statement of various themes, plays a vital part in the unfolding of the drama.
Arabella had its première in this country on February 10, 1955 at the Metropolitan in an English translation by John Gutman.

ACT ONE

There is no overture and the curtain rises almost immediately. The scene is an elaborately-decorated salon in an apartment hotel in Vienna. Adelaide, the Countess Waldner, and a fortuneteller are seated at a table. Zdenka,[1] who is wearing boy's clothes, is sitting at a writing desk at one side of the room. She is looking through a pile of bills, notes, and letters. The ensuing scene is in quasi-recitative.

The fortuneteller informs the Countess that the cards are more encouraging than they were last week. The Countess reacts to the news with eagerness. There is a knock on the door. Adelaide motions to Zdenka and tells her no one is to interrupt. When Zdenka opens the door, someone thrusts a letter into her hand. She makes excuses to the unseen messenger and tells him to come back later. Looking at the letter, she remarks that it is just another unpaid bill. Engrossed in the cards, Adelaide tells Zdenka to put the bill with the others, then agitatedly asks the fortuneteller what else she reads in the cards.

Trying to calm her, the woman says an inheritance is slowly but surely coming closer. Time is too short, wails Adelaide. There is only one hope for this impoverished family: Arabella must land a husband at once. To add to the Countess' distress, the fortuneteller says that Count Waldner is at the moment having extremely bad luck at cards. Almost panic-stricken, Adelaide prays that help may come through Arabella. Then she wants to know if the cards foretell an engagement.

The fortuneteller intones that she sees an officer. Overhearing, Zdenka exclaims, "Matteo!" The fortuneteller shakes her head. This is a stranger, she declares. Adelaide exclaims that if this prediction comes true before next Sunday she will present the fortuneteller with her brooch as a reward.

As though in a trance, the woman goes on to say that the stranger is coming from a distant country. He has been summoned from his home there in the forest by a letter. Adelaide is certain the man is Count Elemer. But why, she wonders, does he hesitate to propose? It is not he—it is the girl who demurs, says the fortuneteller.

Joyously, Adelaide compliments her on being able to read her daughter's character so accurately. Arabella, she says, is refusing out of pride—which is quite like her. Just then there is another knock on the door. Zdenka answers, only to be handed another bill. The fortuneteller glances at her, looks at the cards and then frowns. Now there is another man, she says darkly, who is coming between the daughter and the rich fiancé.

Struck by the Countess' sudden look of despair, the fortuneteller senses something is wrong. Adelaide melodramatically points to Zdenka and cries, "My other daughter!" The fortuneteller stares in surprise.

The Countess then explains that the family is not wealthy enough to bring up *two* young ladies in proper fashion, and so they have allowed

[1] Sometimes called Zdenko by her family, apparently to keep up the pretense of her being a boy.

Zdenka to grow up masquerading as a boy. In spite of that, Zdenka deeply loves her sister and would never harm her. The cards, chants the fortune-teller, never lie . . . here is the officer, there the blond girl . . . two sabres are flashing . . . the rich fiancé draws back. . . . That is the warning. Rising hastily, Adelaide asks the woman to come into her own room—where they can start all over again.

Left alone, Zdenka soliloquizes about the situation ("Sie wollen Alle Geld"). Staring ruefully at the pile of bills, she murmurs that everybody wants money. Some even threaten to sue. Reading one of the letters, Zdenka gasps in surprise: here is someone who writes that the Count and his family are about to leave on a journey. Then, she wails, she will never see him again (meaning Matteo, whom she secretly loves).

Zdenka runs to the door of her mother's room, listens anxiously, and repeats aloud what she overhears: Mama is saying that the officer mentioned by the fortuneteller will not come here again . . . Arabella is too good for him. Zdenka whimpers that now Matteo will commit suicide and then Arabella and everybody else will know how much he loved her.

Deeply troubled, she begins praying in a touching, childlike fashion. She hopes that the journey will be called off, that Papa will win tonight—or perhaps Auntie will die suddenly and leave them a lot of money. And please, God, make Arabella love Matteo very much, so that he can be happy and make the family wealthy again. For this, Zdenka promises, she will renounce her womanhood and wear trousers the rest of her life.

Her prayer is interrupted by a third knock on the door. It is flung open and Matteo himself stalks in, cap in hand. He is in uniform, but without his sabre, and is carrying a bouquet of roses. Zdenka puts them in a vase. Matteo eagerly asks about Arabella. Zdenka says she has gone for a walk—no . . . there is no word for him, no note. Today, Zdenka adds, she and Arabella are to go for a sleigh ride with the three Counts, her current admirers.

Grinding his teeth, Matteo mutters that without Zdenka he would not even know where Arabella is. Zdenka tries to reassure him: Didn't Arabella send him a letter three days ago? It was like a message from heaven, Matteo exclaims, but now she is cold again, like a stranger. Well, says Zdenka with a shrug, that's how girls are . . . they offer more and more while hiding their real feelings.

Impulsively, in a pleading gesture, Matteo grasps Zdenka's arm. In a significant motion—as though afraid to give way to her real feelings toward him—she quickly draws away. He goes on to lament that Arabella seems to look through him "as through empty air." His words are accompanied by an orchestral phrase, heard now for the first time, which recurs as an identifying theme—the theme of "the wrong man." Matteo cries that only two things are left him—a transfer to Galicia or the revolver. With that he storms out, leaving poor Zdenka in tears.

But now who will help Zdenka, she sobs. As for letters, she can forge Arabella's handwriting in her sleep. Yet what good are these forgeries, she reflects, if *I* write them; I must find words to tell Arabella why this man deserves to be loved by her. If I fail in this, Zdenka sighs, then all is lost.

Arabella enters with her companion, whom she dismisses after a moment.

She comes on into the room, notices the roses, and asks if they were brought by a black hussar. When Zdenka tells her they were brought by Matteo, she is no longer interested (here the "wrong man" theme is heard momentarily). She asks who sent the other flowers, the perfumes, and laces. Zdenka says they are from her other admirers—the Counts Elemer, Dominik, and Lamoral. Arabella dismisses them with a flippant jest.

Zdenka implores her sister to consider Matteo's feelings. But that is all over, Arabella retorts, then remarks that there is something strange about Zdenka's interest in the officer. Perhaps, she adds knowingly, it is time for Zdenka to stop this masquerading and become the girl she is. Zdenka declares she will be a "boy" until she dies rather than a proud, heartless coquette.

Then begins a beautiful duet ("Ich red' im Ernst"), in which the leitmotifs that may be labeled "Longing" and "Prince Charming" are interwoven. Arabella sings that she cannot help her feelings: she finds herself interested in a man, then suddenly her heart turns away from him. It happens again and again. Some day, she goes on, the right man will stand before her; she will look into his eyes and all doubting will vanish. She will be as happy and obedient as a child.

Looking at her tenderly, Zdenka takes up the sensuous refrain, singing that her only wish is to help her sister be happy with someone worthy of her. It is as the fortuneteller said: "She is in the light, I am in darkness." Zdenka sings that she will leave, and in going she will bless her dear sister. The two voices bring the duet to a thrilling conclusion.

Suddenly there is the sound of sleigh bells outside. Zdenka exclaims it is Count Elemer's sleigh because she recognizes the sound of the bells. And right behind him, Arabella sings mockingly, will be Dominik and Lamoral. She will have to go along with them because today is Shrovetide Carnival. But only Elemer has come, Zdenka announces. Perhaps, Arabella muses, she must take Elemer as husband. Zdenka vehemently answers no. But the Carnival ends tonight, Arabella says, and she must give her answer. Turning away, Zdenka conjures up the dreadful picture of Matteo as a suicide. She will hold his body in her arms and kiss him for the one and only time.

Meanwhile, Arabella, gazing out of the window, says she has noticed a stranger standing across the street staring at the house. He looked at her keenly as she walked by, Arabella sings, and she almost expected to find flowers from him here when she returned from her walk. The "Prince Charming" motif is heard in the orchestra. With a swift gesture, Zdenka snatches Matteo's roses out of the vase and begs Arabella to hold them. These, she cries, are from the one true lover—she must never take any others. Arabella looks at her in perplexity.

At that moment Count Elemer is announced. Zdenka quietly leaves, and the Count comes strutting in, exuberantly sure of himself. A spirited musical dialogue follows. Elemer announces he and his friends have been drawing lots—and he has won the right to take Arabella for a sleigh ride, then to the Coachmen's Ball this evening.

Arabella pretends to be angry over their drawing lots to decide her fate. It is her fault, says Elemer with practiced gallantry, because the look in her eyes spurred her three lovers to fight for her. But their courtship has left

her heart still unclaimed, she tells the Count. Perhaps—who knows?—she
may meet the right man this very night. Elemer implores her to consider
him alone—and to let his sleigh carry them on the road to happiness.
Arabella quickly agrees to the latter suggestion, but adds that her brother
Zdenko is to come along. They will be ready in thirty minutes. Elemer is
furious, but makes the best of it. Arabella is heartless, he cries as he leaves,
but he adores her.

As soon as he is gone, Zdenka reappears. Arabella tells her to get ready
for the sleigh ride. Suddenly she sees the tall stranger passing by again outside. Both girls watch him.

Just then Adelaide and Count Waldner come in. He is elegantly dressed
but looks somewhat the worse for wear after a bad night. Fussing about,
Adelaide asks the girls to leave, and they do so. Waldner looks at the pile of
bills on the table and sighs unhappily—no letters, only bills. Adelaide complains that he has gambled away all their money, then asks him if he has
written any of his former army comrades for help. Yes, replies Waldner, but
none of them ever answered. He then tells Adelaide that he has written to
an old friend, Mandryka by name. He was very rich and a droll fellow to
boot. Once he had three thousand buckets of salt poured on the streets of
Verona because his current sweetheart wanted to go sleigh riding.

Now he has asked this Mandryka to be "generous," the Count goes on,
and in the letter he enclosed a photograph of Arabella. Perhaps the old fool
will propose marriage. When Adelaide protests against their daughter's marrying an old man, the Count declares that Arabella's eternal flitting about
must stop. Anyway, he adds, there is no other way out.

Adelaide suggests they go to Aunt Jadwiga. She will put them up in one
of her castles—the Count can be steward and she herself will keep house.
And what about our daughters? the Count asks. Well, Zdenka will have to
remain a boy, Adelaide answers, because they are too poor to afford two
daughters. As for Arabella, the cards foretell that she will have a successful
marriage. Meanwhile, grumbles Waldner, they are penniless. Adelaide assures him that something wonderful is bound to happen soon, then sweeps
into her room.

Waldner goes over to the table and glances through the bills again. A
waiter enters and the Count orders cognac. No cognac without cash, says
the waiter. Waldner waves him out. A moment later the waiter returns with
a card. The Count reads it and exclaims joyfully, "Mandryka!"

Mandryka is shown in, with Welko, one of his hussars, at his heels. He is
tall, handsome, about thirty-five, with the intriguing bearing of a foreigner.
Waldner rushes toward him with open arms, then stops short with a gasp of
astonishment. Mandryka courteously asks if he is Captain Count Waldner.
Count—yes, Waldner murmurs, but Captain no longer.

Mandryka motions behind him, and Welko hands him a letter. Then you,
he says, showing it to Waldner, must be the writer of this letter. There are
bloodstains on it, Mandryka goes on. It so happened that his men brought
him the letter while he was bear hunting; a huge beast clawed him and
some of his blood stained the letter. An orchestral phrase imitates the
growling of the bear.

Waldner says he wrote the letter—but to an older man of the same name, a former comrade-in-arms. Mandryka exclaims that the man was his uncle, who is now dead. He himself is the last Mandryka. Again he motions to Welko, who now hands him a photograph. This, he says, was enclosed in the letter. Waldner tells him it is a picture of his daughter Arabella; she is neither married nor engaged, he adds, in answer to Mandryka's question. In that case, says Mandryka, he would like to ask another question.

The two sit down. In a sweeping refrain, Mandryka asks if the Count perhaps enclosed the photograph as a joke. Waldner quickly replies that he thought his old friend might be amused. Did he think, Mandryka goes on, that this might happen: That his uncle, quite beguiled by the loveliness of the picture, might have come to the Count and declared that the man who would not woo so beautiful a creature does not deserve to live? What then?

Waldner, scarcely believing his ears, stammers that it would be an unexpected situation. In rising excitement, Mandryka goes on in a stirring refrain. He is the only Mandryka now, he sings as a fanfare of trumpets resounds in the orchestra. To him belong the forests and villages. Four thousand peasants see to it that he is happy. And now he is imploring a father to give him the hand of a girl of whom he has been dreaming the past fourteen weeks.

As Waldner sits in amazed silence, Mandryka explains he was late in coming to Vienna because his injuries kept him in bed. He forgot his farms, his dairies, and his hunting, and finally sold some of his woodland. As he had heard that Vienna is expensive, he determined nothing was to stand in his way when he came a-courting. And so, he goes on, taking out a huge wallet stuffed with bank notes, his oak forests turned into these pieces of paper. But there are still enough forests left for all his children. Waldner stares pop-eyed at the money.

Rather embarrassed at showing his wealth, Mandryka starts to put the wallet away. Waldner hastily remarks that it interests him very much. With disarming forthrightness, Mandryka takes out a thousand-gulden note and says, "Take some—I mean it!" Here there is a clever effect in the orchestra as the music imitates the natural voice inflections of that phrase. Mumbling that his banker is out of town, Waldner grasps the note with shaking hands. Mandryka offers a second and Waldner takes it.

A brief duet follows. Mandryka asks when he may meet the Countess and her daughter. Immediately, says Waldner, jumping up. Mandryka demurs and suggests they meet later that evening. He bows and starts to leave. With exaggerated courtesy, Waldner escorts him to the door.

In a happy daze, Waldner waltzes around the room, waving the bank notes and asking himself if it is all a dream. In a repetition of the musical phrase, he imitates Mandryka as he said, "Take it—I mean it!" Zdenka comes in, listens to his babbling, and asks what has happened. Scarcely noticing her, Waldner dances out of the room.

Zdenka watches him, sadly shaking her head. His worries are driving him crazy, she murmurs. Suddenly Matteo comes in. He asks if Arabella has left a note for him. Zdenka says he will have it this evening at the Coachmen's Ball. Then with a mysterious air she tells him to stay at his hotel before the ball. Somehow she will bring the note to him there. Matteo quickly leaves. Arabella appears and scolds Zdenka for not being ready. The horses are impatient, she says. Flustered and angry, Zdenka snaps, "The horses—and your Elemer!" She flounces out.

In a reflective phrase, Arabella murmurs the Count's name. Then in a moving refrain ("Das hat so einem sonderbaren Klang"), she tries to analyze her feelings about Matteo and Elemer. Then she muses about the tall stranger. The refrain rises to a brilliant climax as she revels in the thought that she is to be the Queen of the Coachmen's Ball. Zdenka appears, dressed for the ride. The sisters leave as sleigh bells jingle outside. The curtain falls.

ACT TWO

The curtain rises immediately to show a magnificent ballroom in the ornate style of the 1860s. At center is a broad marble staircase, branching off at the top to left and right. Through the archways at the back, couples may be seen dancing. Mandryka and Waldner are standing near the foot of the staircase. Arabella and her mother, flanked by several gentlemen, are slowly descending the stairs. Gazing at Arabella, Mandryka sings that she is an angel sent from heaven. Impetuously he grasps Waldner's hand. The Count winces, saying he won't be able to play cards for three days.

When Waldner prepares to introduce Mandryka, the latter steps back shyly. The Count looks at him in surprise. Adelaide, meanwhile, talks to Arabella about the handsome stranger, but the girl keeps her face averted. As though in a dream, she murmurs that this is the fateful moment. Adelaide looks anxiously into her face, inquiring if she is ill. Arabella asks to be left alone for a moment.

Adelaide walks toward the two men, and a moment later Arabella joins her. After the introductions, Adelaide takes Waldner's arm and literally drags him out of the ballroom. Unable to say a word, Mandryka gazes into Arabella's eyes.

At this point an ingeniously constructed ensemble begins ("Sie seh'n nicht aus") which interweaves some rather complicated stage action with musical dialogue. Somewhat naïvely, Arabella tells Mandryka he does not look like a man who would be interested in gay affairs such as this, and wonders what brought him here. *She* is asking *him* why he came, says Mandryka gallantly. Arabella has a moment of charming confusion.

As the two sit on a divan at one side of the ballroom, Dominik, Elemer, and Lamoral appear at the top of the stairs. First Dominik walks down and asks Arabella to dance. At intervals, the three in turn thus walk down and invite Arabella to dance with them. A waltz theme sounds in the orchestra as they do so.

Despite these interruptions, Arabella and Mandryka continue their conversation. Rather shyly, Mandryka begins to tell Arabella about his past life. In a refrain based on an old Croatian folk tune, he sings about his young wife, who died after they had been married but two short years. Arabella listens sympathetically, then waits for him to go on. Somewhat flustered, Mandryka apologizes for talking like a peasant. But his heart is on fire, he says with sudden fervor, because her photograph has kindled it. Arabella wonders how her photograph happened to reach him in faraway Slavonia.

Mandryka replies in a fiery, lyrical outburst. How he got it does not matter, he begins. The power of her beauty is such that it burns its image on a man's soul. And when that man is a simple person of the forests and the fields, that image takes hold of him completely. Then his mind is made up and nothing can change it.

Astonished at his outburst, Arabella gets up. Mandryka asks her forgiveness for keeping her from dancing. Lamoral now reappears and asks her to dance. She dismisses him and asks Mandryka to sit down again. The beautiful duet continues. Arabella asks him if he has any idea of what her family is like, but Mandryka implies that does not matter. He paints an extravagant picture of what her life will be like if she consents to be his Queen.

Half to herself, Arabella recalls her dream of "the one who is right for her" to a repetition of the theme heard in Act I, where she described that dream to Zdenka. This is how it is to be, she sings—no more doubting, no more asking. In another refrain based on a folk melody, Mandryka imagines the scene of their betrothal if they were living in a village beside the Danube in his native country. She would go to the well behind the house and draw just one goblet of water. Then she would bring it back to him as he stood at the threshold. And thus they would be betrothed in the eyes of God and man. Mandryka utters Arabella's name in a ringing phrase. The duet, dominated by the "Prince Charming" theme, then comes to a magnificent climax as the two pledge their love to each other.

In a complete change of mood, Arabella tells Mandryka that she must now ask him to leave. She would like to dance for an hour or two before she parts forever from the girl she has been. But Mandryka declares that his place is where she is—but she need not say one word to him for the rest of the evening.

To the accompaniment of gay waltz music, coachmen and other guests throng down the marble staircase. Among them are the three Counts and Fiakermilli, a very pretty girl in a bright red dress. Carrying a bouquet, she goes up to Arabella with Dominik at her side. He announces that the Ball awaits the Queen. The Coachmen wish to pay their respects, and Milli will speak for them.

Milli hands her bouquet to Arabella, then speaks her piece in a brash coloratura refrain ("Die Wiener Herrn"). Vienna men, she sings, are all students of the heavenly bodies and they are quick to notice a new star. They name that star the Reigning Queen. Tonight Arabella is the star and Reigning Queen of the ball. Milli concludes the refrain in a dazzling cadenza, and then the waltz music surges up.

The coachmen place Milli on a chair and lift her to their shoulders. Six coachmen, holding long streamers as reins, team up to make a coach-and-six. Holding the reins, Milli drives gaily off. Arabella takes Dominik's arm and goes up the stairs. Mandryka watches her for a moment, then turns away. Adelaide appears.

At the same time, from another entrance, Matteo comes in, followed by Zdenka, who is dressed as a boy in a formal evening suit. The scene continues in ensemble form. Aside, Matteo laments that Arabella has forgotten him; Zdenka vainly tries to comfort him. Adelaide and Mandryka talk about Arabella. Beaming with happiness, Adelaide says she must share her joy with her husband. Telling Mandryka to remain, she goes to look for Waldner. Matteo and Zdenka try to remain unnoticed in the background.

Adelaide and Waldner return; the Count embraces Mandryka, who says he is going to order a champagne supper. He gestures to his three hussars, standing at attention nearby. They order tables brought in. Waldner, saying he doesn't want to interrupt his run of luck at cards, rushes away.

Mandryka calls for champagne—thirty bottles here, thirty there—so nobody will be able to remember if he is a noble disguised as a coachman or a coachman acting like a noble. As tables loaded with food are brought in, Mandryka asks Adelaide if anything is lacking. Adelaide mentions flowers. Mandryka orders one of his hussars to buy up all the flowers in Vienna and bring them here. Arabella shall dance on flowers, he sings—and later, on his very hands. At the conclusion of the refrain, he and Adelaide walk away to join the dancers.

Then follows a quartet passage in which Arabella takes final leave of her three lovers. Tactfully but firmly she informs them one by one that she will always treasure the memory of their affection, but now it has all come to an end. Dominik quietly says good-by and walks slowly away; Elemer protests violently to the last, but Arabella simply leaves him standing alone; Lamoral dances one last waltz with her.

While they are dancing, Matteo comes forward cautiously with Zdenka. A moment later, Mandryka comes back and goes to one of the tables to inspect the service. Zdenka tries to convince the bitter, gloomy Matteo that Arabella even now thinks only of him. Here is proof, she says, taking a letter from her pocket and offering it to Matteo. He refuses it, exclaiming that he knows it is a farewell note.

Mandryka overhears the two talking and turns to watch them. Zdenka begs Matteo at least to touch the letter. Reluctantly he takes the envelope, then gasps in surprise as he feels a key inside. He tears open the envelope. There is no note—only the key. Angrily he asks Zdenka if she is joking.

Scarcely able to control her emotions, Zdenka tells him that this is the key to Arabella's room. In her excitement, she forgets to lower her voice. Matteo wonders if he is losing his mind or has simply not heard correctly. Zdenka swears the key is Arabella's.

Mandryka, about to go up the stairs, hears this; he turns and stares at the two in stupefaction. Moving closer, he hears Zdenka tell Matteo that the key is actually for the room next to Arabella's in their father's suite. Her sister will come to him in a quarter of an hour, because she really loves him and wants to do anything that will make him happy. With that Zdenka quickly leaves. Muttering that nobody can fathom the heart of a woman, Matteo walks away in a daze.

Mandryka looks wildly around, then orders his hussars to go after the man with the key and bring him back here. They hesitate confusedly, not knowing whom their master means. One of them points to Dominik, who has just entered with Adelaide. But Mandryka ignores his question. Desperately trying to understand the situation, he sings that perhaps there are other girls here named Arabella. Wouldn't he be a fool to suppose she would send her key to someone at the ball while she herself is dancing here? He looks at his watch. There are still some moments left of the time he granted her for her last dance, he groans, and already he has been betrayed.

Other couples now drift in. Glaring at them, Mandryka wonders why only Arabella is missing. At that moment, Milli, escorted by Elemer, comes up and asks him as a favor not to deprive the ball of its Queen any longer. He did not lock her up, Mandryka bursts out in fury. The key, he cries, is in the envelope. Suddenly checking himself, he forces a gay laugh and invites everyone to be his guest.

When Elemer asks him where Arabella is, Mandryka orders two of his hussars to go and search all Vienna until they find her. They are to ask her to come here, if she will be kind enough. Then he gulps down a glass of champagne and offers one to Milli. His third hussar hands him a letter. See if there's a key in it, he snaps, but then snatches the letter. Hesitating a moment, he tears it open and begins reading aloud. It is a tender note in which Arabella bids him good night and tells him that from tomorrow on she will be his forever. In scorn and fury Mandryka cries that she has signed it only with a small "a"—for now, of course, she has no time for a loving signature.

Whirling to face the guests, he assumes an air of reckless gaiety, inviting them to drink until they are too drunk to stand. Then he catches Milli in his arms, kisses her violently, and offers to sing a song. She answers with a cadenza. In a spirit of bitter mockery, Mandryka bursts into a wild native drinking song ("Ging durch einen Wald") about a girl who won't surrender to her drunken lover. Milli joins him in the chorus. Pausing to gulp down more champagne, Mandryka finally leaps up on a table to finish off the song. Then he jumps down, takes Milli in his arms again. With a wild shout, he asks what is the price of a key to a Countess' room in Vienna these days.

Adelaide, shocked and bewildered, walks over to him and asks where Arabella is. Reeling, Mandryka replies she didn't condescend to tell him. The guests look on in consternation. Adelaide sends Dominik to look for Count Waldner. A moment later he comes in, followed by three of his gambler friends. He strides over to Mandryka and asks him what has happened. Everything is *comme il faut* Mandryka replies sarcastically. He is no longer acting like a peasant, but like a Viennese nobleman. As for Arabella—well, sometimes Viennese countesses just decide to disappear for a while.

Furiously Waldner turns to Adelaide, who unexpectedly tells her husband that Arabella probably is at home. Very well, then, says Waldner, they will all go home, talk to her, and find out what has been happening. With a grim look at Mandryka, he requests him to come along. Mandryka sardonically remarks that he will consider it an honor and offers Adelaide his arm. Before he leaves he drunkenly invites the guests to enjoy themselves. Lifting their glasses, they toast him in a brief chorus. The others leave as the curtain falls.

ACT THREE

Before the curtain rises, there is a rather long orchestral interlude in which the various themes of the opera are woven into a richly melodic pattern.

The scene is the lobby of Waldner's hotel. It is night. A stairway at left leads up to the second-floor rooms. At right is the reception desk, with the desk clerk sitting behind it. Downstage is a table. Matteo, without his uniform jacket, is discovered at the top of the stairs, leaning over the banister as though looking for something. The entrance bell rings and he disappears. The night clerk opens the door and Arabella enters. She seems to be walking in a dream. Swaying to the rhythm of the waltz theme in the orchestra, she goes over to a divan near the foot of the stairs, sits down and begins to sing about how she will come to Mandryka's home as his bride ("Über die Felder"). The folk-song themes heard before weave through the accompaniment.

They will ride through his fields and his silent forests, she sings, and then his huntsmen will come to meet them. "This is your new mistress," he will tell them, "whom I have brought from Vienna to be my bride. She wants to stay with me forever in my forests." Arabella ends the refrain on a phrase of infinite tenderness, then sits lost in thought.

Matteo reappears at the top of the stairs, sees Arabella and starts in surprise. Scarcely believing his eyes, he slowly descends. Now follows a scene of remarkable dramatic complexity, which Strauss superbly underscores with his music. Two people find themselves in a fantastic situation. Matteo (who now has on his uniform jacket) comes up to Arabella and bows. Both express surprise at finding each other in the lobby. Matteo asks Arabella if she is going out. Replying that she is just returning, she bids him good night and starts up the stairs.

Just returning, Matteo repeats, with amused irony. He starts to say something more, but Arabella tells him that anything else must wait until tomorrow. Matteo cries ardently that he only wants to thank her. Mystified, Arabella asks him why. With a gesture of hopeless confusion, Matteo declares that her cold-blooded play-acting almost smacks of witchcraft. Impatiently Arabella says she does not understand and starts up the stairs again. Barring her way, Matteo says he wants to assure himself that she is still "the same person" she was only a short while ago. A short while ago, Arabella retorts, she was elsewhere. Yes, cries Matteo ecstatically, she well knows where. Angered—and totally unable to fathom the meaning of Matteo's words—Arabella tries to pass by him and go upstairs. Losing control of himself, he roughly grabs Arabella's arm. In a violent outburst, he demands that she look just once more into his eyes to seal the memory of what happened between them in her room.

There is a noise outside and Arabella warns that people are coming. In ringing phrases, Matteo sings that he promised Arabella, as they kissed, that she would be free of him after this night. But it was dark and he could not see her eyes. Now she must look into *his* eyes, so that the promise is sealed. Arabella stares at him in utter bewilderment.

Adelaide, Mandryka and his hussars, followed by Waldner and his three gambler friends, crowd into the lobby. They stop short when they see Arabella and Matteo. Adelaide asks her daughter why she is here. Arabella says nothing is wrong. Mandryka, glaring at Matteo, cries that *there* is the accursed fellow who has the key. Raging, he asks Adelaide's permission to withdraw, turns to one of his hussars and orders him to pack for departure tomorrow.

Going over to Mandryka, Arabella asks why he is so disturbed. She simply met Matteo, an old friend, here and they were talking. She will be glad to tell him all about it later, she adds, quite simply. Mandryka bows stiffly, then turns away. Waldner steps forward and implores Arabella to tell him if Matteo brought her here from the ball. There is nothing to explain about this, she replies, nothing that he does not already know (referring to the fact that she and Mandryka had become virtually betrothed to each other earlier at the ball). Waldner thinks he understands and urges everyone to forget all this fuss.

Implying forgiveness despite her apparent betrayal of his love, Mandryka turns to Arabella and offers to do what he can to help her now. With great dignity, she answers that it is he who should ask forgiveness for doubting her. Glowering at Matteo, Mandryka declares that only a completely stupid man would fail to understand what has happened between a certain girl and an officer this night. At that, Matteo furiously challenges him to defend his rights. Stepping swiftly between the two, Arabella cries that Mandryka indeed has these rights, while Matteo has none whatever. Brokenly, Matteo admits this is true.

But Mandryka insists there is one right Matteo can assert, but that one he refuses to name. Realizing what he means, Arabella angrily asks Matteo if he is cad enough to try to wreck her marriage. Mandryka demands that Matteo speak. When he refuses, Mandryka says the officer bases his right on what has just happened in Arabella's room. Arabella asks Matteo if he has anything more to say to her. Matteo shakes his head. Thereupon, Mandryka sardonically congratulates Matteo on his luck with beautiful women—not to mention his tact.

The excitement grows. Aroused by the altercation, hotel guests crowd to the top of the stairs and look on. Waldner roars for his pistols. Adelaide tells him they have been sold. Arabella gives way to her despair over Mandryka's lack of trust in her. Matteo speaks up, crying that he is to blame for everything. Turning again to Arabella, Mandryka magnanimously declares that Matteo deserves some consideration at her hands. He urges her to confess that the officer is her lover. Arabella hotly denies it. But, Mandryka goes on, with his own eyes he saw Matteo take the key from the boy—Arabella's groom. The realization that Mandryka is referring to Zdenka plunges Arabella into deeper despair. Mandryka furiously asks if he is to spare the man who has destroyed his hopes—and if she intends to marry this man.

When Arabella refuses to answer, Mandryka, in spoken tones, orders two of his hussars to find an armorer and bring back two heavy sabres. Also, he is to find a doctor. Turning to the others, he requests them to withdraw.

Suddenly a beautiful girl in negligee, her hair tumbling in disorder over her shoulders, comes rushing down the stairs. It is Zdenka. In a dramatic scene she confesses everything. One last good-by, she cries, and then she will hurl herself into the river to drown her disgrace. Looking at her, Mandryka gasps that he has seen this face before.

Arabella tenderly takes the sobbing girl in her arms. Zdenka sings that her only thought was for the happiness of her sister and Matteo—and so she managed the rendezvous with Matteo in Arabella's room. Matteo, she goes on, did not know that she, Arabella's sister, was playing him false. Then she turns to Matteo and begs his forgiveness. Quite overcome, Matteo tells her that though the room was in darkness, he now feels that he sensed the truth all along. He gazes passionately into Zdenka's eyes. Mandryka murmurs that he himself can never be forgiven.

At that moment, the two hussars return with two sabres and a box of pistols. Waldner takes one pistol and flourishes it menacingly, but nobody pays any attention to him. Facing Arabella with bowed head, Mandryka, in a dramatic refrain, bitterly reproaches himself, singing that only regret is left him now.

Arabella ignores him. Looking down at Zdenka, who is still in her arms, she sings that her sister has given her a "golden lesson": One must not demand; one must give and love until the day one dies. Like a child, Zdenka voices her complete trust in her sister.

Adelaide, meanwhile, bewails all this misfortune, while Waldner tries to work up courage to propose a duel. Matteo speaks fondly to Zdenka. Mandryka turns to leave, but Arabella's voice stops him. Gently she sings that what has happened was no one's fault and that the bond of good will must now unite them.

Jubilantly, Mandryka takes Matteo by the arm, leads him over to Waldner and implores him to bestow the hand of his younger daughter on the officer. Waldner finally consents; Adelaide dissolves in tears of happiness. Waldner kisses Arabella, shakes Matteo's hand, and nods reassuringly to Zdenka. Then he casually embraces Adelaide and leaves with his fellow gamblers at his heels. The guests on the stairs go back to bed. Adelaide and Zdenka go upstairs. As Zdenka turns, Matteo throws her a lover's kiss. Then he, too, leaves.

Arabella and Mandryka are left alone. Only the hussar Welko waits discreetly in the shadows. Quite casually Arabella asks Mandryka if his servant will bring her a glass of water from the well outside. Then she turns and goes upstairs. Despairingly, Mandryka sinks down at the table, his head in his arms. The hussar comes back with the glass of water on a tray. At Mandryka's order, he takes it upstairs. Mandryka murmurs that perhaps she only meant to mock him.

Suddenly Arabella appears on the stairs, tray and glass in hand, then slowly starts down. The hussar walks behind her. Mandryka turns and sees Arabella; his face lights up. In a tender, impassioned refrain, she sings that she had intended to drink the glass of water and then think no more of him until tomorrow.

But suddenly she knew in her heart that he was waiting here in the dark. Then she no longer needed any kind of drink to refresh her. She takes the glass and hands the tray to Welko, who silently goes out of the lobby. And now, Arabella sings, as she steps down and holds the glass toward Mandryka, she offers this drink, untouched, to her friend in this moment when she takes leave forever from the girl she has been.

Mandryka takes the glass, drains it, then hurls it against the wall. Just as certainly as no one shall ever drink from that glass again, he sings in soaring phrases, he will be hers forever. Mandryka takes her in his arms as the music storms to a blazing climax. As it softly dies away, they kiss passionately. Then Arabella, freeing herself from his embrace, runs up the stairs. Mandryka, pausing a moment below, looks rapturously after her. The curtain falls.

Ariadne auf Naxos

by RICHARD STRAUSS

[1864–1949]

Libretto by
HUGO von HOFMANNSTHAL

CHARACTERS
(*In the Prologue*)

Major-domo	*Speaking role*
Music teacher	*Baritone*
Lackey	*Baritone*
An officer	*Tenor*
Composer	*Soprano*
The Tenor	*Tenor*
Wigmaker	*Baritone*
Zerbinetta, leading lady of the Italian comedians	*Soprano*
Prima donna	*Soprano*
Dancing master	*Tenor*
Arlecchino	*Baritone*
Scaramuccio	*Tenor*
Truffaldino	*Bass*
Brighella	*Tenor*

(*In the Opera*)

Ariadne, daughter of King Minos of Crete	*Soprano*
Naiad	*Soprano*
Dryad ⎬ her companions	*Alto*
Echo	*Soprano*

Arlecchino	*Baritone*	Truffaldino	*Bass*
Zerbinetta	*Soprano*	Scaramuccio	*Tenor*
Brighella	*Tenor*	Bacchus	*Tenor*

Place: Vienna and the island of Naxos
Time: Eighteenth century and antiquity
First performance: Vienna, October 4, 1916
Original language: German

STRAUSS first wrote *Ariadne auf Naxos* for presentation as an interlude in Molière's *Le Bourgeois Gentilhomme*, the adaptation of the ancient Greek legend having been made by von Hofmannsthal. It was presented in that form in 1912. Several years later Strauss prepared a new version of the opera, for which von Hofmannsthal wrote a prologue, discarding entirely the idea of presenting *Ariadne* as an interlude in the Molière comedy. The second version is the one described in the following pages.

Ariadne auf Naxos, one of Strauss's later works, has the romantic lyricism of *Rosenkavalier,* the style to which the composer returned after the stark realism of *Elektra* and *Salome.* It combines music of satiric wit and urbanity with melodic passages of incomparable richness. To be effectively performed, *Ariadne* requires singing actors of superior talent and ability.

PROLOGUE

A large, sparsely furnished salon in the eighteenth-century mansion of a wealthy gentleman of Vienna. There are two doors on each side—the entrances to temporary dressing rooms. At the rear is the "backstage" of a small private theater, with the backdrop—seen in reverse—stretched across the width of the stage. There is great confusion and running about as servants, carpenters, actors, and musicians prepare for the performance of *Ariadne auf Naxos,* which the young composer has been commissioned to write for the entertainment of the wealthy man's guests. The dialogue of the Prologue is carried on partly in recitative and partly in spoken words.

After a brief, melodious prelude, the music teacher rushes in, calling excitedly to the major-domo, who is directing preparations. In a pompous and supercilious manner, the major-domo reminds the music teacher that he is very busy preparing for a grand levee in the home of the richest gentleman in Vienna and obviously has no time to waste in trivial conversation. He deigns, however, to listen briefly. Greatly distressed, the music teacher tells the major-domo he has heard that *Ariadne,* the *opera seria*[1] composed by his pupil, is to be followed by some vulgar *buffa* entertainment to be performed by a troupe of clowns. It is outrageous, the music master fumes, that the effect of his distinguished pupil's exalted work should be nullified by low comedy.

The major-domo sarcastically begs to be permitted to point out that it is the master of the house who decides what is to be presented—not the music-makers he hires to perform their tricks for him. The music teacher may rest assured, he adds, that he and his protégé will get their fees—in addition to a really stupendous bonus. The other ventures to ask where *Ariadne* will be placed in the order of festivities. It will be given first, the major-domo informs him blandly, then the *buffa* performers will appear, and after that there will be a display of fireworks—to begin promptly at nine. With those words the major-domo majestically leaves the room.

As the music master is wondering how he will tell his sensitive and highly temperamental protégé about this unfortunate state of affairs, a lackey enters with an officer. He leads him to the door of Zerbinetta's dressing room. Leering at the officer, the lackey knocks at the door, but the officer roughly pushes him aside, goes in, and slams the door. Muttering that the officer undoubtedly is up to no good, the lackey straightens his liv-

[1] The name given to early forms of opera which later developed into "grand opera."

ery and assumes his usual manner of casual impudence. During this incident the music teacher goes to the door of a dressing room on the other side of the salon, knocks, and enters.

At that moment the composer, a young man obviously thinking of nothing but his music, hurries in, sees the lackey, and excitedly orders him to summon his violins for rehearsal. With stupid insolence, the lackey remarks that the violins have no feet and cannot walk in by themselves. When the composer naïvely tries to explain that he was referring to the players and not the instruments, the lackey rudely interrupts to say that, in any event, the musicians cannot come because they are playing for the master's dinner guests.

Flying into a rage, the composer shouts that his opera begins in a quarter of an hour and that he must have a rehearsal. When the lackey impertinently tells him that he will have to wait until the musicians have finished playing for His Lordship's dinner guests, the composer decides to utilize the time by rehearsing the prima donna who is to play the role of Ariadne. He starts for the door of Zerbinetta's dressing room. Realizing what the situation is, the lackey bars his way, saying that the room is occupied by a lady who must not be disturbed at the moment. Mistaking his meaning entirely, the composer reminds him that he has the right to speak to any of the artists concerned with his opera. With a sneering laugh, the lackey steps aside and goes out of the salon.

Striding to the door, the composer knocks. When there is no answer, he launches into an angry tirade, cursing the lackey for not directing him to the right door ("Eselsgesicht! Sehr unverschämter frecher Esel!"). Suddenly he forgets his anger and begins singing a new refrain for his *Ariadne* which has just come to mind. Feverishly he searches through his pockets for a piece of paper on which to write down the notes. He finds some, but promptly crumples it up and throws it away as he continues singing the strain ("Du allmächtiger Gott"). That, he exclaims triumphantly, will make Bacchus realize that he is a god, not a clown in a panther skin.

He immediately decides to call the singer playing the role of Bacchus and teach him the new part. Joyously singing the melody, he knocks at the second door. It promptly bursts open, and the wigmaker comes flying out with the irate tenor at his heels. At the moment Bacchus is quite ungodlike —a bald gentleman holding a wig of long flowing hair. Pointing to it, he asks the wigmaker how he dare suggest that a great artist make a fool of himself in public by wearing such a monstrosity. The wigmaker retorts that his temperamental outbursts surely indicate that he is descended from a long line of lunatics.

The composer timidly tries to speak to both men, requesting a piece of paper on which to write down some notes. The tenor turns on his heel, stalks back into the dressing room, and bangs the door, while the wigmaker, fuming that his art is unappreciated, dashes angrily away. Zerbinetta, in a brief dancing costume and looking somewhat disheveled, comes out of her dressing room, followed by the officer. They go toward the stage at the back, Zerbinetta remarking that it will be difficult to make the audience laugh after the ordeal of the opera. She coyly asks the officer if he thinks she will be a success, and the officer gallantly obliges with the proper answer.

The music teacher comes out of the dressing room with the prima donna, who wears a wrap over her Ariadne costume. Telling him that she must see the master of the house immediately, she goes back inside. As the composer hurries over to speak to her, the music teacher restrains him, saying that Madame is with her hairdresser and cannot be disturbed. The composer's attention is suddenly attracted by the saucy and charming Zerbinetta, and he asks the music teacher who she is. Conversing privately, they retire to one side of the room as the dancing master minces in, approaches Zerbinetta, and leads her forward. Reassuring her that the audience will be receptive to her comedy, he says contemptuously that *Ariadne auf Naxos* has nothing new to offer in the way of music or ideas and is, in short, a colossal bore.

As they, in turn, retire to the rear, the music teacher is heard telling the composer that the charming young lady is the one who will perform the harlequinade with her troupe after *Ariadne* has been presented. Shocked and incredulous, the composer rages that no one will dare offer such claptrap after the noble spectacle of *Ariadne*. First the people are to be inspired by the profound beauty of his opera, he cries, and then its immortal message is to be driven out of their minds by the low antics of comedians. The incongruity of the situation sets the composer off into hysterical laughter, while the music teacher tries to calm him.

In violent anger the composer pushes him away and launches into a bitter tirade against the gross stupidity of the public ("Ein heiteres Nachspiel! Ein Übergang zu ihrer Gemeinheit!"). He laments that, in the face of this crass indifference and contempt for the ideal, he never again will be able to create a song. Suddenly his mood changes, as it occurs to him that moments of crisis serve their good purpose. A short time ago, he muses good-humoredly, he lost his temper with the lackey—and immediately a new melody came to him. A little later he saw the altercation between the tenor and the wigmaker and was again inspired. The composer begins improvising on his new melody ("Du Venus' Sohn—gibst süssen Lohn"). Wildly excited, he asks the music teacher for a sheet of music paper, sits down at a table, and begins writing furiously.

Zerbinetta comes out of her dressing room with Arlecchino, Scaramuccio, Brighella, and Truffinaldo[2] goose-stepping after her. Seating herself in a chair near the composer, she begins applying rouge, powder, and lipstick, which the four clowns hand her as she calls for them. Arlecchino holds a candle and Brighella a mirror. The composer stops writing, stares at the group for a moment, and then turns to the music teacher with a look of angry distaste. As the music teacher shrugs his shoulders hopelessly, the composer, in another fit of temper, tears the music paper to shreds. Striking a tragic pose, he cries that all mankind is conspiring against him.

The prima donna comes from her dressing room and calls to the music teacher. Noticing Zerbinetta and the comedians, she refers to them with contempt. With a malicious glance at her Zerbinetta loudly remarks to her

[2] Stock characters of *commedia dell' arte*.

companions that their performance certainly should come first, for after an hour of dull opera it will be twice as difficult to make the audience laugh. On the contrary, says the dancing master, who has entered in time to hear her words, the effect will be just the opposite ("Im Gegentheil. Man kommt von Tisch"). The guests, being drowsy after dinner, he argues, will doze through the opera, applaud politely, and then rouse themselves sufficiently to ask what comes next. When they are offered Zerbinetta's merry comedy with its catchy tunes they will be all attention. And when the gentry roll home in their carriages they will remember only the delightful Zerbinetta and her dancing.

Meanwhile the music master is desperately trying to calm the prima donna, who is looking daggers at Zerbinetta. No one will remember anything but her triumph in *Ariadne,* he assures her, and tomorrow she will be the toast of Vienna. Zerbinetta laughs impudently. A crisis is averted when the lackey storms in to announce that dinner is over and that the performance is to begin shortly. There is great commotion. The other members of the cast of *Ariadne*—the tenor and the women playing Naiad, Dryad, and Echo—now enter, while last-minute preparations are made on the stage.

The major-domo rushes in and announces that the master has decided to change the order of the program. Instead of following one another, as originally planned, Zerbinetta's harlequinade and *Ariadne auf Naxos* will be played simultaneously. The performers look at each other in stupefaction. While the tenor, the prima donna, and the music teacher storm over this fantastic idea, the composer, who has been brooding at the table, comes over and anxiously questions the others about what is happening.

When the music teacher groans in protest, the major-domo airily remarks that his master assumes that the performers know their business well enough so that this slight change in arrangements will make no difference. In short, they are to see to it that the *opera buffa* and the *opera seria* are performed simultaneously and completely—and as paid for. He warns that the performance must end at the proper moment, for on the stroke of nine there is to be a display of fireworks in the garden. The music teacher continues to stammer protests, while the composer resignedly murmurs that he was fated to be destroyed by some catastrophe such as this.

The major-domo goes on to say that the master is greatly distressed over the fact that, in a mansion as luxurious as his, there should be displayed the dismal and depressing scenery which is used in *Ariadne*. It is the master's wish, he says, that some of the characters from the comedy appear on the scene to brighten things up. The dancing master immediately agrees that showing a bare, deserted island is decidedly in bad taste.

With a supreme effort at self-control, the composer patiently tries to explain that Ariadne on the desolate island of Naxos is the embodiment of human solitude. If one mortal face appears, the entire effect of the opera will be lost. But the comedy characters will make things much livelier, the dancing master puts in, and at least prevent the audience from going to sleep. Highly pleased with his wit, he executes a pirouette. Unwilling to be drawn into any further argument, the major-domo leaves, warning that the master and his guests will appear directly.

In utter dejection, the composer turns to the music teacher and moans that there is nothing to be gained by staying. The other reminds him that he will at least gain the fifty ducats that will be paid him for writing the opera—which will enable him to live comfortably for the next six months. Sadly shaking his head, the composer walks over to the other side of the room. Approaching the music teacher, the dancing master expresses surprise over the fact that he and his pupil object to the extremely practical arrangements that have been made. It is really very simple, he says, and is merely a matter of eliminating the long, boring passages of the opera and having the performers improvise when necessary. These people are very clever at that sort of thing, he adds.

The music teacher protests that the composer would promptly commit suicide at such a suggestion. Thereupon the dancing master dryly observes that the composer has a choice of hearing his opera performed with a few minor elisions or not hearing it at all. With that he orders a servant to bring an inkpot and pens and tells the music teacher to put his pupil to work on the score. Seating himself at the table, the composer melodramatically clutches the pages of his music to his breast, crying that he would rather burn them than mutilate them. The dancing master, however, finally wins him over by reminding him that greater geniuses than he have been forced to make such sacrifices to have their works performed.

Ordering the music master to see that sufficient cuts are made, the dancing master then prepares to explain matters to Zerbinetta. It will be easy for her, he remarks, because she is an expert at improvisation. Calling Zerbinetta from her dressing room, he takes her to one side while the music teacher, the tenor, and the prima donna gather around the composer, who is furiously crossing out passages of his score. A vastly amusing byplay follows as the prima donna tries to convince the music teacher that the tenor has too much to sing, while the tenor, in turn, whispers to the composer that the prima donna's role is far too long. The music teacher takes them both aside and solemnly assures them—individually—that the role of each will remain intact at the expense of the other.

Meanwhile the dancing master explains the *Ariadne* plot to Zerbinetta. Ariadne, he says, was a princess who eloped with a certain Theseus after saving his life. But Theseus eventually grew tired of her and abandoned her on an island called Naxos. Ariadne, of course, says the dancing master in mock-tragic tones, was brokenhearted and prayed for death. Laughing merrily, Zerbinetta remarks that it was not death she wanted, but another lover.

At those words the composer stops working, looks up at Zerbinetta, and vehemently declares that Ariadne surrenders her heart to one man only and will never relinquish her love until she is vanquished by death. Zerbinetta answers that, instead of death, another young man will come to Ariadne—a young man, she adds, looking at the composer with an alluring smile, full of life and passion like herself. Quite right, says the music teacher, for she meets Bacchus, the god of youth.

But the composer, completely oblivious to Zerbinetta's cynical mockery, tries to explain that Ariadne desires neither god nor mortal, but only death. Ariadne, noblest of women, he declares, seeks nothing but death after the cruel Theseus has left her desolate and alone. Zerbinetta answers the com-

poser's idealistic interpretation with the disillusioned cynicism of a woman
of the world and dismisses his arguments as utter nonsense.

Turning away, she calls her four partners around her and tells them her
version of the plot. Ariadne, a princess who has been jilted, is pining away
on a desert island. They—Zerbinetta and her companions—are five merry
travelers who have come to the island by chance. She tells the clowns that
they are to take their cues from her and improvise their lines. They will
enter and perform whenever the opportunity presents itself.

As the comedians and the music master retire to the stage at the rear, the
composer, still exalted by his dream of Ariadne's sacrifice, sings in glowing
phrases of the mystery of her transformation ("Sie gibt sich dem Tod hin").
This marks the beginning of a moving duet with Zerbinetta. The composer
sings that Ariadne's life is renewed in the embrace of Bacchus, who,
through her love, himself attains his full godhood. Zerbinetta comes close to
him, murmuring tenderly that the idealist had better come down to earth.
When the composer cries out in despair over the mockery and humiliation
that have been heaped upon him, Zerbinetta gently tells him that she will
help him through this hour of trial.

Looking at her wonderingly, the composer asks why she speaks to him in
this manner. In a deliberate attempt to arouse his sympathies, Zerbinetta
sentimentally exclaims that she is misunderstood . . . she plays the coquette, but her heart is weeping . . . she is surrounded by admirers, yet is
utterly alone. Gazing into the composer's eyes, Zerbinetta hints that her interest in him at this moment is born of the fact that she is in love with him.

Naïvely enchanted, the composer impulsively takes the girl in his arms
and ecstatically voices his adoration. Zerbinetta responds with equal ardor
and then, having assured herself of another conquest, adroitly frees herself
and runs into her dressing room. The music teacher now calls the performers to the stage. There is a momentary crisis as the prima donna, seeing
Zerbinetta on the stage in her spangled dancing costume, flatly declares that
she will not set foot on the same stage with a common dancing girl. In a
flash of inspiration, the music teacher assures her that there is no better
place to show the vast gulf that exists between that creature and an illustrious artist like herself. Kissing her hand, the music teacher leads the still
bristling prima donna to the stage.

When he returns to escort the composer into the theater, the young man
impetuously embraces him, crying that his eyes have been opened to a new
world ("Die Tiefen des Daseins sind unermesslich"). In an ecstatic refrain
he gives expression to the emotions inspired by his love for Zerbinetta,
climaxing his declarations with a passionate invocation to music, acclaiming
it as the holiest of arts.

As he stands lost in ardor and exaltation, Zerbinetta appears at the curtains of the stage and whistles sharply for the comedians. Whirling about,
the composer stares dumfounded as Arlecchino, Scaramuccio, Brighella, and
Truffaldino file out of the dressing room and step to the stage. Realizing
that the travesty on his opera actually is to take place as planned, the composer rages over the desecration of his masterpiece. When the music
teacher reminds him that he agreed to the plan, the composer turns on him
with a flood of bitter reproach for having dragged him into a wretched be-

trayal of his ideals. Rather than this, he cries in a dramatic phrase of humiliation and despair, he will freeze and hunger and die in the ideal world of his own making. He rushes distractedly away. The music teacher looks after him, sadly shaking his head as the curtain falls.

ARIADNE AUF NAXOS

The desolate island of Naxos. (In this scene the front of the private stage is shown, with the guests in boxes at either side of the larger stage.) At one side is a cave, at the entrance of which Ariadne lies asleep. Naiad, Dryad, and Echo stand watching her. The classic mood of the scene is reflected in a stately prelude which has the elegiac quality of some of the passages in Gluck's *Orfeo*. The three women murmur that Ariadne weeps in her slumber, never waking, slowly being consumed by the fever of her sorrow. Their voices blend in an exquisite trio interlude ("Ach, wir sind es eingewöhnet"), in which they sing that they have become accustomed to Ariadne's grief, which ceaselessly ebbs and flows like the tides.

They become silent as Ariadne cries despairingly in her sleep and then, raising herself, murmurs incoherently about the world of shadows in which she dwells. The voices of Zerbinetta and the comedians now come from the wings, where they are awaiting their cues. They exclaim over Ariadne's beauty and remark that it will be hard to comfort one who is in such grief and distress. In a long soliloquy, Ariadne, still in her tragic dream, muses over the love of the two beings who were called Ariadne and Theseus ("Ein schönes Paar, hiess Theseus—Ariadne"). As though speaking of strangers, she wonders where the happy lovers have gone—where the maiden who was herself has gone. Naiad, Dryad, and Echo call her name in an effort to awaken her. Still in sleep, Ariadne bids them call no more. Ariadne sleeps serenely and innocently, she says, awaiting the deliverance of death.

From the wings, Arlecchino explains that Ariadne has gone quite mad with grief. Zerbinetta urges him to soothe her with music. The clown thereupon strikes up a simple ditty ("Lieben, Hassen, Hoffen, Zagen"), the burden of which is that madness is a burden more cruel than hope deferred or love unrequited. As Ariadne stares vacantly into space, Zerbinetta murmurs that she has heard nothing of the song. When Arlecchino says that his heart bleeds for Ariadne, Zerbinetta dryly remarks that every beautiful woman he sees seems to have the same effect on his heart.

Ariadne continues in another long soliloquy ("Es gibt ein Reich, wo alles rein ist"). Rising, she sings of the holy land of death, to which the herald Hermes summons the spirits of the pure. Her body, wrapped in the royal garments her mother wove, will soon lie quietly in the cave, which will be her tomb, while her soul, freed from the bonds of earthly sorrow, will follow her new lord to the realms where they will be eternally united.

During her monologue, Naiad, Dryad, and Echo leave the scene. The four comedians ascend to the stage from the front and begin to dance in an absurd attempt to cheer Ariadne. They sing a droll quartet ("Die Dame gibt mit trüben Sinn"), expressing the view that the lady is giving way too easily to grief, which, after all, will disappear in time. Zerbinetta joins them.

After they dance and sing together, Zerbinetta observes that Ariadne is paying no attention and asks the comedians to leave for the moment. They dance into the wings, singing that their efforts at consolation have been in vain.

Approaching Ariadne, who stares dully before her, Zerbinetta bows respectfully and addresses her in a brilliant aria of incredible length and difficulty ("Grossmächtige Prinzessin, wer verstunde nicht"). Though the sorrows of a princess cannot be grasped by a commoner, she begins, they are both women, both moved by feelings that women alone can fathom. Zerbinetta comes nearer in her eagerness to speak, whereupon Ariadne haughtily conceals her face with her veil. The confession of frailty is sweet to a woman, Zerbinetta goes on, and then asks Ariadne why she denies herself the comfort of this confession. Her bitter pride, Zerbinetta says, will only condemn her to dismal solitude, with none to share her secret grief but the rocks and waves.

As though afraid, Ariadne withdraws to the mouth of the cave. Earnestly, yet with disarming simplicity, Zerbinetta continues. She tells the princess that she is not the first to suffer abandonment, loneliness, and heartbreak, for that is the common lot of womankind. There are many deserted islands such as this, she says, and though she herself has lived on them, she does not curse all men for having periodically condemned her to exile. By this time Ariadne has vanished into the cave, but Zerbinetta continues to expound her lighthearted and romantic philosophy of love with ingratiating frankness. She readily grants that men are selfish, faithless, and cruel. Yet the enchantment of love is well worth the anguish, and beyond each disappointment is the ecstasy of another conquest, another romance. In love, men and women deceive and are deceived—and so it is with all lovers of history and legend. As for herself, she welcomes each new lover like a god, Zerbinetta sings in soaring coloratura phrases. At first she is awed and silent in his presence, then is transfigured by the rapture of his first embrace. She ends the aria in a reflective phrase, musing softly that before each new god of love she is a silent and helpless captive.

As she stands lost in thought, Arlecchino comes dancing gaily out of the wings, looks around for Ariadne, and then remarks ironically that Zerbinetta and the lady apparently do not speak the same language. The lady may soon learn, the dancer retorts, that Zerbinetta's language is best suited for a woman. The incorrigible Arlecchino begins making violent love to Zerbinetta and succeeds in kissing her before she is able to free herself from his embrace. As he pursues her, the other three clowns look out from the wings at right and left and call amorously to her. Thereupon Zerbinetta, with a charming show of distress, turns to the audience and asks why it is that, if woman is destined to resist the attentions of men, Providence tempts her with so many varieties of them. She concludes her observation with a brilliant roulade.

The four comedians now come forward and advise her to make no further efforts to cheer Ariadne, as the lady seems determined to refuse all consolation ("Eine Störrische zu trösten, lasst das peinliche Geschäft"). This introduces a delightful ensemble in a sparkling waltz rhythm, and the singing and dancing that follow are in the age-old pattern of Italian masked comedy. Zerbinetta, promptly forgetting Ariadne's woes, devotes herself to her companions. Dancing from one to the other, she coquettes with each one in turn. Brighella, Scaramuccio, and Truffaldino make love to her in traditional clownish fashion, one tripping over the other as they try to embrace her. Arlecchino watches their doltish antics with cynical amusement. The drollery continues until Zerbinetta finally escapes with the sly Arlecchino, who, as always, wins his Columbine. The two reappear at front of the stage and laugh over the frantic efforts of Brighella, Scaramuccio, and Truffaldino to find them. Fuming over Arlecchino's rascally trick in stealing the maiden, the three sadly dance away. Zerbinetta and Arlecchino embrace tenderly and then leave.

The mood of the music immediately changes to the mysterious theme symbolizing Bacchus. Naiad, Dryad, and Echo, hurrying in, exclaim that the young god is approaching and then converse about him in a melodious trio ("Ein schönes Wunder! Ein reizender Knabe!"). They marvel over the handsome youth, the child of a god, who was reared by nymphs to glorious manhood. Then they go on to tell the story of his first adventure—how he and his wild companions sailed to Circe's island. There the enchantress gave them magic wine to drink and then turned them all into swine—all except Bacchus, who defied her fatal spell and stood god-like among the groveling animals.

Going to the mouth of the cave, they call to Ariadne, crying that Bacchus, the wondrous god who escaped the charms of Circe, is approaching. Bacchus is heard in the distance, taunting Circe with his song ("Circe, kannst du mich hören?"). At the sound of his voice Ariadne emerges as though in a trance from the cave. Her three companions softly call to Bacchus, imploring him not to pause in his singing. He appears on a rock above the cave and, unseen by the women, continues in a rather plaintive strain ("Doch da ich unverwandelt"). He wonders why his heart is so strangely sad even though he has triumphed over Circe's wiles.

Ariadne, listening to his voice, hails him as the long-awaited herald of death. As Naiad, Dryad, and Echo urge him to sing on, Bacchus, thinking he still hears the voice of Circe, again taunts her for having failed to ensnare him. He slowly descends from the rock and approaches Ariadne, who covers her face with her hands and cries out the name of Theseus in terror-stricken tones. The three other women bow low before Bacchus and then leave the scene.

Taking her hands from her face, Ariadne looks searchingly at Bacchus and then welcomes him as the herald of death ("Ich grüsse dich, du Bote aller Boten"). This introduces the magnificent duet which brings the opera to a close. In awe and wonder, Bacchus asks if she, too, is a goddess who lures strangers into her abode, plies them with magic wine, and then destroys them with her sorcery. Thinking only of death, Ariadne murmurs that she has waited for him during days and nights of endless despair. Bacchus asks how she knew his name. It was not his name she called in her madness, Ariadne replies, but the name of another. It is no matter now, she continues, for she knows that he who stands before her is the captain of a ship that will carry her to oblivion.

Without understanding, Bacchus asks if she will go with him on his ship.

In tones of resignation and despair, Ariadne replies that she is ready. Then, in mounting terror of death, she asks how he will change her into an immortal. Will he touch her . . . or wave a wand . . . or will he give her a draught of magic wine? Enthralled by her beauty, Bacchus murmurs dreamily that he had forgotten that he spoke of wine. Ariadne speaks of the realm of forgetfulness to which he will soon take her—to the land where all memory of earthly anguish fades away like a dream.

Gradually the meaning of her terror and despair become clear to Bacchus. In an exultant refrain ("Bin ich Gott, schuf mich ein Gott"), he swears on his godhood and by the divine blood that flows in his veins that death will never tear her from his arms. Ariadne cowers back, now certain that death is upon her and that his words are but the magic incantation that conjures up the miracle of death. Overwhelmed, she starts to swoon, but Bacchus takes her in his arms. Not death, but life, has begun, he says quietly, and then passionately kisses her.

The duet surges to a rapturous climax as Ariadne expresses her blissful wonder over the transformation that has taken place, while Bacchus exults that her sorrow has turned to triumph. Pointing to the cave, Ariadne exclaims that the loathsome pallet on which she lay waiting for death has changed to a splendid couch fit for a goddess. Gazing at Bacchus in adoration, she hails the power of his magic. It is her own magic that has wrought the miracle, Bacchus cries, for through her love he has come to realize the full meaning of his godhood. Leading her slowly toward the cave, he sings that the cavern of her desolation will be the retreat where they will share the bliss of their immortal love. As a radiant canopy of mist and stars slowly envelops the lovers, the voices of Naiad, Dryad, and Echo are heard repeating their exhortation to Bacchus to continue his wondrous song.

Suddenly Zerbinetta appears from the wings. Pointing roguishly over her shoulder at the lovers, she softly repeats the phrase in which she summed up her philosophy at the conclusion of her aria—before each new god of love, woman is a silent and helpless captive. Her prophecy has been fulfilled: the god who came to Ariadne was not death, but a new lover. As Ariadne and Bacchus slowly fade from view, their voices blend in rapturous phrases. The curtain falls.

Un Ballo in Maschera
(The Masked Ball)
by GIUSEPPE VERDI
[1813–1901]

Libretto by
ANTONIO SOMMA

Based on the libretto written by the French dramatist Scribe for the opera
GUSTAVUS III, OU LE BAL MASQUÉ
by Daniel Auber

CHARACTERS

Samuele ⎱ conspirators .... *Bass*
Tommaso ⎰

Edgardo, page to King Riccardo........................... *Soprano*
Riccardo, King of Sweden................................... *Tenor*
Renato, secretary to King Riccardo........................ *Baritone*
Ulrica, a sorceress.. *Contralto*
Adelia, wife of Renato.................................... *Soprano*
Silvano, a sailor in King Riccardo's service............. *Bass*
A judge, townspeople, courtiers, maskers, dancers

Place: Sweden
Time: Eighteenth century
First performance: Teatro Apollo, Rome, February 17, 1859
Original language: Italian

UN BALLO IN MASCHERA, like several other Verdi operas, had the distinction of being the center of a political tempest at the time of its scheduled première. It was to have been presented in 1858 under its original title, *Gustavus III*, the plot being based on the events surrounding the assassination of King Gustavus III of Sweden at a court ball in 1792.

While the opera was in rehearsal, Italian revolutionists attempted to assassinate Napoleon III in Paris. In view of the fact that Verdi's opera had to do with a successful conspiracy against royalty, it was promptly banned by the authorities. They suggested to Verdi that he adapt his music to a new libretto, but this he flatly refused to do.

When the controversy came to the attention of the public it touched off vociferous demonstrations in behalf of the composer. Crowds marched through the streets shouting, "Viva Verdi!" Actually his name was being used as a political battle cry by those factions which sought to unite Italy under the leadership of King Victor Emmanuel. Someone had discovered that the letters V E R D I might well represent the slogan "Vittorio Emmanuele, Re D'Italia (Victor Emmanuel, King of Italy).

The problem was finally solved in a rather remarkable way. For the opera's presentation in 1859, Verdi made several changes. The title was changed to *Un Ballo in Maschera*, the locale was shifted from Sweden to Puritan New England, and King Gustavus became Riccardo (or Richard), Earl of Warwick and Governor of Boston. The conspirators Samuele and Tommaso were cast as Negroes, the secretary Renato (or Reinhart) as a Creole, and Ulrica, the sorceress, as a Negress.

In later years it became customary to present the opera with a European setting, usually Naples. Although today the work is frequently performed either with the Naples or the Boston locale, in many opera houses it is given in its original setting: the court of the King of Sweden.

ACT ONE

The palatial audience chamber of King Riccardo. After a brief prelude, a group of officials and gentlemen of the court sing the praises of the King and pledge their loyalty. Samuele and Tommaso, standing at one side with their followers, assert in a sinister undertone that those whom the King has wronged are burning for revenge. He need not think, they warn, that his victims lie forgotten in their graves.

Edgardo,[1] the page, announces the King. Riccardo enters and greets the assemblage, then receives various petitions. He promises that all will receive justice, adding that it is the first duty of those in power to give aid and comfort to their subjects. The page then gives him, for his approval, the list of guests for the forthcoming masked ball. Riccardo says he hopes that none of the court beauties have been overlooked. Seeing the name of Adelia,[2] he exclaims that she is the fairest of the fair, and that her very name fills his heart with joy. These phrases introduce the ecstatic romanza, "La rivedro nell' estasi," in which Riccardo rhapsodizes over his love for Adelia.

An impressive ensemble follows as various persons in the chamber express their sentiments. The conspirators sing that this is not the propitious moment for their plot, as the King is surrounded by his friends. Edgardo and the courtiers observe the look of happiness on the King's face.

Riccardo dismisses the page, who, on leaving, announces Renato. As Renato enters, the courtiers withdraw. The secretary remarks that the King seems troubled. The latter, in an aside, expresses the disturbing thought that this man is the husband of his beloved. The honest Renato wonders why the King seems sad while the city rings with his praises. Riccardo says he is oppressed by a secret woe. When Renato declares he knows the source of the King's concern, Riccardo utters an exclamation of guilty fear. Each, of course, is unaware of the other's real meaning. Renato warns the King that he is no longer safe in his own palace because a certain faction is plotting his death. Relieved, but still concerned, Riccardo asks for further details. When Renato offers to reveal names, the King avers that the matter is, after all, unimportant. Were he to know, he adds, he would be forced to

[1] Sometimes Oscar.
[2] Sometimes Amelia.

shed blood, and that he will not do, for God and his loyal subjects will protect him.

In a dramatic aria, "Alla vita che t'arride," Renato reminds the King that the destiny of thousands depends upon him, and if he were to perish, the pride and glory of the fatherland would perish with him. But Riccardo brushes aside his secretary's warning. Edgardo enters with a judge, who presents a decree of exile for the King's signature. As he peruses it, Riccardo demands the name of the woman who is to be exiled. Her name is Ulrica, a woman of a foreign race, the judge replies. Edgardo interrupts to say that people from near and far—even renowned sages and soothsayers—come to her for advice. The judge declares that this crone's lair is a rendezvous for outlaws and malefactors and insists that the sentence be carried out. When Riccardo, somewhat amused, asks Edgardo for his opinion, the page implores him to intercede. In a florid aria, "Volta la terrea," the page vividly portrays Ulrica as a mighty prophetess who can read good or evil fortunes in the stars and who undoubtedly is in league with the devil himself.

As the aria ends, the judge reiterates that Ulrica must be condemned. Edgardo again implores mercy for her. Riccardo now prepares to announce his decision to the assemblage. When the courtiers have re-entered, he declares that he himself intends to visit Ulrica's hut in disguise and invites his court to accompany him. Renato endeavors to dissuade the King, pointing out that someone may recognize him, but Riccardo deprecates his warning. Edgardo enthuses over the adventure. The King tells the page to make ready a sailor's costume for his disguise. Samuele and Tommaso sneer at Renato's cautious counsel, then gloat over the fact that the King's whim may further their plot.

Riccardo gaily bids all to make the most of this amusing adventure and tells them he will be at the sorceress's den at the hour of three in the morning. Renato promises to keep a watchful eye on the proceedings, while Edgardo jubilantly declares that he proposes to have his own fortune told. Samuele and Tommaso, in a somber undercurrent, utter dire threats. The courtiers express their pleasure over the exciting diversion in store for them, and a tremendous chorus brings the act to a close.

ACT TWO

Ulrica's dwelling, a large hut of rough-hewn timbers.[3] At the left is a steaming cauldron hung on a tripod over a fire. At the rear is a staircase leading above, and at its base a secret door. The hut is crowded with people intently watching Ulrica as she stands before the cauldron. After a weird and somber introduction, the onlookers sing of the evil genie that is soon to appear. Ulrica, stirring her witch's brew, begins the great incantation aria, "Re dell' abisso affretati." Dramatically she bids the monarch of the underworld to appear before her. Three times, she chants, the owl has

[3] The opera was originally written in three acts, this being Scene Two, Act One.

screeched, three times the salamander has leaped through the fire, three times the dead have groaned from the tomb.

Suddenly Riccardo strides in, announcing that he is first to arrive. The women in the crowd, horrified at the interruption, order him away, while Ulrica glares at him. With a careless laugh he walks to the rear and stands in the shadows. A flash of light illumines the hut, and the women gasp in terror. Resuming her incantation, Ulrica sings in primitive ecstasy that the evil genie has come at her bidding, bringing her the terrible power of sorcery that will give her command over human destiny. Her voice now sinks to a hoarse whisper as she demands silence. The effect is one of extraordinary dramatic power.

There is a stir as Silvano, a sailor, shoulders his way through the cowering throng and demands that Ulrica tell his fortune. He relates that as a seaman in the service of the King he has served faithfully and has more than once saved his sovereign's life. After fifteen years, he complains, he has received neither promotion nor increase in pay. What is his reward to be? he asks. Riccardo, in an aside, commends his forthrightness. Ulrica takes the sailor's hand and tells him that he will soon be amply recompensed. Silvano is skeptical, but Ulrica reassures him. Riccardo surreptitiously scribbles a note and slips it, with some money, into the sailor's pocket, stating that he will make *this* prophecy come true. Declaring that Ulrica's optimistic prediction must not go unrewarded, Silvano puts his hand into his pocket. He exclaims in joy when he discovers the money and note of promotion. Ulrica is hailed as a great prophetess.

At that moment there is a knock at the secret door. To Riccardo's surprise, Adelia's servant enters. He tells Ulrica that his mistress is waiting outside and wishes to consult her secretly. Ulrica answers that she must first dismiss the people. She advises her visitors that in order to reveal their fortunes it will be necessary to speak to the oracle alone. After all but Riccardo withdraw, Adelia enters in great agitation. The sorceress asks what troubles her. The torment of secret love, Adelia replies, and then implores Ulrica to pluck from her heart the love of one whom destiny has placed on the throne.

Hearing this, Riccardo is overjoyed. In somber tones Ulrica tells Adelia of a plant possessing the power to control the heart's impulses. Whoever desires this plant must gather it alone at midnight from the fearsome spot in which it grows. Eagerly Adelia asks where she must go, saying that nothing will daunt her. In dramatic, sonorous phrases, Ulrica describes the gallows tree which stands near the west gate of the city ("Della citta all' occaso"). At its base grows the evil plant, flourishing in soil shadowed by the bodies of criminals who have atoned for their sins at the rope's end.

Adelia recoils in horror. Ulrica takes note of her terrified mien, while Riccardo pities her distress. When Adelia vows that she will not shirk her duty, the sorceress directs her to gather the plant this very night. In an aside, Riccardo declares that she shall not go alone. An impressive trio follows. Adelia prays for strength to face the ordeal and implores Heaven to cleanse her heart of its illicit passion ("Consentimi, O Signore"). Ulrica assures her that she will be restored by the magic of the herb. Riccardo passionately avows his love and swears that he will protect Adelia. They are interrupted by the voices of courtiers outside, demanding admittance. Adelia hurries out.

Samuele and Tommaso, Edgardo, and the courtiers, all in disguise, crowd into the hut followed by the townspeople. They urge Ulrica to continue her prophecies. Edgardo inquires about the King, and Riccardo warns the page not to betray his identity. Approaching Ulrica, he asks her to reveal what the future has in store for him. In character with the nautical role he is playing, Riccardo sings the famous *Barcarolle* ("Di' tu se fidele"). Like any sailor, he wonders if his sweetheart is true to him, saying he fears neither wind nor waves, but thinks only of the welcome that awaits him when his ship comes safely back to harbor. The crowd makes a spirited response as he declares that, whatever Ulrica's prophecy, he will hear it unafraid.

The sorceress turns on him with a grim warning that the man who dares mock his destiny may bitterly repent such folly. After a moment's parley as to who will be the first to learn his fate, Riccardo disdainfully holds forth his hand. The sorceress proclaims it the hand of a nobleman and a warrior. True enough, Edgardo remarks impudently. Riccardo silences the page. Suddenly Ulrica lets go his hand and curtly bids him leave and ask no more questions. The others urge her to go on, and as she hesitates, Riccardo commands her to speak.

Thereupon Ulrica cries out that his doom is near. If it is to be a soldier's death, says Riccardo carelessly, he will be grateful. He will die by the hand of a friend—thus it is decreed, Ulrica intones. The crowd exclaims in horror. But Riccardo derides the grim prophecy as idle folly in a mocking strain beginning with the words "E scherzo od e follia." This serves to introduce a quintet which is considered one of Verdi's finest operatic ensemble numbers. Edgardo expresses his fears as Ulrica, glaring at Samuele and Tommaso, repeats her warning of doom, as though reading their thoughts. The conspirators now fear their plot has been discovered.

The ensemble is interrupted when Riccardo asks Ulrica who is destined to slay him. The first man who shakes his hand, she replies. Riccardo promptly holds out his hand to the courtiers, defiantly urging someone to fulfill the prophecy then and there. All shrink back in terror. At that moment Renato enters. The King strides over to him and grasps his hand as the crowd thunders out Renato's name. Samuele and Tommaso, to their great relief, are still beyond suspicion. The crowd proclaims that the prophecy has failed as Riccardo informs Ulrica that the man whose hand he holds is his most trusted friend. Renato then reveals the King's identity. With good-natured sarcasm, Riccardo tells Ulrica that the omniscient genie she conjured up not only failed to inform her of the King's presence but neglected to tell her that she had been put under a decree of banishment that very day. As Ulrica gasps in terror, Riccardo reassures her and gives her a purse. Humbly grateful, Ulrica warns him again that a traitor hovers near. Perhaps more than one, she adds significantly. Samuele and Tommaso, overhearing, are alarmed.

Then from outside come voices hailing Riccardo. Silvano enters with a large group of friends. Pointing to Riccardo, he announces that the King is present and bids all to do him homage. They do so in a ringing chorus, "O figlio d' Inghilterra." All join in the tribute except Ulrica and the conspirators—Ulrica reiterating her dire predictions and Samuele and Tommaso fuming over the fact that the King, thus surrounded by his fawning subjects, is safe from their designs.

ACT THREE

A snow-covered plain, dominated by a gallows.[4] To the accompaniment of the prelude, Adelia appears on the scene and walks hesitantly toward the gibbet. In recitative she says that the sight of the fearful gallows, with the baleful plant at its base, makes her blood run cold. The very sound of her own footsteps frightens her. But she vows that not even the threat of death will deter her from this ghastly errand.

Adelia then sings the dramatic aria, "Ma dall' arido," in which she laments that the glorious love in her heart is about to be destroyed by the evil power of the herb. And when that love is gone, nothing remains, she sighs in despair. Dolefully she bids her heart harden like the very stones in its resolve, then cries out for the surcease that death can bring. Suddenly she gasps in terror as she spies a figure approaching through the gloom. In her panic she imagines that it is an apparition with fiery eyes and grisly countenance. Adelia feverishly prays for protection and then, as the figure draws closer, sinks fear-stricken to her knees.

Riccardo rushes up and takes her in his arms. Distractedly Adelia tries to repulse him, begging him to go. Riccardo ardently replies that he will never leave her because his heart is aflame with love. She tells the King that she must be faithful to another—to the man who would die for his sovereign. Alas, the bitter truth, Riccardo cries. With passionate intensity he tells Adelia that though he is tormented by remorse, he has struggled in vain against his overpowering love for her. In anguish she pleads for death to save her from dishonor. Again she implores Riccardo to go, but he ignores her protests and begs for one word of love.

Yielding to his ardor, Adelia confesses her love for him. Riccardo ecstatically responds. Tenderly Adelia sings that now he must answer both for her honor and her heart, to which Riccardo replies that for her love he will disdain all thoughts of guilt and sacrifice every friendship. In a long, melodious duet, "O qual soave brivido," they pour out their devotion for each other.

Suddenly someone is heard approaching. The King asks who dares come to this place of doom. In the next moment he recognizes Renato. Gasping that it is her husband, Adelia quickly lowers her veil. Renato tells Riccardo that he has come to protect him from traitors who are at this moment in pursuit. The secretary goes on to say that, with his face hidden by his cloak, he had come upon the plotters and had been taken for one of them. He had

[4] Act Two in the original.

overheard one say that he had seen the King on his way to a rendezvous with a mysterious woman; another replied that he intended to interrupt the King's trysting with a sword stroke.

Renato throws his mantle around Riccardo to hide his royal garb, then tells him to flee by a certain pathway. The King protests that he cannot leave his companion, but in an aside Adelia begs him to go at once. Renato, misunderstanding her entreaty, reproachfully asks her if she would deliver the King into the hands of his would-be murderers merely for the sake of her love. Adelia implores Riccardo to make his escape while the way is still clear, but the King vows that he will die before he will leave her. In desperation, Adelia threatens to tear aside her veil. This threat has an immediate effect, and Riccardo turns to speak to Renato, while, in a dramatic aside, Adelia declares that she would gladly die to save her royal lover from the evil fate that stalks him.

Riccardo asks Renato to swear that he will escort his lady safely to the city, that he will not attempt to speak to her or to ascertain her identity, and that he will never try to see her again. The loyal Renato promises unhesitatingly. A spirited trio follows. Renato and Adelia warn of the impending danger and urge the King to flight. Riccardo, fuming against the conspirators, confesses that he too is a traitor. For an illicit love he has shamefully betrayed his truest friend. Were it not for his guilt he would stay and face his enemies.

As Riccardo rushes off, Renato assures Adelia that he will protect her. In the next instant Samuele and Tommaso, with their fellow conspirators, burst upon the scene shouting for vengeance. Renato calls out to them. The conspirators halt in their tracks, exclaiming in baffled fury that he is not the King. The secretary defiantly informs them that the King is safely away, then makes himself known. Samuele ironically remarks that Renato is indeed fortunate to be in the company of so fair a lady. Tommaso adds that he feels obliged to unveil the beauty. Angrily Renato draws his sword. The conspirators are about to attack when Adelia rushes forward to shield Renato. Her veil falls from her face. Horror-stricken, Renato cries out her name. The conspirators are astounded.

Samuele sneers about the guileless husband who unwittingly makes love to his own wife at a secret tryst in the moonlight. He and the others break into sardonic laughter, gloating over how they will regale the whole town with this delectable morsel of court scandal. A powerfully dramatic chorus ensues. Adelia, overwhelmed with grief and shame, laments her wretched fate, while Renato, burning with rage and humiliation, cries that the King has rewarded his devotion with infamy and dishonor. The conspirators, with malicious glee, describe how the gossip will spread through the town.

Interrupting, Renato grimly asks Samuele and Tommaso to come to his home in the morning. When Samuele hints at planning revenge, Renato curtly replies that he will explain his purpose when they meet. Renato coldly tells Adelia that he will keep his promise to escort her to the city, but his words sound to her like a judgment of doom. As the conspirators withdraw, their voices die away to insinuating whispers. The curtain falls.

ACT FOUR

The library of Renato's home.[5] On one wall hangs a great oil painting, a portrait of King Riccardo. After a few measures of introduction the curtain rises to reveal Adelia and Renato. In cold anger he tells his wife that she can expect no mercy—only death. Adelia tries desperately to convince him that what he saw was only the appearance of guilt, not guilt itself. Her protests only goad Renato to greater fury, and he wildly repeats that her doom is sealed. In anguish Adelia kneels before him, begging for one last favor in a moving refrain, "Morro, ma prima in grazia." She asks to see their son once more, so that in her last hour of life she may embrace him.

Renato, moved despite his anger, roughly orders Adelia to her chamber. There in the gloomy silence, he says, she may see her son and think upon her dishonor. Alone, he muses that he will spare his wife and son the consequences of his vengeance. Facing Riccardo's portrait, he cries out in bitter wrath that there is the one whose blood will flow to blot out this disgrace. Then Renato sings the famous aria, "Eri tu che macchiavi," in which he pours out his grief over the treachery of the man whose friendship he had cherished. He recalls his happiness with Adelia when their love was unsullied. In an eloquent, profoundly moving climax, he sings that hope and love are gone forever.

Crushed by despair, Renato stands with bowed head before the portrait. Suddenly Samuele and Tommaso enter. Renato, showing them an official report, abruptly informs them that he has known of their plot against Riccardo. Samuele comments that now Renato will, of course, inform the King. On the contrary, Renato retorts, he wishes to join the conspiracy.

Samuele and Tommaso are dumfounded, but Renato says he will give them a token of good faith. Not only will he aid them in carrying out their bloody plan, he declares, but he will offer his son's life as forfeit if he fails to do his part. To the conspirators this sudden about-face is beyond belief. Renato asks them not to question his motives and repeats that he will join their cause, with his son as hostage. In a brief but dramatic trio the plotters swear that they will stand united in one single purpose: revenge.

At this point Renato asks that he be allowed to strike the fatal blow. Samuele objects, as his father was deprived of his home by Riccardo, and for this he must have his revenge. Tommaso demands the privilege, saying that for ten years he has waited to settle accounts with Riccardo for murdering his brother. Renato finally suggests they draw lots. The three then write their names on separate slips of paper and place them in a vase.

At this tense moment Adelia enters to announce that Edgardo is waiting with an invitation to Riccardo's masked ball. Although surprised, Renato grimly observes that fate must have sent Adelia to him at this moment. Fear-stricken, Adelia voices her premonition of disaster. Renato tells Samuele and Tommaso that Adelia will decide the fateful issue. With sardonic gallantry, he leads her to the vase and invites her to draw one name from it

[5] Act Three in the original.

with her innocent hand. She asks why. Angrily he orders her to obey without further question. In an aside, Adelia murmurs that destiny has forced her hand to a bloody deed.

Dark, somber chords vibrate in the orchestra as Adelia tremblingly takes a slip of paper from the vase and hands it to Renato, who gives it to Samuele. Excitedly Renato asks whom fate has chosen. When Samuele reads his name, Renato exults in vengeful triumph. Adelia cries that the King will fall defenseless before the conspirators' weapons. The four voices join in a dramatic quartet—Adelia voicing her despair over the King's fate, the men rejoicing that their revenge is near.

Renato then admits Edgardo, who presents the King's invitation to the ball. The page assures him that Riccardo will be present, adding that the ball will be an affair of unusual magnificence. Looking sharply at Adelia, Renato promises he will attend with his wife. Samuele and Tommaso, in an aside, note that the masked ball will greatly expedite their plans. Edgardo begins a spirited refrain, "Ah, di che fulgor," introducing the brilliant quintet which closes the act. The page sings of the gaiety and splendor in store for the guests; Adelia bewails the fact that she has become an unwitting accomplice in the plot against the King; Renato, Samuele, and Tommaso exult in the prospect of perpetrating their revenge in mask and domino.

ACT FIVE

A private audience chamber in the King's palace.[6] Riccardo is seated at his writing desk. The orchestra softly plays the melody of his aria in Act One, in which he revealed his love for Adelia. In recitative, the King sings that he will renounce the woman he loves and send Renato back to England, the land of his birth. Adelia shall accompany him. Thus, Riccardo sighs, an ocean will forever separate him from his beloved. Firmly he signs the document, then laments that he has sealed his fate.

In the ensuing aria, "Ma se m'è forza perderti," Riccardo gives vent to his sorrow and despair. He is haunted by the premonition that when Adelia departs not only love but life itself will depart with her. He then prepares to leave for the ball, cheered by the thought that he may see Adelia for at least one more brief moment. Edgardo enters and hands him a note, saying that it is a secret message from a mysterious, masked woman. It informs the King that someone is plotting to kill him during the ball. Riccardo pauses, then resolutely declares that he will attend despite all threats. Expressing his happiness at the prospect of seeing Adelia, he quickly leaves.

The curtains part to reveal the final scene—the great ballroom. The guests sing gaily of the joys of the dance. Samuele, Tommaso, Renato, and their followers appear wearing blue domino costumes set off by a red ribbon. Renato, in conversation with Samuele, expresses doubt that Riccardo will appear, whereupon Samuele fumes that once more they may be cheated of their prey. The secretary warns that they are being watched, indicating the

[6] Originally written as Scene Two of Act Three. Sometimes this is played as Scene One of Act Five and takes place at the front of the stage before the curtain.

masked figure of Edgardo. He approaches the page, and after some banter they unmask each other. Craftily Renato suggests that perhaps Edgardo has slipped away to enjoy the dancing while the King is asleep. The page replies that Riccardo is present, then coolly tells Renato to seek out the King for himself. Renato entreats the page at least to describe the King's costume. In a sprightly aria, "Saper vorreste," Edgardo mocks Renato's questioning. He sings that though he knows well enough where the King is, he will never tell. Renato persists in his efforts to trick Edgardo into betraying the King's whereabouts. Finally he tells the page that before the night is out he must speak to the King on urgent business, implying that Edgardo will be held to account if the meeting is not arranged.

Thus tricked, Edgardo reveals that the King is wearing a black domino with a red rosette. Renato says he has one more question, but Edgardo cuts him short and leaves. Dancers and merrymakers again dominate the scene. Riccardo suddenly appears, thoughtfully watching the throng. In a moment Adelia, dressed in a white costume, hurries to his side. Disguising her voice, she urgently advises him to leave. He asks her if she wrote the warning letter. In answer she tells him that he is in mortal danger and must flee at once. Riccardo asks who she is and why she is so concerned. Adelia, no longer able to control herself, speaks in her natural voice, whereupon Riccardo fervently exclaims that her disguise has been in vain.

To the accompaniment of the graceful rhythm of a mazurka, the two sing an impassioned duet of farewell ("T'amo, si, t'amo, e in lagrime"). Again and again Adelia beseeches Riccardo to escape before it is too late. Ignoring her desperate entreaties, the King reveals that he is going to send her back to England with her husband, then ardently avows his love for her. Passionately they sing their last farewell.

At that instant Renato lunges toward the King, crying out, "And here is *my* farewell!" He fires his pistol at close range, and Riccardo falls.[7] With shouts of rage the crowd closes in on Renato. The dying King, raising himself, commands them to release the assassin. Slowly he draws from his pocket the document assigning Renato to his duties in England and hands it to his secretary. Quietly he assures him that Adelia is innocent. Though he loved her, the King declares, he did nothing to dishonor her name. Renato and Adelia cry out in the anguish of remorse, and the people join in voicing their grief over this tragic denouement.

As Renato bitterly condemns himself, the King forgives all who conspired against him. Summoning his ebbing strength in one last supreme effort, Riccardo utters a ringing phrase of farewell, then falls back dead. As the chorus rises to a powerful climax, the curtain slowly falls.

[7] As originally written, the action calls for Renato to stab Riccardo with a knife, but it has become customary in some opera houses to substitute shooting with a pistol.

Il Barbiere di Siviglia
(The Barber of Seville)
by GIOACHINO ANTONIO ROSSINI
[1792–1868]

Libretto by
CESARE STERBINI

Based on the comedy
LE BARBIER DE SÉVILLE
by the French dramatist Beaumarchais

CHARACTERS

Fiorello, Count Almaviva's servant . . . . *Bass*
Count Almaviva . . . . *Tenor*
Figaro, a barber . . . . *Baritone*
Rosina, ward of Dr. Bartolo . . . . *Soprano*
Dr. Bartolo . . . . *Bass*
Don Basilio, a music teacher . . . . *Bass*
Bertha, Dr. Bartolo's housemaid . . . . *Soprano*
Ambrosius, Dr. Bartolo's servant . . . . *Bass*
A magistrate, a notary, an officer, musicians, and soldiers

Place: Seville
Time: Seventeenth century
First performance: Teatro Argentina, Rome, February 5, 1816
Original language: Italian

THE STORY of *Il Barbiere di Siviglia* is based on the first of a series of three comedies by the eighteenth-century playwright Beaumarchais. The three plays—*Le Barbier de Séville, Le Mariage de Figaro,* and *La Mère Coupable*—are sometimes known as the "Figaro triology" because they have as their hero Figaro, barber and jack-of-all-trades in Seville. The second play formed the basis of Mozart's *The Marriage of Figaro.* Several characters in Mozart's opera appear in Rossini's work. Rossini was not the first to set Beaumarchais's *Le Barbier* to music. Giovanni Paisiello, another Italian composer, had already written an opera, *Il Barbiere di Siviglia* (1776), based on the French comedy.

The impresario of the Teatro Argentina, Duke Cesarini, commissioned Rossini to write two operas for the carnival season of 1816. The first, *Torvaldo e Doliska,* was produced on December 26, 1815. That same day Rossini agreed to have the first act of the second opera—destined to become *The Barber of Seville*—ready on January 20. Time was short, and it was decided to adapt the plot used by Paisiello. Some historians say that Rossini completed the opera in thirteen days; others, in fifteen. In any case, it was written between December 26, 1815, and February 5, 1816.

In view of the continued popularity of Paisiello's work, Rossini realized that his own use of the same plot might incur not only the venerable composer's disfavor but that of the public as well. He wrote Paisiello, requesting permission to use the story and pointing out that the title had been changed to *Almaviva, ossia l'inutile Precauzione* (*Almaviva, or the Useless Precaution*). He also stated that he had required the librettist to make an entirely new versification of the Beaumarchais comedy.

Though Paisiello granted Rossini's request, it did not prevent a fiasco. The entire first act was sung over a bedlam of whistles, catcalls, shrieks, and howls. No one could hear the music except the singers themselves and the players in the orchestra, led by Rossini himself, seated at the piano. The second performance, however, was well received, and within a week the opera achieved the popularity it has maintained for more than 125 years.

The overture to *The Barber* has an interesting history. The one played at the first performance is said to be identical with that which had served for two earlier Rossini operas—*Il Turco in Italia* (*The Turk in Italy*) and *Sigismondo*. When for some strange reason the music disappeared Rossini calmly substituted an overture he had used for at least two other operas—*Aureliano in Palmira* (*Aurelian in Palmyra*) and *Elisabetta, Regina d'Inghilterra* (*Elizabeth, Queen of England*). This one has endured as the opera's overture.

ACT ONE

[*Scene One*]   A square in Seville. Facing it is the house of Dr. Bartolo. There is a second-floor balcony with shuttered windows. As the music softly begins Fiorello enters carrying a lantern and leading a group of musicians. He cautions them to be quiet and they repeat the admonition in chorus. Count Almaviva appears and quietly calls to Fiorello, who assures him that the musicians are ready. The Count commends them, then warns all to be silent. There is a pause while the musicians tune their instruments. In a moment the orchestra begins the air of the Count's serenade to Rosina, "Ecco ridente in cielo."[1]

The Count sings that the dawn's glow is driving away the gloom of night. He bids his loved one rise and fill his heart with joy. He rhapsodizes over the blissful moment of her appearance and of the enchantment she brings to his heart. The aria ends in a florid climax, but Rosina does not appear. Almaviva asks Fiorello if he sees Rosina, then voices his disappointment. The servant reminds the Count that the morning is getting on, whereupon the latter calls to the musicians. Almaviva gives his purse to Fiorello, who starts paying off the players. They are so profuse and long-winded in their

---

[1] Rossini inserted this cavatina for the second performance to replace the ill-fated "Spanish serenade" that Manuel Garcia had insisted on singing on the opening night. The composer had used the cavatina previously in his *Aurelian in Palmyra* and *Cyrus in Babylon*.

thanks that both Almaviva and Fiorello impatiently tell them to be off. All voices blend in a spirited chorus.

A recitative follows. The Count and his servant fret over the noisy musicians, grumbling that they have awakened the whole neighborhood. Almaviva vows he will not leave until he can speak with Rosina, whom he has been secretly watching from afar every morning. He tells Fiorello to leave. He assures himself that he needs only a word with Rosina—and he wants no witnesses. Rosina must have discovered his purpose by this time, he adds, and realizes that he loves her. He resolves to make her his Countess.

Suddenly from the distance comes the rollicking voice of Figaro. The Count wonders who the intruder might be, then decides to hide in a doorway. Figaro appears and begins the famous aria, "Largo al factotum della citta." Make way for the town's most useful citizen, he sings. He is Figaro the barber—a gentleman of parts at the top of his profession. In a word, Fortune's favorite.

He is at everyone's service—anywhere, any time. Ready with scissors, combs, and razors, he awaits his customers. Observe his resourcefulness! He advises lovelorn maidens and ardent swains. Everyone demands and commands—young and old, matron and belle: "My wig! Hurry, a shave! What a headache! Quick—post this letter!" No rest day or night! It is always Figaro-Figaro-Figaro, until he can bear it no longer. Have pity! One at a time, please! It's Figaro here—there, high—low, come—go! Yes, the most illustrious citizen of the town. Bravo, Figaro! The most favored of men! Thus the barber brings his aria to a spectacular close.

In recitative Figaro goes on bragging about himself. It's a great life, he declares—lots of fun and plenty of money. As the result of his distinguished position, not a maid in all Seville can find a husband without his aid, and all the pretty widows give him alluring glances. By day he wields the tools of his trade, by night he strums his guitar. And so he is welcome everywhere.

The Count, meanwhile, wonders where he has seen Figaro before. The barber, catching sight of Almaviva, likewise speculates. Then they greet in mutual recognition. The Count explains that he has come to town incognito and does not wish his presence known. Anyone as clever as Figaro can easily understand why. Figaro instantly agrees, then asks the Count what he is doing in Seville. Almaviva tells him that while strolling along the Prado one evening he saw a very beautiful girl. He discovered that she is the daughter of an old codger of a doctor who lives in this very house. Since he saw her he has spent most of his time beneath her balcony.

Well, says Figaro, that is a rare stroke of luck for the Count. In that very doctor's house, he, Figaro himself, is barber, hairdresser, consultant, and confidant extraordinary. And what is more, that beautiful girl is not the doctor's daughter, but his ward. The Count is overjoyed. Suddenly Figaro cautions silence. The window opens and Rosina steps out on the balcony. Almaviva exclaims in rapture.

If she could only give "him" the letter she holds in her hand, Rosina sighs to herself. Just as she catches sight of the Count and Figaro below, Dr. Bartolo comes bustling out and asks to see the note. Rosina assures him that she has written down the words of a song from *The Vain Precaution*.

The Count and Figaro marvel at her clever ruse. Bartolo asks the meaning of *Vain Precaution,* and the girl explains that it is a new and popular opera. The doctor scoffs at current musical productions, at the stupid public which goes to see them, and the detestable artists who perform them.

Suddenly Rosina exclaims that she has dropped the note and asks Bartolo to get it for her. In an aside she signals the Count, who snatches up the letter and hides in the doorway. Bartolo grumbles that he cannot find the paper. Rosina says that the wind has probably blown it away. Bartolo mutters his suspicions and then roughly orders his ward to go into the house. Rosina laments her misfortune, and Bartolo growls out that the balcony will be walled off tomorrow.

Almaviva exclaims that this turn of events will only strengthen his resolve. Figaro urges him to read Rosina's note. It tells the Count that his visits have been noticed. The doctor is going out, and as soon as he is gone the unknown admirer must somehow identify himself. Although it is impossible to appear on the balcony without her tyrannical guardian, Rosina will make every effort to escape.

Highly pleased with the contents of the note, the Count asks Figaro more about the doctor. Figaro answers that the man is mad, to begin with, and an ill-tempered old skinflint. He is over sixty, yet he is conceited enough to think he can persuade Rosina to marry him—for her money, of course. He tells everyone he is Rosina's future spouse.

Figaro suddenly notices that the door of the house is opening. Out comes Dr. Bartolo, loudly ordering that if Don Basilio arrives he is to wait. He will now arrange his marriage, he mutters to himself as he leaves. Once that is done, there will be no need for Rosina's seclusion.

The Count scornfully observes that if the old fool thinks he will marry Rosina he must be drunk. He asks Figaro about Don Basilio. The barber informs him that Basilio is a crafty, conniving rascal, an unscrupulous matchmaker, and an inveterate chiseler. Yet he is the man, Figaro adds sardonically, who has been hired to teach Rosina the high art of music. The Count remarks that he will make use of him.

The barber now suggests that the Count give his attention to Rosina's wishes as stated in the note. Almaviva decides that he will not disclose his royal identity until he is sure that Rosina loves him for himself alone, not for his rank and money. When he asks Figaro to help him in his campaign the barber tells him he will need no assistance because Rosina is at this very moment standing at her window. All he has to do is to sing a serenade of his own devising, one which will reveal his name and his sentiments.

Almaviva forthwith begins a charming song ("Se il mio nome"), a musical reply to Rosina's letter. He sings that he is Lindoro, who loves her ardently and begs her to say that she loves him in return. Rosina answers him in a tender phrase. Almaviva is in ecstasy over her reply, and Figaro urges him to continue. The second stanza tells Rosina that her Lindoro can offer her neither wealth nor fame but only boundless devotion. He implores her not to scorn what he seeks to give her.

Rosina begins a phrase in answer, then abruptly disappears within. The Count is vexed, but Figaro warns him that someone apparently has entered the house. Impatiently the Count declares that he must see Rosina today at any cost and again asks Figaro to help him. He tells the barber to put his genius to work contriving an entree to the doctor's home. Almaviva says he will pay Figaro well for his trouble—any amount he needs—and bids him get busy. The barber replies that "Signor Lindoro" cannot realize what a magical effect the offer of gold has on his inventive genius.

In a delightfully mock-serious air ("All' idea di quel metallo"), Figaro proclaims that gold stirs his mighty brain into volcanic action. The Count interrupts the barber, advising him to reveal his stupendous thoughts before they overburden his mind. Then, in a brilliant vocal passage, he tells Figaro that if he can successfully carry off this intrigue he will be hailed as the greatest of all barbers.

Figaro suggests that the Count disguise himself as a soldier, reminding him that troops are expected in the town today. The Count approves, remarking that the colonel is a friend of his. What luck! says Figaro. It will be easy to demand quarters at the doctor's house, he explains, because nobody will dare refuse a soldier with good connections. He asks the Count's opinion of his scheme, and Almaviva compliments him on his sagacity. In an amusing duet ("Che invenzione") Figaro joins the Count in praise of himself. The barber interrupts to say that the gold has inspired another brilliant idea. This soldier, he explains, must give the impression that he is drunk. Obviously, anybody in his cups will never be suspected of being a spy. Triumphantly Figaro sings again of his inventive genius, with the Count joining in a continuation of the duet.

They are about to part when the Count asks Figaro where he lives. Figaro answers that there is no mistaking his home—it is the barbershop. Then, in an engaging aria ("Numero quindici a mano manca"), he sings that his shop is at "number fifteen," the left side of the street, four steps up, the door painted white. In the window are displayed five magnificent wigs, as well as wonderful beauty preparations.

You can't miss it, Figaro declares. Keep to the left—remember the five wigs. There he will be. The Count assures the barber that he will be able to find his shop and thanks him for all he has done. Figaro answers that he considers the Count's success as his first duty. Almaviva promises to return with plenty of money. Then the two begin an exultant duet. The Count sings of the bliss of love which this day's planning will bring, while Figaro hails the gold that will soon be clinking in his pockets. As they continue, Figaro reiterates the instructions on how to find his shop, and the Count in his amorous excitement repeats them after him. At the end of the duet the Count leaves and Figaro goes into Dr. Bartolo's house. Fiorello appears and in a brief recitative grumbles that he has been waiting for his master for two solid hours, only to find that he has gone somewhere else. And all because he is in love, Fiorello mutters, going on his way.[2] The curtain falls.

[Scene Two] A drawing room in Dr. Bartolo's home.[3] Large arched french windows lead to a balcony. The curtain rises to reveal Rosina alone in the room. She holds a letter. After a few bars of music suggesting her

[2] Sometimes omitted.
[3] This is sometimes played as Act Two.

trembling heart, she begins the brilliant "Una voce poco fa," one of the best-known arias in the coloratura soprano repertoire.[4] A secret voice is enshrined in her heart—the voice of Lindoro, she sings, and vows that he shall be her love. She will thwart her guardian's plans and will never disclose her love until she has given her hand.

Then Rosina goes on to say that she is by nature very sweet and reasonable—until she is crossed. If she does not get her way she will turn like a serpent, resorting to any kind of trickery to get what she wants. This is a lesson, she warns, that everybody had better learn.

In recitative she wonders where she can find a messenger to deliver her letter, lamenting that she has no one she can trust—always under the eye of that awful ogre, she pouts. Then, while sealing the letter, she recalls that she saw Figaro and the Count talking together. The barber is a decent, accommodating person—he surely will help her. At that moment he enters. He notices her troubled expression and observes that a beautiful girl should always be lighthearted and gay. Of what use is it to be gay, Rosina remarks, when she is hidden away from the world? She might as well be dead, she sighs.

At that Figaro takes her aside and is about to tell her something when the doctor is heard approaching. Figaro quickly hides behind the draperies. Bartolo comes in roaring that Figaro, the villain, has made everybody in his household ill with his potions and medicines. He asks Rosina if she has seen the barber, and she replies that she has just had a very pleasant conversation with him on a number of interesting topics. Bartolo, his suspicions immediately aroused, calls Bertha and Ambrosius and tries to find out from them what Figaro and Rosina have been talking about. He gets nowhere, because Bertha, under the influence of a potion, sneezes helplessly, while Ambrosius, drugged, yawns in the doctor's face.

Bartolo swears vengeance on the barber for this trick. At that moment Don Basilio enters. The doctor tells him that he is determined to marry Rosina tomorrow, fairly or otherwise. Basilio says he understands, then takes Bartolo aside and informs him that he has seen Count Almaviva in the neighborhood. He implies that it is the Count who is wooing Rosina. Bartolo storms at this, but Basilio tells him that he has a foolproof plan for disposing of the Count as a rival. The key to his scheme, says Basilio triumphantly, is slander.

Then Basilio sings the great aria, "La calunnia,"[5] in which he traces the fatal course of slander from the merest sigh of suspicion to the storm of accusation which destroys its victim. The music rises with overpowering effect from the first insinuating notes to its tremendous climax.

Bartolo, however, expresses doubt as to Basilio's scheme and then decides that his own strategy is safer. He asks Basilio to help him draw up the marriage contract immediately. Once he is married, he says, he will put an end to Rosina's intrigue. In an aside Basilio sneers that he is a conceited old

[4] This aria was originally sung in the contralto key because the role was written for low voice. Through the years it gradually became the property of coloraturas.

[5] This aria has been cited as another example of Rossini's "borrowing." It is said to have been adapted from *Sigismondo*.

fool. As they leave the room Figaro emerges, chuckling at the absurdity of Dr. Bartolo's efforts to marry Rosina. As she reappears he tells her that he has astonishing news: Her noble mentor has decided to make himself her adoring spouse! He and Basilio are even now inscribing the marriage papers. Rosina casually remarks that she will have a proper answer for them, then asks the barber whom he met earlier under her window.

Figaro informs her that the stranger is his cousin Lindoro, a personable young man who is studying hard to make a success. Unfortunately he has one sad failing, Figaro goes on gravely. He is hopelessly in love. Rosina expresses great interest and inquires if the young man's ladylove is far away. Nearby, Figaro answers. Then he describes her, enumerating Rosina's own charms and revealing the lady's name by coyly spelling out "Rosina."

Rosina joyously sings that she can scarcely believe that the stranger really loves her—observing, however, that she suspected it all along. Figaro comments admiringly on the girl's cleverness. Excitedly Rosina asks how she may meet her Lindoro at once. Figaro advises her to send him some token—perhaps a short letter. At that Rosina takes a paper from her pocket, saying that the necessary letter has already been written. A duet follows ("Fortunati affetti miei") in which Rosina expresses her rapture over the prospect of meeting her lover, while Figaro comments with amused cynicism on woman's inborn genius for intrigue. The barber leaves as Rosina thanks him for his aid.

Dr. Bartolo returns and with suspicious gentleness asks Rosina what the barber had to say. Warily she answers that it was nothing of importance— Paris fashions, the illness of his daughter Marcellina, and so on. Bartolo suggests that perhaps Figaro brought her an answer to the letter which was "posted" at the window this morning—the "aria" that the wind blew from the balcony. Suddenly he demands to know why her fingers are stained with ink. The girl replies that she burned her finger and applied ink to cure it. Bartolo asks why one sheet of paper is missing from the six that were on the table. Rosina explains that she used one sheet to wrap up candy for Marcellina. Clever! Bartolo sneers, then points out that the pen still has ink on the point. Innocently Rosina says she used it to trace a design on her embroidery.

Bartolo now loses his temper completely and roars at Rosina to be quiet. He bursts into a florid aria ("A un dottor della mia sorte"), berating Rosina for daring to practice her deceptions on a man of his exalted importance. He storms and rants at great length, warning that henceforth he will keep her under lock and key. At the end of the number Bartolo strides furiously from the room. Rosina quietly follows, pausing to remark that the more he objects to her behavior the more she is determined to have her own way.

Bertha now enters, wondering at the uproar. There is a knock at the door and the Count calls from without. Bertha goes to admit him. She is still sneezing. Calling loudly, the Count appears in the uniform of a soldier, pretending to be quite drunk. When Bartolo comes in, the Count takes a piece of paper from his pocket and tries to read Bartolo's name. He repeats it with ridiculous mispronunciations, utterly ignoring Bartolo's shouted efforts to set him right. Drunkenly trying to embrace the old gentleman, the Count says that he is the regimental physician and is to be billeted in Bartolo's house. The doctor splutters in exasperation, while the Count hails him as a true comrade.

At this moment Rosina enters, and an uproarious trio follows. Bartolo desperately protests that he has a paper exempting him from billeting. The Count, managing to reveal his identity to Rosina, declares that he wishes to go at once to his room. Bartolo finally finds the exemption paper and shows it to the Count, who scornfully tosses it aside. The doctor threatens him with his stick, whereupon the Count challenges him to a duel. He takes a stance, calling to Rosina to throw down her handkerchief as a signal for battle.

Deftly he drops a letter as Rosina lets her handkerchief fall. Feigning surprise at seeing the letter, the Count pauses to hand both it and the hand-kerchief to Rosina. Furiously Bartolo demands that Rosina give him the letter. At that point the Count diverts Bartolo's attention, giving Rosina time to substitute a laundry list for the letter. She assures the doctor that it is only a laundry list. Bartolo discovers that it actually *is* a laundry list and is more confused than ever. At this point Bertha and Basilio enter. The din continues in quintet form.

There is a pause in the ensemble as Rosina, resorting to tears, reproaches Bartolo for his cruel suspicions. The doctor moans his remorse as the Count draws his sword. The uproar breaks out again as Rosina restrains the Count from attacking Bartolo. Then in comes Figaro, carrying his barber's basin. He exclaims at the bedlam, saying that it has attracted a crowd outside. In an aside he warns the Count to be careful. But the Count and Bartolo continue to call each other names until Figaro, in mock severity, rebukes Almaviva, at the same time trying to warn him that the guard has been called. Nothing avails, however, and the pandemonium continues.

It ceases abruptly as a thunderous knock is heard. From without come the voice of the officer of the guard and a chorus of soldiers. All in the room express their consternation in a short but dramatic ensemble. Then a guard enters and demands to know who is involved in this fracas. With that the bedlam breaks out afresh as everyone in the room either makes accusations or attempts to explain matters.

They are stopped by the officer, who steps up to Almaviva and tells him he is under arrest. The Count takes the officer aside and reveals to him his rank. Amazed, the officer steps back and salutes. In a short trio ("Fredda ed immobile") Rosina and Bartolo express their bewilderment, while the Count gloats over his coup. The others, voicing their consternation, join in the brilliant ensemble which concludes the act.

ACT TWO

The scene is the same as Scene Two.[6] When the curtain rises Bartolo is alone, musing about the drunken soldier. He concludes that the fellow was sent by Almaviva to find out everything he can about Rosina. There is a knock. Hesitantly Bartolo goes to the door. The Count enters in the guise of

[6] Sometimes played as Act Three.

a music teacher. He greets the doctor with elaborate politeness, and an amusing duet follows ("Pace e gioia sia con voi"). Bartolo becomes so annoyed with the visitor's flowery salutations that he implores him to desist and get to the point. Then he loses his temper altogether and storms that every meddling scoundrel in the world somehow manages to get into his house. The Count, meanwhile, exults that his plan is drawing closer to a successful conclusion.

The Count finally introduces himself as "Don Alonzo," professor of music and pupil of Don Basilio. To add to the deception the supposed pupil is dressed in the same garb as that of his teacher. Basilio, who is ill, has sent him to give Rosina her music lesson. When Bartolo expresses alarm and says he will go to see Basilio, the Count hastily assures him that the music teacher is not seriously ill. Bartolo is instantly suspicious, whereupon the Count whispers that he has just come from Almaviva's apartment. There in the Count's absence he came upon a letter from Rosina addressed to the Count. He lets Bartolo see the letter and suggests that if he could show it to Rosina he could easily convince her that the Count is involved with another woman. That will surely turn her against the Count, he reminds the doctor. Bartolo observes that the scheme is a masterpiece of slander and compliments Don Alonzo on being indeed a worthy pupil of Don Basilio. At that point Bartolo pockets the letter.

As Bartolo leaves to summon Rosina the Count ruefully reflects that he has outsmarted himself by telling the doctor about the letter. He is confident, however, that he will be able to explain everything to his adored one. Rosina then enters and is introduced to the Count—"Don Alonzo"—who tells her that he is substituting for Don Basilio. Now begins the famous lesson scene, in which singers in the role of Rosina customarily interpolate arias of their own choosing.[7] At some point during the scene Rosina and the Count manage to make their plotting known to each other.

As the lesson ends, the Count praises Rosina's voice. Bartolo interrupts to tell them about an aria sung by a famous opera singer of his day, then proceeds to sing it himself ("Quando mi sei vicina"). Figaro enters and imitates the doctor behind his back. The barber then announces that he has come to shave Bartolo and that it must be done today. Tomorrow will not do, he says over Bartolo's protests, because he will be much too busy with his other customers.

Bartolo finally assents, and after some hesitation gives the barber his bunch of keys so that he can get the shaving utensils. Figaro surreptitiously finds out from Rosina which key fits the balcony entrance and removes it. He leaves the room, and a few moments later there is a terrific crash of broken crockery. Bartolo rushes out in great excitement, while Rosina and her "Lindoro" make the most of his absence to pledge their devotion to each other. Figaro returns with the infuriated Bartolo, who fumes that the clumsy barber has broken six plates, eight goblets, and a tureen.

Bartolo no sooner seats himself to be shaved than in walks Don Basilio.

[7] It is said that the trio which Rossini composed for this scene was lost after the première. Instead of writing another he left the number to the discretion of the prima donna.

The two gasp in astonishment. Rosina, Figaro, and the Count voice their dismay, fearing that Basilio will expose the Count's identity by denying that he knows this substitute music teacher, "Don Alonzo." But the Count saves the situation by convincing Dr. Bartolo, in an aside, that as Basilio knows nothing of the letter which is to poison Rosina's mind it will be well to get him out of the house at once.

Thereupon Bartolo suggests that Basilio has a high fever and should never have left his house. The Count and Figaro add their warnings, telling Basilio first that he looks like a corpse and in the next breath that he surely must have scarlet fever. Basilio, completely bewildered, becomes even more so when the Count presses a purseful of money into his hand. Then follows an ingenious ensemble, beginning with a short duet by the Count and Rosina—"Buona sera, mio signore." The others join to bid Basilio good night and good health.

Figaro once more prepares to shave Bartolo, while Rosina and the Count seat themselves at the harpsichord. The barber contrives to stand so that he hides the lovers from Bartolo's view. Presumably engrossed in the music lesson, Rosina and Almaviva plan their elopement at midnight. Figaro diverts Bartolo's attention by spattering soap in his eyes. Unfortunately the Count raises his voice in trying to explain to Rosina how he had to make use of her letter. The suspicious Bartolo overhears, leaps from the chair, and shouts accusations at the conspirators. The three merely mock at his rage, then quickly make their exit, leaving the doctor purple with anger.

Bartolo calls in Bertha and Ambrosius. He sends the manservant off to summon Basilio and orders Bertha to go downstairs and see to it that no one enters the house. The next moment he decides to take care of that himself. Bertha, left alone, sings an aria in which she expresses a number of uncomplimentary opinions about marriage, among which is the observation that every old fool in the world seems determined to wed ("Il vecchietto cerca moglie").

Bartolo re-enters with Basilio, arguing about the "Alonzo" deception. The doctor is sure that Alonzo is the Count's spy, while Basilio is convinced that the man is Almaviva himself. Bartolo insists that the marriage contract be arranged that very evening and sends Basilio off to fetch a lawyer. Rosina enters, and Bartolo suddenly decides on a way to trick his rival. He shows his ward the letter given him by Alonzo, citing it as proof that her lover is unfaithful, that everybody is in league against her, and that she is being betrayed into the hands of Almaviva. Recognizing the letter as her own, Rosina is convinced. Determined to have her revenge, she consents then and there to marry Bartolo.

Rosina reveals that Figaro and "Lindoro" have planned to steal into the house at midnight. She and the doctor plot to capture the intruders, then both leave. With the room momentarily deserted, the orchestra plays a dramatic interlude depicting a thunderstorm. In the half darkness two figures enter from the balcony—the Count and Figaro. They have gained access by means of the key which Figaro took from Bartolo's key ring. Rosina is waiting, and she answers the Count's greeting with scorn and fury. At that point her lover reveals that he is not Lindoro, an emissary of Count Almaviva, but the Count himself. The two then express their rapture in a brilliant duet,

"Ah, qual colpo." Figaro urges them to postpone their love-making for the moment because time is short.

As prelude to the elopement, the three sing the delightful trio, "Zitti, zitti, piano, piano," a warning of the need for caution and silence. As they are about to leave Figaro cries out that the ladder has been taken away from the window. At that moment Basilio enters with the notary who is to draw up the marriage contract between Bartolo and Rosina. Figaro quickly tells the notary to make out the contract as between Count Almaviva and Rosina. The Count takes Basilio aside and offers him a ring as a bribe, emphasizing his offer by flourishing a pistol. The contract is signed, with Figaro and Basilio as witnesses.

The general rejoicing is interrupted by the entrance of Bartolo with a group of soldiers. He orders the Count's arrest, whereupon the latter reveals that not only is Rosina his wife but that he himself is Count Almaviva. In a dramatic aria he sings that Rosina is now out of the doctor's clutches and that all protests are in vain ("Cessa di piu resistere"). Then he expresses his joy at being united with Rosina as the assembled company add their congratulations.

As the ensemble ends, Bartolo turns on Basilio and accuses him of betrayal because he witnessed the marriage contract. Basilio merely replies that the Count's money was too strong an argument. Ruefully the doctor confesses that he unwittingly helped the marriage along by taking the ladder away from the window. That brings from Figaro the ironical comment that it was a "vain precaution." The doctor is consoled, however, when Almaviva tells him he may keep Rosina's dowry. Bartolo philosophically makes the best of the situation and bestows his blessing on the couple. All express their happiness in a short but brilliant chorus which ends the opera.

The Bartered Bride

by BEDŘICH SMETANA

[1824–1884]

Libretto by
KAREL SABINA

CHARACTERS

Hans, the son of Micha by a former marriage....................*Tenor*
Marie, a village girl...*Soprano*
Kezal, a marriage broker......................................*Bass*
Kruschina, a villager, father of Marie........................*Baritone*
Kathinka, his wife..*Soprano*
Wenzel, son of Micha and Agnes................................*Tenor*
Springer, manager of a traveling circus.......................*Bass*
Esmerelda, a dancer...*Soprano*
Muff, a performer...*Tenor*
Agnes, wife of Tobias Micha...................*Mezzo-soprano*
Tobias Micha, a landowner.....................................*Bass*

Villagers, clowns, dancers

Place: A village in Bohemia
Time: Nineteenth century
First performance: National Theater, Prague, May 30, 1866
Original language: Czech

SMETANA is known as the founder of national Bohemian music. An eminent pianist and conductor, he became interested in the rise of the Czech national spirit, which took place during the latter part of the nineteenth century. He was the first to express that spirit in music, and *The Bartered Bride* came to be the Czech national opera. Although written in Czech, it is usually sung in German and its characters listed by their German names.

The brilliant introduction, one of the most popular of operatic overtures, is made up mainly of the themes from the choral numbers in the opera.

ACT ONE

The square of a Bohemian village. At one side is an inn. It is spring, and the time of the annual church festival. Villagers, dancing about in the square, sing a gay chorus hailing the spring ("Seht am Strauch die Knospen springen"). In it is a lighthearted warning against rushing headlong into marriage, thus forfeiting days of youthful freedom. Among the couples in the square are Hans and his sweetheart, Marie. During an interlude in the chorus Hans asks Marie why she is downcast, and she replies that today she is to meet the man whom her parents have chosen to be her husband. Hans tells her to have courage, for nothing can harm a steadfast heart. Then the chorus resumes its exuberant theme. The singing dies away as the villagers leave.

Marie, close to tears, says that the landowner Micha is coming to the village today with his son Wenzel, who will ask for her hand in marriage. Observing that Hans takes the news rather calmly, she asks if he perhaps is thinking of someone else. This he vehemently denies. In a melodious aria Marie sings that she has given him all her love and trust ("Gern ja will ich Dir vertrauen"). If he were to desert her now, she would end her life.

After the aria Marie asks Hans why his past is shrouded in mystery—why he never mentions his home and his childhood. Hans answers bitterly that he would rather not speak of it. He was born of wealthy parents, he relates, but his mother died when he was a child. His father married again, and his second wife, a jealous woman, turned father against son. Eventually he was driven from home to make his own way in the world.

A duet follows in which Hans first laments over his sad fate, while Marie tries to comfort him ("Mit der Mutter sank zu Grabe"). Then, moved by Marie's devotion, he sings that he has found in her love the happiness he had lost. The duet continues in a brighter mood as the lovers exult that all the sorrows of the past will be forgotten when they can finally be united forever. Suddenly Marie exclaims that her father is approaching. After a tender farewell Hans and Marie hurry from the square in different directions.

Kezal, the marriage broker, now appears, followed by Kruschina and Kathinka, Marie's father and mother. In a vigorous refrain Kezal assures them that the marriage arrangements for Marie are as good as made, thanks to his superior wisdom and sagacity ("Alles ist so gut wie richtig"). The parents, however, are still somewhat hesitant about committing themselves on the matter of the marriage contract. Kathinka asks what will happen if Marie should refuse to marry Micha's son, Wenzel. Her consent is not necessary, Kezal answers impatiently; the parents' word is enough as far as he is concerned. Moreover, he continues, there is no good reason for her to refuse. Micha's son is a fine young man, while Micha himself, as they well know, is a highly respected citizen—and worth at least thirty thousand crowns. The dialogue continues in trio form, with Kathinka insisting on knowing all the facts involved, Kruschina admitting that he lacks the courage to contradict his wife, and Kezal bragging about the successful matches he has made.

Kruschina confesses that though he has known neighbor Micha since childhood, he knows little about his two sons, and asks which one the broker has in mind for Marie. Somewhat surprised, Kezal reminds Kruschina that some years ago he promised that Marie would be the wife of Micha's son. There is only one, Wenzel, born of the second marriage, Kezal informs him. The other son, Hans, child of Micha's first marriage, is believed dead. Kezal then proceeds to enumerate Wenzel's virtues and accomplishments in an amusing aria ("Gekommen wär' er mit mir wie gerne"). He explains that Wenzel would have come with him to meet his future bride but for the fact that he is extremely shy. He is, however, a sober, steady lad, with good manners, brains, and a pleasing disposition. The voices of Kruschina and Kathinka again blend with Kezal's as they assure him that they are now convinced of Wenzel's worthiness.

At this point Marie appears, and they tell her that they have been talking about the young man who is to be her bridegroom. Kathinka, who is secretly wary of the proposed match, manages to whisper to Marie that if the young man does not please her she may refuse him. When Marie appears to be thinking things over, Kezal impatiently suggests that they stop wasting time and proposes that the wedding date be set for a month hence.

There is no need for so much haste, Marie retorts, adding that there are certain obstacles in the way. A phrase from her duet with Hans, echoed in the orchestra, indicates her meaning. The truth is, she reveals, her heart has already been pledged to someone else. Kezal snorts that she must forget these childish infatuations, adding that she can trust him to extricate her from any other love affair. But Marie asserts that she and Hans plighted their troth this very day. Her father angrily refuses to sanction it, saying he has already promised her to Micha's son. Thereupon Kezal triumphantly produces the agreement which Kruschina has signed. Marie strikes the paper out of his hand and storms away.

Kruschina, much distressed, tells Kezal that he made a mistake in not bringing Wenzel along, so that his future bride could at least have a look at him. The marriage broker admits he is right but again says that the lad was too shy. He then suggests that the parents talk it over with Micha, who is waiting at the inn. Meanwhile he will try to fetch the bridegroom. The three go on their way. The villagers throng into the square. Some seat themselves at tables, while others dance a lively polka. Everyone finally joins in a rousing chorus ("Durch die Reihen hin zu fliegen"). The curtain falls.

ACT TWO

A room in the village tavern. Hans and a group of village youths are drinking beer. Kezal is seated at a table by himself. The men sing a lusty drinking song ("Wie schäumst du in den Gläsern"). In a solo passage Hans sings that he is thinking of his sweetheart and that love is the only thing worth while. The others, pointing to Kezal, warn Hans to speak cautiously of love when he is around.

At that Kezal comes forward, declaring that love is a mere distraction and makes a fool of a man. Money, and money alone, he proclaims, is the only thing worth having. The chorus continues, with Hans and Kezal joining in to toast love and money respectively. After the rousing climax, village girls throng in, and soon the boys join them in a furiant, a Bohemian peasant dance. When the dance is over, the villagers leave the tavern.

After all have gone, Wenzel timidly comes in. He is a well-meaning, dull-witted young fellow who stutters. The music as well as the words of the aria he now sings—the famous *Stuttering Song* ("Theu—theu—theu—theurer Sohn")—amusingly depicts the difficulty he has in expressing himself. With comical grimaces he sings that his mother has told him he must find himself a wife. He must have courage, she said. But now that he has started out to find one, everyone laughs at him. Shaking his head in bewilderment, he is about to leave when Marie enters.

She asks if he is the lad who is to be the husband of Marie. Stuttering more than ever in his excitement at seeing a pretty girl, Wenzel answers that he is. Marie says that she feels sorry for him, because this girl is a spiteful person who will only make him unhappy by deceiving him. And besides, she really loves someone else. Marie reminds him that there are plenty of other girls in the village to choose from. In the duet which follows she tells Wenzel about a pretty lass who is pining for him ("Ich weiss Euch einen lieben Schatz"). Wenzel says that both Marie and his mother would strenuously object if he married someone else. Marie, he is told, would soon find another, and his mother be pleased with the other bride.

After more persuasion, including a few pretended tears over Wenzel's hesitation, Marie coyly tells him that she herself is the girl who has been pining for him. She asks him if he will make her his wife, and Wenzel finally consents. Thereupon she makes him swear that he will give up the girl named Marie and never try to see her again. At the conclusion of the duet Wenzel clumsily tries to embrace Marie, but she eludes him. Laughing merrily, she runs out of the tavern, with Wenzel stumbling after her.

Kezal now comes in with Hans, who is on the verge of losing his temper over the marriage broker's efforts to make him give up Marie. Reminding Hans that he is a poor young man, Kezal warns him that marriage without money is at best a dubious venture. He asks Hans where his home is. In a poignant phrase he answers that he once lived far away on the banks of the Moldau ("Weit von hier wohnen wir"). Kezal advises him to return to his native village and seek a bride among his own people, but Hans declares that there is an angel here who loves him and she will be his wife. The marriage broker continues his arguments in spirited refrain ("Jeder, der verliebt"). Every lover, he declares cynically, thinks his love is true—until he is deceived. The wise man is he who plays the game for what it is worth and gives it up when it is no longer profitable.

Hans impatiently tells Kezal to be off with his foolish talk, but the marriage broker makes a final effort to win him over. In an ensuing duet he tells the youth that he has a wealthy girl in mind for him ("Weiss ich doch Eine"). In amusing succession he ticks off her possessions—a big farm, dozens of chickens, pigs, horses, and cows. Hans, as though thinking the matter over, repeats the phrases after him in a sort of canon form.

Kezal finally bargains in terms of money, and Hans agrees to give up Marie for three hundred gulden—cash. He will sign a contract to that effect, on one condition: no one else is to marry Marie but the son of Tobias Micha, and it must be so stated in the contract. There is a further stipulation: as soon as Marie and Micha's son are wed, the elder Micha will not be permitted to demand reimbursement from Marie's father. Though Kezal has told Hans that he himself will provide the three hundred gulden, Hans assumes that the marriage broker will try to collect the sum from Micha, saying he is buying off Wenzel's rival. Kezal quickly agrees to Hans's stipulations and then bustles off, reveling in the thought of a fat fee.

Watching him go, Hans muses that Kezal has walked into a trap he tried to bait for someone else. In a charming aria he sings that love will triumph in spite of all duplicity and rejoices that before very long he will be united with Marie ("Es muss gelingen").

Shortly after the conclusion of the aria Kezal returns with Kruschina and a crowd of curious villagers. The marriage broker announces that they are to witness that the contract is all in order. They respond in excited phrases. Kezal begins reading to the effect that the signer relinquishes his bride. Hans steps up and reads the remainder of the clause—that the bride will be relinquished to no one but the son of Tobias Micha, who is to make her his wife and love her devotedly.

When Kezal announces that Hans has sold his bride for three hundred gulden, the villagers comment in shocked surprise. With a flourish Hans signs the contract and then reads aloud his full name, "Hans Ehrentraut." The people express their indignation and dismay in a ringing chorus ("Ach, er hat verkauft seine Braut!").

ACT THREE

Outside the inn, as in the first act. Wenzel comes in, sobbing in distress. In another amusing aria he stutters that courting has brought him nothing but trouble ("O! Was ich mich betrübe!"). The pretty girl who made him promise to give up Marie has deserted him, and now his mother will certainly punish him for having failed to find a wife.

He quickly forgets his troubles, however, when a small traveling circus pulls up in the square, with the villagers crowding around excitedly. Springer, the manager, announces in dialogue the stupendous performances that will be presented—Esmerelda, the famous Spanish dancer, queen of the tightrope; an Indian chief from the Fiji Islands, who is also a man-eating cannibal; and the most wonderful attraction of all—a fierce American grizzly bear that will dance a ballet with Esmerelda. Meanwhile the tent and a tightrope have been set up. To the accompaniment of a vivacious orchestral interlude, usually known as the *Dance of the Comedians*, Esmerelda and the acrobats entertain the crowd in a preview performance.

Wenzel, enchanted by Esmerelda, stands watching her, his mouth agape. Suddenly Muff, who impersonates the Indian chief, rushes up to Springer in great excitement. He tells him that Michel, who plays the role of the grizzly bear, is as drunk as a lord and cannot possibly be revived in time for the performance. Springer wails that the show's best number will be ruined, not to mention his reputation as an artist. Muff suddenly catches sight of Wenzel, who by this time is in transports of delight because Esmerelda has told him she would like to marry him. There, says Muff, is a lad who would fill the bear's hide to perfection.

Telling Muff to prepare for the performance, Springer approaches Wenzel. He tells him that, in view of the fact that he seems to be very fond of Esmerelda, he ought to join the show, and then he will be able to dance with her. But Wenzel answers that he cannot dance, and besides, his mother might see him. Esmerelda assures him that his mother will never recognize him. She and Springer then demonstrate the steps he must do, singing a charming duet as they dance ("Alles geht am Schnürchen"). Noticing that people are approaching, they leave, motioning Wenzel to follow.

He remains behind, trying to practice the dance steps and happily exclaiming over how popular he will be with all the pretty girls when he joins the circus. Just as he is about to leave, Micha and Agnes appear with Kezal. They try to persuade Wenzel to come with them, saying they have chosen a pretty bride for him. Kezal shows him the contract and tells him that if he signs it he will have Marie Kruschina for his wife. Wenzel cries out that he does not want Marie as his wife because she would be cruel to him. Kezal and the parents ask who told him all this foolishness. A pretty girl, Wenzel replies, one who said she loved him very much. When the others ask her name, he looks at them blankly, admits he does not know, and then runs off. The voices of Kezal, Micha, and Agnes blend in a trio as they express their angry determination to bring Wenzel to his senses ("Das sind verwünschte Dinge").

While they are wondering what to do next, Marie rushes in, followed by Kruschina and Kathinka. Marie refuses to believe the story that Hans has betrayed her. Kezal unctuously holds forth the contract signed by Hans and repeats the price agreed upon—three hundred gulden. Overwhelmed by anguish, Marie recalls the tender promises Hans made to her, while a phrase of the first-act love duet echoes in the orchestra. The others urge her to forget the deceitful Hans and find her happiness with Wenzel. Brokenly Marie answers that she will spend the rest of her days in loneliness.

Suddenly Wenzel reappears. Seeing Marie, he cries joyously that she is the very girl who spoke to him this morning and said she loved him. There is general rejoicing among the parents, while Kezal exults that now everything is settled and the marriage contract can be signed at once. But Marie tearfully begs to be allowed a moment to herself. The others, moved by her distress, respect her wish, and in a moving ensemble they counsel her to think matters over ("Noch ein Weilchen, Marie"). They bid her remember that her future happiness is now in her own hands. The ensemble comes to a climax in a sextet as Marie bitterly repeats their words. The parents and Kezal then slowly leave.

In recitative Marie cries that this betrayal is too monstrous to be believed and then pours out her anguish and humiliation in a poignant aria ("Wie fremd und tot ist Alles umher"). Everything is suddenly strange and sad, she sings, and all the joy has gone out of the world. Then her mood changes. Even her grief, she continues, cannot take away the loveliness of spring.

As she stands sadly musing, Hans strides gaily in. Marie replies in scorn and fury to his ardent greeting and then demands to know if he actually signed his name to the contract. Hans readily admits that he did and assures her that she will soon discover that he is not the scoundrel she thinks he is. Marie informs him that she is going to marry Wenzel. At that Hans roars with laughter, which, of course, sends Marie into a rage.

A sparkling duet follows in which Hans implores her to hear his explanation while Marie storms that she will not listen to a word he has to say ("Mein lieber Schatz, nun aufgepasst"). As the quarrel reaches its climax, Kezal walks in and brashly tells Hans that he may have his money as soon as Marie signs the contract. Turning to Marie, he asks if she is willing to marry Micha's son. Before she can answer, Hans cries out that she will marry Micha's son and none other. To Marie's consternation, he makes a bet with Kezal to that effect.

Further thoughts on the matter are expressed in a lively trio ("Gesegnet, wer liebt und auch vertraut"). Hans sings that those who love and trust are blessed, and promises Marie that everything she has lost will be restored to her. Marie gives way to her despair, while Kezal observes that this fellow Hans is either a second Solomon or an out-and-out scoundrel. At the conclusion of the trio Kezal leaves to bring in the witnesses.

Hans again assures Marie that Micha's son will be her husband. She furiously tells him to get out of her sight. As they are glaring at each other, Kezal returns with the parents. The villagers, thronging in after them, express their excitement over the proceedings in a lively chorus. When all have gathered around the marriage broker, Marie comes forward and declares that she will revenge herself for Hans's treachery by obeying the contract to the letter. Thereupon Hans steps forward and sings that this bridal couple will be the handsomest ever seen.

Agnes and Micha, seeing him for the first time, cry out that it is Hans. He tenderly greets his parents, saying that he has returned from his wanderings to make a home of his own. Kezal fumes that he has been tricked, because everyone believes Micha's other son to be dead. Hans tells him there is proof enough that he is alive in the fact that his own parents recognize him. When Agnes gives a hint of her former ill feeling toward her stepson, Hans declares that if he is not wanted here he will go forth again, but this time he will take Marie with him. With that he turns to Marie and asks her to choose between Wenzel and himself. Marie rushes into his arms.

Kezal's wrath over having been outwitted is fanned by the villagers, who taunt him unmercifully in a derisive chorus. Bellowing with rage, he finally rushes away. Suddenly there is a commotion in the distance and someone shouts that the bear has broken loose and is coming toward the square. As the villagers exclaim in alarm, the "bear" appears. Wenzel sticks his head out of the bearskin, grins foolishly at the crowd, and tells them not to be afraid. Agnes scolds him for making a fool of himself and then drags him away by his ear.

Kruschina and Kathinka now turn to Micha with the observation that Wenzel is hardly eligible as a bridegroom and ask him to remember that Hans also is his son. Micha, seeing the obvious logic of their viewpoint, consents to give his blessing to Marie and Hans, who kneel before him. The villagers hail the "bartered bride" and rejoice over the happy denouement in a stirring chorus ("So ist's recht, es freut uns Alle!"). The curtain falls.

La Bohème

by GIACOMO PUCCINI

[1858–1924]

Libretto by
GIUSEPPE GIACOSA *and* LUIGI ILLICA

Based on Henri Murger's novel
SCÈNES DE LA VIE DE BOHÈME

CHARACTERS

Marcello, a painter..*Baritone*
Rodolpho, a poet...*Tenor*
Colline, a philosopher.......................................*Bass*
Schaunard, a musician.......................................*Baritone*
Benoit, a landlord...*Bass*
Mimi, a seamstress..*Soprano*
Parpignol, a vendor of toys.................................*Tenor*
Musetta, a girl of the Latin Quarter........................*Soprano*
Alcindoro, an admirer of Musetta............................*Bass*
Customs guard ....*Bass*
Habitués of the Latin Quarter, merchants, shopgirls, students,
vendors, soldiers, waiters

Place: Latin Quarter of Paris
Time: About 1830
First performance: Teatro Reggio, Turin, February 1, 1896
Original language: Italian

WHEN PUCCINI wrote *La Bohème* he had already achieved renown as the composer of *Manon Lescaut,* which scored a sensational success. *La Bohème,* the composer's fourth opera, won him even greater fame, and he was hailed by many as the successor to Verdi.

The characters of *La Bohème* are said to be fairly accurate portraits of artists and habitués of the Latin Quarter who were friends of Henri Murger during his youthful days as a struggling writer.

ACT ONE

An attic studio in Paris. At right is a large window, giving a view of snow-covered roofs. Next to the window is an empty fireplace. In the center of the room, a table and some chairs. At right, a bed. The curtain rises as the music begins, and we see Marcello at work at his easel, while Rodolpho stands looking out of the window. Both men occasionally draw their coats closer around them, blow on their fingers, and stamp their feet in an effort to keep warm. The music begins brightly and vivaciously and sustains this mood throughout most of the scene. After a brief prelude Marcello stops work on his masterpiece, "The Passage through the Red Sea," to remark that the chilly waters of the Red Sea seem to be running down the back of his neck. Just for that, he adds in mock anger, he will drown a Pharaoh. He makes a few vigorous strokes with his brush, then addresses Rodolpho.

The poet, gazing out of the window, observes that all the chimneys in the neighborhood are dutifully emitting smoke. Meanwhile, their own stove is idling like a lazy scoundrel who is too good to work and fancies himself one of the aristocracy. Marcello reminds him that the stove has had no legitimate payment for a long time. Well, sighs Rodolpho, forests are of little use under snow. Marcello declares that one fact is certain: He is very cold. Rodolpho concurs. It seems, Marcello complains, as though his fingers had been frozen by contact with the stone-cold heart of the perfidious Musetta. The two then briefly philosophize about love, comparing it to a furnace in which man is consumed, while woman—who lighted the fire in the first place—watches the process.

All of which, they conclude, does not obviate the fact that they are freezing to death and starving. Marcello impulsively seizes a chair and prepares to smash it up for kindling. At that moment Rodolpho has an inspiration. He picks up a thick manuscript from the table, saying that genius has fostered a brilliant idea. Marcello enthusiastically suggests burning up his "Red Sea," but Rodolpho objects because it probably would smell too badly. His great play, he says, will warm them. Pretending to be horrified, Marcello exclaims that reading the play will only make them colder.

Rodolpho explains that he is going to feed his play to the flames and thus send its soul back whence it came. The world will somehow have to bear up under the stupendous loss. With that, the two stuff some pages of the manuscript into the grate, light a fire, then bask gleefully in its warmth.

Suddenly the door bursts open and Colline stamps in. Tossing a bundle of books on the table, he grumbles that the pawn shops are closed on Christmas Eve. When he exclaims over the fire Rodolpho informs him in mock grief that his play is feeding the flames. Colline ironically comments that the play is certainly scintillating, while Marcello offers a few harsh words about the entr'actes. As Rodolpho casually tosses Act Two into the fire, however, Marcello is loud in his praises of its profound sentiments. The poet mourns the immolation of its passionate declarations of love. That crackling sound? Kisses burning, Rodolpho sighs sadly. He heaves the rest of the manuscript into the fireplace, saying he wishes to see all three remaining acts at once. The three applaud as the flames soar, then mutter gloomily as the fire dies down. When it becomes only a glow, Colline and Marcello, in mock anger, cry down the author.

Without warning, the door again flies open and two errand boys enter laden with firewood, food, and wine. Rodolpho, Marcello, and Colline gape for a moment in amazement, then make a rush for the food, jubilantly exclaiming that now they will be able to enjoy a holiday feast. Schaunard comes striding in and with a lordly gesture tosses a handful of coins on the floor. More than all the money in the Bank of France, he announces. The others, dumfounded, pick up the coins, believing them to be medallions. When Rodolpho discovers that the coins are stamped with the image of King Louis Philippe, all four ceremoniously acclaim the King.

Schaunard now tells the story of how he came by all this good fortune ("Or vi dirò: quest'oro"), but the others ignore him completely. They set the table, unwrap the food, and stoke up the fire. Schaunard persists in spite of their inattention, explaining that he had learned that a certain Englishman—Lord Somebody-or-other—was looking for a music teacher. He applied, was instantly hired, then inquired when the lessons were to begin. Immediately, the Englishman replied. Then, pointing to a parrot sitting in its cage in the house of a neighbor, he bade Schaunard to play and sing until the bird dropped dead.

For three days, Schaunard goes on, he thumped and shouted to no avail. Suddenly he had an inspiration. With his irresistible charm he won the confidence of the servant girl. At this point there is an amusing interplay of musical dialogue. Rodolpho, Marcello, and Colline, still utterly oblivious of Schaunard's babbling, look about for a tablecloth. They finally decide to use a copy of *The Constitutional,* Rodolpho remarking that they can thus digest food and news at the same time. While they finish setting the table, Schaunard, still at his story, explains that he persuaded the maid to secure a sprig of parsley. And that, he finished triumphantly, had the same effect on the parrot that hemlock had on Socrates.

At that point Schaunard becomes aware that so far as the others are concerned he has been talking to nobody but himself. Highly indignant, he consigns them all to the devil. When they begin wolfing down the food he quickly takes it from the table, declaring that it is to be saved for the gloomy tomorrow. Nobody would think of dining at home on Christmas Eve, he adds, when the Latin Quarter offers its festive delights on every hand. Already the streets are fragrant with appetizing odors. Then there are other tempting attractions, such as the pretty girls. Schaunard's suggestion wins unanimous approval. Tonight, then, he proclaims, they will bow to sacred custom: Drink at home, dine abroad.

With a great flourish they pour out the wine. At that moment there is a knock at the door. It is Benoit, the landlord. After much excited consultation Schaunard lets him in. The four blithely ignore the rent slip in Benoit's hand and greet him with effusive hospitality. Rodolpho immediately plies him with wine. When Benoit says he has come for the rent, his hosts toast his health. Deliberately Marcello shows him the money on the table. Rodolpho and Schaunard are thunderstruck, but Marcello craftily suggests to the landlord that as he has seen the money with his own eyes he may as well relax and enjoy himself.

Taking care to keep Benoit's wineglass filled to the brim, they flatteringly ask him if he is not about the same age as themselves. As Benoit beams at the compliment, Marcello slyly remarks that he saw him making love to a very pretty girl at the Café Mabille one evening. Thereupon the others lustily hail him as a gay dog and a devil of a fellow with the ladies and compliment him on his gallant love-making. Thoroughly befuddled, Benoit brags that, though he was timid when a boy, now in his old age he is at his best. He confesses a weakness for gay young maidens—those who are neither too plump nor—heaven forbid!—too thin. Thin women, he declares, are likely to be catty and ill-tempered. Anyway, they remind him of his wife.

At that the four pretend to be outraged at Benoit's shameless conduct in wantonly deceiving his poor wife. The room must be aired out at once, they exclaim, lest they be contaminated by such immorality. Together they steer the reeling landlord out of the door, melodramatically telling him to be off. In unison they bid him an ironic good night. Roaring with laughter, Marcello announces that now he has paid the last installment on the rent.

Schaunard then reminds his friends that revelry awaits them outside and begins to divide the money. When each pockets his share Marcello holds a battered mirror up to Colline. Now that he has the money, Marcello tells him, he owes it to humanity to get himself a haircut. Colline promises to look for a barber immediately. In an amusing burlesque of "grand opera" exits, Marcello, Colline, and Schaunard announce that they are leaving. Rodolpho, however, says that he must remain behind to complete an article for his magazine, *The Beaver*. It will be a matter of only five minutes, he adds. Schaunard puns that he had better cut the *Beaver's* tale short.

As the three start down the stairs Rodolpho stands at the landing outside the door to light their way with a candle. They descend, good-naturedly cursing the darkness. Suddenly there is a resounding crash, and Colline groans that he has fallen. Rodolpho calls to Colline, asking him if he has managed to kill himself. Colline replies that he is safe. The voices fade.

Rodolpho closes the door, sets the candle on the table, and starts to write. After a few lines he impatiently crumples up the page, throws it on the floor, and murmurs that he is not in the mood. There is a gentle knock at the door, and as Rodolpho rises to answer, the tender "Mimi" theme sounds in the orchestra. Mimi, on her way up the stairs to her room, is heard calling that her candle has blown out. Rodolpho finds her at the door, candle and key in hand. As she hesitates, he urges her to come in. Distressed by her painful coughing, Rodolpho asks if she is ill and exclaims in alarm at her pallor. Mimi gasps that climbing the stairs has taken her breath, then faints in Rodolpho's arms. Her key and candle drop to the floor. Rodolpho places her gently on a chair, sprinkles water on her face, remarks again about her paleness, and gazes at her long and thoughtfully. Slowly she revives. The poet, offering her a glass of wine, invites her to sit closer to the fire. In an aside he marvels at her beauty. Mimi sips the wine, rises, and asks if she may light her candle. After Rodolpho relights it for her they bid each other good night.

As Mimi reaches the door she finds that she has dropped her key. Rodolpho warns her that the draft in the doorway will again blow out her candle, and in the next moment it flickers out. She asks him to light it once more, but as he tries to do so the wind blows out his own light, plunging the room into darkness. Mimi wonders where the key can be, while Rodolpho, unobserved, latches the door. She asks his forgiveness for being such a bothersome neighbor, meanwhile feeling about the floor. Rodolpho gallantly tries to put her at her ease, then drops to his knees to join in the search.

Suddenly he comes upon the key and, with a suppressed exclamation, pockets it. Still pretending to search, he comes closer to Mimi, and in the next moment their hands touch. Mimi exclaims softly. Clasping her hand, Rodolpho begins his great aria, "Che gelida manina." Her hand is cold, he sings softly, and asks her leave to restore its warmth. There is no need to search further in the darkness. Soon the moonlight will flood the room to help them find the key. Meanwhile he will tell her about himself. Mimi, greatly moved, sinks into the chair, and Rodolpho gently lets go her hand. He sings that he is a poet and that he makes his living—such as it is—by writing. Riches he has none, but the beauty of women transports him into a world of fantasy in which he is wealthy beyond the dreams of avarice.

Passionately he tells Mimi that her eyes have stolen away all the priceless jewels of his fancy and the brightest of his dreams. But the loss is nothing, he sings exultantly, for now he has found love. Then quietly he asks Mimi to tell her own story.

They call her Mimi, she begins ("Mi chiamano Mimi"), although her name is Lucia. Her story is brief: She does embroidery to earn her living. The roses and lilies which she stitches are symbols of love and springtime—they are the stuff of dreams and poetry. But why they call her Mimi, she muses, she does not know. She continues that she eats her frugal meals alone, goes to church infrequently but prays often. She spends most of her time in her lonely attic room. But when spring comes, she sings ecstatically, her life then is flooded with sunshine and fragrance. These poor flowers of hers, she adds as an afterthought, have no aroma of their own. There is no more to tell, she concludes simply. For the rest, she is only a bothersome neighbor.

The tender mood of the scene is interrupted by the shouts of Rodolpho's companions urging him to join them. He goes to the window, calls down that he has only three lines still to write, then explains to Mimi that his friends are waiting below. He informs the three that someone is with him in the room and asks them to reserve two places at the Café Momus. The voices of Marcello, Colline, and Schaunard, chanting of Momus, die away.

Mimi and Rodolpho stand alone at the window in a flood of moonlight, and in a rapturous duet ("O soave fanciulla") declare their love for each other. Passionately they kiss. Mimi, freeing herself, reminds Rodolpho that his friends are waiting, then with charming naïveté asks him if she may accompany him. Rodolpho exclaims in delight, then pointedly suggests remaining in the room instead. Fervently Mimi cries that she will stay with him always. When he hints at returning later, however, she is charmingly evasive. Arm in arm, they slowly walk out of the room, singing of their love in ecstatic, soaring phrases. The curtain slowly falls.

ACT TWO

A square surrounded by shops. At one corner is the Café Momus. It is Christmas Eve, and the square is crowded with people. Rodolpho and Mimi are seen strolling. Colline is talking to a clothes mender; Schaunard, before another shop, is bargaining for a pipe and a horn, while Marcello is in the middle of the throng flirting with the pretty girls. Vendors, students, and townspeople sing a spirited chorus urging everyone to buy ("Aranci, datteri!"). Schaunard is heard complaining about the sour notes that the horn gives forth. Mimi says she wants to shop for a hat. Colline expresses satisfaction with his newly mended coat, puts it on, and promptly stuffs the pockets full of books. Marcello invites every girl he meets to make love.

The friends rendezvous in front of the Café Momus. First comes Schaunard, philosophically commenting on the crowd's feverish pursuit of pleasure. Colline joins him, holding up a book and happily proclaiming that he has found a collector's item. A little later Marcello appears. Rodolpho and Mimi arrive, Mimi in transports of delight over her new hat. When Marcello, Colline, and Schaunard are unsuccessful in finding a table out of doors they go inside, while Rodolpho and Mimi continue window shopping. Mimi admires a necklace on display. Rodolpho tells her that he has a rich old aunt, and if the Lord decides to end her days he will be able to buy a much more beautiful necklace.

Shouting and singing, the crowd gradually withdraws from the square. Marcello, Schaunard, and Colline emerge from the café, carrying a table. They seat themselves around it, Colline loftily remarking that, like Horace, he cannot bear rubbing elbows with the masses. Rodolpho and Mimi approach, discussing the pros and cons of jealousy. Phrases of Rodolpho's aria in Act One soar through the music as he talks of his love for Mimi. Schaunard demands privacy while he is dining. Marcello calls for the best of everything. From the distance comes the voice of Parpignol crying his wares.

Rodolpho presents Mimi to his friends. In phrases of striking lyric beauty he tells them her name, saying that she is the Muse who inspires him to his most magnificent expressions of love ("Questa è Mimi"). This soulful peroration brings a burst of cynical laughter from his companions, but they salute Mimi with true gallantry.

A colorful interlude follows as Parpignol appears with his cart, surrounded by a noisy crowd of mothers and children. The urchins pester their mothers for toys—one demands a drum, another a horse. Parpignol moves out of sight with his chattering customers. Marcello asks Mimi if she has received a gift from Rodolpho. Proudly she exhibits her new hat. She has wanted a hat like that for ever so long, she says, and marvels that Rodolpho chose it for her. She declares that the man who can so accurately read a woman's heart is indeed an extraordinary person. A savant, undoubtedly, Schaunard agrees with gentle irony. Colline remarks that Rodolpho is already a poet laureate of love. Oddly enough, Schaunard observes, everything the fellow prates about sounds very convincing. Marcello adds that all you need to do is believe, and the most fantastic dreams come true.

Love, Rodolpho proclaims, is the poet's highest inspiration. Mimi remarks that love can be either honey or vinegar—it is a matter of personal taste. Then in charming distress she exclaims that now she has offended Rodolpho. The others cut short the poet's sentimental protest by calling for a toast. And let the drink be poison, Marcello adds sourly, thinking of Musetta.

In the next moment Musetta imperiously sweeps in, followed by Alcindoro, her wealthy and aging admirer. Those at the table acclaim her beauty. Alcindoro, prancing after her, fumes that he must jump at her bidding like a servant. Musetta confirms this by contemptuously calling to him as though he were a dog. She orders him to secure a table near the others, then sits down facing the other party. Colline comments amusedly about Alcindoro, while Marcello mutters sardonically about the old duffer's "virtuous" companion. When Mimi asks who she is Marcello starts off on a bitter tirade. A brief duet follows between Musetta and Marcello ("Marcello mi vide"). She gives way to her anger at being snubbed by her erstwhile lover and his friends. Marcello describes her to Mimi as a fickle temptress, an insatiable bird of prey which feeds on human hearts. That is why, he declares acidly, he now has no heart—and will someone please pass the ragout!

Furious at Marcello's indifference, Musetta shouts for the waiter, scolds about the food, then hurls her plate to the ground. Alcindoro's efforts to calm her only increase her rage, and the two quarrel violently, to the unalloyed amusement not only of the group at the other table but a passing crowd of shopgirls. The quarrel suddenly sputters out. Musetta, her eyes fixed on Marcello, begins her brilliant aria ("Quando me'n vo'soletta"), in which she describes how everyone turns to marvel at her beauty as she passes by. Marcello can scarcely control himself as she sings that the ardent glances of the men prove that she has ensnared their hearts. In dramatic phrases she exults in her triumphs. Alcindoro rants helplessly. Musetta tauntingly reminds Marcello that he once lost his heart to her. But now, she sings with passionate intensity, he would rather die than admit that she has hurt him.

Mimi remarks that now it is clear that these two are lovers. Rodolpho explains that Musetta spurned Marcello for another. Schaunard and Colline, highly amused, comment cynically on the situation. Stung to fury, Marcello starts to leave but pauses as if transfixed as Musetta cries out that she has conquered him. The voices of the others blend with hers in a melodious quintet. Musetta alternately gibes at Marcello and berates Alcindoro. Mimi and Rodolpho express their sympathy for the unhappy lovers, while Schaunard and Colline continue their flippant comments.

Musetta suddenly screams that her shoe is causing her unbearable pain, makes Alcindoro take it off, and orders him to buy her a new pair immediately. As he distractedly leaves, Marcello realizes the purpose of Musetta's ruse and sings to her ecstatically. They rush into each other's arms as the ensemble comes to a brilliant climax. A moment later the waiter appears with the check. The men look at each other in comic distress, exclaiming that they have no money. Musetta ingeniously solves the problem by telling the waiter that her escort will pay the entire amount when he returns.

From the distance comes the beating of a drum, and the crowd gathers excitedly in the square. In a moment the patrol enters, led by a giant drum major twirling his baton. The crowd hails the marchers in a stirring chorus ("Ecco il tambur maggiore"), and as they go on their way everyone follows. When Musetta, minus her shoe, comically tries to hop along, Marcello and Colline gallantly carry her off on their shoulders. Rodolpho and Mimi follow, arm in arm. Schaunard goes next, merrily blowing his horn. When the square is deserted, Alcindoro rushes in, clutching the neatly wrapped package of shoes. Silently the waiter hands him the check. Alcindoro looks at it, groans, and collapses in a chair. The curtain falls.

ACT THREE

An open space before one of the gates of Paris. At the left is a tavern. Over the door hangs Marcello's "Red Sea" masterpiece, now a tavern sign. A brief prelude in a striking minor mood reflects the gloomy chill of a winter dawn. A group of shivering scavengers rattle the gate, demanding admittance. The sleepy guard finally lets them in. From the tavern come voices of late revelers singing a drinking song ("Chi nel ber trovò il piacer"). Musetta's voice is heard in a merry tune. Carters and farm women, laden with produce, are checked through the toll gate.

As the characteristic theme from Mimi's aria in Act One echoes softly in the orchestra, Mimi herself appears. She pauses a moment, racked by coughing, then asks a guard if there is an inn nearby at which an artist is staying. The guard points to the tavern. At that moment a woman comes out, and Mimi implores her to look for an artist named Marcello and tell him that Mimi wishes to see him. The woman complies. Marcello appears, and Mimi greets him eagerly. He tells her that he and Musetta are staying at the tavern. To pay their lodging, he goes on, Musetta gives singing lessons while he himself now paints tavern signs instead of masterpieces.

Marcello invites Mimi in. When she learns that Rodolpho is there she sobs that she must not enter. In despair she begs Marcello to help her ("Oh, buon Marcello, aiuto!"). Rodolpho, though he adores her madly, refuses to come back to her, she cries. His unreasonable jealousy had made their life together unbearable, Mimi continues bitterly, and she is at a loss for an answer to his cruel accusations. Marcello observes that under the circumstances they would be wise to separate. Mimi sadly agrees and entreats Marcello to help them bring about a parting. Marcello observes that he and Musetta are happy with each other because they can laugh and sing together. Mimi's voice blends briefly with his as she heartbrokenly sings that parting is inevitable.

Marcello says he will go to waken Rodolpho, who, worn out, has dropped off to sleep on a bench. He points him out to Mimi through a window. Marcello expresses alarm at her constant coughing. Mimi gasps that it is unending torture—and now Rodolpho chooses to leave her with the explanation that everything is at an end. At that moment Rodolpho is heard calling Marcello. The painter advises Mimi to conceal herself. Rodolpho comes striding out of the inn. Excitedly he declares that he must part from Mimi. Marcello dryly asks him if that is his latest caprice. Rodolpho dramatically answers that his ardor for Mimi was cooling ("Già un'altra volta credetti"), but one look into her eyes rekindled his passion—to his sorrow. Marcello observes that when love brings tears it is not worth cherishing—with love there must be laughter. He then bluntly reminds Rodolpho that he is unreasonably jealous, ill-tempered, and obstinate.

In an aside Mimi ponders over Rodolpho's rising anger. The poet protests that Mimi is an unfeeling coquette who tries out her charms on every man she sees. Marcello sharply says he does not believe it. Contritely Rodolpho retracts his bitter words. In dramatic, moving phrases he declares that despite his torments he realizes that Mimi is dearer to him than anything else in the world. But there is something more serious, he adds. Mimi is very ill, and he fears she is doomed.

Seeing Mimi approaching, Marcello tries to maneuver Rodolpho away so that she will not overhear. Rodolpho admits that while the terrible cough was slowly destroying her she was forced to share his poverty in his cold, cheerless rooms. Yet she bore everything uncomplainingly. Privation has desolated this fragile flower, he cries out, and now not even his love can save her. Marcello vainly tries to quiet him. Mimi, having overheard, sobs that her doom is sealed.

Weeping, shaken by her cough, Mimi no longer troubles to conceal herself. Wildly calling her name, Rodolpho takes her in his arms. Marcello regrets that she has heard Rodolpho's fateful words. Rodolpho asks Mimi to go into the tavern, but she refuses. Suddenly Musetta's laughter rings out. Marcello, angrily accusing her of playing him false again, rushes inside.

Mimi softly bids Rodolpho good-by ("Addio, senza rancor"). She must go back to the lonely attic room she left at his bidding, she sings, for now love and life are at an end. She asks him to wrap up her belongings—her gold bracelet, her prayer book—and put them aside for her, but tells him he may keep her treasured hat as a remembrance. Then the two join in a profoundly moving duet ("Addio, o dolce svegliare") expressing the anguish of hopeless love and inevitable parting.

The mood of the scene is shattered by the crashing of crockery, and in the next moment Musetta and Marcello come storming out of the tavern. There follows a quartet in which two sharply contrasting moods are combined with striking effect ("Soli l'inverno è cosa da morire!"). Mimi and Rodolpho passionately declare their love for each other and vow that they will wait for another spring before they part. Musetta and Marcello rant furiously at each other. Marcello rages that he will no longer tolerate her incorrigible flirting, while she defies him to stop her. Violently shouting his good-by, Marcello dashes back into the tavern. Musetta, screaming a final imprecation, rushes away. Rodolpho and Mimi slowly walk off. From the distance comes the rapturous ending of their duet. The curtain falls.

ACT FOUR

The attic studio, as in Act One. When the curtain rises Marcello is seen at his easel, Rodolpho at the table. Both are making obvious efforts to appear absorbed in their work. Actually, their thoughts are on Mimi and Musetta. Rodolpho says he saw Musetta riding in a fine carriage. When he asked her about the state of her heart she told him that the lovely velvet she was wearing prevented her from knowing whether it was beating or not. Marcello, with a forced laugh, remarks that he is very happy about it. Rodolpho, in an aside, mutters that Marcello is a faker—he's really raging. Marcello snaps that if "it" is not beating, well and good, and then begins painting furiously. After a moment he reverses the situation by casually mentioning that he saw Mimi riding about like a queen. Rodolpho declares he is overjoyed. Marcello brands him a love-smitten liar.

After another desperate attempt at working, both give up in disgust and stare glumly into space. Marcello turns his back on Rodolpho, takes a rosette from his pocket, and presses it to his lips. The two then sing a melodious duet ("Ah, Mimi, tu più non torni"). Rodolpho grieves over Mimi's perfidy and recalls his lost happiness with her. Marcello sings that his brush refuses to paint anything but two alluring eyes and a laughing mouth. Rodolpho takes Mimi's hat from the table drawer and clutches it to his breast. He and Marcello express their heartbreak in a melodramatic outburst of song.

After a moment Rodolpho, trying to cloak his feelings, asks the time. Marcello jokingly replies that it is the hour for yesterday's dinner. Suddenly Schaunard and Colline enter. Schaunard has four rolls, and Colline has a herring in a paper bag. They place the food on the table and then the four ceremoniously seat themselves as though they were taking their places at a formal banquet. Schaunard places the water carafe in Colline's upturned hat and announces that he has put the champagne on ice. Rodolpho, offering "Baron" Marcello a roll, asks him if he prefers salmon or flounder. Marcello recommends to "Duke" Schaunard a dish of delicious fowl—another roll. Schaunard says he must refuse because he is performing in a ballet this evening. They sip water from a solitary tumbler as though it were rare wine.

Colline rises and pompously informs the others that he has an appointment with the King. The others feign great interest, but Colline declines to divulge the nature of his business at the palace. Schaunard leaps up on a chair, raises the tumbler of water, and proposes a toast. He says he feels a poetic inspiration coming on, but the others shout him down. Undaunted, Schaunard suggests a dance, and they decide it shall be a quadrille. Rodolpho and Marcello pair off, with Marcello playing the damsel. Schaunard and Colline pretend to quarrel, challenge each other, then begin a furious duel with fire tongs and poker. The other two decide to dance a fandango while the duelists are slaying each other.

When the fun is at its height, Musetta suddenly appears, greatly concerned. She says that she has brought Mimi, who was barely able to climb the stairs. Rodolpho and Marcello see Mimi on the landing, help her into the room, and place her on the bed. Mimi begs Rodolpho to let her stay, and he fervently assures her that she may remain forever. Musetta tells the others that she learned Mimi had left her rich friend and had gone away to die alone. She finally found her, more dead than alive. Mimi had whispered that she was dying and implored Musetta to take her to Rodolpho.

Phrases from Mimi's aria in Act One come softly from the orchestra as she sings of her happiness in this reunion. Rodolpho voices his happiness in her return. The others reveal that there is neither food nor medicine for the stricken girl. Schaunard, looking at Mimi, whispers that the end is near. Between spells of coughing Mimi murmurs that her hands are cold and laments that she does not have her muff. Rodolpho sings that he will warm her hands in his. With a pathetic attempt at gaiety Mimi says that she is getting accustomed to her cough, then greets the others. They urge her not to speak. Gently she tells Marcello that he must believe in Musetta's goodness. In answer Marcello quietly takes Musetta's hand.

Leading Marcello to one side, Musetta takes off her earrings and tells the painter to sell them, buy medicine, and find a doctor. Rodolpho seats himself at the bedside. Mimi begs him not to leave her, then closes her eyes. Musetta whispers to Marcello that poor Mimi's requests will probably be her last, and then leaves with Marcello to bring back Mimi's muff.

Meanwhile Colline slowly takes off his beloved coat, holds it out before him, and sings to it a touching farewell ("Vecchia zimarra, senti"). It has served him long and faithfully, he says, and recalls how its pockets have held the treasures of philosophy and poetry. He puts the coat under his arm and starts to leave. He pauses to tell Schaunard that although they have often clashed over their opinions they can at this moment agree on two acts of mercy: to sell the coat and to leave the two lovers to themselves. Deeply moved, Schaunard agrees. As an excuse to leave he picks up the water carafe and then follows Colline.

No sooner has the door closed than Mimi tells Rodolpho ("Sono andati?") that she was only pretending to be asleep because she wanted to be alone with him. There are so many things to say, she goes on. One thought, above all, is as deep and limitless as the ocean: He is her beloved, her very life. She asks Rodolpho if he still thinks her beautiful. Beautiful as the dawn, he replies. Mimi says the simile is wrong—he should have compared her to the sunset. Then, as if in a dream, she sings the poignant phrase from her Act One aria—they call her Mimi, but she does not know why.

In answer Rodolpho sings another phrase of her song, then brings Mimi her frivolous little hat. She exclaims in pleasure as he puts it on her head. As themes from the Act One love music echo through the orchestra they recall incidents of their happy past—how they fell in love, how they looked for the key that night in the darkened attic room. Mimi reminds Rodolpho that he contrived to find it very quickly. Rodolpho gently answers that Destiny guided him. Softly she sings the opening phrases of Rodolpho's song as he held her hand in the darkness.

Suddenly she is racked by a paroxysm of coughing. As Rodolpho cries out frantically, Schaunard hurries in and rushes to the bedside. Recovering momentarily, Mimi reassures them. Musetta and Marcello return, bringing Mimi's muff and a bottle of medicine. Marcello tells Rodolpho that a doctor is on the way. Musetta gives Mimi the muff. Mimi exclaims over it in childlike delight, saying that now her hands will no longer be cold. When she pretends to chide Rodolpho for his extravagance in buying the muff for her, he sobs bitterly. Tenderly she comforts him, saying she will always be near. Then, clasping her hands in her muff, she sighs that now she will sleep.

Rodolpho tiptoes away from the bed and whispers to his companions. Musetta sings a prayer for Mimi, breaking off to ask Marcello to shield Mimi's eyes from the light of the lamp. Rodolpho anxiously consults her about Mimi, and she tries to reassure him. In the next moment Schaunard, who has tiptoed over to the bed, whispers in a voice choked with grief that Mimi is dead. Unseen by Rodolpho, who is draping Musetta's cloak over the window to keep the first rays of the sun from Mimi's eyes, Schaunard gestures to the others.

Rodolpho turns and sees the terror and despair in the faces of his friends.

In fear-stricken tones he implores them to tell him what is wrong. Then, as Marcello brokenly bids him have courage, the terrible realization dawns upon him. Frantically he rushes over to the bed and takes Mimi's lifeless form in his arms. In an agony of grief he cries out her name. Somber, powerful chords thunder forth as the orchestra intones, in minor key, the phrase in which Mimi sang to Rodolpho that she was only pretending sleep.

Boris Godunof

by MODEST PETROVICH MOUSSORGSKY

[1839–1881]

Libretto by the Composer

Based on the drama of the same name by Aleksandr Pushkin

CHARACTERS

Police officer	*Bass*
Mitiukha, a Russian peasant	*Bass*
Prince Vassili Ivanovich Shuisky, court adviser to Boris Godunof	*Tenor*
Andrei Shchelkalof, Secretary of the Duma	*Baritone*
Pimen, a monk and historian	*Bass*
Grigory, a novice (later Dimitri the Pretender)	*Tenor*
Boris Godunof	*Bass*
Hostess of the inn	*Mezzo-soprano*
Missail ⎱ mendicant friars	*Tenor*
Varlaam ⎰	*Bass*
Xenia, daughter of Boris	*Soprano*
Feodor, son of Boris	*Mezzo-soprano*
Nurse to Xenia	*Contralto*
Marina Mnishek, daughter of a Polish landowner	*Mezzo-soprano*
Rangoni, a Jesuit priest	*Bass*
Khrushchof, a boyar	*Tenor*
The Simpleton	*Tenor*
Lavitsky ⎱ Jesuit priests	*Tenor*
Chernikofsky ⎰	*Baritone*

Russian people, soldiers, guards, boyars, pilgrims, children,
ladies and gentlemen of the Polish court

Place: Russia and Poland
Time: 1598–1605
First performance: Marinsky Theater, St. Petersburg, January 24, 1874
Original language: Russian

BORIS GODUNOF is essentially an opera about the Russian people. Although the action centers around certain individuals, it is the spirit of a struggling people that dominates the stage. This spirit finds dramatic expression in the opera's brilliant pageantry and its magnificent choruses. There are few set arias in conventional operatic fashion. The action is carried forward through the medium of recitative and musical dialogue, supported by a complex orchestral accompaniment.

The opera is based on an actual episode in Russian history. Boris Godunof was a minister in the court of Czar Feodor, son of Ivan the Terrible. According to Moussorgsky's plot, Boris contrived the murder of Dimitri, younger brother of Feodor and successor to the throne. When Feodor died, Boris forced the people to demand that he become czar, then took the throne as if in response to the will of the Russians.

Meanwhile Grigory, a young novice, fled to Poland, announced himself as the Czarevich Dimitri, and fomented a revolutionary movement which hastened the downfall and death of Boris. It is interesting to note that historians subsequently absolved Boris of any blame in the death of the boy Dimitri.

Boris Godunof is usually performed from the score prepared by Nikolai Rimsky-Korsakov, who revised the opera in 1896 and again in 1908. The score as Moussorgsky wrote it was published by the Soviet Government in 1928. In this country the opera is usually sung in Russian or Italian.

Boris was given in its original form by the Metropolitan Opera Company during its 1952–53 season.

ACT ONE

[*Scene One*] The courtyard in front of the Novodievichy monastery near Moscow.[1] Boris has gone into retirement here following the death of Czar Feodor. Crowds of people are milling about the courtyard in sullen obedience to the harsh commands of a police officer. The voice of Mitiukha, apparently a minor leader among the people, is heard briefly as he tries to explain why they are being forced to appeal to Boris. The people are leaderless, says Mitiukha, and only Boris can save Russia from ruin. Led by Prince Shuisky, the boyars[2] cross the courtyard and enter the monastery. The people, threatened by the clubs of the police, reluctantly kneel facing the monastery and break into a noisy chorus of entreaty.

Shchelkalof appears at the entrance of the monastery and informs the crowd that Boris refuses to accept the throne. Russia is doomed, he adds in solemn tones, then unctuously prays that Heaven may enlighten the soul of Boris. From behind the scenes comes the chanting of pilgrims approaching the monastery. They enter in a slow procession, exhorting the crowd to hail Boris as their leader. Moving through the kneeling throng, the pilgrims present sacred tokens to the people. When the holy men have disappeared, the police roughly order the people to reassemble at the Kremlin for further demonstrations. The crowd moves off as the curtain falls.

[*Scene Two*] The cell of the monk Pimen in the Chudof monastery.[3] Pimen is writing at a table, while on a nearby cot the novice Grigory lies

[1] In the original score the opera begins with a Prologue, which has two scenes —the scene at the Novodievichy monastery and the *Coronation Scene*. It is customary, however, to present the opera in either three or four acts without a prologue.

[2] Privileged members of the Russian aristocracy, next to the ruling princes. The class was abolished by Peter the Great (1682–1725).

[3] Act One, Scene One, in the original score.

asleep. The monk pauses in reflection as he sings ("Yesho odno poslednje skazanje"—*Pimen's Narrative*), musing that soon his great work of recording the history of Russia will be completed. A murmuring accompaniment seems to follow the movement of his pen as he writes. From behind the scenes comes the soft chanting of the monks.

Suddenly Grigory awakes and sits bolt upright, exclaiming, "Vsje tot-je son" ("Forever that dream"). He frets that he is haunted by a nightmare. Gazing at Pimen, he notes to himself the monk's calm and quiet air as he sits writing his endless chronicles. Grigory then tells Pimen of his dream— how he climbed a long stairway to a high tower and looked down upon a gesticulating throng. The people cursed and derided him. Terror-stricken, he fell, and thus awoke.

Pimen tells the novice that his troubled dreams are but the sign of his youthful restlessness and counsels him to ease his mind with prayer and meditation. But Grigory replies that he chafes at the restrictions of monastic life and longs to escape to the outside world—to savor the thrill of combat and the delights of feasting. The monk answers that the world offers only shallow and illusory pleasures, which are as nothing compared with the holy calm of the cell. Deep in thought, Pimen recalls the days of Czar Ivan the Terrible and his son Feodor—how they lived devoutly and reigned in peace. But now, he concludes in somber tones, Russia is groaning under the heel of a ruthless assassin.

Grigory, fascinated by Pimen's words, says he has been told that the monk witnessed the murder of the Czarevich Dimitri. Pimen thereupon describes how three conspirators slew the boy at the instigation of Boris. The novice asks how old the boy was at the time of his murder. After a moment's thought the monk replies that, had the boy lived, he would be approximately Grigory's own age—and on the throne of Russia. At these words Grigory leaps to his feet in great excitement, but in the next instant controls himself and again assumes the humble mien of a novice.

Pimen, oblivious to his movements, charges Grigory with continuing his chronicles, then slowly leaves the cell. Bells tolling in the monastery summon the monks to matins. Grigory, going to the door, pauses, and then cries out that now all grovel in fear before Boris ("Boris, Boris! Vsje pred toboy trepeshed!"). But the deeds that are being recorded in this lonely cell, he declares gloatingly, will bring down terrible judgment upon the head of the murderous tyrant. The curtain falls.

[*Scene Three*] A square before the Kremlin in Moscow. At one side is the Cathedral of the Assumption. Opposite is the Cathedral of the Archangels. At the rear is the façade of the imperial palace. Now ensues the famous *Coronation Scene* in which Boris is crowned czar. A surging orchestral accompaniment mingles with the reverberation of great bells as a stately procession emerges from the palace and moves toward the Cathedral of the Assumption.

Prince Shuisky and Shchelkalof are seen in the van of the pageant, which includes boyars, palace guards, and dignitaries of church and state. At the steps of the cathedral Prince Shuisky pauses to bid the kneeling throng hail the new czar. The people answer in a thunderous chorus hailing Boris

("Givi i sdravstvuy tsar nash batushka"). As the music rises to a dazzling climax, Boris comes out of the church with his two children. Unheard by the throng that bows before him, he voices the haunting terror of his conscience ("Skorbit doosha"). Feverishly he prays for aid and guidance. Recovering himself, he imperiously bids the people pay homage to the memory of the czars of Russia, then invites all to the royal feast of coronation. Led by Boris, the procession moves across the square to the Cathedral of the Archangels and then proceeds to the palace. The chorus of acclaim rises to a tremendous fortissimo as the curtain falls.

ACT TWO

[*Scene One*]   An inn at the border of Lithuania.[4] After a brief, lively introduction the curtain rises to disclose the hostess of the inn busily engaged in household tasks. She sings to herself a gay, nonsensical little song about a duckling ("Poymala ja siza seleznya"). Her singing is interrupted by the sound of loud laughter and talking outside. She listens and hears two voices unsteadily chanting an appeal for alms to build a church ("Lud christianskiy"). The hostess peers excitedly out of the window and mentions that two holy men are approaching. Opening the door, she bows and scrapes as Varlaam and Missail enter. The two disreputable-looking friars are followed by Grigory, who is disguised in peasant's clothing. He is fleeing Russia because a warrant has been issued for his arrest. The police have learned of his activities in spreading the report that the supposedly slain Dimitri is still alive and should be placed on the throne instead of Boris.

With practiced humility the two friars ask the hostess for wine, and she leaves hurriedly to fetch it. Grigory seats himself at a table and stares into space with an apprehensive and preoccupied air. Varlaam tries to cheer him, but Grigory says he is greatly concerned about reaching the Lithuanian border. When the hostess returns with the wine, Varlaam and Missail greedily fill their glasses. Grigory ignores an invitation to join them.

After a few moments of drinking, Varlaam, waving a bottle, gets to his feet and launches into the famous song about the town of Kazan ("Kack vo gorode beelo vo Kazani"). He tells the story of how Czar Ivan laid siege to the Tartar fortress of Kazan. With great relish he relates how the czar had his engineers dig tunnels under the walls and then roll casks of powder, with fuses sputtering, down the apertures. When the casks exploded, some forty-three thousand Tartars were blown to bits. And that is how Kazan met its fate, Varlaam concludes, taking a long drink from the bottle.

When he notices that Grigory is not drinking, he twits him for remaining sober. Bellowing that he has no use for sobriety, Varlaam proceeds to drink himself into a stupor and finally sinks down at the table, muttering drunkenly as he falls asleep. Missail lurches over to a wooden bench and also drops off to sleep.

Grigory now quietly approaches the hostess and, pointing out of the window, asks where the road leads. To Lithuania, she answers. The border is

4 Scene Two of Act One in the original score.

not far away, but one must be careful of the frontier guards. They are questioning closely all who seek to cross, the hostess says, because they are hunting a fugitive. Varlaam revives momentarily and tries to continue singing. Grigory fears that now he may not be able to get into Lithuania, then asks whom the authorities are looking for. Some thief or other, the hostess answers casually. But they'll never catch him, she adds, for he will undoubtedly make his escape by using the secret path. Obligingly the hostess describes the path in great detail.

She is interrupted by a knock at the door. Complaining that the soldiers are at their searching again, she goes to open it. Entering, the soldiers look sharply at the three visitors. Varlaam and Missail, roused out of their stupor and startled at the sight of the soldiers, immediately offer the information that they are only poor, innocent friars and that this peasant—indicating Grigory—is their companion. Grigory himself explains that he merely led the holy men to the inn and is now preparing to go on his way.

With a deceptive show of sympathy, the officer turns to Varlaam and asks him how he is faring with his almsgathering. Varlaam paints the situation as black as possible, squirming somewhat as the officer eyes him coldly. Suddenly his questioner produces an official document and reads that Czar Boris has ordered a search for a renegade monk, Grishka Otrepief, who has escaped from Moscow. If he is caught he is to be hanged. "Are you the man?" ("Sli-hal-li ti yeto?") the officer asks. Befuddled and frightened out of his wits, Varlaam stammers that he does not know.

The officer, whose ability to read is limited, asks who can read the particulars of the warrant. Grigory volunteers. After a moment's hesitation he begins reading the document, which explains that a traitorous monk, Grishka or Grigory Otrepief by name, has succumbed to the wiles of the devil, fled the Chudof monastery, and is now trying to make his way toward Lithuania. When Grigory reaches the official description of the fugitive, he slyly glances at Varlaam. Pretending to read, he describes the friar in detail. The officer, who has been watching Varlaam closely, promptly orders him seized. Sensing that he is being tricked, the friar fights off the soldiers. Snatching up the document, he shouts that even if he cannot read he can spell out the words letter by letter.

Painstakingly he makes out the description of Grigory, who meanwhile has moved stealthily over to a window. When Varlaam finishes, he stares at Grigory for a moment, then blurts out that *he* is the wanted man. In a flash Grigory whips out his knife and leaps through the window. The soldiers stand for a moment in openmouthed astonishment and then storm after him. There is momentary confusion and uproar as the curtain falls.

[*Scene Two*]   The luxuriously furnished apartment of Czar Boris in the Kremlin in Moscow.[5] Xenia is seated at a table, looking at a picture of a young man. Nearby is her nurse. At another table sits Feodor, absorbed in a book on geography. Xenia sings heartbrokenly of the death of her beloved ("Gdje ti genih moy!"). Feodor's voice now blends with her lamentations as he recites aloud the names of the countries, cities, and seas he is learning

[5] Act Two in the original score.

about. The nurse tries to console Xenia, telling her that she will soon find happiness with a new lover. When the girl does not respond, the nurse attempts to amuse her by singing a song about a flea.[6] It is a story about the flea's friend, the gnat, who labored on the farm of a sexton. One day a greedy cricket invaded the farm and devastated the hayfield. When the gnat tried to beat off the cricket with the handle of a rake, he succeeded only in mortally wounding himself. The flea, trying to carry him home, died of the strenuous effort—and so both the gnat and the flea perished.

Feodor objects to the sad ending of the song and says he will sing a jollier one about Mother Goose. He coaxes the nurse to join him in a game, and the two dance around in a circle, clapping hands and singing nursery rhymes. The game stops abruptly as Boris enters. Observing Xenia's grief, he seeks to comfort her, urging her to forget her sorrow in the companionship of her young friends. Xenia and the nurse leave. Turning his attention to Feodor, Boris listens attentively as the boy comes to his side and tells how he has studied the map of Russia.

With paternal pride the czar praises his son for learning his lessons well. He admonishes Feodor to be diligent, for someday he himself will rule this great country. Feodor goes back to his book. Boris now gives voice to his gloomy forebodings in a dramatic soliloquy ("Dostig ya visshey vlasti"). For five years he has reigned supreme, he muses bitterly, but the success foretold by the soothsayers is only a mockery. All around him are treacherous conspirators. The people, in their blind hatred, heap upon him the blame for all the evils in the kingdom. His soul is torn by remorse and guilt, and he—the mighty czar—must grovel for mercy before God, seeking a moment's peace of mind. Distractedly he sings that the terrible sight of the murdered Dimitri relentlessly haunts his dreams. The drama of the scene is heightened at this point by a menacing, insistent rhythm in the orchestra that seems to suggest the inexorable ticking of the huge clock in one corner of the room. In a paroxysm of anguish, Boris leaps to his feet, then falls heavily into a chair, gasping a prayer for mercy ("O, gospodi, Boje moy!").

There is a commotion outside, with the voices of women rising shrilly. After a moment a court attendant (a boyar) enters to announce that Prince Shuisky desires an interview. The boyar furtively whispers that Shuisky and others have been plotting and have received a messenger from Cracow. Boris furiously orders the messenger's arrest. The boyar hurriedly leaves. Feodor approaches and looks timidly up at his father. Boris forgets his anger as the boy naïvely explains the cause of the disturbance outside. It was all because one of the nurses teased Polly the parrot, Feodor explains. Then Polly flew into a rage and tried to bite her. In compassion and tenderness, Boris embraces his son and thanks him for his story. He exclaims that if he could but live to see the boy succeed him as czar, he would gladly sacrifice the throne. Grimly he warns Feodor that, should he rule, he must guard himself well against wily traitors like Shuisky.

At that point Shuisky enters with a servile bow. Boris turns on him with a flood of contempt and vituperation. Shuisky, however, chooses to ignore

[6] Not the same as the "Song of the Flea," composed by Moussorgsky as an individual vocal number.

the insults and informs Boris that a traitor is plotting a revolution against him and that this renegade has the support of both church and people. Boris demands the plotter's name. As Feodor comes closer to listen, Shuisky, with hypocritical concern, replies that he may well be using the name of Dimitri. That name, Shuisky adds craftily, is one the people well know. Horrified, Boris sends Feodor out of the room.

Confronting Shuisky, Boris commands him to close Russia's borders at once and to prepare for war. In rising excitement he asks the prince if it could be possible for slain children to rise from their graves to haunt a czar. A heaven-appointed Czar of Russia, he adds with a burst of frenzied laughter. Flinging himself upon Shuisky, he forces the prince to relate how he saw the body of the murdered czarevich at Uglich. With evil satisfaction, Shuisky describes the scene in every gory detail. Unable to control himself, Boris commands Shuisky to leave him. He falls into a chair as the prince slinks away. Then follows the intensely dramatic scene in which Boris gives way to the remorse and guilt which torment him.

Almost bereft of reason, he imagines he sees the apparition of the murdered Dimitri approaching. Wildly he denies his guilt and implores the child to spare him this horror. Shaken by his emotions, Boris abjectly prays for mercy as the curtain falls.

ACT THREE

[*Scene One*] The boudoir of Marina Mnishek in Sandomir Castle, Poland. Marina sits looking into the mirror of her dressing table. As a maid combs her hair, the ladies-in-waiting sing that their mistress's beauty enchants all her admirers. She stops them impatiently, saying that she is bored with songs of lovesick swains and longs to hear only of Poland's valiant heroes and their conquests.

Marina dismisses her attendants, then begins a melodious refrain in the characteristic rhythm of a Polish mazurka. She expresses her contempt for the crowds of suitors eternally fawning at her feet ("Kack tomitelno i vyalo"). But there is one, she muses, who has brought new interest and excitement into her life—the young Dimitri from Moscow. He is to play a part in her completely unscrupulous ambitions. She will rob him of his will through her feminine allurements, drive him to overthrow Boris and to proclaim himself czar. Then, as czarina, she will share the throne with him and thus finally have the power and glory she so fiercely craves. Marina ends her song in a burst of triumphant laughter.

At that moment she sees the Jesuit priest, Rangoni, standing in the doorway. With suave humility he asks permission to speak with her. Then follows a long and dramatic colloquy. Insinuatingly the Jesuit tells Marina that it is her holy duty to go to Moscow with Dimitri and help him strengthen the position of the church. To that end, Rangoni goes on, she must use all her womanly charm to make Dimitri a slave to her passion. Then, when he is helpless in her power, she must wring from him a pledge of loyalty to the church. When Marina recoils at the Jesuit's treacherous scheming, the priest violently threatens her with eternal damnation. Groveling in superstitious terror, Marina acquiesces. As Rangoni stands over her exultantly, the curtain falls.

[*Scene Two*] A fountain in the garden of Mnishek Castle.[7] A bright moonlit night. The monk Grigory, now in his guise of the Pretender Dimitri, enters from the castle in the background. Ecstatically he murmurs, "V polnoch v sadu u fontana," repeating Marina's words designating the fountain as their rendezous. Passionately he sings of his longing for her. As he gazes toward the castle, softly repeating Marina's name, Rangoni steps out of the shadows and approaches him.

Dimitri angrily berates the Jesuit for dogging his footsteps. Rangoni answers that he has a message from Marina—she is burning with love for the czarevich and is coming to meet him here. Jubilantly Dimitri sings that she shall accompany him to Moscow in the hour of his triumph. Suddenly suspicious, he turns on Rangoni, warning him not to lie about Marina. The Jesuit assures him of his sincerity, then slyly asserts that Marina is constant in her love despite the jealous gossiping of the court.

Fervently Dimitri avows he is determined to make Marina his queen in defiance of all the courtiers and their slandering tongues. He begs Rangoni to help him win Marina, promising the Jesuit anything he asks in return for the favor. Rangoni unctuously replies that all he desires is to be allowed to remain at Dimitri's side as his friend and counselor. Impetuously Dimitri agrees.

Rangoni interrupts to warn that some of the guests are entering the garden from the castle, and advises Dimitri to conceal himself for the moment. Marina appears, escorted by an aging nobleman. She replies to his lovemaking with cynical banter. There is an interlude of brilliant polonaise music and choral phrases as the guests dance and then sing about the glorious battle in which Poland's heroes will dethrone the usurper Boris.

As Marina re-enters the castle, followed by the throng singing her praises, Dimitri hurries forward in great excitement. He exclaims in distaste at Rangoni's machinations, then gives vent to his jealousy over seeing Marina gazing fondly into the eyes of a doddering noble. He momentarily forswears love and vows to bend all his efforts toward marching to Moscow as a conqueror.

At the height of his heroic exultation Marina approaches and calls his name. Dimitri rushes to her with a passionate cry ("Sdyes moya golubka, krasavitza moya"), which introduces an ardent love duet. At first Marina deliberately jeers at his impassioned declarations of love and chides him for placing his emotions above his ambition. Dimitri, goaded to helpless fury, finally cries that he will conquer alone, and then all the world will laugh in scorn at the woman who spurned the destined Czar of Russia.

Instantly Marina's demeanor changes to one of tenderness and allure. She assures Dimitri that she wants only his love and solemnly pledges her eter-

---

[7] Known as the Fountain Scene, this is sometimes played as Scene Three of Act Two, or Scene One of Act Three. The scene in Marina's boudoir is then omitted entirely.

nal faith ("O, tsarevich, umolyau"). Their voices blend in the rapturous climax of the duet ("O povtori, povtori Marina!"). As they embrace, Rangoni stealthily emerges from his hiding place and joins his voice with those of the lovers in a phrase of evil triumph. The curtain falls.

ACT FOUR

[Scene One] A clearing in the forest of Kromy, not far from Moscow.[8] It is night. After a brief introduction, the shouts of a crowd are heard. Then peasants rush in, dragging the Boyar Khrushchof, whom they have captured. His arms are bound and his clothing torn. The peasants torment him mercilessly. Czar Boris plundered the throne, they sing, and this rascal stole from the plunderer. They push a whimpering crone toward him, saying that so fine a nobleman must not be without a sweetheart. Dancing around their helpless captive, they hail him in mocking chorus ("Oh, oojh i slava-jh tebe boyarinu").

The attention of the mob is suddenly diverted by the appearance of the Simpleton, a sorry figure in rags, wearing a tin pot for a helmet. Fighting off a crowd of teasing children, he seats himself on a rock and begins singing a plaintive, meaningless refrain about the moon and a weeping cat ("Mesyatz yedet kotenok platched"). He takes a coin from his pocket, whereupon the children snatch it from him and run away.

As the Simpleton bewails the loss of his treasure, his cries merge with the voices of the approaching mendicants, Varlaam and Missail. They are heard sardonically chanting the praises of Czar Boris for desolating Russia and oppressing the people. Emboldened by the friars' defiant protest, the peasants join their voices in a fierce chorus in which they pledge their loyalty to Dimitri and swear revenge against Boris.

Now two more voices are heard, chanting in Latin. In a moment the Jesuits Lavitsky and Chernikofsky appear. Shouting furious epithets, the peasants surround the priests and tie their arms with ropes. Incited by Varlaam and Missail, the mob demands that the Jesuits be hanged at once. Still resolutely chanting, the two are dragged off into the forest.

From the distance comes the blare of trumpets. A troop of white-clad soldiers rides into the clearing and is greeted by a lusty chorus acclaiming the Czarevich Dimitri. Dimitri himself shortly appears. He pauses to address the crowd, exhorting all to march with him to Moscow and to victory. As he rides away with his soldiers, followed by the crowd, bells toll wildly from afar off.

Soon the grove is deserted except for the Simpleton. He gets to his feet and turns to stare at the glow of a great fire on the horizon. In wailing tones he sings of the terror and death that are being loosed upon Russia in this night of doom. The curtain falls.

[8] In the original score this is Scene Two of Act Four, and the final scene in the opera. When the opera is presented in three acts, however, it is sometimes Scene One of Act Three, or Scene Two of Act Three.

[*Scene Two*]   The council hall of the Kremlin in Moscow.[9] The Duma, or Council of Boyars, is in special session. Shchelkalof enters and reads the czar's message to the boyars. It proclaims that a betrayer who calls himself the czarevich is leading a revolt against Boris with the aid of certain traitorous boyars. At that the members of the council excitedly denounce the false czarevich and demand that he be executed immediately. Cooler heads observe that he must first be caught.

During the uproar Shuisky enters. With his usual obsequiousness, he apologizes for being late, saying that he is much concerned over the czar. Impelled by anxiety over Boris, Shuisky tells the council, he peered secretly into the royal chamber. There he saw the monarch in the grip of some terrible fear. He seemed to be seeing the apparition of the slain Dimitri and madly prayed for mercy. Over and over he begged the ghost to depart.

As the boyars exclaim in shocked surprise, Boris reels into the chamber. Beside himself with terror, he cowers as though trying to escape from a pursuer. In fear-stricken tones he protests that he is guiltless. Dimitri lives, he mutters, and Shuisky must be punished for spreading the vile lie about his murder.

Suddenly he recovers himself, greets the boyars with his accustomed dignity and authority, and then takes his seat on the throne. Shuisky hesitantly approaches and informs him that a venerable monk is waiting to speak to the czar on a matter of great importance. Boris orders him to be admitted, saying that this holy man may bring some peace to his troubled spirit.

Summoned by Shuisky, the monk Pimen enters. He pauses for a moment at the door, then slowly approaches Boris, who quietly bids him speak. In an impressive aria, "Odnajdi v vetcherniy tchass prishel ko mnye pastuh," Pimen tells his story. He relates that he was visited by an aged shepherd who told him of a miracle. The shepherd explained that he had been blind from childhood. All cures had failed, he said, and he was resigned to eternal darkness. Then in a dream he heard the voice of a young boy bidding him go to the cathedral at Uglich and kneel in prayer at his tomb. The child had said he was the Czarevich Dimitri. The shepherd went immediately to Uglich, and hardly had he prayed than his sight was restored. There before him stood Dimitri.

Boris suddenly clutches at his heart and cries out wildly for help. Great excitement prevails as the boyars crowd around him. Reviving somewhat, Boris calls for his son. Feodor is brought in. He runs to his father's arms, and Boris commands all to leave. Then ensues a moving scene of farewell as Boris sings, "Protshay moy sin."

To the accompaniment of a somber theme in the orchestra, Boris tells Feodor that he will soon take his place on the throne of Russia. He must never seek to learn how his father came to rule, and must guard himself well against traitors. He counsels the boy to pay heed to the will of the people and to rule honorably and justly. Gently he commits Xenia to Feodor's care. Placing his hands upon the boy's head, Boris, in broken phrases, prays for a blessing on his son.

[9] Scene One of Act Four in the original score. When the opera is played in three acts, this is either Scene Two of Act Three or Scene Three of Act Three.

From the distance come the tolling of bells and the chanting of the people as they offer a prayer for their dying monarch. In his final agony Boris cries to Heaven for mercy as boyars and monks enter the council chamber in solemn procession. With a desperate effort the dying czar rises to his feet and commands them to halt. Pointing to his son, he gasps, "Vot vash Tsar!" ("There is your Czar!") A prayer for mercy on his lips, Czar Boris topples from the dais. The curtain falls.

Carmen

by GEORGES BIZET

[1838–1875]

Libretto by
HENRI MEILHAC and LUDOVIC HALÉVY

Based on the story of the same name by the French novelist,
Prosper Mérimée

CHARACTERS

Morales, an officer..*Bass*
Micaela, a peasant girl.....................................*Soprano*
Zuniga, a captain of dragoons...............................*Bass*
Don José, a corporal of dragoons.............................*Tenor*
Carmen, a gypsy girl..*Soprano*
Mercedes ⎫ gypsy companions of Carmen............⎰ *Mezzo-soprano*
Frasquita ⎭ ⎱ *Mezzo-soprano*
Escamillo, a toreador......................................*Baritone*
El Remendado ⎫ smugglers.............................⎰ *Tenor*
El Dancairo ⎭ ⎱ *Baritone*

Cigarette girls, dragoons, an innkeeper, smugglers, dancers

Place: In and near Seville
Time: About 1820
First performance: Opéra-Comique, Paris, March 3, 1875
Original language: French

CARMEN, which is often referred to as an outstanding example of *opéra-comique*, is one of the universal favorites of the operatic stage. In setting Mérimée's story to music, Bizet exploited to the fullest his talent for vivid musical characterization, brilliant orchestration, and dramatic use of "local color." *Carmen* rings true throughout to Spanish temperament and atmosphere.

It has been said that the opera was so dismal a failure that Bizet died not long afterward of sheer humiliation and disappointment. That story has been challenged. It is true that the composer succumbed some three months after the opening, but his death was attributed to physical causes aggravated by overwork.

Carmen was, in fact, moderately well received. Paris was rather cool to it for several reasons. It was not in the conventional operatic idiom of the day. Bizet's use of continuously flowing melody led critics to accuse him of "Wagnerianism," against which there was violent prejudice in Paris at the time. The opera also lacked a happy ending. Finally, Parisian audiences were said to have been shocked by the bohemian character of Carmen her-self.

Although withdrawn from the stage of the Opéra-Comique, *Carmen* was enthusiastically acclaimed in other European capitals a few months after its première. Eventually it won not only the favor of Paris but of the entire operatic world.

The prelude begins with the vigorous rhythm reflecting the festive atmos-phere of the bullfight in the last act. Then comes the stirring refrain of the *Toreador Song*. This is followed by the somber motive of Carmen's tragic destiny—the so-called "fate motive." Just as this builds up to a crescendo it is shattered by an explosive chord. There is a dramatic pause, and the cur-tain rises.

ACT ONE

A public square in Seville. At the right is the entrance to the tobacco fac-tory, at the left, a guardhouse. A bridge spans the rear of the scene. It is noon. Townspeople are crossing the square, and Morales and a number of dragoons are lounging in front of the guardhouse. The soldiers sing about the passing throng. As the brief chorus ends, Micaela enters. Morales calls attention to the comely girl who is approaching, and the guards express lively interest.

Courteously Morales asks Micaela for whom she is looking. A corporal, she replies. Himself, perhaps, suggests the officer hopefully. Micaela ex-plains that she is seeking Don José. Morales says they all know of him but that he does not belong to their company. He is expected soon, the officer continues, because there will shortly be a change of guard. Then he invites her to wait inside the guardhouse. Micaela thanks him but declines, whereupon Morales hastily assures her that she will be in no danger. Micaela answers that she is quite sure of that, but thinks it will be better if she returns later when the relief guard arrives. The soldiers, pressing around, entreat her to stay. She adroitly evades their attentions, gaily bids them good-by, and runs off. Morales remarks philosophically that the bird has escaped and that there is nothing to do but go on watching the crowd as before.

Then begins the bright, martial music of the changing of the guard. The relief detachment is led in by Zuniga and Don José, preceded by a group of street urchins marching along to a merry tune of their own. While the guard is changing, the youngsters march around singing of how they go for-ward like true soldiers, shoulders back and heads high. They imitate trum-pets as they sing.

Morales tells Don José that a pretty girl, with braided hair and dressed in blue, came to the guardhouse looking for him. That must have been Micaela, Don José exclaims. The off-duty guard marches away, with the boys following and singing their gay, piping tune.

In recitative, Zuniga asks Don José if the cigarette girls work in the fac-tory across the square. Don José tells him they do, and adds that they are known to be a flirtatious lot. When Zuniga asks if they are good-looking, Don José confesses that he has never paid any attention to them. Zuniga knowingly remarks that his thoughts are probably wrapped up in a pretty girl in blue, whose name is Micaela. The corporal admits that he loves her very much. He goes on to say that the cigarette girls will shortly appear, and then Zuniga can judge for himself if they are beautiful.

A bell rings and the workers stream out of the factory. First come the men, singing how they wait each noon to make love to the girls ("La cloche a sonné"). Then the girls, smoking cigarettes, stroll into the square. To the accompaniment of a gracefully flowing theme the men describe the alluring movements of the girls as they smoke and compare lovers' words and promises to smoke that ascends to the sky and is gone.

The men wonder why they have not seen Carmen. In the next instant the fate motive flashes in the orchestra and Carmen stands before them. The crowd hails her lustily, the men imploring her to tell when she will give them her heart. Darting a look at Don José, Carmen answers that she does not know—perhaps never, perhaps tomorrow. At any rate, it will not be today.

To a throbbing rhythm, Carmen now begins the well-known *Habanera*. Love is like a bird that will never be tamed, she sings ("L'amour est un oiseau rebelle"). If he does not find your heart to his fancy, all entreaties are in vain. One lover woos with ardent phrases, another with silent adoration—and it is the latter whom Carmen chooses. The chorus repeats her words in a rhythmic chant. Carmen continues that love is like a gypsy, lawless and free. If you do not love her, she will love you nevertheless—and if she loves you, be on your guard. Repeating the refrain, Carmen sings that love is like an elusive bird: just as you think you have caught it, the creature flies away. The *Habanera* ends with a defiant flourish, and the men again beg Carmen to answer their pleas.

As the fate motive again is heard, Carmen starts toward the factory, suddenly turns, and approaches Don José. With an impudent laugh, she takes a flower from her dress, throws it in his face, then runs away. A group of cigarette girls surround Don José and mockingly repeat a strain from the *Habanera*. In a moment the factory bell rings, calling the men and women back to their work.

Don José is left alone. Slowly he picks up the flower, commenting as he wonders about Carmen's brazen gesture. He recalls how the flower sped like a bullet from her hand. The perfume is heady and the flower beautiful, he muses. As for the woman herself, if there are such beings as sorceresses, she most certainly is one.

At that moment Micaela appears and calls his name. Joyously Don José greets her. When Micaela tells him she brings greetings from his mother, he excitedly asks for further news of her. His mother has sent him a letter and some money, Micaela says. Shyly she adds that she has been entrusted with something for him that is far more precious. Eagerly Don José asks her to explain. Micaela replies that whatever has been given her for José, she in turn will give him.

She tells Don José that his mother had kissed her when they left the chapel together and had told her to seek her son in Seville. She bade

Micaela say to her son that his mother thinks of him day and night and forgives his erring ways. The parting kiss she gave Micaela was for her son. Don José voices his emotion in a dramatic phrase. Now, Micaela continues, she will give Don José the kiss his mother sent.

A lyrical duet follows in which the two lovers sing of their tender memories of home and childhood ("Ma mère, je la vois"). The refrain is interrupted by the sinister fate theme. Don José turns abruptly away from Micaela and, in recitative, recalls the evil that strangely menaced him only today. He muses that the kiss his mother sent him from afar has saved him from great danger. What evil? What danger? Thus Micaela anxiously questions him. Don José brushes aside her queries by asking when she plans to return home. She replies that she will see his mother on the morrow.

In a brief but moving air, Don José asks Micaela to give his mother this message: He repents his wrongdoings and hopes she will forgive him. In return for her kiss he sends her the one he now gives Micaela. The two then resume the music of the duet.[1]

As Don José prepares to read his mother's letter, Micaela says she will leave him so that he might be alone. With the music of the duet echoing softly in the orchestra, the corporal utters his thoughts as he reads. His mother need have no fear, he sings, because her prayers will be answered. He loves Micaela and will take her for his wife. He meditates a moment, then in sudden anger his mind reverts to Carmen, the "sorceress," and her flower. He is about to throw the flower away when there is a burst of excitement in the factory. Zuniga rushes out of the guardhouse and asks what has happened. The workers hurry into the square, the women crying for help. They crowd around Zuniga, all chattering at once, some accusing Carmen, others defending her. One group finally takes the bewildered officer aside and tells him the story. Manuelita, one of the cigarette girls, announced that she had decided to buy a donkey, whereupon Carmen remarked that she would be better off buying a broom. Manuelita retorted that Carmen, with all her fine airs, would look well riding on a donkey—with two grooms at her side to chase away the flies. That touched off a hairpulling match, the women add breathlessly.

Zuniga tries to quiet the excited group, then orders Don José to take two soldiers and find out what happened in the factory. The women again begin pestering Zuniga with their noisy arguments. One faction declares that Carmen struck the first blow, the other blames Manuelita. The names are tossed back and forth in an amusing chorus.

Suddenly Carmen appears, escorted by Don José and the two soldiers. Don José tells Zuniga that the two women exchanged blows and that one has been wounded. When Zuniga asks who is to blame, Don José replies that Carmen can tell him. The captain demands an explanation. With deliberate insolence, Carmen begins singing to herself, then replies that even torture could not make her talk. She says that she will defy all his weapons and heaven itself. Zuniga brusquely tells her to save her singing for another

---

[1] The recitative and Don José's following air are sometimes cut. In that case, the first and second parts of the duet are combined and sung without interruption.

time and answer the charges. Carmen retorts that the answer is her own
secret—and she means to keep it. She adds that there is someone near by
whom she loves well enough to die for. Angrily Zuniga warns that she will
do her singing in jail. By way of an answer, Carmen cuffs the first woman
within reach, then resumes her singing with more impudence than ever.
Thereupon Zuniga declares that, as much as he regrets it, he is forced to
bind the arms of this young and charming person. He does so, and puts her
in Don José's charge.

As the captain leaves, Carmen asks Don José where he is going to take
her. He replies that there is nothing he can do but obey orders and take her
to jail. The gypsy calmly informs him that, on the contrary, he will not only
help her but bow to her every whim because he loves her. When Don José
protests, she declares that the flower she gave him has charmed him into
her power. Angrily Don José orders her to be quiet. Instead of obeying, she
begins the alluring *Seguidilla.*

To the accompaniment of its insinuating rhythm she sings that she is
going to dance and drink *manzanilla* at the tavern of her good friend Lillas
Pastia, just outside the walls of Seville ("Près des remparts de Séville"). As
there is no pleasure in going alone, she will take a lover along. But her current lover is gone—the devil knows where—and now her poor heart is as free
as air again. Swains there are by the dozen, but not one of them pleases.
And yet her heart and her soul may be had for the asking.

Meaningfully she observes that Don José has come along at just the right
moment—and so she will go dancing and drinking at Lillas Pastia's with her
new love. Outraged, Don José commands her to be silent. Carmen innocently replies that she was only singing to herself and meant him no
harm. She was just thinking of a certain soldier who is in love with her and
knows she means to do him no wrong. He's not a captain, nor even a lieutenant, but a mere corporal—yet it's all the same to a poor gypsy girl. Yes,
he will do, Carmen adds seductively.

Don José protests that he is going mad. In passionate excitement he
demands to know if she will always be true to him and love him if he
relents. As if hypnotized, he loosens her bonds, again and again demanding
her promise to love him. Deliberately Carmen continues to torment him
with her song, which she ends in brazen triumph.

Zuniga comes out of the guardhouse and gives Don José his orders, warning him to watch Carmen closely. In an aside, Carmen tells the corporal her
plan for escape: At a certain moment she will push him and he must pretend to fall, leaving her unguarded. She reminds him again of their rendezvous. Then, laughing insolently in Zuniga's face, she repeats the refrain of
the *Habanera.* Don José and the soldiers march her off. As they reach the
bridge, Carmen puts her trick into effect and runs away shouting with
laughter. The curtain falls.

ACT TWO

There is a brief entr'acte, which has for its theme an air sung by Don
José later in the act. The curtain rises on Lillas Pastia's tavern. Gypsies and

smugglers are sitting at tables with officers and soldiers. Dancers whirl about to the rhythmic beat of gypsy music. They pause as Carmen begins a fiery gypsy song ("Les tringles des sistres tintaient"). As the music grows wilder and wilder, the dancing begins again in a frenzy of color and movement. Frasquita and Mercedes join Carmen in her song, and the number ends in a riotous outburst of singing and dancing.

Frasquita then announces that it is closing time. Zuniga suggests that she and Mercedes leave with him, but they refuse. He invites Carmen, and she likewise declines. Annoyed at her refusal, he remarks that she looks angry. When she asks why she should be angry, the jealous captain replies that it is probably because of that soldier who was imprisoned for allowing her to escape. Carmen caustically asks if he has been put to death for his crime. Zuniga reveals that Don José has been released, and Carmen exclaims in obvious delight. She and the two other girls bid the disgruntled Zuniga and the soldiers good night with mocking politeness.

Suddenly from outside the tavern come the shouts of a crowd hailing Escamillo. It is a torchlight procession, Zuniga announces from the door. He then invites Escamillo in for a drink, and soon the blustering hero enters. The people crowd into the tavern and toast the bullfighter in a lusty chorus. In response, he sings the famous *Toreador Song*. He describes the great arena, with its vast throng shouting for the hero of the day. The chorus takes up the refrain, singing of the toreador's reward—the hand of his lady-love. Escamillo, continuing his aria, portrays the mad rush of the bull and the agile thrusts of the daring toreador as he stalks his prey. Again the chorus joins him, bringing the number to a stirring climax.

As he ends his song, Escamillo swaggers over to Carmen. He asks her to tell him her name, so that he may repeat it the next time he is in danger. Carmen obliges, but parries his pointed questions about love. Zuniga interrupts to warn her that if she will not come with him now he will return for her later. That will be a waste of time, she replies. The captain scornfully retorts that he is willing to take a chance.

With a flourish of the toreador music, Escamillo struts out, followed by the crowd. Frasquita asks El Dancairo about the plans for a proposed smuggling raid. He replies that the chances for success are good, but that the smugglers will need the expert assistance of the women to carry it out. This is the cue for one of the most delightful numbers in the opera—the scintillating quintet sung by Frasquita, Mercedes, El Dancairo, El Remendado, and Carmen ("Nous avons en tête une affaire"). They expound the theory that in plotting any kind of conspiracy, thievery, or deception, one must first make sure to have the co-operation of women. Their natural gift for duplicity will insure success. Frasquita and Mercedes agree at once to join the smugglers, but Carmen refuses. El Dancairo and El Remendado ask her why, and after much entreaty she finally tells them that she is in love. But they are incredulous. Carmen repeats that she is out of her mind with love. With ingratiating irony, the two smugglers observe that Carmen heretofore has always managed to compromise gracefully between her obligations and affections. She still refuses, saying that this time there can be no compromise. The smugglers plead in vain. Then all resume the refrain of the quintet with its humorous, rapid-fire patter.

El Dancairo, noting Carmen's restless manner, asks if she is expecting someone. She answers that she awaits a soldier who went to prison for her sake. A touching matter, remarks El Remendado cynically, while El Dancairo reminds Carmen that her soldier may very well change his mind about coming.

At that moment the voice of Don José is heard in the distance. He sings a short unaccompanied air (heard previously in the entr'acte) in praise of the brave dragoons of Alcala ("Halte là, qui va là?"). Carmen voices her joy. Frasquita and Mercedes peer outside and comment approvingly, and the two smugglers urge Carmen to ask Don José to join their band. Don José sings another stanza about the dragoons of Alcala as he approaches and enters the tavern. Carmen greets him eagerly. Don José tells her he has been in jail for two months and would gladly have stayed longer for her sake. He ardently assures her of his love.

She teases him by saying that she has just danced for some of his comrades, then taunts him for showing jealousy. Don José admits he is jealous. In gay mockery, Carmen says that now she will sing and dance for Sir Soldier alone. Commanding his attention, she begins a sinuous dance, singing a rhythmic, wordless air to the clicking accompaniment of castanets. Suddenly bugles blare in the distance. Don José stops Carmen and tells her that the retreat is being sounded. She sarcastically remarks that Don José is evidently bored with her singing and dancing and welcomes this interruption. After a moment she resumes her alluring dance. Don José once more restrains her, trying to explain that he must obey the call of duty and go back to quarters.

Carmen turns on Don José in fury. Angrily she reproaches herself for being so stupid as to try to please him with her singing and dancing. She might even have fallen in love with him, she storms. No sooner does he hear the bugle call, Carmen rages as she scornfully parodies the notes, than off he must go. With that she picks up his saber and helmet from the table, flings them at him, and derisively advises him to scamper back to quarters.

Shocked and humiliated, Don José reproaches Carmen for her cruelty. He assures her that he is loath to go—that never has any woman so profoundly stirred his heart. Carmen's reply is again to mock the bugle call and jeer at him for running off the moment he hears the retreat. And *that* is how he loves, she taunts bitterly. As she continues to deride and insult him, Don José declares in ringing, dramatic phrases that he loves her and that she must listen to his words.

Taking her flower from his blouse, he begins the *Flower Song* ("La fleur que tu m'avais jetée"), one of the most famous of tenor arias. This flower, he sings, was his solace in prison. Though withered, its perfume still lingered, and during the night it brought back the vision of her face. Then, tortured by his longing, he cursed the day he first saw her and the destiny that set her in his path. But that was blasphemy, for deep in his heart there was only one desire and one hope—to return to her. From the first moment of their meeting, at her very first glance, she claimed his soul. Don José vows that he has but one single thought: he loves her.

But Carmen sullenly replies that he does not love her, that if he really did he would come away with her at once to her native mountains. There they would be free to love—no commands to obey, no retreat to quarters to heed. Ignoring Don José's desperate protests, Carmen relentlessly continues, as though casting a spell over him. He must follow her to the mountains, she repeats, to freedom beyond the law.

Suddenly Don José tears himself from Carmen's arms, declaring that he will not stoop to the infamy of desertion. His refusal goads Carmen into wild fury. She pours out her hatred for him and bids him good-by forever. In utter despair, Don José sings his farewell and prepares to leave. At that moment there is a knock on the door, and Zuniga is heard calling Carmen's name. She warns Don José to be silent. Zuniga bursts in. Seeing Don José, he makes a sneering reference to Carmen's lack of taste, asking why she chooses a plain soldier when there are officers available. He angrily orders Don José to leave, but the corporal calmly refuses. The captain makes a threatening gesture, whereupon Don José impetuously draws his sword and dares him to fight. Carmen quickly steps between the two men and excitedly summons the gypsies, who pour into the room. El Dancairo and El Remendado swiftly disarm Zuniga. As he stands helplessly between the two, Carmen tauntingly remarks that love has tricked him into arriving at exactly the wrong moment.

She informs him that they will be forced to hold him prisoner for a while to assure their own safety. The two smugglers, sticking their pistols into Zuniga's ribs, suggest with elaborate irony that it is time for him to leave. Merely for a stroll, Carmen explains mockingly. Zuniga assents, remarking that there is no resisting certain methods of argument. Casually he reminds them that there will be a reckoning later. That means war, El Dancairo observes with a shrug, but as things stand now, the captain had better come along without any further talk. The gypsies jeer at Zuniga as he is led away.

Carmen turns to Don José and asks him if he is now willing to join the smugglers. When he resignedly replies that he has no other choice, she chides him for his lack of gallantry. Exultantly she again begins the theme of her song of freedom. The chorus takes up the refrain, closing the act with a stirring ensemble ("Suis-nous à travers la campagne").

ACT THREE

After the entr'acte, a meditative air of quiet charm, the curtain rises on the smugglers' rendezvous in a wild mountain glen near a pass. Some of the band are lying about wrapped in their cloaks. Others enter cautiously to the accompaniment of an impressive, marchlike tune. Then the smugglers begin a dramatic chorus in which they warn of the need for caution as they ply their dangerous trade ("Ecoute, écoute, compagnon"). Danger lurks everywhere, they sing stealthily, and every moment they must be on their guard. The last notes die away in somber silence.

Carmen comes upon Don José staring unhappily down into the valley and asks what he sees. Sorrowfully he answers that down there lives a good, brave woman who still believes him to be an upright man. Bitterly he adds that she is wrong. With cutting sarcasm, Carmen asks who this remarkable woman is. Don José protests at her tone and says he is speaking of his mother. Carmen scornfully advises him to go home at once because he certainly is not suited to the smugglers' trade. She warns that if he does not leave, he will regret it.

Don José is aghast at her callousness in suggesting that they part. As Carmen repeats that they must part, the fate motive is briefly intoned by the orchestra. In rising anger, Don José warns her not to talk thus. She retorts that he will probably kill her for it, then notes the sinister look on his face. When Don José makes no reply, Carmen says indifferently that nothing matters, because Destiny is after all the master.

A little distance away Frasquita and Mercedes are playing cards. They sing a charming duet in which they beseech the cards to tell them who their lovers will be. Frasquita sees her lover as an ardent young man. Mercedes says her wooer is a rich old man who talks of marriage. Frasquita foretells that her young man is going to carry her off to the mountains on his dashing steed. There he will rule as a great chieftain, with hundreds of men to do his bidding. Mercedes boasts that she will have gold and diamonds galore, then triumphantly announces that her aged lover will die and leave her all his vast fortune.

Carmen saunters over and picks up the cards—first a diamond, then a spade. There is a sinister suggestion of the fate motive, followed by sustained descending notes, as Carmen reads her tragic fortune: death—first for her, then for him. To the accompaniment of brooding minor chords she sings of the fateful cards ("En vain pour éviter les réponses amères"). No one can ignore the answers they give. No use to shuffle them—they never lie. If your Destiny is a happy one, every card will foretell good fortune. But if you are fated to die, you may pick up twenty cards and each one will pitilessly repeat your doom. Twice Carmen turns up the cards as the harmonies harshly reverberate in the orchestra. Death—and again Death, Carmen murmurs hopelessly. Frasquita and Mercedes interrupt her as they begin their gay refrain. A striking trio follows, with the two girls singing lightly of their lovers and Carmen reiterating her prophecy of doom.

El Dancairo suddenly appears, announces that the smugglers will try to get through the pass with contraband, and asks Don José to remain behind to guard their stores. He adds that he saw three guards at the pass, and that they will have to be taken care of. Carmen, ordering the men to shoulder their booty, declares that they must and will get through.

A vigorous chorus follows, in which the smugglers explain how they will outwit the guards. As the soldiers are gallant gentlemen, they will not be able to resist the smiles of the women, and while they are thus diverted, the men will pass by with the contraband, unobserved. A moment after the smugglers have left, Micaela appears, searching for Don José. In recitative, she vows to conquer fear and carry out the task imposed on her by his mother. Then, in one of the best-known arias in the opera, "Je dis que rien ne m'épouvante," she voices her determination to accomplish her task. She admits that this wild mountain spot fills her with dread, but offers up a prayer for strength to face the ordeal. She resolves to confront the evil temptress who has lured Don José to his ruin. Her aria ends in a dramatic entreaty for divine guidance.

Suddenly Micaela sees Don José in the distance. She calls his name.

Trembling with fear, she watches him take aim and fire at an unseen target, then conceals herself. A moment later Escamillo comes striding up through the pass, hat in hand. He inspects the bullet hole in the hat and jovially remarks that if the shot had struck a bit lower it would have finished him off. Don José rushes up and demands his name. Escamillo suavely identifies himself.

Don José bids him welcome, but adds that he risked his life coming through the pass alone. The other replies that he is too much in love to worry about such trifles, and that anyone who calls himself a man would certainly risk all to see his ladylove. Don José asks who she is. A gypsy girl, Escamillo tells him, Carmen by name. Don José starts in surprise. The toreador relates that Carmen was in love with a certain soldier who became a deserter in order to be near her. But that's all over now, Escamillo adds, because Carmen's affairs never last more than six months.

Don José sharply asks Escamillo if he is aware of the fact that whoever tries to take a gypsy's woman away must be prepared to pay the price. Escamillo coolly asks what that may be. The slash of a dagger, Don José retorts. Then it dawns upon the toreador that this angry renegade is Carmen's erstwhile lover. Mockingly he expresses his pleasure at meeting his rival. The challenge given, the two sing a dramatic duet as they prepare to duel with daggers ("Enfin ma colère"). They lunge at each other. Escamillo falls, and Don José is about to plunge his knife into his adversary's throat when Carmen, followed by the smugglers, rushes in and stops him.

Escamillo gallantly thanks Carmen for saving his life. Turning to Don José, he observes that the score is even—now—but the winner will be decided "in the next round." El Dancairo interrupts impatiently and tells Escamillo to be off. The toreador pauses to invite all to the bullfight in Seville —particularly those who love him. As he speaks he looks significantly at Carmen. Don José, seeing the glance, makes a threatening gesture, but Escamillo flippantly advises the corporal not to be hasty, then slowly makes his exit, deliberately keeping his eyes on Carmen. Don José lunges at the toreador but is restrained by the smugglers.

He turns on Carmen and warns her not to torment him. El Dancairo urges all to go on their way. Suddenly El Remendado discovers Micaela and drags her from her hiding place. Don José ignores her eager greeting and asks why she has come. To the music of the duet in Act One, Micaela tells him that down in the valley his mother tearfully prays that her son will return to her. She implores Don José to come with her. Sneeringly Carmen advises him to go at once. Stung to fury, Don José accuses her of wanting to get rid of him so that she may follow her new love, the toreador. Wildly he swears that he will never leave Carmen, that death alone can break the chain that binds them. In chorus the smugglers urge him to leave for his own good. Don José brushes Micaela aside and confronts Carmen. He rages that he will force her to bow to the destiny that brought them together and again vows never to leave her. The smugglers appeal to him to heed their warning.

Micaela steps forward, pleading for a final word. Grief-stricken, she tells Don José that his mother is near death and that she wishes to forgive him before she dies. Don José cries out in anguish and prepares to leave with

Micaela. In terrible anger he whirls on Carmen, warning her that they will
meet again. The fate motive underscores the threat in his words.

From the distance comes the voice of Escamillo singing a phrase of the
Toreador Song. Carmen attempts to meet him, but Don José prevents her
with a menacing gesture. The smugglers slowly move off to the marchlike
music heard earlier. The curtain falls.

ACT FOUR

The entr'acte music, flashing with brilliant Spanish rhythms, builds up to
the festive gaiety of the bullfight scene which opens the act. The curtain
rises on a square before the bull ring in Seville. An excited throng is waiting
for the procession into the arena. A shout goes up as the parade approaches,
and the scene glitters with colorful pageantry. Dancers, picadors, ban-
dilleros, officers, and soldiers march proudly by.

A thunderous burst of applause greets Escamillo as he enters with Carmen on his arm. There is a brief but melodramatic duet. The toreador sings
that if Carmen really loves him, she may well be proud of him today ("Si
tu m'aimes, Carmen"). Fervently she answers that she has never loved anyone as she loves him. Their impassioned song is interrupted by the entrance
of the Alcalde, the highest official of Seville. Frasquita and Mercedes approach and warn Carmen that Don José is lurking in the crowd. Carmen
scornfully replies that she is not afraid, and will stay and talk with him. The
crowd surges into the arena. Frasquita and Mercedes follow, and in the
next moment Carmen and Don José stand face to face—alone.

They greet each other curtly. Carmen says that friends have tried to convince her that Don José has come to the arena with the intention of killing
her. Don José quietly replies that he is not here to harm her, only to plead
for her love. He entreats her to forget all their past bitterness and come
away with him to some distant place where they can start life anew. Carmen answers that she will not lie—her mind is made up. All is over between
them.

In a passionate, moving appeal, Don José begs her to allow him to save
her—and, in saving her, save himself. Carmen harshly replies that she knows
he will probably kill her if she refuses, but even that will not break her will.
Their voices blend in a short but intensely dramatic duet, Carmen relentlessly repeating her refusal, Don José frenziedly pleading.

In despair, Don José cries out for her love, but Carmen spurns him with
cruel indifference. Wildly he promises that if she will love him he will join
the smugglers again—will do anything she asks. In a dramatic plea he
implores her not to leave him. Carmen's reply is that she was born free and
she will die free.

There is a sudden fanfare from the bull ring as the shouting crowd hails
the toreador. With an exclamation of pride and joy, Carmen attempts to
rush into the arena. Don José seizes her, sardonically commenting on the
applause for her new lover. Violently he asks if she is really in love with the
toreador. Carmen defiantly answers that even in the face of death she will

admit her love. Another fanfare sounds in the arena, and the throng sings excitedly about the progress of the bullfight.

Again Carmen tries to force her way past Don José. Beside himself with jealous fury, he cries out that he has not pawned his soul for her love only to be scornfully cast aside for his rival. Furiously Carmen tells him either to kill her or let her pass. More cheers come from the arena. Don José curses Carmen and shouts that for the last time he asks her to yield. In answer she takes from her finger the ring he had given her and hurls it away. Don José rushes at her with a terrible cry. As the crowd pours out of the arena singing phrases of the *Toreador Song*, Don José seizes Carmen and plunges his dagger into her heart.

The people draw back in horror as they see him kneeling beside Carmen's body. Then, as the fate motive thunders forth, Don José cries out that it was he who slew her—his own Carmen, whom he adored. The curtain falls.

Cavalleria Rusticana

by PIETRO MASCAGNI

[1863–1945]

Libretto by
GIOVANNI TARGIONI-TOZZETTI *and* GUIDO MENASCI

Based on a short story
CAVALLERIA RUSTICANA
written and later dramatized by the Italian novelist, Giovanni Verga

CHARACTERS

Santuzza, a beautiful peasant girl............................ *Soprano*
Lucia, mother of Turiddu................................. *Contralto*
Alfio, a village teamster..................................... *Baritone*
Turiddu, a young soldier...................................... *Tenor*
Lola, the young wife of Alfio......................... *Mezzo-soprano*
Villagers and peasants

Place: A Sicilian village
Time: Nineteenth century
First performance: Teatro Constanzi, Rome, May 17, 1890
Original language: Italian

CAVALLERIA RUSTICANA, Mascagni's first opera, scored a spectacular success at its very first performance and lifted its composer from obscurity to fame and fortune overnight. It has held its place since then as one of the most popular works on the operatic stage.

At the time Mascagni wrote his masterpiece he was a struggling music teacher in the small Italian town of Cerignola. He had learned, in 1888, that the music publisher Sonzogno was offering a prize for the best one-act opera. Mascagni entered the competition in the hope of securing much-needed funds. He found his inspiration in the libretto by Targioni-Tozzetti and Menasci and forthwith started composing. Early in 1890 he presented his score to the contest judges in Rome, where it was awarded first prize. Its subsequent production made operatic history. The opera is usually presented on the same bill with other short works, such as *Pagliacci*, *Salome*, and *Hänsel und Gretel*.

Ironically titled "Rustic Chivalry," *Cavalleria* deals with anything *but* chivalry. It is a grim story of illicit love and revenge, and the fact that the events take place on an Easter morning adds still further to the dramatic effect.

Action centers around Turiddu, a young soldier, whose mother keeps a wineshop in the village square. When he went away to serve in the army he was betrothed to Lola, but on his return he found her married to Alfio, the teamster. Turiddu, having thus lost Lola, consoled himself by making love to another village girl, Santuzza. Before long he betrayed, then abandoned her, transferring his affections back to Lola, who willingly took advantage of her husband's frequent absences to encourage Turiddu's secret love-making. This tangled state of affairs already exists when the curtain rises.

The orchestral prelude states several themes that are important to the development of the drama. After a quiet opening strain which symbolizes the peace of Easter Day there comes the theme of Santuzza's impassioned pleading for Turiddu's love. The prelude is suddenly interrupted by the voice of Turiddu behind the scenes. To a rhythmic harp accompaniment he sings the *Siciliana*,[1] an amorous serenade in traditional Sicilian style. Turiddu compares Lola's lips to ripe red berries, speaks of the glow of love in her eyes, and likens the color of her cheeks to wild cherries. The man who can win these treasures for himself is indeed lucky. Then in a sinister foreshadowing of disaster Turiddu envisions blood on Lola's doorstep. But even the prospect of dying before her eyes does not frighten him, he sings. Only if Lola were not in Paradise to greet him would he abandon himself to grief. The serenade dies away on long, sustained notes, and the orchestra again takes up the intensely moving themes of the tragedy which is to follow.

The curtain rises to the chiming of bells. We see the deserted square of a village in Sicily. At the right is the entrance of a church; at the left is the tavern and home of Mamma Lucia. It is dawn. As the music becomes brighter and gayer, peasants and villagers cross the square, their voices rising above the orchestral accompaniment in short simple phrases. Some of the people enter the church, while others stroll down the street. Women's voices are heard singing of the joy of Easter Day—of how the caroling of birds and the fresh beauty of awakening spring mingle with tender avowals of love.

As the women slowly enter the scene, men's voices are heard in praise of women's diligence and of feminine charms which ensnare the heart. The men now appear, and all the voices mingle in a tuneful chorus hymning the joys of spring and love. The last notes are charmingly echoed from behind the scenes, as though coming from afar off. The people drift away until the square once more is empty.

Abruptly the mood of the music changes to a somber motif of impending tragedy. As it rises in intensity Santuzza appears and meets Mamma Lucia coming out of her wineshop. The girl inquires for Turiddu. When Lucia asks why she has come to see her son, Santuzza merely repeats her query. Lucia agitatedly replies that she does not know her son's whereabouts, adding she wants no trouble. Desperately Santuzza implores her to have pity—as Christ had pity on Magdalene. She beseeches Lucia to tell her where Turiddu is hiding.

He has gone to fetch wine from Francofonte, Lucia says at last. Santuzza declares that Turiddu was seen in the village only last night. Alarmed,

---

[1] The *Siciliana* is sometimes sung in Sicilian dialect instead of the classic Italian.

Lucia demands to know who told her so, because Turiddu has not been home. Then, touched by the girl's distress, Lucia invites her to come into the house. Santuzza cries that she dare not enter because she has been excommunicated. Fearfully Lucia asks what Santuzza knows about her son, but Santuzza speaks only of the anguish in her heart.

At that moment the music breaks softly into a rhythmic staccato which swiftly grows louder. Whips crack sharply and bells jingle gaily as into the square comes Alfio, the jolly teamster, surrounded by his friends. He strikes up a lusty song about his fine horse, the jingling bells, and the cracking whip ("Il cavallo scalpita"). Rain or shine, he has no cares. The men join in, hailing the carter as a fine fellow who has a trade that none can rival. Joyously Alfio sings of the bliss that awaits him in his Easter reunion with his beautiful wife, Lola. More and more neighbors stop to listen, and soon they, too, join Alfio in a rousing chorus.

As the throng disperses, Lucia greets Alfio, who asks if she still has some of her good wine left. She tells him that Turiddu has gone to the neighboring town to replenish her supply. Again she is contradicted, the teamster stating that he had seen Turiddu that very morning near his cottage. When Lucia exclaims in surprise Santuzza warns her to be quiet. Alfio then goes on his way, exhorting his neighbors to go into church.

Within the church the choir begins the majestic "Regina Coeli." Townspeople in the square slowly assume prayerful attitudes as they answer the choir with Hallelujahs. Then all join in singing the deeply moving Resurrection hymn so appropriate to this Easter morning. Santuzza's voice soars above the chorus as she carries the melody in broad, sweeping phrases to its great climax.

Presently the people enter the church, and finally only two are left—Santuzza and Lucia. In recitative, Lucia asks why Santuzza bade her be silent during her talk with Alfio. Santuzza, in reply, begins the famous aria, "Voi lo sapete," in which she tells the older woman the whole bitter story. She sings that Turiddu, before leaving to serve in the army, was engaged to Lola. He returned only to find her married to another. To console himself, Santuzza goes on, he sought her love, and she loved him madly in return. But Lola, out of envy and jealousy, lured Turiddu to her own arms again. Now, sings Santuzza, nothing is left to her but weeping.

Lucia expresses horror at the evil story told on this holy day. Santuzza cries out that she is accursed and begs Lucia to pray for her soul. She will go once more to Turiddu, she says, and plead for his love. Breathing a prayer for Santuzza, Lucia slowly enters the church, leaving the girl alone in the square.

At that point Turiddu appears, exclaiming in surprise when he sees Santuzza ("Tu qui Santuzza"). He tries to parry her questions as to where he has been and swears that he has just come from Francofonte. Santuzza retorts that she herself saw him in the village. What is more, he had been seen near Lola's home only this morning. Angrily Turiddu accuses her of spying. Santuzza denies it, saying that Alfio himself told the story—and he will spread it through the village.

Trying to bluff his way out, Turiddu berates the girl for being suspicious and orders her away. He denies loving Lola. Santuzza, now beside herself, curses him, and as Turiddu recoils in horror she declares that Lola has lured him away. Then the furious accusations of the two merge in an intensely dramatic duet ("Bada, Santuzza, schiavo non sono"). Violently Turiddu orders Santuzza to be silent, protesting that he will not be enslaved by her jealousy. Unheeding, Santuzza cries that though he may beat and revile her she will still adore him.

Suddenly their words are interrupted by a woman's voice in the distance. With gay mockery she sings about her "king of roses" ("Fior di giaggiolo"), and soon Lola strolls in. Feigning surprise, she asks Turiddu if he has seen Alfio. She ignores Turiddu's embarrassed answer and adds carelessly that Alfio is probably talking with the blacksmith. With deliberate malice Lola asks Turiddu and Santuzza if they are attending services of their own in the square. Turiddu, now completely confused, tries to explain. Santuzza angrily retorts that it is Easter and that God sees all. Lola asks if she is going to Mass. Santuzza replies pointedly that only those should go who are without sin. In brazen irreverence Lola gives thanks to God that she is sinless, whereupon Santuzza sardonically compliments her on her brave words. Turiddu interrupts impatiently and starts to follow Lola into the church. With a sneer she tells him to stay with Santuzza, who now renews her pleas to Turiddu. Blasphemously uttering a blessing on Santuzza, Lola enters the church.

Turiddu furiously turns on Santuzza and the quarrel breaks out afresh, merging once again in an impassioned duet. Santuzza desperately tries to restrain Turiddu from entering the church, imploring him not to leave her ("No, Turiddu, rimani"). Turiddu brutally asks why she persists in spying on him. The duet rises to a blazing climax as Santuzza beseeches Turiddu not to abandon her, while he wrathfully orders her to leave him. Suddenly in wild anger he hurls her to the ground and runs into the church. She screams a curse after him and calls him her betrayer.

Santuzza looks up to find Alfio approaching. Quickly she regains her composure and rises to her feet. The Lord himself sent him at this moment, she says to Alfio. The teamster asks her how far the Mass has progressed. She replies that it is almost over, then significantly adds that Lola and Turiddu are attending service together. Unsuspecting, Alfio asks what she means. In cold fury Santuzza tells him that while he was away making a living Lola was seeking her pleasure with another. Alfio, aghast, demands to know what she is saying. The truth, Santuzza answers simply. Turiddu abandoned her because he could not resist Lola's charms. Alfio threatens to cut out her heart if she is lying. Santuzza retorts that she is not in the habit of lying and then swears by her very dishonor and humiliation that what she says is true.

There is a long pause. Calmly, then, Alfio thanks Santuzza. She expresses shame for having spoken, but Alfio declares that the shame is on the guilty pair. They are caught in the net, and he will have his revenge before the day is out. A stormy duet follows in which Santuzza cries in agony of remorse at having betrayed Turiddu, while Alfio swears terrible revenge

("Infami loro"). At the end of the number both hurry away, leaving the scene completely deserted.

Then follows the famous *Intermezzo*, played by the orchestra while the square remains empty, and this calm, sweet music brings a moment of relief to the opera. But it is like the ominous calm before the storm. Tragedy is impending, and it is only because the lovers are at worship that they have sanctuary from Alfio's revenge.

When the *Intermezzo* ends the villagers and peasants leave the church. They are all in good spirits. A number of them assemble in front of Lucia's wineshop and fill their glasses. The men, singing softly, urge all to go home to the joys of the hearth after the day's religious duties. The women repeat the refrain, then all sing together. Lola and Turiddu now come from the church. Turiddu, indicating the throng, asks Lola gaily if she would pass up the chance to meet with old friends. Lola says she must go home because she has not yet seen Alfio. Turiddu carelessly replies that she will probably see her husband in the square.

He invites the people to have a drink, and then begins the *Brindisi*—the famous drinking song, "Viva il vino spumeggiante." As it ends in a spirited chorus Alfio suddenly appears. He sings a greeting, and his friends lustily respond. Turiddu offers him a glass. Alfio refuses, saying he would not trust a drink given him by Turiddu—it might be poisoned.

Turiddu acknowledges the insult and casually tosses out the wine. Lola utters an exclamation of terror, whereupon the other women persuade her to leave. They hurry away as the two men confront each other. Turiddu asks Alfio if he has anything to say. When the answer is no, Turiddu issues the traditional challenge, placing himself at Alfio's "service." Alfio accepts. Then, according to true Sicilian custom, the two embrace and Turiddu bites Alfio's ear. Alfio significantly remarks that they seem to understand each other.

In a sudden change of mood Turiddu admits he has wronged Alfio and agrees that he deserves to die like a dog. He laments that if he is killed in the duel his "poor Santuzza" will be left without her lover. But, he adds defiantly, he still means to plunge his dagger into Alfio's heart. The teamster coldly warns him to think carefully on what he is about to undertake. He says he will meet Turiddu behind the garden wall, then stalks away.

Turiddu, suddenly panic-stricken, calls his mother to him. He haltingly tells her that he has drunk too much wine, that he is going for a walk to clear his brain. Before he goes he wants her blessing—just as he did when he went away to be a soldier. Then in impassioned phrases he demands Lucia's promise to be a mother to Santuzza—whom he has sworn to cherish —if he should not return ("Voi dovrete fare").

Lucia excitedly asks him the meaning of his strange words. He replies that the wine has set his brain awhirl. Wildly he implores God's forgiveness and begs his mother for one last kiss of farewell. In a final, soaring musical phrase Turiddu again entreats his mother to take care of Santuzza, then rushes frantically away.

Terror-stricken, Lucia tries to follow him, calling his name. Santuzza rushes in and takes Lucia in her arms. People crowd nervously into the square. Suddenly a woman rushes in shrieking: "Turiddu has been murdered!" All cry out in horror; Santuzza and Lucia fall fainting to the ground. The curtain swiftly descends.

La Cenerentola

(Cinderella)

by GIOACHINO ANTONIO ROSSINI

[1792–1868]

Libretto by
JACOPO FERRETTI

CHARACTERS

Cinderella .... *Soprano*
Clorinda .... *Soprano*
Thisbe, her sister................................... *Mezzo-soprano*
Alidoro, a Court Philosopher....................................... *Bass*
Don Magnifico, Baron of Monte Fiascone, father of
    Clorinda and Thisbe................................ *Bass buffo*
Don Ramiro, Prince of Salerno............................... *Tenor*
Dandini, the Prince's valet..................................... *Bass*
Ladies and gentlemen of the court

Place: Salerno, Italy
Time: Legendary
First performance: Teatro Valle, January 25, 1817
Original language: Italian

LA CENERENTOLA is, of course, the Cinderella story—according to Rossini. A man of the world, Rossini had little use for the supernatural. As a result, he deleted certain parts of the legend—the slippers, the pumpkin turned into carriage, the magic transformation at midnight. Yet he has retained the charm of the legend through his music.

The opera has a curious history. Written a year after *Il Barbiere di Siviglia*, it disappeared from operatic repertoire by 1860, then was revived some twenty years ago with the great Spanish soprano, Conchita Supervia. It was revived with outstanding success by the New York City Opera Company in 1953 and 1954.

The overture has a *maestoso* introduction, which leads into an *allegro vivace*, begun in the strings. A modulation into a minor key suggests Cinderella weeping by the fireside, but this soon gives way to the effervescence of the opera's main themes.

ACT ONE

A room in the palace of Don Magnifico. The Baron's two daughters, Clorinda and Thisbe, are fussing about. Clorinda is trying a dance step;

Thisbe, primping in front of a mirror, puts a rose first in her hair, then at her bosom, and studies the effect. In another corner of the room, Cinderella is crouched before the fireplace, blowing up the fire with a bellows to make a pot of coffee boil.

Clorinda, mincing about, sings that no one can dance as lightly as she. Thisbe, busy with the rose, sings that it looks charming in one place, even better in another. The girls sing in identical phrases, Clorinda beginning with "no, no, no, no," and Thisbe with "yes, yes, yes, yes." Then, in a duet, they declare that everyone will virtually swoon at such a combination of grace and artistry. As they pause to admire each other, Cinderella is heard singing softly to herself about a king who became bored with bacherlorhood and set out to find a wife ("Una volta c'era un re"). When he finally narrowed his choice to three, what did he do? He scorned mere physical beauty and chose the most virtuous maiden for his bride. This artless little melody is virtually Cinderella's leitmotiv.

Rudely interrupting, Clorinda and Thisbe tell Cinderella to stop her silly song. What else is there to do but sing, says Cinderella quietly, when one must sit and tend the fire. When she starts her song again, the sisters first mock, then threaten her. At that moment there is a knock at the door. Cinderella opens it. There stands a man in beggar's rags. Actually, he is Alidoro, the Court Philosopher, in disguise.

When he asks for alms ("Un tantin di carita"), the sisters brusquely tell him to be off. This marks the beginning of a sprightly ensemble. As the sisters turn their backs, Cinderella surreptitiously gives the beggar a cup of coffee and some bread. For this kind deed, murmurs Alidoro, she may well be rewarded before nightfall. Meanwhile, Clorinda and Thisbe posture before the mirror. Suddenly they catch sight of Alidoro and exclaim that he has been given something to eat. Angrily they rush over to Cinderella and begin beating her. Cinderella wails for help while Alidoro implores the sisters to stop.

In the middle of the uproar, the door flies open and a group of courtiers enters (having first knocked in vain). In a delightful parody of an operatic "soldiers' chorus," they give their message to the sisters ("O figlie amabali"). They inform the "amiable daughters of Don Magnifico" that Prince Ramiro is on his way to escort them to his palace. There will be singing and dancing. Then the Prince will choose a bride from among the unmarried ladies present. This news throws Clorinda and Thisbe into a frenzy of excitement. They begin bustling about, gathering up their finery to dress for the ball. Each one sings that she is the most beautiful and that Prince Ramiro certainly will choose her. They shout at Cinderella, ordering her to bring their shoes, clothing, and jewels. Poor Cinderella rushes to obey, moaning that the sisters are driving her out of her mind. Alidoro, looking on, remarks that the two obviously are going crazy and that they are due for a surprise.

Meanwhile, the courtiers lustily sing that the contest, soon to begin, will be a triumph for some lucky lady. All the voices bring this ensemble to an exciting finish.

A recitative passage follows. Clorinda gives a coin to Cinderella, who presents it to the courtiers. They bow their thanks and leave. Noticing that Alidoro is still there, Clorinda rudely orders him to get out. Cinderella, taking him to the door, tells him she is sorry she has no money to give him. Leaving, Alidoro tells her that tomorrow she will find happiness.

With everyone out of the way, the sisters begin rushing around again, shouting at Cinderella to bring their ribbons, cloaks, and jewels. When Cinderella addresses them as "sisters," they berate her for daring to consider herself one of them. Cinderella murmurs disconsolately that there is always some new madness to contend with.

At this point, Clorinda and Thisbe decide they must tell their father the exciting news about the ball. They rush to his door, quarreling shrilly over who is to have the honor of breaking the news. While they are at it hammer and tongs, the door bursts open and in walks Don Magnifico. In a towering rage, he roars that his yammering daughters awoke him in the middle of a magnificent dream. The girls placatingly try to kiss his hand, but he brushes them aside as daughters unworthy of a Baron. As he stalks about the room, Clorinda and Thisbe impudently laugh behind his back.

Suddenly Don Magnifico raises his hand for silence and announces that now he will meditate upon his remarkable dream. This he does in a delightfully pompous cavatina, "Mi sognai fra il fosco e il chiaro."

He dreamed, sings the Baron, that he was a donkey—a beautiful, noble donkey. Suddenly he sprouted wings and flew to the top of a bell tower. As he perched there in all his feathered glory, bells began to ring. It was at that point, says the Baron, glaring at his daughters, that their silly chatter woke him up. Calming himself, he goes on. What does the dream symbolize? This: the bells were heralding a joyous occasion in his house—a wedding, of course. The wings were his daughters. The flight to the tower symbolizes his glorious ascent from his plebeian station in life to a higher plane. The donkey? Well, the donkey obviously is himself. The Baron hastily adds that the donkey always has been an ancestral symbol.

In any case, he goes on, one of his daughters will be an extremely fertile queen. As grandfather, he will dandle at least a dozen grandchildren on his knee—to his everlasting glory. Ending with a flourish, the Baron looks with fatuous pride at his daughters. They behave as though they have not heard a single word he has said. In agitated recitative, interrupting each other, they inform their father about the impending visit of Prince Ramiro. The Baron sputters in surprise. Then he bellows at Cinderella to bring him coffee in his room.

Before he goes, he admonishes his daughters to do their best. Remember, he says, half my castle has crumbled into ruins, the other half is about to. The stakes are high and nobility is the prize. With that assertion he leaves. Clorinda and Thisbe go into their own room.

The outside door opens, and Prince Ramiro sticks his head in and looks cautiously around. He is disguised as a groom. To the accompaniment of a figure in the orchestra that reflects the conspiratorial nature of his visit, the Prince tiptoes into the room. In this disguise, he murmurs, he will have a good chance to observe the Baron's beauties. One of them, according to what Alidoro has told him, will make him a perfect wife. Then he bemoans the tyranny of custom that forces him to marry without love and waste his youth on this kind of blind choice.

As he meditates on this, Cinderella, carrying dishes, enters from the

Baron's room. Lost in thought, she sings a phrase of her song about the bachelor king. Suddenly she finds herself face to face with Ramiro. She promptly drops the dishes, runs into her fireside corner and cowers there. Ramiro tries to calm her, then comments on her mysterious beauty in a brief but highly embellished passage, "Un soave non so che."

This introduces a musical dialogue which demands as much coloratura singing of the tenor as it does of the soprano. It is in the typically showy style of the Rossini period. First Cinderella and Ramiro make the point that they are both charmed with each other. Then Ramiro remembers what he is there for, and asks Cinderella where the Baron's daughters are. In the other room, Cinderella says absently, staring at Ramiro. He asks Cinderella who *she* is. Trying to explain, she becomes hopelessly confused.

The man who is her father is not her father. That is, her two sisters . . . her mother was a widow . . . but she was also *their* mother . . . this father is very conceited. . . . And so Cinderella flounders on, making no sense at all—and in a way that completely captivates Prince Ramiro.

Suddenly, from beyond the doors, Clorinda, Thisbe, and the Baron all shout for Cinderella at once. Ramiro asks what in the world is happening. Day or night, Cinderella cries distractedly, these people give her no peace. She goes to answer the summons, singing passionately that she is leaving her heart with Ramiro. The duet comes to a lovely close, and she and the disguised Prince voice their romantic feelings.

As Cinderella leaves, Ramiro remarks that his disguise is a good idea—a woman is more likely to reveal her heart to a groom. But, he wonders, how will his man Dandini play the part of a prince?

The Baron charges into the room, full of apologies, and asks when the Prince will arrive. In three minutes, Ramiro (as the supposed groom) tells him. The Baron bellows to his daughters to hurry, then goes into their room to help things along. Ramiro laughs derisively, then wonders what Alidoro meant when he mentioned the mysterious beauty in this family. There is a commotion outside. "Dandini," Ramiro exclaims.

Magnificently dressed as Prince Ramiro, Dandini makes a grand entrance with his courtiers, who, in a brief chorus, urge him to hurry and select a wife. Clorinda, Thisbe, and Don Magnifico come from their rooms to welcome the royal guest. Dandini pauses to sing some sentimental nonsense, comparing himself to a bee looking for a flower ("Come un'ape"). Up to now, he observes, he has not found what he wants. Meanwhile, the Baron and his daughters bow and scrape.

Dandini acknowledges their salutations with windy compliments, then sidles over to Ramiro and asks him how things are going. Ramiro, in an aside, tells him to get down to business. Dandini promptly turns to the sisters and sings a florid refrain of praise, "Per pietà quelle ciglia."

A typically Rossinian ensemble follows. Clorinda sings that the Prince already is her slave—and Thisbe sings the same. Ramiro wonders where Cinderella has gone. The Baron, noting Dandini's lovesick demeanor, exults that the goose is cooked and a title is as good as won. The courtiers' chorus underscores the ensemble. Dandini goes on with his shameless flattery and is warned by Ramiro not to overdo it.

In his bogus role of Prince Ramiro, Dandini gravely explains that, according to his late father's will, he is to be cut off without a cent unless he marries. For that reason he is here: to find the "delicate morsel" fate has chosen for him. The Baron admires his eloquence.

At that moment, Cinderella enters and gasps in awe at the resplendent Dandini. Ramiro exclaims at the sight of her. Dandini tells the sisters that the courtiers will accompany them to the carriage. They leave. As the Baron, Ramiro, and Dandini are about to follow, Cinderella timidly asks the Baron if she may go to the ball and dance with the Prince for just one hour. The Baron fumes that she is nothing but an ash-can Venus and tells her to be quiet. Ramiro and Dandini try to intercede, but that only enrages the Baron to the point where he raises his hand to strike Cinderella. Clinging to the Baron's arm, Cinderella implores Ramiro and Dandini to help her win her master's consent to go dancing. This uproar continues in quartet form until the Baron manages to free himself from Cinderella's grasp.

Just then Alidoro enters, carrying a large ledger open in his hands. According to his list of marriageable girls, he announces, there are three sisters in the family of Don Magnifico. Now that the Prince is about to choose a wife, the whereabouts of Number Three is requested.

Stammering in confusion, the Baron asks: "Who is this daughter Alidoro is so obligingly giving birth to for him? A third sister, Alidoro replies. She died, the Baron mumbles. Peering at the ledger, Alidoro says that is not the way it is recorded. At that, Cinderella steps forward and shyly announces that, as a matter of fact, she is not dead. Roaring at her to be quiet, the Baron shoves her into a corner. In turn, Ramiro, Dandini, and Alidoro repeat the question: "Did she die?" The Baron gravely answers yes. Shaking his head, Alidoro remarks that the wild look in the eyes of the Baron and Cinderella clearly indicates that their brains are spinning around like a whirlpool on a rampage ("Nel volto estatico").

These words introduce a long ensemble. The Baron, catching hold of Cinderella, hisses that he will kill her if she utters another word. Cinderella cries for help. Ramiro pulls her away from the Baron, who is in turn dragged from the scene by Dandini. Everyone follows in a mad uproar. Cinderella herself dashes into another room.

After a moment Alidoro reappears, wearing a pilgrim's cloak over his Court Philosopher's gown. In recitative, he muses that, while grace and beauty are everywhere at hand, innocence is hard to find. Then, looking toward the door of Cinderella's room, he calls. Cinderella comes out, and in naïve wonder murmurs that Alidoro has called her his "child," when her own father disowns her.

There is no time to talk, says Alidoro. In a few moments a carriage will arrive to take her to the Prince's ball. "Dressed in these rags?" Cinderella cries. At that, Alidoro throws back his pilgrim's cloak and stands before Cinderella in the magnificent robes of the Court Philosopher. As Cinderella gasps, he tells her she will appear at the ball as a great lady, but she must not tell anyone who she is. Love, Alidoro adds, will advise her what to do.

In a happy daze, Cinderella wonders if all this really is happening to her, or if it is only a play. Alidoro answers in an impressive aria, "Vasto teatro è il mondo." Echoing Jacques in Shakespeare's *As You Like It*, Alidoro observes that all the world is a stage and men and women are the players.

Today a man is a feckless Harlequin, beaten and abused. Tomorrow he is an all-powerful lord. Her own role, Alidoro tells Cinderella, is a profound mystery. But now the carriage approaches. Cinderella must go to meet her destined lover. As Alidoro concludes the aria, he takes her by the hand and leads her out of the room. The curtain falls.

The scene changes to a room in Prince Ramiro's palace. Dandini enters, his arms around Clorinda and Thisbe. Following him come Don Magnifico and Ramiro. Dandini loudly compliments the Baron on his learned dissertation on wines, and then invites him to the royal wine cellar. There the Baron can drink his fill, says Dandini, and if he still has his wits left after thirty glasses he will be made the Royal Wine Steward. Don Magnifico is overwhelmed. In an aside he remarks to his daughters that this honor is proof that he can stand on his own merits. Telling them to keep the King amused, the Baron hurries off to the wine cellar.

Meanwhile, Ramiro tells Dandini to find out all he can about the Magnifico and his two daughters. Dandini cynically replies that the latter obviously are a pair of scatterbrained females. Then, aloud, he tells Ramiro to carry out his orders. Picking up his cue, Ramiro bows and leaves. Dandini then gives his attention to Clorinda and Thisbe, each of whom tries to get him away from the other. Somewhat annoyed, Dandini manages to free himself from their clutches. Assuring each girl, in the same breath, that his heart beats only for her, Dandini eventually makes his escape. The curtain falls.

The next scene is the terrace of Prince Ramiro's palace. Don Magnifico, wearing an absurd costume decorated with bunches of grapes, comes in accompanied by a group of courtiers. In a lusty chorus, "Conciosiacossachè trenta botti," they explain what has happened. Don Magnifico has sampled thirty casks, drunk enough for three, and is still on his feet. And so, by royal test and decree, he is duly appointed Royal Wine Steward, Wineglass Manager, President of Grape-Harvesting, and Administrator of Bacchic Revels.

In an alcoholic daze, the Don thanks the courtiers and asks them to put it all in writing, ordering six thousand copies on the spot. The courtiers sit down, take paper and pens, and begin to write. Watching them, Don Magnifico, roaring that all of it must be in capital letters, begins to dictate ("Noi Don Magnifico . . . questo in maiuscole"). In pseudo-legal jargon, he states that, by virtue of his authority, henceforth for fifteen years it will be forbidden to mix water with wine.

With a flourish the courtiers sign their names to the documents, singing they will proclaim this glorious edict throughout the city ("Il pranzo in ordine"). The Don offers a prize of sixty crowns to the person who can drink the most Malaga wine. Bringing the chorus to a roaring climax, Don Magnifico and the courtiers leave.

Dandini and Ramiro tiptoe in and converse in a *sotto voce* duet ("Zitto: piano: senza strepito"). Ramiro asks Dandini what Clorinda and Thisbe are like. Dandini tells him they are not worth bothering about. And as for the third daughter—the one Alidoro recommended to Ramiro—she is the silliest of the lot. Well, then, says Ramiro, let them marry anyone who will have them. As for us, we will play out the comedy.

At that moment Clorinda and Thisbe rush in, all a-flutter, calling for the Prince ("Principino, dove siete?"). This marks the beginning of an ensemble that brings the first act to its close. Both Clorinda and Thisbe fling themselves at Dandini. He fends them off, saying he cannot marry two sisters at the same time. He says he will marry one and bestow the other upon his friend (indicating Ramiro). The sisters recoil at the thought of marrying a lowly servant. Playing his part to the hilt, Ramiro, with mock modesty, says he will do his best to please. The sisters shudder, while, behind their backs, Dandini and Ramiro hugely enjoy the situation.

Suddenly, from outside come the voices of the courtiers urging someone to enter. Alidoro comes in and announces that a mysterious veiled lady is arriving. There is general consternation. Dandini signals Alidoro to bring in the stranger. Cinderella enters, splendidly gowned, her face hidden by a veil. The courtiers follow her. In chorus, they comment on her charms, while Cinderella, Ramiro, and Dandini express their thoughts in florid coloratura passages. Cinderella says she disdains her finery as a capricious gift of fate. The man who chooses her must do so because he loves her for herself alone. Ramiro sings that he recognizes the voice of his beloved, and that it gives him hope. Dandini implores the veiled beauty to reveal herself.

At that, Cinderella lifts her veil. There is an outburst of admiration from all on stage ("Parler, penser vorrei")—except from Clorinda and Thisbe, who are completely nonplused. Cinderella glances secretly at Ramiro, as though she has almost penetrated his disguise. Alidoro, looking at Ramiro, remarks that his plan has succeeded because the Prince already is in love with Cinderella.

The ensemble is interrupted by the entrance of Don Magnifico, who, as usual, is in a state of noisy confusion. He looks around, sees the richly-gowned stranger, then asks his daughters to note her resemblance to Cinderella. Clorinda and Thisbe tell him to take a closer look. Their Cinderella, they point out, is a homely drudge. This girl is much prettier—but still nothing to get excited about. Don Magnifico shrugs, saying Cinderella is now probably at home among the cinders where she belongs. Dandini breaks in to announce that he is hungry. He invites everyone to eat, drink, and dance. Then he will choose the most beautiful girl for his bride. All on stage respond in a long closing chorus, "Andiamo a tavola." The burden of it is that everyone feels this is all a delightful dream. Yet there seems to be an impending catastrophe that will make this dream go up in smoke. The curtain falls.

ACT TWO

A room in Prince Ramiro's palace. Don Magnifico comes storming in with Clorinda and Thisbe. Those courtiers, he fumes, evidently have been laughing at him. This is his excuse to get off an outrageous pun: he will, he says, commit courtier-cide ("cavaliericido"). His daughters take that in stride, and the conversation continues in recitative. The three wonder if the beautiful stranger possibly can be Cinderella. The Don quails at the thought of what will happen if somebody finds out he has squandered his stepdaughter's patrimony. The Prince, say the sisters, is their only hope. Thisbe admits he looks at her, heaves a sigh—then goes away. "What of that," says Clorinda. "When he sees me, he laughs." Both ask Papa for his opinion on this vexing problem. He explains in one of the outstanding arias in the opera, "Sia qualunque delle figlie." It is witty, impudent, and Rossinian to the core.

Even now, sings the Baron, he can see himself as the father of a royal daughter (her marriage to the Prince being a foregone conclusion). Sundry folk approach, asking favors . . . coins are slipped into his hand . . . a beautiful woman, perfumed and powdered, whispers a request. Very good . . . but without silver, he will be stone-deaf. A coin will restore his hearing instantly.

Papa the Magnificent deigns to awaken at noon, and at once his bed is surrounded by petitioners. All of them want something—protection from the law, a job, a professorship, exclusive rights to eel-fishing. Meanwhile, his bed is heaped with favors, from pickles to gold plate. "You bore me," cries the Baron, carried away by his delusions of grandeur. "Get out, all of you!" Concluding the aria, he sweeps majestically from the scene, followed by his daughters.

Ramiro enters. He is still wondering about the lovely lady who resembles the unhappy Cinderella, and remarks that she has also captivated Dandini. There is a noise offstage. He hides. Cinderella hurries in, with Dandini close at her heels. Then Alidoro appears. He, too, hides. Dandini begs Cinderella not to run away from him, because he only wants to talk of love. Cinderella retorts that she loves someone else. When Dandini demands to know who it is, Cinderella replies: "Your groom."

As Dandini gasps in surprise, Ramiro steps from his hiding place with a cry of joy. Alidoro, revealing himself in the background, observes that everything is going according to plan. Then and there Ramiro asks Cinderella to be his bride and impetuously begs her to leave with him at once. But Cinderella, warning him not to follow her, tells the Prince he must first learn all about her. Then she gives him a bracelet from her left arm. He must search for the one who will be wearing its duplicate on her right arm. She will be his bride. With those words, Cinderella quickly leaves.

Puzzled, Ramiro turns to Dandini and asks him what he makes of this situation. Dandini morosely answers that he has suddenly stopped playing the Prince and has become a mere witness. Then Ramiro asks Alidoro what he must do. "Follow your heart," Alidoro replies. At that, Ramiro curtly tells Dandini that indeed he is no longer Prince—this silly masquerade is over. He calls for his courtiers and tells them to get his carriage ready.

Gazing at the bracelet Cinderella has given him, Ramiro expresses his sentiments in the brilliant aria, "Si, ritrovarla io guiro," probably one of the most fantastically difficult tenor arias ever written. It abounds in high C's, with trills and runs of six notes to the beat.

During these vocal gymnastics, Ramiro swears he will find his love. In an accompanying chorus, the courtiers assure him of their sympathy and help. At the conclusion of the number, Ramiro leaves with the courtiers.

Alidoro emerges from his hiding place, remarking that he will arrange to have Ramiro's carriage upset in front of the Baron's home. Dandini comes forward, crestfallen over the sudden change in his fortunes. Then Don Magnifico hurries in and asks Dandini—who he assumes is the Prince—how soon he will make his choice. It is made, Dandini tells him, but it is still a great secret. But who is it, the Baron asks, wild with impatience, Clorinda or Thisbe? Making the most of the situation, Dandini keeps goading the Baron with veiled hints. Swearing him to secrecy, Dandini tells the Baron he is about to let him in on an incredible mystery, "Un segreto d'importanza." What follows is an amusing duet, in which the wily Dandini makes a complete fool of the Baron.

Dandini begins by asking the Baron what dowry he would get if he married one of the Baron's daughters. Says the Baron grandly: Thirty servants, one hundred and sixty horses . . . Dukes, Counts, and Courtiers in attendance by the dozen . . . ice cream at every dinner. Dandini listens attentively, then drops the bombshell. All this has been play acting, he says—he is not Prince Ramiro at all, but merely the Prince's valet. The Baron sputters in baffled rage, vowing he will make the Prince pay dearly for making a fool of him. Dandini blandly advises the Baron to calm himself and suggests he leave at once.

The Baron loudly laments his downfall, while Dandini helpfully offers his services in the event the Baron should want to be shaved or have his hair done. This brings the duet to a close. The Baron storms off and Dandini complacently follows.

Alidoro enters and pauses to remark that destiny, love, and a thunderstorm (which he has conjured up) are all helping his plot along. Then he leaves as the scene ends.

The next scene is a ground-floor room of Don Magnifico's castle. Cinderella, in rags again, is sitting before the fire. She gazes at the bracelet on her arm and sings tenderly of its mate, which she gave to the amorous Prince's "groom." Suddenly there is an uproar outside, and in come the Baron, Clorinda, and Thisbe. They go up close to Cinderella and glare at her malevolently, muttering that there certainly is a resemblance between her and the beautiful stranger at the ball. The Baron roughly orders her to prepare supper. She leaves.

After a musical interlude descriptive of the rising storm, Dandini enters, now in his rightful costume as groom. He announces that Prince Ramiro's carriage has overturned in the street just outside the house. As Don Magnifico glares at him, Prince Ramiro, now the resplendent Prince, comes in. Trying to maintain his dignity, Don Magnifico says he realizes the Prince has come to take away one of his daughters as bride. Then he shouts for Cinderella, ordering her to bring a chair for His Royal Highness. Cinderella brings it in and takes it over to Dandini, still thinking he is the Prince. "To the Prince," growls Don Magnifico, pointing to Ramiro.

Cinderella looks into Ramiro's eyes and suddenly realizes who he is. Overcome, she buries her face in her hands, then tries to rush away. The Prince restrains her, and at that instant sees the bracelet. Joyfully he cries,

"Is it you?" ("Siete voi?"). This marks the beginning of a *maestoso* ensemble in which the mystery of Cinderella is resolved.

The bewildered Baron asks Ramiro for an explanation, but the Prince orders him to be quiet. All on stage comment that the more the knot is untangled the worse the tangle becomes. Fuming with disappointment and anger, the Baron, Clorinda, and Thisbe revile Cinderella and order her out of the house. At that, Ramiro angrily warns the three not to insult the one he loves. He takes Cinderella's hand and announces she shall be his bride.

Don Magnifico, Clorinda, and Thisbe laugh sarcastically at his declaration and tell Cinderella that the Prince is only making a fool of her. The Baron assures the Prince he would be happy with one of his daughters, but Ramiro ironically observes that he himself is much too "plebeian" for either of these highborn ladies. Gently but firmly he takes Cinderella in his arms and asks her to share his throne.

Impetuously Cinderella breaks away, rushes over to the Baron, Clorinda, and Thisbe and tries to embrace them. They rudely thrust her away. Ramiro fumes in anger at their boorishness, while Cinderella abandons herself to her happiness. The others comment in chorus on the general confusion, saying that in the end everybody probably will have to be dragged off to the madhouse.

At length, Ramiro leads Cinderella out. They are followed by Dandini and Don Magnifico. This brings the ensemble to a close. Left alone, Clorinda and Thisbe give vent to their jealous rage. Alidoro strides in and majestically settles accounts with the hateful sisters. He came begging alms, the Philosopher says, but they threw him out. Yet poor "Angelina" (as he calls Cinderella), a miserable servant, befriended him, and now she will be a Princess. Moreover, the Baron owes her an enormous sum of money, because he has wrongly used up her dowry. The castle, crumbling ruin though it is, may have to be sold to pay the debt.

When the sisters ask what is to become of them, Alidoro answers that they have their choice: they can either live out their days in misery or ask pardon at the throne. And this, Alidoro adds significantly, is their last chance.

Clorinda replies in a dramatic aria, "Sventurata! mi credea." It is a bitter thing to be humbled, she sings. She had expected to be a Princess and now she is an outcast. But she decides to make the best of a bad situation. She is young and still pretty, and—who knows?—a husband to her liking may yet come along. Ending the aria on those sentiments, Clorinda leaves. Watching her go, Alidoro observes that it is indeed a hard pill to swallow, but there is no other remedy. He turns to Thisbe and asks what she proposes to do. She philosophically remarks that she will accept her fate. After all, humiliation isn't as bad as dying. With that, she also leaves. Alidoro gives thanks that virtue has triumphed over evil. The curtain falls.

The final scene is the throne room of Prince Ramiro's palace. Cinderella and the Prince, in royal robes, stand before the throne. Dandini is at their side. A little distance away, the Baron stands with downcast eyes. Alidoro enters with Clorinda and Thisbe. Overcome with shame, they cover their faces with their hands. In chorus ("Della Fortuna instabile"), the ladies and gentlemen of the court hail the royal couple, singing that the fickle wheel of fate has spun and stopped. Vanity is punished, goodness is triumphant.

Cinderella turns to Don Magnifico, who falls dejectedly to his knees before her. Though she has now exchanged the cinders of the fireplace for a throne, Cinderella sings, she asks that Don Magnifico still call her "daughter." Ramiro protests, pointing to the sisters.

Gently Cinderella says she bears them no ill will, because she wants her actions to be worthy of a Princess. She turns to the hapless three and spreads her arms in a gesture of forgiveness. They hesitatingly approach. She embraces them.

All in court hail Cinderella's goodness and magnanimity, saying that a throne is an honor far too modest for her. Cinderella sings that never again will she weep by the fire; her days of suffering were only a dream. In a final stirring chorus, "Tutto cangia a poco a poco," all sing that everything in life changes. It is Fortune's own jest to change sadness to joy. The curtain falls.

Les Contes d'Hoffmann

(Tales of Hoffmann)

by JACQUES OFFENBACH

[1819–1880]

Libretto by
JULES BARBIER *and* MICHEL CARRÉ

Based on the writings of Ernst Theodor Wilhelm Hoffmann,
a German composer and author

CHARACTERS

Lindorf, a councilor of Nürnberg...............................*Bass*
Andrès, servant of Stella......................................*Tenor*
Hermann, a student...*Baritone*
Nathanaël, a student..*Tenor*
Luther, a tavern keeper..*Bass*
Hoffmann, a poet..*Tenor*
Nicklausse, his companion...........................*Mezzo-soprano*
Spalanzani, a self-styled scientist and inventor....................*Tenor*
Cochenille, his servant...*Tenor*
Coppélius, another so-called scientist and rival of Spalanzani.......*Baritone*
Olympia, a mechanical doll...................................*Soprano*
Giulietta, a courtesan..*Soprano*
Schlémil, her lover..*Bass*
Dapertutto, a sorcerer......................................*Baritone*
Pittichinaccio, an admirer of Giulietta.........................*Tenor*
Antonia, a singer...*Soprano*
Crespel, her father, a councilor of Munich....................*Baritone*
Frantz, his servant...*Tenor*
Dr. Miracle ....*Baritone*
The voice of Antonia's mother........................*Mezzo-soprano*
Stella, an opera singer....................................*Soprano*
The Muse ....*Soprano*

Students, ladies and gentlemen, servants

Place: Nürnberg, Venice, Munich
Time: Nineteenth century
First performance: Opéra-Comique, Paris, February 10, 1881
Original language: French

OFFENBACH was the acknowledged master of operetta in France during the middle of the nineteenth century. He wrote more than one hundred operettas, staged many of them himself in two Paris theaters of which he was manager, and won considerable prominence as a conductor.

In his last work, *Les Contes d'Hoffmann,* he achieved his desire to write a serious opera but did not live to see it produced.

PROLOGUE

The interior of Luther's tavern in Nürnberg. The taproom, silent and empty, is partially illuminated by moonlight which streams through a window. From behind the scenes comes a ghostly chorus of the *Spirits of Wine and Beer,* "Glou! glou! glou!" It is a song in praise of the delights of drinking. Lindorf enters, followed by Andrès.[1] After some questioning he learns that the servant is carrying a letter from Stella to one of her lovers. He finally manages to bribe Andrès into giving him the letter, discovers that it is addressed to Hoffmann, and finds a key in the envelope. The letter is an ardent love note to the poet, informing him that the key will admit him to Stella's apartment. Lindorf, with a sneer at Hoffmann's amours, murmurs that the poet will not have his rendezvous. In an ensuing aria ("Dans les rôles d'amoureux langoureux") he exults over the power that his devil's soul exercises over his victims. Where others conquer through love, he conquers through fear. Though he is old, he sings, he still is a match for any mooning poet who presumes to be his rival. He decides to wait for Hoffmann, who usually comes to the tavern with his drinking companions. He resolves to see to it that before the evening is over, the poet will be too deep in his cups to keep his rendezvous with Stella.

Luther and several waiters enter to prepare for their patrons. Lindorf withdraws to one corner, where he stands watching. The students, led by Nathanaël and Hermann, burst noisily into the room and strike up a lusty drinking song, "Drig! drig! drig!"[2] As Luther brings their steins he asks Nathanaël about Stella, who is singing in *Don Giovanni* at the opera house adjacent to the tavern. Nathanaël, who, along with his companions, has been attending the performance and has come into the tavern during an intermission, is enthusiastic in his praise of Stella's singing. At this point Hoffmann arrives, followed by Nicklausse. Moody and preoccupied, he sits down at a table, while Nicklausse hums a phrase of an aria from the opera, "Notte e giorno mal dormire." When Hoffmann irritably snaps at him to be quiet, the others twit him about his ill temper. He confesses that the sight of Stella, his former love, has aroused his jealousy and longing. He does not know, of course, about the letter she has sent him, Lindorf having purloined it.

In an effort to cheer him, the students ask him to sing, and he obliges with a song about Kleinzach, a hunchbacked jester in the court of Eisenach ("Il était une fois à la cour d'Eisenach"). Hoffmann's song vividly describes Kleinzach as a hideous figure with a misshapen body, a head that went

[1] The actor playing the part of Lindorf also plays the roles of Coppélius, Dapertutto, and Miracle; the actor playing Andrès also plays the roles of Cochenille, Pittichinaccio, and Frantz.

[2] In some productions the opera begins at this point, the foregoing part of the scene being omitted entirely. In that case the role of Andrès is eliminated.

"cric-crac," and the nostrils perpetually stained with snuff. When the poet goes on to describe the expression on the hunchback's face, his manner suddenly grows tender and he muses instead about the features of a woman. In a passionate aria ("Ah! sa figure était charmante!") he sings about an enchantingly beautiful woman for whom he deserted family and friends and whom he followed into strange lands. His friends listen in surprise. Aroused from his dream by their questions, he completes the ditty about Kleinzach.

Turning to his drink, Hoffmann grimaces over Luther's bad beer and calls for punch. A huge bowl is brought in and lighted, and the students sing a chorus hailing the flaming potion. As the revelry increases, the students gibe at Hoffmann for falling victim to the pangs of love. At that he exclaims that the devil may have his soul if he ever yields to love again. Lindorf speaks up, warning him not to make rash oaths. "Speak of the devil," mutters Hoffmann, looking at him in surprise, and then goes on to describe Lindorf as his personal demon, who manages to be around to annoy him whether he is playing cards, drinking, or loving.

Lindorf suavely taunts Hoffmann about his love affairs. Under the influence of the punch, Hoffmann falls to reminiscing about the women he has loved, the latest being Stella, who, he says, is three loves in one. But there were three other enchantresses, he adds, and then asks the students if they would care to hear the story of his amours. They respond enthusiastically, ignoring Luther's warning that the curtain is going up on the next act of the opera. Lindorf notes with satisfaction that Hoffmann is becoming more and more befuddled. The students settle themselves to listen. The name of his first love, Hoffmann begins, was Olympia. The curtain falls.

ACT ONE

A room in the home of Spalanzani. A large door at the back opens on to a balcony. There are two doors at the sides, one leading to Olympia's room. Spalanzani enters, draws aside the hanging before Olympia's door, and gazes with satisfaction at the mechanical doll, the latest of his inventions. He exclaims that she will help him recoup the money he has lost to the moneylender Elias, and then frets about Coppélius, who is claiming part ownership of Olympia. Hoffmann enters, having come to see the marvelous creature whom Spalanzani refers to as his "daughter." To Hoffmann's considerable bewilderment, Spalanzani says he will make a great physicist of him. Then he bustles off to prepare for the guests whom he has invited to witness the demonstration of the mechanical doll.

Gazing upon the form of Olympia, Hoffmann rhapsodizes over her in the aria "Allons! courage et confiance!" If necessary, he sings, he will become a scientist to win this enchanting creature. Nicklausse enters. Seeing Hoffmann in the familiar throes, he comments on the poet's latest infatuation in a delightful refrain ("Une poupée aux yeux d'émail"). It is a song about a mechanical doll that fell in love with a mechanical bird, but Hoffmann is much too absorbed in Olympia to notice the obvious reference to himself.

He is interrupted in his reverie by Coppélius, who enters carrying a large sack. Finally managing to attract Hoffmann's attention, he introduces himself as a friend of Spalanzani and then shows him his wares. Coppélius, it seems, is a maker of all sorts of instruments, such as barometers, hygrometers, and thermometers. Most remarkable of all, he goes on, is his collection of eyeglasses, and with these words he empties the contents of his sack on the floor. In an amusing air, "J'ai des yeux, de vrais yeux," he explains that with these glasses one may look into the soul—or into the heart—of a woman. Hoffmann snatches up a pair, looks at Olympia, and cries out in delighted surprise. Nicklausse meanwhile hands over the three ducats which Coppélius insistently demands for the glasses.

Spalanzani enters and immediately begins haggling with Coppélius over the ownership of Olympia. Coppélius reminds him that he supplied the doll's eyes from his magic collection, whereupon Spalanzani talks him into accepting five hundred ducats for the eyes—payable in the form of a draft on Elias. The two pseudo-scientists, each complacently assuming that he is successfully cheating the other, bind their bargain with many effusive declarations of friendship. Coppélius, taking his leave, suggests to Spalanzani that he marry Olympia off to the love-smitten fool of a poet.

The guests now enter and praise Spalanzani's hospitality in a vigorous chorus ("Non, aucun hôte, vraiment"). As they walk about, inspecting the sumptuous furnishings, Spalanzani and Cochenille bring in Olympia.[3] The guests enthusiastically admire her, while Hoffmann is captivated by her beauty. Spalanzani introduces her, saying that she will oblige the guests by doing anything they request—she will sing, or play the clavier, the guitar, or the harp. Before anyone can answer, Cochenille, who has meanwhile slipped behind the scenes, calls out for the harp, his call being echoed by another servant.

A harp is immediately brought forth and, as Spalanzani plays an accompaniment, Olympia sings the aria "Les oiseaux dans la charmille" in precise, mechanical tones. Whenever her voice begins to fade out, Cochenille, who stands behind her, touches her shoulder. There is a sound of a spring being wound up, and then the voice continues. At the end of the song the guests crowd around to congratulate Olympia, who stiffly holds out her hands. Spalanzani invites the company to supper. When Hoffmann approaches and asks if he may accompany Olympia, Spalanzani explains that she is tired and would prefer to sit down and rest awhile. He asks Hoffmann if he will remain with her for the moment, and the poet readily assents. Winding up the spring, Spalanzani guides Olympia to a sofa, seats her, and then leaves, chuckling over the thought of Hoffmann's tête-à-tête.

The poet launches into fervent declarations of love, repeating the refrain of the aria he sang when he first entered the room. Occasionally he touches Olympia's shoulder, whereupon she utters an exclamation which he interprets as an ardent sigh. Finally he impetuously takes her hand. This sets a mechanism in motion, and Olympia rises, circles the room, and then moves toward a door, with Hoffmann in excited pursuit. Just as she disappears, Nicklausse enters. Hoffmann, beside himself with joy, shouts to Nicklausse

[3] The actress who plays Olympia also plays Giulietta, Antonia, and Stella.

that Olympia loves him and then rushes out after her. Sadly shaking his head, Nicklausse follows.

Coppélius storms in, shouting that he has been cheated because the moneylender Elias has gone bankrupt. Swearing he will have revenge, he runs quickly into Olympia's room. Spalanzani returns with his guests, who begin dancing to the music of a waltz. Hoffmann waltzes Olympia around the room and out through the door at the back, while the guests comment in chorus on her grace and charm. Suddenly the two reappear, dancing faster and faster. Spalanzani frantically tries to stop Olympia, while Nicklausse, attempting to restrain Hoffmann, is pushed violently back. Spalanzani finally touches the proper spring and Olympia stops instantly. Hoffmann collapses fainting on a sofa. As Olympia sings in brilliant coloratura phrases over the accompaniment of the chorus, Cochenille guides her out of the room.

Nicklausse looks anxiously at Hoffmann, but Spalanzani assures him that only his glasses are broken. As Hoffmann revives there is a loud cracking and crashing behind the scenes. Spalanzani shouts that the doll is broken, and at that moment Coppélius appears, laughing sardonically. Spalanzani flings himself upon his rival and the two struggle furiously, while Hoffmann dashes into Olympia's room. Reappearing with a piece of the doll in his hands, he cries out in bewilderment and despair that his beloved was only an automaton. The guests deride him for his gullibility as the curtain falls.

ACT TWO

The luxurious palace of Giulietta on the Grand Canal in Venice. A brilliant party is in progress. From behind the scenes come the voices of Giulietta and Nicklausse, singing the famous *Barcarolle* ("Belle nuit, ô nuit d'amour"), a sensuous invocation to night and love. Its flowing refrain is echoed by the chorus. As the song ends, Giulietta and Nicklausse enter, and Giulietta seats herself near Hoffmann, who is standing at one side with Pittichinaccio. The poet remarks that the *Barcarolle* is far too melancholy a love song to suit his tastes. He illustrates his own preference by singing a spirited ditty known as the *Couplets Bacchiques* ("Amis, l'amour tendre et rêveur"). The chorus lustily takes up the refrain.

Schlémil appears, followed by Dapertutto. He is bristling with jealousy and almost comes to blows with Hoffmann. Giulietta prevents a quarrel by retiring with him to the card room, where the other guests have now assembled. Hoffmann and Nicklausse are left alone. Nicklausse tells the poet that he proposes to take him away the first moment he shows signs of falling in love with Giulietta. Hoffmann laughingly replies that, unlike Schlémil, he is immune to a courtesan's charms and may the devil damn his soul if he yields to her. He and Nicklausse go into the card room.

Dapertutto, who has been lurking in the background, glides forward, looks after them, and murmurs that Hoffmann will fall victim to Giulietta as all the others have done, for he so wills it. Schlémil, moreover, is to die, and Giulietta will bring about his death. In sinister majesty he holds out his hand, on which glitters an enormous diamond ring. In one of the most dramatic arias in the opera, "Scintille, diamant," he hails its fatal power. This gem, he exults, will make Giulietta his slave.

As he finishes his song, Giulietta enters, her eyes fixed on the ring. Dapertutto, putting it on her finger, commands her to bring him Hoffmann's reflection, just as she has already secured that of Schlémil. In losing their reflections, Dapertutto's victims also lose their souls. Giulietta promises to obey. Dapertutto withdraws as Hoffmann appears. He tells the courtesan that he is leaving because he has lost everything at cards. When he gazes into her eyes, however, he falls completely under her spell and cries out that he will never leave her. She warns him of Schlémil's jealous rage and suggests that he come back to her later in the evening after Schlémil has gone. Hoffmann pours out his love in an ardent refrain ("Ô Dieu, de quelle ivresse").

Taking up a mirror, Giulietta asks him to give her his reflection as a token of his love. Rather amused at her strange whim, he consents. Their voices blend in a passionate refrain ("Si ta présence m'est ravie"). As they are embracing, Schlémil enters. In a fury he calls to the guests, bidding them witness Giulietta's faithlessness. When Hoffmann threatens him, Giulietta restrains the poet. She whispers that Schlémil has the key to her apartment, insinuating that Hoffmann may use it if he can get it. As he is confronted by Schlémil and Pittichinaccio—who is all for killing him on the spot—Dapertutto remarks that he looks pale and hands him a mirror. Horror-stricken, Hoffmann discovers that he has no reflection. But in the madness of his infatuation he cries out that his heart is hopelessly ensnared ("Hélas! mon coeur s'égare encore"). These words introduce a dramatic ensemble. Dapertutto and Pittichinaccio express their contempt for the poet. Giulietta, heartlessly admitting to Hoffmann that the lure of the diamond was stronger than his love, tries to calm him. Schlémil fumes that he will kill his rival, while Nicklausse and the chorus express their pity for Hoffmann for having fallen victim to the treacherous Giulietta.

The strains of the *Barcarolle* are again heard as Giulietta bids her guests good night and retires to her apartment. Schlémil escorts the guests to the gondola landing at the back and then returns to ask Hoffmann why he is not leaving. The poet tells him that he desires a certain key which Schlémil has on his person. Schlémil refuses to give it up and draws his sword. Dapertutto places his sword in Hoffmann's hands, and in another moment Schlémil falls fatally wounded. Flinging away the sword, Hoffmann bends over his dying foe, tears away the key hanging at Schlémil's throat, and rushes through the door leading to Giulietta's apartment. Pittichinaccio satisfies himself that Schlémil is dead and then strolls casually toward the rear. Dapertutto picks up his sword and wipes off the blade.

The *Barcarolle* floats from behind the scenes in a mocking chorus. Giulietta is seen entering a gondola with Pittichinaccio. Suddenly Hoffmann reappears, and Dapertutto sardonically asks Giulietta what she intends to do with the poet. With a gay laugh Giulietta tells Dapertutto that he may have him. Turning to Pittichinaccio, she throws herself in his arms as their gondola glides away. Hoffmann curses her for her treachery. Nicklausse drags him away. The curtain falls.

ACT THREE

An oddly furnished room in the home of Crespel in Munich. Violins are hung on the walls and strange objects of art are seen about. At the rear are two doors, between which hangs a large portrait of Antonia's mother. Antonia, seated at the clavichord, sings a plaintive song ("Elle a fui, la tourterelle"), lamenting that her lover has gone. At the end of the song she sinks into her chair as if fainting. Crespel rushes in. Seeing his daughter's distress, he chides her for breaking her promise not to sing. Antonia answers that she was impelled to do so by thoughts of her mother. Gazing in despair at the portrait, Crespel cries out that when he hears his daughter he is haunted by the unforgettable voice of her mother, a famous singer. Trying to console him, Antonia promises never to sing again. She sadly leaves the room. Crespel worriedly declares that he has noticed the symptoms of the dread consumption that is dooming Antonia. He rants that it is Hoffmann who is responsible for aggravating her condition. He has brought Antonia to Munich so that she could escape the attentions of the poet, and now he learns that Hoffmann has come to the city.

Frantz, the deaf old servant, enters. Crespel tells him that no one is to be admitted, managing to make himself understood by dint of much shouting. When he at length stamps angrily out of the door, Frantz reflects over his master's crotchety ways in an amusing ditty ("Jour et nuit je me mets en quatre"). He complains that he is at his temperamental master's beck and call day and night. Life would be unbearable, he sings, if it were not for the fact that he can take his mind off his troubles by singing and dancing. He is good at both, he brags, and proceeds to demonstrate with such vigor that he falls exhausted into a chair.

Hoffmann and Nicklausse enter. The poet rouses Frantz and sends him to summon Antonia. Nicklausse leaves, saying he will join him later. Hoffmann sits down at the clavichord, looks over the music on the rack, and muses that it is another song about love and its follies ("C'est une chanson d'amour qui s'envole"). This introduces the dramatic duet which ensues as Antonia enters and rushes into Hoffmann's arms. Ecstatically they sing of the happy future which will be theirs after their marriage tomorrow. Hoffmann says that he is disturbed about Antonia's devotion to her music and admits that he is jealous of its attraction for her. She wonders if he is going to forbid her to sing, as her father has done, and then asks him to accompany her in the love song they have often sung together. As their voices blend in a moving climax, Antonia clutches her hand to her heart. Hoffmann is alarmed at her feverish manner. Exclaiming that her father is approaching, Antonia leaves the room. Hoffmann, remarking that he intends to discover the reason for Antonia's mysterious behavior, hides behind the draperies as Crespel enters.

A moment later Frantz announces Dr. Miracle, whereupon Crespel becomes highly excited, moaning that this scoundrel is plotting to kill his daughter as he killed his wife. Miracle suddenly appears. Crespel furiously orders him out, but Miracle pays no attention to him. Turning to the door of Antonia's room, he gestures with the movements of a magician. The door slowly opens. Miracle, as though speaking to the invisible Antonia, bids her be seated, questions her about her age, goes through the motions of feeling her pulse, and then commands her to sing. From the other room comes the voice of Antonia, singing a brilliant cadenza. Miracle murmurs that the girl seems in great pain, observing that it would be tragic indeed if Death were to claim so fair a maiden. When the anguished Crespel implores him to desist, Miracle brings forth several vials of medicine. Holding them between his fingers, he clicks them like castanets, singing that their contents will save Antonia's life. The voices of Crespel and Hoffmann blend with his as they express their anxiety and alarm. Crespel finally succeeds in driving Miracle from the room and then follows after him.

Hoffmann emerges from his hiding place, wondering how he can persuade Antonia not to sing for the sake of saving her life. When she appears he pleads with her, and then, mindful that her father may soon return, takes his leave. As Antonia, reflecting sadly on her plight, sinks into a chair, Miracle suddenly appears behind her. In a dramatic air ("Tu ne chanteras pas?") he exhorts her to be true to the high calling of her art, telling her that it is her destiny to sing. At first she protests, crying that she will gladly relinquish fame and glory for true love. As though seeking help, she turns toward the portrait. As she does so the portrait begins to glow with an eerie light and the voice of her mother is heard, calling on Antonia to obey. Her voice blends with Antonia's and Miracle's in a powerful trio ("Chère enfant! que j'appelle"). Miracle seizes one of the violins hanging on the wall and wildly plays an accompaniment as he urges Antonia to sing. At the fiery climax of the trio Antonia sinks dying on the sofa. The light fades from the portrait, while Miracle vanishes with a burst of mad laughter.

Crespel rushes in and takes his daughter in his arms. Softly she sings a phrase of the song heard at the beginning of the act. Her voice fades as she dies in her father's arms. Hoffmann enters. Crespel, frantic with grief, snatches up a knife and lunges toward the poet, but is restrained by Nicklausse, who appears at that moment. Hoffmann shouts for a doctor, whereupon Miracle appears. He steps over to Antonia's body, feels for a pulse, and then murmurs gloatingly, "Morte!" Hoffmann and Crespel cry out in utter despair. Frantz enters and sinks to his knees beside the body. The curtain falls.

EPILOGUE

The scene shifts back to Luther's tavern, as in the Prologue. With a gesture of finality, Hoffmann tells his listeners that he has finished his story ("Voilà quelle fut l'histoire").[4] Luther enters, saying that the audience in the opera house is acclaiming Stella. In an aside, Lindorf observes that he

---

[4] In some versions Hoffmann muses briefly over his three loves—Olympia, a broken doll . . . Antonia; dead . . . Giulietta. . . . For her, Hoffmann cries, he will repeat a stanza of the song about Kleinzach ("Ah, pour elle le dernier couplet"). The chorus joins him in the refrain. The opera ends at this point.

has nothing more to fear from his rival, for he is now far gone in drink. Nicklausse, suddenly rising as though waking from a dream, exclaims that now things are clear. Hoffmann's three women are really one—Stella. He proposes a toast to her, whereupon Hoffmann shatters his glass, raging that he will do the same to Nicklausse if he dares mention the name of Stella again.

Hoffmann impatiently calls for more liquor, and Luther takes away the punch bowl to refill it. Echoing the chorus about the punch, sung in the Prologue, the students troop into an adjoining room to continue their drinking. Hoffmann remains seated at his table. A light begins to glow around him, and the Muse appears. Tenderly she exhorts him to forget his perfidious loves and disillusioning passions and be true to her who fosters his genius and bestows on him the ultimate reward of greatness ("Et moi? Moi, la fidèle amie"). The impassioned phrases of Hoffmann's song to Giulietta surge up as the Muse speaks. The poet bursts forth ecstatically in a reprise of the song and then collapses in a drunken stupor.

Stella suddenly enters and walks slowly toward the table. As Nicklausse and the students come in from the other room, the singer asks Nicklausse if Hoffmann is asleep. Nicklausse tells her that he is dead drunk and that she has come too late. Lindorf appears. His triumph complete, he looks down at Hoffmann with gloating satisfaction, then offers Stella his arm and leads her away. Just before she leaves, she turns, takes a flower from her bouquet, and throws it at Hoffmann's feet. He looks up and stares blankly at her. The students, clicking their glasses, break into a lusty drinking chorus. The curtain falls.

Così Fan Tutte

by WOLFGANG AMADEUS MOZART

[1756–1791]

Libretto by
LORENZO DA PONTE

CHARACTERS

Ferrando, a young officer in love with Dorabella.................. *Tenor*
Guglielmo, a young officer in love with Fiordiligi.................. *Bass*
Don Alfonso, an elderly bachelor.......................... *Baritone*
Fiordiligi, a lady of Ferrara............................. *Soprano*
Dorabella, her sister................................ *Mezzo-soprano*
Despina, their maid..................................... *Soprano*
    Townspeople, soldiers, singers, musicians, ladies and gentlemen, servants

Place: Naples
Time: Eighteenth century
First performance: Burgtheater, Vienna, January 26, 1790
Original language: Italian

Così FAN TUTTE, which Mozart wrote on commission from Emperor Franz Josef II, is one of the composer's last three operas, having been followed by *La Clemenza di Tito* and *Die Zauberflöte*. Although the work was a comparative failure at its première—mainly due, it is said, to the weakness of the libretto—it contains some of Mozart's most delightful music. The full title of the opera is *Così fan tutte, ossia La Scuola degli Amanti* (*So Do They All, or School for Lovers*).

The sparkling overture prominently states one theme which will be heard near the end of the opera. It is sung by Don Alfonso, Ferrando, and Guglielmo as they express the underlying thought of the opera itself—"Così fan tutte."

ACT ONE

[*Scene One*] A café in Naples. Ferrando and Guglielmo are heatedly arguing with Don Alfonso as to whether or not women are capable of being faithful. The two officers cite their own ladyloves, Fiordiligi and Dorabella, as paragons of womanly virtue and constancy, while Don Alfonso derides their naïve trust in womankind. The argument ensues in the form of a spirited trio ("La mia Dorabella capace non è"). Finally Don Alfonso makes a bet of one hundred sequins that the two young ladies will prove unfaithful when put to the test, and the two lovers enthusiastically accept his challenge. At the end of the scene Ferrando and Guglielmo are already discussing plans for spending the money after they have won it.

[*Scene Two*]   The garden of the villa of Fiordiligi and Dorabella on the Bay of Naples. The sisters, gazing at miniatures of their lovers, sing their praises in a tuneful duet ("Ah guarda, sorella"). As they express impatience because the gentlemen have not yet appeared, Don Alfonso enters and tells them that Ferrando and Guglielmo have been ordered to join their regiment tomorrow. Although they wished to spare their fiancées the painful ordeal of farewell, he continues, they are waiting outside and will appear if the women so desire it. With that he calls in the two officers, and a delightful quintet ensues ("Sento, o Dio!"). Ferrando and Guglielmo pretend to be greatly distressed at this unfortunate turn of events, while the sisters moan that they would rather be slain than part from their lovers. In an aside to Don Alfonso, the two officers declare that such devotion is ample proof of unswerving fidelity, but the Don complacently observes that he still will collect his bet. Embracing the women, Ferrando and Guglielmo assure them of their undying love in a sentimental duet ("Al fato dan legge quegli occhi vezzosi"). Their good-bys are interrupted by the sound of drums in the distance, and Don Alfonso announces that the regiment is preparing to embark.

A troop of soldiers, followed by townspeople, marches in, and we hear a martial chorus. After this the quintet is continued as Ferrando and Guglielmo sing their farewells and the women urge them to write often—"At least two letters a day," as Dorabella says. There is a repetition of the chorus, and then the two men join the ranks and march away. Fiordiligi, Dorabella, and Don Alfonso sing a charming trio ("Soave sia il vento"), voicing the hope that the departing heroes will have fair winds and smooth sailing. When the sisters leave, Don Alfonso expresses satisfaction over the progress of his plot, adding the observation that putting one's trust in women is as futile as sweeping up the sea, planting seeds in sand, or catching the wind in a net.

[*Scene Three*]   A chamber adjoining the rooms of the sisters. Despina enters carrying a tray. In a brief air ("Che vita maledetta"), she complains over the lot of a maid who is kept busy trying to anticipate the whims of two capricious young ladies. Dorabella enters in a state of great emotion. Melodramatically she orders Despina to close the windows and draw the shades, saying that she no longer cares to see light nor to breathe since her lover has gone. Dismissing the maid, she goes on with her lamentations in a dramatic aria ("Smanie implacabili"). After its conclusion Despina returns with Fiordiligi, who expresses sympathy over her sister's distress.

Despina ventures the opinion that the ladies are taking the absence of their lovers much too seriously. Even if they are killed in battle, she observes philosophically, that would mean the loss of only two men, leaving the ladies free to choose from all the other men left in the world. She elaborates on these sentiments in the aria "In uomini, in soldati," after which Dorabella and Fiordiligi, shocked and indignant at such cynicism, stalk out of the room.

Don Alfonso enters and cautiously sounds out Despina as to her views on the dilemmas of her mistresses. The maid agrees that they most certainly deserve the consolation of male companionship. Thereupon Don Alfonso bribes her into aiding him in his plan and forthwith presents two candidates for Despina's approval. They are, of course, Ferrando and Guglielmo, now disguised as Albanians with bushy beards. When Despina, giving no sign that she recognizes the two officers, expresses disapproval over their barbaric appearance, the three plotters conclude that they will be safe from detection by the ladies themselves. Hearing Dorabella and Fiordiligi approach, Don Alfonso conceals himself.

The sisters, aghast at the presence of men in the house, berate Despina for admitting strangers. To their further confusion and alarm, the "Albanians" kneel down before them and ardently declare their love. The dialogue builds up into an amusing ensemble. The outraged demeanor of the ladies reassures Ferrando and Guglielmo of their fidelity, while Despina marvels at the ability of her sex to summon up a convincing show of emotions at a moment's notice. Don Alfonso makes himself known and greets the two Albanians as friends of long standing, warning them in an aside to play their parts according to his cues. The two officers grow more fervent in their pleas. Fiordiligi, exasperated at their persistence, finally orders them out in a dramatic recitative ("Stelle! che dir!"). She then proclaims that her love is as firmly anchored as a rock in the ocean bed and rebukes the strangers for attempting to swerve her affections. These sentiments are expressed in the famous aria "Come scoglio," which is remarkable for its brilliant passages and the extent of its vocal range.

But Fiordiligi's protests only move the strangers to more ardent entreaties, while Don Alfonso intercedes for them as worthy cavaliers and esteemed personal friends. Guglielmo pleads their cause in a mock-serious air ("Non siate ritrosi"), in which he implores the ladies to inspect them carefully and suggest any improvement which would make them more acceptable as wooers. Fiordiligi and Dorabella, unmoved by his gallantry, haughtily sweep out of the room. A gay trio follows ("E voi ridete?"). Ferrando and Guglielmo, satisfied that they now have convincing proof of the ladies' constancy, laugh heartily at Don Alfonso and magnanimously offer to cancel half or even three quarters of the bet. Don Alfonso, dryly observing that the last laugh is the best, declares that the original bet still stands. The men accept his challenge and agree to proceed according to his orders until the next day. Don Alfonso directs them to go into the garden to await further instructions. Before they leave, Ferrando pauses to sing the aria "Un' aura amorosa," in which he discourses on the sustaining power of love.

After he and Guglielmo have gone, Don Alfonso cynically remarks that in a world in which he was certain no woman was ever constant he has actually found two. Despina enters and tells him that the ladies are mooning about in the garden. When he asks her opinion as to whether the two sisters will ever yield to temptation, she replies that it is only a matter of time. She informs him that she has a plan of her own which will break down the defenses of her mistresses and then asks Don Alfonso to have his two swains in readiness in the garden.

[*Scene Four*] The garden of the sisters' home. In a melodious duet Dorabella and Fiordiligi bemoan the absence of their lovers ("Ah! che tutta in un momento"). Their mournful reflections are interrupted by cries of distress, and in another moment Ferrando and Guglielmo—still in their disguises—rush in, followed by Don Alfonso, who appears to be trying to calm them. Declaring that they can no longer live if their love is unrequited, they drink the contents of small vials which they hold in their hands. Don Alfonso tells the horrified ladies that the Albanians have taken poison. Sinking to the ground, the men reproach Dorabella and Fiordiligi for their cruel indifference and then pretend to succumb to the effects of the poison.

Wringing their hands in helpless confusion, the women call for Despina, who, of course, has been looking on unobserved. After properly expressing her alarm, the maid tells the ladies to comfort the victims as best they can while she and Don Alfonso run to fetch a doctor. When they have gone, Dorabella and Fiordiligi kneel beside the men and gingerly feel their pulses and listen for sounds of heartbeats, exclaiming in great distress that signs of life are fading. In asides, Ferrando and Guglielmo express great satisfaction over their solicitude.

Despina, in the disguise of a doctor, returns with Don Alfonso. Muttering Latin phrases, she examines the two victims, feeling their pulses and their brows in a pompous, professional manner. Their condition, the "doctor" announces at length, is obviously the result of a potion they have swallowed. Dorabella and Fiordiligi inform "him" that the two men, distracted by love, drank arsenic. Thereupon the doctor brings forth a huge magnet and with an impressive flourish bids all witness the remarkable curative powers of his great new invention. Holding the magnet over the men's bodies, Despina sings, as though uttering an incantation, "Questo e quel pezzo."

Ferrando and Guglielmo dutifully begin trembling and appear to revive. Staring wildly at Dorabella and Fiordiligi, they ask if they are gazing on angels or goddesses and then pretend to be overjoyed to discover that these are the fair ones for whom they sought to die. The sisters are somewhat taken aback by the enthusiasm of the resuscitated Albanians, and matters are not improved when they implore kisses to make their recovery complete.

Dorabella and Fiordiligi flare up at this impertinence, despite the exhortations of Despina and Don Alfonso that a kiss would be an act of mercy. Ferrando and Guglielmo sing that the ladies' refusal to grant them kisses is a comforting indication of their fidelity. These various sentiments are expressed in a brilliant ensemble which brings the act to a close.

ACT TWO

[*Scene One*] A room in the home of the sisters. Dorabella and Fiordiligi are in conversation with Despina. The maid tries to point out that the ladies are depriving themselves of a great deal of enjoyment by not responding to the wooing of the Albanians. After all, she avers, women are made for love, and men have been supplied by a kind providence to give them the opportunity of loving. She assures her mistresses that the strangers are gallant gentlemen, and that if they have been acting strangely it is due to the effects of the poison they have swallowed. Dorabella and Fiordiligi, evincing some interest, ask how they would be expected to behave toward the gentlemen once they have accepted their company.

Despina explains her theories about the art of love-making in a tuneful aria ("Una donna a quindici anni"). Even a maid of fifteen, she sings, must know the arts of love—the sly glances, coy refusals, tantalizing deceptions—which can make a man her slave. She concludes the aria with an offer to give further advice on these matters if it is desired. After she has left, Dorabella and Fiordiligi rationalize themselves into accepting the attentions of the two Albanians. In the ensuing duet, "Prendero quel brunettino," Dorabella declares that she prefers the "dark one," with his quiet, gentle demeanor, while Fiordiligi decides to take the other, who is blond and vivacious. They amuse themselves by describing how they will exchange sigh for sigh and glance for glance with their suitors.

Their conversation is interrupted by Don Alfonso, who hurries in to ask them to join him at the end of the garden. There at the seashore, he says, they will find entertainment which will be very much to their liking.

[*Scene Two*] A pleasant spot along the seashore, with a small harbor in the background. A flower-festooned boat is seen at anchor, and in the boat are Ferrando and Guglielmo (still as Albanians) with a company of musicians and guests. When Dorabella and Fiordiligi appear, accompanied by Despina and Don Alfonso, the two men sing a melodious serenade ("Secondate, aurette amiche"). They then come ashore and greet the ladies, who respond rather self-consciously. Impatient with the stilted and hesitant manner of the would-be lovers, Despina and Don Alfonso enact for their benefit the meeting of a young lady and her swain, pointing out the niceties of courtship. They then leave the four to themselves.

Fiordiligi pairs off with Ferrando, Dorabella with Guglielmo, and the couples stroll about in the garden. As Fiordiligi and Ferrando disappear among the trees, Dorabella and Guglielmo continue their amorous conversation in the form of a duet ("Il core vi dono"). Guglielmo persuades Dorabella to accept, as a token of his affection, a pendant in the form of a heart. Quickly following up his advantage, he takes off her necklace, from which hangs the miniature of Ferrando, and clasps it about his own neck. With coy declarations of affection, the two stroll away.

Ferrando and Fiordiligi reappear. Ferrando, however, apparently has been unsuccessful in his wooing, for he is being roundly denounced as an evil monster who is trying to lure an innocent maiden into faithlessness and deceit. Fiordiligi scornfully orders him to leave her. He declares his devotion in an impassioned air ("Ah! io veggio quell' anima bella"), and then, with a great show of disappointment, takes his leave.

Fiordiligi reveals her mingled agitation and uncertainty in a dramatic recitative ("Ei parte! Senti! Ah! no!") and aria ("Per pietà, ben mio perdona"). First she expresses her relief over the fact that the stranger has left, thus removing the temptation to which she might otherwise have yielded. Then she confesses that she is torn by unworthy desires and passions and abandons herself to remorse and self-reproach, after which she rushes distractedly away.

The two men return to compare their respective conquests. Ferrando cheers Guglielmo with the information that Fiordiligi rebuffed his love-making at every turn, and congratulates his friend on having so constant a fiancée. Guglielmo, however, is forced to confess that Dorabella appeared receptive to his advances and even gave him Ferrando's miniature in token of her love. Ferrando flies into a rage. Vowing terrible revenge, he starts off, but Guglielmo restrains him, warning him not to commit a rash act that may ruin his life simply because of a woman. In the ensuing aria, "Donne mie, la fate a tanti e tanti," he comments bitterly on woman's fatal instinct for duplicity. At its conclusion he sadly walks away, leaving Ferrando to express his disillusionment and chagrin in the equally dramatic aria, "Tradito, schernito dal perfido cor." Though brokenhearted over Dorabella's perfidy, he confesses that he is still in love with her.

Don Alfonso enters in time to hear these noble sentiments and cynically congratulates the young man on his devotion. Ferrando turns on him angrily, saying he is partly responsible for this unfortunate situation. But Don Alfonso disclaims any responsibility, remarking that Ferrando's anger is only natural under the circumstances. Guglielmo returns at this point and somewhat condescendingly observes that it was only logical that Dorabella should yield to a man of his superior attractiveness. He also reminds Don Alfonso that Fiordiligi's refusal of Ferrando has cost him half his bet. Don Alfonso merely answers that the test is not yet over and warns him not to count his chickens before they are hatched.

[*Scene Three*]   A room in the home of the sisters. Despina is telling Dorabella that she acted in a manner quite natural to a woman. Dorabella frets that she was unable to resist the Albanian's ardent wooing. Fiordiligi enters, highly indignant over the way things have been going. She confesses that she loves her new suitor, but laments that he is not, after all, her Guglielmo. Dorabella advises letting nature take its course, setting forth her reasons in the aria "E' Amore un ladroncello." She observes that the God of Love is very agreeable when one is obedient to his whims, but is a tyrant when crossed. After the aria she and Despina leave.

Left alone, Fiordiligi declares her resolve to remain true to her real lover. As she is musing over the situation, Ferrando, Guglielmo, and Don Alfonso are seen through the open door, watching her from the other room. Suddenly an idea occurs to her. Calling Despina, she tells her to bring from her wardrobe the two swords, helmets, and uniforms which she will find there. When the maid returns, Fiordiligi, after sending Despina away, reveals her plan: she and Dorabella will disguise themselves in the uniforms of their lovers and join them on the battlefield, there to accept whatever fate may be in store for them.

Putting on the uniform, Fiordiligi expresses her eagerness to be off on her adventure as she sings, "Fra gliamplessi, in pochi istanti." This introduces a dramatic duet which follows when Ferrando, seizing the opportunity to avenge himself on Dorabella and turn the tables on Guglielmo, begins making passionate love to Fiordiligi. When he threatens to end his life with the sword she holds, she finally yields. After ecstatically declaring their love, the two leave the room.

Guglielmo rushes in followed by Don Alfonso. The young man is furious over Fiordiligi's infidelity. Ferrando reappears and the two almost come to blows. Don Alfonso restrains them, however, advising them to marry the ladies at once, and thus take advantage of being in the good graces of two acceptable females. In a brief refrain ("Tutti accusan le donne") he sings that women are women and in matters of love they all behave unpredictably— "Così fan tutte" (so do they all). Ferrando and Guglielmo ruefully repeat the phrase with him.

[*Scene Four*] A banquet room, where the two couples are celebrating the approaching nuptials. They are hailed by Despina, Don Alfonso, and a chorus of servants. The lovers then sing to each other of their happiness, the ensemble taking the form of a canon, which Fiordiligi begins with the phrase "E nel tuo, nel mio bicchiero." Only Guglielmo, still smarting under the memory of Fiordiligi's betrayal, fumes that he wishes the others were drinking poison.

Don Alfonso announces that a notary has arrived to officiate at the signing of the marriage contracts. He brings in Despina, who has disguised herself as a notary. She reads the terms of the contract—to the effect that Fiordiligi is to be married to one Sempronio and Dorabella to one Tizio. Just as the contracts are signed, a soldiers' chorus is heard behind the scenes. Don Alfonso leaves to investigate and returns a moment later with the alarming news that the regiment of Ferrando and Guglielmo has returned.

Fiordiligi and Dorabella, panic-stricken, push their would-be husbands into another room, and Despina goes with them. Don Alfonso tries to calm the ladies, assuring them that everything will turn out satisfactorily. Ferrando and Guglielmo, having put aside their disguises in the other room, now appear and fervently greet their fiancées. They explain that their regiment suddenly received orders to return.

The officers feign great concern over the agitation of the ladies, while Don Alfonso notes with satisfaction that the sisters are victims of their own duplicity—as he predicted they would be. Pretending to go into the other room to put down his knapsack, Guglielmo exclaims that a notary is there. Despina thereupon comes forward with the explanation that she has just returned from a masked ball, which she attended in a notary's costume.

During expressions of general consternation, Don Alfonso, in an aside, tells the men to pick up the marriage contracts, which he will let fall. Ferrando snatches up the papers. He and Guglielmo scan them and then turn on the women with expressions of reproach and threats of vengeance on the betrayers. Fiordiligi and Dorabella, overcome with remorse, beg their lovers to kill them, admitting that they have been faithless.

Don Alfonso, gravely informing the officers that tragic proof awaits them in the next room, leads them away. After some moments he returns with the men, who are now again in their Albanian disguises. At this point matters are quickly cleared up. Ferrando explains his identity to Fiordiligi; Guglielmo gives Dorabella the miniature and asks her to return his pendant.

Like the doctor and his fabulous magnet, the officers sing gaily, this "invention" was their own.

The women, however, blame Don Alfonso for most of their troubles. He good-naturedly replies that he merely endeavored to prove his contention that, in matters of love, women the world over are victims of their own frailty. He urges the four to forget past complications and put their trust in each other's love and affection. All six principals join in the joyous closing ensemble of the opera ("Fortunato l'uom"), the theme of which is that the happy man is he who does not allow himself to be distracted by his troubles, but seeks contentment within himself.

Don Carlos

by GIUSEPPE VERDI

[1813–1901]

Libretto by
JOSEPH MÉRY *and* CAMILLE DU LOCLE

Based on the tragedy DON CARLOS
by Johann Christoph Friedrich von Schiller

CHARACTERS

A friar . . . . *Bass*
Don Carlos . . . . *Tenor*
Rodrigo, Marquis de Posa . . . . *Baritone*
Philip II, of Spain, father of Don Carlos . . . . *Bass*
Elizabeth de Valois, Philip's Queen and stepmother
   of Don Carlos . . . . *Soprano*
Theobald, Elizabeth's page . . . . *Soprano*
Princess Eboli . . . . *Mezzo-soprano*
The Countess of Aremberg . . . . *(Mimed)*
A royal herald . . . . *Tenor*
A Celestial Voice . . . . *Soprano*
The Count of Lerma . . . . *Tenor*
The Grand Inquisitor . . . . *Bass*
Nobles and ladies of the Spanish court, grandees, monks, members of the
Holy Office, Flemish deputies, inquisitors, pages, soldiers, magistrates, people

Place: Spain
Time: About 1560
First performance: (first version) Grand Opéra, Paris, March 11, 1867;
                      (second version) La Scala, Milan, January 10, 1884.
Original language: Italian

IN THE HISTORY of Verdi's creative activity, *Don Carlos* falls in the period
between *La Forza del Destino* (1862) and *Aïda* (1871)—sometimes
known as the composer's "middle period." The opera is one of two
Verdi wrote for the Paris Grand Opéra (the other: *I Vespri Siciliani*, 1855).
As produced in its original form in Paris, *Don Carlos* had five acts. Dis-
satisfied with the long libretto, Verdi revised the work with the help of Antonio Ghislanzoni, cutting out the entire first act (the so-called Fontainebleau Scene). He retained the drama of the first version by introducing
a monologue by Don Carlos, based on material in the original first act. This
revised version, in four acts, has remained in operatic repertoire.

Based on Schiller's drama, the opera has for its theme the revolt against
tyranny that swept Europe during the time of Charles V of Spain, grandfa-

ther of Don Carlos. An interesting point is the fact that the Spirit of Charles V, which appears in the guise of a friar at the beginning and the end of the opera, is virtually a dramatic invention of Verdi himself.

There is no overture. The curtain rises after a brief but foreboding introduction.

ACT ONE
(Part One)

The cloister of the monastery of San Giusto (St. Just). At one side is a lighted chapel. Beyond a gilded railing is the tomb of Charles V. At the other side of the stage is an exit; at the back, a door leads to the cloister garden. It is dawn. From the chapel comes the chant of the monks, mourning Charles the mighty Emperor. The voice of a friar, praying before the tomb, rises above the chorus. He laments that Charles claimed the whole world as his kingdom, flaunting his power in the face of the Almighty. The friar asks God's mercy on the soul of the departed Emperor.

Daybreak glowing through the windows reveals Don Carlos wandering about the vaulted cloister. He is pale and haggard. To the tolling of a bell, the monks file out of the chapel, cross the stage, and vanish into the shadows of the cloister.

Don Carlos suddenly stares wildly about, then bursts into an agitated recitative, "Io l'ho perduta." He has lost the woman he loves, he cries—lost her to his own father, who has claimed her as his queen. The joy of which the lovers dreamed as they wandered through the forests of Fontainebleau, in France, has been shattered by a father's ruthless will. In a brief but moving arioso ("Io la vidi"), Don Carlos sorrows over his loss.

The friar reappears and pauses to look at Don Carlos in pity. Don Carlos recoils, exclaiming he sees the ghost of the Emperor, whose spirit, so the legend goes, wanders restlessly through the corridors. At that moment Don Carlos' friend Rodrigo enters. The two greet each other fervently. Rodrigo excitedly tells Don Carlos that the hour of his destiny has struck: the people of Flanders, whom King Philip has enslaved, are rising against tyranny and oppression, and Don Carlos must lead them to freedom. But then Rodrigo notices Carlos' troubled look and asks the reason for it. Carlos thereupon confesses that he is desperately in love with Elizabeth, his father's queen. "Your mother," Rodrigo gasps in disbelief, but says he will stand by his friend. He asks Carlos if the King suspects anything. When Carlos says no, Rodrigo urges him to ask the King at once for permission to go to Flanders. He must forswear his love for the sake of a higher calling—to be the savior of Flanders.

A bell announces the approach of King Philip and his queen. Rodrigo again reminds Carlos that destiny commands. This colloquy is in the form of a duet which comes to a stirring climax ("Dio, che nell'alma") as Carlos and Rodrigo swear to dedicate themselves to liberty and brotherhood.

A fanfare of trumpets signals the entrance of Philip and Elizabeth, who are escorted by the monks. Carlos, controlling himself with an effort, bows before the King, who looks at him sullenly. Elizabeth starts at the sight of Carlos. Scarcely pausing, the King and Elizabeth go toward the chapel. There the King kneels bareheaded before the tomb of Charles V, as the monks repeat the chant heard at the beginning of the act. As the entourage leaves, Carlos and Rodrigo again break out in the refrain of their oath of brotherhood, which ends in a defiant cry of "Liberta!" The curtain falls.

ACT ONE
(Part Two)

Seated around a fountain in the monastery gardens, the Princess Eboli, Theobald (Elizabeth's page), the Countess of Aremberg, ladies in waiting, and pages are awaiting the Queen. One of the pages tunes a mandolin. In a charming three-part chorus, the women sing about the cooling shade of the evergreens. Theobald breaks in with poetic comments on the beauties of nature. Then the Princess Eboli sings that only the Queen of Spain herself may enjoy the sacred delights of this ancient grove. Eboli calls for a song. "Let us," she says, "sing the Saracen Song—the Song of the Veil—which has love for its theme."

To the accompaniment of the mandolin, Eboli (thinking of Don Carlos) sings the *Canzon del Velo* ("Nei gardin del bello"). It tells of an Arab maiden, her charms hidden by a veil, standing in a perfumed garden and gazing at the stars. Mohammed the King steals in, murmurs that he loves her, and offers her a crown and a throne to be his queen. Theobald joins Eboli in a brief refrain that is repeated by the entire chorus in sensuous harmony. Eboli goes on to sing of how Mohammed implores the maid to lift the veil that hides her loveliness, then again offers her his sceptre and his kingdom. His plea is made in spoken words. Without waiting for her answer, Mohammed hails the maid as his queen. The chorus repeats its refrain.

As it ends, Queen Elizabeth enters and is greeted by the women. In an aside, Eboli comments that the Queen seems to be burdened by a secret sorrow. As Elizabeth seats herself beside the fountain Rodrigo appears. Theobald goes to him, whispers a few words, then introduces him to the Queen. Bowing, Rodrigo hands Elizabeth a letter, telling her it is from her mother in Paris. At the same time, he slips a note into the Queen's hand, adroitly shielding it with the letter from the eyes of the women of the court. In an urgent undertone, Rodrigo begs the Queen to read the note. Bewildered, Elizabeth complies.

Rodrigo walks over to Eboli. The two chat about France and the ladies of the court there. Eboli asks if the ladies are as beautiful as people say they are, at the same time archly fishing for compliments. Rodrigo gallantly obliges with both information and flattery. During this exchange, Elizabeth reads the note in recitative. It is from Carlos, and it asks the Queen, "for the sake of the memories that bind us," to confide in the bearer of the note —Rodrigo. She stares at the note in anguish.

Eboli meanwhile asks Rodrigo if he wishes to ask a favor of the Queen. "Yes," he replies, "but not for myself." Eboli leads him before Elizabeth. In a short arioso ("Carlo ch'è sol il nostro amore"), Rodrigo tells Elizabeth that Carlos, realizing the hopelessness of his love for Elizabeth, is about to leave Spain. She alone, Rodrigo says, can give him hope and courage. He entreats the Queen to see Carlos before he leaves. Elizabeth tries desperately to hide her feelings. Eboli, watching her intently, remarks that she once saw a similar look of desperation on Carlos' face as he stood near his stepmother. But Eboli mistakenly assumes that Carlos is suffering because of his love for her and wonders why he tries to hide his emotions.

Rodrigo, in a repetition of the arioso, tells the Queen that Carlos never received from his father the love he needed. One word of comfort from the Queen will make him happy. Elizabeth suddenly makes her decision. With queenly dignity she commands Theobald to summon Don Carlos. Eboli and Rodrigo go to one side and talk together.

Carlos, escorted by Theobald, walks into the room. Theobald, after a few words with Rodrigo, goes into the monastery. Carlos slowly approaches the Queen, not daring to look into her eyes. Rodrigo and Eboli signal the ladies of the court to withdraw. Only the Countess of Aremberg and two attendants remain, standing at a respectful distance. Later, they also leave.

Trying to be calm, Don Carlos says he has come to ask a boon. He says he is haunted by a sense of doom, and the very air he breathes oppresses him. He begs Elizabeth to persuade King Philip to permit his son to go to Flanders. "My son," the Queen murmurs. Carlos recoils as if struck. He entreats her to talk to him as a lover, not as a son. The Queen tries to leave, but Carlos restrains her. A dramatic duet follows ("Prence, se vuol Filippo"). During the scene, Eboli and Rodrigo cross the stage at back, then leave. Elizabeth promises that, if the King gives his consent, Carlos will be on his way tomorrow as Vice Regent of Flanders.

But Carlos ignores her promises, chides her for her coldness toward him, and asks for only one sign of love and pity. In vain Elizabeth tries to calm him, reminding him that she must choose between her love for him and her loyalty to her husband. In tones of anguish, Carlos sobs that he has lost her. Elizabeth, crying that their lost love could have brought them supreme happiness, bids Carlos farewell.

In a sudden strange frenzy, Carlos sings that Elizabeth's words have ended his torment. He cries, "Let me die at your feet," then falls senseless. Elizabeth exclaims that the lover God meant for her is dying before her eyes. Carlos stirs, and in his delirium repeats his avowals of love. Then, reviving, he struggles to his feet and clasps Elizabeth in his arms.

In fury and desperation, Elizabeth tears herself away and storms at Carlos: "Well then, make an end to this. Kill your father and, with your hands stained with his blood, lead me to the altar!"

Carlos glares at her, horror-stricken. Crying that he is accursed, he rushes from the stage. Elizabeth, uttering a phrase of mingled despair and relief, sinks to her knees in prayer.

At that moment Theobald rushes in and announces the King. Philip enters with the Countess of Aremberg, Rodrigo, Eboli, and the court. Philip, moody and ill-tempered, looks for an excuse to vent his rage. Noticing that none of the ladies in waiting are nearby, he turns on Elizabeth and

asks which of her attendants should be with her now. In answer, the Countess of Aremberg comes forward. Glaring at her, the King then and there
banishes her from the court, telling her she is to go back to France at once.

The Countess, bowing, bursts into tears. Looking on, members of the
court murmur that with this edict the King has insulted the Queen herself.
All eyes are on Elizabeth. In a touching gesture, Elizabeth walks over to
the Countess. In an ensuing arioso ("Non pianger, mia compagna"), the
Queen assures the Countess that not even banishment can end their friendship. As a token, she gives the Countess a ring. Looking on, Rodrigo and
the court comment in chorus on the scene.

Philip, watching in sullen suspicion, comments that this show of sentiment only serves to hide Elizabeth's real feelings. The Queen tearfully bids
farewell to the Countess of Aremberg, then leaves with Eboli and the court.
Rodrigo kneels, salutes Philip, then turns to leave. The King stops him, and
pointedly remarks that he knows how to reward those who serve him well.
Rodrigo evasively answers that he is content to do his duty and will always
be ready to draw his sword in the service of Spain.

But the wily King knows that Rodrigo has something else on his mind,
and commands him to speak. Rodrigo answers in a dramatic aria, "O signor, di Fiandra arrivo." He has just returned from Flanders, Rodrigo tells
the King. The land is ravished by fire and sword, and the very rivers run
red with blood. Only by shedding blood, the King says harshly, could he
have crushed the revolt. Death itself will bring prosperity to the people of
Flanders. Rodrigo gasps in astonishment. Look at Spain, the King goes on.
In city and country there is peace—and that selfsame peace he intends to
bring to Flanders.

Yes, Rodrigo retorts, the peace of the sepulchre—the peace that would
make of King Philip another Nero. Then he bursts into a fiery refrain,
"Quest'e la pace." Is this, he asks Philip, what you would give to the world
—a peace that unleashes terror on the land, makes executioners of priests
and bandits of soldiers? Does he want an empire that resounds with curses
against its King? Only one thing, says Rodrigo, can redeem that empire:
Liberty.

In an ominously quiet phrase, Philip remarks that Rodrigo is only a
dreamer. "If you knew men's hearts as I know them," he goes on, "you
would think differently." Then, to the accompaniment of dark descending
chords in the orchestra, Philip warns: Beware of the Grand Inquisitor.

Rodrigo looks at him in bewilderment. Philip tries to divert his suspicions
by asking him if he has a request to make. Rodrigo answers no. But then
the King's feelings get the better of him. He cries out that Rodrigo has
guessed his inner torment—he is a luckless king, an unhappy father, a still
unhappier husband. He confesses he is suspicious of Carlos. Nothing on
earth, he cries, is worth what his own son took from him. As Rodrigo stares
aghast at Philip, the King tells him that the problem of Elizabeth and Don
Carlos is now in his hands, because Rodrigo is the one man he can trust.
With those words, of course, he virtually dooms Rodrigo as a spy. But the
honest courtier is secretly elated, believing that the King has relented toward Carlos. He expresses his elation in a ringing phrase. Then suddenly,

over the dark chords heard earlier, Philip again warns of the Grand Inquisitor. Unheeding, Rodrigo kneels and kisses the King's hand. The curtain falls.

ACT TWO
(Part One)

The garden of Queen Elizabeth's palace in Madrid. A short prelude sets the mood of a calm, clear night. At the rise of the curtain, Carlos is discovered reading a note telling him where to meet for a rendezvous . . . "at midnight, under the laurels by the fountain". . . . Carlos sings ecstatically of the impending meeting with Elizabeth. A veiled figure steals into the garden. It is Eboli, whom Carlos mistakes for Elizabeth. He greets her with a passionate refrain ("Sei tu, bell'adorata"), hailing her as the source of all his happiness and all his misery. The ravishing melodic line continues in duet form as Eboli exults in Carlos' love for her, while Carlos implores her to forget the world and think only of their mutual joy.

But the spell is shattered when Eboli removes her mask. In a shocked aside, Carlos gasps that this is not Elizabeth. Wondering over his sudden change of mood, Eboli asks him if he doubts her love. There is a moment of absolute silence. Then in a passionate outburst, Eboli asks Carlos if he is still unaware of the thunderbolt that is poised to strike him. The duet continues as Carlos answers that he knows his dark destiny only too well. In a repetition of the main theme of the duet, Eboli hints of a sinister conversation between King Philip and Rodrigo, but assures Carlos that she alone can save him because she loves him. Carlos thanks Eboli for her warning, but adds that he cannot return her love. They must remember this meeting as only a beautiful dream. Then it dawns on Eboli that the words of love Carlos has just spoken were meant not for her but for the Queen.

As Carlos recoils at her sudden fury, Rodrigo enters. He tries to calm the raging Princess, saying Carlos does not realize what he is saying. Eboli retorts that now she knows whom Carlos really loves—and what that means. When Rodrigo angrily threatens her, Eboli cuts him short, saying she also knows that Rodrigo is the King's spy. She knows what *he* can do, but he has still to learn her power. And that, says Rodrigo, means. . . . Nothing, Eboli snarls.

Then begins a powerful trio, "Al mio furor sfuggite invano." In a menacing *mezza voce*, Eboli tells Rodrigo she holds his fate in her hands. Rodrigo demands an explanation. Well, then, says Eboli, it is this: she is a tigress, wounded to the heart, and for that she will have revenge. The consequences will be on her own head, Rodrigo cries. The trio gathers intensity as Carlos joins in reproaching himself for the love he bears his mother. Eboli rages for vengeance. Rodrigo demands the reasons for her actions. Venomously, Eboli says that Elizabeth has hidden her sinful love for Carlos behind a mask of piety. Infuriated, Rodrigo draws his dagger. As Carlos leaps to restrain him, Eboli dares him to strike. Rodrigo flings his dagger away. The stormy trio is interrupted at this point, as Rodrigo cries out to God for help in solving this dilemma. Then the trio resumes its wild course as Eboli rages that she will have her revenge, and Carlos, now aware of her treachery, laments his fate. Rodrigo pours out his wrath against Eboli. After the trio's furious climax, Eboli rushes from the scene.

Instantly, Rodrigo, now also aware that Eboli will tell the King everything, urges Carlos to give him any secret documents in his possession. Carlos hesitates, knowing that Rodrigo is the King's confidant, but he hands over the papers as Rodrigo assures him of his loyalty. In climactic phrases the two men reiterate their faith in each other. The curtain falls.

ACT TWO
(Part Two)

A great square before the Cathedral of Our Lady of Atocha, where a milling crowd is gathered. There is a clamor of bells. Excitement rises as monks lead in a group of heretics who are to be burned at the stake. These are the Innovators—those who dared revolt against Philip's tyranny in Flanders. The people burst into a tremendous chorus of praise to the King, "Spuntato ecco il di d'esultanza." There is a sudden, stunned silence as the relentless beat of a funeral march is heard. The condemned march across the stage as the monks chant of the day of doom.

Following this grim procession come Rodrigo, the Count of Lerma, Elizabeth, Theobald, ladies and nobles of the court, heralds, deputies from the Spanish provinces, and grandees. The entire company halts before the closed doors of the cathedral. In a few moments the doors open and King Philip, wearing his crown, strides out, surrounded by monks. Philip tells the people that he has sworn by the crown he wears to destroy all heretics by fire and sword. The crowd shouts its approval. Then all bow in silence as Philip comes down the steps, takes Elizabeth's hand and starts to lead her away.

At that moment six deputies from Flanders, led by Carlos, step forward and kneel before the King. Carlos explains that the men are envoys he has brought from Flanders. In a deeply moving refrain, the deputies implore Philip to free their people in the name of the God who gave the King his power. Philip harshly replies that the Flemish have been faithless to that God, as well as to their King. He curtly orders the guards to take the envoys out of his sight.

From this point on the scene builds into a mighty ensemble ("Su di lor stenda il Re"). Rodrigo, Theobald, Carlos, and the people entreat the King to have mercy, while six friars urge him to punish the vile recreants. Then the assemblage falls silent as Carlos steps forward to ask that he be allowed to prove himself worthy of being the King's son by serving as ruler of Flanders and Brabant. ("Sire! egli è tempo ch'io viva"). Philip turns on him in fury. "You dare ask me," he storms, "to hand you the dagger that will slay me?"

Thereupon Carlos draws his sword and cries out that he will fight for the people of Flanders. The crowd draws back in horror. Philip orders the grandees to disarm Carlos. Not a man moves, and Carlos contemptuously dares them to touch his naked sword. In wild anger the King snatches the sword of the commander of the guards and rushes toward Carlos.

Rodrigo steps between the two. Calmly, but in a voice of authority, he asks Carlos for his sword. Carlos gives it to him. With a bow, Rodrigo hands the sword to Philip. Elizabeth and the people gasp in surprise. Then and there Philip exultantly makes Rodrigo a duke. The chorus of homage to the King is resumed. In a brief interlude, a Celestial Voice commends the souls of the heretics to heaven. The six deputies sing that the tyrant burns the innocent in the name of God. Their lamentations are drowned in a tremendous shout of "Gloria al ciel" as the curtain falls.

ACT THREE
(Part One)

The King's chamber in Madrid. Philip is seated at his littered writing table. It is almost dawn. In recitative, the King voices his thoughts about Elizabeth . . . he knows she has never loved him. Bitterly he recalls how she looked at the greying King the day she came from France. He stares into space, deep in thought. Suddenly he notices the dawn and rouses himself. So the days and nights pass, one by one, he murmurs. Then he launches into the great aria, "Dormiro sol nel manto mio regal." Only in death, he sings, will he find sleep—wrapped in his kingly mantle and laid to rest in the vaults of the Escorial. If only the crown could give a king the power to see into the human heart. But when princes sleep, traitors prowl. Faith and honor count for nothing. Plunged in despair, the King again laments that the Queen does not love him.

Suddenly a powerful unison phrase in the orchestra interrupts his meditations. The Count of Lerma enters and announces the Grand Inquisitor. Two friars lead him before the King. The Inquisitor is 90 years old and blind. Now begins a powerfully dramatic dialogue. Philip tells the Inquisitor that Don Carlos is plotting against his own father. Without hesitation, the Inquisitor asks what punishment Philip desires for his son. The greatest, Philip says. The Inquisitor gives him two choices: exile or death. Philip craftily asks if he will be absolved if he sends his own son to his death. The Inquisitor assures him he will be, adding that everything—even a father's love for his son—must be sacrificed to the Faith. That has been the Law since Calvary.

Then, in a dramatic passage ("Nel ispano suol mai l'eresia domino"), the Inquisitor tells Philip there is one man whose treachery can destroy Spain. That man's crimes make Carlos' treason seem like child's play. And yet, says the Inquisitor, he has refrained from punishing this arch-rebel—and the King as well.

Perplexed, the King says he simply looked for someone in his court who would stand by him in his darkest hour. He found such a person—a loyal man. Sneeringly, the Inquisitor asks how Philip can call himself King if he admits a mere man is his equal. Philip angrily protests this insinuation of weakness. Then the Inquisitor comes to the point of his relentless bargain. First he rebukes Philip for defying the Holy Roman Empire. That the

Church will forgive, he says, if the King will deliver up "Signor di Posa"—Rodrigo.

Philip flatly refuses. The Inquisitor threatens him, but Philip tells him he will tolerate his ruthlessness no longer. Abruptly the Inquisitor changes his tactics. He has crowned two kings in his time, he cries, but now the monarch on whom he has lavished his greatest efforts repudiates him. Why? What does the King expect of him? With that question, the Inquisitor starts to leave.

In sudden terror, Philip cries out, "Peace, Father!" He begs the Inquisitor to forget what has happened. "Perhaps," says the Inquisitor, and walks out of the room. Sinking back in his chair, Philip sings despairingly that thus the throne must always give way before the altar.

A moment later Elizabeth rushes in. She throws herself at the King's feet, crying for justice. She is not safe in her own court, she complains, for someone has stolen her jewel casket. Quietly the King takes a small casket from a nearby table, hands it to Elizabeth, and commands her to open it. She shrinks back, whereupon Philip flings open the lid of the casket. There, lying on top of her jewels, is a miniature of Don Carlos. Elizabeth faces him defiantly. "Yes, there it is," she sings, "and I dare admit it!" ("Io l'oso! si"). From this point on the scene rises to one of the great dramatic climaxes of the opera, involving all four principals.

Elizabeth reminds Philip that he well knew she once was betrothed to Don Carlos. But now she is Queen, and her life has been blameless. Yet there is one who still suspects her—the King himself. She dares him to name the wrong she has done. Philip rages that if she has dishonored him he will kill her. Elizabeth retorts that she can only pity him. Yes, says Philip, with the pity of an adulterous wife.

His brutal accusation so shocks Elizabeth that she faints. Philip strides to the door, flings it open, and calls for some one to assist the Queen. Eboli enters and gasps in terror as she sees the stricken Queen. Rodrigo comes in, sees what has happened, and speaks out impetuously. Is it possible, he asks, that a King who rules half a world cannot keep order in his own house? In a frightened aside, Philip murmurs that Elizabeth is blameless, that some demon is at work here.

Eboli, conscience-stricken, sings that she destroyed the Queen. Rodrigo, looking on, says that the fateful moment has come: what does it matter if, to insure Spain's future glory, one man must die? These sentiments are expressed in trio form until suddenly Elizabeth revives. Her voice joins the others in expressions of remorse and entreaty to Heaven. The ensemble ends when the King abruptly leaves, followed by Rodrigo.

Eboli throws herself at Elizabeth's feet and begs forgiveness. She confesses she planted Carlos' picture in the jewel casket. Hatred and jealousy prompted her, she says, because Carlos spurned her. But she is guilty of yet another wrongdoing, Eboli goes on. She was tempted with the King, and, in order to divert suspicion, placed the portrait among Elizabeth's jewels. In a remarkably dramatic musical passage—marked "pppppp"—Elizabeth makes her reply: tomorrow Eboli must leave the court. The choice: the convent or exile. With that the Queen leaves.

Eboli cries out against this judgment, then expresses her despair in one of the greatest arias in the opera, "O don fatale, o don crudele." She curses the fatal gift of her own beauty, which has brought only sorrow and despair to those around her. Despite herself, she has sacrificed the Queen and Carlos himself to her own wild passion—and tomorrow Carlos is to die. Then suddenly she takes heart. One day is left in which she may save Carlos, she cries. Ending the aria in a soaring phrase, Eboli rushes from the scene. The curtain falls.

ACT THREE
(Part Two)

A dungeon. At the back, a barred window looks on a court where guards are pacing back and forth. Carlos, head in hands, is brooding over his fate. Rodrigo enters, accompanied by guards. Dismissing them, he greets Carlos affectionately. Carlos says he has given up all hope for himself, and now counts on Rodrigo to fulfill the mission he had hoped to accomplish.

But Rodrigo says that the final test of friendship is at hand. Only one thing remains—a final farewell. Carlos stares at him incredulously. In a stirring refrain, "Per me giunto," Rodrigo sings that he is soon to die—and die happily for his friend. Don Carlos, he explains, is no longer in disfavor with the King. The real traitor, the man who incited the Flemish to revolt is— Rodrigo. He goes on to say he was caught with the incriminating documents (those he persuaded Carlos to turn over to him). Now there is a price upon his head. As Rodrigo speaks, two men come down the steps of the dungeon. One is in a friar's habit, the other carries a gun. They whisper and point to Carlos and Rodrigo.

Carlos bursts out that he will tell the King everything. "Never," Rodrigo cries. "It is your duty to live on for the people of Flanders. It is my duty to die for you." At that moment the man with the gun aims at Rodrigo and fires. Rodrigo collapses in Carlos' arms.

In a sweeping refrain, "O Carlo, ascolta," Rodrigo says his farewell to Carlos. Tomorrow, he sings, Carlos' mother will meet him in St. Just. She knows the whole story. As for me, Rodrigo murmurs, I die happy if my dying saves the life of Spain's redeemer. Imploring Carlos to save Flanders, Rodrigo dies in his friend's arms. Carlos throws himself across the body.

Philip enters, looks down at Carlos, and says he will now restore his son to his rightful place. Carlos whirls on him in fury. From now on, he shouts, you have no son. Here, he cries, pointing to Rodrigo's body, is where my heart is. The grandees of Spain crowd around. At the palace gates, the people, incited to mob violence, scream for the blood of the Crown Prince. Philip orders the gates to be opened and the crowd storms in. Eboli, masked, suddenly appears and implores Carlos to flee for his life. Philip points to Carlos and thunders to the people: "There is the traitor!" The Inquisitor, striding through the crowd, denounces Carlos as a heretic. Awed, the people kneel. In a great chorus, the grandees hail the King, while the people, now terrified by the Inquisitor, pray for mercy. The curtain falls.

ACT FOUR

The cloister of St. Just (as in Act One). It is a moonlit night. Somber chords set a mood of tragedy. As an agitated phrase breaks out in the orchestra, Elizabeth enters, approaches the tomb of Charles V, and kneels. Then she sings the moving aria, "Tu che le vanità conoscesti." She asks that the departed Emperor—who has known the vanities of this world and now sleeps in peace—and Heaven as well, heed her prayers. She must find strength to send Carlos on his destined mission. Tenderly she thinks back on France . . . the magic of Fontainebleau and the love she knew there. She expresses the hope that if Carlos ever comes back to the gardens of Spain, Nature herself will sing to him of the love that was theirs in Fontainebleau. Repeating the opening phrases of the aria, she again asks the spirit of the Emperor to heed her prayers.

Carlos enters. Quietly Elizabeth tells him to forget their love and go on living. Somehow, Carlos answers, he will find the strength to do so—but when love dies there is little reason to go on. Elizabeth reminds Carlos of Rodrigo's noble sacrifice. In fiery tones, Carlos vows he will build a monument to his friend on the free soil of Flanders.

The flowers of Paradise itself will smile on this hero, Elizabeth says ("I fior del paradiso"), and these words mark the beginning of a passionate duet. Taking up the refrain, Carlos sings that in his mind's eye he sees the oppressed people raise their hands to him, their redeemer. He will gladly save them; he asks only that Elizabeth weep for him if he dies in the attempt. Pledging her love to him, Elizabeth urges him to go at once. Gently Carlos implores her not to weep. These tears, she says, are tears women shed for the brave. The duet rises to a magnificent climax as Elizabeth and Carlos bid each other farewell forever ("per sempre addio! per sempre!").

At that moment Philip enters, sees the two in their embrace, and echoes sardonically: "Si, per sempre!" ("Indeed—forever!"). He tears the Queen from Carlos' arms, shouting that he will now exact a double sacrifice. Close at his heels, the Inquisitor intones that the Holy Office will do its duty. He orders the guards to seize Carlos.

Fighting off the guards, Carlos retreats toward the tomb of Charles V. Then out of nowhere a friar appears. He reveals himself as the Emperor, in royal crown and mantle. Repeating the phrase heard in the opening scene of the opera, the friar sings that only in heaven can the soul find peace. As Philip and Elizabeth cry out in horror, Charles V leads Don Carlos into the darkness of the tomb. The curtain falls.

Don Giovanni

by WOLFGANG AMADEUS MOZART
[1756–1791]

Libretto by
LORENZO DA PONTE

CHARACTERS

Don Giovanni, a licentious young nobleman................... *Baritone*
Don Pedro, Commendatore of Seville........................... *Bass*
Donna Anna, Don Pedro's daughter.......................... *Soprano*
Don Ottavio, Donna Anna's fiancé............................. *Tenor*
Donna Elvira, a noble lady of Burgos........................ *Soprano*
Leporello, servant of Don Giovanni........................... *Bass*
Zerlina, a peasant girl...................................... *Soprano*
Masetto, a peasant, Zerlina's fiancé............................. *Bass*
Peasants, dancers, musicians, and demons

Place: In and near Seville
Time: Eighteenth century
First performance: National Theater, Prague, October 29, 1787
Original language: Italian

THE OPERA is based on a literary classic that dates back to the Middle Ages—the story of the legendary Spanish lover, Don Giovanni (or, in Spanish, Don Juan), a gallant libertine whose ruthless pursuit of the ladies and whose blasphemous conduct deserve the dramatic punishment he receives.

The overture starts with foreboding chords symbolizing the avenging fate that is finally to overtake Giovanni—chords which are heard again in the last act and which represent the heavy tread of the stone statue as it appears at the door of the Don's home to punish him for his misdeeds. The music then changes to an impetuous characterization of the Don: daring, dashing, pleasure-seeking, heedless of the sorrow he leaves in his wake and deaf to the warnings of retribution to come.

ACT ONE

[*Scene One*] The square before the palace of the Commendatore Don Pedro in Seville. It is about midnight; the moonlight is bright. Leporello is waiting for Don Giovanni, who has secretly entered the house to seduce Donna Anna. The servant, obviously impatient and tired, complains that his master's activities keep him on the go night and day ("Notte e giorno faticar"): He must keep watch while his master makes love to still another lady. The pay is bad; the food is worse. He is too clever for such drudgery. He will leave the Don and become a gentleman himself. But as soon as he hears footsteps approaching his brave words end and he hides himself.

Don Giovanni rushes from the palace, a cloaked figure in the shadows, struggling with Donna Anna, dressed in her night robe. He tries to make his escape, but she clings to his arm, attempting to see his face, demanding to know his name. As she screams for help he threatens her. Meanwhile, the cowardly Leporello crouches in his hiding place, commenting on the fix his master is in but doing nothing about it.

Donna Anna's cries bring her white-haired father, the Commendatore, to the scene. Seeing him approach, she hastily re-enters the palace as her father rushes to her aid, a torch in his left hand and a drawn sword in his right. "Draw and defend yourself!" he commands the Don. Giovanni is reluctant to engage in a duel with so old an adversary, but the Commendatore insists. Nonchalantly knocking the torch from Don Pedro's hands, Don Giovanni calmly parries his thrusts. The fighting grows more serious. Finally Giovanni runs his sword through the old Commandant. Gasping a few words, Don Pedro dies. Leporello, who has been cringing in his hiding place, emerges now and directs some weak wit at his master, who is in no mood for it. "Well done," he comments, "first to seduce the daughter, then kill the father." "He insisted on fighting," Don Giovanni answers. "And did the lady insist too?" Leporello asks slyly. "Silence! breathe not a word," threatens Giovanni, raising his hand to strike. As lights come on in the palace and sounds of commotion are heard Giovanni hurries Leporello away.

Donna Anna rushes from the palace, accompanied by her fiancé, Don Ottavio, sword in hand, and servants carrying torches. They find the slain Don Pedro. "My father!" cries Donna Anna, throwing herself across his body. Ottavio tries to raise her as she cries out her grief in a tragic recitative. At last he leads her away and orders the servants to remove the body of the Commandant. The scene closes with a duet in which Donna Anna, insane with grief, repulses Ottavio ("Fuggi, crudele, fuggi") as he tenderly attempts to console her ("Senti cor mio, deh senti"). He swears he will find the murderer, and together they vow vengeance and call for heaven's aid. The curtain falls as Ottavio leads Anna into the palace.

[*Scene Two*] A desolate road outside the city. It is early the following morning. Leporello is protesting against Giovanni's manner of living and tells him he is a rascal but again assumes his groveling manner when the Don threatens him. Giovanni, the events of the night already gone from his mind, begins to tell Leporello of a new beauty he is pursuing. He is to meet her tonight. Suddenly the Don sniffs the air. "Ah! I detect the odor of femininity." "What a perfect sense of smell," says Leporello. "And a beauty, too, I would say," continues Giovanni. "And what eyesight, too," says Leporello.

A veiled lady comes along the road. "Let us watch her," says the Don, drawing Leporello aside. She sings with bitter sadness of the man who first seduced, then deserted her ("Ah! chi mi dice mai"). The Don's first thought is that he can possibly make another conquest here, especially as she seems to be very sad and in need of consolation. "I must comfort her," he decides. "As he has comforted eighteen hundred others," says Leporello, aside. In offering that consolation, the Don discovers to his dismay that the lady is none other than Donna Elvira, whom he had betrayed years before in Burgos, and that at the moment she is in search of him to take her revenge. She recognizes the Don and upbraids him for deserting her after having declared her his wife forever. He tells her he had good reason. Since she doubts him, he tells her that "this honest fellow" (pushing Leporello forward) will give her a complete explanation. Giovanni escapes while Leporello diverts her attention.

When Elvira discovers that Giovanni has slipped away again, she sadly seats herself. Leporello, unable to escape, tells her not to bother—that Giovanni is not worth the trouble. "But he has betrayed me!" she exclaims. "Console yourself," says Leporello maliciously. "You are neither the first nor the last. Look here." Leporello then goes into the famous comic aria, "Madamina! il catalogo." Taking a book from his pocket, he unfolds, like a map, page after page as he lists the Don's conquests of women: 640 in Italy, 231 in Germany, 100 in France, only 91 in Turkey, but 1,003 in Spain; there are country maids, city girls, countesses, duchesses, old ones, young ones, fat ones, thin ones, rich ones, poor ones. If it is a woman, he makes it his duty to win her, "as *you* well know." By the time he finishes, pages from Leporello's book are stretched across a large part of the stage. Then he runs off.

The insult in the last line of Leporello's aria infuriates Elvira anew. Now that she knows better than ever the nature of the Don, she is determined upon revenge.[1]

[*Scene Three*] A village green near a tavern. It is later the same morning. Joyous festivities, singing, and dancing are in progress. Zerlina, a bright and gay little peasant girl, and Masetto, a thick-skulled but amiable bumpkin, are going to be married, and they merrily sing and dance with their companions ("Giovinette, che fate all' amore").

The audacious Don Giovanni arrives with Leporello. His eye quickly perceives the attractive Zerlina. Leporello also anticipates a wide field for himself among the other girls. Giovanni approaches and makes a great show of friendship toward Zerlina and Masetto. Feigning generosity, he orders Leporello to take the company to his palace nearby and entertain them, and to pay special attention to Masetto. He stays behind with Zerlina. Masetto is reluctant to leave Zerlina, despite Leporello's assurances that Giovanni will "take good care of her." Zerlina, too, says she will be safe, but Masetto continues to protest until the Don touches his sword and tells him to run along. Masetto goes, making servile obeisance to the Don and growling

[1] Sometimes this scene closes with the recitative, "In quali eccessi," and the aria, "Mi tradi quell' alma." In this powerful and dramatic recitative and aria Elvira predicts the doom of Giovanni. Remembering the past, she cannot forget the misery he has caused her, and yet she still loves him. This aria, not originally in the opera, was added by Mozart in 1788, and practice differs widely in placing it. It is more commonly inserted at the opening of the first scene of Act Two; sometimes at the end of Scene Two, Act Two.

jealously at Zerlina ("Ho capito, Signor, si"). Leporello pushes him along.

Giovanni loses no time in making love to Zerlina, even going so far as to propose marriage. Shyly she avoids him at first, but he finally gains her hesitant acquiescence in the charming duet ("Là ci darem la mano"). Meanwhile, Donna Elvira has appeared and is watching everything from the background. As Giovanni is about to lead Zerlina off, Elvira intercepts them, calling Giovanni a scoundrel and declaring that she is just in time to save this poor innocent girl. In spite of his aside to Zerlina that this is just a poor infatuated woman, whom he humors out of pity, Elvira succeeds in exposing his true nature ("Ah! fuggi il traditore"), and leads Zerlina away.

Donna Anna and Don Ottavio arrive as Don Giovanni curses his luck. For a moment Giovanni thinks he is trapped, but when Ottavio greets him by name he knows he is still safe. They have no idea that he is the man who killed Anna's father; in fact, Anna appeals to him to help her find the villain. Relieved to know he is not recognized, he places himself at her service.

Elvira returns at this moment. In the quartet that follows ("Non ti fidar, o misera") she warns Anna and Ottavio against placing any trust in Giovanni's word, but Giovanni maneuvers her aside and whispers to the others that she is demented. Elvira hears him and insists that they must not believe him. Anna and Ottavio do not know what to think, but their suspicions are aroused. Finally Giovanni succeeds in leading Elvira away, telling Anna and Ottavio that he must go now to take care of the poor raving creature but to call on him when they need him.

As he leaves, Anna, in an impressive recitative ("Don Ottavio! son mortal!"), tells Ottavio that she recognizes Giovanni's voice as that of the murderer. Ottavio is horrified that Giovanni, a nobleman and his friend, should be the one. Anna tells him the whole story: how Giovanni entered her chamber, his features hidden, and tried to ravish her; how she fought him off and shrieked for help; how she clung to him to prevent his escape; how her father came and was killed. Leading into the aria, "Or sai, chi l'onore," she calls on Don Ottavio to renew his vow of vengeance for her father's death.

As she leaves, Ottavio still finds it difficult to believe a noble-born friend would be such a villain. He determines to get at the truth. The scene closes as Ottavio steps to the front of the stage for his lovely, quiet aria, "Dalla sua pace," in which he declares that his peace of mind depends on his loved one, Donna Anna.

[*Scene Four*] The garden of Don Giovanni's palace. It is late afternoon of the same day. Leporello enters, still complaining, followed by Giovanni. Leporello tells the Don how he carried out his orders about entertaining the peasants and of the trouble the jealous Masetto gave him. He relates also how Elvira came in with Zerlina and denounced Giovanni at length, while he said nothing till she was finished and could say no more, then led her out and locked the door. In the exuberant *Champagne Aria* ("Finch' han dal vino") Giovanni orders Leporello to summon the peasants for a great party. These country maids are to his taste, he says, and while the others are reveling in wine and dancing he will be adding several more names to his list. Leporello goes off to do as he is told, and Giovanni enters his palace.

Zerlina and Masetto now come upon the scene, Masetto scorning and scolding his peasant love for her attentions to the Don. Zerlina replies to her jealous lover with the coquettish aria, "Batti, batti, o bel Masetto," as she amusingly teases him to good humor, patting his face and kissing him.

Don Giovanni's voice is heard inside as he gives the final orders for the party. Zerlina is flustered and wants to hide. Masetto is immediately suspicious. "You are afraid I shall learn what there is between you," he accuses her. "I shall hide here and see what goes on," he says. Giovanni comes out accompanied by servants. Zerlina draws back into an arbor. The guests arrive. Giovanni is looking everywhere for Zerlina; finally he sees her as she tries to hide. He signals Leporello to take the others inside, while he attempts to lead Zerlina into the arbor. Suddenly confronted by Masetto, he is confused but quickly recovers himself. "Masetto," he says, "you have deserted your bride. Come, join the dancing." They go inside.

At this time three figures come upon the scene in domino costumes, wearing masks over their eyes. They are Elvira, Anna, and Ottavio. They consult together on their plan for vengeance. A minuet drifts out. Leporello comes to open a window and sees them. Mistaking them for revelers, he informs Giovanni, who orders them to be invited in. They accept gladly. Before entering, all three unmask and sing softly the touching, beautiful *Mask Trio* ("Protegga, il giusto cielo"), a prayer to heaven for vengeance. They resume their masks and enter the palace.

[*Scene Five*] The ballroom in Don Giovanni's palace. It is now evening. There are three orchestras. Drinks are flowing freely; Giovanni is paying pretty compliments to the girls, and Leporello is doing much the same. The Don again turns his attention to Zerlina. Masetto is burning with jealousy, while Zerlina flirts with Giovanni. Anna, Elvira, and Ottavio enter, masked, and are made welcome.

One orchestra starts to play. It is the celebrated *Don Giovanni Minuet,* one of the most charming ever composed. Ottavio dances the minuet with Anna. Giovanni draws Zerlina away, ordering Leporello to distract Masetto's attention. A second orchestra breaks into a country dance; a third one starts a waltz. Giovanni swings Zerlina into the country dance. Leporello, feigning solicitude for Masetto, seizes his arms and forces him to waltz with him. As Giovanni and Zerlina pass a door he leads her into the next room. Masetto breaks loose from Leporello, and Leporello goes to warn his master, while Anna, Elvira, and Ottavio closely watch what is going on.

Zerlina's cries for help come from the next room. There is sudden confusion, and all turn toward the door as Zerlina rushes into the ballroom and seeks the protection of the masked trio. Don Giovanni knows he is in a tight spot and plays a comedy. He bursts in, sword in hand, turns to his poor servant, Leporello, and tries to throw the blame on him with threats of punishment. The guests, this time, are not convinced. Ottavio, Anna, and Elvira unmask and confront Giovanni, telling him his lies will help him no longer. The men approach Giovanni threateningly as he leans on his sword. This tumultuous scene ends with the impressive septet, "Trema, trema, scellerato!" as all denounce Giovanni for his crimes, while thunder (sounding his doom) is heard offstage. Still courageous and unrepentant, he only laughs at his fate. Seizing Leporello, he fights off Don Ottavio and escapes.

ACT TWO

[*Scene One*]   A street in Seville in front of Donna Elvira's house. It is night. Donna Elvira is alone. Her recitative ("In quali eccessi") and aria ("Mi tradì quell' alma"),[2] in which she predicts the doom of Giovanni but still proclaims her love for him in spite of the way he has misused her, open this act. Elvira, hearing voices, then enters her house and Giovanni and Leporello come on the scene. Leporello, as usual, is complaining. Giovanni tries to laugh him out of his mood, but Leporello is more persistent this time. The Don has tried to kill him, and that is no joke. Giovanni finally appeases him somewhat with a purse of money. "Well, all right this time," says Leporello, "but you must give up women." "Give up women!" exclaims Giovanni. "Why, I need them more than I need food." "Must you deceive the whole sex, then?" asks Leporello. "It is not deceiving," says the Don. "It is love. But I love all women, and I can't neglect any of them. In their small way of thinking, they call this deceiving."

Well, what now? Leporello wants to know. The Don's roving eye has been attracted to Elvira's pretty serving maid. In order to try his fortune with her, he says, he wants to appear as a servant himself, and so he makes Leporello change cloak and hat with him. Elvira meanwhile has appeared at an upper window and sings the opening of an exquisite trio, "Ah, taci, ingiusto core," as she gazes with melancholy at the moon and tries to quell her heart's rebellious longing for the seducer. Giovanni, ever alert, takes advantage of the situation. Standing behind Leporello, who now wears the Don's hat and cloak, and making appropriate gestures with Leporello's arms, he sings to her of his love. Leporello can hardly refrain from laughing as she falls into the trap and agrees to come down. All this, of course, is to get the mistress out of the house and out of the way, so that Don Giovanni can make love to the maidservant.

While Elvira is on her way down to join him Don Giovanni tells Leporello to take her off somewhere and make love to her. Elvira appears, and Leporello begins to enjoy his assignment. Don Giovanni, acting the part of a street ruffian, pretends to attack them and thus frightens them away. His scheme having worked, the Don picks up his mandolin and begins the *Serenata* to Elvira's maid ("Deh vieni alla finestra").

Just as the girl appears at the window his singing is interrupted by the entrance of Masetto and a crowd of armed peasants seeking Giovanni. Being protected by his disguise as Leporello, he is not alarmed. In fact, he feigns willingness to help in the hunt and rids himself of Masetto's followers by sending them off on fools' errands in all directions ("Metà di voi quà

---

[2] This is now the customary place for this recitative and aria. As noted previously, it sometimes is placed at the close of Scene Two, Act One; sometimes at the end of Scene Two, Act Two. In those cases, this act opens with Leporello and Giovanni entering the scene.

vadano"). He tells Masetto to stay with him, leads him around, off the scene and on again. He asks Masetto if he is resolved upon killing the Don—or wouldn't a beating be sufficient? "I'll kill him and cut him up into pieces," says Masetto. "Show me your weapons," says Giovanni, whereupon the simple peasant hands over his musket and pistol. Thereupon Giovanni unmercifully beats him with the flat of his sword and goes off, leaving the bewildered Masetto groaning on the ground.

Zerlina now appears with a lantern. She hears Masetto's groans. He tells her he was beaten by Leporello or some fiend who looked like him. "I told you your silly jealousy would bring you trouble," says Zerlina. "Where has he hurt you?" Masetto lists the various places in which he is hurt. She sympathizes with him and tends his injuries, and in a lovely aria, "Vedrai carino," consoles him with the pretty thought that love (and particularly hers) can heal all wounds. On this sweet note the curtain falls.

[*Scene Two*]   A courtyard adjoining Donna Anna's house. Leporello, tired of the part he is playing, is trying to escape from Elvira, who still thinks he is Giovanni. "Do not leave me," she cries. Then, trembling with apprehension, she sings the opening lines of a sextet ("Sola, sola, in bujo loco"), while Leporello is groping his way about the courtyard, looking for a way out. He finds an exit, but just as he is about to leave, Don Ottavio and Donna Anna enter through it. She is grieving over her father's death, and Ottavio is attempting to console her. Elvira starts looking for Leporello, who is still searching for a way out. He finds another exit, but again, just as he is about to go out, Masetto and Zerlina enter and confront him. Masetto, Ottavio, Zerlina, and Anna close in on him, thinking he is the Don. They approach him menacingly. Elvira pleads for him, claiming him as her husband. It looks for a moment as though Leporello's life is in great danger, but he whips off the cloak and reveals his identity.

"So it was you who almost killed my Masetto!" cries Zerlina. "Ah, and you have deceived me!" adds Elvira. "You must be wearing those clothes for some mischievous purpose," says Ottavio. As they quarrel about who will punish him, Leporello pleads that the misdeeds are Giovanni's and that anything he has done wrong he has heen forced to do by the Don ("Ah, pietà! Signori miei!"). Then, watching his chance, he escapes.

Ottavio is now convinced beyond any doubt of Giovanni's guilt. As the scene ends Don Ottavio sings the great tenor aria, "Il mio tesoro." This is a calm, smooth melody, and in it he swears to avenge his Donna Anna, for he wishes, above all, to bring her comfort.[3]

[3] In some presentations the scene ends with the sextet. Leporello makes off as soon as he discloses himself, and his aria is omitted. In that case, Ottavio's aria is moved to a later scene.

Following this scene as it is given here is one which Mozart wrote in at a later date, but it is seldom used now. In it, Zerlina, razor in hand, drags in Leporello. She ties him to a chair, and they sing a comic duet ("Per questa tue manine"). While Zerlina goes off to get the others Leporello drags himself off, chair and all.

It is sometimes at this point that Elvira stays after the others have gone in pursuit and sings the recitative, "In quali eccessi," and the aria, "Mi tradi quell' alma," in which she predicts the doom of Giovanni, then proclaims her love for him in spite of the way he has misused her.

[*Scene Three*]   A cemetery. It is about two in the morning. In the rear is a life-size statue of the murdered Commendatore on horseback. Don Giovanni leaps lightheartedly over the wall. "Ah," he cries, "this is a good place to hide. I wonder how Leporello made out with Donna Elvira?"

Just then Leporello scrambles over the wall. He is still frightened from his narrow escape, and angry, but Giovanni is in a frolicsome mood. "I have had some gay adventures since we parted, but I'll tell you only one of them," he laughs. "About a woman, no doubt," says Leporello.

"That's right," answers the Don. He tells how he met one of Leporello's own conquests, who, mistaking him for Leporello because of the clothes, was quite agreeable to his advances. However, she soon became aware of her error and screamed, and he had to run off. Leporello is not amused. "Suppose," he says, "it had been my wife—would you laugh then?" "All the louder," answers the Don.

The moon, meanwhile, has broken through the clouds and shines with a ghostly light on the statue. A solemn voice speaks near them; it is the statue: "Your mirth shall have an end before the morning dawns." "Who spoke there?" asks the Don. Leporello, frightened out of his wits, claims it is a ghost, but Giovanni, grasping his sword, again asks, "Who spoke there?" Again the head of the statue leans forward and says: "Audacious villain, be quiet. Let the dead sleep in peace."

"Someone must be outside," says the Don. Then, with indifference and contempt, he looks up and says: "Isn't this the statue of the Commendatore? Go over and read the inscription." "Oh, excuse me," says the frightened Leporello, "I never learned to read in light so pale." "Read it, I say!" cries the Don threateningly.

Leporello, shaking with fear, reads: "'Here I await vengeance from heaven on him who slew me.'" The reckless Don is not taken aback, though Leporello trembles. He says: "O venerable fool of fools! Tell him to come and have supper with me this evening." Leporello, shaking from head to foot, hangs back, but under the threat of his master's sword he blurts out the invitation in the duet, "O statua gentillisima." "Most noble statue," he begins, but he cannot get it all out. Under the Don's goading he tries again and again and finally succeeds, but almost dies when the statue nods. At this point the brazen Don addresses the statue himself. "Speak if you are able," and he mockingly adds: "Will you come to supper?" The statue answers, "Yes." Still undaunted, the Don drags Leporello off to prepare the meal.

[*Scene Four*]   A small room in Donna Anna's palace. There is a picture of the murdered Commendatore hanging on the wall, with large candles burning at each side. Here once more Don Ottavio is trying to comfort the inconsolable Donna Anna. He urges her to marry him and tells her that the villain, Don Giovanni, will soon be brought to justice. Donna Anna declares she loves him, but until her father's murderer is punished she cannot think of happiness. This is the sentiment of the great aria which closes this scene ("Non mi dir, bel idol mio").[4]

[4] Sometimes Ottavio's great aria, "Il mio tesoro," is sung here instead of at the conclusion of Scene Two of Act Two, as noted at that place.

[*Scene Five*]   Don Giovanni's banquet hall. The Don is seated at a table with two beautiful ladies as his guests. He sings of the pleasures he enjoys. Leporello is serving from a side table filled with good things to eat, occasionally helping himself. Giovanni eats and drinks and teases Leporello. All the while his private orchestra entertains him with music.[5]

Into this gay scene Donna Elvira comes rushing, bringing an entirely different note. She throws herself on her knees and begs Don Giovanni to mend his ways before it is too late—to show just one virtue if he has one. The Don and Leporello just mock her and invite her to stay for supper. She leaves in despair, but just outside the door she screams. The Don orders Leporello to go and see what it is all about. The servant goes to the door, but returns almost speechless with fright. It is the statue he has seen approaching! "Oh, my lord, it is the man of stone. The man in white. Can't you hear his heavy footsteps?"

Loud knocking resounds. The Don orders Leporello to open the door, but the terrified servant's knees tremble so that he cannot obey his master. The Don goes himself, but before he can open it, the wind howls, thunder crashes, the door blows open, and, to the accompaniment of the dramatic chords heard in the overture, the statue in white stone armor enters and stands in the pale light in the doorway. The Don's guests leave hurriedly, and Leporello hides under the table.

"You invited me, Don Giovanni," says the statue, "and here I am." The Don, though amazed, repeats his offer of hospitality and orders Leporello to set another place. The statue, however, refuses, because the spirits of heaven no longer can dine on mortal food. In turn he asks the Don to be *his* guest, and with wicked fortitude Giovanni accepts despite Leporello's pleas from under the table that he should decline on the grounds of a previous engagement. "Give me your hand on it then," says the stone figure, and the doomed man places his hand in that of the statue, which closes upon it like a vise. A cry of horror bursts from Giovanni's lips, and a chill shakes his frame. At last he is impressed—and frightened. Still not so frightened, however, that he will repent when the statue urges him to. "No, no," he cries. "I scorn repentance. Away, you old driveler!" And with this refusal the statue drops Don Giovanni's hand, pronounces him doomed, and sinks into the ground as flames shoot up.

The Don in desperation tries to escape, but every exit to which he rushes is blocked by fire and smoke. Finally the entire scene is enveloped in flames, and Don Giovanni disappears as demons from below proclaim the tortures that await him.

[*Epilogue*]   A road near the cemetery. Anna, Elvira, Zerlina, Ottavio,

---

[5] Although Don Giovanni was supposed to have lived at some indefinite period in the past, Mozart inserted tunes that were popular at the time this opera was first produced: a melody from Martin's *Uno Cosa Rara;* another from Sarti's *I Due Litiganti;* a third from his own *Nozze di Figaro.* This was Mozart's little joke on his contemporaries and on himself. The melodies are parodied, and as the last one begins—it was one of the most popular tunes of the day—Leporello remarks, "I've heard too much of that!"

Masetto, and Leporello all appear. Leporello excitedly relates the events that took place at the Don's palace. In the closing sextet they all rejoice in the justice meted out to the Don, and their closing words may be summarized as: "Thus do the wicked find their end!"[6]

[6] In many presentations this Epilogue is omitted. Originally it was written as part of the last scene: the five enemies of Don Giovanni entering with the police immediately after the death of Giovanni, and Leporello, crawling out from under the table, telling the story of what has happened.

Don Pasquale

by GAETANO DONIZETTI
[1797–1848]

Libretto by the Composer

Suggested by Stefano Pavesi's comic opera
SER MARC' ANTONIO

CHARACTERS

Don Pasquale, a wealthy bachelor............................. *Bass*
Dr. Malatesta, his friend and adviser........................ *Baritone*
Ernesto, Don Pasquale's nephew............................. *Tenor*
Norina, a young widow in love with Ernesto................. *Soprano*
Notary .... *Baritone*
Servants, major-domo, hairdresser, dressmakers

Place: Rome
Time: Nineteenth century
First performance: Théâtre des Italiens, Paris, January 4, 1843
Original language: Italian

THIS DELIGHTFUL OPERA, one of the last Donizetti wrote, has the double advantage of a sparkling score and a witty, interesting libretto. An outstanding example of *opera buffa, Don Pasquale* has outlived many of its contemporaries because of its wealth of charming, vivacious melody and its rich vein of comedy.

The overture begins with the theme of Ernesto's serenade in the third act, and this is followed by the theme of Norina's cavatina in Act One. The two melodies are woven into a musical pattern which reflects the gay mood of the opera.

ACT ONE

[*Scene One*]   A room in the house of Don Pasquale. At the rear is the main entrance. Doors at the sides lead to adjoining rooms. Don Pasquale, sitting in his chair, looks at his watch and frets because it is nine o'clock and Dr. Malatesta has not yet arrived. Then he is heard muttering about his young nephew, who, he vows, will shortly receive the surprise of his life.

His reflections are interrupted by the entrance of Dr. Malatesta. All impatience, Don Pasquale asks the doctor if he has found a bride for him. Malatesta triumphantly announces that he has discovered a lady of surpassing beauty and describes her charms in a tuneful aria ("Bella siccome un angelo"). She is an angel, he says, an angel with black hair, eyes that bewitch, and a smile that enslaves. She is the soul of innocence, demure and kind—in fact, a being expressly created by heaven to make man happy.

Beside himself with joy, Don Pasquale asks her name. Malatesta informs him that the lady is his sister. This news makes Pasquale even happier, and he insists on seeing her at once. Ignoring Malatesta's warning against rushing too impetuously into marriage, Pasquale pushes the doctor out of the room, ordering him to fetch the young lady immediately. In a vigorous aria ("Ah, un foco insolito"), Pasquale exults that the prospect of becoming a bridegroom makes him feel twenty years younger. Already he envisions himself the proud father of six. Greatly pleased, he declares that he will now proceed to put his high-and-mighty nephew in his place. He rubs his hands in satisfaction as he sees Ernesto approaching.

Telling Ernesto to be seated, Don Pasquale begins. With the air of a lawyer questioning a witness, he asks the young man if it is true that he, Pasquale, gave him an opportunity three months ago to marry a wealthy and beautiful lady. Ernesto nods assent. Did he not, Pasquale continues, promise to provide him with an income and make him his heir? And did he not make it clear that if Ernesto refused to marry the lady he would be disinherited and that Don Pasquale himself would marry again? After Ernesto has admitted that all these things are true, his uncle announces that he is repeating the offer.

Ernesto refuses on the spot, saying that he loves Norina and cannot think of marrying anyone else. Don Pasquale snorts that Norina is nothing but a scheming widow, to which Ernesto hotly retorts that though she is poor she is the soul of virtue. The result of the argument is that Don Pasquale declares he will turn Ernesto out of the house for his insubordination. As for himself, Pasquale goes on, he plans to marry.

Staring at him in amazement, Ernesto asks if he is joking. It is no joke, Don Pasquale replies, and then declaims that he, Pasquale da Corneto, being of a sound state of mind and body, is about to take a wife. Though not as young as he once was, Pasquale continues, he still has his youthful vigor, with some to spare. Having thus declared himself, he tells Ernesto to get out of his house as quickly as he can. A long and dramatic duet ensues, beginning with Ernesto's lament that all his hopes have been shattered in one blow ("Sogno soave e casto"). It was only for Norina's sake, he reflects sadly, that he ever desired riches, but now that he is a penniless outcast he must renounce her. Don Pasquale gloats that he has taught this obstinate young upstart a lesson he will never forget.

Ernesto starts to leave but turns back and asks permission to say one word more. Pasquale deigns to listen. Ernesto advises him to seek the counsel of a trusted friend before venturing on so important a step as marriage—someone like Dr. Malatesta. That he has already done, Pasquale answers complacently. Far from objecting, the good doctor encouraged him, for the bride-to-be is the doctor's own sister.

Stunned at the news, Ernesto exclaims that the doctor, whom he considered his friend, has betrayed him by abetting Pasquale's scheme to marry. As Ernesto continues to bewail the fact that all his hopes for marriage with

Norina have been dashed, Pasquale revels in his nephew's discomfiture. After the lively climax of the duet both hurry away.

[*Scene Two*]   Norina's room. Norina is deep in a romantic novel. In a charming cavatina ("Quel guardo, il cavaliere") she reads a tender love scene aloud and then gives herself over to reflections on matters of love. The maid's tender glances, she reads, pierced the heart of her cavalier, and he knelt at her feet and swore eternal fidelity. Smiling to herself, Norina muses that she, too, is well versed in the arts of amorous conquest—the tantalizing smiles, the coy refusals, the thousand feminine caprices which will ensnare a man's heart.

After the aria she wonders why Dr. Malatesta has not returned to tell her what progress he has made in his scheme to deceive Don Pasquale. At that moment a servant brings her a letter. She exclaims as she recognizes Ernesto's handwriting, then reads it with an expression of alarm and dismay. Just as she finishes, Malatesta hurries in to tell her that his plan is succeeding. Norina curtly interrupts him to say that she will have nothing further to do with the affair and then hands him Ernesto's letter, which Malatesta reads aloud in spoken tones. Ernesto writes that his heart is broken. That treacherous villain, Dr. Malatesta, has persuaded Don Pasquale to marry his sister, and as a consequence Pasquale has disinherited his nephew. He will leave Rome immediately, and Europe as soon as he can. He bids Norina farewell forever.

Malatesta dismisses Ernesto's lugubrious message with the remark that it is the usual ranting of a young lover. Ernesto, he says, will not leave Rome, much less Europe. Malatesta declares that he will go to Ernesto shortly and explain the whole scheme to him. When he hears it the young man will be only too happy to remain. In answer to Norina's questions Malatesta explains the details of his plot. When he realized that Pasquale was determined to marry, by way of punishing Ernesto for refusing to marry in accordance with his uncle's wishes, Malatesta decided to change his strategy. Instead of trying to dissuade Don Pasquale, he pretended to encourage him, knowing that this would eventually work to the advantage of Norina and Ernesto. Malatesta states that Pasquale knows that he has a sister in a convent. He proposes to pass off Norina, whom Pasquale has never seen, as his sister Sofronia and present her to Pasquale as his prospective bride. Pasquale, of course, will walk happily into the trap, once he has seen how beautiful Norina is. Malatesta's cousin, Carlotto, is to play the role of notary and perform the mock marriage ceremony. Once Don Pasquale is firmly caught in the bonds of matrimony, it will be Norina's duty to make life so miserable for him that he will do anything to escape. The rest, says Malatesta, will be easy. Norina is delighted with the scheme.

An amusing duet ensues in which Malatesta rehearses Norina in the role she is to play for Don Pasquale's benefit ("Pronta io son"). Norina promises that she will play her part to the utmost, provided it does not involve being unfaithful to Ernesto. Malatesta assures her that he is acting as Ernesto's friend and that this scheme is directed only against Don Pasquale. In a delightful interlude Malatesta instructs Norina how to act the role of a shy and innocent country girl in order to captivate Pasquale. The duet comes to a sparkling climax as Norina and Malatesta revel in the thought of taking revenge on the selfish and domineering Pasquale. As they hurry away the curtain falls.

ACT TWO

A room in Don Pasquale's home. Ernesto enters and disconsolately reflects on his sad fate. Disinherited, driven from home, deceived by his only friend, he is utterly without hope. To make his anguish complete, he must also part forever from Norina. Ernesto gives voice to his sadness in a dramatic aria ("Cercherò lontana terra"). He resolves to go to some distant land and there end his days in sorrow and silence. The memory of Norina will be his only consolation. Even if she gives her love to another, Ernesto declares in a mood of noble renunciation, he will never utter a word of rebuke against her. The realization that Norina is happy will sustain him in his loneliness and grief. Overcome by his emotions, Ernesto walks dejectedly out of the room.

Don Pasquale, splendidly attired, comes in, followed by a servant, to whom he gives the order that no one but Dr. Malatesta and his companion is to be admitted to the house. After dismissing the servant Pasquale swaggers up and down, admiring himself. Pretty good for a man of seventy, he murmurs, and then suddenly checks himself, looking around to make certain no one has heard him mention his age. Hearing footsteps outside, he rushes to the door and opens it.

Malatesta comes in with Norina, who is veiled, timidly following after him. The dialogue takes the form of a delightful trio ("Via da brava! Reggo appena"). Malatesta urges Norina to be brave, while she begs her "dear brother" not to leave her side. She pretends that she is about to faint from sheer fright. Malatesta gravely explains that his poor sister, being fresh from the convent, is naturally shy and confused. Gazing avidly at Norina, Don Pasquale expresses his approval of her gracious bearing and wonders if her face is equally as attractive. Norina, aside, murmurs that she will lead this aging cavalier a merry dance.

The trio is momentarily interrupted when Norina exclaims that she is afraid to be alone and wishes to leave at once. Malatesta assures her that he is nearby, and Don Pasquale as well. As though noticing Don Pasquale for the first time, Norina shrinks back in fear and implores Malatesta to take her away. Pasquale is enchanted by her timidity. At Malatesta's urging Norina curtsies to Don Pasquale. He bows low and then brings forward three chairs. Malatesta seats himself, with Pasquale and Norina on either side.

When Pasquale refers to Norina's veil Malatesta tells him that the young lady would never think of speaking to a man with her face uncovered. He suggests that Don Pasquale converse with her for a few moments, after which, if he still approves, the lady might be persuaded to remove her veil. After a bad beginning Pasquale asks Norina if she likes company and cares about the theater. In the convent, Norina replies, she was always alone, and as for the theater, she does not even know what it means.

Highly pleased, Pasquale implores her to take off her veil. At a command from Malatesta she does so. Pasquale is so smitten with her beauty that he staggers back, gasping in surprise. Scarcely able to speak, he begs Malatesta to ask her if she finds Don Pasquale acceptable. After deliberately prolonging the suspense, Norina timidly answers yes. Pasquale is in transports of joy. When he tells Malatesta to send at once for a notary, the doctor answers that he took the liberty of bringing one along in the event he would be needed. He is waiting outside, he says, and then goes to fetch him.

Malatesta returns shortly with the notary, who seats himself at a table in the center of the room. Taking his place beside the public official, Malatesta begins dictating, in pompous legal terms liberally sprinkled with "et ceteras," the terms of the contract between Sofronia Malatesta and Pasquale da Corneto. Pasquale then takes up the dictation, stipulating that his bride is to have complete possession of all his property and is to be absolute mistress of the house.

When the document is ready Don Pasquale hastily signs his name, while Malatesta leads Norina to the table to sign hers. The notary, looking around, declares that another witness will be necessary. At that moment Ernesto's voice is heard outside, angrily demanding to be allowed to see his uncle. After a moment he bursts in and strides over to Don Pasquale, ignoring Norina and Malatesta, who both look at each other in dismay, realizing that Ernesto has not yet been told of the plot. Ernesto heatedly explains that he came to say good-by and that the servants tried to turn him away like a common beggar.

Pasquale answers that although Ernesto has interrupted important business he has come just in time to serve as witness. With that he calls to Norina, who steps forward. Seeing her, Ernesto gapes in astonishment and then, recovering, is consumed with anger. On the pretext of trying to calm him Malatesta takes him aside, assures him that what is happening is all for his own good, and warns him not to lose his temper ("Ah, figliol, non mi far scene"). From this point on the dialogue continues in the form of a lively quartet. Norina is panic-stricken at the thought that Ernesto, in his rage, may give away the plot. Ernesto cries that this confusion will drive him mad, while Malatesta implores him to believe that this is a scheme to outwit his uncle. Don Pasquale complacently observes that perhaps he may deal more gently with his nephew now that he has been put in his place. As the notary joins the hands of Norina and Don Pasquale, Malatesta leads Ernesto to the table. Still angry and suspicious, he signs the document as witness.

No sooner is the ceremony complete than Norina's manner changes. When Pasquale tries to embrace her she pushes him gently but firmly away. Ernesto laughs at his uncle's embarrassment. The latter furiously orders him out of the house. Norina interrupts to inform Don Pasquale that she will not tolerate such bad manners. As Pasquale gasps at her impudence, she goes on to say that, in view of the fact that Pasquale is much too old to escort her when she goes walking, she has decided to retain Ernesto as her companion.

When Don Pasquale splutters with anger Norina warns him that she is losing patience and will soon resort to other means to enforce her authority.

Pasquale backs away at her threatening gesture. Malatesta tries to calm him, while Ernesto exclaims that at last he is beginning to see the meaning of the plot. Suddenly Norina orders all the servants brought before her. When a major-domo and two servants appear Norina remarks disdainfully that at least the present staff of servants can easily be counted. Informing the major-domo that his salary will be doubled, she orders him to engage new servants at once. They must be young and handsome—about twenty-four will do for the present. Pasquale groans that he will be ruined.

Cutting short his protests, Norina imperturbably continues: There must be two new carriages, eight horses for harness, two for saddle; the house must be reorganized and new furniture purchased. There are a thousand other things, but they can be attended to tomorrow. There is one more item, however, Norina adds, silencing the raging Pasquale with a gesture. Dinner for fifty is to be served promptly at four o'clock. Malatesta and Ernesto, hugely enjoying the situation, remark that the first domestic storm is gathering more swiftly than was expected.

Pasquale demands to know who is to pay for all these commitments. When Norina gives him the obvious answer a violent quarrel ensues over whose word has authority in the house. Pasquale blusters in vain and roars that he has been victimized. Norina, coming close to Ernesto, assures him that it is for his sake that she and Malatesta are taking these stringent measures against Pasquale. Ernesto joyfully replies that all his doubts about her have vanished and then comments with great satisfaction over his uncle's plight. Maneuvering himself between the lovers and Don Pasquale, Malatesta warns them in an aside to restrain their ardor for each other in Pasquale's presence, lest they betray the plot. With the expression of these sentiments the quartet is brought to a vigorous climax and the curtain falls.

ACT THREE

[*Scene One*] A room in Don Pasquale's home, with Norina's apartment adjoining. The room is a confusion of hats, dresses, shawls, shoes, robes, gowns, and other articles of feminine apparel. Don Pasquale, seated at a desk in the midst of the disorder, glares at a huge pile of bills. There is a brief chorus by the servants as they crowd into the room to take the purchases in to Norina. They repeat their orders as relayed by Norina's maid, who stands in the doorway ("I diamanti, presto"). There is much excitement and rushing about until the servants, urging each other to hurry, bustle away on other duties.

Don Pasquale begins adding up the bills, but the staggering totals cause him to lose his temper completely. Tossing the bills into the air, he consigns all this frippery to the devil. He reflects angrily on the fact that he has failed to assert his authority as a husband and resolves to make one more attempt to conquer Norina.

While he is thinking things over Norina hurries out of her apartment and sweeps through the room without even a glance at Pasquale. She is dressed in replendent finery and carries a fan. Controlling himself as best he can, Pasquale quietly asks her where she is going ("Signorina, in tanta fretta").

His words introduce a long duet during which Norina stages another show of temperament to bedevil poor Pasquale. Norina tells him that she is going to the theater, whereupon he rushes to the door and tries to prevent her from leaving. Pasquale makes an insulting remark and Norina retaliates by slapping his face. Outraged, Pasquale fumes that the limit has been reached and that there is nothing left for him to do but hang or drown himself. Norina somewhat regrets having resorted to a blow but observes, aside, that harsh tactics are necessary at the moment in order to ensure the success of the plot.

Again starting for the door, Norina announces she is going. Pasquale tells her not to come back, warning her that she will find the door locked. With malicious sweetness Norina reminds Pasquale that she is young and full of life and cannot be expected to remain always at home. She advises him to heed his years and go to bed, adding that she will return in time to wake him early. At this barbed reference to his age Pasquale storms for a divorce, shouting that anything is better than marriage to a quarrelsome woman.

After the climax of the duet Norina trips gaily out of the room, dropping a letter as she goes. Muttering that it is probably another dressmaker's bill, Pasquale picks it up and begins reading. His jaw drops when he discovers that it is a note to "Dearest Sofronia" from a lover, asking her to meet him at the secret entrance to the garden between nine and ten o'clock that very night. He writes that he will announce his presence with a serenade. Raging that Sofronia is surely trying to drive him mad, Pasquale rings for the servants and sends them off to Dr. Malatesta with the message that he is desperately ill. Wringing his hands, Pasquale staggers from the room.

The servants now come in and sing a pleasing chorus in which they gossip about the exciting events that have taken place since their master has taken a wife ("Che interminabile andirivieni"). There is no end to the confusion and running about, they exclaim, and not a moment's rest from answering bells. It is all worth while, however, because money is plentiful in the household and there are abundant opportunities for lining one's pockets. They go on chattering about the quarrel between Master and Madame at dinner on the matter of going to the theater. It is obvious, they remark, whose word is law in the house. They comment that the handsome young nephew is probably up to some mischief. The chorus ends as the servants warn each other to be cautious and on the alert, so that they may continue to enjoy the advantages of working in this fine house.

After they leave, Malatesta and Ernesto appear, discussing how Ernesto is to play his part at the rendezvous in the garden. They agree that as soon as Malatesta appears with Pasquale, Ernesto is to vanish. Hearing Pasquale approaching, Ernesto hurries away. Malatesta assumes a grave, professional air as Don Pasquale comes in, pale and distraught. Moaning and shaking his head, he goes into a long recital of his woes. He would rather have married Ernesto off to two thousand Norinas than endure this torture, he wails. She has spent half his fortune, flounced off to the theater in defiance of his orders, boxed his ears, and—to cap the climax—she is planning a rendezvous in his own garden with a lover. With that he hands the letter to Malatesta, who pretends to be shocked as he reads it.

Pasquale swears he will get his revenge and explains his plan in an ensuing duet ("Cheti, cheti, immantinenti"). He and Malatesta, accompanied by the servants, will surround the lovers in the garden and surprise them in an embrace. Before they can recover themselves and escape they will be carted off to face the magistrate.

As diplomatically as possible Malatesta proposes his own plan. He reminds Pasquale that Sofronia is, after all, his sister and Pasquale's wife, and that there is nothing to be gained by shouting this scandal from the housetops. He suggests that he and Pasquale go into the garden alone, surprise his wife and her lover, and then threaten to expose the entire affair in court. Faced by the possibility of public disgrace, they will most certainly agree to end their romance.

But Pasquale protests that such a punishment is not harsh enough. If his wife is guilty, he declares, she must leave his house forever. Malatesta then proposes that Pasquale agree to send her away at once if she is proved guilty and to give him, Malatesta, carte blanche in handling the situation from that point on. The plan meets with Pasquale's wholehearted approval. The duet comes to a highly comic climax as the two express their sentiments in rapid-fire patter. Pasquale gloats that his turn for revenge is coming and that his wife will be paid for her highhanded impudence. Malatesta comments, aside, that Pasquale will be neatly caught in his own trap.

[*Scene Two*] The garden of Don Pasquale's home. At one side, steps lead into the house. At the other is a summerhouse. Ernesto is heard singing his serenade—"Com' è gentil," one of the most famous numbers of the opera —to the accompaniment of a guitar. It is a typical Italian serenade in which the impassioned lover, inspired by the soft April night, sings of his longing for his "Nina" and assures her that he will die if she does not come to him. A chorus sings answering phrases and joins in the conclusion of the serenade.

A moment later Norina tiptoes out of the summerhouse and goes to the garden gate. She opens it, admitting Ernesto, who drops the long cloak he is wearing. He and Norina sing an exquisite duet ("Tornami a dir che m'ami"), in which they pour out their longing and love for each other. As the duet ends, Don Pasquale and Malatesta are seen approaching with lanterns. At Norina's warning Ernesto picks up his cloak and moves toward Pasquale's house. Norina starts to run away, screaming in pretended terror. Rushing after her, Pasquale seizes her, flashes the lantern full in her face, and demands to know where her lover is. Norina denies that anyone has been with her. Pasquale rages that he will find the guilty man and begins searching through the shrubbery, with the tentative assistance of Malatesta. Ernesto, meanwhile, slips quietly into the house.

His search unsuccessful, Pasquale again confronts Norina. He rails at her for her brazen deceit and tells her that she is to leave his house at once. Norina saucily reminds him that the house is hers. At this juncture Malatesta steps forward and asks Pasquale to let him handle the situation, reminding him of his agreement. There is an amusing byplay between Norina and Malatesta as he tells her, in asides, what emotion she is to register. She is properly dismayed and then enraged when he tells her that another bride will enter Don Pasquale's house tomorrow. Acting her part with convincing fury, Norina demands to know whose bride the newcomer is. When Malatesta announces that she is Ernesto's bride, Norina, she speaks with scorn and contempt of this designing widow. Pasquale, hearing only the part of the conversation intended for his ears, gleefully voices his approval of the way things are going.

Norina declares that rather than live under one roof with the bride of Ernesto she will leave at once. Pasquale utters an exclamation of joy. But suddenly Norina becomes suspicious. Perhaps, she observes, this marriage is only a trick, adding that she will wait to find out for herself. Turning to Pasquale, Malatesta tells him that unless his wife can be convinced that Norina and Ernesto are actually married she obviously will never leave the house. Thereupon he calls Ernesto and informs him that his uncle has given his consent to his marriage with Norina and will grant him an annual income of four thousand scudi besides.

Scarcely believing his ears, Ernesto asks Pasquale if the good news is true. Malatesta, with a meaningful glance at the supposed Sofronia, warns Pasquale that there is no time for hesitation. For the sake of effect Norina protests the marriage, bringing an immediate assent from Pasquale, who asks that the bride be brought forth at once. Saying that she is already here, Malatesta leads Norina to him. Dumfounded, Pasquale asks where Sofronia is, and Malatesta answers that she is still in the convent.

The bewildered Pasquale then asks Malatesta why he arranged the marriage between him and Norina. Simply because, replies Malatesta, shrugging his shoulders, Don Pasquale was determined to wed. By staging a mock ceremony, Malatesta continues, he has prevented Pasquale from making the mistake—at his age—of actually marrying. While Pasquale denounces them all as traitors, Ernesto and Norina kneel before him and beg him to relent. Pasquale struggles with himself for a moment and then clasps the lovers in his arms.

Malatesta's words of approval of Don Pasquale's magnanimity and good sense ("Bravo, bravo, Don Pasquale") introduce the brilliant finale of the opera. In it the four principals point the moral of the story: The man who takes a young wife in his old age is inviting nothing but trouble and confusion—as Don Pasquale most obligingly has proved. Thus all is well as the curtain falls.

Elektra

by RICHARD STRAUSS

[1864–1949]

Libretto by
HUGO von HOFMANNSTHAL

Based on the tragedies of Sophocles, Euripides, and Aeschylus

CHARACTERS

Five serving maids..........................	{ One contralto / Two mezzo-sopranos / Two sopranos
A woman overseer...	Soprano
Elektra ⎱ daughters of Clytemnestra..................	{ Soprano
Chrysothemis ⎰ and Agamemnon	{ Soprano
Clytemnestra	Mezzo-soprano
Confidante	Soprano
Trainbearer	Soprano
Young servant	Tenor
Old servant	Bass
Orestes, brother of Elektra and Chrysothemis..................	Baritone
Preceptor of Orestes...	Bass
Aegisthus, lover of Clytemnestra.............................	Tenor

Servants

Place: Mycenae
Time: Antiquity
First performance: Hofoper, Dresden, January 25, 1909
Original language: German

IN ELEKTRA Strauss has set to music one of the great legends immortalized by the ancient Greek dramatists. As in the case of his other operas, this work is completely unique in approach and treatment. The music, with its harsh, powerful dissonances, is an integral part of the dramatic action and in many instances is as vital a motivating force as the utterances of the characters themselves. Strauss employs a large number of leading motives in highly complicated forms. The opera makes the most exacting demands on the singers, for with the exception of a few passages of extraordinary lyricism the score is devoid of melodic line in the conventional sense. The entire action of *Elektra* takes place in one act and in one scene.

The interior court of the palace of Agamemnon in Mycenae. At one side are the servants' quarters, at the rear is the palace. In one corner of the court is a well, from which five serving maids are drawing water under the direction of a woman overseer. It is evening. When the curtain rises, the powerful motive of King Agamemnon sounds in the orchestra.

As they work at the well the maids talk among themselves. One inquires after Elektra. Another remarks that this is the hour when she usually laments over her father in tones that echo through the palace. Elektra suddenly appears out of the shadow of a doorway, looks wildly around, then cowers back out of sight, hiding her face with her arm. The maids, who have been apprehensively watching her, relate that when they encounter Elektra she turns on them, snarling and spitting like a cat. She shouts at them to leave her in peace, mingling her incoherent raving with unspeakable insults.

A maid remarks that she cannot understand why the Queen allows this creature to roam about the palace. Another exclaims that if Elektra were her daughter she would keep her under lock and key. One of the others, however, observes that Elektra's lot is hard enough—what with being forced to eat with the dogs and suffering unmerciful beatings at the hands of Aegisthus.

The youngest of the maids startles the others by declaring that she longs to kneel before Elektra, anoint her feet, and dry them with her hair ("Ich will vor ihr mich niederwerfen"). When the overseer roughly pushes her aside and orders her to go within, the maid shouts that though Elektra is forced to live in degradation, clad in beggar's rags, she is the daughter of a king. Not one of those who revile this daughter of Agamemnon, the maid says defiantly, has the courage to face her. The overseer angrily pushes the maid to the door of the servants' quarters. Clinging to the door, the girl screams back to the others that they are not fit to breathe the air Elektra breathes. May they all hang, she rages, for their cruelty and injustice toward her. Struggling with the maid, the overseer finally succeeds in closing the door on her. She exclaims indignantly over the girl's effrontery in daring to defend Elektra, who treats them all like dogs.

One of the other maids says that Elektra has often told them that even dogs would shun the work they are forced to do—endlessly trying to wipe the stains of murder from the palace floor. Elektra speaks of the sin that no water can wash away, another adds. And when she sees the children of the servants, the overseer declares, she reviles them as unclean progeny spawned in a house of murder. Taking up their water jugs, the maids, followed by the overseer, go into the servants' quarters. A moment later the air resounds with the shrieks of the young maid, who is being beaten for defending Elektra.

With the furtive movements of a hunted animal Elektra steals into the deserted court. Obsessed by thoughts of her father, she recalls, in an intensely dramatic soliloquy, the gruesome details of his murder by Aegisthus and her mother ("Allein! Weh, ganz allein. Der Vater fort hinab"). In tones of wild entreaty she calls her father's name, then muses that it was at this very hour her mother and Aegisthus slew Agamemnon in his bath and dragged his naked body away. The eyes that then stared wide in death, she goes on, will once again look upon the guilty pair. With feverish intensity Elektra prays that the avenging spirit of Agamemnon may soon return in triumph to pronounce judgment on the murderers. In that hour of reckoning she will lead the King's horses and his hunting dogs to his tomb as sacrificial thank offerings. She and her sister and Orestes, knowing that the task of vengeance is at last accomplished, will dance in joy. Elektra exults that she herself will leap upon the tomb and dance there in honor of her father. The soliloquy ends with her triumphant cry of "Agamemnon."

As Elektra stands transfixed by her dream of revenge Chrysothemis appears at the door of the palace and softly calls to her sister. Recoiling in momentary fear, Elektra recovers herself and harshly asks Chrysothemis why she has come. When Chrysothemis involuntarily raises her arms before her face in a gesture of protection Elektra cries that it was thus her father raised his arms to ward off the murderer's blows. Shaking with fear, Chrysothemis exclaims that Clytemnestra and Aegisthus are plotting to imprison Elektra in a dungeon.

With a wild laugh Elektra answers that she already knows their evil plans. One does not need to listen secretly at a door to hear these things, she goes on, because the voices of murder and treachery cry aloud in the palace. Beside herself with terror, Chrysothemis wails that she can find no rest because of the torment of her fears. It is Elektra herself, she says, who keeps her imprisoned in this terrible place ("Du bist es, die mit Eisenklammern mich an den Boden schmiedet"). Were it not that Elektra's sleepless hatred keeps the others constantly on their guard, Chrysothemis goes on, she could escape and find the happiness of love and the joy of holding a child in her arms.

When Elektra looks scornfully at her Chrysothemis asks what purpose is served by this endless vigil for revenge. Agamemnon is dead, Orestes is lost —no message about their brother ever comes. Meanwhile she and Elektra, keeping their grim and futile watch within the palace walls, grow older day by day. The fires of hatred consume their youth and beauty. The world outside waits to offer them the precious heritage of womankind—sunshine and singing and the laughter of children. Weeping bitterly, Chrysothemis declares that death is better than this sordid existence.

Elektra contemptuously orders her to be silent. Hearing the sound of excited voices in the palace, she sardonically remarks that the shouting perhaps heralds a birth—or another death. Chrysothemis frantically warns her to leave. Clytemnestra is approaching with death in her eyes, for she has dreamed of Orestes and fear has made her a demon. Staring at the palace, Elektra murmurs that she must speak to her mother. Chrysothemis flees in terror.

An eerie procession is visible through the windows of the palace, which are lighted by the glare of torches. There is a thunder of hoofs and the cracking of whips as animals are driven to the altars for the sacrifice which Clytemnestra has ordered to appease the gods. Then Clytemnestra herself appears at a large window, her swollen features livid in the gleam of the torches. Her eyes are abnormally large and heavy-lidded, and she seems scarcely able to keep them open. She is clad in a purple gown, and her arms and hands glitter with bracelets, amulets, and rings—worn as talismans to ward off evil. Partly supporting herself with an ivory cane set with gems, she leans on the arm of her confidante. Her trainbearer is an exotic, yellow-faced woman whose black hair is drawn tightly back from her forehead, giving her a serpentine appearance.

As Elektra draws herself up to her full height and gazes steadily at the Queen, Clytemnestra suddenly opens her eyes and glares at her daughter. In mingled fear and rage she cries to the gods, upbraiding them for having afflicted her with this strange child whose very look oppresses her. Elektra asks why she storms at the gods, when she herself is a goddess. The confidante and the trainbearer whisper that Elektra is mocking the Queen. Coming closer, Elektra says that she wishes to speak to her mother, but not in the presence of the two despicable creatures who fill her ears with malice and lies.

Turning on the confidante and the trainbearer, Clytemnestra furiously denounces them for their spiteful, venomous gossiping ("Ich will nichts hören!"). They are but the echo of the depraved Aegisthus, she fumes, tormenting her with stories of demons and birds of prey that wait to devour her. Even while they babble that they are speaking the truth, Clytemnestra rages, they incite her to kill and destroy. Growing calmer, the Queen murmurs that she longs to hear words of truth—words that would solace her tortured spirit. Curtly dismissing her attendants, Clytemnestra leaves the window, comes out of the palace, and descends to the court.

A long and dramatic colloquy ensues as she faces Elektra, half hidden in the shadows ("Ich habe keine guten Nächte"). In a voice edged with panic the Queen says that she can no longer sleep in peace. It is because of a terrible dream, against which she has found no protection. Perhaps Elektra, who is wise and knows many things, will tell her how that dream may be dispelled. It is vague and elusive, she goes on, like a shadow in the night, but her fear of it is consuming her like a loathsome disease. Every night at a certain hour she wakes and seems to see, behind the curtains of the bed, a human eye that fixes her with a baleful stare. Surely there must be some sacrifice, animal or human, the blood of which will exorcise this demon.

When the right blood flows, Elektra says slowly, that demon will vanish. Clytemnestra asks if the cleansing blood will be that of a pure animal. An impure animal, Elektra replies with a strange laugh. Terror-stricken by Elektra's mysterious manner, the Queen desperately entreats her to explain her words. The sacrificial offering will be a woman, Elektra says finally, and the ritual will be performed by a man—a stranger, yet one who is known in the palace. When Clytemnestra, somewhat reassured by Elektra's calm demeanor, begs her to explain further, Elektra suddenly asks if she will allow Orestes to return. Clytemnestra starts in surprise. Recovering herself, she says that she has forbidden his return because Orestes, badly treated by those entrusted with his care, has lost his reason. She tried to bribe the boy's guardians to give him the care due a king's son, she adds, but her efforts were in vain.

Elektra accuses her mother of lying and says that the money was sent to persuade the guardians to murder the boy. She declares that she knows Orestes is alive and that Clytemnestra lives in deadly fear of his return. With an attempt at asserting her authority Clytemnestra says that she alone is mistress of the palace and reminds Elektra that she is well guarded against any treachery. She warns her daughter that she will force her to name the sacrificial victim by chaining her in a dungeon and starving her into submission. Suddenly remembering the dream that haunts her, the Queen groans that she must know whose blood can be shed to free her from torment.

At those words Elektra leaps toward Clytemnestra, screaming that it is from the Queen's own veins that the sacrificial blood will flow ("Was bluten muss? Dein eigenes Genick"). In ferocious ecstasy Elektra describes how the avenger will relentlessly follow her into the palace, into her very bedroom. She will flee screaming from room to room, down the great stairs, through the shadowy arches of the hallways, with Elektra and the avenger drawing closer and closer. At last she will fall, only to look up and see the eyes of her murdered husband gazing into her own.

But before the ax falls there will be an awful moment when, like all evil-doers about to die, Clytemnestra will relive all the anguish she has ever known—an eternity of torment compressed into the final second of life. Then the ax will descend. The vile dream will be over, the evil destroyed forever. The horror will be lifted from her own soul, Elektra cries, and she and all other living things can once more shout for joy.

The fearsome prophecy leaves Clytemnestra choking and gasping for breath. As she shrinks away from her daughter the confidante hurriedly appears and whispers to the Queen. A look of bewilderment crosses her face, but in the next instant it gives way to an expression of gloating triumph. Servants crowd about carrying torches, which brilliantly illuminate the scene. The pantomimed movements of the crowd indicate that the message delivered to Clytemnestra is being repeated at her command. The significance of the message is indicated by the motive of Orestes which dominates the orchestral accompaniment to this scene. No word is spoken. With a menacing gesture toward Elektra, Clytemnestra turns and rushes into the palace, followed by her retinue.

Staring after her, Elektra wonders what news could have caused her mother to rejoice. Chrysothemis now comes running madly into the court, shrieking that Orestes is dead. Stunned, Elektra murmurs that it is not true. Chrysothemis gasps that two messengers, an old man and a youth, appeared at the palace gates and told everyone the story. Orestes perished in a distant land, trampled to death by his own horses. Elektra and Chrysothemis, overwhelmed by despair, sink to their knees.

A young servant rushes in, excitedly calling to an old servant, who is following him, to saddle a horse immediately. He must ride at once to Aegisthus with an important message. As the two servants hurry away Elektra rises slowly to her feet. Now they must act—at once—she tells Chrysothemis in tones of suppressed excitement. Chrysothemis stares at her without understanding. As Orestes will never return, Elektra goes on, they themselves must slay Clytemnestra and Aegisthus. She confides that she has secured the ax with which her father was murdered and concealed it, so that it would be ready for Orestes when he returned. She herself will wield the ax, Elektra says, but Chrysothemis must remain near to help her.

Chrysothemis shrinks back in horror. Caressing her arms, Elektra praises their youthful strength and vigor ("Wie stark du bist!"). In sensuous tones she admires the beauty of Chrysothemis's supple body, singing that it is endowed with irresistible power that can crush and destroy. Chrysothemis tries to escape, but Elektra beseeches her to help, promising to serve her in the future as sister and slave in return for her aid. Kneeling before her, Elektra repeats her entreaties with terrible insistence. She attempts to force Chrysothemis to swear that she will meet her in the palace that very night to consummate the murder. Struggling fiercely, Chrysothemis frees herself and escapes into the palace as Elektra wildly curses her.

Murmuring that she will go alone, Elektra begins creeping stealthily along the wall toward the palace. At a spot near the door she stops and begins digging for the ax with her hands, occasionally pausing to look around and listen carefully. As she continues to dig, the young messenger (who is Orestes in disguise) appears in the doorway of the palace, his figure silhouetted against the twilight glow that shines through the windows.

Elektra looks up and springs to her feet. With angry impatience she asks whom he is seeking. The young man replies that he must wait until he is called by the Queen. He and his companion, he says, are bringing her the news of the death of her son Orestes. They themselves saw him perish under the hoofs of his horses. He was the same age as Orestes and his closest friend, the messenger adds.

In poignant phrases Elektra laments that this messenger of woe has come to her with his tidings ("Muss ich dich denn noch sehn?"). Why does he not go to those who would be gladdened by the news? This youth lives, Elektra goes on, while Orestes—a hundred times more noble, a hundred times more deserving of life—is dead. The messenger quietly answers that Orestes loved life too much, and so the jealous gods deprived him of it.

The intensity of Elektra's grief prompts the youth to ask if she is a kin of Orestes and Agamemnon. She is indeed of their blood, she replies. She is Elektra, daughter of Agamemnon. Shaking his head in disbelief, Orestes comes closer, looking at Elektra with intense concentration. Then, realizing that she is his sister, he exclaims in compassion over her pitiful appearance. Elektra recoils under his gaze, imploring him not to look at her beggarly rags.

Drawing close to her, he whispers that Orestes is not dead. He swears by the body of his father, for which, he says, he came here. Her eyes fixed on his face, Elektra asks who he is. At that moment, the old servant, followed by several others, silently approaches. He kneels in homage before Orestes, while the others clasp his hands and his robe. As Elektra staggers back in surprise, Orestes says that though even the hounds of the palace knew him his own sister did not.

Then follows what is known as the *Recognition Scene,* the lyrical climax of the opera. Elektra slowly comes toward Orestes, softly calling his name and then exclaiming in wonder because the figure before her does not vanish like a dream ("Orest! Es rührt sich niemand!"). Passionately she sings that if he is only an illusion he must not go without taking her with him or granting her the release of death. Orestes tries to embrace her, but she repulses him, looking down at her body in shame and disgust. She cries that she is but a sorry shadow of the proud daughter of a king. She was beautiful once—worshiped and desired by all men. But beauty, modesty, virtue— all the attributes of womanhood—were consumed by the fires of revenge.

Her father's spirit imposed upon her the solemn duty of vengeance, and she has lived for that alone.

In exultant phrases Orestes sings that he will take upon himself the task of revenge. Elektra's voice rises in savage ecstasy as she hails Orestes as the man destined to accomplish the work of destruction. They are startled when someone rushes toward them from the palace. It is Orestes's Preceptor, the old man who has come with him in the guise of another messenger. He warns them to be silent, saying that a chance word or false move will undo all their plans. Then he tells Orestes that the Queen is waiting to see the messengers.

The confidante appears, accompanied by a maid carrying a torch. Bowing to the two men, the confidante gestures them to follow her. Orestes shudders with horror as he and the Preceptor go into the palace. Thrusting the torch into an iron ring on the outside of the door, the maid goes in, closing the door after her.

Elektra, wringing her hands, paces back and forth. Suddenly she stops and cries out in a frenzy that she did not have time to give the ax to Orestes. Over the demoniac music of the orchestra comes the piercing shriek of Clytemnestra. Madly screaming to Orestes to strike again, Elektra rushes to the door and stands leaning against it.

Chrysothemis, followed by the serving maids, rushes across the court. In agitated choral phrases the women cry that Elektra is screaming in her sleep—that men have broken into the palace—that assassins have attacked. They halt before the palace door, gazing in terror at Elektra. As they beg her to open the door one of the maids cries out that Aegisthus is approaching. He will kill them all, she wails, if anything has gone amiss in the palace. Panic-stricken, Chrysothemis and the women flee to the servants' quarters.

Aegisthus strides across the court, calling for torches to light his way. Taking the torch from the ring in the door, Elektra runs to meet him. Halting in surprise as she bows before him, Aegisthus exclaims over the strange apparition in his path. Recognizing the figure as Elektra, he asks about the messengers who arrived with the news of Orestes's death. They are now with the Queen, Elektra replies. Aegisthus asks if what they say is really true—that Orestes is dead. The evidence they present in support of their words, Elektra says, proves beyond doubt that they speak the truth.

Aroused to suspicion by the ominous calm in her voice, Aegisthus asks why she speaks to him in these strange tones. She has finally become wise, Elektra answers mysteriously, and has aligned herself with those who are strongest. Thereupon she begs to be permitted to light his way. Torch in hand, she starts toward the door of the palace, then begins moving around Aegisthus in a sinister dance. Reaching the threshold, Aegisthus recoils at the darkness and in a shaking voice asks who the shadowy figures are within the palace. Those who wait to welcome him, Elektra replies. Aegisthus goes inside. A moment later he appears at a window, screaming for help and asking if there is no one to hear him. Agamemnon hears, Elektra shouts fiercely. As the body of Aegisthus is dragged away from the window the curtain clutched in his hand is torn down.

Chrysothemis and the maids run back into the court. Approaching Elektra, Chrysothemis tells her that Orestes is in the palace and that those who have remained loyal to him are rallying to his aid. From within the palace come the sounds of a fierce struggle between the followers of Orestes and those of Aegisthus. Orestes's name is shouted like a battle cry. As the uproar subsides the serving-women rush away, leaving Chrysothemis alone with Elektra, who crouches on the threshold.

When Chrysothemis asks if she hears the sounds of triumph, Elektra, in mad exultation, answers that she hears only the music that comes from within herself ("Ob ich nicht höre? Ob ich die Musik nicht höre?"). She must dance to this music, she says—dance for the thousand triumphant torchbearers who are approaching. But she cannot dance, she moans, for her body is submerged in an ocean of weariness.

Struggling to rise, Elektra, lost in madness, shouts that they are one with the gods ("Wir sind bei den Göttern"). Her words mark the beginning of a brief but fiery duet. The voices of the sisters blend in ringing phrases as they rejoice over the new life that has begun for them through the final act of revenge accomplished by Orestes.

Crying that she must go to embrace her brother, Chrysothemis rushes into the palace. Elektra descends to the court and begins a strange, erotic dance. Chrysothemis reappears, with men and women crowding behind her. She calls to Elektra, who stops and stares at her with unseeing eyes. Then, as though hypnotized, Elektra resumes her dance, calling on all to be silent and join her ("Schweig' und tanze! Alle müssen herbei!"). After a few wild gyrations she falls lifeless. Chrysothemis kneels at her side, looks intently into her face, then runs to the palace door. Pounding on the door, she frantically calls for Orestes. As the Agamemnon motive reverberates in the orchestra, the curtain falls.

L'Elisir d'Amore

by GAETANO DONIZETTI

[1797–1848]

Libretto by
FELICE ROMANI

Based on the French comedy
LE PHILTRE

CHARACTERS

Nemorino, a young peasant.....................................*Tenor*
Adina, a wealthy village girl...............................*Soprano*
Belcore, a sergeant..*Baritone*
Gianetta, a peasant girl......................................*Soprano*
Dulcamara, an itinerant quack doctor...........................*Bass*
Villagers, soldiers, peasants, a notary

Place: An Italian village
Time: Nineteenth century
First performance: Milan, May 12, 1832
Original language: Italian

L'ELISIR D'AMORE, a product of the middle period of Donizetti's creative years, stands with *Don Pasquale* as an example of brilliant *opera buffa*. In addition to its wealth of ingratiating melody, it is especially noteworthy for the character of Dr. Dulcamara, one of the great comedy figures of the operatic stage.

ACT ONE

[*Scene One*] The lawn of Adina's farmhouse on one of her estates near the village. A river, with pleasant open country beyond, is visible in the background. Gathered under a shade tree are Adina, Gianetta, and a group of peasants. Adina is reading a book. It is noon of a fine summer day, and the peasants have come in from the harvest field to rest for a time in the shade. Nemorino is seen standing some distance away, gazing longingly at Adina, with whom he is hopelessly in love. The peasants sing of the pleasure of spending a restful hour in the cool shade ("Bel conforto al meditore").

The chorus is interrupted while Nemorino pours out his adoration for Adina in a melodious aria ("Quanto è bella"). He laments that while Adina is clever and beautiful, he is only a doltish peasant who has neither the wit nor the courage to tell her how much he loves her. The final phrases of his aria blend with the voices of the peasants as they resume their chorus.

Looking up from her book, Adina exclaims over the strange and amusing adventure about which she has been reading. The peasants urge her to read it to them. As Nemorino ventures nearer to listen, Adina reads the story of Tristan and Isolde ("Della crudele Isotta"). It is the familiar tale of how the cruel Isolde spurned Tristan's love and how Tristan finally obtained a love potion from an old sorcerer. When Isolde drank the potion her indifference was instantly changed to burning passion. Adina, Nemorino, and the peasants comment in chorus over this wonderful potion and express the wish that they could find someone who could prepare it for them.

After the chorus, military music is heard in the distance, and soon Sergeant Belcore marches in at the head of a company of soldiers garrisoned in the village. Swaggering up to Adina, he presents her with a bouquet of flowers and, with an air of doing her a great favor, he declares that they are a token of his love. Adina and the women laughingly comment on the sergeant's modesty. Belcore remarks to himself that he seems to be making an impression on Adina—which, of course, is only to be expected, for no woman could resist a handsome officer like himself.

When he asks Adina to surrender to his love, she replies that she is not one to rush hastily into romance. In a vigorous aria ("Più tempo, oh Dio, non perdere") Belcore reminds her that in love, as in battle, delay is dangerous. He loftily advises her to accept his love while this golden opportunity is at hand. Adina laughs at his conceit, while Nemorino, watching from a distance, envies Belcore's overpowering self-confidence in wooing. The peasants sing that Adina is far too clever for Belcore.

At the conclusion of the chorus Belcore asks Adina if his men may rest awhile in the shade. Adina graciously gives her permission, adding that she will give the soldiers some wine. Highly pleased, Belcore murmurs that he is already one of the family. The peasants go back to their work in the fields.

Nemorino hesitantly approaches Adina and asks permission to speak. Sighing that it will be the same sad story again, Adina tells him that, instead of mooning about, he had better go into town and visit his uncle, who is said to be very ill. Nemorino answers that his uncle cannot possibly be suffering as much as he is. He tells Adina that he cannot bear to leave her. She asks what he will do if his uncle dies without leaving him any money. When Nemorino answers that he has no use for money, Adina warns him that he probably will die of hunger. Nemorino sighs that he may as well die of hunger as of love.

Completely losing patience with him, Adina declares that while she prefers his modesty and shyness to Belcore's brash conceit, she is not interested in his love at the moment. Her heart is fancy-free, she says. When Nemorino asks why she is so changeable, she replies in a brilliant refrain ("Chiedi all'aura lusinghiera"), which leads into a long duet. One may as well ask the flowers or the breeze why they change, Adina tells him. A maiden's heart is responsive to every caprice, and her affections veer like the wind. He must give up any thought of ever winning her, she goes on. Nemorino implores her to believe that he can never change, for like the river flows always to the sea, so his affections must find their way to her heart. He can never love anyone but her. Adina tells him that the best cure for his present suffering is to find someone else to love. Change, she assures him, is the best remedy for heartache. Reiterating these sentiments, the two bring the duet to a brilliant close.

[*Scene Two*]   The village square. Sounds of a trumpet are heard in the distance. Hurrying into the square, the villagers look off down the road and, in an excited chorus, exclaim over the magnificent carriage which is approaching ("Che vuol dire cotesta sonata?"). They marvel over the impressive appearance of its occupant, saying that he probably is a baron—or perhaps a marquis. They draw back in awe as the splendid green-and-gold carriage of Dr. Dulcamara drives up. With a majestic flourish Dulcamara stands in the carriage and addresses the crowd in the famous aria "Udite, udite, o rustici." He introduces himself as the greatest medical genius of his age, renowned throughout the universe—and elsewhere—for his remedies.

In rapid-fire patter he goes on to enumerate the virtues of his medicine. It will cure everything from toothache to epilepsy, restore old men to youthful vigor, erase the wrinkles in the cheeks of matrons, and make fair young maidens even fairer. It has been known to relieve a widow of her sorrows and to alleviate the sufferings of lonely hearts. Dulcamara tells his gaping audience that he has traveled a thousand miles for the sole purpose of bringing this miraculous remedy to his friends in his native village. He will make this priceless specific available to them, not for a hundred scudi—not for thirty—not for five—but at the very low price of *one* scudo!

A lively ensemble develops as the villagers crowd around to buy Dulcamara's fabulous cure-all ("Uno scudo! veramente?"). Marveling that this wonderful remedy is being sold so cheaply, they sing that the great Dulcamara will win everlasting fame for his beneficence. The doctor does a brisk business as the chorus comes to a climax. Clutching their bottles of Dulcamara's magic remedy, the peasants go to their homes.

Nemorino, who has meanwhile joined the crowd, now remains behind, timidly approaches Dulcamara, and asks him if he knows of the love potion that was taken by Queen Isolde. Dulcamara promptly informs him that he himself distills this magic stuff. He then shows Nemorino a bottle, which, of course, contains the same liquid he sells under the name of his miraculous cure-all—Bordeaux wine. When Nemorino asks the price, Dulcamara replies that it is ridiculously low for so valuable a concoction. Nemorino remarks that he has only one gold piece. The price exactly, says Dulcamara quickly. The doctor cautions him to shake it well before taking.

An amusing duet ensues as Nemorino fervently thanks Dulcamara for supplying him with the elixir that he believes will solve all his problems ("Obbligato, ah! si obbligato!"). While the gullible Nemorino continues to rejoice over his good fortune, Dulcamara observes, aside, that never in all his travels has he encountered a bigger dunce than this young man. When Nemorino asks him how the elixir is to be taken, Dulcamara gravely warns him that he must be careful not to allow any of the precious vapor to escape. As soon as he uncorks the bottle he must put it to his mouth and drink the stuff down. The elixir, however, will not take effect until the next day, he says, at which time, he adds under his breath, the great Dulcamara will be far away. He also gleefully remarks that he has made this ninny pay a fancy price for ordinary Bordeaux wine. He tells Nemorino not to tell anyone of his purchase, for Dr. Dulcamara has no wish to go to jail for selling love potions.

Nemorino swears he will keep the secret. In a sudden burst of confidence he tells the doctor that he is very much in love with a certain young lady of the village. Dulcamara wishes him all success in his romance. The duet comes to a sparkling climax as Nemorino happily sings that kind fate must have sent the good doctor to him at this crucial moment in his life, while Dulcamara complacently reflects that by the time the so-called elixir is scheduled to work its alleged magic he will be well beyond reach. At the close of the duet he shakes hands with Nemorino and leaves.

As soon as he has gone Nemorino samples the elixir, which is not long in taking effect. After several drinks he begins capering about, singing gaily to himself. Seeing Adina approaching, he stops short. He decides to be aloof with her, relishing the thought of how she will beg for his love tomorrow when the elixir will have brought out all his latent charm. When Adina comes in Nemorino ignores her completely and dances about, singing at the top of his lungs. She wonders if he has lost his mind and then decides that he is only shamming. The two continue to voice their thoughts in a lively duet ("Esulti pur la barbara"). Nemorino sings that though today his heart is aching, tomorrow the tables will be turned. A certain haughty young lady will come begging for his love. Adina, piqued at Nemorino's sudden change from abject pleading to airy indifference, resolves to make him sorry.

The duet is interrupted by the appearance of Belcore, who strides in singing that in love, as in combat, a quick assault brings victory. The dialogue continues in trio form. Murmuring that Belcore arrived just in time, Adina tells the sergeant that his assault on the defenses of her heart is showing signs of success. Overjoyed, Belcore asks when they can be married. In a week, Adina replies promptly, with a malicious glance at Nemorino, who mutters that his plans are going awry. Then the thought of the elixir restores his confidence. He begins laughing merrily as he thinks of how he will sweep Adina off her feet tomorrow before the eyes of the astonished sergeant.

Annoyed by his laughter, Belcore growls that he will give this young puppy the drubbing of his life if he does not leave at once. Adina fumes over Nemorino's impudent defiance. The colloquy ends abruptly as Gianetta rushes in, followed by peasants and soldiers. She breathlessly tells the sergeant that an important message has come for him. As the people crowd around, a courier comes forward and hands Belcore a slip of paper. Reading it, Belcore announces that the company is to march to a new garrison at dawn tomorrow. Nemorino gleefully expresses his satisfaction over this turn of events, while the peasant girls and the soldiers complain about parting.

As Belcore and Adina are making effusive promises of eternal devotion, the sergeant has an inspiration. He suggests that they be married immediately. Nemorino gasps in dismay, a reaction which Adina notes with grim satisfaction. Rushing up to her, Nemorino begs her not to consent, whereupon Belcore roars at him not to meddle.

In a passionate refrain ("Adina credimi") Nemorino implores Adina to wait one more day. The magnificent concluding ensemble of the act is developed from this point. Belcore threatens to tear Nemorino to pieces. Adina tries to calm him, saying that Nemorino is only a harmless bumpkin who has been made reckless by drinking too much. The soldiers and peasants comment that Nemorino must be thoroughly drunk if he imagines he can defy the sergeant. Nemorino meanwhile repeats his entreaties to Adina.

The ensemble comes to a halt as Adina, determined to keep Nemorino on the rack, announces that she wishes to be married at once and tells Belcore to send for a notary. She then invites all to the wedding feast. Plunged into despair, Nemorino wails for Dr. Dulcamara. In the final section of the ensemble ("Fra lieti contenti") the peasants and soldiers rejoice over the festivities in prospect. Belcore and Adina comment that this shock probably will cause Nemorino to lose what little reason he has left. Nemorino, moaning that Adina and the sergeant have made a fool of him, laments that Dulcamara's elixir has left him worse off than he was. After being rudely jostled by the crowd, he rushes away with their taunts ringing in his ears.

ACT TWO

[*Scene One*] A large room in Adina's farmhouse, where the gay wedding feast is in progress. Peasants and soldiers are seated at long tables, while at a smaller table are Dulcamara, Belcore, and Adina. The peasants call for a song ("Cantiamo, facciam brindisi"), and Belcore obliges with a lusty refrain ("Per me l'amore e il vino"), the general sentiment of which is that love and wine go together. In a momentary interlude Adina is heard in an expression of pity for the absent Nemorino.

After the chorus Dulcamara, who has appointed himself master of ceremonies, rises to announce that he has a beautiful barcarolle for two voices which has never been sung before. Taking the music from his pocket, he invites Adina to join him in singing it. Before they begin Dulcamara explains that the song is about Nina, the beautiful lady gondolier, and Signor Tredenti, a gallant but venerable town official. Adina and the doctor then sing a delightful duet ("Io son ricco e tu sei bella"), in which Signor Tredenti implores Nina to marry him for his money. He reminds her that love is fleeting, while gold is permanent. But Nina coyly refuses, saying that the honor is too great for a simple maiden like herself—and, besides, she has given her heart to a much younger lover. As the listeners applaud, Dulcamara remarks that the song suits his own particular style to perfection.

Calling for silence, Dulcamara announces that the notary has arrived. Adina murmurs in dismay that if Nemorino does not appear now, her plans for vengeance will go a-glimmering. She retires to another room with the notary and Belcore, who is in a fever of impatience to sign the marriage contract. The peasants also leave. Remarking that eating interests him much more than nuptial matters, Dulcamara sits down at the table by himself and devotes his attention to the food. His feasting is interrupted by Nemorino, who rushes in and distractedly cries that he must persuade someone to love him today—at once. Muttering that the lad is undoubtedly going crazy, Dulcamara prescribes another bottle of elixir. He assures Nemorino that it will produce results in half an hour. Again in an aside, he remarks that he will be well on his way by that time.

Nemorino implores Dulcamara to give him another bottle. Gladly, says Dulcamara, and then mentions money. When Nemorino tells him that he has none, Dulcamara advises him to go out in search of some, promising to wait at the inn until he returns. Finishing his meal, Dulcamara leaves. Sinking down on a chair, Nemorino disconsolately wails that all is lost.

Just then Belcore comes out of the other room, storming that there is no accounting for the actions of womankind. Though Adina says she loves him, he complains, she has suddenly decided to postpone the wedding until nightfall. Looking around, he notices Nemorino sitting with his head in his hands, muttering to himself. When Belcore asks him what is wrong, Nemorino tells him that he must have money immediately but has no means of getting any. Enlist in the army, says Belcore, and there is a bonus of twenty scudi.

The dialogue continues in the form of a rollicking duet ("Venti scudi! E ben sananti"). Leaping to his feet, Nemorino asks how soon he can have the money. At once, says Belcore. Nemorino, in an agony of indecision, weighs all the possibilities: not only must he leave home and friends—and his beloved Adina—but, worst of all, he may be killed in battle. Belcore merely repeats, "Twenty scudi." If we could only have Adina's love for one day, Nemorino cries, he would be glad to die. Belcore goes on to describe the glories of a soldier's life—including the pleasant diversion of making friends with the pretty canteen girls.

Finally making up his mind, Nemorino signs the enlistment paper which Belcore puts before him. The sergeant countersigns, gives Nemorino the money, and then the two shake hands to bind the bargain. The duet continues with Nemorino wondering how it has come about that he is accepting from his rival the money which he hopes will enable him to win Adina's love. Belcore, looking him over, assures him that a man of his mettle will soon be a corporal. Aside, he exults that he has cleverly made a double bargain—gained a recruit and cleared the field of a rival.

[*Scene Two*] The village square. Gianetta and the peasant girls rush in and, in a delightful chorus ("Possibilissimo, non è probabile!"), chatter excitedly over the astonishing news about Nemorino. The peddler told her in strictest confidence, says Gianetta, that Nemorino's uncle has died and has left him an enormous sum of money. He is now the richest lad in the village and a prize catch for any girl. With vastly amusing effect, the girls caution each other to secrecy about the matter. The chorus ends in a sudden crescendo as they sing that no one else will ever know this delicious secret.

They withdraw to one side as they see Nemorino approaching. He is blithely saying to himself that he has already drunk a quart of Dulcamara's marvelous elixir and is brimming over with confidence ("Dell'elisir mirabile"). This marks the beginning of another gay ensemble. Nothing can thwart him now, Nemorino exults, staggering a little. He stops short and eyes the girls suspiciously as they respectfully bow before him, and then majestically waves them aside. As they begin to shower him with compliments on his good looks, he stares at them openmouthed. Then he decides that his sudden popularity is the result of the elixir. Beaming with joy, he basks in the admiration of the girls.

At this point Adina and Dulcamara come in to find Nemorino surrounded by girls, all flirting shamelessly with him. Noticing the doctor, Nemorino thanks him for prescribing the elixir, saying that the effect is exactly as promised. Dulcamara is dumfounded. Adina rages that she expected to find him crying his eyes out, but instead he is happier than ever.

Looking fondly up at him, Gianetta implores him to come and dance with her on the green. At that all the girls begin clamoring for his attentions. Just as they are about to drag him away Adina calls sharply to him. Muttering that he is being haunted by women, Nemorino goes over to her. Adina snaps that Belcore has told her that for the sake of a few paltry scudi he has enlisted. As Nemorino looks at her indifferently, the girls impatiently urge him to come and dance with them. Nemorino turns to go, but Adina angrily asks him to listen to her.

At that Nemorino, becoming serious, confronts Adina and tells her that he knows very well why she has come to him ("Io gia m'immagino"). His refrain introduces the final section of the ensemble. Now, says Nemorino, the tables are turned, and she is suffering the pangs of unrequited love that have been torturing him. Adina ruefully admits to herself that she is being punished for attempting vengeance. Dulcamara marvels that Nemorino seems to be charming every girl in sight, attesting, of course, to the remarkable power of the elixir. Gianetta and the other girls spitefully remark that Adina expects every man in the village to fall at her feet.

At the conclusion of the chorus Nemorino, escorted by the adoring girls, happily goes off to dance on the green, leaving Adina standing disconsolately with Dulcamara, who then confesses that his magic elixir is responsible for the change in Nemorino. It is the same potion as that taken by Queen Isolde, he says, and he, the great Dulcamara, is the only one who knows how to distill this precious stuff. He explains to the incredulous Adina that Nemorino needed it to win a lady with whom he is madly in love and who has spurned him. To raise the money to buy the elixir, he enlisted in the army.

A long and brilliant duet follows as Adina remorsefully exclaims that she has cruelly rejected Nemorino's honest love ("Quanto amore! ed io, spieta!"). As she laments her ill-considered actions, Dulcamara, aside, declares that he will make the most of this opportunity: Adina must be persuaded to take some of this elixir. Turning to her, he does his best to convince her that if she takes his potion she will have admirers by the hundreds.

But Adina has other and sounder ideas. Assuring Dulcamara that she is very much impressed by the obvious results of his elixir, she explains, in the final section of the duet, that certain feminine arts are much more effective ("Una tenera occhiatina"). Her prescription—which, by the way, will "cure" Nemorino without the slightest doubt—is compounded of tender glances and alluring smiles. There, she says, is her own Elixir of Love. Admitting that his specific is no match for Adina's, Dulcamara declares that he would gladly trade his elixir for hers. After the thrilling climax of the duet, they leave.

Returning from the dance, Nemorino comes into the square. Sadly reflecting on Adina's distress over his unwonted defiance of her, he voices his feelings in the poignant and moving aria "Una furtiva lagrima," a song which is largely responsible for the fact that this opera has maintained its popularity for more than a hundred years. Nemorino recalls how a tear coursed down her cheek when she saw him among the gay crowd of peasant girls. If he could but clasp her in his arms now, he sings in impassioned phrases, he would gladly die.

After he concludes the aria he sees Adina approaching. Despite his magnificent expression of sympathy for her sorrow, Nemorino decides that he will continue to treat her coldly. When Adina greets him and asks how things are going with him, he replies carelessly that he is being pursued by countless women—young and old—all determined to marry him. But he is still biding his time, he adds. When Adina asks him why he enlisted, he answers that he hoped to improve his fortunes. A certain person in the village, Adina says, holds him dear, and for that reason she has bought back the enlistment paper. Nemorino smugly remarks to himself that all this proves what love can do.

Handing him the paper, Adina reveals that through her intercession he is free again ("Prendi, per me sei libero"). This introduces the long and dramatic duet in which the two finally resolve their differences. Adina begins by imploring Nemorino not to leave his home and the friends who love him. Seeing that her pleas apparently are making no impression, Adina bids him farewell, saying that she has nothing more to tell him. Thereupon Nemorino hands back the paper, exclaiming that, as everything has failed and Dulcamara has deceived him, he prefers to perish as a soldier.

This finally brings from Adina the fervent confession that she loves him. In transports of joy, Nemorino pours out his love for her. The two conclude the duet in a passionate exchange of avowals and then stand in an ardent embrace. At this point Belcore comes in. When Adina turns to him and announces that Nemorino is her husband-to-be and that all must be forgiven, the sergeant shrugs his shoulders, philosophically remarking that it is all for the best. Girls by the thousands are waiting for a handsome sergeant like himself.

Very true, interrupts Dulcamara, who has approached just in time to hear Belcore's last remark, provided that the ladies imbibe plenty of his matchless elixir. When Nemorino tells the doctor that he has him to thank for his good fortune, Dulcamara reveals what Nemorino and Adina do not yet know: Nemorino's uncle has died, leaving his nephew the richest man in the village.

Gianetta, who has meanwhile come in with the other girls and the men of the village, steps forward and proudly declares that *she* knew all about the matter. Dulcamara says that he, too, knew the secret, and then informs the crowd that he will tell them another: not only does his miraculous elixir bring lovers together, but it brings riches as well.

Making the most of the situation, Dulcamara calls up his carriage, which has been waiting a little distance away, climbs into it, and begins extolling

the virtues of his magic remedy ("Ei corregge ogni difetto"). This introduces the gay finale of the opera. Crowding around his carriage, the peasants eagerly buy the fabulous Elixir of Love, shouting, "Viva il grande Dulcamara." With every bottle of his Bordeaux wine sold, Dulcamara waves
farewell and rides off in his glittering chariot. The curtain falls.

Die Entführung aus dem Serail

(Abduction from the Seraglio)

by WOLFGANG AMADEUS MOZART

[1756–1791]

Libretto by
GOTTLIEB STEPHANIE

Based on a play by Christoph Friedrich Bretzner

CHARACTERS

Belmonte, a young Spanish nobleman	*Tenor*
Osmin, major-domo in the palace of Selim Pasha	*Bass*
Konstanze, a noblewoman loved by Belmonte	*Soprano*
Blonde, her maid	*Soprano*
Pedrillo, Belmonte's servant	*Tenor*
Selim Pasha	*Speaking role*
Klaas, captain of Belmonte's ship	*Speaking role*
A mute slave	

Palace guards, janissaries, women of the harem, slaves

Place: Turkey
Time: Sixteenth century
First performance: Vienna, July 16, 1782
Original language: German

MOZART was said to have been delighted with the libretto of *Die Entführung* from the very beginning, and he lavished upon it some of his finest music. Stories of Mediterranean pirates who carried off beautiful women to Turkish harems were favorite plot material in Mozart's time and provided the background for any number of operas and plays. It remained for Mozart to create from this material a comic masterpiece, one of the best examples of *Singspiel*.

The "Turkish" themes of the overture set the oriental mood of the opera.

ACT ONE

A square in front of the palace of Selim Pasha, on the shores of the Bosporus, where Konstanze, Blonde, and Pedrillo are being held captive, having been seized by pirates. Belmonte has made his way to the palace in the hope of rescuing his beloved Konstanze. He sings a brief aria ("Hier soll ich dich denn sehen"), in which he expresses the hope that they will soon be reunited.

As he stands in the palace square, pondering on how to gain entrance, Osmin appears carrying a ladder and a basket. He sets the ladder up against a fig tree near the palace door, climbs up, and begins picking the fruit. He cuts a ludicrous figure as he carefully reaches out, balancing his enormous bulk on the ladder. While working, he indulges in sundry reflections about love and women in an amusing aria ("Wer ein Liebchen hat gefunden"). His theory is that he who has a sweetheart must continually overwhelm her with demonstrations of love—and keep her locked up, because if left to herself she will inevitably run off with a rival.

Belmonte approaches and asks Osmin, in dialogue, if this is the Pasha's palace, but the major-domo pays no attention to him. The conversation continues in duet form as Belmonte expresses his impatience with Osmin's serenading. The major-domo finally deigns to answer but adds that he is in a hurry and cannot waste time talking. When Belmonte asks if he may speak to Pedrillo, Osmin flies into a rage, denouncing Pedrillo as a treacherous blackguard whose head properly belongs on a pikestaff. Then he tells Belmonte to be off about his business, warning him not to prowl about the palace trying to steal a maiden. Osmin, using his formidable paunch as a battering-ram, pushes the protesting Belmonte from the scene.

No sooner has Osmin rid himself of Belmonte than Pedrillo appears and proceeds to goad the major-domo into a fury with his taunts. Osmin gives vent to his rage in a vigorous aria ("Solche hergelauf'ne Laffen"), in which he enumerates all the tortures he would like to inflict on this young rogue, then waddles away. Pedrillo is about to leave when Belmonte reappears.

Master and servant joyfully greet each other. Pedrillo tells Belmonte that after he and the two women were captured they were lucky enough to have been purchased by Selim Pasha. Konstanze, he goes on, is now the Pasha's favorite. At this news Belmonte becomes greatly excited, but Pedrillo calms him by saying that Konstanze has steadfastly rebuffed the Pasha's advances. But Blonde, Pedrillo complains, is being pestered by that fat boor of a major-domo, Osmin, to whom she has been given as a slave. The situation is not as black as it might be, however. Pedrillo happens to be in the good graces of the Pasha because of his knowledge of gardening and is at least permitted to speak to Selim's wives when they walk about in the garden. Thus he can easily manage to inform Konstanze of Belmonte's presence. Belmonte is all for carrying the ladies off at once to his ship, which is moored outside the harbor, but Pedrillo warns that they must proceed cautiously. They still have to deal with the eagle-eyed Osmin. Selim Pasha will return shortly from a boating trip with Konstanze. Then, Pedrillo says, he will get Belmonte into the palace by introducing him as an architect, which will immediately arouse the Pasha's interest because architecture is one of his hobbies. Pedrillo now sees the Pasha's barge approaching and leaves to welcome him. Belmonte voices his joy over the prospect of seeing Konstanze again in the aria, "Konstanze! Dich wiederzusehen!"

Soon the Pasha, accompanied by Konstanze and his entourage, appears and is welcomed by a rousing chorus of his janissaries ("Singt dem grossen Bassa Lieder"). Belmonte, and Pedrillo, who has returned meanwhile, conceal themselves. Konstanze is sad and downcast, and the Pasha implores her to tell him why she will not return his love. She finally replies in the brilliant and dramatic aria, "Ach ich liebte, war so glücklich!" Her heart, she confesses, is still with her lover, from whom she was so cruelly torn. The Pasha's concern and tenderness turn to anger as he listens, and he warns her not to try his patience too far. Konstanze begs him to be kind and to give her just a little more time to forget her sorrow. Controlling his jealous rage, Selim answers that he will give her until tomorrow to decide whether or not she will accept his love; after that she may expect no further reprieve. Konstanze sadly leaves. The Pasha muses that the protests and refusals of so lovely a maiden only make her more desirable in his eyes.

Belmonte and Pedrillo now come forward, and Belmonte is duly introduced to the Pasha as a famous architect who has come to offer his services. Selim greets him cordially and makes plans for an interview later. Ordering Pedrillo to show the "architect" to his quarters, the Pasha leaves. Just as Belmonte and Pedrillo are about to go into the palace Osmin appears and bars their way. A lively trio follows ("Marsch! marsch! marsch! trollt euch fort!"). Osmin plants his huge bulk in the doorway and declares that under no circumstances will he allow the other two to enter. Belmonte and Pedrillo are equally insistent on going in, and the argument grows loud and furious. At the climax of the trio they manage to push Osmin aside and make their way into the palace. The curtain falls.

ACT TWO

The palace garden. Osmin's house is at one side. The major-domo is seen in conversation with Blonde, who is upbraiding him for his highhanded manner toward her. She reminds him that she is a European girl, not a Turkish harem woman who can be ordered around at will. In a charming aria ("Durch Zärtlichkeit und Schmeicheln") she points out that tenderness and devotion will win a maiden's love, while tyrannical bullying will not.

Osmin rages that she has been given him as his slave and must obey without question. Blonde jeers at him defiantly. It is unthinkable, she declares, that she, an English girl, accustomed to freedom, should submit to an ugly old Turk—especially when the handsome Pedrillo is nearby. What is more, she intends to rouse the whole harem to rebellion and convince these Turkish women that they need not bow to man's tyranny.

When Osmin begins to threaten her with torture Blonde warns him that, as maid to the Pasha's favorite, she can arrange to have the major-domo soundly beaten for his insolence. With that she orders him to leave. The two wind up their argument in a spirited duet ("Ich gehe, doch rathe ich dir"). Osmin warns her to keep away from that scoundrelly Pedrillo, but Blonde saucily defies him. Osmin storms away.

Blonde sees Konstanze approaching and expresses pity for her. She herself at least has Pedrillo to comfort her, but her mistress has no one to whom she can turn. The maid remains at one side, listening, as Konstanze laments her plight in the moving aria, "Traurigkeit ward mir zum Lose." As she stands in sad reflection, Blonde tries to encourage her to carry on, exhorting her not to lose hope. Konstanze, however, is inconsolable. While the two are talking Blonde sees the Pasha coming out of the palace and quickly leaves.

Resuming his conversation with Konstanze, Selim reminds her that to-morrow is the day on which she must declare her love for him. She turns on him in scorn and fury, asking how he dares command her to love him. She tells him flatly that he can never claim her affection and that even death cannot make her surrender. The penalty will not be death, the Pasha replies ominously, but agonizing torture. At that, Konstanze pours out her defiance in one of the most imposing and difficult numbers in operatic soprano reper-toire, "Martern aller Arten." She sings that she will never love him and that neither the threat of torture nor death can bend her to his will. After its brilliant concluding phrases she sweeps majestically from the garden. Selim, gazing after her, decides that if force will not work, strategy will. He leaves.

Blonde, returning to the scene, is signaled by Pedrillo, who cautiously approaches. He tells her that Belmonte has come to rescue Konstanze, and then describes how he succeeded in getting his master into the palace. Now, he says, freedom is near. He explains that he and Belmonte plan to abduct the women this very night and take them to Belmonte's ship. At midnight they will be on hand with ladders which they will put up at Kon-stanze's and Blonde's windows. Pedrillo then reveals his plan to inveigle Osmin into drinking wine with him before the evening is over. To make doubly sure that danger from that quarter will be eliminated, he gives Blonde a sleeping potion to mix with Osmin's night draught. With a few more words of precaution Pedrillo hurries away. Blonde sings of her joy in the aria, "Welche Wonne, welche Lust," and then she also leaves.

Presently Pedrillo reappears carrying two bottles of wine. He confesses some misgivings about the abduction and wishes it were over. In a spirited aria ("Frisch zum Kampfe") he voices his resolve to meet the situation like a true soldier and plunge into the fray regardless of consequences. While he is thus reviving his courage, Osmin enters, listens for a moment, and then remarks suspiciously that things seem to be going well for Pedrillo. The lat-ter replies that one may as well be merry as bemoan one's fate. Besides, he adds, holding up one of his bottles, here is real cheer and consolation. He pretends to be sorry for Osmin because his Mohammedan vows will not permit him to drink wine and thus share with him the joys of the bottle. Fi-nally he persuades Osmin to take a sip, suggesting that Mohammed proba-bly is much too busy with matters of cosmic importance to worry over whether one Osmin takes a drink of wine.

It is not long before Osmin and Pedrillo are the best of friends, praising the wine in a merry duet ("Vivat Bacchus! Bacchus lebe!"). Pedrillo, of course, remains sober and plies the major-domo with wine until he is re-duced to a helpless stupor. At that stage Pedrillo drags him away. He re-turns a moment later, imitating Osmin's drunken stagger and rejoicing that he has been rendered harmless for the time being at least.

Belmonte appears and Pedrillo tells him that everything has been ar-ranged and that the coast is clear—provided that the wine and the sleeping potion will keep Osmin in a state of unconsciousness until after midnight.

Seeing Konstanze and Blonde approaching, Pedrillo urges his master to explain the situation to his beloved as quickly as possible, for there is not much time left. While Konstanze and Belmonte embrace, Pedrillo takes Blonde aside and re-enacts, in pantomime, how he rendered Osmin helpless.

Belmonte pours out his love for Konstanze in a fervent aria ("Wenn der Freude Thränen fliessen"), and then Konstanze's voice blends with his as she responds with equal ardor. Blonde and Pedrillo, also making their avowals, blend their voices to form the impressive quartet which concludes the act. Things momentarily take a serious tone when Belmonte confesses that he still has some misgivings as to whether or not Konstanze has yielded to the love of the Pasha, but Konstanze's tearful denials convince him that she has been true. Pedrillo, in turn, asks Blonde if she ever encouraged Osmin in his love-making. Blonde answers by boxing his ears. The men are duly forgiven their unworthy suspicions, and the quartet comes to a stirring climax as the four hail the triumphant power of love. The curtain falls.

ACT THREE

[*Scene One*]   The square in front of the Pasha's palace, which is seen at one side. Opposite is Osmin's house. The sea is visible in the background. It is midnight. Klaas, captain of Belmonte's ship, enters carrying a ladder. He is followed by Pedrillo, who quickly sends him off for another ladder. Left alone, Pedrillo, quaking with fear, remarks that these Turks have no sense of humor and have the unpleasant habit of lopping off people's heads for tricks of this sort.

When Belmonte appears Pedrillo tells him that it has been his custom to sing a serenade nightly at about this time and suggests that his master do likewise. Absence of the usual singing, he says, may arouse the suspicions of the janissaries on their rounds. When Pedrillo leaves to investigate the situation in the palace Belmonte supplies a serenade in the form of a florid aria, in which he expresses his confidence in love's power to aid in time of trial ("Ich baue ganz auf deine Stärke").

Pedrillo returns and announces that everything is in readiness for the signal. As Belmonte leaves to keep an eye on the movements of the janissaries Pedrillo stations himself near Osmin's house, beneath Blonde's window, and sings a serenade ("Im Mohrenland gefangen war"). It tells of a maiden held captive by Moors and of a cavalier who came to rescue her. When there is no response Pedrillo sings a second stanza, in which he makes pointed references to the hour of midnight.

At the end of the song Konstanze appears at her window. Pedrillo quickly calls Belmonte, places one of the ladders against the wall and holds it while his master climbs into the window. Shortly after, Belmonte and Konstanze emerge from the door below and rush away. Pedrillo, meanwhile, raises the other ladder to Blonde's window and climbs inside. Just as he disappears, Osmin, accompanied by a mute slave, comes out of his house. Dazed by wine and sleep, the major-domo unsteadily holds up a lantern while the mute pantomimes that he has heard a disturbance. Suddenly the mute notices the ladder and points it out to Osmin. Momentarily jolted out of his stupor, Osmin sends the mute off to bring the guards. Waddling aimlessly about for a few moments, Osmin finally sits down on the lowest rung of the ladder and promptly dozes off.

Pedrillo climbs backward out of the window. Blonde, looking down, cries out that Osmin is below. Suddenly awakening, Osmin looks up, sees Pedrillo, and starts climbing laboriously up the ladder. Pedrillo quickly goes back inside. When Osmin is halfway up, Pedrillo and Blonde come out of the door below and run off, while the major-domo howls with rage. A guard appears and promptly suspects Osmin himself of being the intruder. While Osmin is setting him right about the matter, other guards, having caught Blonde and Pedrillo, drag them back. A few moments later, Konstanze and Belmonte, also having been intercepted, are brought in. Osmin gloats over his victory. When Belmonte tries to bribe him with a purse of gold Osmin scornfully replies that it is not gold he wants, but heads. Ignoring the pleas of the captives for mercy, he orders them taken before the Pasha. In an ensuing aria he relishes his triumph and exults over the thought of his enemies swinging from the gallows ("O! wie will ich triumphiren!").

[*Scene Two*]   A room in the Pasha's palace. Osmin, summoned to explain the disturbance, tells the Pasha that the "architect" whom he hired attempted to steal away Konstanze, while the treacherous Pedrillo, who plotted the abduction, hoped to flee with Blonde. Osmin, of course, takes great pains to point out that the plot was frustrated solely through his own efforts. Konstanze and Belmonte are brought before the Pasha. He denounces Konstanze for her treachery. Admitting her guilt, Konstanze declares that she will gladly die if the Pasha will only spare her lover. Belmonte now steps forward and tells the Pasha that he is of a noble and wealthy Spanish family and is prepared to pay any amount of ransom for the woman he loves. His name, he announces, is Lostados.

Dumfounded, the Pasha asks if he is related to the Commandant of Oran. Belmonte replies that the Commandant is his father. At that, the Pasha cries out in mingled fury and triumph that now he has in his power the son of his bitterest enemy—the man who ruined him, drove him from his homeland, and robbed him of his beloved. He asks Belmonte what his father would do if he were in the Pasha's place. Belmonte indicates with a gesture that the answer is obvious. The Pasha, telling Osmin to follow, leaves with his retinue to prepare the tortures.

Turning to Konstanze, Belmonte bitterly reproaches himself for having brought matters to this sorry conclusion. Konstanze tries to comfort him. In a long and dramatic duet ("Ha! du solltest für mich sterben") the lovers, each trying to shoulder the blame, try to console themselves in the thought that they will soon be united in death.

Blonde and Pedrillo are now led in by guards. Pedrillo trembles at the thought of the tortures that await them, but Blonde philosophically resigns herself to her fate. Suddenly the Pasha and his retinue reappear. Dramatically he pronounces sentence. So great is his hatred of Belmonte's father, he states, that he will not stoop to the kind of revenge which his enemy would demand. Belmonte and Konstanze, therefore, may have their freedom, so that Belmonte may go home and tell his father how Selim Pasha repaid cruelty with kindness. Cutting short the lovers' exclamations of gratitude, Selim prepares to leave. Pedrillo throws himself at the Pasha's feet and begs for mercy for himself and Blonde. When Selim also pardons these two, Osmin is beside himself with rage. The Pasha calms him, dryly remarking that by depriving Osmin of Blonde he is doing the major-domo a great favor.

Belmonte hails the Pasha's greatness and magnanimity in a joyous refrain which is taken up by everyone ("Nie werd' ich Deine Huld verkennen"). The ensemble is briefly interrupted when Osmin, taunted for the last time by Blonde, furiously describes the tortures he would still like to inflict on the four who escaped him. As he rushes off, spluttering with anger, the chorus is resumed. It rises to a climax in a triumphant hymn of praise to the Pasha.

Falstaff

by GIUSEPPE VERDI

[1813–1901]

Libretto by
ARRIGO BOÏTO

Based on Shakespeare's
MERRY WIVES OF WINDSOR AND KING HENRY IV

CHARACTERS

Dr. Caius .... *Tenor*
Sir John Falstaff.. *Baritone*
Bardolph ⎱ Falstaff's henchmen.................................. ⎰ *Tenor*
Pistol ⎰   ⎱ *Bass*
Mistress Meg Page.................................... *Mezzo-soprano*
Mistress Alice Ford...................................... *Soprano*
Nannetta (Anne), her daughter............................. *Soprano*
Dame Quickly .... *Mezzo-soprano*
Ford, a wealthy burgher.................................... *Baritone*
Fenton, a young gentleman in love with Nannetta................ *Tenor*
The host of the Garter Inn
    Townspeople, servants, pages, masqueraders as sprites and witches

Place: Windsor
Time: The reign of Henry IV
First performance: Teatro La Scala, Milan, February 9, 1893
Original language: Italian

FALSTAFF was Verdi's last opera. Written when the composer was eighty, this great comic masterpiece came after a long line of tragic works. In writing the libretto, Boïto took wide liberties with the plot of *The Merry Wives of Windsor,* changing characters and introducing scenes from *King Henry IV* for the sake of operatic convenience. Verdi unified it through his music, however, and fashioned it into a witty and exuberant masterpiece.

ACT ONE

[*Scene One*]　A room of the Garter Inn. Falstaff is seated at a table littered with bottles. Near by are Bardolph and Pistol, his two disreputable henchmen. The knight is in the act of sealing two letters. Dr. Caius comes storming in and confronts him, but for the moment Falstaff utterly ignores him and calls for another bottle of sack. Caius rails at him for having broken into his house, abused his servants, and injured his horse. Falstaff coolly admits everything. The doctor fumes that he will complain to the town council, but Sir John advises him not to make a fool of himself. There is another matter, Caius roars. Bardolph inveigled him into getting drunk with him and that other gallows bird, Pistol, and then, when he was sleeping it off, the two of them stole his purse.

Falstaff gravely asks Bardolph and Pistol if Caius's accusations are true, and they, of course, heatedly deny it. Pistol and Caius turn on each other with a barrage of insults and almost come to blows before Falstaff intervenes. Bardolph serenely observes that Caius's story is merely the figment of a drunken dream. With a magisterial air the knight announces that he has heard the evidence and has come to the conclusion that both parties to the dispute are convinced they are right. With that he tells Caius to depart in peace. The doctor starts for the door, raging that the next time he drinks in a tavern it will be with gentlemen and not a pair of thieving scoundrels. Bardolph and Pistol, singing a sardonic "Amen" in canon form, accompany him as far as the door.

Falstaff rebukes the two for their clumsiness in relieving Caius of his purse, reminding them that the secret of artistic stealing is choosing precisely the right moment ("Rubar con garbo e a tempo"). He then turns his attention to the bill, with which he has just been presented. Tossing his purse to Bardolph, he inquires as to the state of their funds. There is a total of one penny, Bardolph reports. The knight complains that these two sots will most certainly ruin him ("Sei la mia distruzione"). To be sure, Bardolph's glowing nose has long been serving as a beacon to light the three of them from tavern to tavern. But for thirty years now, Sir John recalls, he has been pouring oil in the form of wine into it in prodigious amounts and at monumental expense. The knight is so pained by the thought of this expenditure that he calls for another bottle of sack. After all, he says, it will not do to waste away. Here is his kingdom, he declares, patting his huge paunch, and he must needs extend it.

Apropos of replenishing his purse, Falstaff begins talking about the wealthy burgher Ford. When he mentions Ford's beautiful wife, Bardolph observes that she holds the purse strings. Sir John rhapsodizes over her in an eloquent refrain ("O amor sguardo di stella!"). She looked at him with limpid eyes, he muses, and when she gazed upon his magnificent person her expression seemed to say, "I am Sir John Falstaff's." He mimics a woman's voice in falsetto. And then there is another, he goes on, one Mistress Page, who also idolizes him—and also holds the purse strings. These two, the knight announces, shall be his treasury, his Golconda. With that he hands to Bardolph one of the passionate love letters he has written, with orders to deliver it to Mistress Page. The other he gives to Pistol, telling him to take it to Mistress Ford.

Pistol cringes, remarking that he does not relish the thought of cold steel in his ribs. Bardolph mutters something about honor. Cursing the two for refusing to deliver the two letters, Falstaff orders a tavern page to dispatch them. Turning on his two henchmen, he launches into the operatic version of his famous soliloquy on honor, "L'Onore! Ladri!" Honor, he philosophizes, never filled a belly, nor set a bone, nor replaced a hat, and is at best a mere word. Growing angry, he denounces Bardolph and Pistol as a pair of sniveling cowards who do not even have the right to utter the word and then chases them out of the tavern. The curtain falls.

[*Scene Two*] The garden of Ford's home. Alice Ford and Meg Page are excitedly discussing the love letters they have received. With them is Alice's daughter, Nannetta, and Dame Quickly. When the two women compare letters they discover that they are practically identical in handwriting, phrase, and signature, which is that of Sir John Falstaff. The women are at first shocked at Falstaff's impudence but soon see the ridiculousness of the fat knight's attempts at romance. In a lively quartet they discuss how they will set a trap for him and make him the laughingstock of the town ("Quell'otre! Quel tino! Quel Re delle panice!").

Their conversation is interrupted by the approach of Dr. Caius, Bardolph, Pistol, Fenton, and Ford. As the women withdraw to one side of the garden, the men air their grievances against Falstaff in a quintet ("È un ribaldo, un furbo, un ladro"). Caius is still smarting under the indignities he suffered at Falstaff's hands; Bardolph prates that his "honor" as a soldier impels him to warn Ford that Sir John is plotting against him; Pistol, professing to repent the time he has wasted as Falstaff's henchman and vowing to lead a better life, likewise urges Ford to be on his guard; the young Fenton expresses a desire to give the knight a taste of his sword on general principles. Ford, bewildered by this flood of denunciation, sings that he can make neither head nor tail of the matter because everybody is talking at once. The women, occasionally interjecting their comments, increase the ensemble to nine.

Finally Pistol, in a solo interlude, explains to Ford that Falstaff is planning a rendezvous with his wife, having already written her a letter. The two erstwhile henchmen are quick to add that they refused to deliver the letter. Ford declares that he will see to it that Sir John and his wife do not meet. The four women, chattering among themselves, come forward, and the men express surprise at seeing them. All but Nannetta and Fenton leave.

The two sing a charming love duet ("Labbra di foco! Labbra di fiore!"), in which they revel in the joy of a kiss. Nannetta warns that someone is coming, and Fenton hurriedly leaves. The intruders are Alice, Meg, and Dame Quickly, who are discussing ways to trap Falstaff. Alice tells Dame Quickly to arrange a rendezvous between her and Sir John. Gloating over what they will do with the knight once they have him in their clutches, the women hurry away. Nannetta loiters behind, and a moment later Fenton reappears. They sing another pleasing duet ("Torno all'assalto. Torno alla gara!"). In poetic figures of speech, they sing of returning to the assault in amorous combat. Again interrupted by the approach of several people, the lovers quickly move to another part of the garden.

Bardolph, Pistol, Ford, and Caius return, still absorbed in the problem of Falstaff. Bardolph informs Ford that the knight can be found at the Garter

Inn, and the burgher decides to visit him there in disguise. Bardolph is to introduce him under a false name. Ford then swears Bardolph and Pistol to secrecy. Another sparkling ensemble follows ("Del tuo barbaro diagnostico"). Caius pessimistically observes that, in Falstaff's case, the evil may prove too strong for the cure; Pistol advises plying the knight with wine, which will certainly loosen his tongue—to his own undoing. Ford resolves to win the knight's confidence and then, when he has left himself unguarded, turn the tables on him; Bardolph warns Ford that his adversary is a man of shrewdness and guile and will not easily be caught. Fenton, who returns to join the group, sings that there is little to be gained by getting involved in other people's difficulties, and then declares that his only concern is the love of Nannetta. Having expressed these sentiments, the men go on their way. The four women then reappear and sing a concluding ensemble in which they exult over the trick they are going to play on Sir John. Derisively they repeat a phrase from his letter, "Come una stella sull'immensita!" They burst into merry laughter as the curtain falls.

ACT TWO

[*Scene One*] A room in the Garter Inn, as in the preceding act. Falstaff is sitting in his usual chair, drinking. Bardolph and Pistol are in attendance. Soon Bardolph announces Dame Quickly, who greets the knight with a great show of respect. She asks for a private word with him, and Falstaff dismisses his two henchmen.

Dame Quickly informs Falstaff that Alice has received his letter and is in a state of passionate excitement over him. She wishes him to know that her husband is absent from home every day between two and three, at which time Sir John may visit her. Falstaff tells Dame Quickly to inform Mistress Ford that he will be there at the appointed time. There is another message, Dame Quickly continues. It is from Mistress Page, who likewise is completely bewitched by the eminent knight. With a lordly gesture, Falstaff tosses Dame Quickly a purse and tells her to convey his respects to the two fortunate ladies.

After she has gone, Sir John compliments himself on his irresistible charm in a lusty refrain ("Va, vecchio John, va!"). His pleasant reflections are interrupted by the return of Bardolph, who tells him that a certain Master Brook (Bardolph refers to him as "Messer Fontana") is very anxious to meet him and is willing to offer a bottle of Cyprus wine for the privilege. Falstaff jovially puns that a Fontana (fountain) who spouts wine is indeed welcome. Ford, escorted by Bardolph and Pistol, introduces himself as Master Brook. The two henchmen loiter as close as possible, hoping to eavesdrop, but Sir John soon sends them off.

Ford describes himself as a man of wealth and offers Falstaff a bag of gold if he will help him win a certain Alice, wife of one Ford. In an ardent refrain he sings that though he showers her with every attention, she continues to spurn him ("Io l'amo e lei non m'ama"). Falstaff, elated at this unexpected aid to his own plans, begins singing a fragment of a madrigal

("L'amor che non ci dà mai tregue"). Sir John then asks Ford why he has come to him with his problem. Ford answers that he recognizes Falstaff as a man of the world and a man of action. In an ensuing aria Ford describes the difficulty of his conquest ("Quella crudel beltà"). Alice is pure and unapproachable, he complains, but once she has yielded she will certainly yield again.

Quickly accepting Ford's purse, Falstaff assures him that the conquest is virtually accomplished. In fact, he says, he has already arranged a rendez-vous with Mistress Alice, who sent him a note informing him that her husband is always absent from home between two and three. Dumfounded, the burgher asks Sir John if he knows this Ford. Falstaff responds in a dramatic refrain ("Il diavolo se lo porti all'inferno"), in which he consigns Ford to the devil and asserts that he will make a fine fool of him.

The knight asks Ford to wait until he puts on street clothes and then re-tires to another room. While he is gone, Ford sings an impressive soliloquy ("È sogno? O realta? Due rami enormi"). Scarcely able to comprehend this state of affairs, he rages over the faithlessness of women, reproaching himself for trusting his wife and swearing that he will have revenge. Fal-staff returns, and an amusing scene follows as he and Ford leave the tavern, each insisting that the other take precedence. They compromise by making their exit arm in arm. The curtain falls.

[*Scene Two*] A room in Ford's home. Alice and Meg are waiting for Dame Quickly. She appears presently, and in an amusing refrain tells them about her interview with Falstaff ("Giunta all'Albergo della Giarrettiera"). The knight is unbelievably fat, Dame Quickly relates, and every ounce of him is in love with Alice. He is impatient to walk into the trap and will be at Alice's home between two and three. Alice orders the servants to bring in her large clothesbasket. While other preparations are being made to receive Sir John, Nannetta enters. She is on the verge of tears, and her mother anx-iously asks what is wrong. Nannetta replies that her father insists she marry Dr. Caius. The women indignantly voice their disapproval of such a match and urge Nannetta to refuse. Much cheered by their advice, Nannetta an-nounces that she will not marry Dr. Caius. When the servants bring in the basket, at present filled with soiled linen, Alice tells them that when she calls they are to throw it out of the window into the stream which runs behind the house.

At Alice's direction, her companions bring a lute and a chair, which they place in the center of the room. They also arrange a large screen in one corner. As Alice supervises arrangements she sings a gay refrain saluting the Merry Wives of Windsor and the comedy they are about to play ("Gaje comari di Windsor!"). Dame Quickly, watching at the window, exclaims that the knight is approaching. Alice seats herself in the chair, takes up the lute, strikes a soulful pose, and awaits him.

Sir John enters with a flourish and loses no time in embracing Alice, ex-claiming that now he can die happy. He confesses that he wishes her hus-band had gone on to his reward so that she could become the bride of Sir John. Then he sings an ardent refrain in which he assures her that she is worthy of a king ("Degna d'un Re"). When Alice, unable to resist the temptation, makes a reference to his corpulence, Falstaff obliges her with a description of himself when he was a gallant and slender page in the service of the Duke of Norfolk ("Quand'ero paggio del Duca di Norfolck").

Parrying his ardent advances, Alice reproaches him for being interested in Mistress Page, but Falstaff dismisses the latter with an uncomplimentary remark. Just then Dame Quickly bursts in with the news that Meg Page wishes to see Mistress Ford at once. Sending Falstaff to hide behind the screen, Alice admits Meg.

Raising her voice so that Falstaff will be sure to hear, Meg excitedly tells Alice that her husband has learned that her lover is in the house. He is on his way home, roaring with anger and swearing that he will kill the interloper. While Meg is speaking, there is an uproar outside and Ford comes storming in, followed by Caius, Fenton, Bardolph, and Pistol. Shouting to the others to search the house and watch all the exits, Ford rushes to the basket and begins tossing out all the linen, meanwhile furiously denouncing his wife ("Mi lavi! Rea moglie!"). Finding nothing in the basket, he dashes out to continue his search through the rest of the house.

No sooner has he gone than Meg, Alice, and Dame Quickly drag the quaking Falstaff from behind the screen, stuff him into the basket, pile the clothes on top of him, and slam the lid. While they are thus occupied, Nannetta and Fenton enter and steal unobserved behind the screen, where they again take up their love-making in a brief but charming duet ("Vien qua. Che chiasso!"). The men now come rushing back into the room. Ford, more furious than ever, bellows to Falstaff to come out of hiding. Suddenly they hear the sound of loud kissing behind the screen. Threatening and cursing, the men advance slowly toward the corner of the room. The dramatic ensemble which concludes the act is now built up, beginning with the outcries of Ford and Dr. Caius ("Se t'agguanto! Se ti piglio!").

The men discuss their plan of assault on the screen, while the neighbors, who have crowded in to enjoy the spectacle, add their comments in chorus. Meg, Alice, and Dame Quickly pretend to be attending to the clothes and, as unobtrusively as possible, warn Falstaff to remain quiet. The knight can be heard occasionally, gasping that he is smothering to death.

Above the ensemble come the voices of Nannetta and Fenton, singing passionately of their love in a duet obbligato ("Bella! ridente! Mentre quei vecchi!"). As the ensemble reaches its stirring climax, Ford strides up to the screen and pushes it over, revealing the two lovers in an embrace. Ford rages at Fenton for daring to make love to his daughter. His tirade is interrupted when Bardolph and Pistol shout that Falstaff is in the other room. All the men dash away, while Fenton seizes this opportunity to make his escape.

Alice summons the servants and orders them to throw the basket out of the window. Powerful unison chords sound in the orchestra as they struggle to lift the basket to the sill. Then with a mighty push they send it over, just as Ford and the others reappear. Alice, laughing merrily, takes Ford to the window and points below. The curtain falls.

ACT THREE

[*Scene One*]   The Garter Inn. Falsaff, sitting outside the door, is disconsolately taking stock of his bruises. After calling for a bottle of wine he launches into another famous soliloquy, in which he laments over the barbarous treatment of a gentleman and a knight at the hands of a cruel world ("Mondo ladro. Mondo rubaldo!"). As he sings, the innkeeper brings in the wine. Taking a drink, Falstaff observes that he will mix a little wine with the Thames water he has swallowed. He ceases feeling sorry for himself to revel in the heart-warming effect of wine. A remarkable orchestral effect accompanies his singing. A trill begins almost inaudibly in the strings and gradually swells to a tremendous volume of sound that engulfs the entire orchestra. It symbolizes the glow of the wine spreading through the knight's veins, restoring his good humor.

Just as he attains his usual state of complacency, Dame Quickly comes in. She tells Sir John that she has a message from Alice, but at the mention of her name he recoils. He launches into a tirade against her and all the others involved in his downfall, fuming over the indignities they inflicted on his august person ("Al diavolo te con Alice bella!").

Dame Quickly says that the servants were to blame for his mistreatment, and that Alice is dissolving in remorseful tears, for she still loves him. With that she hands him a letter from Alice. As Sir John reads it, Alice, Ford, Nannetta, Meg, and Caius are seen cautiously approaching in the background to observe the effect of the letter. In it, Alice asks Falstaff to meet her at midnight underneath Herne's Oak in Windsor Park. He is to come disguised as the Black Huntsman. With an exaggerated air of mystery, Dame Quickly tells Sir John that the spot is said to be haunted since the night the original Black Huntsman hanged himself from the oak. The information contributes little to Falstaff's peace of mind.

He asks Dame Quickly to tell him the rest of the story inside the tavern. After the two go in, Alice, mimicking Dame Quickly's voice, goes on with the story of the Black Huntsman, who has two great horns sprouting from his head. In a mock-dramatic refrain she relates that he emerges from his tomb at midnight and goes toward the tree where he met his doom ("Quando il rintocco"). Ford grimly remarks that the sight of the horns on Falstaff will be particularly gratifying. Alice rebukes him for his jealous rage of yesterday and then magnanimously forgives him when he admits his wrongs.

Alice and the others now discuss the roles they will play during the masquerade in which Sir John is to be given a hair-raising reception at Herne's Oak. Nannetta is to be Titania, queen of the fairies; Meg, a wood nymph; Dame Quickly, a sprite. A number of children will act as goblins, sprites, devils, bats, and moths. All will set on Falstaff and torment him for his sins.

As the women are about to leave they overhear Ford promising Caius that he shall marry Nannetta. He tells the doctor to disguise himself as a monk. After the masquerade, he is to lead Nannetta to Ford, who will give them both his blessing. Alice and Meg, going on their way, remark that they will see to it that Ford's ruse is unsuccessful. Dame Quickly comes out of the tavern and follows after the others, reminding Nannetta to prepare the song she will sing as queen of the fairies. The curtain falls.

[*Scene Two*] Windsor Park, at Herne's Oak. It is a bright moonlight night. A fanfare of hunting horns is heard in the distance. Fenton, dressed as Oberon, king of the elves, appears and sings a pleasing serenade ("Dal labbro il canto estasïato vola"). It ends in a duet as Nannetta, approaching from the distance, blends her voice with his. They meet and are about to embrace when Alice steps between them. She hands Fenton a monk's hood and tells him to put it on. Greatly surprised, Fenton asks the reason for this disguise. Alice cryptically remarks that Ford's trickery will be turned to his own disadvantage and their good. With that she tells Nannetta and Fenton to prepare to play their roles. Meg and Dame Quickly appear, and a moment later Alice gives warning that Falstaff is near.

Wearing an outlandish costume, with a pair of horns fastened to his head, Sir John slowly approaches the oak. A clock strikes in the distance. Counting the strokes in a trembling voice, the knight sings a refrain in which he implores the protection of the gods ("Questa è la quercia—Numi proteggetemi!"). As he fearfully gazes around, Alice appears and calls to him. Forgetting his fears, Sir John immediately turns to love-making. When Alice warns that Meg is following her, Falstaff exclaims that the two women may share him. At that moment Meg is heard calling for help, and Alice, pretending to be terror-stricken, urges Falstaff to flee.

Nannetta's voice comes from the distance, bidding the fairies arouse themselves. Falstaff, wailing that it is death to look upon the fairies, falls to the ground in terror. Nannetta, disguised as Titania, appears and, to a rippling accompaniment, sings a delightful air in which she summons her elfin cohorts ("Sul fil d'un suffio etesio"). The children playing the roles of fairies answer in chorus as they throng around her.

Bardolph and Pistol arrive and stumble over Falstaff. They are followed by the others, and then Sir John's torment begins. Joined by the elders, the "fairies" pinch, poke, and generally belabor the poor knight. Unable to raise his vast bulk, he lies helpless under the assault, groaning in anguish. The torture is administered to the accompaniment of a crackling ensemble, the burden of which is that Falstaff is being pricked and pinched for his misdoings ("Pizzica, pizzica, pungi, spilluzzica!").

During the melee Falstaff recognizes Bardolph as one of his tormentors and bellows curses at him. He also catches sight of Ford, who is not disguised. Alice makes it plain to the knight that the "Master Brook" who plotted with him is none other than her husband, which only adds to Sir John's discomfiture. Finally, when all have insulted and abused Falstaff to the limit of their respective vocabularies and have reduced him to whimpering for mercy, they desist and help him to his feet.

Ford then announces that the masquerade will be climaxed by the marriage of the fairy queen. Dr. Caius, obeying instructions, steps forward, leading by the hand a figure in a white veil and a crown of rose leaves. Thereupon Alice leads forth another couple, saying that they too wish to be joined in wedlock. Ford gives both couples his blessing and then orders the disguises removed. There is general consternation as Caius is seen standing with the red-nosed Bardolph, while Nannetta is clasping Fenton's hand. Everyone except Ford and Caius hails the bridal pair in a rousing choral phrase ("Vittoria! Evviva!").

Ford philosophically accepts his defeat and gives the two lovers his blessing. Then Falstaff calls for a closing chorus and forthwith begins a refrain expressing the familiar sentiments—that all the world's a stage and men and women merely players ("Tutto nel mondo è burla"). The chorus builds up in fugal form to a stunning climax. The curtain falls.

Faust

by CHARLES GOUNOD

[1818–1893]

Libretto by
JULES BARBIER *and* MICHEL CARRÉ

Based on Goethe's tragedy
Faust, Part One

CHARACTERS

Faust . . . . *Tenor*
Méphistophélès . . . . *Bass*
Wagner, a young student. . . . . *Baritone*
Valentin, a soldier, brother of Marguerite. . . . . *Baritone*
Siebel, a youth in love with Marguerite. . . . . *Soprano*
Marguerite . . . . *Soprano*
Martha Schwerlein, neighbor and companion of
    Marguerite . . . . *Contralto or mezzo-soprano*
Soldiers, students, villagers, dancers, demons

Place: A village in Germany
Time: Sixteenth century
First performance: Théâtre Lyrique, Paris, March 19, 1859
Original language: French

THE LEGEND of *Faust*, or *Dr. Faustus*, had its beginning in antiquity. It remained for the German poet Goethe to immortalize this drama of the human and the divine in his *Faust*, one of the most stupendous achievements in all literature. The episode of Faust and Marguerite, however, on which Gounod's opera is based, appears only in Goethe's poem and was not part of the legend.

The brief prelude opens with a meditative phrase followed by a short fugue. This leads into the refrain of Valentin's aria in Act Two, after which the prelude comes to a quiet, simple close.

ACT ONE

Faust's study—a gloomy, medieval room. Faust, a venerable and bearded scholar, is seated at a table littered with papers and books. After a somber, reflective phrase in the orchestra, he raises his eyes from the book before him and voices his weariness and despair ("En vain j'interroge"). For years he has queried and searched, but the answer to the riddle of life has eluded him. Faust cries for death and, in sudden resolve, seizes a flask of poison and pours some of it into a goblet. Holding it aloft, he sings that if death will not come to him, he will go forth to seek it. He is about to drink when he hears the carefree singing of villagers outside. Taunted by their gaiety, Faust utters a terrible curse on life and all human aspirations ("Maudites soyez-vous") and calls upon Satan to come to his aid.

There is a vivid flash of light. Méphistophélès stands before him, suavely announcing himself, "Me voici." After a brief colloquy he assures Faust that he can grant him anything he asks—money, fame, power. But Faust scorns all his offers and says he desires only the greatest treasure of them all—his youth.

"Well and good!" the devil replies. When Faust asks the price, Méphistophélès replies that it is but a trifle. Here on earth, he explains, he will do Faust's bidding. Later, in the underworld, Faust will wait upon *him*. When the philosopher hesitates in the face of this grim bargain, Méphistophélès conjures up a vision of Marguerite at her spinning wheel. Faust exclaims in wonder ("O merveille!"), while in the orchestra throbs the passionate theme symbolizing Marguerite.

Impetuously he signs the paper Méphistophélès puts before him. The devil hands him the goblet, saying that it no longer contains poison, but the elixir of life itself. Faust drinks and is instantly transformed into a handsome young man. Méphistophélès tells him that he may see Marguerite that very day. The two then sing a duet hailing the joys of love and beauty now in prospect ("A moi les plaisirs"). They rush out of the study as the curtain falls.

ACT TWO

The square of a German village.[1] A kermis, or fair, is in progress, with villagers, students, and soldiers milling about. A group of students strikes up a rollicking tune in praise of drinking ("Vin ou bière"). This leads into a rousing chorus in which all eventually join.

As all except the students and soldiers leave the square, Valentin and Siebel enter. In recitative, Valentin muses about the medallion given him by his sister Marguerite to charm away danger ("O sainte médaille"). When he expresses concern about Marguerite, who will be left alone when he goes to war, Siebel promises to act as her guardian. Valentin extends his hand to Siebel in thanks and then begins the famous aria, "Avant de quitter ces lieux" (familiarly translated as "Even bravest heart may swell"). Commending his sister to the care of God, he reflects on the sadness of farewell to home and friends, then sings of the glory of victory in battle. After the aria, Wagner, a student, calls for wine and proposes a song. Jumping upon a table, he begins the *Song of the Rat* ("Un rat plus poltron que brave"). He has sung only a few bars when he is interrupted by Méphistophélès,

[1] *Faust* is generally performed in four acts instead of five, as written. This then becomes Scene Two of Act One.

who suddenly appears and politely asks if he may join the group. If Wagner will end his song, the devil says, he will oblige the company with a much better one. Wagner tells him to begin at once. Thereupon Méphistophélès sings the Song of the Golden Calf ("Le veau d'or est toujours debout"). With biting scorn he describes how all men worship gold.

The listeners, although somewhat awed, lustily echo the closing phrases of the song and express their approval. Valentin, however, is suspicious of the stranger. When Wagner hands Méphistophélès a drink, the devil glances at the student's hand and remarks that his life line foretells death in battle. At that, Siebel asks to have his fortune told. Méphistophélès tells the youth that every flower he touches will shrivel and die—particularly the bouquets destined for Marguerite. The mention of her name brings an angry protest from Valentin. The devil coolly tells him to be careful, for his fate too is waiting for him.

Now Méphistophélès exclaims in disgust at the taste of the wine. He strides up to the wine cask used as the tavern sign and strikes it with his sword. As a stream of wine spurts forth, he bids the amazed onlookers to join in a toast to Marguerite. Valentin, infuriated, whips out his sword, whereupon Méphistophélès swiftly draws a circle around himself on the ground with his own weapon. Valentin lunges at Méphistophélès, then draws back, gasping that his sword has been shattered.

Siebel, Valentin, Wagner, and their companions confront Méphistophélès and, holding up the hilts of their swords to form the sign of the cross, they sing the dramatic Chorus of the Swords ("De l'enfer qui vient émousser"). The men regard him warily as they move off.

At that point Faust appears and demands to be taken to the maid he saw in the vision—if, indeed, she is more than a vision. Méphistophélès reassures him, but warns that it will not be easy to win the girl, for Heaven itself protects her. A lofty theme symbolizing divine guidance underscores this thought. But Faust insists that the devil keep his promise.

Méphistophélès declares that Marguerite will soon appear. A smoothly flowing waltz rhythm is heard as he advises Faust to try his luck during the dance. The villagers meanwhile throng into the square, singing as they dance the well-known chorus, "Ainsi que la brise légère." An interlude of musical dialogue follows. Méphistophélès calls Faust's attention to the ardent glances of the maidens, but Faust impatiently bids him be silent—he wishes to be left alone with his thoughts. Siebel enters, voicing his longing for Marguerite. Several girls approach and ask him to dance, but he shyly declines. Faust now spies Marguerite and cries out ecstatically. Siebel rushes forward, calling her name, but Méphistophélès deliberately bars his way. Meanwhile Faust hesitantly approaches Marguerite and asks if he may escort her home. Coolly replying that she is not in need of an escort, Marguerite goes on her way. Faust, though rebuffed, rapturously sings that he loves her ("O belle enfant! Je t'aime!"). Siebel sighs in disappointment. Méphistophélès, who has been observing the scene with obvious relish, sarcastically remarks that Faust apparently needs some lessons in love-making. The waltz music, rising to a glowing climax, brings the act to a close.

ACT THREE

Marguerite's garden.[2] At one side is her cottage. At the rear is a wall with a gate. After a short prelude, Siebel enters. Pausing near a bed of flowers, he sings his melodious serenade imploring the flowers to carry the message of his love to Marguerite ("Faites-lui mes aveux"). But when Siebel picks a bloom it shrivels in his hand. Recalling the stranger's menacing prophecy, he steps swiftly to a small shrine in the garden and dips his fingers in holy water. He picks another flower, exclaiming joyfully as it remains unharmed in his hand. Resuming his serenade, Siebel gathers a bouquet and goes toward another part of the garden.

Faust and Méphistophélès enter through the garden gate. Catching sight of Siebel, the devil warns Faust that his rival is approaching. The youth places the bouquet at Marguerite's door and steals away. Méphistophélès also leaves, while Faust slowly approaches the cottage. Musing on the strange emotion that stirs in his heart, he begins the beautiful aria, "Salut! demeure chaste et pure." Here, he sings, dwells a being of divine innocence, whose humble cottage is blessed with riches beyond measure.

At the conclusion of the aria Faust stands as if spellbound. His reverie is interrupted by Méphistophélès, who appears carrying a casket of jewels. He shows the gems to Faust and then places the casket next to Siebel's flowers. Quickly he leads Faust through the garden gate.

Marguerite now comes from the cottage, reflecting on the comely stranger who spoke to her so gallantly. Deep in thought, she sits at her spinning wheel and sings the ballad of the *King of Thule* ("Il était un Roi de Thulé"). It is the ancient legend about the old and gentle king who treasured a golden cup made in memory of his beloved queen. Throughout the song Marguerite interrupts herself to recall the stranger's gentle voice and manly bearing.

At length she rouses herself from her reverie and thinks of Valentin. After a moment she notices Siebel's bouquet and is touched by this token of his devotion. Then she spies the casket and the key beside it. She unlocks the casket and cries out in surprise and delight at its dazzling array. In childlike excitement, she wonders if she may dare try on the earrings. "Who would not be a coquette?" she murmurs as she finds a mirror in the casket.

Marguerite gives voice to her happiness in the brilliant aria known as the *Jewel Song* ("Je ris de me voir"). With naïve delight she puts on the earrings, holds up the mirror, and asks her reflection if it is really herself whom she sees. Perhaps some magic has transformed her into a princess. If only the handsome lord were here, she sighs, he would find her beautiful beyond compare. She tries on a bracelet, exclaiming that it is like a gentle hand laid on her arm. Joyously she repeats the first theme of her song, bringing it to a thrilling climax as she bedecks herself with jewels. At the end of the aria she remains kneeling before the casket, admiring herself. Martha enters and gapes in astonishment at Marguerite's glittering adornment.

[2] This is Act Two when the opera is played in four acts.

While the two women examine the jewels, Méphistophélès and Faust enter. The devil addresses Martha by name and informs her in lugubrious tones that he is the bearer of bad news: her beloved husband is dead, but sends his parting benediction. Hearing Martha's startled exclamation, Marguerite fears that something is amiss and hurriedly begins taking off the jewels. The four voices then blend in an ensemble in which contrasting sentiments and musical figures are ingeniously interwoven. Marguerite and Faust ponder over the wonder of their awakening passion, while Méphistophélès makes love to Martha, combining his amorous compliments with insulting asides about her age and appearance. Faust impetuously takes Marguerite in his arms. She frees herself and runs away, but he eagerly pursues her. Méphistophélès manages to escape from Martha, who hurries off in search of her new-found cavalier.

Presently Méphistophélès stalks back into the deserted garden. Gloatingly he predicts that the hour of destiny is at hand for the lovers and intones a baleful invocation to night ("O nuit, étends sur eux ton ombre!"). Let blind passion enslave the souls of the lovers, he sings, and may these flowers, now cursed by his hand, work their evil sorcery in Marguerite's heart. With a gesture of malevolent triumph, he vanishes into the gloom.

Faust and Marguerite reappear and pour out their love in an exquisite duet. It begins with Faust's impassioned phrase, "Laisse-moi contempler ton visage" (popularly translated as "Let me gaze on the vision before me"). Marguerite repeats the refrain to sing rapturously of the mysterious enchantment of this night of love. Clasped in each other's arms, the lovers exclaim with passionate intensity, "Eternally!"

Suddenly Marguerite, troubled by a premonition of disaster, begs Faust to leave her lest he break her heart. He finally goes after she promises to see him on the morrow. On his way out of the garden he encounters Méphistophélès, who bids him wait only long enough to hear what Marguerite will say to the stars. At that moment Marguerite flings open her window. Softly she murmurs, "Il m'aime," then, in unrestrained joy, she sings a refrain of such impassioned ecstasy that Faust rushes to her arms. Méphistophélès, watching the lovers, breaks into fiendish, taunting laughter as the curtain falls.

ACT FOUR

[*Scene One*]   After a short and mournful prelude the curtain rises on Marguerite's room.[3] She is seated at her spinning wheel. From outside come the voices of a group of girls, cruelly taunting Marguerite about the lover who ran away. Marguerite sings the dolorous *Spinning Wheel Song*, voicing her love and longing for Faust, even though he has dishonored her.

As she finishes the aria in grief-stricken tones, Siebel rushes in and comments anxiously over her tears.[4] He gently takes her hand and sings the

[3] When the opera is played in four acts, this becomes Scene One of Act Three.

[4] The score indicates that the *Spinning Wheel Song* can be eliminated, in which case the scene opens with Siebel's entrance. In some performances Scene One is omitted entirely, the act opening with the scene in the cathedral.

simple and touching aria, "Si le bonheur à sourire t'invite," recalling how he has shared Marguerite's joys and sorrows. Deeply moved by Siebel's devotion, Marguerite thanks him, then says that she will go to church to pray for her errant lover and the child she will bear him.

[*Scene Two*]   The interior of the cathedral. Organ music vibrates softly as Marguerite enters, kneels, and begins to pray. Suddenly the voice of Méphistophélès calls harshly that she must not pray ("Non! tu ne prieras pas!"). As Marguerite cowers in terror, a tomb opens and Méphistophélès stands before her, thundering that the devils in hell are clamoring for her soul. Marguerite cries out in horror and bewilderment. The choir behind the scenes chants of the awful Day of Judgment ("Quand du Seigneur le jour luira"). As Marguerite prays, Méphistophélès again proclaims her doom, then vanishes. She faints with a piercing cry as the curtain falls.

[*Scene Three*]   A square not far from the cathedral.[5] In the brief but stirring prelude we hear the familiar strains of the *Soldiers' Chorus*. Noisily welcomed by the townspeople, the soldiers, led by Valentin, enter the square. Valentin greets Siebel and asks about Marguerite. Siebel evasively tells him that perhaps she is in the church. Now follows the rousing *Soldiers' Chorus* ("Gloire immortelle de nos aïeux," usually translated as "Glory and love to the men of old"). The men hail the glorious traditions of bravery in combat and describe the joy of returning home. After the chorus, soldiers and townspeople gradually drift away from the square.

Valentin, remaining behind with Siebel, becomes suspicious when the youth tries to dissuade him from entering Marguerite's house. When Siebel finally blurts out, "You must forgive her," Valentin rushes across the square and enters Marguerite's dwelling. Siebel, breathing a prayer for Marguerite, goes toward the church. Faust now appears, followed by Méphistophélès, who is carrying a guitar. They approach Marguerite's house. Flinging back his cloak, the devil strums his guitar and begins his famous serenade ("Vous qui faites l'endormie"). This remarkable song, with its flippant orchestral accompaniment, is a masterpiece of innuendo and insult. Méphistophélès mockingly parodies a lover's song to his "Catherine," advising the lady not to admit her swain until the ring is safely on the proper finger. Though the panting lover begs for kisses, the devil sings, never open the door without the ring. Méphistophélès climaxes his song with a burst of diabolical laughter.

The devil's guffaws bring Valentin rushing from the house, angrily asking the two strangers what they wish ("Que voulez-vous, messieurs?"). His words introduce a fiery trio. Méphistophélès informs him contemptuously that the serenade was not for his ears. Valentin retorts that his sister heard it only too well, then with a blow of his sword knocks the guitar out of the devil's hands. Faust exclaims in surprise as Valentin mentions his sister.

When Valentin asks whom he must fight to avenge his sister's honor, Faust draws his sword. The duel begins. Adroitly aided by Méphistophélès,

---

[5] As originally written, this scene preceded the church scene. It has become customary to play these two scenes in reverse order for the sake of the climactic effect of the *Soldiers' Chorus* and Valentin's death.

Faust finally plunges his sword into Valentin's body. As the stricken soldier falls, the devil looks down at him and snarls that the vaunted "hero" is now stretched on the ground ("Voici notre héros étendu sur le sable"). Swiftly he drags Faust from the scene.

Martha and a crowd of villagers, attracted by the noise of the fight, throng into the square. Horrified, they approach the dying Valentin. Marguerite rushes from the house and kneels at her brother's side, but he roughly repulses her. Siebel tries to comfort her. Raising himself, Valentin wildly accuses his sister of surrendering decency and honor to satisfy her reckless desires. He utters a curse upon her, then falls back dead. Slowly the villagers bare their heads and kneel, murmuring a prayer for his soul. Marguerite falls sobbing upon his body. The curtain descends.

ACT FIVE

[*Scene One*] Walpurgis Night on the Brocken in the Harz Mountains.[6] A chorus of women sings about the souls of the dead who have been released to roam at will on this night of fearful revelry. Méphistophélès leads Faust in and bids him gaze upon the spectacle. At the devil's command, the celebrated beauties of history—Cleopatra, Laïs, Helen of Troy, Phryne, and the Trojan Women—emerge from the mists in a wild, voluptuous dance. Faust drains cup after cup of magic wine, then laughs in drunken disdain at the voice of his conscience. Suddenly he is brought to his senses by a horrible vision of Marguerite with a fiery ribbon encircling her neck like a wound from a sharp blade. In a frenzy he commands Méphistophélès to take him to her.

[*Scene Two*] A prison cell.[7] The music of the prelude is somber and foreboding. As the curtain rises, Marguerite is seen asleep on a pallet of straw. In her madness and despair she has killed her child and has been condemned to death. It is just before dawn on the morning of her execution. Méphistophélès and Faust enter. The demon urges Faust to help Marguerite escape while there is still time—before the break of dawn. Tormented by remorse, Faust ignores him and calls to Marguerite.

Dreamily she murmurs that she hears her lover's voice despite the tormenting laughter of the demons who surround her. Then in ecstasy she sings that she is no longer afraid of death now that he is near. Wildly Faust implores Marguerite to come with him, but cries out in despair when he realizes that she does not hear. Now Méphistophélès strides out of the shadows with the warning, "Away, or you are lost." His words introduce the intensely dramatic trio which concludes the opera ("Alerte! Alerte!").

Marguerite finally sees Méphistophélès as the devil he really is and implores Faust to drive him away. With death upon her, she sings the ex-

[6] This scene depicts, in a spectacular ballet, the lurid revelry held—according to the *Faust* legend—on the first night of May. Gounod composed the ballet for the Grand Opéra version of *Faust* presented in 1869. It is usually omitted in present-day performances.

[7] This is usually played as the final act of the opera.

ultant refrain in which she pleads to be carried to heaven ("Anges purs, anges radieux"). Faust distractedly entreats her to come away with him before it is too late, while Méphistophélès grimly intones that the fatal hour has come. The three voices, repeating the theme in successively higher keys, bring this great trio to an overwhelming climax.

At its conclusion Marguerite turns to Faust and in piercing tones asks him why his hands are stained with blood, then bids him go. "You fill me with horror," she gasps, and dies. Faust utters a terrible cry as Méphistophélès drags him away to his doom, thundering that he is condemned ("Jugée!"). Marguerite's lifeless form is bathed in a golden light, while a majestic chorus of angels is heard proclaiming her redemption ("Sauvée! Christ est ressuscité!"). The curtain falls.

Fidelio

by LUDWIG van BEETHOVEN
[1770–1827]

Libretto by
JOSEF SONNLEITHNER

with subsequent revisions by
STEPHAN von BREUNING *and* GEORG FRIEDRICH TREITSCHKE

Based on a story by Jean Nicolas Bouilly

CHARACTERS

Jaquino, assistant to Rocco....................................*Tenor*
Marcellina, daughter of Rocco............................*Soprano*
Rocco, the jailer...*Bass*
Leonore (disguised as Fidelio), wife of Florestan...............*Soprano*
Pizarro, governor of the prison fortress of Seville.................*Bass*
Florestan, a Spanish nobleman..................................*Tenor*
Don Fernando, Prime Minister of Spain.........................*Bass*
Townspeople, prisoners, soldiers

Place: Seville
Time: Eighteenth century
First performance: Theater an der Wien, Vienna, November 20, 1805
Original language: German

FIDELIO is Beethoven's only opera. He had long wanted to write an opera, and when he at last found a suitable libretto he worked hard on the composition. The first performance, however, was a failure. A year later the opera was presented again with revisions by Beethoven's friend, Von Breuning, who reduced its original three acts to two.

Despite apparent success, Beethoven withdrew it in a disagreement over royalties. *Fidelio* received its third première in 1814, substantially in the form in which it is now given. It was originally written as a *Singspiel* (songplay), with written dialogue. The dialogue passages are occasionally sung in recitative.

Beethoven wrote four overtures to the opera: *Leonore No. 1, Leonore No. 2, Leonore No. 3,* and the *Fidelio.* It is now customary to play the *Fidelio* as the prelude to the opera and the *Leonore No. 3* before the second scene of Act Two.

Florestan has been imprisoned by Pizarro, his political enemy. Pizarro has chained him in a dungeon and has left him to die by slow starvation, meanwhile giving out the report that Florestan has died. Leonore, however, convinced that her husband is still alive, determines to make an attempt to save him. To that end she disguises herself as a man and persuades Rocco, the jailer, to hire her as his assistant. Her plans are somewhat complicated by the fact that Rocco's daughter, Marcellina, falls in love with the handsome youth ("Fidelio") she appears to be.

ACT ONE

The courtyard of the prison fortress. At one side of the scene is the cell building, with its barred windows and doors, and next to it is the gatehouse in which Rocco and Marcellina live. Opposite is a garden. Beside the gate at the back is a small cabinlike building, Jaquino's lodging. Marcellina is ironing at a little table outside the door of her house. Jaquino is hovering about, dividing his time between attending to his duties at the gate and making love to Marcellina. The two sing a sprightly duet in which Jaquino implores Marcellina to marry him, while she scorns his pleas ("Jetzt, Schätzchen, jetzt sind wir allein"). He is finally forced to interrupt his wooing to answer Rocco's summons from the garden. Marcellina, whose mind is on Fidelio, now sings a charming aria voicing her longing for him ("O wär' ich schon mit dir vereint").

Rocco enters, followed by Jaquino. A moment later Fidelio appears. He has just returned from the town, bringing some dispatches for Pizarro, governor of the prison fortress, and a set of chains which have been repaired. Marcellina greets him eagerly, expressing tender concern over the fact that he seems weary from his journey. Rocco, examining the bill for the repair of the chains, commends him for getting the job done at so low a price. In an aside, however, he observes that the youth is putting his best foot forward purely for Marcellina's sake. Much to Leonore's discomfiture, he implies that he approves of the match. For the sake of protecting her disguise, Leonore pretends a romantic interest.

This leads to a striking quartet, "Mir ist so wunderbar," written in canon form. Marcellina rejoices over what she interprets as Fidelio's awakening interest, while Leonore expresses pity for her misguided love. Jaquino laments over losing Marcellina to a rival, and Rocco sings that this union will cheer his declining days. Rocco sends Jaquino off about his duties and then tells Fidelio and Marcellina that he will soon arrange their marriage. He volunteers some practical advice to the young couple in the ensuing aria, in which he points out that money is indispensable to happy married life ("Wenn sich Nichts mit Nichts verbindet").

Leonore thanks him for his interest in her future and then says that she has long wished for an opportunity to show her gratitude by helping him with one of his more arduous duties. She has noticed, she continues, how exhausted and careworn he appears when he returns from attending the prisoners in the subterranean dungeons. To Leonore's joy, Rocco answers that he will arrange to have Fidelio assist him in the future. There is one cell, however, which he will not be permitted to enter. In that one an important prisoner has been kept for two long years, and now he is on the verge of death as the result of his confinement. Leonore suppresses a cry of horror over the thought that this unfortunate man may be her husband. In the trio which follows, Rocco commends Fidelio for his helpful spirit, Marcellina sings that her hopes for marriage may now be fulfilled, and Leonore exults that this turn of events may aid her plans to rescue Florestan.

A vigorous martial strain heralds the approach of Pizarro.[1] Leonore and Marcellina go into the house as Pizarro appears with a detachment of soldiers. Rocco hands him the dispatches brought by Fidelio. Among them Pizarro finds a note warning him that the Prime Minister is coming to inspect the prison because he has heard that certain inmates have been unjustly imprisoned as the result of political conspiracy.

In angry surprise Pizarro exclaims that he must at all costs get rid of Florestan, so that the crime of imprisoning him and spreading the false report of his death will not be discovered. In the great aria, "Welch' ein Augenblick," he declares his resolve to destroy Florestan and gloats that his hour of revenge is at hand. The guards and soldiers, in a choral accompaniment to the latter part of his song, comment that he appears to be planning some dark deed.

Pizarro calls Rocco to him, and a duet follows. First giving the jailer a purse, the governor tries to persuade him to murder Florestan, but Rocco bravely refuses. Pizarro thereupon cries out in fury that he will do the deed himself. He orders Rocco to open the abandoned cistern in Florestan's cell, for there the prisoner's body can be hidden without a trace.

Pizarro and Rocco leave. Leonore, who has overheard the governor's evil plans, rushes from the house and gives voice to her terror and despair in a dramatic recitative, "Abscheulicher! wo eilst du hin!" This is followed by the intensely moving aria, "Komm Hoffnung," in which she declares that her abiding love will give her strength to rescue her husband despite Pizarro's fiendish plot.

After the aria Leonore goes into the garden to seek Rocco. Marcellina and Jaquino appear. There is a moment of comic relief as Jaquino fervently entreats Marcellina to love him—and if she cannot love him, at least marry him. Marcellina impatiently tells him to be silent. Leonore returns with Rocco and persuades him, in the hope of seeing her husband, to allow the prisoners to enjoy a brief moment of sunlight in the courtyard. Rocco leaves Fidelio, Marcellina, and Jaquino to stand guard, while he goes to ask Pizarro if his assistant may accompany him to the subterranean cells.

As Leonore watches closely, the haggard prisoners stumble into the courtyard. They voice their wonder and joy over the sunlight in the moving *Prisoners' Chorus* ("O welche Lust!") and then are led into the garden by Marcellina and Jaquino. Rocco returns with the news that Pizarro not only has sanctioned the marriage of Fidelio and Marcellina but will allow Fidelio to enter the lower cells this very day. Leonore voices her joy in a ringing phrase.

In the ensuing musical dialogue Rocco explains that it will be Fidelio's duty to help dig the grave for the doomed prisoner, whom the governor

[1] The first act is sometimes divided into two scenes at this point, and the music of Pizarro's entrance is played as the prelude to Scene Two.

himself will put to death. Leonore, tortured by the thought that she may be too late to save her husband, steels herself for the ordeal. At that moment Marcellina and Jaquino rush in to say that Pizarro has learned that the prisoners have been allowed out of their cells and is coming to demand an explanation. Fuming with anger, the governor appears and asks Rocco on what authority he released the prisoners. He is somewhat mollified when Rocco answers that he gave them respite in honor of the King's birthday. Pizarro sends the prisoners back to their cells, then orders Rocco to go below and prepare the grave for the victim. The voices of the prisoners and principals, expressing various sentiments, blend in a stirring chorus which concludes the act.

ACT TWO

[*Scene One*] Florestan's cell. In the dim light of a lamp we see him seated on a stone bench. At one side is the abandoned cistern, marked by a heap of rubble. At the rear, seen through a barred opening, is a stair leading down from the cell entrance. After a somber introduction, Florestan, in recitative, resigns himself to death. Then in a dramatic aria he sings that he finds comfort in the thought that he has faithfully performed his duty ("In des Lebens Frühlingstagen"). He imagines he sees Leonore and sings of her in mingled ecstasy and despair. At the end of the aria he falls back half fainting on the bench and lies there motionless.

Rocco and Leonore enter, Leonore shuddering with cold and nervous excitement. Rocco looks at Florestan, finds that he is asleep, then quickly begins clearing away the rubble over the opening of the cistern. In strained suspense he and Leonore converse in musical dialogue as they work. Florestan, roused at length, speaks to Rocco, and Leonore recognizes his voice but with supreme effort restrains herself from speaking.

Florestan asks Rocco who the governor of the prison is, and, when told, he begs the jailer to send someone to Seville to tell Leonore Florestan about his plight. Rocco answers that he dare not take the risk. He refuses Florestan's request for water but offers him a drink of wine. When Leonore gives him the wine Florestan voices his gratitude in the refrain that marks the beginning of a dramatic trio, "Euch werde Lohn in bessern Welten." Florestan sings to Leonore that she will be rewarded in a better world for her kindness, and then declares that her good deed fills him with new hope. Leonore cheers him further by giving him a crust of bread which she had hidden in her clothing. Rocco weighs the danger of thus aiding the prisoner and then expresses concern over the fact that Florestan's life seems hanging by a thread.

Rocco then gives the prearranged signal—a whistle—and Pizarro, who has been waiting nearby, strides into the dungeon. He orders Rocco to send Fidelio away, muttering to himself that he must kill these two also, lest they give away the secret of the murder. The dialogue of the ensuing scene is in the form of a fiery quartet ("Er sterbe! Doch soll er wissen"). Confronting Florestan, Pizarro throws back his cloak and cries out that at last his enemy faces the avenger. Florestan quietly replies that he faces a murderer. As

Pizarro, dagger in hand, rushes toward Florestan, Leonore leaps between the two men, crying out to Pizarro that before he kills Florestan he must first kill his wife. In wild fury Pizarro lunges again, but Leonore holds him at bay with a pistol.

At this climactic moment a trumpet call—the famous trumpet call of the overtures—is heard outside. It is the signal Pizarro had ordered to be sounded at the approach of the Prime Minister. Over an exultant theme in the orchestra the four voices blend in a powerful phrase—Leonore, Florestan, and Rocco expressing relief and gladness, Pizarro cursing in fear and anger.

Jaquino rushes in to announce that Don Fernando and his retinue are at the gates of the fortress. The quartet continues to a brilliant climax. Pizarro leaves with Rocco and Jaquino, while Leonore and Florestan, clasped in each other's arms, sing an ecstatic duet ("O namenlose Freude!"). As Leonore leads Florestan from the dungeon the curtain falls.

[*Scene Two*] The *Leonore No. 3* overture, containing the famous horn call heard in the previous scene, is usually played as a prelude to this scene. Don Fernando and Pizarro are seated on a dais in a great square before the fortress. The townspeople hail the Prime Minister in a stirring chorus. In acknowledging their acclaim, he says he has come to right the wrongs of tyranny and to bring justice to all. The prisoners are brought in by Rocco, who leads Florestan and Leonore forward. Fernando is astounded to see his friend, whom he thought dead. When he sternly demands the reason for Florestan's wretched state Rocco tells him the story of Pizarro's treachery. The governor unsuccessfully tries to implicate Rocco, who is duly exonerated when he convinces the Prime Minister that he was forced to carry out Pizarro's orders under the threat of death.

Don Fernando gives Leonore the key to Florestan's chains and tells her that she is to have the honor of freeing him. In exultant phrases she and Florestan sing of the joy of their reunion, while the people praise her wifely faith and courage in a mighty chorus ("Wer ein holdes Weib errungen"). The curtain falls.

La Figlia del Reggimento

(The Daughter of the Regiment)

by GAETANO DONIZETTI

[1797–1848]

Libretto by
BAYARD *and* JULES H. VERNOY (MARQUIS ST. GEORGE)

CHARACTERS

The Countess of Berkenfeld.......................... *Mezzo-soprano*
Ortensio, her servant... *Bass*
A peasant .... *Tenor*
Sulpizio, a sergeant in the Twenty-first Regiment
    of Napoleon's army... *Bass*
Maria, vivandière of the Twenty-first Regiment................. *Soprano*
Tonio, a young Tyrolese...................................... *Tenor*
A corporal .... *Bass*
A notary .... *Tenor*
The Duchess .... *Mezzo-soprano*
      Soldiers, peasants, ladies in waiting, servants

Place: The Austrian Tyrol
Time: About 1815
First performance: Opéra-Comique, Paris, February 11, 1840 (as *La Fille
        du Régiment*)
Original language: Italian

L A FIGLIA DEL REGGIMENTO was composed by Donizetti during the latter
part of his career. Although it did not achieve the enduring popularity
of his more famous operas, it contains much music that is gay and
ingratiating. The title role was a favorite with such great nineteenth-century
singers as Jenny Lind and Adelina Patti. Although given under its French
title—*La Fille du Régiment*—at its première, the opera is best known by its
Italian title.

There is a lively overture which opens with a fanfare and then continues
with themes reminiscent of the various romantic and martial melodies
prominent in the opera.

ACT ONE

A mountain passage in the Tyrol. At one side is a cottage. In the background a group of peasants are looking down into the valley, following the
progress of a battle. It is the time of the occupation of the Tyrol by Napo-

leon's army. In the foreground the Countess of Berkenfeld, apparently on the verge of fainting, is being attended by Ortensio, her servant. The Countess is greatly distressed over the fact that she is unable to leave her castle in the Tyrol because of the fighting between the Tyrolese and the French. Nearby a number of ladies in waiting are kneeling, their expressions reflecting anxiety and fear. At the present moment there is a lull in the fighting. In an opening chorus the peasants urge everyone to be silent and cautious ("Silenzio! Destrezza ed ardir!"—"L'ennemi s'avance"). The ladies then are heard in a plea for heavenly protection ("Cielo clemente"—"Sainte Madone"). Ortensio assures the Countess that danger is past, and then the voices of the ladies and the peasants join in a chorus of prayer.

Suddenly a peasant stationed as a lookout calls that not a Frenchman is in sight and that safety is now assured. The chorus is resumed as the people express their relief and happiness. At its conclusion the ladies withdraw to the cottage and most of the peasants go back to their homes in the valley. A few remain with the Countess. She is still frightened and in a state of alarm, exclaiming that she has had her fill of warfare. Ortensio starts to say something about her experiences of the past, but the Countess cuts him short. She is undecided on whether to remain in her mountain castle or return to Austria. Ordering Ortensio to find out as best he can what the military situation is, she enters the cottage.

Sulpizio, a sergeant in Napoleon's Twenty-first Regiment, now comes striding in, highly elated over the rout of the enemy. The proclamations make everything clear, he announces to nobody in particular. Whoever holds with the Bavarians is a foe of the French. It is that simple. At that moment a merry "La-la-la" is heard in the distance. Sulpizio exclaims that it is Maria, the daughter of the illustrious Twenty-first. Maria, a pert young lady in the uniform of Napoleon's army, comes in smartly. She and Sulpizio affectionately greet each other. The regiment, says Maria, is everything to her—father, brother, guardian. She does her comrades credit, she avers, because she is a true soldier.

A spirited duet follows ("Io vidi la luce nel camp guerir"—"Au bruit de la guerre"). Maria sings that her joy is in camp life and in battle, while Sulpizio compliments himself on the fact that he has brought her up to be a lady. After joining her in expressing various patriotic sentiments, Sulpizio recalls the day he found her as a baby and how the soldiers immediately adopted her as their child. Then, after she grew to womanhood, they chose her as their vivandière. The duet comes to a climax as Maria and Sulpizio sing the *Rataplan, rataplan* refrain for which the opera is famous.

The sergeant then tells Maria that the regiment is agreed that it is time she found herself a husband. The men have observed, he says, that she has been talking to a young Tyrolean. Maria answers that he is a young peasant who recently saved her life. Just as she is about to explain, there is a commotion in the distance, and shortly afterward the young man himself—Tonio —is dragged in by soldiers. Maria gasps in astonishment. Sulpizio immediately orders him locked up in the guardhouse.

When Maria asks Tonio why he came to this place he answers that it was because he wished to see her. The soldiers declare that he is suspected of being a spy. At that Maria cries that she will not stand idly by while they condemn to death the man who saved her life. She explains that Tonio rescued her after she had fallen into a mountain torrent. The soldiers roar their approval and agree that this young man is brave enough to join the regiment, while Tonio remarks in an aside that joining up will at least assure him of being close to Maria. The soldiers promptly drink a toast to the prospective recruit and then ask Maria to sing her song about the Twenty-first Regiment ("Lo dice ognun"—"Ah! Chacun le sait, chacun le dit"). As the soldiers join in lustily at intervals, Maria extols the incomparable Twenty-first, which has won so many battles that the Emperor himself has taken notice of its prowess.

After the chorus there is a roll of drums calling the soldiers to quarters. Maria attempts to keep Tonio with her, but her efforts are thwarted by Sulpizio, who sends the young man off with two grenadiers as his guards. The sergeant and his men then leave, singing a martial chorus ("Sprona il tamburo"—"Dès que l'appel sonne"). As Maria is lamenting that Tonio has been taken away from her the young man himself rushes in. He explains that he managed to escape from the sergeant and the soldiers. When Maria asks why he returned he gives her the obvious answer in the opening phrase of the love duet which follows ("Perchè v'amo"—"Depuis l'instant où dans mes bras").

Maria is at first skeptical of his avowals, and when he declares that he was determined to give up home and country for her sake she chides him for even thinking of so unpatriotic a sacrifice. He protests that he would gladly die for her sake, to which Maria teasingly answers that a lover should think of living, not dying. At length she decides to believe his fervent declarations, and the duet concludes with the two singing of their future happiness together.

Just as they embrace, Sulpizio returns. He fumes at Tonio for daring to make love to Maria, pointing out that she is destined to marry the bravest man in the Twenty-first—not a Tyrolean peasant. Tonio promptly declares that he will join up, but Sulpizio scoffs at the idea. The young man asserts that he intends to marry Maria and no one else. Sulpizio threatens him, but Tonio laughs in his face and runs off, calling back to Maria that he will meet her later. Maria runs away in the opposite direction before Sulpizio can stop her.

Angry and impatient with Maria, Sulpizio is about to run after her when Ortensio and the Countess appear. The sergeant's temper is not improved when Ortensio calls him "Captain" instead of "Sergeant." Sulpizio barks at him to keep quiet and finally deigns to listen to what the Countess has to say. She requests the favor of an escort to her castle at Berkenfeld. At the mention of the name Sulpizio starts in surprise, exclaiming that it brings back recollections of a certain Captain Robert. It is the Countess's turn to be surprised. When Sulpizio asks if she knew Captain Robert she replies in some confusion that she had a sister who married the captain secretly. They had an infant daughter, and then the mother died. The daughter, Sulpizio breaks in, is Maria, the pride of the Twenty-first Regiment.

He shows proof of Maria's identity by producing a letter written by Captain Robert just before the battle in which he was slain. The letter instructed his servant to carry the child to Berkenfeld Castle, but the servant was himself slain before he reached the castle. Maria was subsequently found by the soldiers, who reared her as their own daughter.

The Countess remarks that she hopes the child has been brought up to be a lady. Sulpizio's enthusiastic assurances on this point are interrupted by the sound of Maria's voice loudly calling to the sergeant to hurry and emphasizing her summons by a succession of lusty soldier's oaths. The Countess, of course, is shocked. When Maria swaggers in the embarrassed Sulpizio introduces her to the Countess, who addresses the girl as her niece. Obviously unimpressed by the fact that the Countess is her aunt, Maria turns to Sulpizio with another oath and demands to know if this means that she must leave her regiment. The sergeant replies that her military career has come to an end. When Maria vehemently protests he shows her the letter, explaining that it is the last will and testament of her father, Captain Robert. It was his wish, Sulpizio says, that Maria be committed to the care of her aunt. Maria reads the letter and is heartbroken. Sulpizio sadly bids her good-by and leaves, while the Countess orders Ortensio to have a carriage in readiness.

There is a fanfare in the distance, and soon the regiment comes marching in to sing the stirring *Rataplan* chorus, the burden of which is the glory of combat and victory. At the conclusion of the chorus Tonio marches in with the French colors conspicuously displayed on his hat. In a vigorous air he informs the soldiers that he has enlisted and is now their comrade ("Amici miei che allegro giorno"—"Ah, mes amis, quel jour de fête"). He admits that he has joined the colors for the love of Maria and then asks permission of her "fathers" to marry her. When they scornfully refuse he assures them that Maria loves him as ardently as he loves her. The soldiers philosophically decide that if such is the case they may as well approve the match. They express sentiments to that effect in an ensuing chorus ("Che scena! che imbroglio!"—"Que dire, que faire"). In florid solo interludes Tonio expresses his joy over their decision.

But his hopes are shattered when Sulpizio reappears and tells him that Maria's days with the regiment are over, for she has been consigned to the care of a relative. Maria sings her farewell in a tender refrain ("Convien partir, o miei compagni d'arme"—"Il faut partir, mes bons compagnons"). An ensemble is built up as Sulpizio, Tonio, and the soldiers voice their sorrow. After the chorus Tonio declares that he will not leave Maria, whereupon Sulpizio reminds him that he has enlisted and must go with the regiment. The ensemble is resumed as the men angrily consign the Countess to the devil for thwarting Maria's romance. Maria and Tonio heartbrokenly bid each other farewell. The Countess sternly orders Maria to come away with her. After the impressive climax of the chorus the soldiers present arms. Maria, though tearful, salutes smartly, passes through the ranks, and then walks up the road at the rear toward the carriage, which is waiting out of sight. Just before she disappears she turns and waves farewell. Tonio rips the colors from his hat and stamps on them as the curtain falls.

ACT TWO

The salon of Berkenfeld Castle. Ortensio ushers in Sulpizio, who has his arm in a sling, evidently having been wounded in a skirmish. He has been given permission to remain at the castle with Maria for the present. Ortensio tells him that the marriage papers have been prepared and that the Duchess will soon arrive with the young Duke, who has been selected as a likely husband for Maria. When Ortensio leaves, Sulpizio frets over the thought that Maria, accustomed to carefree regimental life, now must do whatever she is told and is even obliged to learn the minuet. Maria enters. She is very downcast, and Sulpizio tries to cheer her. She tells the sergeant that the Countess will soon be here to teach her a song which she is to sing at a party this evening. She fumes that she is not interested in singing these dull songs—nor is she interested in barons or dukes. She wants only Tonio. Sulpizio then reveals that Tonio was wounded in action and that there has been no news either of him or the regiment.

At that point the Countess, attired in antiquated finery, sweeps in to rehearse Maria in her song, *Venus Descendeth*, by the eminent Maestro Caffariello. Seating herself at a harpsichord in one corner of the room, the Countess orders Maria to begin. Maria dutifully sings the opening strains of a pompous and sentimental aria about Venus descending at twilight to meet her lover ("Sorgeva il di del bosco in seno"—"Le jour naissait dans le bocage").

Sulpizio murmurs to Maria that such songs were never sung by the regiment. Softly he repeats a phrase of the *Rataplan*, and Maria, without thinking, takes it up. The Countess asks the meaning of this strange interruption. Maria stammers that she has lost her place. She begins again, but after a phrase or two she and Sulpizio again break into the martial refrain of the *Rataplan* ("Egli è la"—"Le voilà, le voilà!").

A lively trio follows. Maria and Sulpizio, caught up in the spirit of the music, march about the room singing of the glories of the Twenty-first, while the Countess does her best to bring Maria back to her aria. The more indignant the Countess becomes over what she terms the vulgarities of a common soldier's song, the more enthusiastically Maria and Sulpizio sing. The trio comes to an end when the Countess storms out. Maria goes to her room. Sulpizio, also about to leave, is met by Ortensio, who tells him that a wounded soldier is outside and wishes to see him. Assuming it is Tonio, the sergeant rushes out.

Maria reappears, lamenting that her fate is sealed. In a moving aria she sings that wealth and position are meaningless to her without true love ("Me sedur han creduto"—"C'en est donc fait et mon coeur va changer"). As she is bewailing her plight she hears the beat of drums outside. In another moment her beloved soldiers, Tonio among them, crowd into the salon, and Maria rapturously welcomes them. The soldiers hail the reunion in a lusty chorus, in which Maria joins. Sulpizio appears and also is enthusiastically greeted.

The sergeant declares that the occasion calls for some drinking. He summons the bewildered Ortensio and orders him to give a bottle of wine to every soldier. He then sends the men into the garden, where they are to be served. He and Tonio and Maria now sing a delightful trio in which they rejoice over the fact that the three of them have been reunited ("Stretti insiem tutti tre"—"Tous les trois réunis"). In the central portion of the number there is a brief change of mood as Tonio and Maria try to make Sulpizio promise that he will plead their cause with the Countess. He warns them that certain complications are involved, but they pay no heed. Finally the trio reverts to its original sparkling theme.

The Countess now comes in. Eying Tonio, she expresses indignation at seeing a grenadier in her drawing room. Maria explains that he is Tonio, whom she loves very much. Tonio starts to speak, but the Countess cuts him short with the announcement that Maria is to marry the Duke of Crackenthorp this very day. Sulpizio protests, but the Countess rebukes him for taking sides against her. The argument ends when the Countess abruptly orders Tonio to leave and sends Maria weeping to her room. Asking Sulpizio to remain, she tells him to lock the door. She then shows him a letter, requesting him to read it aloud. It reveals that Maria is actually the daughter of the Countess—the result of a clandestine romance with a French officer during her youth. The Countess implores Sulpizio to help her persuade Maria to marry the Duke of Crackenthorp for the sake of social position. The sergeant promises to do what he can and then leaves to advise Maria.

The Duchess and the notary are announced. Informing the Countess that her son has been delayed, the Duchess inquires about Maria. The Countess explains that her niece will appear shortly. Sulpizio returns to report that he has had no success with Maria. He suggests that if the girl is told that the Countess is her mother she will not dare disobey. The Countess agrees, and Sulpizio returns to Maria, while the notary announces that the Duke has already signed the marriage contract. It awaits only Maria's signature. Meanwhile the ladies in waiting and others of the court have arrived for the ceremony.

Sulpizio leads in Maria, who tearfully approaches her mother and asks if she must sign. The Countess answers firmly that it is her wish. Just then there is a commotion outside, and in the next moment the soldiers, with Tonio at their head, burst into the room. In a vigorous chorus they assure Maria that they will not permit their "daughter" to be forced into an unwelcome marriage ("Ti rincora, amata figlia"—"Au secours de notre fille"). She is pledged to Tonio, they protest, and she is their own vivandière. There are various expressions of consternation from the ladies.

Maria steps forward and in a dramatic air declares that she cannot repudiate such sincere kindness and affection ("Quando fanciulla ancor l'avverso"—"Quand le destin au milieu"). Her loyalty wins the hearts of not only the court but the Countess as well. Asserting that she will not stand in the way of the lovers' happiness, the Countess gives them her blessing. Sulpizio avows that if it were not for his long mustachios he would reward the

Countess's magnanimity with a kiss. The ladies in waiting are scandalized, but their objections are lost in the brief but stirring ensemble in which all sing a salute to France ("Salvezza alla Francia"—"Salut à la France"). The curtain falls.

Die Fledermaus

("The Bat")

by JOHANN STRAUSS

[1825–1899]

Libretto by
C. HAFFNER *and* F. F. R. GENÉE

Adapted from the play, LE RÉVEILLON, by Henry Meilhac and Ludovic Halévy, based on the comedy, DAS GEFÄNGNIS, by the German playwright Roderich Benedix.

CHARACTERS

Alfred, a singer...*Tenor*
Adele, chambermaid in the von Eisenstein home.................*Soprano*
Rosalinde von Eisenstein......................................*Soprano*
Blind, a lawyer...*Tenor*
Gabriel von Eisenstein..*Tenor*
Dr. Falke, "The Bat"...*Baritone*
Frank, a prison warden.......................................*Baritone*
Ida, sister of Adele.....................................*Speaking role*
Prince Orlofsky, a wealthy young Russian..............*Mezzo-soprano*
Frosch, a turnkey.......................................*Speaking role*
Guests of Prince Orlofsky, dancers, servants

Place: Vienna
Time: Early nineteenth century
First performance: Theater an der Wien, Vienna, April 5, 1874
Original language: German

ALTHOUGH it is part and parcel of the Vienna of more than a century ago, this delightful operetta by Johann Strauss the younger, the "Waltz King," is a perennial favorite. The plot has weathered any number of adaptations. It has been known variously as *Night Birds* (London, 1911), *The Merry Countess* (New York, 1912), *One Wonderful Night* (New York, 1929), *Champagne Sec* (New York, 1933), and *Rosalinda* (New York, 1942). In recent years, with modernized adaptations of the libretto, it has enjoyed great popularity and has become one of the outstanding box-office attractions in operatic repertoire.

The overture, popular in concert repertoire, is a potpourri of the operetta's main themes. After an *allegro vivace* opening, it touches on the following themes: Rosalinde's mock-serious farewell to Eisenstein before he goes off to jail, Eisenstein's wrath when—disguised as the lawyer Blind—he learns how Rosalinde has "deceived" him with Alfred, and the famous waltz which is the core of the operetta itself.

ACT ONE[1]

The home of Gabriel von Eisenstein in the suburbs of Vienna. Behind the scenes, Alfred sings soulfully about his "dove," who has flown ("Täubchen das entflattert ist"). In the manner of moon-struck tenors, of course, he yearns for her return—the dove in this case being Rosalinde, the wife of Gabriel von Eisenstein. His serenade is interrupted by the entrance of Adele, who comes into the room with a letter in her hand.

In the form of a brilliant cadenza, she laughs in glee at what she has read. The letter is from her sister Ida, who is in the ballet. She writes that she has been invited to a magnificent party to be given by the young Prince Orlofsky. Adele must come to the party—she can borrow one of her mistress's dresses for the occasion—and Ida will introduce her to the Prince.

Enchanted, Adele thinks it over and wonders what excuse she can give to get away to the party. If she only were that "dove" Alfred is singing about, she could easily fly there. When, at this point, Alfred bursts into song again, Adele impatiently calls to him to be quiet. Rosalinde enters, hears Alfred, and recognizes the voice as belonging to someone she knew years ago. The fact that he is now close enough to be heard gives her considerable concern.

Adele resorts to an old and not very bright trick. Bursting into tears, she begs permission to go and see her aunt, who is very ill. The ruse fails miserably when Rosalinde tells her maid she cannot have the evening off. The matter is taken up in duet form as Rosalinde repeats her orders and Adele sings about the cruel fate that prevents a lowly serving maid from comforting her only relative in her last hours. Still weeping, Adele leaves.

Rosalinde turns to see Alfred standing in the doorway. She draws back in alarm. Spoken dialogue follows. Alfred dramatically opens his arms to her. When she reminds him that she is married, he replies that doesn't worry him in the least. Rosalinde then tells him her husband may be home any minute, but Alfred says he knows Eisenstein is due in jail this very night. When Rosalinde implores him to leave, Alfred makes her promise to let him visit her while her husband is in jail. Rosalinde promises, and the tenor struts off, theatrically singing "Addio!" Hearing his high notes, Rosalinde almost swoons.

Suddenly there is a commotion outside and Eisenstein storms in with the lawyer Blind at his heels. A vigorous trio ensues ("Nein, mit solchen Advokaten"). Eisenstein berates Blind for bungling his case in court (he had drawn a jail term for talking back to an official). Highly incensed, Blind tries to justify himself as best he can, while Rosalinde tries to placate both men. To put an end to the uproar, Rosalinde advises Blind to leave. Eisen-

---

[1] In current versions, the act is preceded by a curtain speech by Dr. Falke. He explains why he is called "The Bat," and says that now he is about to pay out Gabriel von Eisenstein for a trick Eisenstein played on him at a certain masquerade party.

stein heartily seconds the motion and points dramatically to the door. Sputtering that he will have revenge, Blind rushes away.

Rosalinde soothingly tells her husband not to get excited—his five days in jail will be over in no time. Five days, he roars, is bad enough, but because of that stupid lawyer, three days have been added to his sentence. And what is worse, he must report at the jail this very night or the police will come and fetch him. Rosalinde, with half her thoughts on Alfred, bewails the fate that will separate her from Gabriel for eight whole days. In a repetition of the opening theme of the trio, Eisenstein fumes again over the stupidity of his lawyer. At that moment Blind himself returns.

He hastily assures Eisenstein that he will appeal the sentence and that he is a match for any legal skulduggery being practiced on his client. In support of his assertion, Blind reels off a string of legal terms. Gabriel begs him to desist, while Rosalinde helpfully takes her husband's side as he rants that lawyers do nothing but bring their clients to ruin. Recriminations fly thick and fast as the trio comes to a stormy close. Then Eisenstein boots Blind out of the room.

Dialogue follows. Eisenstein explains to Rosalinde that he talked the jailer into allowing him to come home for a last meal with his wife. Rosalinde is properly grateful. Gabriel rings for Adele, who comes in still sobbing about her poor dying aunt. Eisenstein dryly observes that the aunt has certainly died at least a thousand deaths to date. He then tells Adele to order up a very special dinner and to pack up his clothes—something . . . er . . . appropriate. When both Adele and Rosalinde look at him questioningly, he explains he wants to look his best the first time in jail. Adele, leaving, comes back to announce Dr. Falke.

Entering with a flourish, Dr. Falke suavely compliments Rosalinde on getting rid of her tyrannical husband for eight days, then mockingly congratulates Eisenstein for having three extra days added to his sentence. Rosalinde leaves to help pack up his clothes. When the men are alone, Falke gleefully tells Eisenstein that he has arranged to take him to a glorious party tonight, where Eisenstein will meet some of Vienna's most beautiful women. When Eisenstein protests he has to go to jail, Falke tells him he can go in the morning. But for tonight, there's the party at the villa of the famous Prince Orlofsky, the mad young Russian, whose guests, so they say, take baths in champagne. The Prince, Falke adds, specifically asked him to bring only the gayest and most brilliant people, so. . . . When Eisenstein modestly admits he can fill that bill, Falke agrees: Take Gabriel's genius for practical jokes, for example.

The two then recall the night of the masquerade ball, three years ago, when Eisenstein appeared as a butterfly and Falke as a bat. Falke managed to get thoroughly drunk. Instead of taking him home, Gabriel deposited his friend in the middle of the park to sleep it off. He woke up Sunday morning, in broad daylight, clad in his bat costume and had to walk home with all the passers-by laughing at him. Chuckling, Eisenstein says he will never forget that trick. With a meaning Eisenstein misses entirely, Falke says he won't either. Then he suggests Gabriel take along his watch that strikes the hours—the one he promises to every girl he meets, and gives to none.

This leads into a duet ("Komm mit mir"). To a tantalizing polka accompaniment, Falke paints the picture of the riotous night in prospect, assuring Eisenstein nobody will ever find out. He is to go as the "Marquis Renard." Eisenstein finally convinces himself he can get away with deceiving Rosalinde—and still get to jail on schedule. The two wind up the duet in a merry climax and begin dancing around the room together. Rosalinde comes in and stares at them in amazement. They pass the situation off with a joke and then Falke leaves.

Adele comes in with Eisenstein's "jail clothes"—trousers, shirt, and pajamas, all striped. It is her idea of something "appropriate." But Eisenstein says that in view of the distinguished company he will have in jail—one or two of the nobility, an impresario, a banker, an editor, and so on—it will pay him to look his best. As Falke says, he might make some good contacts. And so, he tells the surprised Rosalinde, it had better be full dress. In great good humor he goes to his room to get ready.

Rosalinde takes due note of the sudden change in his demeanor, but then begins thinking about Alfred again. Adele brings in the dinner on a wheeled serving table. As she arranges the dishes, Rosalinde tells her she may have the evening off to see her aunt, after all. Before Adele can recover from her surprise at this, Eisenstein comes bouncing in, resplendent in full evening dress. He must be off, he tells Rosalinde gaily. As for the dinner, he disdains the thought of food at a time like this. Then, sighs Rosalinde, this is farewell.

This cues in the famous "Farewell" trio ("So muss allein ich bleiben"), one of the most delightful numbers in the score. Rosalinde begins it as she wonders how she will bear the anguish of eight lonely days without her husband. There will be only the empty coffee cup at the breakfast table . . . out of sheer sorrow she will drink her own coffee black and bitter. In a serio-comic phrase, all three express their unutterable sadness over this situation. With hilarious effect, they repeat these lugubrious sentiments in an impudently merry ensemble. At its conclusion, Eisenstein dances off and Adele skips after him.

Alone, Rosalinde murmurs that she wishes she had time to grieve, but she must now think of herself—and Alfred. Adele re-enters with a huge suitcase containing, she explains, "extras in case of emergency." She bids Rosalinde good-by, promising to be back early. No sooner has she gone than Alfred appears. In the face of Rosalinde's half-hearted objections, he dons Eisenstein's dressing gown, cap, and slippers, sits down at the table, and announces that tonight he is going to play the role of Rosalinde's husband. He further scandalizes her by asking what they will have for breakfast next morning. Then he pours wine to the accompaniment of "Libiamo," the drinking song from La Traviata. Rosalinde begs him not to sing, then with a sigh admits she once loved Alfred's singing not wisely but too well.

Lifting his glass, Alfred begins another of the operetta's outstanding numbers ("Trinke, Liebchen, trinke schnell"). Drink up, his song goes, because wine brings sparkle to the eyes and joy to the heart. And never worry about the things in life that can't be changed. Rosalinde joins him in a lilting duet.

This idyllic interlude is interrupted by the sound of voices outside.

Rosalinde frets, but Alfred calmly goes on drinking. The door opens and there stands a man. Bowing to Rosalinde, he introduces himself as Frank, the prison warden. He has come, he says, to escort Herr Gabriel von Eisenstein to jail. As Rosalinde tries to explain the situation, Alfred, feeling his drinks, sings a few phrases of the main theme of the duet. Desperately Rosalinde tries to quiet him, but he sings happily on. When Frank suggests he come along quietly, Alfred offers him a glass of wine. The two join in the closing phrases of the duet, singing it, however, faster and more stridently than it should be sung.

Continuing the ensemble, Frank urges "Herr von Eisenstein" to hurry because it is getting late. Alfred promptly informs him he is *not* von Eisenstein. In an aside, Rosalinde tells him at least to pretend he's her husband for the sake of appearances. Frank begins to smell a rat. This introduces a trio ("Mit mir so spät"). Rosalinde asks Frank how he could possibly suspect her of any impropriety, considering this scene of intimate connubial bliss. Here is the husband in comfortable fireside attire, scarcely able to keep his eyes open. Alfred and Frank duly ponder this ingenious explanation. Finally Frank says he is convinced beyond doubt that this man really is Herr von Eisenstein—and now, will he please come along without wasting any more time? Rosalinde begs Alfred to go for her sake.

Alfred agrees, remarking that he and Rosalinde's husband probably will end up sharing the same cell. Taking full advantage of the situation, he insists on passionately kissing his "wife" farewell. While Frank extols the virtues of his "birdhouse," Alfred and Rosalinde resign themselves to the situation. Thus the trio comes to a close. Frank leads Alfred—still wearing Eisenstein's dressing gown—out of the room. The curtain falls.

ACT TWO

The villa of Prince Orlofsky. A gay party is in progress, with guests milling about. They hail the Prince's hospitality in a rousing chorus ("Ein Souper heut uns winkt"). Adele and Ida come forward and converse briefly. When Ida expresses surprise at seeing her poor chambermaid of a sister at so fashionable a party, Adele reminds her of the letter she wrote inviting her. Ida answers she knows nothing about a letter; somebody obviously has been playing a joke. Adele goes on to tell her sister how she made up the excuse about her dying aunt, and also that she borrowed from her mistress the very dress she's wearing. Ignoring Ida's disapproval of the whole business, Adele says she intends to make some fast friends before the evening is over.

Falke comes up and interrupts their conversation. He has been trying to catch up with Adele all evening and now begins to work fast. He coyly compliments her on the starring role she is to have in a new play. When she asks him what this is all about, he tells her if she plays her part well her career is assured. Adding that he will act as her personal manager, Falke tells Adele that her stage name is to be "Olga." Before Adele can question him further, Prince Orlofsky himself enters.[2] A spoiled, haughty dandy, he affects a monocle and smokes cigarettes in an absurdly long holder. Going over to Falke, he sighs that he is bored to distraction—he cannot laugh, and his billions only make him miserable. He promises Falke a handsome present if he can make him laugh tonight. Done, says Falke. For that very purpose he has prepared a little comedy called "The Revenge of the Bat."

Then Falke introduces Olga and Ida to the Prince. Faintly amused, Orlofsky gives the girls a purse and tells them to try their luck at the gaming table. They leave. Falke then confides that "Olga" actually is the chambermaid of the hero of the comedy. At that instant a servant announces the "Marquis Renard." Greeting Falke, Eisenstein eagerly asks where are all the pretty girls he promised to have on hand. All at the gaming table, Falke says. He then introduces Eisenstein to Prince Orlofsky. The Prince calls for champagne and gathers the guests around him. For their benefit, he explains his philosophy of life in a characteristically arrogant refrain ("Ich lade gern mir Gäste ein"). He likes to invite people to his home, sings the Prince, because they keep him from being bored. His guests may do as they please—*chacun à son goût*—but they must drink and enjoy themselves. The one thing that is not permitted in his home is boredom. He who doesn't drink will have a bottle thrown at his head. As for himself, the Prince sings on, he has seen everything and done everything, and for him only one worthwhile thing remains: *chacun à son goût.*

Spoken dialogue follows. While Eisenstein is busy drinking champagne and ogling the ladies, Falke tells Orlofsky he has invited the "Marquis's" wife. When the Prince observes that is nothing unusual, Falke explains that, in the first place, Eisenstein is not a marquis, and in the second, his wife thinks he is in jail. Orlofsky nods approvingly.

Adele, re-entering from the gaming room with Ida, hands Orlofsky his purse—empty. She and Eisenstein catch sight of each other at the same moment and both stare dumfounded. With a flourish, Falke introduces "Marquis Renard" to the girls. Orlofsky remarks that the Marquis seems quite impressed with Olga. Pulling himself together, Eisenstein asks Olga if she has always been "Olga." Has the Marquis, she asks sweetly, always been the "Marquis"?

Caught completely off guard, Eisenstein stammers that Adele looks exactly like a chambermaid he knows. Adele pretends to be highly insulted, while Orlofsky, Falke, and the others roar with laughter over Eisenstein's *faux pas.* This cues in an ensemble in which the Prince explains to his guests Eisenstein's ridiculous mistake. Then Adele steps forward and begins the famous *Laughing Song* ("Mein Herr Marquis").

With charming impudence Adele suggests that a man as clever as the Marquis should learn to use his eyes to better advantage. It is obvious that a girl like herself, with her face and figure, couldn't possibly be a chambermaid. The good Marquis's blunder is really too funny for words, she sings, ending the refrain in a phrase of rippling laughter which is repeated by the chorus. In a second verse, Adele sings that the Marquis's thoughts obviously

---

[2] This role is customarily played by a mezzo-soprano.

are on some lady's maid, and this has temporarily obscured his vision. The laughing refrain is repeated while Eisenstein squirms.

Dialogue continues. Making the best of things, Eisenstein compliments Adele on her charms and she responds in kind. A servant announces the "Chevalier Chagrin." Aside, Falke explains to Orlofsky that the Chevalier really is Frank, the prison warden. Orlofsky says that now he is beginning to understand the plot. Falke introduces the Chevalier to Orlofsky and then to Eisenstein, who launches into a nonsensical exchange of French phrases with the bogus cavalier, along with some other badinage. Falke then announces the Prince is awaiting a distinguished guest, a Hungarian Countess. Though ravishingly beautiful, she insists on remaining incognito and will come to the party wearing a mask. For Eisenstein's benefit, Falke goes on to say the Countess has an extremely jealous husband—another reason for the mask. It is hoped that everyone, Falke adds pointedly, will respect the lady's desire to remain unknown. All the guests then retire to the garden, leaving Falke and Orlofsky alone. In a moment, the Countess—Rosalinde, of course—arrives.

Warned by Falke that here is *the wife*, Orlofsky discreetly leaves. Rushing over to Falke, Rosalinde asks him if what he wrote in his letter to her is true. She can see for herself, replies Falke, pointing outside—there is Herr von Eisenstein, "serving his term." Rosalinde stares, then gasps in surprise. Not only Eisenstein, she cries furiously, but her own maid, Adele. Then and there she swears dire revenge, but Falke coolly advises her not to start tonight, for the comedy is still to be played out.

As though to underscore his words, Eisenstein comes out of the gaming room followed by Frank and a bevy of giggling girls, all of whom are begging him for his watch. He dangles it tantalizingly before their eyes, adroitly keeping it out of their reach. Rosalinde looks on, smoldering with anger. Frank calls Eisenstein's attention to the Countess, whereupon Gabriel walks over to her, introduces himself, and casually sets his watch chiming. In a stagey Hungarian accent, Rosalinde admires the watch and hints she would like to have it. She then not only traps Gabriel into saying he isn't married but gets him to promise to give her the watch if she will unmask—tomorrow. In the next moment she manages to get the watch away from him. Eisenstein, of course, is completely enchanted, while Rosalinde, aside, fumes over his outrageous flirting just because he considers her—his own wife—a new conquest. Keeping the watch out of his reach, she says she wants to time her heartbeat by its chiming. As Eisenstein attempts to get hold of the watch, Rosalinde laughs triumphantly in a brilliant obbligato. Realizing he has been tricked, Eisenstein bewails his foolhardy gallantry.

Adele, Ida, and the other guests enter. Approaching Rosalinde, Adele invites her to unmask. When Orlofsky reminds her that, in his house, every lady has the right to conceal or reveal as much as she chooses, Adele tartly remarks she isn't sure the lady is a *real* Countess. Thereupon the Countess says the music of her homeland will speak for her. Then she sings the beautiful and moving Csárdas ("Klänge der Heimat"). The song expresses a deep longing of a Hungarian for the homeland, then bursts into the Frischka, a fiery native dance rhythm. It comes to a climax in a brilliant vocal display.

Orlofsky and Eisenstein propose a toast, which is the cue for the well-known *Champagne Chorus,* with its irresistible waltz rhythm. The chorus begins in 2/4 time with "patter" verses sung by Orlofsky, Eisenstein, and Adele. Then follows a refrain in 6/8, in which the principals, all thinking of their own little intrigues, mockingly toast each other and respond with the recurring phrase, *merci, merci, merci.*

Finally Falke offers a toast to "eternal brotherhood," and this introduces the thrilling waltz chorus ("Brüderlein und Schwesterlein"), with its refrain of *dui-du, dui-du,* sung as the guests clink their glasses.

A ballet follows. In the original score it begins with a waltz in Spanish style, changes to a Scotch dance, then to a waltz in the Russian manner. Looking on, the guests break into a polka chorus ("Marianka komm und tanz"), after which the ballet goes into a wild Hungarian dance. In many performances, however, a special ballet—such as *The Blue Danube*—is interpolated.

At its end, Orlofsky steps forward and invites the guests themselves to dance. A Viennese waltz begins, and as the guests swing into the dance they sing a chorus in praise of this night of revelry and wine ("Ha, welch ein Fest"). To the waltz accompaniment there is an exchange of dialogue. Eisenstein and Frank, blissfully drunk on champagne, swear eternal friendship while trying to keep each other from falling down. Rosalinde, Orlofsky, and Falke gleefully speculate on what will happen when the two meet in jail—sober. Frank asks Eisenstein what time it is, which reminds Gabriel that he must get his watch back from the Countess—and also get her to unmask. He promptly makes an attempt, but Rosalinde—with the connivance of the others—neatly puts him off. She cannot unmask, she sings, because she has an unsightly freckle on her nose.

Just as Eisenstein protests that flimsy excuse, the watch strikes six. Momentarily startled into sobriety, Eisenstein and Frank realize they are due at the jail. There is some riotous horseplay as the two shout for their hats and coats and put on the wrong ones. Finally, leaning on each other for support, the two dance tipsily toward the door. Roaring with laughter, the guests watch them go as the curtain falls.

ACT THREE

After a brief orchestral interlude, the curtain rises on an empty stage. The scene is the warden's office in the prison. Some of the cell doors may be seen at the back. In the foreground is Frank's desk, on which are books and papers plus tea cups and a decanter. It is early morning. Offstage, Alfred can be heard singing amorous phrases from grand opera arias and then a phrase from the "Dove" song he sang in the first act. The turnkey Frosch, a heavily mustachioed comedy character, comes in carrying a lantern and a bunch of oversized cell keys. He is hopelessly drunk and very happy. This jail is fine, he mumbles, the whiskey is better, and if that fellow in Number Twelve would only stop his infernal operatics everything would be perfect. He shouts to Alfred to be quiet, then lurches out.

Frank enters, very much the worse for wear, his hat battered and his coat buttoned the wrong way. He too is in a happy daze. As the orchestra takes up the theme of the Act Two waltz, he whistles it softly. He manages to get his overcoat halfway off, then holds it like a dance partner and waltzes unsteadily about. With exaggerated gallantry he stops and bows low to "Olga" and "Ida." As the music echoes the gaiety of Orlofsky's party, Frank sings a phrase or two of the *Champagne Chorus.*

With a heroic attempt to straighten up, he starts making tea, but the effort is too much. Slowly sinking into the chair at his desk, he covers his face with a newspaper and falls asleep. In a moment or two Frosch staggers back in. He rouses Frank by bellowing that he has come to make his report. A comic byplay follows as the two try to figure out what they are talking about. Frosch manages to tell the warden that "Number Twelve" insists on seeing a lawyer. That, says Frank, would be Eisenstein, and he is entitled to a lawyer. The entrance bell rings. Frosch goes to the door, looks out, and reports that two ladies are outside. Frank orders him to let them in. Adele and Ida enter.

Without wasting any time, Adele confesses to Frank that she is not an actress but only Gabriel von Eisenstein's chambermaid. What is more, she borrowed Madame von Eisenstein's dress to wear to the party. Now she would like Frank to put in a good word for her with Eisenstein. So she can keep her job, of course, says Frank. Not at all, Adele retorts—so Eisenstein will persuade his wife to give her chambermaid the dress because it looks so stunning on her. Furthermore, she has decided to permit Herr Frank to "develop" her for the stage. When Frank asks her if she has talent, she sings a song to prove it ("Spiel ich die Unschuld vom Lande").

She can play the innocent country maiden, Adele sings, as convincingly as she can play the proud and haughty queen. As she struts about in the latter role, Ida and Frank imitate a trumpet and drum fanfare. Adele then goes on to show how she can play the bored young wife of an aging Marquis. A handsome Count appears on the scene, and for two whole acts she keeps him at bay. In Act Three she yields, only to be surprised by the Marquis in an embrace with her lover. But the Marquis forgives all, and there is not a dry eye in the theater. Adele ends the song with a brilliant coloratura flourish. Frank loudly applauds her performance.

But before he can make any promises, the entrance bell rings again. Frosch comes in to answer, but Frank goes to see for himself who is calling. He exclaims in dismay when he sees it is the Marquis Renard. Hastily he tells Frosch to get the girls out of the way. As cell Thirteen is the only place vacant, the turnkey gallantly escorts the girls to that "reception room," as he calls it. Eisenstein enters. Dialogue follows in which Frank convinces Gabriel that he is not Chevalier Chagrin, but the prison warden. Gabriel, in turn, tells Frank he himself is no more a Marquis than Frank is a Chevalier, but Herr von Eisenstein. However, Frank has a surprise answer for that. It so happens, says he, that Eisenstein already is in jail, right here in cell Number Twelve. Frank goes on to explain how he arrested the man last night before Orlofsky's party. When Gabriel asks for particulars, Frank obliges: at such and such an address (Eisenstein's own), Eisenstein was in his dressing gown having supper with his wife.

As the truth dawns on him, Eisenstein grinds his teeth in rage. Frank adds fuel to fire by describing how passionately "husband" and wife kissed each other good-by. Eisenstein demands to see this man instantly. No visiting without a permit, Frank curtly informs him. As Eisenstein fumes, Frosch comes in and announces another caller. It's a woman, all done up in veils, he tells Frank. This jail, he mutters, is getting awfully crowded. Frank excuses himself to go and meet the latest arrival, leaving Eisenstein to brood over the fact that Rosalinde has betrayed him.

Frosch re-enters, followed by the lawyer Blind, who is wearing a wig, glasses, and a long coat. He is carrying a brief case. The turnkey leaves, saying he will bring back "Mister Eisenstein." As Blind tries to figure out the situation, Eisenstein turns on him and dresses him down for being a bumbling shyster. He wants to know why Blind is here in the first place. Because Eisenstein sent for him, Blind answers. Realizing who that "Eisenstein" is, Gabriel has a sudden inspiration. He orders Blind to change costumes with him. Snatching the bewildered lawyer's wig, glasses, hat, and brief case, he peels off Blind's coat, pushes him out of the warden's office, and follows.

Frosch comes in with Alfred, who fumes this is no way to treat a famous tenor. Rosalinde enters and Alfred beams with joy, exclaiming that his beloved has come to comfort him in prison. Cutting short his histrionics, Rosalinde tells Alfred her husband will be here shortly, and that it will never do for Alfred to be caught wearing Gabriel's dressing gown. They both agree Eisenstein behaved outrageously in coming to Orlofsky's party. At that moment Gabriel enters, disguised as Blind. Obsequiously he asks if he can be of service, and, in an aside, he mutters that now he will trap the guilty pair.

In an ensuing trio ("Ich stehe voll Zagen"), the complications in which the three are enmeshed are thrashed out. Alfred and Rosalinde sing that obviously the lawyer must have all the facts, but they must use discretion in what they tell him. Eisenstein sings that revenge will be sweet—if he can only bide his time. The facts—he must have all the facts, snaps the lawyer. Alfred explains he was clapped into jail merely for having a late supper with this fair lady here. That is a poor defense, Gabriel bursts out violently in spite of himself. Surprised at his manners, Rosalinde and Alfred remind the lawyer that he is their defender, not their accuser. But Blind angrily warns them to make a full confession. Obviously, the lady was unfaithful to her husband. And just as obviously, Rosalinde and Alfred retort, this lawyer is quite mad. Her husband, Rosalinde goes on, is a scoundrel and a gay deceiver on his own, and when she catches up with him she will scratch his eyes out and sue him for separation. And now, Alfred puts in, how can they make this rascal beg for mercy?

At that, Eisenstein loses all control. Snatching off wig and glasses, he dramatically shouts that he is Eisenstein. There is great consternation. The trio ends uproariously in an exchange of recriminations and expressions of dire vengeance.

These sentiments are continued in ensuing dialogue. But finally Rosalinde brings Gabriel to a full stop by producing his watch and dangling it before his eyes. How can *he* accuse her of deceit, she asks, when she knows exactly what time it is! And doesn't the Marquis, she goes on in her best Hungarian accent, wish to count her heartbeats? Eisenstein groans, cursing himself for being an utter fool. When Alfred affably agrees, Gabriel roars that he is a wife-stealer who—by the way—had better take his hands out of his (Eisenstein's) pockets at once. Alfred calmly tells him to go up to cell Number Twelve and sit out the rest of his sentence—minus the one day which Alfred has obligingly served. Never, says Eisenstein.

Falke comes in, sees the three, and exclaims over the "happy reunion." When Alfred tells him Gabriel refuses to serve the rest of his sentence, Eisenstein declares nobody can prove he *is* Eisenstein. Alfred points out that witnesses are needed because a wife cannot testify against her husband.

Frank, who has just entered, says he can help matters. Calling Frosch, he tells him to bring in the two girls from Number Thirteen. The turnkey drags in Adele and Ida, both furious over being locked up. Rosalinde gasps in surprise. Adele duly identifies Gabriel von Eisenstein and his wife Rosalinde.

Eisenstein merely shrugs, saying the chambermaid is only one witness against him and one doesn't count. In that case, says Frank, stepping forward, he will count himself as another—and there are many more ready to testify. With that, Orlofsky enters, followed by all his party guests.

This cues in the final chorus ("O Fledermaus"). All good-naturedly implore "The Bat"—Falke—to take pity on his victim. Eisenstein, completely bewildered, asks what it all means. Falke explains it was all a joke, staged to pay Eisenstein back for the trick he played the night Falke and Gabriel masqueraded as Butterfly and Bat. Adele, Orlofsky, and Alfred confess they all played their parts to make the joke a success. With a wink, Alfred remarks to Orlofsky that it wasn't all pretense, but what Eisenstein doesn't know won't hurt him.

Gabriel turns to Rosalinde, who embraces him in sweet forgiveness. Frank declares he will underwrite Adele's career to compensate for locking her up in his jail. But Orlofsky says that, as a patron of the arts, he considers that his personal duty. It's his way, he adds, with girls of talent—*chacun à son goût*. Then, in a joyous reprise of the *Champagne Chorus*, the opera comes to a close.

Der Fliegende Holländer
(The Flying Dutchman)
by RICHARD WAGNER
[1813–1883]

Libretto by the Composer

Based on Heine's
MEMOIRS OF HERR VON SCHNABELEWOPSKI
and a novel by Wilhelm Hauff

CHARACTERS

Daland, captain of a Norwegian ship..............................*Bass*
The Steersman of Daland's ship.................................*Tenor*
Vanderdecken, the Dutchman...............................*Baritone*
Senta, daughter of Daland................................*Soprano*
Mary, Senta's nurse...................................*Mezzo-soprano*
Erik, a young huntsman, betrothed to Senta.....................*Tenor*
Norwegian sailors, the crew of the *Flying Dutchman*, village girls

Place: The Norwegian coast
Time: Eighteenth century
First performance: Hoftheater, Dresden, January 2, 1843
Original language: German

WAGNER'S EXPERIENCES during a stormy voyage across the North Sea are said to have inspired him to write an opera based on the legend of the phantom ship. After he had written the libretto he was forced to sell it to secure badly needed funds. A minor composer set Wagner's story to music, but the work failed completely. Wagner meanwhile wrote his own version, finishing it in less than two months.

The opera is of particular significance because in writing it Wagner applied for the first time his theories of "music drama." The unfamiliarity of its musical and dramatic pattern, however, as well as its somber theme, caused it to be coolly received by the public.

According to the legend, Vanderdecken, a Dutch sea captain, tried to sail around the Cape of Good Hope but was beaten back by fierce storms. Infuriated, he swore that he would sail the Cape if it required all eternity to do it. For his profane defiance Satan doomed him to sail the seas forever—unless he could find a woman who would redeem him through love. He was permitted to go ashore once every seven years in search of a woman. The action of the opera takes place during one of the seven-year intervals.

The overture, written after the opera was completed, contains the theme of the Dutchman, strains of the sailors' choruses, the motives of the Curse and Redemption by Love, and Senta's theme.

ACT ONE

A rocky harbor on the Norwegian coast, with a view of the sea in the background. Daland's ship has just anchored during a violent storm, and the sailors are busy on deck, singing as they work. Daland, who has gone ashore to look over the landscape, calls back to the Steersman that the storm drove the ship seven miles from its home port. He recognizes the locality as Sandwike.[1] Coming back on board, Daland sends the sailors to their quarters, tells the Steersman to stand watch, then retires to his cabin.

Seating himself near the helm, the Steersman whiles away the time by singing a ballad about his ladylove ("Mit Gewitter und Sturm"). The smashing of a wave against the side of the ship, indicated by a violent crescendo in the orchestra, interrupts his song. He looks over the side to see if any damage has been done, finds everything safe, and resumes his singing. His voice trails off as he falls asleep.

The storm rises in sudden fury, and in the distance the *Flying Dutchman* appears, its blood-red sails billowing from its black masts. The ship glides alongside the other vessel, and then the anchor is let go with a terrific crash. Startled out of his sleep, the Steersman leaps to his feet. He looks around, hums a few bars of his song, and then sits down and dozes off again. In an eerie silence the crew of the ghost ship brings down the sails and makes everything fast.

Wearily the Dutchman makes his way to shore. Another seven years have gone by, he murmurs, and again the sea has tossed him upon land to resume his eternal quest. In a dramatic aria he describes how he has sailed headlong into danger in a fruitless attempt to find release in death ("Wie oft in Meeres tiefsten Schlund"). But his ship, laden with riches he cannot enjoy, is driven relentlessly on and on. He prays that an angel may rescue him from his terrible doom, then cries out that perhaps only on Judgment Day will he find the oblivion he seeks. His crew echoes the closing phrases of his song.

Daland appears on the deck of his ship, rouses the Steersman, and berates him for falling asleep. The Steersman exclaims in surprise as he sees the other vessel, then hails it through a trumpet. The only answer is an echo. Suddenly Daland catches sight of the Dutchman. Going ashore, he greets the stranger and asks him his name. Identifying himself, the Dutchman tells about his endless travels in an impressive aria ("Durch Sturm und bösen Wind verschlagen"). He begs Daland for a night's lodging in his home, saying he will pay him well for the courtesy.

At a sign from the Dutchman several sailors bring a large chest ashore. He opens the chest before Daland's astonished eyes and shows him a dazzling array of jewels. All are his, the Dutchman says, if he will only give him shelter. To Daland's increasing bewilderment the Dutchman asks him if he will grant his daughter's hand in marriage. Greedily eying the jewels,

[1] It was in the bay of Sandwike that the *Thetis*, in which Wagner sailed from Pillau, Prussia, to London in 1839, sought refuge from a storm.

Daland gives his consent. In an ensuing duet ("Wie? Hör ich recht?") Daland rejoices over this unexpected stroke of good fortune, while the Dutchman expresses the hope that he at last has found a woman who can redeem him.

Meanwhile the weather has cleared and the Steersman shouts that the wind has shifted to the south. Daland tells the Dutchman that they may sail for home at once, but the latter asks him to go on ahead, saying that his crew needs a longer time to rest. The Norwegian vessel sails, with the sailors singing the refrain of the Steersman's song. As the Dutchman goes aboard his own ship the curtain falls.

ACT TWO

The living room of Daland's home.[2] On one wall is a portrait of a bearded young man in Spanish costume. There is a brief introduction, in which we hear the theme of the Steersman's song and a rhythmic sailor's dance. The curtain rises, revealing Mary and a group of girls seated about the fireplace, busy at their spinning wheels. Senta, seated somewhat apart from the others, gazes reflectively at the portrait.

In the expressive *Spinning Chorus* ("Summ' und brumm', du gutes Rädchen") the girls describe how they dutifully toil at their wheels as they wait for their lovers to come home from the sea. Mary chides Senta for idling away her time, while the girls tauntingly sing that she never needs to wait for her lover, for he is a hunter who remains at home. Senta, her eyes fixed on the picture, softly hums the phrase that is her identifying theme. The girls chatter on, remarking that if Senta persists in devoting her attention to the portrait, Erik, her hot-tempered swain, may shoot it from the wall.

Irked by their derisive laughter, Senta angrily tells them that she is tired of their singing. When they ask her to sing her own song, she at first refuses but finally consents to sing the ballad of the Flying Dutchman, familiarly known as *Senta's Ballad* ("Traft ihr das Schiff im Meere an"). As though in a dream she describes the tragic quest of the mariner, and in the dramatic concluding phrases of the aria she feverishly voices the hope that fate has appointed her to save him. The girls exclaim in frightened tones over Senta's wild demeanor.

Erik enters at that moment and, hearing Senta's words, asks in a ringing phrase if she spurns his love. Oblivious to everything in her excitement, Senta does not answer. Mary fumes that if Senta's father were here he would soon drive these foolish thoughts out of her head. Erik informs her that he sighted Daland's ship only a moment ago. Senta joyously greets the news. Mary and the girls bustle about, expressing their happiness in a lively chorus, at the conclusion of which Mary pushes the girls out of the room and follows after them.

As Senta tries to leave, Erik bars her way and implores her to remain,

[2] Wagner wrote the opera in one act, but it was later divided into three for convenience in staging.

crying out, "Bleib', Senta, bleib'l" An impassioned duet follows. Erik begs her to accept his love and forget her mad fantasies about the Dutchman. In answer Senta leads him over to the portrait and asks if his sorrow can match that of the doomed mariner. Erik is in despair as he realizes that she is hopelessly obsessed by the legend of the Dutchman. He tells her of the terrible dream that has been haunting him. In the aria, "Auf hohem Felsen lag' ich träumend," he relates how in his dream he saw a strange vessel come into the harbor. Senta's father came ashore with a dark-visaged seaman—the man in the portrait. Senta rushed into his arms, then boarded the vessel with him and sailed away. In wild ecstasy Senta cries out that she is destined to go with this mariner. Erik, shaken by anguish, rushes from the room.

Staring at the portrait, Senta sings a prayerful phrase. At that moment the Dutchman enters, followed by Daland. Senta cries out in astonishment as she notes the stranger's resemblance to the portrait, then continues to gaze at him as though hypnotized. When Daland rebukes her gently for not greeting her father with her usual embrace she recovers momentarily, takes his hand, and asks who the stranger is. Daland explains in a long mono-logue ("Mögst du, mein Kind"). He tells her that this man has asked for her hand in marriage. He is a rich mariner, and all his wealth will be hers if she consents. Fawningly he bids the Dutchman take note of his daughter's beauty. Observing that the Dutchman and Senta are completely absorbed in each other, Daland, showing his irritation at being ignored, goes out of the room.

Gazing at Senta in awe and wonder, the Dutchman softly sings that here is the maiden of his eternal dreams ("Wie aus der Ferne längst vergang'ner Zeiten"). This introduces a long duet, dominated by the Senta theme, in which the two voice their realization that fate has destined them for each other. At the conclusion of the duet Daland re-enters, saying that the vil-lagers are impatiently awaiting the feast that always marks his return home. It will be the merrier, he adds, if Senta and the Dutchman can announce their betrothal. Senta dramatically affirms that she has consented to be the Dutchman's bride. The scene ends as the three voices blend in an exultant trio.

ACT THREE

The shore of the bay near Daland's home, which is at one side. In the background is the harbor, where Daland's ship and the *Flying Dutchman* are lying side by side. The prelude briefly echoes the Senta motive and the theme of her ballad and then swings into the vigorous rhythm of the *Sailors' Chorus*. The Norwegian ship is ablaze with light when the curtain goes up, and the sailors, in high spirits, strike up the well-known chorus, "Steuer-mann! Lass die Wacht!"

Soon the village girls, carrying baskets of food and drink, emerge from Daland's house and proceed toward the *Flying Dutchman*. Its decks are shrouded in gloom and there is no sign of life aboard. When the Norwegian sailors ask the girls to give them their baskets they reply that the other seamen no doubt are also hungry and thirsty. Drawing close to the *Flying Dutchman*, the girls hail the ship, inviting the crew to eat and drink, but they are greeted by an ominous silence. The Norwegians tauntingly sing that if the sailors refuse food and drink they probably are all dead. Seized by a strange fear, the girls withdraw, whereupon the Norwegians manage to relieve them of their baskets. As the girls return to the house the sailors noisily begin feasting, roaring out another refrain of the chorus.

Suddenly a storm begins to rage around the *Flying Dutchman*, while an eerie bluish flame dances over her decks. Her crew seems to appear out of nowhere, and the men begin to sing in a ghostly chorus. Seven more years have passed, they cry, and they must again set out on their fateful quest. They urge their captain to hurry, mocking him about the bride he has again failed to win. Defiantly they laugh at the storm, singing that their sails are the devil's own, made to last for all eternity. The Norwegians look on, exclaiming in bewilderment. The voices of the two crews join in a stirring climax of the chorus, after which the Norwegians, terrified at the scene aboard the other ship, flee below. There is a burst of savage laughter from the *Flying Dutchman's* crew, and then suddenly everything falls silent.

Senta, greatly excited, rushes out of the house, followed by Erik. Desperately he pleads with her to tell him why she has spurned his love for that of the Dutchman. In a moving aria he implores her to remember the vows they made in the happy past ("Willst jenes Tag's du nicht dich mehr entsinnen"). The Dutchman, meanwhile, approaches and listens with dismay to Erik's words. Feeling that Senta, untrue to Erik, will be false to him as well—and thus deny him redeeming love—he cries out that all is lost. Signaling his crew with a shrill whistle on his pipe, he orders them to set sail.

An intensely dramatic trio follows ("Fort auf das Meer"). Senta tries to convince the Dutchman that she will be faithful to him. He turns from her in despair, singing that he is doomed to continue his wandering because her promise was only a mockery. Erik sings that Senta is in the grip of a fiendish spell and is determined to destroy herself.

In a final effort to dissuade Senta from her purpose the Dutchman tells her that her promise to him was not made before God and that thus she may escape being doomed with him. He warns that the curse upon him has destroyed many another before her. Senta's only answer is that she has always known of his doom and that she must share it with him. Erik desperately calls for help. Daland, Mary, and the village girls come rushing from the house. All recoil in horror when the strange mariner shouts that he is the Flying Dutchman, whose curse is feared over the seven seas. He dashes madly aboard his ship, which sails at once out of the harbor.

Senta, struggling fiercely with Daland, Erik, and Mary, frees herself and runs to the cliff at the water's edge. Exultantly singing that she has been faithful unto death ("Hier steh' ich, treu dir bis zum Tod!"), she throws herself into the sea. The *Flying Dutchman* immediately disappears beneath the waves. Then, as the Redemption theme peals out, Senta and the Dutchman, clasped in each other's arms, rise slowly out of the sea. The curtain falls.

La Forza del Destino

by GIUSEPPE VERDI

[1813–1901]

Libretto by
FRANCESCO MARIA PIAVE

Based on the Duke de Rivas's play
DON ALVARO O LA FUERZA DEL SINO

CHARACTERS

The Marquis of Calatrava...................................... *Bass*
Leonora, his daughter.. *Soprano*
Curra, her maid.. *Mezzo-soprano*
Don Alvaro, a young nobleman of Inca origin................... *Tenor*
The Alcalde of Hornachuelos................................. *Bass*
Don Carlo di Vargas, brother of Leonora...................... *Baritone*
Mastra Trabuco, a muleteer................................. *Tenor*
Preziosilla, a gypsy fortuneteller......................... *Mezzo-soprano*
Brother Melitone, a friar.................................. *Bass*
Father Guardiano, Superior of the convent..................... *Bass*
A military surgeon... *Baritone*
Soldiers, peasants, beggars, pilgrims, monks, dancers,
an innkeeper and his wife

Place: Spain and Italy
Time: Eighteenth century
First performance: St. Petersburg, November 10, 1862
Original language: Italian

THIS OPERA, along with *Un Ballo in Maschera*, marks the high point in what has been called the "second period" in Verdi's career. At this stage his music developed a greater dramatic significance as well as richer and more versatile harmonic patterns.

There is a long and dramatic introduction entitled the *Sinfonia*. It begins with a series of powerful trumpet blasts symbolizing Fate. Then follows a theme in a haunting, uneasy mood that is associated with Leonora. Other dominating themes are those of Leonora's prayer in Act Two and Don Alvaro's entreaty to Don Carlo before the fatal duel in Act Four.

ACT ONE

A paneled hall in the palace of the Marquis of Calatrava in Seville. At the rear are two windows, one of which is open, affording a glimpse of the moonlight outside. Between the windows is a wardrobe. Doors at right and left lead into various rooms. One, toward the back, opens on a terrace. The Marquis has brought his daughter Leonora to the privacy of his palace in Seville to keep her from seeing Don Alvaro, with whom she is in love. Her father bitterly opposes the romance because Don Alvaro is a foreigner with Inca blood in his veins. The Marquis, a proud and haughty Spaniard, refuses to consider him a worthy suitor. Leonora, however, has resolved to elope with Don Alvaro this very night.

The Marquis is bidding Leonora good night. Curra, her maid, waits in the background. Noting that Leonora seems restless and unhappy, the Marquis tries to calm her. He tells her that here she is safe from the attentions of her unwelcome suitor and urges her to leave the cares of the future in his hands. Embracing her affectionately, the Marquis retires to his room. As Leonora, weeping softly, sinks into a chair, Curra begins taking clothing from the wardrobe and packing it in a traveling bag. Leonora sobs that her father's kindness has almost broken her resolve to leave and has brought her to the verge of confessing her plan to elope. Curra reminds her that to have mentioned Don Alvaro's name to her father would have meant her lover's doom.

In a moving soliloquy Leonora grieves over the harsh destiny that forces her to disobey her father for the sake of a tormenting love ("Me pellegrina ed orfana"). Curra warns that it will soon be time to leave. Just then the sound of galloping horses is heard, and in another moment Alvaro, booted and spurred, enters the hall and rushes into Leonora's arms.

A long and dramatic duet begins with Alvaro's passionate greeting ("Ah, per sempre o mio bell'angiol"). He sings that his love for Leonora has made him defy a thousand deaths to rush to her side. The horses are ready, he goes on, and a priest is waiting at the altar. Soon they can be married, and then their glorious life together will begin. But Leonora, losing all her courage, cries that she must see her father once more and begs Don Alvaro to wait until tomorrow. Angry and incredulous, Don Alvaro exclaims that it is clear that she no longer loves him and that now their marriage would be a mockery. At that Leonora vows that she is his forever and will follow him to the end of the world. The duet rises to a feverish climax as the lovers sing that nothing will part them.

As they are about to rush out, the Marquis, sword in hand, storms in, followed by his servants. Don Alvaro draws his pistol, while Leonora rushes to her father and falls on her knees before him. He roughly thrusts her aside. Don Alvaro, declaring that he alone is to blame, puts up his pistol, bares his chest, and tells the Marquis to strike him down. The Marquis, snarling an insult about Don Alvaro's race, orders the servants to seize him. Thereupon Don Alvaro again draws his pistol and warns that no one but the Marquis may touch him. When the Marquis shouts that he will hang for betraying his daughter Don Alvaro swears that Leonora's honor is unsullied. On that assertion, he says, he will stake his life and will face his accuser unarmed. With those words he throws down his pistol. The weapon discharges on striking the floor and fatally wounds the Marquis.

As he falls Leonora rushes to his side, but with his dying breath he utters a terrible curse upon her. Leonora and Don Alvaro cry out in horror and despair. As the servants carry the Marquis to his room Don Alvaro leads the distracted Leonora toward the terrace. The curtain falls.

ACT TWO

[*Scene One*]   The kitchen of an inn in the village of Hornachuelos. At one side is a door leading to the street. At the rear is a fireplace. A stairway leads to a room on a balcony. The innkeeper and his wife are preparing supper. The Alcalde (mayor of the town) is seated beside the fireplace, and at a nearby table a student is sitting alone. The student actually is Don Carlo di Vargas, son of the slain Marquis of Calatrava. He has come to Hornachuelos on the strength of reports that Leonora and Don Alvaro have been seen in the neighborhood, having fled from Seville. Don Carlo has sworn to kill them both in revenge for his father's death and the presumed betrayal of his sister.

At the back of the room several men and women are dancing the *Seguidilla*. A group of peasants and muleteers lounge about, watching them. Soon they break into a brief but lively chorus saluting the muleteers ("Hola! Ben giungi, o mulattieri"). The Alcalde brings the singing and dancing to a halt by announcing that supper is ready. The men and women gather around the tables, and a schoolteacher is prevailed on to say grace.

Don Carlo, remaining apart from the others, stares moodily into space, muttering about the futility of his quest. At that moment Leonora, dressed in men's clothes, comes out on the balcony and catches sight of him. Recognizing him instantly, she quickly returns to her room. Noticing that one of the muleteers, Trabuco, has not joined the others at the table, Don Carlo goes over to him and asks why he is not eating. Trabuco replies that it is Friday and he is fasting. Don Carlo then begins questioning Trabuco about the young man he brought to the inn, but he is interrupted by the entrance of Preziosilla, a gypsy fortuneteller, who comes dancing in. The crowd gives her a hearty greeting and the men invite her to sit with them and tell their fortunes. Don Carlo joins the group.

Preziosilla urges the men to enlist in the Italian army and fight the Germans. Shouting defiance of the enemy, the men enthusiastically promise to join up. The fortuneteller strikes up a martial refrain describing the glories of battle ("Al suon del tamburo"). A stirring ensemble is built up as all respond in chorus. Going from one man to another, Preziosilla reads their palms. In a solo interlude she foretells that this one is destined to be a corporal, that one a captain, another a general. But when she comes to Don Carlo there is a sudden silence. Looking closely at his palm, the fortune-teller says that she sees bad luck. There is more to the prophecy, she goes on softly, for his hand reveals that he is not a student. Dismissing the matter with a mocking phrase, she resumes the gay martial refrain, in which all join.

The people suddenly fall silent as chanting is heard outside and a group of pilgrims is seen passing the inn door. The Alcalde explains that they are making a festival pilgrimage and then asks all in the room to kneel and pray. Their voices blend with those of the pilgrims in an impressive prayer

("Padre Eterno, Signor"). Leonora, who has come out on the balcony at the sound of the chanting, prays that she may be saved from her brother's vengeance.

When the pilgrims have passed, Leonora returns to her room, while the guests go back to the tables. Don Carlo again begins questioning Trabuco about the young traveler, remarking banteringly that he seems to be a shy young man who has not even grown a beard. Trabuco, for reasons of his own, parries Don Carlo's questions and pointedly indicates that he is not interested in other people's personal affairs. Annoyed by Don Carlo's persistent queries, Trabuco finally declares that he is going out to the stable and sleep with his mules. They, he observes, are neither clever nor burdened with learning and will no doubt leave him in peace. The crowd laughs.

When he has gone Don Carlo suggests to some of the others that, as the young traveler does not have a beard, it would be amusing to paint mustachios on him. His hearers are delighted with the idea, but the Alcalde sternly forbids playing that kind of trick on a guest of the inn. Turning to Don Carlo, he remarks that it would be more entertaining if he would tell his own story—who he is and where he is going. Don Carlo obliges in a graceful and rhythmic refrain ("Son Pereda, son ricco d'onore").

His name is Pereda, he begins, and he is an honor student at Salamanca, where he is soon to receive his doctor's degree. At Salamanca, he relates, he made friends with another student, one Don Vargas, who invited him to his home in Seville. When the two arrived there they found that a stranger had abducted Vargas's sister and murdered his father. The two students went from city to city in search of the betrayer but found no trace of him or the girl. Then they heard a report that the girl had perished with her father and that the slayer had fled to America. Don Vargas sailed in pursuit of him. And so, sings Don Carlo, concluding his narrative, he parted from his friend and became a student once more.

His listeners, naïvely thrilled with this exciting tale, repeat his closing phrases in chorus. Preziosilla, apparently suspecting that there is more to Don Carlo's story than he cares to tell, queries him about his "friendship" with Don Vargas. With a knowing laugh she repeats the mocking phrase she sang when she read his palm.

The Alcalde rises and announces that it is time to go to bed. The people begin to leave. Some, however, pause to take up the dance again. Don Carlo, starting for his room, repeats a phrase of his narrative, singing that he is the student Pereda. Preziosilla, watching him, answers with her characteristically flippant phrase. As all sing good night in chorus the curtain falls.

[Scene Two] In the mountains near Hornachuelos. At one side is the entrance to the church of the Madonna degli Angeli, the door of which is closed. A light shines through the window above the door. At the other side is the entrance to the convent. Not far from the door stands a rough stone cross. It is a bright moonlight night.

Leonora, still in male attire, comes in weary and travel-worn. She exclaims in relief at finding the goal of her journey—the convent, where she hopes to take refuge. She thinks of her brother telling his story to the people at the inn and then remembers that he told them that Don Alvaro had fled to America. Now, she cries, her lover has left her alone with her misery. Falling to her knees, she sings a deeply moving prayer in which she implores forgiveness and asks that peace may come to her soul ("Madre, pietosa Vergine"). Her voice soars over the chanting of the friars within the church. Rising, Leonora hesitantly approaches the door of the convent, meanwhile praying for courage and strength.

As Leonora pulls the bell rope a window in the door is opened, and Brother Melitone's scowling face is revealed as he holds up a lantern and peers out. When Leonora asks to be taken to the Superior, Melitone snaps that the convent does not open until five o'clock. Saying that she has come from Father Cleto in the village, she begs Melitone to have pity on her. The friar growls that it is much too early for pity but finally consents to announce her. At length the door is opened and Father Guardiano appears, followed by Melitone. Guardiano dismisses the friar, who retires, grumbling.

The Superior gently asks Leonora why she has come. She makes it known that she is a woman and then begs him to save her, for she is under a curse and fears eternal damnation. When Guardiano protests that such a task is beyond a poor friar Leonora asks if he received a letter from Father Cleto concerning her. In shocked surprise Guardiano exclaims that she must be Leonora di Vargas. He solemnly exhorts her to kneel before the cross.

Devoutly kissing the cross, Leonora sings that already the burden of her father's curse seems to have been lifted from her soul ("Più tranquilla l'alma"). Her refrain leads into a dramatic duet. She tells Guardiano that she desires to enter the convent and devote her life to God. The Superior warns that the life of the penitent is harsh and expresses doubt that Leonora, in her tender youth, could meet its stern demands. But Leonora exults that since she has come to this place she no longer can hear the voice of her father cursing her. In answer to Guardiano's further questions she relates how her lover accidentally caused her father's death and how her brother is determined to kill her in revenge.

When Guardiano suggests that she could perhaps find greater comfort in a cloister Leonora turns to the cross and embraces it, crying that she will never leave its shelter. Guardiano, singing that the will of God must prevail, finally relents. He tells Leonora that she may go to a cave hidden in the rocks, where no human being will ever see her again. With that he calls Melitone and orders him to assemble the friars. In a continuation of the duet Guardiano tells Leonora that she shall enter her penitential cave at dawn. As Leonora expresses her gratitude in soaring phrases, the two voices blend in an impressive climax. Leonora and the Superior enter the convent.

The doors of the church now swing open, revealing the brightly lighted altar and two processions of friars carrying candles. Majestic organ chords peal forth as Father Guardiano leads Leonora, now dressed in a monk's robe, out of the church, with Melitone and the other friars following. They group themselves around the Superior, and Leonora kneels as he raises his hands in blessing, marking the beginning of the great ensemble which concludes the act ("Il santo nome di Dio"). Guardiano proclaims that a penitent has come to the convent to expiate her sins and that she will live in the secret grotto. It will be her refuge forever. Whoever dares invade the grotto, violating the holy solitude of this penitent, will be forever cursed. The friars repeat the curse, "Maledizione, maledizione!"

Bidding Leonora rise, Guardiano tells her to go her way in peace. He and the friars commit her to the protection of the Holy Virgin ("La Vergine degli angeli"). Leonora kisses the Superior's hand and then slowly moves toward the grotto. As Guardiano extends his hands in blessing and the chorus swells to a close, the curtain falls.

ACT THREE

[*Scene One*]   A battlefield near Velletri, Italy. It is night. Don Alvaro, in the uniform of a Spanish grenadier, walks in wearily. He is plunged in gloomy thought. Unseen soldiers, apparently playing cards around a campfire, are heard in a brief chorus as they call out their bids ("Attenti al gioco").

After a mournful orchestral interlude Don Alvaro muses bitterly over his ill-starred existence. He thinks of Seville and of Leonora, whom he believes to be dead. Crying out against the cruel destiny that has haunted him since birth, he reveals something of his past. His father had fought to free his country from foreign domination and had married the last of the Inca princesses in an effort to establish a royal throne and a royal line. But he was overthrown, and he and his wife were put into prison. There Don Alvaro was born, while both parents later perished on the scaffold. Overwhelmed by these tragic memories, Don Alvaro sings the poignant aria, "Oh, tu che in seno agli angeli." He prays to Leonora, imploring her to look down from heaven and take pity on his misery.

At the conclusion of his aria there are sounds of fighting from the direction of the camp, and a moment later several officers are seen running across the background. Alvaro rushes out and returns shortly with Don Carlo. The latter explains that a quarrel broke out during the card game and then thanks Don Alvaro for saving his life. Saying he had just arrived from headquarters, he introduces himself as Don Felice de Borros, adjutant to the commander. Don Alvaro identifies himself as Don Federico Herreros, captain of the grenadiers. Clasping hands, they swear to be friends in life and death ("Amici in vita e in morte"). A bugle call is heard in the distance as a signal for battle. Don Alvaro and Don Carlo rush off as the soldiers are heard in chorus hailing the coming fray.

[*Scene Two*]   A room in the headquarters of the Spanish army in Italy. The noise of battle is heard outside. A surgeon and several orderlies hurry in and rush to the windows to watch the fighting. Peering through a telescope, the surgeon cries that Herreros was leading the charge and has been wounded. The adjutant, he goes on, is now rallying the retreating men. Again they go forward, he exclaims, and now it is the Germans who are in flight. The watchers jubilantly hail the victory, and then the surgeon announces that the wounded Herreros is being brought to headquarters.

Don Alvaro, unconscious, is carried in on a stretcher. At his side is Don

Carlo, his uniform torn and covered with dust. The surgeon, examining Don Alvaro, reports that a bullet has lodged in his chest. Don Alvaro revives and gasps weakly that death is near. Don Carlo, assuring him that the surgeon will save his life, tells him that he will be rewarded with the Order of Calatrava. At the sound of the name Don Alvaro utters an exclamation of surprise. In feverish excitement he tells Don Carlo that he must speak to him privately. At a sign from Don Carlo the surgeon and the orderlies withdraw.

Painfully raising himself, Don Alvaro begins the famous duet, "Solenne in quest'ora." In somber tones he asks Don Carlo if, in this fateful hour, he will carry out one last request. When the other swears he will do so Don Alvaro gives him a key to his valise and tells him to take from it a certain packet of papers and burn them without reading their contents. Deeply moved, Don Carlo promises to do what he asks. In relief and gratitude Don Alvaro sings that now he can die in peace. The duet rises to a powerful climax as Don Carlo, embracing Don Alvaro, tries to give him courage and comfort. After poignant farewells, Don Alvaro is carried into another room, where the surgeon is to operate in an attempt to save his life.

Left alone, Don Carlo recalls Don Alvaro's surprise at hearing the name of Calatrava. Suddenly he is stunned by the thought that perhaps Alvaro is the very man he is seeking. Hastily he unlocks the valise and takes out the packet of papers. For a moment he struggles against the impulse to open them, then remembers his promise to the man who saved his life. Throwing down the packet, he launches into an intensely dramatic monologue in which he voices horror over the evil impulse that is goading him to open the fateful packet and thus dishonor his oath ("Urna fatale del mio destino").

In a frenzy of excitement he again searches through the valise in an effort to find another clue. He comes upon a small box and after a moment's hesitation opens it. There before him is Leonora's picture. As he is gloating over this final proof of Don Alvaro's identity the surgeon opens the door and tells him that Don Alvaro will live. Don Carlo bursts forth into the great aria in which he savagely exults that his archenemy will survive to be the victim of the revenge so long delayed ("Egli è salvo! oh gioia immensa!"). Not only Don Alvaro, but Leonora—wherever she is hiding—will die by his hand. After the fiery climax of the aria Don Carlo rushes away. The curtain falls.

[Scene Three]   The camp at Velletri. Among the tents is a peddler's booth and another where refreshments are sold. It is nearly morning. A patrol marches in, making the rounds of the camp. In a hushed chorus the men describe their guard duties ("Compagni, sostiamo"). Their voices die away as they continue on their rounds.

As the dawn grows brighter Don Alvaro appears. Though recovered from his wound, he lives in dread of the evil fate that seems to be hounding him. While he is reflecting Don Carlo appears, and Don Alvaro greets him warmly. Don Carlo inquires if his wounds have healed, and when Don Alvaro assures him that they have, he asks if he is well enough to fight a duel. As Don Alvaro stares at him in consternation Don Carlo reveals that he knows his real name. A stormy duet follows as Don Alvaro furiously accuses

Don Carlo of having broken his oath ("Sleale! Il segreto fu dunque violato").

Don Carlo retorts that he did not open the packet but that Leonora's picture revealed the secret. Now, he goes on, they will fight it out. Alvaro refuses to fight, saying he will not break the bond of friendship they pledged each other. He protests that the spirits of Don Carlo's father and Leonora will bear witness that he did not kill the Marquis in cold blood. Don Carlo calls him a liar, saying that he has learned that Leonora is not dead. She has fled to relatives in a distant part of the country.

Don Alvaro almost forgets the quarrel in his happiness over the news that Leonora is alive. While Don Carlo threatens that he intends to kill her also, Don Alvaro sings that he will marry his beloved and confer on her his own royal name. But when Don Carlo persists in his threats and insults, Don Alvaro, losing all control, turns on him, crying that *he* shall be the first to die. After the wild climax of the duet the two men begin dueling fiercely. Members of the patrol rush in, separate the combatants, and drag Don Carlo away. Don Alvaro, crying that his every good intention is met with violence, throws away his sword. In a despairing phrase he declares his resolve to seek oblivion in a cloister ("Al chiostro, all'eremo"). Bowed in misery, he walks away.

It is now sunrise and the camp stirs into activity. The scene that follows is an ingenious musical panorama of camp life. The soldiers come out of their tents and busy themselves cleaning their equipment. Vivandières appear and begin selling refreshments to the soldiers. Preziosilla is seen at a booth, telling fortunes. There is a roll of drums and then a spirited chorus in a catchy, martial rhythm ("Lorchè pifferi e temburi"). In a solo passage Preziosilla invites all to have their fortunes told.

Trabuco appears with a box of trinkets, calling to the soldiers to buy or barter ("A buon mercato"). They crowd around him and in a lively chorus haggle over his prices. A number of beggars wander in and stretch out their hands for bread. Some of the younger recruits begin complaining that they were forced to leave their mothers and go to war ("Povere madri deserte"). This introduces an amusing ensemble. The vivandières approach the whimpering recruits and try to cheer them, saying they will gladly act as mothers and sweethearts. Preziosilla, disgusted at this show of weakness on the part of the recruits, pulls them away from the girls and berates them for acting like schoolboys. But everyone takes it in good humor, and soon the vivandières and the recruits begin dancing a tarantella. They sing a merry chorus as they dance ("Nella guerra è la follia").

When the fun is at its height Melitone comes in and looks on disapprovingly. Finally making himself heard, he begins preaching to the people, denouncing them for their sinful and heathenish behavior ("Toh, toh! Poffare il mondo!"). After listening for a while the soldiers shout him down and threaten to beat him. Bellowing dire warnings of doom, Melitone runs away, the soldiers at his heels. Preziosilla saves the friar from a thrashing by snatching up a drum and beating a lively tattoo. As soldiers, recruits, and vivandières gather round her she leads them in the rousing *Rataplan* chorus.

ACT FOUR

[*Scene One*] The courtyard of the convent of Madonna degli Angeli
near Hornachuelos. At one side a door opens onto the road. On the other
side is the door to the cloister. Father Guardiano, reading his breviary,
passes through the courtyard. A motley throng of beggars comes in from
the road. Holding out plates and bowls, they clamor for food.

There is a great uproar as Melitone and another friar carry in a large kettle of soup, which they set down in the middle of the courtyard. The beggars, pushing and shoving, hold up their bowls, each trying to get a larger
portion than his neighbor. Brandishing a soup ladle, Melitone roars at them
to be quiet. Father Guardiano appears and reminds him that he must be
patient with these poor unfortunates, but Melitone fumes that they are a lot
of whining, ungrateful gluttons.

When the beggars sneeringly refer to the soup as "scrapings," Melitone
loses his temper completely and threatens them with his ladle. They wail
that Father Raphael treated them much better. Melitone bellows that the
good Father Raphael evidently had his fill of dispensing charity, for now
the long-suffering Brother Melitone has been left to deal with this rabble. A
humorous ensemble develops. The beggars monotonously repeat that Father
Raphael was an angel ("Padre Raffaele era un angelo"). The louder they
chant his praises, the angrier Melitone becomes, until finally he kicks over
the soup kettle and chases the beggars from the courtyard.

Mopping his brow, he approaches Father Guardiano, who gently rebukes
him for flying into a rage because the beggars seemed to prefer the ministrations of Father Raphael. Thereupon Melitone remarks that Raphael has
been acting strangely of late, staring wildly and talking to himself. Melitone
relates that yesterday he made a joking reference to the dark color of
Raphael's skin and remarked that he was acting like a wild Indian. At that,
Father Raphael ran screaming from his cell.

Melitone asks Father Guardiano the reason for Raphael's strange behavior. Over somber chords in the orchestra Guardiano sings that the burden of
the man's misfortunes and the strain of repentance and fasting have un-
hinged his mind ("Del mondo i disinganni"). The refrain marks the beginning of a striking duet, Melitone repeating Guardiano's words. As the duet
ends a bell rings sharply. Guardiano leaves as Melitone goes to open the
door. Don Carlo, muffled in a cloak, strides in and inquires about a certain
Father Raphael. There are two here, Melitone replies; one is fat and the
other dark and lean. He asks which one is wanted. The demon, answers
Don Carlo. Melitone bustles off to fetch the lean Father Raphael, muttering
that he undoubtedly is the devil in disguise.

While waiting for Father Raphael, who, of course, is Don Alvaro, Don
Carlo exults that now nothing stands between him and his revenge. Don Alvaro, in a friar's robe, appears and gasps in dismay as he recognizes the
other. Don Carlo snarls that now he has found the man whom he has

sought for five long years. A long and dramatic duet follows ("Col sangue sol cancellasi").

Don Carlo cries that Don Alvaro's blood must flow to wipe out the dishonor done to the name of Vargas. As Alvaro is a friar and unarmed, he goes on, he has brought two swords. Don Alvaro refuses to take a sword, whereupon Don Carlo calls him a coward. Controlling himself with a great effort, Don Alvaro kneels before his adversary and implores him to forgive. He swears that Leonora was never betrayed. Don Carlo pours forth insults which he climaxes with a contemptuous reference to Don Alvaro's race.

At that Don Alvaro snatches a sword from Don Carlo. He is about to lunge when he throws the sword away, crying that he will not yield to his baser instincts. Snarling that Don Alvaro is a weakling, Don Carlo slaps his face. Raging that now Don Carlo has sealed his fate, Don Alvaro picks up the sword. The duet comes to a furious climax with the two shouting for death. They rush away to fight their duel in a spot behind the convent.

[*Scene Two*]   A wild rocky place in the mountains not far from the convent. At the rear is a grotto with a door. It is near sunset. Leonora, her pale face bearing the marks of years of suffering and penance, emerges from the grotto. Standing at the door, she voices her desperate longing for peace and forgiveness in the magnificent aria, "Pace, pace mio Dio!" She thinks of Don Alvaro and laments over the cruel fate that parted them. As she goes to the rock where Father Guardiano has left her a few morsels of food she hears the sound of angry voices. She hurries back to the grotto. Her aria ends in a ringing phrase as she calls down a curse on whoever is venturing to disturb her solitude.

Sounds of clashing swords come from beyond the grotto. Suddenly Don Carlo's voice is heard crying out that he is dying and imploring for absolution. Don Alvaro rushes in, sword in hand, shouting that he has again spilled the blood of a Vargas. Wildly he rings the bell at the door of the grotto.

After warning him away from within, Leonora opens the door. She and Don Alvaro stand transfixed as they recognize each other. Then Don Alvaro staggers back, warning Leonora not to approach because his hands are stained with blood. Pointing to the background, he tells her that a man is dying there—it is her brother, whom he was forced to kill. Leonora runs to the spot, while Don Alvaro raves that fate has mocked him again—he has found Leonora, only to meet her when his hands are stained with her brother's blood.

Leonora's voice is heard in a cry of pain, and after a moment she staggers in, aided by Father Guardiano. She gasps that Don Carlo, determined to expiate her sin, stabbed her as she held him in her arms. Don Alvaro curses his destiny. Guardiano exhorts him not to rail against heaven but rather to ask forgiveness ("Non imprecare, umiliati").

This introduces the stirring trio which concludes the opera. The dying Leonora implores Alvaro to seek salvation in prayer. He at first spurns all comfort but at last cries out that heaven has pardoned him. Leonora sings that she will go before him to heaven, where there is no hatred and love alone rules. As Alvaro distractedly begs her not to leave him alone with his guilt Leonora gasps his name and dies. Crushed by despair, Don Alvaro groans, "Mortal" Father Guardiano, lifting his hands in blessing, murmurs that Leonora is with God, "Salita a Dio!" The curtain falls.

Der Freischütz

by CARL MARIA von WEBER

[1786–1826]

Libretto by
FRIEDRICH KIND

Based on a German legend

CHARACTERS

Max, a forester	*Tenor*
Kilian, a young peasant	*Bass*
Caspar, a forester	*Bass*
Cuno, chief forester	*Bass*
Samiel, the Black Huntsman	*Speaking role*
Agathe, daughter of Cuno	*Soprano*
Aennchen, her cousin	*Soprano*
Prince Ottokar	*Tenor*
Hermit	*Bass*

Huntsmen, peasants, bridesmaids

Place: Bohemia
Time: Legendary
First performance: Schauspielhaus, Berlin, June 18, 1821
Original language: German

DER FREISCHÜTZ has been called the most German of all German operas. Its story has all the romantic and supernatural elements characteristic of old Teutonic legends, while the music is imbued with the strongly nationalistic spirit of German folk songs. The opera, an outstanding example of *Singspiel,* is of paramount importance because it marks the beginning of the romantic movement in German music. In reverting to purely Germanic themes, musically and dramatically, Weber broke away from the Italian influence which had pervaded German operatic composition since the middle of the eighteenth century.

The title, which cannot be accurately translated into English, means "The Free-shooter," a marksman who uses charmed bullets. According to the legend, a marksman could secure these bullets by agreeing to give his soul to the devil on a certain date. If, on that date, he could supply the devil with another victim, the marksman could gain a reprieve. There were seven magic bullets. Six could be fired according to the marksman's wishes. The seventh was guided by the devil.

The overture, acknowledged to be one of the finest in operatic literature, begins with a majestic theme in the horns, suggestive of the calm of the forest. It turns suddenly to the sinister theme of the Black Huntsman, which will be heard in Max's aria sung in the first act, then rises to the wild music of the incantation scene of the second act. This gives way to a sustained passage which introduces a theme from Agathe's aria in Act Two. These themes are reiterated in various forms as the overture is brought to a conclusion.

ACT ONE

A clearing before a hostelry in the forest. Max is seated alone at one of the tables outside the door, a mug of beer before him and his gun near by. In the background a crowd of peasants is watching Kilian fire at a target. As he shoots off the last star, they acclaim him with shouts of "Bravo!" Max, obviously angry and distressed, strikes his fist on the table and shouts a grudging "Good luck!" to Kilian. The young peasant comes forward surrounded by his friends, who hail his marksmanship in a rousing chorus ("Viktoria! der Meister soll leben"). Turning away from them, Max fumes over the strange loss of his skill with the rifle. One of the best marksmen in the country, he has been defeated in a shooting contest by an ordinary peasant.

Led by a Bohemian band, the peasants begin marching around the clearing in a victory procession. Kilian holds a huge wreath with ribbons, to which are attached the stars he shot from the target. He and the other peasants pass before Max and indulge in the traditional sport of baiting the loser. In a mocking ditty, Kilian gloats over his victory and jeers at Max for his poor showing ("Schau der Herr mich als König"). The peasants join in a chorus of derision.

Stung to fury by their taunts, Max leaps to his feet, draws his hunting knife, and lunges toward Kilian, shouting a threat. The peasants intervene and drag Max back. At that moment Cuno, Caspar, and a group of huntsmen appear. In dialogue, Cuno demands to know the reason for the dispute. Kilian explains that he was merely making innocent fun of a marksman who cannot hit a target, adding that it is a fine state of affairs when a peasant can outshoot a forester. Max gloomily admits that Kilian is right. At this point Caspar betrays what is on his mind when, in an aside, he mutters his thanks to Samiel. As Max's rival in Cuno's service, Caspar has already called on the Black Huntsman to aid him in his marksmanship.

Cuno sharply rebukes Max because he has nothing to show for an entire month of hunting—and, to top it off, he has lost today's contest. Caspar interrupts to say that Max is under a spell. To rid himself of it, Caspar goes on, Max need only go to a crossroad on a Friday, draw a circle around himself on the ground with his sword or ramrod, and then invoke the Black Huntsman. Cuno angrily silences him, denouncing him as a liar and a troublemaker and threatening him with dismissal as a forester. Turning to Max, Cuno warns him that if he fails in the trial shot tomorrow, he cannot hope to win the hand of Agathe.

Kilian and another hunter ask Cuno to explain the significance of the trial shot. Cuno relates that his great-great-grandfather, also named Cuno, was a forester in the service of the ancestor of the present Prince Ottokar. One day while hunting they came upon a stag, on the back of which a man was tied—a common form of punishment for poachers in those days. Moved by the man's plight, the Prince promised that whoever brought down the stag without injuring the man would be rewarded with the hereditary post of chief forester and have for his dwelling the royal hunting lodge. Cuno performed the feat, and thus the family position and the tradition of the trial shot were established. The present Cuno, wishing to retire, has asked Prince Ottokar to consider Max, betrothed to Agathe, as his successor. Max is to prove his worth at the trial shot to be held the next day.

As Cuno finishes his story, Caspar mutters something about a lucky shot. Looking at him significantly, Cuno remarks that in those days—as now—jealous hunters spread rumors that the successful huntsman used magic bullets. Caspar again mutters Samiel's name. Kilian then tells the legend of the charmed bullets, but Caspar loudly scoffs at this as an old wives' tale. Cuno declares that it is because of the legend that his great-great-grandfather stipulated that a trial shot must be held, so that the candidate for the chief forester's post could be honestly chosen. Turning again to Max, Cuno tries to cheer him, saying that perhaps it is love that has spoiled his aim. Telling the forester that he will meet him at the Prince's lodge at dawn, Cuno prepares to leave with his men.

A spirited ensemble follows, beginning with the refrain in which Max, still a prey to misgivings, expresses his dread of the ordeal of the trial shot ("O diese Sonne"). Cuno sings that his rifle must decide the issue, while Caspar tells him to face the trial like a true forester. Max voices his despair at the thought of losing Agathe. The peasants, in chorus, urge him to have courage. Cuno takes Max's hand in a pledge of good will, then calls his hunters around him and bids them be ready for tomorrow's sport. They respond in a stirring hunting chorus, in which the peasants afterward join ("Das Wild im Fluren und Triften"). At its conclusion Cuno, Caspar, and the huntsmen leave.

Kilian approaches Max and offers his hand in a gesture of renewed friendship. He urges the forester to forget his troubles and dance with the peasant girls, but Max declines. As he looks on, the peasants join in a gay Bohemian waltz. Gathering darkness soon puts an end to the dancing, and Kilian and the other peasants go to their homes. Left alone, Max gives way to his foreboding and despair. In a dramatic aria he recalls how he once roamed the forest, bringing down his quarry with unerring aim ("Durch die Wälder"). Laden with game, he came home to be greeted by Agathe's proud and tender smile.

Somber chords sound in the orchestra as Samiel suddenly becomes visible in the background. While Max sings of the evil fate which seems to be pursuing him, Samiel vanishes. He reappears as Max's aria rises to a dramatic climax. A cruel destiny rules the world, Max cries despairingly, and perhaps God himself has been dethroned. At the word God, Samiel disappears again.

As Max paces about, wringing his hands, Caspar approaches. Noting Max's look of suspicion, Caspar says he returned only to cheer his friend and then prevails on Max to have a glass of wine. While Max is sitting with his head in his hands, Caspar manages to pour some liquid from a vial into one of the glasses of wine, which he pushes over to Max. In an aside, he calls on Samiel for help, and immediately the Black Huntsman appears in the background. Caspar looks around, sees Samiel, and utters an exclamation of surprise, at which Samiel disappears. When Max looks up inquiringly, Caspar hastily proposes a toast to the chief forester. Max drinks unwillingly and then listens with distaste as Caspar launches into a ribald refrain about the joys of wine, women, and song ("Hier im ird'schen Jammerthal"). He virtually forces Max to drink by proposing toasts to Agathe and Prince Ottokar.

Despite the effects of the drugged wine, which Caspar has given Max to make him receptive to his scheme, the forester finally leaps impatiently to his feet and is about to go. Restraining him, Caspar tells him that, out of friendship, he will reveal a huntsman's secret that will make Max the luckiest marksman in the world, thus assuring him of winning Agathe's hand and the chief forester's post at the trial shot.

When Max scoffs at the idea, Caspar points to an eagle soaring far above them, hands Max his rifle, and tells him to fire. Scarcely taking aim, Max fires, and a moment later an enormous eagle drops at his feet. Caspar plucks a feather from the bird and sticks it in Max's hat. Congratulating him on a fine shot, Caspar says that this proof of his marksmanship will not only win the admiration of Agathe but will restore his reputation with the peasants as well. Completely dumfounded, Max demands to know what kind of a bullet it was that brought down an eagle far out of range of the rifle, fired in semidarkness without accurate aim. After considerable hedging, Caspar begins talking about a magic bullet. Max asks him if he has any more left. That was the last one, Caspar answers, but there are more to be had. If Max will meet him at the Wolf's Glen at midnight, he himself will help mold the magic bullets. When Max recoils in horror at the thought of going to that ill-omened spot, Caspar craftily reminds him that his future is at stake. He implies that it is too late for Max to turn back now, because he has already used a charmed bullet. It is strange, he remarks, that Max, having used one magic bullet, hesitates over using more, especially when they may help him to win a lovely bride. Caspar adds with a sneer that the charming young lady who spurned him for Max is not likely to be impressed by her swain's scruples in the matter of bullets. Faced by the possibility of losing Agathe, Max thrusts aside his misgivings and promises to meet Caspar at the Wolf's Glen. With that he hurries away.

Looking after him contemptuously, Caspar launches into a dramatic aria in which he gloats over the success of his trick, exulting that nothing can save Max from his doom ("Schweig'l damit Dich niemand warnt"). In evil glee he calls on the demons to be ready to seize their hapless victim. Concluding his aria in phrases of savage triumph, Caspar rushes into the woods. The curtain falls.

ACT TWO

[*Scene One*] A room in Cuno's house, formerly the royal hunting lodge. The furnishings and decorations—draperies, deer antlers on the walls, and hunting gear—all have the appearance of age, as though they were relics of the past. At the back is a curtained doorway leading to a balcony. At one side is Aennchen's spinning wheel. There is a table, on which is a white dress trimmed in green.

Aennchen, standing on a ladder, is hammering a nail into the wall in order to replace a portrait which has just fallen down. In falling, the picture struck Agathe, who is now removing a bandage from the wound inflicted on her forehead. With a final blow of the hammer, Aennchen, in a charming show of temper, commands the nail to hold fast ("Schelm, halt' fest!"). This introduces a tuneful duet as Aennchen and Agathe discuss the disloyal nail which dropped the illustrious ancestor of the house of Cuno. Carefully straightening the portrait, Aennchen puts the ladder away.

Agathe, watching her cousin, comments on her lightheartedness, saying that once she has known the pangs of love she will take life more seriously. In rippling phrases Aennchen replies that she proposes to enjoy life while she is young, without a thought of care. She reiterates these sentiments, while Agathe laments over the fact that Max is not with her. In this vein the duet is simply and charmingly concluded.

When Agathe continues to fret over Max, Aennchen assures her that he will visit her this evening, for Cuno has permitted him to see his betrothed once more before the trial shot. Agathe comments on the depressing atmosphere of the lodge. Aennchen observes that there are pleasanter places to spend a wedding eve than in an antiquated castle, especially when presumably deceased old gentlemen take to falling down on one's head. For herself, she declares saucily, she likes men young—and alive. With that she sings a delightful aria in which she describes the inevitable course of events which follow when a likely lad meets a maiden ("Kommt ein schlanker Bursch gegangen"). Agathe, meanwhile putting on the green-and-white dress, catches the spirit of the song and joins in singing the last stanza, in which, of course, the man and the maid are bride and groom.

But Agathe's happy mood passes in a moment and she recalls the ominous words of the Hermit, whom she had visited that morning. Giving her the sacred wreath of roses for her bridal, he warned her of impending danger. Perhaps the falling picture was part of the warning, she muses. Aennchen, however, dismisses the matter as a mere coincidence. She suggests that they retire, but Agathe insists on waiting for Max. Taking the roses, Aennchen goes out, shaking her head over the inexplicable vagaries of lovers.

Going to the balcony and looking out into the night, Agathe sings of the calm beauty of the forest in the exquisite melody "Leise, leise, fromme Weise." In an ensuing recitative she describes the thunderclouds gathering over the mountaintops and confesses her fears of the dangers lurking in the forest. She offers a prayer for Max's protection. Then suddenly she sees him approaching, and her fears turn to joy. She expresses her happiness in a brilliant aria, "All' meine Pulse schlagen."

At its conclusion Max rushes in, while Aennchen reappears. Ardently embracing Agathe, Max tells her that he can stay only a moment. She is alarmed over his distraught manner and also puzzled at seeing an eagle feather in his hat. He, in turn, is greatly disturbed about the cut in her forehead, particularly when she tells him it was caused by the portrait, which fell just after the clock struck seven. In an aside, Max notes that it was then that he shot the eagle. Bewildered by his strange actions, Agathe asks if he lost the shooting match. Max points to the eagle feather and replies that, on the contrary, he had extraordinary luck—he brought down an enormous eagle. Agathe exclaims that these great birds of prey fill her with terror. She implores Max not to be overconfident at the trial shot, for she cannot bear to think of what would happen if he should fail.

That is the very reason he must leave at once, Max says, without thinking of his words. He hastily explains that he must go to bring in a stag which he shot near the Wolf's Glen. A dramatic trio ensues as Agathe cries out in terror at the mention of the glen ("Wie? Was? Entsetzen!"). Aennchen exclaims that it is the abode of demons. Taking up his gun and pouch, Max sings that the hunter must be ready to brave any danger. Agathe and Aennchen implore him not to go, but he brushes aside their entreaties. The voices of the three blend in ringing phrases of farewell. Max leaves, but returns a moment later to ask forgiveness for his hasty words. The trio is resumed. Agathe and Aennchen beg him to remember their words of warning, while Max responds that he must obey his destiny. At the conclusion of the trio Max rushes out, while the women retire to their rooms. The curtain falls.

[Scene Two] The Wolf's Glen, a desolate spot in the mountains. At one side is a waterfall, on the other a cave. Blasted trees thrust their stumps up from between the rocks. Ghostly moonlight floods the scene. In the center of the floor of the glen Caspar is arranging a circle of black stones around a skull. Near by is a ladle, a bullet mold, and an eagle's wing. Voices of invisible spirits chant an eerie refrain ("Uhui! Uhui!"). As a distant clock strikes midnight, Caspar completes the circle, takes out his hunting knife, and plunges it into the skull. Waving it around his head, he summons Samiel with an incantation. When the Black Huntsman appears, Caspar kneels before him and abjectly begs for three more years of freedom. In return, he promises to bring Samiel another victim, a brave young huntsman who is willing to bargain his soul for seven magic bullets. Six shall be his, Caspar goes on, but the seventh shall be Samiel's—to slay the hunter's bride. Samiel considers the offer for a moment and then nods. Tomorrow, he decrees coldly, he will either have Max's soul or Caspar's. With that he disappears.

As Caspar staggers to his feet, the skull disappears and in its place stands a hearth with glowing coals. Taking a drink from his hunting flask, Caspar prepares to mold the bullets. He looks anxiously around for Max. The latter suddenly appears at the edge of the glen, staring in horror into its depths. Catching sight of him, Caspar greets him with a sigh of relief and then turns to fan the fire with the eagle's wing. Glancing at the wing, Max murmurs that only yesterday he shot down the eagle with a magic bullet and now it is too late to turn back. Slowly climbing down, he sees the ghost of his mother standing at the side of the waterfall. When he cries out that she is warning him to flee, Caspar laughs sardonically. If Max insists on these foolish fancies, he remarks, let him look again. This time Max sees a vision of Agathe apparently on the verge of throwing herself into the torrent. The terrible sight gives Max the courage of desperation. Shouting that he must save her, he climbs down into the glen.

Clouds now veil the moon, and darkness envelops the scene. Max asks what he must do. He must at all costs remain outside the circle, Caspar tells him, and must make no outcry, no matter what happens. Only if he sees Caspar trembling is he to come to his aid. Then he must step inside the circle and repeat the identical words which Caspar will call out. Caspar then takes the magic ingredients from his pouch and throws them into the ladle— lead, broken glass of church windows, a lapwing's right eye, a lynx's left. As powerful chords reverberate in the orchestra, Caspar intones an unholy invocation to Samiel.

When the mixture in the ladle begins to hiss and bubble, Caspar starts casting the bullets, counting as he pours them out one by one. Between each casting, pandemonium reigns in the glen. Huge black birds swoop over the fire and fan it with their wings. A wild boar crashes through the underbrush near by. A violent tempest roars through the glen. After the fifth bullet, the sound of galloping horses is heard and four fiery wheels roll across the floor of the chasm. Shadowy forms of huntsmen and their hounds, pursuing stags, rush through the air. The huntsmen chant in a ghostly monotone ("Durch Berg und Thal"). As Caspar molds the sixth bullet, a terrific thunderstorm begins to rage. Flames billow up from the earth, which seems to be torn apart by violent convulsions. Shaking with terror, Caspar pours the seventh bullet and then falls to the ground, screaming Samiel's name.

Obedient to his instructions, Max steps into the circle to help him, repeating Samiel's name. At that moment the voice of Samiel is heard. Caspar loses consciousness. A terrible wind whirls Max about. Leaping out of the circle, he grasps the branches of a dead tree. The storm suddenly subsides. In place of the tree the Black Huntsman appears, grasping Max's hand. Max crosses himself, whereupon Samiel disappears. As Max staggers back as though struck, the curtain falls.

There is a brief entr'acte, based mainly on the theme of the hunting chorus, which will be heard in the next act.

ACT THREE

[*Scene One*]   The forest.[1] Max and Caspar are seen talking. Max asks Caspar for another magic bullet, but Caspar says that he had only three to begin with, while Max had four. Saying he has only one left, Max begs

[1] This scene, entirely in dialogue, is usually omitted.

Caspar for his remaining bullet. Caspar, though admitting that he wasted his other bullets on small game, protests that it is only fair that they each keep one for the trial shot. When he refuses to give up his last bullet, Max stalks angrily away. After he has gone, Caspar exults that his ruse has succeeded—Max has been left with the accursed seventh bullet. With that he disposes of the sixth by firing at a fox.

[*Scene Two*]   Agathe's room. It is the day of the trial shot, at which the future of Agathe and Max will be decided. Clad in her bridal dress, Agathe kneels for a moment before a small altar in one corner of the room. Rising, she sings a moving aria in which she commends herself to the protection of heaven on this fateful day ("Und ob die Wolke sie verhülle"). Aennchen then comes in and refers to the terrible storm which raged during the night. Agathe says that she was haunted by bad dreams. She dreamed that she was a white dove and that Max fired at her. As she fell the dove disappeared and she became Agathe again. On the ground a huge bird of prey lay in its own blood. Aennchen, instead of being alarmed, blithely interprets the dream. The white dove, she explains, symbolizes Agathe's white wedding gown, about which she obviously was thinking when she retired. The fact that she remembered the eagle feather in Max's hat accounts for the bird of prey she saw in her dream. And there is the whole explanation, Aennchen concludes gaily. Seeing that Agathe still is frightened and distressed, Aennchen tries to cheer her by telling, in an amusing aria, how her poor aunt was haunted by a dream that came true ("Einst träumte meiner sel'gen Base"). In the dead of night, the story goes, the aunt saw a dreadful apparition with fiery eyes creeping toward her. The monster growled and came closer, with a clanking of chains. The aunt cried for help, and when her servants rushed in with lights they found that the apparition was only Nero, the watchdog. Vexed at Aennchen's mocking attitude, Agathe turns away. Aennchen gently assures her that she is ready to share her every sorrow. In an ensuing aria she urges Agathe to think only of her future happiness and to be gay, as becomes a beautiful bride ("Trübe Augen, Liebchen").

After the aria the bridesmaids appear. Telling them to entertain Agathe with a song, Aennchen leaves to bring in the bridal wreath. The bridesmaids sing the charming *Bridal Wreath* chorus ("Wir winden dir den Jungfernkranz"). It tells the legend of the maiden who wove her bridal veil for seven years while waiting for her lover. As she pined away, thinking he would never return, he came back to her, and every moment of sorrow was repaid with joy.

Aennchen appears carrying a box. She remarks casually to Agathe that the portrait of the old Cuno has fallen down again. When Agathe exclaims that it is another bad omen, Aennchen says that the nail probably gave way because of the trembling of the house during last night's storm. She hands the box to Agathe, who opens it. She utters a cry of horror when she discovers a funeral wreath instead of a bridal garland. Aennchen, concealing her own fright, quickly puts the wreath away, saying that the stupid shopgirl probably is to blame for the mistake.

Agathe, now convinced that misfortune lies ahead, quietly tells Aennchen to make a wreath of the Hermit's white roses. A maiden at the altar or in her coffin, she sighs, wears white roses. With a pretense of gaiety, Aennchen fashions a wreath. She asks the trembling bridesmaids to sing, and they softly repeat the refrain of their chorus. As Agathe leaves, accompanied by Aennchen and the bridesmaids, the curtain falls.

[*Scene Three*] A pleasant forest glade, the scene of the trial shot. At one side are the tents of Prince Ottokar. He is feasting with his huntsmen and members of his court. Max, leaning on his gun, is standing at the entrance to the Prince's tent. On the other side of the clearing Caspar may be seen watching from behind a tree. The Prince and his company emerge from the tents and, holding aloft their glasses, sing the famous *Huntsmen's Chorus* ("Was gleicht wohl auf Erden"). They lustily describe the joys of the chase and the merrymaking which follows.

The chorus over, the Prince turns to the business of the day. He tells Cuno that he approves of his future son-in-law and asks him to tell Max to prepare for the trial shot. As Cuno goes over to speak to Max, Caspar climbs a tree in order to view what he hopes will be the tragic denouement —the death of Agathe and the disgrace of Max. As Cuno returns to the Prince, the latter says he is anxious to see the bride-to-be. Cuno replies that she will soon be present. Turning away from the others, Max takes the final bullet from his pouch, weighs it in his hand, and anxiously examines it. He does not realize, of course, that it is the fatal seventh bullet, which Caspar has managed to leave to him.

Cuno asks the Prince if he will permit the trial shot to be fired before Agathe arrives, for the sake of Max's peace of mind. The young man has been unlucky at shooting recently, Cuno explains, and the presence of his betrothed at the crucial moment might prove too much for his nerves. The Prince acquiesces, remarking that Max seems hardly coolheaded enough for a forester. He relates that as he watched from a distance, Max made three fine shots, but his subsequent attempts have failed miserably. Cuno ruefully admits that Max has made a poor showing. The Prince jovially observes that perhaps neither he nor Cuno would have been at their best on their own wedding day. At any rate, he adds, if Max fails, there is another forester who is entitled to a trial shot.

Realizing that he means Caspar, Cuno stammers a protest, while Max exclaims, in an aside, that Caspar may have kept one magic bullet, with which he may yet win the bride and the coveted position of chief forester. The Prince, however, finally decides to let Max have his shot. Indicating a white dove perched in a treetop, he orders Max to bring it down.

Just as Max takes aim, Agathe, Aennchen, and the bridesmaids appear among the trees. Agathe screams that she is the dove and begs Max not to fire. The dove flutters over Caspar's tree, and Max follows it with his rifle. He fires. The dove flies away. Agathe sinks to the ground with a shriek. Caspar, echoing her cry, falls from the tree.

In an excited chorus the onlookers sing that Max has slain his own bride ("Schaut, er traf die eig'ne Braut!"). Max kneels beside Agathe, who slowly revives and asks if what has happened was all a dream. The people joyfully sing that Agathe's life has been spared. Caspar meanwhile writhes in agony.

Agathe, Cuno, and Max voice their happiness and are joined by the Prince and the chorus.

Visible only to Caspar, Samiel appears. Wildly cursing the Black Huntsman for betraying him, Caspar raises his clenched fist and then falls back dead. Hearing the curse, the people comment in awed tones over so impious a prayer from a dying man. Cuno sings that thus an evildoer is punished by heaven, and the throng echoes his words. Prince Ottokar orders his men to throw Caspar's body into the Wolf's Glen.

As they drag the body away, the Prince turns to Max and commands him to explain these strange happenings. Kneeling before him, Max confesses, in an eloquent refrain, that despair over his failures led him to yield to Caspar's advice to use magic bullets ("Herr! unwerth bin ich Eurer Gnade"). The Prince instantly sentences him to banishment and denies him the hand of Agathe.

As Max gives way to his despair, Agathe, Cuno, and the people implore the Prince to be lenient, but he remains firm. As he sternly orders Max out of his sight, the Hermit comes forward, declaring that a prince must not forget his obligation to be merciful and just. Ottokar invites the Hermit to render a decision, saying he will abide by it. In an air of great dignity, the Hermit warns against judgments dictated by vengeful passions ("Leicht kann des Frommen Herz auch wanken"). He deplores the custom of deciding the fate of a man by means of a trial shot and requests that the trial shot be abolished. As for Max, he asks that the forester be placed on a year's probation, during which he must prove himself worthy.

The Prince agrees to the Hermit's proposals, and the people joyfully hail his magnanimous decision. Turning to Max, he assures him that full justice will be done. Max replies in a ringing phrase of homage to the Prince ("Die Zukunft soll mein Herz bewahren"). The voices of Max, Agathe, Aennchen, Ottokar, Cuno, and the Hermit blend in a sextet as they sing of the justice of the decree. In a brief solo interlude the Hermit exhorts the people to give praise to God. All the voices blend in a great chorus of thanksgiving ("Ja! lasst uns zum Himmel die Blicke erheben"). The curtain falls.

Gianni Schicchi

by GIACOMO PUCCINI

[1858–1924]

Libretto by
GIOACHINO FORZANO

Based on the story of Gianni Schicchi, a citizen of medieval Florence

CHARACTERS

Zita (also called La Vecchia—the Old Woman),
cousin of Buoso Donati, the deceased.................. *Mezzo-soprano*
Marco, son of Simone...................................... *Baritone*
La Ciesca, wife of Marco.................................... *Soprano*
Rinuccio, nephew of Zita...................................... *Tenor*
Simone, cousin of Buoso.. *Bass*
Gherardo, nephew of Buoso..................................... *Tenor*
Nella, his wife... *Soprano*
Gherardino, their son..................................... *Mezzo-soprano*
Betto di Signa, brother-in-law of Buoso....................... *Baritone*
Gianni Schicchi .... *Baritone*
Lauretta, his daughter, in love with Rinuccio................... *Soprano*
Spinelloccio, a doctor... *Bass*
Amantio di Nicolao, a lawyer................................... *Bass*
Pinellino, a shoemaker... *Bass*
Guccio, a dyer... *Bass*

Place: Florence
Time: 1299
First performance: Metropolitan Opera House, New York, December 14, 1918
Original language: Italian

GIANNI SCHICCHI is part of a trilogy of one-act operas which includes *Il Tabarro* and *Suor Angelica*. The hero of the opera is modeled on an actual historical character who lived in Florence at the end of the thirteenth century and whose escapades made him famous.

The bedroom in the home of Buoso Donati, a wealthy Florentine, who has just died. At the four corners of the canopied bed on which the body lies are four lighted candles. In front of it is a candelabrum with three candles unlighted. At one side of the room a staircase leads up to a small balcony. Buoso's relatives, kneeling in prayer, are grouped around the bed. Their occasional outbursts of grief—"Povero Buoso! Povero cugino! Povero zio!"—are obviously forced. Gherardino, a boy of about seven, is seated on the floor, somewhat apart from the others, amusing himself by playing with marbles. Finally he grows restless and is sent out of the room.

Betto, whose threadbare clothing and timid manner mark him as the lowliest of the relations, hesitantly mentions a rumor he has heard about Buoso. It is to the effect that the old man has left most of his possessions—even his mill—to a monastery. In excitement and dismay the relatives appeal to Simone, who, as one-time sheriff of the town, presumably has a constructive opinion about the matter.

Simone ponders a moment and then, with an air of weighty deliberation, declares that if Buoso has filed his will with the town clerk, then all is lost. If, however, the will is still here among his personal effects, the situation may yet be turned to the advantage of the relatives. Instantly there is a mad scramble to find the will, with everyone ransacking cupboards and drawers. Rinuccio, in an ardent strain ("Lauretta, amore mio"), expresses the hope that the document will be found for the sake of his romance. While the others are searching the room he ascends to the balcony and looks through the contents of a chest.

Betto, ignored by everybody, surreptitiously pockets a silver seal and a pair of scissors and finally manages to conceal a silver tray under his coat. There is a momentary uproar as Simone comes upon a document, which, however, proves to be the wrong one. Suddenly Rinuccio, holding up a parchment he has found in the chest, cries out, "Salvati! Il testamento di Buoso Donati!" As he descends the stairs the others rush toward him with hands outstretched, but he holds the document out of their reach. In a brief refrain he reminds them that it was he who found the will ("Zita, l'ho trovato"). He asks Zita, as head of the family, if she will consent to his marriage with Lauretta, in the event that Buoso's legacy provides the clan with wealth. When Zita and the others impatiently assure him that he may marry anyone he likes, he calls Gherardino and sends him off to bring Schicchi and his daughter.

Taking the parchment from Rinuccio, Zita unrolls it and reads the greeting, which is addressed to her and Simone. The latter, murmuring premature thanks to Buoso for his generosity, lights the three candles at the end of the bed. Breathlessly crowding around Zita, the relatives silently read the will as an appropriately dignified theme is given out by the orchestra. But as they read their faces take on expressions of stunned surprise and dismay. Simone slowly walks over to the bed and extinguishes not only the three candles he has just lighted but the other four as well. Turning back to the relatives, he bursts out that the rumor really was the truth ("Dunque era vero!"), and these words introduce an agitated ensemble. One outdoes the other in expressions of envious rage over the fact that the monks and nuns will grow fat on Buoso's wealth. In spiteful mockery they deride each other as disappointed heirs, now left as poor as they were before.

Rinuccio eventually succeeds in quieting them and then says that there is one man who can help—Gianni Schicchi. The relatives, however, assuming that he is concerned only with furthering his romance, scornfully reject his suggestion. At that moment Gherardino rushes in to announce that Schicchi and his daughter are approaching. A vigorous argument now ensues during which Rinuccio stoutly defends Schicchi as a man of resourcefulness and sagacity. He is the type of man, cries Rinuccio, who is a credit to the noble city of Florence. In a melodious aria he rhapsodizes over the city, telling how its splendors attract men of genius and talent the world over ("Firenze è come un albero fiorito"). Gianni Schicchi, he concludes, contributes much to the glory of Florence.

At the conclusion of the aria Schicchi enters with Lauretta, who ardently greets Rinuccio. Schicchi, taking in the situation at a glance, indicates his distaste over the rapacity and pretended grief of the relatives. Zita furiously tries to drive him away, fuming that she will never allow her nephew to marry someone beneath his station. Schicchi, stung to anger, denounces her for her selfish interference, while the two lovers pledge their devotion to each other. The four voices blend in a brief quartet.

Schicchi, disgusted with the wrangling, starts to leave, but Rinuccio implores him to give his attention to the problem of the will. Lauretta adds her entreaties in a touching aria ("O mio babbino caro"). With a deliberate show of unwillingness Schicchi finally takes the will and begins reading. He slowly paces back and forth, and the relatives, their eyes fixed on him, follow in a comical procession. Suddenly he stops as though struck by an idea. He glances at Lauretta and then sends her out on the terrace. When she is out of earshot he asks the relatives if the news of Buoso's death has been given out. Not even the servants know of it, they answer. At Schicchi's bidding they take Buoso's body, along with the candelabrum, into another room.

Just as they are rearranging the bed there is a knock on the door and Spinelloccio, the doctor, announces himself. While the relatives, speaking through the partially opened door, assure the doctor that Buoso is much improved, Schicchi conceals himself behind the bed. Spinelloccio insists on seeing the patient. Schicchi, imitating Buoso's voice, calls out that he is much too tired to see anyone at the moment and tells him to return in the evening. Spinelloccio leaves, first pausing to observe that none of his patients ever dies, thanks to his superior medical knowledge.

Emerging from his hiding place, Schicchi asks if his imitation was convincing. On being assured that it was, he explains his plan in an amusing aria ("Si corre dal notaio"). The relatives are to call the notary at once, telling him that Buoso is at the point of death and wants to make his will. By the time the notary arrives Gianni Schicchi will be in the bed to play the role of Buoso and will dictate the will to the satisfaction of all concerned. The relatives hail Schicchi for his brilliant inspiration.

Then, one by one, they declare their claims to various pieces of Buoso's property—neighboring farmlands—and a loud argument develops over the disposition of the mule, the palace, and the sawmill at Signa. The dispute is interrupted by the tolling of a bell announcing a death. Panic-stricken, the relatives wonder how the news of Buoso's death was made known. Schicchi sighs that now his plans have gone awry. Gherardo hurries out to investigate but returns a moment later with the cheering news that the knell is being sounded for the mayor's Moorish assistant who died of a stroke.

With expressions of happy relief the relatives help Schicchi prepare for his masquerade. Each one, watching his chance, tries to bribe Schicchi into bequeathing him the coveted mule, palace, and mill, and Schicchi solemnly makes them all the same promise. When he is finally arrayed in Buoso's nightgown and cap, Zita, La Ciesca, and Nella push him toward the bed, singing an amusing trio, in which they pretend to coax a little child to go to bed ("Fa' presto, bambino").

Before he gets into bed Schicchi turns to the relatives with a word of advice ("Prima un avvertimento!"). He warns them of the severe penalty which, according to the Florentine law, will be inflicted on all of them if their participation in the fraud is discovered: the right hand cut off—and exile. Gesturing toward the window through which the city is visible, he sings a mock-serious farewell to Florence. It is echoed by all in chorus.

There is a knock at the door. Schicchi jumps into bed and pulls up the covers, while the relatives darken the room. The notary enters, followed by Pinellino and Guccio, who are to witness the will. After appropriate formalities Schicchi begins dictating. The relatives nod approvingly when he assigns a modest sum for his funeral and an equally nominal one for the monastery. There are further expressions of satisfaction as the farmlands are duly disposed of.

When the supposed Buoso comes to the mule, the palace, and the mill, there is a feverish stir of expectancy. These, as well as the house in Florence, he declares, are to be left to his cherished friend, Gianni Schicchi. This brings anguished protests from the relatives, but Schicchi quiets them by repeating the refrain of his adieu to Florence, with its significant reference to waving farewell with a handless arm. He adds to their distress by ordering Zita to reward the notary and the witnesses with a handsome fee out of her own purse. When the will is duly signed and sealed the three leave with effusive expressions of gratitude.

No sooner have they gone than the relatives fling themselves on Schicchi with furious denunciations. Standing up in the bed, he snatches Buoso's stick, which is hanging from a bedpost, and wields it with telling effect. Roaring that the house is now his, he orders them out. As he pursues them around the room they snatch up everything they can lay their hands on and finally rush out, their arms laden with booty. Schicchi dashes after them.

While the music gradually quiets down to rich, sustained chords, Rinuccio and Lauretta go to the rear of the room, where the youth opens a large window, revealing a view of Florence glowing in the sunshine. The lovers sing a beautiful duet ("Lauretta mia") and then stand in a fervent embrace. Schicchi returns with part of the loot, which he drops on the floor. He sees the lovers, oblivious to everything in their rapture. Turning to the audience, he points to the lovers and, in spoken words, asks if Buoso's wealth could serve any better purpose. The relatives, he says, have consigned him to hell for this bit of skulduggery. With all due respect to Dante, he hopes that the audience will acquiesce in the verdict of "Not guilty." Schicchi starts the applause and bows. The curtain falls.

La Gioconda

by AMILCARE PONCHIELLI

[1834–1886]

Libretto by
TOBIA GORRIO (ARRIGO BOÏTO)

Based on Victor Hugo's play
ANGELO, LE TYRAN DE PADOUE

CHARACTERS

Barnaba, a spy of the Inquisition............................*Baritone*
La Gioconda, a street singer................................*Soprano*
La Cieca, her blind mother.................................*Contralto*
Zuàne, a gondolier...*Bass*
Isèpo, a public letter writer...............................*Tenor*
Enzo Grimaldo, a nobleman of Genoa.........................*Tenor*
Alvise Badoero, a chief of the State Inquisition...................*Bass*
Laura, his wife.......................................*Mezzo-soprano*
A monk ....*Baritone*

Townspeople, shipwrights, sailors, monks, ladies and
gentlemen, children, cavaliers, dancers

Place: Venice
Time: Seventeenth century
First performance: La Scala, Milan, April 8, 1876
Original language: Italian

PONCHIELLI, teacher of Puccini, was a gifted musician who is regarded as one of the founders of modern Italian opera. Profoundly influenced by Wagner, he infused his works with a new lyricism and an advanced technique that revitalized the Italian operatic stage. In his own country he became almost as famous as Verdi, but *La Gioconda* was the only one of his operas to bring him universal renown.

The prelude is dominated by a sweeping refrain which is the chief theme of a dramatic air sung by La Cieca in the first act.

ACT ONE
(*The Lion's Mouth*)

The courtyard of the ducal palace in Venice, an imposing building decorated for a holiday festival. It is a spring afternoon. At the rear of the scene is the Giants' Stairway and one of the entrances to the Church of St. Mark.

At one side is the booth of a public letter writer. On a wall of the courtyard is a carved lion's mouth with this inscription: "For Secret Denunciations to the Inquisition against any Person, with Impunity, Secrecy, and Benefit to the State."

The square is filled with an excited crowd of townspeople, sailors, monks, masqueraders, and soldiers, all waiting to see a regatta on one of the canals. They sing a gay chorus and then leave as a fanfare of trumpets and ringing of bells announce the beginning of the race. Barnaba, carrying a guitar as an added touch to his disguise as a merrymaker, stands at one side and cynically regards the throng. When the square is empty he strums his guitar and sings of how a chance phrase spoken by someone in the crowd betrays a fugitive from the Inquisition into his hands. He concludes his evil sere-nade as he voices his desire to snare the greatest prize of all—La Gioconda. At that moment she approaches, leading her blind mother, La Cieca. Bar-naba conceals himself behind a pillar. A trio follows, beginning with La Cieca's words of gratitude to her daughter for taking care of her ("Figlia che reggi il tremulo piè"). Gioconda responds with assurances of her devo-tion, while Barnaba, aside, expresses his uncontrolled desire for the singer.

Gioconda tells her mother to wait at the church while she goes to seek Enzo, a nobleman of Genoa, who has secretly come to Venice in his ship in an effort to see Laura. She was once his betrothed but is now married to Al-vise Badoera of the Inquisition. During his stay in Venice, Enzo met Gioconda, who has fallen in love with him. La Cieca seats herself on the church steps and takes a rosary from her pocket. As Gioconda leaves, Bar-naba intercepts her and tries to force her to listen to his passionate entreat-ies. Fighting him off, she runs away shrieking. At the sound of her voice La Cieca rises and stumbles forward in fear and alarm. As she gropes her way back to her seat Barnaba murmurs that he will use the mother to cap-ture the daughter.

The crowd now returns, singing a vigorous chorus in praise of the winner of the regatta, who is carried in on the shoulders of his friends. His defeated rival, Zuàne, also appears. Barnaba, watching the crestfallen boat-man closely as the people deride him for losing the race, resolves to use him also in furthering his schemes. As some of the crowd withdraws to the Gi-ants' Stairway and noisily begins gambling, the spy approaches Zuàne and tells him that he lost the race because he and his craft were cursed by a sor-ceress. With that he points to La Cieca, who is still seated on the church steps saying her rosary. While he is speaking, Isèpo and a group of sailors draw close and listen. They exclaim in fear as Barnaba tells them that the old witch can see them despite her eyeless sockets. Incited by Barnaba, they venture close to La Cieca and finally seize her, singing in a dramatic chorus that they will burn her at the stake.

At the climax of the chorus, Enzo, disguised as a Dalmatian sailor, rushes in with Gioconda. Drawing his sword, he angrily denounces the crowd for attacking a blind, defenseless old woman. The people, however, grow more violent in their demands for revenge. Enzo tries to fight them off as they press closer, then dashes away to seek the help of his sailors.

The uproar ceases abruptly as the doors of the palace swing open and Al-vise and Laura appear. Laura's face is hidden by a black mask. Alvise sternly rebukes the people for presuming to take the law into their own hands. When they shout that La Cieca is a sorceress Alvise orders her to be brought to trial at once. With a cry of "Pietà! Pietà!" Gioconda throws herself at his feet and begs him to spare her mother. While she is pleading, Enzo and a group of sailors rush in to rescue La Cieca. Rising quickly, Gioconda restrains him. He has meanwhile caught sight of Laura and keeps looking at her with intense interest. Barnaba is quick to note that Laura is returning Enzo's gaze through her mask. Laura now intercedes in behalf of La Cieca, and Alvise frees her. The old woman hands Laura her rosary and thanks her in the impressive aria, "Voce di donna," which contains the theme heard in the prelude. La Cieca asks the name of her benefactress, saying she will remember it in her prayers. When Laura tells her, Enzo, hearing her name, utters an exclamation of joy. At Alvise's bidding all go into the church. Barnaba, watching Enzo, deliberately lags behind and, as Enzo pauses at the door, he steps to his side. He calls him by name—"Enzo Grimaldo, Principe di Santafior [Enzo Grimaldo, Prince of Santafior]." Enzo attempts to deny his identity, but Barnaba cuts him short, saying that he knows his story: He is from Genoa, and there is a price on his head in Venice. . . . He once loved Laura but lost her when she married Alvise. . . . Now he consoles himself with La Gioconda. . . . Just when he had given up all hope of ever seeing her again, he met her—only today—and recognized her in spite of the mask she wore. Forgetting himself for the moment, Enzo ardently sings Laura's name. Thereupon Barnaba tells him that he will arrange matters so that Laura can visit him aboard his ship this very evening. Enzo voices his happiness in a fervent aria ("O grido di quest'-anima").

Barnaba interrupts his rejoicing by revealing that he is a spy of the Inquisition and can doom him then and there. He will spare him, however, he says, because he is saving his revenge for Gioconda, who will now learn how false her lover is. The colloquy ends in a dramatic duet. Enzo sings passionately of Laura, while Barnaba sardonically wishes him good luck on his adventure. Enzo curses the spy as he leaves.

Calling Isèpo, Barnaba dictates a letter to Alvise informing him that Laura plans to flee with Enzo aboard his ship. Gioconda and La Cieca appear at that moment at the door of the church. Overhearing Barnaba, Gioconda cries out in anguish and rushes back into the church.

Taking the letter from Isèpo, Barnaba reads it over and then sings the great aria, "O monumento!" He gloats that he, as spy of the Inquisition, is more powerful than the Doge himself. With a cry of ferocious exultation he puts the letter into the lion's mouth, thus sending it on its way as an official denunciation.

The townspeople and the masqueraders now return, singing and shouting. A dance called the *Furlana* is performed. At its conclusion the voices of the choir are heard in the church and a monk appears to bid the people kneel for vespers. While all kneel and sing a vesper hymn ("Angele Dei") Gioconda and her mother come out of the church and make their way through the crowd. Gioconda grieves bitterly over Enzo's faithlessness, while La Cieca tries to comfort her. The curtain falls.

ACT TWO
(*The Rosary*)

A section of the deck of Enzo's ship, the brigantine *Hecate*, lying at anchor at the shore of a deserted island in a lagoon near Venice. Sailors on deck, calling out orders through speaking trumpets, are answered by others in the rigging and below decks in a mariner's chorus known as the *Marinaresca*.

Barnaba and Isèpo, disguised as fishermen, come alongside in a small boat. In answer to a hail from the ship, Barnaba sings a fisherman's ballad ("Ah, pescator, affonda l'esca"). There is an interlude of recitative in which he informs Isèpo about the number of men in the ship's crew and their armament, and then gives him instructions about posting men in readiness for the attack which is to come later. Sending Isèpo on his way, Barnaba continues his ballad. It is accompanied by the sailors in a chorus, one significant phrase of which is that a siren will soon be caught in the net of the fisherman.

At the end of the chorus Barnaba withdraws. Enzo appears on deck and gives sailing orders to his crew. As they comply they repeat the *Marinaresca*. Enzo sends them off to their quarters and then, standing alone on deck and looking up at the stars, he sings the famous aria, "Cielo e mar!" in which he hails the beauty of the sky and the sea and expresses his impatient longing for Laura.

A boat approaches, and Barnaba's voice is heard hailing Enzo. In a moment Laura appears on deck and rushes into Enzo's arms.[1] Their ecstatic words of greeting are interrupted by Barnaba's mocking "good night" from the darkness beyond the ship as the spy rows away, and Laura exclaims in distress at the ominous sound of his voice. Enzo bids her forget her fears in a tender phrase which introduces their love duet ("Deh! non turbare").

Enzo goes below to prepare for sailing. Overcome by happiness, Laura kneels before a small shrine on deck and sings a prayer to the protecting star of the mariner ("Stella del marinar"). As she sings the closing phrases, Gioconda, wearing a mask, rushes toward her from the bow of the vessel, where she had concealed herself. When Laura, terrified, asks who she is, Gioconda cries out that her name is Vengeance—her rival for Enzo's love. In a tempestuous duet ("Là attesi e il tempo colsi") the two women pour out their contempt and defiance of each other.

Gioconda, dagger in hand, advances toward Laura. Just at that moment she sees a boat approaching. Now a worse fate is in store for her rival, she exclaims, for in the boat is Alvise. Laura, sinking to her knees in terror, lifts up the rosary which La Cieca had given her and begins to pray. At the sight of the rosary Gioconda controls her jealousy, recalling the gratitude she owes Laura. Putting her mask over Laura's face, she helps her escape, sending her home in Gioconda's own boat.

---

[1] In some productions Enzo descends to the shore after his aria, and his meeting with Laura takes place there.

Barnaba, who has brought Alvise, clambers to the deck, finds that Laura has escaped, and curses in baffled fury. He points in the direction in which Laura's boat has gone, calls out to Alvise, and then follows in pursuit. Watching him go, Gioconda cries out that for her mother's sake she has protected the woman who has robbed her of her lover. Enzo hurriedly appears, calling to Laura. Gioconda tells him she has fled. Warning him that he has been betrayed to the Inquisition, Gioconda urges him to flee before it is too late. Enzo furiously upbraids her for daring to suggest that he run from danger. Sailors rush on deck and in an agitated chorus sing that all escape has been cut off. Snatching a torch from the hand of a sailor, Enzo sets fire to the ship. As the flames rise, the vessel slowly sinks. Enzo, about to leap into the sea, sings his farewell to Laura. Gioconda, who has made her way to the shore, laments that even now he thinks only of her rival. In a ringing phrase she declares that she will die with her lover. The curtain falls.

ACT THREE
(*The House of Gold*)

[*Scene One*]   A room in Alvise's palace, the "House of Gold." In a dramatic soliloquy Alvise sings that though Laura succeeded in escaping when surprised at her rendezvous she must pay with her life for dishonoring his name ("Si, morir ella de'l"). Glancing into the adjoining room where his guests are singing and dancing, he contrasts their careless merriment to the grim fate in store for his wife.

Laura enters. She is magnificently gowned, and Alvise greets her with a sardonic compliment on her beauty. Suddenly losing control of himself, he bursts out into violent accusations of infidelity. He seizes Laura and hurls her to the floor, shouting that her hour of doom has come. Desperately she begs for mercy.

Alvise strides to a curtained doorway, tears aside the draperies, and commands her to look upon her new nuptial bed. She recoils in horror as she sees a casket. From behind the scenes come the voices of the revelers in a chorus of mocking gaiety. Thrusting a flask of poison into Laura's hands, Alvise orders her to drink it before the serenade has ended. With that he stalks out of the room.

Gioconda rushes in, snatches the poison from Laura, and gives her a small vial, explaining that it contains an opiate which will produce the semblance of death but will not prove fatal. Laura drinks from the bottle, returns it to Gioconda, and then goes into the room where the casket is placed. Gioconda pours the poison from the flask into the vial, sets the empty flask on the table, and conceals herself behind some draperies. Alvise reappears. He glances at the flask, steps for a moment into the other room to look at Laura's apparently lifeless form, then returns. In grim tones he murmurs that death has claimed her, and then slowly leaves. Gioconda, emerging from her hiding place, cries that she has again saved her rival, this time for Enzo's sake. The curtain falls.

[*Scene Two*] The great reception hall of Alvise's palace. It is thronged with a brilliant company of cavaliers and ladies. While Alvise is welcoming his friends Gioconda enters and mingles with the crowd. The guests, most of whom are masked, sing a stirring chorus in praise of the House of Gold ("Alla Cà d'Oro"). The familiar *Dance of the Hours* is now performed. Groups of dancers come in, each group representing in turn the hours of dawn, day, evening, and night.

When the dance ends Barnaba comes in, dragging with him La Cieca, exclaiming that he caught her in the forbidden room. Gioconda rushes to her mother's side. La Cieca mumbles that she came to pray for the dead, and at that moment a funeral bell tolls. A masked guest steps forward and asks for whom the knell is sounding. Barnaba answers that it is for Laura.

Alvise, annoyed at the sudden hush that has fallen over the festivities, asks who dares be sad when he himself is gay. Thereupon Enzo unmasks and reveals his identity. Furiously Alvise orders Barnaba to see to it that this insolent outlaw is punished. A dramatic and powerful ensemble now follows ("L'un vampiro fatal"). The guests sing that it is as though the cold hand of a vampire had touched them and banished their joy. Gioconda and La Cieca give way to despair, while Barnaba and Alvise resolve to have revenge. In a solo interlude ("Già ti veggo immota") Enzo laments Laura's death. As the chorus continues Gioconda approaches Barnaba and offers to yield herself to him if he will save Enzo. He exultingly agrees to the bargain.

Suddenly there is a pause. Alvise bursts out that now all shall see the wife who has dishonored him. He sweeps aside the curtains of a doorway—another entrance to the room containing the casket—and thunders out that it was he himself who slew his wife ("Miratela! Son io che spenta l'ho!"). Enzo lunges toward him, dagger in hand, but is overpowered by guards. There is a tremendous cry of horror from the crowd. The curtain falls.

ACT FOUR
(*The Orfano Canal*)

The entrance chamber of a ruined palace on an island near Venice. At the rear is a large portico, beyond it the lagoon, and in the far distance may be seen the brightly lighted square of St. Mark. In one corner of the chamber a bed is partly visible behind a screen. On a table is a lantern, beside it a dagger and a flask of poison. Nearby is a couch on which are several pieces of cheap jewelry belonging to Gioconda. She is standing alone, lost in thought, awaiting the arrival of two street singers whom she has hired to secrete Laura from Alvise's burial vault in the city and bring her to the palace. The two men enter at length and place the unconscious Laura on the bed. As they leave, Gioconda begs them to search for her mother, saying that she has not seen her since the grim events at the House of Gold.

She stares at the dagger and the flask and then cries out, "Suicidio!" A long monologue follows. First she determines to take her own life, then, tormented by jealousy, resolves to kill Laura and throw her body into the lagoon. The conversation of two passing gondoliers, however, makes her recoil in horror from the deed. One calls to the other, asking if there is news from the city, where the terrible Inquisition is on a new hunt for victims. The second replies grimly that more corpses are floating in the canal. Gioconda's thoughts turn to Enzo, wondering if he will meet his doom at the hands of the dreaded Alvise. Shaken by passion and despair, she sinks down, weeping bitterly.

Now Enzo appears. He has come to thank her for obtaining his release from prison, where he had been thrown on Alvise's orders. He tells her, however, that his only wish is to go to Laura's tomb. Gioconda thereupon tells him that she has taken Laura from the burial vault. Enzo turns on her in terrible anger, cursing her for being jealous even of the dead. Beside himself with fury, he tries to stab her. In delirious ecstasy Gioconda rejoices that at least she will die by the hand of her lover.

At that moment, Laura, who has revived from the effects of the opiate, appears from behind the screen. Enzo rushes into her arms. Both turn to Gioconda with words of gratitude for saving their lives. From the distance come the strains of the serenade sung in the third act when Alvise commanded Laura to drink the poison. Gioconda tells the lovers that boatmen will soon arrive to take them to a place of safety. When the boat appears and the two prepare to leave, Gioconda places her cloak around Laura's shoulders. In so doing she sees La Cieca's rosary. She kisses it and then repeats the refrain her mother sang when she gave the rosary to Laura. There is a farewell trio ("Sulle tue mani l'anima"), after which Laura and Enzo step into the boat and are rowed away.

Gioconda returns to the table and takes up the flask of poison. Suddenly remembering her terrible bargain with Barnaba, she kneels before a shrine in a corner of the chamber and prays for deliverance. Barnaba enters. Feverishly he anticipates possessing his long-sought prize. As he advances Gioconda goes over to the couch and begins putting on her jewels, saying she must first adorn herself for her lover. Then, confronting Barnaba, she cries out that her body at last is his. With that she stabs herself with the dagger she had snatched up from the table and dies at Barnaba's feet. Barnaba kneels beside her, raging that if this is a jest he has already had his revenge, for last night he strangled her mother. Staring at Gioconda, he gasps that she does not hear ("Non ode piül"). Like a madman, he rushes away. The curtain falls.

Hänsel und Gretel

by ENGELBERT HUMPERDINCK

[1854–1921]

Libretto by
ADELHEID WETTE

Based on a fairy tale of the same name by Grimm

CHARACTERS

Hänsel .... *Mezzo-soprano*
Gretel .... *Soprano*
Peter, their father, a broommaker........................... *Baritone*
Gertrude, their mother................................. *Mezzo-soprano*
The Sandman .... *Soprano*
The Dewman .... *Soprano*
The Witch .... *Mezzo-soprano*
The fourteen angels, woodland voices, children

Place: A forest in ancient Germany
Time: The distant past
First performance: Weimar, Germany, December 23, 1893
Original language: German

HUMPERDINCK'S DELIGHTFUL fairy-tale opera was one of the most important works for the lyric stage to come out of Germany after the era of Wagner. Bases on authentic German folklore, it is truly Germanic in spirit, and in its musical structure it represents a high level of German technique.

The composer met Wagner while the latter was at work on *Parsifal,* and the two became close friends. Humperdinck not only aided in copying the *Parsifal* score but also assisted in preparing the opera for production. His intense admiration for Wagner's work and his close association with him account for the strong Wagnerian influence that is evident, particularly in the score of *Hänsel und Gretel.*

The overture begins with a stately chorale in the horns—the melody of the *Children's Prayer* which dominates the entire opera. This is followed by a lively rhythmic strain which has to do with the spell cast upon the children by the witch. It gives way to a more deliberate melody that will be heard again at the beginning of Act Three, when the children are awakened by the Dewman. These identifying melodies are interwoven with the prayer theme.

ACT ONE

[*Scene One*] A small and sparsely furnished room in the forest cottage of Peter the broommaker. Hänsel sits near the door, busily making a broom. Gretel is seated at the fireplace, knitting. She sings an ancient German folk tune about "Susie," telling of the poor geese who have no shoes. Hänsel, taking up the melody, sings that there is not even a farthing at hand to buy sugar and bread. Impetuously he flings the unfinished broom into a corner and jumps to his feet. If Mother would only come home, he frets. Gretel whimpers that she is terribly hungry. When Hänsel continues grumbling, his sister bids him remember what Father says when Mother complains. To the theme of the prayer the girl repeats the old proverb, "When need is direst, God stretches forth His hand" ("Wenn die Not auf's Höchste steigt"). Gretel then takes up a broom and pretends that she is sweeping out their tribulations, singing a merry little tune as she does so ("Griesgram hinaus"). Hänsel joins his voice in a pleasing duet. But Gretel remembers there is work to be done and warns Hänsel to get busy. He scoffs at the idea, saying he would much rather dance and have fun. Gretel exclaims that she loves to dance—and now they will do so to the little song that Auntie once taught them. Clapping her hands to keep time, Gretel tries to teach Hänsel the steps as she sings ("Brüderchen, komm tanz' mit mir"). She performs for his benefit—first the feet—tap-tap-tap—then the hands—clap-clap-clap. Forgetting their troubles—as well as their work—they dance and sing with carefree abandon, continuing with such vigor that they finally trip over each other and fall to the floor.

As they lie there laughing and out of breath, they hear their mother calling outside. Both spring to their feet in guilty fear. Gertrude storms in, angrily demanding the reason for the uproar. Hänsel explains that it was Gretel's doing, while she in turn blames her brother. Declaring she will thrash the children for not doing their work, Gertrude goes to fetch her stick. In her excitement she knocks over a pitcher of milk on the table.

There goes the pitcher, the Mother wails, and now there is nothing left for supper! Angrily she sends Hänsel and Gretel off to the woods to gather strawberries. She warns that if they dare come back without a full basket they will get the worst beating of their lives. When the children are gone Gertrude sinks sobbing into a chair and bemoans her misfortunes. Pillowing her head in her arms, she sobs herself to sleep.

Then from the distance comes the voice of Peter the broommaker, singing a lusty refrain—"Ra-la-la-la, ra-la-la-la!" As he draws nearer we hear the burden of his song: Hunger is the greatest chef! Carrying a huge basket on his back, Peter bursts in, still roaring his song. Of what use is a great chef, he goes on, when the kettle is empty! As for himself, brandy is the staff of life, he remarks, setting a half-empty bottle on the table. With that he reels over to his sleeping wife and gives her an enthusiastic kiss.

Gertrude wakes up, rubs her eyes in bewilderment, and asks who is making all the din. Peter tries to kiss her again, but she angrily pushes him away and berates him for wasting his time drinking at the tavern. He jovially tells his wife to forget her troubles and begins to unpack his basket. Gertrude exclaims in surprise and delight as he brings forth a tempting array of foodstuffs. Arm in arm the broommaker and his wife dance about the room. As Gertrude prepares supper Peter explains how it all happened. There was a great celebration in the village, he relates, and people were in the mood to buy. He made the most of his opportunity and sold his wares at the highest prices.

Suddenly he asks where Hänsel and Gretel are. In answer Gertrude relates the events of the afternoon—how the milk pitcher came to be broken and how, in anger, she sent the children into the woods. For all I care, she adds spitefully, they can be at Ilsenstein. Horrified, Peter asks his wife if she has not heard of that gruesome spot deep in the forest where the fiend has her lair. In a somber, dramatic aria Peter tells about the "Crust Witch" ("Die Knusperhexe"). At midnight she and her evil brood, astride their brooms, ride on their fiendish errands. During the day, Peter goes on, she lures little children into her Crust Cottage, bakes them into gingerbread children (*Lebkuchenkinder*), then gobbles them up. With a despairing cry for help Gertrude rushes from the house. Peter pauses to pick up the bottle of brandy from the table, then dashes out after his wife. The curtain falls.

[*Scene Two*] Without pause the orchestra begins the prelude, *The Witches' Ride*.[1] The curtain rises on a quiet forest glade, with the gloomy Ilsenstein rising in the background. We find Gretel sitting on a mossy tree trunk making a garland of wild roses, while Hänsel is looking for strawberries among a clump of bushes at the left. The scene gradually darkens.

Gretel sings a song (again a German folk tune) about a little man, wearing a fine purple cloak and a black hat, who stands on one leg all alone in the forest ("Ein Männlein steht im Walde"). Hänsel interrupts, shouting that his basket is full of strawberries. The children turn again to their games, meanwhile eating up all the strawberries. They hear a cuckoo in the distance and amuse themselves by imitating its call. Suddenly they become aware of the gathering darkness, and Hänsel confesses that he does not know the way home. Gretel sobs in terror, thinking she sees a ghost among the trees. Hänsel challenges it with a call which is re-echoed behind the scenes by a chorus of women's voices. The children clasp each other in fright.

At the height of their terror a little gray man with a sack on his back steps through the rising mist, singing that he is the Sandman ("Der kleine Sandmann bin ich—sh!"). He loves little children, he says, and delights in dropping upon their eyes the magic grains that bring deep and restful slumber. The children gradually become calmer as he strews sand over their eyes. They kneel and sing the famous *Children's Prayer*, about the fourteen angels who gather in pairs around their bed to guard them while they sleep ("Abends, will ich schlafen gehn"). At the end of the duet the children sink back upon the ground and fall asleep in each other's arms.

As the orchestra softly echoes the prayer theme total darkness envelops the scene. Suddenly a bright light breaks through the mist, bringing into

[1] Originally written as Act Two.

view a long staircase at the rear. Fourteen angels in flowing garments descend the staircase in pairs, group themselves about the children, then join hands and move about in a slow, dreamlike dance as the curtain falls.

ACT TWO

The prelude begins with a brief phrase which is part of an ancient song-game familiar the world over. It will be heard again later in the act when the Witch sings that someone has been nibbling at her house. Following this comes the dawn motive. After it has been stated the curtain rises. The scene is the same, except that the angels have disappeared.[2]

The Dewman appears and sprinkles drops from a bluebell over the sleeping children to the accompaniment of a little song ("Der kleine Taumann heiss' ich"). He proclaims that he travels with the sun and pries open sleepy eyelids with golden shafts of light. As he wanders off, Gretel sits up and rubs her eyes. Hänsel turns over on his other side and goes back to sleep. In wonder and surprise, Gretel muses at finding herself in the forest. She awakens Hänsel, meanwhile imitating a birdcall. He springs to his feet and gives his own imitation of a rooster's crow. The two voices join briefly in a sparkling duet ("Ti-re-li-re-le, 's ist nichtmehr früh"). The children then tell each other of their wonderful dreams about the guardian angels.

Suddenly they cry out in astonishment. At the back the mists have now cleared, revealing the Witch's house at Ilsenstein. In transports of delight Hänsel and Gretel sing a duet describing the wonders of the gingerbread house ("Von Kuchen und Torten ein Häuslein gemacht"). Hand in hand they tiptoe toward the house. Hänsel, ignoring Gretel's warning, creeps up to the cottage and breaks off a piece from the corner.

With that a voice, singing the phrase of the song-game music heard in the prelude, calls out from within, asking who is nibbling at the house ("Knusper, knusper, Knäuschen, wer knuspert mir am Häuschen?"). Hänsel, startled out of his wits, drops the piece of cake. He asks Gretel if she heard the voice. They decide that it was only the wind, then break off more pieces from the house. At that moment the upper part of the door opens and the Witch peers out, unobserved by the children. While they are merrily feasting the Witch steps quickly out of the house and throws a rope around Hänsel's neck. He cries out in terror and tries desperately to get away, but the Witch merely cackles in fiendish glee. Then she invites the children into the house, promising them all the sweets they can eat. But Hänsel flatly refuses to enter. He cautions Gretel not to mind the Witch, then whispers that they will try to run away.

By that time Hänsel manages to free himself. He and Gretel start to run. Thereupon the Witch draws a stick from her belt, raises it like a wand, and utters her incantation—"Hokus, pokus, Hexenschuss!" Instantly the children are stopped. The scene darkens. As she intones the spell the end of the stick begins to glow eerily. She leads Hänsel into a nearby cage and locks the barred door. Shaking a warning finger at Gretel, who is motionless in the

---

[2] Originally written as Act Three.

grip of the spell, the Witch disappears into the house. Hänsel tells his sister that she must watch carefully everything the Witch does and pretend to obey her. In a moment the Witch returns, bringing a basket of sweetmeats with which to fatten Hänsel. He pretends to be asleep. Then she frees Gretel from the spell and orders her to work about the house.

Hurrying over to the oven, the Witch throws a handful of wood on the fire, slams the door, and rubs her hands in evil delight. Gloatingly she muses on how Gretel is to be "coaxed" into the oven. She will ask her to bend down and look inside. Then, one big push, bang goes the door, and—presto! Gingerbread! In her mad joy over the plan the Witch bestrides a broom and races wildly around the house, chanting a nonsensical refrain about her broomstick horse ("Hopp, Galopp, mein Besengaul!"). Suddenly she stops and dismounts, awakens Hänsel, and tells him to show her his tongue. She examines it closely, smacking her lips. Now then, show me your finger, she orders. Hänsel instead holds forth a small stick, whereupon the Witch complains that he is still much too bony.

Calling to Gretel, she orders her to bring more raisins and almonds for Hänsel. While the Witch is feeding him Gretel cautiously picks up the magic wand and softly repeats the incantation. When the Witch turns to look at the oven, Hänsel, freed from the spell, escapes from the cage. The Witch calls to Gretel and tells her to look into the oven to find out if the gingerbread is ready. Gretel, pretending to be very stupid, asks the Witch to show her how one looks into an oven. Hänsel sneaks closer. As the Witch bends over in front of the open oven the children push her in and slam the door. They shout in mocking imitation of her own words: "Und bist du dann drin—schwaps! Geht die Thür—klaps [One big push, bang goes the door, and—presto]!"

Hänsel and Gretel prance around singing the *Knusperwalzer* (*Crust Waltz*), in which they exult over the death of the Witch. They dance together toward the Witch's house. Hänsel breaks away and rushes inside. In another moment he appears at one of the upper windows and begins throwing down apples, pears, oranges, gilded nuts, and an assortment of sweetmeats. Gretel catches them all in her apron.

All at once the oven begins crackling furiously, then explodes and collapses into smoking debris. Hänsel and Gretel drop their booty in fright and stare in astonishment. They become even more bewildered as a crowd of children, their gingerbread crusts fallen away, throng about them. The strangers, their eyes closed, sing in a soft chorus that now they are forever free ("Erlöst, befreit, für alle Zeit") and urge Hänsel and Gretel to touch them so that they may awaken. Gretel timidly touches the nearest child, who opens its eyes and smiles at her. Eagerly she touches the others, who likewise respond. Hänsel meanwhile waves the Witch's wand and repeats a phrase of the incantation. Instantly the spell is broken. The children rush up to Hänsel and Gretel, join hands, and dance around them, singing a joyful chorus ("Die Hexerei ist nun vorbei").

The ensemble is interrupted by the sound of the broommaker's jolly "Ra-la-la-la" from the distance. As Peter and Gertrude appear their children rush up to them with glad cries of greeting. Two boys then drag from the ruins of the oven the figure of the Witch, now an enormous gingerbread cake.

Peter bids the children observe how the Witch was destroyed by her own evil magic ("Kinder, schaut das Wunder an!")—thus heaven punishes evil.

In a variation of the prayer theme he intones the words of the *Children's Prayer*—"When need is direst, God stretches forth His hand." The children respond in a great chorus. Then, as they join hands and joyously dance around in a circle, the curtain falls.

Lakmé

by LÉO DELIBES
[1836–1891]

Libretto by
EDMOND GONDINET and PHILIPPE GILLE

Suggested by Pierre Loti's novel
LE MARIAGE DE LOTI

CHARACTERS

Mallika, slave of Lakmé	Mezzo-soprano
Hadji, servant of Nilakantha	Tenor
Nilakantha, a Brahman priest	Bass
Lakmé, his daughter	Soprano
Mistress Bentson, a governess	Mezzo-soprano
Rose, cousin and companion of Ellen	Mezzo-soprano
Ellen, daughter of a provincial governor	Soprano
Gerald, a British officer in colonial service	Tenor
Frederic, another British officer	Baritone

Priests, Hindus, officers, merchants, soldiers,
beggars, dancers

Place: India
Time: Nineteenth century
First performance: Opéra-Comique, Paris, April 14, 1883
Original language: French

LÉO DELIBES belongs to the French school of operatic composers who were contemporaries and successors of Bizet. *Lakmé*, Delibes's only successful opera, is written in the typical style of *opéra comique*, with interpolations of spoken dialogue.

The prelude begins with the solemn, powerful chords of the invocation to the goddess Dourga, sung by the Brahman priests in the second act. Then we hear the theme of a sacred dance, several phrases of Lakmé's prayer to Dourga, and the refrain of Gerald's love song to Lakmé. Following another brief reference to the invocation theme, the curtain rises as the music continues into the first act.

ACT ONE

An exotic and colorful garden in India. Toward the rear, almost hidden by the foliage, is a small temple flanked by Brahman images. The garden

and the temple are partly enclosed by a bamboo fence. Not far from the
temple is a stream, with a small boat tied at the bank. As the curtain rises,
Hadji, Mallika, and a group of worshipers are seen before the temple. In a
flowing melody they sing an invocation to Brahma ("A l'heure accou-
tumée"). Nilakantha now appears. He is brooding over the wrong done him
by the foreigners, who have repudiated him and driven him into exile. He
blesses those who have remained faithful to him and assures them that
the wrath of Brahma will strike down their enemies. Nilakantha sings that
the prayers of his daughter are his only source of hope and courage.

From within the temple comes the voice of Lakmé chanting to the Brahman gods ("Blanche Dourga, Pâle Siva, Puissant Ganesa"). As the chorus
responds, Lakmé's voice rises in a soaring obbligato. Soon she appears in
the temple doorway. Nilakantha dismisses the worshipers, who continue
chanting as they withdraw. After a few words, Nilakantha takes leave of his
daughter, commanding Hadji and Mallika to guard her well. The four
voices blend in a short quartet as they invoke the protection of Brahma
("Que le ciel me protège").

Left alone with Mallika, Lakmé prepares to bathe in the stream, removing some of her jewels and placing them on a stone bench. She and her
slave sing a charming duet ("Viens, Mallika, les lianes en fleur"), in which
they describe the calm beauty of the stream shadowed by perfume-laden
jasmine and roses. The mood of the song changes momentarily as Lakmé
expresses concern for her father. Mallika prays that the god Ganesa may
protect him. Their fears forgotten, the two again take up the rippling theme
of the duet. At its conclusion they step into the boat and glide out of sight.

Loud laughter and a confusion of voices are heard as Gerald and Frederic appear on the other side of the bamboo fence. With them are Rose,
Ellen, and Mistress Bentson. There are exclamations of wonder and surprise
at the temple in its strange and mysterious setting. Ellen urges the men to
force apart the bamboo stalks so that they may see what is behind the pali-
sade. The two officers, peering through the cracks, tell the women that they
see the statue of the god Ganesa. Frederic, observing the carved lotus leaf
over the door of the temple, explains that it indicates the dwelling of a
Brahman.

Ellen, determined to see the temple, finally forces aside the bamboos and
steps into the garden, followed by the others. In a combination of spoken
dialogue and recitative they speculate as to the identity of those who live in
this exotic retreat. Frederic informs the party that he knows who the owner
of the temple is, for there has been considerable talk of him in the town. He
emphasizes that their intrusion here is dangerous. When Rose marvels at
the beauty of certain flowers in the garden, the officer warns that death
lurks in their petals, for they are the poisonous *datura stramonium*. He explains that though the plant grows harmless in their native England, it ac-
quires poisonous characteristics under tropical conditions. One taste of a
leaf, he says, would be fatal.

"What a terrible country!" Mistress Bentson exclaims. Frederic then tells
his companions about Nilakantha and his daughter Lakmé, regarded by the
Hindus as a beautiful goddess who must not be profaned by the gaze of
foreigners. A sprightly quintet follows ("Ah! beaux faiseurs de systèmes").

With cynical amusement the visitors argue as to whether a lovely woman has the right to hide herself from the eyes of society. They agree that European and oriental attitudes toward women are vastly different. Frederic concludes the argument with a brief refrain in which he makes the rather obvious observation that no two women in the world are alike.

Ellen suggests that they try to find this goddess Lakmé, but Frederic protests that this would be an unforgivable affront to the Brahman gods ("Je ne dis pas cette sottise"). In a suave refrain he sings that women of Lakmé's station represent the oriental ideal of love—they live for love and know no other law. Ellen, in answering air, spiritedly replies that women of her own race have qualities that are equally commendable ("Ce sont des femmes idéales"). All then resume their argument in a repetition of the quintet.

At the end of the number Frederic urges the party to leave before they are discovered in this sacred place. Suddenly Rose catches sight of Lakmé's jewels. She and the other women exclaim over the beauty of the gems, while Frederic warns that they must not be touched. Although he reminds the women that their presence has desecrated this holy place, and that the Brahmans may try to exact revenge, they are unwilling to leave. After some discussion, Gerald proposes a compromise. He will remain behind to sketch the jewels while the others return to their quarters. His friends then leave.

Gerald, gazing in fascination at the jewels, muses in recitative that merely sketching these gems cannot be so serious a crime ("Prendre le dessin d'un bijou"). This introduces the beautiful aria "Fantaisie aux divins mensonges," one of the outstanding numbers of the opera. Busily sketching, Gerald sings ardently of the vision of loveliness conjured up by the sight of the jewels. After the aria his reflections are interrupted by the voices of Lakmé and Mallika in the distance, singing the theme of their duet. As they enter, Gerald quickly conceals himself behind some bushes.

Lakmé dismisses her slave. In a lyrical aria ("Les fleurs me paraissent plus belles"), she sings that, though she is sad, a great happiness seems to be flooding her heart. The aria concludes on a soft, questioning phrase, "Pourquoi?" Turning to go, Lakmé sees Gerald and cries out in terror for Mallika. The slave rushes in, followed by Hadji. Both excitedly ask her what has happened. Recovering herself, Lakmé answers casually that every sound frightens her today because she has been thinking of her father. She tells the servants to go and seek him. Mallika and Hadji leave.

No sooner have they gone than Lakmé quickly approaches Gerald, who looks at her utterly enraptured. A long and melodious duet ensues, begun by Lakmé as she asks Gerald whence he has come ("D'où viens-tu?"). In sweeping phrases she tells him that he has risked his life by intruding upon this sacred abode and bids him forget that he has looked upon a goddess. When Gerald ignores her warning and replies in phrases of amorous ecstasy, Lakmé asks wonderingly what god there may be who has endowed him with such courage. The god of love, Gerald answers fervently. Under the spell of his ardor, Lakmé confesses that she too knows this god. Bringing the duet to a passionate climax, they invoke the god of love.

Their idyll is shattered as Lakmé cries out that her father is approaching. Distractedly she urges Gerald to flee. He rushes away, and in another moment Hadji, Nilakantha, and a group of Hindus burst into the garden. In fury the priest asks his daughter who has dared profane the temple. Her only reply is a gasp of terror. Nilakantha storms for vengeance as the curtain falls.

ACT TWO

A public square flanked by merchants' booths and tents. An oriental bazaar is in progress, with natives and tourists mingling in a colorful throng. At the rear rises a pagoda. A spirited, rhythmic chorus heightens the festive gaiety of the scene. Mistress Bentson enters and is immediately surrounded by native vendors and beggars. The vendors harass her with entreaties to buy, while the beggars attempt to steal her watch. Highly disturbed and indignant, she is finally rescued by Frederic.

A bell signals the close of the bazaar. Dancing girls now come out of the pagoda and take their places in the square for a series of festival dances. The onlookers comment occasionally in a choral accompaniment to the dancing. At the end of the ballet Nilakantha and Lakmé enter. A rather sinister theme sounds in the orchestra as they mingle with the throng. The priest is disguised as a sannyasi, or Hindu penitent, while his daughter is dressed as a street singer. Mistress Bentson, Frederic, and Rose appear.

Rose calls Frederic's attention to the penitent and his picturesque companion. Frederic explains that while the old man solicits alms his daughter sings ancient ballads that the Hindus love to hear. Gerald and Ellen now approach. Questioned about his afternoon's sketching, Gerald answers that he actually saw the mysterious Brahman goddess. As Ellen pretends to chide her fiancé for his interest in the goddess, a phrase of Lakmé's duet with Mallika runs lightly through the orchestra. In an aside, Frederic informs Gerald that they have been recalled to duty with their regiment.

At length the three women, accompanied by Gerald, leave the square for the governor's palace. Frederic remains. To Ellen's further questioning about Lakmé, Gerald replies casually that she is "mysterious." Rose suddenly turns back to speak to Frederic, saying she knows that the regiment has been ordered to march against a force of rebellious natives. She requests Frederic to keep the news from Ellen in order to spare her anxiety over Gerald's safety. As for herself, Rose adds, she can face the news calmly because she is not concerned with parting from an admirer. In an aside, Frederic comments ardently on her beauty, then promises to say good-by to her before leaving.

To the theme of the invocation to Dourga, Nilakantha enters with Lakmé. Grimly the priest sings that if the hated English realized that this lowly penitent was the man whom they had dishonored and debased, their blood would run cold. Lakmé timidly asks if the god Brahma would condone forgiving an offense. "Never a foreigner's offense!" Nilakantha bursts out angrily. Then, gazing tenderly at his daughter, he continues in an eloquent refrain ("Lakmé, ton doux regard se voile"). Her sadness, Nilakantha sings, is born of the thought that a stranger has desecrated her and that vengeance is tardy. Lakmé, trying to placate him, replies that she is sad only because of his sorrow. The priest, however, determined to revenge himself upon his enemy, bids her sing one of her ballads as a lure to the traitor.

Lakmé then sings the introductory phrases of the aria "De la fille du paria," the famous *Bell Song*. As her voice rises in soaring phrases, the Hindus gather around her to listen. She relates the ballad of the pariah's daughter who rescued a traveler lost in the trackless forest. She saved him from the wild beasts through the enchantment of her magic bell. When the stranger approached to thank her, she discovered that he was none other than Vishnu, the son of Brahma. Since that day, the legend goes, straying travelers can find their way again by listening for the chime of the magic bell.

As Lakmé's voice soars higher and higher in the brilliant passages imitating the sound of a bell, Gerald and Frederic appear at the edge of the throng. "Chante! chante encore!" Nilakantha intones, relentlessly commanding his daughter to repeat her song. Terror-stricken, Lakmé continues. Her voice betrays her fear as she sees Gerald in the crowd. The Hindus murmur among themselves over her look of distress. Again Nilakantha commands her to sing. Falteringly Lakmé tries to go on, then reels as if about to faint. Gerald, crying her name, rushes forward to aid her. In fierce exultation Nilakantha sings that Brahma has destined the guilty foreigner to betray himself. At that moment fifes and drums are heard in the distance. Frederic reminds Gerald that they must answer the call to arms and finally persuades him to leave.

Nilakantha mutters in grim satisfaction that now he knows the culprit. As a detachment of guards marches across the square, Nilakantha calls Lakmé, Hadji, and his followers to him. He then tells them of his plot to kill Gerald. The officer is to be separated from his friends as he watches the procession of the goddess Dourga tonight. Once he is alone, the priest will steal upon him and strike him down. Nilakantha's adherents, in a brief but impressive chorus, express their determination to exact revenge ("Des siens, séparant le coupable"). The priest and his followers withdraw, leaving Lakmé and Hadji alone in the square. The servant, in an effort to console her, sings a simple and touching song ("Le maître ne pense qu'à sa vengeance"). Nilakantha's bitter thoughts have blinded him to Lakmé's tears, Hadji sings. He entreats her to take comfort in his own steadfast loyalty.

Seeing Gerald approaching, she sends Hadji away. The officer rushes to her, and a passionate love duet ensues ("Lakmé! c'est toi"). Overwhelmed by Gerald's fervent protestations, Lakmé implores him to flee with her to a secret rendezvous in the forest, where they both will be safe from all danger. After the ecstatic climax of the duet, she warns that the procession of Dourga is approaching. Tenderly the lovers part.

Led by Nilakantha and the Brahman priests, the procession moves toward the pagoda as the chorus chants the majestic invocation to Dourga ("O Dourga, toi qui renais"). Several statues of the ten-armed goddess are borne on the shoulders of the marchers.

Ellen, Rose, and Mistress Bentson appear, followed by Frederic and Gerald. The latter watches the pageant with a preoccupied air. Lost in his thoughts of Lakmé, he sings of the dream that enthralls his heart. Frederic jestingly tells him that his goddess will never cross his path again, for tomorrow they will be on the march. The crowd gradually disperses. Nilakantha and the Hindus watch Gerald closely as they pass. Then Lakmé appears. As Gerald starts toward her the priest flings himself upon the officer, stabs him, and vanishes.

Lakmé rushes to Gerald's side, screaming that he has been slain. On discovering that he is only wounded, she sings ecstatically that now they will be united forever. The curtain falls.

ACT THREE

A bamboo hut deep in the Indian forest. It is half concealed by a profusion of tropical flowers. Gerald is seen lying asleep. Lakmé, bending over him, sings a soothing lullaby ("Sous le ciel tout étoilé"). Gerald awakes and confusedly recalls the terrible events of the night before—the procession, the sudden attack, and then darkness. Tenderly Lakmé tells him that Hadji carried him to this forest retreat, where nature will help to heal his wounds. Ardently the lovers sing of their future together.

From the distance comes a tuneful chorus ("Descendons la pente doucement"). Lakmé explains that these are the voices of lovers on their way to the magic spring. Those who drink of its waters will enjoy the bliss of eternal love. She then leaves to bring sacred water from the spring.

A moment after she is gone, Frederic appears. He tells Gerald that he found his hiding place by following a trail of blood through the forest. The country is in revolt, he says, and they must join their regiment immediately. But Gerald can think only of Lakmé, and even the mention of Ellen does not move him. "What of your duty and your honor as a soldier?" Frederic asks. At those words Gerald declares that he will be ready to march. Lakmé now returns and Frederic steals away.

Carrying the cup of sacred water, Lakmé sings of how she followed the lovers to the spring, then offers Gerald the cup. She recoils as she sees a new and strange look in his eyes. At that moment martial music sounds in the distance. When Gerald eagerly turns away to listen, Lakmé realizes that she has lost him forever. "All is ended," she murmurs in despair. In a swift, desperate resolve she picks a datura flower from a nearby bush and eats it. Gerald, suddenly aware of what she has done, cries out in horror. Smiling at him tenderly, Lakmé sings, "Tu m'as donné le plus doux rêve." It is the poignant opening phrase of a duet in which the doomed lovers voice their passion and despair. Impetuously Gerald drinks from the cup. Welcoming death, Lakmé and Gerald bring the duet to a deeply moving climax.

As they remain clasped in each other's arms, Nilakantha and his followers rush in. Lakmé cries out in terror, while Gerald begs the priest to kill him. Nilakantha, despite his wild fury, pauses as Lakmé tells him that she and her lover have drunk from the sacred cup together. Feebly she sings that if the gods must have their revenge, let her be the victim. With her dying breath she repeats the impassioned phrase, "Tu m'as donné le plus doux rêve," then dies in her father's arms.

Holding Lakmé's lifeless form, Nilakantha sings in fanatical ecstasy that now she has gone to life eternal. His voice blends with Gerald's despairing cry as the curtain falls.

Lohengrin

by RICHARD WAGNER

[1813–1883]

Libretto by the Composer

Based on a medieval legend

CHARACTERS

King Henry I of Germany...Bass
Count Frederick Telramund of Brabant......................Baritone
A herald...Bass
Ortrud, wife of Count Frederick.......................Mezzo-soprano
Elsa of Brabant...Soprano
Lohengrin, a knight of the Holy Grail...........................Tenor
Gottfried, brother of Elsa
Nobles of Saxony and Brabant, pages, ladies and
gentlemen of the court, attendants

Place: Antwerp
Time: Early part of the tenth century
First performance: Weimar Theater, Germany, August 28, 1850
Original language: German

WAGNER began work on *Lohengrin* in 1845, having gathered material for the libretto from several Teutonic legends dealing with the mythical knight of the Holy Grail. The legend of *Parsifal*, in particular, supplied the background not only for *Lohengrin* but also for the later music-drama, *Parsifal*. In Act Three of *Lohengrin* the knight reveals that he is the son of Parsifal and a knight of the Holy Grail. The Grail knights were the holy warriors whose duty it was to guard the sacred cup in which the blood of the crucified Christ had been poured.

The composer wrote the opera in reverse order, beginning with the third act, and completed it early in 1848. Forced into exile for political reasons, Wagner at length sent the score to Franz Liszt at Weimar and prevailed on him to produce the opera. Wagner himself did not see a performance of it until 1861.

The prelude opens with the ethereal motive symbolizing the Holy Grail. This leads into the refrain of Elsa's prayer in Act One. The music rises to a tremendous climax, then concludes with an exquisite reiteration of the Grail theme.

ACT ONE

An open field on the banks of the Scheldt River, beyond the walls of Antwerp. King Henry is seated on his throne under the Oak of Judgment, surrounded by his Saxon nobles. Facing them some distance away sits Frederick Telramund, with Ortrud at his side. He is attended by noblemen of Brabant.

The King's herald comes forward and signals four trumpeters to sound a fanfare. He announces that King Henry is summoning the men of Brabant to the defense of the German kingdom. Vigorously the Brabantians pledge their loyal efforts in behalf of their country. The King now rises and greets his vassals ("Gott grüss euch"). In solemn tones he tells them that the Hungarian hordes are threatening Germany on the eastern borders. A nine years' truce has expired, and now the Hungarians are clamoring for battle. King Henry says he has come to urge the Brabantians to march with him at once to Mainz and engage the enemy. Turning to Telramund, he asks why Brabant, on which he counted for support in this crucial hour, is torn by civil strife and unrest.

Telramund thanks the King for coming to act as arbiter ("Dank, König, dir, dass du zu richten kamst!"), then gives his explanation. He relates that the Duke of Brabant, on his deathbed, placed in his hands the care of the Duke's two children, Elsa and Gottfried. One day Elsa left the palace with her brother and later returned alone. Gottfried was never found. Convinced by her guilty manner and evasiveness that Elsa was responsible for her brother's disappearance, Telramund continues, he renounced the right to make her his bride—a right granted him by the Duke—and married Ortrud instead. Telramund then charges Elsa with the murder of her brother and claims the throne of Brabant. There is a murmur of surprise and dismay from the people of the court over this alarming state of affairs.

When Telramund hotly continues that Elsa further plotted to rule Brabant with a secret lover at her side, King Henry silences him. The Saxons and Brabantians draw their swords and sing that their weapons will remain unsheathed until the King's judgment on the accused has been proclaimed. The herald summons Elsa.

To the accompaniment of a tender and exalted theme Elsa approaches to take her place before the King. The men softly comment that he who has dared to accuse so pure a being must indeed be certain of her guilt. King Henry asks if she is Elsa von Brabant ("Bist du es, Elsa von Brabant?"). She bows without speaking. When he inquires if she knows the nature of the accusations against her she nods calmly. The King asks if she confesses her guilt ("So bekennst du dein Schuld?").

As if in a trance, Elsa murmurs about her brother. Then she begins the dramatic soliloquy known as *Elsa's Dream* ("Einsam in trüben Tagen"). Lost and alone, Elsa sings, she prayed for help and a cry of anguish burst from her lips. As its echoes died away she sank to the ground in sleep. Then in a vision there appeared before her a knight in shining armor. It is he who will be her champion in this hour of deep distress.

Deeply moved by her strangely exalted manner, King Henry beseeches Telramund to think carefully before he presses his charges any further. In answer Telramund furiously challenges to combat anyone who questions the truth of his assertions. Turning to Elsa, the King asks whom she will choose as her champion. In an ecstatic refrain ("Des Ritters will ich wahren") she repeats that the warrior of her vision shall fight in her behalf. Her hand shall be his reward.

Excitedly the men sing that a royal prize indeed awaits the warrior who will take up this challenge. After a fanfare the herald commands the champion to step forward. There is a long pause. When there is no answer Telramund cries out that his accusations are justified and that he is in the right. Elsa implores the King to sound the call again. Once more it is met with silence. Falling to her knees, Elsa sings the eloquent and moving prayer, "Du trugest zu ihm meine Klage," in which she pleads that her knight may appear. The ladies of her retinue join their entreaties in chorus.

Suddenly the men near the bank of the river cry out that a boat drawn by a swan is approaching. Others join their voices to exclaim that a warrior in resplendent armor is standing in the boat, guiding the swan with reins of gold. The chorus rises to a tremendous crescendo as Lohengrin's boat nears the riverbank. Elsa, standing as if spellbound, does not turn to look. King Henry watches the scene in amazement. Telramund looks on in mingled fear and anger, while Ortrud stares in terror at the swan.

Lohengrin, clad in magnificent armor, stands leaning on his sword as the boat touches the shore. A great shout of welcome bursts from the throng ("Gegrüsst, du gottgesandter Held!"). There is an expectant hush as Lohengrin steps from the boat, then turns and addresses the swan ("Nun sei bedankt, mein lieber Schwan"). He thanks the swan and bids it return to the magic land whence they have come and sorrowfully sings farewell as it departs. The chorus comments in tones of awe.

Lohengrin pays his respects to the King and, as the Grail theme sounds softly in the orchestra, tells him that he has come to protect the maiden who has been grievously accused. Turning to Elsa, he requests the privilege of being her champion knight. Elsa rapturously greets her hero and savior ("Mein Held, mein Retter"). A dramatic colloquy ensues, in which she pledges herself to Lohengrin if he wins in combat. In return he exacts from her the promise that she will never ask his name or seek to know whence he came ("Nie sollst du mich befragen"). When Elsa fervently declares that she will keep faith with him Lohengrin takes her in his arms, crying out that he loves her ("Elsa! Ich liebe dich!").

While the chorus sings softly of the strange enchantment of this scene, Lohengrin escorts Elsa to King Henry, committing her to his care. Swiftly confronting Telramund, he declares that Elsa is guiltless and that the charges are false. When Telramund is warned by his own henchmen not to fight this heaven-sent adversary he answers that he would rather die than prove a coward ("Viel lieber tot, als feig!").

Thereupon the nobles mark off the area of combat. After the herald announces the rules of the contest and the two principals invoke divine aid, King Henry offers a dignified and solemn prayer that right may triumph ("Mein Herr und Gott, nun ruf' ich dich")—known as *König's Gebet*. All intone the prayer in a majestic chorus. As trumpets sound, the King strikes his shield three times with his sword as a signal for the combat.

The two knights lunge at each other, and there is a brief but furious clash of weapons. With a mighty blow Lohengrin strikes Telramund down, then stands over his vanquished foe with the sword point at his throat. In a dramatic phrase the knight sings that he will spare Telramund's life. As the chorus hails the victor with a great shout, Elsa pledges herself to Lohengrin in impassioned phrases ("O fand ich Jubelweisen"). A magnificent chorus of praise and rejoicing follows. It is sung by all except Telramund and Ortrud, who lament their defeat and shame. Overcome by anger and humiliation, Telramund collapses at Ortrud's feet, while Elsa and Lohengrin are borne away in triumph at the brilliant climax of the chorus. The curtain falls.

ACT TWO

The fortress of Antwerp. At the rear is the Pallas, the abode of the knights. Toward the foreground is the Kemenate, or women's chambers. It is night. Lights glow in the windows, and sounds of gaiety come from within. On the shadowy steps of the cathedral opposite the royal dwellings, Telramund and Ortrud are seated. They have been deprived of their royal prerogatives and are clad in beggars' clothing. Telramund is sunk in thought, while Ortrud glares malevolently at the glowing windows. Suddenly Telramund turns upon his wife in bitter wrath, saying that it was her evil sorcery that led him to forfeit his honor in combat.

Ortrud answers him with sneering contempt, remarking that his anger is too late—had he directed it against his foe, they would have been spared this disgrace. Yet one hope is left them, Ortrud says, for she knows the secret of the spell which enabled Lohengrin to conquer. Once the knight reveals his name and race, his magic power will be broken. Elsa alone can draw that secret from him, and she must be persuaded—or forced—to question the knight. Deliberately she goads Telramund to wilder fury by telling him that if he had drawn but one drop of blood from Lohengrin that, too, would have rendered him helpless. In a dramatic and powerful refrain sung in unison Ortrud and Telramund swear that they will exact a terrible revenge ("Der Rache Werk").

As their voices die away to a menacing whisper Elsa appears on the balcony of the Kemenate and stands for a moment in happy reflection. The ardent phrases of her song mark the beginning of what is known as the *Balcony Scene* ("Euch Lüften, die mein Klagen so traurig oft erfüllt"). Ortrud sends Telramund away and in dolorous tones calls to Elsa. Maliciously pretending remorse and repentance, she wails that she meant no harm and that Telramund acted in thoughtless and unreasoning anger. Elsa, moved by her apparent distress, tries to comfort her. She bids Ortrud to wait and hurriedly re-enters the chamber. Alone, Ortrud calls in savage exultation on Odin and Freia, the pagan gods, to aid her in accomplishing her revenge. When Elsa reappears with two ladies in waiting Ortrud kneels before her in servile entreaty. Elsa, in transports of joy over her approaching bridal, assures Ortrud of forgiveness and says she will also seek a word of pardon from her champion.

Craftily Ortrud warns Elsa not to love too rashly and expresses the hope that she may never be deceived in her affections. Though momentarily frightened by the ominous sound of Ortrud's words, Elsa fervently urges her to believe that faith alone can bring happiness in love ("Lass mich dich lehren"). Aside, Ortrud sardonically observes that Elsa's very triumph shall prove her undoing ("Dieser Stolz, er soll mich lehren"). The voices of the two women blend in a brief but impressive duet which brings their colloquy to a close. Ortrud permits Elsa to lead her into the Kemenate. As the women enter the dwelling Telramund appears. Gazing after them, he muses gloatingly that Ortrud's evil sorcery will destroy those who have robbed him of his honor.

Trumpet blasts from various towers of the citadel now herald the dawn. Telramund quickly conceals himself behind an abutment of the cathedral to avoid being seen by the servants who go about their morning duties. Soon the space before the Pallas is filled with courtiers and men from the fortress. In a stirring chorus ("In Früh'n versammelt uns der Ruf") they sing of the glorious events that will mark this day. All then turn to face the herald, who comes out of the Pallas. He proclaims the King's edict branding Telramund a traitor and placing anyone who aids him under the pain of death. The men curse him vehemently. The herald further announces that Elsa's champion has declined the title of Duke and has asked to be named Protector of Brabant. The chorus lustily hails the hero.

After a trumpet call silences the throng the herald informs them that today Elsa's champion invites all to join him in his wedding festivities. Tomorrow, however, they must turn to the stern duties of war. The men pledge their loyalty in an exultant chorus ("Zum Streite säumet nicht!"). While the people and the warriors are milling about in great excitement, four Brabantian noblemen, former henchmen of Telramund, draw aside and sullenly protest among themselves at marching against an enemy who has never challenged them. At that moment Telramund stealthily approaches. He declares that he is resolved to unmask their would-be leader as a pretender and a renegade. Astounded at Telramund's boldness, they warn him against betraying himself and try to shield him from the eyes of the throng.

Four pages now announce Elsa and her bridal retinue. To the accompaniment of a stately refrain the procession emerges from the Kemenate, while the nobles and the populace range themselves on either side of the great court. There is a tremendous chorus of acclaim ("Heil dir, Elsa von Brabant") as Elsa and the ladies move toward the cathedral. In the procession is Ortrud, now clad in royal garments.

Just as Elsa is about to ascend the cathedral steps Ortrud advances and stands before her. In suppressed fury she declares that she will no longer follow like a lowly handmaiden but will force Elsa to relinquish her place. When Elsa angrily rebukes her Ortrud fiercely defies her to speak the name of the knight whose bride she is to be. Perhaps there is good reason, she cries, why he forbids questions about his origin. In a dramatic, sweeping phrase (Du Lästerin! Ruchlose Frau!") Elsa denounces Ortrud's slanderous accusations. She calls upon the assemblage to bear witness that her knight is a stainless champion who spared the life of his treacherous enemy. Furiously Ortrud retorts that this unknown warrior is an evil impostor.

At this point trumpets signal the approach of King Henry, Lohengrin, and their followers, who advance in majestic array from the Pallas. Alarmed by the disturbance, the King and Lohengrin hurry forward. Elsa rushes distractedly into the knight's arms, imploring him to protect her. Imperiously Lohengrin commands Ortrud to leave, then tenderly bids Elsa accompany him to the cathedral.

The procession moves onward. Suddenly Telramund breaks through the throng, confronts the King, and wildly demands to be heard. The warriors cry out against him, while the King orders him to be seized. As the crowd shrinks back in awe at his frenzy Telramund launches into a bitter tirade ("Den dort im Glanz ich vor mir sehe"). He brands Lohengrin a sorcerer and demands that he reveal his name and race. Violently he declares that he who came among them under such mysterious circumstances has much to explain. The people begin murmuring suspiciously.

Lohengrin vehemently replies that no false accusations can impugn his honor. Not even the King, he says, can force him to speak. To one only is he answerable—Elsa. As he utters her name in a ringing phrase he turns to her, only to recoil at her terrified expression. The great closing chorus of the act now begins as the onlookers voice their bewilderment and confusion ("Welch ein Geheimnis muss der Held bewahren?"). Ortrud and Telramund exult that the poison of suspicion is doing its deadly work in Elsa's heart. Elsa herself frantically voices her doubts and fears, while Lohengrin vows that his accusers shall be brought to account.

Led by the King, the nobles crowd around Lohengrin and assure him of their support. Telramund swiftly approaches Elsa and treacherously begs her to betray Lohengrin into his hands. One drop of blood, he tells her, will rob the knight of his protecting magic and also render him powerless to leave her. Elsa distractedly tries to drive Telramund away. Seeing the two in conversation, Lohengrin rushes between them and in a terrible voice commands Telramund to go.

Elsa, stricken with shame at her doubting, sinks to the ground at Lohengrin's feet. Gently he raises her, asking if she wishes to put to him the fateful question. In a moving refrain she answers that love has conquered every doubt ("Mein Retter, der mir Heil gebracht"). Lohengrin thereupon escorts her to the King. As the assemblage hails the bridal pair in the brilliant climax of the chorus, the King leads them to the top of the cathedral steps. Elsa and Lohengrin embrace. In that moment Elsa sees Ortrud standing below with her arm upraised in a gesture of venomous triumph. Controlling herself with a supreme effort, Elsa quickly turns and enters the church with Lohengrin and the King. The curtain falls.

ACT THREE

A richly appointed bridal chamber. At one side is an open casement window. The brilliant prelude, familiar as a concert number, sets the mood for the wedding festivities which open the act. At the conclusion of the prelude doors at the rear open and the bridal procession enters, led by pages carrying lighted tapers. The women escort Elsa, while the men accompany King Henry and Lohengrin. The entire assemblage sings the world-famous *Wedding Chorus* ("Treulich geführt").

Elsa and Lohengrin embrace. Pages remove their robes of state, and then the King approaches and gives the pair his blessing. The men and women, with the King, now retire to the strains of the *Wedding Chorus*. Their voices fade away in the distance as the pages close the doors.

Lohengrin leads Elsa to the couch and tenderly begins the magnificent love duet, "Das süsse Lied verhallt." In passionate phrases soaring over a sensuous orchestral accompaniment the lovers give voice to their rapture. But when Lohengrin ecstatically sings Elsa's name and she responds there is a subtle change of mood. Elsa murmurs that her name sounds sweet on his lips ("Wie süss mein Name deinem Mund entgleitet"), but the harmonies darken when she entreats Lohengrin to allow her to speak his name.

Lohengrin evades her request with fervent protestations of love, singing that all he asks in return for his measureless devotion is her abiding faith in him. But Elsa's mood grows more feverish as she insists that he reveal his secret. When he tells her that he came from realms of light to save her and win her love, she cries despairingly that by those very words she knows her love is doomed. Now, she laments, each day will bring the tormenting fear that he will leave her to return to the enchanted country from which he came. In alarm she imagines she sees the swan returning on its fateful errand. Lohengrin distractedly begs her to cease her questioning, as once again we hear the warning theme associated with the words "Nie sollst du mich befragen." Mad with doubt and fear, Elsa demands to know his name, his destiny, and his race ("Den Name sag' mir an! Woher die Fahrt? Wie deine Art?").

At that moment Telramund and his four henchmen burst into the room with drawn swords. Screaming in terror, Elsa seizes Lohengrin's sheathed sword, which he had placed beside the couch. As she holds the scabbard, Lohengrin draws the sword, whirls about, and kills the onrushing Telramund with one terrible blow. Thereupon the four nobles drop their weapons and kneel at Lohengrin's feet. Elsa faints in his arms.

There is a long, tense pause. Then Lohengrin sadly murmurs that all happiness has ended ("Weh! Nun ist all unser Glück dahin!"). He lifts Elsa to the couch. She revives momentarily and gasps a prayer. Lohengrin then commands the noblemen to bear Telramund's body before the King. Summoning two ladies in waiting, he bids them array Elsa in her bridal finery and escort her to the throne. He slowly leaves the chamber as the stricken Elsa is cared for by her attendants. The dawn grows brighter, and pages extinguish the tapers.

Here the curtain is lowered for a moment. Trumpet calls are heard in the distance. The scene changes to disclose the meadow on the banks of the Scheldt, as in the opening of the opera. In magnificent pageantry King Henry and the nobles arrive with their retinues. They arrange themselves in formal array as the King again takes his place on the throne under the great oak. In a heroic refrain ("Wie fühl' ich stolz mein Herz entbrannt") he bids his followers prepare to march against the foe, then inquires about the hero who is to lead them.

At that point the four nobles enter, carrying Telramund's body on a bier, which is placed before the throne. The King and assemblage exclaim in horror and surprise. Elsa, bowed in sorrow, now appears with her retinue, followed shortly by Lohengrin. Clad in battle armor, he comes forward with solemn dignity as King Henry and the warriors hail him as the hero of Brabant.

Then as the men listen incredulously the knight declares that he cannot lead them into battle. He comes not as warrior but as accuser, he says, and with those words throws back the covering from Telramund's body. Explaining the circumstances of the attack, Lohengrin demands judgment on the slaying of Telramund. In a vigorous chorus the King and the warriors proclaim the justice of his deed.

But there is yet another charge, Lohengrin continues. Dramatically he tells the tense throng that Elsa, through vile treachery, has been betrayed into breaking her promise by asking his name and race. Now, he announces, the destined moment has come to reveal his secret. He does so in the famous aria, "Im fernem Land."

As the exalted Grail theme sweeps through the orchestra he sings of the shining temple on the mountain of Monsalvat, where reposes a sacred cup—the Holy Grail. Its divine power is renewed each year by the visitation of a dove from heaven. The Grail is in the keeping of a company of consecrated knights. It is the duty of these sinless warriors to go forth in the defense of those who are beset by earthly evil. But once the name of the knight is known, he must depart forever from those whom he has redeemed. It was as a knight of the Grail that he himself was sent here, Lohengrin continues. In the ringing climax of his song he proclaims that he is the son of Parsifal, chief among the knights of the Grail, and Lohengrin is his name.

The people murmur in amazement and wonder over his enthralling story. Elsa gives a cry of remorse and approaches Lohengrin with faltering steps. He takes her in his arms as he sings a poignant phrase of sorrow and reproach ("O Elsa! Was hast du mir angethan?"). He mourns the tragic destiny that has destroyed their happiness, then bids her farewell.

Elsa implores him not to leave her. The people add their voices in a dramatic accompaniment to the soaring phrases of her entreaty. But Lohengrin replies that his absence already has provoked the wrath of the Grail and that only in parting can the sin of Elsa's betrayal be expiated. In answer to the plea of the warriors that he remain to lead them against their enemy, Lohengrin turns to King Henry and assures him of a glorious victory.

Tremendous excitement stirs the throng as the swan suddenly appears in the distance. As it reaches the shore Lohengrin greets it in sorrowing tones ("Mein lieber Schwan"). Had but the one year of its bondage elapsed, he sings, the power of the Grail would have restored the swan to human shape. In agony and despair he turns to Elsa. If she had kept faith with him for this one year of trial, he says, so that he could have remained with her, the Grail's might would have sent her brother back to his rightful place at her side.

He then hands Elsa his sword, along with his horn and his ring, bidding her give them to her brother when he at length returns. The sword will protect him, the horn will sound a call for help in time of danger, and the ring will remind him of the champion who came to the defense of his sister. Lohengrin passionately kisses Elsa in farewell, while she stands as if transfixed. In somber tones the people lament his going.

Suddenly Ortrud rushes forward. Tauntingly she bids Lohengrin to return to his home ("Fahr' heim, du stolzer Held"). Now she can tell his unhappy bride the truth. The swan that draws the boat is none other than the transformed heir of Brabant. The chain around its neck is the instrument of sorcery with which she robbed the boy of his human shape.

In fierce exultation she turns on Elsa, saying that but for her betrayal in revealing his name Lohengrin would have freed her brother from the spell at the end of a year. Now the evil enchantment is still in force. The boy must remain a swan—and this very swan will take Elsa's champion away forever. At these words the people cry out violently against Ortrud.

Lohengrin kneels in prayer. Then, as the Grail theme rises triumphantly in the orchestra, the dove of the Grail circles over the boat. The knight swiftly unfastens the chain from the swan's neck, whereupon the swan sinks beneath the surface of the water. At the spot where it disappeared there rises a handsome boy in glittering princely raiment. Leading him forward, Lohengrin asks all to look upon the Duke of Brabant ("Seht da den Herzog von Brabant").

Ortrud screams in terror and falls to the ground. Lohengrin leaps into the boat, and the dove, taking the golden chain in its beak, draws the craft away from the shore. Gottfried slowly approaches Elsa, while the assemblage makes obeisance. As she takes him in her arms she turns her gaze toward the river, calling to her husband ("Mein Gatte! Mein Gatte!"). A bend in the stream momentarily hides Lohengrin. As he reappears, standing in the boat and bowed over his shield, a great cry of sorrow bursts from the throng. The curtain falls.

Louise

by GUSTAVE CHARPENTIER

[1860–1956]

Libretto by the Composer

CHARACTERS

Julien, a poet...*Tenor*
Louise, a seamstress...................................*Soprano*
The Mother ....*Mezzo-soprano*
The Father ....*Bass*
Ragpicker ....*Soprano*
Coal gatherer ....*Contralto*
Noctambulist ....*Tenor*
Junkman ....*Bass*
Paper girl ....*Soprano*
Milk woman ....*Soprano*
Ragman ....*Baritone*
First policeman ....*Tenor*
Second policeman ....*Tenor*
Street sweeper ....*Contralto*
Street arab ....*Soprano*

Painter		*Tenor*
Sculptor		*Tenor*
Songwriter		*Tenor*
First philosopher	Bohemians	*Tenor*
Second philosopher		*Tenor*
Poet		*Tenor*
Student		*Tenor*

Chair mender ....*Contralto*
Artichoke vendor ....*Soprano*
Carrot vendor ....*Tenor*
Bird-food girl ....*Soprano*
Green-peas vendor ....*Tenor*

Blanche		*Soprano*
Marguerite		*Contralto*
Suzanne		*Soprano*
Gertrude	Seamstresses	*Contralto*
Irma		*Soprano*
Camille		*Soprano*
Elise		*Soprano*
Madeleine		*Mezzo-soprano*

Errand girl ....*Soprano*
Old-clothes man ....*Tenor*
Forewoman ....*Contralto*

The King of the Fools. . . . .*Tenor*
      Workers, people of Montmartre, vendors, grisettes, musicians,
                    dancers, children

Place: Paris
Time: About 1900
First performance: Opéra-Comique, Paris, February 2, 1900
Original language: French

GUSTAVE CHARPENTIER is well known for his active interest in the struggles and problems of the working people. *Louise* is remarkable for
its realistic portrayal of people in the humbler walks of life, set
against the background of social conditions prevailing in Paris at the turn of
the century. At the same time Charpentier so infused his score with the
spirit and charm of Paris that the city itself becomes the motivating force in
the opera.

ACT ONE

A rather poorly furnished room of a worker's tenement home in Paris. At
one side, part of the kitchen may be seen. Opposite, a door with a glazed
pane opens into another room. A large window opens onto a balcony, across
from which there is the balcony of an artist's studio. Part of the Paris sky-
line is visible. It is an evening in April. There is a brief introduction, based
mainly on the theme associated with Julien. Standing on his balcony, the
poet sings an ardent refrain ("O coeur ami! O coeur promis!"), which
brings Louise hurrying to her window. A melodious duet follows as she responds to Julien's declarations of love. He reminds her that she promised to
elope with him if her father continued to object to her seeing him, but
Louise denies any such rash intention. Teasingly she inquires how his great
passion for her came into being.

In the air, "Depuis longtemps j'habitais cette chambre," Julien describes
how he lived for a long time in his lonely studio, unaware of his charming
neighbor. When he finally saw her, he continues, he promptly stopped writing verses to fair charmers who existed only in his imagination. Louise, in
turn, recalls the occasions on which she first met Julien. And each time, the
poet interjects, they were interrupted by her old witch of a mother. At this
point the mother steals unnoticed into the room and listens to the impassioned conversation of the lovers. At first she laughs cynically at their ardent protestations, then angrily drags Louise away from the window,
pushes her into the kitchen, and slams the door.

Hurrying back to the window, the mother looks out from behind the
draperies. Julien, thinking she is Louise, begs for one more word of love,
whereupon the mother shouts at him to be quiet. The poet disappears, and
the mother, after glowering for a moment, goes into the next room. Louise,
who has been watching from the partially opened kitchen door, seizes this

opportunity to tiptoe over to the window. Julien shows himself momentarily and holds up a letter, pantomiming that he will send it to her parents. Then he withdraws, singing a phrase of mocking gaiety. Louise hurries back to the kitchen just in time to escape her mother, who re-enters from the other room, bangs the window shut, and then also goes into the kitchen.

There she vents her ill temper on Louise, first giving a sardonic imitation of Julien's love-making, then furiously upbraiding her daughter for wasting her time with a worthless idler. Louise hotly defends him, warning her mother that her spiteful interference will only drive her more quickly into Julien's arms. The mother rages that Louise's father will hear of this. As the quarrel reaches its climax, the sound of footsteps is heard on the stairs. The two women abruptly stop talking and busy themselves with preparing supper. The father enters, holding a letter in his hand. Without any word of greeting, he seats himself at the table, opens the letter, and begins reading. Louise, setting the table, watches him anxiously. Finally he looks up, smiles, and holds out his arms to his daughter, who embraces him affectionately.

Supper is placed on the table and the three begin their meal. The mother complains over the fact that her husband works year after year without any respite. Glaring out of the window toward Julien's studio, she fumes that there are certain lazy good-for-nothings who spend their time singing while honest people toil to make a living. Not everyone can choose his lot in life, the father observes good-naturedly, adding that a good home, health, and a loving family can provide all the happiness anyone may ask. Getting up from the table, he kisses Louise, then catches his wife around the waist and dances about with her. Chuckling contentedly, he sits down by the fire and lights his pipe. The women clear the table and attend to the kitchen duties.

Louise picks up Julien's letter from the table, presses it to her lips, and hesitantly gives it to her father. With a knowing glance at Louise, he rereads it and then casually remarks to his wife that Louise's young man has again asked for her hand. With that the mother breaks out anew in her denunciations of Julien. When Louise flares up in anger, her mother silences her with a vicious slap. The father sternly rebukes his wife for her bad temper, while Louise, sobbing bitterly, sinks into a chair. In a soothing refrain ("O mon enfant"), the father tries to console Louise, assuring her that he and her mother are acting in her best interests in preventing her from rushing headlong into marriage.

But the interminable argument continues, Louise insisting that her heart has told her that Julien is worthy, her father declaring that she is too inexperienced to trust her emotions. The mother further arouses her husband's suspicions by maliciously hinting that Louise and Julien have been meeting secretly. With deep earnestness the father asks Louise to promise that she will abide by her father's wishes if he should refuse Julien. Her disobedience would break his heart, he adds. Touched by his appeal, Louise assures her father that she loves and respects him. Dismissing the matter as though everything had been settled, the father hands Louise the paper and asks her to read the news to him. Louise, fighting back her tears, haltingly begins reading about the brilliant spring season in Paris. The curtain slowly falls.

ACT TWO

[*Scene One*]   A street in Montmartre. At one side is a shed. Opposite is the seamstress's establishment where Louise works. Toward the rear, flights of steps lead downward to other streets and also upward toward the hill of Montmartre. The prelude is a striking musical description of Paris slowly stirring into life at dawn. As the curtain rises a milk woman is trundling milk cans about in her booth under the shed, while near by a young girl is folding morning newspapers. A ragpicker, also a young girl, is pulling rags out of an overturned rubbish basket. A coal gatherer, likewise a young girl, and a junkman are poking about in the refuse.

Their comments—by turns cynical, wistful, and philosophical—are sung above a smoothly flowing accompaniment. A figure in a long black cloak enters and pauses to gaze at the group with a certain condescension. He is the Noctambulist—a reveler on his way home after a round of nocturnal festivity. With mocking gallantry he asks the paper girl for a kiss, but she wearily fends him off. When the milk woman asks who he is, he answers suavely that he is the Pleasure of Paris ("Je suis le Plaisir de Paris") and then throws back his cloak to reveal his resplendent costume.[1] He sings that his mission is to seek out all those who have forgotten what joy is and to grant them the privilege of abandoning themselves again to their desires. With an impudent flourish he goes on his way, rudely pushing aside an old ragman who happens to wander across his path. The old man stumbles and falls heavily. Helped to his feet by the junkman, he looks after the Noctambulist and mutters a curse. He well remembers that scoundrel, the ragman bursts out, for he is the very man who ran away with his daughter. Overcome by anger and grief, he weeps bitterly. The junkman tries to console him, saying that young people, after all, cannot be blamed for preferring the pleasures of Paris to this wretched existence.

Two policemen pass by on their rounds. A street sweeper joins the group and regales her listeners with the story of how she once was the toast of Paris. This is greeted with considerable skepticism by a street arab who has sidled up. He remarks dryly that he has lived in Paris all his life and does not remember Mademoiselle in the days of her glory. After more desultory talk these pathetic outcasts go on their separate ways and vanish into the shadows.

Julien enters with a group of Bohemians, to whom he points out Louise's shop. They advance with elaborate gestures of caution. Louise's mother always brings her to the door, the poet explains. When she has gone, he will talk to Louise and find out if her parents still refuse to give her permission to marry him. If that is the case, he declares, he will simply carry her off. The Bohemians vociferously approve, and then one of them suggests that they crown Louise as their Muse. This idea also is favorably received by all except the two philosophers, who mournfully observe that the Muses have

---

[1] In the original score this costume is described as being symbolic of spring. In present-day productions the Noctambulist is generally in evening clothes.

long since died. The song writer strikes up a serenade ("Enfants de la bohème"), which brings the neighbors to the windows, and soon coins begin to clink on the pavement.

Suddenly Julien exclaims that it is time for Louise to appear and tells his companions to be off. They drift away, their serenade fading in the distance. As Julien frets over whether or not Louise will join him in his daring plan, the vendors appear on the scene. Their voices are woven into a colorful chorus as they cry their wares. Entranced by the medley of sounds, Julien cries that this is the voice of Paris itself—perhaps a triumphant salute to the success of his romance. He withdraws to the shed as the seamstresses appear and go into the shop, chattering among themselves.

Louise and her mother enter, and Julien manages to catch Louise's eye with a furtive signal. The mother crossly bids her good-by at the door of the shop and then goes on her way, looking around suspiciously. As soon as she is out of sight, Julien intercepts Louise and draws her toward the shed. A dramatic colloquy follows. Frightened and confused, Louise struggles to free herself, protesting that her parents have refused to permit her to marry and that she dare not disobey them. Julien begs her to defy their authority and assert her right to freedom and love. Clasping her in his arms, he sings an eloquent refrain entreating her to come with him to Montmartre, the paradise of true lovers ("Ah! Louise, si tu m'aimes"). His intense ardor brings her almost to the point of yielding, but she finally frees herself from his embrace. Promising Julien that someday she will marry him, she kisses him tenderly and then runs into the shop. Julien gazes despondently after her. The old-clothes man and the green-peas vendor pass by, plaintively crying their wares. The curtain falls.

[Scene Two]   The workshop of the seamstresses. The curtain rises after a lively prelude. In a sprightly chorus the girls gossip and chatter about their work, while the forewoman walks among the sewing tables, pausing now and then to give instructions. Louise takes no part in the conversation and does not look up from her work. The girls look at her curiously and speculate among themselves as to the reason for her moody silence. One ventures that it is because she is unhappy at home, but another observes that she is probably in love, an opinion which arouses immediate interest. When several of the girls ask Louise if she is in love, she heatedly denies it. A tuneful ensemble follows as they turn to discussing real or imagined sweethearts and philosophize generally about love. One of them, Irma, sings a charming air in which she rhapsodizes over the alluring voice of Paris, a voice that speaks of love to all who will listen ("Une voix mystérieuse"). There is a touch of ironic symbolism here as some of the older women, who have been listening to the song, mockingly imitate the cry of the vendors of plaisirs, waferlike bonbons which were favorites with Parisians.

The sound of a polka being played by several instruments in the street outside sends the girls rushing to the windows. They exclaim in delight when they see Julien and his companions, who have returned to serenade Louise. She, however, remains at her worktable and tries to hide her embarrassment. Julien's song, which tells about the distant city of his happy dreams ("Dans la cité lointaine"), brings expressions of approval from the girls. Louise listens with increasing agitation as his serenade gradually takes the form of a personal appeal to her. The girls, becoming somewhat bored with the serious mood of the song, try to drown him out with a mocking chorus of disapproval. As he finishes on a phrase of angry reproach for their heartless taunts, the girls dance hilariously about to the rhythm of the music.

Louise, miserable and embarrassed, puts away her work and prepares to leave. Noticing her distraught manner, the girls offer their sympathy. She asks them to tell the forewoman that she is ill and then hurries out. A moment later one girl, still at the window, exclaims that Louise is meeting her young man. The girls shout with laughter as the curtain falls.

ACT THREE

Julien's cottage in Montmartre. At the rear is a hedge, and beyond it a sweeping view of Paris. The prelude, entitled "Dans la cité lointaine," sets the mood of tenderness and passion which dominates the scene that is to follow. It is dusk. Julien is seated on the porch of the cottage, to which he has finally succeeded in bringing Louise. Standing near, Louise gazes at him ardently and sings the famous aria "Depuis le jour," expressing the happiness of her new life with her lover. At the conclusion of her aria they embrace ecstatically. A long and dramatic duet follows. Louise contrasts the blissful freedom of life on Montmartre with the harassing discipline of her home. Though she recalls all the harsh words and bitter recriminations, she thinks of her parents with a certain tenderness and pity. Julien voices the poet's characteristic rebellion against conventional restraint and works himself up to an angry pitch as he denounces the restrictions that society puts upon human behavior.

Meanwhile darkness descends and the lights of the city begin to glow in the distance. The lovers walk to the edge of the garden and gaze in enchantment on the scene. Julien, pointing to the city, sings a fervent refrain ("De Paris tout en fête"), proclaiming that the magical city and his beloved Louise are one and the same in his heart. Overwhelmed by the beauty of the sight, Louise and Julien kneel and stretch forth their arms toward the city as if in a gesture of homage. As the duet rises to a passionate climax, a chorus symbolizing the voice of Paris is heard. Then the flood of music slowly subsides and the lovers walk into the house.

When all is quiet, Julien's Bohemian companions, carrying large bundles, steal into the garden and cautiously approach the house. They begin decorating the front of the cottage with gaily colored streamers and lanterns which they take from the bundles. Other merrymakers carrying torches appear, and soon the scene is filled with a shouting, singing throng, all assembled for a carnival in honor of Louise and Julien. The Noctambulist, dressed in the fantastic costume of the King of the Fools, is borne in on a thronelike chair carried on the shoulders of girls representing Daughters of Joy. In an elaborate ceremony Louise is crowned the Muse of Montmartre, after which the crowd abandons itself to merriment. All join in a magnificent festal chorus.

At the climax of the festivities Louise's mother appears at the back of the garden. The people shrink back in awe as she slowly comes forward and approaches the house. Louise, catching sight of her, runs terror-stricken into Julien's arms. The crowd melts away as if by magic. The mother quietly explains that she has come because Louise's father is very ill and that only the sight of his daughter can restore him to health. In a somber refrain ("Nous avions tout accepté") she goes on to say that though they both resigned themselves to Louise's going, the father was finally broken by his grief. Julien, watching her closely, realizes that she is deliberately working on Louise's sympathies. As though to make the mother's entreaty more poignant, the ragman, muttering vacantly about his lost daughter, wanders through the garden. Deeply moved, Julien allows Louise to go with her mother. Tenderly the lovers bid each other farewell. The curtain falls.

ACT FOUR

The tenement room, as in the first act. Louise is sewing by the open window. The father is seated at the table and the mother is busy in the kitchen. It is about nine o'clock in the evening. The mother brings her husband a cup of tea and urges him to sit by the window where he can enjoy the fresh air. The scene outside is changed now, for the buildings opposite, including Julien's studio, have been torn down. The father is moodily indifferent to his wife's efforts to cheer him. When she suggests, however, that perhaps he went back to his work too soon after his illness, he reveals a flash of his old spirit. These twenty days of idleness, he says, have not impaired his strength, and in that time he has learned to live with his sorrow.

His cheerful mood, however, quickly gives way to despair. In a bitter monologue ("Bête de somme que je suis") he cries out that the lot of the poor toiler is made even more cruel by the selfishness and ingratitude of his children. Louise, aware that his words are meant for her, rises and walks about nervously. One rears a child with loving care, the father goes on harshly, only to have her taken away by some insolent stranger who is concerned with nothing but satisfying his evil desires. In rising anger the father curses the man who has robbed him of his one joy in life.

The mother interrupts his tirade by calling Louise to the kitchen, where she herself continues in the same vein of accusation and reproach. When the kitchen work is done she orders Louise to bid her father good night and go to bed. Louise sullenly obeys. In love and tenderness the father draws her down to him and cradles her in his arms as though she were a little child. He sings a touching lullaby, the Berceuse ("Reste, repose-toi"), pathetically attempting to console his daughter with happy memories of the past. As gently as possible Louise tries to make him understand that he can never win her back by denying her the love and freedom that are rightfully hers.

Louise reminds her parents that they promised to allow her to return to Julien, but they answer that they refuse to sanction anything but an honest marriage. As the dispute reaches a bitter climax the chorus representing the voice of Paris again is heard. Louise turns to the window with an eager cry, listening in growing excitement as the voices seem to draw nearer. In the distance the lights of the town glow brighter. In an ecstatic refrain ("O l'attirante promesse!") Louise hails the city as the symbol of her desires.

Completely under the spell of her emotions, Louise dances defiantly around the room as her parents desperately try to quiet her. She runs to the door, but her father intercepts her. Frantically she cries out for Julien. Beside himself with anger, the father flings open the door and orders her to go. With a scream of terror, Louise rushes out. The glowing horizon of the city is suddenly plunged into darkness.

Stumbling out to the stairs, the father calls after Louise, but there is no answer. Slowly he staggers back into the room, spent and exhausted by his rage. Turning to the window, he shakes his fist at the city and cries out in anguish and despair, "O Paris!" The curtain falls.

The Love for Three Oranges

by SERGEI PROKOFIEV

[1891–1953]

Libretto by the Composer

Based on Count Carlo Gozzi's eighteenth-century Italian comedy
LA FIABA DELL'AMORE DELLE TRE MELARANCIE

CHARACTERS

Tragedians	*Basses*
Comedians	*Tenors*
Lyricists	*Sopranos & Tenors*
Empty Heads	*Altos & Baritones*
Absurdities	*Tenors & Basses*
A Herald	*Bass*
The King of Clubs	*Bass*
The Doctors	*Tenors & Baritones*
Pantalon, the King's Advisor	*Baritone*
Trouffaldino, Court Jester	*Tenor*
Léandre, the Prime Minister	*Baritone*
Tchélio, a magician and protector of the King	*Bass*
Fata Morgana, a sorceress	*Soprano*
Devils	*Basses*
Princess Clarisse, the King's niece	*Contralto*
Sméraldine, servant of Fata Morgana	*Mezzo-soprano*
The Prince, son of the King of Clubs	*Tenor*
Farfarello, a devil	*Bass*
The Cook	*Bass*
Linette ⎤	*Contralto*
Nicolette ⎬ the Princesses hidden in the oranges	*Mezzo-soprano*
Ninette ⎦	*Soprano*
Master of Ceremonies	*Tenor*

Soldiers, courtiers, ladies, guards

Place: Mythical
Time: Legendary
First performance: Chicago, December 30, 1921
Original language: Russian

THE LOVE FOR THREE ORANGES, Sergei Prokofiev's first opera, was commissioned by Cleofonte Campanini, general director of the Chicago Opera Company, in 1919. In rehearsals, singers and musicians alike found the opera too difficult to master, and Campanini abandoned the work. When Mary Garden became head of the company in 1921, she de-

cided to produce the opera. It was sung in French, with the composer con-
ducting. But the complicated libretto, with its bitingly satiric overtones, and
the startling, modern harmonies of the score left the audience of that day
bewildered and unsympathetic. After one performance in Chicago and one
in New York, the opera disappeared from the repertoire.

Then, in 1949, it was revived with outstanding success by New York's
City Center Opera Company, which sang it in English. The libretto was
considerably revised to conform more closely to Carlo Gozzi's *commedia
dell' arte* drama. It was divided into two acts instead of four and the Prologue was spoken. In this form, it has remained one of the most popular
items in the repertoire of the City Center.

The Love for Three Oranges is a sardonic yet delightful satire on grand
opera. With unerring wit and skill, Prokofiev parodies the overblown heroics of conventional operatic plots and music. At times the work is completely nonsensical and wildly farcical, but it emerges as a dazzling musical
fairy tale.

The opera is described here as it was presented in its original performance in Chicago in 1921.

PROLOGUE

In the Prologue, the composer satirizes the theatrical preferences of five
segments of the public, which he characterizes as Tragedians, Comedians,
Lyricists, Empty Heads, and Absurdities. They appear in turn to argue the
respective merits of their own likes and dislikes and finally end up in a
noisy quarrel. The action takes place in front of the curtain.

There is no overture. After an eight-bar introduction, the Tragedians,
waving umbrellas, rush onstage from one wing and loudly demand great
tragedies. Next, the Comedians caper in from the other wing. To the snap-
ping of riding whips, they call for joyous laughter. The Tragedians turn on
the Comedians, attack them with their umbrellas and drive them back. Now
come the Lyricists, waving green branches. Paying no attention to the battle between the Tragedians and the Comedians, the Lyricists take up a position at the center of the stage and sing that they want nothing but ecstasy
and romance.

But in the next moment the Empty Heads rush in and begin to attack the
Lyricists, singing that they want only farces and amusing jokes. They drive
back the Lyricists and then belabor the Tragedians. All four groups, shouting their battle cries in the form of a vigorous chorale, engage in a wild
melee. Into the thick of it march the Absurdities, armed with enormous
shovels. Pushing the others into the wings, the Absurdities call for silence,
then urge all to watch the play that is about to begin—an incomparable
spectacle, worthy of the finest traditions of the theatre. In a melodious
phrase, they proclaim the title of the play: "L'Amour pour trois Oranges."

By this time the Absurdities have chased everyone off the stage. They
themselves climb up into one of the two towers on either side of the pros-
cenium, come out on the battlements, and again call for silence. Then, to a
fanfare of trombones, the Herald steps through the curtain at center stage.

In an imposing phrase ("Pauvre fils!"), he announces that the King of Clubs is in great sorrow. His son and heir is suffering from a grievous illness. The trombone fanfare sounds again and the Herald withdraws. The Absurdities excitedly comment that the play is about to begin. The curtain slowly rises.

ACT ONE

[*Scene One*]   The palace of the King of Clubs. The King, with his confidential advisor, Pantalon, at his elbow, is questioning a group of doctors about the condition of his son. What exactly, the King asks, is wrong with him?

In an amusing patter chorus ("Des douleurs au foie"), the doctors reel off the list of the Prince's ailments: liver pains, lumbago, asthma, headaches, indigestion, weak arteries, softening of the head, a painful cough, poor eyesight, anemia, biliousness, and dizziness. As the King asks what can be done, the doctors continue their dolorous litany. In addition to all this, they report, the Prince has acute melancholia, and the case must be diagnosed as incurable hypochondria.

In despair the King covers his ears. With a wave of his hand he dismisses the doctors, who leave in a funereal procession, chanting, "Incurable!"

Staring at each other in terror, the King and Pantalon repeat the doctors' diagnosis. As the King dolefully enumerates the Prince's afflictions, Pantalon expresses a more hopeful view of the situation. Their conversation continues in duet form. After all, says Pantalon, these doctors know nothing whatever. He gives a mocking imitation of their solemn pronouncements. But the King, inconsolable, worries about who is to inherit his kingdom. Will it be his cruel niece, Clarisse, he wonders. With that he bursts into tears. Pantalon dutifully buries his face in the King's robes and sobs loudly.

Meanwhile, the Absurdities, watching this scene from the tower, comment that the King will lose his royal prestige and dignity if he gives way in this fashion. Pantalon urges the monarch to calm himself. Quieting down a bit, the King murmurs, half to himself, that the only thing that can cure his son is laughter. Well, then, says Pantalon brightly, make him laugh.

The King shakes his head hopelessly, but Pantalon goes on in rising excitement. The Prince must be made to laugh, he insists. But then, he asks, how can the young man possibly be gay when everybody else in the court walks about plunged in gloom? The King's only answer is the moody observation that the Prince never will laugh. At this point an idea pops into Pantalon's head. Now, he says, he knows what is needed: parties, gay festivals—and people who know how to make the Prince laugh. Suddenly Pantalon remembers the name he has been trying to think of all along: Trouffaldino! He literally shouts the name in a ringing phrase.

With the mention of his name, Trouffaldino comes bounding in and eagerly asks if he can be of service. In his best official manner Pantalon tells the Jester he can at this moment be of great service to the King. Trouffaldino thereupon prostrates himself before the sovereign.

Looking down at him thoughtfully, the King says he wishes to arrange

some sort of entertainment that will make the Prince laugh. Scarcely waiting for the King to finish, Trouffaldino assures him this will be done at once
and then he rushes away. The King shows annoyance at Trouffaldino's lack
of manners, while Pantalon, aside, expresses his admiration for the Jester.

Then the King summons his servants and tells them he wishes to see
Léandre, the Prime Minister. At that, Pantalon angrily mutters that he de-
tests Léandre because he is plotting the Prince's death. The Prime Minister
enters and bows before the King, who forthwith orders him to prepare all
kinds of feasts, entertainments, and spectacles. Delighted with the turn of
events, the Absurdities repeat the King's words. Léandre craftily remarks
that all the excitement undoubtedly will tire the Prince unnecessarily. The
King retorts that it is at least worth trying, and repeats his order, which the
Absurdities echo enthusiastically. As the King leaves, the Prime Minister
warns that this plan will only make the Prince's condition worse. Following
the King, Pantalon pauses to snarl, "Traitor!" at Léandre. "Clown," the
Prime Minister sneers.

[*Scene Two*]   The music continues without a break as the stage darkens
and a curtain covered with cabalistic signs is lowered. The entire scene is
played before it in almost total darkness. To a surge of dissonant triplets,
the magician Tchélio suddenly appears. The Absurdities cry out in alarm.
There is a clap of thunder and a flash of lightning, and the form of the
witch Fata Morgana[1] materializes to the accompaniment of eerily wailing
strings. In growing excitement the Absurdities call her name. Now a crowd
of yelling devils throngs the stage. Chanting a weird unison chorus on the
word "Hi!", they bring in a table which they place between the magician
and the witch. Next they bring in oversized playing cards and enormous lu-
minous pictures of the Kings of Clubs and Spades, which glow in the dark.

The devils place the Clubs behind Tchélio and the Spades behind Fata
Morgana. Tchélio deals and the game begins, the two playing their cards to
the beat of the music as the Absurdities exclaim excitedly. Forming a circle,
the devils whirl about the players in a satanic dance. Tchélio loses and cries
out in rage, while Fata Morgana gloats in triumph. Kneeling, the devils do
her homage. The Absurdities, bemoaning the King's defeat, comment that
luck is with Léandre. Now the witch deals and the devils resume their
dance, chanting their demonic chorus. Again Tchélio loses, roaring in fury
as Fata Morgana screams her triumph. The picture of the King of Clubs
grows dimmer, while that of Spades gets brighter. The devils again kneel;
the Absurdities note that Léandre has won another time.

Tchélio deals once more for the final play. Fata Morgana raises her last
card high in the air, then throws it on the table. She bursts into sardonic
laughter as Tchélio bellows curses. Their voices blend with those of the
devils, who servilely repeat the name of Fata Morgana. They then give the
picture of the Spades to the witch and that of the Clubs to the magician.
Fata Morgana calls Léandre's name, while Tchélio growls, "Die!" Holding

---

[1] A fairy celebrated in medieval tales of chivalry. She appears in the Arthurian
legends as Morgan le Fay, a powerful and treacherous necromancer.

the pictures, both vanish, and then the devils carry the card table away. The cabalistic curtain rises as the music continues without pause.

[*Scene Three*] The same as at the end of *Scene One*, with Léandre standing in the same position. To the accompaniment of a rather foreboding figure in the orchestra, he broods that all his plans are meeting with nothing but obstacles. His dark thoughts are interrupted by the entrance of Clarisse, the King's niece, an arrogant, spoiled, scheming young woman.

In a dramatic refrain ("Léandre, sachez ceci"), she reminds the Prime Minister that she is heiress to the King's throne, should the Prince die. She promises Léandre she will marry him if that happens. Léandre's only answer is a low bow.

In what is more or less a repetition of her refrain, Clarisse angrily tells Léandre he is far too calm about this matter. The Prince may well outlive them both in spite of his hypochondria. If Léandre does not take action under the circumstances, Clarisse goes on, he is totally unworthy of her hand and the throne.

Apparently unmoved, the Prime Minister advises her not to get unduly excited—he will gain his objective. As Clarisse utters an exclamation of disgust, Léandre goes to her and whispers in her ear with an exaggerated air of wickedness. In pianissimo tones he confides that he intends to feed the Prince a mixture of "super-tragic" prose, which he will butter the Prince's bread with and also chop up in his soup. Then, concludes Léandre in a boastful phrase, the Prince surely will die of hypochondria.

At this moment the Tragedians come stampeding on the stage. As they did at the beginning of the opera, they blatantly shout for tragedy, murder, and suffering. The Absurdities hastily climb down from their tower and, brandishing their shovels, chase the Tragedians away. The uproar dies down momentarily. Clarisse, leaning close to Léandre, sings insinuatingly that she is not at all impressed by his scheme and that the logical thing to do is give the Prince either opium or a bullet.

As she is speaking, Trouffaldino dances across the back of the stage followed by a motley procession, to the shrill accompaniment of flutes and piccolos. Clarisse asks who the clown is, and the Prime Minister identifies him as one who creates laughter. He has come, Léandre goes on, because the King has ordered him to make the Prince laugh during the great festival tomorrow. This clown, Léandre adds contemptuously, will stand on his head to make the Prince laugh.

In a brief refrain, the Absurdities sing that the Prince will be cured when he can laugh, and everybody will laugh when he is cured. Clarisse and Léandre repeat this thought in a hushed, menacing phrase. In sudden irritation, Clarisse turns on Léandre and berates him for his lack of action.

At that moment a vase falls with a crash from a nearby table. Clarisse and Léandre recoil in terror, then the Prime Minister recovers himself and kicks the table aside. There, crouching on the floor, is Sméraldine, the dusky servant of Fata Morgana. In a terrible rage, Léandre fumes that he will have her hanged for eavesdropping on state secrets.

Ignoring his threats, Sméraldine glides close to him and asks him to listen to what she has to say ("Un instant, Léandre"). Then in warning tones she sings that behind the Prince stands Trouffaldino, behind Trouffaldino stands the all-powerful Tchélio. As a *mysterioso* passage sounds in the orchestra, the magician appears momentarily in a shaft of ghostly light. Léandre stares aghast, but Clarisse only sneers at the apparition.

Remember, she sings ("Eh bien voyez"), tomorrow the festival will indeed begin, and perhaps the Prince will laugh. Well, then, she goes on, it must be either opium or a bullet—and death for this slave Sméraldine. Kneeling before Clarisse and Léandre, Sméraldine implores them to believe that Fata Morgana is really their ally. She will be at the festival and will cast a spell on the Prince so that he will not be able to laugh. Clarisse and the Prime Minister are dumfounded. Sméraldine assures them she is speaking for the witch. Then the music rises to a powerful climax as, with arms outstretched, the three savagely invoke Fata Morgana in trumpetlike unison phrases. The curtain falls.

ACT TWO

[*Scene One*] The Prince's room in the palace. Bundled up in an outlandish array of robes, mufflers, and blankets, the Prince sits slumped in an armchair. On a table beside him is a collection of medicine bottles, glasses, jars, and bowls. Trouffaldino is just finishing what presumably is a comic dance. Turning to the Prince, the Jester asks anxiously, "Is it funny?"

In answer, the Prince shakes his head and groans. Taken aback, poor Trouffaldino wonders if it is possible that he no longer is funny. Twisting about restlessly, the Prince complains that his sight is blurred, he has pains in his head, in his kidneys, in his liver. As he wails in misery, Trouffaldino accompanies him in a plaint of his own ("Qu'inventerais-je encore"): he dances, and the Prince is bored; he jests, and the Prince weeps. Trouffaldino is truly at the end of his tether.

Then the Prince has a coughing spell (comically depicted in a vocal passage). Trouffaldino, holding a basin, observes in alarm that the Prince is coughing up malodorous verses. The Absurdities, looking on, comment that this is all the fault of that scoundrel Léandre, who has obviously made good his threat to feed the Prince some vile, super-tragic poetry. Trouffaldino tells the Prince that a great festival is to be held today for the sole purpose of making him laugh. He entreats the young man to get dressed and go to the celebration without delay. Holding his head, the Prince moans that this is sheer insanity. To add to his discomfort, the Comedians crowd on stage, bleating for comedy and loud laughter. The Absurdities, crying that Trouffaldino alone can cure the Prince of his malady, rout the Comedians with their trusty shovels.

Now from the distance comes the music of a lively march. The Prince petulantly asks for some of his medicine. Ignoring his request, Trouffaldino snatches up a cape and tells the Prince to put it on. In a childish rage, the Prince instead demands fifteen drops of a certain medicine. Exasperated, Trouffaldino hurls the entire collection of medicine bottles out of the window and shouts: "Here is where your drops will go!" As the Prince screams with rage, Trouffaldino throws the cape around him, hoists the struggling hypochondriac on his shoulder and carries him out of the room. The music continues to a stormy climax as the curtain falls.

[*Scene Two*] There is virtually no pause between this scene and the preceding one. The curtain rises on the courtyard of the royal palace. On the veranda are the King, Clarisse, and the Prince, who is swathed in cape and furs. At a little distance are Léandre, Pantalon, and ladies and gentlemen of the court. Trouffaldino, standing in the middle of the courtyard, is acting as master of ceremonies of the festival, directing the proceedings with melodramatic gestures.

To the accompaniment of a fanfare, the Jester announces "Divertisement Number One." A throng of figures with huge grotesque heads appears. They divide into two groups and stage a mock battle which one side finally wins. While the ladies and courtiers hail the performance in a choral phrase, Trouffaldino anxiously asks the King if he saw the Prince laugh. The King sadly shakes his head, as the Prince whines that the noise gives him a headache and the air outdoors is bad for his heart.

Trouffaldino promptly chases the masked figures away and prepares the stage for the next spectacle. Suddenly Fata Morgana appears, disguised as an old woman. Léandre, startled by the apparition, goes up to her and asks her who she is. Identifying herself, the witch says that as long as she is near the Prince cannot laugh. With that she quickly leaves. Staring after her, Léandre ironically salutes her as "the Queen of Hypochondria."

With a flourish, Trouffaldino steps forward. Attendants push two huge fountains toward the center of the court. At Trouffaldino's command, one spouts oil and the other wine. The courtiers applaud approvingly. Then Trouffaldino orders the guards to admit the gluttons and drunkards. The palace gates swing open and a yelling mob, clutching pails, basins, and pots, rushes toward the fountains, trampling each other in their greedy haste. Trouffaldino laughs uproariously at the sight, then checks himself as he remembers the Prince. He looks. The young man still has not laughed. On the contrary, he is crying because he wants to lie down on a nice soft bed.

With a gesture of resignation, the Jester groans that luck is against him. He impetuously orders the guards to chase the gluttons and drunkards away. More and more provoked, Trouffaldino growls about the Prince wanting—of all things—a soft bed.

Just then Fata Morgana comes stumbling on the scene. Finding a convenient target for his ill temper, Trouffaldino turns on her with insulting rudeness. The two promptly clash in a brief but violent quarrel, expressed in duet form. At its climax, the Jester tries to throw Fata Morgana out of the palace, giving her a shove which sends her head over heels.

Staring at her, the Prince suddenly begins chuckling. His laugh, which takes the form of a definite vocal figure, grows louder and louder until at last he is holding his sides and guffawing uncontrollably. In growing wonder the entire court watches the Prince, murmuring that he is laughing at last. Then everyone on stage except Clarisse and Léandre bursts into joyous laughter, which is interpreted in a frenetic choral phrase. With the tension broken, the people begin dancing jerkily about like puppets on a string.

Suddenly the dancers stop and look at Fata Morgana, who is slowly rising to her feet. An ominous shadow seems to envelop the court. With a ferocious cry the witch turns on the Prince, bidding him listen to her curse ("Monstre! Ecoute!"). From all sides comes the swarm of yelling devils. Pointing at the Prince, Fata Morgana intones that he is doomed to love Three Oranges ("Il faut que tu subisses"). He will have no rest day or night until he finds them. Ending her malediction in a thunderous phrase, Fata Morgana vanishes with the devils.

The Absurdities and the people of the court murmur in horror over this catastrophe. As though bewitched, the Prince flings himself about the stage crying, "The Three Oranges!" Trouffaldino and Pantalon try to calm him. Struggling fiercely with them, the Prince babbles that Greonte the witch has the Three Oranges and that he is going to see her at once. Shouting for his helmet and sword, he declares he will take Trouffaldino with him.

The King steps forward and tries to reason with the Prince, but the young man only gets more excited, repeating that Greonte has the Three Oranges and that he must rescue them. Trouffaldino and Pantalon vainly entreat the Prince to be sensible. The four voices spasmodically blend in an ensemble.

When the King changes his tactics and tries to command the Prince to listen, the latter flails his arms about threateningly. The King hastily draws back out of reach, wailing that here is a son who dares raise his hand against his father. Meanwhile the Prince sings in soaring, defiant phrases that the kingdom can go to the devil—he adores only his Oranges.

His father roars that this intolerable situation is all the fault of the vulgar farces just presented at court, whereupon the Empty Heads come skipping in and repeat their vapid clamor for fun and thoughtless laughter. Furiously the King tries to drive them away, but they only mock him with their nonsense. Finally the Absurdities come to the King's aid and scatter the Empty Heads with their shovels.

The uproar quiets down momentarily. Having armed himself for his journey, the Prince now approaches his father. Simply and with dignity he bids him good-by ("Adieu, mon père"), saying that if he stays he may very likely become melancholy again. Shocked at the prospect, the King urges him to be off at once.

Trouffaldino, shaking with fright, stands by waiting for what will happen next. From out of nowhere comes Farfarello, a resplendent devil, waving a pair of bellows. He directs a blast at the backs of Trouffaldino and the Prince, who go flying off the stage. Farfarello follows.

In a mock-operatic climax, the King cries in stentorian tones that all is lost, then falls fainting. Pantalon, in equally melodramatic phrases, bewails the catastrophe that has befallen the country. He faints at the King's side, and the curtain falls.

ACT THREE

[*Scene One*] A desert. Tchélio is discovered drawing magic circles on the ground. He sings a dramatic invocation to the devil Farfarello, to force him to appear. As he concludes on a resounding phrase, Farfarello stands before him. The devil asks Tchélio point-blank if he is a real sorcerer or merely a popular entertainer.

Somewhat taken aback at this insolence, the magician replies that he is an entertainer, of course—but a true sorcerer for all that. Then, drawing himself to his full height, he rumbles majestically that he not only is terrible in his power, but ferocious. He warns Farfarello to be careful, then demands an answer. Very well, says Farfarello imperturbably, ask a question. Melodramatically, Tchélio asks where "they" (meaning Trouffaldino and the Prince) are.

Farfarello explains that at the moment they are lying down. He blew them toward Greonte, the devil goes on, but he himself had to get back to hell—and so the two, having no blast to push them on, simply fell down. Alarmed, Tchélio protests that they may get lost. That, Farfarello points out, is precisely why he keeps blowing them on their way. Making gestures of incantation, Tchélio orders Farfarello to stop all this nonsense at once. With an impudent laugh, Farfarello reminds the magician that he lost at cards, and so now his magic is useless. With that the devil vanishes, leaving Tchélio to grind his teeth in impotent rage.

In another moment Trouffaldino and the Prince come strolling gaily along. There is no more wind, says the Prince, and so the Oranges must be near by. The wind that blew them, Trouffaldino observes solemnly, must have been a cyclone—or at least a monsoon. The Prince ponders a moment, then shrugs off the problem.

Suddenly Tchélio blocks their way and asks where they are going. A colloquy follows in trio form. When the Prince and Trouffaldino answer that they are looking for the Three Oranges, the magician warns that the Oranges are captives of the witch Greonte and are guarded by a ferocious Cook. The Prince merely remarks that he finds this very funny, then tells Trouffaldino to hurry.

Pop-eyed with terror at the thought of their going on, Tchélio cries that this Cook has a great copper ladle and that he can kill with a single blow. Heedless of the warning, the Prince starts off, blithely singing that he loves the Three Oranges. Aware that he cannot deter the Prince, Tchélio turns to Trouffaldino and gives him a magic ribbon. This, he says, may distract the terrible Cook, and then the Prince can make off with the Oranges. If he gets them, Tchélio goes on, he must open them near a spring. Otherwise there will be great tragedy. Trouffaldino politely thanks the magician, but the Prince goes on singing in heedless ecstasy about his dear Oranges. Farfarello bounds onstage, wields his bellows and sends the Prince and Trouffaldino flying off. Making magic signs in their direction, Tchélio intones, "May fate protect them from the ladle" ("Que le sort les garde"). The curtain falls. The music continues into an orchestral interlude that, with its surge of ascending and descending chords, builds up a mood of suppressed excitement.

[*Scene Two*]   The curtain rises to show the courtyard of the castle of Greonte the witch. Farfarello, with blasts from his bellows, is still propelling the Prince and Trouffaldino, who dash full tilt into the courtyard. There they fall headlong, and Farfarello vanishes. Their agitated conversation follows in duet form. Shaking with terror, Trouffaldino looks up and spells out a big sign on the castle walls which reads: "Greonte." It is frightful, the two whimper, certain that death awaits them. Trouffaldino is all for leaving at once, but the Prince insists they must have the Three Oranges.

Recovering somewhat, Trouffaldino remembers that Tchélio said they were to look for the Oranges in the kitchen. The Prince points to a door, and the two sneak up to it with exaggerated caution. Trouffaldino, his teeth chattering, reminds the Prince about the Cook's deadly ladle. Oblivious to danger, the Prince sings ecstatically about his Three Oranges.

Suddenly the kitchen door is shaken violently and noisily from the inside. It is the Cook. Gasping in terror, the Prince and Trouffaldino scramble away and hide in different places not far from the kitchen. Then, as a glissando flashes in the orchestra, the door flies open and the figure of the Cook looms on the threshold. She is a great giant of a woman,[2] brandishing an enormous ladle. There is a majestic fanfare in the orchestra, underscored by a wonderfully descriptive phrase played by the tuba. In a thunderous voice the Cook demands to know who is there. When there is no answer, she begins looking around, discovers Trouffaldino and drags him quaking from his hiding place.

Falling to his knees, Trouffaldino abjectly begs for mercy. The Cook roars that she will make an end of him with her ladle, throw him into the stove, and toss him into the garbage—in that order. Trouffaldino cries that he got here by mistake, then rashly tries to escape. The Cook catches him by the scruff of the neck, growling that she will shake this clown's soul loose from his body for daring to violate the sanctity of her kitchen.

Just then the Cook notices the magic ribbon, which Trouffaldino is wearing around his neck. A trill high in the strings indicates that the ribbon's magic is taking effect—as Tchélio said it would. In a complete change of mood, the Cook admires the ribbon, sighing that she could well lose her head over such a treasure. She asks Trouffaldino who gave him the ribbon. Instantly regaining his cocky self-confidence, Trouffaldino tells the Cook that is a secret. Staring at the ribbon, the Cook asks Trouffaldino with ponderous coyness if he will make her a present of it.

During this conversation the Prince emerges from his hiding place and, in several silent leaps, reaches the kitchen. He goes inside, then reappears a moment later carrying three huge oranges about the size of a man's head. He leaps nimbly out of sight again behind the castle gate.

Sparring for time, Trouffaldino dangles the ribbon temptingly before the Cook's eyes, then hands it to her with a deep bow. He runs off. Completely bemused, the Cook sings in rapture about the beautiful ribbon. Her eyes riveted on it, she gropes for Trouffaldino with outstretched hand. Finding him gone, she murmurs caressingly, "You little devil." The curtain falls. Between this scene and the following one there is another lively orchestral interlude, almost a repetition of the one before *Scene Two*. There is no break in the music as the curtain rises again.

[2] This role is played by a man.

[*Scene Three*]   A desert, the same as in *Scene One* of this act. To a piz-zicato figure in the orchestra, played by the violas, the Prince and Trouffal-dino come plodding in. Pulling on ropes, they drag in the Three Oranges which have now grown large enough to hold a human being.

Groaning with weariness, they wonder how they can go on without the aid of Farfarello's bellows. The Prince says he is so tired he must lie down; Trouffaldino mutters that he is dying of thirst. The Prince advises him to lie down and sleep to restore his strength. Thereupon the Prince himself stretches out on the ground and promptly goes to sleep.

Looking down at him, Trouffaldino launches into a striking monologue—actually one of the few arias of the conventional type in the opera ("Il est drôle, le Prince!"). This Prince, he muses, is a droll fellow—he calmly goes to sleep while his companion is dying of thirst. In rising desperation, Trouffaldino looks around, crying for water. He calls the Prince's name, but the latter sleeps blissfully on. Suddenly Trouffaldino turns to the Oranges. Suppose he should open one, he sings softly—just one of these beautiful, juicy Oranges.

The Jester grasps his sword, then hesitates, admitting he is afraid of what the Prince might do if he found one of the Oranges cut. In the second part of the aria, Trouffaldino tries to rationalize himself into cutting open one of the Oranges. What if he should die of thirst before help arrived? The Prince could not possibly drag these great Oranges any farther by himself. Then all would be lost—the Three Oranges, the Prince, Trouffaldino. Obviously, the sensible thing to do is to eat one of the Oranges. Having thus neatly argued the point, Trouffaldino fervently kisses an Orange, then slices it open with a stroke of his sword.

To a powerful unison passage in the orchestra, a comely young woman in white steps forth. Trouffaldino staggers back, thunderstruck. The young woman introduces herself as Linette. A Princess, murmurs Trouffaldino, in-stead of refreshing orange juice. Immediately the Princess begins to beg for water, gasping that she will die of thirst. There is none, Trouffaldino groans, then in desperation tries to wake up the Prince. Spurred by the Princess's pitiful entreaties, the Jester cuts open another Orange. There is a long sustained chord in the orchestra as a second young woman, also in white, steps out. Her name, she announces, is Nicolette.

While Trouffaldino is still reeling from the shock Nicolette, too, begins begging frantically for water. She is joined in her pleas by Linette, and both stretch out their arms imploringly to Trouffaldino. As he draws back in fear and confusion, the two young women sink to the ground and melodra-matically die before his eyes. Terror-stricken, he dashes away.

No sooner has he gone than the Prince cries out Trouffaldino's name in his sleep, then suddenly wakes up. Looking around for the Jester, he spies the two dead Princesses. Bemused rather than frightened, the Prince mur-murs about the strange sight of two young women lying dead in the desert.

There is a moment's silence and then a march theme begins in the or-chestra. Four soldiers enter in precise military formation. They halt at the Prince's command. He orders them to remove the bodies and bury them at a spot which he indicates. Moving like automatons in strict time with the martial music, the soldiers lift up the Princesses and bear them away. Turning to the remaining Orange, the Prince, parodying the conventional operatic tenor, sings a passionate refrain: "Chére Orange, enfin j'ai le bonheur!" Now, at last, he is alone with his beloved Orange, he sings, then begs her to reveal her secret to him. With a blow of his sword he cuts open the Orange.

A third Princess appears. With regal dignity she announces that she is called Ninette. Falling on his knees, the Prince sings in impassioned phrases that he has been looking for her all his life and adores her beyond all belief. As she responds to his words he wildly embraces her.

But then, like the other Princess, she calls for water. The Prince entreats her to wait until they can make their way to the town. When he starts to lead her away she faints in his arms. Looking on, the Absurdities call out in strong, rhythmic phrases that the Princess must have water immediately. Thereupon, one group brings a pail of water and places it in the middle of the stage. The Prince helps the Princess drink from the pail.

Thanking him fervently, she sings that he has saved her from slavery and that she has been waiting for him a long time. The Prince responds in a beautiful melody ("Non, rien ne pouvait"). Nothing, he tells the Princess, could have kept him away from her. For her love he defied the terrible Greonte, the ferocious Cook, the lethal ladle, and the hell that was the Cook's kitchen. With charming simplicity the Princess assures the Prince of her gratitude and devotion.

At this point the Lyricists drift noiselessly onstage and, in a brief chorus, appeal for romantic dramas, complete with moonlight and flowers. The Absurdities warn them not to disturb the lovers. The Lyricists silently leave.

In gentle tones the Prince asks the Princess to come with him to his palace ("Partons, Princess"), introducing a short duet, one of the loveliest passages in the opera. The Princess answers with the classic feminine excuse that she cannot possibly appear before the King in her present costume. The King has nothing to say about the matter, says the Prince rather huffily. But the Princess urges him to go on ahead, inform the King of her impending visit, and then bring back a royal robe she can wear for the occasion. The Prince replies gallantly that if it is her wish he will bring back the King himself. Tenderly they bid each other farewell, and the Prince leaves. The Princess exclaims softly over her happiness.

The orchestra sounds a quiet, murmurous theme as darkness slowly envelops the scene. The third Princess sits dreaming in the gathering twilight. Suddenly two figures, silhouetted against the fading light, stealthily glide toward her. They are Fata Morgana and Sméraldine.

In excited phrases the watching Absurdities note that Sméraldine is carrying a huge hairpin and that Fata Morgana is with her—a situation that bodes no good. In increasing agitation, remarkably delineated by a succession of ascending quintuplets in the orchestra, the Absurdities rush from their tower and approach Ninette on tiptoe to observe more closely what is happening. Sméraldine steals up behind Ninette and stabs her in the head with the hairpin.

With a long-drawn cry of anguish, Ninette disappears, to be transformed in the next instant into a rat.[3] The animal scampers across the stage and

---

[3] In the revised English version of the opera, Ninette is changed into a pigeon.

out of sight. Terrified, the Absurdities scramble back to their tower and bewail the fate of Ninette.

Sméraldine stands motionless. In commanding tones, Fata Morgana sings that Sméraldine will take Ninette's place and will make it known that *she* is the real Princess. With that Fata Morgana vanishes, and as she does so there comes the sound of martial music. As it grows louder, a strange procession appears, lighted by torches and lanterns. At its head are the King, the Prince, Léandre, Pantalon, courtiers, and guards.

Seeing the supposed Princess, the Prince greets her with a joyous phrase ("Quel bonheur"). When the King exclaims over her suspicious appearance, the Prince looks more closely, then cries out that this woman indeed is not the real Princess. The treacherous Sméraldine insists she is Ninette and warns the Prince that he is bound to her by his own promise. Horrified at the thought, the Prince flatly refuses to marry her.

The King steps forward and declares that the word of a royal Prince cannot be broken—he must marry the "Princess" at once. The courtiers gasp in astonishment as the Prince cries incredulously, "This black woman?" The King peremptorily commands the Prince to offer the Princess his arm, then orders the procession to move on. Crushed by despair, the Prince obeys. The march music continues with sardonic gaiety. Stepping aside momentarily, Léandre and Clarisse gloatingly look on. With malicious glee, Léandre remarks that the Orange was decayed—and so the Princess emerged *black*. He joins arms with Clarisse and the two again fall in with the procession. The curtain falls.

ACT FOUR

[*Scene One*]   The music begins *furioso*. Almost immediately the curtain rises to show the cabalistic curtain seen in *Scene Two* of Act I. Tchélio and Fata Morgana rush in from opposite sides of the stage and almost collide in the center. A violent argument follows in duet form ("Ah! Ignoble sorcière!") as both denounce each other because their evil magic has not been completely successful.

Tchélio sneers that Fata Morgana is unprincipled enough to use the device of a poisoned hairpin. The witch retorts that he, fraud that he is, can only resort to a brightly-colored ribbon to accomplish his sorcery. Heaping mutual abuse, they call down thunder and lightning in an attempt to silence each other. Fata Morgana, being a woman, of course has the last word, shrieking at Tchélio that he is a cheat at cards.

Now the Absurdities come down from their tower, form a double file and close in on Fata Morgana. In an ominous chorus ("Fata Morgana, nous venons parler"), they tell her they have strange news. As the witch leans closer to listen, the Absurdities seize her and push her into one of the towers. Smoke and flame burst forth. Turning to Tchélio, the Absurdities cry that now he can save the royal court. Smugly gloating over his triumph, Tchélio, illumined by a shaft of light, makes gestures of incantation toward the tower where Fata Morgana is imprisoned. The Absurdities, going back to the other tower, take due note of the irony of the situation. The music rises to clashing chords, and then the cabalistic curtain goes up.

[*Scene Two*] The throne room of the royal palace. At one side, the King's throne, with two others beside it—one for the Prince, the other for the future Princess. Ladies and gentlemen of the court crowd in and are herded to one side by the Master of Ceremonies.

Léandre hastily enters, asks the Master of Ceremonies if everything is in readiness, then tells him to draw the velvet curtain that is to hide the thrones until the court ceremonies begin. As the Master of Ceremonies does so, martial music is heard and a procession enters. First comes the King, then the Prince with Sméraldine at his side. Following them are Clarisse, Pantalon, and the guards. The entire ensemble hails the King in a brief chorus ("Gloire à notre Roi!")—which, by the way, is a resounding take-off on standard grand-opera technique.

At the conclusion of the chorus the Master of Ceremonies orders the velvet curtain hiding the thrones to be drawn. There, seated on the throne of the Princess, is an enormous rat the size of a human being. It is, of course, Ninette, transformed by the wicked Sméraldine. The crowd cringes in horror; the courtiers stand their ground and draw their swords. The King and Pantalon, frightened out of their wits, shout for the guards.

All at once, Tchélio appears in a glow of light. Making frenzied gestures of incantation, he commands the rat to turn back into Ninette. Nothing happens. Thereupon the King shouts to the guards to raise their guns. They take aim and fire. The rat turns at once into Ninette and Tchélio vanishes. Everyone hails the miracle. Wild with joy, the Prince rushes over to Ninette, kneels before her and takes her hand.

Completely dumfounded, the King looks at Ninette and then at Sméraldine, asking who the latter is. Trouffaldino, suddenly appearing out of nowhere, tells him. Starting at the name of Sméraldine, the King asks if she is not the accomplice of Léandre. At that, Léandre steps forward and attempts to explain matters, but the King pays no attention to him. At last, he mutters, he is beginning to understand the Prime Minister's treachery. He whirls furiously on Léandre, denouncing him a traitor, to the accompaniment of a powerful unison figure in the orchestra. Clarisse now steps forward and promptly becomes the second target of the royal wrath.

With angry dignity the King ascends the throne. In majestic, ringing phrases, he orders the slave Sméraldine, the traitor Léandre, and his villainous accomplice Clarisse to be hanged at once. All in the court, murmuring in awe at the terrible edict, fall on their knees. Trouffaldino softly pleads for pardon. Pantalon surreptitiously gives him a push and hisses at him to be quiet.

Glaring at the hapless trio, the King commands the guards to bring the rope. As they move closer, Sméraldine makes a break for freedom, with Léandre and Clarisse following. Pandemonium erupts as the guards, Pantalon, Trouffaldino, the Master of Ceremonies, and all the courtiers rush pell-mell after the three. Finally only the King remains standing on the steps of his throne. Ninette, on her throne, bends to the Prince, who embraces her passionately.

As the orchestral accompaniment crackles with a kind of impish glee, the fugitives and their pursuers rush back and forth across the stage. When they stampede out of sight for a moment, Fata Morgana forces open the door of the tower where she has been imprisoned. She glides to the stage center, invokes thunder and lightning, and commands the fugitives to come to her for protection. A trap door opens before her. With the yelling crowd at their heels, Sméraldine, Clarisse, and Léandre come rushing in and leap into the fire and smoke billowing out of the trap door. Fata Morgana follows them.

Clamoring fiercely for the heads of the traitors, the courtiers surround the now vacant spot. The bewildered Absurdities mill about and—not knowing what else to do—hail the King. He responds by commanding everyone to pay homage to the Prince and the Princess. All obey in a brief but thunderous ensemble. The curtain falls.

Lucia di Lammermoor

by GAETANO DONIZETTI

[1797–1848]

Libretto by
SALVATORE CAMMARANO

Based on Sir Walter Scott's novel
THE BRIDE OF LAMMERMOOR

CHARACTERS

Lord Enrico Ashton of Lammermoor, a Scotch nobleman.........*Baritone*
Lucia Ashton, his sister.......................................*Soprano*
Sir Edgardo of Ravenswood, last of his family...................*Tenor*
Raimondo Bidebent, Lucia's tutor.................................*Bass*
Alisa, Lucia's companion............................*Mezzo-soprano*
Lord Arturo Bucklaw, an influential nobleman....................*Tenor*
Normanno, Lord Enrico's captain of the guard....................*Tenor*
    Friends, relatives, pages, soldiers, and servants of Lord Enrico

Place: Scotland
Time: About 1702
First performance: Teatro San Carlo, Naples, September 26, 1835
Original language: Italian

THE NOBLE FAMILIES of Lammermoor and Ravenswood, deadly enemies for many years, have sworn to exterminate each other. Only one member of the Ravenswood clan is left: young and fearless Sir Edgardo. His father was slain by Lord Enrico, who has also taken his lands.

ACT ONE

The park of Ravenswood Castle. The scene is a rocky wooded section, with a lake in the background. A group of guards, headed by their leader, Normanno, are excitedly searching the grounds and talking about a stranger who has been seen prowling about the place.

Lord Enrico enters with Raimondo. He laments to Normanno and Raimondo that he has lost his fortune and is still menaced by his old dispossessed enemy—Edgardo of Ravenswood. He adds, however, that his sister Lucia can save him from ruin if she will marry the man he has chosen to be her husband, but that she dares to refuse. Kindhearted, elderly Raimondo urges him to remember that she is mourning the death of her mother and cannot think of love. "Cannot think of love," sneers Normanno. "Her heart is burning with love." He then relates how Lucia was rescued by a hunter from the attack of a mad bull; that every morning she secretly meets her protector at that very place, near her mother's grave. Enrico asks if he knows the man and Normanno answers that he thinks the mysterious lover is Sir Edgardo.

Enrico is infuriated ("Cruda funesta smania"). Just then some of the guards return to tell that they have seen a man on horseback dash away from the ruined tower. Their suspicions are confirmed: it is Edgardo ("Come vinti"). Enrico's fury rises. He swears vengeance on Lucia and Edgardo ("La pietade in suo favore"), and the guards pledge their support as they all leave. Raimondo has pleaded for Lucia in vain, and he departs despondent.

While the scene darkens somewhat, a lovely harp interlude is heard. Soon Lucia and Alisa, her companion, enter the park to meet Edgardo. Alisa fears Enrico's wrath if they should be discovered. Lucia feels that she must warn Edgardo of his danger. She then tells Alisa how on this very spot, according to legend, a Ravenswood once murdered a maiden who loved him and threw her body into the fountain nearby. Her unhappy spirit still haunts the park. In a beautiful and dramatic aria ("Regnava nel silenzio") she relates how she once encountered this unhappy spirit and was warned by it of a wretched ending to her secret love affair. Alisa begs her to give up Edgardo before some tragedy occurs, but Lucia, her spirits rising, can sing only of the ecstasy of her love for Edgardo ("Quando rapita in estasi"). With misgivings, Alisa sees Edgardo approaching and leaves to keep watch while the lovers are together.

Edgardo begs Lucia's forgiveness for asking her to meet him at such a time, but explains he must leave Scotland that night on a political errand to France. Before he goes, however, he wants to seek peace with her brother and to seal the friendship by asking for her hand. But Lucia knows that Lord Enrico will never consent to their marriage and asks Edgardo to keep their love secret.

Edgardo is resentful. "Is it not enough," he asks, "that he killed my father and stole my heritage? Will only my death satisfy him?" He recites how he had sworn revenge at his father's tomb, but Lucia's love had since cooled his ire ("Sulla tomba che rinserra"). In mounting anger, he states that he can still fulfill his vow.

Lucia, in a state of commingled love and sorrow, persuades him to let love prevail. With sudden determination he asks her to swear to be his forever. He places a ring on her finger as a token of his plighted faith, and Lucia gives him one of her rings as she pledges undying devotion. The act closes with a brilliant love duet as they did each other a tender farewell ("Verrano a te cull'aure").

ACT TWO
(The Marriage Contract)

A hall in Lammermoor Castle. When the curtain rises, several months have elapsed since Edgardo left for France. In the meantime Lord Enrico has been going ahead with a nefarious scheme to separate the lovers. It is not only hatred of the Ravenswood clan that prompts him to plot against

Edgardo, but the fact that he is in desperate financial straits. By arranging a marriage between Lucia and Lord Arturo Bucklaw, he can improve his fortune.

At the beginning of the act we find Enrico talking to Normanno. He tells him he has invited all his friends and kinsmen to celebrate the coming wedding, but he fears Lucia may still refuse to marry Arturo. Normanno calms his fears by reminding him that they have intercepted all the letters between the lovers and have spread a rumor that Edgardo loves another. As they see Lucia approaching, Enrico asks Normanno for the letter which together they have forged in order to make Lucia believe that Edgardo has chosen to marry another. Normanno hands him the letter and then leaves to escort Lord Arturo to the castle.

Presently Lucia enters. She comes forward listlessly, looking fixedly at her brother. He comments on her sad and anguished expression, saying he had hoped to see some signs of happiness. She replies that he knows the cause of her sorrow and implores him to give up his resolve ("Il pallor funesto, orrendo"), but Enrico only bids her forget her lover and pleads with her to accept a noble husband. Lucia will not hear his suggestions and replies that she has already pledged her faith to another. Then the cruel brother produces the forged letter, which he commands her to read, saying that it will prove she has been betrayed. With trembling hands Lucia takes the note and reads. Overcome with horror and dismay, she is about to faint. He rushes to her aid. In a flowing duet she bemoans her misery and wishes for death, while he entreats her to forget her traitorous lover ("Soffriva nel pianto").

Suddenly sounds of festive music are heard. Enrico tells Lucia that the crowds are greeting Lord Arturo Bucklaw, whom he has selected to be her husband. At her insistence that she will not marry but now waits only for death, Enrico in despair confesses to her that unless she consents, his own death and the ruin of the family will result, for he has committed treasonable acts against the king and only Arturo is powerful enough to save him from punishment. His death will be upon her head and his spirit will haunt her ("Se tradirmi tu potrai"). Lucia still insists that death alone is her future.

As Enrico leaves, Raimondo enters. He, too, is now convinced Edgardo is faithless and tells Lucia it is her duty, in her mother's memory, to come to her brother's aid ("Ah! Cedi, cedi"). Lucia is brokenhearted at the prospect of life without Edgardo. Believing he is lost to her forever, and also thinking it is her duty to save her brother, she finally consents ("Guidami tu, tu reggimi"). Weeping, she goes to prepare for the wedding.

Hardly has she left the room when the guests arrive. Arturo, Enrico, Normanno, knights and ladies, pages, squires, guards, and inhabitants of Lammermoor enter, joyfully hailing the coming marriage that will cement the friendship of the Ashtons and the Bucklaws ("Per te d'immenso giubilo"). Arturo proclaims his friendship and his love for Lucia ("Per poco fra le tenebre"). Enrico introduces him to the assembled guests.

Arturo asks for Lucia. Enrico tells him she will be in presently but bids him not to be astonished if she seems grief-stricken, for she is still mourning her mother's death. Lucia enters, supported on the arm of Raimondo and accompanied by Alisa and her other maids-in-waiting. Enrico presents Arturo to the despondent girl. She shrinks from him, but Enrico whispers to her to be cautious and not ruin his plans. He goes to the table where the marriage contract lies. Arturo signs it. Then Raimondo and Alisa lead the trembling Lucia to the table, and, scarcely aware of what she is doing, she signs the deed.

Suddenly the door opens. A stranger appears, his features concealed. He announces himself—"Edgardo!" There is immediate consternation. As Alisa and the ladies lead the swooning Lucia to a seat, there begins one of the most beautiful and powerfully dramatic ensembles ever written—the famous *Sextet*. It opens with Edgardo's questioning phrase, "What restrains me in such a moment?" ("Chi mi frena in tal momento?") It is, of course, only his love for Lucia that keeps him from drawing his sword and wreaking vengeance on his enemies. Even though she has betrayed his faith, he still loves her. Lucia, meanwhile, is consumed by despair; new fears fill Enrico's heart, and he feels compassion for his sister's plight; Arturo, Raimondo, Alisa, and the assembled guests pray that the impending trouble will pass.

Enrico and Arturo order Edgardo away, rushing at him with drawn swords. Edgardo draws too, saying he may die but others will die with him. Raimondo intervenes and bids them put up their swords. Enrico demands to know why Edgardo has come. Edgardo replies that he has come for Lucia, who has sworn faith to him. That vow is canceled, Enrico tells him, and shows him the marriage contract. Edgardo asks Lucia if it is her signature, and she answers that it is.

Edgardo's fury knows no bounds. Stifling with rage, he gives Lucia back her ring and demands his own. Lucia, completely bewildered and hardly conscious of what is going on, takes the ring from her finger. Edgardo snatches it from her, throws it down, and tramples it underfoot.

Lucia swoons. Edgardo is ordered to leave, with a warning that their revenge will seek him out ("Esci, fuggi"). Instead of attempting to defend himself, Edgardo throws away his sword, offers his breast for them to strike, and declares he would gladly perish. Lucia prays for his life. Raimondo, Alisa, and the ladies induce him to flee for the sake of Lucia. After another brilliant concerted number the curtain falls as Edgardo rushes from the hall.

ACT THREE

[*Scene One*]   The great hall of Lammermoor Castle. The first part of the third act is the famous *Mad Scene*. Musically it consists of some of the most beautiful as well as difficult coloratura passages ever composed, while dramatically it portrays a Lucia who cannot help but arouse our pity and sympathy, for in her insanity she believes herself to be with her lover, and so is happy in her madness.

When the curtain rises the hall is well peopled with guests. From adjoining rooms dance music is heard, and also sounds of jubilation ("D'immenso giubilo").

Suddenly Raimondo enters, pale and tense with excitement. He calls to the people to stop their merriment, and, gathering them about him, he tells this tale of horror ("Dalle stanze, ove Lucia"): Hearing a groan of terror from the bridal suite, he swiftly entered to find Arturo dead and Lucia standing triumphantly over his body, still waving the sword with which she had killed him. With glaring eyes fixed on Raimondo, she whispered, "Where is my husband?" and a smile of pleasure flashed over her pale countenance, plainly showing she was bereft of all reason.

He has just finished telling his story to the horror-stricken group when Lucia enters, her disheveled hair coming down over her white gown. She is deathly pale, and evidently unconscious of her surroundings. She thinks she is with her true lover, Edgardo. She imagines she hears his voice. Once again, she thinks, they are in the park, near the fountain. Suddenly she believes the unhappy spirit has risen to separate them. In her bewildered mind they fly to a beautiful altar strewn with roses. She hears celestial harmony. "The tapers are lighted" ("Ardon gl'incensi"), she sings. "There is the priest in his splendid robes. Give me thy right hand, Edgardo," she says in her delirium, "for I am thy bride forever. This blissful moment repays all my suffering." The startled assemblage implores Heaven to have pity on the poor maiden.

Enrico enters angrily and starts to upbraid Lucia for her perfidious crime; but Raimondo draws attention to her pathetic state of mind. He is instantly remorseful. Lucia, believing it is Edgardo who is angry with her, admits she signed the contract, but only because her cruel brother forced her to do so. "I love only you, Edgardo," she says. "Do not leave me."

Now apparently normal once more and realizing that she is dying, she asks them to cast a flower upon her grave but not to weep for her, because she goes to await her true love in heaven ("Spargi d'amaro pianto"). With this aria Lucia falls into the arms of Alisa. Enrico, repenting too late, is overcome with grief. The scene ends with Raimondo assailing Normanno as the cause of all the trouble.

[*Scene Two*]   A section near Edgardo's ruined castle of Wolfscrag. The scene is a weird and eerie place. Lammermoor Castle, brightly illuminated, is seen in the distance, while in the foreground are the tombs of the Ravenswoods. It is night. Here we find Edgardo brooding. He does not know that Lucia has killed her husband and is herself dying. In his great aria ("Fra poco a me ricovero") he sings that he now waits only for an unmourned grave. He is bitter about Lucia's marriage and the happiness he thinks is hers, but anger has gone.

A group of inhabitants of Lammermoor, having left the scene of the tragedy at the castle, enter lamenting. Edgardo asks the cause of their grief, and they recount the whole unhappy story ("Giusto cielo! rispondete"). When he hears that Lucia in her madness is calling only for him, he resolves to see her, but Raimondo, who has come in, restrains him. A tolling bell is heard at that moment. Raimondo tells Edgardo that the bell announces Lucia's death. Edgardo sobs aloud in his grief.

At last realizing the steadfastness of Lucia's love for him, he apostrophizes her pure spirit, declaring that he and she will not be long parted ("Tu che a Dio spiegasti"). Before the others can stop him, Edgardo stabs himself. While his life ebbs away, the saddened onlookers offer a solemn prayer that Heaven may pardon such human errors.

Madama Butterfly

by GIACOMO PUCCINI

[1858–1924]

Libretto by
LUIGI ILLICA *and* GIUSEPPE GIACOSA

Based on John Luther Long's story and David Belasco's play
MADAM BUTTERFLY

CHARACTERS

Goro, a *nakodo*, or marriage broker..............................*Tenor*
B. F. Pinkerton, lieutenant, United States Navy..................*Tenor*
Suzuki, maid to Cio-cio-san...........................*Mezzo-soprano*
Sharpless, American Consul at Nagasaki......................*Baritone*
Madama Butterfly (Cio-cio-san).............................*Soprano*
The Cousin ....*Soprano*
Mother of Cio-cio-san................................*Mezzo-soprano*
Yakusidé, uncle of Cio-cio-san..............................*Baritone*
Commissioner ....*Bass*
Registrar ....*Baritone*
The Bonzo, a Buddhist priest, also an uncle of Cio-cio-san...........*Bass*
Prince Yamadori, a suitor of Cio-cio-san......................*Baritone*
Kate Pinkerton, wife of Lieutenant Pinkerton..............*Mezzo-soprano*
Trouble, Cio-cio-san's child
Relatives and companions of Cio-cio-san, servants

Place: Nagasaki, Japan
Time: Nineteenth century
First performance: La Scala, Milan, February 17, 1904
Original language: Italian

PUCCINI saw a production of Belasco's *Madam Butterfly* in London and decided immediately to use the play as the basis for an opera. He went to particular pains to give the work authentic local color, both dramatically and musically, basing some of his themes on genuine Japanese music.

The first production, however, was a complete failure. For reasons that no one seems to have been able to analyze, it was greeted with expressions of violent dislike. Revised and presented again four months later, the opera was a brilliant success.

ACT ONE

The terrace and garden of the Japanese house which Lieutenant Pinkerton has leased in Nagasaki. It is on a hill overlooking the harbor and the town. Pinkerton expresses surprise and pleasure over the house as Goro scurries about showing him the ingenious arrangement of sliding panels which form the walls. Suzuki and two other servants enter and are introduced to the lieutenant by Goro. Suzuki addresses Pinkerton in flowery phrases, but Goro cuts her short when he observes that the lieutenant is getting bored by her chatter. He sends her and the two others away, then tells Pinkerton about the people who will be present for the signing of his marriage contract. They will include, he says, some two dozen relatives, the American Consul, Japanese officials, and, of course, Butterfly, the bride-to-be.

Sharpless arrives, panting and complaining about the steepness of the climb to the house. Pinkerton orders Goro to set out drinks, and then the two men sit down to talk. The lieutenant explains casually that he has leased the house for nine hundred and ninety-nine years and has bound himself to marriage with a Japanese for the same length of time—with the convenient provision that both the lease and the marriage can be canceled on a month's notice.

In a vigorous air introduced by a phrase from "The Star-Spangled Banner" ("Dovunque al mondo"), Pinkerton describes how the American seafaring man roams the whole world over in devil-may-care fashion, daunted by nothing, making conquests on his own terms. He cites his marriage adventure as an example. Sharpless observes that Pinkerton's philosophy is very convenient but one that eventually will exact its own price. The two men join in a rousing toast to America.

Goro bustles in, overhears Sharpless ask Pinkerton about his bride, and at once offers to provide one for the consul, who laughingly declines the offer. Pinkerton sends Goro off to bring Cio-cio-san. Sharpless remonstrates with him for taking his marriage so lightly, but Pinkerton, in an ardent refrain ("Amore o grillo"), answers that the geisha so enchanted him with her fragile beauty that he resolved to have her. When the consul warns that he may bring sorrow to an innocent and trusting heart, Pinkerton merely proposes another toast—this time to the American girl who will someday be his real wife.

Now the voices of Butterfly and her girl companions are heard in a jubilant chorus, in which we hear the love theme for the first time. Butterfly appears, charmingly introduces Pinkerton to her companions, and then answers questions about her family. They were once wealthy, she says, but now times have changed. At the mention of her father there is a moment of awkward silence, but Butterfly hastens on to explain about her illustrious uncle, the Bonzo. Apologetically she adds that she has another uncle who, unfortunately, is addicted to the bottle. She coyly asks Pinkerton and Sharpless to guess her age, laughing slyly at their astonishment when she reveals that she is only fifteen.

Pinkerton orders Goro to bring forth the refreshments. At that point the relatives arrive, along with the Imperial Registrar and the High Commissioner. Goro officiously takes charge. In a lively, chattering chorus the relatives comment on the Americans and then ceremoniously pay their compliments as they are introduced by Butterfly. Taking Pinkerton to one side, Butterfly shyly asks if she may be permitted to keep certain of her treasures. From the sleeves of her kimono she brings forth a variety of feminine knick-knacks, then finally a long, slender sheath. A brief, somber phrase sounds dramatically in the orchestra. When Pinkerton asks her about the sheath, Butterfly turns away in confusion. Goro steps forward and whispers that it was sent to her father by the Mikado. In further explanation, Goro makes a gesture indicating hara-kiri.

Butterfly then shows Pinkerton a number of figurines, explaining that they are symbolic of the souls of her ancestors. In an impressive refrain ("Ieri son salita") she tells him that for the sake of his love she has repudiated her ancestors and her family. With that she throws the figurines away.

The marriage contract is signed with much ceremony. Sharpless, after a final word of caution to Pinkerton, leaves with the Commissioner and the Registrar. Pinkerton invites the relatives to help themselves to food and drink. In a festive chorus they express their satisfaction, and the sight of Uncle Yakusidé helping himself to the whisky provides considerable amusement.

The celebration is interrupted by the arrival of the Bonzo, who confronts Butterfly and furiously curses her for having renounced the religion of her ancestors. At Pinkerton's threatening command, the Bonzo and the relatives slowly withdraw, shouting denunciations at Butterfly, who buries her face in her hands and sobs bitterly.

As the angry cries die away in the distance, Pinkerton gently takes Butterfly's hands from her face and speaks words of comfort. Twilight approaches. From inside the house comes the sound of Suzuki's voice murmuring evening prayers. Pinkerton gives orders to arrange the house for the night, then seats himself in a chair and lights a cigarette. Suzuki helps Butterfly exchange her wedding dress for a long flowing gown of white.

Butterfly and Pinkerton are left alone, and now the music builds up into the rapturous love duet that concludes the act ("Viene la sera"). Clasped in each other's arms, they gaze up at the starry sky and pour out their ecstasy in the passionate climax of the duet, "Oh, quanti occhi fisi." As they slowly go into the house the curtain falls.

ACT TWO

Butterfly's house. It is three years later. Pinkerton has long since left Nagasaki, and Butterfly has borne him a child. Suzuki is praying before a statue of Buddha, pausing occasionally to ring a prayer bell. Butterfly stands motionless near a screen. Suzuki implores the gods for aid, then shows Butterfly the few coins that are left to buy food. When the maid frets over their plight, Butterfly calmly assures her that Pinkerton will return. He promised, she sings, that he would come back when the robins nest in the spring. In the beautiful aria "Un bel di" she describes the joy that will be hers on the day Pinkerton's ship sails into the harbor.

Butterfly's happy reverie is interrupted by the arrival of Goro and Sharpless. She welcomes the consul graciously and engages in a polite conversation about the state of his health and the weather. Sharpless, ill at ease, waits his chance to speak of the fateful letter he has received from Pinkerton saying that he has an American wife and that his marriage to Butterfly is a thing of the past. The consul stares in surprise when Butterfly asks him when the robins nest in America. Pinkerton assured her, she continues, that he would return with the robins, but they have already nested three times. Sharpless replies with considerable embarrassment that he is not an expert on ornithology, a word which Butterfly naïvely tries to pronounce.

The scene is interrupted by the arrival of the stupid, bumbling Prince Yamadori. Goro, having learned that Butterfly has been deserted, has lost no time in trying to arrange another marriage, and is offering Yamadori to Butterfly as a likely suitor. But she greets the prince's offers with amused contempt. When she reminds him that she is already wed, Goro says that desertion constitutes grounds for divorce. That may be the law in Japan, Butterfly retorts, but not in America. To Sharpless's dismay, she turned to him for confirmation.

After much lugubrious pleading, Yamadori leaves with Goro. Sharpless finally manages to read Pinkerton's letter, and as gently as possible he makes its tragic meaning clear. Butterfly recoils as if struck. After a moment she recovers, hurries from the room, and returns with her baby. In a dramatic and moving air ("Chi vide mai a bimbo"), she proudly tells Sharpless that here is Pinkerton's son. He must be told, she says, and when he knows that his wonderful child is waiting for him, he will allow nothing to stand in the way of his return. Clasping the child in feverish ecstasy, Butterfly sings that perhaps one day the Emperor will pass by and see this boy, with his heavenly blue eyes. He will be so taken by his beauty that he will make him a prince of the kingdom. Sharpless asks the boy's name. His name now is Trouble, Butterfly replies, but when Pinkerton returns it will be Joy. Deeply moved and distressed, Sharpless leaves, promising to tell Pinkerton of his son.

Suzuki bursts in, dragging the whimpering Goro. She tells Butterfly that he has been saying that her baby's father is unknown, and that in America such a child would be held in disgrace. Infuriated, Butterfly threatens to kill Goro with her dagger. Suzuki intervenes and pushes him out of the room.

A cannon booms in the harbor, announcing the arrival of a ship. With the aid of a telescope Butterfly identifies it as the *Abraham Lincoln*, Pinkerton's ship. In wildest excitement, she orders Suzuki to bring all the flowers from the garden to decorate the house. As they arrange the flowers they sing the lovely duet "Scuoti quella fronda di ciliegio," in which they joyously declare that they will rob the cherry tree of all its petals and the garden of all its blooms and scatter them in handfuls over the house in honor of this great occasion. After the duet Butterfly puts on her wedding gown, while Suzuki dresses the baby, then closes the *shosi*, a sliding wall with paper panes, facing the harbor. Butterfly makes three small holes in the *shosi*, one for herself, one for Suzuki, and a third for the baby. In the gathering darkness the women take up their vigil. From behind the scenes comes a melancholy, hummed chorus sung in slow, sweeping phrases over a plaintive melody in the orchestra. Suzuki and the baby gradually fall asleep. The faithful Butterfly remains standing motionless as the humming finally dies away and the curtain falls on this quiet but highly emotional scene.

ACT THREE

The same scene as at the end of Act Two.[1] There is a melodious prelude which echoes the theme of the first-act love duet. From the harbor come the shouts of sailors and the clanking of anchor chains. The early morning sun streams into the house. Butterfly, at length ending her vigil, rouses Suzuki and takes up the baby. At Suzuki's urging she retires to her room to rest.

Pinkerton, his wife Kate, and Sharpless approach. The two men go to the door, while Kate waits in the garden. Suzuki answers at their knock and tells them that Butterfly waited all night for Pinkerton after she had seen his ship in the harbor. Sharpless tells her that they have come to ask her aid in making arrangements for the future care of Pinkerton's child. When Suzuki learns that the strange woman in the garden is Pinkerton's wife, she sinks to the ground, sobbing in despair. A brief, dramatic trio follows ("Lo so che alle sue"). Sharpless implores Suzuki to break the news to Butterfly, assuring her that Mrs. Pinkerton will give the child her loving care. Suzuki begs to be spared this task, while Pinkerton gives way to his remorse.

At length Sharpless persuades Suzuki to go into the garden to meet Kate. He turns on Pinkerton in angry reproach for having caused all this sorrow, and then somewhat contemptuously suggests that he leave without seeing Butterfly in her agony. The lieutenant pauses long enough to sing a heart-broken farewell ("Addio fiorito asil").

Suzuki re-enters with Kate Pinkerton, and at that moment Butterfly appears at the doorway of her room. Suzuki vainly tries to keep her from coming in. Eagerly Butterfly looks for Pinkerton. As she gazes from one to the other, the terrible truth dawns upon her, and she stares at Kate as if hypnotized. Kate tries to approach, but she motions her away. When Kate begs her forgiveness, Butterfly quietly bids her to tell Pinkerton that she will somehow find peace. He may have the child, she says in answer to Kate's request, if he will return for him in half an hour. Kate and Sharpless sadly leave.

The orchestra intones a dolorous theme as Butterfly orders Suzuki to close the doors and draw the curtains and then tells the sobbing maid to join the child in the garden. After a long time Butterfly takes a white veil from the shrine and throws it over the screen. She takes the dagger from its sheath, kisses it, and slowly reads the inscription: "Death with honor is better than life without honor."

She poises the dagger at her throat. At that moment Suzuki pushes the child into the room. In wild anguish Butterfly clasps him to her and sings a poignant farewell to her "little idol" ("Piccolo Iddio"). Brooding chords throb in the orchestra as she seats the child on a small stool, puts an American flag and a doll in his hands, and then blindfolds him. Dagger in hand, she steps behind the screen. In the next moment the knife thuds to the floor and the white veil slides slowly from the screen.

[1] The opera was originally written in two acts. When Puccini revised it he divided Act Two into two parts, which are usually played as Act Two and Act Three.

Butterfly, with the veil around her neck, creeps over to the child and collapses at his feet. She dies as Pinkerton, shouting her name, bursts into the room, followed by Sharpless. Powerful chords sound out the theme of the refrain which Butterfly sang when she mused that the Emperor might admire her beautiful child. The curtain falls.

Manon

by JULES MASSENET

[1842–1912]

Libretto by
HENRI MEILHAC *and* PHILIPPE GILLE

Based on the Abbé Prévost's story
LES AVENTURES DU CHEVALIER DES GRIEUX ET MANON LESCAUT

CHARACTERS

Guillot Morfontain, Minister of France.........................*Bass*
De Brétigny, a nobleman...................................*Baritone*
Pousette ⎱
Javotte ⎰ actresses......................................*Sopranos*
Rosette ⎰
Innkeeper ....*Bass*
Lescaut, member of the Royal Guard........................*Baritone*
Manon Lescaut, his cousin.................................*Soprano*
Chevalier des Grieux......................................*Tenor*
Count des Grieux, his father...............................*Bass*
Soldiers, porters, servants, townspeople, travelers, vendors, gamblers,
croupier, sergeant

Place: Amiens, Paris, and Lettaure
Time: 1721
First performance: Opéra-Comique, Paris, January 19, 1884
Original language: French

MANON was written by Massenet during the summer of 1882 while he was living at The Hague in the same house in which the Abbé Prévost lived when he wrote his novel. The opera tells the story of a charming young French girl who is too anxious for a life of pleasure, too young to know the ways of the world and how to avoid its pitfalls—and yet so artless that we cannot find it in our hearts to condemn her but feel only pity and sympathy as her career winds its course to a degrading and unhappy close.

Before the curtain rises a short prelude briefly states three of the themes of the opera: the gay festival music from the third act; a passionate love theme from the fourth act; and the soldiers' song from the last act.

ACT ONE

The courtyard of an inn at Amiens. When the curtain rises on this picturesque old French courtyard the place is thronged with people waiting for the arrival of the stagecoach. A wealthy old roué, Guillot, and De Brétigny, his young friend, enter, accompanied by three flashily dressed girls, Pousette, Javotte, and Rosette. They call for the innkeeper to serve dinner. The proprietor appears and glowingly describes the meal he has prepared for them, and thereby appeases the impatience of his hungry guests. Servants carrying wine and food follow him as the innkeeper escorts the guests into the inn.

A bell rings. It will soon be time for the arrival of the coach, and the townspeople crowd around. Another person arrives—the devil-may-care Lescaut, who is expecting his young cousin Manon to arrive on the stagecoach on her way to a convent school. He is in his brilliant Royal Guard uniform, and with him are a couple of fellow soldiers. Some good-natured banter takes place between Lescaut and his friends as he sends them off to a wineshop for a drink while he waits for his cousin.

The coach arrives. The street is filled with postilions and porters, carrying bags, boxes, and valises, while the passengers bustle about, identifying their baggage, and the townspeople laugh at the fuss and annoyance of traveling.

Among the passengers is Manon, who looks about with astonishment at the commotion. Lescaut sees her and introduces himself. "You are my cousin?" asks Manon. "Come kiss me then." "With pleasure," answers Lescaut, pleased to find her as beautiful and charming as she is unsophisticated. Manon is quite excited over her first journey, which she describes for Lescaut ("Je suis encore tout étourdie"), telling how she left home, a simple country maid, the sights she saw, and how she wept and laughed in her joy, forgetting that she was on her way to the convent. Then she apologizes for chattering so but explains again it is the first time she has traveled. In this pretty, brief aria we get a glimpse of Manon's character: demure, lively, sometimes sad—but not for long—innocent, and entirely incapable of prolonged serious thought.

As she finishes, the departure bell rings, the crowd reassembles, and amid more bustle and confusion the coach departs. The townspeople disperse, leaving Lescaut and Manon together. "Wait here," says Lescaut, "while I find your luggage." He leaves.

Old Guillot appears from the inn, calling to the landlord for more wine. He sees Manon and tries to make love to her, telling her of his wealth and asking for a word of affection. Manon laughs at him and is joined in the laughter by De Brétigny, Pousette, Javotte, and Rosette, who have followed Guillot. They gaily sing to Guillot to come back with them. As he rejoins them he whispers to Manon that a carriage is coming for him. It is at her service to go where she will. Later she will hear more from him.

Lescaut returns just then and Guillot leaves in confusion. Lescaut is concerned a little about Guillot's speaking to Manon but decides he need not worry about her. The other two guardsmen return to take Lescaut off to the wineshop. Telling Manon that he has some duties to perform, he cautions her against making acquaintances with strangers and tells her not to stir from the spot until he returns ("Regardez-moi bien dans les yeux").

Once again Manon waits alone. Presently Pousette, Javotte, and Rosette appear, and Manon looks at them wistfully. "How happy they must be! Their clothes! Their jewels!" Then sadly she laments that she is being sent

away to a convent and must leave the world and its pleasures behind
("Voyons, Manon, plus de chimères").

A young man—handsome, courtly, aristocratic Des Grieux—enters, and
Manon quickly seats herself in the place indicated by her cousin. At first he
does not observe her. He is thinking of his father, whom he will meet tomorrow. Then he sees Manon. He looks with astonishment, then with
delight, as if a vision has appeared to him. He cannot help but approach
and speak to her. "Pardon me, I have never met you and I shouldn't address you, I know, but my heart has always known you. If I knew your
name . . ." "My name is Manon," she answers. This is the beginning of an
ardent love duet ("Et je sais votre nom"). Then she tells him of herself,
that she is not really a bad girl but is told by her family that she loves
pleasure too well and so is being sent to a convent. Des Grieux will not hear
of her going to a living tomb and persuades her to elope with him.

At this moment Guillot's coachman appears. He has been instructed to
follow Manon's orders. Manon tells Des Grieux that the carriage belongs to
an old man who dared to make love to her. She suggests that they take
their revenge by eloping in the carriage. "We will go to Paris together,"
they sing ("Nous vivions à Paris tous les deux"). "Soon my name will be
yours," Des Grieux says tenderly and is about to embrace her, then recovers
himself and begs her pardon. Looking into his eyes, Manon murmurs that
she is eager to go, but still she wonders if it is wrong to do so. Again they
sing of the bright life that awaits them.

The singing and laughing of Guillot's party are heard, then Lescaut's
voice, returning from the wineshop. Manon and Des Grieux hurry off. Lescaut enters. He is in a sour temper, for he has been gambling and has lost
heavily. Now he finds that he has also lost his cousin. Guillot comes out of
the inn, looking for Manon. Lescaut accuses the old man of stealing her. Attracted by the quarrel, the villagers enter. The innkeeper explains that
Manon and the young man drove away—in Guillot's carriage. The crowd
laughs at the trick played on the rich old roué. Lescaut tries to vent his ire
on Guillot, but Guillot is incensed and swears he will have his revenge on
Manon and on this fool, her cousin, too. The curtain descends as the crowd
continues to laugh at Guillot.

ACT TWO

The apartment of Des Grieux and Manon in the Rue Vivienne, Paris. In
this act the waywardness and weakness of Manon's character become evident as she shifts her affections lightly when a life of greater glamour is
offered. As the act opens Manon and Des Grieux are deeply in love.

After a short musical introduction the curtain rises on a simply furnished
room. Des Grieux is seated before a writing table. Manon comes softly
behind him and tries to read what he is writing. Gently reproaching her, he
says he is drafting a letter to his father but is afraid it will be received in
anger, though he writes from his heart. "Let us read it together," suggests
Manon, and then they read the letter, which describes Manon's charms.

"Do you really think he will consent to our marriage?" she asks. "Yes," he answers. They kiss, and then she tells him to post the letter.

As he is about to go out he notices some fresh flowers and inquires about them. "Who gave them to you?" he asks. "I do not know," she answers. "They were thrown in through the window. They were pretty, so I kept them. I hope you are not jealous." "No, I trust your love," he replies tenderly. "And my heart is entirely yours," she says.

Voices are heard outside. There is a loud knocking on the door. A maid enters, quite frightened, explaining that there are two angry men outside in the uniform of guardsmen. One says he is Manon's cousin—and Manon utters under her breath, "Lescaut!" The other, the maid whispers to Manon, says he is someone who loves her—the state official who lives near here. Manon realizes this must be De Brétigny, who has secretly been sending her flowers.

Then the door bursts open and the two men come angrily in. Lescaut demands satisfaction for the abduction of his cousin, but his blustering manner fails to frighten Des Grieux. Finally he asks in a calmer tone if Des Grieux intends to marry Manon. Des Grieux then explains to Lescaut that he has just written to his father for parental approval of the marriage, and he offers to let him read the letter.

The two go over to the window, where the light is better, and this leaves De Brétigny alone with Manon. This is the opportunity he has been looking for. "Why have you come in this disguise?" she demands. "Are you angry?" he asks. "I am," she answers. "You know that I love him." "I wanted to come in person to warn you," he replies. He tells her that Count des Grieux is determined to separate his son from Manon, and that very evening, in accordance with the Count's orders, the young man is to be carried off by force.

Manon at first is horrified and replies that she will certainly warn her love of the danger that threatens him. But De Brétigny answers her by saying that if she does so it will mean miserable poverty for them both, while if she forsakes Des Grieux, a fortune awaits her. He gives her to understand that he, De Brétigny, can offer her a life of luxury and splendor in keeping with her beauty. The temptation is too much for Manon, and although her reply is indefinite, we can see that her loyalty to Des Grieux has begun to waver. In the meantime Lescaut is satisfied with the letter, and he and De Brétigny leave.

Manon speaks to herself of the torment that tears her heart, while Des Grieux murmurs of his supreme happiness. A servant enters and sets the table for supper. Des Grieux, after a few words with Manon, goes out to mail his letter. Manon is left alone. She decides that for his sake she must give him up; she is no longer worthy of him. But she recognizes her own frailty. She hears the tempter's voice, the promise of gay life. What will the future bring? she wonders.

Gradually she approaches the table on which the meal has been spread by the maid. She sings a charming farewell to the little table which seems to symbolize for her the happiness that they have shared and that she is now tempted to renounce ("Adieu, notre petite table").

Des Grieux returns to find her in tears—tears that flow in spite of her best

efforts to conceal them. In an attempt to comfort her he tells of a dream he
has had. In the beautiful and touching aria, *Le Rêve* ("En fermant les
yeux"), he tells of a little cottage in the country; it is paradise, except that
Manon is not there. "It is a dream," she says. "No," he answers, "it is our
life if you wish it."

A low knock is heard at the door. Manon starts guiltily. "Adieu," she says
before she can stop herself, as Des Grieux goes to send the intruder away.
"Adieu?" he asks, puzzled. A wave of emotion prompts her to cry out
to him not to open the door, but Des Grieux, gently releasing himself from
her embrace, goes to open it. A struggle is heard. Manon runs to the window. Overcome with grief and remorse and realizing that now her happy
hours with Des Grieux are gone forever, she sobs, "My poor Chevalier!" as
the curtain falls.

ACT THREE

[*Scene One*]   The promenade of Cours la Reine, Paris. A dainty minuet
introduces this scene. The curtain rises on a festival. Vendors of all kinds
have set up stalls for their wares. There is a pavilion for dancing. A large
crowd, out for a good time, sings, "It is the fête of Cours la Reine! We
laugh, we drink the King's health, for a whole week!"

Pousette and Javotte, coming out of the pavilion, signal to two young
men in the crowd and go to meet them. Rosette joins them. The minuet
which preceded the act is heard again in the distance. The three girls have
escaped momentarily from the jealous eye of Guillot and are thoroughly enjoying themselves. Pousette and Javotte re-enter the pavilion, and Rosette
goes off.

Lescaut now enters. The vendors try to interest him in their wares. Buying until his arms are full, he declares it is enough and, singing a few sentimental lines to a certain Rosalinde, he goes on his way to do a little
gambling.

Pousette, Javotte, and Rosette reappear. This time Guillot sees them, but
they manage to run off, leaving Guillot to rage about women. He has been
keeping three of them, hoping that at least one will be faithful to him. De
Brétigny has entered, and he twits Guillot about his troubles with the girls.
Guillot expresses contempt for all three of them. Sarcastically De Brétigny
begs Guillot not to steal Manon from him. "Enough jesting," says Guillot.
"I hear that you refused to engage the ballet for a performance at Manon's
house, though she begged you with tears flowing." "That's true," answers
De Brétigny. "Excuse me," Guillot begs, and he goes off, rubbing his
hands, stating that he is about to steal Manon.

The crowd sings gaily of beautiful young women who do nothing, but
who rule the hearts of men. Manon enters. She is recognized by people in
the crowd, and her name is passed around. De Brétigny and several young
men gather around her, paying her compliments. She sings frivolously of
the happy life she leads, every whim satisfied, every desire granted, ready
even to die with laughter on her lips ("Je marche sur tous les chemins").
The crowd cheers, and Manon sings the famous *Gavotte*, in which she

voices her philosophy that life is made for love, laughter, and song, and that we should enjoy these things before the years weigh too heavily upon us ("Obéissons quand leur voix appelle").[1] The crowd takes up the song.

Manon moves off toward the stalls, part of the crowd following her. Count des Grieux enters and is greeted by De Brétigny. The Count tells De Brétigny he has come to Paris to see his son. "The chevalier?" inquires De Brétigny. "Not Chevalier now, but Abbé des Grieux," answers the elder Grieux. "He has entered the Seminary of St. Sulpice." "I am astonished," De Brétigny exclaims, smiling. "What a change!" "It is you who did it," answers the Count, also smiling, "by coming between him and his love." "Speak lower," De Brétigny requests, indicating Manon, who has been coming closer. "I see now why you were so interested in my son's affairs," the Count answers, looking at Manon. He bows and moves away a short distance.

Manon approaches De Brétigny and tells him she has been trying to match the bracelet she is wearing. "I will look for one myself," he replies, and walks off toward the stalls. With De Brétigny out of the way, Manon speaks to the Count. She asks about his son, telling him she is interested because he once loved a friend of hers. (As they talk strains of the minuet are heard in the distance.) She asks how he has borne the separation. Did he ever speak her name? The Count says his son suffered in silence. Does he ever blame her? she asks. No, he assures her, and now his heart is light again; he has learned the lesson every wise man should know: One can forget. "One can forget," she repeats sorrowfully. The Count leaves.

The crowd returns. De Brétigny, Lescaut, and Guillot enter. Guillot has brought with him the ballet to perform, hoping by this favor to win Manon away from De Brétigny. The ballet dances and then mingles with the crowd. Poor Guillot's gallantry is unrewarded, as Manon has been preoccupied during the performance and has seen nothing. She speaks to herself: "No, his life and mine are forever bound. He cannot have forgotten me." Calling for her sedan chair, she gives orders to be taken to St. Sulpice.

As she leaves, the crowd is singing again of the festival of Cours la Reine, and the curtain comes down.

[*Scene Two*]   A reception room of the Seminary of St. Sulpice. An organ is heard in the distance as the curtain rises. The room is filled with people who have just heard the young Abbé des Grieux deliver a sermon, and as they pass on their way out of the seminary they praise his eloquence and his saintly bearing. The elder Des Grieux appears, then the son. The visitors leave. The Count is just as much opposed to his son's becoming a priest as he was to his infatuation with Manon. He tells him he is too young to know life, and pleads with him to marry some worthy girl and go out to face the world. But all the Count's protests have no effect on the young man, who repeats, "Nothing shall prevent me from taking my vows." "Very well," the Count answers, "I shall go and tell everyone we have a saint in the family, though it is doubtful I shall be believed." "Do not mock me, I pray," the

[1] In some presentations the Cours la Reine festival scene is omitted and Manon's *Gavotte* is sung in the Hôtel de Transylvanie scene in Act Four.

son pleads. "One word more," the Count adds. "Since it is not certain that you will be an abbot tomorrow, I am sending you thirty thousand francs. It is a legacy from your mother. Adieu."

Finding himself alone, Des Grieux fervently declares his renunciation, declaring that he will now seek the peace of mind that only heaven can give ("Je suis seul! seul enfin!"). But even at this moment he cannot drive the memory of Manon completely from his mind. He cries out to her image to leave him ("Ah! fuyez douce image").

The sound of an organ is heard in the distance, and a porter arrives to tell Des Grieux it is the hour of service, whereupon he leaves. Almost immediately a veiled figure appears at the outside door. It is Manon. She has left De Brétigny and has come to dissuade Des Grieux from his course of action, which will separate them forever. She asks the porter for the Abbé des Grieux, giving him some money. The porter leaves to find him.

Manon, waiting alone, is greatly affected by the sacred surroundings. In the distance a choir begins to chant a Magnificat. Manon herself prays. By the time Des Grieux comes in she is in a thoroughly repentant mood and tells him tearfully how cruel she was to him and how much she was to blame. Des Grieux is taken aback at seeing her there but tells her coldly his love for her is now dead and that he has banished her forever from his memory. But Manon's charm and fascination begin to have their effect, and as she pleads with him he cries out, "O God, sustain me in this supreme moment!" She tells him she loves him. He replies that those words in such surroundings are blasphemy. But she continues to plead with him, and at last he admits he can no longer struggle against her, that he loves her as much as ever. He takes her in his arms as the music rises to an impassioned climax, and the curtain falls.

ACT FOUR

Hôtel de Transylvanie, a fashionable but notorious gambling house in Paris. The scene is a large, sumptuous, and elegantly furnished hall, decorated profusely with gilt and brilliantly lighted. Scattered around the room are gaming tables, each surrounded by a group of gamblers, while other fashionably dressed men and women are gathered in groups.

We find Lescaut at one of the tables. Also present are Pousette, Javotte, and Rosette. Lescaut wins and sings merrily of his luck. The three actresses sing of the delights of the gambling hall. Guillot comes in. Now Manon arrives with Des Grieux and is joyously greeted by her friends, with the exception of the wealthy old Guillot, who is none too pleased to see Manon with another. They have lost their fortune, and the young nobleman has been persuaded by Manon to come there in the hope of winning it back. He does not like the idea of gambling. But he is still madly in love with Manon, and his poverty is not at all to her liking. He has good reason to worry that her love might turn elsewhere unless he is able to regain his fortune. She urges him on to gamble.

Lescaut also brings pressure to bear as he points out that Manon does not like poverty. He promises Des Grieux that he shall have beginner's luck. Manon pledges her everlasting love. Guillot, too, adds his voice, offering to see if he is always to lose to Des Grieux. Des Grieux sits down to a game with Guillot—and in the meantime Manon abandons herself to the gaiety of the place. She sings of the joys of youth and the music of gold ("Ce bruit de l'or rire et ses éclats joyeux").[2]

Des Grieux finds fortune running in his favor and wins again and again. Guillot becomes more and more bitter at his losses and ends by accusing Des Grieux of cheating. Des Grieux attacks the old man, but the crowd separates them, calling on them to act as gentlemen. "I take you as witnesses," cries Guillot to the assemblage; then, to Manon and Des Grieux: "As for you two, you will soon hear from me." He stalks off.

Lescaut calls for quiet; the croupiers attempt to start up the games; the people speak excitedly of cheating and point to Des Grieux. Manon has become nervous and urges Des Grieux to leave with her, but he replies that if he should leave at this point the others would believe Guillot's accusation justified.

Then a loud knock is heard at the door. The gamblers hide the money. A voice outside calls, "Open—in the King's name!" Lescaut runs out, calling to the others to escape. In comes Guillot, followed by a police officer and several guards.

Guillot points to Des Grieux, saying, "The guilty one is this gentleman," and then, turning to Manon, adds, "And here is his accomplice." To Manon he says, "My regrets, mademoiselle. I told you I would have my revenge." And to Des Grieux: "I have trumped your card, my master. Console yourself if you can." "I will begin by throwing you from the window," answers Des Grieux.

Count des Grieux has entered unobserved. "And I," he asks his son, "will you throw me out also?" When young Des Grieux sees his father standing before him he feels nothing but shame. The Count tells his son he has come to save him from his folly and protect the honor of his family. As Manon sees that her happiness is at an end young Des Grieux pleads for mercy from his father, and the assemblage begs pity for Manon. Guillot gloats; his revenge is complete. Count des Grieux tells everyone he has decided to let justice take its course. He orders the police officer to lead both Des Grieux and Manon away. He adds in an undertone to his son that he will arrange his release soon. When the Chevalier asks what will happen to Manon, Guillot tells him she will go where women of her kind are sent. On hearing this, Des Grieux, in a rage, shouts at them to stand off—he'll defend her. They disarm him, while Manon is seized by the guards. The spectators, touched by her youth and beauty, beg for her release. Manon, fainting, cries, "It is the end. I am dying," while Des Grieux cries out in despair as the curtain falls.

[2] It is at this point that Manon's *Gavotte* ("Obéissons quand leur voix appelle") is sung when the Cours la Reine festival scene is omitted.

ACT FIVE

A lonely spot on the road to Le Havre.[3] After a brief prelude the curtain rises on a dreary stretch of highway. We see a few wind-beaten trees and a mound on which some weeds are struggling for existence. The sea is in the distance. It is evening. Des Grieux, sitting alone beside the road, is desolate at the thought of Manon in chains, among a vanload of prisoners about to be transported to a penal colony. It is along this road the prison van will pass on its way to the port. He has planned to help Manon escape and has arranged with Lescaut to have a force of armed men in hiding to rescue her from the soldiers. But his hopes are dashed to the ground when Lescaut appears and informs him that the men he had hired had run away as soon as they saw the armed soldiers. Des Grieux is incensed and will not believe it.

In the distance the soldiers are heard singing as they draw near. Des Grieux, in desperation, would attack alone, but he is restrained by the more prudent Lescaut, who drags him away. They hide just off the road as a sergeant and a soldier appear, and hear the soldiers speak of the prisoners, saying that one is sick unto death. They mention her name—Manon. Des Grieux is overcome with emotion.

Lescaut takes Des Grieux's purse and steps out. He hails the sergeant and tells him he would like to talk for a moment to Manon, as they are of the same family. The sergeant says it is impossible, but Lescaut gives him some money. The sergeant takes the soldiers away, leaving one with Lescaut. With a little more money Lescaut leads the remaining soldier away, leaving the field clear for Des Grieux.

Manon soon stumbles down the road—a truly pitiful figure, shabbily dressed, footsore, disheveled, hardly more than a ghost of her former self. She cries with joy, however, on seeing Des Grieux and falls in his arms. "You are weeping," he says as they enter the closing duet ("O Manon! Manon! Manon! Tu pleures!"). He tries to comfort her and pictures a happy life with her in some distant country to which they will flee. But Manon knows that her repentance has come too late; she reproaches herself for not having appreciated the loyal affection of Des Grieux. Then, tenderly, as in a dream, she recalls the days they spent together: the inn, the coach, the letter to his father, the little table, the robe he wore when she found him at St. Sulpice.

Joyfully Des Grieux urges Manon to flee with him, for the guard is out of sight and it is night. But it is too late. Her mind wanders amid her dreams. She becomes more and more feeble. Death steals slowly over her like sleep. "Cradle me in your arms," she says. And finally, "It had to be this way—and this is the story of Manon Lescaut." As she falls lifeless, Des Grieux utters a distracted cry and bends over her, sobbing, while the curtain descends.

[3] Written originally as Scene Two of Act Four, this concluding scene is now usually given as a separate act.

Manon Lescaut

by GIACOMO PUCCINI

[1858–1924]

Libretto by the Composer with the aid of
DOMENICO OLIVA, MARCO PRAGA, GIUSEPPE GIACOSA,
LUIGI ILLICA, *and* GIULIO RICORDI

Based on the Abbé Prévost's story
LES AVENTURES DU CHEVALIER DES GRIEUX ET MANON LESCAUT

CHARACTERS

Edmondo, a young student...*Tenor*
Chevalier des Grieux...*Tenor*
Lescaut, sergeant of the King's guards, brother of Manon.........*Baritone*
Geronte de Ravoir, an elderly Parisian gallant.....................*Bass*
Manon Lescaut ....*Soprano*
Innkeeper ....*Baritone*
Dancing master ....*Tenor*
Lamplighter ....*Tenor*
Captain ....*Baritone*

Students, townspeople, singers, dancers, sailors, soldiers, courtesans,
ladies and gentlemen, police, guards

Place: Amiens, Paris, Le Havre, New Orleans
Time: Eighteenth century
First performance: Teatro Reggio, Turin, February 1, 1893
Original language: Italian

MANON LESCAUT and Massenet's *Manon,* both musical settings of Abbé Prévost's tragic story of a pleasure-loving beauty of Paris, have, of course, the same central characters. Puccini's work, however, adheres more closely to the original, with its four acts being, in effect, separate episodes. The opera was Puccini's first outstanding success.

ACT ONE

The curtain rises during the playing of a spirited prelude. We see an inn on a square in Amiens, with a road leading off toward the rear. In front of the inn are tables and chairs. An outside staircase leads to the second floor. The square is filled with students, townspeople, and soldiers. Some are seated at the tables, drinking and playing cards. Edmondo and his companions sing a gay chorus ("Ave, sera gentile, che discendi"). Des Grieux enters, and they invite him to join them, but he at first declines. When they tease him about being unhappy over a love affair he replies with a mock-serious serenade to the girls, "Tra voi, belle," which is heartily applauded. The chorus continues to a sparkling climax.

Lescaut, Geronte, and Manon arrive in the coach from Arras. Manon's beauty brings admiring comments from Des Grieux, Edmondo, and the students. She seats herself at a table, while Geronte and Lescaut go up to their rooms with the innkeeper. Des Grieux approaches, gallantly presents himself, and begins paying her ardent compliments. When she sadly informs him that she is on her way to enter a convent he protests that one so young and beautiful should not be secluded from the world. Their conversation is cut short when Lescaut appears on the balcony and calls to Manon. As she leaves she promises Des Grieux to meet him later. The Chevalier rhapsodizes over her beauty and charm in a fervent aria, "Donna non vidi mai."

Edmondo and the students, who have been watching the scene from a distance, now approach and twit Des Grieux about his love-making. He brushes them aside impatiently and hurries away. As students and girls resume their card playing at the tables Geronte and Lescaut come down the stairs talking about Manon. In answer to Geronte's queries about her Lescaut explains that he is duty-bound to take her to a convent in Paris. After an exchange of complimentary remarks Lescaut invites Geronte to have a drink. He is about to accept, then suddenly excuses himself, saying he wishes to give some orders to the innkeeper. He goes toward the inn as Lescaut joins the cardplayers.

Summoning the innkeeper, Geronte hands him a purse and whispers that he wishes a coach and fast horses ready for departure to Paris within an hour. He also inquires about a rear exit from the inn, and the innkeeper takes him inside to show him. Edmondo, suspicious of Geronte's action, meanwhile has approached and has overheard the conversation. Just as Geronte goes inside Des Grieux appears, and Edmondo tells him what he has heard and suggests that they circumvent the elderly gallant's plans.

While they are talking Manon appears on the balcony and sees Des Grieux. A long and ardent duet follows, beginning with her words of greeting, "Vedete? Io son fedele." Des Grieux responds in impassioned phrases and then reveals that Geronte is plotting to abduct her to Paris. He implores her to flee with him instead. Edmondo approaches and tells them that the carriage is ready. Manon at first objects to the Chevalier's fantastic proposal but finally yields to his fervent pleas. Followed by Edmondo, they rush for the carriage, which is waiting behind the inn.

Geronte appears. Satisfying himself that Lescaut is occupied with playing cards, he looks about for Manon. Edmondo enters and, pointing down the road, laughingly tells Geronte that Manon is already on the way to Paris with the young Chevalier—in the carriage he himself ordered. Furiously Geronte rushes up to Lescaut, tears him away from his cards, and demands that he go in pursuit of his sister. Embarrassed by the derisive comments of Edmondo and the students, Lescaut takes Geronte aside and tries to calm him. He points out that a man of his wealth can easily persuade the luxury-loving Manon to give up her love for a romantic but poverty-stricken student such as Des Grieux. The two go into the inn as the mocking chorus of the students ends in a burst of laughter. The curtain falls.

ACT TWO

Manon's richly appointed room in Geronte's house. True to her brother's prediction, she has yielded to the lure of Geronte's money and has deserted Des Grieux. She is seen seated at her dressing table, attended by a hairdresser. Lescaut enters and gazes at her admiringly. In an appropriately pompous refrain ("Sei splendida e lucente") he compliments himself on having provided Manon with a rich lover in place of the indigent Des Grieux. In an answering air ("In quelle trine morbide") Manon sings that all this luxury cannot replace the passionate devotion of the man she really loves. Thereupon Lescaut tells her that Des Grieux may soon return to her, for he has been taught how to win at the gambling table and may be able to improve his fortunes. Manon expresses her happiness and longing, and the two voices blend in a melodious duet.

A group of singers, engaged by Geronte for Manon's entertainment, now enter and sing a charming madrigal ("Sulla vetta tu del monte"). Manon, bored, dismisses them and turns to welcome a group of aged gallants—friends of Geronte—who have come to pay their respects. Geronte himself enters with a dancing master, and Manon dances a minuet to the great delight of the guests, who praise her in chorus. Carried away by the excitement of the moment, Manon voices her joy in a brilliant refrain ("Lora, o Tirsi"). Geronte and his friends applaud her, then leave for another party, urging her to join them later.

As she prepares to go Des Grieux enters. He answers her ardent greetings with bitter reproach, and a long dramatic duet follows. She is so eloquent and alluring in her entreaties for his forgiveness that his accusation of faithlessness soon changes to fervent declarations of love. The duet rises to a magnificent climax, ending with impressive effect on a pianissimo phrase.

Geronte suddenly returns and finds the lovers in each other's arms. With sardonic gallantry he apologizes for intruding, then coldly rebukes Manon for her fickleness and ingratitude. She taunts him with impudent gaiety. Geronte takes his leave, warning Des Grieux that they will meet again.

Des Grieux implores Manon to flee with him at once, but she is loath to part with her jewels and finery. Lescaut suddenly enters, exclaiming that Geronte has denounced Manon to the police as a wanton woman and that they are coming to arrest her. When Des Grieux frantically begs her to hurry she loses valuable time in gathering up her jewelry and concealing it in her cloak. Outside the police are heard entering the house. Manon locks the door, crying out that they can escape by the alcove, but as they rush toward it three police officers step out from behind the curtains and bar their way. At that moment Geronte and a number of soldiers break open the door. Panic-stricken, Manon drops her cloak, scattering the jewels over the floor. Geronte laughs in malevolent triumph as the police drag Manon away. Des Grieux whips out his sword but is restrained by Lescaut, who warns him that if he is imprisoned no one will be left to help Manon. As Des Grieux distractedly cries out her name the curtain falls.

ACT THREE

A strikingly beautiful prelude recalls the themes of the love duet in the preceding act. The curtain rises on a street near the harbor at Le Havre. A ship at anchor is partly visible in the background, and beyond it is the sea. In the foreground is the corner of a barracks with a barred window. Here Manon has been imprisoned, awaiting deportation to America, along with other outcast women. Guards walk back and forth. It is nearly dawn. Lescaut, talking with Des Grieux in the street outside, tells him of his plan to free Manon, saying he has bribed the guard who is soon to go on duty.

The guard who comes to take over presently moves out of sight at a signal from Lescaut, who then cautiously approaches the window and knocks on the bars. When Manon appears Lescaut hurries away and Des Grieux rushes to the window. Manon reaches out her hands to him, and he kisses them ardently, swearing he will never leave her. He conceals himself in the shadows as the lamplighter appears, singing a rather plaintive tune about a maiden who sold her heart to a king ("E Kate rispose al Re"). The lamplighter gone, Des Grieux tells Manon to be ready when Lescaut returns to release her. The next moment Lescaut comes running in, crying to Des Grieux to save himself because the escape plot has been discovered. Both men rush off down the street. Shouts and sounds of gunfire are heard, and soon the space in front of the barracks is filled with an excited throng.

A detachment of soldiers appears, escorting to the ship the women who are to be deported. With them is Manon. As the roll is called the women line up one by one in front of a guard of marines from the ship. There is an interesting chorale interlude as the onlookers comment on the prisoners, some of whom are defiant, some weeping. Des Grieux, beside himself with grief, approaches as closely as possible to Manon, who heartbrokenly bids him farewell.

When a guard finally pushes Manon toward the ship, Des Grieux, in sudden desperation, tries to free her from his grasp. While they are struggling the ship's captain appears. Des Grieux turns to him, and in a dramatic refrain ("Guardate, pazzo son") he begs to be allowed to sail with Manon, offering to serve as a crew member or even as a menial for the privilege of accompanying her into exile. Moved by his earnest entreaties, the captain consents to take him along. Manon, who has turned to watch the scene, is overwhelmed with joy. Des Grieux rushes into her arms as the curtain falls.

ACT FOUR

A desolate spot on the borders of the French possession of New Orleans. Night is approaching. Manon and Des Grieux, who fled after having landed from the prison ship, have sought refuge in the wilderness. Their clothing is soiled and torn. Des Grieux half carries Manon, who is exhausted and ill from the ordeal. They sing a long and moving duet ("Tutta su me ti sposa"), in which Manon gives way to remorse over the grief and shame that her thoughtless selfishness has brought upon her lover and herself. She implores Des Grieux to leave her to die alone and to save himself, but he declares that he will never part from her.

Finally Manon, overwhelmed by pain and despair, sinks to the ground, urging Des Grieux to go on in search of help and shelter. He hurries off, while Manon, alone in the gathering darkness, voices her terror and hopelessness in a dramatic refrain ("Sola, perduta, abbandonata"). Des Grieux, having searched in vain, returns to find her dying. He takes her in his arms, crying that he will perish with her. Whispering that time will blot out her sins but not her love, Manon expires. Des Grieux collapses at her side. The curtain falls.

Martha

by FRIEDRICH von FLOTOW

[1812–1883]

Libretto by
FRIEDRICH WILHELM RIESE

Based on the Marquis St. George's ballet
LADY HARRIETTE, OU LA SERVANTE DE GREENWICH

CHARACTERS

Lady Harriet, maid of honor to Queen Anne.................... *Soprano*
Nancy, her maid.. *Contralto*
Sir Tristram Mickleford, Lady Harriet's cousin.................... *Bass*
Plunkett, a young farmer................................... *Baritone*
Lionel, his foster brother.................................... *Tenor*
The sheriff of Richmond.................................... *Bass*
Ladies and gentlemen of the court, ladies in waiting, servant girls, farmers

Place: Richmond, England
Time: Eighteenth century, during the reign of Queen Anne
First performance: Imperial Opera House, Vienna, November 25, 1847
Original language: German

MARTHA has been popular on the operatic stage for a hundred years, and its tunes are known the world over. Although it was written by a German, the lightness and elegance of the music are more characteristic of the French school, reflecting the fact that Von Flotow received most of his musical training in Paris. The opera is equally well known in its French, Italian, and English versions.

The overture begins with a rather somber theme and then takes up the sweeping melody of the ensemble at the end of the third act. This is followed by the gay rhythms of some of the country dances heard in the opera. The overture concludes with a repetition, in full orchestra, of the theme of the third act finale.

ACT ONE

[*Scene One*] Lady Harriet's boudoir in Richmond Castle. Attended by Nancy and her ladies in waiting, Harriet is seated at her dressing table. Although young, beautiful, and the darling of the court, Harriet is bored, restless, and unhappy. The women sing a chorus in which they urge her to drive away her melancholy by taking part in the gay whirl of court pleasures ("Darf mit nächtig düstren Träumen"). Nancy shows her the flowers and jewelry Sir Tristram has sent her, but Harriet impatiently tells her maid to take them away. She finally asks the ladies to leave her, saying she is willing to share her joys with them, but not her unhappiness. After repeating the refrain of their chorus, the ladies retire, leaving Harriet and Nancy alone.

Nancy avers that perhaps her mistress is sad because she is in love and then asks if she is pining for one of the courtiers ("Von den edlen Kavalieren"). This introduces a long and melodious duet. Harriet answers that it is not love but sheer boredom that is making her unhappy. The glitter and gaiety of the court and the adulation of the cavaliers mean nothing to her. Nancy opines that the only cure for Her Ladyship's particular malady is a lover. The duet ends in a brilliant vocal display.

The servants announce Sir Tristram Mickleford. He is an aging peer who still fancies himself a great favorite with the ladies, particularly Lady Harriet. Greeting her with elaborate pomposity, Sir Tristram requests the pleasure of her company at the cockfights or the donkey races. Harriet replies that neither interests her. The dialogue continues in the form of a lively trio ("Ha! der Narrheit"). Harriet and Nancy sing mockingly of Sir Tristram's foolish attempts at gallantry and wish that he would leave them alone. Sir Tristram, mistaking Harriet's aversion to his company for maidenly shyness, complacently assumes that she is falling in love with him. Harriet keeps him bustling about the room, opening and closing windows, bringing her smelling salts, and so on, until at last he falls exhausted into a chair.

At the conclusion of the trio a group of country girls pass by outside, singing a merry chorus about the fair ("Wohlgemuth, junges Blut"). Harriet, envying their carefree spirit, asks who they are. Nancy explains that they are servant girls on their way to the Richmond Fair, where, according to the old custom, they will offer their services to the farmers for a year. Harriet remarks that she would like to go to the fair and mingle incognito with the people. The idea is so appealing that she decides then and there to do so. She and Nancy will put on the peasant costumes they wore at the recent ball, while Sir Tristram will disguise himself as a country squire. When Sir Tristram fumes that he, a peer, certainly cannot be a party to such antics, Harriet soon brings him into line by pouting that he does not love her enough. She and Nancy then put him through the steps of a country dance. He cuts a comic figure as he tries to follow the ladies and maintain his dignity at the same time. The "rehearsal" over, Harriet and Nancy, with the protesting Sir Tristram between them, run gaily from the room.

[Scene Two] The fair at Richmond. An excited throng is milling about in front of the gaily decorated tents and booths. The farmers begin a lusty chorus in which they urge the servant girls to appear at their best when the bidding for them begins ("Mädchen, brav und treu"). The girls join them in singing about the traditional terms of the agreement—if the maid accepts the fee offered by the farmer, then the bargain is concluded and she must abide by it for a year. The chorus builds up into a rousing climax as the crowd hails the opening of the fair. At its conclusion the people gradually leave the scene.

Lionel and Plunkett appear. They are discussing the selection of a serving maid. It was their mother's wish, Plunkett says, that the farm be maintained in good circumstances. The men speak of the mother with tenderness
and affection. Plunkett recalls that he, as the stronger of the two, bore the
brunt of boyhood punishments, while Lionel, the foster son, was treated
more gently. He affectionately assures Lionel of his protection and loyalty,
and Lionel expresses his gratitude in a moving refrain ("Ja, seit früher
Kindheit Tagen"). He recalls how his father, exiled, friendless, and ill,
brought him to Plunkett's home. Taking up the story, Plunkett relates that
the father found shelter there until he died, never revealing his name or
past. Before he died he placed on his son's hand a ring, telling him that
when danger threatened he was to show it to the Queen, who would know
what it meant. The voices of the two men blend melodiously as they sing
that they will be guided by a father's wish and will always be loyal to each
other.

Their talk is interrupted as the farmers and servant girls return, all excitedly welcoming the sheriff of Richmond, who is to preside over the bidding
and hiring. With a great show of ceremony he unrolls a scroll and announces the rules in the name of Queen Anne. The people signify that they
understand, and then the sheriff begins calling the girls by name—"Molly
Pitt, Polly Smith, Kitty Bell, Liddy Well, Nelly Box, Sally Fox." He bids
them stand before the crowd and state their qualifications. In solo interludes the girls answer that they can cook and bake and sew, turn the churn,
run the mill, take care of the animals—in fact, there is no farm work they
cannot do ("Ich kann nähen, ich kann mähen"). Bidding begins and the
servants respond. As the farmers and servants crowd around the sheriff all
the voices blend in a stirring ensemble.

Meanwhile, Lady Harriet, Nancy, and Sir Tristram come forward and are
noticed by Lionel and Plunkett, who remark on the attractiveness of the
two servant girls. Sir Tristram bridles when he sees the two farmers staring
at his companions and is all for leaving at once. In a sudden impulse of
deviltry Harriet pretends that Sir Tristram is trying to force her and Nancy
into his service. She begins protesting loudly, whereupon Lionel and Plunkett approach and warn Sir Tristram not to deal roughly with the girls.
The argument attracts a crowd, and soon the other servant girls are pressing around Sir Tristram, shrilly offering their services.

His efforts to extricate himself from the situation are gleefully observed
by Harriet, Nancy, and the farmers and their wives. They voice their
amusement in a continuation of the chorus. Finally Plunkett and Lionel
pluck up enough courage to approach Harriet and Nancy, but are speechless with embarrassment. The four express their reactions in a pleasing
quartet ("Oh! fürwahr! wohl sah ich selten"). The women sing that such
diffidence is indeed rare among the males of their acquaintance, while the
men marvel over the beauty and grace of these prospective servants.

Having recovered from their first shyness, Lionel and Plunkett begin
discussing the work that will be expected of the girls. Indicating Harriet,
Plunkett declares that she can take charge of cleaning the house and the
stables, while her friend can do the cooking and the gardening. Lionel, already struck by Harriet's refined manner, protests that she seems much too

delicate for such heavy work. Plunkett concedes that perhaps she can do the gardening. He tells the women that their wages will be fifty crowns a year, porter to drink on Sundays, and plum pudding on New Year's. Harriet and Nancy lightheartedly agree, accept the fee from the men, and then all four join in a continuation of the quartet.

Sir Tristram appears, still besieged by servant girls, whom he finally quiets by giving them money. Harriet and Nancy, assuming that the afternoon's diversion is at an end, bid the two farmers good-by and start to leave with Sir Tristram. Stepping in their path, Lionel and Plunkett remind them that they accepted the hiring fee and are therefore bound to their new employers. When they protest that they thought it all a joke the men call the sheriff, who repeats the rules for their benefit. Crowding around, the farmers and the servant girls sing a lively chorus, the burden of which is that a bargain is a bargain and that the women have no choice but to comply. Lionel and Plunkett lead the crestfallen Harriet and Nancy to their wagon, while the farmers forcibly prevent Sir Tristram from going to their aid. The chorus comes to a climax as Lionel and Plunkett drive off with their new servants. Sir Tristram struggles with the crowd as the curtain falls.

ACT TWO

The interior of Plunkett's farmhouse. The entrance is at the back and there are doors at either side. Various household objects are seen about, and two spinning wheels are in the corner of the room. It is evening. Lionel and Plunkett come in, followed by Harriet and Nancy, who are thoroughly tired and somewhat frightened. The men tell them that they must go to bed early, for their new tasks will begin at dawn. Before dismissing them Plunkett asks their names. Harriet replies that she is "Martha," while Nancy says her name is "Julia." Looking tenderly at Harriet, Lionel softly repeats her name. Plunkett, however, growls that "Julia" is much too grand a name for a servant girl. Handing her his coat and hat, he orders her to put them away. Nancy promptly drops them on the floor. Plunkett blusters indignantly, while Lionel urges him to treat the girls with more consideration. With that he holds out his hat to Harriet and courteously asks her to take it. She favors him with a disdainful stare. Lionel now joins Plunkett in expressing his astonishment over the unruly behavior of these servants ("Was soll ich dazu sagen?"). This leads into another ensemble, in which all four voice surprise and indignation.

Plunkett then asks the girls to demonstrate their ability with the spinning wheels. Harriet and Nancy laugh merrily over the idea, whereupon Plunkett loses his temper and roars at them to bring the spindles. Frightened into obedience, the women bring the spinning wheels forward. Lionel, helping them, urges Plunkett to be calm. Sitting down at the wheels, Harriet and Nancy awkwardly try to spin as directed by the men. They prove so hopelessly inept that Plunkett impatiently pushes Nancy aside, sits down at the wheel and begins to demonstrate the art of spinning. Lionel sits down at Harriet's wheel and patiently explains the procedure to her.

Now follows the famous *Spinning Quartet* ("Immer munter dreht das Rädchen"). To an accompaniment imitating the rhythmic motion of the treadle, the four sing about the golden thread winding itself on the spindle. At the conclusion of the number Nancy deliberately knocks over her spinning wheel and runs from the room, with Plunkett at her heels.

Harriet tries to run after her but is gently restrained by Lionel. Turning away from him, she muses that she feels a strange misgiving about being alone with this kind and chivalrous young man ("Blickt sein Auge doch so ehrlich"). Her refrain leads into a long and impassioned duet. Lionel also finds himself stirred by strange emotions, and in another moment he is telling Harriet that he loves her. She teasingly remarks that he is much too gentle to be a master and that she is much too contrary to be a servant. Assuring her that he will never ask her to do anything more than sing and enjoy herself, Lionel entreats her to sing for him now. As he impulsively takes from her the rose she is wearing Harriet decides to sing the song she loves best, *The Last Rose of Summer*.[1]

Swept away by the song, Lionel completely dumfounds Harriet by asking her to be his wife, assuring her that he will forget that she is a servant and will look upon her as his equal. The irony of the situation brings a burst of mocking laughter from Harriet. Lionel, deeply hurt, is so fervent and sincere in expressing his wounded feelings that she is overcome with remorse. As Lionel resigns himself to being parted from her forever, Harriet confesses to herself that it will be difficult to say farewell. These sentiments are expressed in the passionate climax of the duet.

As they stand gazing sadly at each other Plunkett comes in, dragging Nancy by the arm. Both are angry and out of breath. Nancy answers defiantly as Plunkett fumes at her for her impudence. Just as he orders both the women to go to bed the clock strikes twelve. There is a sudden change of mood as the four say good night in the lovely quartet known as the *Notturno* ("Schlafe wohl! und mag Dich reuen"). Their differences momentarily forgotten, they sing of the tender emotions stirring in their hearts. Lionel and Plunkett now lock the entrance door and then retire to their own rooms.

No sooner have they gone than Harriet and Nancy discuss ways of escaping. Harriet frets over what the Queen will say when she hears of this escapade. At that moment there is a knock at the window, and Sir Tristram's face appears. Nancy opens the window and he climbs in, informing the women that he has a carriage waiting to take them back to the castle. Pausing briefly to sing good-by to the house that threatened to become their prison, Harriet and Nancy, aided by Sir Tristram, leave via the window. Then comes the sound of carriage wheels and hoofbeats.

A moment later Plunkett is heard calling to the girls that it is time to get up. He suddenly bursts into the room, followed by Lionel. Seeing that Martha and Julia have gone, Plunkett shouts that his new servants have absconded. He roars for his other servants, and when they crowd into the room he offers a pound reward for the capture of the runaways. Lionel, distracted over the thought that Martha has spurned him, rushes out. Plunkett

[1] This is an old Irish air, *The Groves of Blarney*, adapted to Tom Moore's poem.

and his servants sing a lively chorus, declaring that they will leave no stone unturned in their search for the fugitives ("Ruh't nicht, bis sie gefunden"). The curtain falls.

ACT THREE

A rustic inn in Richmond Park. Plunkett and a group of farmers, sitting at a table drinking porter, strike up a lusty chorus in praise of British ale ("Lasst mich euch fragen"). At the conclusion of the chorus hunting horns are heard in the distance. Plunkett informs the others that the Queen is hunting in the park today. He and the men go into the inn.

Nancy appears with a group of ladies dressed in hunting costumes and carrying spears. They sing a brief chorus in which they discuss the hunt in terms of amorous conquest ("Auch wir Frauen, wir kennen"). Nancy elaborates on these sentiments in an amusing ditty about Cupid's unpredictable ways ("Jägerin, schlau im Sinn"). After the number Plunkett comes out of the inn and recognizes Nancy. Addressing her as "Julia," he indignantly asks what she is doing in the royal park in hunting clothes. She haughtily tells him to go on his way. When he tries to force her to come along with him she calls to her companions. Surrounding him, the ladies point their spears at him and sing that they will soon dispose of this intruder ("an dem Frechen lasst uns rächen"). Plunkett finally breaks away and runs, with Nancy and the other ladies at his heels.

Lionel now wanders in. Gazing mournfully at Harriet's rose, which he holds in his hand, he sings a fragment of *The Last Rose of Summer*. Musing that he saw his beloved in a dream, he pours out his loneliness and despair in the famous aria, "Ach! so fromm," better known by its Italian title of "M'appari tutt'amor."[2] In its concluding phrases he dramatically implores Martha to return to him. Throwing himself down on a grassy bank, he abandons himself to sad reflection.

Unseen by Lionel, Harriet and Sir Tristram approach. Harriet, moody and restless, soon makes it clear to Sir Tristram that she wishes to be alone. When he leaves she voices her thoughts about Lionel and her love for him in a wistful refrain ("Hier in stillen Schattengründen"). Lionel, becoming aware of her presence, turns and gasps as he sees his erstwhile servant in the garb of a fine lady. He addresses her as "Martha" and fervently thanks her for returning to him. Determined not to yield to her feelings, Harriet replies scornfully to his fervent protestations of love. Goaded to anger by her disdainful manner, Lionel finally declares that she is his servant and that she must obey her master.

When he tries to detain her she calls for help. Sir Tristram, who has been wandering about nearby, comes running up. He is followed shortly by the men and women of the hunting party. They threaten Lionel with dire punishment for daring to invade the royal park to molest a lady of quality. Harriet and Lionel meanwhile are in despair over the misunderstandings that have developed.

[2] The composer "borrowed" this aria from one of his earlier operas, *L'Ame en Peine*.

At the height of the dispute Plunkett and Nancy appear. The supposed servant girls and their masters stare at each other in utter bewilderment. When Sir Tristram orders Lionel to be seized the young man heatedly insists that the two women were hired as his servants at the fair and that they are bound to him by law. With a sarcastic laugh Harriet asks her friends to forgive this ranting young man—as she herself is willing to do—because he obviously has gone mad.

At that Lionel turns on her and in a sweeping phrase bitterly reproaches her for her mockery and deceit ("Mag der Himmel Euch vergeben"). This introduces the highly dramatic ensemble which concludes the act. In a choral repetition of the refrain sung by Lionel all comment on the unhappy situation. After a stirring climax there is a fanfare of hunting horns announcing the approach of the Queen. Suddenly remembering his ring, Lionel quickly gives it to Plunkett and tells him to take it to the Queen. Guards separate the two men. Horns sound again, and the hunting party strikes up a gay refrain, which blends with the lamentations of Harriet, Nancy, and Lionel in another great choral climax. Lionel is taken away by guards, Harriet and the royal party leave, while Plunkett stands alone, holding up the ring as the curtain falls.

ACT FOUR

[*Scene One*] The interior of Plunkett's farmhouse, as in Act Two. Lady Harriet and Nancy are shown in by a servant. Harriet, excited and anxious, tells Nancy to find Plunkett and tell him of her plan for making amends to Lionel. When Nancy leaves to do her bidding Harriet soliloquizes about how she will soothe Lionel's anguish and assure him of her devotion ("Noch vernahm er nicht die Kunde").

Nancy soon reappears with Plunkett, who confesses that he is somewhat confused by Harriet's message. Explaining that she will try to bring Lionel to his senses by singing the song he loves, Harriet asks the two to leave. After they go she sings *The Last Rose of Summer*, and as she finishes the refrain Lionel appears.

A dramatic duet ensues ("Willst Du mich täuschen"). Harriet eagerly goes toward him, but he greets her with angry reproach for deceiving him and making him an object of ridicule. Imploring forgiveness, Harriet tells him that she herself took his ring to Queen Anne. She recognized the talisman, and now the secret of his past is known. With that she hands him a document containing proof that he is the son of the Earl of Derby, rightful heir to royal titles and lands.

But even this good news does not alleviate Lionel's anger and despair over Harriet's conduct. When she asks pardon for what she has done he accuses her of falseness and treachery and throws the document at her feet. Turning away from her, he laments that all happiness has gone out of his life. Harriet again begs him to forgive her and tries to convince him that their love will triumph and they will yet be happy together. But Lionel rushes away, leaving Harriet remorseful and brokenhearted.

Plunkett, returning with Nancy, notices Lionel running madly from the house and remarks to Harriet that her plan evidently has failed. As though suddenly struck by an idea, Harriet says that there is yet another way in which she can convince Lionel of her love. Asking Plunkett and Nancy to be ready to help her, she hurriedly leaves.

Turning to each other in bewilderment, Plunkett and Nancy ask each other what will happen next. A sprightly duet follows as they begin discussing their own problems ("Ja, was nun?"). Once Harriet's difficulties are ironed out, Plunkett observes sadly, he probably will be left to lead the life of a lonely bachelor. Nancy coyly suggests that he marry one of the pretty girls who were available at the fair. Plunkett replies that he is interested only in one young lady. But she gives herself high-and-mighty airs and, besides, she can neither spin nor cook. Observing that these arts can easily be learned, Nancy hints that she is only waiting for Plunkett to say the proper word. He is about to propose, then suddenly decides that Lionel's affairs come first, because their friendship is sacred. The duet comes to a lively conclusion as Plunkett declares he will soon say the right word and Nancy agrees to give him the proper answer.

[*Scene Two*] Richmond Park. As part of Lady Harriet's plan to rouse Lionel from his despondency and hopelessness, a replica of Richmond Fair is being set up. It is Harriet's hope that if he is brought to the happy scenes in which he first saw his "Martha" a cure will be effected. Farmers and servants, arranging booths and tents, join in a merry chorus ("Hier die Buden, dort die Schenke"). Harriet, dressed as Martha, appears and gives her approval of the arrangements. Nancy, as Julia, runs in and tells Harriet that Lionel is approaching. At a sign from Harriet the servant girls take their places as at the fair and begin the chorus in which they enumerate their accomplishments.

Plunkett arrives with Lionel, who walks with downcast eyes in an attitude of utter dejection. Suddenly he looks up and sees a familiar and happy scene before him. Plunkett, playing his role, calls Martha from the crowd of servant girls and asks what she can do. Looking at Lionel, Harriet answers in a refrain of simple tenderness that she can scorn the world for true love, and this love she offers to him alone ("Ich kann entsagen dem Glanz"). In transports of happiness Lionel takes "Martha" into his arms.

Plunkett turns to Nancy and, in the spirit of the masquerade, asks what her accomplishments are. She demurely replies that she can spin fine linen—and can also make a husband happy. Plunkett pretends to hand her the fee and declares the bargain sealed. Giving Lionel her flowers, Harriet begins the refrain of *The Last Rose of Summer*. Lionel joins her, and then all the voices blend in a thrilling choral climax of the song. The curtain falls.

The Medium

by GIAN-CARLO MENOTTI

[1911–   ]

Libretto by the Composer

CHARACTERS

Monica, daughter of Madame Flora.........................*Soprano*
Toby, a mute..
Madame Flora (Baba), a fake medium.....................*Contralto*
Mrs. Gobineau ⎤   ⎧ *Soprano*
Mr. Gobineau ⎬ séance clients of Baba................⎨ *Baritone*
Mrs. Nolan ⎦   ⎩ *Mezzo-soprano*

Place: A European city
Time: The present
First performance: Brander Matthews Theater, Columbia University, New
                     York City, May 8, 1946
Original language: English

YOUTHFUL, original, and daring, Gian-Carlo Menotti is one of the most
telling personalities in the field of contemporary opera. He has written
eight operatic works, all but one of which (*The Island God*) have had
popular success. Foremost among these is *The Medium,* which has had more
than a thousand performances here and abroad. Musically, it is a blend of
modernism and romanticism. It has no atonal complexities, and Menotti
does not hesitate to spin out a melody when he feels the need for it. Dramatically, the opera is a Grand Guignol shocker. One thing stands out—in
The Medium as in his other stage works: his unerring sense of the theater.
In that respect he is a kind of modern Richard Wagner—he is composer,
librettist, stage director, casting director, and general production consultant.

ACT ONE

The apartment of Madame Flora (Baba). At one side a stairway leading
downward to the street. At right, to the rear, a puppet theater with curtain
drawn. On the rear wall is a large astrological chart which appears trans-
parent when a light is placed behind it. In the center of the room is a table
with an old-fashioned lamp suspended above it. In one corner is a small
statue of the Virgin; a votive candle flickers before it.

The curtain rises after a brief orchestral introduction. It reveals Toby, the
mute, kneeling before a small trunk standing next to the puppet theater.
From the trunk Toby takes a string of beads and brightly-colored pieces of
cloth and makes an outlandish costume for himself. Monica, standing next

to a couch on which lie a white party dress and a filmy veil, looks into a hand mirror and combs her long, flowing hair. She sings a refrain about a queen who confesses to a wicked gnome that she has lost her "golden spindle and thread."

Suddenly she sees the image of Toby in her mirror and turns to him. She warns that Baba will soon come home and find nothing ready. What is more, she sings, Baba will beat Toby if she finds him playing with the things in the trunk. Then Monica is lost in her daydreaming again. She sings about the queen and the gnome who tells her that if she will give him her golden crown he will go and find the lost golden spindle and thread.

Monica now becomes aware of Toby in his fantastic attire. In her childish imagination, she sees him as the King of Babylon. She will be his bride—the princess from a foreign land. She bows to Toby and he bows in return. Impulsively she embraces the boy.

The tender mood of the scene is interrupted by the slamming of the outer door downstairs. With Monica's fumbling help, Toby tries to take off his finery. While they are still struggling to get it off, Madame Flora appears on the stairway and sees them. A passage in recitative follows. Baba launches into a tirade, complaining that Toby is nothing but a half-witted gypsy who wastes his time dressing up in the very things she forbade him to touch. What is more, she fumes, nothing is ready for the clients who will be here shortly for the séance. Coming up into the room, Baba rushes angrily toward Toby, cursing him.

Monica restrains her, calms her a bit, and asks her where she has been. In answer, Baba throws a roll of bills on the table. She got this, she says, by sitting all night long on the doorstep of Mrs. Campi, who has owed her the money for a long time. But the woman is poor, Monica protests. Unheeding, Madame Flora orders her daughter to get ready for the séance.

She helps Monica put on the white dress and veil. Meanwhile, Toby puts the table in its proper position under the hanging lamp. Then he goes to the puppet theater, opens the curtain, and manipulates the hidden levers and cables inside. Testing them, he raises the table off the floor and lowers the lamp. This action takes place to an eerie orchestral accompaniment which builds up to a powerful climax.

The music is abruptly cut off by the ringing of the doorbell. Monica rushes offstage, while Toby dodges into the puppet theater and draws the curtain. Madame Flora herself presses the buzzer to open the door downstairs, then gets a deck of cards and sits at the table dealing a game of solitaire. In a moment, Mr. and Mrs. Gobineau and Mrs. Nolan come up the stairs and into the room. Baba scarcely pays any attention to them. A brief scene in recitative follows.

Baba finally takes notice of Mrs. Nolan and introduces her to the Gobineaus, who had met her only as they entered a moment before. She tells the three to wait until other clients arrive. Then, in trio form, the Gobineaus and Mrs. Nolan explain why they come to these séances. Mrs. Nolan says she wants to speak to her daughter, Doody, who died a year ago when she was only sixteen. Eagerly she asks the Gobineaus if she will be able to hear her child. Mrs. Gobineau nods, adding that Mrs. Nolan even may be able to see her Doody. As Mrs. Nolan exclaims in fear and wonder over the prospect, Baba suddenly gets up and leaves the room.

In a furtive whisper Mrs. Nolan asks the Gobineaus if they have known the medium long. They have been coming here every week for two years, they explain, to communicate with their little boy, who died as a baby. He cannot speak, of course, the Gobineaus add, but they can always hear his happy laugh. Then in a simple, tender refrain, Mrs. Gobineau relates what happened. It was when they lived in France, where they had a garden with a fountain. On their little boy's second birthday they had given him a sailboat. Fighting back tears, Mrs. Gobineau says she cannot remember what happened, but when she looked in the fountain. . . . Her sobs eloquently tell the rest of the story. Her husband does his best to comfort her, saying the boy is happier now.

At that point Baba comes bustling in, announcing it is time for the séance. Mrs. Nolan, almost beside herself with excitement, jumps up from her chair, dropping her pocketbook. Mrs. Gobineau picks it up, helps Mrs. Nolan take off her coat, and leads her to the table. Mr. Gobineau helps Baba place chairs around the table, then locks the doors. Baba switches off the light, leaving only the candle burning in front of the statue of the Virgin. There is a long silence on stage, during which a note sounds softly high in the strings. Then Baba begins to moan, as though in a trance.

Suddenly she is silent. Behind the astrological chart on the wall, Monica's form takes shape in a dim light. To the accompaniment of descending fourths, she begins to sing in ghostly, disembodied tones: "Mother, Mother, are you there?" In a trembling voice, Mrs. Nolan calls to her daughter, while Mrs. Gobineau gently reassures her. Plucking up courage, Mrs. Nolan asks Doody if she can see her father. The voice answers that he is near by. Overcome by the misery of separation, Mrs. Nolan bursts into tears.

Monica then sings a poignant refrain in which she tries to comfort the heartbroken woman. She begs her not to grieve, because the tears of loved ones are like "bitter rain" to those who have died. "Doody" goes on to implore her mother to go home and give away all her belongings and even forget her grave. She is to keep only "the little golden locket."

Mrs. Nolan gasps that she has no such locket. The voice dies away, and the image behind the chart slowly fades. Screaming, Mrs. Nolan rushes toward it, but is restrained by Mrs. Gobineau, who leads her back to her chair. In an exchange of spoken dialogue, Mrs. Nolan insists she must speak to her daughter, while the Gobineaus implore her to be silent so that they may communicate with their son. Baba, playing her role, sighs and moans. When Gobineau tells the medium to send his son to him, Monica is heard imitating childish laughter. Pathetically happy, the parents greet him, then say good-by as the laughter dies away.

The same chord heard earlier sounds high in the strings. There is a gasp of horror from Baba, who springs to her feet and turns on the light. She runs to the stairway, then comes back to the table. Mrs. Nolan and the Gobineaus look at her in consternation. Someone touched her, Baba cries hysterically. Her three clients assure her there is nothing to be afraid of—it has happened before. Panic-stricken, Baba rants that she cannot understand this strange thing. When the Gobineaus and Mrs. Nolan—ironically taking this new visitation as a matter of course—try to calm Baba, she furiously orders them to leave. They put on their wraps and slowly descend the stairway, repeating in a brief trio to the accompaniment of descending fourths: "Why be afraid of our dead?"

A door slams below as they leave. Monica, still dressed in her gown and veil, comes running out. Hysterical with terror, Madame Flora asks for a drink. Monica pours her a glass of whiskey. Flora gulps it down, steadies herself, then tells Monica the séances must stop. The clients are to be given back their money. Monica stares at her mother in amazement. As a succession of foreboding chords sounds in the orchestra, Flora tells Monica that while she was simulating a trance she felt a cold hand around her throat—the hand of a man.

As though goaded to action by her fear, Baba rushes to the puppet theater and tears the curtain aside. There sits Toby, motionless. Glaring at him, Baba cries that he must have been the one who played this horrible trick. While Monica vainly tries to reason with her, Baba repeats that Toby knows everything—that he sees things nobody else sees.

Finally Monica manages to drag Baba away from Toby. Sitting down, she cradles her mother in her arms and begins singing a melancholy song about a black swan. This theme, which seems to be a sort of leitmotif of doom, recurs later. It is a weird lament about a maid who has lost her lover. Her bridal gown is torn, her lamp is lost. She had given her beloved a fiery kiss and a golden ring. Now he looks for the ring at the bottom of the river. Repeating the words of the song, Madame Flora joins with Monica in a duet. This is suddenly broken off as a voice is heard singing the phrase Monica sang during the séance: "Mother, Mother, are you there?"

But Baba alone hears it. Someone must be hiding in the other room, she whimpers, then orders Toby to go and look. He returns a moment later, looks at Baba, and shakes his head. Infuriated, she seizes the boy, forces him to his knees, and commands him to pray. She herself gets the rosary that is hanging from the statue of the Virgin, crouches again at Monica's feet, and begins to intone the *Ave Maria*. Over her spoken tones, Monica softly sings a phrase of her song about the black swan. Suddenly there comes the faint sound of childish laughter. Baba gasps in fear and huddles closer to Monica. The curtain falls.

ACT TWO

After a brief orchestral introduction, the curtain rises to show Madame Flora's apartment, as before. The time is several days later. Monica, seated in front of the puppet theater, is watching Toby give a performance. When the show is over, Monica applauds enthusiastically and Toby comes out to take a bow. Now there will be supper and dancing, Monica announces. Then she begins an appealing melody in a barcarolle-like rhythm. The words are all childish fantasy: Monica, Monica, dance the waltz, to the tune of a trombone and a guitar someone is playing up in the sky. . . .

Toby watches her a moment, then suddenly clutches her arm. As she leans close to him, he desperately tries to make himself understood, then gently touches her face. Intuitively Monica realizes he wants to play this fairy game with her. Kneeling behind him, she makes him play the role of suitor, guiding his gestures while singing his "lines" in a lovely, swaying melody. The lover's heart is bleeding for Monica, so goes the song. He has loved her all his life . . . she is his night and his day.

Monica quickly gets up and stands in front of him in a disdainful pose. Now she is the Queen of Arundel, she sings, and she will have this scoundrel put in chains for daring to speak to her. Quickly shifting back to Toby's role again, she sings the suitor's poetic avowals. Getting into the spirit of the game, Toby translates her words into gestures of his own. Once more she stands in front of him, this time as though yielding to a lover. Then, again in Toby's role, she brings his song to an impassioned climax.

Toby looks up at her adoringly, then buries his face in his arms. Gently stroking his hair, Monica lifts his face and looks into his eyes. In an infinitely tender phrase, she sings that he has the most beautiful voice in the world.

The mood of the scene is shattered by the slamming of the door downstairs. Monica runs off to her room, while Toby slinks into a corner. A moment later, Baba, a bottle in her hands, comes slowly up the stairs. Her hair and clothing are in disarray. She sees Toby and asks him where Monica is. He points to the door of her room. Sitting at the table, Baba orders the boy to come to her. He crawls reluctantly over to her and she puts his head in her lap. With deceptive gentleness, she sings that she has always loved him as her own son. Perhaps she has been harsh with him at times—but, after all, she did take pity on him when he was a starving waif roaming the streets of Budapest. Now, she goes on, they must be good friends. She will never punish him again and, what is more, she will buy him a red silk shirt and a golden scarf.

Then, with a certain menace in her voice, Baba asks if it was he who touched her throat during the séance. Toby sits motionless. Quietly she entreats him to tell what he knows, holding her voice down to a hoarse whisper. Momentarily losing control of herself, she leaps to her feet and screams a curse at the boy. Instantly calm again, she goes on in wheedling tones, but with the same undercurrent of menace. Asking him again if he touched her, she craftily tries to bribe Toby with an offer of the red silk cloth and the beads with which he adorned himself in the opening scene of Act One.

Toby gives no sign of any kind. Baba then goes on to say that perhaps it was not Toby who touched her. But even so, she cries, glaring into his eyes, he knows who did it. Shaking with fright, the mute tries to creep away. Baba catches him by the shirt and rips it off his back. Growing more and more enraged, Baba (in quasi-recitative) tries another tack. Perhaps, she says, Toby would like to marry Monica. Well, then, he may—but only if he will tell Baba what he did or saw that night of the séance. Paralyzed with terror, Toby cowers before her.

Baba, losing all control, screams that she will make him tell. She rushes to the cupboard, snatches up a whip, and lunges at the boy. Trying to escape, he trips and falls helpless. Baba stands over him and beats him savagely.

Meanwhile the doorbell begins ringing loudly and insistently. Finally aware of its sound, Baba stops beating Toby and listens. Her rage has left her spent and panting. Swaying, she walks over to the buzzer and presses it just as Monica comes running in. She looks at Toby lying on the floor, then with an anguished cry runs over to him and takes him in her arms.

The Gobineaus and Mrs. Nolan appear on the stairs as the theme heard during their entrance for the first séance sounds in the orchestra. An ensemble in quartet form follows. As the three politely bid Baba good evening, she brusquely asks why they have come. For the séance, they reply, somewhat surprised. In dark, foreboding tones, Baba then tells them there will be no more séances. There is your money, she adds, throwing it on the table. As her clients stare incredulously, she growls that there never were any séances—it was all a fraud.

But this can't be true, the three insist, because they saw and heard their loved ones—they saw Doody's form and heard Mickey's laughter. At that Baba strides over to the puppet theater, tears aside the curtain, and pulls the cables that raise the table and move the lamp—just as during the séance. Here are the wires, says Baba, and here the hidden microphone. Dumfounded but completely unconvinced, the Gobineaus and Mrs. Nolan shake their heads.

Mrs. Nolan protests she saw her daughter and heard her voice. With an insulting laugh, Baba snatches up the white gauze Monica wore while faking Doody's appearance and says, "There is your daughter!" Then she calls to Monica to let Mrs. Nolan hear her daughter's voice. Over the microphone comes the eerie phrase: "Mother, Mother, are you there?" Mrs. Nolan listens, then shakes her head, saying that is not the same voice she heard. For the benefit of the Gobineaus, Baba then orders Monica to "do the little boy laughing." Monica obediently simulates the childish laughter heard during the séance. But—like Mrs. Nolan—the Gobineaus say it is not the same. Bewildered in turn, Baba asks her clients what further proof of fakery they want.

From this point on the scene builds up to an extraordinary musical and dramatic pitch. Against the themes carried by the voices of Mrs. Nolan and the Gobineaus, Baba's spoken interpolations are like a harsh counterpoint. Mrs. Nolan insists she surely would recognize her own daughter's voice. The Gobineaus say they are equally sure of little Mickey's laughter. The irony of the situation cuts deeper when Baba's clients assure her that even though she thought she was cheating she really was not. Without her guidance, they insist, they would lose everything they love . . . she must allow them to have their séance now, because their dead are waiting for them.

Baba, in blind fury, screams at them to get out and pushes them toward the stairs. As they make their way down, sobbing, she turns on Toby, still huddled in a corner, and orders him to go. Monica enters and intervenes. A dramatic duet follows over an agitated theme in the orchestra. Monica protests that Toby cannot be turned out—he is helpless and unable to take care of himself. Baba repeats that he must go; she cannot stand his haunted look. Then, Monica cries, she will go with him. Her entreaties, mingled with Baba's fierce insistence on Toby's going rise to a powerful climax. In a phrase of deadly warning, Baba orders Toby to go. He slinks down the stairs, turns and looks at Monica. She runs to the banister and impulsively catches his hand in hers. Then Toby vanishes.

Monica turns, sees the puppets scattered on the floor, and picks them up. Baba roughly orders her to her room. Monica goes inside, slamming the door behind her. Baba is left alone. A deep bass note reverberates in the orchestra. Suddenly a ghostly voice sings the phrase of the séance: "Mother, Mother, are you there?" Baba recoils, then rushes to the door of Monica's room and locks it. She then goes to the cupboard, gets the bottle, and gulps down several drinks. Taking the bottle and a glass to the table, she sits down. An insistent trill over a harshly dissonant figure in the orchestra reflects her confused, fear-stricken thoughts.

Staring into space, Baba begins the soliloquy which forms the apex of the opera. Can it be, she murmurs, that she is afraid—she who has seen and heard so many terrible things: women screaming as they were murdered . . . men's hands dripping blood . . . children rotting in filth . . . old men mad with debauchery and young men eaten by disease. . . . But now, when she is sick and old and longs only for peace, she is haunted by these restless ghosts—the dead.

Absently she sings a phrase of Monica's song about the black swan. In spoken tones, Baba tries to reassure herself: there is nothing to be afraid of —one must only laugh at nothingness. A powerful bass figure sweeps through the orchestra as she bursts into a hysterical laugh. In a sudden change of mood, Baba prays to God for forgiveness. Sodden with drink, she falls asleep.

As a sustained chord sounds in the orchestra, Toby appears on the stairs. He tiptoes to Monica's door. The theme of Monica's "duet" with him echoes as he tries the door, then softly scratches on it like an animal. Baba, stirring, knocks over the bottle. Toby leaps behind the couch, but a moment later he creeps over to Monica's door and knocks. When there is no answer he glides over to the trunk and begins to rummage among its contents. He inadvertently lets go the lid, which snaps down noisily.

Baba sits bolt upright. Toby vanishes behind the curtains of the puppet theater. Baba cries out, asking who is there, then calls for Monica. Jerking open a drawer of the table, Madame Flora takes out a revolver. Wild with terror, she glares at the puppet theater screaming, "Answer me or I'll shoot!" The curtain moves slightly. Baba fires into it again and again.

There is a terrible silence. Then, as a series of powerful descending chords surges through the orchestra, a red spot begins to stain the white curtain. Baba screams, "I've killed a ghost!" Toby's hands emerge, clawlike, clutching the curtain. It tears loose under his weight, and his body crashes headlong into the room. As Baba stares at it in hypnotic fascination, Monica pounds on the door of her room, shouting to be let out. Baba goes over and unlocks the door. Horror-stricken, Monica looks at Toby's body, gasps out a call for help, and rushes down the stairs.

Baba slowly kneels beside Toby's body. Looking down into his face, she groans, "Was it you?" As a savage, dissonant phrase thunders in the orchestra, the curtain slowly falls.

Mefistofele

by ARRIGO BOÏTO

[1842–1918]

Libretto by the Composer

CHARACTERS

Mefistofele . . . . *Bass*
Faust . . . . *Tenor*
Wagner, his pupil . . . . *Tenor*
Margherita . . . . *Soprano*
Marta . . . . *Contralto*
Elena (Helen of Troy) . . . . *Soprano*
Pantalis . . . . *Contralto*
Nereus . . . . *Tenor*

Cherubim, mystic choir, celestial phalanxes, penitents, soldiers,
huntsmen, students, townspeople, witches, sorcerers, Greek
chorus, nymphs, Greek dancers, warriors, sirens

Place: Germany and ancient Greece
Time: Middle Ages and antiquity
First performance: Teatro La Scala, Milan, March 5, 1868
Original language: Italian

Boïto, unlike Gounod, based his *Faust* on both the first and second parts of Goethe's poem. Where Gounod's opera ends with the death of Marguerite and the doom of Faust, Boïto's work continues, in Act Four and the Epilogue, to the climax of the original drama—the death and redemption of Faust. Although it is essentially a series of musical and dramatic episodes, Boïto's opera is one of extraordinary lyric beauty. It is remarkable for its adherence to the philosophical concepts of Goethe.

PROLOGUE IN HEAVEN

Masses of clouds. There is a brilliant fanfare of trumpets, sounding a theme which will be heard again at the close of the opera. Other fanfares sound from unseen trumpets to the right, left, and center. These are followed by a stately, hymnlike theme. Invisible choruses—the first and second phalanxes—then sing a paean to the Lord of Creation ("Ave Signor").

Heralded by a mocking scherzo (the *scherzo strumentale*), Mefistofele stalks upon the scene and stands partly in the shadow with his feet on the hem of his cloak. In tones of scornful irreverence he begins a discourse with God ("Ave Signor! Perdona se il mio gergo"). He hopes he will be pardoned for not joining in the fervent praises sung by the celestial choirs, as well as for his general lack of enthusiasm for the Creator's handiwork. Man, he observes with sneering contempt, is a ridiculous creature, hopping about like a cricket and trying to poke his nose among the stars. He struts about, too immersed in his illusions to be aware of his hopeless confusion, and blindly worships reason. In fact, Mefistofele concludes, man has sunk to such a contemptible state that he is no longer interested in tempting him to sin.

In the second section of the Prologue (*Intermezzo drammatico*) voices of an unseen choir, representing the Divinity, ask Mefistofele if he knows Faust. He is the maddest of all men, Mefistofele replies. His craving for knowledge and his tormenting ambition give him no rest. Yet it is possible, the devil avers, to lure even Faust from his contemplation of higher things. Thereupon he makes a wager with God that he can corrupt Faust by giving him a taste of worldly pleasures. Evil, says Mefistofele, will triumph over good. As the heavenly chorus bursts into a *Sanctus*, Mefistofele murmurs that it is pleasant to have an occasional chat with the Old One, and he will take care never to offend him. It is kind of God to talk to the devil in so human a fashion.

Now follows a remarkable vocal scherzo (*scherzo vocale*), sung by an unseen choir of boys representing cherubim from limbo ("Siam nimbi volanti dai limbi"). They sing very rapidly in a monotone, giving the effect of disembodied voices chattering in space. Mefistofele listens for a moment and then remarks with distaste that the droning of cherubim annoys him like the humming of bees. He vanishes. The cherubic voices continue, singing that one day they descended to earth and lost their way, but now, singing and turning, they are spiraling upward to the celestial regions.

The final section of the Prologue, the Psalmodic Finale (*Salmodia finale*), begins with the *Salve Regina* (supplication to the Virgin) sung by spirits and earthly penitents. It builds into an ensemble of magnificent power as the cherubim again join with their chattering chorus, while the heavenly phalanxes blend in with their hymn to the Lord of Creation.

ACT ONE

[*Scene One*] Frankfort-on-the-Main, Easter Sunday. In the background are the city gates, through which crowds are streaming on their way to enjoy the holiday in the country. Bells ring out. A resounding chorus is developed, beginning with a phrase sung by a number of townspeople, who ask others where they are going to spend their holiday ("Perchè di la"). Halberdiers and peasants gather round a booth and call for beer. A friar in a gray habit unobtrusively makes his way through the throng. Some people ignore him, others kneel respectfully as he passes. Excitement stirs the crowd as the Prince Elector appears with his fool, his falconer, cavaliers, ladies of the court, and others of his retinue. They pass and are followed by the throng.

Faust appears, accompanied by Wagner, his pupil. In a brief, melodious air Faust sings of the pleasant weather of early spring and the gaiety of the peasants ("Al soave raggiar"). He is interrupted by a noisy crowd of merrymakers. Wagner remarks that he has no liking for their vulgar antics, and then he and Faust withdraw to the background. The people strike up a lusty chorus ("Juhé! Juhé! Juheisa Juhé!") and begin dancing the *obertas*, a boisterous Polish dance with a mazurka-like rhythm. They sing that the music and the dancing are mingled in wild confusion as lads and lasses whirl about ("Tutti vanno alla rinfusa"). The dance ends in a burst of gay music, and then the people go on their way in the deepening twilight.

Seating themselves on a slope, Faust and Wagner muse over the peace and quiet of evening. After a few moments Faust, with some concern, calls Wagner's attention to the friar, who seems to be slowly circling them, gradually drawing closer. Wagner casually remarks that he is merely a mendicant, but Faust exclaims that he leaves blazing footprints. Though Wagner tries to assure Faust that his fears are merely a figment of his imagination, the philosopher continues to watch the friar in great apprehension. Wagner finally persuades Faust to leave, and as the two go, the friar follows them.

[*Scene Two*]   Faust's study. This change of scene is made very rapidly, without pause in the music. As Faust enters the friar slips in behind him and conceals himself in an alcove. In a beautiful aria ("Dai campi") Faust revels in the serene joy that floods his soul. He reflects how he has walked through the quiet fields and meadows to the cloistered calm of his study. Here he will give himself over to holy thoughts. His fiery emotions have been quieted, and now his mind turns to God. He will seek inspiration from the Holy Writ. At the conclusion of the aria he goes to a lectern and opens his Bible.

As he begins reading the friar rushes shrieking from the alcove. Looking at him in astonishment, Faust remarks that he is quite willing to share his cell with a holy friar and then gently rebukes him for making an unnecessary uproar. But as the friar fixes him with a menacing stare Faust shrinks back in alarm. If he is fiend or phantom, he cries, he will exorcise him with an all-powerful sign. With those words Faust makes the sign of Solomon. Instantly the friar throws off his robe and stands before Faust as Mefistofele, with a black cloak over his arm.

With an ironic bow Mefistofele puts himself at Faust's service. Expressing some amusement at the transformation from humble friar to cavalier, Faust asks the stranger his name. The question, answers Mefistofele, is scarcely worthy of a man of learning. He then describes himself as a part of that power which always thinks evil but achieves good. When Faust asks him to explain his strange words Mefistofele replies in the great aria, "Son spirito che nega." He is the spirit of negation, Mefistofele declares, the spirit which denies all things and troubles heaven by spreading confusion and discord.

His prime creations are ruin and death, and his very name is the synonym for evil. He strides through the universe shouting an insolent "No!" in the face of God and man, hating and destroying, whistling up destruction. At that point he puts his fingers between his lips and whistles shrilly. After a long pause he continues. He is part of darkness and oblivion, the archenemy of light. His sword is ready to strike down the foe in the last great battle between light and darkness, which will plunge the world into endless night. In savage exultation he reiterates that, unchallenged, he hurls his

"No!" in the world's face as he wreaks his devastation. He ends the aria with another piercing whistle.

As Faust stares at him in awe and wonder Mefistofele again tells him that he stands ready to serve. Faust asks what bargain is involved, but Mefistofele tries to evade answering. When Faust insists, however, on knowing the terms, Mefistofele tells him that here on earth Faust will be master and Mefistofele slave, but down in hell their situations will be reversed. Faust remarks that he is not concerned about the future. In an impassioned refrain ("Se tu me doni") he asks Mefistofele to grant him one hour of peace —one moment in which the mysteries of Creation will be revealed to him. If he finds in that moment such supreme joy that he will cry, "Remain, thou art beautiful," then he will gladly sell his soul.

Mefistofele agrees, and Faust takes his hand as pledge to the bargain. In a dramatic duet ("Fin da sta notte") they discuss the terms of the contract. From this night on, Mefistofele proclaims, Faust shall taste every pleasure his heart desires, while Mefistofele will attend him as his faithful slave. Faust jubilantly repeats the words. After the duet Faust asks when they will begin, where and how they will go. With a flourish Mefistofele spreads his cloak. He and Faust vanish. As the music storms to a wild climax the curtain falls.

ACT TWO

[*Scene One*] Marta's garden. Faust, now a handsome cavalier known as Enrico, is talking with Margherita, while Mefistofele is conversing with Marta. The dialogue continues in the form of a quartet, which begins with Margherita's first words to Faust ("Cavaliero illustre e saggio"). In a refrain of charming simplicity Margherita wonders why so illustrious a cavalier as Enrico should deign to speak to a village maid. Faust answers with a passionate avowal and kisses her hand. Margherita shrinks back, saying that her hand is much too rough for a cavalier's kisses. Mefistofele, meanwhile, amuses himself by addressing sardonic gallantries to Marta, who, of course, is completely overwhelmed by his attentions. Rapturously singing of their love, Faust and Margherita retire to another part of the garden.

Watching them go, Mefistofele cynically observes that there is little truth in the proverb which says that wise women do not trifle with love. Marta coyly asks him if he has ever experienced the tender passion, to which Mefistofele replies that he neither knows nor cares what love may be. Marta laughs merrily at his sally as they leave to wander about the garden.

Faust and Margherita reappear, deep in a discussion of religion. The simple Margherita is shocked when Faust tells her that he confesses to no faith. Moved by her bewilderment, he proceeds to give a philosophical explanation of his views. A man, he declares, cannot say "I believe," and yet he dare not say, "I do not believe." Nothing is real. No one, for example, can say what the rapture of love is. Love, life, God—they are but words—empty illusions. Awed and frightened by Faust's cynical denial of the things in which she believes, Margherita tries to leave.

Detaining her, Faust questions her about her home and finally finds an opportunity to ask her if he may visit her there after nightfall. Margherita says that she dare not see him at her home because her mother sleeps lightly, and she would soon find out that her daughter had a lover. Faust gives her a vial containing a potion which, he assures her, will not harm her mother but will bring her sound, peaceful slumber.

Marta and Mefistofele return, and then the four voices blend in the brilliant climax of the quartet. Faust and Mefistofele playfully pursue Margherita and Marta around the garden. When the women are caught, all burst into gay laughter and then sing, in a ringing phrase, "T'amo, t'amo!" As they hurry out of the garden the curtain falls.

[*Scene Two*]   On the heights of the Brocken in the Harz Mountains. A blood-red moon shines down on the desolate crags, and the wind howls dismally. With the help of Mefistofele, Faust climbs toward the summit. In foreboding phrases which are echoed by an unseen chorus Mefistofele urges Faust to climb higher and higher toward the devil's lair. Mysterious flames dance in the air before them. Their voices blend as they sing in a descriptive rhythm about the wildfire that is lighting their way ("Folletto, folletto, veloce"). Finally they reach a peak and stand gazing down into the valley. In savage excitement Mefistofele bids Faust listen to the infernal chorus of witches, who are approaching to begin the orgy of their Sabbath.

In a droning monotone the witches are heard singing that they must hurry so that they will not miss a moment of their hellish revelry ("Rampiamo, rampiamo che il tempo"). As they come nearer the chorus grows louder, and at its climax a horde of loathsome creatures, screaming "Saboè, Saboè," rush wildly into the clearing where Faust and Mefistofele are standing. Striding among them, Mefistofele imperiously commands them to pay homage to their king. Muttering an invocation, they kneel around him in a circle, then posture briefly in a grotesque dance. Seating himself on a thronelike rock, Mefistofele commands the witches to bring him his kingly robes, his scepter, and the world to hold in his hands. While some of the demons invest him with robe and scepter, others slowly circle a caldron in the background, muttering incantations. Then they come forward and present to Mefistofele a globe of glass, intoning that they are bringing him the world.

Holding the globe in his hands, Mefistofele sings the intensely dramatic aria, "Ecco il mondo." Here is the world, he cries, the world that circles aimlessly about the sun, sometimes sated with plenty, sometimes scourged with want. On it crawls a despicable race of men bent on ruin and destruction, flouting God and scorning the devil. The thought of their debased and ignoble deeds makes Mefistofele roar with sardonic laughter. At the end of the aria he hurls the globe to the ground, shattering it to bits. The witches again burst into their mad chorus and whirl about in an orgiastic dance.

Faust, paying no heed to the terrible scene, gazes horrified into the lowering sky, crying that he sees a vision of Margherita, pale as death and bound with chains. Assuring him that it is merely an illusion, Mefistofele urges Faust to turn away from the sight. In passionate despair Faust asks why there is a scarlet line encircling Margherita's throat. She has undoubtedly been beheaded, Mefistofele answers carelessly. As Faust writhes in anguish and remorse, the orgy of the witches' Sabbath rises to its terrible climax, with the witches screeching their infernal cry, "Saboè har Sabbah!"

ACT THREE

A prison cell. Margherita, accused of poisoning her mother and strangling her child, has been condemned to death. She is lying on a pile of straw, awaiting the executioner. Crazed by grief, she voices her wandering thoughts in a poignant aria ("L'altra notte in fondo al mare"). They threw her baby into the sea, she laments, then accused her of slaying the child. Vacantly she muses that her spirit is like a bird that longs to fly far away. Now her thoughts go to her mother. She died in slumber, Margherita murmurs, yet her tormentors are saying that she poisoned her mother. In confusion and bewilderment Margherita prays for mercy.

Mefistofele and Faust appear outside the barred door of the cell. Faust begs Mefistofele to save Margherita, and Mefistofele promises to do whatever he can. The jailers are asleep, he says, unlocking the cell door. He urges Faust to hurry, for his horses are saddled and waiting. As he leaves, Faust rushes into the cell and kneels at Margherita's side. At first she does not recognize him, but little by little fragments of memory come back to her —the street where she first saw him, Marta's garden, the words of love they spoke. Trying to calm her, Faust urges her to come with him.

But Margherita, lost in her madness, only asks why he does not kiss her. He cannot save her, she says, for they have said that she poisoned her mother and strangled her child. Taking Faust's hand, she tells him how she wishes to be buried. Her mother must be placed there, she says, pointing vaguely, where the grass of the churchyard is greenest. Not far away will be her own grave, in which he must place her with her baby on her breast. Faust desperately implores her to flee with him, but Margherita answers that she has no desire to live. In the world beyond the cell door she would be a miserable outcast, driven on relentlessly by her conscience.

A deeply moving duet ("Lontano, lontano") ensues as Faust passionately entreats Margherita to flee with him to a magic land where they can live in bliss forever. Together they sing that they will journey to an enchanted island in a tropical sea, far from all pain and strife.

Suddenly Mefistofele appears outside and Margherita shrinks back in terror. As Faust renews his pleas Mefistofele warns Margherita that the hour of doom is close—it is nearly dawn and the headsman will soon be here. Margherita prays for help, while Faust begs her to flee with him before it is too late. Clinging to Faust in terror, Margherita implores him to save her from the devil, who warns her that if she does not come now he will leave her to the headsman. Shaken by horror, Margherita faints in Faust's arms. Reviving after a moment, she sings softly that the day that is dawning should have been her wedding day, but now it will bring her doom. Freeing herself from Faust's arms, she offers a moving prayer for divine forgiveness and commends herself to the protection of heaven. Mefistofele thunders that she is damned, while Faust cries out in anguish. Staring at Faust, Margherita utters an exclamation of loathing and horror and then falls dead. Faust and Mefistofele rush from the cell. Celestial choirs proclaim that Margherita is saved. As the executioner and his aides appear the curtain falls.

ACT FOUR

Ancient Greece. A beautiful spot on the shores of the Peneus, in the Valley of Tempe in Thessaly. In a setting of lush tropical verdure is a Doric temple. Helen of Troy (Elena) and Pantalis are seen in the background. A group of sirens move alluringly about. Faust is lying half asleep on a grassy slope. The scene is flooded with moonlight.

In an exquisitely sensuous duet ("La luna immobile") Helen and Pantalis sing of the beauty of the motionless moon and the perfumed night, with sylphs and naiads disporting among the swans floating on the river. Faust calls Helen's name in his sleep. At the conclusion of the duet Helen and Pantalis leave, and Faust is momentarily engulfed in shadow. A moment later he appears with Mefistofele, who tells him that this is the night of the classic Sabbath. Fortunately for Faust, he goes on, he has been transported to the fabulous Greece of antiquity, here to enjoy new sensations and experiences. Mefistofele then suggests that they part company.

Enchanted by the scene, Faust revels in his dream of Helen. Ignoring Mefistofele, he walks slowly away. Looking about, Mefistofele mutters that at Brocken, among the fearsome crones, he is sure of his power, but in this shadowy land of antiquity he is lost. He prefers the pungent odors of mountain forests to the perfumes of Greece. Just as he is about to leave, a number of nymphs approach and begin an ancient dance. Mefistofele looks on for a moment, and then with a grimace of distaste he vanishes. As the nymphs move languidly through their dance Helen appears, followed by a group of women who sing a brief refrain in praise of her beauty.

Helen is suddenly tormented by a vision of the fall of Troy. In a dramatic aria ("Notte cupa, truce, senza fine funèbre") she recalls the flaming destruction, the thundering of chariots, and the bloody shambles of battle. She is shaken by remorse at the thought that it was she who betrayed the city into the hands of the enemy and brought about the catastrophe. Her voice dies to a despairing whisper as she muses that where Troy once proudly stood there is only silent ruin.

There is a stir of excitement as Faust, dressed as a knight of the fifteenth century, appears, followed by Mefistofele, Pantalis, and Nereus. Fauns and nymphs dance about them. The women urge Helen to look upon the handsome knight, because on his face love is written. Approaching Helen, Faust kneels before her and rhapsodizes over her beauty in a refrain which marks the beginning of the magnificent finale of the act ("Forma ideal purissima"). Helen marvels that she alone, among all the fabulous beauties of Troy and Argos, has captivated Faust. He pours out his love for her in passionate phrases. Pantalis, Nereus, Mefistofele, and the chorus of nymphs express amazement and wonder over the fact that Helen of Troy and Faust have been brought together by love.

Mefistofele, Nereus, and Pantalis then leave the scene. Helen entreats Faust to tell her how to speak the magic language of love. Faust answers that he listens to his heart and exhorts her to listen to her own. It will reply, "I love thee." They voice their ecstasy in a passionate duet ("Amore! Misterio celeste"). The chorus of women joins them in climactic phrases as they hymn the glories of love. Then the women gradually disperse, leaving Helen and Faust alone. As though in a dream, they murmur that they will go to Arcadia, where, in a calm and peaceful valley, they will live forever in blissful union. As they slowly leave, gazing into each other's eyes, the curtain falls.

EPILOGUE

Faust's study, as in the first act. Its dusty and dilapidated condition indicates that many years have passed. Faust is seated in his chair reading the Bible. Behind him, like a malevolent shadow, stands Mefistofele. The room is dimly lighted by a single lamp. Faust looks up from his book with an ecstatic expression as he recalls the past. Mefistofele gloatingly murmurs that death is near. As Faust muses over his adventures Mefistofele reminds him that he never cried out to any passing moment, asking that it remain. Faust answers that he has probed all of life's mysteries—he has known the love of a village maiden and the love of a goddess—he has learned that the only reality is sorrow and that the Ideal is an illusion. But now, on the brink of death, he has had a vision which has finally brought joy to his heart. He saw a land in which a happy and contented people lived at peace with each other under the protection of wise and just laws. If he could achieve this ideal society for humanity, Faust cries, all his hopes and aspirations would be realized.

As death comes nearer Faust ecstatically sings that the light of heaven is flooding his soul. In anger and alarm Mefistofele mutters that the final battle between good and evil is about to be fought. Swiftly he spreads his cloak, exhorting Faust to come with him to seek new pleasures. But Faust is lost in contemplation of the divine as he listens to the celestial chorus ("Ave Signor degli angeli").

Striding to the alcove, Mefistofele conjures up a vision of sirens voluptuously beckoning to Faust. He desperately urges the philosopher to heed their allurements. But the sirens disappear as the celestial chorus again breaks forth. In this moment of supreme joy Faust cries out at last: "Arrestati sei bello [Remain, thou art beautiful]." As Mefistofele vainly tries to persuade him to turn aside his gaze, Faust, summoning his failing strength, lifts up the Bible. In a ringing phrase he exults that here at last he has found redemption. Over the paeans of the celestial choir he prays for divine mercy. Crying that he has found eternal love, Faust falls dead. Mefistofele rages that he will yet capture his soul, for evil will triumph over good.

Rose petals shower down upon Faust's body. The droning chorus of the cherubim again is heard, as in the Prologue. Cringing under the radiance that is gradually engulfing the scene, Mefistofele slowly sinks into the earth, roaring that the rose petals have paralyzed his limbs and bereft him of his power. Still snarling defiantly, he disappears. The celestial chorus rises to a thunderous climax as the curtain falls.

Die Meistersinger von Nürnberg

by RICHARD WAGNER

[1813–1883]

Libretto by the Composer

Based on actual events in the history of the mastersingers
of sixteenth-century Germany

CHARACTERS

Eva, daughter of Veit Pogner	*Soprano*
Walther von Stolzing, a young knight of Franconia	*Tenor*
Magdalene, Eva's nurse	*Mezzo-soprano*
David, apprentice to Hans Sachs	*Tenor*

Hans Sachs, cobbler		Bass
Veit Pogner, goldsmith		Bass
Sixtus Beckmesser, town clerk		Bass
Kunz Vogelgesang, furrier		Tenor
Fritz Kothner, baker		Bass
Hermann Ortel, soap boiler	mastersingers	Bass
Balthazar Zorn, pewterer		Tenor
Conrad Nachtigall, buckle maker		Bass
Augustin Moser, tailor		Tenor
Ulrich Eisslinger, grocer		Tenor
Hans Foltz, coppersmith		Bass
Hans Schwarz, stocking weaver		Bass

Night watchman .... *Bass*

Journeymen and apprentices of the guilds, burghers,
townspeople, musicians, children

Place: Nürnberg, Germany
Time: Mid-sixteenth century
First performance: Munich, June 21, 1868
Original language: German

THE STORY of *Die Meistersinger* centers around the traditional song competitions held in Germany by the medieval guilds. Artistically inclined craftsmen in the principal cities formed singers' guilds and admitted to membership only those who successfully met the requirements of a song test governed by strict rules relating to rhyme, tune, and subject matter.

One of the most distinguished of the mastersingers was Hans Sachs, who lived in Nürnberg during the early part of the sixteenth century. A shoemaker by trade, he was also a poet of considerable renown. The names of the other mastersingers in the opera were likewise taken directly from history.

The magnificent overture, familiar as a symphonic number, states the dominating themes of the opera—the dignity and authority of the master-singers as exemplified by Hans Sachs, and the love of Eva and Walther.

ACT ONE

In the church of St. Katherine in Nürnberg. At one side, behind an open-work partition, may be seen a section of pews, in which members of the congregation are standing as they sing the final chorale of the service—the *Kirchenchor* ("Da zu Dir der Heiland kam"). The foreground represents the open space in front of the choir. Among the worshipers are Eva and Magdalene. Standing beside a pillar a short distance away is Walther von Stolzing. He intently watches Eva, who glances at him occasionally as she sings. Magdalene, noticing this, looks at her in stern reproof.

As Eva and her nurse leave at the conclusion of the service Walther approaches and earnestly requests Eva to give him an answer to his suit. While Magdalene flutters about anxiously, Eva explains that she is destined to be the bride of the man who wins the mastersingers' contest, which is to be held the next day. During their conversation David enters and draws a curtain across the partition at the back, screening off the rest of the church. When Walther, deeply perturbed at Eva's answer, turns away for a moment, Eva begs Magdalene to help her win her lover, whom she compares to the biblical David of Albrecht Dürer's portrait.

Magdalene repeats the famous biblical name with a sigh of emotion, whereupon David, the apprentice, comes forward and asks who is calling him. He is carrying a ruler and swinging a piece of chalk at the end of a string. In the throes of youthful love for Magdalene, he looks at her ardently as he answers her questions about the preparations he is making. He tells her that he is arranging accommodations for the masters, who are going to hold a preliminary song trial for a number of apprentices trying for membership in the guild. Magdalene advises Walther to make the most of this opportunity and present himself to the masters as a possible candidate for the final competition, where he can perhaps win the beloved Eva as his bride. The lovers manage to arrange for a rendezvous in the evening before the nurse hurries Eva away.

A number of apprentices enter, and David puts them to work. They arrange the benches, set up a special chair for the contestant, and begin building a platform. David meanwhile explains to Walther the details of the song competition, and the knight, deep in thought, seats himself in the contestant's chair. He listens attentively as David tells how he is being taught both versifying and singing by Hans Sachs. To be a master, David says, one must be not only a singer but a poet as well. Walther decides to enter the contest. David now turns his attention to the apprentices, finds that they have built the platform too large, and makes them rebuild it to smaller dimensions. On it they place a chair, a small desk, and a blackboard, then enclose the entire platform with a black curtain. When they have finished they join hands and dance around it, singing a chorus in which they derisively wish Walther good luck in his venture.

They withdraw to a bench at the rear as the mastersingers enter. Walther seats himself on a bench in the foreground. Pogner appears first, accompanied by Beckmesser, who harasses him with entreaties to plead his case with Eva. Walther interrupts to greet Pogner, and Beckmesser looks him over suspiciously, muttering about the prospects of a rival at this crucial moment. Pogner introduces Walther to the others and gives him leave to sing at the preliminary trial.

The roll is called, after which the masters seat themselves. But before they take up the business of the day Pogner speaks to them in a long monologue which is known as *Pogner's Address* ("Das schöne Fest"). He has traveled about Germany and is particularly distressed over the fact that the burghers apparently are held in low esteem by the public. The impression is, he says, that they are interested solely in material things and money-making, to the exclusion of culture and art. To prove to the people that the burghers are not crass materialists, Pogner declares, he is making a special contribution to the annual song competition—he is offering his daughter Eva as bride to the man who wins the contest.

The majority of the burghers voice their approval, but Hans Sachs protests that, in all fairness, the bride should be given some choice in the matter of a husband. The people, too, he adds, are entitled to voice their opinion, particularly as to the qualifications of the singer. When some of the masters express their doubts as to the judgment of the public in matters of art, Pogner suggests, as a compromise, that Eva be permitted to reject the winner of the contest, with the stipulation that only a mastersinger be considered eligible as a future bridegroom. After considerable argument Pogner's plan is adopted.

Pogner now formally introduces Walther as a contestant. The masters ask him where he learned the art of singing, and he replies in the melodious aria, "Am stillen Herd." He studied the art, he says, from the book of the ancient minstrel, Walther von der Vogelweide, and from nature. Sachs expresses his approval, but the others are rather dubious about this unconventional type of training. They ask the knight what subject he will take for his song, and he announces that love will be his theme. He seats himself in the singer's chair. Beckmesser takes his place on the marker's platform, pausing to warn Walther spitefully that he will be allowed only seven mistakes.

Walther's ardent love song ("Fanget an! So rief der Lenz in den Wald"), being a spontaneous expression of his emotions, breaks practically every one of the traditional rules, and violent indications of disapproval are heard from the marker's platform. Despite the furious scratching of chalk on slate, Walther continues undaunted until Beckmesser pulls aside the curtains and holds up the slate, which is covered with chalk marks.

Beckmesser sarcastically enumerates the flaws in the song, and several of the masters add their criticisms. Kothner points out one inexcusable infraction of the rules—Walther rose from his seat as he sang. Hans Sachs protests against the arbitrary judgment of the masters, but he is shouted down by Beckmesser, who gathers his colleagues around him and elaborates on the singer's errors. With the exception of Sachs and Pogner, they are unanimous in their disapproval. Walther, angry and impatient over their haggling, expresses his contempt for their hidebound rules, proclaiming that henceforth he will sing according to the dictates of his heart. With that he strides angrily out of the church.

Sachs, who has listened intently to Walther's song, voices his approval of the knight's talent and courage. Beckmesser calls for an official decision, and the masters signify that the contestant is rejected. Loudly discussing the matter, they leave as the apprentices take down the platform and put away the benches. The voices of the men and boys blend in a lively chorus ("Glück auf zum Meistersingen"). Hans Sachs stands to one side, and as the apprentices remove the contestant's chair he makes a gesture of resignation.

ACT TWO

A street in Nürnberg, intersected at the center by a narrow alley that winds toward the rear, with houses on both sides. On one side of the intersection, toward the foreground, is Pogner's home. Directly opposite is Hans Sachs's shop and living quarters. It is a summer evening. The apprentices are putting up the shutters of the houses, singing as they work. David is attending to the windows of Sachs's shop.

Magdalene comes out of Pogner's house, calls David to her, and asks about the song trial. He tells her that Walther was rejected. The nurse hurries back into the house, while the apprentices dance around David and tease him about talking to Magdalene. He is about to retaliate when Sachs appears and sends him back into the shop. The street becomes quiet again as the apprentices go to their homes.

Pogner and Eva approach arm in arm down the alley, talking about the song competition. They seat themselves on a stone bench under a tree in front of their home, and shortly Magdalene calls them in to supper. As Pogner enters the nurse manages to detain Eva and whisper the news about Walther. Much distressed, Eva decides to appeal to Hans Sachs for advice.

The shoemaker meanwhile has seated himself at his workbench, which David has placed near the door. He closes the lower half of the door, sends David off to bed, and prepares to work. In a long soliloquy ("Wie duftet doch der Flieder") he muses over Walther's song. Eva interrupts his reflections, and an interesting musical dialogue ensues ("Gut'n Abend, Meister"). Sachs reveals his warm affection for Eva, who indicates that she would be well content if the cobbler himself were to win the contest and claim her for his bride. She scornfully dismisses Beckmesser as a suitor. Sachs, touched by her devotion, tells her gently that he himself is much too old for her.

When the talk turns to Walther the cobbler deliberately speaks disparagingly of him. In her annoyance over his remarks Eva is at last betrayed into revealing her true feelings. As she leaves in response to Magdalene's call, Sachs decides with satisfaction that his conjectures about the romance were correct. He withdraws into his shop, leaving the upper half of the door slightly ajar.

Magdalene tells Eva that Beckmesser plans to serenade her this evening with the song he has written for the contest. Just at that moment Walther appears, and Eva rushes to him with an ardent greeting. Walther tells her mournfully that the decision of the mastersingers has put an end to all his hopes. He bursts out in anger and impatience over their blindness and obstinacy, then implores Eva to elope with him. Suddenly the watchman's horn sounds, and Eva tells her lover to hide until he has passed. She runs into the house. In his quaint, medieval chant, the watchman announces that it is ten o'clock, swinging his lantern as he goes on his way. Sachs, having overheard the conversation between the lovers, peers cautiously out, remarking that the two must be prevented from taking so indiscreet a step.

Eva, dressed in Magdalene's clothes, steals out of the house and rushes into Walther's arms. As they start toward the alley Sachs flings open his door, catching them in the light of his lamp. Quickly they dodge into the shadows, Eva warning that they must not be seen by the shoemaker. Walther listens in dismay as Eva tells him that the shoemaker is Sachs and that, far from being his friend, he has taken sides with the other masters against the newcomer. Walther is about to rush over to the shop and demand explanations when Beckmesser comes down the alley.

Pausing in front of Pogner's house, he begins tuning his lute, then looks up at Eva's window, where Magdalene, in Eva's clothes, has seated herself. Thereupon Sachs brings his workbench just outside his door and fits a shoe on the last. Beckmesser is about to begin his serenade when Sachs starts hammering away and bellowing out a lusty refrain, "Jerum! Jerum! Halla-hallo-he!" Beckmesser, trying to control his temper, begs Sachs to be quiet, but the shoemaker replies that he must finish his work. In desperation Beckmesser suggests that Sachs act as marker for his song and pound only when he hears a mistake. He has sung only a few quavering bars of his clumsy ballad ("Den Tag seh' ich erscheinen") when the pounding begins again, and the louder he sings, the faster Sachs pounds. At length Sachs takes the shoe from the last and holds it up in triumph. He sings in praise of the "marker's shoe" ("Mit den Schuhen ward ich fertig schier"), calling it that because he fashioned it while the blows of his hammer recorded the mistakes of a would-be mastersinger. A shoe, like a song, he observes, must be well made. Meanwhile, Beckmesser bellows his serenade at the top of his lungs.

Soon heads pop out of windows, and in an angry chorus the neighbors call for quiet. David looks out of his window and, seeing Beckmesser serenading at the house of his ladylove, rushes out with a club and begins whacking away at his rival. This sets off a tremendous row, in which all the people of the neighborhood—burghers, journeymen, apprentices, women, and children—eventually join.

At the height of the uproar Walther and Eva emerge from their hiding place. Drawing his sword, the knight tries to force a path through the crowd. Sachs rushes from his shop, seizes Walther, and pushes Eva up the steps of her house. Still holding fast to Walther, the shoemaker turns around, manages to catch hold of David, drags both his captives into his shop, and slams the door. Beckmesser, out of David's clutches at last, limps hastily away.

The watchman's horn sounds above the tumult, and the crowd melts away as if by magic. By the time he appears to call out the hour of eleven ("Hört ihr Leut', und lasst euch sagen"), the street once again is deserted and quiet. A full moon rises over the housetops. The themes of the fight and Beckmesser's serenade run softly through the orchestra as the curtain falls.

ACT THREE

The interior of Hans Sachs's shop. The prelude, also a concert favorite, is dominated by the themes associated with Hans Sachs. It is morning, and sun floods the room. Sachs is sitting in a huge armchair, deep in a book. David enters carrying a basket. Seeing that Sachs is unaware of his presence, he takes a piece of pastry and a sausage from the basket and begins to eat.

Startled by the sound of a turning page, he puts aside the food and respectfully takes his place before Sachs. He tells him that he has delivered the shoes to Beckmesser and then tries to make amends for his behavior of the night before ("Ach, Meister, woll't Ihr mir verzeih'n!"). It was all for the sake of Magdalene, he explains, because she has always been so kind to him. Sachs suddenly snaps his book shut and David sinks to his knees in fright. But the cobbler's thoughts are elsewhere. Casually he forgives David, then tells him to repeat his verses for the day. The boy replies with a naïve song about St. John, on whose festival day the song competition is being held ("Am Jordan Sankt Johannes stand"). With his mind still on his encounter with Beckmesser, David sings the first line to the tune of the ill-fated serenade. At Sachs's startled look he corrects himself in confusion. Sachs hears him through and then sends him about his duties.

Left alone, Sachs sings the magnificent aria ("Wahn! Wahn! Überall Wahn!") in which he ponders over the hate and discord that are rife in the world—even here in peaceful Nürnberg. At the slightest pretext, he muses, his good neighbors will strike out at each other in blind anger, as though they were under some mischievous spell. He resolves to turn the folly of the good burghers to some useful purpose.

As he finishes, Walther enters from the other room. Sachs greets him affectionately, and a melodious dialogue follows ("Grüss Gott, mein Junker"). Walther tells Sachs that he had a dream so wonderful that he scarcely dares speak of it for fear that its magic may vanish. Sachs urges him to tell it, saying that man's finest inspirations are born of dreams. In the phrases of the *Prize Song*—sung in its entirety later at the competition—Walther describes his dream, while Sachs, listening with growing excitement, writes it down as he sings. Walther breaks off occasionally to discuss the meaning of the song with Sachs. The shoemaker, realizing that this is the song destined to win the prize, makes certain suggestions as to rhyme and musical form so as to ensure the approval of the masters. He calls for a second stanza and Walther answers with the beautiful refrain in which he describes how the vision of his beloved came to him at close of day ("Abendlich glühend"). It was then that he heard the magic song which now inspires him. Sachs advises Walther to try for the prize, then both leave to prepare for the festival.

Beckmesser now enters. He is resplendent in his festival costume but limps about, groaning in pain from the beating of last night. Muttering in anger and discomfort, he looks stealthily around and finally catches sight of the paper on which Sachs has written Walther's song. Now that scoundrelly Sachs's intentions are clear, he fumes as he examines it, for this proves that he is planning to enter the contest. Hearing the door behind him open, Beckmesser stuffs the paper in his pocket just as Sachs enters.

The shoemaker greets him genially, but Beckmesser angrily accuses him of trying to eliminate him from the competition by deliberately involving him in a street brawl ("O Schuster, voll von Ränken"). He charges Sachs with plotting to clear the field of all rivals so that he can win the hand of Eva. Drawing forth the paper from his pocket, he shakes it under Sachs's nose, sputtering that *here* is proof of the shoemaker's skulduggery. His jaw drops in surprise when Sachs offers him the song as a present. When he finally convinces himself that Sachs is not playing a trick on him, he limps from the shop in triumph, loudly assuring Sachs that he will reward him someday for this noble deed.

As Sachs looks after him, sadly shaking his head, Eva enters. Their conversation ensues in a fine duet ("Sieh, Evchen!"). In charming confusion she tells him that one of her new shoes is too tight. Well aware of her real reason for coming, Sachs kneels down to examine the shoe, and as he does so Walther opens the door and stands in the entrance. He is wearing the splendid costume of a knight, and Eva gasps in delighted surprise. Sachs takes the shoe to his bench, turns his back on the scene, and begins working.

Walther, gazing at Eva in rapture, breaks into the refrain of his dream song, to which Eva listens as if enchanted. Sachs, returning with the shoe, bids Eva to mark the song well, for it is a masterpiece. Overcome by emotion, Eva bursts into tears and throws herself into Sachs's arms. Deeply moved, he gently frees himself and gives her over to Walther.

In a glowing refrain that has in it certain echoes of the *Tristan und Isolde* music ("O Sachs, mein Freund!") Eva pours out her love for Sachs, saying that if fate had not decreed otherwise she would be his bride. Sachs answers rather ruefully that the circumstances remind him of the sad story of Tristan, and that he would prefer to spare himself the role of King Marke. A theme from *Tristan* sweeps through the orchestra to underscore his words.

The entrance of Magdalene and David breaks the mood of the scene. Welcoming them, Sachs proclaims, in an ensuing refrain ("Aha! da streicht schon die Lene"), that a new song has been born and needs christening. He and Eva are to be its godparents, while Magdalene and David are to be witnesses. To make the boy eligible as a witness, Sachs promotes him to journeyman then and there by ordering him to kneel and giving him a box on the ear—the traditional symbol of the bestowal of this new rank.

Eva bursts into a joyous refrain ("Selig, wie die Sonne"), introducing the magnificent quintet which closes the scene. Eva sings that Walther's magic song has banished all her sorrow, while Walther exclaims that it was her love that inspired it. Though rejoicing with Eva, Sachs confesses a pang of regret that her love now belongs to another. Magdalene and David express their happiness over the fact that now they may wed, David having at-tained the rank of a freeman. At its conclusion Sachs bids all to hurry to the festival. The curtain descends as the music continues on a stirring festive theme mingled with the fanfare of trumpets. At its climax the curtain rises on the colorful scene of the song competition.

An open meadow outside Nürnberg, with the river Pegnitz visible in the background. At one side is a raised flag-draped platform for dignitaries and judges of the contest. Gaily bedecked tents and booths line the other side of the open space. Townspeople crowd in upon the scene and are noisily welcomed by the apprentices, who dance about with the girls.

The various guilds now parade in, waving their identifying banners and singing lusty choruses. Then the masters enter in a stately procession and take their places on the platform. When all have gathered, the apprentices silence the throng and Hans Sachs steps forward. He is greeted with a majestic hymn of acclaim, "Wach' auf, es nahet gen den Tag."

In moving tones Sachs acknowledges the greeting ("Euch wird es leicht"), speaks a friendly word to Pogner, and then formally opens the contest. First he calls on Beckmesser, who has been desperately scanning Walther's song in a last-minute effort to memorize the words. The apprentices conduct him to the singer's place, a mound of turf. He stumbles in his excitement, complains that the mound is shaky, and orders the boys to settle it more firmly. Laughing among themselves, they pound it vigorously.

With an exaggerated bow to Eva, Beckmesser launches into his song. He tries to fit the words of Walther's poem to the tune of his serenade, with ludicrous results. Distracted by the snickers of the crowd, he forgets the words and sings on in an aimless panic. As he finishes in a final, desperate effort, the throng bursts into a roar of derisive laughter. Rushing over to the platform, he flings the paper in Sachs's face, shouting that the cobbler tricked him into singing his miserable ditty. Shaking with fury, he storms through the crowd and disappears.

Sachs quietly announces that he merely wrote down the words of the song, which is the inspiration of a distinguished visitor who can sing it as it should be sung. At his command Walther steps forward and sings the great *Preislied (Prize Song)*, the high point of the opera ("Morgenlich leuchtend im rosigen Schein"). It is a poetic description of the miracle which inspired his song. He sings of wandering into a magic garden, where, under an enchanted tree, he saw a beautiful maiden. As he stood beside her he knew that this lovely maiden and his Muse were one and the same. His Muse, he sings exultantly, is Eva, and the music she inspired will transport them both to the heights of Parnassus and to Paradise. The masters and the people, in a choral accompaniment to the final phrases of the song, comment in surprise and wonder at its beauty. Walther is accorded the prize by unanimous acclaim.

Eva places the victor's wreath on his head, then both kneel before Pogner to receive his blessing. When Pogner, however, proffers the knight the gold chain of the Masters' Guild, he spurns it with some show of bitterness. At that Sachs steps forward and in an eloquent refrain ("Verachtet mir die Meister nicht") exhorts him not to scorn the masters' prize. Though their rules may seem stern and unyielding, he continues, it is they who keep sacred the standards of German art. Those who revere that art must safeguard it in time to come, when the land will be threatened by evil from without.

The people echo his words in a triumphant chorus. Eva takes the wreath from Walther's head and bestows it upon Sachs. He, in turn, takes the gold chain from Pogner and presents it to Walther. Pogner kneels before Sachs, while the masters make a gesture of homage. In a dazzling chorus the people hail the beloved shoemaker of Nürnberg ("Heil Sachs! Hans Sachs!").

Mignon

by CHARLES LOUIS AMBROISE THOMAS
[1811–1896]

Libretto by
MICHEL CARRÉ *and* JULES BARBIER

Based on Goethe's novel
WILHELM MEISTER'S LEHRJAHRE

CHARACTERS

Lothario, an Italian nobleman (first seen as a wandering minstrel) . . . . . . *Bass*
Philine, an actress . . . . *Soprano*
Laërtes, an actor . . . . *Tenor*
Giarno, leader of a gypsy band . . . . *Bass*
Mignon, a young girl kidnaped by gypsies, in reality
the daughter of Lothario . . . . *Mezzo-soprano*
Wilhelm Meister, a young student on a tour . . . . *Tenor*
Frédéric, also a student, in love with Philine . . . . *Contralto*
Antonio, a servant . . . . *Bass*
Townspeople, gypsies, peasants, actors, actresses,
comedians, ladies and gentlemen, servants

Place: Germany and Italy
Time: Eighteenth century
First performance: Opéra-Comique, Paris, November 17, 1866
Original language: French

THE COMPOSER of *Mignon* was a brilliant musician and one of the acknowledged masters of *opéra comique*. He wrote a great number of operettas, operas, and ballets, as well as choral works and instrumental pieces. Although he had little faith in *Mignon*, it was enormously successful.

The overture, familiar as a concert piece, is dominated by the theme of Mignon's aria, "Connais-tu le pays?" and the principal motive of Philine's air, "Je suis Titania."

ACT ONE

The courtyard of a hostelry in Germany, with the entrance at one side. On the second floor a door opens on a balcony, from which a staircase leads down to the courtyard. Townspeople and peasants are seated at tables, singing a lively chorus about the joys of drinking and companionship.

Lothario, carrying his harp, wanders in and is invited to one of the tables. The people become quiet and listen as he sings a melancholy air in which he describes his weary, endless search for his lost child ("Fugitif et tremblant"). Some of his listeners comment that this tragedy of the past has driven him partly mad. They try to console him and bid him drink to forget his sorrow.

A number of gypsies enter and begin to dance for the entertainment of the crowd. Philine and Laërtes, coming out on the balcony to watch them, join the others in a gay choral accompaniment to the dancing. At its conclusion Giarno steps forward and announces that Mignon will now perform her famous dance on eggs. He orders Zafari, the fiddler, to play his best tune, while other gypsies spread a carpet on the ground and place eggs upon it. Giarno rouses Mignon, who is lying asleep under a blanket in a gypsy cart, and tells her to get ready to dance. Philine, watching this, asks Giarno if the child is a boy or a girl. "Neither," replies Giarno with a laugh as he throws back the blanket. "It is Mignon."

Climbing out of the cart, Mignon looks sullenly over the crowd and then says that she will not dance. Giarno threatens to beat her, while the gypsies comment in an agitated chorus. As Giarno brandishes his stick, Lothario strides up and puts his arms protectingly around Mignon. Giarno angrily orders him away, and at that moment Wilhelm, attracted by the commotion, rushes to the rescue with drawn pistol. Mignon, in a charming gesture of gratitude, divides her bouquet between Lothario and Wilhelm. Philine and Laërtes, as well as the other onlookers, wonder who this unknown young man may be. Lothario, stirred by the incident to memories of the past, sings about a mysterious knight clad in heavy armor. Mignon offers a prayer of thanks for her deliverance, while Wilhelm muses over this strange adventure.

The crowd gradually scatters, and soon the courtyard is deserted except for Wilhelm and Laërtes. The latter comes down from the balcony, introduces himself, and explains that he and Philine have recently arrived with a theatrical troupe which is now out of employment. Wilhelm, in turn, reveals that he is a student from Vienna. He has become bored with university life, he says, and has decided to see the world. He expresses his carefree philosophy in a florid aria, declaring that he intends to wander through the world as he pleases, tasting all its pleasures ("Oui, je veux par le monde").

The talk soon turns to Philine, and Laërtes warns that she is a heartless flirt who is interested solely in adulation and gaiety. Philine, appearing on the balcony at that moment, overhears Laërtes and with ironical good humor thanks him for singing her praises. The conversation, on the general topic of love, continues in the form of a charming trio, which begins with Wilhelm's comment on Philine's beauty ("Que de grâce et de charmes!").

Philine, making it obvious to Wilhelm that she wishes to see him again, leaves with Laërtes. Mignon approaches and shyly thanks Wilhelm for coming to her aid. In ensuing recitative she tells him as much of her past as she can remember. She has no other name than Mignon, she says. Her mother is dead, and so is the "great devil" who was her first master. All she knows of her past, she continues, is that one summer evening she was seized by a band of men and carried from her home. She recalls her homeland in the famous aria "Connais-tu le pays?" When she sings of a land of warm sunshine and blue skies, where a palace awaits her, Wilhelm concludes that it is Italy.

The scene is interrupted by the appearance of Giarno. Wilhelm decides then and there to buy Mignon's freedom and leaves with the gypsy to arrange the terms. Mignon is beside herself with joy. Lothario enters, and when he tells Mignon that he has come to say good-by she expresses a desire to accompany him on his wanderings. Taking his harp, she sings a song about the free and untroubled flight of the swallows, "Légères hirondelles," which concludes in duet form as Lothario joins his voice with hers. Hearing Philine's laughter behind the scenes, Mignon quickly leads Lothario away.

Philine enters with Frédéric, who is dusting off his riding habit, complaining that he wore out his horse in his hurry to see her. She taunts him coquettishly. They meet Wilhelm and Giarno and learn that Wilhelm has bought Mignon's freedom, an act of kindness which brings warm words of praise from Philine. Satisfied with his bargain, Giarno leaves. Wilhelm is introduced to Frédéric, and while they are talking Laërtes enters with a letter for Philine. It turns out to be an invitation to Philine, Laërtes, and their actor companions to visit the castle of Baron de Rosemberg, Frédéric's uncle. Philine promptly invites Wilhelm to join them, saying that he can assume the role of a poet. She gives Frédéric to understand that he will be decidedly unwelcome, whereupon he rushes away in a jealous fury.

As Philine and Laërtes go into the inn, Mignon rushes up to Wilhelm exclaiming that now she is free she is ready to follow him wherever he goes. Wilhelm tries to dissuade her. Hurt by his rebuff, Mignon declares that she will go with Lothario, who approaches at this moment. The minstrel welcomes her as his companion in a melodious aria ("Viens! la libre vie est douce"). The prospect of committing her to the dubious protection of the old man, however, prompts Wilhelm to change his mind. The three join in a brief trio in which Wilhelm consents to take Mignon, who fervently thanks him ("Envers qui me délivre"). Lothario, again bemused by his dreams, prays that he may be allowed to go on hoping and singing.

Philine and Laërtes, accompanied by the other members of the troupe, emerge from the inn, ready to leave for the castle. The gypsies also prepare to go on their way. The townspeople assemble to bid them good-by, and all join in a stirring chorus. In a solo interlude Philine sings that whoever loves her will follow her, a pointed hint to Wilhelm ("Qui m'aime, me suive"). When he responds by accepting her invitation, she impudently snatches Mignon's bouquet out of his hands. Mignon flares up momentarily in jealous anger. Turning to the gypsies, she bids them farewell, assuring Giarno that she forgives him. The chorus continues to an impressive climax.

ACT TWO

[Scene One] The entr'acte is the familiar gavotte. At the rise of the curtain we see Philine seated at a dressing table in a sumptuously appointed boudoir. With great delight she examines the notes and flowers from various admirers.[1] Laërtes's voice is heard in a merry refrain. He appears shortly and, looking around the room, exclaims over its luxurious appointments. Philine tells him that the baroness has given her the use of her boudoir, whereupon Laërtes banteringly remarks that the baron no doubt has the key. With exaggerated gallantry he strikes up a madrigal, in which he describes the fatal effect of Philine's bewitching glances on the heart of a lover ("Belle, ayez pitié de nous"). Philine teasingly observes that his passionate love-making reminds her of Frédéric.

Wilhelm enters. Laërtes informs him that the troupe will perform *A Midsummer Night's Dream*, by one William Shakespeare, a rather talented playwright. Philine is to play Titania. As he leaves to arrange for the performance he meets Mignon outside the door. She is dressed as a page. In answer to the questioning looks of Philine and Laërtes, Wilhelm explains that, as the girl insisted on remaining with him, he has decided to take her along as his servant. Philine, with deliberate condescension, invites Mignon in, saying that she will have an opportunity to perform her egg dance.

At Wilhelm's urging, Mignon seats herself at the fireside. Philine comments with malicious delight on the spectacle of the master serving the servant, while Mignon smarts under her mocking laughter. As the actress busies herself at making up for her performance, Wilhelm, completely enchanted by her loveliness, stands in attendance. Philine sings a brilliant air describing how her admirers sigh for the privilege of waiting on her ("Je crois entendre"). Wilhelm's voice blends with hers as he sings passionately of her beauty.

Mignon, curled up at the fireside, feigns sleep but watches every move. Wilhelm, lost in adoration, entreats Philine for one word of encouragement. Her reply is a gay, mocking refrain. Mignon, aside, heartbrokenly sings that she longs for sleep so that she may be spared this tormenting scene. The three voices blend briefly, and then Philine and Wilhelm leave.

Resigning herself to the situation for the sake of being near Wilhelm, Mignon soon forgets her troubles in admiration of her luxurious surroundings. Her attention is caught by the cosmetics on Philine's dressing table. She rouges her cheeks, examines the effect in a mirror, and then expresses her delight in a brilliant refrain called the *Styrienne*—"Je connais un pauvre enfant." Then, determined to make the most of this escapade, she goes into an adjoining dressing room to put on one of Philine's costumes.

While she is out of the room Frédéric enters through a window. He expresses his satisfaction at being in the boudoir of his ladylove in the tuneful gavotte "Me voici dans son boudoir." Wilhelm suddenly returns. He stares at Frédéric in mingled surprise and amusement. There is an exchange of words over Philine, the argument coming to a climax when Frédéric draws his sword and challenges Wilhelm as a rival. Just as the two cross swords Mignon, dressed in one of Philine's costumes, rushes in and intervenes.

Frédéric, relishing Wilhelm's discomfiture, puts up his sword and

[1] In the original score an aria, written for the London production, is indicated here. In it Philine voices her pleasure over her romantic conquests ("À merveille! j'en ris d'avance").

swaggers from the room. Seeing Mignon for the first time in appropriate feminine attire, Wilhelm suddenly realizes that she is a beautiful young woman. As diplomatically as possible he points out that he can no longer retain her as his page and tells her that they must part. In a tender aria he bids her farewell ("Adieu, Mignon, courage!"). Mignon sadly sings that she will go back to her old life, wandering about and begging for food. Deeply moved by her despair, Wilhelm realizes that he cannot bear to be parted from her.

Philine returns with Frédéric and comments with mocking disdain on Mignon's appearance. Stung to fury, Mignon rips the lace from the dress and then runs into the dressing room. Frédéric complacently remarks that she is probably jealous of him. Laërtes, costumed for his role as Theseus, enters and announces that the play is about to begin. All leave. Mignon, once more in her gypsy dress, reappears. In a burst of jealous fury, she cries out, "Cette Philine! je la hais [That Philine! I hate her]!" The curtain falls.

[*Scene Two*] The park outside Baron de Rosemberg's castle. At one side is the shore of a small lake. At the rear can be seen the brilliantly lighted windows of the conservatory, where the play is being performed. Mignon appears, gazes at the castle, and laments that Wilhelm is there with her hated rival. Tormented by jealousy and despair, she is about to throw herself into the lake when she hears the strains of a harp.

Lothario enters. On seeing Mignon he first thinks she is his lost daughter, Sperata. Recognizing Mignon and noticing her grief, however, he takes her in his arms and tries to comfort her. In a tender refrain he sings that, like her, he has wandered alone, scorned by the world, to lead a life of suffering ("Pauvre enfant! pauvre créature!"). Their voices join in a duet as they sing of their loneliness and sorrow. Suddenly there is a burst of applause from the conservatory. Tortured by the thought that the acclaim is for Philine, Mignon prays that lightning may set the castle on fire. Distractedly she rushes away. Lothario repeats the word "fire" and slowly walks toward the castle.

The play having ended, members of the audience and the actors—the latter still in their costumes—emerge from the conservatory. In a brief chorus all acclaim Philine for her performance. She comes forward and sings the brilliant *Polonaise*, "Je suis Titania." (A ballet sometimes follows.)

Wilhelm enters, and Philine chides him for not having joined in the chorus of praise. He answers that he is looking for Mignon. As Philine takes him aside, Lothario and Mignon appear. The old man tells her that to avenge her he has set the castle on fire. Wilhelm sees Mignon and eagerly hurries toward her, whereupon Philine approaches and asks Mignon to go into the castle and bring back Wilhelm's bouquet, which she has left behind.

No sooner has Mignon gone inside than Laërtes appears, crying that the castle is on fire. Wilhelm dashes into the burning building. Just as the walls fall into blazing ruins he reappears with Mignon unconscious in his arms. Clutched in her hand is the withered bouquet. The onlookers hail the rescuer in a dramatic chorus as the curtain falls.

ACT THREE

The hall of the Cipriani castle in Italy. At the back is a large door, and on either side are smaller doors through which a lake may be seen in the distance. It is to this castle that Wilhelm has brought Mignon to aid her recovery from the illness which was caused by the harrowing experience of the fire. The hall is deserted as the curtain rises. A harp is heard, and from the distance come the voices of a chorus singing a barcarolle about the soft wind sweeping over the lake ("Au souffle léger du vent"). Lothario appears at the door of the room where Mignon is lying ill and sings the *Berceuse*, in which he muses that Mignon's tormenting fever has subsided and that now angels guard her peaceful slumber ("De son coeur j'ai calmé").

The servant Antonio, carrying a lamp, enters with Wilhelm. He explains that the owner of the castle disappeared many years ago and that the property is now for sale. Wilhelm tells him that he will make a decision on the purchase tomorrow. Antonio leaves. Wilhelm approaches Lothario, who tells him that Mignon is greatly improved. Thereupon Wilhelm declares that he has decided to buy the castle of Cipriani for Mignon. At the mention of Cipriani, Lothario becomes strangely excited. Striding up to a large door at the back, he tries to open it, saying that no one has entered the room for fifteen years. He tries another door, finds it open, and goes through it.

Musing over the old man's mysterious behavior, Wilhelm goes to the door of Mignon's room, and as he softly opens it he hears her speak his name in her sleep. In the well-known aria "Elle ne croyais pas" he voices the hope that when she recovers she will reveal the secret that is troubling her. As he stands in the doorway gazing at her Antonio brings him a letter from Laërtes informing him that Philine has followed him to Italy. He is about to enter Mignon's room when she herself, now awake, steps from her chamber. She looks about in wonder, murmuring that it is as if she had seen this place in a dream. In sudden excitement she calls Wilhelm's name. He hurries to her, and a passionate duet follows ("Je suis hereuse! L'air m'envivre!"). Mignon revels in the thought that the fresh, pure air of this land has renewed her vigor, while Wilhelm begs her to forget the past.

In spite of her rapture, however, Mignon is haunted by the thought of Philine, and as though to justify her fears, Philine's voice is heard in the distance, singing her aria, "Je suis Titania." Wilhelm vainly tries to calm Mignon, assuring her that he loves her alone and that he has forgotten Philine. Mignon bitterly laments that her rival will yet destroy her happiness. Their voices blend in a dramatic climax, after which Mignon, overwhelmed by excitement and fear, faints in Wilhelm's arms.

When she revives, Wilhelm tells her that her fears were imaginary, but Mignon is inconsolable. She calls to Lothario, who enters at that moment. His greeting, "Mignon! Wilhelm! Salut à vous!" introduces the dramatic concluding trio of the opera. The lovers are dumfounded when they see him in the attire of a nobleman. His manner has changed to one of dignity and assurance, his mind having been restored by contact with familiar surroundings. When he announces that he is the owner of the Cipriani castle, Wilhelm, not realizing what has happened, exclaims it is another delusion.

Lothario hands Mignon a small casket and tells her to open it. As she wonderingly examines its contents, Lothario softly calls "Sperata," but it stirs only a vague memory in Mignon's mind. Suddenly she finds a prayer book, and at Lothario's bidding she begins reading a prayer, "O Vierge Marie." After the opening phrase Mignon raises her eyes from the book and repeats the prayer from memory. Excited and shaken by the onrush of memories, she asks what country she is in. Lothario tells her it is Italy. Thereupon she dashes into an adjoining room and after a moment reappears, crying out that she has seen the portrait of her mother. In transports of happiness Lothario greets his long-lost daughter, Sperata, while Wilhelm voices his joy over the reunion. Mignon swoons from sheer ecstasy, but quickly revives. The trio, dominated by the theme of "Connais-tu le pays?" rises to a moving climax as the curtain falls.

Norma

by VINCENZO BELLINI
[1802–1835]

Libretto by
FELICE ROMANI

Based on a play by Alexandre Soumet

CHARACTERS

Oroveso, the Arch-Druid, father of Norma........................ *Bass*
Pollione, the Roman proconsul............................... *Tenor*
Flavio, his centurion... *Tenor*
Norma, high priestess of the Druids......................... *Soprano*
Adalgisa, a temple virgin.................................. *Contralto*
Clotilda, Norma's companion......................... *Mezzo-soprano*
Druids and Druidesses, temple virgins, attendants,
Gallic soldiers, the two children of Norma

Place: Gaul
Time: During the Roman occupation, about 50 B.C.
First performance: Teatro La Scala, Milan, December 26, 1831
Original language: Italian

THE DRUIDS, about whom the story of *Norma* revolves, were members of a religious order which wielded great influence among the ancient tribes of Gaul, Britain, and Ireland. They were regarded as having the gift of prophecy, and all civil and military affairs required their sanction. Their authority was above that of kings and military leaders. Serving in the temples, the Druids were under severe self-imposed discipline. The high priestesses, in particular, committed themselves to rigorous devotion and took the vows of chastity. The high priestess Norma betrayed her vows, loved the Roman proconsul, Pollione, and bore him two children. At the time the story begins Pollione has grown tired of Norma and has become infatuated with Adalgisa, a temple virgin.

The stirring overture opens with a warlike fanfare and then takes up the theme of the opening chorus of Druids and Gallic warriors.

ACT ONE

A clearing in the center of a sacred grove of the Druids. It is dominated by a huge oak tree, with its great branches thickly entwined with mistletoe. Beneath the tree is a large stone altar. To the accompaniment of a grave, martial air, Druid priests and Gallic warriors come into the grove in solemn procession. The last to appear is the Arch-Druid Oroveso. As the men arrange themselves in formal order Oroveso issues his command to the priests, "Ite sul colle, O Druidi." They are to ascend to the mountaintop to watch for the rising of the new moon. When it is sighted, the great bronze shield of the war-god Irminsul is to be struck three times, a signal for the cutting of the mistletoe, the sacred ceremony which Norma is to perform.

The men respond in one of the great choruses for which the opera is famous, "Dell' aura tua profetica." They implore the aid of Irminsul in destroying the Roman legions and driving them from their land. Rome's days are numbered, they cry. As they sing, the men make their way up the paths leading to the mountaintop. Their voices die away in the distance.

When the grove is deserted Pollione and Flavio appear. Flavio reminds the proconsul that Norma has warned them that they risk death in coming to this sacred spot. At the mention of her name Pollione recoils. Flavio, surprised, asks him why he is troubled at hearing the name of the woman he loves. Pollione then confesses that he no longer loves Norma but has become enamored of Adalgisa, a beautiful young virgin of the temple. Norma's vengeance, he admits, would be terrible to contemplate, were she to learn she has a rival. In a dramatic refrain he tells Flavio of a vision ("Meco all'altar di Venere"). He was kneeling with Adalgisa before the altar of Venus in Rome. Her hand was clasped in his, and they were rapturously happy. Suddenly an awful mist enveloped the altar, blotting out the daylight. When he turned to look at Adalgisa, Pollione continues, she had vanished, and only a moan answered his anguished cry for her. Then a terrible voice reverberated through the temple, intoning that thus Norma avenges herself on her false lover ("Norma così facempio, d'amante traditor").

Pollione's narrative is interrupted by a fanfare of Druid trumpets and the booming of the war shield. The voices of the returning Druids are heard in the distance ("Sorta e la luna, o Druidi"). Flavio warns the proconsul to flee, but Pollione cries that he will defy these barbarians. In an ensuing aria he declares that the flame of his new love will not only protect him but will destroy the infidels and their altars ("Me protegge, me difende"). Yielding to Flavio's pleas, he rushes away with him just before the Druids reappear.

Accompanied by virgins and priestesses, the Druids and warriors assemble in the grove and sing a mighty chorus acclaiming Norma and invoking the protection of Irminsul ("Norma viene"). Attended by her retinue of maidens, Norma ascends the steps of the main altar. She is dressed in a flowing robe and on her head is a wreath of sacred flowers. In her hand she carries a golden sickle with which to cut the mistletoe.

She rebukes the Druids for demanding war on Rome without the sanction of divine authority. The fate of Rome, she declares, will be pronounced not by mortals, but by gods. When Oroveso, in angry impatience, asks when Rome's tyranny will cease, Norma replies that the city will be destroyed from within by its own evil. Until that day, she says, there must be peace. With that she cuts a few branches of mistletoe, symbolic of a peace offering, and drops them into a cloth held by priestesses.

Norma then sings the great aria, "Casta Diva." The first part is an entreaty to the pure Queen of Heaven to cleanse the hearts of her people from lawless and warlike emotions, so that peace may prevail. In the second part ("Ah! bello a me ritorna") she voices her distress over the fact that the hatred of the Druids is directed against the man she loves—the proconsul. She expresses her longing for one word from him indicating that his love for her has reawakened. The sentiments of the Druids, dominated by thoughts of vengeance, find expression in a choral accompaniment to her aria. After its climax Norma leaves the grove, the Druids following in procession.

Adalgisa now appears and hesitantly approaches the altar. She laments that, although Pollione's love has caused her to betray her religion, she cannot drive away her thoughts of him. Confused and frightened, she throws herself on the steps of the altar and implores the gods to save her from this fatal love ("Deh! proteggimi, o Dio!"). As she prays Pollione rushes in. He tries to embrace her, but she repels his advances and entreats him to leave. A long and dramatic colloquy follows. Pollione at first reproaches her for spurning him when he willingly would sacrifice himself on the altar of her gods for the sake of her love ("Va, crudele").

Repeating the refrain, Adalgisa sings that the burden of sin weighs heavily on the soul of a maiden whose innocence has been betrayed. Pollione begs her to flee with him to Rome, where they can be forever happy ("Vieni in Roma"). Yielding at length to his fervent entreaties, Adalgisa rushes into his arms, crying that she will follow him no matter what her fate may be. He asks her to meet him at this same spot tomorrow at the same hour, after which they will escape. Their voices blend exultantly as the curtain falls.

The scene changes to Norma's home, a huge rocky cave.[1] Animal skins are hung about the walls. The furniture consists of rough benches and a couch covered with skins. Through the doorway at the back the Druid temple is visible, and beyond it the wild countryside. It is a rude and barbaric scene. Norma comes in leading her two children. With her is Clotilda, her companion. Norma, greatly agitated, confides that Pollione has been recalled to Rome but as yet has given her no sign that she is to go with him. She cries that the thought of his deserting her would drive her to madness. Hearing someone approach, she tells Clotilda to take the children away.

As they are led from the room Adalgisa timidly enters. Noting the girl's troubled demeanor, Norma quietly tells her to approach and unburden herself. Adalgisa then confesses that she has yielded to love and has resolved to flee from the temple. When Norma asks how it happened, Adalgisa describes how she and her lover first met and tells of the ecstasy of her awakening love. Overwhelmed by recollections of her own experience, Norma scarcely seems to hear. She murmurs that she once tasted the same bliss.

Fearing punishment, Adalgisa implores Norma to give her strength to resist the lure of her passion. In answer, Norma embraces the girl and absolves her from her sacred vows. In a tender refrain she describes the joys of love that will be hers ("Ah! si, fa core e abbraccia"). The voices of the

---

[1] *Norma* was originally written in two acts but is sometimes played in four. In that case, this becomes Act Two.

two women blend melodiously as Adalgisa asks Norma to repeat the words she has longed to hear. Norma then asks who her lover is. A Roman, the girl replies, and at that moment Pollione appears in the doorway. Norma is transfixed with horror, while Pollione, gazing at Adalgisa, waits tensely for the storm to break. Adalgisa, bewildered and uncomprehending, looks from one to the other. Confronting the proconsul, Norma breaks into a wild denunciation of his treachery. Cowering in fear, Adalgisa brokenly implores Pollione to explain what has happened.

A fiery trio now ensues. Seizing Adalgisa's arm, Norma forces her to look at Pollione, crying out that this man, in duping an innocent girl, has committed a double crime of deceit and betrayal. Adalgisa, now realizing the enormity of Pollione's offense against the high priestess, sings that the thought of Norma's anguish numbs her own. Pollione implores Norma to let her wrath fall on him alone, declaring that his passion for Adalgisa makes him defy hell itself. He tries to force Adalgisa to go with him, but she cowers terror-stricken in Norma's arms and refuses to leave.

In wild fury Norma then orders Pollione out of her sight ("Vanne, sì, mi lascia indegno"). The proconsul defies her rage, while Adalgisa gives way to despair. As the trio rises to a powerful climax the voices of the Druids are heard in the temple, warning Norma that the god Irminsul is summoning her. Above the surge of voices comes the booming of the shield, the signal for the temple rites. Norma, her arms protectingly around Adalgisa, moves toward the door. With a gesture of baffled fury Pollione rushes away.

ACT TWO

Norma's home.[2] The two children are seen asleep on the couch. During a somber orchestral prelude Norma enters carrying a lamp. In one hand she holds a dagger. Setting the lamp on the table, she gazes wildly at the children, resolving to kill them. Their helpless innocence makes her pause, however, and she voices her love for them in a brief but moving air ("Teneri figli"). Then, remembering that they are also the children of the treacherous Pollione, her hatred returns. But no sooner has she raised her dagger to strike than she falls to her knees beside the bed, sobbing that she cannot kill her own children. Calling Clotilda, she tells her to summon Adalgisa.

When Adalgisa appears, Norma, now determined to end her life, tells the girl to take the children to Pollione in the Roman camp. In a moving refrain she commits the children to Adalgisa's care ("Deh! con te li prendi"). Adalgisa, trying to dissuade Norma from taking her life, cries that she has resolved never to leave the temple. Instead, she will go to Pollione and entreat him to come back to the woman who loves him and who bore his children. When Norma distractedly asks her to leave Adalgisa leads the two children before their mother, bids them kneel, and lifts up their hands in a gesture of entreaty. Then begins the beautiful duet, "Mira o Norma."

---

[2] Act Three when played in four acts.

Adalgisa exhorts the high priestess to let her heart be swayed by a mother's love.

At first abandoning herself to despair, Norma is gradually won over by the fervor of the girl's entreaties. Adalgisa finally convinces her that she has forever rejected Pollione's love and that she will go to him only to plead for Norma. Deeply moved, Norma embraces Adalgisa. Calling Clotilda, she signals her to take the children away. In the lyrical concluding phrases of the duet Norma and Adalgisa pledge their eternal friendship and devotion.

The scene changes to a wild rocky clearing in the sacred forest.[3] The Gallic warriors meet with the Druids to report on the movements of the Romans, and the conference is carried on in a dramatic chorus ("Non parti? Finora è al campo"). The warriors sing that the hated proconsul has not yet withdrawn his forces, and the Druids join them in declaring that they must bide their time until they can strike at the foe with full strength.

Oroveso now appears and informs them that Pollione is to be succeeded by an even more tyrannical commander. The men angrily ask if Norma still counsels peace. Oroveso answers that the high priestess keeps silent. When the men ask what course they are to take Oroveso replies in a dramatic aria ("Ah! del Tebro al giogo indegno"). Though the Romans hold them in bondage, he declares, they must appear to submit meekly while gathering their forces. Then, when the foe is lulled into a false sense of security, they will rise and drive him from the land. Druids and warriors echo Oroveso's sentiments in an accompanying chorus.

There is a change of scene to an open court at the entrance of the temple of Irminsul.[4] In the center of the court is a stone altar. Near it hangs the shield of Irminsul and the club that is used to strike it. Norma, standing near the altar, waits for the return of Adalgisa with the repentant Pollione.

Her hopes are dashed, however, when Clotilda rushes in with the news that Adalgisa's entreaties were useless. Far from yielding, Pollione tried to force her to go with him. Adalgisa managed to escape and flee to the temple, and the proconsul has even tried to pursue her into the sacred precincts.

In a frenzy of rage Norma rushes to the shield and strikes it three times. At this signal for war Oroveso appears, followed by Druids, Druidesses, and warriors, who throng in from all sides. Standing with upraised arms on the altar steps, Norma shouts that the gods have decreed war. The people answer in a fiery chorus ("Guerra! le Galliche selve"), in which they swear to wipe the Romans from the face of the earth.

When the chorus is stilled Oroveso steps forward to say that no sacrifice has been prepared for the altar of the war-god. Norma grimly assures him that the rite will take place. At that moment there is a commotion outside, and Clotilda hastens in, crying that a Roman has desecrated the temple by entering it. As she speaks Pollione is brought in by warriors and led before the altar, where he stands with folded arms, gazing arrogantly at the crowd.

[3] Scene One of Act Four when played in four acts.
[4] Scene Two of Act Four when played in four acts.

Oroveso takes his sacrificial knife from his belt and advances toward the proconsul. Norma snatches the knife from her father's hand and is about to plunge it into Pollione's breast when she pauses. The people murmur in surprise. Announcing that she wishes to question the prisoner to ascertain if some traitor perhaps aided him in gaining access to the temple, Norma asks Oroveso and the others to withdraw. They slowly leave the court.

Dagger in hand, she approaches Pollione. A dramatic duet follows ("In mia man alfin tu sei"). Reminding the proconsul that he is in her power, she tells him that she will spare his life if he will give up Adalgisa. He fiercely refuses. Norma then threatens to kill his children, whereupon he begs her to let him be the victim if she must have revenge. Furious over his refusal to relinquish Adalgisa, Norma declares that the girl must die because the gods demand a sacrifice. At that Pollione kneels before her and entreats her to take his life. Norma scornfully answers that she will torture him to the utmost by sacrificing the woman he loves.

After the stormy climax of the duet Norma turns toward the altar. Desperately the proconsul tries to snatch the dagger away from her. She flings him off, mounts the steps of the altar, and calls to Oroveso and the Druids. Pollione stands transfixed as the people gather to hear Norma's judgment. In ringing tones she cries that she offers a new victim for the sacrifice—a virgin who has not only broken her vows of chastity but has betrayed her country. As the crowd angrily demands her name, Pollione, certain that she will doom Adalgisa, implores Norma not to speak.

Then, answering the roar of the crowd, Norma proclaims that the guilty one is herself ("Son io"). With that she slowly takes the wreath from her head and lets it fall to the ground. Quietly she orders the sacrificial pyre to be prepared. Pollione distractedly protests Norma's self-accusation.

Turning to Pollione, Norma sings that, despite his treachery, her love will bind them together beyond the grave ("Qual cor tradisti"). He replies that he has learned too late the depth of her devotion and begs to be allowed to share her fate. Oroveso and the Druids exhort Norma to repudiate her judgment, saying that it must have been uttered in a moment of madness. But Norma approaches her father and declares that she is guilty beyond hope of pardon. She asks only that he take her innocent children into his care so that they will not be left to the mercy of the Romans. Oroveso refuses.

Kneeling before him, Norma makes a final desperate plea in behalf of her children ("Deh! non volerli vittime"), while several priests come forward holding the black veil of death which is placed over the heads of sacrificial victims. Norma's refrain leads into the powerfully dramatic ensemble which concludes the opera. Oroveso, now yielding to his daughter, promises to protect her children and then asks her to embrace him in farewell. Pollione sings that his only wish is to mount the sacrificial pyre with Norma. The Druids and Druidesses grimly intone that this sacrifice will cleanse their altar and temple of defilement.

Throwing the black veil over Norma's head, the priests command her to go to her doom ("Vanne al rogo"). She embraces Oroveso and then sinks into Pollione's arms. Surrounded by the priests, Norma and Pollione walk slowly toward the pyre. As the chorus rises to a climax the curtain falls.

Le Nozze di Figaro

(The Marriage of Figaro)

by WOLFGANG AMADEUS MOZART

[1756–1791]

Libretto by
LORENZO DA PONTE

Based on Beaumarchais's comedy
LE MARIAGE DE FIGARO

CHARACTERS

Figaro, valet to Count Almaviva.............................*Baritone*
Susanna, fiancée of Figaro and maid to Countess Almaviva........*Soprano*
Dr. Bartolo ....*Bass*
Marcellina, Dr. Bartolo's housemaid.........................*Soprano*
Cherubino, page to Count Almaviva...........................*Soprano*
Count Almaviva ....*Baritone*
Don Basilio, a music teacher................................*Tenor*
Countess Almaviva ....*Soprano*
Antonio, a gardener, uncle of Susanna.......................*Bass*
Don Curzio, a lawyer..*Tenor*
Barbarina, daughter of Antonio..............................*Soprano*

Peasants, townspeople, servants

Place: The palace of Count Almaviva, near Seville
Time: Seventeenth century
First performance: Burgtheater, Vienna, May 1, 1786
Original language: Italian

ALTHOUGH *Le Nozze di Figaro* is a sequel to *Il Barbiere di Siviglia*, it was the first play of the Figaro trilogy to be produced as an opera. Rossini's *Il Barbiere* did not come along until some thirty years later. The principal characters, of course, appear in both operas. Rosina, who was wooed by Count Almaviva in *Il Barbiere*, appears in *Figaro* as the count's wife. Figaro, who has become the count's valet, is planning to marry Susanna, maid to Countess Almaviva. Don Basilio appears again as a music teacher, while Dr. Bartolo, still sulking over his failure to win Rosina and her fortune, continues his plotting against Figaro.

The brilliant overture is familiar to all concertgoers.

ACT ONE

Figaro's apartment, not yet completely furnished. Susanna is trying on a hat, critically observing the effect in a mirror. Figaro is measuring the room. In a brief duet Susanna asks Figaro his opinion of the hat, while he tries to divide his attention between measuring and giving Susanna the proper answer ("Cinque, dieci, venti, trenta").

In recitative he explains that he is trying to find out if the room will accommodate the bed which the count has given them as a wedding gift.[1] Susanna promptly objects to using this room as their bedroom. The two argue the matter in an ensuing duet in which Figaro points out how convenient the arrangement would be, with the count's apartment on one side and the countess's on the other ("Se a caso madama la notte ti chiama"). Should they call at night, it would be but two steps to their respective doors. Suppose, Susanna retorts, the count should send Figaro on a journey for a few days. It would be very convenient for his lordship to have Susanna's room but two steps from his own.

To Figaro's complete astonishment, Susanna reveals that the count is infatuated with her and is determined to take advantage of his feudal rights as master of the house (the right to woo a maid in his service before she is wed to another servant). Susanna leaves to answer the countess's ring.

Now it is clear, muses Figaro, why he and Susanna have been asked to accompany the count to London, where he is to serve as minister. He expresses his thoughts on the matter in the well-known aria "Se vuol ballare, Signor Contino." If that is the way Sir Count wishes to dance, sings Figaro, he shall be glad to play the tune. Meanwhile he has a few tricks of his own up his sleeve. At the conclusion of his aria he leaves.

Bartolo and Marcellina enter, discussing the contract signed by Figaro stipulating that he will either pay back the money he borrowed from Marcellina or marry her. The two then plot to turn the count against Susanna, in the hope that he will support Marcellina in her attempts to marry Figaro. In a spirited aria Bartolo describes how he will launch a campaign of vengeance that will bring this scoundrel Figaro to his knees ("La vendetta!"). After he stalks pompously from the room Marcellina encounters Susanna returning from the countess's room with one of her mistress's dresses and a ribbon. The two women address each other with studied courtesy and then, in a sparkling duet, proceed to exchange feminine insults ("Via resti servita"). Finding herself no match for Susanna, Marcellina rushes furiously from the room.

While Susanna is still calling choice sarcasms after her, Cherubino enters. The page, in great distress, explains that the count, having caught him with his arms around Barbarina, is about to send him away. He cannot bear to leave, he sighs, because of his current passion for the countess. Susanna is to be envied, he goes on ardently, because she is always near his beloved.

[1] In present-day performances most of the recitatives are given in spoken dialogue.

Cherubino manages to snatch the countess's hair ribbon out of Susanna's hands, offering in exchange a love song he has just written. It is a song for all the beautiful women in the world, he exclaims, and then sings the charming and amorous serenade "Non so più cosa son."

Susanna warns him that the count is approaching, and Cherubino quickly hides behind an armchair. Almaviva seats himself in the armchair, much to Susanna's alarm, and adds to her confusion by making love to her. As he tries to persuade her to meet him in the garden that night, Basilio's voice is heard outside. The count starts to go behind the chair, whereupon Cherubino, screened by Susanna, deserts his hiding place and slips into the chair. Susanna flings the countess's dress over him just as Basilio enters.

Looking around suspiciously, Basilio asks Susanna if she has seen the count, adding that Figaro is looking for him. He continues with insinuating references to the count's attentions to Susanna and hints at her flirtation with Cherubino. He advises her to warn the page to restrain his affection for the countess, because it is becoming obvious to everyone in the palace. At that the count emerges angrily, and an excited trio follows ("Cosa sento!").

When the count orders Basilio to bring the page to him at once, Basilio smugly protests that the boy meant no harm. Susanna almost faints, but manages to prevent the two men from leading her to the armchair. Basilio deliberately keeps harping on the subject of Cherubino. The count tells how he caught the page in Barbarina's room only yesterday. Demonstrating how he found the culprit, he walks over to the chair and pulls away the dress, only to find Cherubino in virtually the same predicament.

Angry and chagrined, Almaviva determines to call in Figaro and tell him that Susanna has been deceiving him with Cherubino. He changes his mind, however, when he realizes that the page overheard him making love to Susanna herself only a few moments ago. To hide his confusion he turns angrily on Cherubino, but is interrupted by the entrance of a group of peasants carrying flowers and singing the praises of the count. With them is Figaro, holding a bridal veil.

He explains that the demonstration is honoring the count for having revoked the laws of feudal privilege, adding that he and Susanna wish to be the first to take advantage of his enlightened action by being married this very day. He requests the count to place the bridal veil on Susanna's head in token of his blessing. Almaviva, well aware of Figaro's ruse, asks that the wedding celebration be postponed until evening. Then, he murmurs in an aside, he will thwart Figaro's plans by bringing Marcellina on the scene. The peasants withdraw as they repeat their chorus. Cherubino begs the count not to be too harsh with him, and Susanna and Figaro add their entreaties. Determined to send the page away from the castle, Almaviva decides to give him the post of ensign in his regiment, with the stipulation that he join immediately. The count and Basilio leave.

Figaro offers Cherubino some parting advice in an amusing aria, "Non più andrai," a delightful parody on military heroics. He tells the page that he must now give up his amorous exploits for the sterner duties of war and describes the glories of coming back as a hero—assuming, of course, that he will be lucky enough to come back alive. Joined by Susanna, they march off in mock-military style. The curtain falls.

ACT TWO

The countess's apartment. At one side is the entrance door of the apartment and near it the door of an adjoining room. On the other side is the door of the dressing room. At the rear is a window. In the moving aria "Porgi amor" the countess laments that the count no longer loves her. Susanna enters, and the two discuss Almaviva's wayward affections. They are interrupted by Figaro, who informs them that the count, nettled because Susanna has thwarted his romantic schemes, has gone over to the enemy—that is, Marcellina. But, says Figaro, he means to trap the count in his own intrigues. Basilio has been sent to the count with an anonymous letter warning him that the countess has arranged to meet an admirer in the garden tonight during the ball. Meanwhile Susanna is to ask the count to meet her in the garden at the same time, but Cherubino, dressed as a girl, will go in her place. The countess will then surprise her husband and thus have him at her mercy. While he is preoccupied with his difficulties, Susanna and Figaro will be quietly married. The three plotters decide to act at once, because the count is away hunting. Figaro goes to fetch Cherubino, and as he leaves he repeats a phrase of his aria, "Se vuol ballare, Signor Contino."

When the page arrives to try on Susanna's clothes, he is persuaded to sing another one of his compositions. With Susanna accompanying him on the guitar, he sings the famous aria "Voi, che sapete," in which he describes how he is tormented by the pangs of young love. While the countess compliments him on his singing, Susanna locks the door of the apartment and then goes into the dressing room. Cherubino shows the countess his commission, and she remarks in surprise that it still lacks the official seal.

An amusing scene now follows, in which Susanna, having brought out a dress, gives Cherubino a lesson in feminine mannerisms. She explains how he is to act in the delightful aria "Venite inginocchiatevi." The page proves so adept at imitation that Susanna is quite overwhelmed by his charm. The countess discovers that he has bound her ribbon around his arm to bandage a cut. She asks to have it back, but is touched by his ardor when he implores to be allowed to keep it. Susanna goes into an adjoining room to bring a new ribbon. In her absence Cherubino declares his love to the countess.

His avowals are interrupted by a knock at the door, and the count's voice is heard outside. Cherubino rushes into the dressing room and locks the door, while the countess, trying to control her agitation, opens the apartment door. Almaviva enters with Figaro's letter in his hand. He first demands to know why the door was locked, then asks her to explain the letter. As he watches her suspiciously, there is a noise in the dressing room. The countess explains that Susanna is trying on her wedding gown.

A lively trio follows. The count orders Susanna to come out, while the countess warns her to stay inside. Susanna, who has meanwhile slipped unnoticed out of the adjoining room and is hiding in an alcove, calmly appraises the situation. When the countess refuses to open the dressing-room door, Almaviva furiously declares that he will bring tools to force the door, then orders his wife to come with him. As they leave, the count locks the apartment door from the outside.

Cherubino bursts out of the dressing room. When Susanna tells him that he is locked in the apartment, he rushes panic-stricken to the window and jumps out. There is a tremendous crash below. Susanna looks down, sees that he has made his escape, then runs into the dressing room and locks the door just as the count and the countess re-enter. Unaware that Cherubino has fled, the countess confesses that it was the page who locked himself in her dressing room. In a fury Almaviva forces his wife to give him the key, unlocks the door, and, drawing his sword, commands Cherubino to come out.

Susanna appears, demurely greeting the count, who stares at her in be-wilderment, while the countess nearly faints in surprise and confusion. When the count rushes in to search the room, Susanna assures the countess that Cherubino has safely escaped. Making the most of the situation, the countess roundly upbraids her husband for his suspicions. Abjectly he begs her forgiveness. As to the anonymous letter, the countess and Susanna de-cide to make an end to their plotting and confess that Figaro wrote it.

They have almost succeeded in placating the count when in walks Figaro. Questioned by Almaviva, he denies writing the letter. The countess and Susanna, having failed to warn him in time, try to pass the letter off as a joke. They implore the count to put no further obstacles in the way of the marriage. Almaviva fumes because Marcellina has not arrived.

To make matters worse, Antonio the gardener now enters. He is quite drunk and is carrying a broken flowerpot. He loudly complains that for some time a variety of rubbish has been flung out of the castle windows into his flower beds. Now the limit has been reached: someone threw down a man. Susanna and the countess, in a desperate aside, implore Figaro to save the situation. He makes an attempt by declaring that he him-self jumped out of the window. When Antonio remarks that the man he saw seemed much smaller and younger, the count angrily exclaims, "Cheru-bino!" Figaro quickly says that the page evidently returned on horseback, because he left for Seville this morning. Antonio says that he saw no horse fall from the window.

Figaro, in growing panic, repeats that it was he who jumped. He tells the count that he was waiting for Susanna when he heard the count outside. Fearing his master's wrath because of the letter, he made his escape via the window. He limps about, saying he hurt his ankle.

At this crucial point Antonio shows Figaro a paper which he found in the flower bed. The count snatches it away, and the others are horrified to dis-cover that it is Cherubino's commission. Figaro stammers that the page left it with him because it had not yet been stamped with the official seal. Com-pletely out of patience, Almaviva tears up the document.

Matters are now brought to a climax with the appearance of Marcellina, Dr. Bartolo, and Don Basilio, who present Figaro's contract to the count and demand that the barber be made to fulfill his obligations. The count, seeing his opportunity to revenge himself on Susanna and Figaro, promises to give the matter proper consideration. A brilliant ensemble ends the act.

ACT THREE

A hall in the palace, decorated for the wedding festivities. The count, pacing about, is musing on the complicated state of affairs of his household. When his back is turned the countess and Susanna enter, the countess urging her maid to arrange a rendezvous with her husband in the garden. She herself will then meet him there. When Susanna mentions Figaro, the countess suggests leaving him out of things for the moment.

The countess steals away, and Susanna approaches Almaviva, overhearing him say to himself that he will force Figaro to marry Marcellina. At that Susanna makes herself known and calmly tells him that she will buy off Marcellina with the dowry the count himself has promised her. She lures him into again declaring his love for her. They arrange the meeting in the garden as they sing the charming duet that begins with the count's fervent expression of his love, "Crudell perchè finora."

Almaviva now leaves as he hears Figaro approaching. Unfortunately, he overhears Susanna exclaim to Figaro that now they have won their campaign. In fury over Susanna's perfidy, the count resolves to thwart her plans. Even though they have bought off Marcellina, he fumes, he will persuade Antonio not to allow his niece to marry Figaro. He will arouse the gardener's exaggerated sense of family pride by telling him that Figaro is of dubious parentage. Then, in the imposingly dramatic aria "Vedrò mentr'io sospiro," he swears he will have revenge.

He is about to go when he encounters Marcellina, the stammering lawyer Don Curzio, Bartolo, and Figaro. Then and there Marcellina's suit is to be settled, Don Curzio having decided that Figaro's contract is valid—he must either pay his debt or marry Marcellina. Figaro protests that he is of noble birth and cannot marry without the consent of his parents. Unfortunately, he continues, he was stolen from them in babyhood, but he has proof of his identity in a certain birthmark. Marcellina asks him if it is under his right elbow. Figaro answers that it is, whereupon Marcellina joyfully exclaims that she is his mother and Bartolo his father—to Bartolo's acute discomfiture.

Another ensemble number follows. Figaro and his parents fondly greet each other, while Don Curzio and Almaviva express surprise and disappointment. Susanna runs in with money to pay Figaro's fine, only to find him embracing Marcellina. Storming that Figaro is deserting her for her rival at the crucial moment, she boxes his ears. During the ensuing sextet, however, things are explained to her satisfaction. After the number Curzio and the count leave, muttering darkly that the happiness of the others will be short-lived. Marcellina and Bartolo decide on a double wedding and give Figaro back his contract, along with a purse, as a dowry. Susanna hands him the money which was to pay the fine. They all leave happily together.

Barbarina enters with Cherubino, who has returned secretly from Seville.

In order to conceal his presence from the count, he decides to dress himself as a girl and join the flower maidens in presenting bouquets to the countess. The two go on their way, and then the countess enters, expressing deep concern about the probable results of Susanna's rendezvous with the count. In the beautiful, stately aria "Dove sono" she recalls the happiness of the past with her husband and voices the fervent hope that she may win back his love. After the aria she leaves to look for Susanna.

The count appears briefly with Antonio, who, showing him Cherubino's cap, insists that the page has returned. The countess, re-entering with Susanna, tells her she must write a note to the count, definitely fixing the time and place for the rendezvous. The engaging *Letter Duet* follows ("Che soave zeffiretto"). Susanna, writing at the countess's dictation, repeats the words after her in answering phrases. Instead of sealing the letter, they use a pin, writing on the paper that the pin is to be returned with the bearer.

Susanna hides the note in her dress as the peasant girls approach for the flower ceremony. Singing a brief chorus, they present bouquets to the countess, who, catching sight of Cherubino in girl's costume, remarks on "her" resemblance to the page. Antonio, entering with the count, makes his way through the crowd to Cherubino, snatches off his girl's hat, and puts the soldier's cap on his head. There is great consternation, and the count threatens Cherubino with dire punishment. Thereupon Barbarina naïvely reminds the count that he promised her, in return for kisses and embraces, to grant anything she asked. She then requests his permission to marry Cherubino. Confused and embarrassed, Almaviva makes an evasive answer, and to himself he fumes that every move he makes works to his own disadvantage.

Figaro enters, gaily bidding all to prepare for the wedding dance. The count and Antonio, trying to trap him, present Cherubino, saying that the page has admitted jumping from the window. But Figaro imperturbably remarks that one man can leap from a window as well as another.

As the music of the bridal march begins, the count and countess seat themselves on a dais to welcome the wedding guests, who sing a chorus of praise as they march by. They then dance a fandango, during which Susanna secretly gives the count her letter. In opening it he pricks his finger with the pin, which he lets fall. Figaro, dancing near by, takes due note of this and observes to Susanna that the count evidently has received a letter from another admirer. The count invites the people to the wedding celebration which is to be held in the evening. They sing joyfully of the festivities in prospect.

ACT FOUR

The garden of the palace, with arbors to the right and left. Barbarina enters carrying a lantern, and in a plaintive aria ("L'ho perduta") she laments over something she has lost. Figaro and Marcellina appear. Barbarina tells them that she has lost the pin which the count gave her to take back to Susanna with the message that it was to remind her of the "pine tree."

Figaro, assuming, of course, that his fiancée is deceiving him with the count, rushes furiously away, swearing to revenge himself on the whole race of womankind. Marcellina, remarking that women must act together in their own interests, declares that she will warn Susanna.[2] Marcellina leaves, and Figaro reappears to sing his stormy aria, "Aprite un po' quegl' occhi" ("Open your eyes a little"), in which he voices his disillusionment and gives vent to his rage over woman's conniving and deceit. After the number he conceals himself in the background.

The countess and Susanna, dressed in each other's clothing, now enter, followed by Marcellina, who whispers that Figaro is near by. Deliberately raising their voices, the countess and Susanna talk about the rendezvous, and then the maid asks to be left alone. She sings the beautiful aria "Deh vieni, non tardar," an ardent expression of her love, not for the count but for Figaro, who she knows is listening.

As he looks on from his hiding place, raging over Susanna's treachery, Cherubino comes upon the scene. Obeying his natural impulse to woo every pretty woman he meets, he promptly begins making violent love to Susanna, not knowing, of course, that it is the countess in disguise. An exciting ensemble follows. While the countess is trying to fend off the page, the count rushes in with an ardent greeting to the supposed Susanna. Just as Cherubino tries to kiss her, the count interposes himself, and the page kisses him instead. He turns to slap Cherubino but hits Figaro, who has rushed into the melee at this point. The page makes his escape.

Figaro and Susanna now withdraw to different parts of the garden, while the count makes ardent love to his own wife, thinking she is Susanna. He gives her a ring as a pledge of his devotion. Figaro returns in time to see the count lead the disguised countess toward the arbor at the right. Lurking about in the darkness, Figaro encounters Susanna and, believing her to be the countess, tells her that now they both may trap the faithless pair. Susanna tries to disguise her voice, but in an unguarded moment she forgets, and Figaro realizes who she is. He deliberately continues the masquerade and, addressing her as the countess, passionately declares his love. Susanna, provoked to fury, boxes his ears. Figaro happily accepts the blows, convinced by this show of temper that Susanna really loves him.

The count now enters looking for the supposed Susanna, who has meanwhile eluded him. Figaro, catching sight of him, kneels before his "countess" in an exaggerated gesture of adoration, then both he and Susanna rush for the arbor to the left of the stage. Almaviva captures Figaro and shouts furiously for his servants. As Basilio, Bartolo, and Curzio rush in, he denounces his valet and declares that he will now unmask his partner in infidelity.

Storming into the arbor, the count drags forth, in comical procession, Cherubino, Barbarina, Marcellina, and Susanna. The others, seeing Susanna still dressed as the countess, are dumfounded. As Susanna begs the count to

[2] Following this, in the original score, is an aria for Marcellina, after which there is a short scene involving Figaro, Bartolo, and Basilio, then an aria for Basilio. Because of their relative unimportance—musically and dramatically—these scenes are generally omitted.

forgive her, the countess herself emerges from the right-hand arbor. The situation now becomes clear to Almaviva. Thoroughly chastened and repenting his jealous suspicions, he implores his wife's forgiveness and is duly pardoned. All voice their joy over the happy denouement.

Orfeo ed Euridice

by CHRISTOPH WILLIBALD von GLUCK

[1714–1787]

Libretto by
RANIERI CALZABIGI

Based on the Greek legend

CHARACTERS

Orfeo .... *Contralto*
Amor, god of love .... *Soprano*
L'ombra felice (A Happy Shade) .... *Soprano*
Euridice .... *Soprano*

Nymphs, shepherds, shepherdesses, demons, Furies,
Happy Shades, attendants, ballet

Place: Greece and the Underworld
Time: Antiquity
First performance: Hofburgtheater, Vienna, October 5, 1762
Original language: Italian

ORFEO ED EURIDICE, generally considered the oldest opera in modern repertoire, is one of the great milestones in the development of opera. During the seventeenth century opera had become artificial and highly stylized and was rapidly being reduced to a mere vehicle for showing off the vocal accomplishments of individual singers. In *Orfeo,* Gluck abolished the florid, conventional forms and made music and drama mutually dependent on each other. It represented a return to the simple technique of the Florentines and did much to revitalize opera, both musically and dramatically.

Two versions of the opera are generally performed—either the original, or the revised, which Gluck prepared for the Paris première in 1774. The part of Orfeo, originally written for a male contralto, was rewritten for tenor. The role is now generally sung by a female contralto. Certain arias and ballet numbers were added to the original for the Paris production.

ACT ONE

The tomb of Euridice, wife of the Greek minstrel, Orfeo. It is set in a grove of laurel and cypress trees. Shepherds, shepherdesses, and nymphs, placing garlands and funeral vases on the tomb, sing a chorus of lamentation ("Ah! se intorno a quest'urna funesta"). They call upon the spirit of Euridice to look down in pity on her sorrowing husband. Seated under a nearby tree, Orfeo repeats Euridice's name in poignant phrases. He bows in silent grief as the mourners repeat the chorus.

At length Orfeo requests his friends to leave him, saying he wishes to be alone with his sorrow. After circling the tomb in stately procession the mourners disperse. Gazing at the tomb, Orfeo eloquently voices his despair ("Chiamo il mio ben così"). He grieves that his beloved wife lies silent in the bonds of death and does not answer his anguished call. His entreaties to the gods are borne away on the wind. He speaks her name, but only Echo answers. The hills and valleys, the trees and flowers—nature itself repeats the name of Euridice, but there is no reply.

Maddened by grief, Orfeo rages against the gods for their heartless cruelty in taking his wife from him. Springing to his feet, he resolves to defy the gods and journey to the Underworld in search of Euridice. He is certain that the rulers of the infernal regions will listen to his pleas and grant what he asks. As he speaks, Amor, the god of love, appears and tells him that the gods, moved by his sorrow, will allow him to descend to the realm of the dead and claim Euridice. In an ensuing aria ("Dalla cetra tua dolci tuoni") Amor bids him take his lyre and present his plea in song to the rulers of the Underworld. They will be unable to resist his singing and will permit him to bring Euridice back to earth with him. Amor goes on to say, in recitative, that the gods impose this condition: Orfeo must not look at his wife while he leads her back to earth. If he does she will be lost to him forever. Amor then sings another aria ("Gli sguardi tratieni"), in which he exhorts Orfeo to face the ordeal with bravery and courage.[1] At the conclusion of the aria Amor leaves.

In recitative Orfeo reflects that the joy of being reunited with his wife is tempered by the harsh conditions imposed by the gods. He is tortured by the thought of Euridice's confusion and anger when he keeps his face averted. For a moment he quails at the dangers in prospect but then cries that he will risk losing Euridice again rather than live without her. In a dramatic aria ("Addio, o miei sospiri") he declares that he will thrust aside all misgivings, walk bravely through the portals of hell, and boldly force the infernal powers to restore Euridice to him.[2] As he rushes away the curtain falls.

ACT TWO

[*Scene One*]   The portals of the Underworld, beyond which can be seen the lurid glow of hellish fires, occasionally obscured by billowing clouds of smoke. A fearful crowd of Furies stands guard before the gates. There is a short prelude with a heroic theme symbolizing Orfeo's steadfast courage. Harp arpeggios then herald his approach. Hearing these tones, the Furies break out in a harsh unison refrain ("Chi mai dell'Erebo foralle caligini"), demanding to know what rash mortal dares approach the portals of the Underworld.

[1] Sometimes omitted.
[2] This aria is omitted in some versions, the act ending with Orfeo's preceding recitative.

At the sight of Orfeo they dance frantically about and then launch into a repetition of the chorus, in which they describe the horrors that await the luckless mortal intruder—Cerberus, the three-headed watchdog of the infernal regions, and the fierce Eumenides, spirits of retribution with writhing serpents in place of hair. The orchestral accompaniment imitates the barking of Cerberus and the wild cries of the Furies.

During a moment of silence, Orfeo, singing to a flowing harp accompaniment, begins his plea ("Deh placatevi con me!"). His entreaties for mercy are met with thunderous shouts of "No!" from the Furies. In sweeping phrases Orfeo pleads with them to take pity on him, for his soul is racked with pain. Growing quieter under the spell of his music, the denizens of hell ask, in a somber chorus ("Misero, giovane, che vuoi, che mediti"), why he has come to this place of horror and death. When Orfeo answers that he, like them, is suffering endless torment, they murmur that his anguish inspires feelings they have never known—feelings of mercy and compassion. If they had ever been tortured by grief over one who is loved and lost, Orfeo cries, their hearts would now be moved to pity.

The power of Orfeo's music finally triumphs. Slowly the throng before the gates of hell parts to make way for him. They softly intone that his singing has mastered them ("Le porte stridano su'neri cardini") and then, in a sudden dramatic outburst, command the portals to be opened. As they continue to sing in hushed tones that Orfeo has triumphed, he walks with firm step into the infernal regions. The ballet, *Dance of the Furies*, now follows, after which the curtain falls.

[*Scene Two*[3]] The Elysian fields. In an enchanting pastoral scene flooded with a golden radiance, Happy Shades move in a slow, dreamlike dance (the ballet known as the *Dance of the Happy Shades*) to the accompaniment of some of the most exquisite music in the literature of opera. After the dance Euridice (sometimes a Happy Shade) sings a beautiful aria describing the peace and serenity of Elysium, where all earthly sorrow is forgotten ("È quest' asilo ameno e grato"). A chorus of Shades reiterates the theme.

As the music dies away in the orchestra Orfeo appears. Enthralled by the scene, he expresses his wonder and awe in the profoundly beautiful aria, "Che puro ciel! che chiaro sol!" He revels in the dazzling sunlight, the invigorating air, and the celestial harmonies which seem to fill the entire universe. Yet even these scenes, he cries, cannot lift the burden of sorrow from his soul. Only the sight of Euridice can restore his happiness.

From the distance come the voices of the Shades, assuring Orfeo that Euridice will be returned to him. Then follows a brief ballet, during which Euridice appears, her face hidden by a veil. In a recitative Orfeo implores the Shades to allow her to approach. Repeating the chorus, they bid Euridice go to her spouse and share with him the bliss of reunion. As they lead her to Orfeo the curtain falls.

[3] In some versions this is Act Three.

ACT THREE

[*Scene One*] A region between the Elysian fields and the earth.[4] A strange, uncertain light illumines the scene. Orfeo appears, leading Euridice by the hand and gently urging her to hasten on their journey ("Ah! vieni Euridice"). A dialogue in recitative ensues. Mindful of his agreement with the gods, Orfeo keeps his face averted. Bewildered by his apparent aloofness and unconcern, Euridice asks if his love for her has grown cold, or if perhaps her beauty has faded. Haunted by the fear of losing her, Orfeo evades her questions, telling her they must think only of escaping from this place. Euridice bitterly reproaches him for having lured her on with promises of a happy life on earth, then piteously implores him to grant her but a single look. Orfeo struggles desperately against the temptation to gaze upon his wife.

When all entreaties prove futile Euridice turns away, saying that she does not want the freedom that Orfeo has won for her. In an ensuing duet ("Su, e con me vieni") Orfeo beseeches her to trust him and to allow him to lead her out of the realm of death. But Euridice answers that she will go no farther, lamenting that she has been rescued from death only to find new sorrow awaiting her—the sorrow of unrequited love. In recitative and ensuing aria ("Che fiero momento") she continues to bewail Orfeo's silence and indifference. Their voices blend as Orfeo gives way to his despair.

Unable to resist Euridice's anguished pleading, Orfeo cries out that he will defy the gods. He turns to his wife and takes her in his arms, and at that moment Euridice dies. Orfeo is frantic with grief and remorse. In the famous aria, "Che farò senza Euridice?"—one of the most profoundly moving melodies in all opera—he laments that he has lost his beloved Euridice forever. Brokenheartedly calling her name, he vows that he will not remain on earth without her.

Declaring that he will join her in death, Orfeo draws his sword. Just as he is about to plunge it into his heart Amor appears and thrusts the weapon aside. Orfeo has proved his courage and constancy, Amor proclaims, and the gods have ordained that Euridice is to be restored to him. The god of love then leads Euridice forward and tells Orfeo to continue his journey back to earth. They go on their way hand in hand as the curtain falls.

[*Scene Two*] The court of the Temple of Love. Orfeo, Euridice, and Amor, surrounded by a great throng of attendants, move toward the altar in the background to the music of a majestic ensemble, introduced by Orfeo's refrain hailing the triumph of the god of love ("Trionfi Amore, e il mondo serva intiero"). In brief solo passages Amor and Euridice sing that love's rapture will heal the heart wounded by suspicion and distrust.

As Orfeo and Euridice ascend to the raised throne behind the altar a series of dances are performed. During an interlude, Amor, Euridice, and Orfeo hymn the bliss of true and noble love in a beautiful trio ("Gaudio son al tuore queste pene dell'amor"). A final ballet brings the opera to a close.

[4] Act Four in some versions.

Otello

by GIUSEPPE VERDI

[1813–1901]

Libretto by
ARRIGO BOÏTO

Based on Shakespeare's tragedy
OTHELLO, THE MOOR OF VENICE

CHARACTERS

Montano, Otello's predecessor as governor of Cyprus..............*Bass*
Cassio, Otello's lieutenant....................................*Tenor*
Iago, Otello's ensign...*Baritone*
Roderigo, a Venetian gentleman................................*Tenor*
Otello, a noble Moor in the service of Venice....................*Tenor*
Desdemona, Otello's wife......................................*Soprano*
Emilia, Iago's wife and Desdemona's companion...........*Mezzo-soprano*
Lodovico, Ambassador of Venice................................*Bass*
A herald ....*Bass*

People of Cyprus, Venetian soldiers and sailors, innkeeper,
servants, Venetian ladies and gentlemen

Place: A seaport in Cyprus
Time: Late fifteenth century
First performance: La Scala, Milan, February 5, 1887
Original language: Italian

THE OUTLINE of the opera's story follows closely Shakespeare's tragic play, *Othello*. Turkey is threatening the supremacy of the Venetian state in the Mediterranean and has launched an attack against the Venetian-held island of Cyprus. The Duke of Venice has sent out a fleet under Otello, an exceptionally brilliant general, who is also governor of Cyprus.

There is no overture. The curtain rises quickly after a few introductory bars.

ACT ONE

An open square outside Otello's castle overlooking the sea. In the foreground is a tavern and in the background a quay. It is night and a storm is in full blow with much thunder and lightning. A ship has been sighted and identified as Otello's. A large crowd of people, including many soldiers, has gathered, all looking anxiously out to sea. Among the crowd are Iago, Roderigo, Cassio, and Montano.

The opening chorus describes the storm and voices the fear that the ship will be wrecked on the rocks. Iago, in an aside to Roderigo, says he would just as soon see the ship go down. But the danger passes and Otello comes safely ashore, followed by soldiers and sailors. In a brief solo beginning with the exclamation "Esultate!" he announces his overwhelming defeat of the Turks. The crowd cheers and sings of victory as Otello enters his castle, followed by Cassio, Montano, and the soldiers. The storm now subsides and the people start to build a bonfire.

Iago talks with Roderigo, a young gentleman who is much in love with Desdemona, Otello's wife. Roderigo is in despair over the hopelessness of his love, but Iago tells him to have courage and patience, for Desdemona will soon tire of Otello. Iago professes his friendship for Roderigo, adding that he hates Otello, though serving him and posing as his friend. Cassio re-enters and Iago points to him while pouring forth his scorn and envy. Cassio had been made Otello's lieutenant, a post Iago coveted for himself. Iago instead was named Otello's ensign, a lower post. It is this slight that has made Iago, in his burning ambition, hate Otello. He takes Roderigo aside to tell him more.

The bonfire has been lighted and the festive crowd sings of the brightly burning flame ("Fuoco di gioia"). As the firelight dies, servants set out colorful Venetian lanterns in the arbor adjoining the tavern. The soldiers gather about the tables and Iago, Roderigo, and Cassio join them in drinking. After several rounds Iago urges Cassio to have another beaker of wine, but Cassio at first refuses, saying he has had enough. Iago then toasts the fair Desdemona and Cassio joins in the praise of her beauty. This fits in well with Iago's scheming. Now he works on Roderigo's passion and jealousy, telling him that Cassio, too, seeks Desdemona's love, and he cleverly points out how Cassio has just exalted her. "We must make him drink," Iago tells Roderigo. "If he drinks he is ruined."

Pressing more wine on Cassio, Iago surges into the rollicking yet sinister *Brindisi*, or drinking song ("Inaffia l'ugola!"). The chorus takes up the song. Cassio sings and drinks, gradually becoming so befuddled with wine he can sing no more. Iago had kept the song going for just this purpose. Having already slyly built up an active resentment to Cassio in the mind of Roderigo, he now urges him to provoke the drunken Cassio to combat so that an uproar will result and thus arouse Otello.

At this point Montano arrives to tell Cassio it is time for him to stand guard. He is concerned when he sees Cassio's condition, and Iago plays upon his apprehension, telling him that Cassio is always that way before going to sleep. Meanwhile Cassio has grown boisterous and quarrelsome. Roderigo provokes a fight by laughing at him. Montano attempts to intervene, telling Cassio he is drunk, whereupon Cassio draws his sword and attacks Montano.

Iago sends Roderigo off to sound the alarm, then turns to the furiously fighting pair and hypocritically orders them to stop. Montano is wounded. Finally the alarm sounds and Otello appears, followed by men with torches. The fighting ceases.

Otello demands an explanation. Iago innocently claims that he cannot understand it. They were as the closest of friends, then suddenly, as if mad, they drew their weapons. Cassio, ashamed, has nothing to say.

Awakened by the tumult, Desdemona enters. Otello, in great anger, dismisses Cassio from his service for provoking the disturbance. This, of course, is just what Iago had hoped to accomplish. Otello dispatches Iago to quiet the city and Montano is assisted into the castle. The crowd disperses.

Otello and Desdemona are left alone. The act closes with a tender love duet ("Gia nella notta densa") in which the Moor and Desdemona recall the hours they spent together when he beguiled her with his stories of danger and hardship in battle, and she thus came to love him. Their joy overwhelms them. Three times Otello kisses Desdemona ("Un bacio . . . un bacio . . . ancora un bacio") to the accompaniment of the kiss motive, the words and music of which are repeated at the very end of the opera with such telling effect. The storm clouds have now passed and the scene is bathed in moonlight. With their arms about each other Desdemona and Otello return to the castle as the curtain falls.

ACT TWO   •

A room on the ground floor of Otello's castle. At the rear an arched doorway leads out to a garden. When the curtain rises Iago is conversing with Cassio, telling him that Desdemona is usually to be found in the garden at noontime and that his best chance of mending his fortune lies in persuading her to plead his cause before Otello. "She is our general's general and of a kind nature. She will obtain your pardon."

Cassio agrees that Iago's plan is a good one and walks into the garden to await Desdemona. Iago gazes after him with a look of contempt and then, as Cassio disappears among the trees, gives voice to his cynical and altogether contemptible philosophy of life, singing the famous Credo ("Credo in un Dio crudel che m'ha creato"). This is an extremely effective aria that reveals the full treachery and villainy of his character. He believes in a cruel God who has fashioned him in His own image. He believes that life is made but to feed death and that good, honest men are only wretched actors whose so-called virtues—pity, love, unselfishness, and honor—are but falsehoods. (The text of the Credo, incidentally, is Boïto's own invention and doesn't occur in Shakespeare's play.)

Iago pauses as Desdemona comes into the garden, then calls out softly to Cassio, "Go to her. This is the moment." Cassio approaches her. While Iago expresses his satisfaction in the progress of his plot, Cassio and Desdemona walk back and forth at the end of the garden in earnest conversation.

Iago's luck continues. He sees Otello approaching but pretends not to. Leaning against a column and staring toward the garden, he talks as though to himself: "I don't like that." His words arouse Otello's curiosity. The Moor glances out into the garden just as Cassio and Desdemona are disappearing from view. He quickly turns to Iago, asking if that was not Cassio with his wife. Iago answers evasively and craftily arouses the Moor's suspicions by means of hints and continued questions. He asks, for instance, if Cassio knew of Otello's passion for Desdemona in the days when he wooed her. Otello answers: "Yes, why do you ask?" "Just for the satisfaction of my thought," replies Iago. "I did not think he knew her then." "Oh yes," says Otello, "he was often my messenger to carry tender words to her." Iago murmurs: "Indeed," as if to imply that Otello had been too trusting.

Otello sees that Iago has something on his mind and begs him to come out with it; but Iago again replies in riddles, telling him to beware of jealousy, "the green-eyed monster which doth mock the meat it feeds on." Furiously Otello says he will cast aside suspicion and jealousy and will require proof before he doubts. Playing up to his mood, Iago agrees that proof is needed. "Watch closely," he advises, "so that your faith may be restored or your suspicions confirmed."

At this point Desdemona returns to the garden, surrounded by women, children, and sailors who bring her flowers and gifts. They sing Desdemona's praises, accompanying themselves on mandolins and small harps ("Dove guardi splendono"). This scene emphasizes the noble gentleness of Desdemona's nature and the utter contrast between her character and that of the unprincipled, scheming Iago. Otello's attitude toward her softens.

At the conclusion of this little scene Desdemona comes through the archway from the garden into the house, followed by her serving woman, Emilia, who is Iago's wife. Desdemona, of course, knows nothing of the suspicion which Iago has planted in Otello's mind, and in a generous-hearted way begs her husband to reinstate Cassio. He tries to avoid the subject, but she insists. This only seems to arouse Otello's suspicions still further. He begins to think Iago is right and that Desdemona might actually be in love with Cassio. She notices the troubled look on her husband's face and, being a loving wife, asks if he is ill. "Are you not well?" "I have a pain upon my forehead here," he answers. She tries to soothe him by binding her handkerchief around his head, but Otello rudely snatches the handkerchief and throws it to the floor. Desdemona is astonished and dismayed, especially as the handkerchief she offered him was his own first gift to her—a handkerchief with little strawberry designs on it. Emilia recovers the handkerchief.

A dramatic quartet follows in which Desdemona declares her love for Otello and begs forgiveness if she has ever offended him ("Se inconscia, contro te, sposo, ho peccato"). The Moor tells himself that his heart is broken and his golden dream of love scattered in the dust. Iago, who has seen Emilia pick up the handkerchief, demands that she give it to him. Suspicious that he is up to some wicked scheme, she refuses, but he grasps her arm and snatches it from her. He gloats that now he has them in his meshes, while Emilia prays to God to save them from disaster.

Otello orders them all to leave him. Iago admonishes Emilia to say nothing of the incident. Desdemona and Emilia leave, but Iago moves only to the door at the rear as Otello throws himself into a chair and cries out the grief that is in him. Behind him, Iago carefully examines the handkerchief, then puts it away, saying: "Trifles are as good proof as holy writ to the jealous. I will lose this napkin in Cassio's house and let him find it." He watches Otello with grim satisfaction. "The Moor already changes with my poison." Then, approaching Otello cordially: "General, no more of that."

Otello accuses Iago of causing his grief by arousing his suspicion. " 'Tis better to be much abused than but to know it a little," he states. In a touching melody he says farewell to peace of mind, to his thoughts of fame, to his whole military career ("Ora e per sempre addio sante memorie").

Iago pretends to soothe Otello's feelings. This merely infuriates Otello, who throws himself on Iago. Grasping him by the throat and throwing him down, he demands that he prove his accusations. Iago, rising, feigns wounded vanity that his honest efforts should thus be treated, and he is reluctant to speak. He allows Otello to press him for proof. Finally he tells of spending the night with Cassio recently and hearing Cassio murmur of his love for Desdemona in his sleep ("Era la notte, Cassio dormia, gli stavo accanto"). He goes still further: "Have you not sometimes seen a handkerchief spotted with strawberries in your wife's hand?" "It was my first gift to her," answers Otello. "I have seen it in Cassio's hand lately," Iago states. Otello is now beside himself with jealousy. He kneels, lifts his arms heavenward, and cries out a great oath of vengeance ("Si, pel ciel marmoreo giuro!"). Iago's duplicity at this point is almost unbelievable. As Otello is about to rise, he holds him down and, kneeling beside him, he too swears to avenge himself upon those who have wronged Otello. Their voices blend in ringing phrases, and upon this duet the curtain falls.

ACT THREE

The great hall of the castle. At one side is a large portico. At the rear is a terrace. The room is vast and richly appointed. At one side is a raised throne.

After a brief orchestral introduction the curtain rises on Otello and Iago in the hall. From the portico a herald announces that a galley bringing ambassadors to Cyprus has been sighted. Otello dismisses the herald and, turning to Iago, urges him to go on with the tale he has been telling. Iago explains to Otello that he has agreed to meet Cassio very shortly in the great hall of the castle, and that if Otello wants proof of Desdemona's guilt he should hide and listen. As Desdemona approaches, Iago leaves, but he makes one last reference to the handkerchief with the strawberry design.

Desdemona comes into the hall, and in one of the most dramatic scenes in the opera, Otello tries to trap her into confessing her love for Cassio. Desdemona's innocence and the Moor's unreasoning suspicion are displayed in a duet ("Dio ti giocondi"). Desdemona attempts to speak again in behalf of Cassio, but Otello, claiming a cold, asks to borrow her handkerchief. She offers one, but of course it is not the handkerchief with the strawberry pattern. He asks for the one that was his gift to her, but she tells him she does not have it with her. Warning her of great woe if she loses it, Otello says his mother received it from an Egyptian charmer who put a spell on it. He insists that she fetch it, but Desdemona replies that it is a trick to prevent her from speaking for Cassio. She, of course, is moved simply by pity for a fine, brave officer who in a weak and thoughtless moment had endangered his career; but to Otello it seems as if her mind were always on Cassio. He grows even more wild-eyed and insistent. In spite of her earnest assurances of fidelity, he calls her false. Poor Desdemona does not understand this fury. She falls on her knees to assure him of the purity of her love for him ("Esterrefatta fisso lo sguardo tuo tremendo"), but Otello is in no mood to listen or believe.

Sending her rudely away, he utters his sorrowful soliloquy ("Dio! mi potevi scagliar tutti i mali della miseria"). Singing hardly above a whisper, he reveals how completely heartbroken he is now that his illusions have been shattered.

Iago returns and hurriedly whispers to Otello to watch and listen from behind a column, for Cassio is coming. Otello retires out of sight, and as Cassio walks in, Iago begins his craftily planned conversation, which is designed to torture Otello's mind still further. He cunningly induces Cassio to talk of his affairs with Bianca, a woman of the town, but speaks her name so softly that Otello cannot hear it. As they indulge in their half-whispered conversation punctuated by laughter, Iago keeps Cassio at a distance where Otello can hear only snatches of what is said, knowing that Otello will think Cassio is talking of Desdemona. Cassio mentions in an undertone that he has found a lady's handkerchief in his room and wonders how it came there. Iago asks to see it, and he holds it behind him so that Otello can view it from his hiding place. In the trio that follows ("Quest' è una ragna"), Iago pretends to sense a true romantic symbol in the handkerchief. Cassio takes it back from Iago and admires it too while Otello swallows the "proof," doubting not the slightest now that Desdemona has betrayed him.

There is a flourish of trumpets and a cannon shot, the signal of the arrival of the ships from Venice. Iago hurries Cassio off to avoid having him meet Otello in the great hall. In a murderous rage Otello strides from his hiding place and asks Iago to tell him how he can slay Cassio. Iago fans his anger by recalling Cassio's laughter and the reference to the handkerchief. Otello orders Iago to procure poison to kill Desdemona that very night, but Iago advises him instead to strangle his wife as she sleeps. Otello signifies his approval of this method of vengeance, while Iago remarks that he himself will "take care" of Cassio. Impetuously the Moor raises Iago to the rank of lieutenant on the spot, and Iago sardonically thanks him. He announces that the ambassador from Venice is approaching and suggests that Desdemona be present in order to avoid any suspicion. Otello agrees and directs Iago to call her.

During this dialogue, shouts of greeting from those aboard the ships are heard outside. Now the company enters the great hall and in an imposing chorus hails Otello as the "Lion of San Marco." In the forefront of the throng are Iago, the Venetian ambassador Lodovico, Roderigo, Desdemona, and Emilia. Lodovico sings a formal greeting to Otello and hands him a parchment. Otello acknowledges the message, kisses the seal of the scroll, opens it, and begins to read.

Meanwhile, Lodovico pays his respects to Desdemona and she responds. In an aside to Emilia she comments on Otello's angry demeanor. Iago joins the group with a bland greeting to Lodovico, who asks for news of Cassio. Iago replies that Cassio has incurred Otello's displeasure, whereupon Desdemona predicts that the lieutenant will soon be restored to favor. Otello, overhearing this remark, is instantly suspicious. He mutters threateningly to

Desdemona while pretending to read the parchment. Desdemona is bewildered, but Lodovico says casually that Otello has misunderstood. Iago deliberately repeats Desdemona's remark about Cassio, and with innocent sincerity Desdemona says she would do her utmost for Cassio out of her affection for him.

Still pretending to read the document to Desdemona, Otello warns her in a fierce undertone to hold her tongue. Distressed, Desdemona asks his forgiveness. In uncontrollable fury Otello bursts out, "Silence, demon!" and raises his hand as if to strike his wife. Lodovico holds him back while the crowd exclaims in horror. Otello orders Cassio to be brought in, then softly tells Iago to watch Desdemona when the lieutenant enters. In shocked amazement at Otello's conduct toward Desdemona, Lodovico seeks an explanation from Iago. He unctuously shrugs his shoulders and asks to be spared from expressing his opinion.

Cassio enters, and Otello again warns Iago to watch closely. The Moor announces loudly that the Doge has recalled him to Venice. In an aside he snarls an insult to Desdemona. Roderigo, frustrated in his love for Desdemona, cries out in despair. Otello goes on to proclaim that Cassio will succeed him as governor of Cyprus. At those words Iago curses in angry surprise, realizing that Otello's departure will spoil his plans. The Moor and Cassio signify their obedience to the senatorial decree. In a whisper Otello calls Iago's attention to Cassio's discomfiture. He again addresses the company—pausing for another sarcastic aside to Desdemona—declaring that the city's defenses will be left in Cassio's hands. Lodovico, pointing to the stricken Desdemona, implores Otello to speak some word of comfort. Otello's only answer is that they will sail tomorrow.

Suddenly, in wild fury, he seizes Desdemona, orders her to kneel, then hurls her to the ground. In the confusion Otello drops the parchment. Iago snatches it up and slyly reads it. Desdemona, helped to her feet by Emilia and Lodovico, then begins the tragic aria in which she laments the loss of Otello's love ("A terra!—si, nel livido"). She cries out that she lies helpless in the dust and already feels the icy hand of death. She mourns Otello's tender greeting, his smile, his kiss. Nothing now can dry her tears. The aria is continued over the accompaniment of a dramatic chorus in which all join. Those in the throng comment on Otello's mad behavior, then attempt to console Desdemona. Iago approaches and urges Otello to take his revenge on Desdemona before his wrath cools, while he himself swears to kill Cassio. Then turning to jeer at Roderigo, he reminds him that if Otello leaves for Venice, Desdemona will be out of his reach forever. He conspires with Roderigo to murder Cassio in order to prevent Otello's departure from Cyprus and warns him to do as he is told, sneering at him for being a weakling and a coward.

As the chorus rises to a tremendous climax Otello violently orders everyone to leave. The throng falls back in terror. When Desdemona rushes toward Otello imploringly, he turns on her with a terrible curse. The people flee, and Desdemona is led away by Emilia and Lodovico.

Otello and Iago remain alone. Mad with anger, Otello cries for blood and rants about the handkerchief. Convulsed by his rage, he falls fainting to the ground. Iago looks down at him and remarks that the poison is beginning to work. From outside the castle come the shouts of the throng, hailing Otello. In a powerful, unaccompanied musical phrase, Iago exults that at this moment no one could prevent him from grinding his heel into Otello's face. The crowd again hails the "Lion of Venice." Iago points to the prostrate Otello and in arrogant, venomous triumph sings: "Ecco il Leone!" ("Behold the Lion!"). The curtain falls.

ACT FOUR

There is a short orchestral interlude, based on the plaintive theme of the *Willow Song*, which Desdemona sings later in the act. The curtain rises on Desdemona's bedroom. Near the bed is a prie-dieu, and above it the image of the Madonna. A candle burns on the table. Emilia, helping Desdemona as she prepares to retire, inquires about Otello. Desdemona says that he has ordered her to await him. She directs Emilia to make up the bed with her wedding sheets. If she should die, the maid is to use one of the sheets for Desdemona's shroud.

Desdemona seats herself before her mirror and quietly begins a recitative in which she tells the sad story of her mother's maid, Barbara, whose lover went mad. She sang a song of "Willow" to console herself. This evening, Desdemona muses, the song keeps running through her mind. Then she begins the mournful melody of the *Willow Song* ("O Salce! Salce!"). Desdemona gives her ring to Emilia and asks her to guard it. She takes up the song again, then suddenly stops to listen, imagining she hears a sigh or a knock at the door. It is only the wind, Emilia says.

Desdemona ends her song in a simple, unaccompanied phrase of infinite sadness. She bids Emilia good night. Her eyes are aching, she says, and wonders if that foretells weeping. There is a long quiet note in the orchestra, and Desdemona again whispers, "Good night." As Emilia is about to go, Desdemona, shaken by a premonition of doom, pours out an impassioned phrase of farewell. She embraces Emilia, who then leaves her. Desdemona kneels at the prie-dieu and sings a profoundly moving prayer to the Madonna, the quiet, beautiful *Ave Maria*. For several moments she remains in a prayerful attitude, then goes to the bed and lies down.

As the orchestra begins a sinister, foreboding theme, Otello steps through a secret door. He lays his scimitar on the table, pauses before the candle, looks at Desdemona. He blows out the candle and stalks toward the bed. Parting the curtains, he gazes for a long time on his sleeping wife, then kisses her three times as the kiss motive sounds in the orchestra. Desdemona awakes and calls his name. With sinister deliberation Otello asks if she has prayed this night—if there is any unforgiven crime on her conscience—for he does not wish to kill her soul. Terror-stricken, she pleads for mercy.

Otello warns Desdemona to think upon her sins, but she sobs that her only sin is the love she bears Otello. Must she die because of that love? she asks in desperation. Furiously Otello accuses her of loving Cassio. Desdemona denies it. Otello says he saw her handkerchief in Cassio's hands. Ignoring Desdemona's frantic protests, Otello scornfully tells her not to perjure herself on her deathbed by denying her guilt.

Desdemona implores Otello to call Cassio and thus establish her innocence. Otello retorts coldly that Cassio is dead. As Desdemona voices her despair, Otello rages like a madman at her tears, which he imagines are for Cassio. Desdemona begs the Moor to banish, not to kill, her. As Otello curses her in maniacal fury, Desdemona entreats for one moment more to pray. With a terrible cry Otello strangles her.

There is a knock at the door. The clamor of the orchestra dies down to somber, brooding chords as Otello, looking down at his wife, intones, "Calma, come la tomba" ("Calm as the grave"). More knocking is heard at the door. Emilia rushes in with the news that Cassio has killed Roderigo and that Cassio himself still lives. Desdemona stirs in her death agony and cries out that she is dying guiltless. Horror-stricken, Emilia asks who has done this deed. Desdemona gasps that she herself has done it but that she is innocent. Then she dies.

Otello cries out that Desdemona lies and that he himself has killed her. He tells Emilia that Iago proved to him that Desdemona was unfaithful with Cassio. When Emilia brands Otello a fool for believing Iago, the Moor threatens her. Emilia rushes to the door and loudly calls for help. Lodovico, Cassio, and Iago come in. Emilia denounces Iago's perfidy to his face. Montano enters at that moment and adds the news that Roderigo, before he died, confessed his part in the plot against Otello and exposed Iago's treachery. When Otello calls on Iago to answer the charge, Iago dashes for the nearest door and escapes.

Otello strides to the table, picks up his scimitar, and in an agony of remorse calls down lightning from heaven. Lodovico tries to take his sword, but Otello fends him off. Softly, as if to himself, he sings that although he has still another weapon this moment alone seals his doom. He drops the sword, goes to the bed, and looks upon Desdemona. In a final, tragic monologue he mourns her evil fate. Swiftly he draws a dagger from his doublet and stabs himself. Cassio, Lodovico, and Montano exclaim in horror.

Then Otello sings the Italian equivalent of Shakespeare's immortal lines: "I kissed thee ere I killed thee; no way but this, killing myself. . . ." He sinks upon the bed and, as the kiss motive throbs in the orchestra, he sings the impassioned phrases: "Un bacio, un bacio ancora, un altro bacio!" ("A kiss, again a kiss, and yet another kiss!"). Otello falls dead across Desdemona's body and the curtain slowly descends.

Pagliacci

by RUGGIERO LEONCAVALLO

[1858–1919]

Libretto by the Composer

CHARACTERS

Canio, head of a troupe of strolling players ("Pagliaccio," First
  Clown, in the play) ....*Tenor*
Nedda, his wife ("Columbine" in the play) ....*Soprano*
Tonio, an actor ("Taddeo," Second Clown, in the play) ....*Baritone*
Peppe, or Beppe, an actor ("Harlequin" in the play) ....*Tenor*
Silvio, a villager, lover of Nedda.............................*Baritone*

Peasants and villagers

Place: Montalto, province of Calabria, Italy
Time: Between 1865 and 1870
First performance: Teatro dal Verme, Milan, May 21, 1892
Original language: Italian

IN THE minds of opera lovers *Pagliacci* is inevitably linked with *Cavalleria Rusticana*, for these two operas have provided a favorite double bill for years. The careers of Leoncavallo and Mascagni, in fact, bear a remarkable similarity. Each achieved lasting fame with a single opera, while their other works sank into comparative obscurity. It is said that the success of *Cavalleria Rusticana* inspired Leoncavallo to write his opera.

"Pagliacci" was the name given to the mimes and comedians who were the trade-mark of the strolling players of sixteenth-century Italy. The plot is in the familiar play-within-a-play pattern, in which the actors suddenly assume real-life roles. In this instance, the on-stage play is the pantomime of old Italian comedy, with its well-known characters of Columbine, Harlequin, and Clown. Leoncavallo once wrote that in Montalto, the town of his boyhood and the locale of the opera, an actor killed his wife after a performance. The composer's father was judge at the trial. The episode made so deep an impression that Leoncavallo later immortalized it in *Pagliacci*.

The prelude begins with a vivacious theme descriptive of the festive spirit which accompanies the visit of the strolling players to the village on the day of the Feast of the Assumption. Next we hear a brief strain of the aria, "Ridi, Pagliaccio," sung by Canio at the end of Act One. This is followed by several bars of the love music sung by Nedda and Silvio. Then the music reverts to the staccato of the opening phrases.

PROLOGUE

Tonio, the hunchbacked clown, steps before the curtain to sing the *Prologue* ("Si può? Signore! Signori!"). Announcing himself ("Io son il Prologo"), he explains that, in this old play, the author is presenting something true to life. Inspired by poignant memories ("Un nido di memorie"), the playwright wrote down his thoughts to the cadence of his sobs and tears. The result will be a pageant of powerful human emotions. In a ringing phrase Tonio cries, "Andiam! Incominciate [Come then! Let the play begin]!"

ACT ONE

A sunlit village street. At one side a small traveling theater has been set up. From the distance come the sound of a trumpet and the thumping of a drum. Villagers enter, shouting that Pagliaccio has returned. They pause to stare at Tonio, who sullenly lies near the steps leading up to the small stage. The townspeople sing a chorus of welcome ("Viva Pagliaccio") as Canio, Nedda, and Peppe, dressed in their familiar pantomime costumes, enter in a donkey cart. Canio pounds his big drum for silence and then invites the crowd to attend the play about the great Pagliaccio, which is to be given in the evening. As Canio climbs down from the cart Tonio limps up to help Nedda alight, but Canio roughly pushes him aside and boxes his ears. The crowd laughs derisively, and some urchins begin to tease Tonio. He strikes out angrily at them, then retreats into the theater, muttering threats against Canio. Peppe drags away the cart.

Several villagers invite Canio to drink with them. Peppe promptly invites himself. Throwing down his whip at the steps of the theater, he rushes inside to take off his costume. Canio asks Tonio if he is coming along. The hunchback replies that he must first take care of the donkey. One of the villagers hints that Tonio only wants to remain behind so that he can make love to Nedda. Canio, suppressing his anger, sings that if he, as Pagliaccio, found his ladylove with a rival, he would either trounce them both, or make the best of it and perhaps get a beating into the bargain. But were he to find Nedda in such a situation, he says, the end of the play would be much different.

Nedda, aside, exclaims in alarm. Canio, recovering himself, says he adores his wife, and as proof gives Nedda a kiss. The men leave. Soon the villagers appear on their way to vespers, and now follows the well-known *Chorus of the Bells* ("Din, don, suona vespero"). It fades gradually as the people wander off.

Nedda, left alone, recalls Canio's strange outburst and wonders if he suspects her. Dismissing the thought, she muses about the birds, wheeling in the sunshine ("O che bel sole"). This introduces the famous *Ballatella*, one of the best-known soprano arias in operatic repertoire. Nedda sings of the free and joyous flight of the birds ("Stridono lassù").

At the end of her aria Tonio appears, telling her that he was so enthralled by her singing that he could not leave to join the other men. When he ardently declares his love Nedda tells him to save his love-making for the stage. Stung to fury by her insolence and contempt, he advances threateningly, whereupon Nedda snatches up Peppe's whip and slashes him across the face. Shouting that he will have his revenge, Tonio limps away.

In another moment Silvio appears at the wall behind the theater. The love theme vibrates in the orchestra. When Nedda tells him about Tonio, Silvio implores her to end this wretched existence and go away with him. The two voices blend in a long and moving duet[1] ("Silvio! a quest'ora"). While they are singing Tonio steals in, listens for a moment, then slinks away. At last Nedda yields, promising to meet Silvio that night when the play is over.

Tonio and Canio appear just in time to hear Nedda call after the fleeing Silvio that she will be his tonight and forevermore ("A stanotte—a per sempre tua sarò!"). Canio springs forward with a cry of rage. Nedda tries to bar his way as he leaps over the wall in pursuit of Silvio, while Tonio laughs gloatingly. Canio returns. Dagger in hand, he confronts Nedda, demanding the name of her lover. When she coolly refuses to answer he lunges toward her. Peppe, who has been busy behind the theater, rushes forward on hearing the commotion. Just in time he leaps between the two, wrenches the knife out of Canio's hand, and hurls it away. He begs Canio to control himself, for the people are already leaving the church and are coming to see the play.

Tonio, also trying to calm Canio, advises him to bide his time, for the lover may come to the play and there betray his identity. Peppe tells Canio to put on his costume and bids Tonio to beat the drum to announce the performance. He and Tonio retire behind the theater.

Canio, standing alone, sings the great aria, "Vesti la giubba," voicing the tragic fate of the clown. On with costume and make-up! The public pays and must be amused. If Harlequin steals your Columbine, laugh—and win the applause! Change your tears into laughter, Clown—"Ridi, Pagliaccio!" As the orchestra repeats the powerful theme of his lament Canio staggers up the steps of the theater and disappears inside. The curtain falls.

ACT TWO

After a brief intermezzo the curtain rises on the same scene as Act One. It is evening of the same day. While Peppe blows a trumpet and Tonio beats the drum, the people seat themselves on benches arranged in front of the theater. In a lively chorus the villagers express their excitement over the play. Silvio enters and cautiously approaches Nedda, who is passing around a plate for admission money. She whispers that she will be at the rendezvous, then continues on her rounds. A bell rings backstage, and the play begins.

We see a small crude stage, where Nedda, dressed as Columbine, is

[1] Because of the length of this number an optional cut is indicated in the score.

seated at a table. The orchestra plays a minuet which continues as accompaniment to the scene. Columbine sings that her husband Pagliaccio will come home late this evening, then frets because the servant Taddeo has not returned from the market. From behind the scenes comes the voice of Peppe, as Harlequin, singing his serenade, "O Columbina, il tenero fide Arlecchin [O, Columbine, here waits your faithful Harlequin]."

After the serenade, Tonio, costumed as Taddeo, enters carrying a market basket. Columbine asks him if he has brought the chicken, whereupon Taddeo kneels down before her and bids her look in the basket. Then he makes ardent love to her. Ignoring him, Columbine goes to the window and signals outside. With deliberate emphasis Tonio sings that Columbine is the soul of innocence—as pure as the driven snow ("È casta al par di neve!"). Harlequin, carrying a bottle of wine, climbs through the window, sneaks up behind Taddeo, gives him a kick, and tells him to be off. The goodhearted Taddeo offers to stand guard for the lovers and then exits.

Columbine and Harlequin sit down at the table and feast gaily on the chicken and wine. Harlequin gives Columbine a sleeping potion for Pagliaccio. Taddeo bursts in and warns the lovers that Pagliaccio is approaching. Harlequin leaps out of the window. Just as Canio—now Pagliaccio—enters, Nedda repeats, as part of the play, her parting words to Silvio—"A stanotte —e sempre tua sarò."

Canio's anger gives a harsh edge to the familiar accusations of infidelity which are part of the play. Tonio, taking up his cues as Taddeo, calls from outside with sardonic emphasis that Columbine could not possibly utter a falsehood. Canio commands Nedda to tell him her lover's name. When she reproachfully exclaims, "Pagliaccio," Canio cries out, "Pagliaccio non son [Pagliaccio no longer]!" In a dramatic aria he sings that his honor as a man must be revenged and bitterly reproaches himself for having loved a woman who is not worth all the anguish she has caused him.

Nedda taunts that if he considers her so worthless he may send her away, whereupon Canio declares that she will remain here until she names her lover. Trying desperately to continue the play, Nedda, singing to the accompaniment of a gavotte, assures Canio that nothing tragic has happened. But Canio cries out that Nedda either will name her lover or die. The villagers voice their bewilderment at the strange scene. Peppe tries to rush toward the furious couple but is restrained by Tonio.

Suddenly Canio, shouting "Il nome," stabs Nedda. Silvio draws his dagger and rushes to the stage. As Nedda, with her last breath, gasps out his name, Canio whirls and buries his knife in Silvio's heart. He drops his knife, then gasps the closing lines of the tragedy: "La commedia è finita [The comedy is ended]!" The curtain falls.

Parsifal

by RICHARD WAGNER

[1813–1883]

Libretto by the Composer

Based on Wolfram von Eschenbach's poem
PARSIFAL
a fourteenth-century manuscript known as the
MABINOGION
and Chrétien de Troyes's
PERCIVAL LE GALOIS, OU CONTES DE GRAIL

CHARACTERS

Gurnemanz, an elderly knight of the Grail	*Bass*
Four esquires	{ *Sopranos* *Tenors*
First knight	*Tenor*
Second knight	*Baritone*
Kundry, part sorceress, part mortal woman	*Soprano*
Amfortas, King of the knights of the Holy Grail	*Baritone*
Parsifal	*Tenor*
Titurel, father of Amfortas, former King of Monsalvat	*Bass*
Klingsor, a sorcerer	*Bass*

Knights of the Grail, boys and youths, Flower Maidens
of Klingsor's garden

Place: In and about the castle of Monsalvat in the Spanish Pyrenees
Time: Middle Ages
First performance: Festspielhaus, Bayreuth, July 26, 1882
Original language: German

WAGNER regarded *Parsifal* as something beyond mere theatrical entertainment. Because of its profound theme—the spiritual redemption of man through the sacrifice of a Saviour—he designated it as a consecrational festival play and expressly prohibited its performance at any other theater than the Festspielhaus at Bayreuth. Its first presentation outside Bayreuth was in New York in 1903, and it was not introduced to European opera houses until 1914.

The magnificent prelude, familiar as a symphonic piece, states the motives which underlie the central idea of the Holy Grail. First we hear the theme of the Eucharist, after which there emerges the Grail theme—with its *Dresden Amen*—symbolizing the sacred cup of communion. These are followed by the motive of faith and the motive of the lance.

ACT ONE

A shadowy forest grove near the castle of Monsalvat. At one side is a road leading to the castle. At the rear is a lake. It is dawn. Gurnemanz and two esquires are seen asleep under a tree. At the sound of a stately fanfare from the castle Gurnemanz awakens and rouses the esquires, who kneel with him in morning prayer as the horns sound forth the faith and Grail themes. Gurnemanz orders the esquires to prepare to assist Amfortas when he is brought to the lake to bathe the spear wound in his side. Two knights enter, and Gurnemanz inquires as to the King's condition, expressing the hope that the balm which the knight Gawain has found will help heal him. The knights answer that Amfortas lay in sleepless agony all through the night. Gurnemanz sadly muses that only one remedy and one man can heal the wound. The knights ask him to explain, but at that moment a galloping rhythm sounds forth in the orchestra and the esquires exclaim that the sorceress is approaching.

Kundry rushes in. She is an eerie figure in a rough, black gown, with her hair flying and eyes staring in wildest excitement. She hands Gurnemanz a small vial of balsam, crying that if this does not heal Amfortas, then all the potions of Arabia will be of no avail. With that she falls exhausted to the ground.

Amfortas is borne in on a litter carried by knights. Racked by pain, he voices the hope that the lake's pure waters will relieve his agony. A knight tells him that Gawain did not find the herb for which he sought and has ridden forth again to look farther. Deeply troubled, Amfortas sings in the music of the promise motive that he must wait for the one who is destined to save him—the Innocent Fool. Gurnemanz hands him Kundry's flask, bidding him try the potion. When Amfortas tries to thank Kundry she sullenly answers that she wants no words of gratitude. At the King's signal the knights continue on their way to the lake.

The esquires, going about their duties, look contemptuously down on Kundry, who is still cowering on the ground, and jeer that her potion will do more harm than good. Gurnemanz rebukes them, pointing out that Kundry faithfully performs her duties as messenger to Grail knights on faroff battlefields. Since she has found refuge in Monsalvat, he goes on, she seeks to expiate her past sins through devoted service.

In answer to the questions of the esquires concerning Amfortas and Kundry, Gurnemanz launches into a long monologue ("O wunden-wundervoller heiliger Speer!") recalling the legend of the Grail. He relates how Titurel, while fighting pagan hordes, was visited by a host of angels, who gave into his keeping the sacred chalice from which Christ drank at the Last Supper, and the spear which pierced His side as He hung on the cross. Titurel then built Monsalvat as a sanctuary for these treasures and recruited a band of sinless knights to guard them. These guardians are the knights of the Holy Grail, whose duty it is to ride forth into the world and fight on the side of justice and mercy.

Klingsor sought admission to the Grail company but was refused because

he could not conquer his evil instincts. Enraged and determined on revenge, Klingsor gave himself over to heathen magic and learned the arts of
sorcery. He transformed a deserted spot near Monsalvat into a luxurious
garden and peopled it with surpassingly beautiful and voluptuous women,
the loveliest of whom was Kundry. These creatures enticed a number of
Grail knights into the garden, where Klingsor kept them as slave-warriors.
Amfortas, who was made ruler of Monsalvat by the aging Titurel, took up
the sacred lance and invaded Klingsor's domain in an attempt to destroy the
sorcerer and free the knights. Kundry, however, tempted him and betrayed
him into Klingsor's hands, whereupon the sorcerer seized the monarch's
spear, plunged it into his side, then fled with the weapon. Amfortas made
his way back to Monsalvat, where he has since been lying tortured by the
wound which will not heal.

Klingsor now has the sacred lance and is plotting to gain control of the
Grail itself. Only he who retrieves the spear can release Monsalvat from the
evil which has brooded over it since the day of Amfortas's tragic encounter
with Klingsor. One day, Gurnemanz goes on in the conclusion of his narrative, when the wounded Amfortas was praying for help, a celestial voice
spoke to him, saying that his redeemer will be an Innocent Fool, made wise
through compassion.

Suddenly cries of alarm are heard in the direction of the lake. Knights
and esquires rush forward, their eyes on a swan fluttering overhead. The
bird plunges to the ground. As a knight steps forward and pulls an arrow
from its body Parsifal is dragged in. The knights and esquires, pointing to
the bow he is carrying, cry out that it was he who killed the swan. Gurnemanz asks him if he is guilty. As the Parsifal motive peals out, the youth
unhesitatingly admits shooting the bird. In majestic anger Gurnemanz denounces him for this wanton killing. Overcome with shame and remorse, Parsifal snaps his bow in two and hurls away his arrows.

Gurnemanz questions Parsifal further but receives only vague answers.
The youth says that he does not know who his parents are, nor anything
about his origin. He does not even know his own name. Gurnemanz, though
irked by his apparent stupidity, is determined to learn more about him. He
curtly orders the knights to return to the King, who is still at his bath. They
leave, while the esquires carry the swan away.

In response to Gurnemanz's queries Parsifal finally says that he remembers that his mother's name was Herzeleide (Heart's Sorrow) and that
his home always has been in the forest. He made his own bow, he explains,
to protect him from wild animals. Gurnemanz remarks on his noble bearing
and wonders why his mother did not provide him with better weapons.
Kundry, who has been crouching at one side, suddenly interrupts. The lad
was reared fatherless, she says harshly. His father was Gamuret, who was
slain in battle. The boy's mother, seeking to shield him from a warrior's
fate, kept him hidden from the world and did not teach him the use of
arms.

Listening to her in growing excitement, Parsifal exclaims that he recalls a
troop of knights in shining armor passing through the forest. He followed
after them for many days. Kundry breaks in to say that the youth encountered men and beasts in his wanderings and that men learned to fear him in

the fury of combat. In naïve wonder Parsifal asks who it is that fears him. The evil ones, Kundry replies. Puzzled at this, Parsifal desires to know who, then, is good. The mother whom he has deserted, Gurnemanz says gently. The boy's mother is dead, Kundry declares. She herself was asked by the dying woman to bear her last greeting to this fool. Furious at her contemptuous tone, Parsifal flings himself at Kundry. Gurnemanz rushes to her aid and rebukes the youth. Shaken by his outburst, Parsifal sinks to the ground in a faint. Kundry aids Gurnemanz in reviving him, then makes her way to a thicket in the background and disappears.

The knights are seen in the distance carrying Amfortas back to the castle. Gurnemanz helps Parsifal to his feet and starts off with him in the direction of the castle, musing to himself that this innocent youth may well be the Grail's destined redeemer.

Now follows what is generally referred to as the *Transformation Scene*.[1] As Parsifal and Gurnemanz begin walking the scene gradually changes to the accompaniment of an orchestral interlude in which the themes of the cry of the Saviour, the bells of Monsalvat, and the Eucharist predominate. The two men climb through a rocky pass and disappear. As the Grail theme soars up through the sound of the bells of Monsalvat, the huge hall of the castle, with its vaulted dome, becomes visible. Parsifal and Gurnemanz enter. In the center are two long tables, extending from the front of the scene to the rear. Knights of the Grail enter and seat themselves at the tables in preparation for the Communion Feast, hailing the ritual in a majestic chorus ("Zum letzten Liebesmahle").

Amfortas is brought in and carried to a couch at the center of the hall toward the rear. Before it is a stone altar on which stands the shrine of the Grail, draped with a cloth. The litany of the Holy Grail is intoned in an intensely moving chorus ("Den sündigen Welten"), which is sung by a choir of youths at the middle height of the dome and a boys' choir at the top.

At the conclusion of the chorus the voice of Titurel is heard as though issuing from a tomb. He exhorts Amfortas to perform the office of Holy Communion, and in so doing expiate his guilt. As the esquires move forward to uncover the Grail, Amfortas stops them with the cry, "Lasst ihn unenthüllt [Leave it undisclosed]!" He launches into a long monologue of bitter self-reproach, protesting that his guilt has rendered him unworthy of this sacred task. He prays for divine forgiveness, so that he may die in peace.

Spent by his confession, he falls back in a faint. The voices of the invisible choir exhort him to put his faith in the Innocent Fool who will come to redeem him, while the knights urge him to perform the holy office. The esquires uncover the golden shrine, take out a crystal cup, and set it before Amfortas, who slowly revives. He remains with bowed head before the chalice, while the theme of the Eucharist sings softly in the orchestra. The scene gradually grows darker until it is enveloped in complete blackness.

Suddenly the cup begins to glow in a wine-colored light which spreads through the darkness. Amfortas lifts it up and moves it from side to side in

[1] Wagner's original stage directions called for moving scenery to give the illusion of the journey from the grove to the castle. In present-day productions the curtain is generally lowered for a scene change.

a gesture of consecration. Titurel's voice is heard in an exultant phrase. Then Amfortas sets the cup on the table, while its glow fades and the scene again brightens. The esquires replace the cup in the shrine, then pass the Bread and Wine for the Communion Feast.

Gurnemanz, who has seated himself at the table with the knights, motions to Parsifal to sit beside him and partake of the Bread and Wine. The youth, who has been watching the scene as though spellbound, neither moves nor speaks. The knights join with the invisible choir in singing of the Last Supper ("Blut und Leib der heil'gen Gabe"). At the conclusion of the chorus the knights advance to the center, embrace each other, and then prepare to leave. Amfortas, with his wound torn open as the result of his feverish ecstasy, is borne groaning from the hall, followed by the company. Parsifal, transfixed by the scene, puts his hand to his side in a convulsive movement as he hears Amfortas's cry of pain. Gurnemanz approaches and asks him if he has understood what he has just seen. As though his senses were dulled by pain, Parsifal shakes his head and does not answer. In angry impatience Gurnemanz drives him out of the hall through a side door and then follows after the knights. From far above in the dome a voice repeats the theme of the Innocent Fool. It is answered in a soft phrase by the invisible choir. The curtain falls.

ACT TWO

The open top of the tower of Klingsor's castle. Steps at one side lead up to the battlements. Objects used in the performance of magic arts are scattered about. In the brief but dramatic prelude we hear the motives of Klingsor, the magic, and Kundry. As the curtain rises Klingsor is seated before a magic mirror into which he gazes to see events of the future. He murmurs with evil satisfaction that the Innocent Fool is making his way to the castle. With mysterious motions and incantations he summons Kundry, who seems to rise up from the black depths beyond the tower at the back. She moves as though in sleep. Gradually awakening, she utters a cry of terror at the sight of Klingsor. He jeers at her for humbling herself in the service of the knights and then reminds her that she is still in his power. Now that he wields the sacred spear, he adds, he will enslave the holy knights as well.

But now he must be on his guard, he continues, for one who is more dangerous than any of the knights is on his way to the castle. He is the Innocent Fool, and Kundry must tempt him to his ruin as she did the knights. When Kundry recoils in horror Klingsor warns that he is master and must be obeyed. Ignoring her protests and lamentations, he goes to the battlement to observe Parsifal's approach. He takes up a horn, blows a signal, then commands the enslaved knights below to give battle to the intruder. With savage delight he describes how the confused and stupefied warriors are routed by the youth, exclaiming over the lad's fearlessness and his prowess with the sword. Kundry, now helpless in the grip of Klingsor's spell, vanishes, shrieking, to prepare herself to lure Parsifal to his doom. Gazing down from the battlement, Klingsor gloats that Parsifal will soon be his slave.

At a gesture from the sorcerer the tower disappears and in its place is a lush, tropical garden. Parsifal, standing on the ramparts at the rear, gazes on the scene in awe and wonder. The Flower Maidens, beautiful young girls dressed in light flowing garments, enter in great excitement. In an agitated chorus they lament that their knightly lovers have been wounded by a cruel intruder. Seeing Parsifal, they curse him for bringing this sorrow upon them.

Parsifal, completely enchanted by their beauty, advances slowly. The maidens shrink back in fear, but when they see that he does not intend to harm them they draw close to him. Their hostile manner changes to gaiety and delight over his handsome features and friendly demeanor. Soon they move about him in a sensuous dance, and in an alluring chorus they invite him to share the delights of love with them. At first Parsifal gently fends them off. Finally, annoyed by their voluptuous entreaties, he impatiently orders them away and turns to leave the garden.

At that moment Kundry's voice, tenderly singing Parsifal's name, comes from the depths of the garden. The youth pauses in astonishment, murmuring that his mother once called to him thus in a dream. At the sound of Kundry's voice the Flower Maidens withdraw to the castle, regretfully bidding Parsifal farewell. Kundry gradually becomes visible in the background. Now in the disguise of a ravishingly beautiful woman, she is lying on a bed of flowers, her arms temptingly outstretched.

Wonderingly the youth asks why she called him by the strange name of Parsifal. Kundry answers that it is a name she coined from the one his father gave him—"Falparsi"—signifying innocence in folly and folly in innocence, and to tell him this at long last, she has come to the garden. In an ensuing monologue ("Ich sah das Kind an seiner Mutter Brust") Kundry tells Parsifal of his mother, Herzeleide, and the events of his youth. The narrative is dominated by the Herzeleide theme. Kundry deliberately stirs his emotions by telling him that his mother died of a broken heart when he left her to roam about in the world.

As Parsifal gives way to his remorse, Kundry, pretending to console him, draws him to her side with tender caresses. Parsifal laments that in his folly he has forgotten his mother's love, then is suddenly haunted by a torturing thought. As the theme of Amfortas's agony flashes through the orchestra he presses his hand to his side.

Kundry, gathering him in her embrace, sings that by confession to her he will absolve himself of the sin against his mother. Obedient to her wish, Kundry goes on, she has come to teach him love. With that she presses her mouth to his in a long, passionate kiss, while the magic motive sweeps through the orchestra.

Suddenly Parsifal, clutching his hand to his heart, leaps to his feet with a terrible cry of pain ("Amfortas! Die Wunde!"). As though in a delirium, he raves that the spear wound is burning in his side, then in feverish ecstasy he recalls the scene of the Communion. In rising frenzy he cries out that he hears the agonized voice of the Saviour calling on him to redeem the Grail from the thralldom of sin.

Using all her powers of seduction, Kundry tries to turn his thoughts to her. In a sudden flash of understanding Parsifal exclaims that it was with these very caresses that Kundry tempted Amfortas and lured him to his doom. Furiously he struggles out of her embrace. Kundry turns on him in bitter reproach, asking why—if he is indeed the appointed redeemer—he does not save her. In the intensely dramatic aria ("Seit Ewigkeiten harre ich deiner") she tells of the curse that is upon her. At the Crucifixion she looked on the Saviour and laughed at His agony. Since that day she has been condemned to wander about the earth, seeking one who will redeem her from the curse. But always when she is in reach of salvation the fatal, mocking laughter seizes her and dooms her again to torment and frustration. Distractedly she implores Parsifal to take her in his arms for but one hour so that she may find atonement.

Parsifal answers that were he to yield to her they both would be damned forever. He can redeem her only if she will cleanse her heart of its carnal desires. Now at last, he sings, he knows the torment of humanity's struggle between good and evil. At these words Kundry exults that her kiss has bestowed manhood's wisdom on Parsifal. Her love, she tells him, can make him a god and at the same time deliver her from the curse of her laughter. Parsifal consents to help her if she will lead him to Amfortas. Furiously Kundry refuses, declaring that she will leave the fallen monarch to his ruin. Moreover, she warns that she will use the spear that wounded him against Parsifal himself if he dares to spurn her love. In a final desperate effort she tries to embrace Parsifal, but he pushes her violently away.

Leaping to the battlement, she shouts for Klingsor. Turning back to Parsifal, she cries upon him the curse that will doom him to wander, like herself, over the earth in an endless quest for salvation. Klingsor springs upon the battlement with the sacred lance upraised. He hurls it, but it remains motionless in the air above Parsifal's head. There is a remarkable orchestral effect here as a harp glissando vividly portrays the spear's flight toward its target. Parsifal grasps the weapon and makes the sign of the cross with it, proclaiming in ringing tones that the sorcerer's spell is broken forever.

Instantly Klingsor vanishes and the castle collapses into ruins, while the garden is transformed into a desert. Kundry falls to the ground with a despairing cry. Parsifal, leaving the scene of desolation, pauses and turns to her, saying that she will know where to find him. The curtain falls.

ACT THREE

A meadow at the edge of a forest near Monsalvat. At one side is a rude hut. It is an early morning in spring. The introduction reflects the mood of despair that hangs over Monsalvat and then states the theme descriptive of Parsifal's wanderings. As the curtain rises, Gurnemanz, greatly aged and clad as a hermit, comes out of the hut. Hearing groans issuing from a thicket at the edge of the woods, he goes to investigate. He finds Kundry lying unconscious on the ground, carries her into the clearing, and tries to revive her. Finally she opens her eyes and utters a cry of alarm. She is dressed in the rough robe of a penitent, and there is a marked change in her demeanor. Her feverish, excited manner has given way to a calm humility. She looks at Gurnemanz for a long time in silence. When he expresses surprise at her seeming lack of gratitude toward him for saving her life she only mutters, "Dienen—dienen [Service—service]."

Gurnemanz sadly tells her that now the knights have no need for her services. They go no more to distant battlefields and are fending for themselves in the forest like wild animals. Without a word Kundry busies herself about the hut, then goes to bring water from a nearby spring. While there, she sees a stranger approaching and points him out to Gurnemanz. After a moment Parsifal enters. He is clad in black armor, with the visor of his helmet closed, and carries a spear. Slowly, as if deep in thought, he seats himself on a grassy slope. He remains silent when Gurnemanz questions him. The old man tells him that he has come to a holy place where it is forbidden to carry weapons, especially on this day of all days—Good Friday.

Thereupon Parsifal thrusts his spear into the earth, places his sword, shield, and helmet beside it, and kneels before his weapons in prayer. Gurnemanz is astonished to find that he is the youth who killed the swan. Kundry also indicates that she knows the knight—and his spear as well. Parsifal rises at length and approaches Gurnemanz. Recognizing him, he holds out his hand in greeting. In answer to the old man's questions he tells his story ("Der Irrnis und der Leiden Pfade").

Hounded by a curse, he relates, he wandered over the earth seeking the Holy Grail, which he has sworn to restore to its rightful power. He fought many a battle but never once profaned his spear by using it in combat. Now at last he has reached his goal with the sacred lance unstained. Gurnemanz exults over the miracle that has brought the knight to Monsalvat to perform his destined task. He then tells Parsifal of the sad plight of the knights—how Amfortas, tortured by physical and spiritual agony, refuses to perform the rite of Holy Communion and is obsessed with the desire for death. The knights, deprived of the sacred food, have lost their strength and can no longer go forth into combat. Gurnemanz says that he himself has retired to a hermit's hut to wait for death, while Titurel, having been denied the Grail's sustaining power, has died like any mortal.

Parsifal cries out that he is to blame for the misery and suffering inflicted on the company of the Grail. Shaken by anguish and remorse, he sinks unconscious to the ground. Gurnemanz and Kundry bear him gently to the spring and remove his armor. Reviving, Parsifal asks if he may now see Amfortas. Gurnemanz tells him that they both will go to the castle today to attend the funeral rites for Titurel, during which Amfortas is to serve Holy Communion. As he speaks, the somber burial theme sounds in the orchestra.

To the accompaniment of the baptism theme Kundry and Gurnemanz perform a ceremony symbolic of purification. They anoint Parsifal's head and feet with the contents of a small golden vial which Kundry takes from her gown. Gurnemanz then baptizes Parsifal with water from the spring, after which the knight baptizes Kundry. Shaken by sobs, she remains on her knees before him. Gazing about him, Parsifal exclaims over the fresh beauty of the spring morning, and now the great music of the *Good Friday Spell* surges up from the orchestra. Over the music Gurnemanz sings to Parsifal of the meaning of Good Friday—the day when all mankind looks up in gratitude and joy at the cross, where humanity was redeemed by love's sacrifice. Kundry raises her eyes to Parsifal with an expression of humble entreaty. In compassion and tenderness he kisses her on the forehead.

Bells sound in the distance, while in the orchestra the theme of Titurel's burial begins. Gurnemanz brings his Grail mantle from his hut and, with Kundry's help, places it around Parsifal's shoulders. The knight takes up his spear, and then he and Kundry follow Gurnemanz to the castle. The scene changes gradually as in the first act, while the burial theme throbs powerfully in the orchestra. As the bells toll louder the hall of the Grail comes into view.

From one side a procession of knights enters carrying Titurel's coffin. From the other side comes a second procession of knights bringing in Amfortas. The two groups sing antiphonally. Amfortas is borne to the couch behind the altar, while the coffin is placed in front of it. The knights entreat Amfortas to perform the office of Communion, but his only answer is an expression of anguish. Titurel's coffin is opened, whereupon a cry of lamentation rises from the assemblage. Painfully raising himself, Amfortas entreats the spirit of his father to intercede for him in heaven, so that he may be granted the boon of death. The knights crowd toward him, begging him to reveal the Grail.

Frantic with pain and remorse, Amfortas leaps from the couch, tears aside his robe, and bares his wound. Wildly he begs the knights to slay him, the vilest of sinners, and thus bring about the Grail's redemption. As the knights draw back in terror and dismay Parsifal strides forward and places his spear point on Amfortas's wound, declaring that the weapon that caused the wound now heals it ("Nur eine Waffe taugt"). The King, his anguish suddenly turned to joy, reels back and is supported by Gurnemanz. Parsifal sings that his sins have been forgiven and that through the King's suffering the Innocent Fool has received the gift of wisdom.

As the Parsifal motive thunders out, the knight proclaims that he has brought back the sacred lance, which now has been purified by the very blood it once drew. He orders the shrine to be uncovered and the Grail chalice brought forth. Parsifal kneels before the altar. Again the hall darkens, while the cup glows with its mysterious roseate light. The voices of the knights blend with the invisible choir in an exultant hymn of praise to the redeemer. As a piercingly brilliant ray from above illumines the chalice a white dove flutters down from the dome and hovers over the head of Parsifal. Kundry, her eyes fixed on the knight, sinks to the ground and dies. Parsifal raises the chalice in the gesture of consecration. The motives of faith and the Grail soar upward as the curtain slowly falls.

Pelléas et Mélisande

by CLAUDE ACHILLE DEBUSSY

[1862–1918]

Libretto by
MAURICE MAETERLINCK

Adapted from Maeterlinck's play of the same name

CHARACTERS

Mélisande . . . . *Soprano*
Golaud, grandson of King Arkel . . . . *Baritone*
Geneviève, daughter of Arkel, mother of Golaud and Pelléas . . . . *Contralto*
Arkel, King of Allemonde . . . . *Bass*
Pelléas, Golaud's half-brother . . . . *Tenor*
Yniold, Golaud's young son . . . . *Mezzo-soprano*
Physician . . . . *Bass*
Women servants, an unseen chorus of sailors, an unseen shepherd,
three old men

Place: The mythical kingdom of Allemonde
Time: Legendary
First performance: Opéra-Comique, Paris, April 30, 1902
Original language: French

IN MUSICAL STRUCTURE and dramatic concept *Pelléas* is unlike any other opera. There are no set arias, most of the singing being in the form of flexible recitative. The subtle symbolism of the plot has its counterpart in the complex harmonies which Debussy uses to delineate his characters and to motivate dramatic situations. The music progresses through each act in an unbroken chain, with scenes being "bridged" by orchestral interludes. Debussy's opera has been called the most important operatic development since the era of Wagner. Paradoxically enough, it represents, in certain aspects, a return to the simple lyricism of the Florentines, who invented opera.

ACT ONE

[*Scene One*]   A forest in the kingdom of Allemonde. Mélisande is seen sitting at the edge of a well, mournfully gazing into its depths. Golaud appears. In the opening recitative phrases he reveals that he has been hunting in the forest and is pursuing a wounded animal which has escaped him ("Je ne pourrai plus sortir"). He fears that he has gone so far astray that not even his hounds will be able to find him.

As he is about to go on in search of a path out of the forest, he hears a sob. Turning back, he sees Mélisande. Wonderingly he approaches, touches her on the shoulder, and asks why she is weeping. Mélisande springs to her feet in terror and starts to run away. Golaud tries to calm her, but she implores him not to touch her. Overwhelmed by her loveliness, Golaud involuntarily steps nearer, whereupon Mélisande cries out that if he touches her she will throw herself into the well.

Stepping back, Golaud assures her that he will not harm her and then asks if someone has wronged her. The whole world has wronged her, Mélisande sobs distractedly. Golaud tries to learn where she has come from, but Mélisande answers incoherently that she ran away from a distant place and is lost.

A glittering object at the bottom of the well attracts Golaud's eye, and he asks Mélisande what it is. She replies vaguely that it is a crown which "he" gave her—it fell into the water as she wept. After trying unsuccessfully to find out who gave her the crown, Golaud offers to retrieve it, but Mélisande wildly declares that if he attempts to do so she will throw herself into the well. At his promise to leave the crown where it is, she grows calmer and asks his name. He tells her that he is Golaud, grandson of King Arkel. With naïve frankness, Mélisande observes that his hair and beard are turning gray. He is a giant, she murmurs, looking up at him. Golaud, fascinated by her eyes, asks if she ever closes them. Yes—at night, Mélisande answers simply.

When she asks Golaud what brought him to the forest, he explains that he was following a boar which he had wounded during the hunt. Telling her that it will soon grow dark, Golaud urges her to come with him, but she shrinks back, saying she will remain in the forest. Though she finally tells him her name, she refuses to go with him. He warns her that it will soon be very dark and cold here in the forest. Yielding at last to his entreaties, she asks where they will go. Golaud softly answers that he does not know, for he too is lost. As he and Mélisande slowly leave, the curtain falls.

[Scene Two] A room in King Arkel's castle.[1] Geneviève, seated at the king's side, is reading aloud a long letter from Golaud to Pelléas telling about Mélisande ("Voici ce qu'il écrit"). The letter describes how Golaud met Mélisande in the forest and how she seemed to be haunted by a terrible fear. At times she sobs like a child, Golaud writes, and though he has been married to her for six months he knows no more about her than when he found her. He asks Pelléas to prepare the castle for his return with his bride. If Arkel consents to receive Mélisande, Pelléas is to place a light on the tower of the castle overlooking the sea. Golaud writes that if he does not see the light from his ship as he approaches the harbor, he will sail away and never return.

Reflecting on the letter, the half-blind Arkel muses that thus destiny takes its course. Until now, he sings, Golaud has always heeded his advice ("Il avait toujours suivi"). He had sent Golaud to win the hand of the Princess Ursula because he did not think it good for his grandson to live alone after

[1] During all scene changes the music continues without interruption.

his wife's death. That marriage would have joined two houses and would have ended many ancient feuds. But Golaud, it seems, has decided otherwise. Resignedly the king says he will not object, because he is not one to fly in the face of destiny. Geneviève laments that Golaud has changed—he seems even to have lost his love for his little son Yniold.

While they are talking, Pelléas comes in weeping. He explains that he has received a letter from his friend Marcellus, who writes that he is dying. He knows the very day on which he is to die and begs Pelléas to come to him before it is too late. But Arkel tells him that he must not leave the castle because of Golaud's imminent return. And besides, the king continues, Pelléas's own father is lying at the point of death here in the castle, and a son's first duty is to his father. Arkel then leaves with Geneviève, who reminds the sorrowing Pelléas to put the light in the tower for Golaud.

[*Scene Three*]   In front of the castle. Mélisande and Geneviève appear. Mélisande comments on the dark and gloomy forest that surrounds the castle, and Geneviève tells her that in some places the trees are so thick that one cannot see the sun. But one becomes accustomed to the gloom as time goes by, Geneviève sighs, adding that she has lived in the castle for forty years. She calls Mélisande's attention to an opening among the trees through which the sea is visible. As they go toward it, Pelléas appears. He has been looking at the sea, where it is light, he says, and Geneviève replies that she and Mélisande, too, have been looking for the light. Pelléas observes that there will be another storm, like those of the past several days. And yet the sea is so calm, he muses, so calm that one could sail away now and never return.

The chanting of sailors comes from the harbor in the distance ("Hoé! hisse hoé!"). Mélisande exclaims that a ship is putting out to sea. For a time the rising mists obscure the vessel, but when it finally comes into view Mélisande recognizes it as the one in which Golaud brought her to the castle. She wonders why it is sailing when a storm threatens. Perhaps it will be shipwrecked, she says, watching it disappear in the distance. The voices of the sailors float back in a dying phrase.

Telling Pelléas to lead Mélisande back to the castle, Geneviève leaves to look after Yniold. After the two stand for a moment looking out at the sea, Pelléas suggests that they go back by way of the path along the cliffs. He reaches out his hand to her, but she tells him that her hands are full of flowers. Then he must take her arm, Pelléas insists, coming close to her, because the path is steep and it is getting very dark. As they go, Pelléas tells Mélisande that tomorrow he may leave the castle. She asks why, but he does not answer. The curtain falls.

ACT TWO

[*Scene One*]   A well in the castle park. Pelléas, standing with Mélisande beside the well, tells her that its waters have magic powers and can cure blindness. It is called the "Blindman's Well." But since the king himself has lost his eyesight, Pelléas goes on, the blind come no more to be cured. He reflects for a moment over the brooding silence of the forest and then asks Mélisande to sit with him on the marble edge of the well. With the charming artlessness of a child, Mélisande lies down on the stone and stares into the water, murmuring that she wants to see the bottom of the well. No one has ever seen it, Pelléas tells her, because it is as deep as the sea. But one could see a shining object in the water, Mélisande persists, peering downward. Pelléas cautions her not to lean over too far, but she says that she wishes to dip her hands into the water. Ignoring Pelléas's warning, she leans so far over that her hair falls down and trails in the water. It is longer than her arms, Mélisande observes softly, longer even than she is.

Watching her with a certain amused wonder, Pelléas recalls that Golaud also sat beside her at a well. He asks her what she said to Golaud. Mélisande replies that she does not remember. He too wanted to kiss her, she adds with naïve coquetry, but she refused him. As she talks she removes Golaud's ring from her finger and begins tossing it in the air and catching it. No sooner has Pelléas warned her not to play with the ring over the water when it slips out of her fingers and falls into the well. A glissando in the orchestra marks its fall.

Mélisande exclaims in childlike distress, but Pelléas makes light of the matter. Perhaps it will be recovered someday, he consoles, and, if not, another can be found. In wistful regret, Mélisande sings that the ring never will be found again, nor will there ever be another ("Non, nous ne la retrouverons plus"). Pelléas says they must go back to the castle before someone comes to look for them. He reflects that the clock struck twelve just as the ring fell into the well. Mélisande asks him what they are to tell Golaud about the ring. The truth, Pelléas answers. They walk slowly away as the curtain falls.

[Scene Two] Golaud's room in the castle. Golaud, who has been injured, is lying in bed. Mélisande is attending him. Saying he is convinced his injuries are not serious, Golaud tells about the accident that befell him ("Ah! Ah! tout va bien"). As he was riding in the woods, listening to a distant clock striking twelve, his horse suddenly bolted and dashed head-on into a tree. Flung from his saddle, he lost consciousness. When he revived it seemed as though the whole forest was lying across his body, and his heart felt as though it had been torn asunder. But his heart is sound and strong, he says confidently, and he has survived the ordeal without serious harm. Mélisande hovers anxiously over him, trying to make him comfortable. She urges him to sleep, saying that she will watch at his side. But Golaud declares he does not need any further care and forbids her to tire herself by waiting on him.

Suddenly Mélisande weeps. Deeply distressed, Golaud tries to find out why she is grieving. He asks if someone has offended her—Pelléas, or perhaps even the king. Sobbing bitterly, Mélisande answers that the gloomy atmosphere of the castle is making her ill. She would like to go far away with Golaud, she says softly, because she feels that she will not live much longer.

Golaud gently rebukes her for such childish fears and then again asks if she is disturbed over Pelléas. He has noticed, he adds, that his brother does not often speak to her. Mélisande avers it is because he does not like her.

Golaud tells her that she must not be offended. Pelléas is still young, and his ways are strange. But it is not Pelléas who is causing her unhappiness, Mélisande exclaims. It is this castle and all the people in it. They have all grown old, and there is no sunshine nor any joy in living. Touched by her distress, Golaud takes her hands and draws her gently to him. He starts in surprise and alarm when he notices that his ring is not on her finger. He demands to know what she has done with it. Frightened and confused, Mélisande stammers that it slipped off her finger while she was at the seashore gathering shells for Yniold. The tide rose so rapidly that she did not have time to recover it, she explains hastily.

Golaud excitedly commands her to go back at once and look for the ring. She does not realize what it means to him, he exclaims, adding that he would rather have given up all his possessions than to have lost the ring. When Mélisande shrinks in fear at the thought of going to the seashore alone, Golaud orders her to take Pelléas with her. He will not sleep, he says, until the ring has been recovered. Weeping in fright and despair, Mélisande leaves.

[Scene Three]   At the mouth of a cave at the seashore. It is night. Pelléas appears, leading Mélisande. Peering into the cave, Pelléas decides that they must wait until the moon breaks through the clouds so that it will light their way. It is very dangerous to walk there in the dark, Pelléas continues, for just inside are two bottomless pools, with only a narrow path between. Mélisande must enter, however, he advises, so that she will be able to describe the cave to Golaud. Pelléas then tells her of the beauties of the cave—its strange recesses and glittering rock formations. As the moon appears he takes Mélisande's hand and leads her slowly inside. They will go only as far as the moon's light shows them the path.

Looking around, they suddenly see three ragged old men asleep under a projecting rock. Mélisande cries out in terror. Gazing at the gaunt, starved creatures, Pelléas murmurs that there is famine in the land. He wonders why these poor victims have come to this cold and gloomy cave to sleep. As though seized by a strange panic, Mélisande turns and runs out of the cave, crying that they can come back another day. As Pelléas follows, the curtain falls.

ACT THREE

[Scene One]   A tower of the castle. It is night. Mélisande, seated at a window, is combing her hair, which falls loosely over her shoulders and hangs down from the casement. Mélisande observes that her long hair reaches to the very foot of the tower. As she slowly continues combing, she sings a phrase of a childish song ("Saint Daniel et Saint Michel").

Pelléas comes along the pathway under the window, sees Mélisande, and greets her fondly. Her hair, he murmurs, is like a glowing light. He implores her to lean out farther so that he can see it better. When she bends lower, Pelléas looks up into her face and rapturously sings her name.

He entreats her to let him kiss her hand in farewell, for tomorrow he must go away.

Mélisande answers that she will not give him her hand unless he promises to stay. Assuring her that he will not go, Pelléas eagerly reaches up to grasp her hand. As she bends down to him her hair falls over him in a shining cascade. A beautiful duet ensues as Pelléas rhapsodizes over Mélisande's hair ("Oh! qu'est-ce que c'est? Tes cheveux"). It is in his hands, at his mouth, and in his arms, he cries, and he will never let it go. He sings of it as a golden deluge sweeping over his heart. Mélisande gently implores him to let go her hair, but Pelléas declares that he will hold her captive all night long. Ecstatically she murmurs his name. Pelléas sings that he is kissing her hair and that each kiss travels along the strands until it reaches her. As Mélisande tries to disengage herself, her white doves fly out of the tower and flutter about. Mélisande anxiously entreats Pelléas to release her, fearing that her doves will lose themselves in the darkness and never return.

Suddenly she whispers that Golaud is approaching and then tries to tear herself away. Pelléas says softly that she cannot go because her hair is entangled in the branches of a bush. The two wait thus as Golaud comes along the path. He looks up at Mélisande in utter bewilderment and then stares incredulously at Pelléas. As though bemused, he murmurs that they are like two children. With a strange, nervous laugh he rebukes them gently for playing in the dark. Taking Pelléas by the arm, he slowly leads him away.

[*Scene Two*] The subterranean vaults of the castle. Golaud appears, followed by Pelléas. Warning Pelléas to be careful, he inquires if he has ever visited these vaults, and Pelléas answers that he came here once long ago. Golaud points out the stagnant pools of water and remarks about the overpowering stench of death. Taking Pelléas's arm, he leads him to the brink of a deep pit in the floor and in foreboding tones asks his brother if he can see the pit at his feet. In a low voice Pelléas answers that he can see almost to the bottom. He starts in surprise as a ray of light flashes into the depths. Golaud says quietly that it is only the light from his lantern. Drawing back, Pelléas gasps that the foul air is choking him. In silence the two turn and make their way out of the crypt.

A brief but vividly descriptive orchestral interlude marks the passage of Golaud and Pelléas from the reeking gloom of the underground chamber to the sunshine above. The brooding chords give way to sweeping arpeggios as the scene is changed.

[*Scene Three*] A terrace at the entrance of the vault. Hurrying out on the terrace with Golaud, Pelléas voices his relief and joy in being able to breathe the fresh air again in a lyrical refrain ("Ah! je respire enfin!"). He contrasts the foul mists of the vault to the invigorating breeze that is blowing from the sea and marvels over the beauty of trees and flowers bathed in the noonday sun. Looking toward the castle, he exclaims that he sees his mother and Mélisande at the window.

Golaud, who has been watching Pelléas in silence, now tells him that he overheard his conversation with Mélisande at her window. It is not to occur again, he warns. Mélisande must be spared any excitement or shock, for she is soon to become a mother. There have been other times, Golaud goes on, when it seemed as though there might be something between Mélisande and Pelléas, but from now on he is to remain out of her sight as much as possible. His avoidance of her must not be too obvious, however, Golaud adds as he and Pelléas leave.

[*Scene Four*] A place outside the castle, near the windows of Mélisande's apartment. Golaud comes in with Yniold, sits down on a stone bench near the windows, and takes the boy on his knee. With fatherly affection, he chides Yniold for having deserted him for his little mother Mélisande. They are now sitting near her window, he says, looking up, and perhaps at this very moment she is kneeling at her evening prayers.

Golaud quietly begins questioning Yniold about Mélisande and his uncle Pelléas. The boy says he has often seen them together—mostly when his father is away. Yes . . . they quarrel sometimes . . . it is about a door that should not remain open. . . . As the child's attention begins to wander, Golaud, in rising emotion, grips his arm. Yniold cries out in pain and begins whimpering. Hastily trying to calm him, Golaud promises him a bow and some arrows. When Yniold becomes quiet again, Golaud continues his questioning. Though confused and vague, the child's answers throw Golaud into a torment of suspicion. Golaud asks what Pelléas and Mélisande say when they talk together. They talk mostly of himself, Yniold answers, and sometimes of Father, and they always weep together in the dark. Golaud asks if he has seen them kiss. They kissed once, the boy says, once when it rained. Showing how they kissed, Yniold laughingly kisses his father on the mouth. He draws back quickly, exclaiming that his father's beard has scratched him, and then wonders why it has grown so gray.

Suddenly a light appears in Mélisande's room. Yniold, plaintively crying that he is afraid of the dark, implores his father to take him inside to the light, but Golaud tells him that they must remain here for a little while. He asks the boy if he would like to look in and see his mother. When Yniold eagerly answers yes, Golaud, warning him to be very quiet, holds him up to the level of the window. He asks the boy what he sees, and Yniold replies that his mother and Uncle Pelléas are in the room. They are not looking at each other, he says, and they are not speaking. They are looking at the lamp and they do not shut their eyes. Golaud's suppressed fury and despair seem to communicate themselves to Yniold. Crying in fear, he struggles to be let down. Golaud lowers him to the ground and leads him away as the curtain falls.

ACT FOUR

[*Scene One*] A room in the castle. Pelléas and Mélisande meet. Pelléas tells her that he has just come from his father, who has taken a new hold on life and is now out of danger. He relates that his father gazed into his eyes and told him that he had the serene look of one who does not have long to live. He advised his son to go away on a journey. Now that his father is recovering, Pelléas comments, the whole castle seems to be awakening to new life.

Hearing someone approaching, Pelléas quickly asks Mélisande to meet him at nightfall beside Blindman's Well. After tonight he will never see her again, because he is going away in obedience to his father's request. Surprised and dismayed, Mélisande says that she does not know the meaning of his going. As the footsteps outside sound louder, Pelléas hurriedly leaves by another door.

Arkel comes in. In an impressive soliloquy he tells Mélisande that the recovery of Pelléas's father will banish the gloom that has enveloped the castle ("Maintenant que le père de Pelléas"). Looking at her affectionately, he says that he has pitied her because she has been submerged in the dismal atmosphere of a sickroom. She has the strange look of one who is expecting some terrible doom, he continues. Now, however, everything will be changed. Philosophizing over the situation, Arkel asserts that those who have youth and beauty bring new life to things around them. He is certain that Mélisande is destined to assure a happier future for those in the castle.

Arkel tenderly asks her to kiss him, saying that those who are old long for a touch of freshness and beauty to drive away the thoughts of impending death. As Mélisande stands with downcast eyes, Arkel asks if she is afraid of his aged lips. He entreats her to come closer, so that he may at least look at her loveliness.

Without warning, Golaud strides into the room. Obviously wild with anger, he is trying to control himself. He mutters that Pelléas will leave tonight. Arkel notices blood on Golaud's forehead and asks what has happened. Golaud replies that he scratched himself while making his way through a thorny hedge. Arkel tries to wipe off the blood, but Golaud roughly pushes him aside, saying he has come to look for his sword. Mélisande tells him that it is lying on the prie-dieu and goes to bring it to him. Turning to Arkel, Golaud tells him that the body of another peasant, who apparently died of starvation, has been found on the seashore. He complains that all the victims of the famine presumably will come to the castle grounds to die. Snatching the sword from Mélisande's hands, he inquires with brutal sarcasm why she looks at him in fear. Perhaps, he sneers, she is seeking something in his eyes, while she herself hides the secrets of her own eyes from him.

He bids Arkel look at Mélisande's beautiful eyes. The old king observes that they are the eyes of innocence. As innocent as those of a lamb, Golaud snarls, and perhaps God himself could learn innocence from them. As for himself, Golaud says, he knows as much about eternity as he knows about the secrets behind those eyes. Wildly he tells Mélisande to shut them, lest he himself close them for her. He commands her to take her hands from her throat, for he has not threatened her. Then, in a terrible outburst of fury, he seizes her hair and forces her to her knees.

At last, he raves, her long hair will serve a purpose. Grasping it, he wrenches her from side to side. In his frenzy he thinks of Absalom, caught by his hair in a tree. Shouting, "Absalom! Absalom!" he forces Mélisande helplessly to the floor and then bursts into mad laughter. Arkel, horrified at his actions, rushes up and forces him to desist. Golaud suddenly becomes quiet. In cold fury he mutters that Mélisande may do as she likes. It is of no concern to him, for he is too old and has no desire for spying. Exhausted by his rage, he staggers out of the room. Mélisande, overwhelmed by humiliation and despair, weeps bitterly. Looking down at her in sorrow and compassion, Arkel murmurs that if he were God he would take pity on the hearts of men. As the curtain falls, the orchestra underscores the tragic mood of the scene in a powerful climax.

[*Scene Two*]   Near a fountain in the park. Yniold is seen futilely trying to move a stone behind which his golden ball has rolled. He voices his thoughts in a striking monologue which continues throughout the scene ("Oh! cette pierre est lourde"). The stone is heavier than the whole world, he complains as he pushes and tugs. He can see his golden ball, he says, but his arm is not long enough to reach it.

Then his attention is distracted by the bleating of sheep. Looking through the trees toward the road, he exclaims over the many sheep in the flock. They are all pushing toward the right side of the road, he sings, and now the shepherd is throwing stones at them to make them go to the left. The bleating ceases, and Yniold calls out to the shepherd, asking him why the sheep have become quiet. The shepherd is heard answering that it is because they are not going to the fold. Yniold asks where they are going, but the shepherd is too far away to hear. Looking around, Yniold sees that it is getting dark. Pondering over the sheep, he aimlessly wanders away.

Shortly after Yniold has disappeared Pelléas approaches the fountain. He reflects that this is the last time he shall ever see Mélisande. He has tempted fate by meeting her, he sings, and wonders if perhaps it would be better to leave without seeing her again. But he resolves to see her once more, so that he can tell all the things that he has wanted to tell her. Then Mélisande approaches. Eagerly calling her name, Pelléas tells her to come out of the moonlight into the shadow with him ("Viens ici, ne reste pas au bord du clair de lune"). This marks the beginning of their impassioned duet of farewell. Pelléas asks why she has come so late—in an hour the castle gates will be locked. Mélisande explains that she stayed to comfort Golaud, who had been troubled in his sleep by evil dreams. Then when she hurried out of the castle she tore her gown on a doornail and thus was further delayed.

Pelléas exclaims that she is like a poor, hunted bird, trembling and out of breath. Smiling tenderly, he asks her to come nearer. This is the last time they will ever meet, he says softly, and he must tell her now what is in his heart. With that he takes her in his arms and kisses her. In a simple, unaccompanied phrase Pelléas murmurs that he loves her, and Mélisande whispers her answer. Their hushed voices in the tense silence give a strikingly dramatic effect to this climactic moment of the opera.

In awe and wonder, Pelléas sings that their fiery passion has broken its fetters at last. He marvels that Mélisande has spoken fateful words in a voice that seemed to come from the end of the world. When Mélisande reveals that she loved him from the moment they first saw each other, Pelléas seems scarcely able to understand. He asks if she is saying this merely to make him happy during their final moments together. She will not lie to him, even though she lies to his brother, Mélisande answers simply.

Pelléas sings in rapturous phrases of the music of her words and the enchantment of her beauty. He has searched for beauty everywhere, he declares, but only today has he found it. She is the loveliest woman in all the world, he cries. He entreats her to step out into the moonlight, so that they both may see how happy they are. But Mélisande draws back, protesting that she is closer to him in the dark. Pelléas is disturbed by her air of sadness and anxiety.

From the distance comes the sound of grating locks and clanking chains as the castle gates are closed. Gazing at each other in mingled joy and resignation, Pelléas and Mélisande sing that now their fate has been sealed—now everything is lost, everything is won ("Tout est perdu, tout est sauvé!"). Heedless of danger, the lovers remain clasped in each other's arms as a passionate theme surges through the orchestra.

Mélisande exclaims that she heard a noise among the trees, but Pelléas says that is only the beating of her heart. For a moment they stand together in the moonlight, gazing at their lengthening shadows. Then Mélisande whispers that Golaud is lurking behind a tree—there, just beyond the end of their shadow. Pelléas turns and sees him. He has his sword, Mélisande warns. Pelléas murmurs that he does not have his own. Releasing her, he urges her to run away while he detains Golaud. He has seen everything, Pelléas whispers, and will surely kill them both.

Mélisande warns that Golaud is coming toward them. Pelléas cries out for a final kiss, and they clasp each other in a feverish embrace. Golaud flings himself upon Pelléas and strikes him dead with a blow of his sword. Crying out in terror and despair, Mélisande flees into the woods. Golaud strides after her as the curtain falls.

ACT FIVE

Mélisande's room in the castle. Mélisande is lying in bed. At her side are Arkel, the physician, and Golaud, who gravely wounded himself with his sword after wounding Mélisande. Brought back to the castle, she gave birth prematurely. The physician assures Golaud that Mélisande will not die of the minor wound he inflicted. Arkel expresses misgivings over her chances for recovery. It is the way she sleeps, he says, gazing down at her anxiously. She sleeps as though her soul were already cold. Tortured by remorse, Golaud moans that he killed Pelléas without reason. They kissed, he murmurs, but they were like brother and sister, not like lovers. When his voice rises in anguish, the physician adjures him to be quiet, for Mélisande is waking.

Opening her eyes, Mélisande looks up at Arkel and asks him to open the window so that she may look at the sun setting over the sea. After a moment of silence Mélisande inquires if there is someone else in the room, and Arkel answers that another person is present. He will do her no harm, the old king says, and she must not be frightened—the other person is Golaud. Mélisande asks why he does not come to her. Golaud staggers over to the bed. Mélisande murmurs that he is so changed that she scarcely knows him. Golaud begs Arkel and the physician to leave him alone with Mélisande for a moment.

Golaud desperately implores Mélisande to forgive him ("Mélisande, as-tu pitié de moi"). Everything that has happened has been his fault, he goes on remorsefully, and now death is near. But there is one thing he must know: Did she love Pelléas? Mélisande's answer is a simple "Yes," and then she asks if Pelléas is in the room. The tortured Golaud demands to know if it was a guilty love. Neither she nor Pelléas sinned, Mélisande replies. Golaud warns her not to lie at the moment of death and then frantically beseeches her to tell the truth.

Mélisande, her eyes closed, does not answer, but lies as though dead. Looking up, Golaud sees Arkel and the physician watching from the door. As they both hurry to the bed Golaud says that his questions have been in vain and that he will die without knowing the truth. Horrified at Mélisande's deathly look, Arkel asks Golaud what he has done to her. Golaud murmurs that he has killed Mélisande. Suddenly opening her eyes, Mélisande whispers that winter is coming because it is growing cold. The sun is going down into the sea very slowly, she says, and that is a sign of winter. She is afraid of the cold. Arkel brings her child to her, but she cannot lift her arms to take it. She too will weep, Mélisande says, looking at her baby.

The women servants file into the room and line up against a far wall. Golaud demands to know why they have come, but they do not answer. In the final agony of death, Mélisande raises her arms. Golaud frenziedly calls her name and then implores Arkel and the physician to give him another moment alone with her. Restraining him, Arkel exhorts him not to disturb her. The soul, he sings in an intensely moving phrase, must take its leave in silence ("Il ne faut plus l'inquiéter").

At that moment the women servants all kneel. Approaching the bed, the physician feels Mélisande's pulse and then turns away. Arkel muses wonderingly that there was no sound of her going. Golaud sinks down at the side of the bed and sobs in anguish. Arkel tells him gently that he must leave Mélisande to the silence that is now hers. She was a strange creature, he muses, sad and lonely and silent, as are all the people of the world. She looks more like her child's elder sister than its mother.

With the child in his arms, Arkel slowly leaves. The child must live on—now it is the turn of this poor little one, he sings softly. The music dies away on a tender and melancholy phrase as the curtain falls.

Peter Grimes

by BENJAMIN BRITTEN

[1913–   ]

Libretto by
MONTAGU SLATER

Based on a narrative poem, THE BOROUGH, by George Crabbe, an
English poet of the eighteenth century

CHARACTERS

Hobson, carter and town constable..............................*Bass*
Peter Grimes, a fisherman......................................*Tenor*
Swallow, a lawyer..*Bass*
Ned Keene, apothecary and quack............................*Baritone*
The Rev. Horace Adams, the Rector.............................*Tenor*
Bob Boles, fisherman and Methodist............................*Tenor*
Mrs. Sedley (sometimes called Mrs. Nabob), widow
   of an East India Company merchant...................*Mezzo-soprano*
Ellen Orford, widow and schoolmistress.......................*Soprano*
Captain Balstrode, retired skipper..........................*Baritone*
Auntie, proprietress of "The Boar"..........................*Contralto*
Niece One ⎱...*Soprano*
Niece Two ⎰
Dr. Thorp ....*Silent*
Boy (John), Grimes' apprentice................................*Silent*
Townspeople and fisherfolk

Place: The Borough, a fishing village on the East Coast of England
Time: About 1830
First performance: Sadler's Wells Theater, London, June 7, 1945
Original language: English

BENJAMIN BRITTEN, one of England's foremost contemporary composers
of opera, wrote *Peter Grimes* in fulfillment of a commission from the
Koussevitsky Music Foundation. The work has been called the major
English contribution to opera since the time of Purcell, and one that put
England back into the operatic firmament after two hundred years.

Peter Grimes is the story of a man who doesn't "fit in." He is "different"
—and therefore an object of suspicion among his fellow townspeople. It
reflects the classic struggle between the individualist and society. There is
another element of conflict in the opera—expressed by Britten himself when
he said he "wanted to express awareness of the perpetual struggle of men
and women whose livelihood depends upon the sea."

Though in the modern idiom, with an equal share of flowing melody and harsh dissonance, *Peter Grimes* is somewhat in the pattern of Verdi's *Otello*. There are set numbers, bridged by recitatives (as contrasted to the continuous line of Wagnerian music drama). Scenes and acts are linked by six orchestral interludes, played while the curtain is down. These are sometimes heard in concert form.

PROLOGUE

The curtain rises almost immediately to reveal a room in Moot Hall, the town hall of The Borough. A coroner's inquest is about to begin, and the hall is filled with townspeople, all talking excitedly. At a table in front sits Swallow, the lawyer. Hobson, the town constable, calls the name of Peter Grimes. The fisherman, who has been waiting among the crowd of villagers, steps forward.

Lawyer Swallow, reading from a legal document, states that the inquest has been called to investigate the death of Grimes' apprentice, a boy named William Spode. His body, the report reads, was brought ashore by Grimes from his boat, the "Boy Billy." Swallow asks Grimes if he wishes to give evidence. Peter nods. Hobson holds out a Bible, and Peter swears the familiar oath (intoning on a single note): ". . . the whole truth and nothing but the truth."

But when Swallow asks Grimes to tell the story in his own words the fisherman remains silent. Consulting the record, Swallow asks Grimes why he headed his boat for London on that fatal day. Grimes explains that he had a big catch, too big to sell in The Borough. Then a storm blew his boat off its course. He and the boy were at sea three days, and they ran out of drinking water. The boy then died, lying there among the fish. When that happened, Grimes goes on, he threw the fish overboard and steered for home.

In answer to Swallow's sharp questioning, Peter says that when he landed he immediately told Ned Keene, the apothecary, about the boy's death. There was a great deal of excitement when the news got around . . . somebody called the parson, Horace Adams . . . fisherman Bob Boles started shouting. Then, says Swallow, picking up the thread of the story, Grimes was cornered by a group of townsmen, only to be rescued by "Auntie." Next, Swallow goes on, he was abusive to a very respectable woman of the town. At that, Mrs. Sedley steps forward, whereupon Swallow identifies her as the injured party. Glaring at her, Grimes snaps that he doesn't like meddlers.

The townspeople, hanging on to every word, comment in a brief chorus that when women gossip, some unfortunate victim will not sleep at night. Hobson roars for silence. Swallow now wants to know if it is true that widow Ellen Orford, the schoolmistress, helped Grimes carry the boy's body home.

Ellen comes forward. The onlookers, eager for scandal, murmur in chorus that when you shut your eyes, you can't tell truth from lies. Hobson vainly tries to quiet them. Ellen patiently explains to Swallow that she was only trying to help. Swallow rebukes her for having anything to do with a brutal fellow like Grimes. Then he turns to Grimes with a stern warning. He advises the fisherman not to get another boy apprentice, but to hire a man who can take care of himself. The coroner's verdict, Swallow continues, is that William Spode died accidentally. But people remember things like that, the lawyer adds darkly. There is an ominous murmur from the crowd.

Peter speaks up, saying he must have an apprentice to help him run his boat. Then get a woman to take care of him, says Swallow. That, Grimes answers, is exactly what he intends to do—but not until he has cleared his name. Then and there he asks for a trial. Over the chorus of the townspeople, Peter sings that he will thrust the simple truth down the throats of the gossipers. Scorning him, Swallow struts out, and Hobson clears the hall. Ellen and Peter are left alone.

They converse in unaccompanied recitative. Ellen entreats Grimes to come to her home and talk things out. He answers bitterly that she herself will become an outlaw if she is seen with him. Ellen gently bids him have courage, assuring him they can work together to restore his good name. The sun will shine again . . . there will be new shoals of fish to catch. . . . Somberly Peter sings that the dead will always be witness. Then, in a moving unison passage, Ellen and Peter sing that the pain they both feel is drawing them together in a bond of friendship. The curtain falls as the music continues without interruption into Interlude I.

Subtitled "Dawn," this interlude begins meditatively in the flutes and strings, then becomes livelier to portray the town awakening to the day's work. It continues without a break as the curtain goes up, and forms a background for the opening chorus.

ACT ONE

[*Scene One*] A street corner in The Borough, before morning high tide, several days later. One street leads down to the breakwater and the sea, which can be seen in the background. Ned Keene's apothecary shop is on one corner, opposite is Moot Hall. Next to it is the tavern called "The Boar." Fishermen are turning a capstan to pull a boat out of the water. Women mending nets leave off to take baskets of fish from the men who are disembarking. All sing a unison chorus welcoming the fishermen, who can now warm their insides with fiery gin at the bars. Auntie appears at the door of her tavern and invites the men inside. All go in except the stern Methodist, fisherman Boles, who warns that Auntie's gin is poison.

Captain Balstrode, sitting on the breakwater, taunts Boles good-naturedly about his abstinence. Looking toward the harbor, the women sing about the urchins at play, scrambling over the boats. Balstrode chases them away as a second boat is hauled in. A dignified figure comes down the street, ceremoniously tipping his hat. It is Dr. Thorp, who heads straight for "The Boar."

Suddenly Balstrode sweeps the sea with his binoculars and calls out that sea horses are in sight. The wind, he says, is now holding back the tide, but there will be trouble if it shifts. In a rather foreboding choral interlude the fisherfolk sing that then the greedy waves will swallow not only the shore line but their homes as well.

The attention of the villagers is momentarily attracted to the scene in front of "The Boar," where Mrs. Sedley has just encountered the Rector and is bidding him a haughty good morning. Auntie's irrepressible "nieces" call a cheery greeting to the Rector, who answers in considerable embarrassment. Swallow appears and is similarly greeted. From the door of his shop, Ned Keene calls to Auntie that he is coming over tonight to visit with the nieces. Boles glumly warns that the impending storm will soon cool his base passions. This colloquy goes on above the chorus of fisherfolk who sing that the sea has only contempt for the strength and bravery of those who are at its mercy.

There is a sudden silence as the voice of Peter Grimes is heard offstage, calling for someone to help him with his boat. Boles gruffly shouts back that Grimes can haul it in himself. But when Peter appears, rope in hand, Balstrode and Keene take it from him, make it fast to the capstan, and begin hauling in. A short ensemble follows, involving Balstrode, Auntie, Boles, and Keene. Balstrode says he wants to help because the tide is turning. Keene remarks that the storm probably will drown the town gossip. Boles and Auntie sing that the wisest course is to take neither side of the argument, but then Boles self-righteously proclaims that Peter Grimes must be shunned by all respectable people. The four voices blend in a dramatic phrase, concluding this brief passage just as the boat is hauled into view, with Grimes walking beside it.

Keene tells Grimes he has found an apprentice at the workhouse; all Grimes has to do is send Hobson over with a note to fetch the boy. The apothecary calls Hobson and tells him what he is to do, but Hobson answers that his cart is already full. Keene blusters that Hobson is to do as he is told. Boles breaks in to deplore the fact that in a Christian country children can be sold for cash. Hobson stubbornly insists that he has his own errands to do and asks Keene to find some other way to bring the boy from the workhouse. Onlookers who have crowded around mutter agreement with Hobson.

Suddenly Ellen breaks through the crowd and offers to go along with Hobson and bring the boy back. The crowd exclaims in surprise. The boy will need help and comfort so late at night, says Ellen in explanation. In chorus, the townspeople reproach her for trying to help Grimes, warning that she will share the blame for his misdeeds. Ellen turns on them in majestic anger. In a ringing refrain, she repeats the Biblical admonition: Let him who is without sin cast the first stone. Let the Pharisees and Sadducees pass self-righteously by. She will show them how a poor schoolteacher can face her responsibilities. Shamed into silence, the crowd slinks away. Ellen leaves with Hobson.

Only Ned Keene and Mrs. Sedley are left on the scene. Beckoning Ned, Mrs. Sedley asks him if he has her sleeping pills. He tells her he is out of stock, but that Hobson is to bring a new supply in his cart when he returns tonight. Ned asks the woman to meet him later at "The Boar." As she leaves, he sneers that one more dose of laudanum probably will land her in the madhouse.

At that moment there is a warning cry from Captain Balstrode, who calls out that the wind has veered and the tide is rising. This leads into one of the big dramatic choruses of the opera, in which the villagers express the fear that is always uppermost in their minds: the spring tide, with the gale behind it, will eat away the shore line—as it has steadily for years—and finally engulf the village. The chorus ends in a desperate supplication: "O tide that waits for no man, spare our coasts."

As the chorus ends, the fisherfolk scatter, most of them retreating through the swinging doors of "The Boar." Finally only Balstrode and Grimes are left. Then follows a lengthy conversation between the two in duet form. Unmindful of the storm, Peter keeps working at his boat. Balstrode asks him if he prefers the storm to the company in Auntie's parlor. Peter replies he is used to being alone. If that is so, says Balstrode, why not ship out on a merchantman that will take him across the sea—far out of reach of the gossipers. But Peter only answers that he would miss the familiar scenes and the faces of his acquaintances.

In this very town, Balstrode reminds him, mothers frighten their children by threatening to sell them to Peter Grimes. There is a forceful, dramatic effect here when Peter repeats this thought precisely in the phrase Balstrode has sung, but in an enharmonic change of key. Then, Balstrode goes on, there is that coroner's verdict, which casts suspicion on Grimes in the death of his apprentice.

In dramatic phrases, against an agitated figure in the orchestra, Peter tries to explain. On that evil day, he says, he turned his heavily-laden boat into the storm. Gigantic waves poured over the gunwales. At the height of the storm the apprentice became ill and died before his eyes. Then he had to sail home—alone—with the dead child. Balstrode nods sympathetically. This storm is all to the good, he murmurs, because it prompts Grimes to confess and clear his conscience—never mind what the villagers say.

Defiantly Peter cries that he will answer the scandalmongers. They scorn him as a dreamer, but he has an answer for them: they think only of money. Very well. He will get a new apprentice and fish the sea dry. Then he will sell his catches, become a rich merchant, and marry Ellen Orford. Balstrode urges Peter to marry her now, because she'll have him without any money. Peter retorts that he does not want Ellen to marry him out of pity. In that case, Balstrode remarks, it will be the same story all over again —only with a new apprentice. The wind now rises to a shrieking gale, and the two men's voices rise with it in angry argument. Grimes roars that he has made up his mind and scorns Balstrode's advice. The Captain pleads with him to take shelter from the storm. In a ringing phrase, Peter sings that the storm is here—and here he, too, will stay. With a gesture of resignation, Balstrode goes into the tavern.

There is a sudden lull in the storm. Staring out to sea, Peter sings quietly that there is one harbor that will shelter him from all terror and tragedy: Ellen's all-embracing love. The curtain falls.

There is only a moment's pause, and then the orchestra launches into Interlude II ("The Storm"). Its furious tempo depicts the hurricane force of the gale. As it comes to a raging climax, in a series of powerful, dissonant descending chords, the curtain rises.

[*Scene Two*] The interior of "The Boar." It is a typical country pub, with tables and a log fire. Auntie is just opening the door to admit Mrs. Sedley. They both push the door shut with all their might against the wind. Conversation follows in recitative. Auntie tartly reminds Mrs. Sedley that it is past closing time and asks her why she has come. To keep an appointment with Mister Keene—and to find shelter from the storm, Mrs. Sedley replies. The women eye each other suspiciously during a rapid exchange of insults. Finally Auntie tells Mrs. Sedley to sit down in a corner out of sight, and just then Balstrode and a group of fishermen struggle through the door.

Balstrode curses the gale. With a warning nod, Auntie indicates Mrs. Sedley. Balstrode sees her and apologizes for his language. Auntie explains why Mrs. Sedley has come. The Captain nods, then orders drinks, brushing aside Auntie's protest that it is past closing time.

At that moment Boles and other fishermen enter, Boles crying out that the tide has broken through over the Northern Road. Just then the wind tears the door out of his grasp and a tremendous gust howls into the room, wrenching open the shutters of a window and breaking a pane of glass. Balstrode upbraids Auntie for leaving her windows "naked," and follows up with a coarse jest about her two "nieces." The jest is no sooner out of his mouth than the two girls come running down the stairs. Both are hysterical with fright, and they express their feelings in a ludicrous parody of a canon. They wouldn't mind the wind, they whimper, if it didn't howl so. Looking them over with amused contempt, Balstrode suggests to Auntie that she gets some new "relations" who aren't afraid of storms.

Auntie wrathfully turns on him and tells him to mind his manners. While the two nieces gabble aimlessly, Mrs. Sedley frets over being marooned in this terrible place. More fisherfolk make their way inside, and one of them shouts that there has been a landslide up the coast.

Boles rises from the table where he has been sitting, proclaims he is drunk, and promptly gets into a fight with Balstrode over one of the girls. As he swings drunkenly, Balstrode easily overpowers him and plumps him back into his chair. Tavern talk, the Captain observes calmly, should never descend to fisticuffs—live and let live. All those present repeat these eminently moral sentiments in a brief ensemble.

Then the door flies open again, and this time Ned Keene and a group of fishermen come in. Keene says that the cliff directly back of Grimes' hut has fallen down and that the road there is under water. Mrs. Sedley fumes that Hobson is already half an hour late and that she will stay not a minute longer in the middle of this drunken brawl. Keene remarks that if she wants her pills she will have to stay.

Again the door bursts open. There stands Peter Grimes. He advances slowly into the room, a wild glare in his eyes. Mrs. Sedley promptly faints into Keene's arms. The tavern patrons, murmuring "speak of the devil," shrink back. There is an ominously vibrating note deep in the bass, then a long silence. In quiet, sustained tones, Peter begins to express his thoughts aloud, as if he were all alone. He speaks in poetic fantasy of the stars, the earth, and fate, and asks wonderingly: "Who can turn the skies back and begin again?"

At this point, in a sudden change of key, the final ensemble of the act begins. The tavern brawlers murmur that Grimes is either mad or drunk, and they are all for throwing him out. Above the chorus are heard phrases sung by the various principals. The nieces sing that Grimes' gloomy words are enough to sour the beer. The drunken Boles, despite Balstrode's efforts to stop him, staggers up to Grimes and abjures him to "see the light" before it is too late. Peter impatiently pushes Boles aside. Babbling that Grimes is involved in killing boys, Boles picks up a bottle and swings at Peter's head. Balstrode knocks the bottle out of Boles' hand; it shatters on the floor. Auntie frantically tries to quiet the melee. Balstrode helps her by calling for a song. Thereupon Keene steps forward and begins a round: "Old Joe has gone fishing." Auntie takes up the theme. In due course, Balstrode, the two nieces and Boles join in, and finally everyone in the tavern is roaring out the song. As the round builds up into a rousing chorus, Peter's voice is heard over the rest in a kind of obbligato.

At the feverish climax of the chorus, the door swings open. Ellen, Hobson, and a young boy—Grimes' new apprentice—stagger into the room. They are soaked to the skin and spattered with mud. Hobson gasps that the bridge is down. Ellen stands shivering. The two nieces rush over to the boy, but Ellen fends them off.

Peter steps forward and tells the boy to come along home. Auntie cries out that his home has been washed away, but Peter ignores her. As the boy hesitates, Ellen gently takes him by the hand and tells him to go along home with Peter. In anger and scorn the fisherfolk cry: "Do you call that home?" Flinging the door open, Peter leads the boy out into the raging storm. The curtain falls.

ACT TWO

The act is prefaced by Interlude III ("Sunday morning"). The music establishes the serene, sunny mood of The Borough on a calm, clear Sunday morning. It is interesting to note that the melody for violas and cellos becomes the theme of Ellen's first song in the scene that follows. The music of the Interlude continues without interruption as the curtain rises.

[Scene One]   A street in The Borough, as before. At one side is the entrance to the village church. Villagers stand in a group outside the church door; others are coming toward it. As the church bells begin to ring, Ellen and John, Grimes' new apprentice, cross the street against the crowd of churchgoers and walk toward the beach. Looking out over the sea, Ellen sings a joyous refrain ("Glitter of waves and glitter of sunlight"), reflecting the happiness she feels this Sunday morning when men and women go to church with uplifted hearts to worship God. She sits down on the breakwater; the boy plays quietly near by. Ellen tries to get him to talk, but he only smiles and says nothing.

From the church come the voices of the congregation singing a hymn: "Now that the daylight fills the skies." In the ensuing scene, the composer achieves one of the most striking musical effects in the opera. In essence, it is a vocal concerto: Ellen, talking to the boy, sings in solo against the harmonies of the congregation, chanting the service of worship.

When the boy remains silent about his past, despite Ellen's gentle coaxing, she tells him that she herself can fill in the picture. Perhaps he was not too unhappy in the workhouse, after all. As a schoolteacher, she sometimes thought that the lives of children were lonely but carefree. But once she learned to know children, she found they had sorrows of their own—simple, but deeply felt. Ellen goes on to tell the boy that, now he is here, Peter Grimes can make a new start.

From the church comes the voice of the Rector reciting the service, with the congregation making response. Ellen suddenly notices a tear in the boy's coat. When she asks him how it came to be torn he says nothing and tries to hide the place with his hand. Entreating the boy to explain, Ellen looks closer, then unbuttons his shirt and looks at his neck. At that moment, Mrs. Sedley comes by on her way to church. Seeing Ellen talking excitedly to the boy, she stops to eavesdrop. Meanwhile, Ellen opens the boy's shirt and gasps in alarm at the bruise on his neck. That means the beatings, for which Grimes is notorious, have begun again. In a poignant phrase, Ellen voices her despair over Grimes' senseless violence.

Then Ellen gently draws the boy to her. He is not too young, she murmurs, to know what hardships and torments are. But she bids him enjoy himself while he can on this beautiful, sunny day . . . storms will come, to be sure, but afterward there will be quietness and rest.

The tempo of the church service quickens as the choir begins the *Magnificat:* "Oh all ye works of the Lord, bless ye the Lord." This sudden change of mood cues in the entrance of Grimes, who comes striding up from the harbor. He sees the apprentice and orders him to get aboard the boat, then explains to Ellen that he has sighted a shoal of fish and wants to put out his nets at once. Ellen protests that it is Sunday and that the boy is entitled to a rest on this day. Grimes' only answer is to growl another order to the boy, and when Ellen tries to intervene, Peter shouts at her angrily: "Leave him alone. He's mine!"

Ellen desperately implores Peter to be quiet. Coming close to him, she asks why he drives himself so relentlessly. To buy a home, to buy respect, to buy freedom from the gossipers and scandalmongers, Peter bursts out fiercely. In ironic contrast to his violent outcry comes the hushed monotone of the choir chanting the *Credo*.

Quietly Ellen asks Peter how the boy got the bruise on his neck. Peter shrugs off the question. Torn by doubt, Ellen wonders if they were right in trying to defy the village and fight their way back to respectability. In rising anger, Grimes pushes her roughly aside. If it is wrong to struggle and wrong to hope, he cries, then the scandalmongers are right, after all.

Ellen answers that even with all the fish in the sea he cannot buy peace of mind nor protection from the gossips. Giving way completely to her despair, she sobs, "Peter, we've failed!" With a cry of mingled fury and anguish, Peter strikes Ellen, knocking her workbasket out of her hands. For a moment he stares at her, horrified at what he has done. Then he turns fiercely on his apprentice and drives him toward the boat. Weeping bitterly, Ellen goes in the opposite direction.

No sooner are the three gone than Auntie, Ned Keene, and Boles—who have been watching from a window of "The Boar"—rush out talking excitedly. Auntie brands Ellen a fool for wasting tears on Grimes. Keene exclaims that Peter is mad, and at his "exercise." The fanatic Boles intones that the fisherman is in terror of the Lord's flaming sword. They continue their remarks in trio form.

More and more people now come out of their houses and out of the church, all crowding into the village green and discussing the strange behavior of Grimes. Their voices merge into a striking chorus, the central theme of which is this couplet: "What do you suppose? Grimes is at his exercise." The phrase is repeated by villagers walking two by two about the green. In brief solo passages, various individuals smugly moralize over Grimes' misdoings, while the gossip continues full blast.

Boles makes his way to the steps of the church and declares he wishes to speak. This problem, he begins, concerns everybody. He rants about the inhuman apprentice system, then demands to know why the Rector, as guardian of public morals, ignores the evil that flowers at the very door of his church.

While he is speaking, Ellen comes in to gather up the contents of her workbasket, strewn about when Peter knocked it out of her hand. Auntie helps her and then invites her into the tavern. Pointing with quivering finger, Boles shouts that Ellen Orford can explain everything. The Rector, raising his hand for silence, asks Ellen to speak. As Ellen stares at him in bewilderment, the villagers, incited by Boles, clamor that Ellen must explain. The schoolmistress steps forward. There is a long dramatic pause.

She and Grimes, Ellen begins sorrowfully, had planned a new start in life. It was to be built around the new apprentice, whom they would protect from all hardship and danger. Her listeners do not let her finish her sentences. They interrupt either with words of encouragement or vicious accusation. This introduces one of the great ensemble scenes of the opera. First the Rector voices unctuous disapproval. Mrs. Sedley, Keene, and Swallow speak contemptuously of Ellen's plans to help Grimes and the boy. Balstrode angrily turns on the gossips and tells them to mind their own affairs. Boles noisily interjects that the "danger" Ellen means to protect the boy from is merely another name for murder. That word touches off a mob reaction among the rest of the villagers, and they now add their accusations. Whoever besmirches the good name of The Borough, they babble, will suffer the consequences.

Crushed by their taunts, Ellen cries out in anguish over the hardness of their hearts, and Balstrode alone shares her feelings. The accusations of the crowd grow louder; there is a burst of savage laughter as the villagers deride Ellen's talk of kindness. The music rises to a stormy climax as the crowd screams "Murder!"

The Rector steps forward and asks Swallow if they should go and see Grimes in his hut. Mrs. Sedley and the nieces step forward and maliciously offer to give evidence. Balstrode protests, but Swallow, Boles, and Keene shout him down. Yet in the next moment all the men refuse to allow the women to go along. Boles himself roughly shoves the nieces aside and tells them to get back to the gutter where they belong. Swallow orders Hobson to fetch the drum for the march. He runs off and comes back in a moment with the drum.

Led by Swallow, the villagers—now a shouting, hysterical mob—start for Grimes' hut. To the pitiless beat of the drum, they chant that now gossip will be put on trial . . . now the rumors either will die or sweep through the land like a destroying wind. They will kill the slander or the sin, the frenzied villagers cry, and what is now to be accomplished can never be undone. The throng disappears, leaving Ellen, Auntie, and the nieces on the empty stage.

The music subsides into a dejected, minor mood which marks the beginning of an impressive trio—actually sung by the four people on the stage (the two nieces sing in unison). The music reflects the merging thoughts of the four characters involved, divergent though they are. The central theme of the trio is the phrase: "Shall we smile or shall we weep, or wait quietly till they sleep?" In "variations" on this theme, the women sing that all men are children and all women are mothers—this is an old truth that never changes. The trio ends in a soaring phrase as the women look sadly after the grim procession on its way to Grimes' hut. The curtain slowly falls as the music continues into Interlude IV, the *Passacaglia*. (This is a seventeenth-century Italian dance-form in triple rhythm, a classical musical device.) It concludes without interruption as the curtain rises on the next scene.

[*Scene Two*] Grimes' hut, an upturned boat fashioned into crude but fairly comfortable living quarters. Though bare of furniture, it is shipshape, with fishing gear all about. There are two doors—one, at the back, opens on the cliff above the sea; the other, downstage, opens on the road in front of the hut.

Th young apprentice stumbles into the room, pushed violently through the door by Peter, who storms in after him. Peter's first words, "Go there!" are uttered in a wild cadenza. Obviously enraged, the fisherman goes over to a shelf where some clothing is piled, takes down sea boots, sou'wester, and oilskins, and throws them at the boy. Shaking the apprentice roughly, Grimes orders him to put on the clothing at once. Sobbing with fright, the boy tries to obey. Grimes, abruptly controlling himself, puts a steadying hand on the lad's shoulder.

Peter goes over to the cliff door, flings it open, and looks down into the boiling sea below. He orders the boy to bring the nets. Then, in an impassioned monologue, he gives way to his wild thoughts. He will fish the sea dry, Grimes sings, sell his catch, and make a lot of money. He will then ram the villagers' evil gossip down their throats, marry Ellen, and settle down to the life of a respectable citizen.

Suddenly he turns and sees the apprentice crouched on a coil of rope. Again in a rage, he tears off the boy's coat, flings a jersey at him, and tells him to put it on. Then Peter continues, more quietly. He sings that he and Ellen will have a home—a haven safe from storms. In a strange ecstasy he imagines the happiness they will share, the happiness he has read in the stars.

But all at once Peter's mood changes. Dead fingers, he cries bitterly, can tear the dream down, and now the voices of the dead have come back to haunt him. As Peter's voice rises to a feverish pitch, there comes the sound of a drum. It is Hobson's drum, signaling the approach of the villagers.

The sound sets Grimes thinking of the other apprentice. He relives the night of the boy's death on the boat. The drumbeat grows louder, and Grimes begins to hear the voices of the villagers. In blind fury he turns on the boy cowering in the corner. In his half-demented state, Peter confuses the apprentice with the boy who drowned, accusing the lad of conniving against him. The voices come closer. In mounting terror, Grimes shouts at the boy that he is to "blame for everything."

Hysterical with fear, the boy begins dragging nets and tackle to the cliff door, with Grimes urging him along. As the procession reaches the hut, the chorus rises to an awesome climax, repeating its malevolent refrain: "We shall strike to kill, at the slander or the sin." There is a thunderous knock at the other door. In his desperate haste to flee, Grimes pushes the boy. He falls screaming through the open cliff door and disappears. Peter throws the tackle after him and climbs down out of sight.

In the next moment, the Rector, Swallow, Keene, and Balstrode burst through the other door, shouting for Grimes. They rush over to the cliff door and stare into the darkness below, speculating that Grimes probably keeps his boat down there. Then they look about the hut and grudgingly admit that the place is neatly kept. Swallow pompously observes that the present state of things in the hut gives the lie to Borough gossip. He advises everyone to go home and stop meddling—and will the last one to go please close the door . . . ? All the others meekly leave—all except Balstrode.

He waits until Swallow himself has gone, then carefully examines the boy's Sunday clothes, which are scattered about. He goes to the other door, closes it, and quickly crosses to the cliff door. After a moment's hesitation, he climbs down out of sight, just as Grimes did. The curtain falls quickly.

ACT THREE

[*Scene One*]   Before the rise of the curtain we hear Interlude V played in the orchestra. It is meditative, in a minor key; octave skips high in the strings suggest the shrill cries of gulls wheeling above a desolate sea. The Interlude dies away into quiet chords, then suddenly the music changes to the gay rhythm of a barn dance. The curtain rises to show the green before Moot Hall several days later. A dance is going on, and happy laughter sounds above the music. Across from Moot Hall, "The Boar" is brightly lit. As the festivities continue there is a steady procession of young men between the Hall and the tavern.

Suddenly one of the nieces scampers giggling down the outside stairway of Moot Hall. Close behind her is Swallow, who is clumsily trying to make love to her in ridiculous legal jargon. The second niece appears just in time to save the other from the lawyer's clutches. They teasingly sing that there is safety in numbers and that things are better "when the tête-à-tête's in three."

Swallow, ignoring their saucy behavior, continues his avowals in a solemn repetition of his refrain, singing that he will take his appeal all the way up to the House of Lords, if need be. The three express these sentiments in a brief trio, at the end of which Swallow manages to catch hold of the first niece. He starts leading her to "The Boar." By a quick-witted ruse, the second niece helps the first to get away from Swallow, leaving the lawyer fuming at the door of the tavern. With an exclamation of disgust, he goes inside, while the girls run back up the Moot Hall stairs.

They are halfway up when Keene comes out of the door at the top of the stairs. Shrieking with laughter, the two girls run and hide behind one of the boats on the beach. He starts after them, but at that moment Mrs. Sedley appears. The music of the barn dance changes at this point to a slow waltz, which continues throughout the ensuing conversation.

Mrs. Sedley begins by telling Keene that Peter Grimes' apprentice has disappeared. Ned shrugs off this news impatiently. Behind their backs, meanwhile, the two nieces sneak back to the dance. In deep conspiratorial tones, Mrs. Sedley goes on to say that for two days she has been watching and waiting. All the clues, she says in malicious triumph, point to Grimes as the boy's murderer. Keene angrily tells her she is far too eager to accuse. It is murder most foul, Mrs. Sedley goes on, in sepulchral tones, and she will make it known. When she tries to cross-examine Ned, he bursts out that this is either madness or the effect of laudanum. Exasperated with the woman, he turns on his heel and goes into the tavern, slamming the door in her face.

The band music changes here to a merry hornpipe. Dr. Thorp comes out of the tavern. Mrs. Sedley tries to approach him, but he adroitly dodges, tipping his hat. Then the Rector and a group of burgesses come down the stairs of Moot Hall. Mrs. Sedley hides in the shadow of the building. With the music of the hornpipe as accompaniment, the Rector and the burgesses sing a melodious chorus of good night, dominated by solo passages sung by the Rector. As they all go their separate ways, the music of the band fades out.

From the shadows comes the foreboding voice of Mrs. Sedley, reveling in her dire suspicions of murder. She draws deeper into the shadows as Ellen and Balstrode come slowly up from the beach. They are talking earnestly together about the disappearance of Grimes and the apprentice. Ellen shows Balstrode the boy's jersey, saying she found it at the water's edge. Balstrode examines it in the light of his lantern.

Pointing to the anchor embroidered on the jersey, Ellen sings in a moving refrain that this bit of embroidery has become a symbol in her life. When she was a child, sewing was merely a way to pass an idle hour. As a grown woman, she embroidered things for children, thinking of it as weaving some happiness into their lives. And now, by a strange caprice of fate, her embroidery has become a clue in a terrible mystery.

In utter dejection she murmurs that everything is hopeless now. Balstrode tries to give her courage, saying they must not turn their backs on a friend in such desperate need. Ellen momentarily takes hope. Her voice blends with Balstrode's as they both vow to stand by Grimes and the boy. The two slowly leave; Balstrode murmurs to himself that now they can only wait—the answer to the mystery is "beyond life."

In "The Boar," the music starts up again. Mrs. Sedley runs to the tavern door, pushes it open, and excitedly calls for lawyer Swallow. She comes face to face with Auntie, who tells her Swallow is busy. This is official business, snaps Mrs. Sedley, and demands to see the lawyer at once. Auntie calls her a meddling busybody, and then the two begin quarreling furiously. At the height of the shouting, Swallow comes between them. Hurling imprecations, Auntie goes back inside the tavern and slams the door.

Mrs. Sedley suddenly looks toward the beach and points dramatically, crying out that Grimes' boat is back. Swallow gasps in amazement, then shouts back into the tavern for Hobson. When the constable appears, Swallow orders him to start a search at once for Grimes. The lawyer rushes back into the tavern. With evil glee, Mrs. Sedley gloats that murder—the noblest of crimes, and her hobby—is at hand and she is ready.

Meanwhile, Hobson's shouts for helpers bring the villagers stampeding out on the green. As though under a demonic spell, they begin to sing that he who holds himself apart, him they will destroy. This introduces the great climactic ensemble of the opera. Repeating the threatening words over and over, the villagers whip themselves into a frenzy. Lusting for revenge, they howl with insane laughter as they vow to make the murderer atone for his crime. The chorus comes to a terrifying climax with a shout of "Peter Grimes!" Then the crowd rushes headlong into the night. The curtain quickly falls. Interlude VI ("Moonlight") follows immediately. Its weird, unearthly harmonies give the impression of doom and madness to come. At the end of the Interlude the curtain rises.

[*Scene Two*] The same as before, several hours later. There is a thick fog. The distant cries of the searchers mingle with the sound of foghorns.

Suddenly Grimes staggers in, wild-eyed and obviously out of his mind. In disjointed phrases he talks of the boy who died, rants about the gossipers, and calls to Ellen for help. He shouts a defiant curse, then listens breathlessly as he hears the searchers calling his name. He screams the name back at them, and then his voice trails off into silence.

As he stares unseeing into space, Ellen and Balstrode approach. They stand for a moment watching, then Ellen goes up to him. Gently she tells him they have come to take him home. Grimes gives no sign of recognition. The voices of the searchers grow fainter, but their call of "Peter" continues with terrible insistence. Over these sounds, Peter sings the poignant refrain he sang in the first act after his meeting with Ellen: "What harbor shelters peace." His voice fades away, as do the distant voices of the villagers. Their call of "Peter" changes from a harsh cry to a whisper of tender entreaty.

Balstrode takes Peter by the arm and tells him he will help him with the boat. Sensing what Balstrode is about to do, Ellen utters an anguished cry of protest. But Balstrode tells Peter to sail until he loses sight of Moot Hall, then sink the boat. Without a word, Peter gets into the boat. Balstrode watches him for a moment, waves good-by, then takes Ellen's arm and gently leads her away.

Dawn slowly brightens the sky. As the orchestral accompaniment begins high in the strings, The Borough stirs to the tasks of another day. Shutters are thrown open. Some of the searchers straggle wearily home across the green. As people begin to go about their routine work, the chorus of women sings that another day has begun. Swallow enters and tells a group of fishermen that the Coast Guard reports a boat sinking far out at sea—too far out for rescue. The men stare indifferently over the water and then absently sing a few bars of a chantey. Auntie and Boles also appear and gaze out to sea. Auntie asks what is happening. "Nothing I can see," Boles replies. With a shrug, Auntie remarks, "One of those rumors."

All on stage now join in the majestic closing ensemble: "In ceaseless motion comes and goes the tide." As the voices die away on a descending phrase vividly descriptive of the ebbing tide, the curtain falls.

Rigoletto

by GIUSEPPE VERDI

[1813–1901]

Libretto by
FRANCESCO MARIA PIAVE

Based on Victor Hugo's drama
LE ROI S'AMUSE

CHARACTERS

The Duke of Mantua...*Tenor*
Borsa, a courtier...*Tenor*
The Countess Ceprano...............................*Mezzo-soprano*
Rigoletto, the Duke's jester, a hunchback......................*Baritone*
Count Ceprano, a nobleman.......................................*Bass*
Marullo, a courtier...*Baritone*
Count Monterone, a nobleman...................................*Baritone*
Sparafucile, a professional assassin.............................*Bass*
Gilda, daughter of Rigoletto..................................*Soprano*
Giovanna, Gilda's nurse............................*Mezzo-soprano*
A page ....*Soprano*
A herald ....*Baritone*
Maddalena, sister of Sparafucile............................*Contralto*
Courtiers, ladies and gentlemen of the court, servants

Place: Mantua, Italy
Time: Sixteenth century
First performance: Teatro La Fenice, Venice, March 11, 1851
Original language: Italian

VICTOR HUGO'S DRAMA of intrigue, treachery, and revenge at the court of François I of France greatly impressed Verdi as material for an operatic plot. Asked to write an opera for the Teatro La Fenice, he insisted that Piave prepare a libretto based on the play. Although the rather insinuating title, *Le Roi s'amuse,* was changed to *La Maledizione* (*The Curse*), the libretto provoked difficulties with the censor. Because of current political unrest, the authorities deemed it unwise to present a story of royal decadence and philandering. Consequently the locale of the opera was changed to the palace of the Duke of Mantua, a petty Italian nobleman, and the opera was retitled *Rigoletto*. Both Verdi and the authorities were satisfied. He wrote the opera in about six weeks, and the production was a spectacular success.

The first theme we hear in the brief prelude is that of the curse laid upon Rigoletto by Count Monterone. This somber, brooding music gives way to a brilliant, rhythmic strain as the curtain rises.

ACT ONE

[*Scene One*]   The glittering ballroom in the palace of the Duke of Mantua. It is thronged with cavaliers and their ladies. Some are dancing. The Duke, in conversation with Borsa, enters. He tells the courtier about a beautiful girl whom he has been observing at Mass for the past three months. He has learned that she lives in a remote part of town and that each night a mysterious stranger is admitted to the girl's home. The Duke then turns his attention to the ladies in the room, exclaiming that Count Ceprano's wife is the most beautiful of all. Borsa warns that Ceprano may overhear him and inform a "certain lady" of his roving eye. "That would be most unfortunate," is the Duke's rejoinder. He sums up his cynical philosophy about women in the graceful and carefree aria, "Questa o quella." One woman is as welcome to him as another, he sings. Fidelity has no appeal for the true lover, who cherishes his freedom to rove. He scorns the husband's jealous fury and mocks the lover's rage.

The guests now begin a minuet, and the Duke gallantly leads the Countess Ceprano forward to be his partner. Much to her discomfiture, he proceeds to make violent love, then escorts her out of the room before Ceprano's very eyes. Rigoletto, who has entered just in time to mark the Duke's exit, sneers at Ceprano's anger and embarrassment. The Count strides out of the room to follow the Duke. Rigoletto joins the courtiers, who exclaim in malicious glee over his sallies about the Duke's latest amorous exploit. The jester then limps away, while the courtiers laugh uproariously. There is a brief interlude during which the guests join in the *perigourdine,* a stately court dance. The courtiers remain at one side, looking on.

Suddenly the music changes to the spirited refrain heard at the beginning of the scene. Marullo enters, hurries up to the courtiers, and tells them that Rigoletto has decided to play the lover—he has a young sweetheart. "An elegant Cupid," the courtiers observe sarcastically. At that moment the Duke reappears, followed by Rigoletto. The Duke asks his jester how to dispose of Ceprano, because the Countess has completely ensnared his heart. The jester suggests that the Duke carry off the Countess. As for Ceprano, he says viciously, let him be arrested or beheaded.

Ceprano, who has re-entered, overhears the conversation and exclaims in fury. Rigoletto continues to torment Ceprano until he threatens to draw his sword. The jester's cruel raillery brings an angry warning from not only the Duke but the courtiers as well, but Rigoletto boasts that no harm can touch him.

These various sentiments introduce a dramatic chorus as the courtiers join their voices to sing "Vendetta del pazzo!" They all turn on Rigoletto, declaring that they will no longer tolerate his evil jests. He arrogantly repeats that he is safe from their vengeance. The mood of the music

changes as the dancers crowd in from the other rooms. The entire ensemble
sings about the festivity and merriment that rule the evening.

As the chorus ends, the voice of Count Monterone is heard outside, demanding admittance. With an angry exclamation he bursts into the room
and accuses the Duke of dishonoring his daughter. Goaded to fury by
Rigoletto's taunts, the Count challenges the Duke to condemn him to death,
saying that his curses will haunt the betrayer and that he will demand
vengeance from God himself.

Angrily the Duke orders the Count's arrest. Monterone, whirling on
Rigoletto, thunders, in ringing tones, "You who laugh at a father's anguish,
be accursed!" Rigoletto recoils with a gasp of horror. The entire assemblage
denounces Monterone for interrupting the festivities, and they order him to
leave. Monterone reiterates his curse, while Rigoletto voices a foreboding of
disaster. The Count is led away by guards and the people follow him out of
the room. The curtain falls.

[*Scene Two*[1]] A deserted street near Rigoletto's house. At the side of
the house is a walled courtyard with a door leading into it from the street.
In the courtyard is a tree. The balcony of the house rises above the wall,
with a stairway leading from it to the courtyard. Across the street is another
high wall, over the top of which the gable of Count Ceprano's house is
visible.

Rigoletto, muffled in his long cloak, comes slowly down the street. Ominous chords reverberate in the orchestra as he recalls Monterone's curse—
"Quel vecchio maledivami." Sparafucile approaches and introduces himself
as a man who can properly dispose of an enemy or a rival. There are such,
he adds significantly. "Inside there," says Sparafucile, nodding his head toward Rigoletto's house, "you have a woman. . . ." Rigoletto, fearing that
the man may know about Gilda, quickly asks him his price for killing a
nobleman. The price is as may be, Sparafucile answers casually. At any
rate, half must be paid in advance.

The assassin goes on to explain that, with the aid of his beautiful sister,
he lures his victims to his tavern on the outskirts of the town and there
quietly dispatches them. Telling Rigoletto he may be found at this spot
nightly, Sparafucile slinks away, murmuring his name.

Rigoletto, staring after him, sings a bitter soliloquy ("Pari siamo"). "We
are equal—the murderer and I," he reflects. "He strikes with a knife by night,
I with a malicious tongue by day." In despair the jester cries out that nature, in her cruel caprice, has created him as a monstrous caricature of a
man ("O uomini! o natura!"). Then he pours out his hatred and contempt
for the courtiers. Finally shaking off these tormenting thoughts, he enters
the courtyard.

The music becomes livelier as Gilda rushes out of the house and embraces her father. After they affectionately greet each other ("Figlia!" "Mio
padre!") their voices blend in a long and melodious colloquy. Gilda entreats
him to tell her of the secret grief that seems to overshadow their lives.

[1] Originally written in three acts, *Rigoletto* now is generally played in four,
and this then becomes Act Two.

Evading her question, he asks her if she has left the house today. When Gilda replies that she has gone only to Mass, he is reassured.

Earnestly Gilda begs Rigoletto to tell her about her mother. Yielding at length to her pleas, he tells her, in a touching refrain, that her mother died long ago ("Deh non parlare al misero"). Now, he says, they are left alone, surrounded by enemies and threatened by a strange curse. Their voices blend in a moving climax as they express their sorrow over the past and pledge their devotion to each other.

Gilda then wishes to know why she is not allowed to go into the city. Greatly agitated, Rigoletto asks if she has ever ventured beyond the neighborhood. In an aside, Gilda, thinking of the handsome stranger she has seen at church, betrays a twinge of conscience. Her father warns her never to leave home. Calling Giovanna, the nurse, he orders her to keep close watch over Gilda, who assures her father that all will be well.

Stepping out through the courtyard door, Rigoletto looks carefully up and down the street. As he does so, the Duke, disguised as a student, steals up behind the jester and enters the yard through the door without being noticed either by Rigoletto or Gilda. Before Rigoletto re-enters, the Duke tosses a purse to Giovanna with a gesture to be quiet and then conceals himself behind the tree. He is astounded when the jester comes back and addresses Gilda as his daughter. In poignant phrases the two bid each other good-by. After Rigoletto has left, Gilda muses about her unknown admirer. As she sings the Duke comes forward, signaling Giovanna to leave. Kneeling before Gilda, he declares his love in a phrase which completes her sentence and begins on the note Gilda has just sung ("T'amo, ripetilo!").

This introduces an impassioned duet in which they both confess their love. Eagerly Gilda asks the Duke his name. Walter Maldè, a humble student, the Duke replies. At that moment Count Ceprano and Borsa are seen cautiously approaching the house. They satisfy themselves that it is the home of Rigoletto, then withdraw. Giovanna rushes in, saying she heard footsteps. Gilda tells the nurse to lead the Duke out through the house. The lovers tenderly bid each other farewell.

Gilda, gazing after him, ecstatically repeats the name he gave—"Walter Maldè." Then she begins the famous aria, "Caro nome che il mio cor," a brilliant and rhapsodic expression of her newly awakened love. At the end of the aria Gilda goes into the house and reappears shortly after on the balcony, carrying a lantern to light her lover on his way. Softly she repeats several phrases of her aria, her voice trailing off into silence as she re-enters the house.

Meanwhile, Ceprano, Marullo, Borsa, and other courtiers have stealthily gathered in the street below. There they encounter Rigoletto returning home. In the dark street he does not recognize them. Marullo identifies only himself and says they have come to abduct Ceprano's wife. Rigoletto, who has been nervous at finding the courtiers so near his own home, is relieved and agrees to join them. He consents to mask himself, as the others are disguised. Marullo places a mask over his eyes and at the same time slips a handkerchief over the mask. Rigoletto, thinking he wears only the mask, remarks that it has grown very dark. Taking advantage of his confusion, the conspirators lead him to his own house and tell him that he is going toward Ceprano's. They explain that he is to hold the ladder up to the wall.

As the courtiers force their way into the house they sing a striking chorus ("Zitti, zitti, moviamo a vendetta"), in which they exult over their trick on Rigoletto. At the end of the ensemble some of the courtiers emerge carrying Gilda, gagged and bound. Now from the distance comes the muffled voice of Gilda calling for help, then a shout of triumph from the conspirators.

Rigoletto, still at the foot of the ladder, puts his hands to his face and discovers that his eyes are bandaged. He tears off the handkerchief and mask. In the light of a lantern left by the courtiers he catches sight of Gilda's scarf. Like a madman, he rushes into the house and reappears, dragging the bewildered Giovanna. For a moment Rigoletto's frenzy leaves him choking and speechless. Finally he bursts out in tones of anguish "Ah! la maledizione [The curse]!" He collapses, fainting, as the curtain falls.

ACT TWO

A room adjoining the Duke's chambers in the palace.[2] The Duke enters and in an excited soliloquy discloses that he returned to Gilda's house only to find the door locked and the premises deserted. In a brief but melodious aria the Duke voices his sincere longing for Gilda ("Parmi veder le lagrime"). His tender musings are interrupted by the entrance of the courtiers, who, in a spirited chorus ("Scorrendo uniti remota via"), inform him that they succeeded in abducting Rigoletto's maiden. When they reveal that they have brought the girl to the palace the Duke ardently sings of his joy over the prospect of seeing his beloved again. At the end of the number he hurries from the room, leaving the courtiers gaping in astonishment over his unusual demeanor.

From behind the scenes comes the voice of Rigoletto in a phrase of careless gaiety. As he enters the courtiers mockingly bid him good morning. Rigoletto looks furtively around for possible signs of his daughter's presence, hiding his anxiety by singing to himself as he limps about. He spies a handkerchief lying on the floor at the back of the room. Surreptitiously picking it up, he glances at it, then mutters that it is not Gilda's.

When Rigoletto asks about the Duke the courtiers answer that he is still sleeping. They likewise evasively answer the Duchess of Mantua's page, who has just entered. All this subterfuge finally rouses Rigoletto's worst suspicions. Confronting the courtiers, he cries that the girl must be in the chamber with the Duke and demands that they give him back his daughter. "His daughter!" the courtiers exclaim in astonishment. As the jester lunges toward the door of the chamber the courtiers bar his way. At this point Rigoletto sings the intensely dramatic aria ("Cortigiani, vil razza dannata"), denouncing the treachery of the courtiers. Again he tries to force his way into the chamber, crying, "Open the door, murderers!" Rigoletto then wildly implores the courtiers to give him back his child. The great aria ends with a cry for mercy—"Pietà, signori!"

[2] Act Three when given in four acts.

As the courtiers look contemptuously down at the jester the door of the chamber suddenly opens and Gilda rushes out. She throws herself into her father's arms. Joyously he greets her, then becomes alarmed at her tears. "I am disgraced, Father!" she gasps. As Rigoletto recoils in horror she pathetically begs him to hide her shame. He turns on the courtiers and commands them to leave. A single note repeated insistently in the orchestra lends striking emphasis to his words.

Flinging himself into a chair, Rigoletto orders Gilda to speak. In the brief aria which introduces the dramatic closing scene of the act ("Tutte le feste al tempio") she confesses meeting her youthful admirer, then tells how she was torn from her home and brought to the palace.

Rigoletto is shaken with horror. In a duet reminiscent of the one in the first act, father and daughter attempt to console each other. Rigoletto declares that they must leave the palace at once. Just at that moment Monterone, surrounded by guards, crosses the room on his way to prison. Dramatically he pauses before a portrait of the Duke, saying that his curse has been in vain, for the Duke still triumphs in his sins. As the guards lead Monterone away Rigoletto calls after him that vengeance is not far off. Glaring at the Duke's portrait, Rigoletto swears revenge, while Gilda prays that she may be able to protect the man she loves. Their voices blend in a duet of thrilling power. As they both rush from the room the curtain falls.

ACT THREE

Sparafucile's inn, partly in ruins, on the outskirts of Mantua.[3] The stage setting shows both the interior, with a broken staircase leading to a loft, and the road in front of the inn. The Mincio River is visible in the background. Sparafucile is seated at a table inside the tavern, cleaning a leather belt. Rigoletto and Gilda, standing in the roadway, are talking excitedly.

The jester asks his daughter if she still loves the Duke. "Always," she replies, whereupon Rigoletto bids her peer into the tavern through a chink in the wall. At that moment the Duke, dressed as a soldier, comes in calling loudly for a room and some wine. While he is being served he sings the brilliant aria, "La donna è mobile [Woman is fickle]," which vividly characterizes him as a gay philanderer. He sings that woman's affections are as wayward as the breeze, and he who tries to capture her heart does so to his sorrow.

Sparafucile enters, places a jug of wine and glasses on the table, then knocks on the ceiling with the hilt of his sword. At that signal Maddalena comes down from the upper room. The Duke promptly tries to embrace her, but she evades him. Sparafucile steps outside and asks Rigoletto if he is to kill the victim immediately or later. Rigoletto tells him to await instructions. Sparafucile walks away toward the river.

Then begins the great Rigoletto quartet, "Un dì, se ben rammento mi." The Duke, inside the tavern, woos Maddalena, who coyly responds. Outside, Gilda and Rigoletto express their humiliation and anger. The conflict-

[3] Act Four when given in four acts.

ing sentiments are skillfully blended to bring the quartet to a magnificent climax.

Rigoletto tells Gilda to don boy's clothing and ride to Verona, where he will meet her. When she leaves, Sparafucile reappears. Rigoletto pays the assassin half his fee, then says he will return at midnight to carry the body to the river. Thunder rumbles in the distance as he goes, while behind the scenes a humming chorus gives the effect of the rising wind of the storm.

As Sparafucile re-enters the Duke informs him that he has decided to stay at the inn overnight. Sparafucile offers the Duke his own room, then leads him upstairs. When Sparafucile returns, Maddalena, now completely under the spell of the Duke, desperately tries to persuade her brother not to kill him. While they are arguing, Gilda, wearing a man's costume, with boots and spurs, appears outside. She sings that her love for the Duke has drawn her here despite her father's orders to leave, then peers into the tavern.

Maddalena sings to Sparafucile that she adores the Duke and cannot let him die. In answer Sparafucile tosses her a large sack and harshly orders her to mend it so that it will hold the victim when he is borne off to the river. Maddalena suggests that Sparafucile murder Rigoletto instead of the Duke when the hunchback returns to pay the rest of his fee. Gilda is beside herself with horror.

Sparafucile finally compromises by agreeing to substitute for the Duke the first person who arrives at the inn before midnight. A brief but dramatic trio follows. Gilda prays desperately for help; Maddalena exults that the stormy night will aid her plan; Sparafucile reiterates the terms of his compromise. The storm increases in violence. A clock strikes. Determined to sacrifice herself for her lover, Gilda knocks at the inn door. As Sparafucile answers she tells him that she is a stranger and has lost her way. She enters, and Sparafucile flings himself upon her with drawn dagger.

There is a musical interlude which depicts the storm rising to a furious climax, then slowly subsiding. As the sounds of the storm die away Rigoletto approaches, grimly musing that the hour of revenge has come at last. The clock strikes midnight as he knocks at the door of the inn. Sparafucile answers, then drags forth the sack in which he has placed Gilda's body. Rigoletto pays him the rest of the fee, takes up his burden, and starts for the river. Suddenly he hears the Duke's voice singing the refrain of "La donna è mobile." He listens as if hypnotized, and as the Duke's voice dies away in the distance he tremblingly tears open the sack, only to find his dying child.

Gilda suddenly stirs in her death agony and calls to her father. Quietly she tells him that she has sacrificed herself for the man she loved. Her voice blends with Rigoletto's in a final duet of farewell, and then she dies in her father's arms. Brokenly the jester sobs, "My Gilda! Dead!" In a paroxysm of despair he bursts out, "Ah! la maledizione!" He collapses over the body of his child as the theme of the curse reverberates in a mighty fortissimo. The curtain falls.

Der Ring des Nibelungen

by RICHARD WAGNER

[1813–1883]

Libretto by the Composer

Based on Germanic, Scandinavian, and Icelandic sagas,
particularly the *Nibelungenlied* (*Nibelungen saga*)

DAS RHEINGOLD

CHARACTERS

Woglinde	} Rhinemaidens	Soprano
Wellgunde		Soprano
Flosshilde		Mezzo-soprano
Alberich, king of the Nibelungs		Bass
Fricka, wife of Wotan		Mezzo-soprano
Wotan, ruler of the gods		Bass-baritone
Freia, sister of Fricka, Goddess of Youth and Beauty		Soprano
Fasolt	} giants	Bass
Fafner		Bass
Froh	} brothers of Freia	Tenor
Donner, the thunder god		Baritone
Loge, the fire god		Tenor
Mime, brother of Alberich		Tenor
Erda, the earth-goddess		Mezzo-soprano

Place: Legendary Germany
Time: Antiquity
First performance: Munich, September 22, 1869
Original language: German

WAGNER began work on the prose poem of *Der Ring des Nibelungen* in 1848, with the writing of *Siegfrieds Tod* (*Siegfried's Death*), which embodied the core of the drama. But after completing it he realized that it required prefatory explanation and therefore wrote *Der Junge Siegfried* (*The Young Siegfried*). Finding it necessary to preface this poem (which became the present *Siegfried*) with still more explanatory material, he wrote *Die Walküre* and then *Das Rheingold*. The original *Siegfrieds Tod* became *Die Götterdämmerung*. Wagner completed the *Ring* poem in 1852, and in 1853 began composition of *Das Rheingold*, which he designated as the prologue to the drama. The entire score of the *Ring* was completed in 1872. The first complete performance of the *Ring* cycle took place at the Festspielhaus, Bayreuth, in August 1876.

The prelude to *Das Rheingold* is remarkable for the fact that it continues for 135 measures without a change of key. It is presumably symbolic of the calm, undisturbed depths of the Rhine and the elemental state of creation at the time the drama opens. This striking passage embodies what may be considered the first *leitmotiv*, or leading motive, of the *Ring* drama. Although it does not occur again in its original form, a number of other leading motives are constructed out of its harmonic element—that is, the perfect major chord. Among those which will be recognized are the motives of *Rhinemaidens, Gold, Norns, Destruction of the Gods, Rainbow, Sword, Ride of the Valkyries,* and *Brünnhilde's Sleep.* The first leading motive of *Das Rheingold* becomes strongly apparent at the end of *Die Götterdämmerung,* when the ring is finally engulfed by the Rhine. The simple, strong chord that dominates the music symbolizes the return to the primordial state of creation.

Because of the vast and complicated plot of the *Ring,* there are numberless other leading motives that symbolize characters and dramatic situations. As developed by Wagner, the leading motive was not merely a musical imitation of characteristic sounds, such as the galloping of horses, the sound of laughter, or the roaring of the wind. Wagner's leading motives—he was not the first nor the only one to use them—express in music the psychological factors of a dramatic situation as well as the identifying characteristics of an individual. A given motive will be heard not only when a character appears on the scene but also when that character is linked with a certain dramatic situation. Thus, in Act Two of *Die Walküre,* when Fricka rebukes Wotan for allowing Siegmund to steal Hunding's wife, we hear leading motives of persons or things as they are referred to in the conversation—*Hunding, Sword, Ring, Love, Spring,* and *Treaty.*

[*Scene One*] The rocky bed of the Rhine.[1] In the greenish-blue depths of the river the Rhinemaidens are swimming about at play. As they glide to and fro, Alberich, an evil-looking misshapen dwarf, emerges from the shadows at the base of the rocks and begins to climb upward, gazing in fascination at the mermaids. His passion stirred by their beauty, he tries awkwardly to lure them into his grasp, but they only laugh at his efforts. The dwarf curses in fury as they elude him.

Suddenly a yellowish light begins to glow at the peak of one of the largest rocks, and the Rhinemaidens, swimming around it, hail the gold of the Rhine. They sing that their father, who imposed on them the duty of guarding the treasure, told them that a ring forged from it would make its owner lord of all the world. But only he who is willing to renounce love forever can forge this ring.

Alberich, staring up at the gold, listens as if hypnotized, then climbs slowly toward the top of the rock. Reaching it at last, he shouts his renunciation of love, then tears the gold loose from the rock. Clutching the treas-

[1] The opera is in one act and four scenes and is generally given without lowering the curtain. Scene changes are indicated by cloud and mist effects as the stage is darkened. Sometimes the opera is divided into two acts at the end of Scene Two.

ure, he scrambles down from the rock and disappears, while the Rhinemaidens pursue him with angry cries. The waters recede as darkness envelops the scene and a thick mist begins to rise. When it clears and the stage gradually brightens again, a mountaintop becomes visible. At one side of an area of flat rocks Wotan and Fricka are lying asleep.

[Scene Two]   The morning light discloses, in the background, the shining castle of Walhalla, the newly built home of the gods, above the valley of the Rhine. Wotan and Fricka awake as the stately Walhalla motive sounds in the orchestra. Wotan, gazing proudly at the castle, declares that a dwelling worthy of the gods, built by the giants Fasolt and Fafner, at last is completed. Fricka reminds him that he has offered her sister Freia to the giants as payment for building the castle and bitterly reproaches him for his evil bargain. She adds that this castle, instead of satisfying Wotan's lust for power and glory, seems to have sharpened his desire for wandering about the world bent on conquest. When she accuses him of being heartless and cruel toward her, he retorts that there is proof enough of his devotion in the fact that he sacrificed one of his eyes to win her as his bride.

At that point Freia appears, imploring protection from the giants, who are now coming to claim their fee. Wotan, very much disturbed, fumes that Loge, his clever and crafty adviser in affairs of state, should be present, because he has devised a plan to ransom Freia. Confronted by the giants, the god spars for time, suggesting that they ask for some other reward. In angry surprise, they remind Wotan that the contract was written on his sacred spear and that as chief of the gods he must keep his word. Just as they start toward Freia her brothers, Donner and Froh, rush in. With his hammer upraised, Donner threatens the giants, but Wotan steps between the quarreling gods.

To the accompaniment of the Magic Fire music, Loge appears. Wotan, attempting to shift from himself the blame for the rash agreement with the giants, tells Loge that he would never have heeded his advice on the matter if the fire god had not promised him to find some way out of the contract. Loge, somewhat taken aback, points out that Fasolt and Fafner have satisfactorily performed their task and now may justly claim their fee. Furthermore, he says, he has wandered over the earth seeking some treasure that could be given them in place of Freia. But nowhere, he says, did he find a treasure for which men would be willing to sacrifice the love of womankind.

One man alone, the evil Alberich, has renounced love for gold, continues Loge, and he then tells the gods how the Nibelung king stole the hoard and forged the magic ring. Loge adds that he promised the Rhinemaidens he would present to Wotan their plea to restore their treasure. But Wotan, his thoughts on the ring and its terrible power, listens carefully as Fricka, Donner, and Froh—prompted by the wily Loge—counsel him to steal the treasure from Alberich. The Rhinemaidens, Fricka says scornfully, deserve their fate.

Fasolt and Fafner now offer to abrogate the contract and relinquish Freia if Wotan will agree to give them Alberich's treasure instead. Wotan contemptuously refuses, whereupon the giants seize Freia and carry her off. Transfixed with horror, the gods stare helplessly after her.

Loge, watching the others, cries out that they are growing pale and old before his eyes. Then he realizes what has happened. He tells Wotan that, because the Goddess of Youth and Beauty has been taken away, the gods are doomed to mortal old age. He warns that they will now be deprived of the golden apples from the tree which she guarded and with which they sustained their immortality. Spurred to action by the plight of the gods, Wotan decides to descend to Alberich's lair in search of the treasure that can ransom Freia.

Bidding the gods wait until he returns, Wotan follows Loge through an opening in the rocks and disappears. Clouds of smoke darken the scene. The Magic Fire music surges up and then gives way to a rhythmic figure as the beating of hammers on anvils is heard. A red glow flickers through the murk. Finally the smoke lifts and a gloomy cavern becomes visible. This is Nibelheim, the home of the Nibelungs, deep in the earth.

[*Scene Three*] Alberich enters, dragging the yelping Mime by his ear and abusing him for not having finished his forging. As Mime is being cuffed about he drops a piece of metalwork that somewhat resembles loosely woven chain mail. It is the tarnhelm, which makes its wearer invisible. The strange Tarnhelm motive sounds in the orchestra. Mime tells Alberich that he must keep it awhile longer because it is not quite completed. Examining it closely, Alberich says he can find no flaws, then angrily accuses Mime of plotting to keep the tarnhelm for himself. To test its power, he puts it on his head and instantly vanishes, a puff of smoke appearing in his place. Mime looks distractedly about as he hears Alberich's voice, then wildly tries to ward off invisible blows. We hear savage, exulting laughter, and then the voice fades as Alberich goes to his slaves deep in another part of the cave.

Wotan and Loge now make their way into the cave, come upon Mime crouching in the shadows, and lift him to his feet. Sobbing in pain and terror, the dwarf tells them how Alberich forged the magic ring and with its aid discovered unlimited treasure in the earth. He has set the Nibelungs to digging up the hoard for him, giving them no rest night or day. Mime also explains about the tarnhelm.

At that point Alberich reappears, driving before him a group of Nibelungs burdened with gold, which they pile up at one side of the cave. The tarnhelm is hanging at his belt. Catching sight of Wotan and Loge, he drives Mime and the other dwarfs back into the cavern, ordering them to dig up more gold. Howling under his blows, they disappear.

Eying the gods suspiciously, Alberich asks why they have come. Wotan replies that they have heard of Alberich's wonderful treasures and would like to see for themselves. Through subtle flattery, Loge finally leads Alberich into boasting how, with the aid of his ring and his gold, he will rule not only the whole world but the gods as well. Craftily Loge asks what good all this gold would do him if someone should steal the ring and thus deprive him of his power. Alberich replies that with his tarnhelm he not only could make himself invisible but could assume any shape he pleases. Thus anyone who tried to steal the ring could never escape him.

Loge deliberately expresses doubt as to the power of the tarnhelm, whereupon Alberich puts it on and becomes a great snake, which writhes and hisses on the ground before the gods. They pretend to be terrified. When Alberich resumes his human shape, Loge asks if he can change himself into a small creature as well as a large one—say, for example, a toad. Alberich again vanishes, and the gods see a toad crawling on a nearby rock.

Instantly Wotan puts his foot on the creature, while Loge snatches up the tarnhelm. Alberich, changed back to his own shape, curses and struggles under Wotan's foot. Tying him securely, the gods drag him out of the cavern. The scene darkens, fires glow through billowing smoke, and the sound of the hammers again is heard. The characteristic rhythmic beat in the orchestra is superseded by the Walhalla motive as the smoke lifts and the scene grows brighter. Once more we see the mountaintop near Walhalla, but the clinging mists hide the castle in the background.

[Scene Four] Wotan and Loge, dragging Alberich, enter through a pass in the rocks by which they had descended to Nibelheim. The dwarf curses in helpless rage as Loge taunts him unmercifully. Wotan tells him that he may buy his freedom with the hoard. To himself Alberich mutters that as long as he has his ring he can replenish his treasures at will, and thus the price of freedom will not, after all, be too dear. Asking Loge to loosen his right hand, he raises the ring to his lips and utters an incantation that brings his slaves up from the depths with the treasure. No sooner have they been sent back below than the gods declare that they will keep the tarnhelm as part of the ransom. As Loge tosses it on top of the mound of gold, Alberich shouts that they are a brace of greedy scoundrels, saying to himself, however, that he can easily force Mime to make him another.

Loge asks Wotan if the prisoner may now be released. In answer, the god points to the ring and demands it as the final item of ransom. Frantically Alberich protests, accusing Wotan of treachery and cynical lack of respect for the terms of a bargain. He warns that whoever robs him of his ring will be forever accursed. With a sneer at his warning, Wotan ruthlessly pulls the ring from Alberich's finger, slips it on his own, and gazes at it in triumph.

He tells Loge to set Alberich free. Staggering to his feet, the dwarf shouts his terrible imprecation. Let this ring, acquired by a curse, bring anguish and death to all who possess it, he intones. Warning Wotan again that he shall never escape the ring's curse, Alberich disappears. Loge remarks sardonically on his "blessing," while Wotan stares at the ring as if hypnotized.

Suddenly Loge exclaims that Fasolt and Fafner are approaching with Freia. At that moment Fricka, Donner, and Froh enter, and Loge proudly shows them the hoard. The giants, with Freia between them, confront Wotan, who tells them that the ransom is ready. Thrusting their staffs into the ground on each side of Freia as a measure of her height and width, they order the gods to pile up the gold until it hides her from their sight. When all the gold has been placed in front of her, Fafner says he can still see Freia's hair and orders the tarnhelm to be thrown on top of the heap. Sullenly the gods obey. Fasolt, examining the mound, exclaims that he cannot part with Freia as long as he can see her eyes through one small hole that remains unfilled. The ring on Wotan's finger, he says, must serve to hide her completely from his sight. At Wotan's flat refusal to give up the ring, Fasolt drags Freia from between the two staves and starts to take her away.

While the gods plead desperately with Wotan a light begins to glow in a crevasse at the side of the clearing, and Erda, the earth-goddess, rises out of the ground. In ominous tones she sings that she is the all-wise goddess who knows all that has happened and all that is to be ("Weiche, Wotan, weiche!"). Through her three daughters, the Norns, who spin the web of fate, Wotan has gained his wisdom. But she herself has come to warn him that the gods are doomed. He must give up the ring. Slowly Erda disappears into the earth.

Suddenly resolved, Wotan raises his spear, orders the giants to release Freia, then throws the ring on top of the hoard. Freia is joyously embraced by the gods. In the next moment the giants begin quarreling furiously over the division of the spoils. Loge maliciously advises Fasolt to take the ring and give the rest of the treasure to Fafner. Fasolt snatches the ring, whereupon Fafner kills him with a blow of his staff and tears it from his grasp. The gods exclaim in horror, while Wotan muses uneasily that the curse has already begun its work. He resolves to go to Erda for further counsel.

Fricka, noting her husband's troubled look, urges him to go to the castle, where he can find respite from his cares. Wotan orders Donner to dispel the mists which still hide the castle. Donner summons up a thunderstorm, calls Froh to help him, and then both vanish in the swirling clouds. Meanwhile Fafner drags away the body of Fasolt and the sack containing the treasure. The blows of Donner's mighty hammer are heard in the distance; lightning blazes and thunder rolls. As the Rainbow theme soars up from the orchestra, the clouds lift, revealing a shining rainbow bridge that arches from the castle across the valley to the feet of the gods. Over the accompaniment of the Walhalla motive, Wotan proclaims that the shining fortress will be called Walhalla ("Abendlich strahlt"). He takes up a sword which Fafner, in dragging away the treasure, has left behind, points with it toward Walhalla as the Sword theme rings out, and bids the gods follow him to their destined abode. Hand in hand with Fricka, he starts across the bridge. Only Loge remains behind, remarking cynically that the gods will think themselves safe in their new home. He muses that perhaps it would be better to go his own way rather than join the gods in their fool's paradise of self-complacency. He will think it over, he decides, then casually follows after the gods.

From below comes the poignant lamentation of the Rhinemaidens, bewailing the loss of their gold. Wotan looks uneasily downward and orders Loge to quiet them. When he calls down to the Rhinemaidens in jeering tones, the gods laugh and continue on their way. The sorrowing voices of the maidens are engulfed in the triumphant Walhalla motive as the curtain falls.

DIE WALKÜRE

CHARACTERS

Siegmund } Wälsungs, mortal son and daughter of Wotan........ { *Tenor*		
Sieglinde }		*Soprano*

Siegmund ⎱ Wälsungs, mortal son and daughter of Wotan........ ⎰ *Tenor*
Sieglinde ⎰ ⎱ *Soprano*
Hunding, husband of Sieglinde.................................*Bass*
Wotan ....*Bass-baritone*
Brünnhilde, daughter of Wotan and Erda,
   eldest of the Valkyries.................................. *Soprano*
Fricka, wife of Wotan............................... *Mezzo-soprano*

Gerhilde ⎫
Ortlinde ⎪
Waltraute ⎪
Schwertleite ⎪ Valkyries, other daughters of   ⎧ *Sopranos,*
Helmwige ⎬   Wotan and Erda.................... ⎨ *mezzo-sopranos,*
Siegrune ⎪   ⎩ *and contraltos*
Grimgerde ⎪
Rossweise ⎭

Place: Legendary Germany
Time: Antiquity
First performance: Munich, June 26, 1870
Original language: German

WOTAN, realizing that Alberich would make every effort to get the magic ring away from Fafner, usurp world power, and then destroy the gods, was forced to take action to forestall his enemy. In order to safeguard Walhalla, he gave to his nine daughters, the Valkyries, the task of bringing from the world's battlefields the bodies of the bravest heroes. Transformed into immortals, they served as protectors for the gods.

Meanwhile Wotan has been ranging over the earth seeking the hero who would recover the ring from Fafner. The giant had dragged the hoard into a cave in the forest, where, in the form of a dragon, he was guarding his loot. Wotan now hopes that his earthly son Siegmund will be the one to wrest the treasure away from Fafner. (Siegmund and Sieglinde were Wotan's children by a mortal woman, with whom he lived for a time in the guise of Wolfe, or Wälse, creating the race of Wälsungs.) At the time *Die Walküre* opens, Siegmund, fleeing from a hostile forest tribe, has found refuge in the home of Hunding.

ACT ONE

A primitive dwelling in the forest, built of rough logs around a huge tree which branches up through the rafters. From the trunk protrudes the hilt of a great sword. At one side of the room is a fireplace, and at the back are large double doors. The fury of the storm raging outside is vividly portrayed in the brief prelude. At its climax the doors swing open and Sieg-mund enters. Exhausted and out of breath, he staggers over to the hearth, flings himself down on a large bearskin, and lies there motionless.

Sieglinde enters from another room and exclaims in surprise as she sees the stranger. As she bends over him for a closer look, Siegmund revives and calls for water. Sieglinde brings him a beaker made of horn, and while he drinks, the Love motive sounds in the orchestra. Gazing at her intently, he asks who she is. Sieglinde replies that she is the wife of Hunding and that this is his home. Siegmund explains that, in combat with enemy tribesmen, his sword and shield were destroyed and he was forced to flee. As he goes on with his story, Sieglinde gives him mead to drink for further refresh-ment.

His strength somewhat restored, Siegmund rises and starts to leave. When Sieglinde invites him to rest awhile, he answers sadly that he must go in order to spare this household the misfortune that seems constantly to pursue him. Sieglinde observes that he could not bring trouble to the place where trouble itself dwells. The two pause as though spellbound, gazing at each other with growing ardor as the Love motive again sounds forth.

They are interrupted by the entrance of Hunding, who mutters a surly greeting and eyes Siegmund suspiciously. Abiding by the traditional rules of hospitality, however, he invites Siegmund to share his meal, noting with increasing surprise the close resemblance between the stranger's features and those of his wife. In answer to Hunding's questions, Siegmund explains more about himself. He is called Wehwalt (Woeful), he says, and he is of the tribe of Wälsungs (Wolfings). For a time he lived happily in the forest with his father, Wälse (Wolfe), his mother, and his twin sister. One day he and his father came home from the hunt to find their home burned to the ground and the mother murdered. They searched the ruins, but found no trace of the sister. The perpetrators of this deed, Siegmund says, were the Neidings, a hostile tribe that had long been feuding with the Wälsungs. He relates that his father was eventually slain in combat, leaving his son to wander alone through the forest, doomed to misery and defeat.

Siegmund then tells how one day he went to the rescue of a maiden who was being taken by her tribesmen to the house of a man they were forcing her to marry. After a furious combat in which the girl herself perished, Siegmund says, he was forced to flee for his life.

Hunding springs to his feet, angrily exclaiming that those whom Sieg-mund had attacked were his own kinsmen, and that now his enemy is under his roof. He offers Siegmund sanctuary for the night, but warns him to be ready to defend himself in the morning. With that Hunding orders Sieg-linde to prepare his night drink and leaves the room. His wife, following him, tries unobtrusively to direct Siegmund's eyes to the sword in the tree. Siegmund, however, fails to read the meaning of her glances.

Alone, Siegmund laments that he is unarmed in the house of his foe and wonders why he does not have the sword which his father promised he would find in his hour of need ("Ein Schwert verhiess mir der Vater"). But his thoughts soon turn to Sieglinde's beauty. He does not notice how the gleam from the dying fire is occasionally reflected in the hilt of the sword in the tree.

As the fire flickers out, leaving the room in darkness, Sieglinde re-enters and steals to Siegmund's side, whispering that she has mixed a sleeping potion with Hunding's drink. She then tells how she was forced to marry Hunding, and how, during the wedding feast, a one-eyed stranger entered the house unbidden. With a single stroke he thrust a great sword into the tree, saying that it would belong to the warrior who could draw it forth again. Siegmund leaps to his feet in great excitement. Ardently Sieglinde sings that she longs for someone to unsheathe the sword and avenge her, then rushes into Siegmund's arms.

At that moment the doors at the rear swing open, showing the forest flooded with spring moonlight. Siegmund sings rapturously of love and spring in the beautiful aria "Winterstürme wichen dem Wonnemond," which Sieglinde answers in the equally ecstatic refrain, "Du bist der Lenz." They discover that they are Wälsungs—brother and sister—and are overwhelmed with joy at their reunion. Siegmund now realizes that it was his own father who thrust the sword into the tree and that he himself is destined to draw it forth.

Siegmund repeatedly cries "Wälse" in powerfully swelling and rising tones, then, hailing the sword ("Nothung! So nenn' ich dich Schwert!"—"Needful, I name this sword!"), he wrenches it free. He and Sieglinde passionately embrace, then rush out into the night. The curtain falls.

ACT TWO

A desolate mountain overlooking a deep ravine. Wotan, clad in full armor and carrying a spear, is standing in the foreground. Before him is Brünnhilde in the armor of a Valkyrie. He orders her to summon the other Valkyries and ride to the aid of Siegmund, who must soon face Hunding in combat. Brünnhilde climbs to a rocky ledge in the background and there sings her magnificent battle cry, "Hojotoho!" Looking down the valley, she informs Wotan that Fricka is approaching, then leaves as she continues her battle call.

Fricka angrily confronts Wotan, and a dramatic colloquy follows. Bitterly she reproaches him for permitting Siegmund to steal Hunding's wife. As the Goddess of Marriage, whose duty it is to see that nuptial vows are kept inviolate, Fricka demands that Wotan punish the guilty lovers. Wotan protests that the gods are sorely in need of a mortal champion who can perform a service that they themselves cannot accomplish. For that task, says the god, he has destined Siegmund, and that is why he is protecting him. Fricka denounces Wotan for shielding a sinful mortal, then forces him to promise that he will doom Siegmund.

She stalks away just as Brünnhilde rides up the pass. Curtly she tells the Valkyrie that Wotan has made his decision. Brünnhilde quietly approaches her father, who is overwhelmed by humiliation and despair. Trying to console him, she puts aside her shield and weapons and kneels before him. In a long monologue Wotan tells his daughter of his tragic attempts to regain the ring. He reveals how first he went to Erda for counsel, won her love, and sired nine daughters—the Valkyries, who have brought to Walhalla the heroes appointed for its defense. Then he reared Siegmund as a lawless warrior and gave him a magic sword in the hope that he would recover the ring. But now the ring's fearful curse will strike again, because Fricka has forced him to deny Siegmund protection in his coming encounter with Hunding.

Glory and power are gone, Wotan says bitterly, and now there remains only the dismal end. The gods are doomed and Alberich will triumph. That loathsome dwarf, Wotan goes on, has bought a woman with his gold, and she will soon bear him a son who will carry on his evil work. But he, chief of the gods, can find no one who will aid him in redeeming the world. In savage irony the god consigns Walhalla and its power to the Nibelungs with his blessing.

When he tells Brünnhilde that Siegmund must die, she desperately pleads for his life. Her entreaties rouse Wotan to violent anger. Roughly ordering her to obey, he strides from the scene. For a long time Brünnhilde stands motionless, overcome by horror and despair. At last she takes up her weapons and walks slowly to the top of the rocky height. From there she sees Siegmund and Sieglinde in the valley below. She watches them for a while, then sadly descends from the peak and disappears.

The lovers, exhausted by their flight, make their way painfully up through the pass. Sieglinde, beside herself with fear and remorse, begs Siegmund to leave her so that she might die alone in her shame. Delirious with terror, she imagines that Hunding's dogs are about to spring at her with wide-open jaws. With a piercing cry she faints in Siegmund's arms. Cradling her in his embrace, he seats himself and gazes at her in tenderness and concern.

Brünnhilde slowly approaches and stands before him, calling him by name as the Fate motive sounds in the orchestra ("Siegmund, sich' auf mich!"). To the accompaniment of the Death motive, Siegmund asks who she is. Gravely she tells him that only heroes destined to die in battle may gaze upon her, and that she has come to take him to Walhalla. When Siegmund asks if Sieglinde may go with him, Brünnhilde says that he must part from her forever. Thereupon Siegmund flatly refuses to go, saying that he proposes to defend his beloved and himself with his magic sword. Wotan has disenchanted the sword, Brünnhilde says, and he is fated to be slain by the pursuing Hunding. Impetuously Siegmund raises his sword and cries out that he will kill Sieglinde and then himself rather than part from her. Won over by Siegmund's brave defiance, Brünnhilde promises to aid him in the fight despite Wotan's command. Warning him to prepare for battle, she rushes away.

Hunding's horn is heard in the distance. Siegmund tenderly kisses the sleeping Sieglinde, then strides toward the heights to meet his foe. Lightning blazes and thunder crashes as the two men come face to face. Brünnhilde is seen hovering near Siegmund, trying to protect him with her shield. Suddenly a reddish glow breaks through the clouds, revealing Wotan with his spear pointed at Siegmund. Brünnhilde falls back in terror. Just as Siegmund aims a deadly blow at Hunding, his sword is shattered against Wotan's interposing spear, and, defenseless, he is killed by Hunding.

During the fight Brünnhilde rushes to Sieglinde, lifts her to her horse, tethered near by, and rides away. Wotan stands for a moment looking down at Siegmund. Then, at a contemptuous gesture of his hand, Hunding falls dead. Furiously vowing punishment for Brünnhilde, the god disappears. The curtain falls.

ACT THREE

The prelude is the thrilling and powerful *Ride of the Valkyries*, during which the curtain rises on a rocky mountain summit bordered by pines. Storm clouds, torn by the wind, swirl across the dark sky. On the highest peak three of the Valkyries await the arrival of the others, who are seen coming through the sky with the bodies of heroes slung across their saddles. The war maidens laugh in savage glee as they exclaim that the horses, carrying heroes who were foemen on the battlefield, rear at each other as though imbued with the hatred of combat.

Suddenly they see Brünnhilde approaching and are dumfounded when they discover that she is carrying not a warrior but a woman, Sieglinde. Brünnhilde tells her sisters about the fight, saying that Wotan, in terrible anger, is pursuing her to punish her for attempting to aid Siegmund. She begs the Valkyries to give her one of their fresh horses, but they refuse, fearing Wotan's wrath.

While the increasing roar of the storm heralds Wotan's approach, Sieglinde begs the Valkyries to save her. They tell her to flee eastward to a cave deep in the forest where Fafner sleeps on his gold. Wotan shuns that spot and will never pursue her there. Brünnhilde bids her have courage, for she is to bear a son who will be the world's most glorious hero—Siegfried. She hands her the fragments of Siegmund's sword. Sieglinde thanks her ecstatically, then makes her escape.

At the height of the storm Wotan strides in. The Valkyries, retreating farther up the mountain height, surround Brünnhilde and try to conceal her. In majestic anger the god commands Brünnhilde to stand before him. Her sisters beg Wotan to be merciful. He proclaims that henceforth Brünnhilde will no longer be a Valkyrie and furiously orders her sisters to have nothing more to do with her, under the pain of similar punishment. The eight Valkyries flee in terror, while Brünnhilde, crushed by despair, falls at Wotan's feet.

For a long time Brünnhilde and Wotan remain motionless. The storm subsides, the weather clears, and a calm twilight descends. Then follows the magnificent scene of farewell. Brünnhilde eloquently tries to justify her actions, but her father insists she must be punished. She shall be placed in a deep sleep upon this mountaintop until the rightful hero awakens her. Resigned to her fate, Brünnhilde begs him to protect her in her helpless slumber with a wall of fire.

Overcome by his love for her, Wotan clasps her in his arms and sings his heartbreaking song of farewell ("Leb' wohl, du kühnes, herrliches Kind!"). At its conclusion he gently kisses her eyes, singing with infinite sadness, "So

küsst er die Gottheit von dir" ("Thus the god takes away your godhood").
Slowly she loses consciousness.

Wotan carries her to a grassy slope under a great tree, closes her helmet,
lays her spear at her side, and covers her with her shield. He then calls to
Loge, commanding him to encircle the sleeping maiden with fire. He strikes
a nearby rock three times with his spear. To the accompaniment of the
thrillingly descriptive Magic Fire music, the flickering flames leap forth,
ringing Brünnhilde's rock. In the tones of the prophetic Siegfried motive,
Wotan, standing in lonely majesty on the lofty eminence, against a background of smoke and fire, holds forth his spear and sings that he who fears
this weapon shall never break through the flames. While the Sleep motive
wells up through the Fire theme, Wotan turns for a moment to gaze in tenderness and sorrow on Brünnhilde, then vanishes. The curtain falls.

SIEGFRIED

CHARACTERS

Mime . . . . *Tenor*
Siegfried . . . . *Tenor*
Wanderer (the god Wotan in disguise) . . . . *Bass-baritone*
Alberich . . . . *Baritone*
Fafner (the dragon) . . . . *Bass*
Forest bird . . . . *Soprano*
Erda, the earth-goddess . . . . *Contralto*
Brünnhilde . . . . *Soprano*

Place: A legendary forest in Germany
Time: Antiquity
First performance: Festspielhaus, Bayreuth, August 16, 1876
Original language: German

SIEGFRIED introduces the central character of the great *Ring* drama. The young Siegfried, son of Siegmund and Sieglinde, has been reared by Mime, the dwarf, in his cavelike home deep in the forest. Sieglinde, fleeing after the death of Siegmund in combat with Hunding (recounted in *Die Walküre*), has been found wandering in the forest by Mime. He took her to his dwelling, where she died giving birth to her son. Now grown to early manhood, Siegfried is about to take up his role of "world hero," destined to triumph because he is oblivious to fear and has learned the meaning of love.

The prelude briefly sounds the dark and mysterious Mime motive and then is dominated by an insistent, pounding rhythm suggestive of hammer strokes. The Slavery motive is heard, while the Sword motive cuts through momentarily. The curtain rises as the music continues without pause.

ACT ONE

Mime's crude cave home in the forest. At one side is a natural stone abutment which serves as a forge, and over it is a bellows. Before the forge is an anvil, at which Mime is working. Swinging his small hammer to the rhythm of the music, he beats futilely away at the blade of a sword. In weariness and disgust he rages over the utter futility of his efforts ("Zwangvolle Plage! Müh' ohne Zweck!"). He fumes that every sword he makes is promptly shattered by the headstrong youth for whom he fashions it. Completely out of patience, he throws down the blade. Staring at it gloomily, he muses that if he could but forge together the broken sword *Nothung* (*Needful*), his troubles would be over. Having this mighty weapon, he could persuade that reckless devil of a boy to slay the dragon Fafner for him and recover the Nibelung hoard which the dragon guards with his body. Then, Mime gloats, he would gain possession of the ring and be master of the world.

Complaining about his hard lot, Mime goes back to work. At this point
Siegfried comes storming in, leading a bear by a rope. He sets the bear on
Mime and roars with laughter at the dwarf's frantic efforts to escape. When
he has had enough of this sport he drives the bear out of the cave, remarking that the animal proved pleasanter company than Mime. Taking up the
sword on which Mime has been working, Siegfried smashes it to pieces
against the anvil, raging at the dwarf for being too stupid to forge a
weapon he can use. He sits down on a stone bench and lapses into a sulky
silence.

Mime, warily staying out of reach, tries to placate him and finally offers
him a dish of food. Siegfried knocks the dish from his hand, whereupon the
dwarf launches into a querulous tirade. Has he not lavished fatherly care
and devotion on this boy, fed and clothed him, taught him all he knew?
And now what is his reward? Nothing but ingratitude and abuse! Siegfried
retorts that the only thing he ever learned from Mime was a loathing for
Mime himself. He wonders what impels him to return to the cave at all—
when the birds and the beasts of the forest are friendlier than Mime could
ever be.

Siegfried further annoys the dwarf by his persistent questioning. The animals, he says, live happily together—the male, his mate, and their offspring.
The little ones, he has noted, resemble their parents, while he himself
knows only a whining, repulsive dwarf as "Father." Fortunately, says
Siegfried, he does not in the least resemble him and, what is more, does not
believe that Mime is his father. Excitedly he demands to know who his parents are. When Mime tries to evade the question, Siegfried takes him by the
throat and cries that he will force the answer from him.

The terrified dwarf thereupon tells Siegfried that long ago he came upon
a woman lying helpless and ill in the forest. He took her to his cave, where
she gave birth to a child and then died. But before her death, Mime relates,
she told him that the child was to be called Siegfried and that she was
Sieglinde. Of Siegfried's real father, Mime continues, he learned only that
he was killed in combat. When Siegfried asks Mime to produce some proof
to substantiate this fantastic story, Mime shows him the sword blade, broken in two. And this, wails Mime, remembering to feel sorry for himself
again, was his sole reward for his deed of mercy.

In great agitation Siegfried cries that these fragments shall be forged into
his rightful sword. He commands Mime to mend it for him, threatening him
with the worst beating of his life if he fails. With that the youth rushes off
into the forest, leaving Mime moaning that all his Nibelung's craft and skill
will never be able to fashion this hero's sword.

The dwarf, overcome by despair, huddles in front of the anvil. Then, as
an impressive passage of chords vibrates in the orchestra, the Wanderer appears at the entrance of the cave. He wears a long dark cloak and a wide-
brimmed hat, which droops over the missing eye, and carries a great spear.
After solemnly introducing himself to the frightened Mime, he explains that
he has been wandering over the world and has learned much of its wisdom.
The dwarf ungraciously tells him to be on his way, but the Wanderer, ignoring the remark, strides over to the hearth and sits down.

He observes after a moment that he has discovered in his travels that man is sorely lacking in wisdom. Mime, eying him suspiciously, remarks that he is well content with the wits he possesses. Thereupon the Wanderer proposes a contest of brains, offering his head as forfeit if he fails to answer any three questions Mime asks him. The dwarf agrees, musing that he will certainly trap this interloper in his own folly. First, asks Mime, what race inhabits the depths of the earth? The Nibelungs, replies the Wanderer. Alberich, their ruler, plundered the earth of its gold. With it and the aid of a magic ring, he hoped to enslave all mankind. Mime asks who rules the earth's surface. The giants Fasolt and Fafner ruled there, the Wanderer replies. They gained possession of Alberich's hoard, and in a quarrel over the spoils Fafner slew Fasolt. Fafner, in the form of a dragon, now guards the hoard. For his third question, Mime asks who rules the skies. The Walhalla motive peals through the orchestra as the Wanderer replies that the gods rule above. Wotan is their monarch. He holds a spear hewn from the world ash, and on it are graven sacred edicts governing man's conduct. With this spear Wotan rules over gods, Nibelungs, and giants alike.

Now, says the Wanderer, settling himself more comfortably, it shall be Mime's turn. First, who are those with whom Wotan is most severe, yet loves above all others? The Wälsungs, answers Mime. Best-beloved were Siegmund and Sieglinde and Siegfried, their son. The Wanderer then asks what sword Siegfried must have to slay Fafner and recover the hoard. "Nothung!" cries Mime, in gleeful self-confidence. The third question— Who will reforge the broken sword Nothung?—throws the unsuspecting dwarf into a panic. Chattering in fear, he admits that he cannot answer.

The Wanderer tells him that only he who knows no fear can mend the sword. Regarding Mime with quiet amusement, the visitor remarks that he will leave his host's head as a prize for the fearless one. With that he leaves.

Mime, staring into the forest, gives way to his panic, conjuring up horrible dangers. Overcome by terror, he hides in a corner. In another moment Siegfried bursts in, demanding to know if the sword is ready. By way of excuse, Mime says that he has been too concerned with fears for Siegfried's sake to give his attention to the sword. When Siegfried asks the meaning of fear, the dwarf says he will take him to Neidhöhle, the lair of the dragon, where he will learn this important lesson.

Impetuously Siegfried orders Mime to fashion the sword, so that he may be on his way. Mime wails that he is not equal to the task. Fuming at the dwarf, Siegfried picks up the broken weapon and declares that he will forge this sword himself. He builds up the fire and prepares the mold. As he works he sings the jubilant *Forge Song* ("Nothung! Nothung! Neidliches Schwert!"). Mime watches with gloating satisfaction, then begins preparing a magic brew. With this he proposes to poison Siegfried after the lad has slain Fafner and gained possession of the hoard.

Finally the great sword is finished. Siegfried cools it in water, then brandishes it triumphantly aloft. Striding over to the anvil, he splits it from top to bottom with a powerful blow. Laughing joyously, he runs out of the cave. The curtain falls.

ACT TWO

A dark forest glade. The motives of Fafner, the Ring, the Curse, and Destruction are woven into the gloomy measures of the prelude. Barely visible at the rear is the mouth of a huge cave. Alberich crouches in the shadows, watching by Fafner's cave in the hope that he may recover his lost hoard. Heralded by mysterious flashes of light, the Wanderer appears. Alberich recognizes him as Wotan, his ancient foe, and curses him as a troublemaker. The god himself, he taunts, is being haunted by the fear that the Nibelungs will regain possession of the ring—with obvious consequences.

The Wanderer replies that Mime at this very moment is leading to the cave one who will win the ring—a youth who knows no fear. He suggests that Alberich try to persuade Fafner to give up the ring before the inevitable occurs. Obligingly he awakens Fafner. Alberich calls into the cave that he will be content to let the dragon keep the hoard if he will but surrender the ring. The dragon merely growls back that the treasure is his by right of possession. Wotan laughs at Alberich's disappointment, then disappears with a word of warning. Glaring after him, Alberich savagely vows revenge. He vanishes among the rocks.

The scene grows lighter as the day dawns. Siegfried enters, his sword tied at his waist. Mime shuffles after him, cautiously peering about. Seating himself under a lime tree, Siegfried asks if he is now to have his lesson in fear. Mime points out the cave and tells the youth about the dragon. Its breath is deadly poison, and one drop of its saliva will corrode flesh and bones, says the dwarf in awed tones. It can pulverize a man's bones with a flick of its tail, Mime goes on. This remarkable beast, declares Siegfried, will soon feel the sword Nothung in its heart. He derides Mime for offering him all this nonsense in place of a useful lesson on fear and impatiently tells him to take himself off into the forest. Mime goes, saying he will wait at the nearby spring.

Siegfried lies down under the tree and indulges in pleasant reflection on the beauty of the woodland. The orchestra begins the wonderfully descriptive music familiarly known as the *Forest Murmurs* (*Waldweben*). Dismissing the unpleasant thoughts of the cringing dwarf, Siegfried muses tenderly about the mother he has never known. A birdcall from the branches above interrupts his thoughts. Intrigued by its song, he fashions a pipe from a reed and tries to blow an answering call. But the notes—amusingly played off-key in the orchestra—bring no response. Siegfried finally gives up and, raising his hunting horn to his lips, sounds his famous *Horn Call*.

At this Fafner awakes and drags his fearsome dragon's body out of his cave. Siegfried whirls and, facing the beast, remarks with an amused chuckle that his efforts have attracted the attention of a handsome stranger indeed. Fafner roars, shows his teeth, and asks who dares interrupt his slumbers. Siegfried mockingly asks the beast if it can teach him fear. Bellowing with rage, the dragon spews out its poison, while smoke pours from its nostrils. Adroitly avoiding the poisonous spume, Siegfried leaps forward to attack.

He lunges at the dragon's tail, then, when the beast rears in pain, turns and drives his sword into its heart.

With its dying breath the dragon asks Siegfried who incited him to this murderous deed. He answers that it was the dragon's own threat that impelled him to use his sword in self-defense. Fafner now realizes that Alberich's ancient curse on the ring has at last struck him down. He warns Siegfried that the one who plotted this deed is planning the youth's death also. Siegfried asks Fafner if *he* knows the riddle of his birth, then reveals his name. The dragon repeats the name and slumps down dead.

Siegfried now pulls his sword from the body and in so doing gets the dragon's blood on his hand. He exclaims that it burns and involuntarily puts his hand to his lips. Through the magic of the blood he finds that he can understand the language of the forest bird, which at that moment begins to sing again. The bird tells him that within the cave is the coveted hoard. Its chief treasures are the tarnhelm, which will help him to accomplish mighty deeds, and the ring, which will bestow world power on its wearer. Thanking the bird for its kind advice, Siegfried enters the cave.

Alberich and Mime now return, and the moment they meet, a violent quarrel ensues over the hoard. Mime is wild with fury when Alberich refuses to share the ring and the tarnhelm and claims the entire treasure for himself. At the height of the argument Siegfried reappears with both the ring and the tarnhelm. He examines them closely, then puts the ring on his finger and hangs the tarnhelm from his belt. The forest bird begins to sing again, telling Siegfried that the taste of the dragon's blood will henceforth enable him to divine the real meaning behind Mime's deceitful words.

A remarkable dialogue follows. The dwarf himself assumes that he is deceiving Siegfried with cunning flattery. However, we hear Mime's words as Siegfried understands them—that he intends to render Siegfried helpless with poison brew, lop off his head with the sword, and then take possession of the ring and the tarnhelm. Mime recoils in angry surprise when the youth's answers show that he understands the true meaning of the words. Nevertheless he extends the drinking horn containing the poison. Siegfried strikes him dead with a single blow of his sword. From the distance comes Alberich's savage, mocking laughter. Siegfried drags the dwarf's body into the cave, then barricades the opening with the carcass of the dragon. The *Curse Motive,* reverberating in the orchestra, reminds us that the ring's curse has claimed another victim.

Wearied by his efforts, Siegfried throws himself down under the lime tree and muses on his loneliness and the mystery of his past. Once more the forest bird sings. It tells Siegfried of Brünnhilde, who lies asleep on a great rock on a mountain height, ringed by flames. Only he who has never known fear can break through the flames and win this glorious maid for his bride. He himself is this hero, Siegfried cries jubilantly, because he had never learned the lesson of fear. Excitedly he implores the bird to lead him to Brünnhilde's rock. The *Fire Music* and the Siegfried motive sound triumphantly as he rushes away to follow the bird's receding voice. The curtain falls.

ACT THREE

A wild, rocky glen. The brief prelude dramatically states the motives of the Gods' Need and the Treaty, rising to a fiery crescendo with the theme of the Twilight of the Gods. A storm is raging as the curtain rises. Wotan, still in his Wanderer's garb, enters and pauses before a cavernous opening in the rocks. He calls out to Erda, the earth-goddess. An eerie light shimmers in the cavern, and Erda rises slowly from the ground. A long discourse follows. Wotan seeks to learn from the all-wise goddess how the inexorable processes of fate may be halted. Erda pointedly suggests that he ask his own daughter, Brünnhilde, who also was endowed with godlike wisdom. When Wotan reveals how he has punished Brünnhilde—imprisoning her in sleep behind a barricade of flame—Erda berates him for his harshness. She points out that he, with grievous sins on his own conscience, is hardly in a position to punish so severely.

Wotan, however, stubbornly continues. The wisdom that Erda long ago implanted in his heart, he says, has brought him not peace and confidence, but dismay and confusion. Now she must tell him how to conquer the despair that is engulfing his soul. In the face of Erda's evasive reply, Wotan resigns himself to his fate. There is a long pause. Then Wotan somberly declares that he is no longer concerned with the imminent doom of the gods. Siegfried, the hero without fear, has won the ring. With its aid he will also win Brünnhilde, and by that deed of love will redeem the world. As he bids Erda return again to her eternal sleep, she sinks slowly back into the earth.

Wotan, seeing Siegfried approaching in the distance, sits down to await him. The youth rushes in, anxiously following the forest bird, which flutters about for a moment and then disappears. Catching sight of Wotan, Siegfried asks the way to the fire-encircled rock. Instead of answering, Wotan questions the youth, and Siegfried tells him about Mime and killing the dragon with his sword. Asked who forged the sword, Siegfried replies that he himself did it. Wotan wishes to know who first made the fragments out of which he fashioned this sword. Siegfried says that he does not know, adding that the weapon was certainly of no use to him in fragments. That is obvious, remarks Wotan with a good-natured laugh.

Siegfried, rather irked at the stranger's bantering manner, curtly tells him that he has no more time for idle talk. He expresses curiosity, however, about Wotan's appearance, particularly over the fact that he has only one eye. Wotan's devious explanations serve only to make Siegfried more impatient, and he at length orders the god to let him pass on his way to the rock.

In majestic anger, Wotan bars his way. He bids Siegfried look up at the mountain height, where the glow of a great fire is seen. There the maiden slumbers, he says, but he who dares approach her will be consumed by the flames. Siegfried scornfully attempts to push Wotan aside, whereupon the god holds his spear before him, blocking his path. As Siegfried angrily draws his sword, Wotan warns that this spear once shattered the very sword Siegfried holds in his hands—and will do so again. In a sudden flash of understanding, Siegfried cries out that now at last he faces his father's enemy. Thus his sire will be avenged, he storms, and with a mighty blow splinters the shaft of the spear. There is a blaze of lightning and crash of thunder. Wotan vanishes.

Exultantly Siegfried turns toward the fiery mountain, from which the flaming tide appears to be descending closer. Lifting his horn to his lips, Siegfried blows his horn call, then plunges straight toward the flames. A glowing mist envelops the scene, while the *Fire Music* swells and surges in the orchestra.

When the mist clears we see the sunlit mountain summit where Brünnhilde lies asleep under a huge fir tree. It is the same setting as that of the closing act of *Die Walküre*. The Sleep motive whispers high in the strings. Siegfried appears from behind a rock and gazes on the scene, overcome with amazement. He first notices a fully caparisoned horse near by. Slowly he approaches the sleeping figure in armor and helmet partly hidden by a great shield.

Gently he lifts the shield, gazing in fascination upon the face of the warrior. He carefully cuts through the fastenings of the breastplate with his sword, then lifts off the armor. Completely dumfounded, he discovers that the warrior is a beautiful woman. Siegfried is suddenly gripped by a profound foreboding which he recognizes as fear. Crying wildly for help, he sinks down at Brünnhilde's side.

After a moment he slowly rises, his eyes fixed on Brünnhilde's face. Overwhelmed by her enchanting beauty, he bends down and kisses her passionately on the mouth. Brünnhilde, awakened, hails the sunlit world about her in an ecstatic flood of song. She turns to Siegfried with the soaring phrase, "Siegfried! seliger Held!" ("Siegfried! Blessed hero!"). Joyously she greets him as the son of the mother whom she befriended in defiance of Wotan.

Siegfried, shaken by the unfamiliar emotion of love, answers her in mingled wonder and rapture. Impetuously he tries to embrace Brünnhilde. She recoils in terror, realizing that in taking away her armor the hero has taken away her godhood. She is no longer a Walküre, but a mortal woman. Desperately she entreats Siegfried to leave her, crying out that she does not want mortal embraces. He sweeps aside her pleas with passionate declarations of his love. Helpless before his ardor, Brünnhilde surrenders, singing that she will follow him to her doom. Jubilantly she bids adieu to Walhalla and the splendor of the gods. Brünnhilde and Siegfried blend their voices in a magnificent duet as they sing of the love that overwhelms them in the dawn of their new world—transfiguring love that laughs at death ("Leuchtende Liebe! lachender Tod!"). They are clasped in each other's arms as the curtain falls.

Die Götterdämmerung

(The Twilight of the Gods)

CHARACTERS

First Norn ⎫		*Contralto*
Second Norn ⎬ daughters of Erda...................		*Mezzo-soprano*
Third Norn ⎭		*Soprano*
Siegfried		....*Tenor*
Brünnhilde		.*Soprano*
Gunther ⎱ Gibichungs—children of Gibich and Grimhilde........		⎰ *Bass*
Gutrune ⎰		⎱ *Soprano*
Hagen, their half brother, son of Grimhilde and Alberich.............		...*Bass*
Waltraute, a Valkyrie................................		.*Mezzo-soprano*
Alberich		..*Bass*
Woglinde ⎫		*Soprano*
Wellgunde ⎬ Rhinemaidens.........................		*Mezzo-soprano*
Flosshilde ⎭		*Contralto*

Vassals, warriors, and women

Place: Legendary Germany
Time: Antiquity
First performance: Festspielhaus, Bayreuth, August 17, 1876
Original language: German

PROLOGUE

BRÜNNHILDE'S ROCK (the same as in the closing scenes of *Die Walküre* and *Siegfried*).[1] It is night. From below, in the background, comes the glow of the fire that encircles the rock. In the dim, bluish light of the foreground the three Norns are visible. The First Norn unwinds from about her body the golden cord of Fate, ties one end to a pine tree, and then passes it along to the others. As they weave, the destinies of gods and men are decided.

The First Norn sings that one day, as she was weaving beside the spring at the foot of the world ash tree, Wotan appeared and exchanged one of his eyes for a drink of the waters of wisdom. Then he broke a branch from the tree and fashioned a great spear, after which the tree withered and the spring dried up. The Second Norn takes up the story. Winding the cord around a rocky projection, she tells how Wotan engraved on his spear the sacred treaties that gave him world power, and how afterward the spear was shattered by Siegfried. Wotan then returned to Walhalla and commanded the heroes to cut down the ash tree. The Third Norn, catching up the end of the cord, concludes the narrative. The branches of the tree were hewn into pieces and piled up like a rampart around Walhalla. There, the

[1] The opera, written in a prologue and three acts, is sometimes cut because of its great length, the prologue being played as the first scene of Act One.

Norn intones, Wotan and his hosts await their doom, which will come when flames obliterate both rampart and castle.

Completing the prophecy, the Norns sing that Wotan will one day plunge his broken spear into the breast of Loge, whom he has bound by magic to Brünnhilde's rock. He will then pull the spear flaming from the fire god's wound, hurl it upon the ramparts of Walhalla, and thus kindle the destroying fire. In frightened tones the Norns exclaim that the sharp edges of the rock are cutting the cord. As they lament that the world's evil and Alberich's curse are severing the strands, the cord suddenly snaps. The Fate motive sounds in the orchestra. The Norns tie themselves together with the torn cord and then disappear, crying that they must now return to their mother Erda.

Dawn slowly brightens over the rocky height. Soon Brünnhilde and Siegfried appear, heralded by their characteristic motives, after which we hear the music played as the introduction to the concert version of *Siegfried's Rhine Journey*. Brünnhilde leads her horse, Grane, by the bridle. Siegfried is clad in armor. In a heroic refrain ("Zu neuen Thaten, theurer Helde") Brünnhilde sings that Siegfried must now go forth to triumph for her. With fateful insight, she reveals she is haunted by the thought that, in sending him forth to conquer, she may lose his love. She has given him divine wisdom at the cost of her godhood. Now she has only mortal love to offer him, and he, as a mortal man, may one day spurn that love. She begs him never to forget their pledges of love. Siegfried promises to accomplish glorious deeds in her behalf, and as a token of faith he gives her the magic ring. In exchange she gives him Grane.

At the end of an ecstatic duet Siegfried, leading Grane through a cleft in the rocks, begins his journey down the Rhine valley. Brünnhilde watches him go, waving to him joyously as his horn call sounds from the distance. The curtain falls during the playing of the familiar *Rhine Journey* music, which continues into the Hagen motive as the curtain rises again.

ACT ONE

The castle of the Gibichungs on the Rhine.[2] Gunther, King of the Gibichungs, is seated on his throne with his sister, Gutrune. They are in conversation with Hagen, who is seated at a table before them. Hagen observes that neither Gunther nor Gutrune is married, and expresses concern about the future of the race of Gibichungs. He would have Gunther marry Brünnhilde, the fairest of women, he says, but her destined bridegroom is the world's greatest hero, Siegfried. Only he was brave enough to penetrate the ring of magic fire that girded the mountain peak on which she lay. Hagen then relates the story of Siegfried's origin and his adventures, adding that a hero of such stature should be the husband of Gutrune. Gunther angrily rebukes him for mocking him with dreams of a bride he cannot win.

At that point Hagen takes Gunther aside and tells him of his evil plan. When Siegfried, journeying down the Rhine, visits the Gibichungs' castle,

[2] Sometimes played as Scene Two of Act One.

he can be given a magic potion which will not only put him in Gunther's power but will cause him to forget Brünnhilde and fall in love with Gutrune. Once in the grip of the spell, Siegfried can be persuaded to win Brünnhilde for Gunther in return for taking Gutrune as his own bride.

While they are talking Siegfried's horn call sounds in the distance, and shortly the boat carrying Siegfried and his horse approaches the riverbank. The Curse motive thunders out as he leaps to the shore on his horse. Dismounting, he enters the castle and is greeted by the Gibichungs. Hagen quietly signals Gutrune to retire to her room. Gunther puts his lands, his vassals, and himself at Siegfried's disposal. Siegfried, in return, can offer nothing but his strong muscles and his sword. Moving close to him, Hagen remarks that it has been told that Siegfried has won the Nibelungen hoard. He had forgotten that, Siegfried answers carelessly, because the gold was of no use to him. All he kept of the hoard, he goes on, pointing to the tarnhelm hanging from his belt, was this bit of metal network. He does not know what it is for, he adds. Hagen, saying that it represents the Nibelungs' finest piece of craftsmanship, explains its magic power and then asks Siegfried if he has any other treasure. A ring, Siegfried replies, which is now on the hand of a woman. Gunther betrays great excitement. While he and Siegfried are in conversation, Hagen unobtrusively opens the door of Gutrune's room. She comes out carrying a drinking horn containing the magic potion. Handing it to Siegfried, she courteously invites him to drink.

The draught instantly erases from his mind all memory of Brünnhilde, and he gazes at Gutrune with passionate intensity. Confused and embarrassed by his ardor, she withdraws to her room. Siegfried promises to set out at once to win Brünnhilde for Gunther, saying that, by means of the tarnhelm, he will woo her in Gunther's form. For this service, Gunther assures him, Gutrune shall be his bride. The two men then prick their arms, mix their blood with wine, and drink, swearing an oath of blood brotherhood as their voices blend in a vigorous duet ("Blühenden Lebens labendes Blut"). He who breaks the oath, they proclaim, must pay forfeit with his heart's blood. Hagen declines to drink, saying that his blood is too cold for so fiery a potion.

Taking up their weapons, Siegfried and Gunther leap into the boat and row away on their adventure. Gutrune reappears momentarily, looks after them, and sings Siegfried's name in ecstasy. Hagen, taking up his shield and spear, seats himself in the doorway and watches the two men leave. Sardonically he wishes them godspeed, gloating that their quest for Gunther's bride will bring him the ring ("Hier sitz' ich zur Wacht"). The curtain falls, while the music continues without pause into an interlude dominated by the somber themes of the Nibelungs' Destruction and Triumph. The Gold and Ring motives are heard, and then the Brünnhilde motive. Here the curtain rises again on Brünnhilde's rock—the same scene as the Prologue.[3]

Brünnhilde, gazing in rapture at the magic ring on her finger, is startled by the sound of thunder. As the *Ride of the Valkyries* echoes in the orchestra, Waltraute rides up in wild excitement. Eagerly Brünnhilde asks if she has come with a message of forgiveness from Wotan. Giving Waltraute no

[3] Sometimes played as Scene Three of Act One.

opportunity to answer, she sings exultantly that Wotan's stern sentence was a blessing in disguise, for it brought her the boon of love.

The Valkyrie impatiently silences her and tells why she has come. In what is known as *Waltraute's Narrative* ("Seit er von dir geschieden") she describes, virtually in the words of the Norn's prophecy, how Wotan and the gods are awaiting their downfall. Wotan has said that if Brünnhilde will give the ring back to the Rhinemaidens, Alberich's curse will be broken and the peace of Walhalla assured. Waltraute implores Brünnhilde to give up the ring, but Brünnhilde replies that she will never part with this token of her hero's love, even though it means the destruction of the gods. With a cry of warning and despair Waltraute rides away.

The glow of the fire encircling the rock now grows brighter, with the flames leaping into view to the accompaniment of the Magic Fire music. Brünnhilde, looking down into the valley, ecstatically hails the approach of Siegfried. In a moment he appears, but Brünnhilde recoils in terror and bewilderment as she sees a stranger standing before her. With the tarnhelm on his head, hiding most of his face except his eyes, Siegfried has assumed Gunther's shape. In a disguised voice he tells Brünnhilde that he is Gunther and has come to claim her as his bride. He seizes her and, after a fierce struggle, tears the ring from her finger and then forces her into a cave at the base of the rock. Before he himself enters he unsheathes his sword and—now in his natural voice—cries that the weapon will guard Gunther's bride.

ACT TWO

Before the entrance hall of the Gibichungs' castle, which is at the right. The sloping bank of the Rhine at the left. To the rear rises a mountain height, on which great stone altars to Wotan, Fricka, and Donner are visible. It is night. Hagen, spear and shield in hand, sits motionless beside one of the pillars of the hall, waiting for the return of Siegfried and Gunther. Alberich is kneeling before him, his hands on Hagen's knees. A strange and somber dialogue follows, throughout which Hagen stares unseeing before him, as though in a trance. Beginning in soft, mysterious tones ("Schläfst du, Hagen, mein Sohn?"), Alberich tells him the story of the ring's curse, then makes him swear that he will regain the ring. The dwarf's voice dies away as he vanishes in the shadows.

Dawn breaks. Hagen is roused by Siegfried, who appears suddenly, explaining that the tarnhelm instantly transported him from Brünnhilde's rock. Gunther and his bride, he says, are following in the boat. Gutrune enters and is joyously greeted by Siegfried. Triumphantly he relates how he won his way to Brünnhilde's side and how his sword helped him keep sacred the oath he swore with Gunther. Telling Hagen to summon the vassals for the wedding festivities, he goes into the hall with Gutrune.

Hagen sounds an oxhorn and calls out to the vassals of the Gibichung ("Hoiho! Hoiho! Hoiho!"), and soon the riverbank is thronged with men responding in a vigorous chorus. The hero Siegfried, Hagen proclaims, has won a Valkyrie as a bride for Gunther, and he himself will wed Gutrune. He invites them all to the wedding feast. Meanwhile the boat bearing

Brünnhilde and Gunther approaches, and as it touches the shore the vassals cheer.

Gunther proudly leads forth Brünnhilde. She walks beside him with bowed head, her pale features betraying her misery and humiliation. Siegfried and Gutrune, attended by ladies-in-waiting, come from the castle to greet them. Shaken with horror, Brünnhilde sees the ring on Siegfried's finger. She cries out that Gunther forced her to become his bride and tore the ring from her hand, then demands to know why it is now on Siegfried's finger. Gunther, completely confused, protests that he did not give the ring to Siegfried. Wild with anger, Brünnhilde turns on Siegfried and accuses him of betraying her and robbing her of the ring. But Siegfried, still under the influence of the potion, stares at the ring, saying that he wrested it from a dragon, not from the hand of a woman. Thereupon Hagen steps forward, also accuses Siegfried of betrayal, and demands vengeance in Gunther's name. Completely unconscious of his guilt, Siegfried declares that he kept faith with Gunther and that his sword Nothung was the guardian of his trust.

At that Hagen holds forth his spear and demands that Siegfried take an oath upon it. Siegfried places his fingers on the spear point and swears that he was never wed to Brünnhilde ("Helle Wehr!"). Livid with rage, Brünnhilde rushes to the spear and dedicates it to the destruction of Siegfried because of his betrayal and perjury. Unmoved by her fury, Siegfried embraces Gutrune, then gaily invites all to the wedding celebration. He leads Gutrune into the castle, and the people follow.

Brünnhilde, Gunther, and Hagen remain to plan their revenge. When Hagen asks Brünnhilde how he may bring about Siegfried's death, she reveals that with her magic arts she has made the hero invulnerable to attack —all but his back, which he never turns on a foe. That, then, will be the target for his spear, Hagen says malevolently. Gunther, however, thinking of Gutrune, rebels at murdering Siegfried. Hagen whispers that his death will give the Gibichungs possession of the ring. Gutrune need never know how her hero died, he goes on, for tomorrow there will be a great hunting party, during which Siegfried will be killed by a wild boar. As the voices of the plotters blend in a dramatic expression of revenge, the wedding procession emerges from the castle, with the vassals bearing Gutrune and Siegfried on their shields. Hagen compels Brünnhilde to join the procession with Gunther.

ACT THREE

A forest clearing on the bank of the Rhine. The Rhinemaidens are frolicking about in the water. Siegfried appears on the riverbank, spies the mermaids, and asks them if they have seen the animal he has been trailing. Teasingly they ask if he will give them his ring if they tell him where his quarry is hiding. At his refusal, they taunt him for being miserly. When they find that he is determined to keep the ring, however, their cajolery turns to earnest entreaty, and they warn him that the ring's curse will strike him down that very day. Siegfried's voice blends with theirs in a melodious ensemble as he expresses his contempt for the advice of women.

The Rhinemaidens swim away. Siegfried hears the horns of the hunting party and sounds an answering call. Soon Hagen and Gunther appear, followed by their vassals carrying game. The hunters prepare to feast on their kill. Siegfried tells how he lost track of his quarry and came at length to the bank of the Rhine, where three mermaids told him that he was destined to be killed before nightfall. Gunther, terror-stricken, looks at Hagen, who casually hands Siegfried wine containing a potion that will restore his memory.

As the hunters gather about the campfire, Hagen asks Siegfried to tell of his exploits. When Siegfried, his mind cleared by the potion, relates how he braved the flames and claimed Brünnhilde as his bride ("Mime hiess ein mürrischer Zwerg"), Gunther leaps to his feet in horror. At that moment two ravens circle slowly above and then fly away toward the Rhine. As Siegfried turns to watch them, Hagen plunges his spear into his back. Siegfried falls on his shield, while the murderer vanishes into the darkness. In the final agony of death, Siegfried raises himself and sings a poignant farewell to Brünnhilde.

Now follows the magnificent music of Siegfried's Funeral March, which traces in its themes the hero's past and the overwhelming tragedy of his death. The sorrowing vassals lift the shield to their shoulders and slowly move off in a dramatic cortege. Rising mists from the Rhine gradually envelop the scene during this interlude. When they clear away we see the hall of the Gibichung castle, as in Act One.

Gutrune, tortured by a premonition of disaster, starts in fear at the sound of a hunting horn in the distance. The hunting party approaches. Transfixed with horror, Gutrune watches the vassals bring in Siegfried's body and place it in the middle of the hall. When Hagen tells her that Siegfried was killed by a boar, she utters a wild cry of grief and faints over the body. After a moment she revives and accuses Gunther of the murder, but he cries out that Hagen is guilty. In savage defiance, Hagen admits the deed. Siegfried, he declares, swore falsely on his spear, and that very spear has now revenged his betrayal. Shouting that the ring is his by right, he flings himself on Gunther and kills him with a blow of his sword. As he turns to snatch the ring from the hand of the dead Siegfried, the lifeless arm rises slowly, as if in a gesture of warning. The clamoring throng stands frozen with horror.

Brünnhilde now approaches, and with majestic scorn she bids the people cease their childish lamentations because they are unfit for a great hero. Gutrune cries out that Brünnhilde was the cause of all her misfortune, whereupon Brünnhilde tells her contemptuously that she, Gutrune, was never Siegfried's wife, but a mere interloper. Realizing that she too is a victim of Hagen's treachery, Gutrune curses him, and then, crushed by despair, sinks over Gunther's body.

Brünnhilde commands the vassals to build a pyre on the riverbank and to bring to her Siegfried's horse. As the men obey, she looks down upon the hero and pours out her love and sorrow in a heartbreaking strain ("Wie Sonne lauter strahlt mir sein Licht"). Raising her eyes, she bids the gods look upon what they have destroyed, then draws the ring from Siegfried's finger and puts it on her own. She looks toward the Rhine and sings that the Rhinemaidens may soon claim from her ashes their precious ring, cleansed at last of its curse. At her command the two ravens perched near the riverbank start their flight back to Wotan with the message that his doom is upon him. Brünnhilde bids them pause at the fire-encircled rock and tell Loge to join the gods in their final hour. With that she snatches a torch from the hand of a vassal and hurls it upon the pyre, which bursts into flame.

Grane, Siegfried's horse, is led forward. To the music of the great *Immolation Scene*, Brünnhilde hails Siegfried in death, then rides into the flames. The fire billows up fiercely and seems to devour the entire hall, while the terrified onlookers crowd to the foreground. When the flames die down the Rhine surges up in a mighty flood, bearing the Rhinemaidens on its crest. On seeing them, Hagen leaps like a madman into the river to gain the coveted ring, crying, "Zurück vom Ring!" ("Away from the Ring!"). The Rhinemaidens drag him beneath the waves, then reappear, with Flosshilde holding up the ring in a gesture of joyous triumph.

The Rhine subsides. In the distance a glow breaks through a dark band of clouds, revealing Walhalla and Wotan with the gods about him, facing their flaming doom. The music storms to a great climax on the Rhine and Walhalla themes, then dies away as the motive of Redemption by Love soars high in the strings. The curtain falls.

Roméo et Juliette

by CHARLES GOUNOD

[1818–1893]

Libretto by
JULES BARBIER *and* MICHEL CARRÉ

Based on the tragedy by Shakespeare

CHARACTERS

Tybalt	*Tenor*
Paris	*Baritone*
Capulet	*Bass*
Juliette, his daughter	*Soprano*
Mercutio	*Baritone*
Roméo	*Tenor*
Gregorio, retainer to the Capulets	*Baritone*
Gertrude, Juliette's nurse	*Mezzo-soprano*
Friar Laurence	*Bass*
Stephano, Roméo's page	*Soprano*
Benvolio, retainer to the Montagues	*Tenor*
Duke of Verona	*Bass*
Friar Jean	*Bass*

Adherents of the houses of Capulet and Montague,
ladies and gentlemen, servants

Place: Verona
Time: Fourteenth century
First performance: Théâtre-Lyrique, Paris, April 27, 1867
Original language: French

SHAKESPEARE'S PLAY was set to music by such composers as Zingarelli, Bellini, and Berlioz, but Gounod's version is the only one which has endured in operatic repertoire. Although it is considered musically inferior to *Faust*, it has maintained its place in public favor since the day of its première. For the sake of operatic conventions, Gounod's librettists took considerable liberties with the play, omitting several characters and adding one—Stephano.

PROLOGUE

After a brief introduction the curtain rises to reveal the entire cast of principals on the stage. In the chorus, "Vérone vit jadis deux familles rivales," they comment on the feud between the Capulets and the Montagues of Verona and on the tragic love of Roméo and Juliette.

ACT ONE

The ballroom of the Capulet palace, where guests are assembled for a masked ball in celebration of Juliette's birthday. A lilting waltz chorus ("L'heure s'envole") reflects the gay mood of the scene. Tybalt enters with Paris. Commenting on the brilliant company, Tybalt remarks that Paris is destined to claim the fairest of them all as his bride. Paris observes rather casually that he hopes his heart will awaken to love. There is a stir as Capulet and Juliette appear, the guests marveling over her beauty. She expresses her excitement over the ball in a sparkling air ("Ecoutez! Ecoutez!"). In a jovial refrain ("Allons! jeunes gens!") Capulet urges all to enjoy themselves to the utmost, and the assemblage responds in an exuberant chorus.

Roméo, Mercutio, and some of their followers enter. Mercutio is all for removing his mask and making himself known to the Capulets, but Roméo restrains him. He has not come to quarrel, he says, but only because he has had a dream. It is probably a message from Queen Mab, Mercutio observes flippantly. By way of explaining his remark he sings the *Ballad of Queen Mab*, telling of the fairy queen who brings disturbing dreams and perplexing illusions. Roméo, although he listens to the song with some amusement, is haunted by a feeling of impending misfortune and is anxious to leave the palace of his enemies before trouble arises. Suddenly he espies Juliette and is completely captivated by her beauty. He watches her as she walks among the guests with Gertrude. The nurse compliments her on her betrothal to Paris, but Juliette can think only of the gaiety of the moment and the enchantment of spring. She gives voice to her feelings in the well-known valse, "Ah! je veux vivre dans le rêve."

As Gregorio appears and asks the two women to join the guests at supper Roméo manages to detain Juliette. A charming duet now follows ("Ange adorable"), in which Roméo gallantly pays court and Juliette answers with disarming coquetry. Their conversation is interrupted by the approach of a courtier, whom Juliette identifies as her cousin Tybalt. Roméo learns to his dismay that he has been talking to Capulet's daughter. He murmurs a word of greeting to Tybalt and then hurriedly leaves. Gazing after him, Tybalt angrily exclaims that he recognizes the stranger by his voice as Roméo and swears that he will kill him. As he rushes away Juliette voices her foreboding of the disaster that may be engendered by this meeting with Roméo. She leaves to join the guests.

Roméo, having been rejoined by Mercutio, returns to the ballroom on his way out of the palace. He is in despair because the woman he loves is the daughter of a Capulet. Mercutio, seeing Tybalt and Paris approach, warns that there may be trouble ahead. As the enemies, their hands on their sword hilts, warily regard each other, Capulet and his guests reappear. Roméo and Mercutio leave. Capulet, unaware that the two masked figures are foemen, sternly forbids Tybalt to follow them. Turning to his guests, the host once again urges them to dance. Gaiety rules the scene as they repeat the refrain of the waltz chorus. The curtain falls.

ACT TWO

The garden of the Capulet palace. At one side is the balcony window of Juliette's room. Roméo enters cautiously, invoking the protection of the night. Behind the scenes Roméo's followers sing a brief chorus in which they mockingly wish him success on his romantic conquest. Gazing up at Juliette's window, Roméo exclaims in rapture as he sees a light ("L'amour! Oui, son ardeur"). In an ensuing aria ("Ah! lève-toi, soleil") he compares Juliette's beauty to the rising sun, which pales the stars with its radiance. Juliette, appearing on the balcony, laments that her lover bears the name so hated by the Capulets. In the phrase "O Roméo! pourquoi ce nom est-il le tien?" she sings the operatic version of the famous line, "O Romeo, Romeo! wherefore art thou Romeo?" An impassioned colloquy follows as Roméo makes himself known and the lovers pledge their eternal devotion.

They are interrupted by the sound of angry voices in the distance. Roméo hides in the shadows of the garden as Gregorio and a group of Capulet followers rush in, exclaiming in an agitated chorus that their quarry has eluded them. Encountering Gertrude, they explain that they are seeking a Montague page who has been seen on the palace grounds. The nurse assures them that she will keep watch for the intruder. Thanking her with exaggerated gallantry, the courtiers go on their way.

When all is quiet the lovers resume their conversation. Juliette asks Roméo to name the day on which they can be wed or else—if he is merely wooing lightly—to leave her forever. This brings a fervent declaration of love from Roméo. Gertrude's warning voice is heard inside, but Roméo implores Juliette to remain for yet another word of love. Their voices blend in an exquisite refrain ("De cet adieu si douce est la tristesse"—the equivalent of the poignant words of the play, "Good night, good night! Parting is such sweet sorrow!"). Juliette retires while Roméo sings his adieu in the strain heard at the opening of the act. The curtain falls.

ACT THREE

[Scene One] Friar Laurence's cell, where the marriage of Roméo and Juliette is to take place. The religious mood of the scene is established by the stately theme in the prelude. Roméo enters, and the wise old friar, noting his excited manner, asks if he is troubled by love. Assuring him that such is the case, Roméo tells him about Juliette. Friar Laurence is considerably alarmed to learn that he is enamored of a Capulet. Juliette and Gertrude enter, and the ceremony takes place at once. As the lovers kneel before the friar he begins the ritual with the impressive prayer, "Dieu, qui fit l'homme à ton image." Roméo and Juliette make their responses and exchange the vows of matrimony. At the conclusion of the ceremony the four voices blend in a beautiful quartet expressive of the happiness over this union ("O pur bonheur!"). The curtain falls.

[*Scene Two*] A square before the Capulet palace. Stephano enters, fretting that he has not seen his master since yesterday and wondering if he is still in the palace of his enemy. In brash defiance he sings a taunting serenade ("Que fais-tu, blanche tourterelle, dans ce nid de vautours?"), in which he makes pointed references to a turtledove held captive in a nest of vultures. The dove, he sings impudently, may soon be set free. The song has the desired effect—it brings Gregorio and a group of Capulets storming from the palace. There is an exchange of insults, and Stephano and Gregorio draw swords. At that moment Mercutio enters, rushes to Stephano's aid, and is confronted by Tybalt. The two immediately cross swords. Roméo appears, whereupon Tybalt sardonically tells Mercutio that this adversary will receive preference. In fury he turns on Roméo, who starts to draw his sword and then sheathes it again. He speaks placatingly to Tybalt, assuring him that he bears him no hatred. At that, Mercutio, rebuking Roméo for retreating before the enemy, exclaims that if Roméo will not uphold the honor of the Montagues he himself will do so. In vain Roméo tries to restrain him. The Capulets and the Montagues confront each other and pour out their hatred and defiance in a dramatic chorus ("Capulets! Montagues! race immonde!"). At its climax Tybalt and Mercutio lunge at each other and Mercutio falls mortally wounded, crying out the famous phrase, "Que le diable soit de vos deux maisons [A plague on both your houses]!" Roméo orders his followers to carry the dying Mercutio away, whirls on Tybalt, and runs him through. As he falls Capulet rushes from the palace, followed by people of the court. They look on in horror as Capulet bends over Tybalt, who, with his dying breath, cries for revenge. While the Capulets are lamenting their defeat, the Duke of Verona strides in. Both factions press toward him, clamoring for justice. Denouncing Roméo, the Duke orders him banished from Verona and then exacts an oath of allegiance from the Capulets and Montagues.

In an eloquent refrain ("Ah! jour de deuil") Roméo bitterly laments the irreparable harm done by this day's violence. It is repeated in a majestic chorus. The Duke warns Roméo to leave the city before nightfall, but Roméo vows that he will defy death to see Juliette once again. As the Capulets clamor for revenge the curtain falls.

ACT FOUR

Juliette's chamber, to which Roméo has come at the risk of his life to say farewell. Juliette assures him that she forgives him for killing Tybalt, for it was he who provoked the quarrel. Ardently she declares her love, and then the two sing a glowing duet ("Nuit d'hyménée!") in which they rhapsodize over the enchantment of the night. After its ecstatic climax Roméo sadly murmurs that he hears the song of the lark heralding the day on which they must part. It is not the lark, Juliette replies, but the nightingale, singing her song of love. Roméo takes her in his arms, and they remain in a rapturous embrace as a passionate theme throbs in the orchestra. Freeing herself, Juliette exclaims that now day has dawned and Roméo must flee. Their voices blend once more in despairing farewells, and Roméo hurriedly makes his escape.

Gertrude enters in great excitement and warns Juliette that her father and Friar Laurence are coming to see her. The dialogue continues in the form of a quartet ("Juliette! Ah! le ciel soit l'ouél"). As Capulet enters with the friar he expresses surprise at finding Juliette awake. He tells her that out of respect for Tybalt's wishes she is to be married at once to Paris. Bidding the friar to prepare Juliette for the nuptial vows, Capulet leaves to welcome the wedding guests.

In despair Juliette implores the friar to aid her in this trying hour. He asks if she is afraid of death, to which she unhesitatingly replies that she would rather die than live in dishonor. Thereupon the friar hands her a small vial. In a dramatic air ("Buvez donc ce breuage") he bids her drink the potion, which will produce the semblance of death for one day. Those who seek to awaken her, he goes on, will say that she is dead, but the angels will answer that she only sleeps. Friar Laurence promises that when night comes he will bring Roméo to her, and then, the effects of the potion having worn off, they can flee together. Juliette agrees to the plan and assures the friar of her complete trust in him. After he has gone Juliette drinks the potion, then exclaims over the chilling effect it produces. Taking up a dagger, she resolves to kill herself if the potion does not accomplish its purpose. In the aria, "Amour, ranime mon courage," she prays for courage to face the ordeal, momentarily imagines she sees the avenging apparition of Tybalt, and, finally conquering her fears, vows she will be faithful to Roméo even in death.[1]

Paris, Capulet, Gertrude, Friar Laurence, and a throng of guests now enter for the nuptial procession. They greet Juliette in a chorus known as the *Epithalamium* ("O Juliette, sois heureuse!"), in which they exhort her to be happy in her marriage to Paris. Juliette and Gertrude blend their voices with the others as they lament that the union with Roméo is destined never to be fulfilled.[2]

As they crowd around Juliette, Capulet steps forward and tells his daughter that her hour of supreme happiness has arrived ("Ma fille, cède aux voeux du fiancé"). Crying that hate alone has prompted this marriage and that the grave will be her wedding chamber ("La haine est le berceau"), Juliette totters and falls insensible at the feet of her father. The curtain falls.

ACT FIVE

The burial vault of the Capulets. Juliette, in her deathlike slumber, lies on a bier in the center of the chamber. After a brief prelude in the form of an instrumental chorale there is a scene before the curtain, in which Friar

[1] In some performances Act Four ends here.
[2] This number is frequently omitted in performance.

Laurence is informed by Friar Jean that Roméo's page was attacked and wounded by the Capulets while on his way to deliver the message explaining about the potion. Friar Laurence immediately dispatches Friar Jean in all haste to Roméo.

There is a brief orchestral interlude, wonderfully descriptive of Juliette's sleep. Roméo enters the tomb, gazes upon his bride, whom he believes to be dead, and marvels that even death has not robbed her of her loveliness ("Salut! tombeau! sombre et silencieux"). In a transport of grief he embraces Juliette and then drinks poison from a vial he has brought with him. As he slowly succumbs Juliette revives. Bewildered and unbelieving, they greet each other and in a poignant refrain ("Dieu de bonté!") give thanks for their reunion.

Juliette cries out in alarm at Roméo's sudden paroxysm of agony. He gasps that he took poison because he believed her to be dead. As approaching death clouds his mind, Roméo recalls, in the refrain of the farewell duet, their tender words about the lark and the nightingale. Frenziedly Juliette asks if there is no poison left for her. Crying out that there is another way, she draws a dagger from the folds of her gown and plunges it into her breast. With a final prayer for forgiveness ("Seigneur, pardonnez-nous") Roméo and Juliette die in each other's arms. The curtain falls.

Der Rosenkavalier

(The Rose Bearer)

by RICHARD STRAUSS

[1864–1949]

Libretto by
HUGO von HOFMANNSTHAL

CHARACTERS

Count Octavian Rofrano, a young Viennese nobleman.......*Mezzo-soprano*
The Marschallin, Princess von Werdenberg.....................*Soprano*
Mohamed, her young Negro servant
Major-domo to the Princess.................................*Tenor*
Baron Ochs von Lerchenau....................................*Bass*
Attorney ....*Bass*
Milliner ....*Soprano*
Vendor of animals...*Tenor*
Widow

Three orphans................................... $\left\{ \begin{array}{l} \textit{Soprano} \\ \textit{Mezzo-soprano} \\ \textit{Alto} \end{array} \right.$

Singer ....*Tenor*
Flautist
Head cook
Hairdresser
Valzacchi, an intriguing Italian............................*Tenor*
Annina, his companion.....................................*Alto*
Leopold, Baron Ochs's personal servant

Four footmen to the Princess........................... $\left\{ \begin{array}{l} \textit{Two tenors} \\ \textit{Two basses} \end{array} \right.$

Four waiters.. $\left\{ \begin{array}{l} \textit{One tenor} \\ \textit{Three basses} \end{array} \right.$

Herr von Faninal, a wealthy merchant, recently
   admitted to the nobility....................................*Baritone*
Mistress Marianne Leitmetzer, Sophie's duenna................*Soprano*
Major-domo to Faninal.....................................*Tenor*
Sophie, daughter of Faninal................................*Soprano*
Innkeeper ....*Tenor*
Police commissioner ....*Bass*
Guests, musicians, servants, coachmen, stableboys, children, a doctor

Place: Vienna
Time: During the reign of Maria Theresa of Austria in the eighteenth century

First performance: Hofoper, Dresden, January 26, 1911
Original language: German

IN DER ROSENKAVALIER, Strauss turned from the harsh realism of *Salome, Elektra,* and other works in the *verismo* style to romance and lyricism. Subtitled *A Comedy for Music,* the opera contains some of the composer's wittiest and most ingratiating melodies. Its waltz tunes are favorites in concert repertoire.

The brief introduction concerns itself principally with the themes associated with Octavian and the Princess and also states the theme symbolizing their love.

ACT ONE

The boudoir of the Princess von Werdenberg. At one side, in an alcove, is a large curtained four-poster bed. At the other side of the room are large folding doors which lead to an antechamber. At the back, in the center, is a small door, a private entrance. It is late morning and the sun streams in through windows overlooking a garden. The Princess is lying in bed. Only her hand and arm, emerging from the sleeve of her lace nightgown, are visible.[1] Count Octavian, her seventeen-year-old lover, kneels on a footstool beside the bed and addresses her in impassioned phrases ("Wie Du warst! Wie Du bist!"). The Princess answers the Count's exaggerated expressions of devotion with mingled affection and amusement. Octavian frets that the day has dawned. Rushing impetuously to the windows, he draws the curtains, exclaiming that he must hide his beloved from other men's eyes. When a bell tinkles outside he strikes a heroic pose and proclaims that no one shall enter.

At a warning word from the Princess, however, Octavian conceals himself behind a screen near the bed. As he does so the private door at the back opens and Mohamed, the little Negro servant, enters with the Princess's morning chocolate. While he busies himself with putting his tray on a table, the Princess, in an excited whisper, tells Octavian to get his sword, which he has left lying on a chair. Octavian manages to retrieve the sword without being seen by the servant. The latter brings the table forward, places it before a sofa, and then, with a ceremonious bow in the direction of the bed, he trips out.

When all is quiet again the Princess rises, puts on a dressing gown, and sits at the table, where she is joined by Octavian. With mock severity she scolds him for being indiscreet enough to leave his sword lying about in a lady's boudoir. He immediately becomes the tragically misunderstood lover, but the Princess affectionately forgives him. She addresses him as "Quinquin," while he calls her his "Bichette." Over the chocolate they discuss the Field Marshal, who is away on a hunting trip in Croatia. Half-teasingly, the

[1] In some versions the Princess is seated in a chair.

Princess remarks that only last night she dreamed that her husband came home. Octavian fumes with jealousy. When the Princess speaks reassuringly to him, he asks why she has a troubled look. The Field Marshal, answers the Princess, sometimes travels very rapidly.

Even as she is speaking there is a noise outside, and the Princess exclaims in dismay that perhaps the Field Marshal actually is coming home. Octavian, drawing his sword, runs to the doors of the antechamber but is warned back by the Princess, who tells him that out there the footmen are waiting. He runs to the small door, but the Princess calls him back, saying that the private passage also is blocked. At her urgent bidding Octavian hides behind the curtains of the bed. Meanwhile the uproar outside is growing louder. The Princess goes to the door, listens for a moment, and then suddenly laughs with relief as she recognizes the voice of Baron Ochs. Turning toward the bed, she calls to Octavian, telling him that the danger is over. She warns him to remain hidden for the present to avoid being seen by the footmen. Ochs is heard angrily arguing with the major-domo outside.

Puzzling over the reason for the Baron's visit, the Princess recalls that she received a long letter from him several days ago—which she neglected to read. The Baron, she says to Octavian, has undoubtedly come to talk about some matters mentioned in the letter. At that point Octavian, dressed as a maid, emerges from behind the bed. Curtsying, he addresses the Princess in Viennese street dialect. Delighted with his clever disguise, the Princess tells him to leave through the antechamber and walk boldly past the footmen.

The doors are now flung open and the portly Baron stalks in despite the frantic efforts of the footmen to bar his way. He greets the Princess with elaborate gallantry and then looks with a connoisseur's glance at Octavian. He was certain, he says, glaring at the footmen, that the Princess would welcome him despite the early hour. People of quality pay little attention to the time of day when they are in the mood to go calling. There was the Princess Brioche, for example, the Baron goes on, with whom he once chatted while she was in her bath.

The Princess, dismissing the footmen, explains that they were merely obeying orders—she had been suffering from a touch of migraine and did not wish to see any visitors. When she notices the Baron's persistent interest in Octavian the Princess remarks that the "girl" is her new maid, Mariandel. Her country ways, she hopes, will not be too displeasing to the Baron. He exclaims that he is delighted with the young lady. Catching the Princess's knowing look, Ochs hastily changes the subject. He asks if the news of his impending marriage, which he announced in his recent letter, came as a surprise. The Princess adroitly manages to conceal the fact that she never read the letter and, pleading a lapse of memory, asks the name of the bride-to-be. During this conversation, Octavian, despite signals from the Princess to leave the room, deliberately keeps himself within the Baron's range of vision. He looks at the maid with longing glances, at the same time trying to continue his talk with the Princess.

The bride-to-be, says the Baron, is the daughter of one Faninal, who recently has been elevated to the nobility and has been put in charge of provisioning Her Majesty's armies in the Netherlands. Looking over the Baron's shoulder, the Princess again impatiently signals Octavian to go. The

Baron, misunderstanding her look, hastens to explain that his affianced is pretty, convent-bred, and an only child, whose father, by the way, is in indifferent health. Moreover, he owns twelve houses and a palace. As the conversation goes on the Baron catches sight of Octavian backing toward the door with the serving tray. Determined to detain the maid, Ochs says that he is hungry, and the Princess orders "Mariandel" to serve him. As he helps himself greedily he looks Octavian over with vulgar approval, muttering amorous proposals in asides.

Ochs tells the Princess that, with her permission, he and his retinue will remain at her palace overnight and then move to the White Horse Inn tomorrow. One of his first duties will be to observe the traditional custom of sending a messenger to his bride-to-be with a silver rose as pledge of his love. He asks the Princess to recommend a proper emissary, and she promises to make some suggestions in the morning. The Baron also asks if he may have a few words with her attorney on the matter of property settlements.

When the Princess endeavors to send Octavian out to summon the attorney, the Baron, grimly determined not to let the maid out of his sight, warns that so young and innocent a child should not be permitted to mingle with the footmen. At that moment the major-domo comes in and announces that the attorney is waiting outside, along with the head cook, the steward, a singer and a flautist recommended by the Duke of Silva, and the usual assortment of morning visitors. While he is speaking to the Princess, Ochs maneuvers Mariandel to the other side of the room and invites her to have supper with him. She coyly demurs.

Dismissing the major-domo, the Princess sees the Baron talking to Mariandel and twits him about taking his fun where he finds it—even on the eve of his marriage. Marriage, answers the Baron, does not mean that he must curb his hunter's instincts. The chase, he says, is the sport of noblemen. In a lilting refrain he goes through the entire category of amorous conquest and expounds at length on the comparative charms of German and Bohemian girls ("Dafür ist man kein Auerhahn und kein Hirsch"). The Princess occasionally interjects a gently sarcastic comment.

Mariandel, pretending to be greatly impressed, listens for a while and then, unable to control herself, bursts out laughing at the Baron's pompous self-esteem. Assuming that the maid is admiring him, Ochs imperturbably brags away. The dialogue continues in trio form as the maid expresses her pretended confusion over the Baron's attentions, while the Princess cautions Ochs to leave her alone. He suddenly asks the Princess if he may take Mariandel to be maid to the Baroness. She would be most acceptable, he says, because he is convinced she has blue blood. The Princess dryly compliments him on his discernment. Ochs observes that it is not unusual for people of position to have servants with a touch of royalty in them. His own servant—a duke's son—has Lerchenau blood as blue as his own. He is outside, the Baron explains, waiting to bring in the silver rose.

As though suddenly struck with an idea, the Princess sends Octavian to bring a medallion from the jewel case in her dressing room. When Octavian returns the Princess shows Ochs the picture it contains and asks if this young nobleman would qualify as the bearer of the silver rose. The Baron enthusiastically approves. The Princess takes pains to point out the strong resemblance between the Count—younger brother of the Marquis Rofrano—and Mariandel. Astonished at the similarity, the Baron hints that it is possibly the result of an amorous adventure on the part of the Marquis. The Princess, implying that she understands, says that the apparent kinship between the Count and the maid prompts her to keep Mariandel in her service. The conversation ends when the Princess finally dismisses the maid. The Baron tries to follow her out, but Mariandel neatly slams the door in his face.

The Princess now turns her attention to her morning interviews. Pandemonium reigns as the folding doors are again flung open, admitting the strange assortment of people who have been waiting. The throng includes the attorney, the head cook, a scullion, the milliner, the scholar, the animal vendor, Valzacchi and Annina, a widow and her three orphans, a tenor, and a flautist. First the three orphans, garbed in black, approach the table where the Princess is seated and appeal melodramatically for help in the name of their noble, departed father. The milliner enthuses over the style and beauty of her selection of hats, while the animal vendor exhibits his apes, dogs, and parrots. During the melee the Princess manages to introduce her attorney to the Baron, who is standing at one side of the room. The scholar approaches the Princess with the idea of showing her a book, but Valzacchi brushes him aside and holds forth a copy of a local scandal sheet. After he enumerates the lurid accounts of murders and poisonings it records the Princess impatiently tells him to be off with his trash. The three orphans and the widow, meanwhile having been given a purse, kiss the Princess's hand, whine their thanks, and make their way out.

Now the hairdresser and his assistants bustle in, elbow the others out of the way, and give their attention to the Princess's coiffure. In the meantime the tenor and the flautist come forward. As the flautist plays a cadenza the singer strikes a pose and then launches into a florid Italian serenade, "Di rigori armato." While he is singing three oafish individuals enter. They are obviously ill at ease in their liveries and are apparently quarreling among themselves. They turn out to be the Baron's body servant, his almoner, and his chasseur. The servant is carrying a morocco jewel case. All three awkwardly make their way over to the Baron and then stand nearby awaiting instructions.

Ochs is deep in a whispered conversation with the attorney over dowry matters. When the attorney tries to point out to him that the "morning gift" (a gift from husband to wife on the day after the wedding) is customarily given by the groom to the bride, and not vice versa, Ochs loses his temper and begins shouting. The tenor plunges on into the second stanza of his song, but just as he braces himself for the high note of the climax the Baron emits a shout of rage and bangs his fist on the table. Startled out of his wits, the tenor stops short. With a placating gesture the Princess calls the singer to her and permits him to kiss her hand as a sign of approval. The tenor and the flautist then withdraw, the tenor glaring at the Baron, who acknowledges the look with a gesture of contemptuous indifference.

The hairdresser by this time has completed the Princess's coiffure. She examines the effect in a mirror and then chides the hairdresser for having made her look middle-aged. In great agitation he and his assistants begin changing the coiffure. Valzacchi and Annina now make their way over to the Baron and fawningly offer their services. They are ready to perform any task, they tell him. They will be glad, for example, to report on the activities of his bride-to-be—where she goes, with whom she dines, to whom she writes. At first the Baron tries to ignore the couple but finally tells them they may try their skill by gathering some information about a maid named Mariandel, who is in the service of the Princess von Werdenberg. With that he walks away and turns his attention to the Princess, who has meanwhile dismissed the hairdresser.

At a sign from the Baron the servant steps forward to give the Princess the case containing the silver rose. He is about to open it when the Princess tells him to set it aside for the moment, saying she will look at it later. She promises the Baron to inform Count Octavian at once about carrying the rose to his bride-to-be, then announces it is time for her to go to Mass. Ochs ceremoniously takes his leave, with all the others—the attorney, his three servants, and the two Italians—trooping after him. The major-domo retires, while the footmen close the doors.

Musing alone, the Princess expresses her contempt for the vulgar pomposities of the Baron but soon dismisses these unpleasant thoughts. Gazing again into her mirror, she abandons herself to melancholy reflections on her passing youth in an exquisite refrain ("Kann ich mich auch an ein Mädel erinnern"). She recalls the past when she, a young girl eager for life—much like the Baron's affianced—suddenly found herself bound in wedlock. But that was long ago, and soon they will be referring to her as "the old Princess."

Her train of thought is broken by the entrance of Octavian, dressed in riding habit. He greets the Princess ardently and then expresses concern over her troubled, preoccupied air. When she gently repulses his embraces he excitedly cries that some fatal change has taken place in her heart. In poignant phrases she unburdens her thoughts to him ("Oh sei Er gut, Quinquin"). All things, she tells him, must come to an end. In a tender refrain ("Die Zeit im Grunde"), she sings that time takes its inexorable toll of beauty and that she knows someday he will desert her for someone younger and lovelier. Octavian protests that such a thing can never be. He will love her and her alone forever. The Princess goes on to say that only those who make the most of their happiness when it comes to them, and are prepared to relinquish it when it is over, are spared the pain and grief of regret. At last she quietly tells Octavian that he must go. Perhaps this afternoon he may meet her in the park and ride beside her carriage. Stunned and uncomprehending, Octavian slowly walks out of the room. No sooner has he gone than the Princess cries in remorse and anguish that she allowed him to go without a single kiss.

Distractedly she rings for her four footmen and orders them to call Octavian back. They return after a moment and report that the Count rode away like a madman and that they shouted after him in vain. Dismissing them, the Princess calls in Mohamed. She gives him the morocco case and tells him to carry it to the Count Rofrano with the message that inside it he will find the silver rose. He will understand, she adds softly. Mohamed quickly leaves. The Princess appears lost in thought as the curtain falls.

ACT TWO

A room in the home of Herr von Faninal. There are doors to right and left, with a door at the center rear leading into an anteroom. On either side, toward the back, in the rounded corners of the room, are two large fireplaces. It is the day on which the messenger is to bring the silver rose to Sophie. Faninal, about to take leave of his daughter, is loud in his rejoicing. Marianne, looking out of the window, comments excitedly on the new family carriage which is drawing up outside. As Faninal lingers with Sophie his major-domo reminds him that social custom does not permit the father of the bride-to-be to remain in the house when the messenger arrives with the silver rose. Pausing long enough to assure Sophie that when he returns he will be escorting the noble lord of Lerchenau, Faninal hurries away. Sophie, overwhelmed by the thought of being the wife of the great Baron, sings a prayer in which she asks God to make her worthy of so exalted a union ("In dieser feierlichen Stunde"). Marianne, still at the window watching the carriage depart, is in such a state of excitement that Sophie has difficulty concentrating on her prayer.

No sooner has Faninal's carriage gone than shouts of "Rofrano" come up from the street below, and Marianne exclaims that the Count's splendid equipage is approaching. This is too much for Sophie's self-control, and she rushes to the window. She stares in childish awe as the footmen shout Rofrano's name and Marianne describes the Count's magnificent appearance. A moment later the door at the center is flung open and Octavian walks in. He is dressed in a glittering costume of white and silver and in his hand he holds the silver rose. He is followed by his retinue, all in splendid livery.

For a moment Sophie and Octavian, each enchanted by the other's beauty, stand looking at each other without moving. Then follows the ceremony of the *Presentation of the Rose*. With royal grace and dignity Octavian approaches and hands the rose to Sophie. The exquisite theme of the rose is played upon strings, flutes, harps, and celesta. It is reiterated during the ensuing dialogue between Octavian and Sophie, which now begins as Octavian says he is bringing a token of love in behalf of his kinsman, the Baron von Lerchenau ("Mir ist die Ehre, widerfahren"). Sophie smells the rose and marvels at its wonderful scent. Octavian explains that a few drops of Persian perfume have been poured upon it. Gazing into each other's eyes, the two sing in passionate phrases of the mysterious enchantment of this moment ("Dahin muss ich zurück"). They sing that the memory of it will last throughout eternity.

Movements among the servants interrupt their brief reverie. Octavian's footman hands the jewel case to Marianne, who takes the rose from Sophie and places it in the case. This she gives to the major-domo, who withdraws with the other servants. Sophie and Octavian seat themselves, while

Marianne sits down a little distance away. A graceful waltz theme begins in the orchestra and continues throughout the colloquy that follows.

Sophie observes that she knows all about Octavian, having read of him in *The Mirror of Nobility*. He is seventeen years and two months old, she says, and his given names are Octavian Maria Ehrenreich Bonaventura Fernand Hyacinth. She also knows that he is called Quinquin by his closest friends—including some of the court beauties. With winsome naïveté she tells him how happy she is over the prospect of marriage, adding that she feels sorry for such lonely bachelors as himself. Octavian marvels at her freshness and innocence. Sophie confides more of her views on marriage and then tells Octavian with disarming forthrightness that he is the most gallant and pleasing gentleman she has ever met.

This charming conversation is interrupted by the arrival of Faninal and the Baron. The latter is followed by a coterie of his uncouth servants, who stumble awkwardly into the room. Presented to Sophie, the Baron kisses her hand in a carelessly patronizing manner that makes the girl shrink back in distaste. Octavian fumes in annoyance. Completely ignoring Sophie, Ochs turns to Faninal and remarks over the strange similarity between Octavian and his younger sister, whom he describes to Faninal with a knowing leer. When Sophie fumes over the Baron's lack of manners and makes a reference to his pock-marked face, Marianne simpers that Ochs is a fine figure of a man and a prize catch indeed.

Faninal offers the Baron some old Tokay to drink to the bride's health and the Baron deigns to accept. Turning to Octavian, he observes that occasionally one may show consideration to those of the lower classes, provided one keeps them in their places. The Count acidly compliments him on his superior wisdom. Finally taking notice of Sophie again, Ochs leads her over to a divan and tries to make her sit on his knee. His coarse demonstrations of affection infuriate Sophie, while Octavian looks on in suppressed fury. Vastly amused by the girl's distress, Ochs declares that he prefers a show of spirit in a young filly rather than meek acquiescence. Faninal, looking on, revels in the thought of a Count and a Baron under his roof at one and the same time and wishes, for the benefit of his neighbors, that the walls were made of glass.

Enraged and embarrassed by the Baron's behavior, Sophie finally manages to free herself and leaps to her feet. As the Baron rises and attempts to catch her in his embrace, Octavian, scarcely able to control his rage, crushes the wineglass he holds and hurls the pieces to the floor. Marianne, hurrying to pick up the fragments, exclaims delightedly over the Baron's diverting informalities.

When Sophie, now beside herself with anger, tries to make the Baron desist, he observes complacently that she will eventually learn how fortunate she is to be the object of his affections. In a mocking waltz refrain he assures her that with him no room is too small, without him the day is a bore ("Mit mir, mit mir, keine Kammer dir zu klein"). With that he tries once more to embrace her, but she violently pushes him away.

Meanwhile the attorney has entered, followed by a clerk carrying a sheaf of papers. Faninal brings them both forward. Seeing the attorney, Ochs immediately goes to him, pausing to suggest to Octavian that he entertain the young lady for the moment. He adds coarsely that he has no objection to a bit of love-making, for the more a young girl knows about it, the better. Indicating to Faninal that he is to follow at the regulation three paces, Ochs strides out of the room. The attorney and clerk follow likewise. A footman closes the side door through which they have left and then goes into the anteroom, leaving the door open.

Octavian hurries over to Sophie and indignantly asks if she actually intends to marry that ruffian. Sophie declares that she will never marry the Baron and begs Octavian to help her. They are momentarily interrupted by an uproar in the anteroom, where two of Lerchenau's servants have caught one of Faninal's maids. Faninal's major-domo rushes in. With Marianne's help he manages to free the girl from the clutches of the servants and takes her away.

With Marianne gone, Sophie more urgently entreats Octavian to help her. Octavian promises to do so but tells her that in order to save them both she must have courage. Sophie is in raptures when Octavian speaks of her and himself together ("Für uns zwei"). In the next moment he takes her in his arms and a beautiful duet ensues ("Mit Ihren Augen voll Thränen"). Sophie sings that she feels safe and happy in his arms because he came in her hour of direst need and saved her from despair. Octavian answers that it is as though they had loved once before in some magic dream and now have met again, never to be parted.

During the closing phrases of the duet Valzacchi and Annina emerge from the recesses of the two fireplaces in the corners of the room. Stealing up behind the lovers, Annina clutches Sophie's arms while Valzacchi pinions Octavian's hands behind his back. As the two struggle with their captives they scream loudly for Baron Ochs. He comes rushing in. The two Italians free Sophie and Octavian and bow low to the Baron.

Ochs orders Sophie to explain. She stammers some reply. Octavian, advancing defiantly, tries to speak to the Baron. With amused contempt the latter compliments Octavian on his youthful courage, saying that it reminds him of his own mettlesome youth. Even when Octavian finally manages to make him understand that Sophie is determined not to marry him, the Baron refuses to take him seriously. He seizes Sophie's hand and tries to lead her into the other room to sign the marriage contract.

Losing his temper completely, Octavian, his hand on his sword, plants himself in front of the Baron, declaring that he shall not leave the room. Sophie meanwhile frees her hand from the Baron's and takes refuge behind Octavian. Violently denouncing the Baron for his churlishness, Octavian draws his sword. At that, Ochs's courage rapidly oozes away. Putting his fingers to his mouth, he whistles shrilly for his servants. When they come trooping in Ochs grows brave again and blusters that he will not be intimidated by a mere boy. First looking around to make sure that his servants are behind him, he takes a step forward. Octavian rushes at him. The Baron draws his sword, and as he awkwardly tries to defend himself Octavian wounds him slightly in the upper arm.

The servants make a rush for Octavian, but he sends them scampering with a sweep of his sword. Ochs bellows that he has been murdered, while his servants shout for sponges and bandages. Valzacchi and the almoner help Ochs to a chair and take off his coat. Faninal's servants rush in and immediately begin quarreling with the Baron's retinue. Their outcries blend in an agitated chorus. Sophie and Octavian try to give each other courage. When the pandemonium is at its height Faninal bursts in, with the attorney at his heels. Learning from Annina that Sophie and Octavian were surprised in an ardent embrace, Faninal groans in anguish. Wringing his hands, he rushes over to the Baron, roaring to his servants to ride for a doctor. In one breath he laments that the Baron's precious blood is being spilled and in the next he rails at Octavian for his hotheaded attack. The dialogue is punctuated by the Baron's howls of pain.

Octavian courteously tells Faninal that he is sorry for the disturbance but that his own daughter can testify he was not to blame. When Faninal turns furiously on Sophie she calmly tells him that after the Baron's outrageous behavior she refuses to consider him as her future husband. Faninal breaks out into loud lamentation over the terrible scandal that now threatens his house. Spluttering with rage, he shouts to Sophie that she shall marry the Baron. With as much humility as he can muster under the circumstances, he turns to Octavian and requests him to leave at once. Octavian bows, retrieves his hat, which has been badly trampled, and then tries to delay his going long enough to have a word with Sophie.

The doctor, who has meanwhile arrived and examined the Baron's arm, makes it known that the wound is not serious. Sophie, seeing that Octavian is leaving, declares that she will lock herself in her room and starve to death before she will marry the Baron. Faninal growls that he will put her into a carriage by force and pack her off to church. Then, retorts Sophie, she will jump from the coach—or, if she is forced to the altar, she will say "No" instead of "Yes." It is either "Yes" at the altar or the convent, Faninal shouts, and then orders her out of his sight. He refuses to listen to her final plea for forgiveness. The major-domo herds the Faninal servants out of the room. Octavian quickly steps over to Sophie, whispers that she will hear from him later, and then leaves. Marianne bundles Sophie out.

Faninal scurries over to the Baron and embraces him, whereupon Ochs again howls with pain. This throws poor Faninal into even worse confusion. He is so distracted by the thought of Sophie's refusal that he scarcely heeds the Baron's request for wine. Fuming that he will be master in his own house, Faninal stamps out. Soon a footman comes in and serves wine to the Baron, who leans wearily back in his chair.

When Ochs raises the glass to his lips the movement causes a twinge in his arm, which sets him to cursing Octavian and swearing he will have revenge. His threats are comically echoed by his servants, who shake their fists in the direction of the door through which Octavian left. The doctor pours the Baron more wine and he gulps it down. Under the influence of the wine Ochs's humor returns. Ordering the servants to prepare his bed, he downs another glass of wine, then begins humming the refrain of the waltz theme ("Ohne mich"). Its rhythm continues throughout the remainder of the scene.

Annina comes cautiously in and hands Ochs a letter. He glances sharply at it and then orders his servants to withdraw. First he tells Annina to look in his coat pocket for his glasses but suddenly decides not to trust her. He tells her to read the letter. Taking up the waltz refrain, Annina begins reading ("Herr Kavalier! Den morigen Abend hätt i frei"). It is from Mariandel, saying that she will be free tomorrow night. She is very much taken with the Baron and hopes that he has not forgotten her. She awaits an answer.

The Baron, overjoyed, sings that he has all the luck of the Lerchenaus. Musing over the prospect of this delectable conquest, Ochs orders Annina to bring writing materials later to his room, where he will write the hoped-for answer. He completely ignores her obvious hints that a reward is in order for her services. Going out, Annina makes a gesture signifying that she proposes to have her revenge on the Baron for his stinginess. The Baron, one arm in a sling, a wineglass held aloft in the other hand, sings and waltzes about the room in happy anticipation of his meeting with Mariandel. The curtain falls.

ACT THREE

A large room in an inn. At one side, in a curtained-off alcove, is a bed. At the other side, toward the front, is a door leading into another room. At the back, a fireplace with a mirror above it, a blind window, and a door leading into a corridor. On one side a window looks into the street. Before the fireplace is a table with places for two. There is a large candelabrum on the table, another on a sideboard, and a number of sconces on the walls.

An elaborate pantomime opens the scene. Annina, in mourning dress, is being attended by Valzacchi, who arranges her veil and retouches her make-up. An old woman brings in Octavian, dressed as a girl, and introduces him to Annina and Valzacchi. Octavian lifts his skirt—revealing his riding boots underneath—reaches into his pocket, and brings forth a purse which he throws to Valzacchi. The two Italians, now recognizing Octavian, help him arrange his costume. Five questionable-looking men enter and stand near the door. A clock strikes. Valzacchi, taking out his watch, indicates that the time has come. Octavian and the old woman, who is his "duenna," quickly take their leave. Valzacchi then rehearses the five individuals in popping in and out of various trap doors and wall panels at a given signal. Satisfied with their performance, he sends them to their places and begins lighting some of the candles. A waiter and a serving boy come in to help him. From another part of the inn are heard the strains of a waltz.

Valzacchi opens the door at the back and the Baron enters. One arm is still in a sling. With his good hand he leads in Mariandel. As the Baron looks around, Mariandel runs to the mirror and begins arranging her hair. The innkeeper, followed by several waiters, appears and anxiously inquires if the Baron desires any changes—perhaps a larger room or more candles. But Ochs, already annoyed by the many candles which are being lighted, goes about snuffing as many as he can reach. He listens impatiently to the music and then sharply tells the innkeeper that he did not order an orchestra. He is about to have it stopped but suddenly changes his mind and permits the orchestra to continue. As to the waiters, he says, he will not need them—his own servant will take care of his wants. Valzacchi pushes them out of the room. The Baron tells him that he will be well rewarded if he manages to cut down the bill for all this. Bowing and scraping, the Italian leaves.

Mariandel and the Baron sit down at the table and the servant pours wine. Ochs then signals him to leave, but the fellow is so interested in his master's romance that he has to be signaled several times before he obeys. Then, to the accompaniment of the delightful waltz refrains for which the opera is famous, the Baron begins what he thinks will be a most satisfying conquest. The amorous colloquy begins with the phrase Mariandel sings when she refuses to drink any wine ("I' trink kein Wein").

The coy Mariandel keeps the Baron in a fever of uncertainty and impatience. She runs over to the alcove, peeps through the curtains, and exclaims over the size of the bed. When Ochs leads her back to the table and seats her again she looks up at him soulfully and laments that he is promised to another. Assuring her that she may trust him completely, he tells her to look upon him as a highborn gentleman who merely wishes to have a pleasant supper with a pretty girl. Leaning back, Mariandel looks up at him provocatively. Ochs bends over for the first kiss, but as he does so he recalls the resemblance between Mariandel and Octavian. For a moment he almost gives way to terror, then recovers and makes another attempt at a kiss. This time he is interrupted by a head popping out of a trap door in the floor and then disappearing. When the Baron gasps and points to the floor Mariandel innocently asks him what is wrong. Muttering something about being feverish, the Baron mops his brow and gulps down his wine.

The servant enters, and as the door opens the sound of the music from the other part of the tavern floats into the room. As the servant pours more wine and then reluctantly leaves, Mariandel assumes an attitude of deep dejection. The music, she says, makes her very sad. Life is short and fate is cruel, she murmurs. Soon, all too soon, she will die, and the Baron will die, and not a tear will be shed for either of them. Much distressed, the Baron asks her if wine always affects her in this manner. He then suggests that perhaps her bodice is too tight and makes tentative efforts to remedy the situation. Mariandel, however, adroitly rebuffs him.

At that point the Baron, complaining of the heat, takes off his wig. As he looks around for a place to put it faces suddenly leer at him from the walls and the bed curtains. Shaking with fear, Ochs picks up a bell from the table and rings it wildly. The blind window at the back flies open to reveal Annina, standing with arms outstretched to the Baron and crying out that he is her husband. She sweeps into the room, followed by Valzacchi, who pretends to restrain her. The innkeeper and the waiters rush in through the door.

Confronting the Baron, Annina declares that she is his wife and that the law must restore him to her. Pretending to notice Mariandel for the first time, Annina wails that what her friends have been saying is, alas! only too true—this scoundrel already has a *second* innocent maiden in his clutches. Ochs, now convinced he is going mad, groans helplessly as Annina addresses him as her dear "Leopold." The innkeeper and the waiters commiserate loudly with the poor wronged wife. Things are brought to a climax when four small children burst in. Crying, "Papa!" they rush to the Baron, who wrathfully beats them off with a napkin. Octavian finds the opportunity to ask Valzacchi if Faninal has been sent for, and the Italian replies that he will soon be here.

As Ochs bellows orders to clear the room of the maniacal crew that is pestering him, the innkeeper warns him to be careful, for the local police deal harshly with bigamists. The Baron snorts contemptuously at this. Rushing to the window, he yells for police, and shortly a police commissioner and two constables appear. When Ochs haughtily orders the commissioner to drive the rabble out the officer tells him to hold his tongue until he is spoken to. While the commissioner is interrogating the innkeeper the Baron stumbles about looking for his wig. The innkeeper explains that the gentleman is the Baron von Lerchenau, but the skeptical commissioner asks if there is anyone else who can identify him. Ochs points to Valzacchi, saying that his "personal secretary" can testify. Valzacchi promptly denies knowing anything.

Mariandel suddenly runs around the room as though trying to escape. The commissioner demands to know who she is. When the Baron tries to pass her off as his bride-to-be the commissioner immediately orders him to disclose her father's name and residence. Helplessly trapped, Ochs says that the girl is Mistress Faninal, daughter of Herr von Faninal.

The words are scarcely out of his mouth when Faninal walks in. The Baron holds his head in his hands and groans. Faninal asks why he has been summoned to rescue his noble son-in-law from a common tavern. While Faninal is answering the commissioner's questions Ochs edges over to Mariandel and tries to hide her behind him. Asked if Faninal is the father of the girl, the Baron says that this man is not Herr von Faninal, but only a cousin. Faninal, however, insists that the Baron is his son-in-law, saying he can still recognize him despite his bald head. Pressed further by the commissioner, Ochs lamely admits that the other gentleman is the young lady's father. Thereupon the commissioner asks Faninal if he still denies that he is the father of the young lady described as his daughter. Noticing Mariandel for the first time, Faninal furiously denies that she is his daughter.

The Baron tries unsuccessfully to bluster his way out. Faninal, in a towering rage, sends for Sophie, who has been waiting outside. When she appears Faninal points to the Baron and bids his daughter look on her future husband—trapped in a low-class tavern with a maiden he was trying to ruin, his morganatic wife, and his four children. When Sophie observes with obvious delight that she never looked upon him as her future husband, Faninal moans in anguish over the disgrace that has fallen upon him. All the servants who have crowded into the room comment in a brief choral phrase on the scandal. They are answered in a hollow echo by those whose heads suddenly appear from wall panels and trap doors.

Losing all control, Faninal rushes at the Baron with upraised fist and then suddenly collapses. Attended by Sophie and the innkeeper, he is carried from the room by footmen. The Baron suddenly finds his wig, puts it on, and assumes some of his accustomed self-confidence. He makes a visible effort to ignore Annina and the four children, who remain in the room. Nonchalantly taking Mariandel by the arm, the Baron starts to leave, but the commissioner stops him, saying he has more questions to ask. He orders the room cleared, and only Annina and the children remain. The Baron says he will explain things later on and states that he will marry the young lady. Mariandel, however, tears herself away from him and tells the commissioner she has a statement to make to him privately. At a sign from the commissioner the two constables flank the Baron and force him to one side of the room.

Octavian and the commissioner walk over to the curtained alcove. The Count whispers something to the officer which brings a look of mingled surprise and amusement to his face. As the Baron watches in anger and astonishment, Mariandel slips behind the curtains. A moment later her clothes come flying out piece by piece. The commissioner calmly gathers them up, while Octavian shows his head through the opening of the curtains. The Baron, shouting that he must go to the young lady's aid, struggles desperately with the constables.

Suddenly the innkeeper rushes in and announces that the Princess von Werdenberg is coming. With majestic dignity the Princess walks in, followed by her retinue. She looks about her with a faintly distasteful air. Octavian gasps, while Ochs, mopping his brow, deferentially approaches her. Ignoring him for the moment, the Princess speaks to the commissioner, whom she recognizes as a former orderly of her husband, the Field Marshal. Just as she turns questioningly to the Baron he hears a step outside. Hastening to the side door, he stands with his back to it as though trying to prevent someone from entering. Sophie's voice is heard saying she has a message from her father.

Despite Ochs's efforts to keep the door closed, Faninal's servants force it open and Sophie storms in. Octavian, who has meanwhile emerged from the alcove in male attire, whispers to the Princess that this is the girl to whom he brought the rose. Then he dodges back into the alcove. Sophie furiously tells the Baron that she is through with him once and for all. Moreover, she goes on, if he dares come near Faninal's palace he will do so at his own risk. With that she turns on her heel and goes out. The Baron attempts to follow but is restrained by two footmen.

The Princess walks over to him, taps him on the shoulder, and advises him to leave while his reputation as a gentleman is still reasonably intact. Turning to the commissioner, she says, in tones of finality, that the entire affair has been merely a game. Taking the hint, the commissioner bows respectfully and leaves with his two constables. Sophie meanwhile returns. Octavian reappears from behind the curtains, and the Baron, staring at him, now realizes who his Mariandel really was. Gradually the true state of affairs dawns upon him. Your true sportsman, he says, can always appreciate a good joke. He endeavors to make light of matters, saying that, so far as Faninal and Sophie are concerned, he is willing to forgive and forget.

When he asks the Princess's permission to tell Faninal she curtly tells him to leave immediately. More than that, he must renounce his marriage plans. The Baron fumes in helpless anger. At that point the details of the masquerade are revealed to him. Valzacchi comes in and summons his hirelings from their places behind trap doors and panels, while Annina takes off her mourning veil and wipes the make-up from her face.

And now Ochs finds himself confronted by the landlord with a bill in his hand. Behind him is a motley assortment of musicians, waiters, and coachmen. Realizing that he has been cornered, the Baron tries to force his way out but finds himself confronted by Annina, who impudently repeats the refrain he sang when he boasted about having all the luck of the Lerchenaus. In an amusing chorus the landlord and all the others present their claims ("Entschuld'gen Euer Gnaden"). Waiters, musicians, coachmen, and stableboys crowd around him, bawling their demands. Finally, aided by his servant, the Baron fights his way to the door and rushes out, the mob at his heels.

The Princess, Octavian, and Sophie are left alone. Very ill at ease, Octavian tries to explain to the Princess how he came to be involved in the doings at the inn. Sophie, observing his ardent looks, reflects bitterly over the Princess's remark that everything was merely a game. The Count, she sighs, was merely mocking her with his declarations of love. The Princess, wisely realizing the turn which affairs have taken, tells Octavian to go to Sophie. Hesitantly he walks over to her. At first the girl reproaches him for toying with her heart when his own so obviously belongs to the Princess. Octavian fervently assures Sophie that he loves her alone. Though scarcely daring to believe what she hears, Sophie finally is convinced.

Watching the two for a moment in sadness, the Princess approaches Sophie and looks at her intently. When she comments on the girl's distraught look Sophie answers that it is because of her father's humiliation and the Baron's shameful insults. With quiet humor the Princess says that she has a remedy for her father's bruised feelings: She will invite him to ride to his home in her own coach. As for Sophie's own distress, she goes on, Octavian no doubt has the proper cure.

Octavian, overwhelmed by the thought of the Princess's renunciation, can only murmur words of gratitude. Then, in an eloquent phrase of resignation and sorrow, the Princess begins the magnificent trio which is the climax of the opera ("Hab' mir's gelobt, ihn lieb zu haben"). She recalls how she resolved bravely to face the fateful moment when Octavian would give his love to another. Yet, she laments, she did not believe that moment would come so soon. But here they stand—she, alone, and the youth she adored with his new love. And now *they* are all in all to each other. Sophie sings that she should kneel at the Princess's feet in gratitude for the holy joy that has been bestowed upon her. The Princess has given her this youth, yet kept part of him from her. But one thing she knows—she loves him. Octavian wonders if he should dare ask the Princess to explain the riddle of this new enchantment. But perhaps that question is the very one he must not ask. All perplexity vanishes, he sings exultantly, when he looks into Sophie's eyes.

After the fiery climax of the trio the Princess walks slowly from the room. The lovers do not realize that she has gone. Clasped in each other's arms, they pour out their love in passionate phrases ("Ist ein Traum, kann nicht wirklich sein"). As they stand lost in their embrace, the Princess reenters with Faninal. Faninal approaches Sophie, pats her cheek with paternal affection, and observes philosophically that youth will have its way. Then he and the Princess leave. Sophie and Octavian repeat the refrain they sang a moment ago. As their voices soar to the high notes of its climax, Octavian gathers Sophie in his arms. The theme of the silver rose sounds in the orchestra. Octavian kisses Sophie, and as he does so her handkerchief falls from her hand. The lovers hasten from the room.

For a moment the stage is empty. Then Mohamed, the little turbaned Negro boy, comes in holding a candle. He looks around, finds the handkerchief, holds it up, and then silently trips out to the final, swift phrases of the music. With this artistic and appealing touch the curtain falls.

The Saint of Bleecker Street

by GIAN-CARLO MENOTTI

[1911–   ]

Libretto by the Composer

CHARACTERS

Assunta	Mezzo-soprano
Carmela	Soprano
Maria Corona, a subway newsstand vendor	Soprano
Her idiot son	Acting role
Don Marco, the parish priest	Bass
Annina, a young girl	Soprano
Michele, her brother	Tenor
Desideria, a neighborhood "outcast"	Mezzo-soprano
Concettina, a child	Acting role
Salvatore, fiancé of Carmela	Baritone

A young man, an old woman, a bartender, First Guest,
Second Guest, a nun, a young priest, neighbors, friends, policemen

Place: New York
Time: The present
First performance: Broadway Theatre, New York, December 27, 1954
Original language: English

ALTHOUGH as contemporary as New York's Broadway itself, *The Saint of Bleecker Street* is essentially a *verismo* opera, much in the earlier style of *Carmen, Cavalleria Rusticana, Louise,* and *La Boheme.* While its theme is deeply religious, it is at the same time a blood-and-thunder opera, one on which Menotti has lavished his lyrical and dramatic gifts. As it is a story about the hopes and joys and sorrows of simple people, the music is simple, direct, and powerful. There are arias with the long melodic line, and there is fine choral writing. The most "operatic" of Menotti's works to date, *The Saint* was acclaimed as a "smash hit" on Broadway and was awarded the Pulitzer Prize. Heavy operating expenses, however, caused its closing after a comparatively short run. It was subsequently presented abroad and bore promise of becoming a standard item in modern operatic repertoire. The work is in three acts and five scenes.

ACT ONE

[*Scene One*]   A shabby tenement in Bleecker Street, on New York's lower East Side. At rear, a door leading to a hallway; on either side of it are a stove and an iron bed. At stage right is the door to Annina's bedroom. Next to it is an elaborately-decorated altar with a picture of the Virgin.

The curtain rises to reveal a group of neighbors standing or kneeling in a group around Assunta, who leads them in chanting the Litany ("Rosa Mystica, Ora pro nobis"). At its conclusion, dialogue follows in quasi-recitative. A young man tiptoes to Annina's door and peers into her room. In hushed tones, the others ask him what is happening. Why don't they bring her out, they whisper impatiently. She weeps and moans, the young man says, and her eyes are glassy like those of a dead person . . . her visions have begun. In chorus, the neighbors implore Annina, daughter of Christ, to come and heal them.

An ensemble ensues as the neighbors, weary and frustrated, fall to bickering among themselves. It begins as Maria Corona, the shabbily-dressed newspaper vendor, complains that she has been waiting all day and is tired. At her side is her idiot son, staring vacantly into space and clinging to her skirt. Maria grumbles that these miracles of healing never happen.

Assunta and Carmela chide her for her lack of faith. Carmela says Annina made her walk again after three years; she must be a saint, because every Good Friday she suffers the agony of Our Lord. Continuing in duet form,[1] she and Assunta recount the miracles that have happened: Annina saw Saint Michael and Saint Peter and the Holy Virgin . . . and once the Devil set her clothing on fire.

Then a violent argument develops between a young woman and Maria, who hurl insults at each other. In chorus, the other neighbors pray that Annina may soon receive the sacred wounds and bring to them the blessing of the Lord. The ensemble rises in intensity, then comes to an abrupt stop as Don Marco, the priest, suddenly appears in the doorway of Annina's room.

In quiet but firm tones, he declares Annina's vision has begun. Annina will now be brought out, he says. She is very ill, and if she receives the stigmata, everyone must be very gentle with her. If they dare touch her bleeding wounds, Don Marco warns sternly, he will throw them all out. He tells them to pray. All in the room kneel and, in choral form, sing another portion of the Litany, "Salve Virgo florens."

The priest goes back into the bedroom, then reappears followed by two neighbors who are carrying Annina. She is as pale as death and barely conscious. The two men place her gently in a large armchair at the center of the stage. For several moments Annina sits motionless, her eyes closed. Chanting softly, the neighbors strain forward to look at her.

Suddenly she utters a piercing cry, underscored by a blaring trumpet note in the orchestra, and writhes as though in terrible pain. Then Annina begins the intensely moving aria, "Oh, sweet Jesus, spare me this agony," in which she relives the Crucifixion. As she stares with unseeing eyes, she describes the hill of Calvary, the drunken throng jostling for a better view of the grim procession. Now come the soldiers, surrounding Christ staggering under the burden of the cross. In frenzied tones, Annina describes how

[1] An interesting example of Menotti's use of time changes to co-ordinate the rhythms of words and music. In this comparatively brief duet there are four different time signatures: 4/4, 2/4, 5/4, and 3/4.

He quivers under the blows of the whip, His face stained by bloody sweat.

The mood of the music suddenly changes as Annina looks anxiously around as though searching for someone in the crowd. There, in a group of weeping women, is the Holy Virgin, she sings. Her sorrow is heavier than the cross. Annina begs the other women to take her home. The aria, in its high-C ending, rises to a climax of anguish as Annina, in her frenzied imagination, sees Christ nailed to the cross. She falls exhausted back into the chair. Her clenched hands slowly open. In the palm of each is the bleeding stigmata.

Beside themselves with excitement, the neighbors crowd around the chair, all clamoring to touch Annina. Don Marco, Assunta, and Carmela vainly try to keep them away. The voices of the crowd mingle in shrill entreaty as they describe their afflictions and struggle to be the first to be healed.

The uproar comes to a sudden halt as the door to the hallway is flung open and Michele bursts into the room. A powerful, four-note figure is reiterated in the bass as he furiously orders the neighbors to get out and leave his sister alone. The crowd shrinks back in fear. Carmela steps forward and tries to calm him, telling him Annina is very ill. Michele comes over to his sister and tenderly strokes her hair. Then he whirls savagely on the neighbors and drives them out of the room. As they go they sing a brief chorus asking God's mercy on the sinful brother.

Slamming the door, Michele turns to face Don Marco. Angrily he reminds the priest that he is not wanted in this house. A vigorous duet ensues. Don Marco answers quietly that he is here only because Annina needs him. She needs a doctor, not a priest, Michele snaps. Trying to reason with him, Don Marco tells him he must not give way to doubt. Michele says he loves his sister and knows she is a sick child, not a saint. He scoffs at the superstitions of the poor deluded folk who try to forget their misery in looking for miracles that will never happen. Then he asks the priest outright if he himself believes in all this.

Annina believes, Don Marco answers simply, and she must be guided. In rising anger, Michele retorts that he alone will guide his sister, and again warns the priest to stay away. Don Marco, in a ringing refrain, replies that it is not he who is Michele's rival, but God Himself. God's power is greater than the avalanche or the raging fire, and His decrees are beyond the understanding of human beings. His love is overwhelming and beyond resisting. At the conclusion of the refrain, Don Marco walks slowly out of the room and Michele slams the door after him. The curtain falls.

[*Scene Two*]   An empty lot between two tenements. At the back it is enclosed by a sagging wire fence with a gate in the middle. Over the gate are arches of electric lights. The street beyond also is festooned with lights, typical of the decorations in streets of Italian neighborhoods in New York on feast days. The present decorations are in honor of the Festival of San Gennaro.

Seated on crates inside the lot, downstage, Annina and Carmela are sewing gold paper stars on the white dress worn by Concettina, a thin little girl of about five, who is dressed as an angel. At a window of one of the tenements, Assunta is seen rocking her baby as she sings a lullaby, "Canta ninna, canta nanna." It is late afternoon.

Several women in gay holiday dresses come out of the door of the tenement at stage right and, in recitative phrases, greet Annina and Carmela. When they ask Annina if she will join the procession, she replies that her brother won't allow it. Expressing their displeasure, the women leave. Coaxing the restless Concettina to be patient, Annina and Carmela finally sew the last star on her dress. Then they fit a paper crown on her head. Free at last, the girl runs toward the street, crown already askew and wings flapping. Annina and Carmela are left alone.

A duet follows. In a flowing 12/8 refrain, Carmela tells Annina that she is going to break her promise to take the veil, as Annina intends to do. The reason, she goes on in painful shyness, is that she is going to be married in May. She tried to resist . . . she prayed hard—but she kept thinking of "the boy" even while she was praying. His name is Salvatore and he is very nice. Bursting into tears, Carmela says that last week he asked her to marry him and she said yes.

Smiling at her tenderly, Annina rejoices over the news. She assures Carmela that God will not be angry with her because, after all, she made her promise not to God, but only to Annina. Happy again, Carmela invites Annina to her wedding. Yes, Annina replies quietly, if Carmela will come to hers—on the day when she will put on a white veil and become the bride of Christ.

A trio now develops as Assunta appears on the scene. Overhearing Carmela ask Annina if she still has a chance to go to heaven, Assunta laughs cynically. When you have six children and a drunken husband, she says, you will surely go there. Assunta then asks Annina if she has ever caught a glimpse of heaven.

In a lyrical refrain, Annina answers that she has not seen heaven. But once in the night, Michael the Archangel came to her. She asked him if she could see the gates of Paradise. When she awoke, there they were, with Saint Peter standing beside them. She asked him what she would find behind the gates. There, said Saint Peter, she will "eat golden bread and wear sun-woven clothes." Carmela's voice joins Annina's as both sing about the wonders of Paradise.

Their reverie is interrupted when Maria Corona comes running in from the street, with her idiot son stumbling after her. She tells Annina there is trouble ahead. The Sons of San Gennaro are angry because Annina refuses to take part in the procession. They have vowed to take her away by force if Michele tries to stop them.

When the other three women urge Annina to hide, she says quietly that her only fears are for Michele. Assunta, saying she will try to find Michele and bring him here, hurries away. Approaching Annina, Maria Corona says she will defend her to the death, because Annina touched her poor son and now he has begun to speak. Pathetically, she tries to show Annina proof of the miracle, coaxing the boy to say "Mamma." He can utter only a grotesque distortion of the word.

At that moment Michele strides in through the gate, glowers at Maria and her son and Carmela, then orders them away. He and Annina are left alone, and a dramatic duet ("Oh, dear Michele") begins to the accompaniment of strongly accented descending minor chords. Michele implores her to try to understand that he loves her and is trying to protect her. He asks her if she really believes she is a saint. She has never said she is, Annina replies. Why, then, Michele asks, does she allow these sick people to come to her in the hope that they can be healed?

She cannot help that, Annina answers with childlike simplicity. She does not ask to be believed—but she herself beliefs. Trying a different tack, Michele asks if she remembers how her schoolmates made fun of her and called her a "numbskull." Annina nods. Well, then, Michele goes on, why should God have chosen *her*, of all people? Annina's answer is simple: because she loves Him. Lost for the moment in ecstasy, Annina sings that there is only one thing she knows and desires: to be the bride of God.

Never, cries Michele violently, she shall never take the veil. In mounting excitement, he tells Annina he will take her away from these streets and these people, from this place where young people are still slaves to the superstition-ridden past. But Annina only replies that she will lead him to the City of God. Haunted by the realization that she is withdrawing into a world he cannot reach, he desperately implores her not to leave him. Without her, he sings, he will be a lost beggar in a strange land. Annina's voice blends with his in a stunning climax as she sings that she will pray to the Archangel Michael to be his guide.

Suddenly the arches over the street light up and a procession comes into view. First come barefoot women, holding lighted candles, then men holding religious banners. All sing a festival chorus, "Veglia su di noi." Annina tries to get Michele to go inside out of sight, warning that there will be trouble because she has not joined the procession. But Michele defiantly refuses to leave.

A band, following the religious procession, blares out a march. Just then five or six young men swiftly come into the yard, close in on Michele, and overpower him. Despite his fierce struggles, they drag him over to the fence and chain him to it by his wrists. Then they lift Annina to their shoulders and join the procession. Sobbing with rage, Michele screams curses after them. His imprecations are lost in the lusty chorus of the marchers ("Tu che tutti puoi") as they pass by carrying a huge effigy of San Gennaro.

Michele, head bowed, sags against the fence. Two small children, wearing gay paper hats, look at him curiously, then run into one of the tenements. As the last of the procession disappears and the music dies away, a dark-haired, voluptuous girl in a vivid red dress appears in the doorway of the tenement at stage left. It is Desideria.

For a moment she stands there, looking at Michele. Then she walks over and releases his wrists. As he slumps forward, sobbing bitterly, she takes him in her arms and kisses him passionately on the mouth. A brooding minor chord reverberates as the curtain falls.

ACT TWO

An Italian restaurant in the basement of a house on Bleecker Street. It is gaily decorated for a wedding party. At stage right is a bar; on the same side is a door marked "Banquet Room." At stage center are chairs and tables; toward the back is a raised area used as a dance floor. A huge juke box stands in one corner. Visible through a window at the rear are steps leading up to the street.

The curtain rises to show Carmela and Salvatore posed with the wedding guests in an old-fashioned, formal grouping to have their wedding picture taken. The photographer takes a flash-bulb picture, and then the group breaks up laughing and cheering. The juke box blares out a dance tune. Teasing and joking, some of the younger guests push Carmela and Salvatore into each other's arms and force them to dance. Painfully embarrassed, they go through the motions, while the onlookers comment outspokenly in a lusty chorus ("Never was there such a pair").

A waiter brings in wine. All take glasses. A young man jumps on a chair, raises his glass high, and toasts the bridal couple in an old Italian folksong, "Hai l'occhio nero nero della quaglia." The chorus roars out a repetition of the refrain. A second young man follows with another song, "Il giglio t'ha donato," with the chorus again joining in. Then Michele, too, jumps up on a chair and serenades the pair with a third song, "Sei tutta bianca." The crowd cheers him vociferously.

Now the waiter brings in the wedding cake from the banquet room. Holding it high for everyone to see, he starts marching back into the banquet room again, followed by the guests. In a moment all are gone except Carmela and Salvatore and Annina, who stands almost hidden in a corner.

Annina calls softly to Carmela, who comes over to her arm in arm with Salvatore. Feeling the effects of the wine, she is giggling happily. She coyly teases Salvatore, who tries to look stern. In a tender refrain, which echoes the theme of the girls' duet about Annina's dream of Paradise in Act One, Annina tells Salvatore he must promise always to love Carmela and be good to her. They were to take the veil together, she sings, in a lyrical ¾ refrain, but here she is a bride "with a red rose bush in her heart and black stars in her eyes." Overcome with emotion, Carmela rushes sobbing into Annina's arms.

A guest now comes out of the banquet room and calls the bridal couple. Salvatore and Carmela go inside with Annina. Only the bartender, polishing glasses, is left on the stage. Then, as a somber theme sounds in the orchestra, Desideria walks slowly into the restaurant. Going over to the bar, she asks where Michele is. The bartender gestures toward the banquet room. Tell him I want to see him, Desideria says curtly. The bartender eyes her suspiciously, then goes into the banquet room. Desideria pours herself a drink and walks around nervously, obviously trying to gain control of herself.

Michele comes in from the banquet room. For a moment he and Desideria look at each other in silence. A dramatic colloquy ensues. Michele asks her why she has come. Her mother has driven her out of the house, the girl replies, sarcastically adding that her lover is busy singing at other girls' weddings.

Michele recoils at that. Changing her tone, Desideria pleads with him to understand. She has become an outcast because she loves him, she says bitterly, while he is still accepted by their neighbors and friends. Michele warns her not to try to change him. He never asked for her love, she offered it, he reminds her rather brutally.

But the argument continues as Desideria persistently demands proof of his love. Michele hotly insists that he loves her and is proud of it. They face each other, both helplessly at an impasse; a somber phrase in the orchestra mirrors their despair. Snatching up a glass and a bottle of wine, Michele sits down at a table and begins drinking. If he loves her, Desideria says with ominous intensity, he can prove it by taking her into the banquet room with him. No, says Michele, he must think of Annina.

At that Desideria turns on him in a furious outburst. Annina . . . always Annina, she storms. All she can do is light candles for his soul—and ruin his life. She does not love her brother, she only pities him. Let her go her own way, Desideria begs, and take my love instead. It is not a holy dream, she sings to the accompaniment of sustained, chromatically ascending chords, but as real as the earth itself. Michele, angry and uncertain, declares there is nothing he can do—Annina needs him. Desideria protests in vain. As they talk, the happy singing of the guests comes from the banquet hall like an ironic antiphony.

Desideria again asks Michele if he will take her inside. When he does not answer, she continues her pleading in an eloquent, sensuous refrain. One word, she sings, can turn love into wounding hate. And the one who bears the scar will weep alone . . . will weep tears that leave a poisoned trail. Those who share an earthly love, she goes on as the music mounts in intensity, must make the most of it. To hide it is to invite the terrible vengeance that only thwarted love can inflict.

With a gesture of hopelessness, Michele gets up, takes the girl by the hand, and starts toward the banquet room. At that moment Don Marco appears and bars his way. There is a brief and bitter exchange of words as the priest warns Michele not to take Desideria in and Michele defies him. It comes to a climax when Michele lunges toward Don Marco with upraised fist. Just then Annina, with the guests at her heels, rushes out of the banquet room and grabs Michele's arm. Seeing Desideria, the guests make insulting remarks. Salvatore, confronting Michele, lashes out at him for always causing trouble.

Pushing Annina away, Michele pours himself a glass of wine and defiantly faces the angry crowd. He expresses his bitterness and contempt in a magnificent aria. "I know you all hate me," he begins. He never asked for their love, he storms, only their understanding—and that they denied him. Who are they to judge, he asks them, when they blindly live like strangers in the land that has given them a home? He accuses them of being ashamed of their birthright, of being ashamed to say "I am Italian." But he will not share their false contentment, he cries. He will be a part of this new world and still be proud of his Italian heritage. Perhaps if he could see that "sweet, sad country" just once, Michele sings in phrases of surging melody, it would rekindle his pride—and make him forget their eyes. A high C climaxes the aria. With that he hurls the wine into the faces of the guests, then sinks down at a table and buries his face in his arms.

Some of the guests look scornfully down at Michele, then walk slowly out of the restaurant. Don Marco, gently putting his hand on Michele's shoul-

der, murmurs that his bitterness has made him judge his friends falsely.
Carmela sobs in Salvatore's arms, and Annina tells him to take her home.
The bridal couple leave. Only a few guests remain in the room.

Annina goes hesitantly up to Michele and puts her hand on his head. He
looks up and brokenly asks her forgiveness. Gently she tells him to come
home with her. At that, Desideria, who has been watching, steps forward.
Consumed by jealous rage, she cries that now she knows why Michele will
not marry her: it is not Desideria he loves—it is *she*. With a wild glare in
her eyes, she points to Annina.

When the full horror of her accusation dawns upon Michele, he staggers
back as if struck. Then in cold fury he advances on Desideria, crying that
she lies and demanding that she take back what she has said. As though
demented, Desideria laughs in his face and repeats the accusation. As
Michele slowly comes toward her, the girl moves back toward the bar,
where she finally stands cornered. Beside herself with fury, she screams the
words again and again: "You love her! You love her!"

With his body pressed against Desideria's, Michele frenziedly shouts at
her to be quiet. Suddenly he snatches a knife from the bar and plunges it
into the girl's back. With a strange, questioning look on her face, Desideria
staggers a few steps, then collapses on the floor. As the onlookers scream in
terror, Annina kneels down and takes the girl in her arms. Michele races out
of the restaurant, knocking over chairs as he goes. The bartender rushes to
the telephone and calls the police. Crowded on the steps leading to the
street, people can be seen staring curiously.

In Annina's arms, Desideria gasps that she is dying. Stroking her forehead gently, Annina tells her not to be afraid. Desideria's body convulses in
a spasm of terror and pain; then she becomes calm. In tones that grow
gradually weaker, she repeats a prayer after Annina. Murmuring the word
"love," she sinks back in death. Sobbing heartbrokenly, Annina clasps
Desideria's body to her breast. Police sirens are heard outside. As a policeman is seen forcing his way through the crowd on the steps, the curtain
falls.

ACT THREE

[*Scene One*]   A gloomy, deserted station of the New York subway. At
back, a stairway leads to the street. At stage left, a newsstand, with its interior facing the audience. At stage right is an iron partition with a turnstile
marking the exit from the subway itself. It is early morning; snow is sifting
down the street stairwell. From below comes the rumble of passing subway
trains, interpreted by a running bass figure in the orchestra. As the curtain
rises, Annina, wrapped in a shawl, is seen at the foot of the street exit, anxiously waiting for someone. In the newsstand, Maria Corona bustles about.
She leads her son inside the stand, buttons his coat, then sends him up to
the street with a bundle of papers.

Going up to Annina, she tries to comfort her. Michele will surely come,
she says. And certainly Don Marco won't betray him to the police because

the boy asked for help at the confessional. She leads Annina inside the newsstand, which is warmed by a small kerosene stove. Annina silently huddles beside it.

In recitative, Maria chatters about seeing Michele's picture in the papers. She shows Annina an old Italian newspaper and begins reading the story of the tragedy. Shuddering, Annina begs her not to go on. Maria then sings a rather amusing ditty ("And to think that all my life,") lamenting that she has never got her picture in the papers in all the twenty-five years she has been selling this "trash."

With considerable relish she recalls the story of one Marinella, who "stabbed her sister-in-law twenty times with a rusty kitchen knife." They printed a picture of Marinella in a bathing suit and called her the "protagonist of a drama of jealousy." In whimsical resignation, Maria sighs that she is old and ugly, and will have to kill somebody to get her picture in the papers. Meanwhile, Annina falls asleep with her head against Maria's shoulder. Again the music imitates the rumble of the passing trains.

Suddenly Don Marco comes down the stairway from the street. He looks quickly around, goes back up the stairs, then returns followed by Michele. Pointing to Annina, the priest warns the boy not to upset her, because she is very ill. He then turns and leaves.

Sunk in despair, Michele leans against the wall and buries his face in his hands. Maria, seeing him, rouses Annina, who runs over to him and flings herself into his arms. A deeply moving duet follows. Leading Annina over to a bench beside the newsstand, Michele takes her hands in his. He will never find peace again, he groans. Annina tells him he must give himself up. That he will never do, Michele declares, then laments that in one terrible moment all his hopes and dreams were shattered. Only Annina is left now, and he must fight on for her.

As gently as she can, Annina tells him she is very ill and will die before very long—her voices have told her so. Those voices lie, Michele bursts out, and she must forget them. Quietly, but with intense conviction, Annina says she is going to take the veil. He will never consent to that, Michele cries in anguish. How can she cast aside her own brother, he asks, just when he needs her most? Noticing several passengers watching him curiously, he goes over into the shadows and lights a cigarette.

As though to underscore the tragedy of the scene, Maria sings a mournful refrain ("These for him are days of weeping") about what the stars predict for Michele. She reads from an astrology magazine she has picked up from the newsstand. Tears and a long journey for any man born in July under the sign of cancer, she sings sadly. It is all in the stars . . . in the stars. Her voice trails into silence.

Slowly Annina walks over to Michele, and the duet continues. Everything —and nothing—has changed, she begins quietly. She has waited this long only because her brother is dear to her, but now she must go to her Love. She can no longer help him, she says over his stricken pleas. Suddenly suspicious, he asks if she believes Desideria's terrible accusation. Annina gasps out a denial. Then why, Michele begs to know, can she no longer help him?

She must heed the call of God, Annina says in increasing excitement. Now there is no turning back . . . and by serving God, perhaps she can save her brother. Desperately Michele implores her to wait a little longer. No, answers Annina firmly, her mind is made up; nothing can change it. Michele makes one more frantic plea. This is good-by, Annina cries. Staring at her wildly, Michele shouts that she will be followed forever by his curse. Then he runs like a madman out of the station. With an anguished cry, Annina staggers to the foot of the stairs, where she collapses sobbing. Maria tries vainly to comfort her. The curtain falls.

[*Scene Two*]   Annina's apartment, as in Act One. Wrapped in a shawl, Annina sits in the armchair at the center of the stage. Her eyes are closed, and she is deathly pale. A nun sits next to her. A little distance away, Carmela is being comforted by Salvatore. In a corner, Assunta, Maria Corona, and her son kneel in prayer with a group of women. Assunta chants the *Agnus Dei*, and the women respond in chorus.

At its conclusion, Annina softly calls to Carmela and asks if there has been any news. Not yet, answers Carmela. Her voices have told her, Annina murmurs restlessly, that she is to take the veil today . . . but perhaps she may not live until tonight. Carmela does her best to comfort her.

In sudden excitement, Annina cries that if permission comes today, she will have no bridal dress to wear. Tenderly Carmela says she has a surprise for her and tells her to close her eyes. When Annina does so, Carmela gets her wedding dress from a closet and places it on Annina's lap. Opening her eyes, Annina gasps in astonishment and pleasure. She thanks Carmela and asks her to place the dress on the chair next to her.

There is commotion outside, and then a young priest hurries in with a letter, which he hands to Don Marco. The women crowd around. The priest looks at the letter, then goes over to Annina. In a phrase of solemn triumph, he tells her that the Church has granted her permission to take the veil. Ecstatically Annina sings that her voices have told her she will die tonight— but now she will die a bride.

Spent by emotion, she sinks back into her chair. Assuring Don Marco she will be ready, she tells him to prepare for the ceremony. She asks Carmela to leave her for a while so that she may pray. At Carmela's request, Don Marco motions the women to leave the room. They crowd outside in the hall. The priest kneels in front of the altar next to the doorway of Annina's room.

Then in a sudden transport of ecstasy, Annina sings in soaring phrases that her hour of joy has come at last. She implores Death to wait only a little while longer before he brings the "eternal night for his eternal love." Suddenly she calls for Carmela again and asks if her crown and bridal veil are in readiness. Carmela reassures her. Annina expresses fear that her strength may not last. In a repetition of the foregoing phrase, she begs Death to wait.

With Carmela's help, she walks slowly to her room. The nun follows, carrying the bridal dress. During the ensuing scene,[2] Don Marco, with the help of the young priest, prepares for the ceremony of the taking of the

[2] This is considered by the composer as *Scene Three*, although the stage action continues without interruption.

veil. Meanwhile, the neighbors crowd back into the room, some of them carrying lighted candles. In an agitated ensemble, they discuss the fact that Michele has been seen in the neighborhood. They fear that he may try to stop Annina from taking the veil.

Overhearing, Don Marco tells Salvatore to keep watch by the door and prevent Michele from interfering if he shows up. Then the priest continues preparations for the ceremony, placing many candles on the altar and lighting them. In a brief chorus, the neighbors talk excitedly about what will happen if Michele should appear.

Now Carmela comes in and announces that Annina is ready. There is a moment of tense silence. Then Annina walks into the room. She is dressed as a bride and holds a lighted candle in her hand. As the chorus begins to chant the Mass, the nun walks slowly to meet her, and Annina kisses her hand. The nun leads the girl across the room to a folding screen, which the nun places so that it hides Annina from those in the room.

At the altar, meanwhile, Don Marco chants the Mass, the chorus responding with the *Kyrie*. The ceremony of the taking of the veil then follows in realistic detail.[3] Annina knocks twice on the screen and is asked the prescribed questions by the priest. After she answers, the nun leads her from behind the screen to the center of the stage. There the nun removes Annina's wreath of blossoms. Annina prostrates herself, her arms outstretched in the form of a cross. As the nun covers her with a black cloth, Don Marco intones that she is now dead unto the world: until now she has been known to the world as Annina; henceforth she shall be called Sister Angela. A triumphant choral phrase underscores his words.

The nun takes away the black cloth and helps Annina to her knees. As though hypnotized, she gazes at the holy image on the altar. At that moment Michele lunges into the room. Salvatore and a neighbor bar his way and struggle fiercely with him. Annina neither sees nor hears. In a frenzied outburst, Michele begs Annina to listen to him while there is still time . . . why leave a world that is so in need of love? And he himself, he cries brokenly, needs her love now more than ever. There is a moment of utter silence. Annina kneels motionless.

In quiet but authoritative tones, Don Marco requests Michele to allow his sister to take her leave of the world in peace. Then, continuing the ceremony, he approaches Annina and performs the rite of the cutting of her hair, symbolizing the complete renunciation of worldly things. Carmela, Maria, and Assunta chant softly. Michele falls sobbing on his knees. Controlling himself with an effort, he stands up again and stares in utter amazement at the rest of the ceremony.

Now standing at the altar, Don Marco tells Annina to come forward and receive the ring of faith, the ring of the bride of Christ. Everyone kneels except Michele. Her head covered by a black veil, Annina starts toward the

3 Menotti here points out that under special circumstances "ecclesiastical authorities may grant permission to conduct certain religious rites in . . . a private home. The ritual of these rites is prescribed: it is taken from ancient Hebrew, Greek and early Christian texts and psalms. Their ceremonial applications are both symbolic and actual, and their meaning is contained verbatim in the text."

priest in a last desperate effort. One step; another. Then she sinks slowly to the floor. Carmela catches her as she falls. No one moves. Don Marco kneels beside her, lifts her lifeless hand, and reverently slips the gold ring on her finger. As the music dies away high in the strings, the curtain falls.

Salome

by RICHARD STRAUSS

[1864–1949]

Libretto by
HEDWIG LACHMANN

Based on Oscar Wilde's dramatic poem
SALOME

CHARACTERS

Narraboth, a young Syrian captain of the guard..................*Tenor*
A page to Herodias.......................................*Contralto*
First soldier ....*Bass*
Second soldier ....*Bass*
Jokanaan (John the Baptist)..............................*Baritone*
A Cappadocian ....*Bass*
Salome, daughter of Herodias............................*Soprano*
A slave ....*Soprano*
Herod, Antipas, Tetrarch of Judea........................*Tenor*
Herodias, his wife.................................*Mezzo-soprano*
Five Jews ....⎰ *Four tenors*
⎱ *One Bass*
First Nazarene ....*Bass*
Second Nazarene ....*Tenor*
Executioner

Place: The grand terrace in the palace of Herod
Time: About 30 A.D.
First performance: Hofoper, Dresden, December 9, 1905
Original language: German

IN SALOME, Strauss achieved his first important success as a composer of opera. It caused a sensation because of the pathological nature of its subject and the daring harmonic innovations employed in the delineation of subtle psychological reactions. Strongly influenced by Wagner, Strauss uses the technique of the leading motive—identifying the principals of the drama with a characteristic musical phrase—and also the method of superimposing the vocal line on an uninterrupted flow of orchestral accompaniment.

The entire action of *Salome* takes place in one scene. At one side is the entrance to the banquet hall of Herod's palace. Opposite is a massive gateway. In the center of the terrace a barred grating covers the mouth of a large well—the dungeon in which Jokanaan is confined. It is night, and the terrace is flooded with pale moonlight.

First we hear the Salome motive and then the voice of Narraboth, who is talking to the page. The captain looks with burning eyes toward the banquet hall, where Salome is feasting with Herod and his court, and marvels over her beauty. The page warns him not to gaze upon her so ardently, for evil consequences are sure to follow. But the infatuated Narraboth cannot keep his eyes from the Princess. Suddenly from the depths of the well comes the voice of Jokanaan, intoning the Scriptural prophecy, "Nach mir wird Einer kommen der ist stärker als ich [After me cometh One mightier than I]." Several soldiers approach and discuss the prisoner, saying that he is a holy man and a prophet. No one, however, remarks a soldier, can understand the meaning of his strange words.

Presently Salome appears. Restless and troubled, she sings that she can no longer bear the look in Herod's eyes or the brutish revelry of the guests. The cool night air gradually calms her and, gazing up at the moon, she muses softly over its chaste beauty. Jokanaan's voice breaks in on her reverie. Startled, Salome asks the soldiers who cries out in these strange tones, and they reply that it is the prophet. Narraboth approaches and tries to divert her attention by suggesting that she rest in the garden. Meanwhile a slave informs her that Herod wishes her to return to the banquet table, but she angrily declares that she will not go back.

Ignoring Narraboth's plea that she go inside, Salome continues to question the soldiers about the prisoner. She asks them if he is old, and they answer that he is a young man. The Princess listens in tense silence as Jokanaan's grim, foreboding voice is heard again, and then says that she desires to speak to the prophet. One of the soldiers tells her that Herod has said that no one, not even the high priest, is to speak to the prisoner. Completely heedless of his warning, Salome orders the soldiers to bring the prophet before her. She goes over to the well and peers into its black depths. Fiercely she repeats her command, but the trembling soldiers answer that they cannot obey.

Gliding close to Narraboth, she tries to cajole him into granting her request. If he will carry out her wishes, she says in seductive tones, perhaps she will throw him a flower or even smile upon him tomorrow when she passes his post of duty. Helpless under the spell of her tantalizing pleas, Narraboth orders the prophet to be brought forth. There is an orchestral interlude in which the music builds up to the impressive theme of prophecy associated with Jokanaan. The grated cover of the well is thrown back and the prophet emerges, a majestic figure in the rough garb of a pilgrim.

In ringing tones Jokanaan utters strange words of imprecation. Salome, drawing back in awe, asks Narraboth the meaning of his words, but he cannot tell her. Then the prophet bursts forth into a terrible denunciation of Herodias, branding her as the incarnation of evil and depravity, a woman whose sins have infected the very earth itself. Salome is first horrified, then fascinated, and cannot take her eyes from his face. Narraboth desperately pleads with her to leave, but she only answers that she must look more closely on the prophet.

Regarding her with fierce scorn, Jokanaan asks the soldiers who this woman is. Salome tells him that she is the daughter of Herodias. The prophet wrathfully orders her to leave, but Salome, her eyes fixed on his face, sings that his voice is music in her ears. When he exhorts her to go into the wilderness and seek redemption she sings amorously of the beauty of his body. She apostrophizes his hair and his mouth and then voluptuously begs him for a kiss. Narraboth, mad with jealousy, steps between Salome and Jokanaan and kills himself. The Princess does not even look down as he falls. Jokanaan pleads with her to seek the Redeemer on the shores of Galilee and kneel at His feet to ask forgiveness for her sins. Her only answer is a frenzied supplication for a kiss. Thundering that she is cursed, the prophet turns away and descends into the dungeon. When the grating is lowered into place Salome stares into its depths with an expression of ferocious triumph.

Herod and Herodias appear, followed by their drunken, glutted court. The King asks for Salome, his feverish manner betraying his passion for her. Herodias sharply rebukes him for gazing longingly at his stepdaughter. Herod, paying no heed to her words, cries that the moon is like a woman driven mad by desire. Suddenly he slips in a pool of blood and recoils as he sees the body of Narraboth. A soldier informs him that the captain killed himself. Recalling that the Syrian had looked ardently at Salome, he orders the body to be taken away.

As the accompaniment vividly portrays the sound of rushing wind Herod cowers in fear, gasping that mighty wings are beating in the air around him. Herodias, looking at him in cold scorn, remarks that he looks ill. Recovering himself, Herod retorts that it is Salome who has a stricken look. Cajolingly he invites the Princess to eat and drink with him, but she curtly refuses. Herodias gloats over the King's discomfiture at being spurned.

Jokanaan calls out from the dungeon that the appointed hour has come, whereupon Herodias furiously orders the soldiers to quiet him. When Herod protests she taunts him, saying that he is afraid of the prophet, reminding him that he has failed to turn him over to the Jews. The five Jews then approach and ask that Jokanaan be given into their hands. Herod brusquely refuses, saying that the prisoner is a holy man who has seen God. Thereupon the Jews vehemently denounce Jokanaan as a blasphemer, protesting that no one since Elias has seen God. Herod contradicts them, and a long and involved theological argument ensues. It is built up into a strikingly dramatic chorus.

At its climax the voice of Jokanaan breaks through as he prophesies the coming of the Saviour. Two Nazarenes begin to discuss some of the miracles that have been performed by this mysterious leader, one of the most remarkable being the raising of the dead. At this Herod starts in alarm and then excitedly declares that this terrible miracle will be forbidden by royal decree. Jokanaan goes on to foretell the doom of Herodias and the fearful day of reckoning that shall soon dawn for the kings of the earth. Wild with anger, Herodias demands that her accuser be silenced.

Herod, who has been staring intently at Salome, asks her to dance for him. The Queen forbids her to dance, and Salome demurs. The King, however, pleads with her and tries to tempt her by offering to give her anything she asks. Despite the angry protests of Herodias, Salome acquiesces, but first she forces Herod to swear that he will grant her anything she desires. As the ominous theme of the rushing wind again sweeps through the orchestra Herod whimpers that he hears the sound of wings. His mounting fears goad him into frenzy, and he tears the chaplet of roses from his head, shouting that they are burning like a crown of fire. He falls back exhausted. The voice of Jokanaan, repeating his dark prophecy of doom, continues like a relentless undercurrent. Slaves meanwhile prepare Salome for her dance, and then she performs the *Dance of the Seven Veils*.[1]

After its wild climax she stands poised for a moment at the mouth of the dungeon, then flings herself at Herod's feet. In feverish ecstasy he asks her to name her wish. A single note quivers high in the strings as Salome begins speaking. With venomous sweetness she demands the head of Jokanaan on a silver platter.

Herod cries out in unbelieving horror, while Herodias applauds her daughter as her worthy offspring. Frantically Herod offers her his precious gems, his peacocks, the mantle of the high priest, the veil of the sanctuary, begging her not to ask for the head of the holy man of God. Salome is obdurate and with savage intensity repeats her request. Shaken by fear and despair, Herod finally sinks back in his chair as if in a faint. Herodias quickly draws the execution ring from his finger and hands it to a soldier, who takes it to the executioner. Herod revives, misses the ring, and wails that its absence bodes terrible misfortune.

Creeping over to the dungeon, Salome watches the executioner descend, then listens intently. When she hears no sound she furiously orders the executioner to strike, cursing him for the delay. Through the gathering darkness the arm of the executioner suddenly can be seen emerging from the well, bearing aloft the platter with the severed head. Seizing it, Salome begins her terrible song of frustrated passion and lust, "Ah! Du wolltest mich nicht deinem Mund küssen lassen!" In life he would not let her kiss his mouth, she cries, but she will kiss it now. The eyes that looked upon her in anger are closed forever, and the tongue that so fiercely denounced her is silent. But she still lives, Salome exults, and then, caressing the head, she again apostrophizes Jokanaan's body.

Herod, stricken with terror at the monstrous sight, turns to leave. Salome murmurs that now at last she has kissed the mouth of the prophet. The kiss had a bitter taste, she muses. In mad exultation she cries out again that she has kissed Jokanaan's mouth, and at that moment a ray of moonlight breaks through the clouds and illumines her. Herod whirls, stares at her in utter horror, and then commands his soldiers to kill her. They crush Salome beneath their shields. The curtain falls.

[1] In some productions this is performed by a dancer instead of by the singer.

Samson et Dalila

by CAMILLE SAINT-SAËNS

[1834–1921]

Libretto by
FERDINAND LEMAIRE

Based on the
BOOK OF JUDGES

CHARACTERS

Samson, leader of the Israelites..*Tenor*
Abimelech, Satrap of Gaza.....................................*Bass*
High Priest of Dagon..*Baritone*
First Philistine ....*Tenor*
Second Philistine ....*Bass*
A messenger of the Philistines................................*Tenor*
An old Hebrew..*Bass*
Dalila, priestess in the Temple of Dagon.................*Mezzo-soprano*
Hebrews, Philistines, people of Gaza, dancers

Place: Gaza, Palestine
Time: 1136 B.C.
First performance: Grand Ducal Theater, Weimar, December 2, 1877
Original language: French

SAMSON ET DALILA has elements of both oratorio and opera by reason of its biblical story and the wealth of choral effects combined with powerful dramatic characterization. Although Saint-Saëns wrote more than a dozen other operas, this one alone has survived as his masterpiece. Its première at Weimar was arranged by Franz Liszt, who was impressed by the composer's musical ability and encouraged him in his career. As musician, composer, and author, Saint-Saëns was one of the most brilliant figures in the musical life of nineteenth-century France.

Before the curtain rises we hear a chorus of lamentation sung by the Hebrews who have been enslaved by the Philistines ("Dieu d'Israël, écoute la prière"). They implore God to lead them out of bondage, and in their deep misery they wonder if the Almighty has turned a deaf ear to their pleas. Their cities have been destroyed, they wail, and their altars defamed, but no one comes to help them. The feverish orchestral theme that accompanies the chorus continues as the curtain rises.

ACT ONE

A public square in the city of Gaza. At one side is the portal of the Philistine Temple of Dagon. The Jews, kneeling before it in prayer and supplication, again break out into despairing entreaties. As they rail against heaven for ignoring their cries Samson strides forward and faces the people. In a vigorous refrain he exhorts them to raise their voices to God in praise, not protest ("Arrêtez, ô mes frères"). He proclaims that God is speaking through him when he says that the day of liberation is at hand.

The people answer Samson in powerful choral interludes. At first they scoff at his words of encouragement, complaining that the God who led their fathers out of Egypt has now deserted His people. Samson fiercely rebukes them for their blasphemous lack of faith. With dignity and eloquence he assures them that the God of Israel is still their champion and will deliver them from the enemy. Listening more and more attentively to his words, the people finally take courage and then respond in a stirring choral passage in which they sing that Samson's words are indeed inspired by God ("Ah! le souffle du Seigneur").

While they are listening to their leader, Abimelech, Satrap (governor) of Gaza, appears, followed by a body of Philistine soldiers. Gazing with angry contempt on the crowd, he asks how they dare disturb him with their outcries ("Qui donc élève ici la voix?"). He advises them to cease their rebellion and submit to their masters, saying that they can never hope to break their bonds. Abimelech sneeringly defies their God to set them free, declaring that the God of Israel flees before the power of the Great Dagon as the dove flees before the hawk.

In an answering refrain Samson angrily denounces Abimelech for his tyranny and warns him that the powers of heaven itself are gathering to strike down the oppressor ("C'est toi que sa bouche invective"). The hour of reckoning is at hand, he cries, while the Hebrews repeat his warning in chorus. Although Abimelech threatens them with death, the Hebrews, taking courage from Samson, continue to defy him. Goaded to fury, Abimelech rushes at Samson with drawn sword. Samson wrenches the weapon out of his hand and runs him through. The Philistine soldiers try to go to Abimelech's aid but fall back in wild disorder before Samson's onslaught. Brandishing the sword, Samson leads the Hebrews from the square.

The uproar brings the High Priest of Dagon rushing from the temple. Gazing in horror at the body of Abimelech, he rages that the Israelites must be destroyed to a man in punishment for this murderous deed. Cringing before his wrath, the Philistine soldiers retreat from the square. Two Philistines who remain with the High Priest tremblingly sing that an icy fear has clutched their hearts and has left their hands powerless to lift their weapons. The High Priest furiously denounces them for their cowardice. At that moment a messenger rushes in with the news that the Hebrew army, led by Samson, has put the Philistines to rout and is spreading terror and destruction through the countryside. In panic-stricken tones the two Philistines and the messenger cry that there is nothing left but flight to some distant land where they can hide their shame. The High Priest, beside himself with fury, calls down a terrible curse on Samson and the Israelites ("Maudite à jamais soit la race"). His voice blends with those of the two Philistines and the messenger as they sing that they must desert their altars and flee to the mountains. Taking up the body of Abimelech, they hurry away.

The Hebrew men and women, with Samson at their head, now return from battle to the accompaniment of majestic, sustained chords that sound forth like a fanfare. In a simple yet highly dramatic choral passage sung by the old men, the Hebrews voice their thanks for victory and liberation ("Hymne de joie").

The mood of the scene changes abruptly as Dalila and a procession of maidens carrying wreaths and garlands come out of the temple. In a melodious chorus they pay tribute to the conquering hero ("Voici le printemps nous portant des fleurs"). After the chorus Dalila approaches Samson and in seductive tones invites him to come with her to her rendezvous in the valley of Sorek, where all the delights of love await the hero who has conquered her heart ("Je viens célébrer la victoire"). This introduces a dramatic trio. Samson, fascinated by Dalila's beauty, prays that he may be kept from falling victim to her charms. An old Hebrew warns that if he yields to this woman she will lead him to his destruction. The trio is interrupted as the maidens begin moving around Samson in a sensuous, pagan dance in which Dalila joins. Gazing provocatively at Samson as she dances, she sings of how she will wait for her lover in the flower-scented valley ("Printemps qui commence"). The voice of the old Hebrew blends with hers as he reiterates his warning. Samson, struggling against his desires, is unable to take his eyes from Dalila. Tantalizing him with looks and voice, she ends her dance and moves slowly toward the temple. As she goes inside, followed by the maidens, the curtain falls.

ACT TWO

The home of Dalila in the valley of Sorek. Set in a garden, it is surrounded by luxuriant tropical foliage. The calm mood of early evening is established by the smoothly flowing music of a brief prelude. Dalila, clad in magnificent oriental attire set off by sparkling jewels, is seated on a bench near the door. In a brief recitative she muses that when Samson comes to her in this retreat her hour of revenge will be at hand. She then sings the passionate aria in which she invokes the aid of the god of love in destroying the archenemy of her people ("Amour! viens aider ma faiblesse!"). She prays that her wiles may poison his heart, rob him of his strength, and leave him helpless in the hands of his enemies. The aria ends in a descending phrase of menace and triumph. As Dalila sits musing in the gathering darkness, distant lightning flashes accentuate the foreboding mood of the scene.

The High Priest now appears, saying that he has come in the name of Dagon to talk to her about Samson. A dramatic dialogue follows. Inspired by Samson's strength, the High Priest says, the Hebrews have turned against their masters, and the Philistines are in a state of abject terror. When Dalila betrays her anger over the fact that Samson's courage has cowed the Philistines, the High Priest craftily arouses her to greater hatred by saying that Samson is openly boasting that her efforts to ensnare him have failed. In ominous tones Dalila assures the High Priest that the hero will find her charms irresistible and that she will soon have him helpless in her arms.

Highly gratified at the effect of his words, the High Priest offers Dalila all the wealth of Dagon's temple if she will deliver Samson into his hands. Gold is worthless to her, Dalila answers disdainfully. Vengeance alone will suffice, for her hatred of Samson rivals that of the High Priest. Three times she has tried to ring from him the secret of his mighty strength, Dalila continues, but each time he tore himself from her ardent embraces without betraying himself. But this night he will yield, she promises, for Samson is a slave to passion. Her voice blends with the High Priest's in an exultant duet as they anticipate victory over Samson and the rebellious Hebrews ("Il faut, pour assouvir ma haine"). Learning that Samson is expected momentarily, the High Priest takes his leave.

Leaning against a pillar, Dalila awaits the hero. A restless theme murmurs in the orchestra as she muses anxiously over the possibility that he may not come to her. It grows darker and thunder rumbles in the distance. Finally Samson, groping his way through the darkness, approaches the house, muttering that his accursed love is driving him on against his will and judgment. Seeing him at last, Dalila greets him with an impassioned phrase, "C'est toi! mon bien-aimé!" Torn between loyalty to his people and his love, Samson tries to repel her embraces, saying that he cannot disobey the Lord's commands.

Spurred by his hesitation and uncertainty, Dalila adds the persuasion of tears to her allurements, sobbing that her heart will break if Samson scorns her love. When he implores her not to weep she sings enticingly of the hours of bliss they have had together—bliss that is as nothing compared with the joys of their future. As the dialogue continues the sounds of the rising storm reflect the tumult in Samson's heart. At last, carried away by his passion, Samson cries out that he loves her because destiny has decreed it. Dalila exultantly responds in the famous aria, "Mon coeur s'ouvre à ta voix." In sensuous phrases she sings of the joy that floods her heart at the sound of his words. Their voices blend ardently in a repetition of the final phrases of the aria.

Now certain of victory, Dalila insinuatingly asks Samson to tell her the secret of his great strength, which she so much admires. But Samson, though shaken by his emotions, implores her not to ask that question, saying that he dare not betray the source of the power bestowed upon him by his God. The music rises to a wild climax as Dalila cajoles and implores, while Samson, begging her to desist, tries to tear himself from her embrace. Suddenly, with a cry of fury, Dalila pushes him away ("Lâche! coeur sans amour!"). Shouting at him to go, she hurries toward the house. Lightning blazes as the storm reaches its height. Raising his hands in a gesture of helplessness and despair, Samson slowly follows Dalila into the house. There is a tremendous crash of thunder. Soldiers are seen cautiously surrounding the house. Dalila suddenly appears at the window, calling on the Philistines to help. As the soldiers rush in we hear the voice of Samson crying out that he has been betrayed. In the fatal moment of surrender he has told Dalila that the secret source of his strength is his hair. Dalila has cut it off, leaving him at the mercy of the Philistines. As shouts of triumph come from within the house the curtain falls.

ACT THREE

[*Scene One*]　The courtyard of the prison at Gaza. Samson, blinded by his captors, is chained to a mill. As he walks wearily in a circle, turning the millstone, he prays for courage to bear his pain and disgrace ("Voici ma misère, hélas!"). From beyond the prison come the bitter reproaches of the Hebrews, once more made captive through the downfall of their great leader ("Samson, qu'as-tu fait du Dieu de tes pères?"). Overcome by shame and agony, Samson calls on God to take his life in atonement for the misery of the people whom he has betrayed. The denunciation of the Hebrews continues in a relentless chorus, until at last Samson falls on his knees, wretchedly praying for mercy. While he is praying the jailers come in, take off his chains, and drag him away. The curtain falls, with the music continuing in a brief interlude while the scene is changed.

[*Scene Two*]　The great hall in the Temple of Dagon, its vaulted roof supported by two great pillars. There is a sacrificial altar and a large statue of Dagon. It is dawn. The temple is already crowded with worshipers. The High Priest appears, followed by Philistine dignitaries. Dalila then comes in with a group of dancing girls garlanded with flowers and carrying goblets of wine. They repeat the chorus sung to the victorious Samson in the first act. After the chorus there is a wild *bacchanale*.

As the dancers are being applauded Samson is led in by a little child. He has been brought in so that the Philistines may amuse themselves by mocking their vanquished enemy. Greeting him with sneering raillery, the High Priest urges Dalila and the worshipers to pay homage to this hero of the Israelites. Dalila, goblet in hand, approaches Samson and in a dramatic refrain gloats over her victory ("Laissez moi prendre ta main"). Mocking his blindness, she offers to take his hand and guide him. When he recoils at her touch she reminds him that once he dared everything to be at her side. The passion that she roused in him proved his undoing, she goes on, and betrayed him into telling her the secret of his great strength. Now, Dalila, her god, and her people have been revenged. With bowed head Samson murmurs brokenly that he defamed his love by bestowing it on Dalila.

The High Priest tauntingly asks Samson to repeat the passionate avowals he made to Dalila, so that all may hear how a hero loves. If Samson's God will restore his sight, the High Priest declares, he himself will worship the God of the Israelites instead of Dagon ("Allons, Samson, divertis nous"). Raising his sightless eyes, Samson prays that some rebuke from heaven may answer this impiety and reveal the power of the Lord of Hosts in the hour of shame and dishonor ("Tu permets, ô Dieu d'Israël"). The worshipers mock his prayer with a burst of jeering laughter.

Calling to Dalila to aid him, the High Priest begins the sacrificial rite in honor of Dagon. As they pour libations on the flaming altar they sing, in canon form, an impressive invocation to Dagon ("Gloire à Dagon vainqueur!"). The worshipers respond in exultant phrases, calling on their god to restore the altars and fields despoiled by the Hebrews. Then the High Priest commands the child to guide Samson between the two great pillars. There the defeated champion of the Israelites is to climax this ceremony by kneeling in obeisance to Dagon. After the child has led him to the spot Samson quietly tells him to leave the temple at once. The child runs off. As the flames of the altar leap higher, the invocation of the Philistines rises in a triumphant chorus ("Gloire à Dagon!").

Gripping the pillars with his arms, Samson prays for one final burst of strength to destroy the pagan rabble before him ("Souviens-toi de ton serviteur"). Ending his prayer with a high, ringing phrase, Samson wrenches at the two pillars, which begin to sway and crumble. There is a scream of horror from the throng as the temple crashes down upon Samson and the Philistines. The curtain falls.

Simon Boccanegra

by GIUSEPPE VERDI

[1813–1901]

Libretto by
FRANCESCO MARIA PIAVE *and* ARRIGO BOÏTO

Based on a drama by Antonio Garcia Gutiérrez

CHARACTERS
In the Prologue

Paolo Albiani ⎱ commoners, leaders of the ⎰ *Bass*
Pietro ⎰ people's party in Genoa . . . . ⎱ *Baritone*
Jacopo Fiesco, a nobleman of Genoa . . . . *Bass*
Simon Boccanegra, a corsair, or pirate, serving
the republic of Genoa . . . . *Baritone*

In the Opera
(*Twenty-five years later*)

Amelia Grimaldi (Maria, daughter of Simon Boccanegra) . . . . *Soprano*
Gabriele Adorno, a nobleman of Genoa, betrothed to Amelia . . . . *Tenor*
Amelia's maid . . . . *Soprano*
Pietro, now courtier to the Doge of Genoa . . . . *Bass*
Jacopo Fiesco, now disguised as Andrea . . . . *Bass*
Simon Boccanegra, now the Doge of Genoa . . . . *Baritone*
Paolo Albiani, now courtier to the Doge . . . . *Bass*
Captain of the palace guard . . . . *Tenor*
Courtiers, commoners, sailors, senators, ladies and gentlemen
of the court, people of Genoa

Place: Genoa
Time: Fourteenth century
First performance: Teatro La Fenice, Venice, March 12, 1857
Original language: Italian

SIMON BOCCANEGRA, another product of Verdi's "second period," was not received favorably by the public, presumably because of the somber and tragic nature of its plot. In 1881 Verdi revised the score and Arrigo Boïto the libretto, and the opera was presented anew. This production likewise failed to stir much enthusiasm. It has been successful in revival, however, because some of its music is conceded to be among the finest that Verdi ever wrote.

PROLOGUE

A square before the Church of San Lorenzo in Genoa. At the right is the palace of Jacopo Fiesco. It is night. Paolo and Pietro are talking in a secluded corner of the square. As leaders of the people's party, they are eager for power and are conspiring to elect a puppet of their own choice as Doge of Genoa. The election is to be held the following morning. Paolo insists that the logical candidate is Simon Boccanegra, because he has become a hero in the eyes of his fellow townsmen by reason of his exploits as a corsair. Pietro agrees, then leaves to arouse the sentiment of the populace in Simon's behalf.

Simon enters, and Paolo urges him to accept the candidacy. When he hesitates Paolo craftily mentions the name of Maria. She is Fiesco's daughter, whom Simon loves and who has borne him a child. Simon has taken the child to a secret hiding place while Maria is being held prisoner in the palace by her father. Infuriated because Simon, a commoner and a pirate, has dared to love his daughter, Fiesco is burning for revenge. When Paolo reminds Simon that, as Doge, he will be able to rescue Maria from Fiesco's palace, he consents to run for office and promises Paolo a share in his rule. The two withdraw to one side as Pietro returns with a crowd of seamen and laborers.

Pietro tells the crowd that a worthy candidate has been found, and then Paolo steps forward to announce the name of Simon Boccanegra. He deliberately sets about to inflame the crowd against Fiesco, leader of the hated nobility. Indicating the palace, he tells the men that there the nobleman keeps his beautiful daughter as a wretched prisoner. They comment in a spirited chorus, then promise to support Boccanegra, singing his name as they leave the square.

Fiesco, shaken with grief, comes out of the palace and in the great aria, "Il lacerato spirito," laments that Maria has died. From within comes a mournful chorus of women chanting the *Miserere*. Simon, crossing the square, encounters Fiesco. Kneeling before him, he begs that the enmity between them be ended for the sake of the love he bears Maria. But Fiesco refuses to make peace, denouncing Simon for dishonoring his name. He will forgive only if Simon will give up his own daughter, Maria's child. That he cannot do, Simon answers, and then relates how he went to the distant place where he had left the child in care of a nurse, found that the nurse had died and that the baby had disappeared. Fiesco tells him that now there can never be a reconciliation and abruptly leaves him.

Simon, determined to see Maria, rushes into the palace, and in the next moment we hear his cry of anguish as he finds her dead. Crushed by horror and despair, he reappears, only to be confronted by a shouting throng. Led by Paolo and Pietro, they acclaim him as their new leader, while Fiesco, watching from a distance, curses in fury. Simon, stunned by grief, turns to the palace and murmurs that it is a tomb. Paolo cries triumphantly that it is a throne. The curtain falls.

ACT ONE

[*Scene One*]   The garden of the Grimaldi Palace outside Genoa twenty-five years later. It is dawn. Amelia, a young and beautiful girl, stands alone in the garden. In a melodious aria ("Come in quest'ora bruna") she recalls her childhood in a humble cottage, so unlike the luxurious palace in which she now lives. She exclaims in delight as she hears the voice of her lover, Gabriele Adorno, a young nobleman. In a moment he appears, and they greet each other in impassioned phrases.

Amelia tells Gabriele that she has been disturbed at seeing him in conversation with Andrea (Fiesco in disguise) and others of the court. Gabriele hints that they are planning an uprising against the Doge but bids her forget her misgivings for the moment. They sing an ardent duet ("Vieni a mirar la cerula"). Looking at Genoa in the distance, Amelia sings that though the city is under the rule of Gabriele's enemy she will banish misgivings and think only of love. Gabriele sings that Amelia's love is like a shining light. No thought of evil feuds must cast a shadow over her radiance.

They are interrupted by the entrance of Pietro, who tells them that the Doge, returning from the hunt, asks if he may pause at the castle to rest. Amelia consents, but when Pietro has gone she warns Gabriele that the Doge is coming to ask her to marry Paolo, his favorite courtier. She urges her lover to speed plans for their own wedding, then goes into the palace. Andrea appears, and Gabriele asks his consent to marry Amelia. Andrea replies that Gabriele must first know the secret of Amelia's past. He then relates that Amelia is not a Grimaldi by birth but an orphan who inherited the cell of the real Amelia Grimaldi when she died in a nunnery. The orphan was given Amelia's family name in order to keep the nobleman Grimaldi's property from confiscation after he had been exiled from Genoa for plotting against the Doge. The voices of the two men blend dramatically as Andrea gives his consent to the marriage and Gabriele expresses his gratitude. They leave quickly as a fanfare announces the arrival of the Doge.

He enters the garden, and Amelia appears to welcome him. He informs her that he has pardoned the Grimaldis so that she and her kinsmen need no longer live in exile. Amelia answers that she is well content with her lot, for she has found love, and she tells him about Gabriele. She adds that Paolo also is seeking her hand in marriage, but only for the sake of the Grimaldi wealth. But she is not a Grimaldi, Amelia goes on, telling the Doge how she was reared by an aged nurse in a cottage by the sea near Pisa. The nurse left her a locket with a picture of her mother.

Greatly excited, the Doge shows her a picture of Maria Fiesco, whom he had loved and lost twenty-five years ago. Amelia produces her locket. They find that the pictures are identical, and the Doge now realizes that Amelia is his own daughter, Maria Boccanegra. They voice their joy over their reunion in a dramatic duet ("Figlia, tal nome palpita").

Amelia goes into the palace. As Simon blissfully watches her Paolo enters and asks if Amelia has given her consent to the marriage. Glancing at him contemptuously, Simon curtly tells him to give up his hopes of marrying Amelia, then follows after his daughter. Paolo glares after him in baffled fury. Pietro approaches, and Paolo, saying that his suit has failed, tells him that he has decided to kidnap the girl. He instructs Pietro to make ready his ship, so that Amelia may be carried off to the home of Lorenzo, another member of their faction. They both leave as the curtain falls.

[*Scene Two*]   The Doge's council chamber in Genoa. Simon Boccanegra is seated on his throne. At one side are the nobles, on the other the commoners, including Paolo and Pietro. In discussing affairs of state, Simon announces that a messenger has come from Venice with an offer of peace between the two cities, but the councilors clamor for war.

Deliberations are interrupted by a tumult outside. Paolo steps to the balcony of the chamber and reports that a rioting mob is approaching the square in pursuit of two men. There are cries of "Morte [Death]!" Simon rushes to the balcony and exclaims in surprise as he sees Gabriele and his companion, Fiesco, whom Simon recognizes only as a member of the rival faction. In an aside Pietro warns Paolo to flee. Simon, catching sight of him as he tries to steal out of the chamber, orders the doors locked, saying that anyone who tries to leave will be considered a traitor. Paolo, confused and frightened, stops in his tracks.

In another moment an angry mob bursts into the room, dragging Gabriele and Fiesco and demanding death for the murderer. Imperiously Simon quiets the mob and orders Gabriele to explain the reason for the uproar. In answer Gabriele admits that he killed Lorenzo because he kidnaped Amelia Grimaldi. Before he died, Gabriele goes on, the abductor confessed that he had been incited to the deed by someone in a position of great power. When Simon asks the man's name Gabriele replies that Lorenzo died before he could speak it. Suddenly suspicious of Simon, Gabriele wildly accuses him of abducting Amelia and then lunges at him with drawn dagger. At that moment Amelia rushes in and throws herself between the two men.

She begs Simon to spare Gabriele's life. In a moving refrain she tells about her abduction ("Nell'ora soave che all'estasi invita"). She relates that she was seized by a band of men and taken to Lorenzo's home. When she warned Lorenzo that the Doge would show him no mercy when he learned about his part in the abduction the man became panic-stricken and released her at once. Looking meaningfully at Paolo, she says that there is a man in this very chamber who deserves a worse fate than that meted out to Lorenzo. As Paolo squirms under her gaze the commoners and nobles, drawing their swords, begin shouting accusations.

Simon strides forward and in an impressive aria ("Plebe! Patrizi!") implores the councilors to reconcile their differences for the sake of the republic. The people softly comment on the eloquence of his plea. Amelia approaches Fiesco and begs him to be prudent. Gabriele surrenders his sword to Simon, who orders him to remain in the castle until this affair can be settled. Then Simon suddenly calls out to Paolo, who has been trying to escape in the crowd, commanding him, as a high officer of the state, to curse the man who plotted the abduction with the phrase, "Sia maledetto!"

The assembly echoes the words, and Paolo, shaken with terror at the realization that he must curse himself, repeats "Sia maledettol" The curtain falls.

ACT TWO

A room adjoining the Doge's apartment in the ducal palace. Through doors at either side the lights of the city are visible. Among the furnishings of the room are a high-backed chair and a table, on which stand a decanter of water and a drinking bowl. Paolo, talking with Pietro, orders him to bring Gabriele and Fiesco from their cells. Left alone, Paolo sings a dramatic monologue ("Me stesso ho maledetto") in which he broods over the curse he was forced to pronounce upon himself. Swearing revenge, he brings forth a vial of poison and pours its contents into the drinking bowl.

When the prisoners are brought in Paolo tries to persuade Fiesco to kill the Doge while he sleeps, but Fiesco scorns so dishonorable a revenge. Angrily Paolo orders him back to his cell. He rouses Gabriele to fury by vile insinuations about the Doge's relations with Amelia. Locking the door on one side of the room, Paolo starts to leave by the other door. Warning Gabriele that now he must fight for Amelia or die, he leaves, locking the door behind him.

In a ringing aria ("Sento avvampar nell'anima") Gabriele gives vent to his fury and jealousy, raging that the man who caused the death of his father is now his rival in love. With her own key Amelia opens the door which Paolo had first locked, comes in, and a dramatic colloquy follows. When Gabriele accuses her of being faithless, Amelia protests that her love for the Doge is pure and begs Gabriele to have faith in her devotion to him.

Amelia hears the Doge approaching. Gabriele swears he will kill him, but Amelia finally persuades him to conceal himself in the room, as all escape has been cut off. Simon enters, and the girl begs him to allow her to marry Gabriele. He refuses, saying that Gabriele is his enemy and a conspirator against his government. At length, however, he agrees to yield if Gabriele will promise to desert his fellow conspirators.

Gently he bids Amelia leave and then wearily seats himself at the table. He pours water from the decanter into the bowl and drinks, remarking that even water tastes bitter to him who reigns. Gradually he falls asleep. Gabriele steals from his hiding place and stands over the sleeping Doge. Calling on the spirit of his slain father for courage to kill his enemy, he raises his dagger. He is about to strike when Amelia rushes in and interposes herself between him and her father.

Simon awakens. Shaking off the first effects of the poison, he springs to his feet. A dramatic trio ensues. Simon cries that Gabriele has well avenged his father, not with the dagger but by robbing him of his daughter. Gabriele, astounded to hear that Simon is the father of his loved one, kneels before the Doge and implores his forgiveness, while Amelia prays that her father may grant her lover mercy.

Now from the distance comes the chorus of the Doge's enemies. Simon orders Gabriele to join his erstwhile fellow conspirators outside, but he now refuses. The Doge then bids him try to persuade the rebels to make peace. Gabriele consents, saying that if he fails he will return to fight at the Doge's side. Simon promises him Amelia's hand. As the chorus rises to a great climax Simon and Gabriele draw their swords and prepare for the attack. The curtain falls.

ACT THREE

In the ducal palace. At the rear is an open balustrade with a view of Genoa, lighted as though for a festival, and beyond it the sea. From outside come the voices of a throng hailing the Doge for his victory over the rebels. The revolt, in which Paolo and Fiesco traitorously took part, has been quelled.

The captain of the guard enters. He orders Fiesco brought before him and gives him back his sword, thus restoring his freedom. Paolo now enters under guard. He tells Fiesco that he has been condemned to death but reveals in an aside that he has poisoned Simon Boccanegra. Hearing the bridal chorus outside, Paolo cries out that Gabriele Adorno is now marrying the girl whom he himself carried away. As Fiesco recoils at this final confession of treachery the guards drag Paolo away. Simon appears, and Fiesco withdraws into the shadows. The captain of the guard steps to the balcony and announces to the throng outside that the Doge has ordered the festival lights extinguished out of respect for those who have died in the rebellion.

Somber chords throb in the orchestra as Simon muses over the strange fever that has seized him, and voices his premonition of doom. He looks over the city, watching the lights gradually go out. Fiesco strides forward, singing in grim triumph that his revenge is at hand. A powerfully dramatic scene now follows as he reveals to Simon that he is Fiesco, his mortal enemy. Simon, fighting off death, tells him that Amelia is his daughter, Maria, and the nobleman's own granddaughter. Stunned by the revelation, Fiesco cries out to Simon that he has been poisoned by a traitor and bitterly laments that the peace they now can make has come too late.

Gasping, Simon sinks into a chair, just as Maria and Gabriele enter, followed by bridal attendants, senators, and ladies and gentlemen of the court. Gently Simon tells Maria he is dying. She and Gabriele, crushed by horror and sadness, kneel at his feet. With a tremendous effort Simon rises, places his hands on their heads, and blesses them. As he falls back into his chair the onlookers express their sorrow in an impressive chorus. Maria, Gabriele, and Fiesco join their voices in grief and anguish.

Simon, with his dying breath, orders the senators to crown Gabriele as Doge and asks Fiesco to see that this is done. Calling Maria's name, he dies. Fiesco steps to the balcony and announces the news to the people. In hushed accents they repeat Boccanegra's name and, to the solemn tolling of bells, chant a prayer for his soul. The curtain falls.

La Sonnambula

by VINCENZO BELLINI

[1801–1835]

Libretto by
FELICE ROMANI

CHARACTERS

Lisa, hostess of the village inn.............................. *Soprano*
Alessio, a young peasant in love with Lisa..................... *Bass*
Amina, a village maiden..................................... *Soprano*
Teresa, owner of the village mill, foster mother of Amina......... *Soprano*
Elvino, a young farmer betrothed to Amina.................... *Tenor*
Notary .... *Tenor*
Count Rodolpho, lord of the manor........................... *Bass*
Villagers and peasants

Place: A village in the mountains of Switzerland
Time: Nineteenth century
First performance: Teatro Carcano, Milan, March 6, 1831
Original language: Italian

L A SONNAMBULA, one of the great operatic favorites of the nineteenth century, contains some of the finest examples of Bellini's gift for facile, limpid melody. Written in an era that produced some of the foremost singers of Italian opera, it provides abundant opportunity for vocal display, at the same time having the advantage of a simple, natural story.

ACT ONE

[*Scene One*] The village square, with Lisa's inn at one side. In the background is a picturesque mill with a water wheel. A narrow, rather ramshackle bridge, spanning the stream at a point above the water wheel, leads from a flight of stone steps on one side to a dormer window of the mill. Mountains are visible beyond the village.

From the distance come the voices of peasants on their way to the village to celebrate the marriage of Amina, the most popular girl of the village, to Elvino, a well-known young farmer. The peasants are singing a festive chorus in honor of the bride-to-be ("Viva Amina"). At the sound of their voices Lisa, hostess of the inn, comes to the door and listens with an expression of displeasure and resentment. After the chorus she voices her thoughts in a florid aria ("Tutto è gioia"), in which she asserts that the joyous nuptial chorus fills her heart with bitterness. It is the bitterness of jealousy, for she was once loved by Elvino. Now she must hide her real feelings behind a smile and pretend to be happy with the others.

Soon the peasants appear, continuing their chorus as they throng into the square. Among them is Alessio, a young rustic, who hurries over to Lisa and ardently greets her. Although Lisa makes it plain that his attentions are unwelcome, Alessio persists in declaring his affections and speaks enthusiastically of the day when they too will be married. Hearing the shouts of more villagers coming into the square, Alessio turns away. Much to Lisa's annoyance, he leads them in a chorus of tribute to Amina's beauty ("In Elvezia non v'ha rosa"). While the peasants sing that Amina's loveliness shames not only the flowers but the stars and the dawn as well, Lisa fumes over the homage paid to her rival.

Greeted by the shouting crowd, Amina appears, accompanied by Teresa, her foster mother. The bride-to-be thanks her neighbors and friends for their good wishes and weeps tears of joy as she expresses her gratitude to Teresa for her kindness and care. Exclaiming that she is the happiest person in the world, Amina proceeds to describe the rapture of being in love in the melodious aria "Come per me sereno." At its conclusion she impetuously embraces Teresa and then, in an ensuing refrain ("Sovra il sen"), she sings that mere words cannot express the bliss that is in her heart.

The peasants comment approvingly on these sentiments, after which Alessio, acting more or less as their spokesman, steps forward and with naïve pride tells Amina that he arranged the entire celebration in her honor —it was he who wrote the music of the bridal chorus and invited the guests. Graciously thanking him, Amina promises that he will be amply rewarded for his good offices when he claims Lisa as his bride. At those words Alessio turns hopefully to Lisa, who disdainfully remarks that she is interested only in maintaining her freedom. Amina gently tells her that she does not realize what happiness love can bring, to which Lisa cynically answers that the delights of love very often turn to bitterness.

The conversation is interrupted by the appearance of the notary, who informs Amina that Elvino will arrive presently. A moment later Elvino makes his way through the throng and asks Amina's forgiveness for having made her wait. In a brief refrain ("Perdona, o mia diletta") he explains that he paused at the church to pray to the memory of his mother, asking her blessing on his marriage. The notary meanwhile has seated himself at one of the tables in front of the inn and has drawn up the marriage contract. After the ceremony of signing the document, Elvino slips the ring on Amina's finger and, in an ardent refrain, bids her treasure it always as the bond that unites them in love ("Prendi: l'anel ti dono"). He also gives her a bouquet of flowers. A tender duet follows as Amina passionately avows her love ("Sposi—oh, tenera parola!"). Words cannot express her adoration, she sings ("Ah! vorrei trovar parola"), to which Elvino responds that her tender looks and smiles say more than words can tell ("Tutto in quest' istante"). Lisa's voice blends with theirs in the closing phrases of the number as she gives way to her jealousy over their happiness.

As Elvino turns to the people and invites them to the wedding ceremony which is to be held the next day, the sound of galloping horses and the cracking of whips comes from beyond the square. A few moments later a handsome stranger in an officer's uniform strides through the crowd, approaches Lisa, and asks how far it is to the manor. Lisa tells him that it is three miles farther on, adding that he could not hope to reach there before nightfall because of the bad condition of the roads. She advises him to spend the night at the inn. Looking around, the stranger muses over the familiar landmarks—the mill, the fountain, the fields. In an impressive aria ("Vi ravviso") he abandons himself to the memories which these scenes bring back to him. Though they inspire pleasant recollections, he reflects, they also bring the pain of knowing that the happy days of his youth are gone, never to return. In an accompanying chorus the villagers comment that the visitor, evidently no stranger to the village, seems to be harboring some secret grief.

After standing for a few moments as though lost in thought, the officer—who, of course, is Count Rodolpho, lord of the manor—turns to the villagers and asks the reason for the celebration. The people tell him about the wedding which is to be held the next day and point out Amina as the bride. Approaching her, Rodolpho compliments her on her beauty and then goes on to say that she reminds him of someone who once was very dear to him—someone whom he loved and lost many years ago ("Tu non sai con quei bel gli occhio"). This refrain leads into an ensemble in which Lisa comments rather spitefully that Amina seems able to charm any man she meets, while Elvino remarks that his betrothed seems unduly attentive to the stranger. The villagers comment that the visitor must be a nobleman, for such gallant manners are not common to country swains.

When Elvino observes to Rodolpho that he seems familiar with the countryside, the count replies that in his early years he lived with the lord of the manor. Teresa informs him that the lord died four years ago. He had a son, Teresa continues, who disappeared and was never heard of again. Thereupon Rodolpho says that he has come to bring the people of the manor news about the lost child—he is still alive. When the villagers express the hope that they will see him, Rodolpho gravely assures them that they will.

Meanwhile it has grown darker and a shepherd's pipe is heard in the distance. Teresa urges the villagers to go to their homes, warning that it will soon be time for the dreaded phantom to appear. In reply to Rodolpho's questions about the ghost, the people explain in a dramatic chorus ("A fosco cielo, a notte bruna"). Every night, they relate, a ghostly figure in white, with its hair and gown streaming in the wind, walks through the streets of the town. It looks about with staring eyes, and whoever meets that gaze is stricken with fatal enchantment.

Rodolpho scoffs at the story, telling the villagers that the ghost is merely an illusion or a shadow. They earnestly assure him that they have seen it with their own eyes. When it passes, they say in awed tones, the water stops flowing in the millrace and the fountain, and not a leaf stirs. Watchdogs cringe in fear, while owls make the night hideous with their shrieks. With an amused smile the count declares that he will attempt to solve the mystery of the phantom during his stay, adding that, unless his conjectures are wrong, they will soon see the last of it.

Saying that he wishes to retire, the count turns to go into the inn. The villagers bid him good night and slowly leave the square. Taking Amina's hand, Rodolpho expresses the hope that the love she has chosen will make her happy, whereupon Elvino, somewhat annoyed at the count's affectionate manner, declares that no love can rival that which he has for his bride. After the count goes inside, Elvino coldly turns away from Amina and starts to leave. Amina asks if he is going without a word of good night, to which Elvino sarcastically replies that perhaps the stranger's tender farewell was sufficient. He was most courteous and kind, Amina avers, bewildered at Elvino's sullen manner. A quarrel threatens as Elvino mutters that the stranger behaved like a lover.

Surprised and hurt by Elvino's unreasonableness, Amina accuses him of being jealous. In a passionate refrain ("Son geloso del zefiro amante") Elvino cries that he is jealous of the wind that caresses her hair and the sun that shines upon her. Reassured by his fervent declarations, Amina forgives him his momentary doubts and suspicions. Their voices blend in brilliant phrases as they renew their pledges of love and devotion to each other ("Ah, mio bene! Ah, constante"). Tenderly saying good night, they leave the square.

[*Scene Two*] The count's bedroom at the inn.[1] At one side is the entrance door, at the other, a bed with a table beside it. Another door leads to an adjoining room. At the rear are large french windows, through which the moonlight streams. Rodolpho, alone, muses that he is content to stay at the inn for the time being because the surroundings are pleasant, the villagers agreeable, and the hostess charming and attractive. His reflections are interrupted when Lisa enters to ask if the count is satisfied with the accommodations. When Rodolpho expresses surprise over the fact that his identity has been discovered, Lisa tells him that the villagers are on their way to the inn to do him honor and modestly adds that she wishes to be the first to pay her respects.

Rodolpho answers that he is flattered by the interest of one so charming and confesses that he is quite taken with her beauty. Lisa coyly responds to his compliments and looks at him in a manner designed to encourage his romantic inclinations. Just at that moment, however, there is a noise outside the window. Exclaiming in alarm, Lisa hurries into the adjoining room. In her excitement she drops her scarf, which the count picks up and places on the bed.

To his great astonishment, the count sees a ladder being placed against the balcony of the french window. A moment later a young woman wearing a white nightdress and holding a lighted candle in her hand climbs up, slowly opens the window, and walks into the room. Rodolpho murmurs that this must be the ghost he has been hearing about ("Che veggio? Saria questo il notturno fantasma?"). His comments and the young woman's trancelike utterances continue in duet form. As the count recognizes the "phantom" as Amina, she calls Elvino's name, and Rodolpho immediately realizes that she is sleepwalking. Coming toward him, Amina, dreaming of Elvino, offers the count her hand to kiss. Saying that there is nothing he can do to awaken her, Rodolpho goes over to the french windows and carefully

[1] In some versions this is Act Two.

closes them. As he does so Lisa comes out of the other room, utters an exclamation of shocked surprise at seeing Amina, and steals out of the room without attracting the count's attention.

Dreaming of the marriage ceremony, Amina murmurs about her friends gathered around the altar and exclaims in childlike wonder over the gleaming candles. Raising her right hand, she swears that she will love Elvino forever. Rodolpho, touched by her innocence and simplicity, watches her without moving. Ecstatically crying to Elvino that now she belongs to him, Amina comes toward Rodolpho with arms outstretched, imploring for a kiss. Avoiding her embrace, the count quickly steps to the door, but turns back when he hears voices outside. Amina, still deep in slumber, goes to the bed and lies down. Rodolpho steps out of the french windows, closes them after him, and disappears.

Led by Alessio, the villagers push open the door of the bedroom and enter on tiptoe. Having learned that Rodolpho is lord of the manor, they have come to bid him welcome. In hushed voices they sing that he surely will not take offense at being awakened under these circumstances ("Osservate; l'uscio è aperto"). Cautiously approaching the bed, they are dumfounded to see a young woman lying there. Looking at each other, they slyly comment on this remarkable discovery. About to leave, they are startled by the sound of angry voices outside, and a moment later Elvino bursts into the room, followed by Lisa and Teresa.

A long and dramatic ensemble follows, beginning with the phrase sung by Elvino as he exclaims in anger and disbelief over Lisa's assertion that Amina is in the count's bedroom ("E menzogna"). Lisa maliciously points to the bed and tells Elvino to look for himself. Awakened by the uproar, Amina exclaims in bewilderment and confusion. Seeing Elvino, she rises and goes to him, but he repulses her, furiously denouncing her heartless betrayal on the eve of their marriage. The villagers, promptly concluding that Amina has been unfaithful, add their denunciations.

Amina, completely at a loss to understand the situation, throws herself into Teresa's arms and sobs that she has done nothing wrong ("D'un pensiero, e d'un accento"). Elvino's voice blends with hers in a duet obbligato as he gives way to his humiliation and anger. Teresa does her best to convince him that Amina is innocent, assuring him that the truth will soon come to light. In a gesture of protection and comfort, she picks up Lisa's scarf from the bed and puts it gently around Amina's shoulders. The villagers continue to express their sympathy for Elvino.

There is great consternation when Elvino suddenly cries out to Amina that he will never marry her and tells her to go to her new lover ("Non più nozze; al nuovo amante"). The ensemble continues to a fiery climax as Amina distractedly protests her innocence, while Elvino rages that the voice he once loved to hear now fills him with hate. As he and Amina both lament that their happiness has been blighted forever, Lisa gloats over the misery she has brought upon her rival. With her arms protectingly around her foster daughter, Teresa tries to comfort her with assurances that she believes in her innocence. Elvino rushes away, and Teresa slowly leads Amina out of the room, with the villagers following, as the curtain falls.

ACT TWO

[*Scene One*] A pleasant spot in a valley between the village and the manor.[2] The peasants are on their way to the manor to ask the count's aid in clearing Amina's name. In a tuneful chorus ("Qui la selva è piu folta ed ombrosa") they declare that they will rest for a while in the shade and then discuss how they will state their case to the count. They decide that they will bow low—so as to show proper respect—and then say that poor Amina, once beloved by everyone in the village, is now scorned by all and crushed by sorrow ("Signor Conte . . . la povera Amina"). They will then plead with him to tell the truth of the matter and help restore Amina's good name. If successful in their plea, they will rush back to the village, bringing to Amina the cheering news. Having decided on their course of action, the villagers continue on their way.

Amina now slowly approaches, leaning on Teresa for support. She also has decided to go to the count and beg him to intercede for her, but is too weary and faint to go any farther. With assurances that the villagers will do their best to help her, Teresa urges her to return home. Amina looks up and sees Elvino's home in the distance, and the sight inspires tender recollections of the happy days of the past ("Vedi siam noi presso il poder d'Elvino").

As Amina sobs brokenheartedly, Teresa exclaims that Elvino is approaching. Oblivious to everything in his despair, he voices his thoughts in a poignant refrain ("Tutto è sciolto"), lamenting that he has been bereft of all hope. Timidly coming close to him, Amina begs him once more to listen to her, but he turns on her with a flood of bitter reproach. In angry, ringing phrases ("Pasci il guardo e appaga l'alma") he tells her to be content with having shattered his happiness, leaving him a prey to anguish. In a burst of rage he seizes Amina's hand and tears the ring from her finger.

Almost fainting from grief and shame, Amina sinks back in Teresa's arms. At that moment the villagers rush in, exclaiming that the count has declared that Amina is guiltless and that he is on his way to the village to speak in her behalf. But Elvino, consumed with anger, pays no heed to them. Turning to Amina, he voices his thoughts in the great aria "Ah! perchè non posso odiarti." Though she has betrayed him, he cannot hate her, he cries, and then expresses the hope that she will find happiness with another lover. In a choral accompaniment the villagers urge him to wait for the count, who will reveal the truth and put matters right. Ignoring them, Elvino disconsolately sings that though Amina has proved faithless he can never forget his love for her. At the conclusion of the aria he sadly goes on his way. Teresa and Amina, followed by the villagers, depart in another direction.

[*Scene Two*] Outside Teresa's mill.[3] A torrent of water is rapidly turning the mill wheel. Lisa appears, followed by the ever-hopeful Alessio. As

[2] In some versions, Scene One of Act Three.
[3] In some versions, Scene Two of Act Three.

usual, Lisa refuses to listen to his love-making and impatiently tells him to be off. Alessio warns Lisa—who is now planning to persuade Elvino to marry her—that her hopes are in vain, for definite proof of Amina's innocence has come to light. When Lisa sneers at his warning, Alessio declares that he will not stand idly by while she carries on her intrigues. He will have his revenge for being spurned, he says, by telling the count and the whole village of her plotting.

Their conversation is interrupted by a crowd of villagers, who rush in to tell Lisa that Elvino has announced his intention to marry her. Crowding around, they congratulate her in a brief chorus ("Lisa è la sposa"). With malicious glances at Alessio, Lisa exults over her victory in a gay and mocking refrain ("De' lieti auguri a voi"). In a choral accompaniment the villagers hail the new bride-to-be as Alessio expresses his disappointment and chagrin.

While Lisa is reveling in her triumph, Elvino comes in. Asking Lisa's pardon for having spurned her, he says that his love for her has reawakened and then invites her to go to the altar with him. Just as the couple start for the church the count appears and asks Elvino where he is going. To the altar with Lisa, Elvino replies. The count requests him to wait and hear his story. Amina, he declares, is innocent of any wrongdoing. Elvino reminds him that he saw Amina with his own eyes, asleep in the count's bedroom. Rodolpho admits that she was there, then startles everyone by asserting that she was fast asleep when she entered his room.

When Elvino looks at him in utter disbelief, Rodolpho explains the phenomenon of somnambulism ("V'han certuni che dormendo"). There are certain persons, he says, who walk and talk in slumber, completely unaware of their actions. Elvino hears him out and then scornfully remarks that this is merely a tale invented for the purpose of making Amina appear innocent. Ignoring the count's angry rebuke for doubting his word, Elvino takes Lisa's arm and starts to go. The villagers prepare to follow, talking among themselves about the count's fantastic story.

At that moment Teresa comes out of the mill and entreats the crowd to be quiet lest they awaken Amina, who, exhausted by her sorrow, has finally fallen asleep. Seeing Lisa and Elvino arm in arm, she asks them where they are going. To the church to be married, replies Lisa triumphantly, adding that no one can say that *she* was ever found asleep in a nobleman's bedroom at midnight. Turning on her in anger and scorn, Teresa takes Lisa's scarf from the folds of her dress and holds it before her, crying that she found it in the count's bedroom. As Elvino stares at Lisa in stunned surprise, Teresa challenges the count to deny that the scarf was in his room. But Rodolpho can only murmur in consternation.

An ensemble is built up as Elvino upbraids Lisa for her treachery and cries out that there is neither faith nor love left anywhere on earth. Teresa continues to denounce Lisa for her heartless deceit, while Rodolpho comments that Lisa's burning cheeks bear witness to her guilt. Lisa herself cries that everyone is turning against her and bitterly repents her wrongdoing. The villagers express their complete bewilderment over this strange turn of events. After the ensemble rises to a powerful climax the voices subside to a dramatic pianissimo as Elvino expresses his hopelessness and despair in a descending chromatic phrase.

Turning to the count, Elvino distractedly asks whom he can trust, since all have proved false. Rodolpho entreats him to believe that Amina is guiltless and tells him that he is doing her a great wrong by doubting her. As Elvino asks where he will find proof of her innocence, Rodolpho clutches his arm and points to the roof of the mill.

Elvino and the startled throng look up to see Amina, a lamp in her hand, emerge from a dormer window and walk along the edge of the roof toward the bridge. Her trancelike movements indicate that she is walking in her sleep. The crowd kneels and begins to pray softly as Amina starts across the bridge. As she reaches a point above the churning mill wheel, a decayed board breaks under her weight. The lamp falls from her hand as she lurches forward and then recovers herself. There is a gasp of terror from the crowd. Finally she reaches the other side, comes slowly down the stone steps, and stands among the people.

As they stare at her she murmurs that she hears the chime of wedding bells and then piteously laments that she has lost the one she loved. Protesting that she has done no wrong, Amina kneels and prays for Elvino's happiness. Rising suddenly, she feels for the ring on her finger, crying that though Elvino has snatched it from her, he cannot tear his image from her heart. Taking from her bosom the bouquet Elvino gave her, she mourns over the withered flowers in a poignant aria ("Ah! non credea mirarti").

She laments that the flowers, deprived of sunlight and rain, fade and die, like the bliss of love, in one brief summer day. Perhaps the rain of her tears, she sings softly, may restore their loveliness. The count, meanwhile restraining Elvino with great difficulty, warns him to do whatever she asks. Still in her dream, Amina comes toward him, requesting him to return the ring. At the count's direction, Elvino places it upon her finger. Amina turns toward Teresa, asking for her embrace. Prompted by Rodolpho, Teresa takes Amina in her arms, while Elvino kneels before her. Now she is ready to be awakened, the count declares. The shouts of the villagers rouse Amina from her sleep.

Looking around in bewilderment, Amina covers her face with her hands, begging the people not to disturb her dream. Taking her in his arms, Elvino tells her to look upon her husband. Amina utters a cry of rapture. The general rejoicing is expressed in an exultant chorus ("Vanne al tempio").

Amina voices her joy in the great aria "Ah! non giunge uman pensiero," one of the most brilliant and difficult numbers in operatic soprano repertoire. Sweeping aside all thoughts of sorrow, Amina rejoices that the evil dream of hatred and suspicion has been dispelled, leaving the blissful reality of love which she and Elvino will share forever. In a choral accompaniment the villagers wish her happiness and urge her to hasten to the altar. The aria and the ensemble rise to a glittering climax as the curtain falls.

Tannhäuser

by RICHARD WAGNER

[1813–1883]

Libretto by the Composer

CHARACTERS

Heinrich Tannhäuser, a minstrel knight..........................*Tenor*
Elisabeth, niece of the Landgraf.............................*Soprano*
Venus, Goddess of Love....................................*Soprano*
Hermann, Landgraf of Thuringia...............................*Bass*

Wolfram von Eschenbach		*Baritone*
Walther von der Vogelweide		*Tenor*
Biterolf	minstrel knights..............	*Bass*
Heinrich der Schreiber		*Tenor*
Reinmar von Zweter		*Bass*

A young shepherd...*Soprano*
Four noble pages.....................*Two sopranos and two contraltos*
The Three Graces, sirens, naiads, nymphs, bacchantes, nobles,
knights, ladies, and pilgrims

Place: Near Eisenach, in Thuringia, Germany
Time: Early in the thirteenth century
First performance: Dresden, Germany, October 19, 1845
Original language: German

FOR THE BASIS of this great opera of medieval German legend we must look partly to history, partly to mythology, and partly to Wagner's own rich imagination. The action takes place in Thuringia, where stands the mighty castle of the Wartburg. Near the castle is the hill known sometimes as the Horselberg, sometimes as the Venusberg (Hill of Venus), because, according to legend, it was beneath this hill that the goddess Venus had her abode. Wagner himself visited the castle of the Wartburg, and he took his story from the ancient traditions that centered around this picturesque old-world edifice where, six centuries earlier, the knight minstrels, or minnesingers, were said to have gathered in its great hall for tournaments of song.

The opera revolves around one of these legendary knight minstrels, the passionate, quarrelsome Tannhäuser. Seeking refuge from the griefs of the world, Tannhäuser has left his earthly existence to live under the magic spell of Venus, Goddess of Love. As the opera opens, Tannhäuser has been with Venus a year and a day.

This story of sacred and profane love offered Wagner wonderful opportunities for colorful scenes, rich music, and striking contrasts—as, for example, between the seductive spell of Venus and her supernatural realm and the simple nobility of the fervent band of pilgrims, whose march comes to us again and again in the opera.

The opera opens with the familiar overture, beginning with the solemn *Pilgrim's Chorus*. As it reaches the sensuous melody of the *Venusberg Music*, the curtain rises on the opening scene that takes place in the weird and supernatural grotto in the interior of the Venusberg, where the goddess holds court and preys upon the souls of men.

ACT ONE

[*Scene One*] The Hill of Venus. When the curtains first part they disclose an alluring scene. In the farthest visible background of an apparently endless cave a bluish lake is seen in which naiads are bathing, while sirens are reclining on its banks. In the center are groups of dancing nymphs. Reclining on mounds at the sides are caressing couples, some of whom join the dances of the nymphs in the chorus of the scene. In the foreground Venus is reclining on a couch, surrounded by the Three Graces. Kneeling before her is Tannhäuser. The cave glows with a strange roseate light.

A train of bacchantes rushes from the rear of the cave in a tumultuous dance. They dart wildly through the groups of nymphs and couples, inciting them to the frenzied and voluptuous *Bacchanale*. The dancers suddenly pause and listen to the beautiful singing of the *Chorus of Sirens*, then resume their dance, which rises to the wildest excitement in the famous *Venusberg Music*.

When the frenzy is at its height a sudden weariness comes over the dancers. The couples separate and rest near the entrance of the cave. The bacchantes disappear as a mist gathers and spreads with growing density, gradually enveloping the sleepers. Only a small space in the foreground now remains visible, where Venus, Tannhäuser, and the Three Graces are seen. The Three Graces perform their dance interpretive of the stories of Europa and the White Bull and Leda and the Swan as these scenes loom up in the background. Then they depart, leaving only Venus and Tannhäuser.

Suddenly Tannhäuser raises his head as though starting from a dream. Venus draws him back again, caressingly. She asks the knight what is troubling him, and he replies that he dreams of the life he left on earth. At her insistence he takes up his harp and sings passionately his *Hymn to Venus* ("Dir töne Lob!"). But he sings also that he is weary of the life of the senses which he has been leading and finally begs for freedom from her spell so that he may return to earth, with its mingled pain and pleasure. Angry that her love is praised, yet scorned, she cries that he shall not go. Tannhäuser insists that fate impels his choice.

Venus, with a cry, turns away from him, burying her face in her hands. She seeks gradually to win Tannhäuser's glances again and turns toward him with a seductive smile, singing "Beloved one, come [Geliebter, komm]!" Sirens are again heard singing softly in the distance. Venus once more draws Tannhäuser lovingly to her and tries to charm away his restlessness. With great emotion he takes his harp and once more sings her praises ("Stets soll nur dir") but still begs to be released. Then Venus, in great fury, threatens him. She tells him he will be scorned on earth, an outcast, and that his Christian God will never forgive him. Tannhäuser replies simply that he places his faith in the Virgin Mary. At mention of the name of the Blessed Virgin, the unholy spell is broken. With a cry, Venus shrinks and vanishes. Cymbals crash, and there is complete darkness while the scene changes.

[*Scene Two*] A valley near the Wartburg. Tannhäuser suddenly finds himself in the midst of a peaceful valley, with the sun shining and blue skies above. His life in the Venusberg is over. In the background looms the mighty Wartburg, with a winding mountain path leading down from it. In the foreground is a shrine to the Virgin. From a nearby hill comes the tinkle of sheep bells. On a small rise a young shepherd reclines, playing on his pipe. He sings a pastoral folklike tune to Holda, Goddess of Spring ("Frau Holda kam aus dem Berg hervor").

A company of pilgrims passes in the distance on their journey to Rome, and the *Pilgrim's Chorus* is heard as the wayfarers thread their way down the mountain path. The shepherd, hearing their song, stops his playing and listens reverently. Waving his cap, he calls out to them to breathe a prayer for him when they reach Rome.

All the while Tannhäuser has been standing spellbound, awed at the beauty of the scene. Deeply overcome, he falls to his knees in prayer as the procession passes by the Virgin's shrine and disappears down the mountain road. The shepherd also goes his way, and the sheep bells are heard fainter and fainter in the distance. Tannhäuser remains on his knees, absorbed in fervent prayer. Tears choke his voice. He bows his head to the ground and seems to weep bitterly. Distant bells chime as the chant of the pilgrims dies away.

Then comes a sound of hunting horns, drawing nearer and nearer. A group in hunting dress comes upon the scene. It is Hermann, the Landgraf, with his retinue. In this group is Wolfram, who recognizes his old friend Tannhäuser. Astonished, Tannhäuser rises hastily and bows in silence to the Landgraf, who welcomes his long-lost favorite. Tannhäuser answers their questions vaguely and speaks of having traveled in strange lands. He tries to avoid them, saying he is doomed to roam alone, but they press him to stay. When Wolfram mentions the lovely Princess Elisabeth's name, Tannhäuser stands entranced. Wolfram sings ("Als du im kühnem Sange") that Elisabeth has been grieving for him and his songs ever since he left the Wartburg and has not entered the hall of minstrels during his absence. He appeals to Tannhäuser to return. The music of this appeal is especially impressive as the others add their entreaties to Wolfram's. Tannhäuser is deeply touched. He throws himself into Wolfram's arms, greets the minstrels in turn, and bows to the Landgraf, giving his joyful consent to rejoin his old comrades ("Ha, jetzt erkenne ich sie wieder").

Other members of the Landgraf's hunting party come upon the scene. The Hunters sound the horns. Tannhäuser then gladly rejoins them as they set off for the Wartburg and the coming song tournament, singing in chorus ("Er kehrt zurück den wir verloren!").

ACT TWO

The Hall of Minstrels in the Wartburg. Through the spacious opening at the rear we have an open view of the courtyard and the valley below. Elisabeth enters and rapturously greets the hall, overjoyed that Tannhäuser's voice is now to glorify it once again, in the lovely aria "Dich, theure Halle."

As Elisabeth finishes, Tannhäuser is led by Wolfram through the open doorway at the rear, into the hall. For a time he stands leaning against a pillar and then throws himself impetuously at the feet of Elisabeth. In timid confusion, the maiden bids him rise, tells him that this hall is *his* domain, which he has conquered with his songs. Gently Elisabeth asks where he has been. Tannhäuser, slowly rising, pleads that a veil be thrown forever between yesterday and today, for Heaven has wrought a change in his spirit. "I praise the power that wrought it from out my heart's recesses [Ich preise dieses Wunder aus meines Herzen's Tiefe]!" Elisabeth sings. Tannhäuser and Elisabeth are fervently reunited in the duet "Gepriesen sei die Stunde."

Wolfram has remained in the background. He realizes now that his own hopes for Elisabeth are gone. His grave and dignified self-forgetfulness forms a curious contrast to the rapture of Tannhäuser and Elisabeth.

As Tannhäuser and Wolfram leave, the Landgraf makes his appearance, welcoming Elisabeth to the place she has shunned so long and proclaiming her queen of the coming song contest. He tells her that all the nobles will be there, because once again her hand will bestow the victor's wreath.

The court now gathers with much pomp. Four pages announce the arrival of the various groups of guests. The knights, nobles, ladies, and attendants enter and are received by the Landgraf and Elisabeth. This is an inspiring scene of pageantry and ceremony as the music of the *Tannhäuser March* wells up to its tremendous climax. The chorus of knights and nobles sings "Freudig begrüssen wir die edle Halle," joined by the chorus of ladies. The lords and ladies take their places on one side of the great hall of song, the Landgraf and Elisabeth occupying the two seats of honor.

The minstrels now enter, greeting the assembly in stately fashion, and take their places on the opposite side of the hall. The Landgraf rises and announces that Love will be the theme of the song contest and that the hand of Elisabeth herself shall be the prize to the winner ("Gar viel und schön ward hier in dieser Halle").

The contest begins. The four pages collect from each singer a folded slip of paper bearing his name. The slips are placed in a gold cup, which is presented to Elisabeth. She selects one of the papers, hands it to the pages, and in quartet they announce the name. Wolfram is the first chosen. He sings with power and eloquence his *Eulogy of Love* ("Blick' ich umher"). It is a song of placid love for Elisabeth, in which he says he will worship her from afar. He is well applauded by the minstrels and nobles.

During Wolfram's singing Tannhäuser's attitude is one of impatience and scorn. Suddenly his expression turns to exquisite delight. He rises as though dreaming. He seeks the strings of his harp, and an uncanny smile indicates that a strange emotion has control of him. Then he powerfully sweeps the strings, his whole being betraying that he hardly knows where he is. He even seems unaware of Elisabeth as he boastfully sings of sensual passion. There is general consternation in the assembly. Chaste Elisabeth is startled with conflicting emotions of rapture and anxious surprise. Biterolf—a hot-headed knight—arises quickly and angrily rebukes Tannhäuser, but Tannhäuser, with ever-increasing vehemence, asks Biterolf what *he* knows of such bliss and reiterates his view of love. The nobles, now in great excitement, think he has gone mad. Biterolf draws his sword. The Landgraf, however, calls for order.

Wolfram tries to calm the rising excitement with a second eulogy to love ("O Himmel! Lass' dich jetzt erflehen!"). Tannhäuser, forgetting himself completely, bursts into the *Hymn to Venus* ("Dir Göttin der Liebe"), crying out that he alone among that company of dull mortals has tasted the fullness of love, that Venus alone can teach love. There is general disorder and horror, for they all realize now that Tannhäuser has visited the Venusberg.

The ladies leave the hall in great dismay. Elisabeth, pale and trembling, alone remains. The Landgraf, knights, and minstrels have left their seats and are conferring together. Tannhäuser, standing aloof, remains silent, as though in rapture. The knights and nobles now press toward him angrily with drawn swords, threatening to kill him for his blasphemy. Elisabeth rushes between them, staying their hands, and all stand back in amazement as she shields Tannhäuser. Again they try to close upon the minstrel, and again Elisabeth intervenes, telling them it is not for them to judge him, that he must have his chance to earn heavenly salvation ("Zurück von ihm!"). She pleads that she, who is crushed and wronged, will pray for his soul.

Tannhäuser is now overcome with shame and contrition and, falling to the floor, prays for mercy on his soul. The Landgraf, with great solemnity, steps into their midst and pronounces judgment ("Ein furchtbares Verbrechen ward begangen"). Tannhäuser is banished from the realm. The Landgraf suggests that the knight join a band of pilgrims who are about to leave to seek absolution at Rome, while Elisabeth calls attention to the comforting promise of the *Pilgrim's Chorus*, which echoes up from the valley.

A sudden ray of hope inspires Tannhäuser. He throws himself at Elisabeth's feet, devoutly kisses the hem of her robe, and strides out to join the pilgrim band, calling in exultation, "To Rome!" The chorus of nobles repeats the words, and Elisabeth looks on in despair and pity as the curtain falls.

ACT THREE

A valley near the Wartburg. It is the same peaceful scene in which Tannhäuser found himself after he had left Venus. Elisabeth has waited hopefully and prayerfully for Tannhäuser's return from his pilgrimage, but in vain. Several months have gone by, and the erring knight has not returned.

Twilight is approaching. Before the shrine to the Virgin, Elisabeth, clothed in white, kneels in prayer. Wolfram approaches from a woodland path and stops as he becomes aware of Elisabeth's presence. He muses on her incessant prayers that Tannhäuser will return forgiven ("Wohl wusst' ich hier sie im Gebet zu finden").

From the distance comes the song of a band of pilgrims. Elisabeth rises eagerly. We hear the beautiful *Pilgrim's Chorus* gradually growing louder as the band of penitents, passing by the shrine, makes its way slowly down through the valley. Elisabeth has been anxiously watching for Tannhäuser among the returning pilgrims, but he is nowhere to be seen. She falls upon her knees once more and prays to the Blessed Virgin that she be set free of this life and that Tannhäuser's sin be forgiven. This is the fervent aria *Elisabeth's Prayer* (*Elisabeth's Gebet*—"Allmächt'ge Jungfrau").

For a long time she remains kneeling, then slowly rises, as if in a trance. Wolfram approaches to speak to her, but she bids him be silent, and by gesture expresses to him her heartfelt thanks for his faithful love. Her way now leads to heaven, where she has a high purpose to fulfill. She does not want him to accompany or follow her. Slowly ascending the footpath leading toward the Wartburg, she disappears from view. The valley darkens with the approach of night. The faithful Wolfram seats himself at the foot of the hill and begins to finger softly on his harp. As the evening star shines in the distant sky he sings to it, asking that it bless and guide Elisabeth ("O du mein holder Abendstern"). This *Song to the Evening Star* is one of Wagner's loveliest melodies.

In the darkening night a stumbling figure appears in ragged pilgrim dress. It is Tannhäuser. His face is pale and drawn, and he comes with faltering steps, supported by a staff. Wolfram asks how he dares return unforgiven. Tannhäuser declares wildly that he is on his way to the Venusberg again. Wolfram asks in horror if he has not been to Rome. Tannhäuser bitterly answers yes. As Wolfram inquires what took place there, Tannhäuser seats himself in despair. Wolfram is about to sit beside him, but Tannhäuser waves him away, saying that he is accursed. He tells how the Pope had absolved all the other pilgrims but had turned upon him with a grim denunciation. If you have tasted of the forbidden delights of the Venusberg, the Pope had said, then you are doomed forever. Even as the staff I hold in my hand can never burst into bloom, so your soul can never be reborn, nor your sins redeemed. Forsaken by all, Tannhäuser cries, he can find welcome only from Venus. Yes, he is again on his way to the Venusberg. Wolfram tries to stop him in his godless raving.

Light clouds now gradually veil the scene. Tannhäuser calls aloud for Venus. A confusing whirl of dancing forms becomes visible to the strains of the *Venusberg Music* as Venus appears, reclining upon her couch, singing her delirious and seductive melody. He is about to go to her, but Wolfram restrains him and begs him to gain his soul's salvation. The two knights struggle violently. Tannhäuser will not listen to Wolfram's entreaties. Just as Tannhäuser tears himself loose, crying that the heavens are closed to him, Wolfram tells him that salvation is his because an angel prays for him —Elisabeth. Tannhäuser stands spellbound. He repeats the name, "Elisabeth," as his mind turns once more to the true and pure love of this gentle princess. Venus cries out, "Woe! I have lost him [Weh! Mir Verloren]!" and the vision disappears.

The clouds gradually darken, and through them bright torchlights gleam. Then, as the first streaks of dawn begin to glow, a funeral procession winds its way down from the Wartburg into the valley. Pilgrims, followed by the minstrels, bear an open bier on which lies the body of Elisabeth. They are followed by the Landgraf, knights, and nobles, singing that Tannhäuser has been absolved through Elisabeth's love. Wolfram now leads Tannhäuser to the bier of Elisabeth. Sinking down beside it, he cries, "Holy Elisabeth, pray for me!" and dies.

One by one the torches are extinguished and the scene is illumined by the pale, clear morning light. A chorus of young pilgrims enters, singing of the miracle they have seen. With them they have brought the Pope's staff, which has miraculously blossomed with new green leaves—a token of God's forgiveness. As they sing of Tannhäuser's redemption, the curtain falls.

Thaïs

by JULES MASSENET

[1842–1912]

Libretto by
LOUIS GALLET

Based on the novel by Anatole France

CHARACTERS

Palemon, an old cenobite monk	Bass
Athanaël, a young cenobite	Baritone
Nicias, a wealthy young man of Alexandria	Tenor
A servant of Nicias	Baritone
Crobyle ⎱ his two beautiful slave girls	⎰ Soprano
Myrtale ⎰	⎱ Mezzo-soprano
Thaïs, actress and courtesan of Alexandria	Soprano
La Charmeuse, a dancer	Soprano
Albine, an abbess	Mezzo-soprano

Cenobites, friends of Nicias, actors, dancers, citizens
of Alexandria, nuns

Place: Thebes, Alexandria, and the Egyptian desert
Time: Fourth century
First performance: Grand Opéra, Paris, March 16, 1894
Original language: French

NEXT TO *Manon, Thaïs,* written some ten years later, is probably the best known of Massenet's operas. Like most of his music, the opera reveals the composer's gift for rich, sensuous melody and effective dramatic characterization. The most familiar music in the opera is perhaps the *Meditation,* an orchestral interlude which has long been a concert favorite.

ACT ONE

[*Scene One*] The huts of the cenobites, a monastic order, on the banks of the Nile. Seated about a table in the open, Palemon, oldest of the monks, and twelve others are eating their frugal evening meal—bread, salt, hyssop, and honey. One place at the table is vacant. It is that of Athanaël, one of the younger brethren. Palemon rises and gives thanks for the food. As the other monks make their responses one of them mentions Athanaël in his prayer. In answer to their questions about the absent brother, Palemon tells them that he soon should be returning from Alexandria. Only last night, Palemon goes on, he dreamed he saw the young monk hastening home.

While the others repeat his name in awed tones Athanaël appears. He walks slowly and painfully, as though worn by exhaustion and suffering.

The cenobites greet him eagerly and then comment among themselves regarding his careworn appearance. Sitting down at his place, he pushes away the food they offer him. Seemingly a prey to torturing thoughts, he suddenly declares that Alexandria is being corrupted by an evil and dissolute woman—Thaïs. The monks ask him to tell them about her. In a somber refrain Athanaël begins the story of his first meeting with her ("Hélas! enfant encore"). He relates that in his youth he went to visit Thaïs, but at the very threshold of her house God prevented him from entering and yielding to sin. In feverish tones he cries that he must save her soul.

Trying to calm him, Palemon advises him to have nothing to do with the people of this godless age, who will only destroy him with their wickedness. He then urges Athanaël and the others to retire. After a brief prayer ("Que les noirs démons de l'abime") the monks go into their huts. Lying down on a pallet in front of his rude abode, Athanaël commends his soul to God and then falls asleep. The scene is gradually enveloped in darkness.

As an exquisite melody soars from the orchestra Athanaël's vision materializes in the background. A huge theater in Alexandria becomes visible. On the stage, Thaïs, in the role of Aphrodite, moves in a voluptuous dance. Prolonged applause and shouts of "Thaïs" are heard faintly, as in a dream. As Thaïs brings her dance to a wild climax the vision fades and day dawns.

Athanaël awakens and springs to his feet, crying out against the torment of his dream ("Horreur! Ténèbres éternelles!"). Prostrating himself, he launches into a feverish prayer in which he sings that the terrible vision was a sign from God that he is to go to Alexandria and save the soul of Thaïs ("Toi qui mis la pitié dans nos âmes"). Calling the other cenobites around him, he tells them that he is going back to the city to save Thaïs from eternal damnation. Palemon at first tries to dissuade him but finally allows him to go. The monks accompany him for a short distance, then kneel in prayer as Athanaël takes his leave of them. His voice dies away in the distance as he prays for courage and strength ("Esprit de lumière et de grâce").

[Scene Two]   The palm-shaded terrace of the home of Nicias in Alexandria. The city and the sea are visible in the distance. Off the terrace is a banquet room. Athanaël hesitantly approaches. A servant of Nicias bars his way and rudely tells him to do his begging elsewhere. Athanaël requests him to inform Nicias that an old friend has come to see him. The servant at first tries to drive him away but cringes at Athanaël's imperious command and goes to summon his master.

Looking out over the city, Athanaël sings a dramatic monologue in which he laments that Alexandria, the fair city of his youth, has fallen upon evil days ("Voilà donc la terrible cité!"). In the climax of the aria he implores the angels of heaven to cleanse the city of its sin.

In sharp contrast to Athanaël's lamentation come the voices of women, blending in phrases of mocking gaiety. Soon Crobyle and Myrtale, two lovely slave girls, appear escorting their master, Nicias, a wealthy and pleasure-loving Alexandrian. A cynical and worldly philosopher, he is at the same time kindly and generous. Seeing Athanaël, he runs to him and embraces the monk affectionately, greeting him as a former colleague among the philosophers. With a good-natured gibe at Athanaël's unkempt appearance Nicias inquires the reason for his visit.

The monk asks if he knows Thaïs. Very well indeed, replies Nicias with a laugh. He has sold practically all of his possessions, down to his vineyards and his mill, for a few days of her companionship. But even all this wealth, he adds ruefully, cannot tempt her to remain with him. Athanaël then tells Nicias that he has come to save the soul of Thaïs and persuade her to enter a convent.

With cynical amusement Nicias reminds the monk that Thaïs has all Alexandria at her feet. Moreover, she is a high priestess of Venus, a goddess who cannot be defied with impunity. Athanaël declares that God will protect him. Nicias, with an air of humoring his friend, tells him that Thaïs is coming to his house for a banquet this evening after her performance at the theater. There he may see this beauty whom he proposes to convert. Athanaël asks if he may borrow some suitable attire for the banquet. Nicias orders Crobyle and Myrtale to provide clean robes for his friend and to make him presentable for the festivities. At a sign from the women the servant brings robes and perfumes. As the two men continue talking Crobyle and Myrtale, laughing merrily, pour perfume on the monk's head and comb out his ragged beard. Nicias remarks that under their ministrations Athanaël is beginning to look as he did in the days of his youth ("Je vais donc te revoir brillant").

This marks the beginning of an interesting ensemble. Obsessed with his self-imposed mission, Athanaël endeavors to keep the conversation on the subject of Thaïs. As the slaves adorn him they remark over his flashing eyes and handsome features. When they coax him to remove his tattered monk's robe he pushes them impatiently aside. Nicias urges him to make the most of the attentions that are being showered upon him. With the help of their master, the slave girls finally persuade Athanaël to don a richly colored robe, and then they put bracelets on his arms and sandals on his feet. In the climax of the ensemble Crobyle and Myrtale marvel that this monk is as handsome as a god, Nicias comments approvingly, and Athanaël prays for strength to accomplish his task.

Shouts are heard in the distance. Looking toward the city, Nicias announces that Thaïs is approaching. A group of actors and philosophers, all friends of Nicias, arrive on the terrace, and shortly afterward Thaïs herself appears. She is hailed in majestic choral phrases. After greeting her Nicias invites his friends to go into the banquet room. As Thaïs starts to follow the others Nicias detains her. Gazing at him with a mocking smile, she remarks that tonight she will sit at his banquet table for the last time. Nicias muses that their idyl has endured only a week. Their voices blend in sweeping phrases as they sing that tomorrow they will be nothing to each other but a name ("Demain, je ne serai pour toi qu'un nom").

At that point Athanaël returns from the banquet room with several of his erstwhile friends, with whom he is in earnest discussion. Catching sight of Thaïs, he stands as though transfixed. She likewise notices him and remarks to Nicias that she remembers having seen him before. Nicias tells her that Athanaël is a philosopher who took holy vows and went into the desert to live as a monk. This man, he continues, has come to save her soul. Puzzled, Thaïs asks what doctrine he teaches. Athanaël, who has meanwhile come close to her, answers that he teaches contempt of the flesh and atonement for sin.

Gazing at him in mingled curiosity and wonder, Thaïs declares that she knows no law but love. When Athanaël angrily accuses her of blasphemy she answers him in a sensuous, enticing refrain ("Qui te fait si sévère"). She wonders why he has denied himself the pleasures which the world has to offer and asks him why he has not drunk deep of passion. Alluringly she invites him to taste the pleasures of life, the guests repeating her phrases in an impressive chorus.

Athanaël cries out that he will not be tempted and that he will follow Thaïs to her very palace door to bring her salvation. As the guests mock and deride him he fiercely denounces their sinfulness. Finally Thaïs rushes forward, assumes a seductive pose of the dance of Aphrodite seen in the vision, and then challenges the monk to come to her home and defy the power of the goddess she serves—Venus. As Athanaël recoils in horror and rushes out, the curtain falls.

ACT TWO

[*Scene One*] A room in the house of Thaïs. She comes in with a group of friends. Weary and preoccupied, she soon tires of their company and dismisses them. Alone in her room, she voices her disillusionment in a dramatic soliloquy ("Ah! je suis seule, seule enfin!"). She muses sadly on her loneliness and on the shallow, tiresome people who surround her, and then continues her reflections in the beautiful aria, "Dis-moi que je suis belle"— known as the *Air du miroir*. Gazing into her mirror, she demands that it assure her that her loveliness will last forever. She is horrified at the thought that perhaps someday she may be old and ugly. With passionate intensity she prays to Venus, imploring her to promise that Thaïs will be young and desirable until the end of time ("Vénus, invisible et présente!").

As she finishes her invocation she sees Athanaël standing in the doorway, watching her intently. Graciously inviting him in, Thaïs remarks that he has kept his word to seek her out at her home. Athanaël murmurs a prayer for strength to withstand her temptations. Gazing at Thaïs, he marvels at her beauty, exclaiming that she is indeed worthy to be conquered for the Lord. Mistaking his zeal for ardor, Thaïs warns the monk not to love her. Athanaël cries out that he loves her in a way that she does not yet understand. His love is for her soul alone, and that love will bring her new and profound joy. Thaïs mockingly assures him that all the raptures of love are familiar to her.

In fanatical ecstasy Athanaël declares that he will cleanse her heart of its shameful, earthly love and will lead her into the way of eternal life. At those words, Thaïs, remembering her prayer to Venus for eternal beauty, looks at the monk in mingled fear and awe. For the sake of this strange love, she murmurs, she will yield to him. Going over to her statue of Venus, she lights the perfumed incense in the burner before it and, as though performing a sacred rite, begins intoning her invocation to the goddess. The incense rises about her in a cloud. Athanaël, tormented by her beauty, prays that her charms may be veiled from his sight.

Shaken by his emotions, he tears off the robes that cover his tunic, crying out that he, Athanaël, a holy monk of the desert, will curse the bonds of flesh that hold Thaïs captive ("Je suis Athanaël, Moine d'Antinoé!"). In thunderous tones he commands her to rise from the tomb of her living death in degradation and sin. Seized by an unreasoning fear, Thaïs prostrates herself before him and begs for mercy. She implores him not to blame her because destiny made her beautiful and distractedly entreats him to save her from death. Athanaël triumphantly assures her that she will be the bride of Christ and will have eternal life. In ecstatic phrases Thaïs sings of the strange new joy that is flooding her soul.

At that moment the voice of Nicias is heard in the distance, calling out to Thaïs that he has come for one last kiss. Thaïs cringes at the words and exclaims in disgust at the thought of his pagan caresses. Nicias's voice is heard again, singing with careless gaiety that tomorrow he will be only a name to her. Thaïs asks Athanaël to tell her erstwhile lover that she no longer cares for the pleasures he has to offer. Athanaël declares that he will stand guard at her door and wait there until she is ready to go with him.

In a sudden change of mood Thaïs turns on the monk, crying that she is Thaïs, the courtesan, and Thaïs she will remain. Protesting that she wants nothing of Athanaël or his God, she bursts into wild laughter that breaks into hysterical sobbing. As Athanaël looks at her in anger and surprise, the curtain falls.

Between the foregoing scene and the next, the famous *Meditation* is played by a solo violin with soft orchestral accompaniment. The music symbolizes the spiritual regeneration of Thaïs.

[*Scene Two*]   In front of the house of Thaïs. Near the door is a small ivory statue of Eros, with a lighted lamp in front. Athanaël is lying asleep on the pavement not far from the doorway. In the house next to that of Thaïs, Nicias and his friends are carousing. The windows are brightly lighted and sounds of music and gaiety come from within. Thaïs, holding a lamp, comes out of her house. She looks around, sees Athanaël, and goes over to him.

The monk awakens as she softly calls to him. With deep humility she tells him that she has wept and prayed all night long, and now her soul is filled with a blinding light. In its radiance she sees clearly how empty and meaningless her past life has been. Saying that she is ready to obey his every command, she asks him what she must do. Athanaël tells her that she must go with him to the Albine convent in the desert ("Non loin d'ici, vers l'occident"). There, in penance and meditation, she will purge herself of her sins and find divine happiness. He himself will take her to Albine, the abbess, who will consecrate her to the Lord. Thaïs joyfully sings that she is ready to go.

Athanaël then sternly tells her that she must first destroy everything that binds her to the past—her house, her possessions, and the images that are symbolic of her shameful life. As Thaïs meekly goes to comply with his command she pauses before the statue of Eros at the door. Taking it up, she asks Athanaël, in an appealing refrain, if she may be allowed to keep only this image of the god of love ("Cette image d'ivoire"). She has done her best to serve this gentle god, Thaïs sings, and regrets only those moments when she disobeyed him by not giving herself wholly to love. With disarming simplicity she tells Athanaël to take the image to some monastery, where it may inspire those who look upon it to think of love and thus turn to God. It was a gift from Nicias, she adds softly.

In a violent outburst Athanaël curses Nicias as the source of corruption and evil and then smashes the statue to bits on the pavement. Everything must be destroyed, he shouts; everything that connects her with the past must be devoured by flames and thus consigned to oblivion. Shocked and frightened by his rage, Thaïs repeats his foreboding words in a dramatic unison phrase ("Que tout ce qui fut moi retourne à la poussière"). Slowly she follows the monk into the house.

Nicias and his companions, laughing and singing, come out of the other house. Flushed with wine, Nicias urges all to continue the revelry, proclaiming that at the gaming table he has won back thirty times the price he paid for the love of Thaïs. The crowd hails his good fortune. Nicias calls for dancers and entertainers, for more torches and wilder music. Nothing is real but life, he cries exultantly, and folly triumphs over wisdom. The dancers then appear and perform a series of ballets.

The entertainment is brought to a climax with the entrance of a beautiful dancer, La Charmeuse. At Nicias's command, Crobyle and Myrtale, playing musical instruments, accompany the dance with a lovely duet ("Celle qui vient est plus belle"). At intervals La Charmeuse pauses to sing obbligato phrases. After her dance the ballet reappears and brings the festivities to a close in a whirl of abandoned revelry. The guests hail the dancers in a tremendous choral outburst of "Evohè!"

Suddenly all eyes turn to the house of Thaïs as Athanaël emerges carrying a torch. Nicias and his friends, assuming that Thaïs has added the monk to her list of conquests, shout his name in delighted surprise. Hurling the torch to the ground, Athanaël tells them that the shameless Thaïs who was their favorite is dead. Behold the new Thaïs, he cries. At those words Thaïs comes out of her house, walking slowly with bowed head. Her hair is flowing loosely over her shoulders and she is wearing a coarse, plain tunic. The crowd gasps in astonishment. Within the house smoke is beginning to billow up and the glare of flames can be seen.

When Athanaël exhorts her to come with him and leave the city forever, Nicias and the crowd burst into a chorus of protest ("Jamais! Non! L'emmener!"). This marks the beginning of the dramatic ensemble which concludes the act. The people voice their dismay and anger over the fact that the monk is taking their beloved Thaïs away. When Nicias tries to restrain her Athanaël roughly pushes him aside, crying that unholy hands must not defile this child of God. The people stare in horror at the flames which are consuming Thaïs's home with all its treasures and then turn fiercely on Athanaël, threatening to kill him. A stone hurled by someone in the crowd strikes Athanaël in the face. Laughing in savage glee, the crowd presses closer to Athanaël and Thaïs, determined to tear her away from the monk. Nicias does his best to protect the two as the people clamor for Athanaël's death. Finally he reaches into his purse and flings a handful of coins among the crowd. As they scramble for the money Nicias turns to Thaïs and bids her farewell in a ringing phrase, warning her that she will never be able to forget the life she has deserted ("Adieu, Thaïs! En vain tu m'oubliéras!"). The crowd surges back, clamoring for more gold. Nicias flings out another handful, while Thaïs and Athanaël make their escape. As Thaïs's house collapses into flaming ruins, the curtain falls.

ACT THREE

[Scene One] An oasis in the desert. At one side is a well shaded by palms. Nearby is a shelter for travelers. Beyond the oasis the white walls of the Albine convent gleam in the blinding desert sun. During a murmurous orchestral interlude several women come to the well for water and then leave. Soon Athanaël and Thaïs appear. Utterly exhausted, Thaïs begs the monk to allow her to rest awhile. But he relentlessly drives her on, declaring that she must punish her body so that she may be cleansed from sin. She who was once the delight of pagans, he goes on fiercely, is now dedicated to God, and she must learn to despise the flesh as she once worshiped it. With fanatical zeal he exhorts her to repent.

On the verge of fainting, Thaïs implores him to let her rest. Taking her in his arms, Athanaël leads her into the shade. His manner grows tender as he sings that the sight of her torn and bleeding feet have awakened his pity ("Ah! des gouttes de sang coulent"). Overcome with remorse over his harshness, he falls weeping at her feet and then passionately sings her name.

Thaïs, musing that her name sounds sweet on his lips, is ready to go on, but Athanaël says he will first bring her water and fruit so that she may be refreshed. Pointing to the white walls of the convent in the distance, he tells her that there is her goal. When Athanaël goes, Thaïs reflects over his kindness in a tender refrain ("O messager de Dieu"). She rejoices that the peace which he has brought to her soul triumphs over bodily pain. Athanaël returns and gives her a cup of water and some fruit. Their voices blend in a melodious duet as they rejoice in the consolation of food and drink and then express the exaltation of their spiritual union ("Baigne d'eau mes mains et mes lèvres").

They are interrupted by the sound of chanting in the distance. Looking toward the desert, Athanaël exclaims that the Abbess Albine and the nuns are approaching. When they arrive at the oasis Athanaël greets the abbess with great dignity. In a solemn refrain he tells her that he has brought a repentant sinner to the fold to be consecrated to God ("La paix du Seigneur soit avec toi").

He leads Thaïs to the abbess, who embraces her. Saying that his task is now over, Athanaël takes leave of Thaïs, exhorting her to be diligent in penitence and prayer. Deeply moved, Thaïs expresses her gratitude to him for saving her soul and then bids him farewell forever ("Adieu pour toujours!"). Athanaël recoils at the words. As she leaves with the abbess Thaïs sings that they will meet again in heaven. Gazing after her as though spellbound, Athanaël sorrowfully muses on her going. Tormented by the thought that he is never to see her again, he cries out in anguish. As he gazes longingly after her the curtain falls.

[*Scene Two*] The huts of the cenobites, as in Act One. It is sunset. Heavy storm clouds are hanging in the west. The monks comment in chorus on the gathering storm ("Que le ciel est pesant!"). At Palemon's direction they bring in their supplies of corn and fruit to protect them from damage. One of the monks asks about Athanaël, and another replies that he has fasted for twenty days.

As they are talking Athanaël appears. Gaunt and haggard, with staring eyes, he takes no notice of the others as he walks among them and approaches Palemon. As the monks withdraw Athanaël implores Palemon to remain with him. In a dramatic refrain he confesses the tortures of the spirit he has undergone since his experience with Thaïs ("Tu sais, O Palemon"). He saved the soul of Thaïs, he cries, only to be tormented by dreams of her ravishing beauty. All the lovely creatures of history are concentrated in his vision of Thaïs, and this vision gives him no rest day or night. Shaken by his passion, he falls at Palemon's feet. The old monk sadly reminds him of how he warned against mingling with the people of this sinful age. Embracing him in a pathetic gesture of comfort, Palemon leaves.

Athanaël prays silently for a moment and then lies down on the pallet in front of his hut. Thaïs appears to him in a vision, tantalizingly repeating the words she spoke to him at their first meeting at the home of Nicias, "Qui te fait si sévère." As Athanaël, in his dream, frantically calls her name, she vanishes with a burst of sardonic laughter.

Ghostly voices now chant that Thaïs of Alexandria is doomed to die ("Thaïs va mourir"). Starting from his sleep, Athanaël springs to his feet, gasping the words he heard in the dream. In an intensely dramatic aria he rages over the purposeless cruelty of a world in which so lovely a being as Thaïs is permitted to die. Crying that he loves her and must see her once more, he rushes out into the storm. The curtain falls.

A descriptive musical interlude depicts the journey of Athanaël to the convent of Albine. At its conclusion the music gradually subsides to chords that reflect the religious quiet of the convent.

[*Scene Three*] The garden of the convent. Thaïs, near death, lies in the shade of a fig tree. Albine and the nuns are kneeling around her, intoning a prayer ("Seigneur ayez pitié de moi"). The abbess, looking at Thaïs, muses that three months of praying and penance have destroyed her body but redeemed her soul.

Suddenly Athanaël appears at the entrance to the garden. He is wildly excited but controls himself with an effort when Albine approaches to welcome him. The nuns meanwhile group closer around Thaïs and screen her from Athanaël's sight. Albine tells the monk that it is well that he has come to pronounce his blessing upon the holy woman whom he brought to the convent, because she is on the threshold of eternity. At that moment the nuns move away and Athanaël sees Thaïs.

He falls down with an agonized cry and then drags himself over to where Thaïs is lying. Brokenly he calls her name. Opening her eyes, Thaïs quietly greets him. An intensely moving duet ensues as she asks him if he remembers the soul-inspiring journey to the convent ("Te souvient-il du lumineux voyage"). In the ecstasy of death she sings of the peace and contentment he brought to her soul by teaching her the meaning of divine love.

Athanaël sings that he can think of nothing but her pagan beauty and of his hunger for her, which could only be satisfied by her love. Frenzied by the realization that he has destroyed what he most desired, Athanaël declares that his exhortations were lies and that truth is only in earthly beauty and passion.

Raising herself, Thaïs sings that she sees before her the splendors of Paradise, where she will be eternally at peace. Wildly repeating that he loves her, Athanaël implores her not to die. In rapturous tones Thaïs sings that now she sees God. As she falls back lifeless, Athanaël sinks at her side with a desolate cry ("Morte! pitié!"). The curtain falls.

Tosca

by GIACOMO PUCCINI
[1858–1924]

Libretto by
LUIGI ILLICA *and* GIUSEPPE GIACOSA

Based on Victorien Sardou's drama
La Tosca

CHARACTERS

Cesare Angelotti, an escaped political prisoner.................... *Bass*
A Sacristan .... *Baritone*
Mario Cavaradossi, a painter...................... *Tenor*
Floria Tosca, a famous opera singer........................ *Soprano*
Baron Scarpia, chief of the Roman police..................... *Baritone*
Spoletta, a police officer...................................... *Tenor*
Sciarrone, a gendarme... *Bass*
A young shepherd... *Bass*
Jailer .... *Bass*
Cardinal, the executioner Roberti, judge, clerk, sergeant,
infantryman, Swiss Guards, townspeople

Place: Rome
Time: June 1800
First performance: Teatro Constanzi, Rome, January 14, 1900
Original language: Italian

THE STORY of *Tosca* takes place at the time when Rome was torn by fierce political strife between the Bonapartists and the monarchists. In setting to music Sardou's drama of violence, intrigue, and passion, Puccini infused his natural lyricism with powerful dramatic expression.

ACT ONE

The interior of the Church of Sant' Andrea della Valle, in Rome. On one side a grilled gate closes off the entrance to the Attavanti chapel. On the other side stands an easel, partly covered, on which is an uncompleted portrait of a woman, supposedly a Magdalen. Scattered about are painter's implements, and a basket near by.

There is no prelude. After a brief phrase of harsh chords symbolizing Scarpia, chief of police, the curtain rises. Angelotti, unkempt and breathless, and dressed in prison garb, enters in desperate haste. Muttering that he has escaped his pursuers, he steals over to a pillar at which is a shrine to the Madonna, finds a key hidden there by his sister, unlocks the door of the chapel, and disappears inside.

To the accompaniment of a sprightly melody the Sacristan enters, carrying a handful of paintbrushes. He is a rather strange character, afflicted with a nervous jerking of his head and shoulders. Pattering over to the easel, he grumbles about the dirty paintbrushes and expresses surprise that the painter is not there. He looks into the basket, and, finding that the food in it is untouched, he concludes that Cavaradossi will soon return. At the sound of the Angelus the Sacristan kneels and intones a prayer in Latin.

Mario enters and takes up his work at the easel. The Sacristan, staring at the portrait—a beautiful woman with blond hair and blue eyes—exclaims that it is the likeness of the woman who has been praying daily at the shrine of the Madonna. Mario smiles and says that her lovely face inspired him. Laying down his brush, he takes a miniature of Floria Tosca from his pocket. In the beautiful aria "Recondita armonia" he compares the two beauties—Tosca's hair is dark, the Magdalen's blond; Tosca's eyes are black, the other's blue. The Sacristan, in accompanying phrases, expresses pious disapproval over these worldly sentiments. He busies himself awhile with cleaning brushes, notes with sly satisfaction that Mario has not touched his food, then leaves.

As Mario continues painting, Angelotti comes cautiously out of the chapel and approaches. The painter finally recognizes his friend and cries out in happy surprise. Quickly he locks the door of the church. Angelotti tells him that he has escaped from the prison of Sant' Angelo, and Mario eagerly offers to help him. At that moment Tosca's voice is heard outside. Giving Angelotti the basket of food, Mario pushes him into the chapel, warns him to be quiet, and then opens the door to admit Tosca.

Annoyed at having been kept waiting, she rebuffs Mario's embraces and inquires suspiciously if the beautiful lady of the portrait has been here. Mario denies that he has had any visitors and goes on with his painting. When she asks him to come to her cottage in the evening, he answers with a preoccupied air, which she notes with irritation. She forgets her misgivings, however, in the passionate duet which follows ("Non la sospiri la nostra casetta"). Tosca describes the bliss that she and her lover will share at the cottage, and Mario answers ardently.

Glancing nervously at the chapel, he tells Tosca as gently as possible that she must now leave him to his work. As she prepares to go she looks at the portrait and remarks rather spitefully that the Magdalen is too beautiful. Suddenly recognizing her as the Marchioness Attavanti, Tosca cries out in jealous fury that *there* is the reason for all these furtive movements behind locked doors. A fiery duet ensues as Mario tries to convince her that her suspicions are groundless. She responds amorously as her mood changes, then implores him to make the Magdalen's eyes black like her own, instead of blue. Extorting a promise from Mario to be faithful, she hurries away.

Mario calls Angelotti from the chapel. The fugitive reveals, much to the painter's surprise, that the Marchioness Attavanti is his sister and that she has hidden clothing under the altar to disguise him in his escape from the terrible Scarpia. Mario gives him the key to his villa and tells him of a secret passageway to his cellar, where he will be safe. Taking the bundle of clothing from under the altar, Angelotti is about to leave. Just then several cannon shots are heard, and Mario exclaims that the escape has been discovered. He decides to guide Angelotti to his home.

The Sacristan rushes in and is surprised to find Mario gone. He is followed shortly by a noisy crowd of choirboys and acolytes, to whom he announces that Bonaparte has been defeated. In honor of the event, he continues, there will be a great *Te Deum,* and a new cantata will be sung by Floria Tosca. The boys greet the news with much shouting and singing.

The uproar ceases abruptly as Scarpia enters the church, followed by Spoletta and other police officers. He orders the boys to prepare themselves for the service, then informs the trembling Sacristan that he is on the trail of an escaped prisoner who has been traced to the church. Searching the chapel, he finds a fan bearing the crest of the Marchioness Attavanti. He catches sight of the portrait and exclaims in surprise on recognizing the features of the marchioness. The Sacristan tells him it was painted by Mario Cavaradossi. That name is familiar to Scarpia, for Cavaradossi is under suspicion as a Bonapartist, and is also known to him as Tosca's lover.

A police officer comes from the chapel with the empty basket. The Sacristan babbles stupidly that Cavaradossi did not have the key to the chapel, so could not have eaten his meal there. Scarpia, listening carefully, concludes that it was Angelotti who ate the food and that Cavaradossi is implicated in his escape.

Tosca, prompted by misgivings about Mario's fidelity, returns to the church. Scarpia quickly hides behind a pillar and orders the Sacristan, standing near the easel, not to move. When Tosca asks him about Mario, he mumbles some reply and hurries away. Scarpia quietly approaches and with oily flattery commends her piety. There are some, he continues, who enter the church only to profane it by using it as a lovers' rendezvous. Carelessly holding up the fan, he remarks that some fair lady evidently dropped it in her haste to leave when surprised in a tryst.

Horrified, Tosca sees the Attavanti crest. She tries to hide her jealous fury, but, goaded by Scarpia's insinuations, she finally threatens to have revenge on her rival. Unctuously he reproaches her for giving way to her anger in a holy place. Tosca, weeping with humiliation, now leaves, while Scarpia, pretending to be distressed at her grief, escorts her to the door.

As he returns, Spoletta emerges from a hiding place. Scarpia orders him to follow Tosca and to meet him later at the Farnese Palace to report on her movements. Standing alone in the nave, the wily chief of police gloats over the success of his evil plan. The cardinal enters and the *Te Deum* begins. In a grim obbligato to the chanting, Scarpia sings the soliloquy known as the *Te Deum,* in which he savagely exults over the prospects of a double triumph—Tosca's embraces and Cavaradossi's downfall. The curtain falls.

ACT TWO

Scarpia's apartment in the Farnese Palace. He is dining alone at a table near a window above the palace courtyard. Nervously he muses that Cavaradossi and Angelotti will soon be swinging from the same gallows.

From below comes the sound of music being played at the celebration in honor of General Melas's reported victory over Bonaparte, at which Tosca is to be the soloist. Scarpia rings for Sciarrone, orders him to tell Tosca that Scarpia is expecting her after the cantata, then gives the gendarme a note to take to her. In a dramatic monologue ("Ha più forte sapore") he sings that he scorns the gentler arts of love and finds his pleasure in ruthlessly possessing what he desires.

Spoletta now appears to make his report. Shaking with fear, the officer explains that he and his men searched Cavaradossi's villa but found no trace of Angelotti. Scarpia's fury subsides, however, when Spoletta tells him that he has brought the painter back as a prisoner. He orders Cavaradossi to be led before him, along with the executioner Roberti, a judge, and a clerk.

As Scarpia waits, Tosca's voice, accompanied by the chorus, is heard in the beginning of the cantata. Mario is brought in, angrily demanding to know why he has been seized. With menacing suavity, Scarpia questions him about Angelotti. When he accuses Mario of hiding the fugitive in his villa, Mario resolutely denies everything. Tosca's voice, soaring over the choir in the stately measures of the cantata, serves as accompaniment to the dialogue of the two men until Scarpia abruptly cuts off the sound by closing the window.

Relentlessly Scarpia questions, but Mario continues to defy him. Tosca, greatly excited, bursts into the room and rushes into her lover's arms. In an aside he warns her not to reveal any information about the villa. Scarpia, springing to his feet, tells Mario that the judge is waiting to hear his confession in an adjoining room—in reality the torture chamber. Mario is led away, followed by Roberti, the judge, the clerk, and Sciarrone. Scarpia calls after Roberti that he is to proceed in the usual way, pending further instructions. Sciarrone, entering the torture chamber last, closes the door behind him, while Spoletta stations himself before the outer door of the room.

Adopting a casual air, Scarpia begins questioning Tosca about the villa. She insists that no one but Mario was there. At that Scarpia calls out to Sciarrone, asking if the witness has made any statement. None, replies the gendarme, whereupon Tosca, unaware that her lover is being tortured, flippantly remarks that this questioning is useless. Scarpia quietly tells her that a truthful answer may save her lover agony. Tosca gasps in horror as he thunders that at this very moment Mario's head is encircled by a spiked band of steel that is being tightened at intervals, bringing the blood spurting from his veins at every denial. A groan from behind the door underscores Scarpia's words.

Tosca makes her way over to the door and calls out to Mario, whose tormented voice is heard cautioning her to keep silent. Wildly she curses Scarpia for his brutality, but he merely compliments her sardonically on her dramatic performance. Suddenly he commands Spoletta to open the door and, as Tosca recoils at the sight of the torture, he harshly repeats his question: "Where is Angelotti?"

Frantically Tosca begs Mario to allow her to speak, but the painter, between his cries of pain, forbids her. As a fearful cry of agony bursts from

Mario's lips, Tosca, unable to control herself, gasps out the location of Angelotti's hiding place. Instantly Scarpia orders the torture stopped, and soon Mario, bleeding and unconscious, is brought into the room and placed on a couch. Tosca kneels sobbing at his side. After a few minutes have elapsed he revives and asks weakly if he revealed the secret. As Tosca assures him he did not, Scarpia loudly repeats to Spoletta the words she spoke a moment earlier.

In a torment of pain and fury, Mario curses Tosca for her betrayal. At that moment Sciarrone rushes in with the news that Bonaparte has defeated General Melas at Marengo. A brief but stormy trio ensues ("L'alba vindice appar"). In delirious ecstasy Mario exults over the victory, while Tosca endeavors to calm him. Scarpia pours out his hatred for this defiant rebel and orders him to a cell. Tosca struggles desperately with the guards but is finally pushed aside as Mario is taken away.

Smiling triumphantly, Scarpia sits down at his table, offers Tosca a glass of wine, then resumes his meal. Watching him a moment with loathing and disgust, Tosca asks him his price. Scarpia answers in the great aria "Mi dicon venal." His enemies, he declares, call him corrupt and mercenary. But where a beautiful woman is concerned, he does not stoop to talk in sordid terms of money. Tosca's beauty has so enthralled him that her very hatred has made him resolve to possess her. His price, Scarpia proclaims, coming toward her in passionate excitement, is Tosca herself. As she shrinks from him in unbelieving horror, a roll of drums is heard. In another hour, says Scarpia, after they listen in silence, her lover will die. Tosca pours out her anguish in the magnificent aria "Vissi d'arte." She has always lived only for her art and for love, Tosca laments, harming no one, helping the poor, praying devotedly. And now, in her darkest hour, God has deserted her. Kneeling before Scarpia, she makes a final desperate plea, but he only reiterates his lecherous proposal.

Spoletta suddenly rushes in to tell Scarpia that Angelotti killed himself with poison at the moment of capture. Scarpia orders his body hung from the scaffold. "And Cavaradossi?" asks Spoletta. Scarpia turns to Tosca with a questioning look. Crushed with humiliation, she nods her head.

Thereupon Scarpia informs Spoletta that there will be a mock execution. "Just as we did with Palmieri," he says, looking intently at the officer, who, as he leaves, signifies that he understands his meaning. Scarpia agrees to permit Tosca to come to the scene of the execution and inform Cavaradossi of his reprieve. She further inveigles him into giving her a passport for Mario and herself. While he is at his desk writing out the passport, Tosca goes to the table and takes the glass of wine he has poured for her. Carefully she picks up a knife from the table, hiding it behind her as she turns to watch Scarpia. Stamping the passport, he springs to his feet and advances toward Tosca with arms outstretched.

As he tries to embrace her, she plunges the knife into his chest, whispering fiercely, "Here is Tosca's kiss." He dies at her feet. With her eyes on Scarpia's face, she wets a napkin with water from a carafe and washes her fingers. Searching for the passport, she sees it clutched in Scarpia's lifeless hand. A sudden, harsh crescendo sounds in the orchestra as she wrenches it free and hides it in her dress. While the Scarpia motive echoes softly, Tosca places one lighted candle at the right of Scarpia's head and another at the left, takes a crucifix from the wall and lays it on his breast. She steals from the room and the curtain falls.

ACT THREE

The roof of the prison castle of Sant' Angelo. On a table at the left stands a lantern, and next to it is the prison register book. On one wall is a crucifix with a lamp beneath. At the right is a trap door. It is just before daybreak on the morning of Cavaradossi's supposed execution. No one is on the scene. After a quiet prelude, sheep bells tinkle in the distance and we hear the plaintive song of a shepherd. It dies away as church bells ring for matins.

The jailer enters through the trap door and seats himself at the table. Soon Cavaradossi is brought in by a sergeant and an infantryman, who leave after the sergeant signs the register. Mario requests permission to write a farewell letter and offers the jailer a ring in return for the favor.

As he writes, the theme of the first-act love duet sweeps through the orchestra. Laying down his pen, he recalls his blissful past with Tosca in the poignant aria "E lucevan le stelle." Overwhelmed by despair, he breaks into sobs, burying his face in his hands. Tosca is brought in, and the two are left alone. Excitedly she shows him the passport. When Mario sees Scarpia's signature, he looks darkly at Tosca. In a fiery aria ("Il tuo sangue o il mio amore volea") she relates how she killed Scarpia, staining her hands with his blood. Mario takes her hands in his and comforts her in an ardent refrain ("O dolci mani").

Tosca then explains that the firing squad will use blank cartridges and that he must pretend to fall dead when the soldiers fire. There is a final duet as they sing of the happiness of the future, concluding with poignant, unaccompanied phrases as Spoletta appears with the firing squad.

Cavaradossi is led to the wall. Smilingly he refuses a blindfold. Tosca withdraws some distance away and faces him. The firing squad is lined up, and Spoletta raises his sword. Tosca covers her ears with her hands. The sword descends, there is a burst of fire, and Mario falls. The sergeant steps forward to administer the *coup de grâce*, but Spoletta stops him. After covering the body, the officer and soldiers leave.

Tosca cautiously approaches, warning Mario not to move. Making sure that the soldiers have gone, she calls his name, first softly, then more desperately when he does not answer. She flings back the cover, sees that he is dead, and falls over his body with a terrible cry. Suddenly angry shouts are heard below, and in a moment Spoletta and Sciarrone clamber hastily through the trap door. The officer flings himself on Tosca, shouting that she will pay for Scarpia's murder. She violently hurls him back. Crying, "Scarpia, avanti a Dio!" ("Scarpia, we meet before God!"), she throws herself over the parapet. The curtain falls.

La Traviata

by GIUSEPPE VERDI

[1813–1901]

Libretto by
FRANCESCO MARIA PIAVE

Based on Dumas's play
LA DAME AUX CAMÉLIAS (CAMILLE)

CHARACTERS

Violetta Valery, a courtesan.................................... *Soprano*
Dr. Grenvil, Violetta's physician............................... *Bass*
Marquis d'Obigny, a nobleman................................. *Bass*
Flora Bervoix, friend of Violetta......................... *Mezzo-soprano*
Baron Douphol, rival of Alfredo.............................. *Baritone*
Gastone, Viscount of Letorieres.............................. *Tenor*
Alfredo Germont, lover of Violetta............................ *Tenor*
Annina, Violetta's maid.............................. *Mezzo-soprano*
Giorgio Germont, father of Alfredo........................... *Baritone*
Salon guests, masqueraders, dancers, and servants

Place: In and near Paris
Time: About 1700
First performance: La Fenice Theater, Venice, March 6, 1853
Original language: Italian

L A TRAVIATA is the story of the tragic romance of Violetta Valery, a beautiful courtesan of Paris, and Alfredo Germont, a sincere and poetic young man of a respectable provincial family.

Verdi wrote *La Traviata* in 1853 while at work on another opera, *Il Trovatore*. Although Verdi usually devoted about four months to the composition of an opera, he completed *La Traviata* in four weeks. Its first performance was a complete failure. It was performed in modern costume, an innovation which aroused the distaste of the audience. The leading tenor was hoarse. The soprano cast as Violetta was a fat prima donna, and when Dr. Grenvil announced in the last act that the heroine was dying of consumption, the audience howled with laughter.

La Traviata was next presented about a year later, the period of the opera being put back from 1850 to 1700 and costumed accordingly. The performance was an outstanding success, and since then *La Traviata* has been a favorite of opera lovers.

There is a short prelude dominated by two themes. The first is associated with Violetta's fatal illness and death and is heard again in the introduction to the fourth act. The second is the haunting, impassioned melody of Violetta's parting from Alfredo near the close of Act Two.

ACT ONE

The richly furnished drawing room of Violetta Valery in Paris. The music reflects an atmosphere of festivity, for the pleasure-loving Violetta is giving another of the brilliant parties which have made her famous in Parisian society. About the room are several tables lavishly laden with food and drink.

Although afflicted with a grave illness, Violetta is determined to ignore the precarious state of her health in a ceaseless round of enjoyment. We first see her seated on a sofa, talking to Dr. Grenvil and several friends. Guests begin to arrive, among them Marquis d'Obigny, Flora, Violetta's closest friend, and Baron Douphol. Musical dialogue follows in which Violetta vivaciously welcomes her guests, and they inquire solicitously if she really has the health and strength for revelry. Violetta replies that she lives for pleasure alone, that Pleasure is the only physician who can heal her.

At that moment Gastone, Viscount of Letorieres, enters with Alfredo Germont, who is presented to Violetta as one of her latest admirers and who, in fact, is deeply in love with her. She receives him graciously, yet with a trace of coquetry, then invites her guests to be seated at one of the tables. She herself sits between Alfredo and Gastone. The latter tells her of Alfredo's infatuation, but Violetta discourages any sentiments other than friendship. Baron Douphol, Violetta's jealous admirer (later revealed as Alfredo's bitter rival), sings in an aside to Flora that he instinctively dislikes Alfredo.

There is a round of toasts, and Alfredo is prevailed upon to sing a drinking song. Other guests crowd into the drawing room to listen as he begins the famous "Libiamo, libiamo, ne' lieti calici." It is a catchy refrain in waltz time praising the joys of youth, love, and wine. Alfredo's eyes are on Violetta as he sings, and she joyously takes up the melody in response. Then the entire chorus joins in to bring the song to a rousing conclusion.

Violetta now invites her guests to dance and rises to lead them to the ballroom. Suddenly she sways and appears on the verge of fainting. There is a flurry of alarm, but Violetta explains that it is only a dizzy spell. She assures her guests that she will join them shortly. Alfredo remains with her, deeply concerned. "These nightly revels," he warns, "will one day be fatal." He implores her to be more mindful of her health, expressing a wish that he might always be near to take care of her. Violetta laughingly tries to brush aside his solicitous attentions.

Then in a tender and moving melody, "Un di felice," Alfredo tells Violetta of the first day he saw her. For more than a year, he sings, he has been hopelessly in love. Violetta, now realizing that he is passionately sincere in his avowals, is profoundly moved and replies that she is unworthy of such great love.

"I have only friendship to offer," Violetta tells him. "I live for love and liberty and use my friends only to serve my pleasure. If you do not care to be one of them, forget me."

Alfredo's declaration of love and Violetta's insistence on her own unworthiness are united in a beautiful duet. Although Alfredo persists in his love, he finally promises to say no more about it and turns to leave the room. Violetta calls him back, takes a flower from her breast, and tells him he may see her when it fades. Rapturously Alfredo takes the flower and kisses Violetta's hand.

The guests, weary of dancing and merrymaking, drift back into the drawing room to thank Violetta for the good time they have had and assure her they are always ready to be her companions in gaiety. Alfredo and the guests depart and Violetta is left alone.

In a recitative she meditates on the happenings of the night. She thinks of Alfredo's deep and abiding love in contrast to the empty flattery of her fair-weather friends. She ponders the choice between a life of quiet happiness with him and her own hectic, meaningless existence. Then she begins the tender, expressive aria, "Ah, fors'è lui che l'anima solinga ne' tumulti." It is a confession to herself that she has at last learned the meaning of real love. Overwhelmed by the thought, Violetta stands pensively.

In another instant her mood changes. "Folie, folie [What folly]," she sings as she is stung by the realization that such love can never be, that her loneliness and helplessness make Paris a vast, empty desert in which she is condemned to live and die. These thoughts are sung in a short recitative. Then Violetta bursts into the dazzling aria, "Sempre libera degg'io folleggiare di gioja in gioja." The scintillating coloratura passages reflect Violetta's determination to abandon herself solely to pleasure. She will forget Alfredo's love by pursuing new joys, each wilder and fiercer than the last.

Suddenly her song is interrupted by the sound of Alfredo's voice outside. He repeats the passionate melody in which he declared his love earlier in the act. Violetta stands as if hypnotized, then bursts forth again into the glittering phrases of her aria. This brilliant climax brings the first act to a close.

ACT TWO

A room on the ground floor of a country home near Paris.[1] After a short orchestral introduction Alfredo enters, attired in hunting costume. Putting away his gun, he sings in recitative about the idyllic happiness of his life with Violetta. He rejoices that she so willingly gave up the gaiety and excitement of Paris, where she had reigned as a social queen, to be with him in the seclusion of the country. In a melodious aria Alfredo recalls how Violetta tamed his wild and youthful passions and revealed to him the calm depths of mature love ("De' miei bollenti spiriti"). Her devotion has been a source of unbelievable joy and inspiration.

His thoughts are interrupted by the entrance of Annina, Violetta's maid, obviously in a state of agitation. In response to Alfredo's questions, Annina says she has just returned from Paris, where, on Violetta's orders, she has

[1] The opera was first written in three acts, and this was Scene One of Act Two.

sold some of her mistress's personal possessions to pay the heavy household expenses. Unwillingly the maid reveals that two thousand louis are still needed. Shocked and startled by this state of affairs, Alfredo announces that he will go to Paris at once to raise the money. He sends Annina away with a warning not to reveal to Violetta the purpose of his journey.

In a florid and dramatic aria Alfredo voices his humiliation and remorse for having lived like a drone on Violetta's money. He bitterly reproaches himself for his thoughtlessness, swears he will make amends before another day dawns, then rushes distractedly from the room.

Violetta enters, looking for Alfredo. Annina informs her that he has gone to Paris for a day. A servant hands Violetta a letter, which she reads with an amused smile. It is an invitation to a ball from Flora Bervoix, Violetta's former Parisian companion. Violetta carelessly tosses the letter aside with the comment that Flora will look for her in vain.

Now a dignified, elderly gentleman is shown into the room. He introduces himself as Alfredo's father and brusquely accuses Violetta of luring his son to ruin. Angered by the elder Germont's charge, Violetta starts to leave, then turns and sits down. She denies that Alfredo is lavishing his money on her and hands her visitor a legal paper prepared for the sale of her possessions. Germont, although somewhat abashed, points out that her past still casts a shadow over her life and Alfredo's. Violetta replies that her deep love for Alfredo has blotted out her past sins.

Germont's attitude softens. With dignity and restraint he tells Violetta that he has come to ask her to make a great sacrifice. Violetta, suddenly fear-stricken, faces Germont, saying she foresees the end of her happiness. Germont sings the aria in which he reveals that his daughter's plans for marriage are threatened by the scandal of Alfredo's intimate friendship with Violetta. She replies that she is willing to give up Alfredo until after his sister's wedding. Germont insists that it must be forever. In an intensely dramatic aria, Violetta protests that giving up Alfredo is impossible ("Non sapete quale affetto"). She is already beset by illness, and separation from the man she loves will only hasten her doom. The only other alternative, she cries, is death.

In an effort to induce Violetta to release his son, Germont now resorts to a different strategy. He reminds her that when time has destroyed her youth and beauty Alfredo's love will be destroyed with them. The years will thus bring nothing but sorrow and regret. She will find her own happiness, Germont adds, only in the happiness she can bring to both his children by her great renunciation.

The somber, minor key of the music underscores Violetta's anguish as she realizes the hopelessness of the situation. Weeping, she asks Germont to tell his daughter that for the sake of her future happiness Violetta's heart has been broken. Now she awaits the father's command. Germont says she must tell Alfredo that she no longer loves him. Violetta warns that Alfredo will not believe her, and if she attempts to leave him he will follow her. Then she thinks of a plan. She tells Germont that his son will be restored to him but that the separation will break Alfredo's heart too. Shaken and distressed by the bitterness of the sacrifice he has demanded of the lovers, Germont asks Violetta how he can repay her for her noble act.

Only death can end her agony, Violetta sings. Her remaining hope is that Alfredo will not curse her memory but will understand that she has made this supreme sacrifice for his sake alone. Brokenhearted, she bids Germont farewell, while he goes into the garden to await his son.

Violetta sits down to write a letter to Alfredo, but no sooner has she sealed it than he himself enters. She attempts to hide the letter, and Alfredo is momentarily puzzled by her confusion. He tells Violetta that he has received a stern note from his father, who is expected to arrive any moment. Unaware, of course, of the scene between Violetta and the elder Germont, Alfredo attempts to reassure her by saying that when his father sees her he, too, will love her. She counsels him first to meet his father alone. She will wait in the garden during the interview and later plead with Germont in her own way. Scarcely able to conceal her despair, Violetta asks Alfredo again and again to say that he loves her. Alfredo ardently replies, mystified by her tears. Then regaining control of herself, she bids him farewell to the intensely passionate music of the theme previously heard in the prelude of the opera.

Alfredo is left alone. He reflects on Violetta's devotion, then picks up a book and tries to read. Nervous and impatient, he puts it quickly aside. The servant enters hastily to tell him that Violetta and her maid have taken a coach for Paris. Alfredo assumes that she has gone to arrange for the sale of her possessions, a contingency which he thinks Annina will prevent. A messenger enters with a letter for Alfredo. He tears it open and staggers as he reads Violetta's message of farewell. With a tortured cry he turns to go and finds himself in the arms of his father. Sinking down at the table, Alfredo buries his face in his hands in utter despair.

In the great aria, "Di Provenza il mar," Germont, in majestic, sweeping phrases, recalls Alfredo's happy childhood in Provence by the sea. Gently he implores his son to return home, where he can find solace for his grief in the sympathy and kindness of his family.

Suddenly a dark suspicion crosses Alfredo's mind, rousing him to jealous fury. He is certain that Baron Douphol has persuaded Violetta to betray him. In vain his father pleads with him to forget Violetta and return home. As Germont's entreaties rise to a dramatic climax, Alfredo discovers Flora's invitation, which is still lying on the table. This confirms his suspicions and he furiously swears vengeance. Alfredo rushes madly from the stage, followed by his father.

ACT THREE

The luxurious mansion of Flora Bervoix in Paris.[2] Another gay party is in progress. Prominent on the scene are a gaming table and another large table set with refreshments and decorated with flowers. As in the first act, the music is lively and festive.

Flora, Marquis d'Obigny, Dr. Grenvil, and other guests engage in musical dialogue. The hostess promises her friends a night of brilliant revelry,

[2] Originally Scene Two of Act Two.

then announces that Violetta and Alfredo are expected. The Marquis, however, informs her that the lovers are separated and that if Violetta appears it will be with Baron Douphol, not Alfredo. The others are incredulous. Just then some of the masqueraders come in.

First we hear a delightful chorus of women gypsies. Some have wands and others tambourines with which they beat time as they sing. They invite the guests to hold out their hands so that they may have their palms read. One group reads Flora's hand and tells her there is a rival in the offing. Others of the chorus read the palm of the Marquis. They laughingly inform him that no one will ever accuse him of being constant in his love affairs. In sprightly music Flora and the Marquis indulge in a bit of banter. Flora brands D'Obigny a gay deceiver, while he in mock seriousness swears he is true to her alone. Then both join the gypsies in a carefree song.

The music takes on a new rhythm as Viscount Gastone and others make a colorful entrance as Spanish matadors and picadors. They sing the tale of a brave young picador whose ladylove promised him her hand only if he succeeded in killing five bulls in one day. This feat the daring young man accomplished and so proved his love. Everyone joins in a chorus of joyous revelry, while the gypsies beat time with their tambourines and the picadors with their staves, creating a stirring rhythmic effect.

At the end of the number Alfredo enters and is hailed by the gathering. Flora inquires about Violetta. He curtly answers that he is not concerned, then strides over to the gaming table to join the others at cards. A moment later Violetta enters on the arm of Baron Douphol. Flora welcomes her and thanks the Baron for bringing Violetta back to her friends. In an aside Douphol tells Violetta that Alfredo is present and grimly warns her not to speak to him. In a poignant musical phrase, which is repeated several times later in this scene, Violetta expresses foreboding and anxiety over the inevitable meeting of Alfredo and Douphol.

Taking Violetta aside, Flora asks her what has happened. Alfredo, winning consistently at the gaming table, sings with contemptuous indifference that whoever is unlucky in love is lucky at cards. He pointedly announces that he intends to retire to the country again with his winnings, to lavish them on someone who once shared his life there but has temporarily deserted him. Violetta gasps at the remark while Gastone begs Alfredo to spare her feelings. Angrily the Baron starts to address Alfredo. Violetta, in an aside to the Baron, threatens to leave him if he causes trouble. Alfredo disdainfully recognizes the Baron. With suave malice Douphol compliments Alfredo on his luck, then offers to play him at cards. Alfredo coolly accepts the challenge. The premonitory theme is again heard as Violetta voices her fear of the outcome of this contest.

Douphol stakes one hundred louis. Alfredo wins. They double the stakes and again Alfredo wins. The tension mounts as the guests discuss Alfredo's luck, while Flora comments that the night promises to be an expensive one for the Baron. The situation is saved by a servant's announcement that supper is served. The guests withdraw to the banquet room. For the third time we hear the theme of Violetta's apprehension and distress. Alfredo and Douphol face each other alone. Alfredo asks his adversary if he wishes to continue the game, but the Baron replies that he will take his revenge later. Alfredo scornfully offers to meet the Baron at any game he chooses.

The stage is momentarily empty. Suddenly Violetta re-enters, greatly excited. She has asked Alfredo to come to her but fears that his hatred will make this interview useless. Alfredo appears and the two unhappy lovers are face to face. Violetta implores him to leave, warning him of the Baron's jealousy. Alfredo retorts that he and the Baron are mortal enemies and taunts her with the threat that he may kill Douphol. In vain Violetta tries to convince Alfredo that her anxiety is for him alone and again beseeches him to leave. Alfredo merely jeers at her terror and says he will leave only if she promises to go with him. Frantic with despair, Violetta answers that a fatal promise forces her to refuse his request. With mounting fury Alfredo demands to know who exacted the promise. In a desperate lie Violetta answers that it was Douphol and that she made the promise because she is in love with the Baron.

Raging, Alfredo rushes to the doors, throws them open, and calls in the guests. As they excitedly crowd around him he points to Violetta and hurls his accusations. He tells them that she attempted to buy his love by lavishing her possessions on him. He blindly accepted because of his real love for her. Now that he has unmasked her infamous scheming, he calls on the guests to witness that he is paying her back in full. Mad with anger, he hurls the purse containing his winnings at the feet of Violetta, who faints in the arms of Flora and Dr. Grenvil.

In a thrilling, dramatic chorus, Violetta's friends denounce Alfredo's brutal insults and angrily order him to leave. The elder Germont, who entered just as Alfredo was finishing his tirade, now steps forward. He vehemently reproaches Alfredo and renounces him as his son. Alfredo cringes at his father's words and in a tense aside voices his remorse for his shameless conduct.

Then begins the magnificent closing chorus of the act, in which all join. Flora, Gastone, the Marquis, Germont, and the others attempt to console Violetta, who is slowly reviving. Baron Douphol, burning for revenge, challenges Alfredo to a duel. Alfredo himself, in humiliation and despair, cries out that he has forever lost the one he loves. Over the music of the chorus Violetta sings to Alfredo—softly at first, then with passionate intensity. Someday, she says sorrowfully, he will know how great her sacrifice has been and how deeply he has wronged her. Despite the dark tragedy of their misunderstanding, she will love him forever. As the chorus ends in a tremendous flood of sound, Germont slowly leads Alfredo away, followed by the Baron. Flora and Dr. Grenvil support Violetta as she leaves. The remaining guests slowly depart and the curtain falls.

ACT FOUR

Violetta's modest apartment in Paris.[3] Ravaged by illness, Violetta lies asleep on her bed, at the side of which stands a table with a decanter, a

[3] Originally Act Three.

glass, and several vials of medicine. Annina, the maid, is drowsing by the fireplace. The windows are shuttered and a night lamp is burning. The orchestral introduction softly intones the theme of Violetta's illness and impending death.

Violetta awakens, calls to Annina, asks for a glass of water, then learns that it is seven o'clock in the morning. She asks Annina to open the shutters. As the maid does so, she sees Dr. Grenvil approaching below. Violetta tries to rise but falls back exhausted. As she is helped to her feet by Annina, Dr. Grenvil enters and they both assist her to a nearby sofa. With pathetic gratitude Violetta welcomes the faithful doctor, who asks if she is feeling better. She answers that though she is weak her mind is at peace. She has found solace and spiritual strength in prayer. When she informs Grenvil that she has slept soundly, he cheerfully assures her that recovery is not far off. With a sad smile Violetta feigns to accept this professional consolation. As the doctor leaves he answers Annina's whispered question with the grim truth: Violetta's death is only a matter of hours.

Annina turns back to her mistress with forced cheerfulness, bidding her have courage. Violetta says she hears sounds of revelry in the streets, whereupon Annina reminds her that it is carnival time. Musing on the poor unfortunates who are doubtless among the pleasure-mad throng, Violetta asks Annina how much money is left. When Annina tells her that twenty louis remain, Violetta directs the maid to keep ten for herself and distribute the other ten among the needy in the streets. She assures Annina that whatever money is left will be sufficient for her needs, then asks her to find out if a letter has arrived.

When Annina leaves, Violetta takes a letter from her bosom and reads it aloud in a hollow voice as the orchestra softly plays the music of the love theme. It is a message from the elder Germont: Alfredo and the Baron fought a duel—the Baron was wounded but is recovering. Alfredo has gone abroad, but Germont has revealed to him the meaning of Violetta's great sacrifice. Soon Alfredo will come to beg her forgiveness. Germont bids her have faith in a happier future. Violetta stops reading and the tender theme in the orchestra dies out incompleted.

Despairingly Violetta sings that she has waited in vain. She looks at her reflection in a mirror and is horrified at the change illness has made in her features. Despite Dr. Grenvil's reassuring words she realizes that the weakness which seizes her is fatal. Then Violetta begins the tragic and moving aria in which she bids farewell to the world ("Addio! del passato"). Her cherished hopes are shattered—friendless and utterly alone, she awaits a grave which shall be unmarked by cross or flower.

As the last note dies away like a sigh, a bacchanalian chorus of revelers outside harshly breaks in on Violetta's mood of sorrow and resignation. In ironic contrast the merrymakers sing lustily in praise of the fine, fat bull which is traditionally led to slaughter to provide the carnival feast. The revelers finally move on. Suddenly Annina enters, scarcely able to suppress her excitement. Hesitantly she asks Violetta to remain calm because a wonderful surprise is in store. In feverish suspense Violetta asks if it is Alfredo. Annina nods. The door is flung open and in another moment the lovers are in each other's arms, pouring out their love and longing in an ecstatic burst of song.

The music gradually grows quieter, and then follows the famous duet, "Parigi, o cara." Alfredo tenderly sings of how he will take Violetta to the country, far away from Paris, to restore her to health and happiness. Alfredo's rapturous promises revive Violetta and she echoes the melody as she rejoices over the end of her sorrow. In tranquil simplicity the duet comes to a close. Violetta asks Alfredo to go to church with her so that they may give thanks for their reunion. Suddenly she falters, and Alfredo is alarmed at her pallor. It is nothing, Violetta says reassuringly, only the shock of supreme joy after so much sorrow. With a desperate effort Violetta fights off her weakness, tries to put on a dress Annina hands her, but collapses helplessly. Panic-stricken, Alfredo orders Annina to get the doctor. Violetta instructs the maid to say that Alfredo has returned and that now she wants to live. When Annina leaves, Violetta, with calm resignation, tells Alfredo that if his return cannot restore her to health, nothing on earth can save her.

Suddenly the thought of dying so young spurs her to anguished protest against her fate. Frantically Alfredo attempts to give Violetta courage, and their voices again unite in a dramatic duet. At its climax Violetta sinks back upon the bed—now within a few moments of the end. Annina, Dr. Grenvil, and the elder Germont rush in. Alfredo's father has come to beg Violetta's forgiveness and give his consent to the marriage of the lovers. Stricken with remorse as he realizes it is all too late, he reproaches himself for having wronged Violetta.

For a parting gift Violetta gives Alfredo a miniature of herself. Alfredo cries out that she must not die; and his father joins him in an expression of agonized grief. Violetta gently continues, bidding Alfredo to give the miniature to the maiden he may someday marry. It will be a token of Violetta's prayers for them. There follows a short but strikingly melodic quintet in which the persons in this tragic scene express their individual sorrow ("Cara, sublime vittima"). It is suddenly interrupted as Violetta, with that false strength which sometimes comes just before the end, sings deliriously that her pain is gone and life is returning. The love theme soars high and clear in the orchestra. With a final cry of ecstasy Violetta falls back, lifeless. The others express their profound grief. Dr. Grenvil, feeling Violetta's pulse, signifies that all is over. The final curtain falls.

Tristan und Isolde

by RICHARD WAGNER

[1813–1883]

Libretto by the Composer

Based on the medieval legend of
TRISTAN AND ISOLDA

CHARACTERS

A young sailor...*Tenor*
Isolde, a princess of Ireland................................*Soprano*
Brangäne, lady in waiting to Isolde.....................*Mezzo-soprano*
Tristan, a knight of Cornwall...............................*Tenor*
Kurvenal, henchman to Tristan...........................*Baritone*
Melot, courtier to King Marke.............................*Tenor*
King Marke of Cornwall.......................................*Bass*
A shepherd ....*Tenor*
A helmsman ....*Baritone*
Knights, soldiers, attendants, sailors

Place: Aboard a ship, Cornwall, and Brittany
Time: A medieval period
First performance: Royal Court Theater, Munich, June 10, 1865
Original language: German

IN 1857 WAGNER resolved to discontinue temporarily his work on *Der Ring des Nibelungen* and forthwith halted the composition of *Siegfried*. He turned to the writing of *Tristan und Isolde*, plans for which had been occupying his mind since about 1854. The score was completed in 1859, but six years elapsed before this great masterpiece was given its première. After repeated postponements it was performed under the baton of the brilliant conductor, Hans von Bülow, before young King Ludwig of Bavaria, Wagner's patron, and an audience of notables. Although the advanced musical ideas of *Tristan* were generally beyond the grasp of the public hearing it for the first time, the opera was enthusiastically applauded. Primarily it represented an artistic triumph rather than a popular success.

The introduction eloquently states several underlying musical motives of the opera. It begins with the themes of confession of love and desire, then moves on to the love-glance motive. Gathering intensity, the music sweeps on, through the themes of the love drink, the death potion, and the magic casket, to the motive symbolizing the longing of the lovers for the release of death. The first theme is again interwoven as the music builds up to a tremendous climax, after which it subsides to a meditative restatement of the love-suffering-longing motive.

ACT ONE

The deck of the ship in which Tristan is bringing Isolde from Ireland to be the bride of his uncle, King Marke of Cornwall. We see a royal pavilion erected near the bow of the ship. It is decorated with luxurious tapestries and enclosed at the rear with great hangings. At one side is a couch, on which Isolde is reclining. Her face is dark with anger and dejection. Brangäne, standing near an opening of the curtain, is looking toward the sea.

From the lookout's post high up on the mast comes the voice of a sailor singing a rollicking chantey about an Irish maid he left behind. The words strike Isolde's ears like a taunt, and she rises from the couch with an exclamation of annoyance at this fancied insult. Impatiently she asks Brangäne how far they have journeyed. When the lady in waiting replies that the ship will land in Cornwall by evening Isolde abandons herself to bitter reflection. She, daughter of a line of mighty sorcerers who could command the elements, has contented herself with brewing magic potions to heal her bitterest enemy. In a burst of rage she calls on the wind and waves to destroy the ship and all who sail in it. Brangäne, much distressed, tries to calm her mistress's anger. Isolde cries out that she is suffocating and orders Brangäne to draw aside the hangings.

A large part of the main deck now becomes visible. Sailors are busy at their tasks; men-at-arms are seated about. Lost in thought, Tristan stands alone, looking out over the water. Kurvenal sits near him. The lookout's voice is again heard as he sings his chantey with its characteristic sea motive. Isolde glares at Tristan, scornfully remarking that this fabulous hero—he who has only death in his heart—lacks the courage to face her. The somber death motive gives menace to her words. She tells Brangäne to inform Tristan that she wishes to see him—and it is a command, not a request.

As the sea motive sounds out in a strong rhythmic beat from the orchestra, Brangäne timorously approaches Tristan, who is startled from his reverie by a warning word from Kurvenal. Brangäne delivers her message. Tristan courteously answers that when the ship lands he will be proud to fulfill his duty and escort Isolde to King Marke. He adds that, at the moment, he cannot leave the helm. Kurvenal brashly interrupts to observe that the knight Tristan is not a man to be ordered about by a woman. He sings a sturdy refrain ("Herr Morold zog zu Meere her"), in which he jeeringly relates how Morold, the Irish lord who was to wed Isolde, tried to collect taxes from Cornwall. For his pains the brave Tristan cut off his head and sent it back to Ireland. The sailors lustily repeat the refrain.

Angrily Brangäne leaves, while Tristan tries to restrain his henchman. Closing the curtains behind her, Brangäne re-enters the pavilion and tells Isolde of Tristan's refusal and Kurvenal's insult. In fury Isolde recalls the fateful events in Ireland. Tristan, badly wounded in the fight with Morold, came to Ireland to be healed by Isolde's magic arts. He called himself Tantris, but Isolde soon found out his real identity. She noted that a piece was missing from the edge of Tristan's sword and that a broken fragment of steel taken from the head of Morold exactly fitted into the sword blade. Thereupon Isolde came sword in hand to the stricken Tristan, resolved to kill him in revenge. But the knight looked into her eyes and left her powerless to kill. Isolde restored the knight to health and sent him home to Cornwall. This great hero repaid her kindness, Isolde continues sardonically, by returning to claim her as the bride of his graybeard uncle, King Marke. Savagely Isolde reproaches herself for her weakness in showing mercy to Tristan.

Brangäne tries to calm and console Isolde by pointing out that as King Marke's bride she will be Queen of a great realm. Isolde betrays her real feelings when she speaks of the torment of living near Tristan in unrequited love. The loyal but naïve Brangäne, assuming that Isolde is concerned about the success of her marriage, hastily assures her that the magic potions provided by Isolde's mother will make marital happiness certain.

Isolde, obsessed with thoughts of revenge and death, orders Brangäne to bring the casket containing her mother's preparations. She takes from it a vial of poison and tells Brangäne that this is the only magic potion she desires. The maid is horror-stricken. Meanwhile there is a great stir on deck as the sailors prepare the ship for landing. Kurvenal strides into the pavilion and tells Isolde that his liege lord bids her make ready to greet King Marke. Isolde coldly replies that before Tristan may lead her to the King he must first seek her forgiveness for his overbearing conduct. Kurvenal grimly promises to inform Tristan accordingly.

In rising desperation Isolde thinks of suicide. She fervently embraces Brangäne, pauses in sudden resolve, then commands Brangäne to prepare the poison cup. Tristan, she intones, will drink with her the cup of atonement. When Brangäne tries to dissuade her Isolde answers with angry sarcasm. Truly, she says, her mother has provided her with helpful libations. One above all will give surcease from deepest pain—the death potion. With brooding intensity Isolde sings the death motive. As she orders Brangäne to prepare the drink Kurvenal enters to announce Tristan.

The Tristan motive thunders in the orchestra. Quietly the knight steps into the pavilion, greeting Isolde with the words, "Begehrt, Herrin, was ihr wünscht [Noble lady, what is your wish]?" In answer, Isolde observes harshly that the noble Tristan has evidently forgotten the chief tenets of knighthood—to make amends for wrongs he has done and to seek forgiveness of his enemies. She reminds him that the blood feud between them has not yet been erased. Furiously she condemns Tristan for his wanton murder of Morold and swears she will yet have revenge.

With great dignity Tristan offers her his sword. In cold contempt Isolde observes that King Marke would hardly welcome as his bride the murderess of his most trusted knight. Then, pretending to cast aside thoughts of revenge, she asks Tristan to drink the cup of peace with her. The chorus of sailors breaks in sharply. With an impatient gesture Isolde commands Brangäne to hand her the drink. Tristan softly voices his premonition of the fate that awaits both him and Isolde in the cup.

Isolde proffers the beaker, saying scornfully that Tristan may now tell his lord that he has drunk of the cup of friendship with this fair bride who saved his life. Confused and shaken, Tristan excitedly shouts an order to the sailors, then takes the cup. With a ringing phrase of despair and resignation he drinks. Isolde watches for a moment, then tears the cup from his hands, drains it, and flings it away. They stand transfixed as the love theme begins whispering in the orchestra. As the music rises in intensity they gaze at each other in unbelieving wonder. With passionate outcries they rush into each other's arms. From another part of the ship comes a chorus of sailors hailing King Marke. Brangäne, watching the lovers, laments her fateful ruse of substituting the love potion for the drink of death. Oblivious to everything, Isolde and Tristan pour out their love for each other.

While all the men on board acclaim King Marke in a thunderous chorus, Tristan stares uncomprehendingly toward the shore. Brangäne quickly places the regal mantel over Isolde's shoulders. In sudden terror Isolde asks her, "Ha! welcher Trank [Ah, what was the potion]?" When Brangäne answers that it was the love drink, Tristan and Isolde cry out in mingled ecstasy and despair. The curtain falls.

ACT TWO

The garden of King Marke's palace in Cornwall. The brief introduction is dominated by the tense, agitated theme of anticipation. It is night. A torch burns at the entrance of Isolde's apartments, off a balcony at the rear. The horns of King Marke's hunting party sound in the distance. Brangäne gazes apprehensively toward the forest, then back at the doorway. Isolde enters hurriedly. Lost in rapture, she sings of her impatience to be in Tristan's arms. Brangäne, haunted by fear and remorse over her deed, vainly tries to bring Isolde to her senses. She warns that Melot, though posing as a friend, is planning some treachery and that this hunting expedition is part of his evil plan. But Isolde derides her fears and commands her to extinguish the torch as a signal for Tristan to approach. When Brangäne protests, lamenting bitterly over mixing the love potion, Isolde sings that destiny has brought her and Tristan together. Impetuously she throws the torch to the ground as the theme of anticipation sweeps through the orchestra. Brangäne, disturbed and uneasy, mounts an outer flight of steps to a turret where she may watch and warn the lovers of the return of King Marke and his huntsmen.

Isolde looks eagerly beyond the ramparts and hopefully waves her scarf, the symbolical scarf motive accompanying her movements. The music grows wilder as she sees Tristan and signals him in fervid excitement. At its climax Tristan rushes in. They embrace in utter ecstasy and sing in exultant tones of the miracle of their love. The storm of their passionate utterances gradually subsides. Tristan slowly leads Isolde to a grassy slope. Gazing into each other's eyes, they sing the magnificent love duet, "O sink hernieder, Nacht der Liebe."

When they pause Brangäne's warning voice floats from the tower ("Habet Acht"). It is lost again as Tristan and Isolde continue their duet.

In the intensity of their passion they cry for death, so that they may be forever united beyond the reach of the world.

The flood of love music stops suddenly at its height. A harsh chord crashes in the orchestra. Brangäne screams in terror. Kurvenal runs in shouting a warning to Tristan. Then King Marke and his huntsmen, led by Melot, stride in. Brangäne hurries to Isolde's side. Tristan springs up and stands before her, shielding her form with his cloak. For a long moment no one moves or speaks, while in the orchestra the motives of love's transfiguration and the coming of day mingle softly.

Tristan is the first to break the silence, murmuring, "Der öde Tag—zum letzen Mal [Wretched dawn—for the last time]!" Melot smugly exults that his ruse has successfully trapped the lovers. King Marke turns on Tristan with a flood of bitter reproach for betraying his friendship and trust. In helpless bewilderment he asks why fate has dealt him this cruel blow. To that question, Tristan says dolorously, there is no answer. He asks Isolde if she is prepared to follow him into the land of night to which he now must go. When Isolde answers in the affirmative Melot cries out that he will avenge this final insult to the King. Drawing his sword, he challenges Tristan, who accepts with cold contempt. He hurls himself at Melot, then deliberately allows his adversary to wound him. Kurvenal and Isolde rush to him as he sinks to the ground, while King Marke restrains the treacherous Melot. The King Marke motive thunders forth as the curtain falls.

ACT THREE

The rocky courtyard of Tristan's castle, Kareol, in Brittany. At the rear is a watch tower commanding a view of a broad waste of ocean. Before the curtain rises there is a brief prelude in which the motive of suffering and longing is combined with the rising wail of the desolation theme.

Tristan, gravely wounded, lies motionless on a couch. Kurvenal is at his side, watching him closely. From beyond the ramparts comes the plaintive and melancholy sound of a shepherd's pipe. Soon the young shepherd appears and inquires if Tristan still sleeps. Were he to awake, Kurvenal answers sadly, it would be only to die. He bids the shepherd watch closely for any sign of a ship on the horizon, and directs him to change his sad piping to a merry tune, should a vessel heave in sight.

Tristan revives, and in answer to his confused questions Kurvenal explains how they made their way to Tristan's castle—that after the duel he carried his master to the ship which brought them home. Here in his homeland, Kurvenal assures him, his wounds will quickly heal. But Tristan now sinks into delirium, calling wildly for Isolde and raving against the light of day, which he associates with his doom.

When he again becomes quiet Kurvenal goes on to tell him that he has dispatched a servant to Cornwall to bring Isolde, so that she who once before had restored Tristan to health may do so again. In poignant phrases Tristan expresses his gratitude for Kurvenal's loyalty, having shared with him joy and sorrow and even betrayal. One thing only this loyal friend cannot share—the fearful pain of love in his heart. In his feverish excitement Tristan imagines that Isolde's ship is approaching.

He tries to rise but falls back exhausted. Listening to the shepherd's mournful piping, he murmurs that he had heard this dirge long ago at the death of his mother and father and that its refrain is interwoven with his own fate. Again the madness of pain overcomes him, and in a spasm of anguish he curses the love potion. Frenziedly crying out that the ship is approaching, he implores Kurvenal to go to the rampart. As Kurvenal, deeply distressed, tries to calm him, the shepherd's piping changes to a gay and sprightly tune. Kurvenal springs to the rampart and joyously describes the approach of the ship. Tristan orders him to meet Isolde.

In a paroxysm of ecstasy and pain Tristan raises himself, rips away his bandages, and struggles to his feet. Isolde appears, calling his name, as the motive of love's longing soars up in a tremendous crescendo. Tristan sinks into her arms. There, tenderly breathing her name, he dies. Isolde, stunned, kneels beside his body. Bitterly she laments that death has robbed her of the bliss of this reunion. She collapses, fainting, at Tristan's side.

Kurvenal, who has been watching horror-stricken, is roused by the shepherd's warning that another vessel is coming. Looking seaward, Kurvenal recognizes it as King Marke's ship. Hurriedly he and the shepherd attempt to barricade the gate at the entrance to the courtyard. In another moment there is a confusion of sounds and the clashing of swords from below the rampart. Brangäne is heard calling for Isolde. Melot rushes up, and Kurvenal kills him with a blow. When King Marke and his followers storm the barricade Kurvenal attacks them furiously. While they are fighting, Brangäne makes her way to Isolde. Soon Kurvenal, fatally wounded, staggers over to Tristan's couch and falls dead. King Marke gazes down on the scene, murmuring brokenly, "Todt denn Alles—Alles todt [Now all—all are dead]."

Isolde revives. Brangäne explains to her that she had confessed mixing the love potion and that when King Marke heard her story he came in all haste to Brittany to forgive Isolde. In grief-stricken tones the King adds that he had absolved Tristan of all blame and was prepared to give him Isolde as his bride. But death alone has triumphed, he cries out in sorrow and despair.

With her eyes fixed on Tristan's face, Isolde begins her magnificent and heart-rending song of farewell, the *Liebestod* ("Mild und leise wie er lächelt"). As her voice soars in the exaltation of approaching death, the themes of bliss, parting, and transfiguration surge through the orchestra to an overwhelming climax. Isolde sinks upon Tristan's body—the lovers reunited at last in death. King Marke raises his hands in blessing over the dead. The music dies away high in the strings. The curtain falls.

Il Trovatore

by GIUSEPPE VERDI

[1813–1901]

Libretto by
SALVATORE CAMMARANO

Based on Antonio Garcia Gutiérrez's play
EL TROVADOR

CHARACTERS

Ferrando, captain of the palace guard
and henchman of Count di Luna............................*Bass*
Inez, companion to Leonora.................................*Soprano*
Leonora, a titled lady-in-waiting to the Queen
in a court of Aragon.......................................*Soprano*
Count di Luna, a nobleman in the same court................*Baritone*
Manrico, the troubador, an officer in the service of the
Prince of Biscay, and brother of Count di Luna.............*Tenor*
Azucena, a gypsy woman.....................................*Mezzo-soprano*
Ruiz, an officer in the service of Manrico.................*Tenor*
Soldiers in the service of Count di Luna and Manrico, guards, gypsies, a
messenger, a jailer, nuns, palace attendants

Place: Aragon and Biscay, in Spain
Time: Fifteenth century
First performance: Teatro Apollo, Rome, January 19, 1853
Original language: Italian

IL TROVATORE, Verdi's seventeenth opera, was composed in what has been termed his "second period" (1851–53), during which he also wrote *Rigoletto* and *La Traviata*. These operas firmly established his position as the greatest of Italian operatic composers. *Il Trovatore* has enjoyed uninterrupted success from the day of its première, and its melodies are perhaps more widely known than those of any other opera.

ACT ONE
(*The Duel*)

[*Scene One*]   A chamber adjoining the apartments of Count di Luna in Aliaferia Palace. Soldiers are on guard, while a group of di Luna's servants wait outside the chamber door to be assigned to their duties. Ferrando warns the servants to remain awake and watchful, for the count may return at any moment from his nightly vigil under the window of his ladylove,

Leonora. The officer reveals that the count is much perturbed over the recent appearance of a rival on the scene—a certain troubador. This information, however, fails to interest the weary servants, who request Ferrando to help them keep awake by telling the story of Garcia, brother of Count di Luna. As the retainers and soldiers gather round, Ferrando begins his narrative ("Di due figli vivea"), which reveals events prior to the time of the opera.

One day long ago the nurse to the younger of two children of Count di Luna (the present count's father) found a gypsy woman bending over the baby's bed. The screams of the nurse brought the servants, who drove the gypsy away despite her protests that she had come only to read the child's horoscope. The child, however, fell victim to a wasting illness as the result of a spell cast upon him by the gypsy, who was later captured and burned at the stake for her sorcery. The gypsy's daughter, burning for revenge, stole the count's other child and hurled him upon the flames that were consuming her mother. Although there was no witness to the terrible deed, so Ferrando's story goes, the charred bones of a child were found in the ashes. The grief-stricken count clung until his death to the conviction that his child was still alive. As he lay dying he charged his older son (the present Count di Luna) to devote his life to the search of his brother.

In foreboding tones Ferrando goes on to say that the tortured spirit of the gypsy haunts the castle to this day in various grisly shapes. In fact, one of the servants who struck the gypsy on her way to the stake had died in a state of madness that night as the clock struck twelve, the result of being haunted by her spirit in the form of an owl. A bell strikes midnight, and the listeners curse the witch. Servants and soldiers then resume their places of duty, and the curtain falls.

[Scene Two]   In the garden of the Aliaferia Palace. It is night. Inez, entering the garden with Leonora, reminds her that she is awaited by the queen. Leonora, however, can think only of her mysterious admirer. She tells Inez that she first saw the knight at a tournament, where he appeared in black armor, with a shield that bore no identifying device. He vanquished all his opponents in the lists, and Leonora placed the victor's crown upon his brow. But with the outbreak of civil war in the land, the knight vanished as suddenly as he had come. In a melodious aria ("Tacea la notte placida") Leonora relates the sequel to the story—how the knight, now in the role of an ardent troubador, has returned to sing passionate serenades beneath her window. In rapturous phrases Leonora declares her love for him. Inez expresses the hope that Leonora's love will not be in vain. The two voices blend in the closing phrases of the song as the women enter the palace.

Count di Luna now steps out of the shadows, gazes up at Leonora's window, and sings of his love in fervent phrases. Just as he is ascending the staircase to the palace he hears the notes of a harp and exclaims in fury that it is the troubador. The voice of Manrico is heard in a brief but lyrical serenade ("Deserto sulla terra"). Leonora hurries out of the palace and stands for a moment on the staircase, peering into the gloom of the garden. She sees the count muffled in his cloak. Mistaking him for Manrico, she rushes into his arms with a passionate cry.

At that moment she hears Manrico's angry exclamation, "Infida [Faithless one]!" As she gasps out "Qual voce [That voice]!" a ray of moonlight reveals the visored knight standing before her. A fiery trio now ensues. Freeing herself from the count's embrace, Leonora kneels before Manrico and in confusion and despair implores him to believe that her ardent words were meant for him. He gently reassures her, while the count furiously demands that his rival identify himself. In answer, Manrico raises his visor. The count rages at the impudence of this henchman of Urgel of Biscay, archenemy of Aragon, in daring to cross the boundaries of the kingdom. Manrico coolly taunts di Luna and defies him to call out his guards. When Leonora tries to intercede, the count, in a stormy refrain ("Di geloso amor sprezzato"), swears he will have Manrico's life and reproaches Leonora for her deception. Manrico continues to defy him, while Leonora resigns herself to death for the sake of her love. After the tremendous climax of the trio the two adversaries draw swords and rush away to fight. Leonora swoons. The curtain falls.

ACT TWO
(The Gypsy)

[*Scene One*] A gypsy camp in the mountains of Biscay. Azucena is huddled before a fire. On a cot near by is Manrico, wrapped in his cloak, his helmet put aside. He is holding his sword, gazing at it thoughtfully. As the dawn grows brighter the gypsies begin to move about. The men go to their forges, take up their hammers, and swing them in rhythm as they break into the stirring *Anvil Chorus* ("Chi del gitano i giorni abbella?"). They pause in their work to ask the women to bring wine, and then the chorus takes up the lusty song in praise of women, wine, and the carefree life of a gypsy.

The mood of the scene changes with dramatic swiftness as Azucena begins the great aria "Stride la vampa." Obsessed by the terrible memory of her mother's execution, she sings of how the victim was dragged to the pyre and how her screams of pain mingled with the jeers of the vengeful throng. The gypsies, who have gathered around Azucena, try to console her. Oblivious to their attentions, she turns to Manrico and fiercely commands him to avenge her ("Mi vendica"). Manrico is mystified at her insistence on revenge. One of the gypsies now reminds his companions that they must be on their way to forage for food in the neighboring villages. They all leave the camp to the strains of the *Anvil Chorus*.

Manrico bids Azucena continue her story. Grimly the gypsy says that her mother was burned at the very spot on which Manrico is now standing. With an exclamation of horror he moves away. In somber tones Azucena tells how she tried vainly to reach her mother's side as the brutal guards drove her to the stake. Through the smoke and flames came the dying cry for vengeance, and that cry has haunted Azucena day and night. Desperately resolved to avenge her mother, she stole the younger child of the old

Count di Luna and carried him to the pyre. The child's cries momentarily aroused her pity. But then the fearful vision of her mother's agony began to torment her, Azucena sings in tense, whispered tones. Her voice gradually rises to a wild crescendo as she relates how she hurled the baby into the flames, only to discover that in her madness and confusion she had sacrificed her own child, whom she had brought to the scene of the execution. Azucena's voice dies away in a brooding, tragic phrase as she sinks to the ground spent with fury and despair.

When Manrico shakes off the sinister spell of Azucena's story, he tries to unravel the mystery of his own birth. Now aware that the gypsy had destroyed her only child, he reasons that she is not his mother. When he asks whose son he really is, Azucena insists excitedly that he is her son. She reminds him that she has given him a mother's love—that she rescued him from the battlefield of Petilla, where he had lain half dead from wounds, and nursed him back to health.

Manrico recalls how he, sole survivor of his company, had faced the hated Count di Luna's men and had been badly wounded. Why, then, Azucena asks vindictively, had he spared the life of this treacherous enemy in the duel over Leonora. Manrico replies that some mysterious impulse had stayed his sword at di Luna's throat. In an impressive air ("Mal reggendo all'aspro assalto") he sings that when the count lay at his mercy a strange voice warned him not to kill. In vengeful fury Azucena exhorts Manrico to strike down his foe mercilessly, should they meet again. Manrico's voice blends dramatically with hers as he vows to plunge his dagger into di Luna's heart at their next encounter.

A horn call is heard in the distance. Manrico sounds an answer, and in a moment a messenger appears with a letter from his henchman, Ruiz. Manrico reads that Castellor fortress has fallen to them and that he has been ordered to take over its defenses. But the letter contains other startling news. Leonora, having heard the false report that Manrico has been killed in battle, has abandoned the world and is preparing to enter a convent this very day.

In great excitement Manrico tells Azucena that he must leave immediately. Feverishly the gypsy implores him not to go, but Manrico brushes aside her entreaties, saying that nothing can part him from Leonora. Their colloquy ends in a dramatic and powerful refrain. Manrico finally tears himself from Azucena's grasp and rushes away. The curtain falls.

[Scene two] Outside a convent near Castellor fortress. It is night. Count di Luna, Ferrando, and a company of their men stealthily approach. In recitative, di Luna tells Ferrando that his burning passion for Leonora has driven him to this desperate attempt to carry her away from the convent by force. He expresses his tormenting love for her in a fervent aria ("Il balen del suo sorriso").

As the count finishes his song a bell tolls. Ferrando explains that it is the signal for the ceremony at which Leonora will become a nun. The count plans to intercept Leonora before she can take her holy vows and orders Ferrando and the men to conceal themselves. In a hushed chorus the men assure their leader that his orders will be carried out. In another impassioned aria ("Per me ora fatale") he again declares his resolve to possess

Leonora. As di Luna and his men withdraw to places of concealment, their voices die away in tense, rhythmic phrases.

From within the convent come the voices of the nuns chanting of Leonora's renunciation. The sustained, solemn notes float above the staccato phrases sung by the count and his followers in a continuation of their chorus. Again the voices fade away, and all is silence. Chords sound softly in the strings as Leonora enters with Inez and a group of women attendants. Inez laments the parting from her mistress, who endeavors to comfort her. In a brief but exalted refrain Leonora commends herself to God. Suddenly the count strides forward crying that she is destined only for the altar of marriage. As Leonora and the other women exclaim in shocked surprise, Manrico enters.

Leonora rushes into his arms, singing that she scarcely dares believe that Manrico is standing before her ("E deggio e posso crederlo?"). Her refrain introduces the brilliant chorus of the act. While her ecstatic tones soar high over the ensemble, Manrico and di Luna pour out their hatred for each other and prepare to fight. The nuns sing that heaven has sent Manrico at this moment to save Leonora. Ferrando and his men warn Manrico that he is tempting fate by opposing the count. Soon Ruiz and Manrico's men rush in, and a fierce encounter ensues. Manrico fights his way to Leonora's side while his men force the count and his adherents to retreat. The nuns make their way to the shelter of the convent. As the chorus rises to a great crescendo the curtain falls.

ACT THREE
(*The Gypsy's Son*)

[*Scene One*]   The camp of Count di Luna, whose tent is seen at one side. In the background can be seen the ramparts of Castellor, to which Manrico has taken Leonora. The count is now besieging the fortress, and his soldiers are busily preparing for an attack. Ferrando addresses them briefly, assuring them of rich booty if they take Castellor. The soldiers answer in a spirited chorus ("Squilli, echeggi la tromba") in which they sing of their eagerness for combat and the glorious fruits of victory. Their voices fade into the distance as they march away.

Count di Luna emerges from his tent and gazes at Castellor. Bitterly he muses that Leonora is there in the embraces of his hated rival. In a burst of fury he swears revenge, then passionately sings Leonora's name. Ferrando comes rushing in with the news that the guards have seized a gypsy prowling about the outskirts of the camp. She is suspected of being a spy. Azucena is dragged in by the guards, who roughly urge her on as she pleads for mercy. The count orders her to be released and begins questioning her. Asked where her home is, Azucena replies that, after the manner of gypsies, her home is wherever she happens to be. She has lately come from Biscay, she adds, which brings an exclamation of surprise from both the count and Ferrando.

In a moving refrain ("Giorno poveri vivea") Azucena recalls her life in Biscay with her son, who was her only joy. But he disappeared, she continues, and since that day she has wandered everywhere in search of him. Ferrando, who has been watching her closely, remarks that he notes a strange familiarity about her features. Count di Luna asks the gypsy if she remembers that some fifteen years ago the child of a nobleman was stolen and carried off into the mountains of Biscay. Azucena, startled, asks di Luna if he was that child. The count replies that the baby was his brother. When the count persists in his questioning, Azucena vehemently denies that she knows anything about the theft of the child. Ferrando, noting her rising terror, declares that she is the sorceress who hurled the count's brother into the flames. Angrily di Luna orders the guards to seize her. When Azucena, distractedly calling for help, cries out "O Manrico, o figlio mio [O Manrico, my son]!" di Luna fiercely exults that now he has the mother of his rival at his mercy.

Azucena implores her tormentors to let death put an end to her misery. Suddenly she turns on di Luna and in a fierce whisper warns him that an angry God will strike him down for this injustice. The voices of Azucena, di Luna, Ferrando, and the guards blend dramatically. Azucena reiterates her warning, the count ordains death for the sorceress, and Ferrando and the guards consign her to the eternal fires of hell. At the conclusion of the chorus the guards drag the gypsy away. The curtain falls.

[*Scene Two*]   A chamber in the castle of Castellor. At the rear is a balcony, beyond which can be seen the tents of di Luna's camp. It is the day set for the marriage of Leonora and Manrico. Leonora, however, is restless and apprehensive over the impending attack of the count's forces. In an effort to reassure her, Manrico sings the beautiful aria "ah si, ben mio," in which he promises that even if he should die on the battlefield he will be faithful to her beyond the grave. The sound of organ music drifts from the chapel of the castle. Leonora and Manrico pledge their eternal love to each other in a brief but eloquent duet ("L'onda de' suoni mistici").

Their idyll is interrupted as Ruiz bursts into the room and excitedly bids Manrico look toward di Luna's camp. There, he says, the gypsy woman is being led in chains to the stake. Manrico reels in horror, then turns to Leonora and gasps that the gypsy is his mother. Recovering himself, he orders Ruiz to prepare his men for an attack upon the camp. As Ruiz leaves, Manrico begins the famous aria "Di quella pira," one of the most dramatic numbers in the opera. In ringing tones he vows to save his mother from a fiery death. Fervently he bids Leonora adieu, declaring that he cannot forsake his mother now. Leonora heartbrokenly sings farewell.

Ruiz and the soldiers enter, armed and ready for battle. In a powerful chorus they pledge themselves to follow Manrico to the rescue of his mother. He and the soldiers rush away to the blaring of trumpets as the curtain falls.

ACT FOUR
(*The Torture*)

[*Scene One*]   At the battlements of the Aliaferia Palace. A prison tower with barred windows rises at one side. It is night. Manrico and Azucena are imprisoned in the tower, having been brought there after Manrico's unsuccessful attempt to rescue his mother. Not only were Manrico and his followers defeated by di Luna, but Castellor itself was stormed and taken. Leonora and Ruiz fled to the safety of the mountains, but Leonora has returned to Aliaferia in a desperate effort to save Manrico.

As the curtain rises Leonora and Ruiz, their faces hidden in their cloaks, cautiously approach the ramparts of the castle. Leonora dismisses Ruiz. On her right hand Leonora wears a ring containing poison. She gazes at it for a moment, murmuring that this guardian will protect her from all harm. Raising her eyes to the tower, she muses in recitative about her imprisoned lover. Then in a tender and passionate aria ("D'amor sull'ali rosee") Leonora voices the hope that Manrico will be sustained by the assurance of her love for him.

At the end of her song a bell tolls ominously. From within the castle come the voices of men chanting a *Miserere* for the doomed prisoner, introducing one of the most famous ensemble numbers in all opera. To the accompaniment of softly throbbing chords in the orchestra, Leonora expresses her terror and despair in broken, sobbing phrases. Then from the tower comes the voice of the troubador in the sweeping phrases of the great aria "Ah! che la morte ognora." He frets that death is too slow in bringing him release, and bids farewell to Leonora. The voices of the lovers rise above the chanting of the chorus as, unseen by each other, they pour out their devotion.

After the ensemble surges to a tremendous climax, Leonora sings a fervid refrain ("Tu vedrai che amore in terra") in which she resolves to make one final attempt to save her lover. She then withdraws as the count appears with several attendants. He indicates the spot where Manrico is to be beheaded and his mother burned at the stake. When the attendants leave, di Luna laments that he has been unable to find any trace of Leonora.

Thereupon Leonora steps out of the shadows and stands before him. A stormy musical dialogue follows. The count answers Leonora's anguished pleas for Manrico's life with violent refusals. When she kneels abjectly before him, di Luna cries out that his only desire is to prolong his rival's torment. Half mad with despair, Leonora finally promises the count that she will be his if he will grant Manrico's freedom. She asks only that she be permitted to go to Manrico and tell him that he has been spared.

Before the count can reply, a guard appears. As di Luna turns to speak to him Leonora swiftly raises the ring to her lips and swallows the poison concealed under the jewel. In low tones she murmurs that the count will claim only her cold and lifeless body. When di Luna turns back to her, saying he will spare Manrico's life, Leonora sings in feverish exaltation ("Vivrà! Contende il giubilo"). The count, mistaking her ardor and excitement, sings triumphantly that his heart's desire at last has been granted. The two voices join in ecstatic phrases at the climax of the scene. Leonora and the count hurry into the tower. The curtain falls.

[*Scene Two*]   The dungeon in the prison tower. Azucena lies on a pallet, with Manrico at her side. They try to comfort each other. Azucena exults that she will yet escape her captors because death will claim her before she can be led to the stake. Then, as the theme of her "Stride la vampa" aria echoes in the orchestra, Azucena is seized by the tormenting recollection of her mother's death. She rises in wild terror from her pallet as she relives the scene. Shaken and exhausted, she sinks into Manrico's arms.

Gently he bids her seek comfort in sleep. Azucena sings a plaintive refrain which introduces the tender duet "Ai nostri monti," popularly known as "Home to our mountains." She and Manrico envision a happy return to their homeland. With Manrico kneeling beside her, Azucena gradually falls asleep. The music softly dies away.

Without warning, the door of the dungeon opens and Leonora steps inside. The lovers rush into each other's arms with exclamations of rapture. Tearing herself from Manrico's embrace, Leonora frantically implores him to leave at once. He refuses to go without her. Leonora's agitated demeanor arouses Manrico's suspicions, and he demands to know at what price she has obtained his freedom. Before she can answer he furiously denounces her for having made an unholy bargain with di Luna. Heedless of her protests, he bitterly reproaches her for her faithlessness. Azucena's voice is interwoven with their angry phrases as in her dreams she again sings of returning home to her beloved mountains.

Leonora collapses at Manrico's feet as the poison begins to take effect. In blind anger he orders her to leave, but when he sees the agony in her face he takes her in his arms and distractedly beseeches her to speak. Leonora gasps that she has taken poison and that death is near. In a torment of remorse and grief, Manrico implores her forgiveness.

Count di Luna enters. Seeing Leonora in Manrico's arms, he cries out in fury. Leonora bids farewell to Manrico, who brokenly repeats his entreaties to be forgiven. The count rages that he will have revenge on both for this ultimate deception. With a last cry of farewell, Leonora dies in the arms of Manrico.

The count now orders the guards to lead Manrico to his execution. His parting words, "Ah, madre, addio [Ah, Mother, farewell]!" rouse Azucena. Dazed and bewildered, she rises and staggers toward the window, calling for her son. In ferocious triumph the count thunders that Manrico is dying on the scaffold. With that Azucena turns on the count and reveals her terrible secret—Manrico was his brother ("Egli era tuo fratello"). Exultantly she sings that her mother is revenged at last. She falls unconscious as Count di Luna cries out in horror and despair. The curtain falls.

Turandot

by GIACOMO PUCCINI

[1858–1924]

Libretto by
GIUSEPPE ADAMI *and* RENATO SIMONI

Based on Schiller's version of a play of the same name by
Count Carlo Gozzi

CHARACTERS

A mandarin .... *Baritone*
Liù, a young slave girl..................................... *Soprano*
The Unknown Prince (Calaf)................................ *Tenor*
Timur, his father, an exiled Tartar King....................... *Bass*
Ping, the Grand Chancellor................................ *Baritone*
Pang, the General Purveyor................................. *Tenor*
Pong, the Chief Cook..................................... *Tenor*
The Emperor Altoum..................................... *Tenor*
Princess Turandot, his daughter .... *Soprano*
The Prince of Persia....................................... *Tenor*
Pu-Tin-Pao, the executioner
  Imperial guards, priests, mandarins, officials, executioner's assistants, the
  eight Wise Men, slaves, musicians, ghosts of the dead, soldiers, the people
  of Pekin

Place: Pekin
Time: Legendary
First performance: Teatro La Scala, Milan, April 25, 1926
Original language: Italian

PUCCINI died before he could complete *Turandot*, his last and—in the opinion of many—his greatest opera. The score was finished by his friend, Franco Alfano, who worked from sketches left by the composer. Puccini's own music ends near the close of the first scene of the third act, shortly after the suicide of Liù. It is related that Arturo Toscanini, who conducted the première, abruptly halted the performance at this point, turned to the audience, and announced that there the composer had put down his pen.

In its general technique of composition and complicated harmonic structure, *Turandot* reveals an advance over Puccini's earlier operas. The highly flexible forms of musical utterance delineate the action with maximum effectiveness, and there is superb fusion of music and drama. Through it all there runs a vein of opulent Puccinian melody that makes *Turandot* one of the most profoundly beautiful scores in the literature of opera.

ACT ONE

Before the walls of the Imperial Palace in Pekin. At one side are huge semicircular bastions, flanking a great door carved with figures of unicorns and phoenixes. Near the door an enormous bronze gong hangs between two arches. Fixed to poles on top of the wall are the heads of those who failed to give the answers to the three enigmas put by Princess Turandot—a test which she required of every man who presented himself as a suitor. Beyond the palace the Celestial City glows in the light of the setting sun.

In the square in front of the great door is a vast crowd of people, all looking silently up at a mandarin standing on top of the bastions, reading an imperial decree ("Popolo di Pekino! La legge è questa"). It is ordained, he proclaims, that Turandot the Pure will become the bride of the royal suitor who can solve the three enigmas which she will propound. The penalty for failure is death. The Prince of Persia, being the latest to answer unsuccessfully, is condemned to die at the rising of the moon. Having delivered the proclamation, the mandarin stalks away.

As though seized by frenzy, the crowd howls for death, calling on the executioner to hasten to his task ("Muoia! Noi vogliamo il carnefice"). Threatening to drag him out of bed if he does not hurry, the crowd surges toward the door. There they are met by guards, who brutally force them back. Shrieking in panic, the people retreat, trampling each other in their efforts to escape the blows.

Liù, the young slave girl, is seen kneeling beside an old man crouched on the ground. She is heard calling for help and crying that her aged master has been thrown to the ground. A young man—the Unknown Prince—makes his way to her through the crowd. He bends to look at the old man and then mutters an exclamation of surprise as he recognizes his father. The old man is Timur, exiled king of the Tartars, and his rescuer is Calaf. Exiled like his father, Calaf calls himself the Unknown Prince to conceal his identity from his enemies. Liù, who served as a slave in Timur's palace, is secretly in love with Calaf.

The two men weep with joy at being reunited, and then Calaf, with Liù's assistance, leads Timur to one side. The crowd stampedes back into the square, yelling that the executioners have arrived. A group of fierce-looking men in bloodstained rags appear on the wall, dragging a huge sword. Others bring in a grindstone and prepare to sharpen the weapon. Timur meanwhile tells Calaf that when he fled from his kingdom, following the defeat of his forces by rebels, Liù faithfully remained at his side and cared for him. When Calaf asks her why she endured the hardships of exile, she shyly replies that it is because one day in the palace he favored her with a smile.

Their words are lost in the harsh tones of a chorus sung by the executioner's assistants as they sharpen the great sword ("Arrota! Che la lama guizzi"). As the sparks fly from the wheel, they chant that the sword, bathed in blood and flame, is never idle while Turandot commands. They call to the hapless lovers to come and embrace the shining blade, as cold and fatally beautiful as the princess herself. A powerful ensemble is built up as the crowd repeats their words. In savage glee the assistants sing that when a suitor sounds the gong, indicating that he has come to woo the princess, they sharpen the sword, for they know that the luckless fellow will hear the three enigmas and then die. The people join in their exultation, bringing the ensemble to a ferocious climax as they acclaim Princess Turandot.

When the assistants leave to take the sword to the executioner, the people rush to points of vantage to await the rising of the moon, at which time the victim will be lead out to die. In a macabre chorus they call on the moon to appear ("Perchè tarda la luna? Faccia pallida"). With its rising, their excitement increases, and they begin yelling for Pu-Tin-Pao. The death procession finally appears, led by a group of children wailing the funereal chorus in unison ("La sui monti dell'Est"), an adaptation of an ancient Chinese melody. They chant meaninglessly about the stork singing in the mountains of the East, and of the thousand voices that implore the princess to return so that the flowers may bloom again.

The children are followed by priests, mandarins, and officials, and after them, walking alone, comes the victim—the young and handsome Prince of Persia. When he is led to the spot where he is to die, the executioner stalks in, his great sword on his shoulder. The sight of the unfortunate prince stirs the capricious crowd to pity, and in an ensuing chorus ("O giovinetto! Grazia") they ask mercy for the victim as fervently as they had cried for his death. The Unknown Prince adds his entreaties. He calls for the heartless Princess Turandot to appear so that he may curse her.

No sooner has he spoken than Turandot walks slowly across the top of the wall. Gasping in wonder at her beauty, the Unknown Prince buries his face in his hands as though blinded by a light. There is a moment of silence. Turandot raises her hand in a commanding gesture to signal the death sentence, the executioner bows, and the procession moves slowly onward to the chanting of the priests. The crowd pushes through the great door, while Turandot re-enters the palace.

Timur, Liù, and Calaf are left standing alone in the square, with Calaf staring up at the top of the wall as though hypnotized. Exclaiming in feverish ecstasy over the beauty of the princess, he starts walking toward the door, while Liù and his father try to restrain him. Struggling out of their grasp and wildly crying Turandot's name, Calaf runs toward the gong to strike it as a signal that he has come as a suitor. His cry is echoed within the walls of the palace in an agonized phrase as the Prince of Persia screams Turandot's name. It is followed by the sound of a blow and a succession of horrified exclamations from the crowd watching his execution.

For an instant Calaf stands transfixed, then his mad desire again takes possession of him. Just as he is about to fling himself against the gong three strange, masked figures bar his way. They are Ping, Pang, and Pong, the Emperor's ministers.[1] In a striking trio ("Fermo! che fai? T'arresta!") they

[1] Ping, Pang, and Pong are operatic adaptations of traditional characters of *commedia dell' arte*, the old Italian masked comedy.

berate him for his rashness and folly. Pointing to the door, they warn him that it leads to the abattoir where the royal victims are spiked, skinned, and beheaded. With impatient scorn they tell him to go back to his own country and find someone who will oblige him by lopping off his head—if that is what he desires.

Calaf's voice is added to the ensemble as he demands to be allowed to pass. The ministers fume that all the graveyards in Pekin are full and that there already are enough lunatics in China who insist on losing their heads. And for a mere princess, at that, they exclaim with humorous gestures of incredulity, a creature who is nothing more than a woman with a crown on her head. Ping advises him to shun all women or—if he must have feminine company—to marry a hundred. Then he will have Turandot's charms multiplied a hundred times. Ignoring him completely, Calaf again tries to force his way through the door.

At that moment a group of lightly clad young women—Turandot's maids—come to the edge of the wall and warn those below to be silent. In a melodious chorus they sing that the princess is sleeping and that the night is fragrant with her perfume ("È l'ora dolcissima"). Blustering that the Emperor's illustrious ministers are not to be addressed in that manner, Ping, Pang, and Pong order the women to be off.

Calaf meanwhile stands lost in thought, murmuring about Turandot. The ministers exclaim that he has gone crazy, while Timur groans that his son is past all hearing and heeding. Crowding closely around him and affecting the singsong speech of a child reciting a poem, the ministers repeat the warning they have uttered so many times—Turandot's enigmas can never be answered . . . they are obscure as night . . . they are more impenetrable than iron, bronze, or rock, and so on. To give emphasis to their words, the voices of Turandot's dead lovers come out of the darkness. Their ghosts seem to float through the air as they urge Calaf to flee and then despairingly wail their declarations of love for Turandot.

With weary insistence the ministers try to convince Calaf that his dream of possessing Turandot is utter madness. Everything is illusion, they observe, and nothing exists except the oblivion to which he will be consigned as an unsuccessful suitor. When Calaf reiterates that he will win Turandot's love, the ministers turn and point to the top of the wall, where, at that moment, the executioner is thrusting the head of the Prince of Persia on a spike. *There* is her love, they remark sardonically.

Timur now adds his entreaties, asking desperately if there is no voice to which his son will listen in his insane folly. Liù approaches and, in a poignant refrain ("Signore, ascolta"), begs him to heed her words. She thought only of him during these bitter days of exile, she says, and that thought sustained her. If he dooms himself by becoming Turandot's suitor, Timur will lose his beloved son and she will lose her last and only hope. She will have only the memory of his smile, she sobs.

Calaf tenderly answers, gently telling her not to cry ("Non piangere, Liù"). If she treasures the memory of the smile he once gave her, he says, she can show her gratitude by remaining with his father and making his cruel exile easier through her care. This is the plea of one who can no longer smile, he concludes in a ringing phrase.

Ping, Pang, and Pong again approach him. Their final words of appeal mark the beginning of the thrilling ensemble which brings the act to a close ("Ah! per l'ultima volta"). Timur and Liù beg him not to desert them. Calaf raves that he will listen to no one because he hears the princess calling to him. In desperation Timur and Liù try to drag him away, and the ministers add their own efforts. But Calaf struggles free, shouting that he must go to meet his destiny. The voices of an unseen chorus join the ensemble, warning that a fate as mysterious as it is cruel awaits the rash lover.

Turning toward the palace, Calaf shouts that his tortured senses cry with one voice the name of Turandot. Like a madman he rushes to the gong, seizes the hammer, and violently strikes three times, each time calling aloud Turandot's name. Timur and Liù cower in fear. Ping, Pang, and Pong, exclaiming that it is futile to reason with a lunatic, run away. Death dances when the gong sounds, they cry with a burst of sardonic laughter. Calaf remains standing by the gong, staring at the palace, as the curtain falls.

ACT TWO

[*Scene One*]   A pavilion enclosed on three sides by a large curtain decorated with fantastic Chinese figures. There is an entrance in the center and one at either side. Ping sticks his head through the center opening, looks to right and left, and then calls in a loud whisper to Pang and Pong. They enter with exaggerated dignity, followed by three servants, each of whom carries a lantern—one red, one green, and one yellow. Placing the lanterns on a low table in the center of the room, the servants withdraw to the rear. The dialogue throughout the entire scene is in the form of a trio, which Ping begins by remarking that, as the gong has been sounded again, they can prepare either for a wedding or a funeral ("Poichè il funesto gong"). They go on talking ironically about festive lights and funeral lanterns, palanquins and coffins, nuptial hymns and requiems—everything properly in keeping with sacred custom.

The ministers lament that China slept serenely for seven thousand centuries—until the birth of Turandot. Since the reign of the princess there has been nothing but bloodshed and the festival entertainments have followed an unvarying pattern—three sounds of the gong, three enigmas, and the pleasant spectacle of rolling heads. Taking up scrolls which the servants have placed on the table, the ministers begin reading in lugubrious tones the impressive toll of Turandot's unfortunate suitors. In the year of the mouse, six; in the year of the dog, eight; in the present year of the tiger, the total already is thirteen—counting the latest, though he still has his head.

They complain comically about the hard lot of the Emperor's ministers of execution. Ping speaks longingly of his house on a lake in Honan, which he never has time to visit; Pang sighs for his estate in Tsiang; while Pong wails that he has a beautiful garden near Kiù which he probably will never see again. Groaning about a world full of lunatic lovers, they reminisce about the sorry procession of wooers they have seen led to the headsman—Prince Samarcanda, Sagarika of India, the Mussulman, the Prince of Kirghiz. They listen gloomily as the voices of the executioner's assistants come from within the palace, singing their bloodthirsty chorus as they sharpen the sword. Murder, endless murder, the ministers wail, murder that will eradicate the entire race if this orgy of decapitation is not halted.

Half seriously, half in bitter irony, Ping prays for the night when the murderous princess will finally yield to love. With appropriate gestures the three describe how they will prepare the nuptial chamber. Intrigued by the possibility of Turandot's surrender, Ping, Pang, and Pong sing melodiously of the new era, when the icy heart of the princess will have been melted by passion ("Non v'e in Cina, per nostra fortuna"). Then the days of blood lust will be a thing of the past, and the mighty Turandot, who rules with an iron hand over a vast realm, will be powerless under the spell of kisses. On that night of miracles she will listen enraptured to words of love, and peace will reign again in China.

But they are soon jarred out of their pleasant reverie by sounds of activity in the palace, indicating that the grim ceremony is about to begin again. Ping exclaims that they have been daydreaming while trumpets and drums signal the possible doom of another victim. Cynically observing that they will now go to enjoy this infamous spectacle, the ministers hurry away.

[Scene Two] A great square at the foot of a broad marble staircase leading up to the Imperial Palace. The staircase has three wide landings on which servants are placing brightly colored lanterns. Incense drifting up from braziers hangs like a mist over the scene. At the top of the marble steps stand the eight Wise Men, tall, old, and dignified. Each one holds three sealed scrolls of silk, on which are written the answers to Turandot's enigmas. Mandarins in their blue and gold robes of state come out of the palace and take their places on the staircase.

The people of Pekin, gathered in the square, gape at the magnificent array of dignitaries and comment among themselves in brief choral phrases ("Gravi, enormi, venerandi"). A shout goes up as Ping, Pang, and Pong, in their yellow ceremonial robes, take their places. A majestic theme sounds in the orchestra as the clouds of incense roll away to reveal the Emperor Altoum seated on his throne at the head of the staircase. The people prostrate themselves, then hail the Emperor in a thunderous outburst of sound ("Diecimila anni al nostro Imperatore").

The Unknown Prince walks through the crowd and pauses at the foot of the great stairway. Timur and Liù, who have followed him, remain at one side. The Emperor, a white-haired, shriveled old man, gazes down at Calaf and speaks in a thin, quavering voice. The ensuing colloquy between him and Calaf is carried on without accompaniment. Saying that he is bound by a terrible oath which has stained his scepter with blood, the Emperor exhorts the Unknown Prince to leave at once and save his life. Calaf answers that he desires to face the ordeal. The Emperor begs him not to throw his life away, but Calaf merely makes the same reply in identical musical phrases. With a gesture of hopelessness, the Emperor orders the trial to proceed.

After a trumpet fanfare a mandarin reads the conditions of the test. When he has finished, Turandot, preceded by her attendants, comes out of the palace and walks slowly toward the throne. She looks contemptuously down at Calaf, who controls himself with an effort and gazes steadily into her eyes. Children's voices are heard chanting Turandot's praises.

After a moment of silence Turandot launches into a long soliloquy ("In questa Reggia, or son mill'anni e mille"), accompanied occasionally by the comments of the crowd, murmured in chorus. Centuries ago, she begins, the pure and beautiful Princess Lo-u-ling, her revered ancestor, lived in this palace and ruled the land in peace and serenity. Then the King of Tartary invaded China with his savage hordes, conquering and despoiling the land. Princess Lo-u-ling was dragged from the palace and brutally slain by a stranger—a stranger like himself, Turandot adds, glaring at Calaf.

For that foul crime, she continues, she has sworn to take revenge on all the princes of the earth. Lo-u-ling's murder has kindled an unquenchable fire of hate in her heart against all men, and she is resolved that no man will ever possess her. There are three enigmas, she proclaims fiercely, and one is Death. One is Life, Calaf shouts back in joyous defiance.

Turandot thereupon sets forth the first enigma ("Nella cupa notte vola un fantasma iridescente"): At night a glowing phantom wings its way over the world. It dies with the rising of the sun and is reborn each night. The answer, says Calaf, is Hope. The eight Wise Men consult their scrolls and signify that the answer is correct. Concealing her surprise, Turandot descends halfway down the staircase and proclaims the second enigma ("Guizza al pari di fiamma"): It is like a flame, feverish and intense, which subsides only with the coming of death. Dreams of triumph and conquest cause it to glow with passionate fire. It has the fiery color of sunset.

Calaf hesitates. The Emperor, Timur, Liù, and the crowd breathlessly urge him on. Suddenly he looks up at the princess and cries that the answer is Blood. As the Wise Men consult their scrolls again and nod their heads there is a tremendous uproar from the crowd. Turandot furiously orders the guards to beat the people into silence with their whips. She then rushes down the stairs to Calaf, who falls to his knees. Bending over him, her face close to his, she speaks the third enigma with venomous emphasis ("Gelo che ti dà foco"): A being of ice and fire. The freedom she grants is slavery, and to be her slave is to be a king.

In a spasm of terror, Calaf buries his face in his hands, but in the next instant he springs to his feet, crying exultantly that the victory is his. Proudly he gives the answer—Turandot. The crowd acclaims him in a ringing chorus ("Gloria, o vincitore"). As though stricken, Turandot drags herself up the staircase, kneels before the throne, and begs her father to save her from the stranger ("Figlio del cielo"). The Emperor intones that the oath is sacred. Turandot rages that she will never submit, but her father's only answer is to remind her of the oath. The people clamor that the princess must give her love to the stranger as a reward for his courage.

Glaring down at Calaf, Turandot asks if he wants her with her heart full of hatred, unwilling and defiant in his embrace. Calaf resolutely answers that he desires her to yield only in love. Then he stuns the princess by declaring that he will release her from her oath. He has solved three enigmas, he continues, and now he will propound a single riddle to Turandot ("Il mio nome non sai"): His name is unknown to her. If she can tell him his name before dawn, then at dawn he will forfeit his life. Turandot stares at him for a moment as though in a trance, then makes a gesture of assent. The Emperor and the court rise. Commending the prince for his courage, the Emperor welcomes him to the palace, adding that it is his hope that he may call the young man his son at tomorrow's dawn. As Calaf proudly ascends the staircase the people chant the Imperial Hymn in praise of the Emperor ("Ai tuoi piedi ci prostriamo"). The curtain falls.

ACT THREE

[Scene One] The beautiful gardens of the palace. The glow of many incense burners is reflected in the statues of gods and goddesses. At one side, before the entrance of Turandot's apartments, is a pavilion hung with an embroidered curtain. Seated on the steps of the pavilion, Calaf listens to the voices of the heralds as they go about the city proclaiming Turandot's order that no one may sleep tonight in Pekin ("Questa notte nessun dorma in Pekino"). Everyone will perish, they declare, unless the name of the Unknown Prince is brought to Turandot before dawn.

In one of the loveliest melodies in the opera, Calaf muses that the princess, too, lies sleepless in her chamber, haunted by the riddle that he alone can answer ("Tu pure, o Principessa"). But in the morning he will whisper his name to her with a kiss that will unite them forever in love. An unseen chorus of women repeat a strain of his song as they lament that they are doomed because they do not know the prince's name. Calaf climaxes his refrain with a ringing phrase of triumph.

Shadowy figures are seen moving about in the garden. More and more appear, and at last they resolve themselves into a large crowd of people, led by Ping, Pang, and Pong. A dramatic ensemble follows as the ministers and the people try to persuade Calaf to tell them his name so that they may be saved from unspeakable torture. Ping begins by telling Calaf to stop stargazing and give heed to the terrible doom that threatens Pekin ("Tu che guardi le stelle"). First the ministers try to tempt him with beautiful young women, who are brought before him alluringly clad in thin veils. At the ministers' command, they surround him with voluptuous gestures.

When Calaf impatiently pushes them away, the ministers order slaves to bring forth chests heaped with shining gold and glittering gems. Scarcely looking at the treasures, Calaf exclaims that he has no desire for wealth. Failing to tempt the prince with these offerings, the ministers declare that they will help him escape from Pekin to empires far out of reach of the vengeful Turandot. He will then have the satisfaction of knowing that he is the only man who not only conquered Turandot but escaped with his life. The crowd desperately begs him to flee so that they may follow him to safety. Harassed by their clamorous entreaties, Calaf prays for the dawn, so that the ordeal may be ended.

But the uproar only grows louder as the ministers and the people describe, in an agitated choral passage ("Straniero, tu non sai"), the hideous tortures that Turandot has devised for those who disobey her. Calaf shouts them down, declaring that their entreaties are useless—he must and will have Turandot. Maddened by terror and frustration, the people lunge toward Calaf with daggers upraised, screaming that they will force him to speak his name.

At that moment loud cries come from beyond the garden, with voices shouting that the name is known. A group of soldiers drags in Timur and Liù, both of whom have been mercilessly beaten and are bleeding. As Calaf runs toward them, frantically crying that they do not know his name, Ping recognizes them as the two who were talking to Calaf the day before.

Ping turns and sees Turandot coming out of the palace. As the people hail her and prostrate themselves, Ping approaches and tells her that the two captives know the prince's name, adding that the necessary devices are at hand to tear that name from their lips. With an exclamation of horror, Calaf starts toward his father to protect him. Sneering contemptuously at the prince, Turandot commands Timur to speak. Dazed by pain, the old man can do nothing but look at her beseechingly.

Suddenly Liù runs toward Turandot, crying that she alone knows the name. The crowd shouts with relief, while Calaf fiercely rebukes her for speaking. Gazing at him ardently, Liù quietly says that she will keep his name forever as her most cherished secret. The people, frantic with disappointment, howl for her death. While some of the soldiers grapple with Calaf and bind him with chains, others seize Liù and begin torturing her. Ping bends over her and with relentless insistence orders her to speak the name. As Liù sinks back, almost fainting from pain, Turandot commands the soldiers to release her. Struggling to her feet, Liù staggers toward the pavilion and there collapses. Looking down at her, Turandot asks wonderingly who has inspired her with so much courage.

Liù answers in a poignant refrain ("Principessa, l'amore!"). It is love that has given her strength, a secret love for the prince who is her lord. By her silence, Liù continues, she will give him to the princess, and it will be her ultimate gift. She calls on the soldiers to torment her as they will, saying that thus she will sacrifice herself on the altar of love.

For one moment Turandot is held spellbound by Liù's simple, unshakable resolution. In the next, however, her cruelty asserts itself and she commands the ministers to continue the torture. As Ping and the crowd howl for the executioner, Liù tries frantically to escape. Hemmed in by the crowd, she runs back to Turandot. In a final burst of defiance, she cries that the princess, too, will be conquered by the prince's love ("Si, Principessa! Ascoltami!"). As for herself, she will die so that he may triumph at last. Whirling on a soldier standing near by, Liù snatches a dagger from his belt and stabs herself. She staggers toward Calaf, looks at him with compassion and tenderness, and falls dead at his feet. With an anguished cry Calaf kneels beside her.

There is deep silence as a mournful strain echoes in the orchestra. The spell is broken as Turandot wrenches a whip out of the hands of an executioner's assistant, goes over to the soldier from whom Liù snatched the dagger, and strikes him savagely across the face. Timur, stunned by despair, kneels at Liù's side and brokenly calls her name. The crowd recoils in superstitious terror as he wails that Liù's spirit will demand atonement for the injustice of her death. As maids cover Turandot's face with a veil, the people, fearing that the avenging spirit may return in the form of a vampire, pray to Liù's soul, asking mercy and forgiveness. The body is carried away, with Timur, bitterly lamenting, walking beside it and holding Liù's hand in his. Ping, Pang, and Pong, murmuring that they have been stirred to unfamiliar feelings of pity, slowly leave. The crowd follows, repeating the prayer to the spirit of Liù, ending with the phrase "Oblia! Liù! Poesia!"[2]

Calaf and Turandot are alone. In a powerful refrain accompanied by the orchestra in unison, Calaf commands the princess to lift her veil and look upon the innocent blood that was spilled in her behalf ("Principessa di morte! Principessa di gelo!"). With those words he rushes to her and tears the veil from her face. This marks the beginning of the fiery duet during which Turandot finally surrenders. At first she warns him away, crying that she is not a mortal, but a goddess, who must not be defiled by the touch of human hands. When Calaf advances with arms outstretched, she protests that she will never yield. Ignoring her angry remonstrances, Calaf takes her in his arms and passionately kisses her. In triumph and ecstasy he declares his love. Overwhelmed by his ardor, Turandot, her eyes filled with tears, softly answers that she has been vanquished at last. Voices come from the shadows of the garden, softly singing that new and holy life is awakening with the dawn.

When Calaf hails the miracle of her first tears, Turandot confesses, in an eloquent refrain, that her first sight of him brought the premonition that she would be conquered by his love ("Del primo pianto, si, straniero, quando sei giunto"). Calaf fervently declares that she will be his forever. Thereupon the princess asks him not to seek any further triumph, but to leave her and take the mystery of his name with him. There is no longer any mystery, Calaf answers, because now he will give her his name and his life. Calaf, son of Timur, is his name, he cries. Realizing that he has successfully defied her, and that now her power is broken forever, Turandot momentarily gives way to anger over this final blow to her pride. Suddenly a fanfare of trumpets comes from the distance, signaling that the moment of the final trial has come. Imperiously Turandot commands Calaf to appear with her as her conqueror before the people. They turn and leave the garden.

[*Scene Two*]   The square before the staircase, as in Act Two. In the background the palace glows in the light of the rising sun. The Emperor is seated on his throne, surrounded by his court. Calaf stands at the foot of the staircase, and behind him is the crowd. After the people acclaim the Emperor, Turandot approaches the throne and tells her father that she has learned the stranger's name. Facing toward Calaf, she declares in soaring tones that his name is Love. Calaf runs up the staircase and into Turandot's outstretched arms. Delirious with joy, the people dance about and scatter flowers, shouting a thunderous invocation to love ("O sole! Vita! Eternità!").

[2] It is at this point that Puccini's music ends.

Wozzeck

by ALBAN BERG

[1885–1935]

Libretto by the Composer

Based on the tragedy of the same name by the German dramatist
Georg Büchner.

CHARACTERS

Captain ....*Tenor buffo*
Wozzeck ....*Baritone*
Andres, friend of Wozzeck...............................*Lyric tenor*
Marie, mistress of Wozzeck................................*Soprano*
Marie's baby son..*Singing voice*
Margret, neighbor of Marie...............................*Contralto*
Doctor ....*Bass buffo*
Drum Major ....*Dramatic tenor*
First Apprentice ....*Low bass*
Second Apprentice ....*High baritone (or tenor)*
Idiot ....*High tenor*
Soldier ....*Tenor*
Soldiers, apprentices, servant girls, wenches, children

Place: A town in Germany
Time: Post–World War I
First performance: State Opera, Berlin, December 14, 1925
Original language: German

WOZZECK is probably the first full-length opera written in atonal form —that is to say, a form in which melody and harmony are unrelated to a fundamental key. As a result, the work breaks away completely from operatic tradition. There are no set arias or ensembles. With the exception of an occasional melodic phrase, the vocal line is in the form of *Sprechstimme* or "song-speech," which is similar to, but freer than, recitative. The opera's three acts, subtitled respectively *Exposition, Dénouement,* and *Catastrophe,* are divided into musical episodes which bear such names as Suite, Passacaglia, Fantasie and Fugue, Invention on a Theme, and so on.

Berg was a disciple of Arnold Schönberg, chief exponent of the atonal school and inventor of the twelve-tone scale system. He added the elements of emotion and humanity to Schönberg's rather cold, mathematical technique.

Although the opera stirred violent controversy—and even riots—wherever it was performed, it became popular in Europe. It was introduced into

American repertoire with a performance by the New York City Center Opera Company on April 3, 1952. *Wozzeck* is in a mood of unrelieved tragedy, which is given relentless force by Berg's atonal style. Further impact is inherent in the instrumentation, which is scored for chamber orchestra, military band, and a tavern orchestra of violins. Instruments include the bombardon (a bass instrument of the trumpet family), accordion, and an out-of-tune piano.

ACT ONE
(*Exposition*)

[*Scene One*]   The Captain's room in the barracks. It is early morning. The Captain is seated in front of a mirror, and Wozzeck is shaving him. The two converse in *Sprechstimme* (song-speech) to a continuous musical accompaniment, which is in the form of a suite.

Pompous and domineering, the Captain warns Wozzeck to go more slowly and take his time, because the soldier's nervous movements are beginning to make him dizzy. Wozzeck is forced to leave off shaving while the Captain composes himself. Then the latter begins lecturing. First he wants to know what Wozzeck intends to do with the ten minutes he saved by hurrying. The Captain reminds the soldier that he has at least thirty more years to live—a matter of three hundred and sixty months, so many days, hours, and minutes. What's to be done with all that time?

Poor Wozzeck can only mumble, "Yes, Captain." The thought of eternity frightens him, the Captain goes on. He is terrified when he thinks of the whole world revolving in one short day. And for that very reason he cannot watch a mill wheel turn without being seized by melancholy. Wozzeck merely nods his head and repeats, "Yes, Captain," in a single-note phrase. To make matters worse for Wozzeck, the Captain keeps nagging at him. A man with a clear conscience, says he, always takes his time. When Wozzeck remains silent, the Captain impatiently orders him to talk about something— the weather, at least. Wozzeck makes some sort of reply. After a feeble attempt at joking about the wind blowing south-north, the Captain takes a hypocritical, moral tone and remarks that Wozzeck has a child who does not have "the blessing of the church."

In his simple way, Wozzeck answers that God probably will not hold the poor little worm to account just because "amens" were not said before he was born. After all, the Lord did say: "Suffer little children to come unto Me." These surprising words catch the Captain off his guard and he flies into a rage. He demands to know what Wozzeck means by that kind of talk. In a sudden outburst of despair ("Wir arme Leut!"),[1] Wozzeck cries that poor folk like himself are always in need—and the greatest need is money. Just let one of the poor try to bring a child into the world rightfully and morally—and see what happens. If he were a lord, says Wozzeck, he could afford to be virtuous. But people like himself are doomed to be unblessed

[1] This is perhaps the most important leitmotif of the whole opera. The phrase, "We poor people," sums up Wozzeck's frustration and despair.

in this world and the next. And if they ever do get to heaven they will probably be put to work making thunder.

Rather frightened at all this, the Captain soothingly assures Wozzeck that he is a worthy man, then warns him about thinking too much. Always take the middle of the road, the Captain advises, and always go slowly. Without a word Wozzeck leaves, and the curtain falls.

[Scene Two] The music continues without pause into an orchestral interlude which briefly restates the themes of the first scene, then rises to an agitated climax. At that point the curtain rises swiftly. It shows an open field with the town in the distance. Wozzeck and his friend Andres are cutting brush. Looking apprehensively at the darkening sky, Wozzeck mutters that this place is accursed. Andres calmly goes on with his work, singing a brief hunting song ("Das ist die schöne Jägerei"), a sort of folk tune about the joys of a huntsman's life. But Wozzeck interrupts with his gloomy comments about the accursed woods, where the mists float above the grass like a shroud. And among the grass, Wozzeck goes on, there rolls a man's head. Once a man picked it up, thinking the object was a hedgehog. Three days later the man was in his coffin.

Andres twits Wozzeck about being afraid, then breaks once more into his huntsman's song. Wozzeck mutters wildly about the strange things moving in the woods. Andres vainly tries to calm him. Suddenly Wozzeck stares at the setting sun, crying that a great fire is rising from earth to heaven. Trying to bring him to his senses, Andres slowly leads Wozzeck away. The latter mutters to himself, "The world is dead." As military music sounds faintly in the distance the curtain falls.

[Scene Three] A room in Marie's home. Standing at the window with her child in her arms, Marie imitates the sound of a drum and excitedly tells the boy the band is approaching. Margret, a neighbor, comes by and calls Marie's attention to the handsome Drum Major. Noticing Marie and the Drum Major exchanging warm glances, Margret comments maliciously on the fact. To herself, Marie sings a phrase about how fine soldiers are. But when Margret remarks that Marie's eyes are sparkling, Marie turns on her in fury, and the two exchange bitter insults. The altercation ends abruptly when Marie slams down the window. Hugging her child to her breast, Marie sings a tender lullaby ("Mädel, was fangst du jetzt an?"), one of the rare melodic passages in the opera. It has a vague, aimless theme that echoes Marie's own deep sadness—the maiden who has a child but no wedding ring. The lullaby dies away on a descending phrase. A brief instrumental interlude repeats the opening strain of Marie's song as she sits deep in thought.

Suddenly there is a knock on the window and Marie jumps up in alarm. She opens the window, sees Wozzeck, and tells him to come in. He tells her he must report to the barracks. Still under the spell of the woods, he mumbles incoherently about the darkness, about the fires rising from the land, about a mysterious shape in the heavens. Here the music becomes harsh and formless, in powerful contrast to the tender melodic aspect of Marie's lullaby. Completely bewildered, Marie shows Wozzeck his child in an effort to distract his thoughts. Wozzeck does not even look at the boy, but rushes wildly away. Frightened and alone, Marie gives way to terror. It is dark, she wails, as dark as though one were blind. Clasping the child to her, she rushes to the door with a wild cry of anguish. The curtain falls swiftly and a brief interlude follows.

[*Scene Four*] The Doctor's study. It is a sunny afternoon. Wozzeck comes in, and the Doctor rushes to meet him. (It is interesting to note that the ensuing dialogue is carried on against a background of a twelve-tone passacaglia which continues through twenty-one well-defined variations. The theme is first stated by the cello recitative which accompanies the Doctor's opening words.) The Doctor—who has Wozzeck's permission to experiment on him in return for money to support Marie and his child—begins by berating his "patient" for not following instructions. He accuses the man of coughing openly on the street, barking like a dog. Is it for such antics, the Doctor asks, that he is to pay three groschen a day?

When Wozzeck tries to explain that he simply did what nature forced him to do, the Doctor shouts that he himself has proved that the muscles obey only the human will. In short, when Wozzeck coughs he is misbehaving again. Then the Doctor launches into the subject of the experimental diet: beans for the present—nothing but beans. Next week a bit of leg of mutton. Then will come a revolutionary medical innovation: albumen, fats, carbohydrates, and oxyaldehydanhydridum!

At this point the Doctor for some reason again loses his temper and fumes at Wozzeck. He suddenly checks himself, feels his own pulse. Anger is bad for one's health, he babbles, then assures himself he is quite calm. Trying to help matters, Wozzeck attempts to explain what he calls his own "nature"—which he himself cannot understand. But he only gets hopelessly tangled in his explanations, then suddenly begins to rant as before about the darkness and the red flames in the west. Flinging wide his arms, he despairingly calls the name of Marie. The next moment he lowers his voice almost to a whisper and tells the Doctor about the world that is bursting into flames, the terrible voices that haunt him, and the toadstools that grow in circles in the forest.

Listening carefully, the Doctor nods and announces triumphantly that Wozzeck shows signs of an excellent aberration. Very good. Wozzeck shall have an extra bonus for this. But for the present, the Doctor declares, he must be sure to go on living as before—shaving the Captain, catching lizards, eating those beans.

Yes, Wozzeck answers, he will faithfully do everything the Doctor orders him to do, because he needs the money for his wife. The Doctor rubs his hands in satisfaction. Now that he has this magnificent aberration to work with, he can prove his hypothesis and become immortal. His cry, "Immortality," is underscored by the twenty-first variation of the passacaglia, given out in chorale form by the orchestra with overwhelming effect.

A sardonic embodiment of quackery, the Doctor suddenly becomes very calm and professional. Going up to the unfortunate Wozzeck, he asks to see his tongue. Wozzeck meekly obeys, and the curtain falls.

[*Scene Five*]   The street before Marie's house. It is evening. Marie is admiring the Drum Major, who is strutting before her. She murmurs that he has the chest of a steer and the beard of a lion . . . she is the proudest of women. But wait until Sunday, says the Drum Major, when he'll wear his plumes and his white gloves. The Prince himself says, "There's a splendid chap!"

Marie goes up to him with a tantalizing gesture. The Drum Major catches her in a passionate embrace and she struggles fiercely in his arms, then breaks loose. Looking down at her, the Drum Major marvels at the "devil" in her glance. With that he embraces her again, almost savagely. Marie stops struggling. "Have your own way," she cries, "it's all the same to me!" The two rush into the house. As the curtain slowly falls on the empty stage, the music rises to a great crescendo, then dies away to a tremulo in the strings. (This scene, brief though it is, is one of the most important in the opera. Marie's seduction by the Drum Major sets off the tragic chain of events which now follow.)

ACT TWO
(*Dénouement*)

[*Scene One*]   Marie's room on a sunny morning. Holding the sleeping child on her lap, Marie looks at her reflection in a broken piece of mirror and admires two earrings she is wearing. The music begins in a sonata form which carries through the entire scene. Marie marvels at the glistening stones ("Was die Steine glänzen") and wonders what they are. Then she tries to remember what "he" said. When the child cries and disturbs her thoughts, she crossly threatens him with the bogeyman. With an eerie, almost mischievous air, she sings a brief strain ("Mädel, mach's Lädel zu!"). It is a warning to a maid to keep her lattice shut, because a roving sprite may come by and lead her away to Gypsyland.

Frightened, the boy hides his head against his mother and sits very still. Marie, again looking into the mirror, once more gives voice to her thoughts. She wonders if the earrings are gold. Poor folk she muses, have only a broken piece of mirror—but she has just as rich and red a mouth as those noble ladies whose mirrors stretch from floor to ceiling. They and their handsome, hand-kissing husbands! The boy wakes. Irritably Marie tells him the sandman is coming. "See, there he is on the wall," she exclaims, flashing the mirror. The boy huddles close to her and is quiet again. Unnoticed, Wozzeck comes in and stands behind Marie, who looks down at the cringing child to see the effect of the "mirror game" on him. Suddenly aware of Wozzeck, Marie springs up, places the child on the chair, and covers up her earrings with her hands.

Wozzeck asks what she is hiding that glistens so. Earrings, Marie stammers. She found them. . . . When Wozzeck questions her suspiciously, she flares up in self-defense. He speaks placatingly, then looks down at the boy. Sadly he murmurs that the poor mite always sleeps—but even in sleep there is moisture on his brow. So it is always, he cries bitterly, nothing under the sun but work; even in sleep the poor must sweat—wretched folk that they are! (Here again is the phrase, "Wir arme Leute!"—Wozzeck's leitmotif.)

In a sudden change of mood, reflected by a calm sustained chord in the orchestra, he hands Marie some money, saying it is his pay from the Captain and the Doctor. With that, he leaves. Left alone again, Marie cries in bitter self-accusation that she is a bad woman and that she may as well commit suicide. Everything in this world, she sings in a poignant phrase, has gone to the devil—husband, wife, child. The curtain quickly falls. The music storms on into an interlude which is climaxed by a harp glissando.

[*Scene Two*] A street. The Captain and the Doctor meet. In this scene the structure of the music changes to a fugue with three themes—identifying the Captain (heard at the beginning of the opera), the Doctor (heard in *Scene Four* of Act One) and, later, Wozzeck. The dialogue is satiric and mocking.

Strolling along, the Captain addresses the Doctor as Mister Coffin-Nail. The Doctor—in a frantic hurry, as usual—greets the Captain as Sir Drill-Angel and asks him where he is going at so slow a pace. Hastening to catch up with the Doctor, the Captain asks him why he is hurrying. No time, says the Doctor, pushing on. The Captain warns the other that he will surely run his legs off at the rate he is going. By this time the Captain is panting, while the Doctor is standing stock-still, staring fixedly at him. The Captain begs the Doctor to help him save a human life, then whispers something to him. The Doctor repeats aloud, "A woman, dead within four weeks—cancer." Casually he adds that he himself has had twenty such cases, all dead within four weeks. "Don't frighten me that way," the Captain whimpers. "Many people die of fright."

Eyeing the Captain in a coldly professional manner, the Doctor remarks that he has all the signs of imminent apoplexy. Yes, he goes on, it might well happen within four weeks, and the progress of the illness would be most fascinating. And if, God willing, the tongue should become paralyzed, then we shall do some more immortal experimenting.

Beside himself with terror, the Captain clutches the Doctor's arm, crying he will not let him go, because people have died of fright and he needs help. The Captain begins coughing violently. Already he can see the mourners, he gasps, all weeping and all saying, "He was a good man!" Alarmed by the Captain's outburst, the Doctor tries to distract his thoughts from this morbid subject—and just at that moment Wozzeck comes by. When the Doctor calls to him, Wozzeck salutes, hurries on a few paces, then stops, and comes back.

The Captain, now himself again, remarks facetiously that Wozzeck runs by like a razor slicing the world. Then, abashed by Wozzeck's confused and helpless expression, the Captain looks at the Doctor's beard and lamely continues with his joke. Wozzeck, he says, runs as if all the beards of all the University professors needed shaving, and he would be hanged if one single hair. . . . At this point the fugue is resumed again, as at the beginning of the scene.

Musing about the fine long beards of the professors, the Captain whistles meditatively. The Doctor, looking at him, quotes a line about "a fine long beard beneath the chin," and remarks that the Roman poet Pliny spoke of that. Divining each other's thoughts about the Drum Major, the two proceed to make the hapless Wozzeck the butt of their merciless ridicule. Now of course, says the Doctor, Wozzeck has a faithful wife. Leering, the Captain adds that if Wozzeck has never found a hair from a fine long beard in his porridge, perhaps he has found it on two red lips. Oh, yes, the Captain goes on, *he* knows what love is. Then, suddenly serious, he looks at Wozzeck and remarks that he has turned pale.

Wozzeck, his impotent anger welling up within him, says the Captain is pleased to make fun of him—but he should remember that for some the earth can become so hot that hell is cold by comparison. Alarmed, the Doctor tries to feel Wozzeck's pulse. Still glaring at the Captain, Wozzeck jerks his hand away, crying out to the Captain that anything is possible. The Captain, quailing before Wozzeck's rage, tries to placate him with soft words, while the Doctor continues with his idiotic "diagnosis" of Wozzeck's condition: "Stiff facial muscles, stony stare. . . ." Their words merge in a discordant trio, out of which rises Wozzeck's heart-rending cry: "One might better end it all by hanging—then, at least, one would know where one is." With that, he rushes madly away. Looking after him, the Captain and the Doctor express their bewilderment over this strange creature.

This fellow, says the Captain fatuously, depresses him. A good man is grateful to God, and so has no need of courage. With an obvious reference to Wozzeck's failings, he adds, "Only a scoundrel . . ." He walks over to the Doctor, who, expecting another of the Captain's earlier outbursts about his fear of dying, beats a hasty retreat. Leaving the stage, the Captain sings the word "scoundrel" behind the scenes. Curtain.

[*Scene Three*] The street in front of Marie's home on a cloudy, dismal day. Marie is standing outside her door. The music of this scene is in the form of a largo and is scored for chamber orchestra. Wozzeck enters, rushes up to Marie, and stares at her wildly. In spoken tones he mutters that he sees nothing—but one *should* see it and hold it in one's hands. Where is the sin, he raves, so stinking that it would smoke the very angels out of heaven? But yet, Wozzeck goes on, Marie has a rosy mouth . . . a mouth without blemish.

As Marie shrinks back in terror, Wozzeck, as though bemused, says she is as beautiful as sin itself. Suddenly he points to the threshold, strikes the pose of a soldier at attention, and screams, "There! is that where he stood—like this?" Well, says Marie, regaining her composure, she does not own the street, and people may stand where they please. Wozzeck again demands to know if it is here she saw "him." Marie's insolent answers finally shatter Wozzeck's self-control and, shouting a curse, he rushes at her with upraised fist.

Defiantly Marie warns him not to touch her, saying she would rather have a knife in her body than have his hand laid upon her. Her own father never dared, she hisses, even when she was but ten years old. With that she whirls and goes into the house. Staring after her, Wozzeck repeats in an awed whisper, "Rather a knife!" ("Lieber ein Messer!"). With a gesture of hopelessness, he murmurs that man is an abyss, and when one looks into that abyss one becomes dizzy. Wozzeck staggers away. For a moment the stage is empty. The full orchestra states the theme of the largo, which is carried on by successively fewer instruments until finally only four are playing. At this point the curtain slowly falls. In the next few measures the clarinet takes up the rhythm of a slow country dance in three-quarter time.

[Scene Four]   The orchestral dissonances of the accompaniment here portray the tonal vagaries of drunken tavern musicians. Instrumentally, the scene corresponds to the "scherzo" of the symphonic pattern of Act Two. The curtain rises slowly on a tavern garden. Apprentices, soldiers, and servant girls are milling about, some dancing while others watch.

The First and Second Apprentices weave drunkenly about the dance floor, talking in maudlin phrases. One says he has on a shirt which isn't his; the other says his soul stinks of brandy. The two then lugubriously pledge eternal friendship and commiserate over the fact that the world is such a dreary place—in the usual manner of inebriates. Most of the crowd stop to watch their antics.

Now the band strikes up another tune and the dancers begin again. Among them are Marie and the Drum Major. Wozzeck rushes in, sees the couple, and cries out in rage. As Marie dances by, singing with impudent abandon, Wozzeck sinks to a bench near the dance floor and glares at her and the Drum Major. In jealous torment he asks why God does not black out the sun at such a sight as this . . . they twist and turn in their shamelessness . . . the woman is all fire . . . the man despoils her with his touch, and she merely laughs. In a frenzy, Wozzeck screams a curse. He is about to rush at Marie and her partner when the music finishes and the dancers scatter. Wozzeck sits down again.

Apprentices and soldiers break into a lusty chorus about the happy life of a huntsman ("Ein Jäger aus der Pfalz"). Andres, who had come in with Wozzeck, snatches a guitar from one of the men in the band and begins to direct the singing like a chorus master. He offers a verse of his own about the "darling daughter" who flirts with coachmen and stable boys. The others then finish off the chorus.

Andres hands the guitar back to the bandsman, sees Wozzeck sitting near the door, and goes over to him. The two converse briefly. Andres can make little sense out of Wozzeck's moody answers and finally asks him if he is drunk. No such luck, says Wozzeck. Andres shrugs and turns away.

At that point the First Apprentice, arousing himself from his drunken stupor, climbs on a table and begins preaching to the crowd in a mocking parody of a sermon ("Jedoch, wenn ein Wanderer"). The accompaniment itself is a parody of a chorale.

The Apprentice orates as follows: "Suppose a wanderer in space and time should suddenly ask God, 'Why is Man?' Verily, brethren, it is well that God made him. How else would the farmer, the cooper, the tailor, and the doctor make a living, if they did not have to serve Man? How would the tailor exist if God had not made Man ashamed of his nakedness? What would happen to the soldier and the master of the house if men were not determined to become experts at killing each other? Therefore, brethren, have no fear—everything is perfection. Remember only that all is vanity and money corrupts." Lapsing into his drunken stupor again, the Apprentice mumbles that his soul stinks of brandy. Roaring with laughter, his listeners pick him up and carry him away. Shouting a phrase of the huntsman's song, the crowd moves to the dance floor.

As the band begins to tune up, the Idiot suddenly appears and sidles up to Wozzeck, who is still sitting alone on the bench. When Wozzeck becomes aware of the creature's muttering, he angrily asks him what he wants. The Idiot babbles that he smells blood. Blood, Wozzeck repeats confusedly. Just then the tavern band begins again and Marie and the Drum Major dance by. Staring at them, Wozzeck sings that everyone seems to be twisting and turning in a red mist. The curtain quickly falls while the waltz music continues as an interlude between this scene and the next. It rises swiftly to a crescendo and then stops suddenly.

[*Scene Five*] The guard room of the barracks at night. Andres and Wozzeck are asleep on a wooden pallet. Before the curtain slowly rises we hear the "snoring chorus" of sleeping soldiers, based on the three-chord structure heard in *Scene Two* of Act One. This continues until the rise of the curtain reveals the entire barrack room.

Suddenly Wozzeck tosses restlessly, moaning that he cannot sleep. The other soldiers stir but do not awaken. Tormented by his jealous thoughts, Wozzeck frets that every time he closes his eyes he sees *them* dancing and hears the fiddlers . . . and in between there is a bright flashing, like a knife blade. Andres sleepily tells him to be quiet. In his anguish, Wozzeck prays, singing in a descending phrase: "And lead us not into temptation. . . ."

At that moment the Drum Major staggers in, very drunk. Loudly he brags about the woman he has been making love to, a woman with a beautiful body and burning eyes, who is built to breed smart drummer boys. The soldiers, all ears at this, sit up to listen. Andres asks who she is. Ask Wozzeck, there, says the Drum Major, then hands Wozzeck a bottle of brandy and orders him to drink. Wozzeck disdainfully looks away, whistling softly to himself.

This enrages the Drum Major. Flinging himself on Wozzeck, he shouts that he will rip his tongue from his throat and wrap it around his neck. Wozzeck struggles fiercely as the Drum Major begins to choke him, but finally sinks down exhausted. Letting go, the Drum Major staggers to his feet. He pulls the bottle from his pocket, takes a drink, then looks down contemptuously at the prostrate soldier. He's black and blue, the Drum Major mumbles drunkenly, *now* let him whistle. With that he turns and lurches out of the door. Wozzeck raises himself, crawls painfully over to his bed, and slumps down on it.

A soldier turns, looks at Wozzeck curiously and remarks that this one "has had it." A deep bass note sounds ominously in the orchestra as Andres mutters that Wozzeck is bleeding, and Wozzeck himself sighs hopelessly, "One after another" ("Einer nach dem Andern"). The curtain falls.

ACT THREE
(*Catastrophe*)

[*Scene One*] Musically, this scene consists of seven brief variations on a two-part theme, which is first stated in the accompaniment to the opening phrase of Marie's soliloquy. The curtain rises to show Marie's room. Sitting alone at a table with her child beside her, she is reading the Bible by candlelight. In spoken words ("Und ist kein Betrug"), she begins reading the passage: "And out of his mouth there came forth neither deceit nor falsehood." In an impassioned phrase she betrays the torment of her conscience: "Lord, look not on me!" Then she turns the pages and reads on about the adulteress whom the Pharisees brought before Jesus and to whom He said, "Go forth and sin no more" (John 8: verses 3 to 12). Marie buries her face in her hands. The child huddles closer to her and looks up into her eyes.

The boy's look stabs her to the heart, she murmurs, then peevishly pushes him away. Go, and proudly face the sun, she says, and then in the next moment she tenderly takes the boy in her arms and begins telling him a story. Once upon a time, she says, there was a poor little child who had neither father nor mother. There was no one left in the world—only the child, hungry and crying. . . .

Marie breaks off suddenly, turns to the Bible, and begins reading the passage in which Mary Magdalene washes the feet of Jesus with her tears and then anoints them with ointment (Luke 7: verses 37 to 50). In anguish she bursts out: "Lord, as thou hadst compassion on her, have compassion on me also!" The curtain slowly falls.

[*Scene Two*] A path beside a pool in a forest. It is night. Marie and Wozzeck enter. (Throughout this entire scene a B-natural sounds in the orchestra, starting in the contrabass and continuing through the middle and high registers. This is the "keynote," so to speak, of the murder scene.) Following Wozzeck along the path, Marie says the town is still some distance away, and they must hurry. Wozzeck tells her to sit down and rest. She unwillingly obeys. How long, he asks, has it been since they met? Three years come Whitsuntide, Marie answers. Grimly he asks another question: How much longer will this go on? Marie scrambles angrily to her feet. With a strange, mad laugh, Wozzeck pulls her down into his arms and passionately kisses her. In a poignant phrase, he sings he would trade heaven and the hope of eternal bliss for the privilege of always kissing her that way—but now he must not.

He notices she is shivering. The dew of night is cold, Marie whispers. Wozzeck mutters darkly that she will never notice the cold dew of morning. There is a long, ominous silence. The two watch the moon rise, and Marie murmurs that it is blood-red. Like a blood-red iron, Wozzeck says, drawing a knife. In the next instant he flings himself upon Marie, plunges the knife into her throat, and—above the thunderous roll of tympani in the orchestra—cries fiercely, "If not I, then no one!" With a piercing scream for help, Marie dies. Rising, Wozzeck looks down at her body for a moment, then rushes away like a madman. Curtain. The single note of B-natural, sounding through the entire orchestra, continues as an interlude. It is punctuated by a rhythmic figure that carries into the next scene.

[*Scene Three*] A shabby, ill-lighted tavern. Apprentices and girls are dancing a wild polka. Among the dancers is Margret. Wozzeck, glass in hand, sits at one of the tables. Dance away, he shouts, the Devil will get you soon enough. Then he breaks into a song about three horsemen riding along the Rhine. Forgetting the words, he jumps up impatiently, catches Margret, and dances a few steps with her. Then he drags her over to his table, pulls her down on his lap, and begins fondling her. When she struggles to get away, he asks her to sing. To the accompaniment of an out-of-tune piano, Margret sings a brief refrain ("In's Schwabenland, da mag ich nit"). I'll not fare to Swabia and wear long dresses, the song goes, because long dresses and pointed shoes are not for servant girls.

For some reason, this enrages Wozzeck. He rants about going barefooted to hell, then announces that he wants to fight. Suddenly Margret notices blood on his hand. First feigning surprise, Wozzeck stammers that he cut himself on his right hand. This talk of blood attracts the attention of the dancers, who crowd around. Imitating Wozzeck's voice, Margret asks him how blood got on his right elbow. In a desperate attempt to explain, Wozzeck says he wiped his hand there. In a ringing phrase, Margret sings that there is a smell of human blood here. Trapped and panic-stricken, Wozzeck leaps to his feet crying, "Am I a murderer? Someone else will pay the Devil!" He rushes away. Some of the onlookers ironically ask how he could have wiped his right hand on his right elbow. In a brief ensemble, all repeat that Wozzeck's hands smell of human blood. The curtain falls swiftly while the chorus is still singing, its theme being taken up in a brief orchestral interlude.

[Scene Four] This scene is based on a six-tone chord in a wide variety of forms. The curtain rises to show the forest path beside the pool, as in Scene Two. Wozzeck staggers in, then stops suddenly to look for something. Launching into the climactic soliloquy of the opera—partly spoken, partly sung—he gasps, "The knife—where is the knife?" ("Das Messer—wo ist das Messer?") He comes upon Marie's body and sings brokenly: "What is that crimson cord around your neck . . . was it paid for with your sin, like the gold earrings?" Then he starts searching frantically for the knife, crying that he must find it before it betrays him. He comes upon it at the edge of the pool and hurls it into the water.

As he stares at the spot where the knife sank, the moon breaks blood-red through the clouds. Terror-stricken, Wozzeck raves that the moon will betray him . . . the knife is too close to the shore . . . the bathers may find it, or the mussel hunters. His reason completely gone, Wozzeck wades into the pond, gasping that he must wash himself in blood . . . the water itself is blood. He struggles on until the waves of the pond close over his head.

As the music continues in a vividly descriptive chromatic figure, the Doctor enters, followed by the Captain. They both stare at the water, listening. The Doctor says he hears a sound. That is the water calling, says the Captain. It is a long time, he adds, since anyone drowned in this pond, and that sound is not good to hear. He tries vainly to drag the Doctor away, but the latter keeps listening intently, saying he hears groans as though someone were drowning at this moment. The Captain comments on the uncanny appearance of the blood-red moon and the gray mists. Still listening, the Doctor whispers that the groaning is getting softer . . . now it is gone. Finally the Captain pulls the Doctor away. The curtain falls. The music continues into another long interlude which reiterates all the important thematic forms used throughout the opera in relation to Wozzeck.

[*Scene Five*] In front of Marie's house. It is a bright, sunny morning and children are playing happily about. Marie's son is astride a hobbyhorse on a stick. The children sing a ring-around-a-rosy tune, playing the familiar game. It is interrupted when other children rush onstage and in breathless, frightened tones say that everyone has gone "out there." One child goes up to Marie's son and tells him his mother is dead.

Enchanted with his hobbyhorse, the boy is oblivious to everything. Talking among themselves, the other children say the boy's mother is lying in the path beside the pool. They rush off to look. Meanwhile, the little boy rides about, shouting happily. Suddenly he realizes he is alone. Puzzled, he looks around, then gallops off on his hobbyhorse after the other children. The curtain falls.

Die Zauberflöte

(The Magic Flute)

by WOLFGANG AMADEUS MOZART

[1756–1791]

Libretto by
EMANUEL SCHIKANEDER *and*
JOHANN GEORG METZLER (GIESECKE)

Based on Liebeskind's oriental story
LULU, ODER DIE ZAUBERFLÖTE

CHARACTERS

Tamino, an Egyptian prince	*Tenor*
Three Ladies, attendants of the Queen of Night	{ *Two Sopranos* / *Mezzo-soprano*
Papageno, a birdcatcher	*Baritone*
The Queen of Night	*Soprano*
Monostatos, a Moorish slave in the palace of Sarastro	*Tenor*
Pamina, daughter of the Queen of Night	*Soprano*
Three Genii	{ *Soprano* / *Mezzo-soprano* / *Contralto*
A priest, Speaker of the Temple of Isis	*Baritone*
Sarastro, High Priest of the Temple of Isis	*Bass*
First priest	*Tenor*
Second priest	*Baritone*
Two Men in Armor	{ *Tenor* / *Baritone*
Old Woman, later Papagena	*Soprano*

Priests of the temple, attendants, slaves

Place: In and near the Temple of Isis in Egypt
Time: About the period of Rameses I
First performance: Theater auf der Wieden, Vienna, September 30, 1791
Original language: German

DIE ZAUBERFLÖTE, written by Mozart at the age of thirty-five, not long before his death, is considered by many to be his finest opera. In it he combined simple German folk tunes and classic operatic writing with brilliant effect. The plot is a curious hodgepodge of political satire, the symbolism of Freemasonry, and naïve humor, set against an Egyptian background.

The Temple of Isis, more or less the focal point of the action, represents Freemasonry. Sarastro is its High Priest. Pamina, typifying the Austrian people, finds refuge in the temple from her wicked mother, the Queen of Night, said to have been identified with the Empress Maria Theresa, who was actively opposed to Freemasonry. Prince Tamino is presumably symbolic of the Emperor Joseph II, who was comparatively liberal in his attitude toward the order. The trials by fire and water imposed on Pamina and Tamino, the conflict between light and darkness, and the ultimate triumph of good over evil are all inherent in the Masonic philosophy.

The brilliant overture is an established favorite in the concert repertoire. Prominent in it is a series of impressive chords sounded three times in groups of three, said to be symbolic of the knocking at the door of the temple as part of the Masonic rites of initiation. They will be heard again during the temple scene.

ACT ONE

[Scene One] A wild rocky pass near the Temple of Isis. Prince Tamino, dressed in Japanese hunting costume and carrying a bow but no arrows, rushes down the pass.[1] He is being pursued by a ravenous snake. Tamino implores the gods to deliver him from the fangs of this monster, then falls fainting to the ground. Just as the serpent is about to attack him the temple doors open and the Three Ladies rush to his aid. They kill the snake with their silver spears. In a melodious trio they rejoice that they have saved Tamino ("Sie ist vollbracht, die Heldenthat"). They gaze fondly down at Tamino and comment on his handsome looks. Their Queen must be informed at once, they finally decide. An amusing colloquy follows, in which each of the Three Ladies urges the other to hasten to the Queen while offering to stand guard over the stricken youth. As none of the three makes a move, they resign themselves to leaving together and ardently bid the unconscious Tamino farewell.

After they re-enter the temple Tamino revives, looks wildly about, and is startled to see the serpent dead at his feet. As he wonders where he is he hears someone approaching down the pass. Tamino quickly conceals himself behind some trees. From the orchestra comes a sprightly refrain, punctuated by a flutelike phrase of five ascending notes. Soon Papageno appears. He is dressed in a fantastic, brightly colored bird costume, and on his back is a large cage containing birds. He carries a pipe of Pan, on which he plays his whimsical five-note call. Without further ado he sings a gay ditty ("Der Vogelfänger bin ich ja"). He explains that he sets his traps, blows on his pipe, and the birds come flocking round. In a second verse he muses on how pleasant it would be if he could set his traps for pretty maidens.

With a final flourish on his pipe he starts for the temple. Tamino intercepts him, and dialogue ensues in which each questions the other. Tamino asks Papageno who he is. A man like himself, Papageno replies. In turn, Tamino reveals that he is a prince of a far-off country, then asks Papageno

[1] In most productions Tamino is dressed in a modified Greek costume. Also, he sometimes appears with one arrow left. This he shoots at the serpent but misses.

who reigns here. The birdcatcher answers that he knows nothing about this country. His business, he says, is to catch birds for the Queen of Night, in payment for which the Three Ladies bring him food and drink. Tamino exclaims excitedly over mention of the Queen.

Papageno, frightened and suspicious of Tamino's manner, tries to hide his fear by warning that he has the strength of a giant when aroused. Tamino, thinking that perhaps Papageno is one of the Queen's mystic entourage, asks him if he killed the snake. Therefore Papageno—first making certain that the snake is dead—boasts that he strangled the monster with his bare hands.

At this point the Three Ladies appear and overhear Papageno's lurid bit of fiction. Sternly they tell him that today he is to have only water instead of wine to drink and a stone instead of bread. One of the Ladies fastens a padlock to his mouth and informs him that it is his punishment for lying. Turning to Tamino, they explain that it was they who saved him from the serpent. They hand him a portrait of the daughter of the Queen of Night. The three then leave, taking Papageno along.

Gazing at the portrait, Tamino, in a tender aria ("Dies Bildnis ist bezaubernd schön"), sings that if he could but find this lovely creature he would ardently declare his love and then she would be his forever. At the finish of the aria the Three Ladies appear to tell Tamino that the Queen of Night has decided to grant his wish. If he is as brave as he is comely, the Queen has told her attendants, he is worthy of the task of saving her daughter. The Three Ladies then reveal that the Queen's daughter is being held captive by a wicked sorcerer. As Tamino eagerly urges the Ladies to guide him to the sorcerer's lair there is a crash of thunder and the Queen of Night stands before him.

In recitative the Queen tells Tamino that he need have no fear because he is pure in heart. In a moving aria ("Zum leiden bin ich auserkoren") she relates how her daughter was carried off by the sorcerer. Dramatically she imposes on Tamino the task of rescuing the girl. As the thunder crashes again the Queen and the Three Ladies vanish.

Tamino, astounded, wonders if he has been dreaming. He is about to leave when Papageno enters. Dolefully he points to his padlock and hums in lieu of speech. Tamino says he can do nothing for him. Thereupon the Three Ladies appear, saying that the Queen has ordered Papageno to be freed. They remove the padlock and warn him not to do any more lying. A quintet follows ("Dies Schloss soll deine Warnung sein"), in which they moralize over the evils of lying. The Ladies hand Tamino a golden flute, saying that it will give him power over human emotions and move the hardest heart to love.

Papageno is informed that he is to accompany Tamino to the palace of Sarastro. In terror Papageno protests, saying that this fiend will have him plucked, fried, and tossed to his hounds. The Ladies assure the birdcatcher that the Prince will protect him. The Prince can go to the devil, Papageno retorts, pointing out that Tamino might decide to desert him. At that the Ladies hand him a set of chimes with a warning that no one but himself must play upon them. In a brief but charming ensemble ("Silberglöckchen") the Ladies, Tamino, and Papageno sing that the chimes, if rung when danger threatens, will dispel all harm. When Tamino and Papageno ask who is to lead them to Sarastro's palace the Ladies tell them that three wise and fair youths will act as their protectors. The quintet is concluded as all sing farewell. The curtain falls.

[*Scene Two*]   An elaborate Egyptian room in Sarastro's palace. Monostatos suddenly appears, dragging in Pamina.[2] He threatens her with death, but she ignores her own plight and laments that her mother will die of grief. Monostatos orders other slaves to chain the girl. Resisting his advances, she then falls fainting on a couch. The Moor, on leaving, encounters Papageno, who has wandered into the palace quite by accident. An amusing duet follows ("Hu! das ist der Teufel sicherlich!"). Each is terror-stricken at the sight of the other, and they both beg each other for mercy. Panic-stricken, they finally dash off in opposite directions.

As Pamina revives, Papageno reappears. Approaching Pamina he addresses her (in dialogue) as the daughter of the Queen of Night and tells her he is Papageno. Just to make sure that she is the Queen's daughter he compares her with the portrait given him by Tamino.

When Pamina asks Papageno where he got the portrait he tells her about Tamino. He's a fellow who calls himself a prince, the birdcatcher says. He was given the portrait by the Queen and commanded to rescue her daughter. No sooner did he see the portrait than he fell in love with the original, Papageno goes on, and he will be here shortly to save her. Pamina says they must hurry because Sarastro will soon be home from the hunt. Papageno observes that he knows only too well what will happen to them if they are caught. The fact that Papageno has her portrait convinces Pamina that the birdcatcher is not one of Sarastro's minions. And besides, she says, she knows by looking at Papageno's face that he has a kind heart. "A kind heart, yes," Papageno agrees sadly, "but no Papagena to appreciate it." Now follows a beautiful duet ("Bei Männern, welche Liebe fühlen"), in which Pamina and Papageno sing of the magic power of love.

[*Scene Three*]   A sacred grove with three massive doorways, above which are inscribed, respectively, *Temple of Wisdom*, *Temple of Reason*, and *Temple of Nature*. Tamino is led in by the Three Genii, each carrying silver palm branches. In a trio ("Zum Ziele führt dich diese Bahn") they bid him go forward to victory, remembering always that he must be firm, patient, and silent. He asks them if he will now be able to rescue Pamina. In answer they repeat their exhortation, "Be firm, patient, and silent." Manliness will bring him victory, they proclaim as they leave.

Tamino tries to enter the Temples of Reason and Nature, but each time he is turned away by a warning voice from within. Finally, in answer to his knock at the Temple of Wisdom, a venerable priest appears. When the priest asks Tamino why he has come he replies that he seeks revenge upon the tyrant Sarastro, whose cruelty has caused a woman to suffer. "Could Sarastro but reveal to you his true purpose!" the priest exclaims. "Is he not

2 In some performances three slaves first reveal in dialogue, before Monostatos actually enters, that Pamina is his captive.

the thief who tore Pamina from her mother's arms?" Tamino cries. The priest bids him be calm and in a phrase of great dignity tells him that only when he is inspired by friendship and love may he enter the temple to be united with Pamina.

Within the temple voices chant softly that Tamino will soon see Pamina and that she still lives unharmed. Joyfully thanking the gods for guiding him to the temple, he puts the magic flute to his lips and begins playing. But when Pamina, contrary to his expectations, does not appear, Tamino frets in disappointment. Again and again he plays his flute and calls her name. Suddenly, from the distance he hears the five-note tune of Papageno's Panpipe. Excitedly he sings that perhaps Papageno has found Pamina, then rushes off.

No sooner has he disappeared than Pamina and Papageno hurry in from the opposite direction. They are being pursued by Monostatos. In a duet ("Schnelle Füsse, rascher Muth") they reassure themselves that they will elude their pursuer. Could they but find Tamino, they sing, all would be well. When Pamina cries out his name Papageno says he will send forth a call on his Panpipe. His notes are immediately answered by a flute in the distance. Joyously Pamina and Papageno exclaim that now they can hasten to Tamino's side.

But Monostatos, mockingly repeating the last phrase of their duet—"Nur geschwinde, nur geschwinde [Hasten, hasten]!"—leaps into their path and bars their way. Exultantly he sings that he has them in his power at last, then calls to his slaves to put the fugitives in chains. Thereupon Papageno remembers the chimes and begins playing a delightfully rhythmic refrain. Instantly under the spell of the music, Monostatos and his slaves begin dancing in droll fashion as they happily sing in chorus ("Das klingt so herrlich"). Like automatons, Monostatos and his crew dance harmlessly away to Papageno's music.

Gratefully Pamina and Papageno sing of the magic power of the chimes. Then from the distance a chorus is heard hailing Sarastro. Trembling, Papageno asks Pamina what they are to say to the High Priest. Pamina resolves to speak only the truth. Sarastro enters in a majestic procession, accompanied by priests, attendants, and slaves. In a stirring chorus ("Es lebe Sarastro") they acclaim him as their mentor and idol. Falling to her knees before him, Pamina confesses that although she had long planned to seek her freedom her real reason for fleeing was to escape the attentions of Monostatos. In a stately melody ("Steh' auf, erheitre dich, Liebe") Sarastro answers. Gravely he tells her that though he cannot compel her to love he cannot grant her freedom.

When Pamina pleads to be freed for her mother's sake, Sarastro angrily replies that he dare not return her to this woman, for she is wicked and false. Monostatos now appears, leading in Tamino. Tamino and Pamina rush ecstatically into each other's arms, but Monostatos roughly parts them. Fawning before Sarastro, the Moor lies that Tamino and his companion, the birdcatcher, tried to abduct Pamina from the palace. But he, brave fellow that he is, prevented it, Monostatos goes on, hinting modestly that some sort of reward no doubt is in order. Sarastro dryly agrees. The reward, he announces, will be seventy-seven lashes. Monostatos is led away, loudly protesting. The chorus hails the justice of the great Sarastro's decision.

Sarastro orders Pamina and Tamino to be veiled, led into the Temple of the Ordeal, and prepared for the sacred ceremonies. Papageno, also veiled, is led off with Tamino, while Sarastro conducts Pamina to the door of the temple. A mighty chorus in praise of virtue and justice concludes the act.

ACT TWO

[*Scene One*]   A palm grove dominated by a tall obelisk. To the grave measures of the *March of the Priests*, Sarastro and the priests enter and arrange themselves in a circle. In dialogue Sarastro announces that Prince Tamino waits at the northern gate of the temple. He seeks to pierce his veil of darkness so that he may see the light. The solemn chords heard in the overture sound forth. Sarastro informs the priests that the gods have destined Pamina and Tamino for each other, and for this reason he took Pamina from her mother, who was bent on destroying the temple. Tamino himself shall now aid in thwarting her evil designs. Sarastro orders Pamina and Tamino to be brought to the temple porch.

As the Speaker leaves and the other priests gather around Sarastro he sings the impressive aria, "O Isis und Osiris," invoking the blessings of the gods on the novitiates. Solemnly echoing his words, the priests follow him out of the temple. The curtain falls.

[*Scene Two*]   Before the temple. Two priests lead in Tamino and Papageno, remove their veils, then withdraw. In dialogue Tamino and his companion discuss this stage of their initiation. The priests return shortly to question them. Tamino says that he is prepared for the ordeal. Papageno asserts that he is mainly concerned with getting enough to eat and drink—and perhaps a loving wife into the bargain. The priests inform him that Sarastro will provide him with a feathered companion. He may look upon her during these trials, one priest says, but he must not speak to her. To Tamino the priests likewise say that he may see Pamina, but they impose silence. As the two prepare to leave they sing a brief duet ("Bewahret euch vor Weibertücken"), warning of women's wiles.

Papageno complains about the darkness, but Tamino counsels forbearance. Suddenly the Three Ladies appear, lighting their way with torches. A spirited quintet ensues ("Wie! Ihr an diesem Schrecksort!"). The Three Ladies try to persuade Tamino and Papageno to flee with them to the Queen of Night by describing the dire fate in store for them if they remain in the palace of Sarastro. Tamino warns Papageno not to listen to them, declaring that the brave man will not be swerved from his purpose by idle chatter.

Within the temple the priests thunder in angry chorus that the sacred precincts have been profaned by the presence of women. They consign the interlopers to hell, whereupon the Three Ladies sink into the earth with cries of lamentation. Papageno grovels in fear. The Speaker and the two priests then reappear and, in dialogue, commend Tamino for resisting temptation. He and Papageno are again veiled and led away. The curtain falls.

[*Scene Three*]   The garden of Sarastro's palace. Pamina is seen sleeping. Monostatos creeps in, gazes fondly upon the Princess, and then sings an amorous lament ("Alles fühlt der Liebe Freuden"). Everybody in the world except himself, he sighs, has someone to love. He decides that he will make love while he can to this radiant beauty. But as he approaches Pamina there is a flash of lightning and a loud clap of thunder, and the Queen of Night appears. Pamina awakes and calls to her mother. Monostatos slinks away.

The Queen asks Pamina what has happened to Tamino. He is to become one of the elect of the temple, Pamina tells her. The Queen fumes that now she can never regain her daughter. When Pamina implores her mother to take her away the Queen exclaims that she is powerless, for she no longer possesses the "sevenfold shield of the sun." Pamina's father, at his death, gave the shield to Sarastro, who wears it now. The Queen hands Pamina a dagger, imperiously commanding her to kill Sarastro and bring back the shield.

As Pamina recoils in horror the Queen begins the brilliant aria "Der Hölle Rache kocht in meinem Herzen." Furiously the Queen orders Pamina to slay Sarastro, threatening to disown her if she disobeys. At the end of the aria the Queen vanishes, leaving Pamina staring fearfully at the dagger in her hand. Monostatos re-enters, takes away her dagger, and tells her that the only way she can save her mother and herself is by agreeing to love him. Pamina flatly refuses. In fury Monostatos raises the dagger. At that instant Sarastro strides in and drives the Moor off.

Tearfully Pamina implores Sarastro not to punish her mother. Sarastro replies that if Tamino proves worthy in his trials all will be well with Pamina and her mother. He then sings the magnificent aria, "In diesem heil'gen Hallen." In the sacred temple, Sarastro declares, the hand of brotherly love guides the erring one and the foe finds forgiveness. As Sarastro leaves the curtain falls.

[*Scene Four*[3]]   A great hall. Tamino and Papageno are led in by the Speaker and two priests to undergo a further trial, the test of silence. When Papageno complains that he is thirsty an old crone brings him a cup of water. The talkative Papageno cannot resist the temptation to chat with the Old Woman. Thereupon ensues an amusing dialogue during which, to Papageno's dismay, she declares that she is his sweetheart. Finally telling her his name, he asks hers. Just as she is about to answer there is a roll of thunder. She disappears.

The Three Genii now enter. They bring in a table laden with food and drink, then give Tamino his flute and Papageno his chimes. In a charming trio ("Seid uns zum zweitenmal willkommen") they remind the novices that the flute and bells will protect them. They urge the two to refresh themselves. With a warning to maintain silence, the Genii disappear.

Papageno promptly devotes his entire attention to the food, while Tamino plays his flute. Pamina enters and eagerly greets him. Sadly Tamino shakes his head and with a gesture bids her leave. Pamina voices her de-

[3] Sometimes the opera is played in three acts instead of two, and this scene becomes Scene One of Act Three. In other three-act versions Scene Five becomes the opening scene of the third act.

spair at his apparent indifference in a moving aria ("Ach, ich fühl's, es ist verschwunden"). When Tamino still remains mute Pamina disconsolately leaves.

Three blasts of the trumpet now summon Tamino and Papageno to the crypt beneath the temple for further trials. The birdcatcher, unwilling to leave the table, is dragged off by Tamino. The curtain falls.

[*Scene Five*]   The inner shrine of the sacred order in the crypt beneath the temple. Sarastro and the priests enter and sing the impressive chorus, "O Isis und Osiris." They invoke the gods and hail the approaching climax of Tamino's ordeal. After the chorus Tamino and Pamina, veiled, are led in. Sarastro bids them say their final farewells because Tamino still must undergo two more stern trials.

A dramatic trio ensues ("Soll ich dich, Theurer, nicht mehr sehn?"). Pamina voices her fear of dangers ahead, but Sarastro assures her that she will see her lover again. Tamino resolutely declares that he will bow to the will of the gods. Sarastro and the priests depart as Tamino and Pamina are led off in opposite directions.

When all are gone Papageno enters, calling in frightened tones for Tamino.[4] Thoroughly bewildered, the birdcatcher is confronted by the Speaker, who sternly tells him that because of his unworthiness he shall never know the bliss of the chosen ones. Papageno replies that his sole desire at the moment is a glass of wine. In the next moment a glass is placed in his hands.

Papageno drinks deeply and then, accompanying himself on his chimes, sings a delightful song ("Ein Mädchen oder Weibchen wünscht Papageno sich"). If he had either a maiden or a wife, he sings, he would be her devoted slave.

No sooner has he finished his song than in comes the Old Woman to whom he had spoken previously. Before his startled eyes she turns into a young girl, his birdlike counterpart. "Papagena!" he cries. Just as he is about to embrace her the Speaker enters and bars his way, saying he is not yet worthy. The priest drags Papagena away, while Papageno follows, protesting loudly. The curtain falls.

[*Scene Six*]   A palm garden near the temple. The Three Genii enter and sing a hymn to the sun ("Bald prangt, den Morgen zu verkünden"). As they sing they see Pamina approaching. Mad with grief over being parted from Tamino, she prepares to stab herself with the dagger given her by her mother (having retrieved it meanwhile from Monostatos). The Three Genii intervene just in time. They assure her that she will soon see her lover and offer to lead her to him. As she expresses her gratitude her voice blends with theirs in a melodious quartet ("Zwei Herzen, die von Liebe brennen"). The Genii and Pamina then leave. The curtain falls.

[*Scene Seven*]   Two rocky caves with grilled gates. Behind one gate a fire glows; behind the other water is visible. Between the gates is a great

---

4 Sometimes this is played as a separate scene.

doorway before which stand two men in black armor. During a brief but somber prelude Tamino is brought in by the priests. The two armored men, singing in powerful octaves, proclaim that he who treads this stern path must be purified by fire, water, air, and earth ("Der, welcher wandert diese Strasse").

As Tamino is about to enter he hears Pamina calling. A short trio ensues ("Ja! das ist Paminens Stimme!"). Tamino rejoices over the prospect of meeting Pamina, while the Men in Armor declare that she has proved herself worthy of him. When she is brought in she rushes into Tamino's arms. Then, clasping hands, the lovers prepare for the trial by fire and water. Pamina bids Tamino play the magic flute, which, she now reveals, was carved long ago by her father. The Two Men in Armor now join the pair in an exultant quartet hailing the magic power of the flute ("Ihr wandelt durch des Tones Macht").

To the accompaniment of a stately march Tamino and Pamina walk safely through the fire and water, Tamino playing his flute. As they finish the tests the temple gates swing open and the two enter. From within come the voices of the priests hailing the redeemed couple ("Triumph! du edles Paar!"). As Sarastro and the priests conduct them to the inner shrine the curtain falls.

[*Scene Eight*] A garden. Papageno comes in, plays on his Panpipe, and disconsolately calls for Papagena. He sings a doleful song ("Weibchen! Täubchen, meine Schöne!"), lamenting that he is the most wretched man on the face of the earth. Taking a rope from his belt, he prepares to hang himself, at the count of three, from a nearby tree. Slowly counting, "One—two—two and a half," he manages to postpone the hanging long enough to permit the Three Genii to come on the scene and dissuade him altogether. When he wails that nothing can soothe his aching heart, they suggest that he play his chimes. This he does eagerly, singing "Klinget, Glöckchen, klinget!" He implores the bells to work their magic and bring his sweetheart to his side. Meanwhile the Three Genii, unnoticed by Papageno, bring forth Papagena, then tell the birdcatcher to turn and look. In transports of joy he greets his mate at last, and a delightful love duet follows. The birdlike creatures sing of their future happiness as man and wife. First there will be a little Papageno, then a little Papagena. Then another little Papageno, and so on ad infinitum. The duet closes with the pair happily chattering each other's name.

[*Scene Nine*] A dark and gloomy spot not far from the temple. The Queen of Night, the Three Ladies, and Monostatos approach, determined to make one last assault on the temple and carry off Pamina. But as they are about to put their plans into effect there is a blaze of lightning and a tremendous crash of thunder. The five people representing the thwarted forces of evil sink into the earth. In a descending musical phrase they voice their last despairing cry: "We are plunged into eternal night."

A brief musical interlude follows, during which the scene becomes bathed in a brilliant light, bringing into view Sarastro, the priests, Tamino,

Pamina, and a great host of temple adherents. Sarastro, sole possessor of the "sevenfold shield of the sun," proclaims in a short recitative that light has conquered darkness. The entire assemblage then breaks out into a mighty chorus ("Heil sei euch Geweihten!"). As it rises to a glorious climax the curtain falls.

PART II

HOW TO ENJOY AN OPERA

To ENJOY ANYTHING, you must first understand it. As for opera, there are at least three main avenues to understanding even before you see a performance: reading the story, studying the libretto, hearing the music—either on records or in an instrumental transcription. Reading the story is really of first importance. It is the essential framework for the music, and no appreciation of an opera is complete if the story is confused and unclear to the listener.

At the outset, you should be warned that many opera plots are weak and illogical. Some are full of obscure symbolism (Debussy's *Pelléas et Mélisande*), some wholly in the realm of legend (Wagner's *Der Ring des Nibelungen*), some—particularly those of the modern school—are as puzzling as a non-objective painting (Thomson's *Four Saints in Three Acts*, which consists mostly of unintelligible words, or intelligible words that seem to have no relation to each other). But an opera must begin somewhere, and you will find, when you later listen to the music, that the composer has clothed the plot with meaning, excitement, and drama.

Learning about opera need not stop with simply reading the stories themselves. In fact, the more you know about opera and its relation to other forms of culture, the more you will enjoy it. Books that have been written about it cover every phase of the subject—there are biographies of composers, analyses of music, critical essays on individual operas, translations of lyrics and explanations of plots, stories by and about famous operatic personalities. This kind of reading will help you relate opera to its own time. To life, in other words. Know who the artist is, what he thinks, and where he stands in relation to the world about him—and you know his work.

Probably the ideal way to study an actual opera before seeing it performed is to follow the musical score while listening either to a radio broadcast or to recordings. That, of course, presupposes a knowledge of music. If you live in one of the larger cities, it is likely that operatic scores and libretti are available at libraries, as well as recordings of operas and facilities for listening to them. Recordings and radio broadcasts make it possible for anyone interested in opera today to familiarize himself not only with the important choruses and arias of an opera but with the entire work. Moreover, with abridged versions of certain operas now being performed for television, it is possible to *see* a work as well.

If it happens that the score is too difficult for you to follow, then the most important requisite is the libretto. Admittedly, standard translations of operas do not always make particularly interesting reading, but at least they provide some idea of what the story is about. In the main, grand-opera translations are stiff and stilted, for it is next to impossible to render into understandable vernacular the poetic flowing phrases constructed primarily for singing. Operas of the *verismo* school—*Cavalleria Rusticana, La Bohème, Louise, Pagliacci*—come off better in translation because emotions and sentiments are more realistically expressed. Wagnerian translations are generally ponderous and highly involved, due to the difficulty of translating the complicated prose which the composer created to suit his dramatic requirements. The full effect of Wagner's surging cadences and resounding alliterations can be appreciated only by those who understand German.

But in the absence of a detailed paraphrase of the lyrics of an opera, it will generally pay you to labor through a libretto in order to know what the plot is really about. In the love duet between Elsa and Lohengrin in the third act of *Lohengrin,* for example, dark and somber chords suddenly interrupt the flood of glorious love music. The real meaning of this change of mood will be utterly lost on the listener unless he knows that at this point Elsa asks the forbidden question—Lohengrin's name. In *Traviata,* Violetta's abrupt change from the tender, reflective mood of the "Ah, fors e lui" to the abandon of the "Sempre libra?" will mean little to anyone who does not know that it symbolizes a gesture of repudiation and despair—Violetta thrusts aside her thoughts of Alfredo's love and resolves to abandon herself to the life of gaiety she knows will doom her.

Familiarity with the lyrics will also help you to recognize and understand the leitmotif, or leading motive. This is a way of "spotting" a character musically, and is used extensively by such composers as Weber, Wagner, and Bizet. Wagner is its chief exponent. If, in listening to the *Ring* operas, for example, you learn to associate the utterances of the characters with certain motives as they are stated in the orchestra, the various elements of music and drama gradually fall into proper perspective in relation to the plot. After repeated hearings of Wagnerian operas, you may find that the composer's closely integrated system of leitmotif makes reference to the libretto unnecessary. Likewise, in *Carmen* the dramatic Fate motive associated with the gypsy becomes more eloquent and forceful at each hearing.

In many instances the enjoyment of opera can begin, not with the rise of the curtain, but with the first bars of the overture. Not every operatic overture, it is true, is written with a serious purpose. Early composers usually assumed that the audience would talk before the curtain went up, and they contented themselves with writing inconsequential music that merely served as a background for conversation. In writing *Salome* and *Elektra,* Richard Strauss eliminated the overture altogether, on the theory that the abrupt rise of the curtain would instantly capture the attention of the audience. It does—as you will learn when you see these operas.

Certain other composers, however, have designed their overtures to state the important themes of their operas and to establish the proper emotional mood. Thus the overtures to *Le Nozze di Figaro, Die Meistersinger, The Bartered Bride,* or the Leonore overtures of *Fidelio* fully prepare the listener for what he is about to see and hear on the stage.

One of the important things about understanding and enjoying opera is the recognition of certain irreconcilable differences between it and the spoken drama. To these differences the operagoer must learn to adjust himself. There is the view that opera is merely the stepchild of the arts—a sort of mongrel offspring of ballet, music, and drama. Granted that it is not a pure art form, familiarity with it will soon lead you to realize that it is a highly complicated and specialized form of expression.

Opera rarely approaches the detached realism of drama. A play can be intellectual—in the manner of Shaw, Ibsen, or T. S. Eliot, let us say—and still retain enough of an extrovert element, so to speak, to carry its subtleties over the footlights. But opera must remain emotional because music is emotional. No one in real life, for instance, would pause to express his feelings in the lengthy soliloquies which are sometimes the high point of operatic performances. Yet the magnificent soliloquies of Gérard in *Andrea Chénier*, or of Hans Sachs in *Die Meistersinger*, or of Iago in *Otello* do not seem long-winded or out of place. They are profound and to the point because the music frees emotional expression from the confines of mere speech.

If it seems to you that opera singers move in slow motion and with unnecessary formality of gesture, remember that they must synchronize with the orchestral accompaniment not only vocally but physically. When a performer sings a long phrase on a single word, his gestures must be timed accordingly. Correctly synchronized, the gestures will not seem awkward. Operatic acting is difficult, and only the most accomplished and versatile performers can make it convincing. Over and above all else is the singing, which imposes certain limitations on movement and gesture and makes strenuous physical demands on the performer. Artists singing the leading roles in *Tristan und Isolde*, for example, have been known to lose as much as five pounds during a performance.

When opera is viewed within the scope of its own possibilities and limitations, it becomes endlessly fascinating. It offers comedy, tragedy, pageantry, and romance in a repertoire that is almost inexhaustible. In *American Opera and Its Composers*, Edward Ellsworth Hipsher says: "In the Bibliothèque Nationale in Paris are the scores of 28,000 operas; yet of this prodigious number, less than 200 are found in the standard repertoire of the great opera houses of the world." Even if no one ever writes another opera, there is still a vast storehouse of lyric wealth available.

Opera is unusual in its appeal to both old and young alike, and with its gods and goddesses, its kings and queens and clowns, has a special appeal for children. As the eminent basso, Ezio Pinza once said: "Children are born with a subtle sense of fantasy. If one plays along with it, opera is just their meat." They approach opera with simple directness—a god is a god, a witch is a witch, a dragon is a dragon. They wisely leave to their elders any musical problems involving such characters.

In *The Child and His Music*, Hazel G. Kinscella and Elizabeth M. Tierney suggest that "an ideal introduction to opera is a study of *Hänsel und Gretel*. The plot is plausible and picturesque, the stage action simple and pleasantly melodic. An informal performance can be done in the schoolroom without scenery, costumes or stage accessories."

Another opera recommended is one by Benjamin Britten—*Let's Make an Opera*. During its first scene, children of an imaginary household talk about opera and then decide to write and produce one themselves. This they do. "Many small operatic scenes," say Kinscella and Tierney, "can be staged in schoolrooms in much the same way as Britten's work. They may be based on actual world events, local history, favorite selections from child literature, legends or folk tales. All that is needed is a simple story in which something actually happens. Children may select appropriate music from familiar songs and recordings."

What children like in operatic music covers a surprisingly wide range. On the basis of actual experimentation and study, here is a sampling: Music from Reginald de Koven's *Robin Hood;* the Children's Chorus from Act One of *Carmen;* the contest scene from the last act of *Die Meistersinger;* Polka and Fugue from Weinberger's *Schwanda;* Entrance of the Gods into Valhalla, from Wagner's *Rheingold.* Favorite recordings in the modern vein include Prokofiev's *Peter and the Wolf* and Douglas Moore's *The Emperor's New Clothes* (based on the Hans Christian Andersen tale). The child who is thus led into the world of opera is bound to develop intelligent standards of taste as he grows up.

You will find that many people are inclined to accept traditional opinions about operas—that *Traviata, Trovatore* and *Aïda* are barrel-organ music, that *Lucia di Lammermoor* is an opera for twittering coloraturas. Some of these notions have prevailed for a long time and are the result either of the most casual acquaintance with opera or no familiarity at all. When you completely understand opera, your perspective changes.

Once you have heard enough opera to make comparisons and to formulate your own standard of values, stick to your own opinions. You have a perfect right to prefer to listen to the music of Mozart's *Zauberflöte* on the radio or recordings rather than see it on the stage, if you think the plot interferes with your enjoyment of the music. On the other hand, once you know the plot framework upon which the music revolves, and accept it for what it is, you will almost certainly be better able to appreciate the performance.

There are many kinds of operas, and no one who has developed any discrimination is going to like all of them—just as no one likes all of the novels he reads, the paintings he sees, or the lectures he hears. But the most certain route to wider appreciation of music and opera is surely through increased knowledge. To enjoy the true depth and beauty of opera, you must consciously develop your understanding of the form.

The section of this book called "A Brief History of Opera" is a starting point. In its brief analyses of periods and types of operatic music, and in its discussions of aims and purposes of composers and librettists, you will be able gradually to orient yourself. Before you listen to an opera—indeed, even before you read the libretto or the story in brief—it will be wise to find out when it was written and by whom. Knowing even a little about the period and the composer may give the opera itself deeper meaning and considerably enhance your appreciation.

Just as knowing the background of an opera will make it more interesting, so familiarity with the music will add to your enjoyment. Before you go to a performance or before listening to an opera broadcast, take time to listen to recordings of the music that are available. No one can catch all of the nuances of great music at first hearing, and the person who is already somewhat familiar even with only the important arias has thus prepared himself for new pleasures when he hears the music in its complete operatic setting.

Sincere people are often puzzled and sometimes antagonized when they go to an opera and are bored or disappointed, simply because they haven't bothered first to acquire even a little knowledge about it. There is an unfortunate number of such people, and one is always tempted to remind them that the little effort it takes to understand the fundamentals of opera is a small price to pay for the pleasure they seek. To enjoy any activity, you must know something about the forms and rules. You can't expect to enjoy a baseball game if you can't tell a foul ball from a double play. The pleasures of great literature come only after a long and difficult apprenticeship in the art of reading. Appreciation of a painting presupposes some familiarity with that art form, though pictorial representation is so much a part of our daily lives that we often forget that taste in art is acquired.

Certainly all pleasure arising in the arts demands of the participant some background, some foundation in education. Opera, principally because it is a complicated art form difficult to produce, is somewhat more removed from common experience than other arts. But obstacles that may have interfered with wide public appreciation in the past have been greatly reduced in recent years by the perfection of techniques of television, radio broadcasting, and recording. Today the difficulties that remain are easily surmounted by anyone interested enough to make the effort, and with constantly increasing opportunities to hear and see opera, the rewards are greater than ever before.

When you have the knowledge and understanding properly to enjoy opera, it is for you to decide the way you enjoy it most. Can you attend a performance and lose yourself in the make-believe of the stage while absorbing the music? Then do so. Do you prefer the complete performance via radio—or an abridged version via television—having read the story earlier? Many others do too. Do you want only the recordings of outstanding excerpts? Or recordings of complete operas? Let no one tell you one is better than the other or replaces the others. You are the judge. Your enjoyment is a personal thing, and with understanding, your pleasure is secure.

PART III

A BRIEF HISTORY OF OPERA

O PERA was born in Italy at the end of the sixteenth century. Actually, the influences that led to its birth are rooted in antiquity. Centuries ago, when actors declaimed the mighty dramas of Sophocles, Aeschylus, and other tragic poets of Greece, they were sometimes accompanied by stringed and wind instruments. An integral part of the play was the chorus, which chanted a commentary on the action of the drama. It was inevitable, of course, that music and drama should eventually serve each other, but several centuries went by before musical minds achieved that happy combination.

We shall see in this brief history that the development of opera as we know it today involves a process of revolution and evolution that has been going on for more than three hundred years. Opera grew out of a revolt against the highly complicated polyphonic writing of the sixteenth century. The "rebellion" was accomplished near the beginning of the seventeenth century in Italy by Jacopo Peri in his opera *Dafne*, in which single-voiced recitative replaced the contrapuntal madrigal style, with its five, six, or even seven separate vocal parts. The influence of this rebellion, spreading northward from Italy through Europe, motivated—or at least vitalized—other forces, which then began moving in parallel direction.

In England, during the reigns of James I and Charles I in the early years of the seventeenth century, the court masques—elaborate allegorical presentations declaimed, mimed, and danced to the accompaniment of incidental music—led to the development of the recitative. In 1617 the London-born Italian, Nicolo Laniere, set to music a masque written by Ben Jonson. The influence of this work, however, was temporary, and the real progenitor of opera in England is acknowledged to be Henry Purcell, whose work appeared some decades later.

As for Germany, the first signs of Italy's musical invasion appeared at Dresden about 1627. Heinrich Schütz, a German who had studied at Venice, composed an opera on the libretto of *Dafne*, which Peri had used. As might be expected, it was in the Italian style and—as was true in England—this first German effort at opera had only a temporary influence. It served, however, to put operatic forces in motion.

In France the story was different. Because of their peculiar sensitivity to drama, the French did not take readily to Italian opera, in which vocal elements were emphasized at the expense of dramatic principles. They prided themselves on a preference for French techniques, in which plot and action were given a more important place. True French opera was developed in the mid-seventeenth century by Jean Baptiste Lully, ironically enough, a Florentine, and under the aegis of the renowned *Académie Royale de Musique*, founded under the patronage of Louis XIV. France resisted Italian influence until the time of the Revolution.

By the end of the seventeenth century Italian opera was flourishing in England and Germany—and imitated in France, but not at the cost of dramatic principles. Singers from Italy traveled all over the continent and to England, popularizing Italian opera and style of performance. It was the "golden age" of singers, for opera, under the influence of such composers as Alessandro Scarlatti, was written primarily for exhibition of the voice and with little thought to dramatic entertainment. Sometimes known as the "oratorio era," because operas were virtually concert performances with the singers in costume, it extended, roughly, from the production of Scarlatti's *Pompeo* in Naples, in 1684, to the presentation of Gluck's *Orfeo ed Euridice* in 1762.

With *Orfeo* came the second revolution in opera. By balancing musical and dramatic values, Gluck took it out of the category of costumed oratorio and gave it a new significance. It is interesting to note that the lines of Italian and French influence converged in Gluck's operas. His later works molded the pattern of French grand opera, which had been in the process of development under Lully and Rameau.

After Gluck, the progress of opera was profoundly affected by the newly born Romantic movement and the political changes wrought by the French Revolution. These cultural and social upheavals ushered in the era of opera that pulsed with the new spirit of romanticism and nationalism—the names of Mozart, Beethoven, Meyerbeer, Rossini, Donizetti, and Weber glittered in the operatic firmament. Then, at the climax of the Romantic epoch, the cycle of operatic revolution began again with Wagner and Verdi. As in the case of Gluck, it was a matter of cutting through artificiality and superficiality to essential musical and dramatic values.

Russia was left more or less untouched by operatic changes and trends until the latter part of the eighteenth century, when Italian opera was introduced in Moscow and St. Petersburg. The nineteenth century saw a return to native music, and the beginning of Russian opera is generally dated from the production of Michail Glinka's *A Life for the Czar* in 1836. The spirit of nationalism that first showed itself in Glinka's opera was fostered by the composers known as "The Five"—Alexander Borodin, Mily Balakirev, César Cui, Modest Moussorgsky, and Nikolai Rimsky-Korsakov. Pre-eminently nationalistic, they resisted Italian influence and gave their works native flavor through the infusion of the melodies and rhythms of Russian folk songs.

The epoch of the third revolution extends from the end of the nineteenth century into our own time. Opera turned from romanticism to *verismo*—realism—and then went through impressionism and objectivism to modern experimental forms.

The development of opera as an art form should be viewed—like that of any other art form—against the broader background of civilization itself. Certain important events in the history of human progress influenced its growth and change from time to time. The Renaissance, for example—one of the milestones of civilization—set in motion certain artistic forces which brought opera into being. The Renaissance began in 1453, when the Turks captured Constantinople. For eleven centuries the city had been the seat of eastern Christianity, and there a coterie of great Greek scholars had brought the arts and sciences to a fine flowering. When Constantinople became the capital of the Ottoman Empire, these artists, scientists, and philosophers scattered to different parts of the world. The closest place of safety was

Italy, and it was there that most of these distinguished refugees fled. Thus it was that Italy became the cradle of the Renaissance.

The Renaissance brought immediately to Italy a revival of the classic learning of the Greeks and Romans in all the arts but one—music. It was a relatively easy matter to return to the simplicity and directness of classical antiquity in the other arts, because they had lain neglected during the Middle Ages and presented no obstacle to outside influence. Music, however, had grown and developed to high stature, and actually medieval influence carried over a century and a half into the Renaissance. The revolt in music, as we have noted, was a revolt against the complicated polyphony of the day, as exemplified by the church music of Palestrina and the madrigalists.

In Florence, more than a hundred years after the dawn of the Renaissance, there lived a group of musical scholars who were devotees of the art of ancient Greece. This group included Jacopo Peri, Vincenzo Galilei (the father of Galileo, the astronomer), and Giulio Caccini, and they had as their patron Count Giovanni Bardi, a wealthy Florentine nobleman. The Bardists, as they were sometimes called, sought to re-create the power and splendor of the Greek drama and to heighten its effect with musical accompaniment.

Restless, radical thinkers—like all men of the Renaissance—they revolted against the involved polyphonic writing that had become the high musical art of the sixteenth century. Determined to give music the same elemental and powerful simplicity of the Greek drama, the Bardists went to the other extreme—from the intricate, multivoiced structure of the madrigal to the single vocal line. That was recitative, and recitative was the beginning of opera.

The first work written in the revolutionary style of the accompanied recitative was Peri's *Dafne*, produced for a private audience in 1597. It may be said to be the first opera ever put on a stage. Peri's *Euridice*, written in collaboration with Caccini, was *publicly* produced in 1600, and this is generally recognized as the date of the birth of opera. *Euridice* was in five acts, each concluding with a chorus, and the dialogue was in the form of accompanied recitative. There was also an aria, introduced by an instrumental passage.

Mention should be made here of a work which is sometimes considered an important forerunner of opera. That is *Amfiparnasso*, written in 1594 by Orazio Vecchi, a composer of madrigals and church music and one of the great masters of the polyphonic period. It is a musical setting of a Comedy of Masks—the *commedia dell' arte*—and is written in five-part madrigal form, with three acts and fourteen scenes. *Amfiparnasso* was *not* acted, only sung. It is interesting to note that the work was produced in New York City as recently as 1933.

There were other forms of music in the thirteenth, fourteenth, and fifteenth centuries which had the seed of opera in them. Secular and religious composers injected certain drama qualities into their music, as did the *trouvères* (poet-musicians) of northern France and the players in the mystery and miracle plays of England.

Opera, as "invented" by the Florentines, won the favor of the musical world, and *Dafne* and *Euridice* long served as models for other composers. In the hands of composers like Claudio Monteverdi, who wrote *Ariadne* and

Orfeo, and Pietro Francesco Cavalli, a Venetian with some forty operas to his credit, opera made significant strides. Monteverdi revolutionized music by establishing the tonal system and contributed to the development of the recitative by giving it a more flexible accompaniment. Among Cavalli's important contributions was the introduction of the comic character into opera, a popularizing influence which took opera out of its sphere of austere classicism and brought it closer to the people. This innovation of Cavalli's appeared in his *Doriclea*, produced in 1645.

Monteverdi and Cavalli not only widened the emotional and dramatic scope of opera but its orchestral requirements as well. They scored their works for larger orchestras and introduced melodic passages to break up the continuous recitatives. It is interesting to note that even at this stage the irresistible impulse for melody showed itself, despite the rules of severe simplicity that governed the recitative. In the works of Monteverdi and Cavalli, for example, there appeared long melodious passages on a single vowel, devices which were later to be used with spectacular effect by Scarlatti and Händel.

As opera gradually won popular attention, there was an increasing demand for public performance. In 1637 the first public opera house was opened in Venice. Up to that time opera audiences had been small in size and aristocratic by nature. By 1700 there were no fewer than eleven opera houses in that city, then renowned as Italy's operatic capital. There, and in other opera houses which were built in the principal cities of Italy, was offered an extensive repertoire of works by Monteverdi, Pietro Cavalli, Marc Antonio Cesti, Giacomo Carissimi, and other early composers.

The late seventeenth century saw a surprising development in opera. Whereas the inventors of opera had disdained melody, composers now began developing melodies of the most formalized sort. The emphasis shifted from simple and direct dramatic utterance, and opera became a medium for sheer vocal display. The principal reason was that Italy, fountainhead of opera, produced the best singers—performers with tremendous vocal resources and magnificent tone quality. There is little doubt that singing as an art, though later developed throughout the world, was cradled in Italy in the seventeenth and eighteenth centuries. Opera was written mainly to give these singers a chance to show off. The logical medium for vocal prowess was, of course, the long sustained passages, and thus the aria was born. Eventually it developed into a rigid pattern: a first section, a contrasting middle section, and then a recapitulation of the first section. Opera finally degenerated into a succession of arias and choruses at the sacrifice of intelligible plot and dramatic content.

Typical of this trend in operatic writing were the works of Alessandro Scarlatti (1659–1725), composer of some one hundred and fifteen operas, who is regarded as the true founder of Italian opera. With Scarlatti, vocal display came first; for the most part, simple musical accompaniment would suffice. He added an orchestral embellishment to the aria in the form of an introduction, an interlude, and a postlude. Scarlatti set a style for operatic composition that remained in vogue for nearly a century. It is known as *opera seria*.

While opera was flowering in Italy, a native type of this art form was springing up in France and Germany. In France, opera grew out of the ballet, which had as its chief exponent Jean Baptiste Lully (1632–1687), a Florentine who became court composer to the king of France. He is considered the founder of true French opera, and his *Les Fêtes de l'Amour et de Bacchus*, produced in 1672, is an important operatic milestone. Lully was the first to introduce brasses into the orchestra. He did opera a particularly good turn by pruning away the florid, meaningless arias of the Scarlatti school. Putting the plot in its proper perspective and emphasizing scenic values, Lully gave French opera the individuality that has characterized it ever since. After Lully came Jean Philippe Rameau, a famous French organist and composer. He enriched opera musically by giving it greater harmonic variety and fuller orchestral background.

The rise of opera in Germany was largely under Italian influence, and practically every German court had its Italian opera company, or one functioning under Italian direction. A native form of opera, called the *singspiel* (*songplay*), however, flourished in the folk theaters of small communities. Simply defined, *singspiel* is a musical play in which the vocal interludes are connected by spoken dialogue. In its general pattern it is analogous to English *ballad opera*, Italian *opera buffa*, and French *opéra bouffe*. These four forms, incidentally, all had their origin in the medieval miracle and mystery plays of the fifteenth century. *Singspiel* reappeared later in a highly refined form in works of Beethoven and Mozart, while composers such as Pergolesi, Donizetti, and Rossini brought *opera buffa* to a peak of perfection. *Opéra bouffe* of France developed into the form later known as *opéra comique*, of which *Carmen* and *Faust* are typical examples. *Ballad opera* of England projected its influence into the late nineteenth-century operas of Gilbert and Sullivan.

True national opera was nurtured in North Germany, particularly in Hamburg, where the first German opera house was opened in 1678. One of its initial attractions was the première of what may be considered the first native German opera, *Adam und Eva*, by Johann Theile (1646–1724). Two popular composers who contributed to the musical and dramatic progress of opera during this era—although they wrote in the Italian idiom—were Reinhart Keiser and Johann Adolph Hasse, both with about one hundred operas apiece to their credit. The foremost composer of the day was Georg Frederic Händel (1685–1759). He wrote several operas in Germany, but reached the peak of his brilliant career in London, where he completely dominated the operatic scene. Händel was an exponent of the formalized *opera seria* developed by Scarlatti, with its emphasis on the aria as a vehicle for vocal display. The Scarlatti-Händel period, in fact, can be called the epoch of the aria. It was also the era of the *castrati*, adult male sopranos and contraltos whose brilliant vocalization made them the pampered stars of the operatic stage.

In England, before the advent of Händel, opera had achieved no particular importance. Henry Purcell (1658–1695), one of the most gifted of the seventeenth-century English composers, had written *Dido and Aeneas* and *Dioclesian*, both of which showed extraordinary promise. Purcell's tragically early death at the age of thirty-seven virtually changed England's operatic history. With no truly English champion, opera remained under the influence of Händel and the Italian school. Eventually there was a reaction to the stilted Italianate style. It came in the form of ballad opera, typified by Gay's *The Beggar's Opera*, produced in 1728. Curiously enough, the music for this opera, which achieved tremendous popularity, was composed by John Pepusch, a German expatriate. After the success of *The Beggar's Opera* scores of other ballad operas were composed, establishing a traditional English form which persisted through the works of Gilbert and Sullivan. Prominent among later composers identified with opera in England were Michael William Balfe, who wrote *The Bohemian Girl*, William Vincent Wallace, composer of *Maritana*, and Henry Rowley Bishop, composer of *Clari*, which contains one of the world's best-known songs, "Home, Sweet Home."

By the time the eighteenth century dawned, opera had progressed through an artistic cycle and was ripe for rebellion. The refreshing inventiveness and spontaneity of the Florentines had long ago given way to highly stylized and conventional forms. Composers were practically under an obligation to write a certain number of arias for each singer so that each artist could strut to his heart's content. There was even a standardization of libretti, oddly reminiscent of the standardization of the aria in the preceding century. Whenever a composer wanted a libretto he would simply apply to Pietro Metastasio, an Italian poet who was the foremost librettist of the period. Some of his texts were set to music as many as thirty or forty times by various composers. The effect of this assembly-line technique may well be imagined.

This was the state of affairs when Gluck and Mozart appeared on the scene and altered opera's destiny. Christoph Willibald, Ritter von Gluck (1714–1787), who had become one of Germany's greatest composers in the Italian style, was the first to break with tradition. In middle life he suddenly discarded the accepted forms as the result of contacts with the musical life of Paris and Vienna. His *Orfeo ed Euridice* (1762) marks the beginning of his rebellion, as we noted earlier. It expressed his conviction that opera must have dramatic coherence and that the music must serve the plot, not merely a singer's ego. In his insistence on dramatic values, Gluck was going back to the sound ideals of the Florentines, as did later great performers of opera—Verdi, Wagner, and Debussy.

When *Orfeo* was rather coolly received in Vienna, Gluck went to Paris, where, under the patronage of Marie Antoinette, he launched a campaign in behalf of his new ideas. He promptly ran head-on into the musical reactionaries, who roared long and loudly against the iconoclast. The musical world was divided into two camps. Champions of the operatic status quo were led by Nicola Piccinni, a leading composer of conventional opera. They opened violent attacks on the "radical" Gluck, and the epic feud between the Gluckists and the Piccinnists was on. Some accounts say that the war became so bitter that it reached the stage of physical violence. At any rate, the situation finally came to a climax in 1779, when the directors of the Paris Opéra commissioned both Gluck and Piccinni to write an opera based on *Iphigénie en Tauride*. Gluck's version won by popular acclaim and his triumph marked the beginning of a new epoch in opera.

Although Gluck infused opera with new life and meaning, it remained essentially in the tradition of Peri and Scarlatti, as far as subject matter was concerned. The first to break out of this pattern was Wolfgang Amadeus Mozart (1756–1791). He turned from the lofty Olympian themes of antiquity to contemporary life for his plots, endowing his characters with natural human emotions. Although strongly influenced by the Italian school, Mozart, like Gluck, avoided showy vocalization and made his music conform to the vital dramatic elements in the plot. He wrote some of his operas in Italian simply because that language was the most musically adaptable to his purposes. The new musical and dramatic concepts expressed in *Don Giovanni*, *Le Nozze di Figaro*, and *Die Zauberflöte* make those operas symbolic of one of the most significant periods in operatic history. *Die Zauberflöte* had the innovation of spoken dialogue, and in this respect it classed as a glorified example of *singspiel*.

Mozart represents not only the dawn of the Romantic period in opera but reflects the new spirit of enlightenment that was awakening in Europe at the time. It was the spirit Rousseau was talking about when he preached nature and the individual man. It was expressed in the dramas of Beaumarchais when he favored the middle class at the expense of the nobility.

In addition to the reforms of Gluck and Mozart, another purging influence on opera during the eighteenth century was *opera buffa*. This form of lyric drama gradually became identified with between-the-acts diversions presented at performances of *opera seria*. Gradually acquiring a status of its own, *opera buffa* relied for its effects largely upon a comic plot of a contemporary or topical nature. It was therefore free of many of the restrictions of conventional opera, and was fertile soil for satiric characterization. Important composers of the eighteenth and nineteenth centuries turned to *opera buffa* and its naturalistic approach to life because it offered greater dramatic and musical freedom. Some examples of *opera buffa* at its best are Giovanni Pergolesi's *La Serva Padrona*, Mozart's *Così Fan Tutte*, Donizetti's *Don Pasquale*, and Rossini's *Il Barbiere di Siviglia*. It should be mentioned that another Italian composer, Giovanni Paisiello, wrote another *Il Barbiere di Siviglia* some decades before Rossini, and it ranks high on the list of *opera buffa*. Paisiello, who wrote more than one hundred operas, had a tremendous vogue in Italy during the eighteenth century.

The Romantic movement found eloquent expression in *Fidelio*, by Ludwig van Beethoven (1770–1827). Although it is grounded in the classic tradition, it has revolutionary fire and spirit. Like Mozart, Beethoven used spoken dialogue, thus carrying on the tradition of the *singspiel*. The emotional intensity of the Romantic movement was heightened by the social upheavals that stirred Europe at the end of the eighteenth century and the beginning of the nineteenth. Artistic revolt against classicism, the newly awakened spirit of chivalry and adventure, the preoccupation with the picturesque—all these manifestations were akin to the revolutionary mood which found its outlet in the Napoleonic wars. Romanticism and revolution virtually merged into one dynamic force that affected human destiny and the arts alike. In opera it found its expression in the passionate and heroic themes of works by Cherubini, Spontini, Auber, Rossini, Meyerbeer, Halévy, and Weber. They were concerned with human problems and aspirations, and delineated them against backgrounds of spectacular pageantry.

Operatic works reflecting the spirit of this exciting epoch won varying degrees of permanence in repertoire. Maria Luigi Cherubini, distinguished Italian composer who became head of the Paris Conservatoire, won considerable fame with *Les Deux Journées* and *Faniska*. Gasparo Spontini, also an Italian, and an important figure in the German operatic world of the time, was highly successful with *La Vestale, Fernando Cortez,* and *Agnes von Hohenstaufen,* the last-mentioned more or less after the style of Weber. The French school, with its emphasis on dramatic verities, was prominently represented. François Fromental Elie Halévy scored a great success with *La Juive,* and the opera has survived in repertoire. Others of importance include Etienne Nicolas Mehul (*Joseph*), Daniel François Esprit Auber (*Masaniello, Fra Diavolo*), and François Adrien Boieldieu (*Le Calife de Bagdad, Jean de Paris, La Dame Blanche*). The last-mentioned opera contains the famous song "Robin Adair." The works of both Auber and Boieldieu were favorites with American audiences of the early nineteenth century.

Head and shoulders above these composers, however, was Giacomo Meyerbeer (Jakob Liebmann Beer) (1791–1864), who seemed to concentrate in his works the dominant German, Italian, and French influences of the early Romantic era. Meyerbeer typifies the penchant of the Romanticists for pageantry, melodrama, and themes of high tragedy. He won such tremendous successes with *L'Africaine, Les Huguenots,* and *Robert le Diable* that he became the undisputed monarch of the operatic kingdom.

In Italy the new Romantic influence was reflected in the works of the foremost composers of the period—Gioachino Antonio Rossini (1792–1868), Vincenzo Bellini, and Gaetano Donizetti. While they carried on the tradition of the Italian school, with its emphasis on vocal virtuosity, they responded to the contemporary spirit in their versatility of plot treatment. The most brilliant spokesman for Romanticism in Italy was Rossini. One of his important operatic innovations was doing away with the thinly accompanied *secco* (dry) recitative peculiar to *opera buffa*. Rossini embellished these explanatory interludes with fuller orchestral accompaniment, which avoided monotony and made for smoother transition. In his last opera, *Guillaume Tell,* written under the influence of the French school, Rossini departed radically from his earlier style. This opera, with its melodrama and pageantry, has a serious revolutionary theme that is in sharp contrast to the satiric mood of his other works.

When composers turned away from the abstractions of classicism, they demanded more theatrical realism in their libretti. The need for sounder and more cogent libretto writing was amply supplied by the French dramatist Eugéne Scribe. As prolific as Metastasio before him, Scribe was an expert in stagecraft and extraordinarily inventive in the matter of plot mechanics. It was said of him that, at a moment's notice, he could write lines or create a scene that would not only meet the needs of the plot but fit perfectly into the pattern of the music as well. Scribe wrote libretti for Meyerbeer, Halévy, Auber, Cherubini, Gounod, Donizetti, and Verdi. At this period, also, opera underwent a change not only musically and dramatically but scenically. The classic background of the abode of the gods was discarded in favor of realistic settings which accurately portrayed the locale of the plot.

In general, composers of the early nineteenth century advanced opera by developing several types from earlier forms. Thus, out of the *opera buffa*, the ingenious French devised a more elaborate form called *opéra comique*, in which comedy was made to serve the larger aims of drama. It is characterized by variety of subject matter, interludes of spoken dialogue, and versatility of musical and dramatic treatment. The *singspiel* of Germany blossomed into *romantic opera* under Weber's influence, while the old *opera seria*, embellished by Spontini and Meyerbeer with vivid stage display and orchestral coloring, became *grand opera*.

The Romantic epoch was vitalized by the spirit of nationalism that spread through Europe during the nineteenth century. The acknowledged master of the movement in music was Carl Maria von Weber, who represents the high tide of German nationalism. Thoroughly Germanic in spirit and concept, his operas are full of romantic fervor and melodrama. *Der Freischütz*, produced in 1821, took Germany by storm, and from then on Weber superseded all other operatic composers in public favor. He was one of the most powerful influences of the nineteenth century.

Although somewhat overshadowed by Weber, other composers reflected the new Germanic spirit in operas that were widely popular during the period. Chief among these was Heinrich Marschner, a close friend of Weber, whose *Hans Heiling* was long a favorite. Ludwig Spohr, not only a composer but a great violinist and conductor, wrote *Zemire und Azor* and *Jessonda*. Spohr was an associate of Richard Wagner and produced *Der Fliegende Holländer*. Gustav Albert Lortzing delighted German audiences with his light operas such as *Zar und Zimmermann* and *Der Wildschütz*.

The nationalistic spirit gradually spread through eastern Europe and found voice in the operas of Czechoslovakia, Poland, Hungary, and Russia. Bedřich Smetana caught the vigor and exuberance of his people in *The Bartered Bride*, which became the Czech national opera. In Poland there was Stanislaw Moniuszko, whose *Halka* was the first Polish opera. The pioneer of national opera in Hungary was Ferencz Erkel, with operas such as *Hunyády Laszlo* and *Bank Bán*.

In Russia the Romantic era was marked by stirrings of revolt. Nationalism came to life as the people turned on their oppressors, threw aside the restraints of provincial existence, and became aware of a world outside Russia's borders. Such works as *Russalka*, by Alexander Dargomijsky (1813–1869), and *Russlan and Ludmilla* and *A Life for the Czar*, by Michail Glinka (1804–1857), heralded musical nationalism. Operas which further developed it include *Eugin Onegin*, by Peter Ilyich Tschaikowsky (1840–1893), *Prince Igor*, by Alexander Borodin (1834–1887), *Le Coq d'Or*, by Nikolai Rimsky-Korsakov (1844–1908), and *Boris Godunof* by Modest Moussorgsky (1835–1881).

Meanwhile there appeared on the operatic scene two composers who brought the Romantic movement to the pinnacle of its expression and who shaped the future of opera. They are Giuseppe Verdi (1813–1901) and

Richard Wagner (1813–1883), both of whom instituted the most significant reforms in operatic composition since the time of Gluck and Mozart.

Although Verdi's earlier operas adhered to the conventional Italian style, his lyric gift and instinct for dramatic values infused Italian opera with a strong quality of realism and restored the balance of music and plot. As Verdi progressed in his career, the conventional arias of his earlier works gave way to a more continuous melodic line, which was given more prominent orchestral support. His final works, *Otello* and *Falstaff,* represent the welding of music and drama in a technique that closely approaches that of Wagner.

"Wagner," says Ernest Newman in his *Wagner As Man and Artist,* "was one of those dynamically charged personalities after whose passing the world can never be the same as it was before he came—one of the tiny group of men to whom it is given to bestride an old world and a new, but to sunder them by a gulf that becomes ever more and more impassable; one of the very few who are able so to fill the veins of a whole civilization with a new principle of vitality that the tingle of it is felt not only by the rarer but by the commonest of spirits—some new principle from which, whether a man like it or not, he will find it impossible to escape."

The operatic craftsmanship and musical nationalism of the early Romanticists paved the way for the greatest genius in the history of opera. In his early days he had absorbed the influences of such composers as Spontini, Cherubini, Auber, and Meyerbeer, and he raised the German nationalism of Weber to a high plane of development. It is in his later works—the *Ring* operas, *Die Meistersinger, Tristan und Isolde,* and *Parsifal*—that he reached his goal. That was the creation of a revolutionary form of opera—the music-drama. He replaced the traditional operatic aria and connecting recitative with an "endless chain" of musical speech which is an integral part of a complex orchestral accompaniment.

Wagner also perfected the leitmotif, or leading motive. This device is a melodic or harmonic figure associated with a dramatic situation, a particular person, or a motivating thought. Where earlier composers, such as Weber, used the leitmotif merely as a musical label to identify a character or an idea, Wagner altered the structure of the motif itself to conform to the progress of the drama. It should be pointed out here, however, that Wagner was a musician first and dramatist second. As creator of his own plots, he fashioned the drama to fit the music, not the music to fit the drama. Wagner symbolizes the next great operatic reform after the Florentines: drama and music are components of an artistic whole, with each created to serve the purpose of the other.

After Verdi and Wagner brought the Romantic era to a brilliant climax, a new influence began to make itself felt in the economic and cultural life of the people. The great strides made by science and industry during the last decades of the nineteenth century ushered in the era of Materialism. Interest was centered in the struggle of man for material benefits, and in the arts this preoccupation with the individual led to a naturalistic portrayal of the details of human existence.

In opera there was, naturally, a period of transition, marked by the works of composers under the influence of Wagner. He, of course, had many imitators, few of whom were successful. Engelbert Humperdinck (1854–1921) used the rudiments of music-drama technique with pleasing effect in *Hänsel und Gretel*. Arrigo Boïto (1842–1918) and Amilcare Ponchielli (1834–1886) were among the first in Italy to adapt advanced musical ideas, and are considered by some as founders of modern Italian opera. Boïto applied certain Wagnerian techniques to his fantastic and beautiful *Mefistofele*, a setting of the Faust legend, while Ponchielli's *La Gioconda* shows the modern influence in its richness of orchestration, bringing the accompaniment on a plane of equal importance with the voice.

The impact of Wagnerian ideas on composers like Georges Bizet (1838–1875) and Camille Saint-Saëns (1835–1921) was very evident. Bizet's *Carmen*, in fact, at first was frowned on by the French as being too Wagnerian, while Saint-Saëns's *Samson et Dalila* was kept from the stage of the Paris Opéra for a number of years for the same reason. Charles Gounod (1818–1893), another composer of the transition period, reveals in his emphasis on lyrical elements more of the Verdian influence. To the transition group may be added the names of Ambroise Thomas (1811–1896) and Jules Massenet (1842–1912).

Materialism somewhat dimmed the emotional glow which had pervaded opera during the Romantic era, but the lyric stage lost none of its power. Realism gave the drama more impact, the music more incisiveness. The effect of preoccupation with the individual and his problems is well illustrated by *Louise*, by Gustave Charpentier. Although set against a romantic background—like *Carmen*—it is a realistic and sometimes uncompromising picture of lower levels of Parisian life.

In Italy the new realism found voice in the *verismo* school of composers—Leoncavallo, Mascagni, Giordano, Wolf-Ferrari, and Puccini. Though in most cases the plots were starkly realistic, the Italians, with their natural impulse of melody, clothed the expressions of violent emotions in rich trappings of harmony.

After the turn of the century, composers seemed to turn to a more symphonic style, with the vocal line serving as an accompaniment. The music served to express subtle moods and psychological reactions rather than sentiment or emotion. In that respect opera turned toward Impressionism, which had first made its influence felt in painting. Among the first to use this newer technique was Richard Strauss. Operas such as *Salome* and *Elektra* show projections of Wagnerian techniques to which he added certain dramatic and musical concepts of his own, while the psychological problems posed in these operas reveal traces of the Impressionistic influence. In that period Strauss reflected a preoccupation with the erotic and the pathological, as did composers such as Alban Berg and Franz Shreker. But Strauss broke out of the pattern with *Rosenkavalier*, which brims over with a lusty, extrovert spirit and exuberant melody.

One of the most remarkable operas of the twentieth century is Claude Debussy's *Pelléas et Mélisande*. In its use of the leitmotif it is Wagnerian; in its psychological nuances and subtle delineation of moods it is Impressionistic. At the same time *Pelléas* marks another return to the Florentines in the perfection of its blending of music and drama.

Taken as a whole, European operatic composition of the twentieth century reveals several trends. Some composers show the influence of Wagnerian reform, under which they have developed distinct styles of their own. In this category may be named such men as Italo Montemezzi (*L'Amore dei Tre Re*), Ildebrando Pizzetti (*Fra Gherardo*), Ottorino Respighi (*La Campana Sommersa*). Later twentieth-century composers forged into experimental fields with interesting results. A trend toward absolute objectivity is revealed in *Christoph Colomb,* by Paul Claudel and Darius Milhaud, in which stage action is supplemented by movie projection. Men like Arnold Schönberg (*Die glückliche Hand*) and Alban Berg (*Wozzeck*) turned to atonality in music and expressionism in plot. Others whose innovations have attracted attention include Paul Hindemith (*Neues vom Tage*), Jaromir Weinberger (*Schwanda*), Ernest Krenek (*Jonny spielt auf*), Kurt Weill (*Dreigroschenoper*), and Dmitri Shostakovitch (*Lady Macbeth Mtsenskago Uyezda—Lady Macbeth of Mtsensk District*). One interesting trend in European opera is in the direction of the old forms, as though opera, in the fourth century of its existence, were completing a full circle. A notable example of this is Strauss's *Ariadne auf Naxos,* which interestingly combined elements of Florentine technique, *opera buffa,* and *opera seria.*

The development of opera in America was shaped—as it was in Europe—by economic and cultural trends. The harsh struggle for existence in the pioneer days left little opportunity for the amenities of civilization. Yet, with the gradual establishment of communities, the desire for entertainment and relaxation asserted itself, and the theater of the day met the demands of the public with importations of English ballad operas, which were long in vogue. The popularity of ballad operas, however, aroused the ire of some of the sterner citizens, who protested that the "strolling Comedians" presenting these entertainments were "propagating vice and immorality." These moral objections, in fact, led indirectly to the use of the term "opera house" for the first time in America, in August 1787. It was applied to the Southwark Theater, in Philadelphia, by the way of removing the taint that clung to the professional title of "theater," with all that it implied in the form of worldly entertainment.

During the colonial period there were interesting attempts at native opera, among which may be mentioned *Flora; or, Hob in the Well* (1735), usually cited as the first performance of native opera in America; *Tammany; or, The Indian Chief* (1794), an opera on an Indian subject by James Hewitt; *Edwin and Angelina* (1796), by the French-born Victor Pelissier, and *The Saw Mill; or, A Yankee Trick* (1824), by Micah Hawkins. The popularity of musical attractions may be gauged by the fact that the Hallam family, an American theatrical troupe, was active from about 1735 until 1800 with a repertoire of some two hundred operas and musical plays.

There were, so to speak, operatic repercussions of the French Revolution in this country which were felt principally in New Orleans. Many musical artists who fled the war in Europe made their way to that city, with the result that it became the center of French drama and opera, and its audiences were among the first to see the *opéra comique* works of Boieldieu and Auber. In the 1830s operas by these composers were given in abridged form in New York by artists who came northward from New Orleans. Called an "American Paris," New Orleans was an operatic center rivaling New York and Philadelphia in the eighteenth century and during the early part of the nineteenth. It was virtually a French provincial city in which was reproduced the cultural life of Paris and, as for opera, it remained a completely French institution.

Operatic history in New Orleans centered in the Théâtre d'Orléans, built in 1813. Destroyed by fire and rebuilt four years later, it was known as the finest theater in America. For close to half a century it provided operatic performances on a level of professional excellence that almost approached that of the foremost European lyric theaters. The repertoire was the standard one of the period and included—besides Boieldieu and Auber, mentioned previously—works of Halévy, Meyerbeer, Verdi, Rossini, Spontini, and Mozart. New Orleans opera was important for its influence on opera in Philadelphia and New York, by virtue of the fact that experienced artists from the Théâtre d'Orléans gave performances in those cities. It was not until the mid-nineteenth century, when New York became the mecca for foreign artists, that New Orleans lost its place as the operatic capital of America.

Opera benefited by the fact that the invention of the steamship more closely linked Europe and America. Original opera companies were imported from Europe and there was an influx of European musical personalities into this country. Many arrived under encouragement from Lorenzo da Ponte, Mozart's famous librettist, who had come to America at the beginning of the century. In 1825 the famous Manuel Garcia operatic troupe arrived to inaugurate the first season of grand opera in New York.

It is an interesting fact that a desire for opera in English manifested itself in America in the eighteenth century. Edward Ellsworth Hipsher, in his *American Opera and Its Composers*, states: "From that eventful February 8, 1735, when the opera of *Flora; or, Hob in the Well* was produced at Charleston, South Carolina . . . till the end of the century, Opera in English held undisputed sway." The preference was so strong that attempts made toward the end of the century to introduce French opera outside of New Orleans met with little success. In 1793 a New York company was presenting an entire repertoire of operas in English.

The cause of opera in the vernacular, however, suffered a serious blow with the arrival of Garcia's troupe, one member of which was his daughter, who, as Marie Malibran, was to become one of the greatest singers of the day. Garcia and his colleagues represented the best in Italian operatic art, which was then at high tide in Europe. They quickly built up a following and threatened the supremacy of opera in English. In the 1830s, however, there were performances in English of such operas as *Fidelio*, *Sonnambula*, and *Robert le Diable*. Another interesting phase of the battle of opera was introduced with the establishment in New York of the Italian Opera House by da Ponte. One of the first opera houses, *per se*, in America, it was supported by subscribers in the manner of later organizations of that kind, and the operas were performed by noted Italian singers. In competition with it, however, was a company giving operas in English. After a two-year period of intense rivalry, the English company emerged triumphant. Balfe's *Bohe-*

mian Girl, introduced to American audiences in 1840, is said to have inspired the Philadelphian William Henry Fry to write *Leonora,* which is considered the first real American *grand opera.* Another important composer of this period was George F. Bristow, who wrote the grand opera *Rip Van Winkle,* presented in New York in 1855. Both composers are important in American operatic history for their championship of American music.

During the middle of the nineteenth century the influx of foreign singers gradually crowded singers of English opera from the stage, leaving the field to French, Italian, and German performers. Then came the epoch of the "star system," when the opera-going public clamored to hear the fabulous performances of such artists as Patti, Sembrich, Malibran, and Nilsson. In the face of their vocal accomplishments, the language in which they sang was a matter of indifference to their listeners. The custom of opera in foreign tongue firmly established itself, and opera in English lost ground it has never regained.

Opera moved westward with the tide of territorial expansion. During the 1850s Chicago became an operatic center of the Middle West, with English and Italian companies playing there. During the Gold Rush days opera invaded San Francisco, and affluent patrons heard some of the famous stars such as Jenny Lind, Patti, and Malibran in performances of standard operas. It was the fantastic era of sudden wealth, when the society that followed on the heels of lusty prospectors demanded spectacular entertainment and enthusiastically acclaimed even as "high-brow" a form as opera. Opera lovers whose pockets were literally bulging with new-found wealth sometimes threw chunks of raw gold on the stage as tokens of appreciation of an operatic favorite. A colorful chapter in the history of the Gold Rush days was the famous Central City Opera House, Central City, Colorado, built in 1878. Opera troupes from the East, on their way to the Coast, stopped there to give performances that were applauded to the echo by bearded miners and resplendently attired patrons. Some of the greatest dramatic actors of the day, including Sarah Bernhardt and Tommaso Salvini, played at the Opera House during its nine-month season. When the boom passed, the glory and glitter faded, but the Opera House has survived to the present day as an important cultural institution.

Industrial and economic development after the Civil War established a wealthy society which was able to support opera in its most lavish form. Opera houses were built in all the larger cities—Philadelphia, Boston, Cleveland, Cincinnati, St. Louis—and opera became an important part of society life. The present Metropolitan Opera House was opened in 1883, and in ensuing years European artists came to this country in greater numbers than ever before. In 1884, Leopold Damrosch organized a season of Wagnerian operas, and the repertoire was repeated yearly until 1891. During this period, representing the high tide of German opera in America, Anton Seidl, who had been Wagner's assistant at Bayreuth, conducted the first American performances of *Die Meistersinger, Tristan und Isolde,* and the *Ring.*

Although foreign operas were consistently popular in all parts of the country during the nineteenth century, native American opera was in continuous existence. Pioneer composers such as Hewitt, Hawkins, Fry, and Bristow had their successors in men like Charles Wakefield Cadman (*Shan-*

ewis), Frederick Shepherd Converse (*The Pipe of Desire*—presented at the Metropolitan in 1910, the first American opera by a native composer to be given there), Walter Damrosch (*Cyrano de Bergerac*), Reginald de Koven (*Robin Hood, Canterbury Pilgrims*), Victor Herbert (*Natoma*), and Horatio Parker (*Mona*).

Conspicuous among contemporary American grand-opera composers are Deems Taylor (*The King's Henchman, Peter Ibbetson*), Louis Gruenberg (*Emperor Jones*), and Howard Hanson (*Merry Mount*). These works were regarded as having made important musical and dramatic contributions to the progress of opera, and their initial presentations—in the early thirties in this country—were acclaimed. They have not, however, established a place for themselves in grand-opera repertoire.

Virtually the only grand opera presented in America during that period which has lasted in repertoire is *Wozzeck*, by the Viennese composer Alban Berg. It had premières in Philadelphia and New York in 1931. *Wozzeck* is a grim tragedy of murder and madness, set to an unorthodox combination of traditional and modern music. Some consider it an operatic milestone as important as *Pelléas et Mélisande;* others dismiss it as sheer insanity. Yet it has enduring power as a new operatic form.

The depression and the social upheaval that swept America during the first half of the thirties were reflected in opera just as they were in the drama. Playwrights and composers turned again to stark realism, to the harsh realities of hunger, poverty, and frustration. To match such dramas as *One Third of a Nation* or *Class of '29*, there was Marc Blitzstein's opera, *The Cradle Will Rock*. The plot centers around the efforts of steel workers to organize a union. The opera had its première in New York on June 15, 1937, under hectic circumstances. Because of its political overtones it was banned at the last moment from a WPA theater on Broadway. Producers scurried around, found another vacant theater, and there the opera was performed without scenery or costumes. Blitzstein himself played the score, sitting at a piano on the stage. One New York critic compared the work, in its realistic approach to social problems of the day, to Charpentier's *Louise*.

An opera in an entirely different vein was produced at about the same period. This was *Porgy and Bess*, by George Gershwin. It had its première in Boston on September 30, 1935. *Porgy and Bess* is rich in folklore of the South, and Gershwin planned it as a *native* American opera. Critics consider it a hybrid—somewhere between opera and musical comedy. Hybrid or otherwise, it has been performed time and again by singing companies throughout the country. Lately, it achieved spectacular success abroad.

The period of the thirties also marks the emergence of a composer who gave opera freshness and renewed vitality. That composer is Gian-Carlo Menotti, Italian by birth, American by adoption. The first of his works was *Amelia Goes to the Ball*, expertly written in the old *opera buffa* style. He followed that with *The Old Maid and the Thief*, in the same vein. Then came *The Medium*, in quite different, modern style, with spiritualism as its theme. Following these, Menotti wrote *The Consul*, which is really in the pattern of grand opera. Its theme is the tragedy of the displaced person and his struggle to cope with a world that is cynically indifferent to his fate.

Here Menotti makes effective use of *singspiel*, simple melody, traditional aria forms, and modern dissonances.

Among the most important of Menotti's operatic works is *Amahl and the Night Visitors*, the first opera expressly written for television. It had its television première on Christmas Eve, 1951, and has since been performed by opera companies. From the première of *Amelia Goes to the Ball*, in 1937, to the première of *The Saint of Bleeker Street*, in 1954, is a span of 17 years, a period in which Menotti made a lasting contribution to the cause of opera in America.

The matter-of-fact realism of operatic works of the thirties seems to have paved the way for a return to the *verismo* school of writing. Composed mostly in the modern idiom, opera today sticks more or less to facts and spurns romantic flights of fancy. When it is not harshly realistic, it is satiric. *Il Prigioniero*, for example, a one-act opera by Luigi Dellapiccola (1947) has for its theme the torture of a political prisoner. *L'Apostrophe*, a comic opera by Jean Françaix (1950) is based on one of Balzac's *Droll Stories*. *Trouble in Tahiti*, by Leonard Bernstein is in the American jazz idiom. *The Trial* (*Der Prozess*), a full-length opera by Gottfried von Einem, is based on a novel by Franz Kafka. It depicts one man's struggle against totalitarian despotism, which finally destroys him.

In the forefront of present-day operatic composers, along with Menotti, is England's Benjamin Britten. He has contributed two grand operas (*Peter Grimes, Billy Budd*), a chamber opera (*The Rape of Lucretia*), and an *opera buffa* (*Albert Herring*). Although not yet securely in opera repertoire, they are performed from time to time in this country. One of the most important premières in recent years in America was that of *The Rake's Progress* by Igor Stravinsky. It was first presented at the Metropolitan (in English) on February 14, 1953. It opened in this country to mixed reviews, and while at first it was acclaimed by the public, it gradually lost favor and, although still in the repertoire, it is rarely given. At any rate, all of the above, since they are in English, do help to keep alive the healthy controversy over opera in that language.

One organization that lends weight to the argument for opera in English is the New England Opera Theatre—or NEOT, as it is known in Boston, where the company puts on its performances. Under the direction of Boris Goldovsky, NEOT presents restudied versions of classic and modern operas in English. Goldovsky has introduced such unconventional methods as having singers turn their backs to the conductor during rehearsals—so they will not get into the habit of staring into the pit during performances instead of acting. He has the actors analyze their actions offstage to find out what motivates their entrance on cue.

The NEOT chooses for performance little-known operas like Mozart's early satire on opera, *La Finta Giardiniera* (written when he was 12), presented as *The Merry Masquerade*. The company's repertoire also includes Mozart's *Idomeneo* and Rossini's *The Turk in Italy*.

On the basis of what has already been presented on television, this medium is certain to loom large in the future of opera. The possibilities—as with the presentation of dramas—are limitless. Already, standard operas adapted for television presentation in English include *Madama Butterfly*,

Pique Dame, Pagliacci, Carmen, Il Tabarro, Gianni Schicchi, Macbeth, The Marriage of Figaro, The Taming of the Shrew, Pelléas et Mélisande, and *Salome.* Obviously, this is only a beginning. The future of opera on television is in the hands of those producers who have the necessary taste, talent, and imagination to exploit its possibilities.

In opera, as in human history, "the Past is Prologue." The techniques of the Florentines and the achievements of later creators and "reformers"— Monteverdi, Lully, Gluck, Mozart, Verdi, and Wagner—comprise a treasure house of operatic theory and principle from which composers of today draw their inspiration. We have seen how the tide of lyricism, gathering force in 1600, swept northward from Italy into Europe and England, thrust eastward into Russia, and surged westward into the New World. In the three and a half centuries of opera's existence it has made a definite impact on Western civilization.

Opera has gained a permanent place in America's culture. There are no fewer than six major opera companies in the United States today, as well as a great many smaller organizations that give performances ranging from the oldest and most conservative repertoire to the newest experimental forms. Still to be reckoned with is the impact of television on opera. There, in the making, may well be a new chapter in operatic history.

PART IV

THE BALLET IN OPERA

THE ASSOCIATION of ballet and opera throughout the history of both arts has sometimes been casual, sometimes intimate. These two streams of artistic expression have merged at various periods, flowed together for a time, then have divided to continue on their separate courses. Despite the fact that ballet and opera have, on innumerable occasions, occupied the same stage at the same time, they have maintained their identity as separate art forms. Of the two, ballet is the older.

In 1570, for example—more than a quarter of a century before the Florentines began their experimentation with musical forms that led to the invention of opera—Jean Antoine de Baïf founded the Academy of St. Cecilia. It was comprised of musicians and poets who conducted researches into antique musical forms, experimented in welding metrical forms to music, and made a study of dancing, with particular reference to the inauguration of choreographic reforms. The Academy, though comparatively short-lived, served as a model for later institutions of the same kind, particularly the famous *Académie Royale de la Musique et de la Danse*, which played so significant a part in the development of ballet and opera in Europe from the time of its founding in 1661. The members of Baïf's Academy responded to the spirit of the Renaissance by directing their interests to the pure classic forms of the Greeks, just as the Florentines did later. In other words, both ballet and opera owe much of their initial development to the same force—the Renaissance.

In the dramas of the Greeks the chorus and the ballet were one. Groups moved in stately cadences that coincided with the rhythm of chanted verses and the musical accompaniment. In the ensuing centuries, dance forms were adapted to religious rites, seasonal festivals, court fetes, and formal spectacles. Then came the colorful court masques of the fourteenth and fifteenth centuries—popular in Italy, France, and England, in which countries they were developed into spectacles of unbelievable magnificence. In France the masques took the form of *ballet-comique*. One of the most memorable was the *Ballet Comique de la Reine*, produced in 1581 at the court of Catherine de Medici, then the wife of Henry II. This remarkable presentation, which lasted five hours and was said to have cost more than six million francs, is an important event in the history of theatrical dancing because it marked the first time that a court masque adhered to a dramatic plan taking the form of a plot. The artistic principles involved in its production contributed to the further progress of ballet and opera.

After the time of the *Ballet Comique de la Reine*, development of dancing centered in France. The Italians, meanwhile, concentrated their attention on opera. The two streams were brought together through the introduction of Italian opera in Paris, largely through the efforts of Cardinal Mazarin, who produced Italian works there from 1645 to 1647. The determination of the French to resist the Italian influence—apparently out of national pride and an inborn love of their own native drama—led to the development of national French opera.

The guiding spirit of the movement was Jean Baptiste Lully, whose works mark the beginning of opera in France. He appeared under the patronage of Louis XIV, who, as an accomplished dancer, may well be considered the founder of modern ballet. Lully, himself a remarkable combination of dancer, composer, musician, and impresario, co-ordinated the elements of opera and ballet into a semblance of dramatic unity. He was primarily a musician, and the operatic forms he created in such works as *Les Fêtes de l'Amour et de Bacchus* (1672) and *Le Triomphe de l'Amour* (1681) remained virtually unchanged in France until the advent of Gluck a century later. Though many of his works were called ballets, they were really operas in which considerable opportunity was given for the introduction of dances.

In addition to his artistic accomplishments, Lully was adept at court politics and managed, through some rather unscrupulous conniving, to gain the king's permission to establish the Royal Academy of Music, which he later combined with the Academy of Dance (*Académie Royale de la Musique et de la Danse*). Modeled somewhat along the lines of Baïf's Academy, it became one of the artistic shrines of Europe, where only the greatest dancers, musicians, poets, and scenic designers practiced their arts. The progress of opera in France can be traced in the history of the Academy, which was in continuous existence for more than two hundred years. More works were produced there during the eighteenth and nineteenth centuries than in any other place in Europe, and among its operatic milestones are the productions of Rameau, Gluck, Auber, Rossini, and Meyerbeer.

After the era of Louis XIV and Lully there was a long interval of comparative inaction. Despite the tacit resistance of the French to Italian influence, the lyric stage felt the effect of Italian works. The importance of dramatic and poetic elements became less, while the emphasis on music increased. The public, however, still demanded dancing with its opera, with the result that there was introduced into opera a type of choreographic invention that came to be known as Opéra-Ballet. It remained in vogue during the first half of the eighteenth century.

Another important figure in ballet was Jean Philippe Rameau, a composer and musical theorist who first gained prominence through publication of several treatises on harmony. Although his music was somewhat academic and difficult, he soon acquired a following which set itself up in opposition to those who preferred Lully's style. As a theorist, Rameau stylized the Opéra-Ballet and gave it precise and exact form. His motives and melodies were clearly enunciated and his rhythms sharply marked, so that there was never any disparity between the music and the dance forms that were inherent in the rhythms. In his careful adherence to form and dramatic principle, Rameau may be considered a forerunner of such later music-dramatists as Gluck, Wagner, and Stravinsky.

In the period after Rameau the Opéra-Ballet more or less atrophied into conventional and academic forms and suffered from a lack of co-operation among its creators. The composer, the librettist, the *maître de ballet*, and the scenic artist strove to promote their respective achievements without any attempt to co-ordinate or unify their efforts for the sake of dramatic coherence. The negative influence of this trend manifested itself in weak libretti and undue emphasis on individual performers.

Reform was eventually brought about by a man who is highly important in the history of ballet and opera—Jean Georges Noverre. Born in 1727, he became *Maître de Ballet* at the Paris Opéra at an early age. Noverre broke the pattern of stage dancing which had been created by Lully during the founding of the Académie and which had been left intact by Rameau. At one point in his career he went to Vienna, where he became friendly with Gluck. The importance of Gluck's reforms in opera may be compared with Noverre's in the ballet. Noverre demanded stronger libretti and music of greater variety, in order to give the ballet more dramatic impact—just as Gluck had insisted on closer attention to dramatic elements in opera.

Noverre's dramatic ballets had a strong influence in operatic acting. His choreographic technique gave the *corps de ballet* significance as an integral part of the action, not merely as accompaniment to solo performers. When this technique was applied to opera, it meant that the role of the chorus was made increasingly important. The kinship of ballet movement to acting on the lyric stage lies in the fact that in both ballet and opera movements must be synchronized with the music.

Noverre's ideas influenced choreography and operatic stage direction from his own time through the nineteenth century. His techniques and theories found able exponents in such men as Salvatore Vigano, Carlo Blasis, Charles Louis Didelot, Marius Petipa, and Michel Fokine. During the latter part of the eighteenth century and the beginning of the nineteenth Vigano and Blasis were instrumental in establishing the tradition of the classical ballet that has endured to the present time. The later history of the ballet is linked to the Russian school, which exploited the techniques and styles of the French and the Italians to an impressive degree. Charles Louis Didelot, trained in France in the tradition of Noverre, brought French techniques to the Russian stage. After Didelot came Marius Petipa, who is credited with creation of the classical repertory of the Russian ballet. He was a contemporary of Tschaikowsky, who was a keen student of ballet and had an artistic comprehension of the type of music it needed. He willingly adapted himself to the limitations imposed on music by gesture and pantomime and set a style of ballet composition that is a lasting contribution to the art of the dance.

The relation of ballet to opera during the nineteenth century was sometimes one of expediency, sometimes one in which the ballet appeared to the advantage of the opera. In many cases the ballet was introduced merely as divertisement, as, for example, an entertainment during a court spectacle, a peasant dance, a festival scene, and so on. The production of Wagner's *Tannhäuser*, it will be remembered, touched off the famous controversy over ballet. At the Paris Opéra it was an unwritten law that there must be a ballet in the second act. One of the fantastic reasons for this was that the members of the Jockey Club, young bloods of Paris society, never arrived at the theater before the second act, and they demanded a ballet which featured their favorite dancers. Wagner flatly refused to consider a second-act ballet, arguing that the proper place for it was in the *bacchanale* of the Venusberg scene in the first act. The final concession he made was an elaboration of this scene. The Jockey Club took its revenge in hissing and booing, and the Paris première of *Tannhäuser* was, of course, a failure.

In other instances, however, the ballet was an important element of the opera itself. The role of the mute heroine of Auber's *La Muette de Portici* is played by a *prima ballerina*. In Meyerbeer's *Robert le Diable* there is the spectacular ballet of the dead nuns. Some of the most thrilling moments in Boïto's *Mefistofele* and Gounod's *Faust* come when the ballet performs the fantastic dances of the witches during their orgies on the Brocken. Likewise Rimsky-Korsakov's *Sadko* is famous for its undersea ballet.

Some productions of his *Le Coq d'Or* depend solely upon the ballet for the presentation of the action. The opera required singers who can dance and dancers who can sing. This combination is rarely available, and *Le Coq d'Or* is generally given with the ballet miming the action and the singers grouped at the sides of the stage. In such operas as Borodin's *Prince Igor* and Stravinsky's *Petrouchka* were articulated the new ideas and techniques of Michel Fokine, one of the great contemporary contributors to the art of the dance.

Interesting ballet techniques have been introduced in some of the experimental operatic forms of the twentieth century. One remarkable example is Richard Strauss's *Ariadne auf Naxos*—actually part of Hugo von Hofmannsthal's version of Molière's *Le Bourgeois Gentilhomme*. This was presented as a play with ballets, which, incidentally, was Molière's original intention. Strauss composed ballet music based on that originally written by Lully for Molière's play (Lully himself danced in the first production) and wrote *Ariadne* as an epilogue to the play itself. In his libretto von Hofmannsthal ingeniously combined the play and the opera by having Monsieur Jourdain order an opera and an Italian comedy of masks for the entertainment of his guests and then insist that both be played simultaneously. In a later version von Hofmannsthal severed all connection with the Molière play and wrote material for a new first act, to which Strauss composed the music. In this form *Ariadne auf Naxos* was revived in New York in 1946 with much success. Strauss wrote two other ballet-operas—*Legend of Joseph*, produced by Serge Diaghileff, and *Schlagobers*.

Modern opera appears to be bringing ballet into closer relationship. As Edward J. Dent observes in his excellent book, *Opera*, ". . . it is . . . the tendency of the present day to produce opera more and more in the spirit of ballet. Opera, by virtue of its music, stands nearer to ballet than to drama, even to poetic drama. Wagner, when he wrote that operatic gesture was derived from ballet, was expressing his contempt for both, but . . . it is obvious that the Wagnerian system of acting could never have come into existence but for the dramatic ballets of Noverre. And the modern ballet, as exemplified by Kurt Jooss's *Chronica*, has become so serious and tragic that modern Wagnerian production may well seek to learn something from it."

The realistic trend in contemporary opera, as revealed in such works as Darius Milhaud's *Christoph Colomb*, Manuel de Falla's *El Amor Brujo*, Paul Hindemith's *Neues vom Tage*, and Alban Berg's *Wozzeck*, demands a type of operatic acting that can best be delineated with ballet techniques. No longer is it possible for stars and chorus to withdraw to either side of the stage and suspend the action of the opera while the ballet entertains the audience with assorted leaps, pirouettes, and *entrechats* in the classic manner.

Although modern opera is largely concerned with experimental forms, the tendency toward achieving greater dramatic coherence through the medium of ballet action—thus bridging movement and music—seems to foreshadow a return to the principles enunciated by the great reformers and creators, such as Lully, Rameau, Vigano, Blasis, and Fokine. Generally it may be said that ballet has forged ahead of opera in finding new forms of dramatic expression. Innovations and techniques developed in America by such groups as the Ballet Caravan, Ballet Theatre, the Denishawn School, and the American Ballet have been interestingly adapted to the lyric stage, particularly in semi-operatic productions such as *Porgy and Bess* and *Oklahoma*. Although far from grand opera, these adaptions may well be the forerunners of major works in which ballet and opera will be fused into an art form of unparalleled versatility and dramatic power.

SELECTED READING GUIDE

American Opera and Its Composers, Edward Ellsworth Hipsher. Philadelphia. Theo. Presser Company.
  Beginnings of opera in America, American composers and their operas.

Miniature History of Opera, Percy Scholes. London. Oxford University Press.
  Carefully selected highlights of opera history in a brief but scholarly survey.

Opera, Edward J. Dent. New York. Penguin Books.
  History plus comment on enjoyment of opera, ballet in opera, operatic singing and acting, and opera in English.

Our American Music (3rd ed.), John Tasker Howard. New York. Thomas Y. Crowell.
  Opera in relation to general musical developments in America. Discusses important American composers.

The Life of Richard Wagner (4 vols.), Ernest Newman. New York. Alfred A. Knopf.
  This biography is not only the story of the composer's life and works, but virtually a history of the era in which he lived.

The Opera and Its Future in America, Herbert Graf. New York. Norton.
  Reviews European history of opera, then turns to American scene, discussing opera in relation to social and cultural trends.

The Perfect Wagnerite, George Bernard Shaw. New York. Brentano's.
  Provocative essays on the philosophy of *Der Ring des Nibelungen.*

A Short History of Opera (2 vols.), Donald Jay Grout. New York. Columbia University Press.
  A history of opera from its sources to modern times, for layman or music scholar.

The Opera Reader, compiled and edited by Louis Biancolli. New York. McGraw-Hill.
  A chatty, informative discussion of operas and composers.

Opera Comique, Martin Cooper. London. M. Parrish.
  Traces origins of *opera comique,* analyzes its style, and explains how it differs from grand opera and operetta.

French Grand Opera, William Loran Crosten. New York. King's Crown Press.
  Discusses the role of French composers in the development of opera and their contributions to its progress.

Walt Whitman and Opera, Robert D. Faner. Philadelphia. University of Pennsylvania Press.
  A discussion of opera and its relation to poetry. The great American poet Whitman was intensely interested in opera from the standpoint of musical speech.

The Tales of Hoffmann, a study of the film, Monk Gibbon. London. Saturn Press.
  An interesting and vivid account of how Offenbach's opera was made into a full-length film, a spectacular example of how opera can be adapted to the medium of the screen.

Opera for the People, Herbert Graf. Minneapolis. University of Minnesota Press.
  Opera and its problems as viewed by one of today's leading operatic stage directors.

Makers of Opera, Kathleen O'Donnell Hoover. New York. H. Bittner.
A discussion of how operas came into being.

A Front Seat at the Opera, George Marek. New York. Allen, Towne & Heath.
"Close-ups" of performers and performances.

Behind the Gold Curtain, Mary E. Peltz. New York. Farrar, Strauss.
Backstage at the Metropolitan.

Opera Production for Amateurs, Harold Smethhurst. London. Turnstile Press.

Problems of Opera Production, Walter W. Volbach. Fort Worth. Texas Christian
University Press.

The Rise of English Opera, Eric W. White. New York. Philosophical Library.

The International Cyclopedia of Music and Musicians, Oscar Thompson. New York.
Dodd, Mead.
A reference book by an eminent scholar and musicologist.

The Victor Book of Operas, Louis Biancolli and Robert Bagar. New York. Simon
& Schuster.
This includes a discography.

The Complete Book of 20th Century Music, David Ewen. New York. Prentice-
Hall.
Brief but authoritative analyses of musical compositions written since 1900
(including operas), biographies of composers, critical evaluations.

The Child and His Music, Hazel Gertrude Kinscella and Elizabeth M. Tierney.
University Publishing Company, Lincoln, New York, Dallas, Kansas City.
Contains practical suggestions on how to introduce children to opera and how
to stimulate their interest in it.

The Magic World of Music, Olga Samaroff Stokowski. New York. Norton.
A book that explains opera and its origins in terms of a delightful fantasy.

Accents on Opera, Boris Goldovsky. New York. Farrar, Strauss & Young.
Brief essays and analyses of operatic plots and musical themes, with musical
notations.

Milton Cross' Encyclopedia of the Great Composers and Their Music. New York.
Doubleday.
While this is concerned primarily with composers of all types of music there
are numerous references to operatic works. There is such information as the
date of the première and a brief analysis of the plot as well as a discussion
of the music.

SUPPLEMENTARY READING

I am a Conductor, Charles Munch. Translated from the French by Leonard Burkat. New York. Oxford University Press.
> Autobiographical volume by the conductor of the Boston Symphony Orchestra, detailing some of his musical experiences and giving his views on the relationship between the batonist, the musician, and the world of art.

America's Music: From the Pilgrims to the Present, Gilbert Chase. New York. McGraw-Hill.
> A study, illustrated with musical examples, of the development of music in America from the psalm-singing of the Puritans to the compositions of Charles Ives.

The Agony of Modern Music, by Henry Pleasants. New York. Simon & Schuster.
> A highly controversial and provocative book by the former music editor of the Philadelphia Evening Bulletin. Mr. Pleasants argues from the point that "modern music is not modern and is rarely music."

MISCELLANEOUS READING

The world of opera is peopled with colorful personalities, and for that reason autobiographies and biographies invariably make interesting reading. Below is a representative selection of books that afford glimpses of the other side of the footlights.

Galli-Curci's Life of Song, C. E. La Massena. New York. The Paebar Company.

Impresario, Solomon Hurok. New York. Random House.

Jean de Reszke, Clara Leiser. New York. Minton, Balch and Company.

Memoirs of an American Prima Donna, Clara Louise Kellogg. New York. G. P. Putnam's Sons.

Memoirs of a Singer, Minnie Hauk. London. A. M. Philpott, Ltd.

Midway in My Song, Lotte Lehmann. Indianapolis. Bobbs-Merrill.

My Path Through Life, Lilli Lehmann. New York. G. P. Putnam's Sons.

Painted Veils, James Gibbons Huneker. New York. Modern Library.

Prima Donna, Pitts Sanborn. London. Longmans, Green and Co.

Such Sweet Compulsion, Geraldine Farrar. New York. Greystone Press.

Index